INTERNET & WORLD WIDE WEB

HOW TO PROGRAM

SECOND EDITION

Deitel™ Books, Cyber Classrooms, Complete Training Courses and Web-Based Training published by Prentice Hall

How to Program Series

Advanced Java™ 2 Platform How to Program
C How to Program, 3/E
C++ How to Program, 3/E
C# How to Program
e-Business and e-Commerce How to Program
Internet and World Wide Web How to Program, 2/E
Java™ How to Program, 4/E
Perl How to Program
Visual Basic® 6 How to Program
Visual Basic® .NET How to Program
Visual C++® .NET How to Program
Wireless Internet & Mobile Business How to Program
XML How to Program

Multimedia Cyber Classroom and *Web-Based Training* Series

(for information regarding Deitel™ Web-based training visit **`www.ptgtraining.com`**)

Advanced Java™ 2 Platform Multimedia Cyber Classroom
C++ Multimedia Cyber Classroom, 3/E
C# Multimedia Cyber Classroom, 3/E
e-Business and e-Commerce Multimedia Cyber Classroom
Internet and World Wide Web Multimedia Cyber Classroom, 2/E
Java™ 2 Multimedia Cyber Classroom, 4/E
Perl Multimedia Cyber Classroom
Visual Basic® 6 Multimedia Cyber Classroom
Visual Basic® .NET Multimedia Cyber Classroom
Visual C++® .NET Multimedia Cyber Classroom
Wireless Internet & Mobile Business Programming Multimedia Cyber Classroom
XML Multimedia Cyber Classroom

The Complete Training Course Series

The Complete Advanced Java™ 2 Platform Training Course
The Complete C++ Training Course, 3/E
The Complete C# Training Course, 3/E
The Complete e-Business and e-Commerce Programming Training Course
The Complete Internet and World Wide Web Programming Training Course
The Complete Java™ 2 Training Course, 3/E
The Complete Perl Training Course
The Complete Visual Basic® 6 Training Course
The Complete Visual Basic® .NET Training Course
The Complete Visual C++® .NET Training Course
The Complete Wireless Internet & Mobile Business Programming Training Course
The Complete XML Training Course

.NET Series

C# How to Program
Visual Basic® .NET How to Program
Visual C++® .NET How to Program

Visual Studio® Series

Getting Started with Microsoft® Visual C++™ 6 with an Introduction to MFC
Visual Basic® 6 How to Program
C# How to Program
Visual Basic® .NET How to Program
Visual C++® .NET How to Program

For Managers Series

e-Business and e-Commerce for Managers

Coming Soon

e-books and e-whitepapers

To communicate with the authors, send email to:

`deitel@deitel.com`

For information on corporate on-site seminars and public seminars offered by Deitel & Associates, Inc. worldwide, visit:

`www.deitel.com`

For continuing updates on Prentice Hall and Deitel & Associates, Inc. publications visit the Prentice Hall Web site

`www.prenhall.com/deitel`

INTERNET & WORLD WIDE WEB

HOW TO PROGRAM

SECOND EDITION

H. M. Deitel
Deitel & Associates, Inc.

P. J. Deitel
Deitel & Associates, Inc.

T. R. Nieto
Deitel & Associates, Inc.

PRENTICE HALL, Upper Saddle River, New Jersey 07458

Library of Congress Cataloging-in-Publication Data

Deitel, Harvey M
Internet and World Wide Web : how to program / H.M. Deitel, P.J. Deitel. --2nd ed.
p. cm.
Includes bibliographical references and index.
ISBN 0-13-030897-8
1. Internet programming. 2. World Wide Web. I. Deitel, Paul J. II. Nieto, T.R. (Tem R.) III. Title
QA76.625 .D47 2001
005.2'76--dc21 2001045144

Vice President and Editorial Director: ***Marcia Horton***
Acquisitions Editor: ***Petra J. Recter***
Assistant Editor: ***Sarah Burrows***
Project Manager: ***Crissy Statuto***
Editorial Assistant: ***Karen Schultz***
Vice President and Director of Production and Manufacturing, ESM: ***David W. Riccardi***
Executive Managing Editor: ***Vince O'Brien***
Managing Editor: ***David A. George***
Assistant Managing Editor: ***Camille Trentacoste***
Director of Creative Services: ***Paul Belfanti***
Creative Director: ***Carole Anson***
Chapter Opener and Cover Designer: ***Tamara Newnam***
Manufacturing Manager: ***Trudy Pisciotti***
Manufacturing Buyer: ***Lisa McDowell***
Marketing Manager: ***Jennie Burger***

Upper Saddle River, New Jersey 07458

Printed in the United States of America

10 9 8 7 6 5 4 3 2 1

ISBN 0-13-030897-8

Prentice-Hall International (UK) Limited, *London*
Prentice-Hall of Australia Pty. Limited, *Sydney*
Prentice-Hall Canada Inc., *Toronto*
Prentice-Hall Hispanoamericana, S.A., *Mexico*
Prentice-Hall of India Private Limited, *New Delhi*
Prentice-Hall of Japan, Inc., *Tokyo*
Pearson Education Asia Pte. Ltd., *Singapore*
Editora Prentice-Hall do Brasil, Ltda., *Rio de Janeiro*

To our aunt and our grand aunt

Rochelle Deitel

Thank you for being
the special person that you are.
You make every day special
for everyone around you.

Love,
Harvey and Paul

To the Pighetti family: Danielle, Joe, Sharon, Amy and Tom

For your kindness, warmth and company.
For the holidays, fantastic meals and gifts.
For being the special, wonderful family that you are.
Thank you for opening your home and hearts to me.

Tem R. Nieto

Trademarks

Contents

Illustrations

3 Photoshop® Elements

12 JavaScript: Objects

13 Dynamic HTML: Object Model and Collections

14 Dynamic HTML: Event Model

15 Dynamic HTML: Filters and Transitions

20 Extensible Markup Language (XML)

21 Web Servers (IIS, PWS and Apache)

23 Wireless Internet and m-Business

29 PHP

30 Servlets: Bonus for Java™ Developers

32 e-Business & e-Commerce (on CD)

33 Multimedia: Audio, Video, Speech Synthesis and Recognition

34 Accessibility

Preface

Live in fragments no longer. Only connect.
Edward Morgan Forster

Welcome to the exciting world of Internet and World Wide Web programming. This book is by an old guy and two young guys. The old guy (HMD; Massachusetts Institute of Technology 1967) has been programming and/or teaching programming for 40 years. The two young guys (PJD; MIT 1991 and TRN; MIT 1992) have been programming and/or teaching programming for over 20 years. The old guy programs and teaches from experience; the young guys do so from an inexhaustible reserve of energy. The old guy wants clarity; the young guys want performance. The old guy seeks elegance and beauty; the young guys want results. We got together to produce a book we hope you will find informative, challenging and entertaining.

The explosion and popularity of the Internet and the World Wide Web creates tremendous challenges for us as authors, for our publisher—Prentice Hall, for instructors, for students and for professionals.

The World Wide Web increases the prominence of the Internet in information systems, strategic planning and implementation. Organizations want to integrate the Internet "seamlessly" into their information systems and the World Wide Web offers endless opportunity to do so.

New Features in Internet & World Wide Web How to Program: Second Edition

This edition contains many new features and enhancements including:

- ***Full-Color Presentation***. The book enhances LIVE-CODE™ examples by using full color. Readers see sample outputs as they would appear on a color monitor. We have syntax colored all the code examples, as many of today's development environments do. Our syntax-coloring conventions are as follows:

```
comments appear in green
keywords appear in dark blue
literal values appear in light blue
XHTML text and scripting text appear in black
ASP and JSP delimiters appear in red
```

- ***XHTML***. This edition uses XHTML as the primary means of describing Web content. The World Wide Web Consortium deprecated the use of HTML 4 and replaced it with XHTML 1.0 (Extensible Hypertext Markup Language). XHTML is derived from XML (Extensible Markup Language), which allows Web developers to create their own tags and languages. XHTML is replacing HTML as the standard for marking up Web content because it is more robust and offers more features.
- ***Chapter 19, Macromedia® Flash***.™ Flash is a cutting-edge multimedia application that enables Web developers to create interactive, animated content. Through hands-on examples, we show how to add interactivity, sound and animation to Web sites while teaching the fundamentals of Flash and *ActionScript*—Flash's scripting language. The chapter examples include creating interactive buttons, animated banners and animated splash screens (called *animation pre-loaders*).
- ***Chapter 20, Extensible Markup Language (XML)***. Throughout the book we emphasize XHTML, which derived from XML and HTML. XML derives from SGML (Standardized General Markup Language), whose sheer size and complexity limits its use beyond heavy-duty, industrial-strength applications. XML is a technology created by the World Wide Web Consortium for describing data in a portable format. XML is an effort to make SGML-like technology available to a much broader community. XML is a condensed subset of SGML with additional features for usability. Document authors use XML's extensibility to create entirely new markup languages for describing specific types of data, including mathematical formulas, chemical molecular structures and music. Markup languages created with XML include XHTML (Chapters 4 and 5), MathML (for mathematics), VoiceXML™ (for speech), SMIL™ (the Synchronized Multimedia Integration Language for multimedia presentations), CML (Chemical Markup Language for chemistry) and XBRL (Extensible Business Reporting Language for financial data exchange).
- ***Chapter 23, Wireless Internet and m-Business***. We introduce the impact of wireless communications on individuals and businesses. The chapter then explores wireless devices and communications technologies and introduces wireless programming. The *Wireless Application Protocol (WAP)* is designed to enable different kinds of wireless devices to communicate and access the Internet using the *Wireless Markup Language (WML)*. WML tags mark up a Web page to specify how to format a page on a wireless device. WMLScript helps WAP applications "come alive" by allowing a developer to manipulate WML document content dynamically. In addition to WAP/WML, we explore various platforms and programming languages on the client, such as *Java 2 Micro Edition (J2ME)*, *Qualcomm's Binary Runtime Environment for Wireless (BREW)*, the enormously popular Japanese *i-mode* service, *Compact HyperText Markup Language (cHTML)* and *Bluetooth™ wireless technology*.

- ***Server-Side Technology***. We present condensed treatments of six popular Internet/ Web programming languages for building the server side of Internet- and Web-based client/server applications. In Chapters 25 and 26, we discuss Active Server Pages (ASP)—Microsoft's technology for server-side scripting. In Chapter 27, we introduce Perl, an open-source scripting language for programming Web-based applications. In Chapters 28 and 29, we introduce Python and PHP—two emerging, open-source scripting languages. In Chapters 30 and 31, we provide two bonus chapters for Java programmers on Java™ servlets and JavaServer Pages™ (JSP).
- ***Chapter 34, Accessibility***. Currently, the World Wide Web presents many challenges to people with disabilities. Individuals with hearing and visual impairments have difficulty accessing multimedia-rich Web sites. To rectify this situation, the World Wide Web Consortium (W3C) launched the *Web Accessibility Initiative (WAI)*, which provides guidelines for making Web sites accessible to people with disabilities. This chapter provides a description of these guidelines. We also introduce *VoiceXML* and *CallXML*, two technologies for increasing the accessibility of Web-based content.
- ***Appendix F, Career Opportunities***. This detailed appendix introduces career services on the Internet. We explore online career services from the employer and employee's perspective. We suggest sites on which you can submit applications, search for jobs and review applicants (if you are interested in hiring people). We also review services that build recruiting pages directly into e-businesses. One of our reviewers told us that he had just gone through a job search largely using the Internet and this chapter would have expanded his search dramatically.
- ***Appendix G, Unicode***. This appendix overviews the *Unicode Standard.* As computer systems evolved worldwide, computer vendors developed numeric representations of character sets and special symbols for the local languages spoken in different countries. In some cases, different representations were developed for the same languages. Such disparate character sets made communication between computer systems difficult. XML and XML-derived languages, such as XHTML, support the Unicode Standard (maintained by a non-profit organization called the *Unicode Consortium*), which defines a single character set with unique numeric values for characters and special symbols in most spoken languages. This appendix discusses the Unicode Standard, overviews the Unicode Consortium Web site (**`unicode.org`**) and shows an XML example that displays "Welcome to Unicode!" in ten different languages!

Some Notes to Instructors

Why We Wrote *Internet & World Wide Web How to Program: Second Edition*

Dr. Harvey M. Deitel taught introductory programming courses in universities for 20 years with an emphasis on developing clearly written, well-designed programs. Much of what is taught in these courses are the basic principles of programming with an emphasis on the effective use of control structures and functionalization. We present these topics in *Internet & World Wide Web How to Program: Second Edition,* the way HMD has done in his university courses. Students are highly motivated by the fact that they are learning six leading-edge scripting languages (JavaScript, VBScript, Perl, Python, PHP and Flash ActionScript) and a leading-edge programming paradigm (object-based programming). We also teach Dynamic HTML, a means of adding "dynamic content" to World Wide Web pages. Instead of Web pages with only text and static graphics, Web pages "come alive" with audios, videos, animations, interactivity and three-dimensional moving images. Dynamic HTML's features are precisely what businesses and organizations need to meet today's information processing requirements. These programming languages will be useful to students immediately as they leave the university environment and head into a world in which the Internet and the World Wide Web have massive prominence.

Focus of the Book

Our goal was clear: produce a textbook for introductory university-level courses in computer programming for students with little or no programming experience, yet offer the depth and rigorous treatment of theory and practice demanded by traditional, upper-level programming courses and professionals. To meet this goal, we produced a comprehensive book that teaches the principles of control structures, object-based programming, various markup languages (XHTML, Dynamic HTML and XML) and scripting languages such as JavaScript, VBScript, Perl, Python, PHP and Flash ActionScript. After mastering the material in this book, students entering upper-level programming courses and industry will be well prepared to take advantage of the Internet and the Web.

Using Color to Enhance Pedagogy and Clarity

We have emphasized color throughout the book. The World Wide Web is a colorful, multimedia-intensive medium. It appeals to our visual and audio senses. Someday it may even appeal to our senses of touch, taste and smell! We suggested to our publisher, Prentice Hall, that they publish this book in color. The use of color is crucial to understanding and appreciating many of the programs we present. Almost from its inception, the Web has been a color-intensive medium. We hope it helps you develop more appealing Web-based applications.

Web-Based Applications Development

Many books about the Web concentrate on developing attractive Web pages. We discuss Web-page design intensely. But more importantly, the key focus of this book is on Web-based applications development. Our audiences want to build real-world, industrial-strength, Web-based applications. These audiences care about good looking Web pages, but they also care about client/server systems, databases, distributed computing, etc. Many books about the Web are reference manuals with exhaustive listings of features. That is not our style. We concentrate on creating real applications. We provide the LIVE-CODE™ examples on the CD accompanying this book (and at **`www.deitel.com`**) so that you can run the applications and see and hear the multimedia outputs. You can interact with our game and art programs. The Web is an artist's paradise. Your creativity is your only limitation. However, the Web contains so many tools and mechanisms to leverage your abilities that even if you are not artistically inclined, you can create stunning output. Our goal is to help you master these tools so that you can maximize your creativity and development abilities.

Multimedia-Intensive Communications

People want to communicate. Sure, they have been communicating since the dawn of civilization, but computer communications have been limited mostly to digits, alphabetic characters and special characters. The next major wave of communication technology is multimedia. People want to transmit pictures and they want those pictures to be in color. They want to transmit voices, sounds and audio clips. They want to transmit full-motion color video. At some point, they will insist on three-dimensional, moving-image transmission. Our current flat, two-dimensional televisions eventually will be replaced with three-dimensional versions that turn our living rooms into "theaters-in-the-round." Actors will perform their roles as if we were watching live theater. Our living rooms will be turned into miniature sports stadiums. Our business offices will enable video conferencing among colleagues half a world apart, as if they were sitting around one conference table. The possibilities are intriguing, and the Internet is sure to play a key role in making many of these possibilities become reality. Dynamic HTML and Flash ActionScript are means of adding "dynamic content" to World Wide Web pages. Instead of Web pages with only text and static graphics, Web pages "come alive" with audios, videos, animations, interactivity and three-dimensional imaging. Dynamic HTML's and Flash ActionScript's features are precisely what businesses and organizations need to meet today's multimedia-communications requirements. There have been predictions that the Internet will eventually replace the telephone system. Why stop there? It could also replace radio and television as we know them today. It is not hard to imagine the Internet and the World Wide Web replacing newspapers with electronic news media. Many newspapers and magazines already offer Web-based versions, some fee based and some free. Increased bandwidth makes it possible to stream audio and video over the Web. Both companies and individuals run their own Web-based radio and television stations. Just a few decades ago, there were only a few television stations. Today, standard cable boxes accommodate about 100 stations. In a few more years, we will have access to thousands of stations broadcasting over the Web worldwide. This textbook may someday appear in a museum alongside radios, TVs and newspapers in an "early media of ancient civilization" exhibit.

Teaching Approach

Internet & World Wide Web How to Program: Second Edition contains a rich collection of examples, exercises and projects drawn from many fields to provide the student with a chance to solve interesting real-world problems. The book concentrates on the principles of good software engineering and stresses program clarity. We avoid arcane terminology and syntax specifications in favor of teaching by example. The book is written by educators who spend much of their time teaching edge-of-the-practice topics in industry classrooms. The text emphasizes good pedagogy.

LIVE-CODE™ Teaching Approach

The book is loaded with hundreds of LIVE-CODE™ examples. This is how we teach and write about programming, and is the focus of each of our multimedia *Cyber Classrooms* as well. Each new concept is presented in the context of a complete, working example immediately followed by one or more windows showing the example's input/output dialog. We call this style of teaching and writing our ***LIVE-CODE™ approach***. *We use the language to teach the language.* Reading these examples is much like entering and running them on a computer.

Internet & World Wide Web How to Program: Second Edition "jumps right in" with XHTML in Chapter 4, then rapidly proceeds with programming in JavaScript, Microsoft's Dynamic HTML, XML, VBScript/ASP, Perl, Python, PHP, Flash ActionScript, Java Servlets and JavaServer Pages. Many students wish to "cut to the chase;" there is great stuff to be done in these languages so let's get to it! Web programming is not trivial by any means, but it is fun, and students can see immediate results. Students can get graphical, animated, multimedia-based, audio-intensive, database-intensive, network-based programs running quickly through "reusable components." They can implement impressive projects. They can be more creative and productive in a one- or two-semester course than is possible in introductory courses taught in conventional programming languages, such as C, C++, Visual Basic and Java. [*Note*: This book includes Java Servlets and JavaServer Pages as "bonus chapters;" it does not teach the fundamentals of Java programming. Readers who want to learn Java may want to consider reading our book, *Java How to Program: Fourth Edition*. Readers who desire a deeper, more developer-oriented treatment of Java may want to consider reading our book, *Advanced Java 2 Platform How to Program*.]

World Wide Web Access

All the code for *Internet & World Wide Web How to Program: Second Edition* (and our other publications) is on the Internet free for download at the Deitel & Associates, Inc. Web site

`www.deitel.com`

Please download all the code, then run each program as you read the text. Make changes to the code examples and immediately see the effects of those changes. A great way to learn programming is by programming. [*Note*: You must respect the fact that this is copyrighted material. Feel free to use it as you study, but you may not republish any portion of it in any form without explicit permission from Prentice Hall and the authors.]

Objectives

Each chapter begins with a statement of *Objectives*. This tells students what to expect and gives students an opportunity, after reading the chapter, to determine if they have met these objectives. This is a confidence builder and a source of positive reinforcement.

Quotations

The learning objectives are followed by quotations. Some are humorous, some are philosophical and some offer interesting insights. Our students enjoy relating the quotations to the chapter material. Many of the quotations are worth a "second look" *after* reading the chapter.

Outline

The chapter *Outline* helps the student approach the material in top-down fashion. This, too, helps students anticipate what is to come and set a comfortable and effective learning pace.

15,836 Lines of Code in 311 Example LIVE-CODE™ Programs (with Program Outputs)

Each program is followed by the outputs produced when the document is rendered and its scripts are executed. This enables the student to confirm that the programs run as expected. Reading the book carefully is much like entering and running these programs on a computer. The programs range from just a few lines of code to substantial examples with several hundred lines of code. Students should run each program while studying that program in the text. The examples are available on the CD and at our Deitel (**`www.deitel.com`**) and Prentice Hall Web sites (**`www.prenhall.com\deitel`**).

714 Illustrations/Figures

An abundance of charts, line drawings and program outputs is included. The discussion of control structures, for example, features carefully drawn flowcharts. [*Note*: We do not teach flowcharting as a program development tool, but we do use a brief, flowchart-oriented presentation to specify the precise operation of JavaScript's and VBScript's control structures.]

466 Programming Tips

We have included programming tips to help students focus on important aspects of program development. We highlight hundreds of these tips in the form of *Good Programming Practices, Common Programming Errors, Testing and Debugging Tips, Performance Tips, Portability Tips, Software Engineering Observations* and *Look-and-Feel Observations.* These tips and practices represent the best we have gleaned from a combined seven decades of programming and teaching experience. One of our students—a mathematics major—told us that she feels this approach is like the highlighting of axioms, theorems and corollaries in mathematics books; it provides a foundation on which to build good software.

86 Good Programming Practices

Good Programming Practices call the students' attention to techniques for writing programs that are clearer, more understandable and more maintainable.

143 Common Programming Errors

Students learning a language—especially in their first programming course—tend to make certain errors frequently. Focusing on these Common Programming Errors helps students avoid making the same errors. It also helps reduce long lines outside instructors' offices during office hours!

48 Performance Tips

In our experience, teaching students to write clear and understandable programs is by far the most important goal of a first programming course. However, students want to write the programs that run the fastest, use the least memory, require the smallest number of keystrokes or dazzle in other nifty ways. Students care about performance. They want to know what they can do to "turbo charge" their programs. Therefore, we include Performance Tips to highlight opportunities for improving program performance.

31 Portability Tips

There is a strong emphasis today on portability (i.e., on producing software that will run on a variety of computer systems with few, if any, changes). Achieving portability requires careful and cautious design. There are many pitfalls. We include numerous Portability Tips to help students write portable code.

118 Software Engineering Observations

The Software Engineering Observations highlight architectural and design issues that affect the construction of software systems, especially large-scale systems. Much of what the student learns here will be useful in upper-level courses and in industry as the student begins to work with large, complex real-world systems.

31 Testing and Debugging Tips

This "tip type" may be misnamed. When we first decided to incorporate Testing and Debugging Tips, we thought these tips would be suggestions for testing programs to expose bugs and suggestions to remove those bugs. In fact, most of these tips tend to be observations about capabilities and features that prevent bugs from getting into programs in the first place.

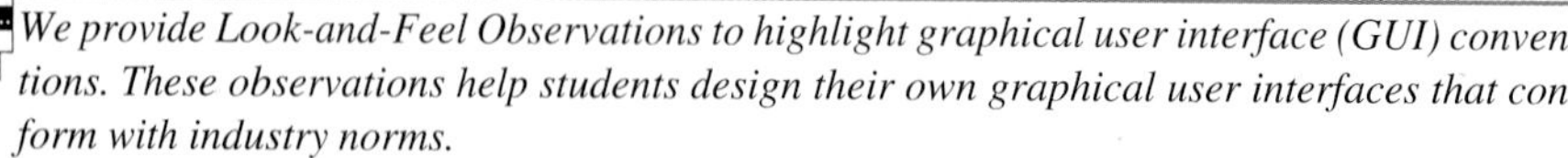

9 Look-and-Feel Observations

We provide Look-and-Feel Observations to highlight graphical user interface (GUI) conventions. These observations help students design their own graphical user interfaces that conform with industry norms.

Summary (1274 Summary bullets)

Each chapter includes additional pedagogical devices. We present a thorough, bullet-list-style *Summary* of the chapter. On average, each chapter contains 37 summary bullets that help students review and reinforce important concepts.

Terminology (2921 Terms)

In the *Terminology* section, we include an alphabetized list of the important terms defined in the chapter—again, further reinforcement. On average, there are 86 terms per chapter.

652 Self-Review Exercises and Answers (Count Includes Separate Parts)

Extensive self-review exercises and answers are included for self-study. They provide the student with a chance to build confidence with the material and to prepare for the regular exercises. Students should attempt all the self-review exercises and check their answers.

633 Exercises (Solutions in Instructor's Manual; Count Includes Separate Parts)

Each chapter concludes with a substantial set of exercises, including simple recall of important terminology and concepts; writing individual statements; writing small portions of functions; writing complete functions and scripts; and writing major term projects. The large number of exercises across a wide variety of topics enables instructors to tailor their courses to the unique needs of their audiences and to vary course assignments each semester. Instructors can use these exercises to form homework assignments, short quizzes and major examinations. The solutions for the vast majority of the exercises are included in the *Instructor's Manual* and on the disks *available only to instructors* through their Prentice-Hall representatives. [***NOTE*: Please do not write to us requesting the instructor's manual. Distribution of this publication is strictly limited to college professors teaching from the book. Instructors may obtain the solutions manual only from their regular Prentice Hall representatives. We regret that we cannot provide the solutions to professionals.**] Solutions to approximately half the exercises are included on the *Internet & World Wide Web Multimedia Cyber Classroom: Second Edition* CD (available in bookstores and computer stores; please see the last few pages of this book or visit our Web site at **`www.deitel.com`** for ordering instructions).

Approximately 6657 Index Entries (with approximately 8208 Page References)

At the back of the book, we have included an extensive *Index* to help students find any term or concept by keyword. The *Index* is useful to people reading the book for the first time and is especially useful to practicing programmers who use the book as a reference. Most of the terms in the *Terminology* sections appear in the *Index* (along with many more index items from each chapter). Students can use the *Index* in conjunction with the *Terminology* sections to be sure they have covered the key material of each chapter.

"Double Indexing" of All LIVE-CODE™ Examples and Exercises

Internet & World Wide Web How to Program: Second Edition has 311 LIVE-CODE™ examples and 633 exercises (including parts). Many of the exercises are challenging problems or projects requiring substantial effort. We have double indexed each of the LIVE-CODE™ examples and most of the more challenging projects. For every source-code program in the book, we took the file name and indexed it both alphabetically and as a subindex item under "Examples." This makes it easier to find examples using particular features. The more substantial exercises are indexed both alphabetically and as subindex items under "Exercises."

Bibliography
An extensive bibliography of books, articles and online documentation is included to encourage further reading.

The student should have two key projects in mind while reading through this book—developing a personal Web site using XHTML markup and JavaScript coding, and developing a complete client/server, database-intensive Web-based application by using techniques taught throughout this book.

Software Included with Internet & World Wide Web How to Program: Second Edition

The CD-ROM at the end of this book contains Microsoft Internet Explorer 5.5, Microsoft Agent 2.0, Adobe® Acrobat® Reader 5.0, MySQL 3.23, Jasc® Paint Shop Pro™ 7.0 (90-day evaluation version; this product is included as a bonus—it is not described in the book), ActivePerl 5.6.1, ActivePython 2.1, PHP 4.0.5 and Apache Web Server 1.3.20. The CD also contains the book's examples and an HTML Web page with links to the Deitel & Associates, Inc. Web site, to the Prentice Hall Web site and to the Web site that contains the links to the Web resources mentioned in the chapters. If you have access to the Internet, this Web page can be loaded into your World Wide Web browser to give you quick access to all the resources. We especially would like to thank Jasc Software for providing a trial version of their graphics and photo editor; again, this product is not discussed in the book, but a tutorial can be found at their Web site, **`www.jasc.com`**.

If you have any questions about the software on the CD, please read the introductory documentation on the CD. We will post additional information on our Web site **`www.deitel.com`**. If you have any technical questions about the installation of the CD or about any of the software supplied with Deitel/Prentice Hall products, please e-mail **`media.support@pearsoned.com`**. They will respond promptly.

On our Web site, we provide installation instructions for ODBC, MySQL, IBM VoiceServer SDK 1.5, Microsoft Internet Information Services (IIS), Microsoft Personal Web Server (PWS), Apache Web server, Microsoft's MSXML 3.0 Parser, Perl, Python, PHP, World Wide Web Consortium's Validation Service (both for XHTML and Cascading Style Sheets), IBM Voice Server SDK 1.1, Java 2 Platform Standard Edition, the Microsoft Agent character Wartnose. We also illustrate how to create a database in MySQL and Microsoft Access.

Ancillary Package for Internet & World Wide Web How to Program: Second Edition

[*NOTE*: Please do not write to us requesting the instructor's manual. Distribution of this publication is strictly limited to college professors teaching from the book. Instructors may obtain the solutions manual only from their regular Prentice Hall rep-

resentatives. We regret that we cannot provide the solutions to professionals.] *Internet & World Wide Web How to Program: Second Edition* has extensive ancillary materials for instructors teaching from the book. The Instructor's Manual CD contains solutions to the vast majority of the end-of-chapter exercises and a test bank of multiple choice questions (approximately 2 per book section). In addition, we provide PowerPoint® slides containing all the code and figures in the text. You are free to customize these slides to meet your own classroom needs. Prentice Hall provides a *Companion Web Site* (**`www.prenhall.com/deitel`**) that includes resources for instructors and students. For instructors, the Web site has a Syllabus Manager for course planning, links to the PowerPoint slides and reference materials from the appendices of the book (such as the operator precedence chart, character sets and Web resources). For students, the Web site provides chapter objectives, true/false exercises with instant feedback, chapter highlights and reference materials.

Internet & World Wide Web Programming Multimedia Cyber Classroom: Second Edition *and* The Complete Internet & World Wide Web Programming Training Course: Second Edition

We have prepared an interactive, CD-ROM-based, software version of *Internet & World Wide Web How to Program: Second Edition*, called the *Internet & World Wide Web Programming Multimedia Cyber Classroom: Second Edition.* It is loaded with features for learning and reference. The *Cyber Classroom* is wrapped with the textbook at a discount in *The Complete Internet & World Wide Web Programming Training Course: Second Edition.* If you already have the book and would like to purchase the *Internet & World Wide Web Programming Multimedia Cyber Classroom: Second Edition* separately, please call 1-800-811-0912 and ask for ISBN# 0-13-089559-8. Please be sure to give the name of the product as well to avoid errors.

The CD includes an introduction with the authors overviewing the *Cyber Classroom*'s features. The 311 LIVE-CODE™ example programs in the textbook truly "come alive" in the *Cyber Classroom.* If you are viewing a program and want to execute it, simply click the lightning bolt icon and the program will run. You will see—and hear for the audio-based multimedia programs—the program's outputs. If you want to modify a program and see and hear the effects of your changes, simply click the floppy-disk icon that causes the source code to be "lifted off" the CD and "dropped into" one of your own directories so that you can edit the text and try out your new version. Click the speaker icon for an audio that talks about the program and "walks you through" the code.

The *Cyber Classroom* also provides navigational aids, including extensive hyperlinking. With its browser-based front-end, the *Cyber Classroom* remembers recent sections you have visited and allows you to move forward or backward in that list. The thousands of index entries are hyperlinked to their text occurrences. You can key in a term using the "find" feature and, the *Cyber Classroom* will locate occurrences of that term throughout the text. The *Table of Contents* entries are "hot," so clicking a chapter name takes you to that chapter.

Students appreciate the hundreds of solved problems from the textbook (about half of the book exercises) that are included with the *Cyber Classroom.* Studying and running these extra programs is a great way for students to enhance their learning experience.

Students and professional users of our *Cyber Classrooms* tell us they like the interactivity and that the *Cyber Classroom* is an effective reference, due to the extensive hyperlinking and other navigational features. We recently received an e-mail from a person who said that he lives "in the boonies" and cannot take a live course at a university, so the *Cyber Classroom* was the solution to his educational needs.

Professors tell us that their students enjoy using the *Cyber Classroom*, spend more time on the course and master more of the material than in textbook-only courses. Also, the *Cyber Classroom* helps shrink lines outside professors' offices during office hours. We have published the *Cyber Classrooms* for most of our books.

Acknowledgments

One of the great pleasures of writing a textbook is acknowledging the efforts of the many people whose names may not appear on the cover, but whose hard work, cooperation, friendship and understanding were crucial to the production of the book.

Other people at Deitel & Associates, Inc. devoted long hours to this project.We would like to acknowledge the efforts of our full-time Deitel & Associates, Inc. colleagues Abbey Deitel, Sean Santry, Laura Treibick, Rashmi Jayaprakash, Cheryl Yaeger, Ben Wiedermann, Kate Steinbuhler, Matthew R. Kowalewski, Christine Connolly, Betsy DuWaldt and Christi Kelsey.

- Abbey Deitel, a graduate of Carnegie Mellon University's Industrial Management program, and President of Deitel & Associates, Inc., co-authored the security section of Chapter 32.
- Sean Santry, a graduate of Boston College with a major in Computer Science and Philosophy, and Director of Software Development at Deitel & Associates, Inc., co-authored Chapters 30 and 31. In addition, he revised Chapters 6 and 20.
- Laura Treibick, a graduate of the University of Colorado at Boulder with a major in Photography and Multimedia, co-authored Chapters 3 and 19. In addition, she revised Chapters 2 and 33 and edited Chapter 25.
- Rashmi Jayaprakash, a graduate of Boston University with a major in Computer Science, co-authored Chapter 21 and Appendix G. In addition, she revised Chapters 3, 4, 22, 23, 26, 32 and 34.
- Cheryl Yaeger, a graduate of Boston University with a major in Computer Science, and Director of Microsoft Software Publications at Deitel & Associates, Inc., revised Chapter 27.
- Ben Wiedermann, a graduate of Boston University with a major in Computer Science, co-authored Chapter 28.
- Kate Steinbuhler, a graduate of Boston College with a major in English and Communications, and co-Editorial Director at Deitel & Associates, Inc., co-authored Chapters 23, 32 and Appendix F.
- Matthew R. Kowalewski, a graduate of Bentley College with a major in Accounting Information Systems, and Director of Wireless Development at Deitel & Associates, Inc., co-authored Chapters 19 and 23.
- Christine Connolly, a graduate of Boston College Carroll School of Management with a major in Marketing and Finance, and Director of Public Relations and Advertising at Deitel & Associates, Inc., revised Chapters 23 and 32.

- Betsy DuWaldt, a graduate of Metropolitan State College of Denver with a major in Technical Communications (Technical Writing and Editing), and Editorial Director at Deitel & Associates, Inc., revised Chapters 1, 2, 3, 4, 5, 6, 19, 21, 22, 23 and 32.
- Christi Kelsey, a graduate of Purdue University Krannert School of Management with a major in Management and Information Systems, and Director of Corporate Training at Deitel & Associates, Inc., edited Chapters 2, 4, 5, 25, 32 and 34.
- Peter Brandano, a graduate of Boston College with a major in Computer Science, contributed to Chapters 23, 33 and 34. He also created the majority of examples in Chapter 19.

We would also like to thank the participants in our Deitel & Associates, Inc. College Internship Program.[1]

- Peter Lavelle, a senior in Computer Information Systems at Bentley College, revised Chapters 4, 5, 23, 25, 29 and 33. He also converted all HTML-based code in the book to XHTML.
- Gary Grinev, a freshman in Computer Science at the University of Connecticut at Storrs, helped edit the Bibliography and Chapters 1, 21 and 23. He tested all LIVE-CODE™ examples on Netscape Communicator 6, Internet Explorer 5.5 and Internet Explorer 6 (beta). He assisted with the ancillary questions and the installation instructions.
- Zachary Bouchard, a junior in Economics and Philosophy at Boston College, revised Chapters 4, 5 and 6, and he created questions for Chapters 4, 5, 6, 14 and 16. He solved the exercises for Chapter 20, updated all code examples to XHTML 1.0, and converted all code examples for the *Cyber Classroom* and for the *Instructor's Manual* to XHTML.
- Reshma Khilnani, a junior in Computer Science and Mathematics at Massachusetts Institute of Technology, contributed to Appendix G and assisted with the ancillary questions for the test bank and the companion Web site.
- Mary Pacold, a sophomore in Computer Science at the University of Illinois at Urbana-Champaign, assisted with the ancillary questions for the test bank and the companion Web site. She wrote the installation instructions for various software products.
- Lauren Trees, a graduate of Brown University in English, revised Chapters 23 and 32.
- Andrew Jones, a fifth-year student at Dartmouth College, co-authored Chapter 29. He also contributed to Chapter 27.

---

1. The *Deitel & Associates, Inc. College Internship Program* offers a limited number of salaried positions to Boston-area college students majoring in Computer Science, Information Technology, Marketing or English. Students work at our corporate headquarters in Sudbury, Massachusetts full-time in the summers and (for those attending college in the Boston area) part-time during the academic year. Full-time positions are available to college graduates. For more information about this competitive program, please contact Abbey Deitel at **deitel@deitel.com** and visit our Web site, **www.deitel.com**.

- Elizabeth Rockett, a senior in English at Princeton University, edited Chapters 1, 2, 3, 21, 22, 23, 33 and 34.
- Barbara Strauss, a senior in English at Brandeis University, co-authored the security section of Chapter 32. She also edited Chapters 6, 21, 22, 34 and Appendix G.
- A. James O'Leary, a sophomore in Computer Science and Psychology at Rensselaer Polytechnic Institute, co-authored the security section of Chapter 32.
- Joshua Modell, a freshman at Duke University, formulated exercises for Chapter 32. He helped design the PowerPoint slides.
- Christina Carney, a senior in Psychology and Business at Framingham State College, researched URLs for the Internet and World Wide Web Resources section.
- Amy Gips, a sophomore in Marketing and Finance at Boston College, researched quotes for Chapters 3, 19, 23, 29 and 31.

Moreover, we would like to thank Su Zhang, Marina Zlatkina, Carol Treibick, Ana Rodrigues and Muni Jayaprakash for providing translations in Appendix G.

We would also like to acknowledge the following people who contributed to the first edition of *Internet & World Wide Web How to Program*: Jacob Ellis, an undergraduate student at the University of Pennsylvania, worked on Chapter 2, 3 and 4. David Gusovsky, an undergraduate student at the University of California at Berkeley, worked on Chapter 2, 4, 5, 6, 11, 12, 15, 16, 17, 18, 27 and 33. Robin Trudel, an independent consultant, co-authored Chapter 25 of the first edition. Chris Poirier, a senior at the University of Rhode Island, worked on Chapter 27 for the first edition.

We are fortunate to have been able to work on this project with the talented and dedicated team of publishing professionals at Prentice Hall. We especially appreciate the extraordinary efforts of our computer science editor, Petra Recter, her assistant Crissy Statuto and their boss—our mentor in publishing—Marcia Horton, Editor-in-Chief of Prentice-Hall's Engineering and Computer Science Division. Camille Trentacoste and her boss Vince O'Brien, did a marvelous job managing the production of the book.

The *Internet & World Wide Web Programming Multimedia Cyber Classroom: Second Edition* was developed in parallel with *Internet & World Wide Web How to Program: Second Edition*. We sincerely appreciate the "new media" insight, savvy and technical expertise of our editor Karen McLean. She did a remarkable job bringing the *Internet & World Wide Web Programming Multimedia Cyber Classroom: Second Edition* to publication under a tight schedule. Michael Ruel did a marvelous job as production manager. Mark Taub (their boss) is our e-publishing mentor and guides all our efforts in *Cyber Classrooms*, *Complete Training Courses*, Web-based training, e-books and e-whitepaper publications.

We owe special thanks to the creativity of Tamara Newnam Cavallo (**smart_art@earthlink.net**), who did the art work for our programming tips icons and the cover. She created the delightful bug creature that has become our corporate mascot.

We sincerely appreciate the efforts of our second edition reviewers:

Internet & World Wide Web How to Program: Second Edition Reviewers
Richard Albright (University of Delaware)
Joan Aliprand (Unicode Consortium)
Race Bannon (Information Architects)
Paul Bohman (WebAIM)

Steve Burnett (RSA)
Carl Burnham (Southpoint.com)
Sylvia Candelaria de Ram (Editor, Python Journal)
Shane Carareo (Active State)
Kelly Carey (West Valley College)
Chris Constentino (Cisco Systems Inc., PTR Author)
Kevin Dorff (Honeywell)
Fred Drake (PythonLabs)
Jonathan Earl (Technical Training and Consulting)
Amanda Farr (Virtual-FX.net)
Avi Finkel (WhizBang! Labs)
Seth Fogie (Donecker's, PTR Author)
Steven Franklin (UC Irvine)
Charles Fry (thesundancekid.org)
Phillip Gordon (Berkeley)
Christopher Haupt (Adobe)
Auda Hesham (CUNY)
Damon Houghland (Author of PTR book "Essential WAP for Web Professionals")
Bryan Hughes (Adobe)
Jeff Isom (WebAIM)
John Jenkins (Unicode Consortium)
Simon Johnson (Shake Communications Pty Ltd)
Alwyn Joy (Whiz Networks Pvt. Ltd.)
Ankur Kapoor (MIND UR Web)
Elizabeth Lane Lawley (RIT)
Mike Leavy (Adobe)
Ze-Nian Li (Simon Frasier University)
Luby Liao (University of San Diego)
Maxim Loukianov (SoloMio Corp.)
Marc Loy (Consultant)
Rick McGowan (Unicode Consortium)
Julie McVicar (Oakland Community College)
Jasmine Merced (PerlArchive.com)
Mark Michael (Kings College)
Scott Mitchell (Consultant)
Dan Moore (XOR, Inc.)
Charles McCathie Neville (W3C)
Simon North (Synopsys)
Dr. Cyrus Peikari (VirusMD Corp., PTR Author)
Steven Pemberton (CWI, Amsterdam)
Shep Perkins (Fidelity Select Wireless Portfolio)
Corrin Pitcher (DePaul University)
Paul Prescod (Active State)
Keith Roberts (Prentice Hall PTR Author "Core CSS")
Rama Roberts (Sun)
Chad Rolfs (Adobe)

Robert Rybaric (PRO-INFO Systems)
Devan Shepherd (Shepherd Consulting Services)
Steve Smith (ASP Alliance)
M.G. Sriram (HelloBrian Corp.)
Dan Steinman (Consultant)
Vadim Tkachenko (Sera Nova)
Guido Van Rossum (python.org)
Nic Van't Schip (vanschip.com)
Ken Whistler (Sybase; Unicode Consortium)
Monty Widenius (MySQL)
Jesse Wilkins (Metalinear Media)
Michael Willett (wavesys.com)
Bernard Wong (Microsoft)
Ed Wright (Jet Propulsion Laboratory)

We would also like to thank our first edition reviewers.
Kamaljit Bath (Microsoft)
Sunand Bhattacharya (ITT Technical Schools)
Jason Bronfeld (Bristol-Myers Squibb Company)
Bob DuCharme (XML Author)
Jonathan Earl (Technical Training and Consulting)
Jim Gips (Boston College)
Jesse Glick (NetBeans)
Jesse Heines (UMass Lowell)
Shelly Heller (George Washington University)
Peter Jones (SUN Microsystems)
David Kershaw (Art Technology)
Ryan Kuykendall (Amazon)
Hunt LaCascia (Engenius, Inc.)
Yves Lafon (W3C)
Daniel LaLiberte (W3C/Mosaic/NASA)
Wen Liu (ITT)
Marc Loy, (Java Consultant/Cyber Classroom)
Dan Lynch (CyberCash)
Massimo Marchiori (W3C)
Simon North (XML Author)
Ashish Prakash (IBM)
Rama Roberts (SUN Microsystems)
Arie Schlessinger (Columbia University)
Deb Shapiro (Computer Learning Centers)
MG Sriram (GoMo Technologies)
Sumanth Sukumar, (IBM Transarc Labs [HTTP / AFS & DCE DFS])
Scott Tilley (University of California, Riverside)
William Vaughn (Microsoft)
Michael Wallent (Microsoft)
Susan Warren (Microsoft)
Stephen Wynne (IBM Transarc Labs/Carnegie Mellon University)

Under a tight time schedule, our reviewers scrutinized every aspect of the text and made countless suggestions for improving the accuracy and completeness of the presentation.

We would sincerely appreciate your comments, criticisms, corrections and suggestions for improving the text. Please address all correspondence to:

deitel@deitel.com

We will respond promptly. Well, that's it for now. Welcome to the exciting world of Internet and World Wide Web programming. We hope you enjoy your look at leading-edge computer applications development. Good luck!

Dr. Harvey M. Deitel
Paul J. Deitel
Tem R. Nieto

About the Authors

Dr. Harvey M. Deitel, CEO of Deitel & Associates, Inc., has 40 years in the computing field including extensive industry and academic experience. He is one of the world's leading computer science instructors and seminar presenters. Dr. Deitel earned B.S. and M.S. degrees from the Massachusetts Institute of Technology and a Ph.D. from Boston University. He has 20 years of college teaching experience including earning tenure and serving as the Chairman of the Computer Science Department at Boston College before founding Deitel & Associates, Inc. with his son Paul J. Deitel. He is author or co-author of several dozen books and multimedia packages and is currently writing many more. With translations published in Japanese, Russian, Spanish, Traditional Chinese, Simplified Chinese, Korean, French, Polish, Italian and Portuguese, Dr. Deitel's texts have earned international recognition. Dr. Deitel has delivered professional seminars internationally to major corporations, government organizations and various branches of the military.

Paul J. Deitel, Executive Vice President of Deitel & Associates, Inc., is a graduate of the Massachusetts Institute of Technology's Sloan School of Management where he studied Information Technology. Through Deitel & Associates, Inc. he has delivered Internet and World Wide Web courses and programming language classes for industry clients including Compaq, Sun Microsystems, White Sands Missile Range, Rogue Wave Software, Stratus, Fidelity, Cambridge Technology Partners, Lucent Technologies, Adra Systems, Entergy, CableData Systems, NASA at the Kennedy Space Center, the National Severe Storm Laboratory, IBM and many other organizations. He has lectured on for the Boston Chapter of the Association for Computing Machinery, and has taught satellite-based courses through a cooperative venture of Deitel & Associates, Inc., Prentice Hall and the Technology Education Network. He and his father, Dr. Harvey M. Deitel, are the world's best-selling Computer Science textbook authors.

Tem R. Nieto is a graduate of the Massachusetts Institute of Technology where he studied engineering and computing. Through Deitel & Associates, Inc. he has delivered courses for industry clients including Sun Microsystems, Compaq, EMC, Stratus, Fidelity, Art Technology, Progress Software, Toys "R" Us, Operational Support Facility of the National Oceanographic and Atmospheric Administration, Jet Propulsion Laboratory, Nynex, Motorola, Federal Reserve Bank of Chicago, Banyan, Schlumberger, University of

Notre Dame, NASA, various military installations and many others. He has co-authored several books and multimedia packages with the Deitels and has contributed to virtually every Deitel & Associates, Inc. publication.

About Deitel & Associates, Inc.

Deitel & Associates, Inc. is an internationally recognized corporate training and content-creation organization specializing in Internet/World Wide Web software technology, e-business/e-commerce software technology and computer programming languages education. Deitel & Associates, Inc. is a member of the World Wide Web Consortium. The company provides courses on Internet and World Wide Web programming, object technology and major programming languages. The founders of Deitel & Associates, Inc. are Dr. Harvey M. Deitel and Paul J. Deitel. The company's clients include many of the world's largest computer companies, government agencies, branches of the military and business organizations. Through its publishing partnership with Prentice Hall, Deitel & Associates, Inc. publishes leading-edge programming textbooks, professional books, interactive CD-ROM-based multimedia *Cyber Classrooms*, satellite courses and Web-based training courses. Deitel & Associates, Inc. and the authors can be reached via e-mail at

deitel@deitel.com

To learn more about Deitel & Associates, Inc., its publications and its worldwide corporate on-site curriculum, see the last few pages of this book and visit:

www.deitel.com

Individuals wishing to purchase Deitel books, Cyber Classrooms, Complete Training Courses and Web-based training courses can do so through

www.deitel.com

Bulk orders by corporations and academic institutions should be placed directly with Prentice Hall. See the last few pages of this book for worldwide ordering details.

The World Wide Web Consortium (W3C)

Deitel & Associates, Inc. is a member of the *World Wide Web Consortium (W3C)*. The W3C was founded in 1994 "to develop common protocols for the evolution of the World Wide Web." As a W3C member, Deitel and Associates, Inc. holds a seat on the W3C Advisory Committee (the company's representative is its Chief Technology Officer, Paul Deitel). Advisory Committee members help provide "strategic direction" to the W3C through worldwide meetings. Member organizations also help develop standards recommendations for Web technologies (such as HTML, XML and many others) through participation in W3C activities and groups. Membership in the W3C is intended for companies and large organizations. For information on becoming a member of the W3C visit **www.w3.org/Consortium/Prospectus/Joining**.

1

Introduction to Computers and the Internet

Objectives

- To understand basic computer science concepts.
- To become familiar with different types of programming languages.
- To understand the evolution of the Internet and the World Wide Web.
- To understand the roles XHTML, JavaScript, Dynamic HTML, Active Server Pages, Perl, Python, PHP, Java servlets and JavaServer pages have in developing distributed client/server applications for the Internet and the World Wide Web.
- To preview the remaining chapters of the book.

Our life is frittered away by detail ... Simplify, simplify.
Henry Thoreau

What networks of railroads, highways and canals were in another age, networks of telecommunications, information and computerization...are today.
Bruno Kreisky, Austrian Chancellor

My object all sublime
I shall achieve in time.
W. S. Gilbert

He had a wonderful talent for packing thought close, and rendering it portable.
Thomas Babington Macaulay

Outline

1.1 Introduction

Welcome to Internet and World Wide Web programming! We have worked hard to create what we hope will be an informative, entertaining and challenging learning experience for you. As you read this book, you may want to refer to our Web site

`www.deitel.com`

for updates and additional information on each subject.

The technologies you will learn in this book are fun for novices, while simultaneously being appropriate for experienced professionals who build substantial information systems. *Internet and World Wide Web How to Program, Second Edition* is designed to be an effective learning tool for each of these audiences. How can one book appeal to both groups? The answer is that the core of this book emphasizes achieving program *clarity* through the proven techniques of *structured programming*, *object-based programming* and—in the optional Java sections—*object-oriented programming*. Beginners will learn programming the right way from the beginning. We have attempted to write in a clear and straightforward manner.

Perhaps most importantly, the book presents hundreds of working examples and shows the outputs produced when these examples are rendered in browsers or run on computers. We present all concepts in the context of complete working programs. We call this the *live-code™ approach*. These examples are available in three locations—on the CD-ROM inside the back cover of this book, by download from our Web site **www.deitel.com** and on our interactive CD-ROM product, the *Internet and World Wide Web Programming Multimedia Cyber Classroom: Second Edition*. The *Cyber Classroom*'s features and ordering information appear in the last few pages of this book. The *Cyber Classroom* also contains answers to approximately half the exercises in this book, including short-answer questions, small programs and many full projects. Our boxed product, *The Complete Internet and World Wide Web Programming Training Course, Second Edition*, includes the *Cyber Classroom*.

The early chapters introduce computer fundamentals, the Internet and the World Wide Web. We show how to use software packages for browsing the Web and for creating images for the Web. We present a carefully paced introduction to computer programming, using the popular JavaScript programming language. In this book, we will often refer to "programming" as *scripting* for reasons that will soon become clear. Novices will find that the material in the JavaScript chapters presents a solid foundation for the deeper treatment of scripting in VBScript, Perl, Python and PHP in the later chapters. Experienced programmers will read the early chapters for a review of technologies and find that the treatment of scripting in the later chapters is rigorous and challenging.

Most people are familiar with the exciting things computers do. Using this textbook, you will learn how to command computers to perform specific tasks. *Software* (i.e., the instructions you write to command the computer to perform *actions* and make *decisions*) controls computers (often referred to as *hardware*), and JavaScript is one of today's most popular software development languages for Web-based applications.

Computer use is increasing in almost every field of endeavor. In an era of steadily rising costs, computing costs have been decreasing dramatically because of rapid developments in both hardware and software technologies. A computer that filled large rooms and cost millions of dollars just two decades ago can now be inscribed on the surfaces of silicon chips smaller than fingernails, costing perhaps a few dollars each. Silicon is one of the most abundant materials on earth—it is an ingredient in common sand. Silicon chip technology has made computing so economical that hundreds of millions of general-purpose computers worldwide are helping people in business, industry, government and in their personal lives. The number of computers could easily double in a few years.

This book will challenge you on several levels. Your peers over the last few years probably have learned C, C++, Visual Basic® or Java™ as their first computer programming language. Indeed, the Advanced Placement Examination administered to high school students wishing to earn college credit in computer programming is now based on C++ (switched recently from Pascal, a programming language widely used at the college level for two decades and soon to be switched to Java). Until recently, students in introductory programming courses learned only the methodology called structured programming. You will learn *both* structured programming and the exciting newer methodology called *object-based programming*. After this, you will be well-prepared to study the C++ and Java programming languages and learn the even more powerful programming methodology of *object-oriented programming* (which we include in the bonus Java chapters on servlets and

JavaServer Pages). We believe that object-oriented programming will be the key programming methodology at least for the next decade.

Today's users are accustomed to applications with graphical user interfaces (GUIs). Users want applications that use the multimedia capabilities of graphics, images, animation, audio and video. They want applications that can run on the Internet and the World Wide Web and communicate with other applications. Users want to move away from older file-processing techniques to newer database technologies. They want applications that are not limited to the desktop or even to some local computer network, but that can integrate Internet, World Wide Web components and remote databases as well. Programmers want all these capabilities in a truly portable manner so that applications will run without modification on a variety of *platforms* (i.e., different types of computers running different operating systems).

In this book, we present a number of powerful software technologies that enable you to build these kinds of systems. The first part of the book (through Chapter 20) concentrates on using technologies such as Extensible HyperText Markup Language (XHTML), JavaScript, Dynamic HTML, Flash and Extensible Markup Language (XML) to build the portions of Web-based applications that reside on the *client side* (i.e., the portions of applications that typically run on Web browsers such as Netscape's Communicator or Microsoft's Internet Explorer). The second part of the book (through Chapter 34) concentrates on using technologies such as Web servers, databases, Active Server Pages, Perl/CGI, Python, PHP, Java servlets and JavaServer Pages. Programmers use these technologies to build the other major portion of Web-based applications, the *server side* (i.e., the portions of applications that typically run on "heavy-duty," complex computer systems on which an organization's business-critical Web sites reside). Each of these terms will be introduced in this chapter and carefully explained throughout the book. Readers who master the technologies in this book will be able to build substantial Web-based, client/server, database-intensive, "multi-tier" applications. We begin with a discussion of computer hardware and software fundamentals. If you are generally familiar with computers, you may want to skip portions of Chapter 1.

1.2 What Is a Computer?

A *computer* is a device capable of performing computations and making logical decisions at speeds millions, even billions, of times faster than human beings can. For example, a person operating a desk calculator might require a lifetime to complete the hundreds of millions of calculations a powerful personal computer can perform in one second. (Points to ponder: How would you know whether the person had added the numbers correctly? How would you know whether the computer had added the numbers correctly?) Today, the world's fastest *supercomputers* can perform hundreds of billions of additions per second, and computers that perform a trillion instructions per second are already functioning in research laboratories!

Computers process *data* under the direction of sets of instructions called *computer programs.* Computer programs guide the computer through orderly sets of actions specified by people called *computer programmers.*

The various devices, such as the keyboard, screen, disks, memory and processing units, that comprise a computer system are referred to as *hardware.* Regardless of differences in physical appearance, virtually every computer may be envisioned as being divided into six *logical units* or sections. These are as follows:

1. *Input unit.* This is the "receiving" section of the computer. It obtains information (data and computer programs) from various *input devices* and makes the information available to the other units so that the information can be processed. Most information is entered into computers today through keyboards, "mouse" devices and disks. In the future, most information will be entered by speaking to computers, by electronically scanning images and by video recording.
2. *Output unit.* This is the "shipping" section of the computer. It takes information processed by the computer and sends it to various *output devices* to make the information available for use outside the computer. Information output from computers is displayed on screens, printed on paper, played through audio speakers and video devices, magnetically recorded on disks and tapes and used to control other devices.
3. *Memory unit.* This is the rapid access, relatively low-capacity "warehouse" section of the computer. It retains information entered through the input unit so that the information may be made available for processing. The memory unit also retains information which has already been processed until that information can be placed on output devices by the output unit. The memory unit often is called either *memory, primary memory, primary storage* or *random access memory (RAM).*
4. *Arithmetic and logic unit (ALU).* This is the "manufacturing" section of the computer. It is responsible for performing calculations, such as addition, subtraction, multiplication and division. It contains the decision mechanisms that allow the computer, for example, to compare two items from the memory unit to determine whether or not they are equal.
5. *Central processing unit (CPU).* This is the "administrative" section of the computer. The CPU acts as the computer's coordinator and is responsible for supervising the operation of the other sections. The CPU tells the input unit when information should be read into the memory unit, tells the ALU when information from the memory unit should be utilized in calculations and tells the output unit when to send information from the memory unit to certain output devices.
6. *Secondary storage unit.* This is the long-term, high-capacity "warehousing" section of the computer. Programs or data not being used by the other units are normally placed on secondary storage devices (such as disks) until they are needed, possibly hours, days, months or even years later. Information in secondary storage takes longer to access than information in primary memory. The cost per unit of secondary storage is much less than the cost per unit of primary memory.

1.3 Types of Programming Languages

The computer programs that run on a computer are referred to as *software*. Programmers write the instructions that comprise software in various programming languages, some that the computer can understand and others that require intermediate translation steps. The hundreds of computer languages in use today may be divided into three types:

1. Machine languages
2. Assembly languages
3. High-level languages

Any computer can directly understand only its own *machine language*. Machine language is the "natural language" of a particular computer and is defined by the hardware design of that computer. Machine languages generally consist of strings of numbers (ultimately reduced to 1s and 0s) that instruct computers to perform their most elementary operations one at a time. Machine languages are *machine dependent* (i.e., a particular machine language can be used on only one type of computer). Machine languages are cumbersome for humans, as illustrated by the following section, in which a machine-language program adds overtime pay to base pay and stores the result in gross pay.

```
+1300042774
+1400593419
+1200274027
```

As computers became more popular, it became apparent that machine-language programming was too slow and tedious for most programmers. Instead of using strings of numbers that computers could directly understand, programmers began using English-like abbreviations to represent the elementary operations of the computer. These abbreviations formed the basis of *assembly languages*. *Translator programs*, called *assemblers*, were developed to convert assembly-language programs to machine language at computer speeds. The following section of an assembly-language program also adds overtime pay to base pay and stores the result in gross pay, but more clearly than its machine-language equivalent.

```
LOAD BASEPAY
ADD  OVERPAY
STORE GROSSPAY
```

Although such code is understandable to humans, it is incomprehensible to computers until translated to machine language.

Computer use increased rapidly with the advent of assembly languages, but programming in these still required many instructions to accomplish even the simplest tasks. To speed the programming process, *high-level languages* were developed, in which single statements could be written to accomplish substantial tasks. The translator programs that convert high-level language programs into machine language are called *compilers*. High-level languages allow programmers to write instructions that are similar to everyday English and contain commonly used mathematical notations. A payroll program written in a high-level language might contain the statement:

```
grossPay = basePay + overTimePay
```

From this, it is easy to see that programmers find high-level languages more desirable than either machine languages or assembly languages. C, C++, Visual Basic and Java are among the most powerful and most widely used high-level programming languages.

The process of compiling a high-level language program into machine language can take a considerable amount of computer time. *Interpreter* programs were developed to execute high-level language programs directly, without the need for compiling those programs into machine language. Although compiled programs execute faster than interpreted programs, interpreters are popular in program-development environments, in which programs are recompiled frequently as new features are added and errors are corrected. In this book, we study six key programming languages: JavaScript, WMLScript, VBScript, Perl, Python and PHP (along with many other languages including XHTML, XML, WML) and—in the bonus chapters—we use Java. Each of these *scripting languages* is processed by interpreters. You will see that interpreters have played an especially important role in helping scripting languages achieve their goal of portability across a variety of platforms.

Performance Tip 1.1

Interpreters have an advantage over compilers in the scripting world. An interpreted program can begin executing immediately as soon as it is downloaded to the client's machine, whereas a source program must first be compiled before it can execute.

1.4 Other High-Level Languages

Only a few high-level languages have achieved broad acceptance, out of the hundreds developed. IBM Corporation developed *Fortran* (FORmula TRANslator) from 1954–1957 for scientific and engineering applications that require complex mathematical computations. Fortran is still widely used.

A group of computer manufacturers and government and industrial computer users developed *COBOL* (COmmon Business Oriented Language) in 1959. Commercial applications that manipulate large amounts of data are programmed in COBOL. Today, about half of all business software is still programmed in COBOL. Approximately one million people are actively writing COBOL programs.

Basic was developed in 1965 at Dartmouth University as a simple language to help novices learn programming. Bill Gates implemented Basic on several early personal computers. Today, *Microsoft*—the company Bill Gates created—is the world's leading software development organization. Gates has become one of the world's wealthiest people, and Microsoft is included in the list of prestigious stocks that form the Dow Jones Industrials—from which the Dow Jones Industrial Average is calculated as a measure of stock market performance.

1.5 Structured Programming

During the 1960s, many large software development efforts encountered severe difficulties. Software schedules were typically late, costs greatly exceeded budgets and the finished products were unreliable. People began to realize that software development was a far more complex activity than they had imagined. Research activity in the 1960s resulted in the evolution of *structured programming*—a disciplined approach to writing programs that are clearer than unstructured programs, easier to test and debug and easier to modify. Chapters 7–9 discuss the principles of structured programming.

One of the more tangible results of this research was the development of the Pascal programming language by Professor Nicklaus Wirth in 1971. Pascal, named after the 17th-century mathematician and philosopher Blaise Pascal, was designed for teaching structured programming in academic environments and rapidly became the preferred programming language in most universities.

The Ada programming language was developed under the sponsorship of the United States Department of Defense (DOD) during the 1970s and early 1980s. Hundreds of separate languages had been used to produce DOD's massive command-and-control software systems. DOD wanted a single language that would fulfill most of the department's needs. Pascal was chosen as a base, but the final Ada language is quite different from Pascal. The language was named after Lady Ada Lovelace, daughter of the poet Lord Byron. Lady Lovelace is generally credited with writing the world's first computer program, in the early 1800s (for the Analytical Engine mechanical computing device designed by Charles Babbage).

One important capability of Ada is called *multitasking*, which allows programmers to have many activities running simultaneously. Java, through a technique called *multithreading*, also enables programmers to write programs with parallel activities. Other widely used high-level languages such as C and C++, generally allow programs to perform only one activity at a time (although they can support multithreading through special-purpose libraries).

1.6 History of the Internet

In the late 1960s, one of the authors (HMD) was a graduate student at MIT. His research at MIT's Project Mac (now the Laboratory for Computer Science—the home of the World Wide Web Consortium) was funded by ARPA—the Advanced Research Projects Agency of the Department of Defense. ARPA sponsored a conference at which several dozen ARPA-funded graduate students were brought together at the University of Illinois at Urbana-Champaign to meet and share ideas. During this conference, ARPA rolled out the blueprints for networking the main computer systems of about a dozen ARPA-funded universities and research institutions. They were to be connected with communications lines operating at a then-stunning 56Kbps (i.e., 56,000 bits per second)—this at a time when most people (of the few who could) were connecting over telephone lines to computers at a rate of 110 bits per second. HMD vividly recalls the excitement at that conference. Researchers at Harvard talked about communicating with the Univac 1108 "supercomputer" at the University of Utah to handle calculations related to their computer graphics research. Many other intriguing possibilities were raised. Academic research was on the verge of taking a giant leap forward. Shortly after this conference, ARPA proceeded to implement the *ARPAnet*, the grandparent of today's *Internet.*

Things worked out differently from what was originally planned. Rather than the primary benefit of researchers sharing each other's computers, it rapidly became clear that enabling the researchers to communicate quickly and easily among themselves via what became known as *electronic mail* (*e-mail*, for short) was the key benefit of the ARPAnet. This is true even today on the Internet, as e-mail facilitates communications of all kinds among millions of people worldwide.

One of the primary goals for ARPAnet was to allow multiple users to send and receive information simultaneously over the same communications paths (such as phone lines). The network operated with a technique called *packet-switching*, in which digital data was sent in small packages called *packets*. The packets contained data address, error control and sequencing information. The address information allowed packets to be routed to their destinations. The sequencing information helped reassemble the packets (which, because of complex routing mechanisms, could actually arrive out of order) into their original order for presentation to the recipient. Packets from different senders were intermixed on the same lines. This packet-switching technique greatly reduced transmission costs compared with the cost of dedicated communications lines.

The network was designed to operate without centralized control. If a portion of the network should fail, the remaining working portions would still route packets from senders to receivers over alternate paths.

The protocols for communicating over the ARPAnet became known as *TCP—the Transmission Control Protocol*. TCP ensured that messages were properly routed from sender to receiver and that those messages arrived intact.

As the Internet evolved, organizations worldwide were implementing their own networks for both intraorganization (i.e., within the organization) and interorganization (i.e., between organizations) communications. A wide variety of networking hardware and software appeared. One challenge was to get these different networks to communicate. ARPA accomplished this with the development of *IP*—the *Internetworking Protocol*, truly creating a "network of networks," the current architecture of the Internet. The combined set of protocols is now commonly called *TCP/IP*.

Initially, Internet use was limited to universities and research institutions; then the military began using the Internet. Eventually, the government decided to allow access to the Internet for commercial purposes. Initially, there was resentment among the research and military communities—these groups were concerned that response times would become poor as "the Net" became saturated with users.

In fact, the exact opposite has occurred. Businesses rapidly realized that they could tune their operations and offer new and better services to their clients, so they started spending vasts amounts of money to develop and enhance the Internet. This generated fierce competition among the communications carriers and hardware and software suppliers to meet this demand. The result is that *bandwidth* (i.e., the information carrying capacity) on the Internet has increased tremendously and costs have decreased significantly. It is widely believed that the Internet has played a significant role in the economic prosperity that the United States and many other industrialized nations have enjoyed recently and are likely to enjoy for many years.

1.7 Personal Computing

In 1977, Apple Computer popularized the phenomenon of *personal computing*. Initially, it was a hobbyist's dream, but computers quickly became economical enough for people to buy for personal use. In 1981, IBM, the world's largest computer vendor, introduced the *IBM Personal Computer*, making computing legitimate in business, industry and government organizations.

However, these computers were "stand-alone" units—people did their work on their own machines and then transported disks back and forth to share information (this was called "sneakernet"). Although early personal computers were not powerful enough to timeshare several users, these machines could be linked together in computer networks, sometimes over telephone lines and sometimes in *local area networks (LANs)* within an organization. This led to the phenomenon of *distributed computing*, in which an organization's computing, instead of being performed strictly at a central computer installation, is distributed over networks to the sites at which the bulk of the organization's work is performed. Personal computers were powerful enough to handle the computing requirements of individual users and to enable the basic communications tasks of passing information back and forth electronically.

Today's most powerful personal computers are as powerful as the million dollar machines of two decades ago. Desktop computers—called *workstations*—provide individual users with enormous capabilities. Information is easily shared across computer networks in which some computers, called *servers*, offer common stores of programs and data that may be used by *client* computers distributed throughout the network—hence the term *client/server computing*. Today's popular operating systems, such as Unix, MacOS, Windows NT, Windows 2000 and Linux provide the kinds of capabilities discussed in this section.

1.8 History of the World Wide Web

The *World Wide Web* allows computer users to locate and view multimedia-based documents (i.e., documents with text, graphics, animations, audios or videos) on almost any subject. Even though the Internet was developed more than three decades ago, the introduction of the World Wide Web is a relatively recent event. In 1990, *Tim Berners-Lee* of CERN (the European Laboratory for Particle Physics) developed the World Wide Web and several communication protocols that form the backbone of the Web.

The Internet and the World Wide Web surely will be listed among the most important and profound creations of humankind. In the past, most computer applications executed on "stand-alone" computers (i.e., computers that were not connected to one another). Today's applications can be written to communicate with hundreds of millions of computers. The Internet mixes computing and communications technologies. It makes our work easier. It makes information instantly and conveniently accessible worldwide. Individuals and small businesses can receive worldwide exposure on the Internet. It is changing the nature of the way business is done. People can search for the best prices on virtually any product or service. Special-interest communities can stay in touch with one another and researchers can learn of scientific and academic breakthroughs worldwide.

1.9 World Wide Web Consortium (W3C)

In October 1994, Tim Berners-Lee founded an organization—called the *World Wide Web Consortium (W3C)*—devoted to developing nonproprietary, interoperable technologies for the World Wide Web. One of the W3C's primary goals is to make the Web universally accessible—regardless of disability, language or culture.

The W3C is also a standardization organization. Web technologies standardized by the W3C are called *Recommendations*. W3C Recommendations include the Extensible HyperText Markup Language (XHTML), Cascading Style Sheets (CSS), HyperText Markup Language (HTML; now considered a "legacy" technology) and the Extensible Markup Language (XML). A recommendation is not an actual software product, but a document that specifies a technology's role, syntax, rules, etc. Before becoming a W3C Recommendation, a document passes through three phases: *Working Draft*—which, as its name implies, specifies an evolving draft, *Candidate Recommendation*—a stable version of the document that industry may begin implementing and *Proposed Recommendation*—a Candidate Recommendation that is considered mature (i.e., has been implemented and tested over a period of time) and is ready to be considered for W3C Recommendation status. For detailed information about the W3C Recommendation process, see "6.2 The W3C Recommendation track" at

www.w3.org/Consortium/Process/Process-19991111/process.html#RecsCR

The W3C is comprised of three *hosts*—the Massachusetts Institute of Technology (MIT), Institut National de Recherche en Informatique et Automatique (INRIA) and Keio University of Japan—and over 400 *members*, including Deitel & Associates, Inc. Members provide the primary financing for the W3C and help provide the strategic direction of the Consortium.

The W3C homepage (**www.w3.org**) provides extensive resources on Internet and Web technologies. For each Internet technology with which the W3C is involved, the site provides a description of the technology and its benefits to Web designers, the history of the technology and the future goals of the W3C in developing the technology. This site also describes W3C's goals. The goals of the W3C are divided into the following categories: User Interface Domain, Technology and Society Domain, Architecture Domain and Web Accessibility Initiatives.

1.10 Hardware Trends

The Internet community thrives on the continuing stream of dramatic improvements in hardware, software and communications technologies. In general, people expect to pay at least a little more for most products and services every year. The exact opposite has been the case in the computer and communications fields, especially with regard to the hardware costs of supporting these technologies. For many decades, and with no change in the foreseeable future, hardware costs have fallen rapidly, if not precipitously. This is a phenomenon of technology, another driving force powering the current economic boom. Every year or two, the capacities of computers tend to double, especially the amount of *memory* they have in which to execute programs, the amount of *secondary memory* (such as disk storage) they have to hold programs and data over the longer term and the processor speeds—the speed at which computers execute their programs (i.e., do their work). The same has been true in the communications field, especially in recent years, with the enormous demand for communications bandwidth attracting tremendous competition. We know of no other fields in which technology moves so quickly and costs fall so rapidly.

When computer use exploded in the sixties and seventies, there was talk of huge improvements in human productivity that computing and communications would bring about. However, these productivity improvements did not materialize. Organizations were spending vast sums on computers and distributing them to their workforce, but without the expected productivity gains. It was the invention of microprocessor chip technology and its wide deployment in the late 1970s and 1980s which laid the groundwork for the productivity improvements of the 1990s that have been so crucial to economic prosperity.

1.11 Key Software Trend: Object Technology

One of the authors, HMD, remembers the frustration that was felt in the 1960s by software development organizations, especially those developing large-scale projects. During his undergraduate years, HMD had the privilege of working summers at a leading computer vendor on the teams developing time-sharing, virtual-memory operating systems. He remembers it as a great experience for a college student. In the summer of 1967, however, reality set in when the company "decommitted" from commercially producing the particular system that hundreds of people had been working on for many years. It was difficult to get this software right. Software is "complex stuff."

Hardware costs have been declining rapidly in recent years, to the point that personal computers have become a commodity. Unfortunately, software development costs have been rising steadily as programmers develop ever more powerful and complex applications without significantly improving the underlying technologies of software development.

There is a revolution brewing in the software community. Building software quickly, correctly and economically remains an elusive goal at a time when demands for new and more powerful software are soaring. *Objects* are essentially reusable software *components* that model real-world items. Software developers are discovering that using a modular, object-oriented design and implementation approach can make software development groups much more productive than is possible with previous popular programming techniques, such as structured programming. Object-oriented programs are often easier to understand, correct and modify.

Improvements to software technology did start to appear with the benefits of structured programming (and the related discipline of *structured systems analysis and design)* being realized in the 1970s. It was not until the technology of object-oriented programming became widely used in the 1980s, and especially in the 1990s, that software developers finally felt they had the tools to make major strides in the software development process.

Actually, object technology dates back at least to the mid-1960s. The C++ programming language, developed at AT&T by Bjarne Stroustrup in the early 1980s, is based on two languages: C, which was initially developed at AT&T to implement the Unix operating system in the early 1970s and Simula 67, a simulation programming language developed in Europe and released in 1967. C++ absorbed the capabilities of C and added Simula's capabilities for creating and manipulating objects.

Before object-oriented languages appeared, programming languages (such as Fortran, Pascal, Basic and C) focused on actions (verbs), rather than things or objects (nouns). This style of programming is called *procedural programming.* One of the key problems with procedural programming is that the program units programmers create do not mirror real-world entities effectively, so they are not particularly reusable. We live in a world of objects. Just look around you. Cars, planes, people, businesses, animals, buildings, traffic lights and elevators are all examples of objects. It is not unusual for programmers to "start fresh" on each new project and wind up writing similar software "from scratch." This wastes resources as people repeatedly "reinvent the wheel."

With object technology, properly designed software tends to be more reusable in future projects. Libraries of reusable components such as *MFC (Microsoft Foundation Classes)* and those produced by Rogue Wave and many other software development organizations can greatly reduce the effort it takes to implement certain kinds of systems (compared with the effort required to reinvent these capabilities on new projects).

Some organizations report that software reuse is not, in fact, the key benefit they derive from object-oriented programming. Rather, companies indicate that object-oriented programming tends to produce software that is more understandable, better organized and easier to maintain. These improvements are significant, because it has been estimated that as much as 80% of software costs are not associated with the original efforts to develop the software, but are in fact, attributed to the evolution and maintenance of that software throughout its lifetime. Whatever perceived benefits object orientation offers, it is clear that object-oriented programming will be the primary programming methodology for at least the next decade or two.

Software Engineering Observation 1.1

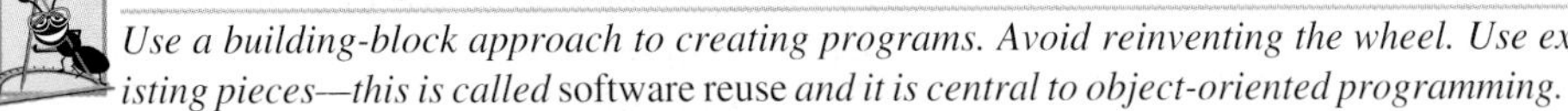

Use a building-block approach to creating programs. Avoid reinventing the wheel. Use existing pieces—this is called software reuse *and it is central to object-oriented programming.*

[*Note*: We will include many *Software Engineering Observations* throughout the text to explain concepts that affect and improve the overall architecture and quality of a software system, and particularly, of large software systems. We also highlight *Good Programming Practices* (practices that can help you write programs that are clearer, more understandable, more maintainable and easier to test and debug), *Common Programming Errors* (problems to watch out for so you do not make these same errors in your programs), *Performance Tips* (techniques that will help you write programs that run faster and use less memory), *Portability Tips* (techniques that will help you write programs that can run, with little or no modification, on a variety of computers), *Testing and Debugging Tips* (techniques that will help you remove bugs from your programs and, more important, techniques that will help you write bug-free programs in the first place) and *Look-and-Feel Observations* (techniques that will help you design the "look" and "feel" of your graphical user interfaces for appearance and ease of use). Many of these techniques and practices are only guidelines; you will, no doubt, develop your own preferred programming style.]

Performance Tip 1.2

Reusing proven code components instead of writing your own versions can improve program performance, because these components normally are written to perform efficiently.

Software Engineering Observation 1.2

Extensive class libraries of reusable software components are available over the Internet and the World Wide Web. Many of these libraries are available at no charge.

1.12 JavaScript: Object-Based Scripting for the Web

JavaScript provides an attractive package for advancing the state of programming language education, especially at the introductory and intermediate levels. JavaScript is an object-based language with strong support for proper software engineering techniques. Students learn to create and manipulate objects from the start in JavaScript. The fact that JavaScript is built into today's most popular Web browsers is appealing to colleges facing tight budgets and lengthy budget-planning cycles. Bug fixes and new versions of JavaScript are available on the Internet, so colleges can keep their JavaScript software current.

Does JavaScript provide the solid foundation of programming principles typically taught in first programming courses—the intended audience for this book? We think so.

The JavaScript chapters of this book are much more than just an introduction to the language. The chapters also present an introduction to computer programming fundamentals, including control structures, functions, arrays, recursion, strings and objects. Experienced programmers will read Chapters 7–12 quickly and master JavaScript by reading our live-code™ examples and by examining the corresponding input/output screens. Nonprogrammers will learn computer programming in these carefully paced chapters by reading the code explanations and completing a large number of exercises. We do not provide answers to all exercises, because this is a textbook—college professors use the exercises for homework assignments, labs, short quizzes, major examinations and even term projects. We do, however, provide answers to about half of the exercises in the companion product to this book called *The Internet and World Wide Web Programming Multimedia Cyber Classroom, Second Edition.* If you have the book and would like to order the CD separately, please check our Web site or the last few pages of the this book.

JavaScript is a powerful scripting language. Experienced programmers sometimes take pride in creating strange, contorted, convoluted JavaScript expressions. These make programs more difficult to read, test and debug. This book is also geared for novice programmers; for them we stress program *clarity.* The following is our first *Good Programming Practice*:

Good Programming Practice 1.1

Write your programs in a simple and straightforward manner. This is sometimes referred to as KIS ("keep it simple"). *Do not "stretch" the language by trying bizarre uses.*

You will read that JavaScript is a portable scripting language and that programs written in JavaScript can run in many different Web browsers. Actually, *portability is an elusive goal.* Here is our first *Portability Tip* and our first *Testing and Debugging Tip*:

Portability Tip 1.1

Although it is easier to write portable programs in JavaScript than in many other programming languages, differences among interpreters and browsers make portability difficult to achieve. Simply writing programs in JavaScript does not guarantee portability. The programmer occasionally needs to deal directly with platform variations.

Testing and Debugging Tip 1.1

Always test your JavaScript programs on all systems for which the programs are intended.

Good Programming Practice 1.2

Read the documentation for the JavaScript version you are using to access JavaScript's rich collection of features.

Testing and Debugging Tip 1.2

Your computer and interpreter are good teachers. If you are not sure how a feature works even after studying the documentation, experiment and see what happens. Study each error or warning message and correct it.

1.13 Browser Portability

Ensuring a consistent look and feel on client-side browsers is one of the great challenges of developing Web-based applications. Currently, a standard does not exist to which software developers must adhere when creating Web browsers. Although browsers share a common set of features, each browser can render pages differently. Browsers are available in many versions (1.0, 2.0 etc.) and on many different platforms (Unix, Microsoft Windows, Apple Macintosh, IBM OS/2, Linux etc.). Vendors add features to each new version that result in increased cross-platform incompatibility issues. Clearly it is difficult, if not impossible, to develop Web pages that render correctly on all versions of each browser. This book attempts to minimize these problems by teaching XHTML, which is widely supported by browsers.

This book focuses on platform-independent topics such as XHTML, JavaScript, Cascading Style Sheets, database/SQL/MySQL, Apache Web server, Perl/CGI, Python, PHP and XML. However, it also features many topics that are Microsoft Windows-specific, including the Internet Explorer 5.5 browser, the Adobe PhotoShop Elements graphics package for Windows, Dynamic HTML, multimedia, VBScript, Internet Information Services (IIS), database access via ActiveX Data Objects (ADO) and Active Server Pages (ASP).

Portability Tip 1.2

The Web world is highly fragmented which, makes it difficult for authors and Web developers to create universal solutions. The World Wide Web Consortium (W3C) is working toward the goal of creating a universal client-side platform.

1.14 C and C++

For many years, the Pascal programming language was preferred for introductory and intermediate programming courses. The C language evolved from a language called B, developed by Dennis Ritchie at Bell Laboratories. C was implemented in 1972, making C a contemporary of Pascal. C initially became known as the development language of the Unix operating system. Today, virtually all new major operating systems are written in C and/or C++. Over the past two decades, C has become available for most computers and is generally considered to be hardware independent.

Many people said that C was too difficult a language for the courses in which Pascal was being used. In 1992, we published the first edition of *C How to Program* to encourage universities to replace Pascal with introductory C courses. The students were able to handle C at about the same level as Pascal, but we discovered that there was one noticeable difference: Students appreciated that they were learning a language (C) likely to be valuable to them in industry. Our industry clients appreciated the availability of C-literate graduates who could work immediately on substantial projects, rather than first having to go through costly and time-consuming training programs.

Bjarne Stroustrup developed C++, an extension of C, in the early 1980s. C++ provides a number of features that "spruce up" the C language, but more importantly, it provides capabilities for object-oriented programming. C++ is a hybrid language: it is possible to program in either a C-like style (procedural programming) in which the focus is on actions, or an object-oriented style (in which the focus is on objects) or both.

One reason that C++ use has grown so quickly is that it extends C programming into the area of object orientation. For the huge community of C programmers, this has been a powerful advantage. An enormous amount of C code has been written in industry over the last several decades. Because C++ is a superset of C, many organizations find it to be an ideal next step. Programmers can take their C code, compile it, often with nominal changes, in a C++ compiler and continue writing C-like code, while mastering the object paradigm. Programmers then can migrate portions of the legacy C code into C++, as time permits. New systems can be entirely written in object-oriented C++. Such strategies have been appealing to many organizations. The downside is that even after adopting this strategy, companies tend to continue producing C-like code for many years. This, of course, means that they do not realize the full benefits of object-oriented programming and continue to produce programs that are confusing and hard to maintain due to their hybrid design. C and C++ have influenced many programming languages such as Java, Microsoft C# and JavaScript, which adopted syntax similar to C and C++ to appeal to C and C++ programmers.

1.15 Java

Intelligent consumer electronic devices may be the next major area in which microprocessors will have a profound impact. Recognizing this, Sun Microsystems funded an internal corporate research project that was code named Green in 1991. The project resulted in the development of an object-oriented, C- and C++-based language, which its creator, James Gosling, called Oak, after an oak tree outside his office window. It was later discovered that a computer language already in use was named Oak. When a group of Sun employees visited a local coffee shop, the name *Java* was suggested, and it stuck.

The Green project ran into some difficulties, the marketplace for intelligent consumer electronic devices was not developing as quickly as Sun had anticipated. Worse yet, a major contract for which Sun competed was awarded to another company. The Green project was in jeopardy of being cancelled. By sheer good fortune, the World Wide Web exploded in popularity in 1993, and the people on the Green project saw the immediate potential to use Java as a Web programming language. This breathed new life into the project.

Java allows programmers to create Web pages with dynamic and interactive content, to develop large-scale enterprise applications, to enhance the functionality of *Web servers* (software that provides the content we see in our Web browsers), to provide applications for consumer devices (such as wireless phones and personal digital assistants) and much more.

In 1995, we were carefully following Sun's development of Java. In November 1995, we attended an Internet conference in Boston in which a representative from Sun gave a rousing presentation on Java. As the talk proceeded, it became clear to us that Java would play an important part in developing Internet-based applications. Since its release, Java has become one of the most widely used programming languages in the world.

In addition to its prominence in developing Internet- and intranet-based applications, Java is certain to become the language of choice for implementing software for devices that communicate over a network. Do not be surprised when your new stereo and other devices in your home will be networked together using Java technology! Although we do not teach Java in this book, we have included as a bonus for Java programmers Chapters 30, Java Servlets and 31, JavaServer Pages. The reader interested in learning Java may wish to read our texts, *Java How to Program, Fourth Edition* and *Advanced Java 2 Platform How to Program.*

1.16 Internet and World Wide Web How to Program

In 1998, we saw an explosion of interest in the Internet and the World Wide Web. We immersed ourselves in these technologies, and a clear picture started to emerge in our minds of the next direction to take in introductory programming courses. *Electronic commerce*, or *e-commerce*, as it is typically called, began to dominate the business, financial and computer industry news. This was a total reconceptualization of the way business was conducted. We were faced with a dilemma: Should we be writing programming language principles textbooks or writing textbooks focused more on these enhanced capabilities that organizations want to incorporate into their information systems? We still wanted to teach programming principles, but we felt compelled to do it in the context of the technologies that businesses and organizations needed to create Internet-based and Web-based applications. With this realization, *Internet and World Wide Web How to Program* was born and published in December of 1999.

Internet and World Wide Web How to Program, Second Edition teaches programming languages and programming language principles. In addition, we focus on the broad range of technologies that will help you build real-world Internet-based and Web-based applications that interact with other applications and with databases. These capabilities allow programmers to develop the kinds of enterprise-level, distributed applications popular in industry today. Applications can be written to execute on any computer platform, yielding major savings in systems development time and costs. If you have been hearing a great deal about the Internet and World Wide Web lately, and if you are interested in developing applications to run over the Internet and the Web, then learning the software-development techniques discussed in this book could be the key to challenging and rewarding career opportunities for you. Please be sure to check out our Appendix F, Career Resources.

This book is intended for several academic markets, namely, the introductory course sequences in which C++, Java and Visual Basic are traditionally taught; upper-level elective courses for students who already know programming and as a supplement in introductory courses, where students are first becoming familiar with computers, the Internet and the Web. The book offers a solid one- or two-semester introductory programming experience or an extensive one-semester upper-level elective. The book is also intended for professional programmers in corporate training programs or for doing self-study.

In this book, you will learn computer programming and basic principles of computer science and information technology. You also will learn proven software-development methods that can reduce software-development costs—top-down stepwise refinement, functionalization and especially object-based programming. JavaScript is our primary programming language, a condensed programming language that is especially designed for developing Internet- and Web-based applications. Chapters 7–12 present a rich discussion of JavaScript and its capabilities, including dozens of complete, live-code™ examples followed by screen images that illustrate typical program inputs and outputs.

After you have learned programming principles from the detailed JavaScript discussions, we present condensed treatments of six other popular Internet/Web programming languages for building the server side of Internet- and Web-based client/server applications. In Chapters 25 and 26, we discuss Active Server Pages (ASP)—Microsoft's technology for server-side scripting. In Chapter 27, we introduce Perl—throughout the 1990s, Perl was the most widely used scripting language for programming Web-based applications and is certain to remain popular for many years. In Chapters 28 and 29, we introduce Python and PHP—two emerging scripting languages. In Chapters 30 and 31, we provide two bonus chapters for Java programmers on Java servlets and JavaServer Pages (JSP). We will say more about these exciting server-side programming languages momentarily.

We will publish new editions of this book promptly in response to rapidly evolving Internet and Web technologies. [*Note:* Our publishing plans are updated regularly at our Web site **www.deitel.com**. The contents and publication dates of our forthcoming publications are always subject to change. If you need more specific information, please e-mail us at **deitel@deitel.com**.]

1.17 Dynamic HTML

Dynamic HTML is geared to developing high-performance, Web-based applications in which much of an application is executed directly on the client rather than on the server. Dynamic HTML makes Web pages "come alive" by providing stunning multimedia effects that include animation, audio and video. What exactly is Dynamic HTML? This is an interesting question, because if you walk into a computer store or scan online software stores, you will not find a product by this name offered for sale. Rather, Dynamic HTML, which has at least two versions—Microsoft's and Netscape's—consists of a number of technologies that are freely available and are known by other names. Microsoft *Dynamic HTML* includes XHTML, JavaScript, Cascading Style Sheets, the Dynamic HTML Object Model and Event Model, ActiveX controls—each of which we discuss in this book—and other related technologies. Netscape *Dynamic HTML* provides similar capabilities.[1] Microsoft *Dynamic HTML* is introduced in Chapters 13–18.

1.18 Tour of the Book

In this section, we take a tour of the subjects you will study in *Internet and World Wide Web How to Program, Second Edition*. Many of the chapters end with an Internet and World Wide Web Resources section that provides a listing of resources through which you can enhance your knowledge and use of the Internet and the World Wide Web. In addition, you may want to visit our Web site **www.deitel.com** for additional resources.

Chapter 1—Introduction to Computers and the Internet

In Chapter 1, we present historical information about computers and computer programming and introductory information on the Internet and the World Wide Web. We also overview the technologies and concepts discussed in the remaining chapters of the book.

Chapter 2—Microsoft® Internet Explorer 5.5[2]

Prior to the explosion of interest in the Internet and the World Wide Web, if you heard the term *browser,* you probably thought about browsing at a bookstore. Today "browser" has a whole new meaning—an important piece of software that enables you to view Web pages. The two most popular browsers are Microsoft's Internet Explorer and Netscape's Commu-

1. Microsoft Dynamic HTML and Netscape Dynamic HTML are incompatible. In this book, we focus on Microsoft Dynamic HTML. We have tested all of the Dynamic HTML examples in Microsoft Internet Explorer 5.5 and Netscape® Communicator® 6. All of these examples execute in Microsoft Internet Explorer; most do not execute in Netscape Communicator 6. We have posted the testing results at **www.deitel.com**. In this book, the material we present in Chapter 19, Macromedia® Flash™, executes properly in both of the latest Microsoft and Netscape browsers.
2. We provide a comparable chapter on Netscape Communicator 6 at **www.deitel.com**.

nicator. Throughout this book, we use Internet Explorer 5.5, but we provide a solid introduction to Netscape Communicator 6 at **www.deitel.com**. Using tools included with Internet Explorer, we demonstrate how to use the Web. These tools include, but are not limited to, the Web browser, e-mail, newsgroups (i.e., where users can post messages on a variety of topics to the general public) and instant messaging, which allows users to communicate over the Internet in real time. This chapter shows readers unfamiliar with the World Wide Web how to browse the Web with Internet Explorer. We demonstrate several commonly used features for searching the Web, keeping track of the sites you visit and transferring files between computers. We also discuss several programs included with Internet Explorer. We demonstrate sending and receiving e-mail, and using Internet newsgroups with Microsoft *Outlook Express*. We demonstrate MSN *Instant Messenger*, which enables almost instant conferencing with friends, family and coworkers. We demonstrate Microsoft *NetMeeting* and Microsoft *Chat* for having live meetings and discussions with other people on the Internet. The chapter concludes with a discussion of browser *plug-ins* that provide access to the ever-increasing number of programs and features that make browsing more enjoyable and interactive.

Chapter 3—Adobe® PhotoShop® Elements

The Internet and World Wide Web are rich in multimedia content. Web pages contain colorful graphics, sounds and text. Graphics are an essential element of Web-page design that convey visual information about a site's contents. In this chapter, we introduce *Adobe PhotoShop Elements*, a graphics software package that contains an extensive set of tools and features for creating high-quality graphics and animations. These tools and features include filters for applying special effects and screen capturing for taking "snap shots" of the screen. Chapter examples demonstrate creating title images for a Web page, creating a navigation bar that contains a series of buttons used to connect a Web site's pages and manipulating images by using advanced photographic effects. We focus on creating and manipulating the two most popular image formats used in Web documents: *Graphics Interchange Format (GIF)* and *Joint Photographic Expert Group (JPEG)* files. [*Note*: Readers can download a 30-day evaluation copy of PhotoShop Elements from **www.adobe.com/support/downloads**. The chapter examples were developed using that version of PhotoShop Elements.]

Chapter 4—Introduction to XHTML: Part 1

In this chapter, we unlock the power of Web-based application development by introducing *XHTML*—the *Extensible Hypertext Markup Language*. XHTML is a *markup language* for identifying the elements of an XHTML document (or Web page) so that a browser can render (i.e., display) that document on a computer screen. We introduce basic XHTML Web-page creation using a technique we call the live-code™ approach. Every concept is presented in the context of a complete working XHTML document. We render each working example in Internet Explorer and show the screen outputs. We present many short Web pages that demonstrate XHTML features. Later chapters introduce more sophisticated XHTML techniques, such as *tables*, which are useful for formatting information retrieved from a database. We introduce XHTML *tags* and *attributes*, which describe the document's information. A key issue when using XHTML is the separation of the *presentation of a document* (i.e., how the document is rendered on the screen by a browser) from the *structure of the information in that document* (i.e., the information the document contains). This chapter introduces our in-depth discussion of this issue. As the book proceeds, you will be able to create appealing and powerful Web pages and Web-based applications. Other topics in this chapter include incorporating text, images and special characters (such as copyright and trademark symbols) into an XHTML document, validating an XHTML document to ensure that it is written correctly, placing information inside *lists*, separating parts of an XHTML document with horizontal lines (called *horizontal rules*) and linking to other XHTML documents on the Web. In one of the chapter exercises, we ask readers to mark up their resume with XHTML.

Chapter 5—Introduction to XHTML: Part 2

In this chapter, we discuss more substantial XHTML elements and features. We demonstrate how to present information in *tables* and how to gather user input. We explain and demonstrate *internal linking* and *image maps* to make Web pages more navigable and how to use *frames* to display multiple XHTML documents in a browser. *XHTML forms* are one of the most important features introduced in this chapter—forms display information to the user and accept user input. By the end of this chapter, readers should be familiar with the most popular XHTML tags and features used to create Web sites.

Chapter 6—Cascading Style Sheets (CSS)

Web browsers control the appearance (i.e., the rendering) of every Web page. For instance, one browser may render an **`h1`** (i.e., a large heading) element in an XHTML document differently than another browser. With the advent of *Cascading Style Sheets (CSS)*, Web developers can control the appearance of their Web pages. CSS allows Web developers to specify the style of their Web page's elements (spacing, margins etc.) separately from the structure of their pages (section headers, body text, links etc.). This *separation of structure from content* allows greater manageability and makes changing document styles easier and faster. We introduce *inline*, *embedded* and *external* style sheets. Inline style sheets are applied to individual XHTML elements, embedded style sheets are entire style sheets placed directly inside an XHTML document and external style sheets are style sheets located outside an XHTML document.

Chapter 7—JavaScript:[3] Introduction to Scripting

Chapter 7 presents our first JavaScript *programs*[4] (also called *scripts*). Scripting helps Web pages "come alive." Web developers dynamically manipulate Web-page elements through scripting as clients browse Web pages. Chapters 7–12 present JavaScript, which is then used in Chapters 13–18 to manipulate Web-page content. We present the key fundamental computer-science concepts of JavaScript at the same depth as we do in our other books on

3. Netscape created JavaScript; the Microsoft version is called JScript. The two scripting languages are similar. Netscape, Microsoft and other companies cooperated with the European Computer Manufacturer's Association (ECMA) to produce a universal, client-side scripting language, which is referred to as ECMA-262. JavaScript and JScript each conform to this standard.

4. The book's JavaScript examples execute in Microsoft Internet Explorer 5.5. We have tested these examples on the following clients: Internet Explorer 5.5, Internet Explorer 6 Beta and Netscape Communicator 6. For those few examples that do not execute in Netscape Communicator 6, we have (when possible) created Netscape Communicator 6 equivalent examples. These examples and the test results are available at **`www.deitel.com`**.

conventional programming languages (such as C, C++, C#, Java and Visual Basic), but in the exciting context of the Internet and World Wide Web. Using our live-code™ approach, we present every concept in the context of a working JavaScript program that is immediately followed by the screen output. The chapter introduces nonprogrammers to basic programming concepts and constructs. The scripts in this chapter illustrate how to output text to a browser and how to obtain user input through the browser. Some of the input and output is performed using the browser's capability to display predefined *graphical user interface (GUI)* windows (called *dialogs*). This allows nonprogrammers to concentrate on fundamental programming concepts and constructs rather than on GUI components and on GUI *event handling*. Chapter 7 also provides detailed treatments of *decision making* and *arithmetic operations*.

Chapter 8—JavaScript: Control Structures 1

Chapter 8 focuses on the program-development process. The chapter discusses how to develop a working JavaScript program from a *problem statement* (i.e., a *requirements document*). We show the intermediate steps using, a program development tool called *pseudocode*. The chapter introduces some simple control structures used for decision making (**`if`** and **`if/else`**) and repetition (**`while`**). We examine countercontrolled repetition and sentinel-controlled repetition and introduce the increment, decrement and assignment operators. Simple flowcharts illustrate graphically the flow of control through each of the control structures. This chapter helps the student develop good programming habits in preparation for the more substantial programming tasks in the remainder of the book.

Chapter 9—JavaScript: Control Structures 2

Chapter 9 discusses much of the material JavaScript has in common with the C programming language, especially the *sequence*, *selection* and *repetition* control structures. Here, we introduce one additional control structure for decision making (**`switch`**) and two additional control structures for repetition (**`for`** and **`do/while`**). This chapter also introduces several operators that allow programmers to define complex conditions in their decision-making and repetition structures. The chapter uses flowcharts to illustrate the flow of control through each of the control structures, and concludes with a summary that enumerates each of the structures. The techniques discussed in this chapter and in Chapter 10 constitute a large part of what has been traditionally taught in universities under the topic of structured programming.

Chapter 10—JavaScript: Functions

Chapter 10 takes a deeper look inside scripts. Scripts contain data called *global* (or *script-level*) *variables* and executable units called *functions*. We discuss JavaScript functions, programmer-defined functions and *recursive* functions (i.e., functions that call themselves). The techniques presented in Chapter 10 are essential to produce properly structured programs, especially large programs that Web developers are likely to build in real-world, Web-based applications. The *divide-and-conquer* strategy is presented as an effective means for solving complex problems by dividing them into simpler, interacting components. The chapter offers a solid introduction to recursion and includes a table summarizing the many recursion examples and exercises in Chapters 10–12. We introduce *events* and *event handling*—elements required for programming graphical user interfaces (GUIs) in XHTML forms. Events are notifications of state changes, such as button clicks, mouse clicks, pressing keyboard keys, etc. JavaScript allows programmers to respond to various events by coding functions called *event handlers*. This begins our discussion of *event-driven programming*—the user drives the program by interacting with GUI components (causing *events such as mouse clicks*), and the scripts respond to the events by performing appropriate tasks (*event handling*). The event-driven programming techniques introduced here are used in scripts throughout the book. Dynamic HTML event handling is introduced in Chapter 14. Chapter 10 contains a rich set of exercises that include the Towers of Hanoi, computer-aided instruction and a guess-the-number game.

Chapter 11—JavaScript: Arrays

Chapter 11 explores the processing of data in lists and tables of values. We discuss the structuring of data into *arrays*, or groups, of related data items. The chapter presents numerous examples of both single-subscripted arrays and double-subscripted arrays. It is widely recognized that structuring data properly is as important as using control structures effectively in the development of properly structured programs. Examples in the chapter investigate various common array manipulations, searching arrays, sorting data and passing arrays to functions. This chapter introduces JavaScript's **`for/in`** control structure, which interacts with collections of data stored in arrays. The end-of-chapter exercises include a variety of interesting and challenging problems, such as the *Sieve of Eratosthenes* and the design of an airline reservations system. The chapter exercises also include a delightful simulation of the classic race between the tortoise and the hare.

Chapter 12—JavaScript: Objects

This chapter discusses *object-based programming* with JavaScript's built-in objects. The chapter introduces the terminology of objects. We overview the methods (functions associated with particular objects) of the JavaScript **`Math`** object and provide several examples of JavaScript's string-, date- and time-processing capabilities with the **`String`** and **`Date`** objects. An interesting feature of the **`String`** object is a set of methods that help a programmer output XHTML from a script by enclosing strings in XHTML elements. The chapter also discusses JavaScript's **`Number`** and **`Boolean`** objects. Many of the features discussed in this chapter are used in Chapters 13–18 to illustrate that every XHTML element is an object that can be manipulated by JavaScript statements. Many challenging, yet entertaining, string-manipulation exercises are included.

Chapter 13—Dynamic HTML:[5] DHTML Object Model and Collections

A massive switch is occurring in the computer industry. The procedural programming style used since the inception of the industry is being replaced by the object-oriented style of programming. The vast majority of new software efforts use object technology in one form or another. The scripting languages we discuss in this book usually manipulate existing objects by sending messages that either inquire about the objects' attributes or ask the objects to perform certain actions. In this chapter, we continue the discussion of object technology

---

5. Microsoft Dynamic HTML and Netscape Dynamic HTML are incompatible. In this book, we focus on Microsoft Dynamic HTML. We have tested all of the Dynamic HTML examples in Internet Explorer 5.5 and Netscape Communicator 6. All of these examples execute in Internet Explorer, but do not execute in Netscape Communicator 6. We have posted the testing results at **`www.deitel.com`**. In this book, we also present Macromedia® Flash™, which executes in Internet Explorer and Netscape Communicator 6.

by presenting Microsoft's Dynamic HTML object model. As Internet Explorer downloads a Web page from a server, it converts each element to an object. Objects store data (their attributes) and perform functions (their methods). Through scripting languages such as JavaScript, you can write commands that *get* or *set* (i.e., read or write) an object's attributes. You can also write commands that invoke an object's methods. The chapter exercises provide the opportunity to program the classic "15-puzzle" game.

Chapter 14—Dynamic HTML: Event Model
We have discussed how scripting can control XHTML pages. Dynamic HTML includes *event models* that enable scripts to respond to user actions. This allows Web applications to be more responsive and user friendly, and can it reduce server load—a performance concern we discuss in Chapters 21–31 on server-side programming. With the event model, scripts can respond to a user moving or clicking the mouse, scrolling up or down the screen or entering keystrokes. Content becomes more dynamic, while interfaces become more intuitive. We discuss how to use the event model to respond to user actions. We provide examples of event handling, which range from mouse capture to error handling to form processing. For example, we call the **`onreset`** event to confirm that a user wants to reset the form (i.e., the GUI in which the user inputs data). For one of the chapter exercises, the reader creates an interactive script that displays an image alongside the mouse pointer. When the mouse pointer is moved, the image moves with it.

Chapter 15—Dynamic HTML: Filters and Transitions
Internet Explorer includes a set of filters that allow developers to perform complex image transformations entirely in the Web browser without the need for additional downloads from a Web server. Filters are scriptable, so the developer can create stunning, customized animations with a few lines of client-side JavaScript. We introduce the **`fliph`** and **`flipv`** filters, which mirror text and images horizontally and vertically. We explain the **`gray`**, **`xray`** and **`invert`** filters, which all apply simple transformations to images. We introduce many of the filters that apply effects such as shadows, transparency gradients and distortions. Internet Explorer enables *transitions* that are similar to transitions between slides in PowerPoint-like presentations. The **`revealTrans`** filter applies visual effects such as *box in*, *circle out*, *wipe left*, *vertical blinds*, *checkerboard across*, *random dissolve*, *split horizontal in*, *strips right up* and *random bars horizontal*. This chapter also introduces the **`blendTrans`** filter, which allows you to fade in or fade out of an XHTML element over a set interval.

Chapter 16—Dynamic HTML: Data Binding with Tabular Data Control
This is one of the most important chapters in the book for people who want to build substantial, real-world Web-based applications. Businesses thrive on data, and Dynamic HTML helps Web developers build data-intensive applications. With *data binding*, data does not reside exclusively on the server. Data are sent from the server to the client, and all subsequent manipulations of the data occur on the client. Data can be maintained on the client in a manner that distinguishes the data from the XHTML markup. Manipulating data on the client improves performance by eliminating server activity and network delays. Once data is available on the client, the data can be *sorted* (i.e., arranged into ascending or descending order) and *filtered* (i.e., selected according to some criterion) in various ways. We present examples of each of these operations. To bind external data to XHTML ele-

ments, Internet Explorer employs software capable of connecting the browser to live data sources, known as *Data Source Objects (DSOs)*. Several DSOs are available in Internet Explorer—in this chapter, we discuss the most popular DSO, *Tabular Data Control (TDC)*.

Chapter 17—Dynamic HTML: Structured Graphics ActiveX Control
Although high-quality content is important to a Web site, it does not attract or maintain visitors' attention like eye-catching, animated graphics. This chapter explores the *Structured Graphics ActiveX Control* included with Internet Explorer. The Structured Graphics Control is a Web interface for the *DirectAnimation* subset of Microsoft's *DirectX* software. DirectAnimation is used in many popular video games and graphical applications. This control allows you to create complex graphics containing lines, shapes, textures and fills. In addition, scripting allows the graphics to be manipulated dynamically. The exercises at the end of the chapter ask the reader to create three-dimensional shapes and rotate them.

Chapter 18—Dynamic HTML: Path, Sequencer and Sprite ActiveX Controls
In this chapter, we discuss three additional DirectAnimation ActiveX controls available for Internet Explorer: the *Path Control*, the *Sequencer Control* and the *Sprite Control*. Each of these controls allow Web developers to add animated multimedia effects to Web pages. The Path Control allows the user to determine the positioning of elements on the screen. This is more elaborate than CSS absolute positioning, because the user can define lines, ovals and other shapes as paths along which objects move. Every aspect of motion is controllable through scripting. The Sequencer Control performs tasks at specified time intervals. This is useful for presentationlike effects, especially when used with the transitions discussed in Chapter 15. The Sprite Control creates Web animations. We also discuss, for comparison purposes, animated GIFs—another technique for producing Web-based animations.

Chapter 19—Macromedia® Flash™: Creating Interactive Web Pages
Macromedia Flash[6] is a cutting-edge multimedia application that creates interactive content for the World Wide Web. Through hands-on examples, this chapter shows how to add interactivity, sound and animation to Web sites, while teaching the fundamentals of Macromedia Flash and *ActionScript*, Flash's scripting language. The chapter examples include creating interactive buttons, animated banners and animated splash screens (called *animation preloaders*). The exercises ask the reader to create a navigation bar, a spotlight effect and a morphing effect. The morphing effect exercise in particular is a wonderful illustration of the power of Flash. Readers will enjoy watching text transform into a shape and back.

Chapter 20—Extensible Markup Language (XML)
Throughout the book, we have been emphasizing XHTML. This language derives from SGML (Standardized General Markup Language), which became an industry standard in 1986. SGML is employed in publishing applications worldwide, but it has not been incorporated into mainstream computing and information technology curricula. Its sheer size and complexity limit its use beyond heavy-duty, industrial-strength applications. The Ex-

6. Many browsers, including Internet Explorer 5.5 and Netscape Communicator 6, support Macromedia Flash content. All of the functionality in this chapter has been tested on, and properly works on both Internet Explorer 5.5 and Netscape Communicator 6. Some Web developers prefer Flash to Dynamic HTML. Some use both.

tensible Markup Language (XML) is an effort to make SGML-like technology available to a much broader community. XML, a condensed subset of SGML, contains additional features for usability. XML differs in concept from XHTML. XHTML is a markup language, and XML is a language for *creating* markup languages. XML enables document authors to create their own markup for virtually any type of information. As a result, document authors use this extensibility to create entirely new markup languages to describe specific types of data, including mathematical formulas, chemical molecular structures, music and recipes. Markup languages created with XML include XHTML (Chapters 4 and 5), MathML (for mathematics), VoiceXML™ (for speech), SMIL™ (the Synchronized Multimedia Integration Language, for multimedia presentations), CML (Chemical Markup Language, for chemistry) and XBRL (Extensible Business Reporting Language, for financial data exchange). XML is a technology created by the World Wide Web Consortium for describing data in a portable format. XML is one of most important technologies in industry today and is being integrated into almost every field. Every-day, companies and individuals are finding new and exciting uses for XML. In this chapter, we present examples that illustrate the basics of marking up data using XML. We demonstrate several XML-derived markup languages, such as MathML, CML, *XML Schema* (for checking an XML document's grammar), *XSLT (Extensible Stylesheet Language Transformations,* for transforming an XML document's data into an XHTML document) and Microsoft's *BizTalk*™ (for marking up business transactions). The reader interested in a deeper treatment of XML may want to consider our book, *XML How to Program.*

Chapter 21—Web Servers (IIS, PWS and Apache)

Through Chapter 20, we have focused on the client side of Web-based applications. Chapters 21–31 focus on the server side, discussing many technologies crucial to implementing successful Web-based systems. A Web server is part of a *multitiered application*—sometimes referred to as an *n*-tier application. A three-tier application contains a *data tier (bottom tier), middle tier* and *client tier (top tier).* The bottom tier is an organization's database. The middle tier receives client requests from the top tier, references the data stored in the bottom tier and sends the requested information to the client. The client tier renders a Web page and executes any scripting commands contained in the Web page. A crucial decision in building Web-based systems is which Web server to use. The *Apache Web Server* and Microsoft *Internet Information Services (IIS)* are the two most popular Web servers used in industry. Each of these is an "industrial-strength" server designed to handle the high volumes of transactions that occur in real-world systems. They require considerable system resources and administrative support. To help people enter the world of server programming, Microsoft provides *Personal Web Server (PWS)*—a scaled-down version of IIS. In this chapter, we provide a brief introduction to IIS, PWS and Apache. We provide installation instructions for these Web servers at **www.deitel.com**. We discuss how to request XHTML, ASP, Perl, Python and PHP documents from these Web servers when using Internet Explorer. The chapter concludes by listing some additional Web servers that are available on the Internet. *[Note: The world of server software is complex and evolving quickly. Our goal in this chapter is to give you a "handle" on setting up and using server-side software. Deitel & Associates, Inc., does not provide software support for these servers. We suggest that you browse the Web sites we list at the end of this chapter for organizations that may provide such support.]*

Chapter 22—Database: SQL, MySQL, DBI and ADO
The vast majority of an organizations' data is stored in databases. In this chapter, we introduce databases as well as the *Structured Query Language (SQL)* for making database queries. The chapter also introduces *MySQL*, an open source, enterprise-level database server, and highlights several key features of this database server. We provide a list of data objects that access MySQL through various programmatic libraries called *database interfaces* (DBIs). We specifically discuss DBIs for Perl, Python and PHP. In addition, a brief discussion of Microsoft's version of data storage, called *universal database access (UDA)*, is provided. A key UDA component is ActiveX Data Objects (ADO), which we introduce in this chapter and use in Chapter 25, Active Server Pages. ADO provides a set of objects used by Microsoft languages such as Visual Basic, Visual C++, C# and Active Server Pages to interact with databases. We list additional resources related to MySQL and Microsoft Access at **`www.deitel.com`**.

Chapter 23—Wireless[7] Internet Technology
In Chapter 23, we discuss the impact of wireless communications on individuals and businesses. We investigate mobile business applications such as shipping and tracking. We explore location-identification technologies and the services they enable, including wireless marketing and advertising. Privacy issues, related to the ability to locate a user, are carefully examined. The chapter then explores wireless devices and communications technologies and introduces wireless programming. The *Wireless Application Protocol (WAP)* is designed to enable different kinds of wireless devices to communicate and access the Internet using the *Wireless Markup Language* (*WML*). WML tags mark up a Web page to specify how the page is to be formatted on a wireless device. WMLScript helps WAP applications "come alive" by allowing a developer to manipulate WML document content dynamically. In addition to WAP/WML, we explore various platforms and programming languages, such as *Java 2 Micro Edition (J2ME)*, *Qualcomm's Binary Runtime Environment for Wireless (BREW)*, *i-mode*, *Compact HyperText Markup Language* (*cHTML)* and *Bluetooth™ wireless technology.*

Chapter 24—VBScript
JavaScript has become the de facto standard for *client-side scripting*. All major browsers support this language, which has been standardized through the *European Computer Manufacturers Association* as *ECMA-262*. *Visual Basic Scripting Edition* (VBScript) is a scripting language developed by Microsoft. Although it is not supported by many leading browsers, *plug-ins* help some of those browsers understand and process VBScript. VBScript, however, is the most widely used language for writing Active Server Pages (ASP)—a server-side technology we discuss in Chapters 25 and 26. Chapter 24 prepares you to use VBScript on the client side in Microsoft communities and in Microsoft-based *intranets* (i.e., internal networks that use the same communications protocols as the Internet). It will also prepare you to use VBScript to program Active Server Pages in the next two chapters.

Chapter 25—Active Server Pages (ASP)
This chapter introduces Microsoft's Active Server Pages (ASP), the first of the six server-side software development paradigms we discuss. Active Server Pages can be programmed in a variety of languages—by far the most popular is Microsoft's VBScript (Chapter 24). Active Server Pages implement middle-tier business logic. In this chapter, we introduce the

7. The reader interested in a deeper treatment of wireless Internet programming may want to consider our book, *Wireless Internet and Mobile Business How to Program*.

reader to *dynamic content generation* (i.e., the process by which a scripting language generates an XHTML document, an XML document etc.). Chapter examples include a wide range of server-side programming topics, such as writing text files, querying an Access database and using server-side ActiveX controls to extend Web server functionality. Key examples include an ASP document that allows users to create Web pages, a guestbook application and an ASP document that displays information about the client's browser. This is a crucial chapter for those readers who want to implement Web-based applications by using Microsoft technologies.

Chapter 26—Case Study: Active Server Pages and XML

In this chapter, we build on the material presented in Chapter 25 by creating an online message forum using ASP. Message forums are "virtual" bulletin boards in which users discuss a variety of topics. The case study presented allows users to post messages to an existing forum and to create new forums. Each forum's data are stored in XML documents that are dynamically manipulated using ASP. This chapter ties together many of the technologies presented earlier in the book, including XHTML, CSS, ASP, XML and XSLT. Chapter exercises ask the reader to modify the case study to delete individual messages from a forum and to delete individual forums.

Chapter 27—Perl and CGI[8] (Common Gateway Interface)

Historically, the most widely used server-side technology for developing Web-based applications has been Perl/CGI. Despite the emergence of newer technologies such as Active Server Pages (Chapters 25 and 26), Python (Chapter 28), PHP (Chapter 29), Java Servlets (Chapter 30) and JavaServer Pages (Chapter 31), the Perl community is well entrenched, and Perl will remain popular for the foreseeable future. Chapter 27 presents an introduction to Perl/CGI, including many real-world, live-code™ examples and discussions, and demonstrations of some of the most recent features of each of these technologies. Key examples demonstrate how to interact with a MySQL database and *regular expressions* (i.e., statements that efficiently search strings for patterns of characters).

Chapter 28—Python[9]

In this chapter, we introduce Python, an interpreted, cross-platform, object-oriented, general-purpose programming language. We begin by presenting basic syntax, data types, control structures and functions. We then introduce *lists* (i.e., data structures similar to a JavaScript array), *tuples* (i.e., immutable lists) and *dictionaries*, which are high-level data structures that store pairs of related data items. String processing and regular expressions are discussed, as is *exception handling*, which provides a structured mechanism for recovering from run-time errors. Chapter examples include implementing an XHTML registration form and showing how to use *cookies* (i.e., small text files written to the client machine). In addition, a three-tier Web-based example queries a MySQL database for author information.

8. The reader interested in a deeper treatment of Perl and CGI may want to consider our book, *Perl How to Program.*
9. The reader interested in a deeper treatment of Python may want to consider our book, *Python How to Program.*

Chapter 29—PHP

In this chapter, we introduce PHP, another popular server-side scripting language for Web-based application development. Similar to Perl and Python, PHP has a large community of users and developers. We begin the chapter by introducing basic syntax, data types, operators and arrays, string processing and regular expressions. Chapter examples include form processing and business logic, connecting to a database and writing cookies. The chapter examples include a three-tier Web-based application that queries a MySQL database.

Chapter 30—Java™ Servlets (Bonus Chapter for Java Developers)

Java servlets represent a fifth popular way of building server-side Web-based applications. Servlets are written in Java (not JavaScript), which requires a substantial book-length treatment to learn. We do not teach Java in *Internet and World Wide Web How to Program: Second Edition*. This chapter (from our book *Advanced Java 2 Platform How to Program*)[10] is provided as a "bonus chapter" for readers familiar with Java. Readers who want to learn Java may want to consider reading our book *Java How to Program, Fourth Edition*.

Chapter 31—JavaServer™ Pages (Bonus Chapter for Java Developers)

In this chapter (from our book *Advanced Java 2 Platform How to Program*), we introduce *JavaServer Pages (JSP)*—an extension of Java servlet technology. JavaServer Pages enable Web-application programmers to create dynamic Web content, using familiar XML syntax and scripting with Java. Using JavaServer Pages, Web-application programmers can create *custom tag libraries* that encapsulate complex and dynamic functionality in XML tags. Web-page designers who are not familiar with Java can use these custom tag libraries to integrate information from databases, business-logic components and other resources into dynamically generated Web pages. This chapter is provided as a "bonus" chapter for readers familiar with Java. Readers who want to learn Java may want to consider reading our book *Java How to Program, Fourth Edition*.

Chapter 32—E-Business and E-Commerce

Chapter 32 explores the world of e-business and e-commerce. It begins by discussing the various business models associated with e-businesses. These include storefronts, auctions, portals, dynamic pricing, comparison shopping and demand-sensitive and name-your-price models. We also discuss the management and maintenance of an e-business, which includes advertising and marketing, accepting online payments, securing online transactions and understanding legal issues. We address such topics as branding, e-advertising, customer relationship management, e-wallets, micropayments, privacy and copyright. We also discuss security topics, including public-key cryptography, *Secure Socket Layer (SSL)* and wireless security. The final section in this chapter discusses the emergence of XML and how it enables the standardization of business transactions worldwide.

Chapter 33—Multimedia: Audio, Video, Speech Synthesis and Recognition

This chapter focuses on the explosion of audio, video and speech technology appearing on the Web. We discuss adding sound, video and animated characters to Web pages (primarily using existing audio and video clips). Your first reaction may be a sense of caution, because these

---

10. This book also discusses Java 2 Enterprise Edition, Java 2 Micro Edition (J2ME), XML, Peer-to-Peer, Java3D, security, Java Database Connectivity (JDBC), Jini and many other advanced topics.

are complex technologies about which most readers have had little education. You quickly will see how easy it is to incorporate multimedia into Web pages and control multimedia components with Dynamic HTML. Multimedia files can be large. Some multimedia technologies require that an entire multimedia file be downloaded to the client before the audio or video begins playing. With *streaming audio* and *streaming video* technologies, audio and video can begin playing while the files are downloading, thus reducing delays. Streaming technologies are popular on the Web. This chapter demonstrates how to incorporate the *RealNetworks RealPlayer* into a Web page to receive streaming media. The chapter also includes an extensive set of Internet and Web resources that discuss interesting ways in which designers use multimedia-enhanced Web pages. This chapter introduces an exciting technology called *Microsoft Agent* for adding *interactive animated characters* to an XHTML document. *Agent characters* include *Peedy the Parrot, Genie, Merlin* and *Robby the Robot,* as well as those created by third-party developers. Each character allows users to interact with the application, using more natural human communication techniques such as speech. The agent characters accept mouse and keyboard interaction, speak and hear (i.e., they support speech synthesis and speech recognition). With these capabilities, your Web pages can speak to users and can actually respond to their voice commands! Microsoft Agent is included on the CD-ROM that accompanies this book. The chapter exercises ask the reader to create a karaoke machine and to incorporate an agent character into a Web page.

Chapter 34—Accessibility

Currently, the World Wide Web presents a challenge to individuals with disabilities. Multimedia-rich Web sites are difficult for text readers and other programs to interpret, especially for deaf users and users with visual impairments. To rectify this situation, the World Wide Web Consortium (W3C) launched the *Web Accessibility Initiative (WAI),* which provides guidelines for making Web sites accessible to people with disabilities. This chapter provides a description of these guidelines, such as the use of the `<headers>` tag to make tables more accessible to page readers, the `alt` attribute of the `<img>` tag to describe images, and XHTML and CSS to ensure that a page can be viewed on any type of display or reader. We also introduce *VoiceXML* and *CallXML,* two technologies for increasing the accessibility of Web-based content. VoiceXML helps people with visual impairments to access Web content via speech synthesis and speech recognition. CallXML allows users with visual impairments to access Web-based content through a telephone. In the chapter exercises, readers create their own voicemail applications using CallXML.

Appendix A—XHTML Special Characters

This appendix shows many commonly used XHTML special characters, called *character entity references* by the World Wide Web Consortium (W3C).

Appendix B—Operator Precedence Chart

This appendix contains a JavaScript operator precedence chart.

Appendix C—ASCII Character Set

This appendix contains a table of the 128 ASCII alphanumeric symbols.

Appendix D—Number Systems

This appendix explains the binary, octal, decimal and hexadecimal number systems. It shows how to convert between bases and perform mathematical operations in each base.

Appendix E—XHTML Colors

This appendix explains how to create colors by using either color names or hexadecimal RGB values. Included is a table that matches colors to values.

Appendix F—Career Resources

The Internet presents valuable resources and services for job seekers and employers. Automatic search features allow employees to scan the Web for open positions. Employers also can find job candidates by using the Internet. This greatly reduces the amount of time spent preparing and reviewing resumes, as well as travel expenses for distance recruiting and interviewing. In this chapter, we explore career services on the Web from the perspectives of of job seekers and employers. We introduce comprehensive job sites, industry-specific sites (including sites geared specifically for Java and wireless programmers) and contracting opportunities, as well as additional resources and career services designed to meet the needs of a variety of individuals.

Appendix G—Unicode®

This appendix introduces the *Unicode Standard*, an encoding scheme that assigns unique numeric values to the world's characters. It includes an XML-based example that uses Unicode encoding to print a welcome message in 10 different languages.

Well, there you have it! We have worked hard to create this book and its optional interactive multimedia *Cyber Classroom* version. The book is loaded with hundreds of working, live-code™ examples, programming tips, self-review exercises and answers, challenging exercises and projects and numerous study aids to help you master the material. The technologies we introduce will help you write Web-based applications quickly and effectively. As you read the book, if something is not clear or if you find an error, please write to us at **deitel@deitel.com**. We will respond promptly, and we will post corrections, clarifications and additional materials on our Web site

www.deitel.com

Prentice Hall maintains **www.prenhall.com/deitel**—a Web site dedicated to our Prentice Hall textbooks, multimedia packages and Web-based e-learning training products. For each of our books, the site contains "Companion Web Sites" that include frequently asked questions (FAQs), sample downloads, errata, updates, additional self-test questions, Microsoft® PowerPoint® slides and other resources.

You are about to start on a challenging and rewarding path. We hope you enjoy learning with *Internet and World Wide Web How to Program, Second Edition* as much as we enjoyed writing it!

1.19 Internet and World Wide Web Resources

www.deitel.com

Please check this site for updates, corrections and additional resources for all Deitel & Associates, Inc., publications.

www.learnthenet.com/english/index.html

Learn the Net is a Web site containing a complete overview of the Internet, the World Wide Web and the underlying technologies. The site contains much information appropriate for novices.

www.w3.org
The World Wide Web Consortium (W3C) Web site offers a comprehensive description of the Web and where it is headed. For each Internet technology with which the W3C is involved, the site provides a description of the technology, its benefits to Web designers, the history of the technology and the future goals of the W3C in developing the technology. This site is of great benefit for understanding the technologies of the World Wide Web.

www.ukans.edu/cwis/units/coms2/class/intro/index.htm
This University of Kansas Web site gives a comprehensive overview of the Internet and World Wide Web, with an interactive slide presentation of each topic covered.

members.tripod.com/~teachers/index.html
This site introduces novices to the Internet and the World Wide Web, targeting users who will be surfing the Web in a classroom setting.

www.ed.gov/pubs/OR/ConsumerGuides/internet.html
The U.S. Department of Education's Consumer Guide provides a clear, concise tutorial on the structure, content and compatibilities of the Internet and the Web.

SUMMARY

[Note: Because this chapter is primarily a summary of the rest of the book, we have not provided a summary section. In each of the remaining chapters, we provide a detailed summary of the points covered in that chapter.]

TERMINOLOGY

ActionScript
Active Server pages (ASP)
ActiveX Data Objects (ADO)
Ada
ALU (arithmetic and logic unit)
Apache Web Server
arithmetic and logic unit (ALU)
ARPA
ARPANet
array
assembly language
bandwidth
Basic
Binary Runtime Environment (BREW)
bottom tier
browser
C
C++
CallXML
Cascading Style Sheets (CSS)
central processing unit (CPU)
client
client/server computing
client-side scripting
COBOL
compiler
computer
computer program
computer programmer
cookie
CPU (central processing unit)
data binding
Data Source Object (DSO)
data tier
database
Database Interface (DBI)
disk
divide-and-conquer strategy
dynamic content
Dynamic HTML
ECMA-262
e-commerce
editor
event-driven programming
execute phase
filter
filtering data
Fortran
function
hardware
high-level language
i-mode

input device
input unit
input/output (I/O)
Internet
Internet Explorer 5.5
Internet Information Services (IIS)
interpreter
intranet
IP (Internet Protocol)
Java
Java 2 Micro Edition (J2ME)
Java Servlet
JavaScript
JavaServer Pages (JSP)
JScript
KIS (keep it simple)
live-code™ approach
machine language
memory unit
method
Microsoft
Microsoft Agent
Microsoft's Internet Explorer Web browser
middle tier
multimedia
multitasking
multithreading
MySQL database
Netscape's Communicator
object
object-based programming (OBP)
object-oriented programming (OOP)
output device
output unit
Pascal
Path Control
Perl
personal computing
Personal Web Server (PWS)
PhotoShop Elements
PHP
presentation of a document
primary memory
problem statement
procedural programming
programming language
Python
reusable components
regular expression
secondary storage unit
Sequencer Control
server-side scripting
software
software reuse
sorting data
speech
Sprite Control
streaming audio and video
structure of a document
Structured Graphics Control
structured programming
Sun Microsystems
syntax error
TCP (Transmission Control protocol)
TCP/IP
top tier
transition
translator program
Unicode
Unicode Standard
VBScript (Visual Basic Scripting Edition)
VoiceXML
W3C Recommendation
Web server
Wireless Markup Language (WML)
WMLScript
World Wide Web (WWW)
World Wide Web Consortium (W3C)
XHTML (Extensible Hypertext Markup Language)
XHTML form
XML (Extensible Markup Language)

SELF-REVIEW EXERCISES

1.1 Fill in the blanks in each of the following statements:

a) The company that popularized personal computing was __________.
b) The computer that made personal computing legitimate in business and industry was the __________.
c) Computers process data under the control of sets of instructions called __________.
d) The six key logical units of the computer are the __________, __________, __________, __________, __________ and __________.

e) The three classes of languages discussed in the chapter are _________, _________ and _________.

f) The programs that translate high-level language programs into machine language are called _________.

1.2 Fill in the blanks in each of the following statements:

a) The _________ programming language was created by Professor Nicklaus Wirth and was intended for academic use.

b) One important capability of Ada is called _________; this allows programmers to specify that many activities are to occur in parallel.

c) The _________ is the grandparent of what is today called the Internet.

d) The information-carrying capacity of a communications medium like the Internet is called _________.

e) The acronym TCP/IP stands for _________.

1.3 Fill in the blanks in each of the following statements.

a) The _________ allows computer users to locate and view multimedia-based documents on almost any subject over the Internet.

b) _________ of CERN developed the World Wide Web and several of the communications protocols that form the backbone of the Web.

c) _________ are essentially reusable software components that model items in the real world.

d) C initially became widely known as the development language of the _________ operating system.

e) In a client/server relationship, the _________ requests that some action be performed and the _________ performs the action and responds.

ANSWERS TO SELF-REVIEW EXERCISES

1.1 a) Apple. b) IBM Personal Computer. c) programs (or scripts). d) input unit, output unit, memory unit, arithmetic and logic unit, central processing unit, secondary storage unit. e) machine languages, assembly languages, high-level languages. f) compilers.

1.2 a) Pascal. b) multitasking. c) ARPAnet. d) bandwidth. e) Transmission Control Protocol/ Internet Protocol.

1.3 a) World Wide Web. b) Tim Berners-Lee. c) Objects. d) Unix. e) client, server.

EXERCISES

1.4 Categorize each of the following items as either hardware or software:

a) CPU
b) compiler
c) ALU
d) interpreter
e) input unit
f) an editor program

1.5 Why might you want to write a program in a machine-independent language instead of a machine-dependent language? Why might a machine-dependent language be more appropriate for writing certain types of programs?

1.6 Fill in the blanks in each of the following statements:

a) Which logical unit of the computer receives information from outside the computer for use by the computer? _________.

b) The process of instructing the computer to solve specific problems is called __________.
c) What type of computer language uses English-like abbreviations for machine language instructions? __________.
d) Which logical unit of the computer sends information that has already been processed by the computer to various devices so that the information may be used outside the computer? __________.
e) Which logical unit of the computer retains information? __________.
f) Which logical unit of the computer performs calculations? __________.
g) Which logical unit of the computer makes logical decisions? __________.
h) The level of computer language most convenient to the programmer for writing programs quickly and easily is __________.
i) The only language that a computer can directly understand is called that computer's __________.
j) Which logical unit of the computer coordinates the activities of all the other logical units? __________.

1.7 Fill in the blanks in each of the following statements:
a) The two most popular World Wide Web browsers are Netscape Communicator and Microsoft __________.
b) A key issue when using XHTML is the separation of the presentation of a document from the __________ of that document.
c) A function associated with a particular object is called a __________.
d) With the advent of __________ Style Sheets, you can now take control of the way the browsers render your pages.
e) The data of an object is also referred to as that object's __________.
f) Visual effects such as *Box in*, *Circle out*, *Wipe left*, *Vertical blinds*, *Checkerboard across*, *Random dissolve*, *Split horizontal in*, *Strips right up* and *Random bars horizontal* are all examples of Internet Explorer 5.5 __________.
g) The process of arranging data into ascending or descending order is called __________.

1.8 Fill in the blanks in each of the following statements:
a) The __________ Control allows you to perform tasks at specified time intervals.
b) With __________ audio and video technologies, audios and videos can begin playing while the files are downloading, thus reducing delays.
c) The __________ scripting language has become the *de facto* standard for writing server-side Active Server Pages.
d) The acronym XML stands for the __________ Markup Language.
e) The two most popular Web Servers are __________ and __________.
f) In a three-tier Web-based application, the __________ tier renders a Web page and executes scripting commands.
g) MathML and CML are markup languages created from __________.

Microsoft® Internet Explorer 5.5

Objectives

- To become familiar with the Microsoft Internet Explorer 5.5 (IE5.5) Web browser's capabilities.
- To be able to use IE5.5 to search the "world of information" available on the World Wide Web.
- To be able to use Microsoft Outlook Express to send and receive e-mail.
- To be able to use Microsoft NetMeeting for online conferences with friends and colleagues.
- To be able to use the Internet as an information tool.

Give us the tools, and we will finish the job.
Sir Winston Spencer Churchill

We must learn to explore all the options and possibilities that confront us in a complex and rapidly changing world.
James William Fulbright

Outline

2.1 Introduction to the Internet Explorer 5.5 Web Browser

The Internet is an essential medium for communicating and interacting with people worldwide. The need to publish and share information has fueled the rapid growth of the Web. *Web browsers* are software programs that allow users to access the Web's rich multimedia content. Whether for business or for personal use, millions of people use Web browsers to access the tremendous amount of information available on the Web.

The two most popular Web browsers are Microsoft's *Internet Explorer* and Netscape's *Communicator*. This chapter focuses on the features of Internet Explorer (IE5.5) to view, exchange and transfer information, such as images, messages and documents, over the Internet. We provide an equivalent chapter-length treatment on Netscape Communicator 6 at our Web site, **www.deitel.com**.

2.2 Connecting to the Internet

A computer alone is not enough to access the Internet. In addition to Web browser software, the computer needs specific hardware and a connection to an Internet Service Provider to view Web pages. This section describes the necessary components that enable Internet access.

First, a computer must have a *modem* or *network card*. A modem is hardware that enables a computer to connect to a *network*. A modem converts data to audio tones and transmits the data over phone lines. A network card, also called a *network interface card* (*NIC*), is hardware that allows a computer to connect to the Internet through a network or a high-speed Internet connection such as a *cable modem* or a *Digital Subscriber Line (DSL)*.

After ensuring that a computer has a modem or network card, the next step is to register with an *Internet Service Provider* (ISP). Computers connect to an ISP using a modem and phone line or a NIC using DSL or cable modem. The ISP connects computers to the Internet. Many college campuses have free network connections available. If a network connection is not available, then popular commercial ISPs such as America Online (**www.aol.com**), Microsoft Network (**essentials.msn.com/access**) and NetZero (**www.netzero.com**) are alternatives.

Bandwidth and cost are two considerations when deciding on which commercial ISP service to use. Bandwidth refers to the amount of data that can be transferred through a communications medium in a fixed amount of time. Different ISPs offer different types of high-speed connections, called *broadband connections* that include DSL, cable modem, *Integrated Services Digital Network (ISDN)* and the slower *dial-up connections*, each of which has different bandwidths and costs to users.

Broadband is a category of high-bandwidth Internet service that is most often provided by cable television and telephone companies to home users. DSL is a broadband service that allows computers to be constantly connected to the Internet over existing phone lines, without interfering with voice services. However, DSL requires a special modem that is acquired from the ISP. Like DSL, cable modems enable the computer to be connected to the Internet at all times. Cable modems transmit data over the cables that bring television to homes and businesses. Unlike DSL, the bandwidth is shared among many users. This sharing can reduce the bandwidth available to each person when many use the system simultaneously. ISDN provides Internet service over either digital or standard telephone lines. ISDN requires specialized hardware, called a *terminal adaptor (TA)*, which is usually obtained from the ISP.

Dial-up service shares an existing telephone line. If the computer is connected to the Internet, users usually cannot receive voice calls during this time. If the voice calls do connect, the Internet connection is interrupted. To prevent this, users often have an extra phone line installed, dedicated to Internet service.

Once a network connection is established, IE5.5's **Internet Connection Wizard** (ICW) can be used to configure the computer to connect to the Internet. Access the ICW through the **Start** menu. Select the **Accessories** option in the **Programs** menu, then **Communications** and **Internet Connection Wizard**. Use the connection information provided by the ISP and follow the instructions in the ICW dialog (Fig. 2.1). Click **Tutorial** to learn more about the Internet and its features. Once ICW finishes, the computer can connect to the Internet.

2.3 Internet Explorer 5.5 Features

A Web browser is software that allows users to view certain types of Internet files in an interactive environment. Figure 2.2 shows the Deitel Web page on the Prentice Hall Web site using IE5.5 Web browser. The *URL (Uniform Resource Locator* or *Universal Resource Locator*), is **http://www.prenticehall.com/deitel/** found in the **Address** bar. The URL is the address of the Web page displayed in the browser window. Each Web page on the Internet is associated with a unique URL. URLs usually begin with **http://** , which stands for *HyperText Transfer Protocol* (*HTTP*), the industry standard for transferring Web documents over the Internet.

Several methods are available to navigate between different URLs. In one method, a user clicks the **Address** field and types a Web page's URL. The user then presses *Enter* or clicks **Go** to request the Web page located at that URL. For example, to visit *Yahoo!'s* Web site, type **www.yahoo.com** in the **Address** bar and press the *Enter* key. IE5.5 adds the **http://** prefix to the Web site name because HTTP is the protocol used for the Web.

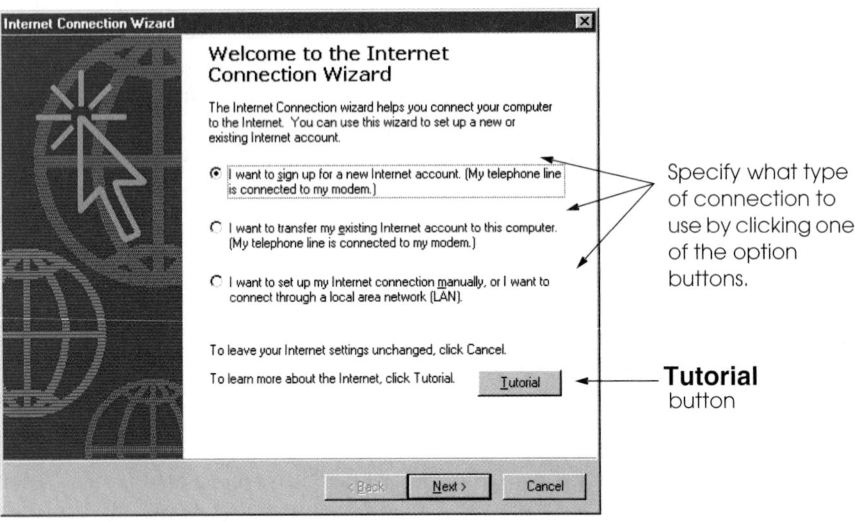

Fig. 2.1 Using the **Internet Connection Wizard** to access the Internet.

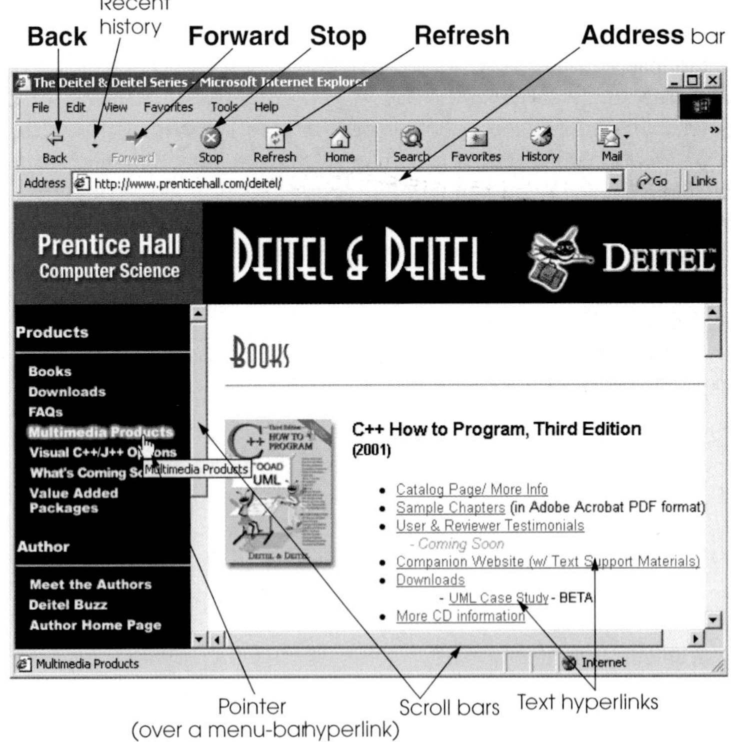

Fig. 2.2 Prentice Hall Web site. (Courtesy of Prentice Hall, Inc.).

Another way to navigate the Web is via visual elements on Web pages called *hyperlinks* that, when clicked, load a specified Web document. Both images and text may be hyperlinked. When the mouse pointer hovers over a hyperlink, the default arrow pointer changes into a hand with the index finger pointing upward. Often hyperlinked text appears as a different color than the text that is not hyperlinked. Originally used as a publishing tool for scientific research, hyperlinking creates the effect of the "Web."

Hyperlinks can reference other Web pages, e-mail addresses and files. If a hyperlink is an e-mail address, clicking the link loads the computer's default e-mail program and opens a *message window* addressed to the specified recipient's e-mail address. E-mail is discussed later in this chapter.

If a hyperlink references a file that the browser is incapable of displaying, the browser prepares to *download* the file by prompting the user for information. When a file is downloaded, it is copied onto the user's computer. Programs, documents, images and sound files are all examples of downloadable files.

IE5.5 maintains a *history* list of previously visited URLs in chronological order. This feature allows users to return to recently visited Web sites easily.

The history feature can be accessed several different ways. The simplest and most frequently used methods are to click the ***Forward*** and ***Back*** buttons located at the top of the browser window (Fig. 2.2). The **Back** button reloads the previously viewed page into the browser. The **Forward** button loads the next URL from the history into the browser.

When users view frequently updated Web pages, they should click the **Refresh** button to load the most current version. If a URL is not loading correctly or is slow, click the **Stop** button to stop loading the Web page.

The user can view the last/next nine URLs visited by clicking the down-arrows immediately to the right of both the **Back** and **Forward** buttons; the user can then request a page at a given URL by clicking that URL.

Clicking the **History** button (Fig. 2.3) divides the browser window into two sections: the **`History`** window and the content window. The **History** window lists the URLs visited in the past 30 days.

The **History** window contains heading levels ordered chronologically. Within each time frame (e.g., **Today**) headings are alphabetized by site directory name. This window is useful for finding previously visited URLs without having to remember the exact URL. Selecting a URL from the **History** window loads the Web page into the content window. The **History** window can be resized by clicking and dragging the vertical bar that separates it from the content window.

URLs from the history are displayed in a drop-down list when a user types a URL into the **Address** bar. This feature is called *Autocomplete*. Any URL from this drop-down list can be selected with the mouse to load the Web page at that URL into the browser (Fig. 2.4).

For some users, such as those with dial-up connections, maintaining a connection for long periods of time may not be practical. For this reason, Web pages can be saved directly to the computer's hard drive for *off-line* browsing (i.e., browsing while not connected to the Internet). Select **Save As** from the **File** menu at the top of the browser window to save a Web page and all its components (e.g., images, etc.).

Individual images from a Web site can also be saved by clicking the image with the right mouse button and selecting **Save Picture As...** from the displayed *context menu* (Fig. 2.5).

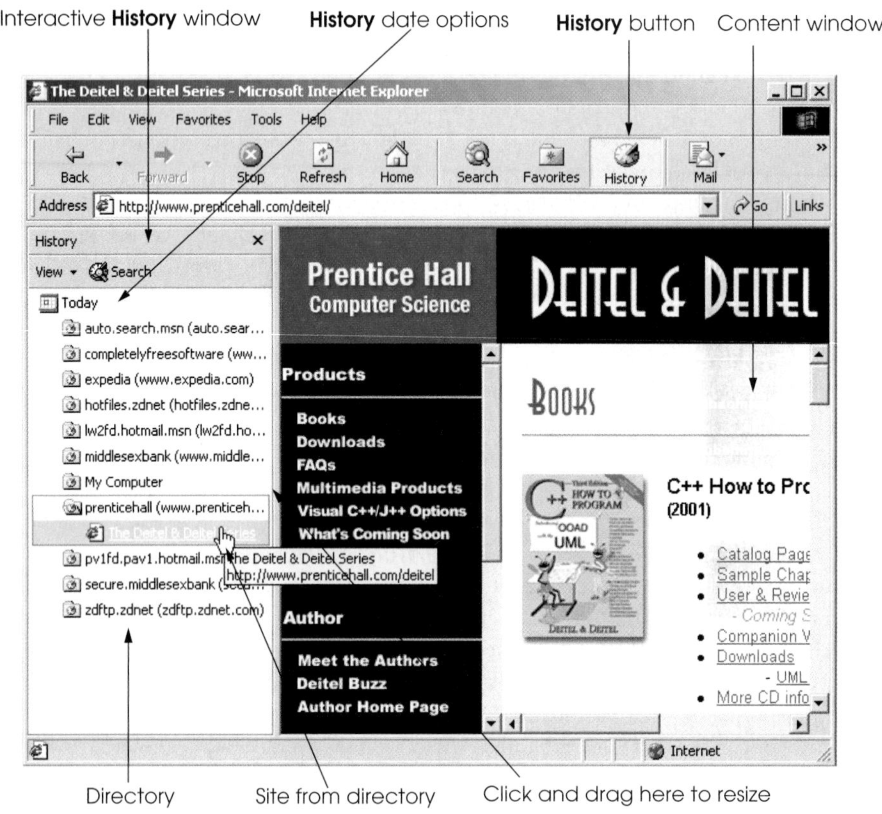

Fig. 2.3 Using the **History** menu to navigate to previously visited Web sites (Courtesy of Prentice Hall, Inc.).

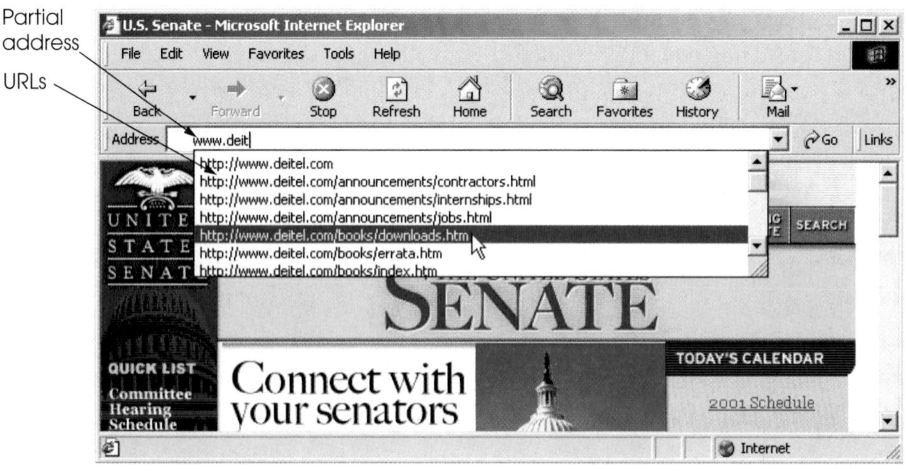

Fig. 2.4 Using the *Autocomplete* feature to enter URLs.

Fig. 2.5 Saving a picture from a Web site. (Courtesy of Prentice Hall, Inc.)

2.4 Searching the Internet

The Internet provides a wealth of information on virtually any topic. You might think that the volume of information would make it difficult for users to find specific information. To help users locate information, many Web sites provide *search engines* that explore the Internet and maintain searchable records containing information about Web sites. This section explains how search engines work and discusses two types of search engines.

Search engines such as *Google* (**www.google.com**), *Yahoo!* (**www.yahoo.com**), *Altavista* (**www.altavista.com**) or *HotBot* (**www.hotbot.com**) store information in data repositories called *databases*, which allow for quick retrieval of information. When the user enters a word or phrase, the search engine returns a list of hyperlinks to sites that satisfy the search criteria. Each search-engine site has different criteria for narrowing searches such as publishing date, language and relevance. Using multiple search engines may provide the best results.

Other sites, such as *Microsoft Network* (**www.msn.com**), use *metasearch engines*, which do not maintain databases. Instead, they send the search criteria to other search engines and aggregate the results. IE5.5 has a built-in metasearch engine that is accessed by clicking the **Search** button on the toolbar (Fig. 2.6). As with the history feature, the browser window divides into two sections, with the **Search** window on the left and the content window on the right. Several predefined searching categories are provided. Type the keyword for which you are searching and click the **Search** button. The search results appear as hyperlinks in the search window. Clicking a hyperlink loads the Web page at that URL into the content window.

2.5 Online Help and Tutorials

Web browsers are complex pieces of software with rich functionality. Although browser vendors make every effort to produce user-friendly software, users still need time to familiarize themselves with each Web browser and its particular features. Answers to frequently asked questions about using the Web browser are included with IE5.5. This information is accessible through the online tour and built-in help feature available in the **Help** menu (Fig. 2.7).

When **Tour** is selected from the **Help** menu, the Web browser loads a document from Microsoft's Web site. The page features an expanded version of the tour available from the **Internet Connection Wizard**. The tour includes an overview of the Internet, browsers and IE5.5.

A good source for locating help about a specific feature is the **Contents and Index** menu item accessible through the **Help** menu. When **Contents and Index** is selected, the ***Microsoft Internet Explorer Help*** dialog is displayed. The **Contents** tab organizes the help topics by category, the **Index** tab contains an alphabetical list of **Help** topics and the **Search** tab provides capabilities for searching the help documents.

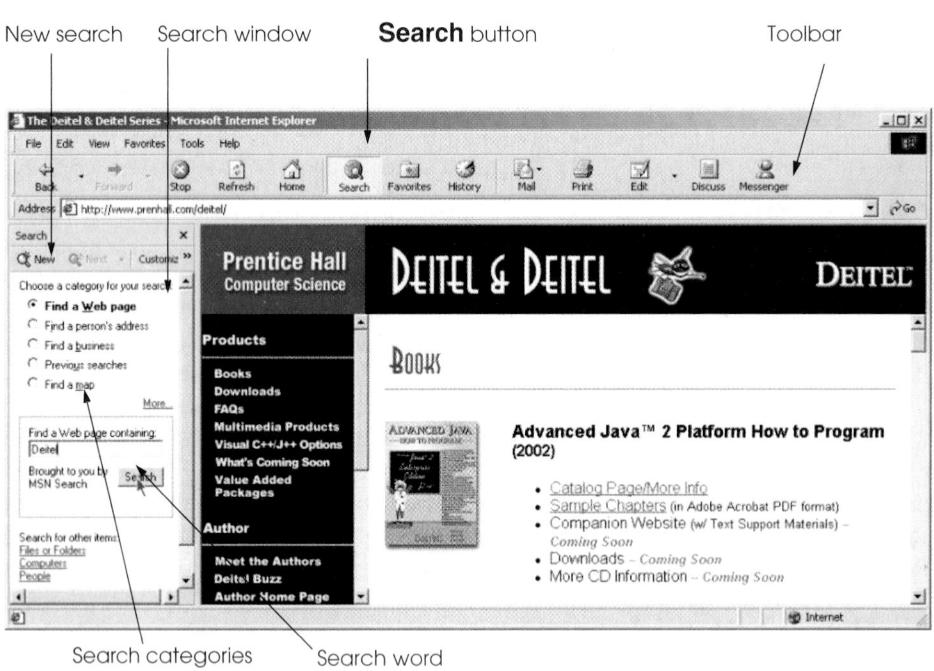

Fig. 2.6 Searching the Internet with IE5.5. (Courtesy of Prentice Hall, Inc.)

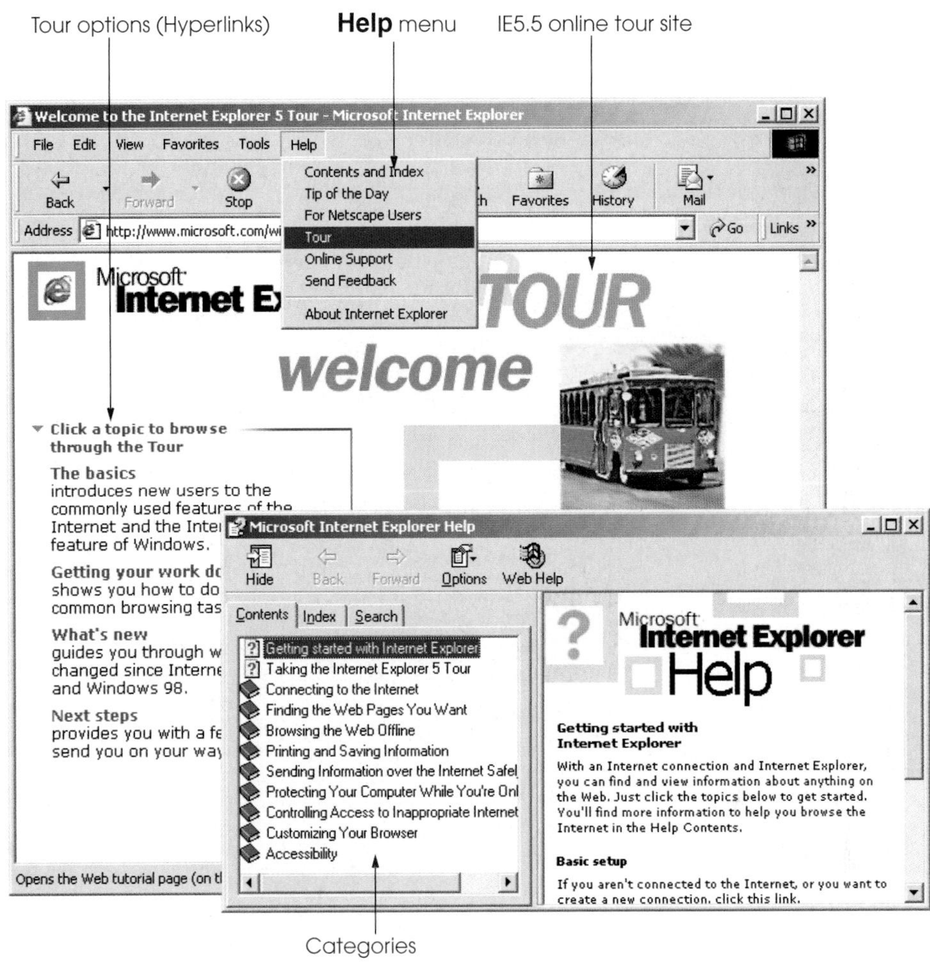

Fig. 2.7 IE5.5 online **Tour** and **Help** windows.

2.6 Keeping Track of Favorite Sites

As users browse the Web, they often visit certain sites repeatedly. Internet Explorer provides a feature called *favorites* for bookmarking such sites (Fig. 2.8). Any page's URL can be added to the list of favorites using the **Favorites** menu's **Add to Favorites...** command.

Favorites can be categorized by grouping them into folders and can be accessed at any time by selecting them with the mouse. Favorites can be renamed, moved and deleted in the **Organize Favorites** dialog. This dialog is displayed when **Organize Favorites...** is selected from the **Favorites** menu. For each favorite, the **Organize Favorites** dialog displays information about how frequently that page is visited. Favorites may also be saved for off-line browsing.

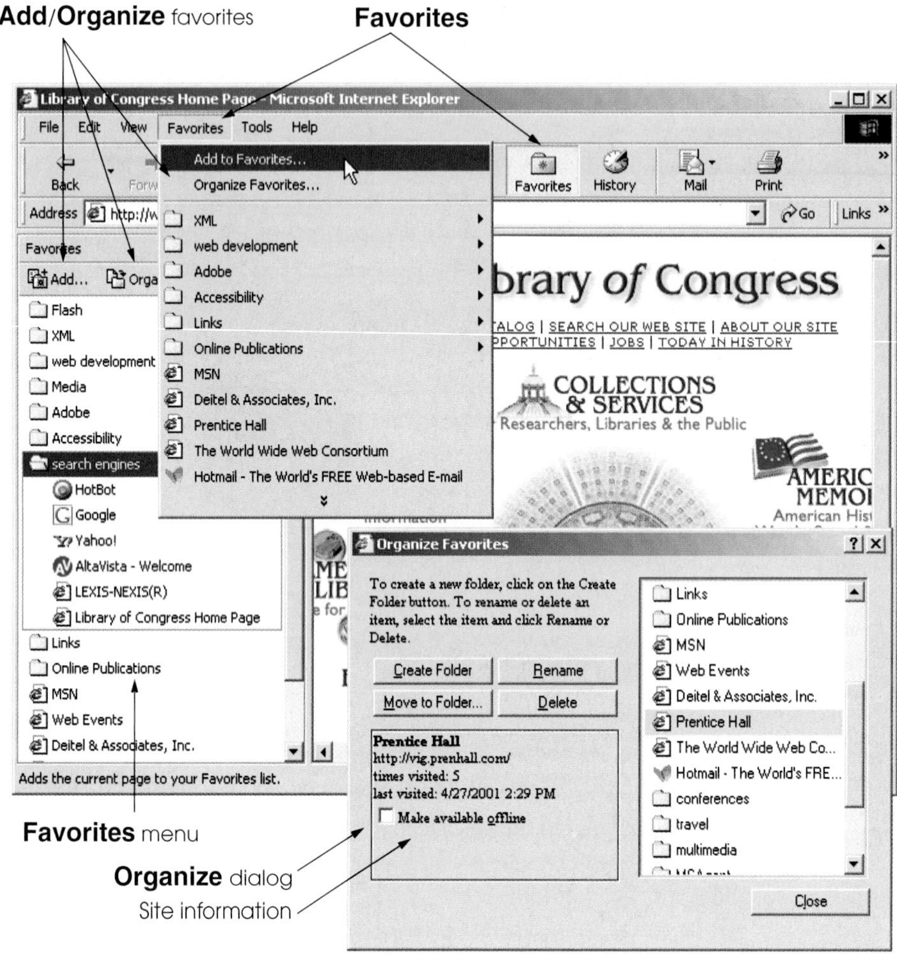

Fig. 2.8 Using the **Favorites** menu to organize frequently visited Web sites. (Courtesy of Library of Congress.)

2.7 File Transfer Protocol (FTP)

As mentioned earlier, files from the Internet may be copied to a computer's hard drive by a process called *downloading*. This section discusses the types of documents commonly downloaded from the Internet and methods of downloading them.

The most common Internet downloads are *applications* (i.e., software that performs specific functions such as word processing) and *plug-ins*. Plug-ins are specialized pieces of software that extend other applications, such as IE5.5, by providing additional functionality. An example of an IE5.5 plug-in is the *Acrobat Reader*® from *Adobe*®, *Inc.* (**www.adobe.com**), which allows users to view *PDF* (*Portable Document Format*) documents that otherwise cannot be rendered by the browser. Another popular plug-in is *Macromedia Shockwave*, which adds audio, video and animation effects to a Web site. To view sites enabled with Shockwave, visit **www.shockwave.com**. Normally the browser prompts the user to download a plug-in when one is needed. Plug-ins may also be downloaded from CNET (**www.download.com**) or from **www.plugins.com**. These sites have large, searchable indexes and databases of almost every plug-in program available for download on the Internet.

When browsing the Web, downloading is initiated by clicking a hyperlink that references a document at an *FTP* (*file transfer protocol*) site. FTP is an older, but still popular, protocol for transferring information, especially large files, over the Internet.

An FTP site's URL begins with ***ftp://***, rather than **http://**. FTP sites are typically accessed via hyperlinks (Fig. 2.9), but can also be accessed by any software that supports FTP. Such software may or may not use a Web browser.

When the browser is pointed to an FTP site's URL, the contents of the specified site directory appear on the right side of the screen, with FTP information on the left. Two types of icons appear in the directory: files and directories. Files are downloaded by right clicking their icons, selecting **Copy to Folder...** and specifying the locations where the files are to be saved.

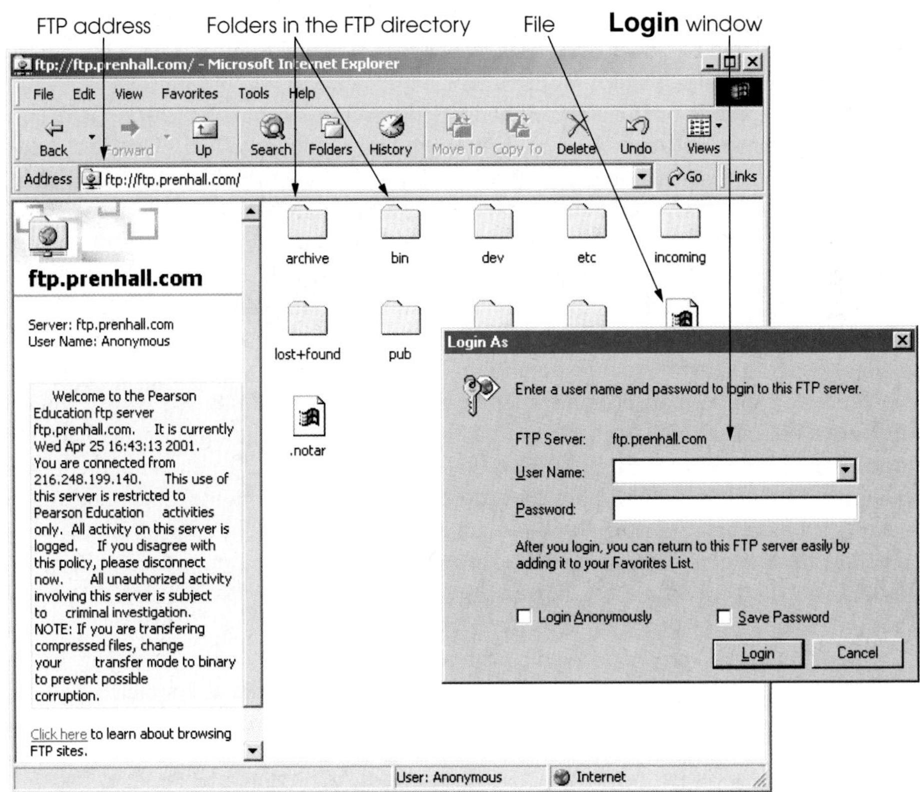

Fig. 2.9 Using IE5.5 to access an FTP site.

When a user visits an FTP site, IE5.5 sends the user's e-mail address and name (which is set by default to **anonymous**) to the site. This procedure occurs on FTP sites with *public access*, where any user is permitted access. Many FTP sites on the Internet have *restricted access*; only users with authorized user names and passwords are permitted to access such sites. When a user is trying to enter a restricted-access FTP site, a dialog like the one in Fig. 2.9 is displayed, prompting the user for login information.

Transferring a file from the local machine to another location on the Internet is called *uploading* and can be accomplished using the FTP protocol. To place information on a Web site, the files must be uploaded to a specific restricted-access FTP server (this is dependent on the ISP). The process involves uploading the file to a directory on the FTP site that is accessible through the Web.

2.8 Outlook Express and Electronic Mail

Electronic mail (*e-mail* for short) is a method of sending and receiving formatted messages and files over the Internet to other people. Depending on Internet traffic, an e-mail message can go anywhere in the world in as little as a few seconds. Internet Service Providers issue e-mail addresses in the form *username@domainname* (e.g., **deitel@deitel.com**). Many e-mail programs are available, such as *Pegasus Mail* and *Eudora*. This section introduces Microsoft's *Outlook Express* (Fig. 2.10).

Outlook Express's opening screen is divided into three panes: **Folders**, **Contacts** and a content pane. **Folders** contains directories for organizing e-mail. **Contacts** contains online contacts added using the MSN Messenger Service, which allows users to send text and voice messages over the Internet. We discuss the MSN Messenger Service in detail in Section 2.10. When starting Outlook Express for the first time, it is necessary to provide information about your ISP connection and e-mail accounts. This dialog asks for the names of the incoming and outgoing *e-mail servers*. These names are addresses of servers located at the ISP that administer incoming and outgoing e-mail. The server addresses can be obtained from the network administrator.

More than one e-mail account may be managed with *Outlook Express*. Click the **Accounts** option in the **Tools** menu to add new accounts. This displays the **Internet Accounts** dialog shown in Fig. 2.10. This dialog lists all accounts (a number of predefined accounts appear in this dialog). Click the **Add** button in the upper-right corner of the dialog to add a new account. Selecting **Mail** sets up an e-mail account. The screen shots in Fig. 2.11 show the e-mail account setup dialog at various points in the setup process. Selecting **News** sets up a *newsgroup* account. Newsgroups allow users to post and respond to messages on a wide variety of topics.

Outlook Express provides a graphical interface (Fig. 2.12) for managing e-mail accounts. When messages are received, they are saved on the local computer. Outlook Express checks for new messages several times per hour (this frequency can be changed depending on a user's preference). When a new e-mail message arrives, it is placed in the **Inbox**.

Outlook Express contains buttons for creating e-mails, replying to e-mails and forwarding e-mails. The right side of the window contains a chronological list of e-mails from the selected folder (Fig. 2.12).

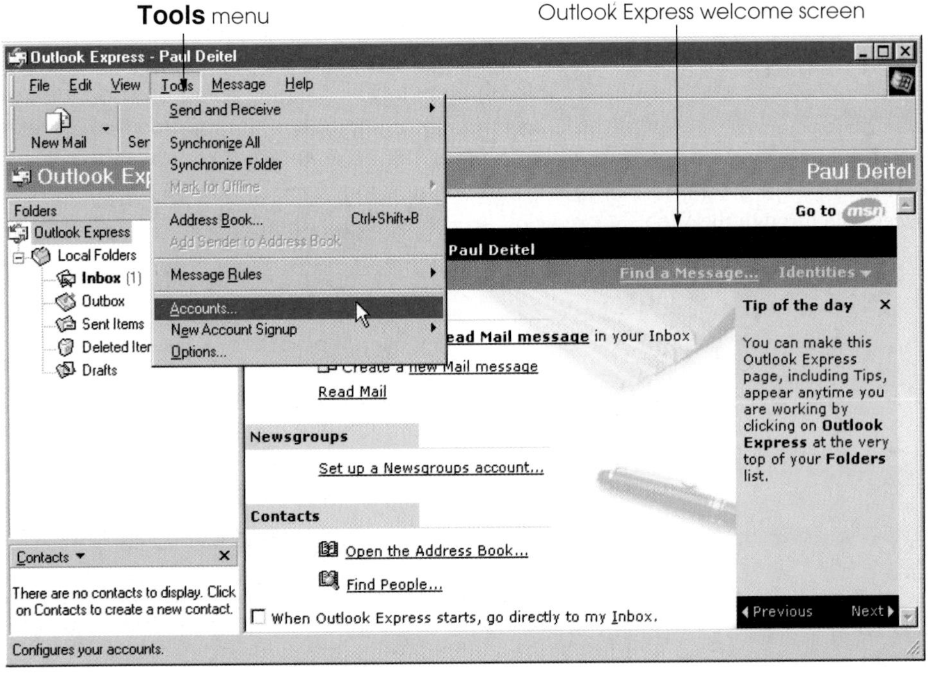

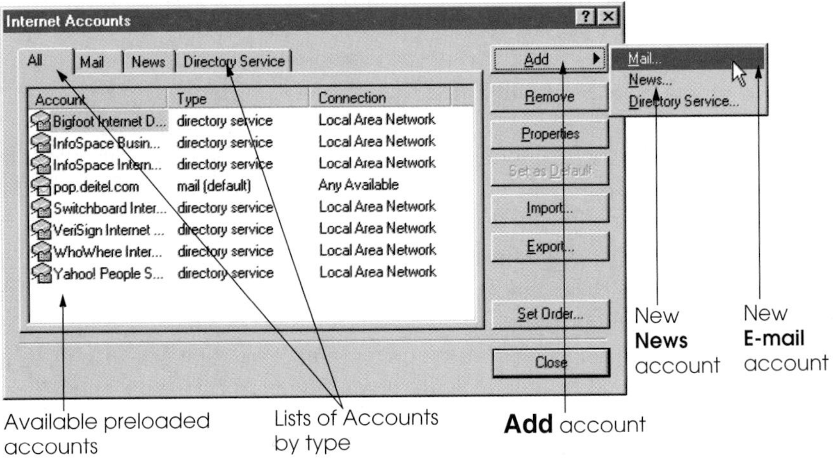

Fig. 2.10 *Outlook Express* opening screen and the **Internet Accounts** dialog.

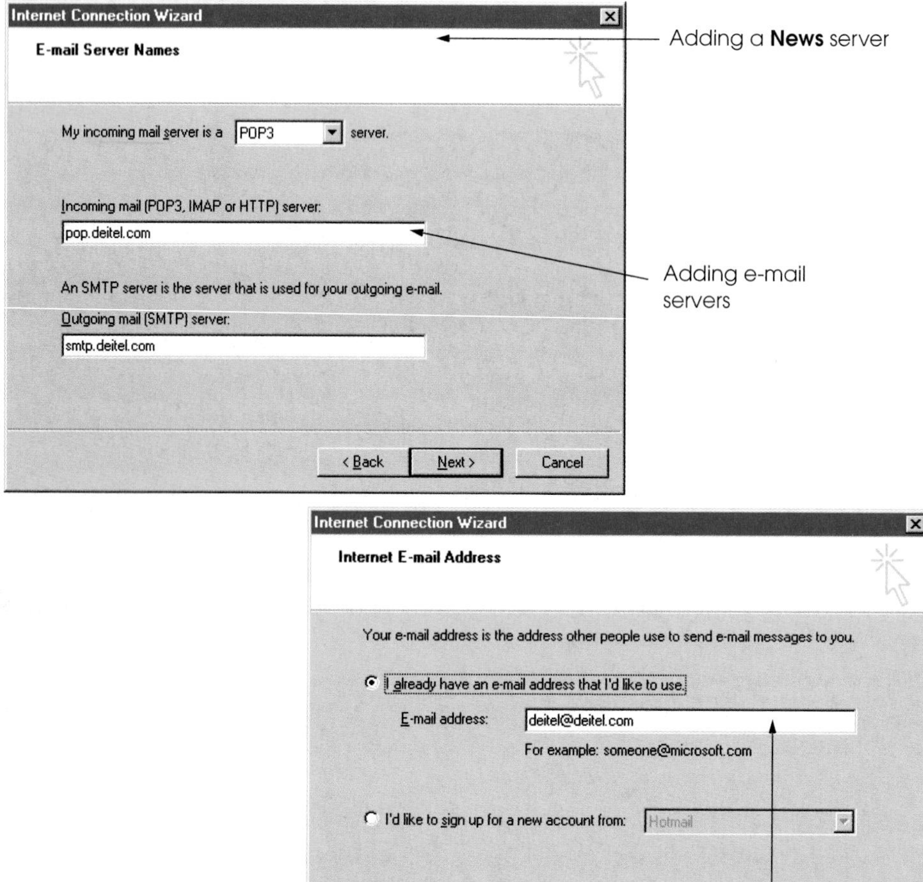

Fig. 2.11 Adding e-mail and news accounts in Outlook Express.

E-mail messages can be organized by sender or by subject. Click **From** in the message list to sort by sender. Click **Subject** to sort by subject. Selecting an e-mail in the message lists displays the e-mail's contents in the bottom portion of the right pane. Double clicking an e-mail opens a new window containing the e-mail's contents. To reply to or forward an e-mail, select the e-mail and click the appropriate button (e.g., **Reply**, **Forward**, etc.). E-mails can be moved from one folder to another by dragging and dropping the message into the appropriate folder.

The *address book* stores names and e-mail addresses of people with whom you communicate frequently. Click the **Addresses** button (Fig. 2.12), or select **Address Book...** from the **Tools** menu, to display the **Address Book** dialog (2.13).

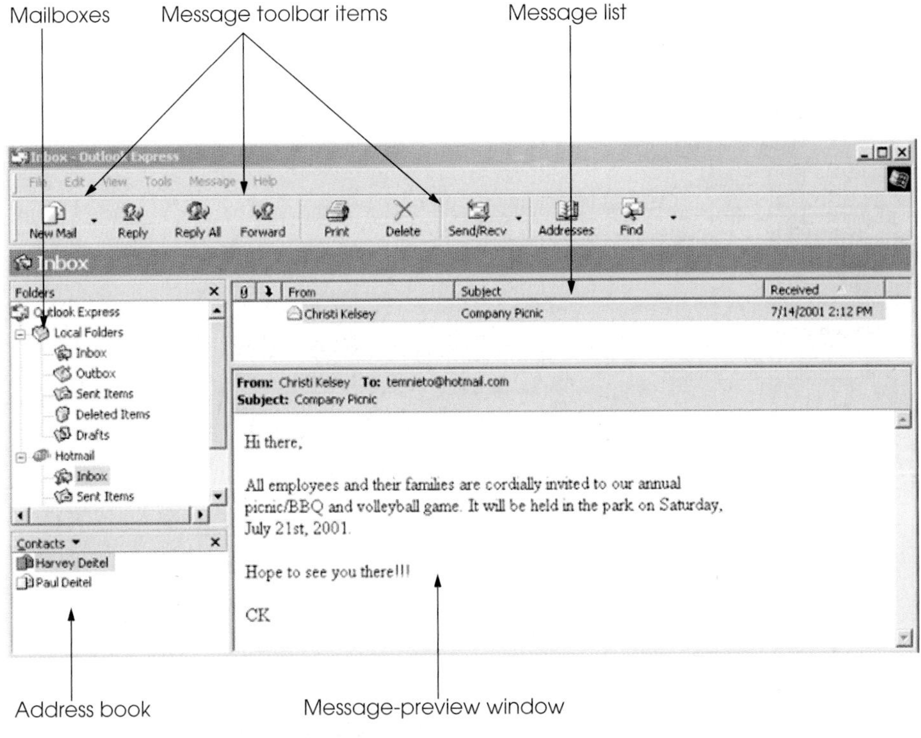

Fig. 2.12 Outlook Express e-mail main screen.

A message can be sent to anyone in the list by highlighting that person's entry, clicking the **Action** button and selecting **Send Mail**. This sequence opens a blank e-mail message addressed to the selected recipient. To add a new contact, click the **New** button and select **Contact**. This displays the **Properties** dialog (Fig. 2.13) where information is input.

When composing an e-mail, the dialog of Fig. 2.14 is used. The e-mail address of the intended recipient is placed in the **To:** field. If the e-mail is being sent to multiple recipients, separate each address by a semicolon (**;**). The **Cc:** (carbon copy) field is for sending e-mails to people who, although the e-mail is not addressed to them directly, may be interested in the message. The *priority* of the e-mail can be changed by clicking the **Priority** button on the toolbar. High-priority e-mails are flagged (typically with an exclamation point) to emphasize its importance.

The e-mail's text is typed in the message body. Text can be formatted (e.g., by changing font size, color, style, etc.) using the buttons above the message body. Clicking **Send** sends the e-mail.

2.9 NetMeeting

Internet Explorer 5.5 is bundled with two programs for communicating with people over the Internet using text, audio (with a microphone) and video (with a camera). The first of these programs, *NetMeeting*, is designed for business- and work-related collaborations.

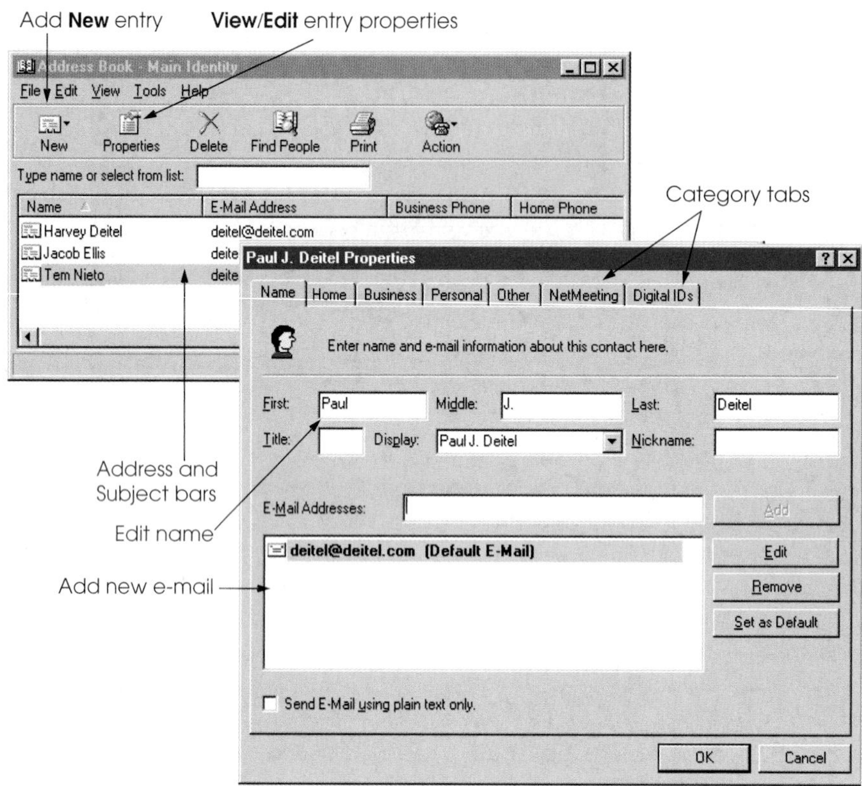

Fig. 2.13 Adding and modifying names in the **Address Book**.

NetMeeting enables communication among groups of people via textual and visual aids such as sound (using a microphone connected to your computer so you can speak with people) and video (using video cameras to transmit live video). In addition, NetMeeting has four main tools which individuals can use to enhance their meeting sessions: *chat*, *sharing*, *file transfer* and *whiteboard*. Sharing is used to describe the method NetMeeting uses to share program files (e.g., programs installed or applications downloaded and stored on a computer) between to users. Built-in mechanisms are available for group editing of files and for sharing diagrams via the *whiteboard*, a drawing application that allows *sharing* visual effects with others in the meeting. *File transfer* allows one user to download and save an application or file from one computer to another so that the new information can be permanently stored on the user's system without losing the information once the NetMeeting session is ended. Finally, *chat* allows users to send and receive text, images, video or audio messages instantaneously.

Microsoft provides users with direct and indirect ways to use NetMeeting. To start a NetMeeting, select the **Start** menu, **Accessories**, **Communications** and click **NetMeeting**. Once NetMeeting is launched, the NetMeeting user interface with appear with all program options and meeting choices (Fig. 2.15).

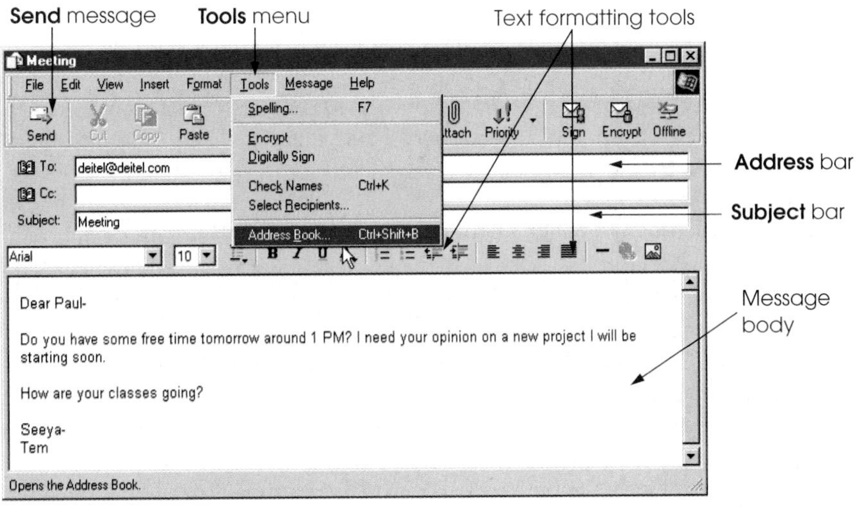

Fig. 2.14 Composing a message with Outlook Express.

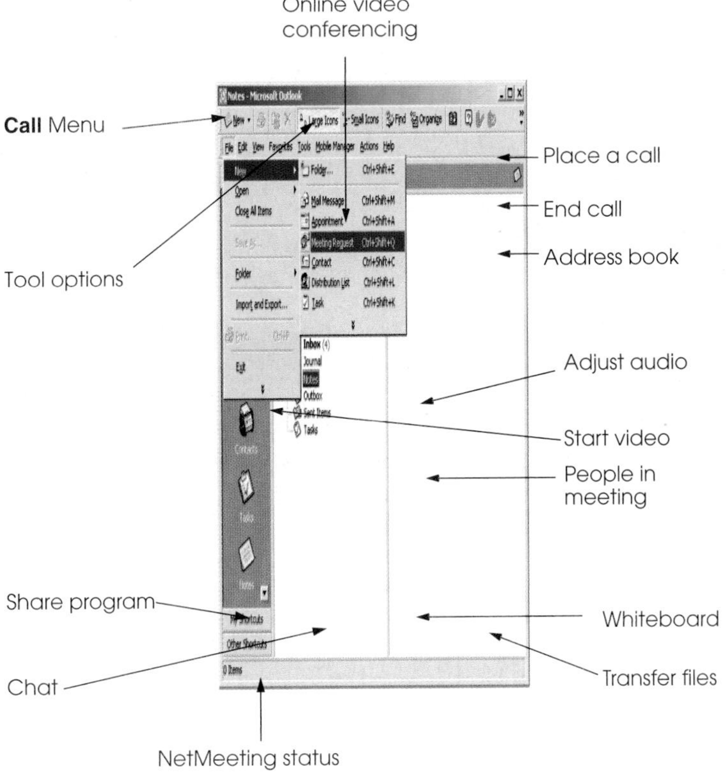

Fig. 2.15 NetMeeting User Interface.

Users can select two options from the `Call` menu, **New Call...** or **Host Meeting...**.If a user opts to place a new call, the user is prompted by the **Place a Call** box (Fig. 2.16) to enter the individual's name they wish to contact, security preference and where the call will occur (e.g., over the network, MSN directory, etc.). Users can also select the **Address Book** icon to find a contact already stored in their personal address database. The **Address Book** in NetMeeting works the same as the address book in Outlook Express.

If a user wishes to contact multiple users at one time, then a user can host a meeting. Meetings allow users to interact in the same communications environment at one time without the need to establish multiple individual connections (i.e., making a new call to each meeting participant). When a new meeting session is opened for the first time on a computer, it asks the user to set the initial options, such as contact information and security preferences (i.e., only accept incoming calls or can only place outgoing calls to other users) as shown in on the right in Fig. 2.17. The user hosting the meeting must establish a meeting name and password that will be used only by those members participating in the meeting. In addition, users have the options to restrict certain uses of meeting tools (e.g., sharing, whiteboard, file transfer and chat).

An indirect way to use NetMeeting is through Microsoft Outlook e-mail. Outlook allows users to establish NetMeeting sessions for specific times and dates in the future, similar to a conference call on a telephone. From the Outlook menu, select **File**, **New**, **Meeting Request** (Fig. 2.18) and users are taken to the **Meeting** screen (Fig.2.19).

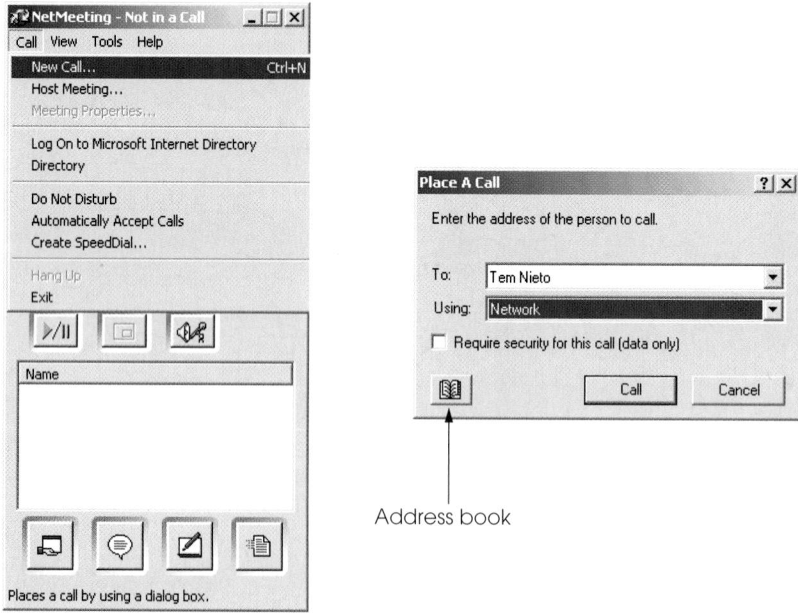

Fig. 2.16 Placing a new call to another user in NetMeeting.

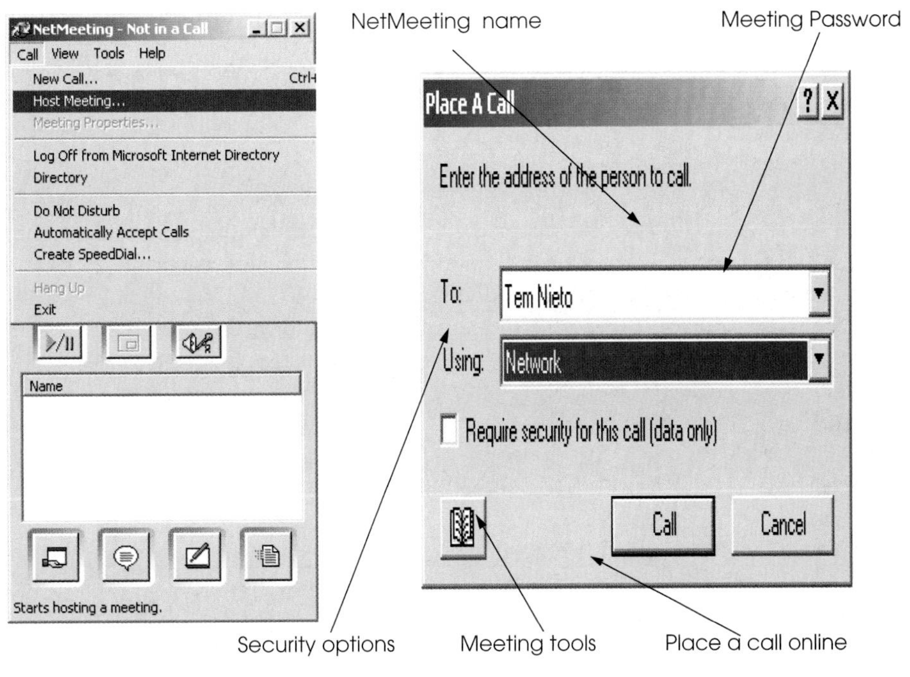

Fig. 2.17 Hosting a new NetMeeting or Joining an existing one.

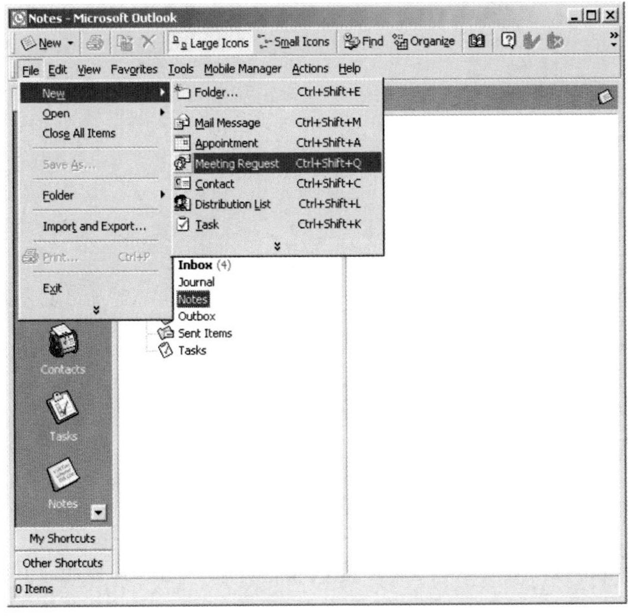

Fig. 2.18 Using Microsoft Outlook to set-up a NetMeeting.

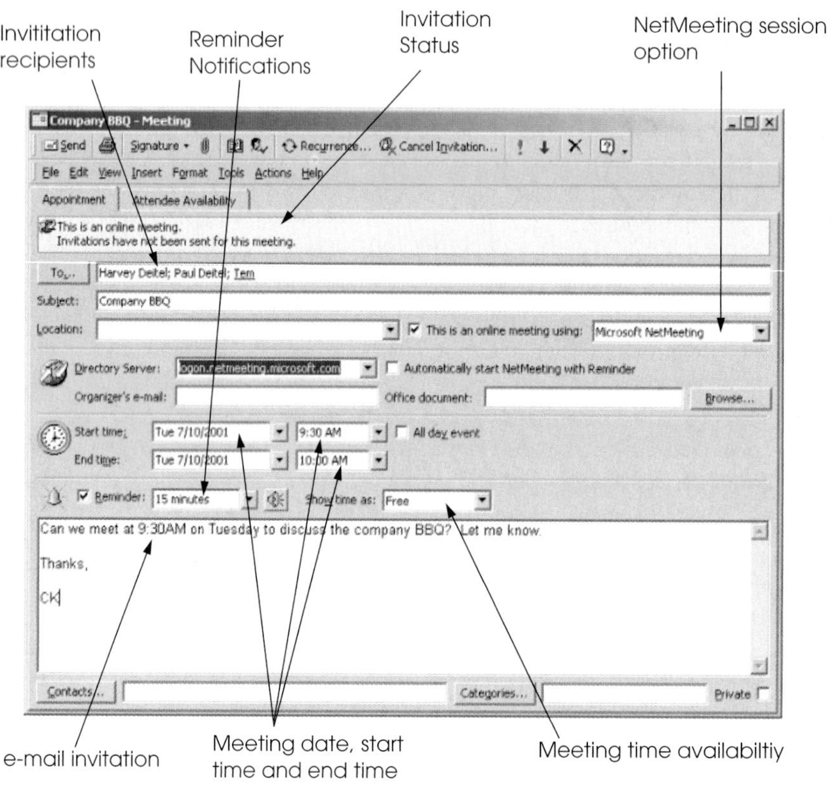

Fig. 2.19 Sending invitations through Microsoft Outlook for a NetMeeting session.

Users then specify who to invite to the NetMeeting session. Also, users can specify other meeting options such as the date, time, location and host e-mail address. Users then e-mail invitations and maintain a record of all the responses. Users can receive notifications daily, hourly, etc. to remind them of upcoming meetings sessions. When the pre-determined date and time for the NetMeeting session arrives, NetMeeting launches automatically and begins a new session with those users that accepted invitations. Microsoft Outlook does not directly establish this session, but is used more as a planning tool to notify and manage contact information for the session

NetMeeting can be an effective tool for enhancing work-related meetings and conferencing for individuals in different geographic locations or as an alternative form of communications and informative collaboration. However, NetMeeting is not as popular as other forms of messaging. Typically, it is used in conjunction with more popular forms of instant messaging services such as Microsoft's MSN Messenger Service.

2.10 MSN Messenger Service

MSN Messenger Service is a program that establishes live chats among *Microsoft Passport* holders. To begin using MSN Messenger, a free *passport account* must be created with Microsoft at **www.passport.com**. This passport supplies a free messaging service and a free e-mail account. Different domain names or account types can be created including **hotmail.com**, **msn.com** and **passport.com**. Once registered, users must go to **http://messenger.msn.com** and follow the instructions to download MSN messenger. When the download is complete, users sign into MSN messenger using their newly created or existing passport account (Fig. 2.20)

Once signed-in, users can link their MSN Messengers to those of friends, family and business associates also running MSN Messenger. MSN Messenger users can communicate only with other MSN Messenger users. However, users can send e-mail messages via Messenger to invite others to download the service.

MSN Messenger offers a direct link for users to communicate in a text-based chat. Users can initiate text and audio chat sessions with other users through the MSN Messenger interface. The service is compatible with Microsoft NetMeeting and offers easy access to the conferencing tool. A user only needs to select the **Invite** option to initiate a conference using Microsoft NetMeeting.

Double click the name of a contact that is currently online to initiate a chat session (Fig. 2.21). A chat opens, allowing two-way text communication. Once a chat session has been initiated, other contacts can be added to the conversation by using the **Invite** feature. Users can also transfer files over the MSN messenger, eliminating the need to send an e-mail message.

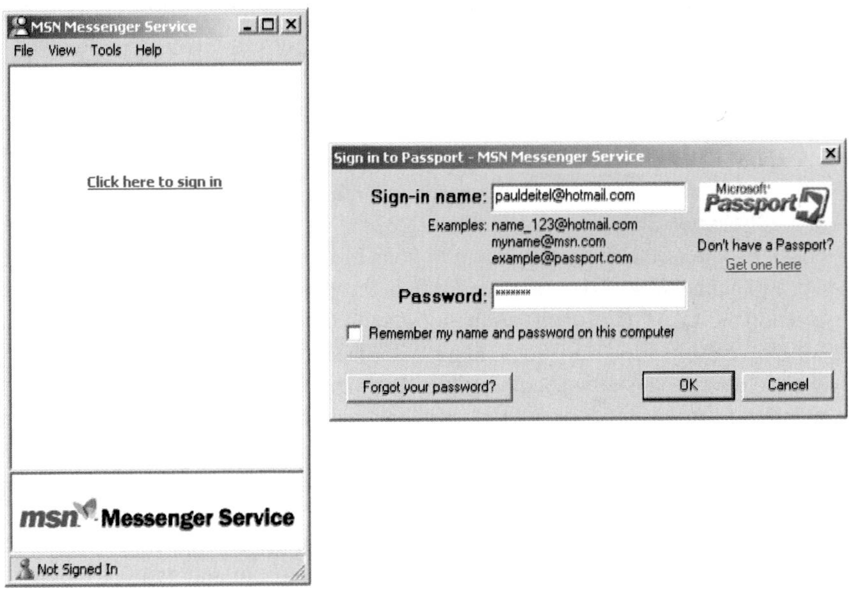

Fig. 2.20 Sign-in screen for access to MSN Messenger.

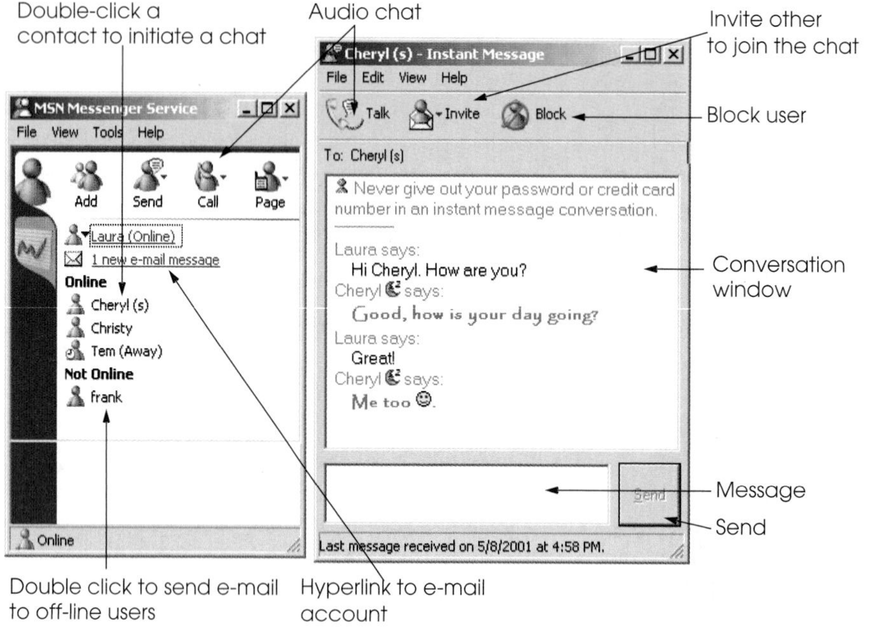

Fig. 2.21 Chatting with MSN Messenger Service

A contact may be blocked using the **Block** feature. The **Block** feature makes a user appear offline to blocked users. Have fun meeting and chatting with new people; however, be careful about revealing personal information to users you do not know.

2.11 Customizing Browser Settings

Internet Explorer 5.5 has many default settings that determine how sites are displayed, how security measures are applied and how outputs are rendered. Most of these settings are located in the ***Internet Options*** dialog (Fig. 2.22).

Consider some of the more significant options that affect your browsing experience. If you are browsing the Web with a slow connection, the page download time can be decreased by deselecting the ***Load Pictures*** setting, located under the **Advanced** tab. Toggling this setting off prevents the browser from loading Web-page images. Images can require considerable time to download, so this toggle could save time during browsing sessions.

Default programs used for common Internet procedures such as sending e-mail are set in the **Programs** tab. Specifying these settings causes the designated programs to execute when there is a need for their respective technologies while browsing. For example, if Outlook Express is designated as the default e-mail program, every time an e-mail hyperlink is clicked, Outlook Express opens an e-mail message dialog directed to the designated recipient.

The security level for IE5.5 can be set under the **Security** tab. There are four levels of security. The most lenient level permits downloading and *cookies* (files that are placed on the computer by Web sites to retain or gather information about the user); the strictest level renders a constant flow of alerts and alarms about browsing security.

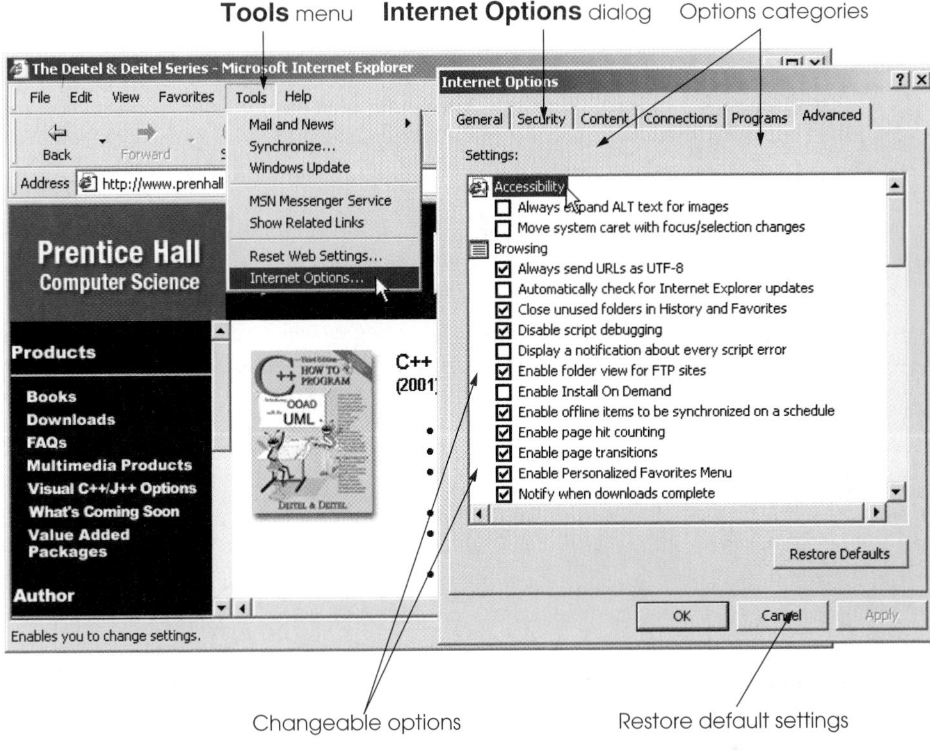

Fig. 2.22 Changing the **Internet Options** in IE5.5.

A personal home page can be specified under the **General** tab. The home page is the Web page that loads when the browser is first opened and appears when the **Home** button at the top of the browser window is clicked.

History options also may be adjusted in this category. By clicking the **Settings...** button, the amount of disk space to be reserved for Web page *cache* can be set. The cache is an area on the hard drive that a browser designates for saving Web pages for rapid, future access. When a page is viewed that has been visited recently, IE5.5 checks if it already has some elements on that page saved in the cache, to reduce download time. Having a large cache can considerably speed up Web browsing, whereas having a small cache saves disk space. Caching can sometimes cause problems, as Internet Explorer does not always check to ensure that a cached page is the same as the latest version residing on the Web server. Clicking the **Refresh** button at the top of the browser window remedies this problem by forcing Internet Explorer to retrieve the latest version of the Web page from the Web site. Once the **Internet Options** are set, click **Apply** and click **OK**.

In this chapter we introduced the features of Internet Explorer 5.5 and showed how to search the Internet, send e-mail, and conference with friends and co-workers. In the next chapter we introduce Adobe's PhotoShop Elements and show how to create your own graphics.

SUMMARY

- Web browsers are software programs that allow users to access the Web's rich multimedia content.
- The two most popular Web browsers are Microsoft's Internet Explorer and Netscape's Communicator.
- A computer alone is not enough to access the Internet. In addition to Web browser software, the computer needs specific hardware and a connection to an Internet Service Provider to view Web pages.
- A modem is hardware that enables a computer to connect to the Internet. A modem converts data to audio tones and transmits the data over phone lines. A network card, also called a network interface card (NIC), is hardware that allows a computer to connect to the Internet through a network or a high-speed Internet connection such as a cable modem or a Digital Subscriber Line (DSL).
- Bandwidth and cost are two considerations when deciding on which commercial ISP service to use. Bandwidth refers to the amount of data that can be transferred through a communications medium in a fixed amount of time. Different ISPs offer different types of high-speed connections, called broadband connections that include DSL, cable modem, Integrated Services Digital Network (ISDN) and the slower dial-up connections, each of which has different bandwidths and costs to users.
- Broadband is a category of high-bandwidth Internet service that is most often provided by cable television and telephone companies to home users.
- DSL is a broadband service that allows computers to be constantly connected to the Internet over existing phone lines, without interfering with voice services. However, DSL requires a special modem that is acquired from the ISP.
- Cable modems enable the computer to be connected to the Internet at all times. Cable modems transmit data over the cables that bring television to homes and businesses. The bandwidth is shared among many users.
- ISDN provides Internet service over either digital or standard telephone lines. ISDN requires specialized hardware, called a terminal adaptor (TA), which is usually obtained from the ISP. ISDN service has limited availability.
- Once a network connection is established, IE 5.5's **Internet Connection Wizard** (ICW) can be used to configure the computer to connect to the Internet.
- The URL is the address of the Web page displayed in the browser window. Each Web page is associated with a unique URL. URLs usually begin with **`http://`**, which stands for HyperText Transfer Protocol (HTTP), the industry standard for transferring Web documents over the Internet.
- Several methods are available to navigate between different URLs. In one method, a user clicks the **Address** field and types a Web page's URL. The user then presses *Enter* or clicks **Go** to request the Web page located at that URL.
- Another way to navigate the Web is via visual elements on Web pages called hyperlinks that, when clicked, load a specified Web document. Both images and text may be hyperlinked.
- Hyperlinks can reference other Web pages, e-mail addresses and files. If a hyperlink is an e-mail address, clicking the link loads the computer's default e-mail program and opens a message window addressed to the specified recipient's e-mail address.
- When a file is downloaded, it is copied onto the user's computer. Programs, documents, images and sound files are all downloadable files.
- IE5.5 maintains a list of previously visited URLs. This list is called the history and stores URLs in chronological order.

- The **History** window contains heading levels ordered chronologically. Within each time frame headings are alphabetized by site directory name. This window is useful for finding previously visited URLs without having to remember the exact URL.
- URLs from the history are displayed in a drop-down list when a user types a URL into the **Address** bar. This feature is called Autocomplete. Any URL from this drop-down list can be selected with the mouse to load the Web page at that URL into the browser.
- Web pages can be saved directly to the computer's hard drive for off-line browsing (i.e., browsing while not connected to the Internet). Select **Save As** from the **File** menu at the top of the browser window to save a Web page and all its components (e.g., images, etc.).
- Individual images from a Web site can also be saved by clicking the image with the right mouse button and selecting **Save Picture As...** from the displayed context menu (i.e., pop-up menu).
- Search engines explore the Internet and maintain searchable records containing information about Web sites. This section explains how search engines work and discusses two types of search engines.
- Metasearch engines do not maintain databases. Instead, they send the search criteria to other search engines and aggregate the results. IE5.5 has a built-in metasearch engine that is accessed by clicking the **Search** button on the toolbar.
- As users browser the Web, they often visit certain sites repeatedly. Internet Explorer provides a feature called favorites for bookmarking such sites.
- Plug-ins are specialized pieces of software that extend other applications, such as IE5.5, by providing additional functionality. Normally the browser prompts the user to download a plug-in when a plug-in is needed.
- FTP (file transfer protocol) is an older protocol for transferring information, especially large files, over the Internet. An FTP site's URL begins with `ftp://`, rather than `http://`. FTP sites are typically accessed via hyperlinks, but can also be accessed by any software that supports FTP.
- FTP sites with public access allow any user access. Many FTP sites on the Internet have restricted access; only users with authorized user names and passwords are permitted to access such sites.
- Transferring a file from the local machine to another location on the Internet is called uploading and can accomplished using the FTP protocol.
- Electronic mail (e-mail for short) is a method of sending and receiving formatted messages and files over the Internet to other people. Internet Service Providers issue e-mail addresses in the form username@domainname. Many e-mail programs are available, such as Pegasus Mail, Messenger, Eudora and Microsoft's Outlook Express.
- Outlook Express provides a graphical interface for managing e-mail accounts. When messages are received, they are saved on the local computer. Outlook Express checks for new messages several times per hour (this frequency can be changed depending on a user's preference). When a new e-mail message arrives, it is placed in the **Inbox**.
- The address book stores names and e-mail addresses of people with whom you communicate frequently. Click the **Addresses** button, or select **Address Book...** from the **Tools** menu, to display the **Address Book** dialog.
- A message can be sent to anyone in the list by highlighting that person's entry, clicking the **Action** button and selecting **Send Mail**. This sequence opens a blank e-mail message addressed to the selected recipient.
- Internet Explorer is bundled with two programs for communicating with people over the Internet using text, audio (with a microphone) and video (with a camera). NetMeeting shares files; built-in mechanisms are available for group editing of files and for sharing diagrams via the whiteboard,

a drawing application that allows sharing visual effects with others in the meeting. MSN Messenger Service is a program that establishes live chats among Microsoft Passport holders.

- Internet Explorer has many default settings that determine how sites are displayed, how security measures are applied and how outputs are rendered.
- Default programs used for common Internet procedures such as sending e-mail are set in the **Programs** tab of the **Internet Options** dialog. Specifying these settings causes the designated programs to execute when there is a need for their respective technologies while browsing.
- The security level for IE5.5 can be set under the **Security** tab of the **Internet Options** dialog. There are four levels of security. The most lenient level permits downloading and cookies (files that are placed on the computer by Web sites to retain or gather information about the user); the strictest level renders a constant flow of alerts and alarms about browsing security.
- A personal home page can be specified under the **General** tab of the **Internet Options** dialog. The home page is the Web page that loads when the browser is first opened and appears when the **Home** button at the top of the browser window is clicked.
- History options also may be adjusted in the **General** tab of the **Internet Options** dialog. By clicking the **Settings...** button, the amount of disk space to be reserved for Web page cache can be set. The cache is an area on the hard drive that a browser designates for saving Web pages and their elements for rapid, future access.

TERMINOLOGY

Address bar
Address Book
Adobe Acrobat Reader
anonymous
applications
Autocomplete
Back button
bandwidth
broadband connection
cable modem
cache
chat
context menu
cookie
database
dial-up connection
Digital Subscriber Line (DSL)
download
electronic mail (e-mail)
e-mail server
Favorites
file transfer
File Transfer Protocol (FTP)
Forward button
Help menu
high-priority message
History
home page
HyperText Transfer Protocol (HTTP)
hyperlink
Inbox
Integrated Services Digital Network (ISDN)
Internet Connection Wizard (ICW)
Internet Explorer 5.5 (IE5.5)
Internet Options
Internet Service Provider (ISP)
Macromedia Shockwave
message window
metasearch engine
modem
Microsoft Internet Explorer
Microsoft NetMeeting
Microsoft Outlook Express
MSN Messenger Service
Netscape Communicator
network
network administrator
network card
network interface card (NIC)
off-line browsing
Passport
Portable Document Format (PDF)
priority
public access
Refresh
restricted access

sharing
Search
search engine
Security
security level
terminal adaptor (TA)
uploading
Universal Resource Locator (URL)
Web browser
whiteboard

SELF REVIEW EXERCISES

2.1 Fill in the blanks in each of the following statements:

a) The two most popular Web browsers are __________ and __________.
b) A browser is used to view files on the __________.
c) The location of a file on the Internet is called its __________.
d) The element in a Web page that, when clicked, causes a new Web page to load is called a __________; when your mouse passes over this element, the mouse pointer changes into a __________ in IE5.5.
e) The list IE5.5 keeps of visited URLs is called the __________.
f) You can save an image from a Web page by right clicking the image and selecting __________.
g) The feature of IE5.5 that provides options for completing URLs is called __________.
h) The feature of IE5.5 that enables the user to save URLs of frequently visited sites is called __________.

2.2 State whether each of the following is *true* or *false*. If the statement is *false*, explain why.

a) A whiteboard is a drawing application that allows sharing visual effects with others in a NetMeeting.
b) Plug-ins must be downloaded and installed to use them.
c) NetMeeting and MSN Messenger are identical programs that do the same thing, but look different.
d) FTP is a popular Internet mechanism by which files are uploaded and downloaded.
e) You can access any FTP site by logging in as **`anonymous`**.

ANSWERS TO SELF-REVIEW EXERCISES

2.1 a) Internet Explorer, Netscape Communicator. b) Internet and the Web. c) URL. d) hyperlink, hand. e) history. f) **Save Picture as...**. g) *Autocomplete*. h) **Favorites**.

2.2 a) True. b) True. c) False. NetMeeting is geared more for business use and includes many features that facilitate the sharing of information. MSN Messenger is intended for more casual, "chat" use. d) True. e) False. Many FTP sites are restricted and do not admit the general public.

EXERCISES

2.3 Expand the following acronyms, and include a description of each:

a) HTTP
b) FTP
c) URL
d) DSL
e) PDF
f) ISP

2.4 Use Internet Explorer's FTP capability to access both **`ftp.cdrom.com`** and **`sunsite.unc.edu`**. List the directory output for both sites.

2.5 Open a passport at **`passport.msn.com`**. Then log onto MSN Messenger Service, and initiate a conversation with a friend.

2.6 Log on to a NetMeeting server and initiate a conversation with a friend.

2.7 Go to **`www.shockwave.com/software/shockwaveplayer`** and download the Shockwave Player to your computer. Use the shockwave plug-in to view shockwave content from this site.

2.8 Download the Adobe Acrobat Reader from **`www.adobe.com/products/acrobat`**. Once the reader is installed, visit **`www.prenhall.com/deitel`** and download the Deitel Buzz.

Photoshop® Elements

Objectives

- To explore the basics of Photoshop Elements.
- To be able to design images for Web pages.
- To learn how colors are represented in image files and what "color mode" and "transparency" are.
- To understand the techniques of layering, selection, image slicing and other image-preparation processes.
- To understand the difference between graphic file formats.
- To be able to take screen shots using screen capture technology.

Now follow in this direction, now turn a different hue.
Theognis

Beware lest you lose the substance by grasping at the shadow.
Aesop

Before a diamond shows its brilliancy and prismatic colors it has to stand a good deal of cutting and smoothing.
Anonymous

Outline

3.1 Introduction

The most successful Web pages use both text and graphics to enhance the user experience. The graphic design of a Web page can greatly influence the amount of time a user spends at a site. For instance, if a company's Web site contains only text, it may not produce as many online sales. Web site graphics, such as buttons, banners or product images, define the user experience and distinguish a company's site from its competition. While many images are available free for download on the Internet, creating original images helps make a Web site unique. This chapter teaches basic image-creation techniques for producing attractive, user-friendly Web pages.

This chapter introduces Adobe® Inc.'s *Photoshop Elements*—an easy-to-use graphics package that offers the functionality of more expensive packages at an economical price. Graphics such as title images, banners, buttons and advanced photographic effects all can be created using this program. A 30-day free-trial version of Photoshop Elements is available at **`www.adobe.com/support/downloads`**.[1] The full version may be purchased at this site.

3.2 Image Basics

Photoshop Elements is best taught by example. This chapter provides several examples that illustrate how to use Photoshop Elements' tools and functions. This section examines the basic steps for creating original images.

---

1. Caution: Do not change the clock settings of a computer after installing Photoshop Elements. Doing so causes the 30-day trial to expire, immediately disabling the program. Photoshop Elements cannot be re-enabled, even by reinstalling it.

Begin by opening Photoshop Elements. When the program first opens, the ***Quick Start*** menu appears in the center of the screen and presents several options (Fig. 3.1). Some options include creating a new file, opening an existing file or acquiring an image from an outside source such as a scanner or a digital camera. This window appears when the program is started, but also may be accessed at any time through the **Window** menu by selecting **Show Quick Start**. The **File** menu also opens new or existing files.

Click **New** in the **Quick Start** menu to open the ***New*** dialog (Fig. 3.2), to begin creating an image.

The **New** dialog specifies initial image settings and appears each time a new image file is created. The initial image settings include **Height** and **Width** and the units in which these are measured. The dialog sets the image *resolution*. Resolution is a measurement of image clarity and is measured in *pixels* per unit—every image in Photoshop Elements is composed of a grid of dots called *pixels,* which store color information.

Performance Tip 3.1

Higher image resolutions result in better image clarity. However, higher resolutions produce larger file sizes. The standard resolution for the Web is 72 pixels per inch.

The **New** dialog sets an image's **Background Color** and *color* **Mode**. The three color modes available are *red-green-blue (RGB)*, *grayscale* and *bitmap*. Color mode determines the number of colors that Photoshop Elements uses to compose an image. RGB and grayscale are the most commonly used color modes for creating Web graphics. Color images use the RGB mode and black-and-white images use the grayscale mode.

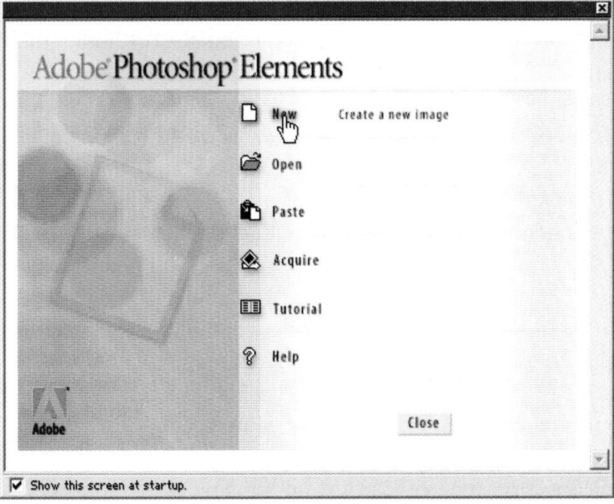

Fig. 3.1 Photoshop Elements **Quick Start** menu. (Adobe and Photoshop are either registered trademarks or trademarks of Adobe Systems Incorporated in the United States and/or other countries.)

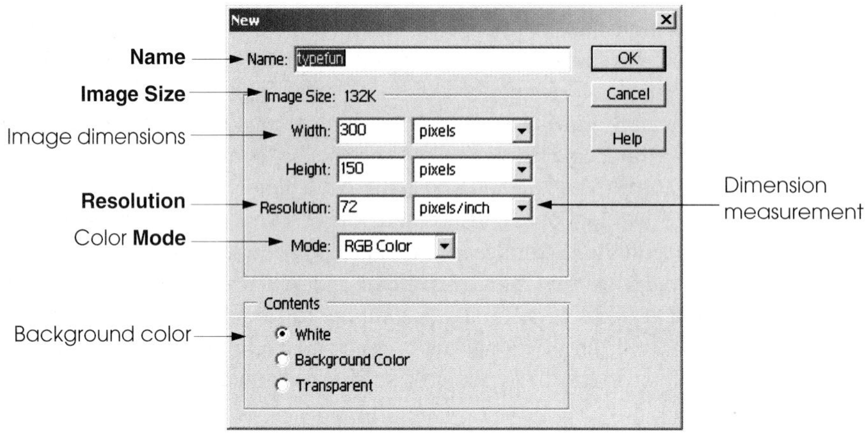

Fig. 3.2 Creating a new image in Photoshop Elements. (Adobe and Photoshop are either registered trademarks or trademarks of Adobe Systems Incorporated in the United States and/or other countries.)

In RGB mode, each pixel in the image is assigned an *intensity value* for the *primary colors in light* (i.e., red, green and blue) that create a color range of 16.7 million colors when combined in different intensity values from 0 (full saturation) to 255 (no saturation). This spectrum is comparable to that of human vision and is adequate for developing screen images. For instance, a bright-blue pixel might have a red value of 16, a green value of 20 and a blue value of 200. Grayscale model uses only *neutral grays* which have identical red, green and blue values. The bitmap mode uses only black and white.

Create a new image by entering **`typefun`** in the **New** dialog's **Name** field. Set the image width to **300** pixels, the height to **150** pixels and the resolution to **72** pixels per inch by typing the numbers into the **Width**, **Height**, and **Resolution** fields. Choose the measurement units from the drop-down lists.

Select the **RGB Color** mode from the color **Mode** drop-down list. Set the **Background Color** to white by clicking the **White** radio button in the **Contents** frame. These settings can be changed at any point during the image-editing process. The background color is the image's initial color. Click **OK** to create the new file **`typefun`**.

A new *image window* opens in the development environment with the name **typefun** in the title bar (Fig. 3.3). The development environment is the gray area that contains the *toolbox*, *palettes* and image window. The toolbox is the vertical window to the left of the image window that contains different tools to create images. Palettes are windows that contain different image-editing options. The ***Hints*** palette is open by default.

The development environment can be customized to suit users' preferences. For instance, the image window may be resized by clicking and dragging any of the sides or corners. Also, the palettes, toolbox and image window can be dragged to different locations. Selecting **Reset Palette Locations** from the **Window** menu restores the default development environment settings.

Palettes, located inside the *palette well*, are windows that contain image editing and effects options. A palette is opened by clicking its tab in the palette well, and is closed by clicking outside the palette. Palettes may be organized in different ways to make image editing easier. Several palettes can be open at one time by clicking and dragging their tabs out of the palette well and into the development environment. Palettes outside the palette well remain open until they are closed by clicking the **x** button in the upper-right corner of the palette. Palette locations may be restored to their default locations by selecting **Reset Palette Locations** from the **Windows** menu. Different palette options will be discussed shortly.

The toolbox contains *selection*, *editing*, *painting* and *type tools* that add to or subtract graphic elements from images. The *active tool* applies changes to an image and is highlighted in the toolbox. Only one tool can be active at a time. Tips for using the active tool are found in the *status bar* at the bottom of the screen or in the **Hints** palette.

The two squares at the bottom of the toolbox represent the two *active colors*—the foreground color and the background color. These squares are called *swatches*. Click the foreground color swatch to display the ***Color Picker*** dialog (Fig. 3.4) that allows the user to select the foreground or background color. Colors are selected based on the *HSB (Hue, Saturation, Brightness)* model or the RGB (Red, Green, Blue) model. These color models form the 16.7 million colors available in the RGB model based on combinations of their three primary values. Both color models produce the same colors except that they measure color differently.

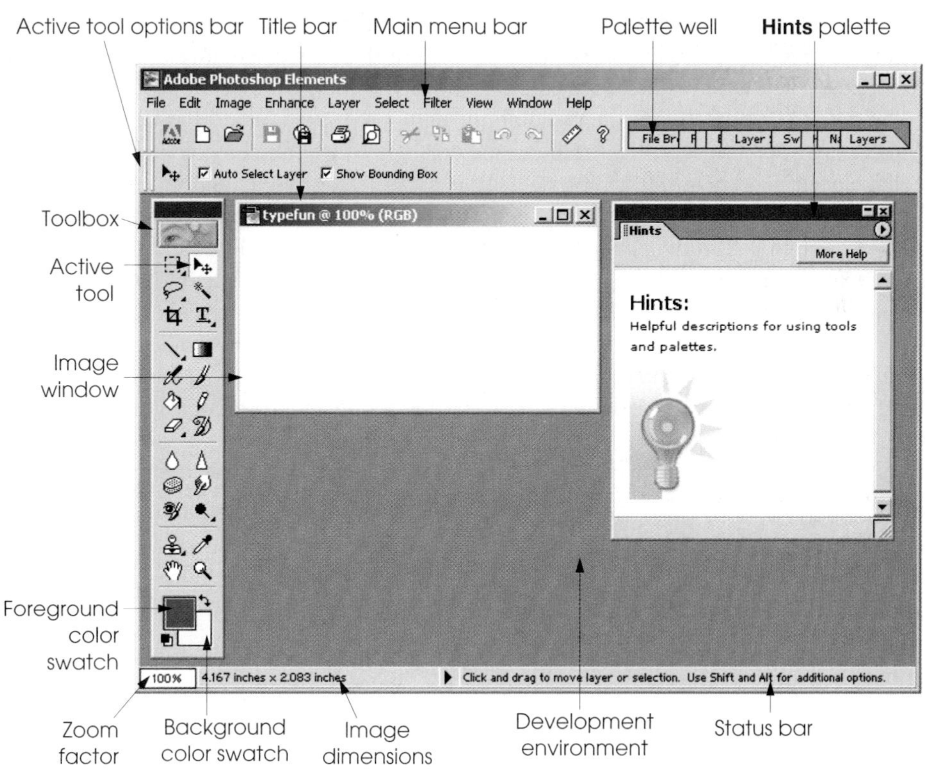

Fig. 3.3 Photoshop Elements development environment. (Adobe and Photoshop are either registered trademarks or trademarks of Adobe Systems Incorporated in the United States and/or other countries.)

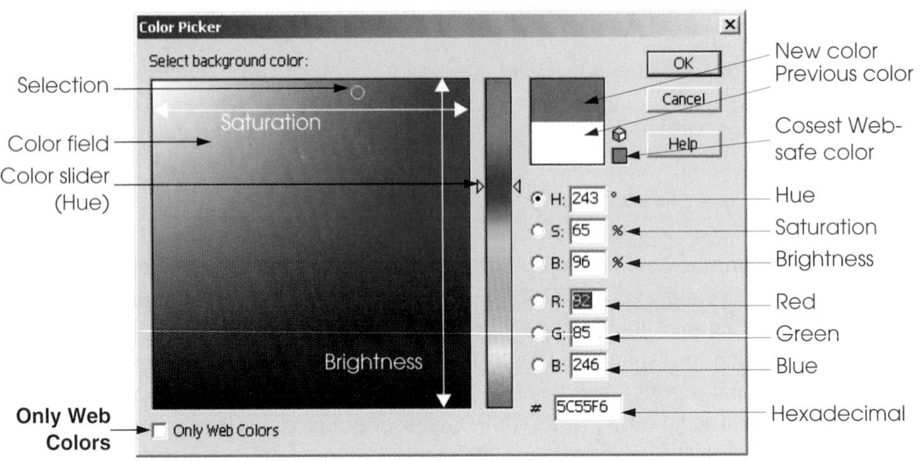

Fig. 3.4 Selecting a color using the **Color Picker** dialog. (Adobe and Photoshop are either registered trademarks or trademarks of Adobe Systems Incorporated in the United States and/or other countries.)

Hue is selected for the HSB model from the vertical color slider in the **Color Picker** dialog (Fig. 3.4). Hue is measured in degrees from 0–360 representing the colors of the *color wheel*. The color wheel is a theoretical model that shows how colors are created from combinations of the three primary colors in light—red, green and blue. *Saturation* is a color's intensity measured in the percentage of gray that the color contains. Saturated colors appear more vivid; less saturated colors appear dull. *Brightness* is a color's relative lightness or darkness and is measured in the amount of black or white a color contains.

RGB color selection is based on the same principle as the RGB color mode, in which each pixel has a red, green and blue value between 0 and 255 assigned to it. When RGB values are entered into the **Color Picker**, the HSB values change to reflect the selection.

The **Color Picker** allows the user to choose colors from a *Web-safe palette*, restricting color selection to the 216 colors that are cross-platform (e.g., Windows, Macintosh and UNIX) and cross-browser (e.g., Internet Explorer and Communicator) compatible.

Portability Tip 3.1

Web-safe colors should display in almost the same way in any browser on any platform. However, some color inconsistencies do occur between colors on different platforms and browsers. It is a good idea to try to choose only Web-safe colors when designing original images for the Web.

Look-and-Feel Observation 3.1

Too many colors make a site look confusing and erratic. Pick three or four main colors to use as the prominent colors for images and text.

When selecting a foreground or background color, either click inside the color field on the desired color or enter that color's numerical values. The **Color Picker** dialog allows the user to choose colors based on *hexadecimal* notation. Hexadecimal notation is equivalent to RGB notation except that it uses a 6-digit combination of the numbers 0–9 and the letters A–F to represent the 256-color range for each red, green and blue specification. The first two digits are the red value, the second two are the green value and the last two are the blue value—00 signifies the least intensity and FF the greatest intensity. For more information on hexadecimal notation, see Appendix D, Number Systems.

Portability Tip 3.2

It is easy to tell if a color is part of the Web-safe palette by examining its hexadecimal notation. The hexadecimal notation for any Web-safe color contains only the digits 00, 33, 66, 99, CC and FF for each red, green and blue value.

Select a foreground color by adjusting the color slider to the desired hue, then pick the color from the color field and click **OK**. This color displays in the foreground color swatch of the toolbox.

The following example shows how to place text into an image and how to apply special effects to that text. Select the *type tool* from the toolbox by clicking the tool containing the capital letter **T**. Notice that the active tool options bar changes to reflect the new active tool (Fig. 3.5).

Similar to word-processing programs, the type options bar allows the user to alter text properties such as *font face*, *font weight* and *alignment*. For this example, choose **Helvetica 30 point bold** and click the image with the type tool. A cursor appears indicating the point where the text begins. Type in two lines of text and select it with the cursor. Type properties may be changed when text is selected. For instance, double clicking the type color swatch in the type options bar changes the type color.

Be sure to have the ***Anti-aliased*** checkbox selected in the type options bar. *Anti-aliasing* is a process that smooths edges on scalable fonts and other graphics by blending the color of the edge pixels with the color of the background on which the text is placed. Fonts can look jagged without anti-aliasing (Fig. 3.6).

Once the text is typed, it can be moved with either the type tool or the *move tool*. The move tool is indicated by an arrow with cross hairs (Fig. 3.7). As soon as the move tool is selected, a *bounding box* with side and corner *anchors* appears around the text. Anchors are the small boxes that appear on the edges of a bounding box. Clicking and dragging the anchors resizes the contents of the bounding box.

Select the move tool and click anywhere within the bounding box. Drag the text to the center of the image window. Click and drag any anchor to resize the text. Dragging a corner anchor while pressing the *Shift* key resizes the bounding box contents proportionately.

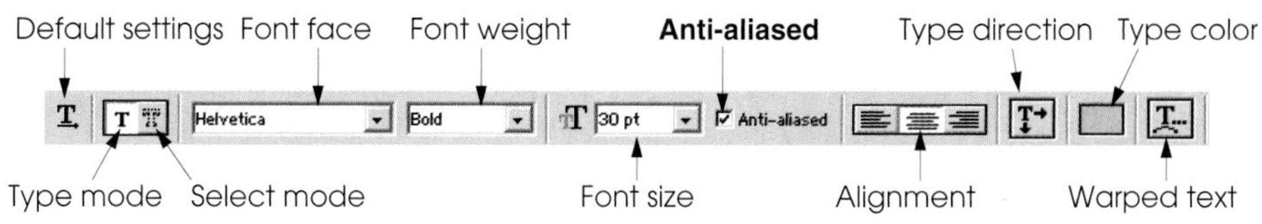

Fig. 3.5 Type options bar. (Adobe and Photoshop are either registered trademarks or trademarks of Adobe Systems Incorporated in the United States and/or other countries.)

Fig. 3.6 Example of anti-aliasing. (Adobe and Photoshop are either registered trademarks or trademarks of Adobe Systems Incorporated in the United States and/or other countries.)

Photoshop Elements has several options for applying special effects to text and images. Click and drag the ***Layer Styles*** tab out of the *palettes well* to open the ***Layer Styles*** *palette*. If this palette tab is not visible in the palettes well, it can be opened by selecting **Show Layer Styles** from the **Window** menu. The **Layer Styles** palette offers a variety of effects that can be applied to text or shapes. Select **Drop Shadows** as the style type from the drop-down list inside this palette (Fig. 3.8).

Next select **Low** as the type of drop shadow from the style selection. A drop-shadow effect is applied to the text. Any layer style can be removed by selecting the ***Default Style*** from the **Layer Styles** palette.

A user can edit an effect, such as a drop shadow in two ways. The first is by selecting **Scale Effects...** from the **Layer Style** submenu of the **Layer** menu. The scale adjustment in the **Scale Effects** dialog increases or decreases the intensity of any layer effect. Scale the low drop shadow to **31** percent (Fig. 3.8).

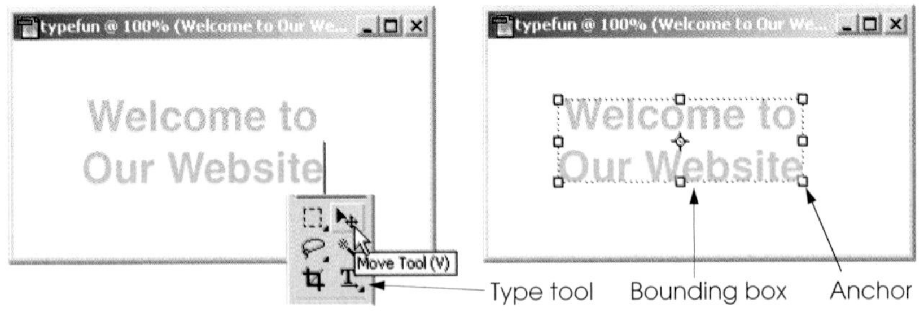

Fig. 3.7 Adding text to an image. (Adobe and Photoshop are either registered trademarks or trademarks of Adobe Systems Incorporated in the United States and/or other countries.)

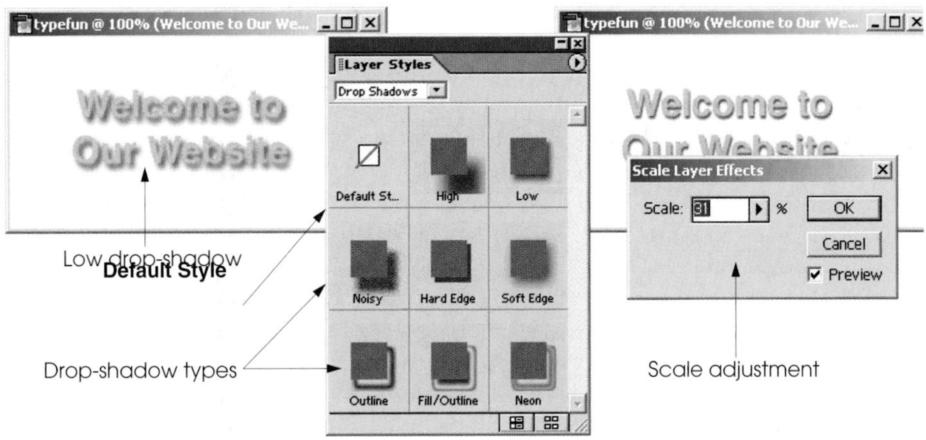

Fig. 3.8 Adding a drop shadow to text with the **Layer Styles** palette. (Adobe and Photoshop are either registered trademarks or trademarks of Adobe Systems Incorporated in the United States and/or other countries.)

The second way to adjust a layer style is through the ***Layers*** *palette*. Drag the **Layers** palette out of the palette well. This palette controls the use of *layers* in Photoshop Elements. Layers organize the different components that compose an image. The *active layer* is highlighted in blue in the **Layers** palette. When using tools or applying special effects, only the active layer is affected. Notice that the text occupies its own *type layer* indicated by a **T** on its layer in the **Layers** palette (Fig. 3.9). Having the type on its own layer enables it to be edited independently of any other part of the image. Click the type layer in the **Layers** palette to activate it. The ***f*** symbol in the blue area of the type layer indicates that the layer has a style applied to it. Double click the ***f*** to open the ***Style Settings*** dialog (Fig. 3.9).

Different options are available depending on the type of style applied to the layer. Set the drop shadow ***Lighting Angle*** to **120** degrees and the ***Shadow Distance*** to **3** pixels. The **Lighting Angle** controls the direction of the light source creating the shadow. The **Shadow Distance** determines the size of the drop shadow. Press **OK** to apply these changes.

Text also can be warped to conform to a shape. Select the type tool from the toolbox to reveal the **Type** options bar. Click the **Warp text** button in the **Type** options bar indicated by a **T** with an arc beneath it (Fig. 3.10).

The **Warp Text** dialog allows the user to select different shapes. For this example, select **Flag** from the **Styles** drop-down list and set the **Bend** slider to **+50%**. The three sliders modify the bend, horizontal distortion and vertical distortion of the text shape, respectively. The text changes to reflect the selection in real time in the original image window; however, the change is not applied until **OK** is clicked in the dialog.

The next step is to create the effect of *transparency*. Transparency allows the background of the Web page to show through in the white portions of the image. Recall that when this file was created, the background color was set to white. A transparent background could have been specified. Creating a transparent background at this stage requires using the **Layers** palette (Fig. 3.11).

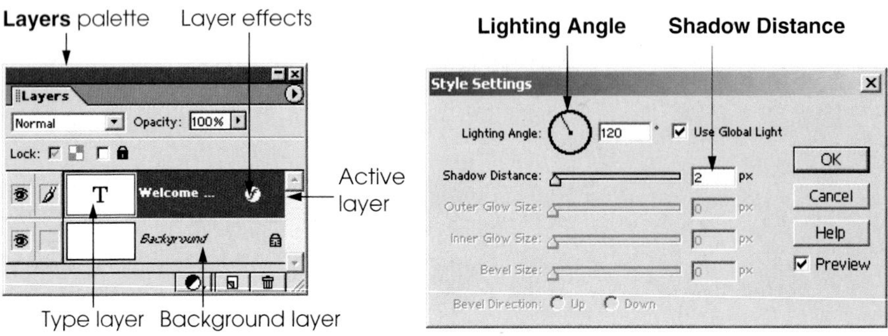

Fig. 3.9 Customizing layer effects. (Adobe and Photoshop are either registered trademarks or trademarks of Adobe Systems Incorporated in the United States and/or other countries.)

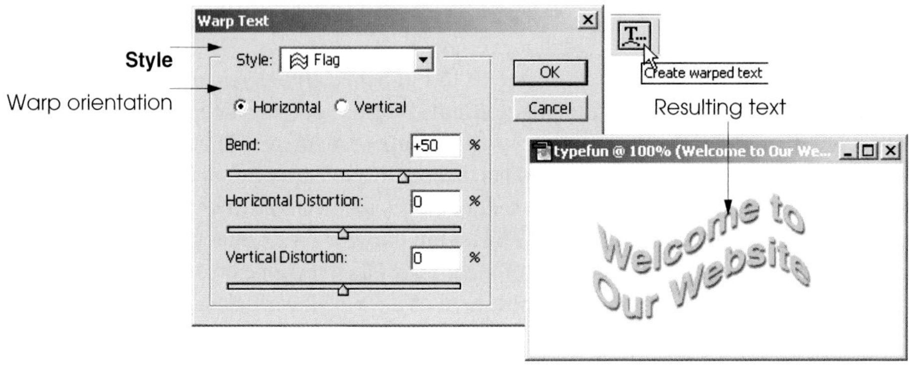

Fig. 3.10 **Warped Text** dialog. (Adobe and Photoshop are either registered trademarks or trademarks of Adobe Systems Incorporated in the United States and/or other countries.)

New layers are transparent by default. The type layer is transparent with the exception of the type and its effects. Deleting the white background layer makes the image background transparent. Select the background layer in the **Layers** palette to make it the active layer. Click the **Trashcan** button to delete this layer. The new image should have a gray and white checkerboard background, representing transparency. When the image is placed in a Web document, the background color of the Web page appears in the transparent parts.

Photoshop Elements provides an option for saving images for the Web. Choosing **Save for Web...** option, located under the **File** menu, opens a dialog **Save for Web** dialog. This dialog allows the user to determine the file format and color settings for saving an image. The original image appears on the left side of the dialog and the *optimized* version appears on the right (Fig. 3.12). Information about the graphic file, including file type, file size, estimated download time and the *number of colors*, appears for each image.

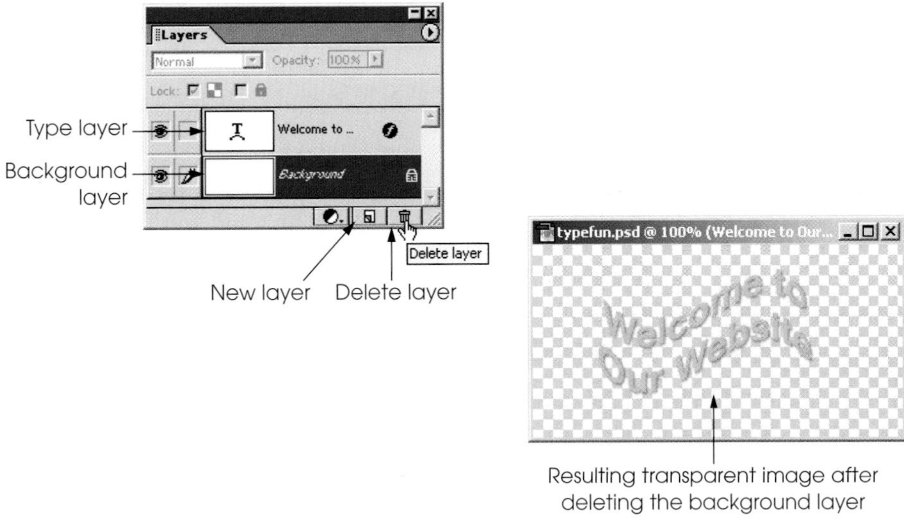

Fig. 3.11 Deleting a layer using the **Layers** palette. (Adobe and Photoshop are either registered trademarks or trademarks of Adobe Systems Incorporated in the United States and/or other countries.)

The optimized version is a preview of what the image will look like after it is saved. The different optimization settings such as file type, *compression quality* and number of colors the image utilizes, are all set in the **Save for Web** dialog. The file type determines the *compression* Photoshop Elements uses to save an image. Compression is defined by an algorithm that Photoshop Elements uses to save file data. The compression quality is the accuracy of the compression algorithm and determines the quality of the saved image.

The number of colors an image contains also affects the image quality. The more colors an image uses, the higher the image clarity. The number of colors may only be selected with certain file types.

Reducing the number of colors or the compression quality may decrease file size, thus lessening the image's download time. Optimization is the process of finding the correct balance between the number of colors, the compression quality and the file size such that the download time is ideal for the target audience.

Different file formats are appropriate for different types of graphics. The *GIF* (Compuserve Graphics Interchange Format) format preserves transparency (saving pixels void of color information), making GIF ideal for transparent Web graphics such as **`typefun`**. Other file formats are discussed later in this chapter. Select **GIF** from the file type drop-down list. Make sure that the **Transparency** box is checked in the **Save for Web** dialog; otherwise, the image will not be saved as a transparent image.

When saving transparent images, it is important to choose a *matte color* with the **Matte** selector. A matte color optimizes the effect of transparency by blending the transparent edge pixels with the color so that the graphic blends into the page without having jagged edges. It is ideal to select a matte color that closely matches the background color of the Web page into which the image is placed. Select a matte color and notice the change to the optimized image.

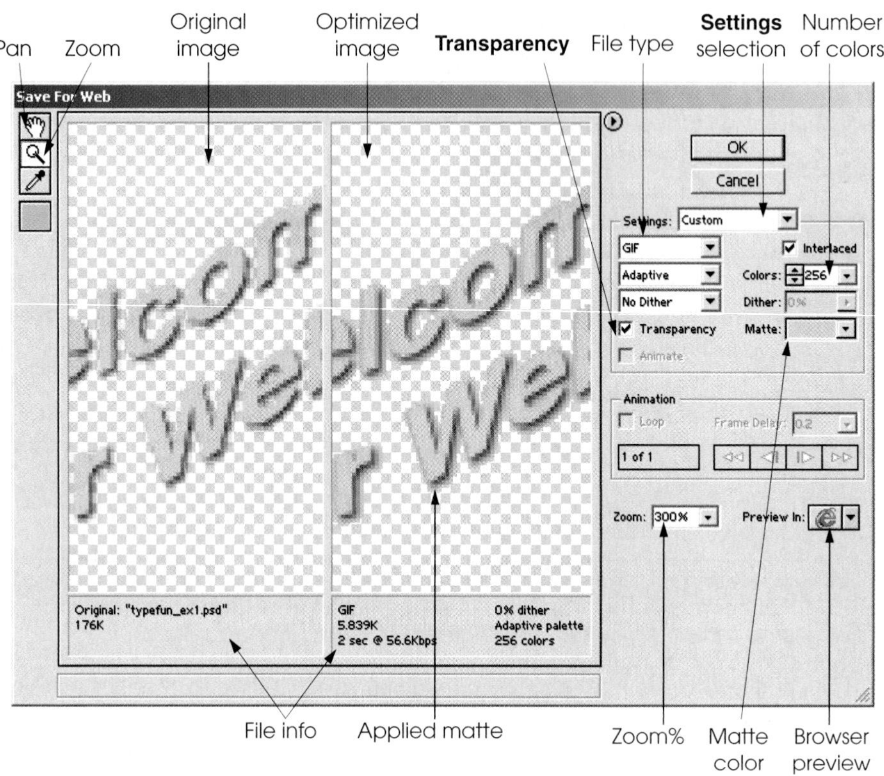

Fig. 3.12 Adding a matte color to a transparent GIF in the **Save for Web** dialog. (Adobe and Photoshop are either registered trademarks or trademarks of Adobe Systems Incorporated in the United States and/or other countries.)

An image may be previewed in a Web browser by clicking the *browser preview* button before it is saved. This option creates a temporary Web document with the image embedded. The background color of the preview is the **Matte** color. This preview also provides information about the image such as file format, image dimensions, file size and file settings. Close the browser window to return to Photoshop Elements and click **OK** in the **Save for Web** dialog. Choose a descriptive name for the file so that it is easily identified when it is placed in a Web document. Inserting images into Web pages is introduced in Chapters 4 and 5.

3.3 Vector and Raster Graphics

Photoshop Elements creates and edits two types of graphics that are standard for Web design—*raster* and *vector*. A raster image is composed of pixels organized on a grid. Each pixel in a raster image is stored as a particular combination of colors when it is saved. If the size of a raster image is increased, the image editing program adds pixels in a process called *interpolation*. Interpolation lowers the image quality, making raster images *resolution dependent*. Raster graphics are ideal for images that have subtle gradations of colors such as photographs and original artwork, or images created with the raster tool set in Photoshop Elements. Raster tools are discussed in the next section.

A vector graphic is not stored as a grid of pixels. Instead, a vector graphic is created by a set of user-determined mathematical properties called *vectors*. These properties include a graphic's dimensions, attributes and position. Examples of vector graphics in Photoshop Elements are text created with the type tool and shapes created with the *shape tool*. The shape tool can create rectangles, ellipses, polygons, lines and custom shapes. Vector images exist as individual objects that can be edited separately from one another. They can also be resized without losing clarity because vector information is stored as sets of instructions instead of groups of pixels. It is this characteristic which makes vector graphics *resolution independent*. Vector graphics are ideal for creating solid areas of color and text; however, they cannot handle the image quality of photographs or other color-complex images. Figure 3.13 demonstrates the difference between scaling raster and vector graphics. The raster image becomes *pixelated* while the vector does not lose any clarity.

3.4 Toolbox

Photoshop Elements offers tools which simplify the image-composition process. The toolbox, which appears by default on the left side of the editing area, groups these tools by editing function. The names of the different tools are highlighted in Fig. 3.14.

Photoshop Elements provides *navigation tools* that aid the user in the editing process. The *magnifying glass* is a navigation tool that *zooms in* on an image. Click and drag with the magnifying glass tool to zoom into a particular area. Click a spot to zoom in with that spot centered in the image window. Hold down the *Alt* key while clicking to zoom out. The shortcut for zooming in is *Ctrl*+ (plus) and the shortcut for zooming out is *Ctrl*– (minus).

Clicking and dragging with the *hand* tool pans from one side of an image to the other. This tool is useful when an image is large or when an image is magnified. The hand tool is accessible at any time by holding down the *Spacebar* key.

Some tools have *hidden tools* beneath them in the toolbox. A small triangle in the lower-right corner of the tool button indicates hidden tools. The *marquee tool*, the *type tool* and the lasso tool have hidden tools beneath them. Click and hold the tool button to reveal hidden options.

Fig. 3.13 Raster and vector graphics scaled. (Adobe and Photoshop are either registered trademarks or trademarks of Adobe Systems Incorporated in the United States and/or other countries.)

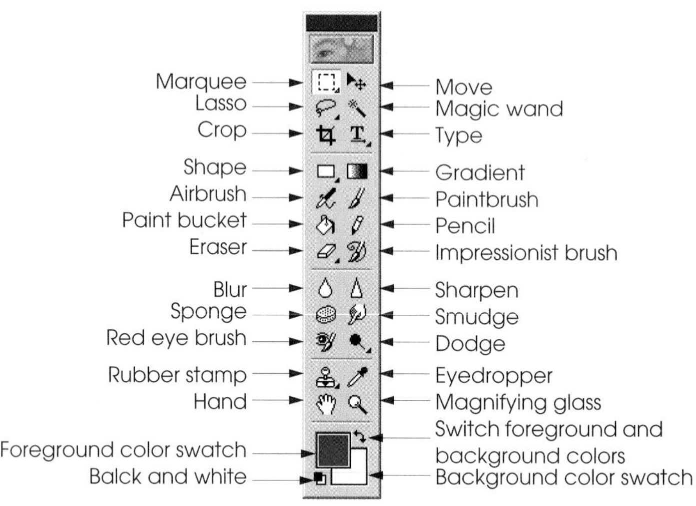

Fig. 3.14 Photoshop Elements Toolbox. (Adobe and Photoshop are either registered trademarks or trademarks of Adobe Systems Incorporated in the United States and/or other countries.)

3.4.1 Selection Tools

The *selection tools*—the "marquee", "lasso" and "magic wand"—create a border called a *marquee*. A marquee bounds a selected area of pixels that can be modified by *filters*, moved or have their colors adjusted. Filters are special effects that perform uniform changes to an area of pixels. A selection marquee is moved by dragging it with a selection tool. Moving a selection marquee with the move tool moves the pixels bounded inside the marquee, leaving the area the selection previously occupied transparent, revealing any layers beneath (Fig. 3.15).

The *rectangular marquee* and the *elliptical marquee* tools select areas of pixels. The default marquee is the rectangular marquee tool and the elliptical marquee is hidden beneath it. These tools may be constrained to either a perfect circle or square by pressing the *Shift* key while clicking and dragging.

The *lasso tools* (regular, polygonal and magnetic) allow the user to customize a selection area. The *regular lasso*, the default, draws a freehand marquee around an area of pixels, following every move of the mouse. Clicking and dragging the *magnetic lasso* tool, hidden behind the regular lasso, traces a selection area by adhering to the edges of an object in an image. The magnetic lasso finds the edges by the difference in pixel color. The *polygonal lasso* draws straight-edged selections by clicking at the selection corner points. Figure 3.16 illustrates the selections using the various lasso tools.

The *magic wand* tool selects areas of similarly colored adjacent pixels. The *tolerance* setting increases or decreases the pixel color range that the magic wand selects (Fig. 3.17). The **Magic Wand** options bar provides the tolerance settings.

The selection tool option bars help customize selection areas (Fig. 3.18). A selection can be added to, subtracted from or intersected with another selection with these options. These options also may be used while toggling between different selection tools.

Fig. 3.15 Moving a selection with the move tool. (Adobe and Photoshop are either registered trademarks or trademarks of Adobe Systems Incorporated in the United States and/or other countries.)

Selection with the regular lasso

Selection with the magnetic lasso

Fig. 3.16 Drawing selection areas with the lasso tools. (Adobe and Photoshop are either registered trademarks or trademarks of Adobe Systems Incorporated in the United States and/or other countries.)

The next example shows how to use the selection tools to create a blurred frame for an image so that it gradually blends into the background color of a Web page. Open the file **`eiffel.jpg`** located in the Chapter 3 examples directory on the CD-ROM that accompanies this book. Choose the rectangular marquee tool from the toolbox and set the *feathering* to 8 pixels in the **Marquee tool** options bar. Feathering blurs the edges of a selection so the pixels inside the selection blend with the pixels outside the selection. The number of pixels, in this case, determines the amount of blur around the selection's edge. The effects of feathering a selection are shown in Fig. 3.19.

Click and drag the rectangular marquee tool from the upper left to the lower right of the photograph, leaving some space between the edge of the picture and the selection. Any selection may be removed or modified. Clicking the image with any of the selection tools while a marquee is active, removes the marquee. Notice that the corners of the selection are rounded, indicating that it is feathered. The image on the left in Fig. 3.19 has selection feathering set to 0.

Fig. 3.17 Changing the magic wand tolerance to affect the size of a selection. (Adobe and Photoshop are either registered trademarks or trademarks of Adobe Systems Incorporated in the United States and/or other countries.)

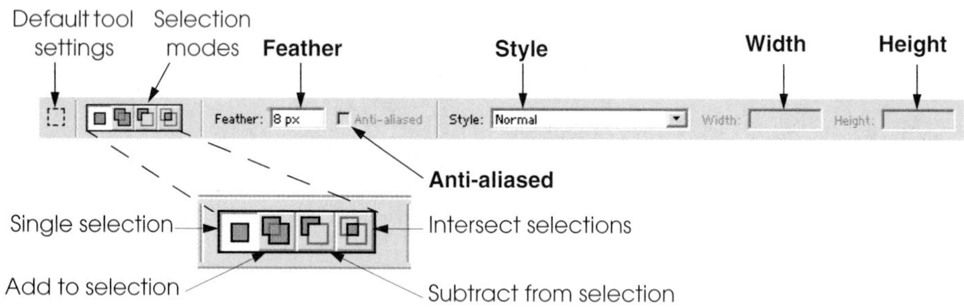

Fig. 3.18 Making multiple selections using the selection tool options bar. (Adobe and Photoshop are either registered trademarks or trademarks of Adobe Systems Incorporated in the United States and/or other countries.)

Select **Inverse** from the **Select** menu or use the shortcut *Ctrl+Shift+I* to *invert* the selection. *Inverting* selects all the pixels outside the current selection marquee. Click the foreground color and choose RGB **204**, **0**, **1** or **#CC0033** in the **Color Picker** dialog. Choose **Fill...** from the **Edit** menu. The **Fill** dialog (Fig. 3.20) presents several options for filling a selection or layer. For this example, set the fill to **Foreground Color**, leave the *blending mode* set to **Normal** and click **OK**. The shortcut to fill any selection with the foreground color is *Alt+Backspace*. Alternatively, pressing *Ctrl+Backspace* fills a selection with the background color. These shortcuts only work with the *normal blending mode*. The blending mode determines how color interacts with the image color to which it is applied. Blending modes are explored in a later example.

Look-and-Feel Observation 3.2

*Changing the blending mode in the **Fill** dialog produces different blending effects between the border and the image. Test the different blending modes to view the differences.*

Feathering set to 0 pixels

Feathering set to 8 pixels

Fig. 3.19 Feathering a selection. (Adobe and Photoshop are either registered trademarks or trademarks of Adobe Systems Incorporated in the United States and/or other countries.)

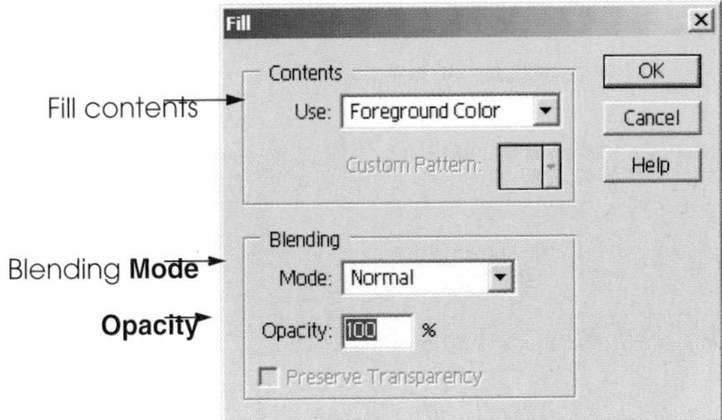

Fill the feathered selection

Fig. 3.20 Filling a selection with color. (Adobe and Photoshop are either registered trademarks or trademarks of Adobe Systems Incorporated in the United States and/or other countries.)

Choose **Deselect** from the **Select** menu or use the shortcut *Ctrl+D* to remove a selection marquee. As in the first example in which we created the file **`typefun`**, this image is saved for the Web. This time save the file in *JPEG* (Joint Photographic Experts Group) format, by selecting **JPEG** as the file type in the **Save for Web** dialog. JPEG is a format commonly used on the Web for saving photographic-quality images.

The JPEG format allows the user to specify the quality of the image being saved. For this image, set the quality to 50, which is medium quality. Most JPEG images intended for the Web are saved as medium or low quality to reduce their file size. JPEG images are previewed in a Web browser in the same way as GIF files. Choose RGB **204**, **0**, **1** or

#CC0033 as the matte color so that the background color of the preview Web page is the same as the blurred frame around the photograph (Fig. 3.21).

3.4.2 Painting Tools

The second group of toolbox tools are the *painting tools,* which apply color to an image in simulated brush strokes or in constrained shapes. *Paintbrush* and *airbrush* are raster tools that draw with virtual paintbrush or airbrush strokes by clicking and dragging them on the image area. Different brush size and stroke options are selected in the options bar.

The *paint bucket* tool adds the foreground color to selections or areas of similarly colored pixels. The pixel selection process for this tool is the same as the selection process for the magic wand tool. The paint bucket tool fills large areas with color.

Another interesting way to fill an area with color is with the *gradient* tool. The gradient tool fills an area with a progression of colors (Fig. 3.22). The area to be filled must be selected with one of the selection tools before a gradient is applied to it, otherwise the gradient fills the entire canvas. Click and drag with the gradient tool, in the direction of the gradient movement to create patterns of color. Gradients can be created in many shapes and colors depending on which options are selected in the **Gradients** options bar.

Fig. 3.21 Previewing the feathered image in a Web browser. (Adobe and Photoshop are either registered trademarks or trademarks of Adobe Systems Incorporated in the United States and/or other countries.)

The following example shows the different uses of the painting tools, *filters* and type tools to create a title image for a Web page. Filters alter the appearance of a selection or an entire raster layer by applying uniform changes to every pixel. Create a new image that is 200 pixels high, 600 pixels wide with a white background in RGB mode. Select RGB **153, 204, 255** or **#99CCFF**, a light blue, as the foreground color and RGB **0, 0, 153** or **#000099**, a darker blue, as the background color. Fill the background layer with the foreground color by using the shortcut *Alt+Backspace*. This shortcut works on an entire layer if no selection is made. Next choose the paintbrush tool and select a *brush size* of **13** from the **Paintbrush** options bar. Several brush types and sizes are available in this options bar, including some that are hidden. The hidden brushes are found in different categories under the **brush** drop-down list (Fig. 3.23). This brush menu may also be accessed by right clicking in the image area with any of the paint-brush tools.

Feel free to experiment with these different brushes. For this example, it does not matter which brushes are used because painting will be distorted. Painting tools always paint with the foreground color. For this example, we want to paint with the dark blue background color. Make the background color become the foreground color by clicking the *switch foreground and background* arrow found directly above the background color swatch in the toolbox. Once the colors are switched, paint randomly on the canvas with the dark blue color (Fig. 3.24).

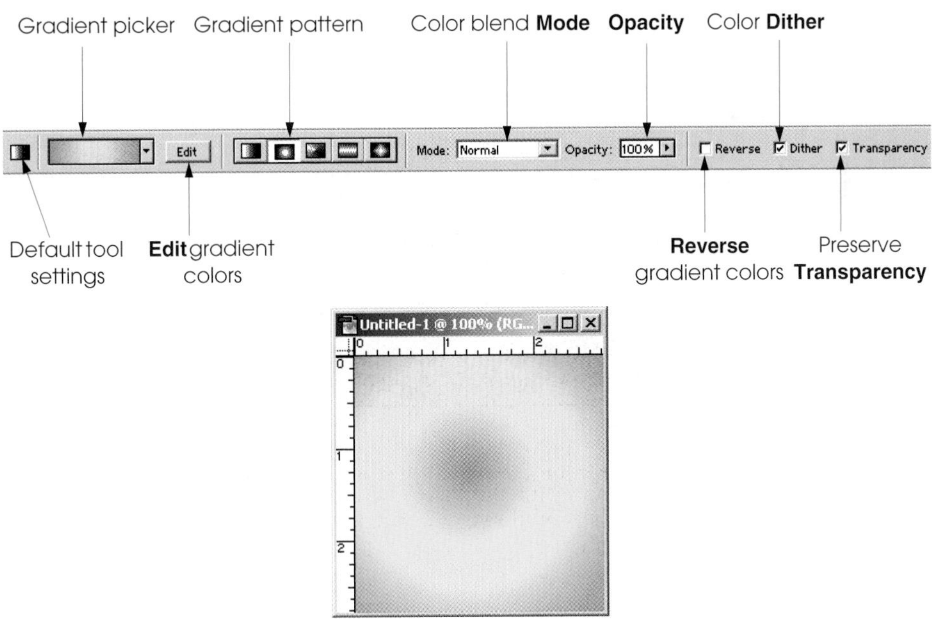

Fig. 3.22 Using the gradient tool. (Adobe and Photoshop are either registered trademarks or trademarks of Adobe Systems Incorporated in the United States and/or other countries.)

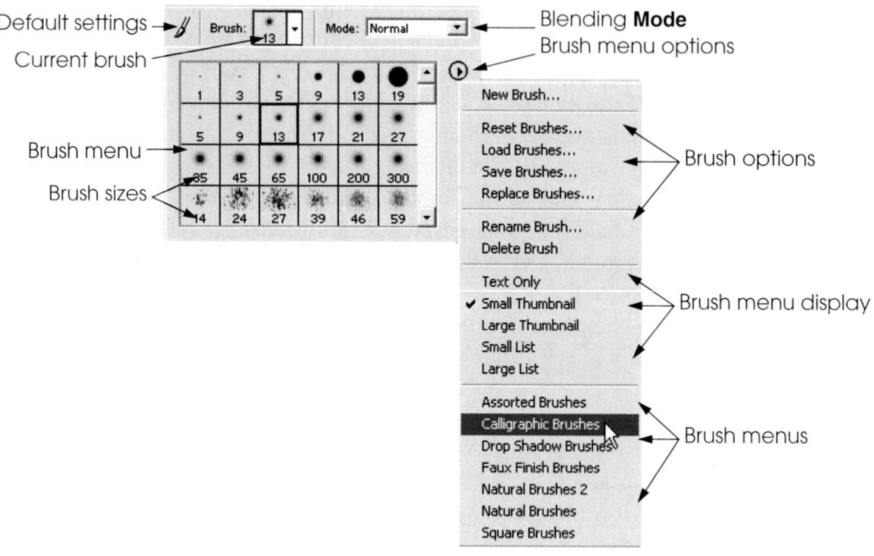

Fig. 3.23 Brush options. (Adobe and Photoshop are either registered trademarks or trademarks of Adobe Systems Incorporated in the United States and/ or other countries.)

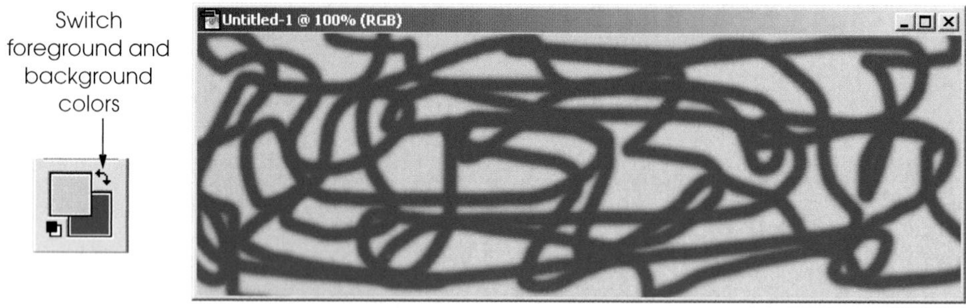

Fig. 3.24 Painting with the paintbrush tool. (Adobe and Photoshop are either registered trademarks or trademarks of Adobe Systems Incorporated in the United States and/or other countries.)

This "painting" will eventually become a design that fills the title text. Designs can be created by using one of Photoshop Elements' many filters. Begin to create the pattern by choosing **Liquify...** from the **Filters** menu. The *liquify* filter distorts an image by modifying color placement. When the **Liquify** dialog opens (Fig. 3.25), choose a *brush size* of

50 with a *brush pressure* of **50**. The brush size determines the area affected by the filter. The brush pressure determines the filter's intensity. Click and drag in the painted area to apply the liquify filter. Eight different modes for the liquify filter can be selected with buttons along the left side of the dialog. The default mode for this tool is *warp*, however, feel free to experiment with the other modes. If a mistake is made, click **Revert** to change the image back to its original appearance.

The liquify filter is one of the few filters that creates its effects based on the artistic input of the user, making it more like a tool than an actual filter. Most of the other filter effects are performed uniformly on image pixels. Continue to click and drag with the liquify brush until a design is created. Press **OK** to apply the filter to the original image.

Performance Tip 3.2

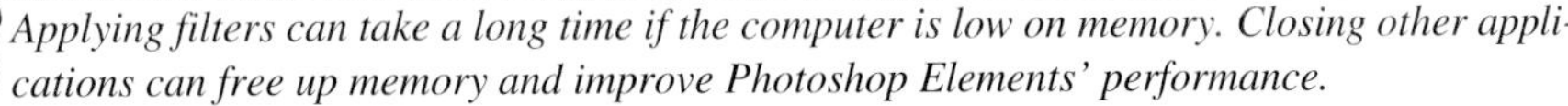

Applying filters can take a long time if the computer is low on memory. Closing other applications can free up memory and improve Photoshop Elements' performance.

The next step is to define the text area to which the design is applied. Instead of creating regular text, we want to create a selection marquee in the shape of text. Select the type tool and choose the *type selection* option from the type options bar. The type selection tool is indicated by a dashed line **T** (Fig. 3.26). Choose a font face of **Brush Script** with font size **150** point (type the font size). The purpose of using the type selection tool instead of the regular type tool is to capture the pattern inside the selection boundaries of the type. Then the selection can be separated from the rest of the pattern and placed onto a new layer. Set the alignment for the type selection tool to *center* and click the middle of the image. The image turns red, indicating that a text selection is being made. Type the word "Welcome." The background remains red and the type shows through in the original blue color (Fig. 3.26).

Fig. 3.25 Using the **Liquify** filter to create a pattern. (Adobe and Photoshop are either registered trademarks or trademarks of Adobe Systems Incorporated in the United States and/or other countries.)

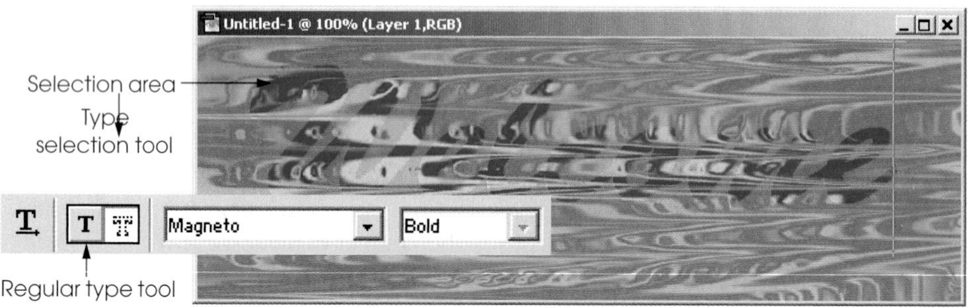

Fig. 3.26 Using the type selection tool to create a title image. (Adobe and Photoshop are either registered trademarks or trademarks of Adobe Systems Incorporated in the United States and/or other countries.)

The selection is not applied until another tool is chosen. For this example, select the move tool to apply the selection. The move tool creates a bounding box around the selection.

Separate the text from the background by copying its contents to a new layer. Use the **Layer via Copy** (*Ctrl+J*) function found under the **New** submenu of the **Layer** menu to create a new layer with the contents of a selection. Even though the text exists in its own layer, it is still not visible because it is hidden by the background layer. Turn off the background layer *visibility* by opening the **Layers** palette and clicking the layer's visibility button (Fig. 3.27). A layer is not deleted when the visibility is turned off; it is only deactivated so that contents of other layers can be better identified. The copied text in the new layer should be the only visible element.

The next step is to crop out the background area using the *crop* tool located in the toolbox next to the type tool. Click and drag with the crop tool to make a *crop box* that eliminates the extra background area. The area being cropped turns gray and a bounding box with anchors surrounds the remaining area (Fig. 3.28). Adjust the bounding box that eliminates the background area around the word. Once the crop selection is set, press the *Enter* key to crop the image.

The next step in creating the title image is to give the word a layer effect to raise it off the page. Select the background layer in the **Layers** palette if it is not already selected. As in the first example, open the **Layer Styles** palette. Instead of applying a **Drop Shadow**, this time choose **Bevels** from the style-selection drop-down list. Apply the **Simple Sharp Inner** bevel to the "Welcome" layer (Fig. 3.29).

The last step is to create a color border to outline the text. Choose the **Magic Wand** tool and click outside the word, selecting the transparent area. Add spaces inside the **o, e** and **l** by either clicking the **add to selection** button in the **Magic Wand** options bar (Fig. 3.18) or holding down *Shift* while clicking the letter spaces with the magic wand tool. Next, invert the selection so that the word is selected instead of the transparent background (*Ctrl+Shift+I*). Create a line with an even pixel weight along the selection by choosing ***Stroke*** from the **Edit** menu. The **Stroke** dialog has options for stroke width, stroke color, stroke location, blending mode and opacity (Fig. 3.29).

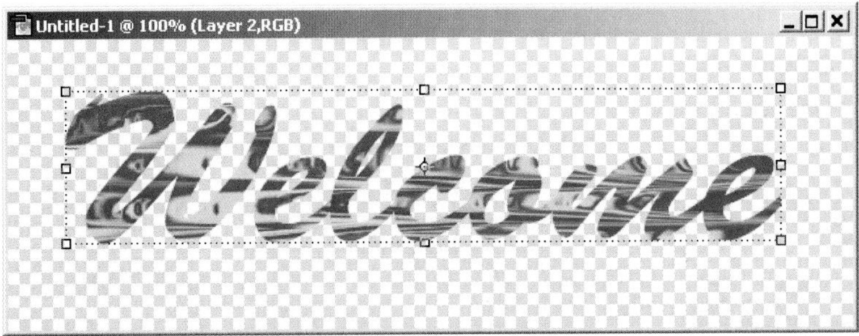

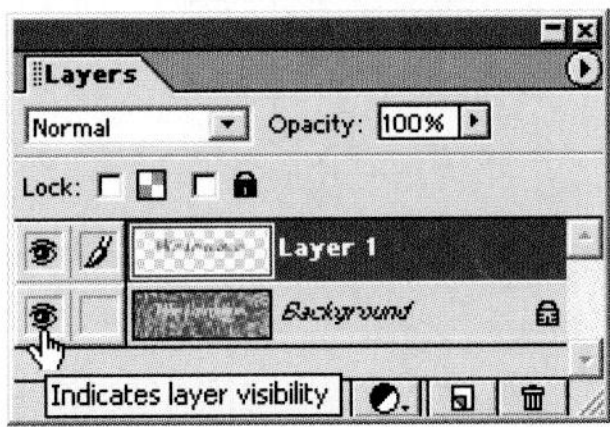

Fig. 3.27 Turning off layer visibility in the **Layers** palette. (Adobe and Photoshop are either registered trademarks or trademarks of Adobe Systems Incorporated in the United States and/or other countries.)

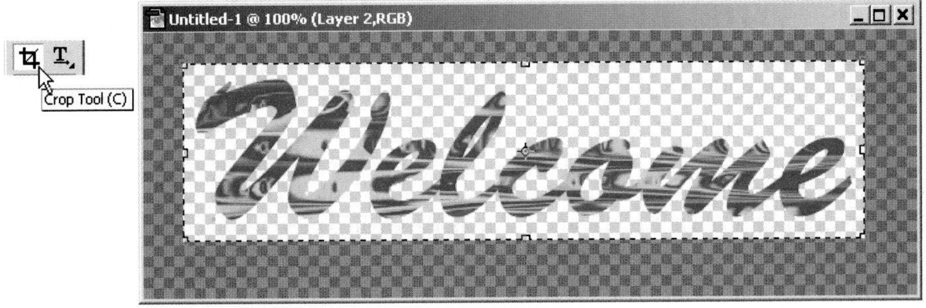

Fig. 3.28 Using the crop tool to eliminate excess image area. (Adobe and Photoshop are either registered trademarks or trademarks of Adobe Systems Incorporated in the United States and/or other countries.)

Set the *line weight* to 3 pixels and ***Location*** to center in the **Stroke** dialog. The stroke **Color** defaults to the current foreground color, and can be changed by double clicking the stroke swatch. Make sure that the **Preserve Transparency** box is unchecked, otherwise the stroke will not appear in the transparent area around the word. Click **OK**.

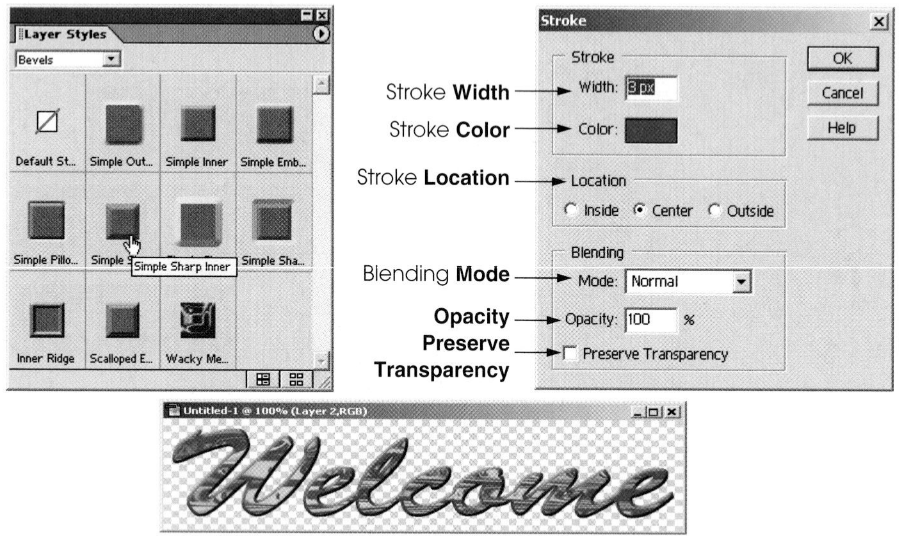

Fig. 3.29 Applying a simple inner bevel and a stroke selection. (Adobe and Photoshop are either registered trademarks or trademarks of Adobe Systems Incorporated in the United States and/or other countries.)

3.4.3 Shape Tools

The *shape* tool draws vector shapes filled with color. Unlike raster graphics in the same layer, vector graphics can be edited independently from one another. Every time a shape tool is used, a new vector *shape layer* is created. Shape layers contain only shapes created with the shape tool and cannot contain raster graphics. The shape tool's default setting is a rectangle; however the shape can be changed to an ellipse, polygon, line or custom shape with the shape tool options bar. The options change depending on the selected tool (Fig. 3.30).

To demonstrate the shape tool, we will create a navigation bar. Each button on the bar is created as a vector shape with the shape tool and converted into a raster graphic to create the navigation bar.

Create a new file that is 625 pixels wide and 100 pixels high. For guidance when creating the navigation bar, turn on the grid by choosing **Show Grid** from the **View** menu. This option helps to space the buttons evenly. The settings for the grid are changed in the **Grid Preferences** dialog by choosing **Grid...** from the **Preferences** submenu of the **Edit** menu. Set the grid lines to appear for every pixel and set the grid line color to light blue.

Choose a new foreground color to become the color of the buttons. The navigation buttons are created as a series of duplicate rectangles. Select the shape tool from the toolbox and select the rectangle tool from the **Shape tool** options bar. Create a rectangle that fills a little less than 1/4 of the image width, approximately 15 grid squares, as shown in Fig. 3.31.

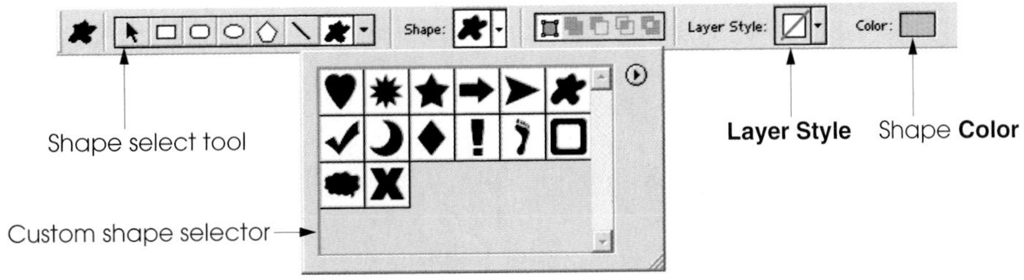

Fig. 3.30 **Custom shape** options bar. (Adobe and Photoshop are either registered trademarks or trademarks of Adobe Systems Incorporated in the United States and/or other countries.)

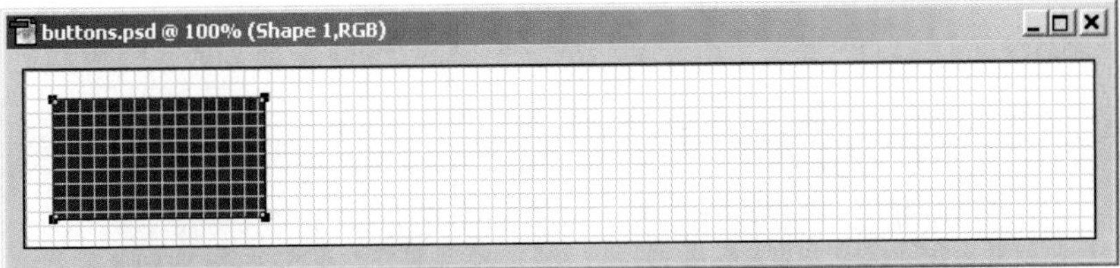

Fig. 3.31 Creating a rectangle with the shape tool. (Adobe and Photoshop are either registered trademarks or trademarks of Adobe Systems Incorporated in the United States and/or other countries.)

Duplicate this rectangle three times (once for each link in the navigation bar). Select the *shape select* tool, indicated by an arrow, from the **Shape** options bar. Copy the rectangle to the *clipboard* by clicking the copy button in the main menu bar (Fig. 3.32) or use the shortcut *Ctrl+C*. The clipboard is an area of temporary memory in the computer in which text and graphics can be stored for immediate reuse. The *paste* command places the information from the clipboard into a document. Use the paste button or the shortcut *Ctrl+V* to paste the rectangle from the clipboard back into the main image. This new rectangle is placed directly on top of the existing rectangle in the same vector layer. Drag the new rectangle next to the original using the shape select tool. Space the rectangles two grid lines apart. Repeat the copy and paste step two more times to create the four navigation bar buttons (Fig. 3.33).

If the rectangles were placed unevenly, adjust their position using the shape select tool. It is also possible to use the **Undo** command in the **Edit** menu, or the *Ctrl+Z* command to correct mistakes. Actions can be undone as far back as the last time the image was saved by using the ***History*** *palette*. The **History** palette (Fig. 3.34) displays every action performed since the last save. Selecting an action in the palette creates a preview of the image if that action were undone. Click the **trashcan** button in the **History** palette to undo an action permanently.

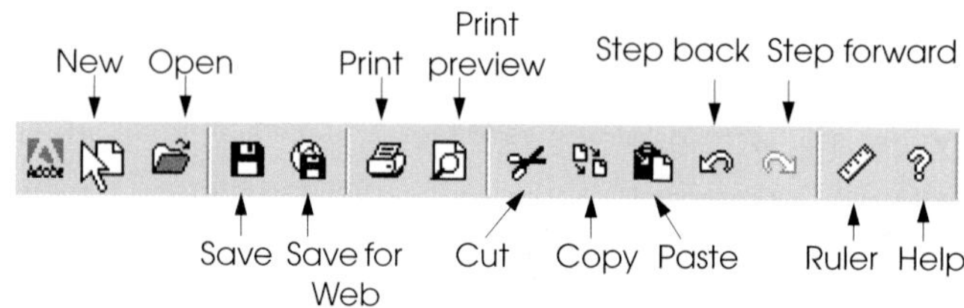

Fig. 3.32 Using the main menu bar to copy and paste. (Adobe and Photoshop are either registered trademarks or trademarks of Adobe Systems Incorporated in the United States and/or other countries.)

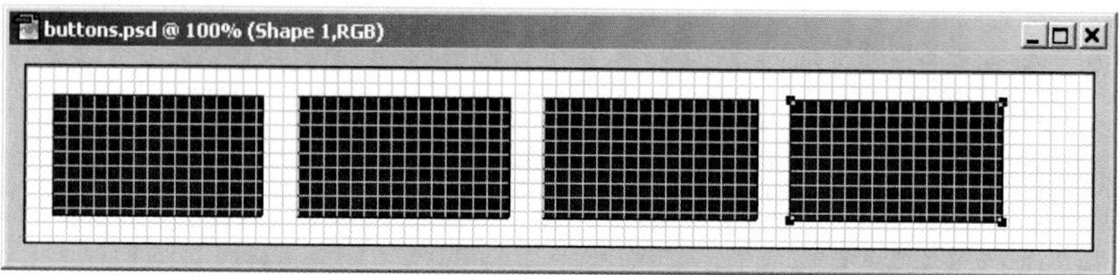

Fig. 3.33 Creating multiple rectangles with the move shape tool. (Adobe and Photoshop are either registered trademarks or trademarks of Adobe Systems Incorporated in the United States and/or other countries.)

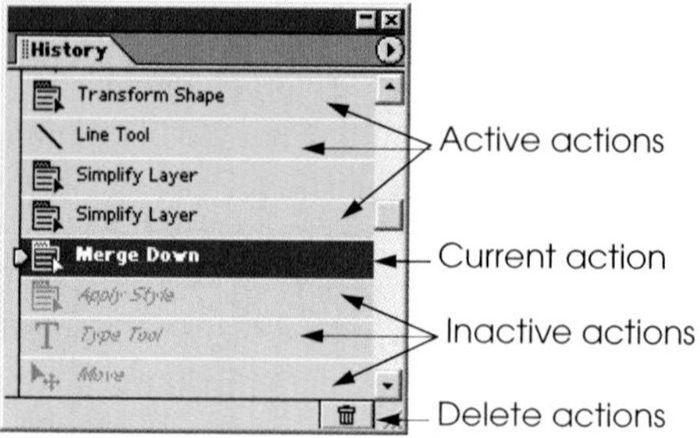

Fig. 3.34 Using the **History** palette to reverse actions. (Adobe and Photoshop are either registered trademarks or trademarks of Adobe Systems Incorporated in the United States and/or other countries.)

The rectangles should now be in a straight line and evenly spaced. The next step is to change the shape of the rectangles uniformly, turning them into parallelograms by *skewing* the rectangles with the *transformation* option to tilt them along the horizontal or vertical axis. To achieve this, select all the rectangles by clicking each with the shape select tool while holding down the *Shift* key. All rectangles are selected simultaneously when each has a shape selection box around it. Apply a skew transformation by selecting **Skew** from the **Transform Shape** submenu of the **Image** menu. During the skew transformation a bounding box encloses all four rectangles. Hover near the top center anchor until a two-way arrow appears. Click and drag the bounding box two grid lines to the right, transforming the rectangles (Fig. 3.35).

All four rectangles slant to the right when the mouse is released. Transformations are not applied until the *Enter* key is pressed, so if the shapes do not look correct, the transformation still can be changed.

A *navigation bar* effect is created by connecting the buttons. For this example, the buttons will be connected by a heavy-weight line created with the *line shape* tool. The line shape tool is located in the **Shape tool** options bar between the *polygon* tool and the *custom shape* tool. Set the line weight for the line tool to **20** pixels in the tool options bar. Click and drag from left to right with the line shape tool, creating a line in a new vector layer (Fig. 3.36).

The outline of the four parallelograms connected with the line outlines the navigation bar. Apply a bevel to these shapes to make them appear as buttons; however the steps to do this are more complicated than applying layer styles to text or shapes alone. First the rectangles and line layers must be converted from vector shape layers into regular raster layers. Then they must be merged together so the buttons and line are treated as one area of pixels.

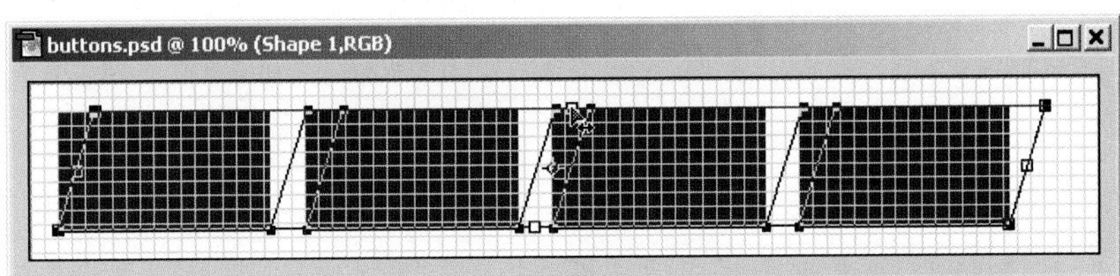

Fig. 3.35 Applying the skew transformation. (Adobe and Photoshop are either registered trademarks or trademarks of Adobe Systems Incorporated in the United States and/or other countries.)

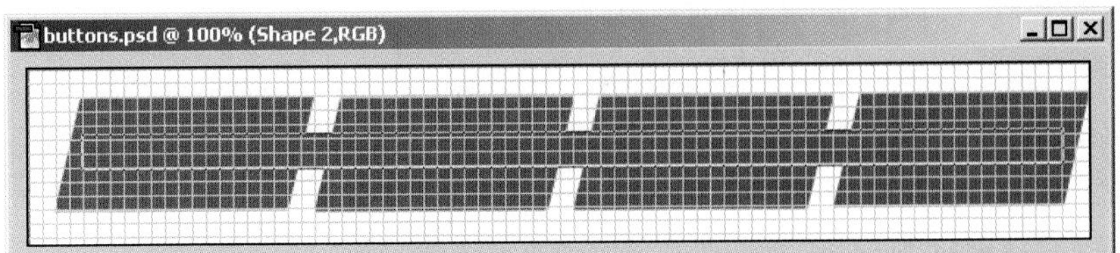

Fig. 3.36 Line added to link the skewed rectangles together. (Adobe and Photoshop are either registered trademarks or trademarks of Adobe Systems Incorporated in the United States and/or other countries.)

Open the **Layers** palette and select the line layer. Change both the line layer and buttons layer into regular raster layers separately by choosing **Simplify Layer** from the layer options menu (Fig. 3.37). Both the line and the parallelograms are no longer individual vector objects. Instead they are raster areas of pixels.

The next step is to merge the line layer with the rectangles layer so when the bevel is applied, it is applied uniformly around the perimeter of the navigation bar. Merge the layers by selecting the line layer in the **Layers** palette and choose **Merge Down** from the **Layer options** menu. Merging two raster layers unifies their contents into a combined area of pixels. Next, layer styles may be applied to the navigation bar. Create the button effect by applying a simple sharp inner bevel with the **Layer Styles** palette.

The navigation bar is completed by adding titles to the buttons. Select a large font face and type the following button labels: **Links**, **News**, **Files** and **E-mail**. Center the type over the buttons with the move tool (Fig. 3.38). This example uses font face Courier, bold, italic at 30 point.

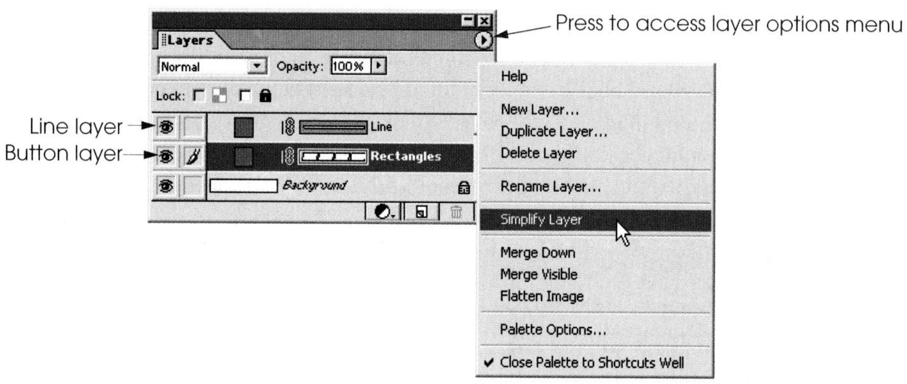

Fig. 3.37 Simplifying a shape layer using the **Layers** palette. (Adobe and Photoshop are either registered trademarks or trademarks of Adobe Systems Incorporated in the United States and/or other countries.)

Fig. 3.38 Navigation bar. (Adobe and Photoshop are either registered trademarks or trademarks of Adobe Systems Incorporated in the United States and/or other countries.)

There are a few ways to implement a navigation bar on a Web page. One way is to create *hot spots* which are sensitive to the mouse and link to different locations. Another way is to break apart the navigation bar into separate buttons through a process called *image slicing*. Image slicing creates smaller individual images from an original larger image. First turn the grid back on and turn off the visibility of the background layer. Reduce the file size by eliminating the unnecessary background area with the crop tool.

Select each button with the rectangular marquee tool and then copy the selection contents into a new document. First check to make sure that *snap* is on by checking **Snap** in the **View** menu. The snap option makes selections adhere to grid lines. Click and drag the rectangular marquee tool using the grid as a guide to select only the links button (Fig. 3.39).

Copy the contents of the selection to the clipboard by choosing **Copy Merged** from the **Edit** menu. This command copies pixels within the selection from all visible layers. Open a new file with a transparent background. The default height and width should match the contents of the clipboard, so do not change them. Now paste the links button into the new file (*Ctrl+P*) to be saved as a transparent GIF. Repeat these steps for each of the buttons (Fig. 3.40). These files are ready to be inserted into a Web document by rebuilding the navigation bar.

3.5 Layers

One of the most important features of Photoshop Elements is the ability to edit images in *layers*. Any image can be composed of many layers, each with its own attributes and effects. Each element of an image can be moved and edited independently if kept in its own layer. Layers are sometimes complicated; however, they ultimately save time in the overall process. The concept of layers is somewhat like *animation cells*. An animator uses separate layers of transparencies to create a scene so that each item can be edited individually.

Fig. 3.39 Slicing an image with the rectangular marquee tool. (Adobe and Photoshop are either registered trademarks or trademarks of Adobe Systems Incorporated in the United States and/or other countries.)

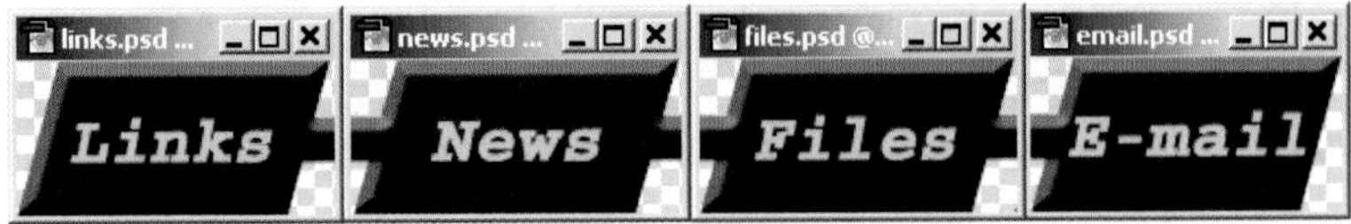

Fig. 3.40 Sliced image as individual buttons. (Adobe and Photoshop are either registered trademarks or trademarks of Adobe Systems Incorporated in the United States and/or other countries.)

Photoshop Elements has three categories of layers: *vector*, *raster* and *adjustment*. Each object on a vector layer is an independent element that is stored as a set of properties. Raster layers exist as a grid of colored pixels. Editing elements in raster layers affects all other parts of that layer. Open the file **`arches.psd`** located in the Chapter 3 examples directory on the CD-ROM that accompanies this book. This file shows the different types of layers.

Portability Tip 3.3

The **`psd`** *extension, which stands for Photoshop Document, is a file format that is specific to Adobe image editing programs. This file format supports layers, making it ideal for images that are in the middle of the editing process and for archiving. Web documents do not support this file format.*

This file has several different layers which can be seen individually in the **Layers** palette. The layers are arranged hierarchically, with the uppermost layer at the top of the list. The active layer is highlighted in blue (Fig. 3.41).

Click the ***New Layer*** button in the **Layers** palette to create a new raster layer. Only raster layers are created with the **New Layer** button. Vector layers are created when a vector tool such as the type or shape tool is used. The difference in the ways vector and raster information is stored prevents these two types of graphics from existing on the same layer.

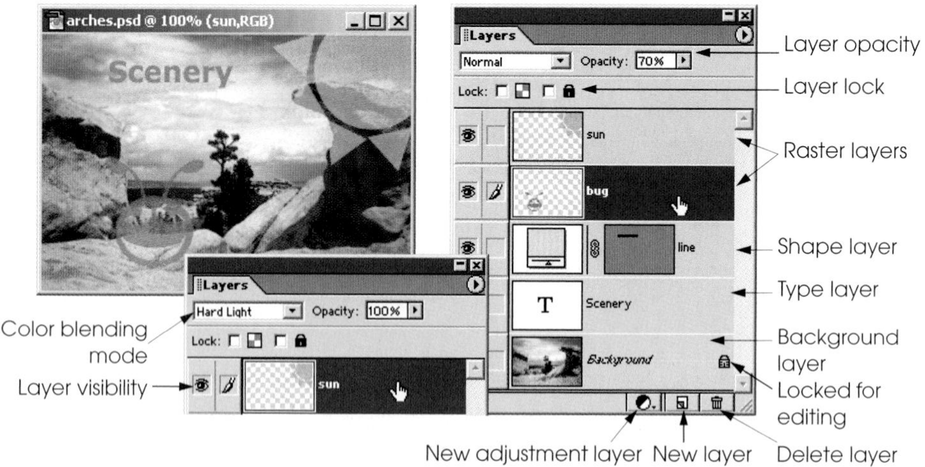

Fig. 3.41 Layers in the **Layers** palette. (Adobe and Photoshop are either registered trademarks or trademarks of Adobe Systems Incorporated in the United States and/or other countries.)

Each layer occupies one row in the palette. A row displays that layer's name, its position relative to other layers and several properties that modify the function of the layer. It is a good idea to name each layer for the objects it contains to make it easier to remember what layers effect what images. Select the **Arrange** submenu from the **Layers** menu to move a layer up or down in the hierarchy. Layers also can be dragged up or down in the hierarchy inside the **Layers** palette.

The *background layer* is always a raster layer anchored to the bottom of the image. The *layer order*, *color blending mode* and *opacity* cannot be changed on the background layer. Convert the background layer into a regular raster layer by double clicking **Background** in the **Layers** palette. The displayed dialog provides the option of renaming the layer. Renaming a background layer converts it to an independent raster layer. Files with transparent backgrounds do not have background layers. Instead the bottommost layer is an independent raster layer named **Layer 1**.

The *layer opacity* is the measure of a layer's transparency, given as a percentage. The **Bug** layer in **`arches.psd`** (Fig. 3.41) has an opacity of 70% making the layer beneath it visible through the bug. An opacity of 0% makes the layer completely transparent.

The *color blending mode* determines how a layer is affected by painting or editing tools. The blending mode for the **Sun** layer in **`arches.psd`** is set to **Hard Light**, affecting the image in the **Sun** layer as if a spotlight were pointed at it. There are several blending modes from which to choose. Select the **Sun** layer from the **Layers** palette. Try applying different blending modes by changing the selection in the blending modes drop-down list in the **Layers** palette, and note the varying effects.

Adjustment Layers allow color adjustments to be made to the layer beneath it without affecting color in the other layers. An adjustment layer acts as a preview of what a particular adjustment would look like if directly applied to a layer, without making any permanent changes. Select the background layer in the **Layers** palette for the **`arches.psd`** file. Create an adjustment layer by clicking the **New Adjustment Layer** button (Fig. 3.42). The new adjustment layer is placed directly above the selected layer.

When the **New Adjustment Layer** button is pressed a menu opens allowing the user to choose the type of adjustment. Choose ***Hue/Saturation*** from this menu to open the **Hue/Saturation** dialog. Change the hue to **+121** and the saturation to **+45**, then click **OK** to apply the adjustment to the background layer. Notice that the adjustment only affects the background layer. If the visibility of an adjustment layer is turned off, the layers beneath appear as if no changes were made.

3.6 Screen Capturing

Screen capturing is a widely used technique to create images from a screen display. The process takes the content of a screen and "captures" it so that the capture can be used as an image. For instance, the diagrams in this chapter that show actual windows and tools from Photoshop Elements were all created using screen capturing. Screen capturing in Photoshop Elements works like the copy and paste functions—when performing a screen capture, the image is copied to the clipboard until it is pasted into a document.

Press the *Print Screen* key on the keyboard, found above the *Delete* and *Insert* keys, to capture the entire screen area. Pressing this button copies the screen contents to the clipboard. Open a new image in Photoshop Elements. The default dimensions for the new image are the same as the screen capture on the clipboard. Then paste the screen capture into the new image. (*Alt+Print Screen* captures only the active window).

3.7 File Formats: GIF and JPEG

The three major file formats for images on the Web are *GIF*, *JPEG*, and *PNG*. Each format has a specific use when saving images for the Web. Web developers and designers need to know the differences between these formats to optimize download times and user compatibility.

The *Graphics Interchange Format (GIF)*, developed by CompuServe, is based on a 256-color palette. GIF is best used for screen captures, line drawings, graphics with sharp edges and images with transparency. When reducing colors to the 256 available in the GIF file format, Photoshop Elements performs *dithering* on the image. Dithering simulates the desired color with a color from the GIF palette. GIF is a *lossless* format, meaning that the picture quality is not reduced by the *compression algorithm*. The compression algorithm is the formula that a file format uses to store file information.

Performance Tip 3.3

A GIF file is typically larger than a JPEG file. If server space is a problem and the image has many more than 256 colors, the JPEG format is preferable.

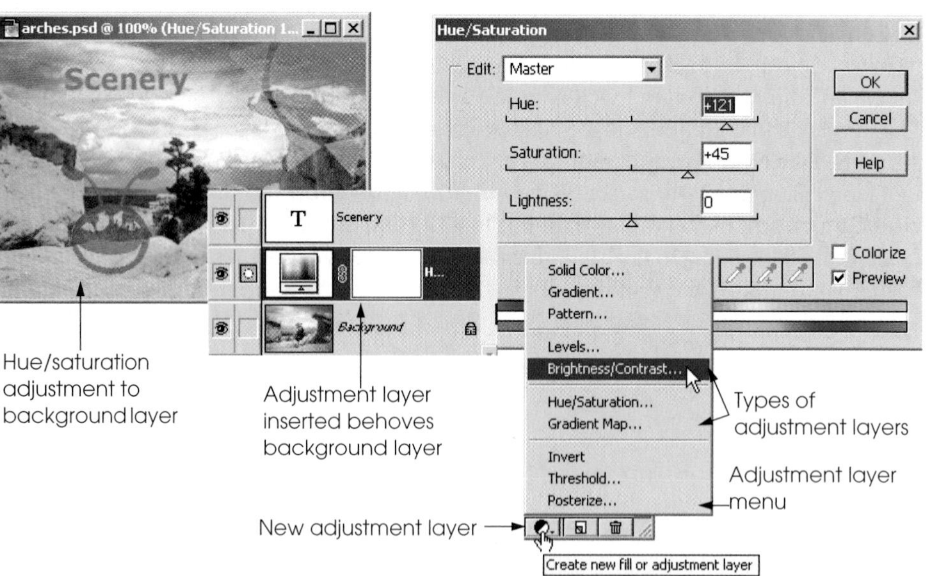

Fig. 3.42 Adjusting the hue and saturation using an adjustment layer. (Adobe and Photoshop are either registered trademarks or trademarks of Adobe Systems Incorporated in the United States and/or other countries.)

Dithering may be effective, but often it destroys the quality of an image that has color complexity. Such richness is characteristic of real-world images such as photographs, scanned images and computer art created with 3-D rendering programs. Images that are "color complex" are better-suited to the JPEG format. However, this format is not without limitations. JPEG is a *lossy* format (i.e., saving an image in this format gradually reduces the quality of the image due to loss of color information). The JPEG compression algorithm handles sharp edges and abrupt changes poorly.

Performance Tip 3.4

The JPEG format has scalable compression. When saving a JPEG image, in the **Save Options** *dialog, sliding the compression slider to the right causes the image to retain high quality, but the file size also remains large. Sliding the compression slider to the left causes the file size to decrease, but image quality suffers. This graduated scale helps to find a good balance between file size and image quality.*

One feature that GIF and JPEG share is *interlacing* (in GIF terminology) or *progressive encoding* (in JPEG terminology). Interlacing or progressive encoding creates a rough image preview at the beginning of the download process. The image clarity then gradually increases as the image loads. This behavior often keeps the user's attention while a page loads. Interlacing is specified in the **Save for Web** dialog. Non-interlaced images download at the highest quality and are ideal for images that have small file sizes.

Performance Tip 3.5

Do not place too many interlaced images on any one Web page; doing so slows page rendering.

A newer image standard is making its mark on the Web. The *Portable Network Graphics (PNG*, pronounced *ping*) format was developed in response to a decision by the UniSys corporation to start charging royalties on the GIF format, on which UniSys holds a patent. PNG is a suitable replacement for both GIF and JPEG because it has the better qualities of both formats. For example, PNG can encode in *RGBA*—the A stands for *alpha transparency*, which makes images transparent against any background, similar to opacity. The PNG file format solves many problems that previously existed with transparency. An image with both color complexity and transparency could not be saved as a transparent GIF or a JPEG. The PNG file format supports millions of colors as well as transparency. This makes it a great alternative for both GIF and JPEG. Photoshop Elements supports the PNG format, as do the latest versions of both Netscape Communicator and Internet Explorer. Web developers increasingly are using the PNG file format. For more information on the PNG format, visit **`www.w3.org/Graphics/PNG`**.

3.8 Internet and World Wide Web Resources

Many resources are available on the topic of using Photoshop Elements to create images for Web pages. A good resource is the *interactive help file* packaged with Photoshop Elements. This help file covers almost every function Photoshop Elements has to offer. The interactive help file is accessed by clicking the question mark button on the main menu bar. Also check out **`www.adobe.com`** (Adobe Inc.'s home page) to stay up-to-date on general information about Photoshop Elements. The majority of information on the Web, however, is available at user-run sites offering information and tutorials. For example, **www.photoshop-cafe.com** has excellent in-depth tutorials, for both Photoshop beginners and for experts who want to explore new techniques. Another site for tutorials is located at **www.planetphotoshop.com**. Keep in mind that many Photoshop tutorials are written for different versions of Photoshop other than Elements; however, many of the main concepts carry over to the Elements version. If looking for more diverse effects than those included in Photoshop Elements, new filters can be downloaded for free from sites such as **www.plugins.com/plugins/photoshop**. Plug-in filters, brushes and fonts are installed to the hard drive of the computer under the Photoshop Elements directory.

SUMMARY

- The most successful Web pages use both text and graphics to enhance the user experience.
- Adobe Inc.'s Photoshop Elements is an easy-to-use graphics package that offers the functionality of more expensive packages at an economical price.
- The **File** menu is used to open new or existing files.
- Initial image settings, such as image height and width, image resolution and background color are specified in the **New** dialog that appears every time a new image file is created.
- Every image in Photoshop Elements is composed of a series of dots called pixels organized in a grid.
- The number of pixels-per-unit measure is called the image resolution. The resolution is set in the **New** dialog.
- The three color modes available are RGB, Grayscale and Bitmap, of which RGB and Grayscale are the most commonly used for creating Web graphics.
- Red, Green and Blue are the primary colors in light which when combined in different intensity values from 0 (black) to 255 (white), create a color range of 16.7 million colors.
- Palettes are opened by clicking their tabs in the palette well. Each palette contains options for image editing and effects.
- The toolbox contains selection, editing, painting and type tools that are all used to modify existing images or to create new ones.
- The two squares at the bottom of the toolbox are the two active colors—the foreground color and the background color.
- The **Color Picker** dialog is where the foreground or background color is selected.
- A Web-safe palette refers to the 216 colors that are cross-platform and cross-browser compatible.
- Hexadecimal notation is the color code used in most Web documents to define font and background colors.
- Anti-aliasing is a process that smooths image edges by blending the color of the edge pixels with the color of the background on which the text is being placed.
- The move tool moves an object or resizes a selected object.
- The **Layer Styles** palette offers a variety of special effects that can be applied to text or shapes.
- Photoshop Elements uses layers so that items can be edited independently.
- Type layers are indicated by a **T** in the **Layers** palette.
- Clicking the **Trashcan** button in the **Layers** palette deletes the active layer.
- The **Save for Web...** option sets the file format and color strategy for saving an image based on certain Internet standards.

- GIF (Compuserve Graphics Interchange Format) is a file format that preserves transparency (saving pixels void of color information), making GIF appropriate for transparent Web graphics.
- Photoshop Elements creates and edits two different types of graphics that are standard for Web design—raster and vector.
- Raster images are composed of pixels organized on a grid.
- Vector images exist as individual objects that can be edited separately from one another.
- The selection tools—the lasso, magic wand, and marquee tools create a border called a marquee which bounds a selected area of pixels that can be modified by filters, moved or have color adjustments made.
- Feathering blurs the edges of a selection such that the pixels inside the selection will blend with the pixels outside the selection.
- Inverting a selection selects all the pixels outside the current selection marquee.
- A selection is filled with a color by choosing **Fill...** from the **Edit** menu.
- Patterns can be created from scratch by using one of many filters.
- The type selection tool, indicated by a dashed line **T** in the **Type** options bar, creates a marquee selection in the shape of text.
- The crop tool eliminates unnecessary image area.
- The shape tool is a vector tool that draws precise shapes filled with a particular color.
- Paste a clipboard item into an image by using **Paste** button or the shortcut *Ctrl+V*.
- Image slicing creates smaller images from an original larger image by separating it into pieces.
- Layers organize the different parts of an image.
- Photoshop Elements has three categories of layers: vector, raster and adjustment.
- The active layer is highlighted in blue in the **Layers** palette.
- Each layer occupies one row in the palette which displays the layer's name, its position relative to other layers and several properties that modify the function of the layer.
- Adjustment layers allow adjustments to be made to the layers beneath them without affecting any of the pixels in the lower layers.
- Photoshop Elements performs screen captures and adds the convenience of being able to edit them.
- The two major file formats used for images are GIF and JPEG.
- GIF is best used for screen captures, line drawings and other graphics with sharp edges.
- JPEG is ideal for images with "color complexity" such as photographs and original art.
- The PNG file format supports millions of colors as well as transparency, making it an effective alternative to both GIF and JPEG.

TERMINOLOGY

active layer
active tool options bar
adjustment layer
alignment
alpha transparency
anchor
animation cells
anti-alias
background color
background layer
blending mode
bounding box
brightness
browser preview
brush pressure
brush size

clipboard
color blending mode
color mode
Color Picker
color wheel
compression algorithm
compression quality
constrain proportions
Copy
Copy Merged
crop tool
custom shape tool
Deselect
development environment
dithering
drop shadow
elliptical marquee
feathering
file size
fill selection
filter
font
font face
font weight
foreground color
GIF (Graphics Interchange Format)
gradient tool
grayscale color mode
grid
hexadecimal
hidden tools
History palette
hot spots
HSB color model
hue
image slicing
image window
interlacing
interpolation
invert selection
JPEG (Joint Photographic Experts Group)
lasso tool
layer
layer opacity
layer order
layer styles
Layers palette
line tool
line weight
Liquify filter
lossless format
lossy format
magic wand tool
magnetic lasso
magnifying glass tool
marquee tool
matte
matte color
move tool
multiple selections
New Layer
New Layer via Copy
normal blending mode
opacity
optimize
paintbrush tool
palette
palette well
paste
Photoshop Document (`psd`) extension
pixel
PNG (Portable Network Graphics)
polygon tool
polygonal lasso
primary colors in light
progressive encoding
`psd` extension
raster layer
rectangular marquee
regular raster layer
Reset Palette Locations
resize
resolution dependent
resolution independent
Revert
RGB color mode
RGB color model
saturation
Save for Web
screen capture
selection tools
shape layer
shape tool
skew
status bar
stroke selection
swatches
tolerance
toolbox
transform

transparency
transparent GIF
type layer
type selection tool
type tool
vector layer
warped text
Web-safe palette

SELF-REVIEW EXERCISES

3.1 Fill in the blanks in each of the following statements:

a) The __________ palette is used to organize different image components.

b) A __________ is the dashed line that indicates a selection.

c) A full screen capture is performed by hitting the __________ button.

d) Selection __________ is when the pixels inside the selection are blended with the pixels outside the selection.

e) The **Fill** command is found under the __________ menu.

3.2 State whether each of the following is *true* or *false*. If the answer is *false*, explain why.

a) The best file format to save a transparent image is GIF.

b) Raster images do not lose image quality when they are enlarged.

c) The three main types of layers are transparent, color and drawing.

d) The type selection tool creates a marquee selection in the shape of text.

e) Hexadecimal color notation produces different colors than the RGB color notation.

ANSWERS TO SELF-REVIEW EXERCISES

3.1 a) **Layers**. b) marquee. c) *Print Screen.* d) feathering. e) **Edit**.

3.2 a) True. b) False. Raster images lose image quality as they are enlarged because of pixels being added in the interpolation process. c) False. The three main types of layers are vector, raster and adjustment. d) True. e) False. Hexadecimal produces the same colors as the RGB color notation.

EXERCISES

3.3 Create a vertical navigation bar (145 × 350 px) with six different-colored, identical-shaped, elliptical navigation buttons. Name these buttons **About Us**, **News**, **Portfolio**, **Programs**, **Events** and **Contact**. Give the buttons a simple inner bevel. Slice the image into six different files and save each button as a transparent GIF.

3.4 This exercise uses several of the filters which Photoshop Elements has to offer, all of which can be found in the **Filters** palette in the palette well. Create a title image (500 × 150 px) with a transparent background. Choose white as the foreground color and a medium green as the background color. Using the type selection tool, type in the title of a Web page and center the selection on the page. Expand the borders of the selection by one pixel by choosing **Expand** from the **Modify** submenu of the **Select** menu. Apply the clouds filter. To create a texture, apply the grain filter, with grain intensity set to **40**, the contrast set to **50**, and the grain type to regular. Now apply the watercolor filter with the brush detail set to **14**, the shadow intensity set to **0** and the texture set to **1**. Finally, apply the glowing edges filter with the edge brightness set to **4** and the smoothness set to **1**. Stroke the text selection with yellow, a pixel weight of **2**, inside the selection. Save the image as a transparent GIF.

3.5 Create a new image (250 × 250 px) with a white background. Create five separate ellipses with the ellipse shape tool on five separate shape layers. Make each ellipse a different color. Make the ellipses overlap one another in several places, but not completely. For each layer, change the blending mode to multiply (from the drop-down list of the **Layers** palette). Save the image for the Web.

3.6 Create a new image (500 × 150 px) with a white background. Apply the render clouds filter. Apply the chrome filter with detail set to **4** and smoothness set to **7**. Using the text selection tool, type "Chrome" with a large, heavy font. With this selection, make a new layer via copy. On the new layer, apply a simple outer bevel. Select the background layer and add a contrast adjustment layer to it. Increase the brightness to **+50**. Now select the type layer. Change the color balance by choosing **Hue/ Saturation** from the **Color** submenu of the **Enhance** menu. With the **Colorize** checkbox selected, adjust the hue to **245**, the saturation to **50** and the lightness to **17**. Save the image for Web as a JPEG.

3.7 Discuss the differences between the GIF, JPEG and PNG file formats and when each should be used.

3.8 Define the following terms: Interlacing, tolerance, matte, feathering, Web-safe palette, filter and image slicing.

Introduction to XHTML: Part 1

Objectives

- To understand important components of XHTML documents.
- To use XHTML to create World Wide Web pages.
- To be able to add images to Web pages.
- To understand how to create and use hyperlinks to navigate Web pages.
- To be able to mark up lists of information.

To read between the lines was easier than to follow the text.

Henry James

High thoughts must have high language.

Aristophanes

Outline

4.1 Introduction

Welcome to the world of opportunity created by the World Wide Web. The Internet is now three decades old, but it was not until the World Wide Web became popular in the 1990s that the explosion of opportunity that we are still experiencing began. Exciting new developments occur almost daily—the pace of innovation is unprecedented by any other technology. In this chapter, you will develop your own Web pages. As the book proceeds, you will create increasingly appealing and powerful Web pages. In the later portion of the book, you will learn how to create complete Web-based applications.

In this chapter, we begin unlocking the power of Web-based application development with *XHTML*[1]—the *Extensible Hypertext Markup Language*. In later chapters, we introduce more sophisticated XHTML techniques, such as *tables*, which are particularly useful for structuring information from *databases* (i.e., software that stores structured sets of data), and *Cascading Style Sheets (CSS)*, which make Web pages more visually appealing.

Unlike procedural programming languages such as C, Fortran, Cobol and Pascal, XHTML is a *markup language* that specifies the format of text that is displayed in a Web browser such as Microsoft's Internet Explorer or Netscape's Communicator.

One key issue when using XHTML[2] is the separation of the *presentation of a document* (i.e., the document's appearance when rendered by a browser) from the *structure of the document's information*. Over the next several chapters, we will discuss this issue in depth.

---

1. XHTML has replaced the HyperText Markup Language (HTML) as the primary means of describing Web content. XHTML provides more robust, richer and extensible features than HTML. For more on XHTML/HTML visit **www.w3.org/markup**.
2. As this book was being submitted to the publisher, XHTML 1.1 became a World Wide Web Consortium (W3C) Recommendation. The XHTML examples presented in this book are based upon the XHTML 1.0 Recommendation, because Internet Explorer 5.5 does not support the full set of XHTML 1.1 features. In the future, Internet Explorer and other browsers will support XHTML 1.1. When this occurs, we will update our Web site (**www.deitel.com**) with XHTML 1.1 examples and information.

4.2 Editing XHTML

In this chapter, we write XHTML in its *source-code form*. We create *XHTML documents* by typing them in with a text editor (e.g., *Notepad*, *Wordpad*, *vi*, *emacs*, etc.), saving the documents with either an ***.html*** or ***.htm*** file-name extension.

Good Programming Practice 4.1

Assign documents file names that describe their functionality. This practice can help you identify documents faster. It also helps people who want to link to a page, by giving them an easy-to-remember name. For example, if you are writing an XHTML document that contains product information, you might want to call it **products.html**.

Machines running specialized software called *Web servers* store XHTML documents. Clients (e.g., Web browsers) request specific *resources* such as the XHTML documents from the Web server. For example, typing **www.deitel.com/books/downloads.htm** into a Web browser's address field requests **downloads.htm** from the Web server running at **www.deitel.com**. This document is located in a directory named **books**. We discuss Web servers in detail in Chapter 21. For now, we simply place the XHTML documents on our machine and open them using Internet Explorer as discussed in Section 4.3.

4.3 First XHTML Example[3]

In this chapter and the next, we present XHTML markup and provide screen captures that show how Internet Explorer 5.5 renders (i.e., displays) the XHTML. Every XHTML document we show has line numbers for the reader's convenience. These line numbers are not part of the XHTML documents.

Our first example (Fig. 4.1) is an XHTML document named **main.html** that displays the message "Welcome to XHTML!" in the browser.

The key line in the program is line 14, which tells the browser to display "Welcome to XHTML!" Now let us consider each line of the program.

Lines 1–3 are required in XHTML documents to conform with proper XHTML syntax. For now, copy and paste these lines into each XHTML document you create. The meaning of these lines is discussed in detail in Chapter 20, Extensible Markup Language (XML).

Lines 5–6 are *XHTML comments*. XHTML document creators insert comments to improve markup readability and describe the content of a document. Comments also help other people read and understand an XHTML document's markup and content. Comments do not cause the browser to perform any action when the user loads the XHTML document into the Web browser to view the document. XHTML comments always start with **<!--** and end with **-->**. Each of our XHTML examples includes comments that specify the figure number and file name, and provide a brief description of the example's purpose. Subsequent examples include comments in the markup, especially to highlight new features.

Good Programming Practice 4.2

Place comments throughout your markup. Comments help other programmers understand the markup, assist in debugging and list useful information that you do not want the browser to render. Comments also help you understand your own markup when you revisit a document for modifications or updates in the future.

3. All of the examples presented in this book are available at **www.deitel.com** and on the CD-ROM that accompanies this book.

```
1  <?xml version = "1.0"?>
2  <!DOCTYPE html PUBLIC "-//W3C//DTD XHTML 1.0 Strict//EN"
3     "http://www.w3.org/TR/xhtml1/DTD/xhtml1-strict.dtd">
4
5  <!-- Fig. 4.1: main.html -->
6  <!-- Our first Web page  -->
7
8  <html xmlns = "http://www.w3.org/1999/xhtml">
9     <head>
10       <title>Internet and WWW How to Program - Welcome</title>
11    </head>
12
13    <body>
14       <p>Welcome to XHTML!</p>
15    </body>
16 </html>
```

Fig. 4.1 First XHTML example.

XHTML markup contains text that represents the content of a document and *elements* that specify a document's structure. Some important elements of an XHTML document include the ***html*** element, the ***head*** element and the ***body*** element. The **html** element encloses the *head section* (represented by the ***head*** *element*) and the *body section* (represented by the ***body*** *element*). The head section contains information about the XHTML document, such as the *title* of the document. The head section also can contain special document formatting instructions called *style sheets* and client-side programs called *scripts* for creating dynamic Web pages. (We introduce style sheets in Chapter 6 and we introduce scripting with JavaScript in Chapter 7.) The body section contains the page's content that the browser displays when the user visits the Web page.

XHTML documents delimit an element with *start* and *end* tags. A start tag consists of the element name in angle brackets (e.g., **<html>**). An end tag consists of the element name preceded by a **/** in angle brackets (e.g., **</html>**). In this example lines 8 and 16 define the start and end of the **html** element. Note that the end tag on line 16 has the same name as the start tag, but is preceded by a **/** inside the angle brackets. Many start tags define *attributes* that provide additional information about an element. Browsers can use this additional information to determine how to process the element. Each attribute has a *name* and a *value* separated by an equal sign (**=**). Line 8 specifies a required attribute (**xmlns**) and value (**http://www.w3.org/1999/xhtml**) for the **html** element in an XHTML document. For now, simply copy and paste the **html** element start tag on line 8 into your XHTML documents. We discuss the details of the **html** element's **xmlns** attribute in Chapter 20, Extensible Markup Language (XML).

Common Programming Error 4.1

Not enclosing attribute values in either single or double quotes is a syntax error.

Common Programming Error 4.2

Using uppercase letters in an XHTML element or attribute name is a syntax error.

An XHTML document divides the **`html`** element into two sections—head and body. Lines 9–11 define the Web page's head section with a **`head`** element. Line 10 specifies a **`title`** element. This is called a *nested element*, because it is enclosed in the **`head`** element's start and end tags. The **`head`** element also is a nested element, because it is enclosed in the **`html`** element's start and end tags. The **`title`** element describes the Web page. Titles usually appear in the *title bar* at the top of the browser window and also as the text identifying a page when users add the page to their list of **Favorites** or **Bookmarks**, which enable users to return to their favorite sites. Search engines (i.e., sites that allow users to search the Web) also use the **`title`** for cataloging purposes.

Good Programming Practice 4.3

Indenting nested elements emphasizes a document's structure and promotes readability.

Common Programming Error 4.3

XHTML does not permit tags to overlap—a nested element's end tag must appear in the document before the enclosing element's end tag. For example, the nested XHTML tags **`<head><title>hello</head></title>`** *cause a syntax error, because the enclosing* **`head`** *element's ending* **`</head>`** *tag appears before the nested* **`title`** *element's ending* **`</title>`** *tag.*

Good Programming Practice 4.4

Use a consistent **`title`** *naming convention for all pages on a site. For example, if a site is named "Bailey's Web Site," then the* **`title`** *of the main page might be "Bailey's Web Site—Links," etc. This practice can help users better understand the Web site's structure.*

Line 13 opens the document's ***`body`*** element. The body section of an XHTML document specifies the document's content, which may include text and tags.

Some tags, such as the *paragraph tags* (**`<p>`** and **`</p>`**) in line 14, markup text for display in a browser. All text placed between the **`<p>`** and **`</p>`** tags form one paragraph. When the browser renders a paragraph, a blank line usually precedes and follows paragraph text.

This document ends with two closing tags (lines 15–16). These tags close the **`body`** and **`html`** elements, respectively. The ending **`</html>`** tag in an XHTML document informs the browser that the XHTML markup is complete.

To view this example in Internet Explorer, perform the following steps:

1. Copy the Chapter 4 examples onto your machine from the CD that accompanies this book (or download the examples from **`www.deitel.com`**).
2. Launch Internet Explorer and select **Open...** from the **File** Menu. This displays the **Open** dialog.
3. Click the **Open** dialog's **Browse...** button to display the **Microsoft Internet Explorer** file dialog.

4. Navigate to the directory containing the Chapter 4 examples and select the file **main.html**, then click **Open**.
5. Click **OK** to have Internet Explorer render the document. Other examples are opened in a similar manner.

At this point your browser window should appear similar to the sample screen capture shown in Fig. 4.1. (Note that we resized the browser window to save space in the book.)

4.4 W3C XHTML Validation Service

Programming Web-based applications can be complex and XHTML documents must be written correctly to ensure that browsers process them properly. To promote correctly written documents, the World Wide Web Consortium (W3C) provides a *validation service* (**validator.w3.org**) for checking a document's syntax. Documents can be validated from either a URL that specifies the location of the file or by uploading a file to the site **validator.w3.org/file-upload.html**. Uploading a file copies the file from the user's computer to another computer on the Internet. Figure 4.2 shows **main.html** (Fig. 4.1) being uploaded for validation. Although the W3C's Web page indicates that the service name is **HTML Validation Service**,[4] the validation service is able to validate the syntax of XHTML documents. All the XHTML examples in this book have been validated successfully using **validator.w3.org**.

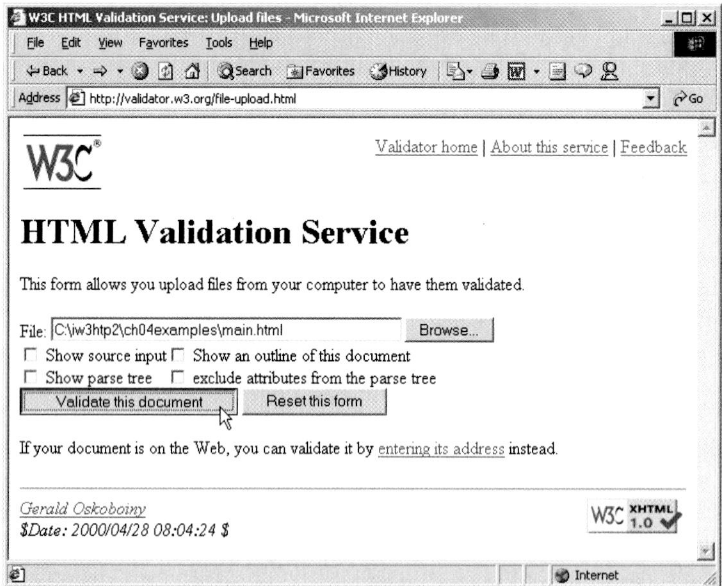

Fig. 4.2 Validating an XHTML document. (Courtesy of World Wide Web Consortium (W3C).)

4. HTML (HyperText Markup Language) is the predecessor of XHTML designed for marking up Web content. HTML is a deprecated technology.

By clicking **Browse...**, users can select files on their own computers for upload. After selecting a file, clicking the **Validate this document** button uploads and validates the file. Figure 4.3 shows the results of validating **`main.html`**. This document does not contain any syntax errors. If a document does contain syntax errors, the Validation Service displays error messages describing the errors. In Exercise 4.13, we ask readers to create an invalid XHTML document (i.e., one that contains syntax errors) and to check the document's syntax using the Validation Service. This enables readers to see the types of error messages generated by the validator.

Testing and Debugging Tip 4.1

Use a validation service, such as the W3C HTML Validation Service, to confirm that an XHTML document is syntactically correct.

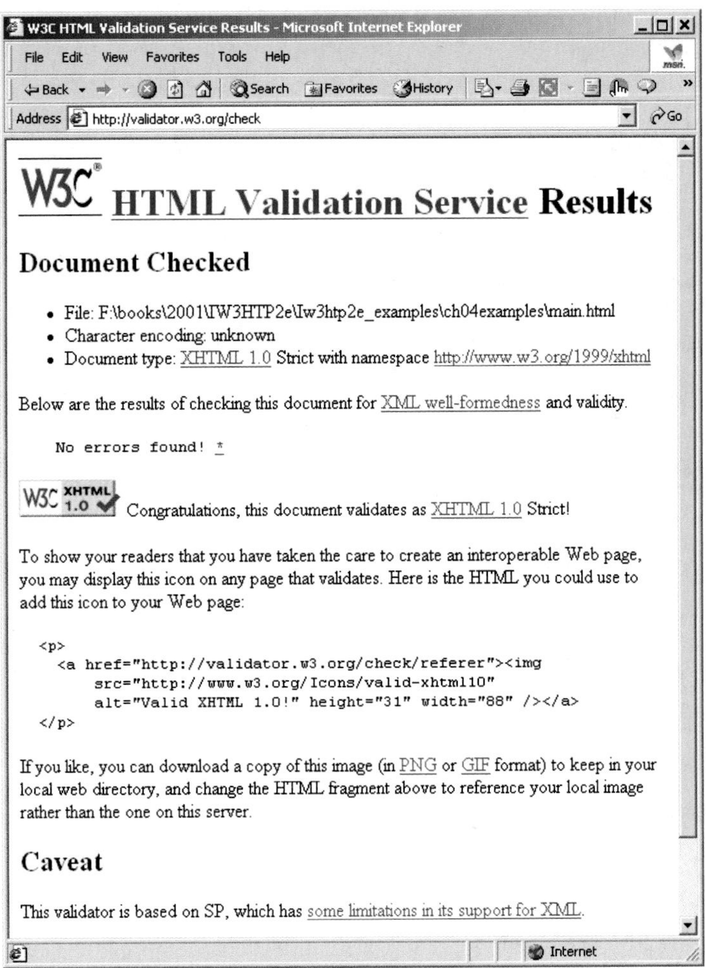

Fig. 4.3 XHTML validation results. (Courtesy of World Wide Web Consortium (W3C).)

4.5 Headers

Some text in an XHTML document may be more important than others. For example, the text in this section is considered more important than a footnote. XHTML provides six *headers*, called *header elements*, for specifying the relative importance of information. Figure 4.4 demonstrates these elements (**h1** through **h6**).

Portability Tip 4.1

The text size used to display each header element can vary significantly between browsers. In Chapter 6, we discuss how to control the text size and other text properties.

```
<?xml version = "1.0"?>
<!DOCTYPE html PUBLIC "-//W3C//DTD XHTML 1.0 Strict//EN"
   "http://www.w3.org/TR/xhtml1/DTD/xhtml1-strict.dtd">

<!-- Fig. 4.4: header.html -->
<!-- XHTML headers         -->

<html xmlns = "http://www.w3.org/1999/xhtml">
   <head>
      <title>Internet and WWW How to Program - Headers</title>
   </head>

   <body>

      <h1>Level 1 Header</h1>
      <h2>Level 2 header</h2>
      <h3>Level 3 header</h3>
      <h4>Level 4 header</h4>
      <h5>Level 5 header</h5>
      <h6>Level 6 header</h6>

   </body>
</html>
```

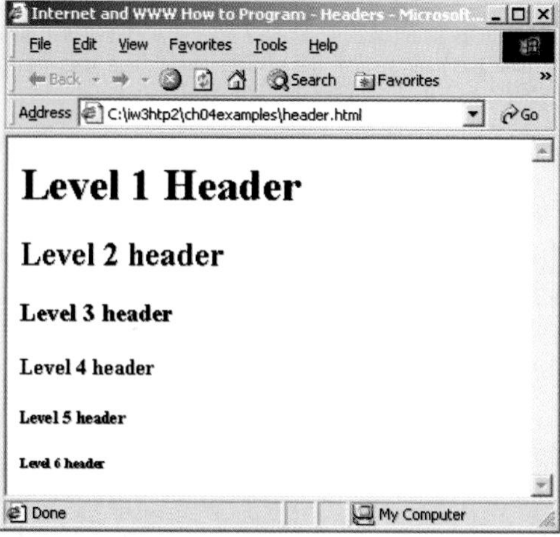

Fig. 4.4 Header elements **h1** through **h6**.

Header element **h1** (line 15) is considered the most significant header and is rendered in a larger font than the other five headers (lines 16–20). Each successive header element (i.e., **h2**, **h3**, etc.) is rendered in a smaller font.

Look-and-Feel Observation 4.1

Placing a header at the top of every XHTML page helps viewers understand the purpose of each page.

Look-and-Feel Observation 4.2

Use larger headers to emphasize more important sections of a Web page.

4.6 Linking

One of the most important XHTML features is the *hyperlink,* which references (or *links* to) other resources such as XHTML documents and images. In XHTML, both text and images can act as hyperlinks. Web browsers typically underline text hyperlinks and color their text blue by default, so that users can distinguish hyperlinks from plain text. In Fig. 4.5, we create text hyperlinks to four different Web sites.

```
<?xml version = "1.0"?>
<!DOCTYPE html PUBLIC "-//W3C//DTD XHTML 1.0 Strict//EN"
   "http://www.w3.org/TR/xhtml1/DTD/xhtml1-strict.dtd">

<!-- Fig. 4.5: links.html         -->
<!-- Introduction to hyperlinks -->

<html xmlns = "http://www.w3.org/1999/xhtml">
   <head>
      <title>Internet and WWW How to Program - Links</title>
   </head>

   <body>

      <h1>Here are my favorite sites</h1>

      <p><strong>Click a name to go to that page.</strong></p>

      <!-- Create four text hyperlinks -->
      <p><a href = "http://www.deitel.com">Deitel</a></p>

      <p><a href = "http://www.prenhall.com">Prentice Hall</a></p>

      <p><a href = "http://www.yahoo.com">Yahoo!</a></p>

      <p><a href = "http://www.usatoday.com">USA Today</a></p>

   </body>
</html>
```

Fig. 4.5 Linking to other Web pages (part 1 of 2).

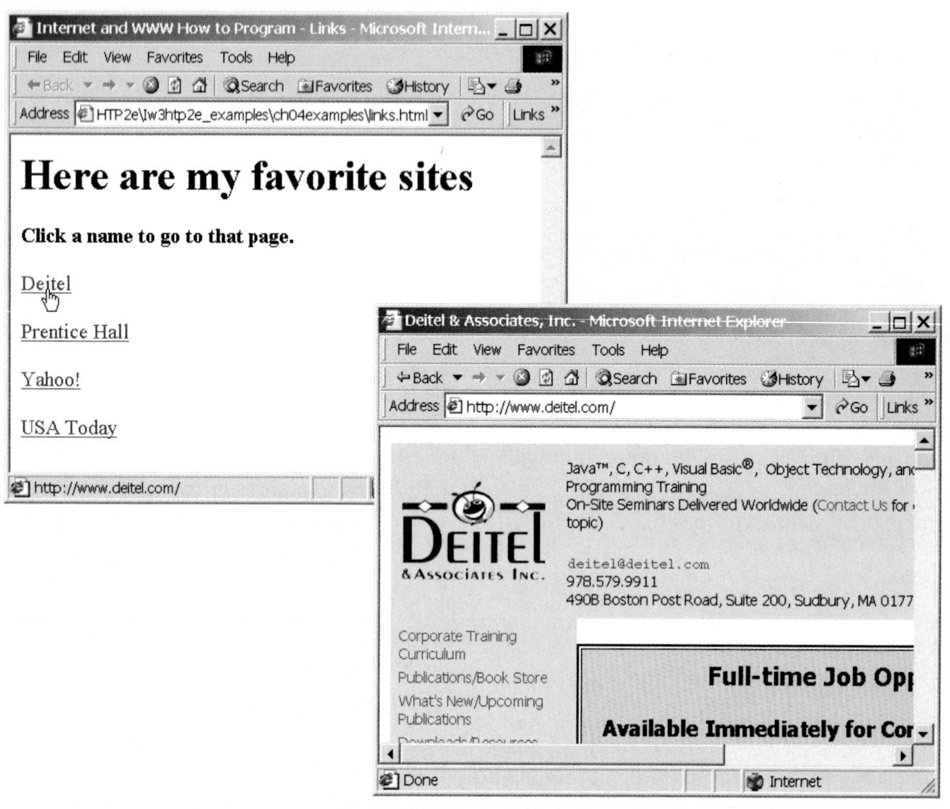

Fig. 4.5 Linking to other Web pages (part 2 of 2).

Line 17 introduces the **`<strong>`** tag. Browsers typically display text marked up with **`<strong>`** in a bold font.

Links are created using the **`a`** (*anchor*) *element*. Line 20 defines a hyperlink that links the text **`Deitel`** to the URL assigned to attribute ***`href`***, which specifies the location of a linked resource, such as a Web page, a file or an e-mail address. This particular anchor element links to a Web page located at **`http://www.deitel.com`**. When a URL does not indicate a specific document on the Web site, the Web server returns a default Web page. This pages often is called **`index.html`**; however, most Web servers can be configured to to use any file as the default Web page for the site. (Open **`http://www.deitel.com`** in one browser window and **`http://www.deitel.com/index.html`** in a second browser window to confirm that they are identical.) If the Web server cannot locate a requested document, the server returns an error indication to the Web browser and the browser displays an error message to the user.

Anchors can link to e-mail addresses using a ***`mailto:`*** URL. When someone clicks this type of anchored link, most browsers launch the default e-mail program (e.g., Outlook Express) to enable the user to write an e-mail message to the linked address. Figure 4.6 demonstrates this type of anchor.

```
<?xml version = "1.0"?>
<!DOCTYPE html PUBLIC "-//W3C//DTD XHTML 1.0 Strict//EN"
   "http://www.w3.org/TR/xhtml1/DTD/xhtml1-strict.dtd">

<!-- Fig. 4.6: contact.html  -->
<!-- Adding email hyperlinks -->

<html xmlns = "http://www.w3.org/1999/xhtml">
   <head>
      <title>Internet and WWW How to Program - Contact Page
      </title>
   </head>

   <body>

      <p>My email address is
         <a href = "mailto:deitel@deitel.com">
            deitel@deitel.com
         </a>
         . Click the address and your browser will
         open an e-mail message and address it to me.
      </p>
   </body>
</html>
```

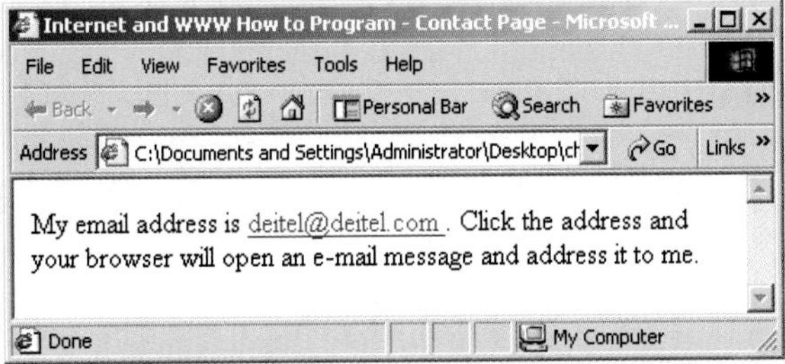

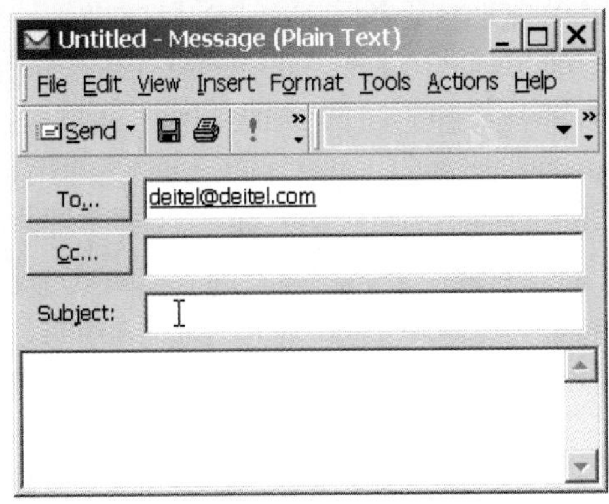

Fig. 4.6 Linking to an e-mail address.

Lines 17–19 contain an e-mail link. The form of an e-mail anchor is **<a href = "mailto:***emailaddress***">**…**</a>**. In this case, we link to the e-mail address **deitel@deitel.com**.

4.7 Images

The examples discussed so far demonstrated how to mark up documents that contain only text. However, most Web pages contain both text and images. In fact, images are an equal, if not essential, part of Web-page design. The two most popular image formats used by Web developers are Graphics Interchange Format (GIF) and Joint Photographic Experts Group (JPEG) images. Users can create images using specialized pieces of software such as Adobe PhotoShop Elements (discussed in Chapter 3) and Jasc Paint Shop Pro[5] (**www.jasc.com**). Images may also be acquired from various Web sites, such as **gallery.yahoo.com**. Figure 4.7 demonstrates how to incorporate images into Web pages.

Lines 15–16 use an ***img*** element to insert an image in the document. The image file's location is specified with the **img** element's ***src*** attribute. In this case, the image is located in the same directory as this XHTML document, so only the image's file name is required. Optional attributes ***width*** and ***height*** specify the image's width and height, respectively. The document author can scale an image by increasing or decreasing the values of the image **width** and **height** attributes. If these attributes are omitted, the browser uses the image's actual width and height. Images are measured in *pixels* ("picture elements"), which represent dots of color on the screen. The image in Fig. 4.7 is **183** pixels wide and **238** pixels high.

```
1  <?xml version = "1.0"?>
2  <!DOCTYPE html PUBLIC "-//W3C//DTD XHTML 1.0 Strict//EN"
3     "http://www.w3.org/TR/xhtml1/DTD/xhtml1-strict.dtd">
4
5  <!-- Fig. 4.7: picture.html   -->
6  <!-- Adding images with XHTML -->
7
8  <html xmlns = "http://www.w3.org/1999/xhtml">
9     <head>
10       <title>Internet and WWW How to Program - Welcome</title>
11    </head>
12
13    <body>
14
15       <p><img src = "xmlhtp.jpg" height = "238" width = "183"
16             alt = "XML How to Program book cover" />
17          <img src = "jhtp.jpg" height = "238" width = "183"
18             alt = "Java How to Program book cover" />
19       </p>
20    </body>
21 </html>
```

Fig. 4.7 Placing images in XHTML files (part 1 of 2).

5. The CD-ROM that accompanies this book contains a 90-day evaluation version of Paint Shop Pro™.

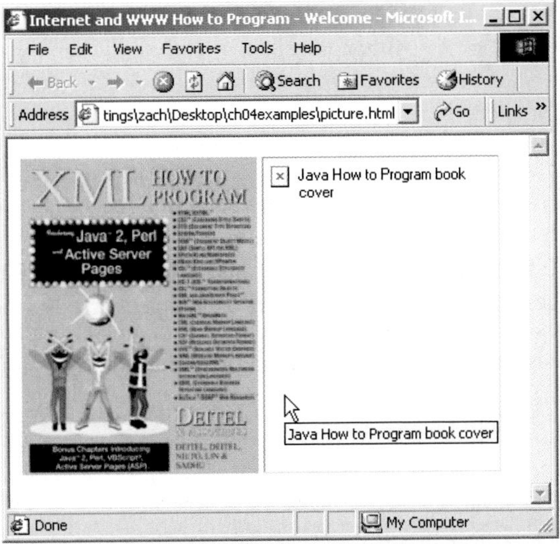

Fig. 4.7 Placing images in XHTML files (part 2 of 2).

Good Programming Practice 4.5

Always include the **width** *and the* **height** *of an image inside the* **<img>** *tag. When the browser loads the XHTML file, it will know immediately from these attributes how much screen space to provide for the image and will lay out the page properly, even before it downloads the image.*

Performance Tip 4.1

Including the **width** *and* **height** *attributes in an* **<img>** *tag can result in the browser loading and rendering pages faster.*

Common Programming Error 4.4

Entering new dimensions for an image that change its inherent width-to-height ratio distorts the appearance of the image. For example, if your image is 200 pixels wide and 100 pixels high, you should ensure that any new dimensions have a 2:1 width-to-height ratio.

Every **img** element in an XHTML document has an **alt** attribute. If a browser cannot render an image, the browser displays the **alt** attribute's value. A browser may not be able to render an image for several reasons. It may not support images—as is the case with a *text-based browser* (i.e., a browser that can display only text)—or the client may have disabled image viewing to reduce download time. Figure 4.7 shows Internet Explorer 5.5 rendering the **alt** attribute's value when a document references a non-existent image file (**jhtp.jpg**).

The **alt** attribute is important for creating *accessible* Web pages for users with disabilities, especially those with vision impairments and text-based browsers. Specialized software called *speech synthesizers* often are used by people with disabilities. These software applications "speak" the **alt** attribute's value so that the user knows what the browser is displaying. We discuss accessibility issues in detail in Chapter 34.

Some XHTML elements (called *empty elements*) contain only attributes and do not markup text (i.e., text is not placed between the start and end tags). Empty elements (e.g., **img**) must be terminated, either by using the *forward slash character* (**/**) inside the closing right angle bracket (**>**) of the start tag or by explicitly including the end tag. When using the forward slash character, we add a space before the forward slash to improve readability (as shown at the ends of lines 16 and 18). Rather than using the forward slash character, lines 17–18 could be written with a closing **</img>** tag as follows:

```
<img src = "jhtp.jpg" height = "238" width = "183"
   alt = "Java How to Program book cover"></img></p>
```

By using images as hyperlinks, Web developers can create graphical Web pages that link to other resources. In Fig. 4.8, we create six different image hyperlinks.

```
<?xml version = "1.0"?>
<!DOCTYPE html PUBLIC "-//W3C//DTD XHTML 1.0 Strict//EN"
   "http://www.w3.org/TR/xhtml1/DTD/xhtml1-strict.dtd">

<!-- Fig. 4.8: nav.html              -->
<!-- Using images as link anchors -->

<html xmlns = "http://www.w3.org/1999/xhtml">
   <head>
      <title>Internet and WWW How to Program - Navigation Bar
      </title>
   </head>

   <body>

      <p>
         <a href = "links.html">
            <img src = "buttons/links.jpg" width = "65"
               height = "50" alt = "Links Page" />
         </a><br />

         <a href = "list.html">
            <img src = "buttons/list.jpg" width = "65"
               height = "50" alt = "List Example Page" />
         </a><br />

         <a href = "contact.html">
            <img src = "buttons/contact.jpg" width = "65"
               height = "50" alt = "Contact Page" />
         </a><br />

         <a href = "header.html">
            <img src = "buttons/header.jpg" width = "65"
               height = "50" alt = "Header Page" />
         </a><br />

```

Fig. 4.8 Using images as link anchors (part 1 of 2).

```
37          <a href = "table.html">
38             <img src = "buttons/table.jpg" width = "65"
39                height = "50" alt = "Table Page" />
40          </a><br />
41
42          <a href = "form.html">
43             <img src = "buttons/form.jpg" width = "65"
44                height = "50" alt = "Feedback Form" />
45          </a><br />
46       </p>
47
48    </body>
49 </html>
```

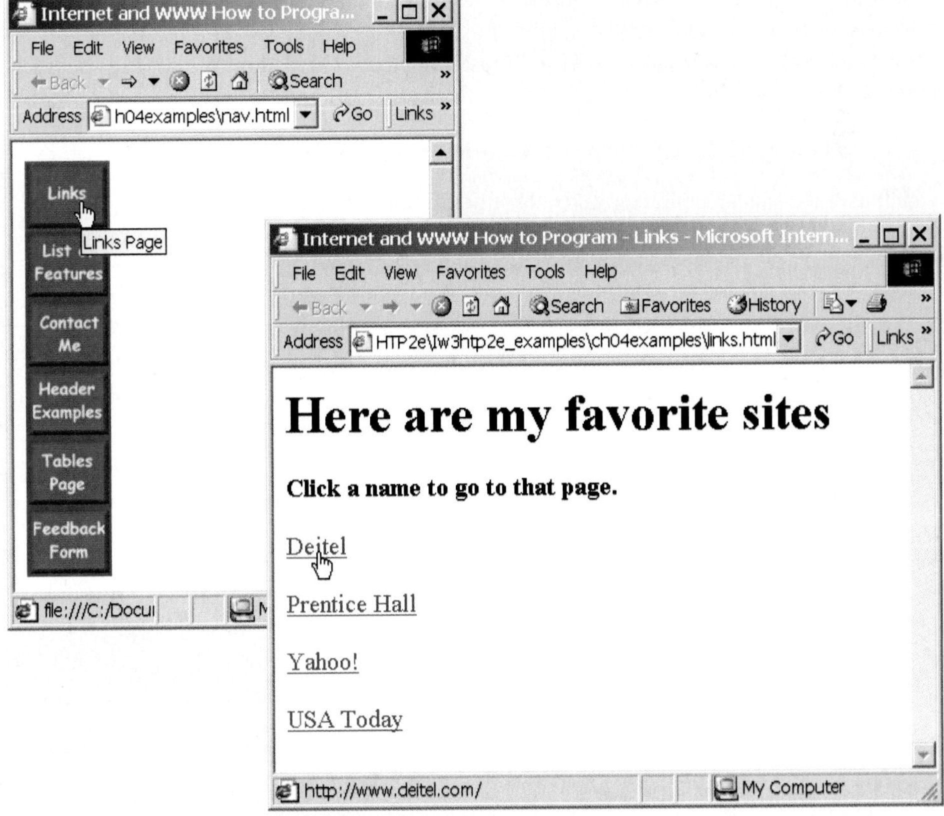

Fig. 4.8 Using images as link anchors (part 2 of 2).

Lines 17–20 create an *image hyperlink* by nesting an **`img`** element nested in an anchor (**`a`**) element. The value of the **`img`** element's **`src`** attribute value specifies that this image (**`links.jpg`**) resides in a directory named **`buttons`**. The **`buttons`** directory and the XHTML document are in the same directory. Images from other Web documents also can be referenced (after obtaining permission from the document's owner) by setting the **`src`** attribute to the name and location of the image.

On line 20, we introduce the **br** *element*, which most browsers render as a *line break*. Any markup or text following a **br** element is rendered on the next line. Like the **img** element, **br** is an example of an empty element terminated with a forward slash. We add a space before the forward slash to enhance readability.

4.8 Special Characters and More Line Breaks

When marking up text, certain characters or symbols (e.g., **<**) may be difficult to embed directly into an XHTML document. Some keyboards may not provide these symbols, or the presence of these symbols may cause syntax errors. For example, the markup

```
<p>if x < 10 then increment x by 1</p>
```

results in a syntax error because it uses the less-than character (**<**), which is reserved for start tags and end tags such as **<p>** and **</p>**. XHTML provides *special characters* or *entity references* (in the form **&*code*;**) for representing these characters. We could correct the previous line by writing

```
<p>if x &lt; 10 then increment x by 1</p>
```

which uses the special character ***<*** for the less-than symbol.

Figure 4.9 demonstrates how to use special characters in an XHTML document. For a list of special characters, see Appendix A, Special Characters.

```
<?xml version = "1.0"?>
<!DOCTYPE html PUBLIC "-//W3C//DTD XHTML 1.0 Strict//EN"
   "http://www.w3.org/TR/xhtml1/DTD/xhtml1-strict.dtd">

<!-- Fig. 4.9: contact2.html       -->
<!-- Inserting special characters -->

<html xmlns = "http://www.w3.org/1999/xhtml">
   <head>
      <title>Internet and WWW How to Program - Contact Page
      </title>
   </head>

   <body>

      <!-- special characters are entered -->
      <!-- using the form &code;          -->
      <p>
         Click
         <a href = "mailto:deitel@deitel.com">here
         </a> to open an e-mail message addressed to
         deitel@deitel.com.
      </p>

      <hr /> <!-- inserts a horizontal rule -->

```

Fig. 4.9 Inserting special characters into XHTML (part 1 of 2).

```
27        <p>All information on this site is <strong>&copy;</strong>
28           Deitel <strong>&amp;</strong> Associates, Inc. 2002.</p>
29
30        <!-- to strike through text use <del> tags   -->
31        <!-- to subscript text use <sub> tags        -->
32        <!-- to superscript text use <sup> tags      -->
33        <!-- these tags are nested inside other tags -->
34        <p><del>You may download 3.14 x 10<sup>2</sup>
35           characters worth of information from this site.</del>
36           Only <sub>one</sub> download per hour is permitted.</p>
37
38        <p>Note: <strong>&lt; &frac14;</strong> of the information
39           presented here is updated daily.</p>
40
41     </body>
42  </html>
```

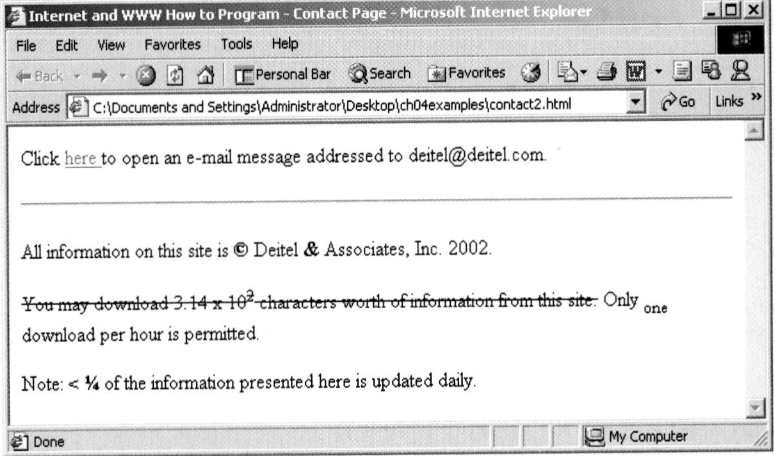

Fig. 4.9 Inserting special characters into XHTML (part 2 of 2).

Lines 27–28 contain other special characters, which are expressed as either word abbreviations (e.g., **amp** for ampersand and **copy** for copyright) or *hexadecimal (hex)* values (e.g., **&** is the hexadecimal representation of **&**). Hexadecimal numbers are base 16 numbers—digits in a hexadecimal number have values from 0 to 15 (a total of 16 different values). The letters A–F represent the hexadecimal digits corresponding to decimal values 10–15. Thus in hexadecimal notation we can have numbers like 876 consisting solely of decimal-like digits, numbers like DA19F consisting of digits and letters, and numbers like DCB consisting solely of letters. We discuss hexadecimal numbers in detail in Appendix D, Number Systems.

In lines 34–36, we introduce three new elements. Most browsers render the ***del*** element as strike-through text. With this format users can easily indicate document revisions. To *superscript* text (i.e., raise text on a line with a decreased font size) or *subscript* text (i.e., lower text on a line with a decreased font size), use the ***sup*** and ***sub*** elements, respectively. We also use special characters **<** for a less-than sign and ***¼*** for the fraction 1/4 (line 38).

In addition to special characters, this document introduces a *horizontal rule*, indicated by the **<hr />** tag in line 24. Most browsers render a horizontal rule as a horizontal line. The **<hr />** tag also inserts a line break above and below the horizontal line.

4.9 Unordered Lists

Up to this point, we have presented basic XHTML elements and attributes for linking to resources, creating headers, using special characters and incorporating images. In this section, we discuss how to organize information on a Web page using lists. In Chapter 5, we introduce another feature for organizing information, called a table. Figure 4.10 displays text in an *unordered list* (i.e., a list that does not order its items by letter or number). The *unordered list element* **ul** creates a list in which each item begins with a bullet symbol (called a *disc*).

Each entry in an unordered list (element **ul** in line 20) is an ***li*** (*list item*) element (lines 23, 25, 27 and 29). Most Web browsers render these elements with a line break and a bullet symbol indented from the beginning of the new line.

```
1  <?xml version = "1.0"?>
2  <!DOCTYPE html PUBLIC "-//W3C//DTD XHTML 1.0 Strict//EN"
3     "http://www.w3.org/TR/xhtml1/DTD/xhtml1-strict.dtd">
4
5  <!-- Fig. 4.10: links2.html                   -->
6  <!-- Unordered list containing hyperlinks -->
7
8  <html xmlns = "http://www.w3.org/1999/xhtml">
9     <head>
10       <title>Internet and WWW How to Program - Links</title>
11    </head>
12
13    <body>
14
15       <h1>Here are my favorite sites</h1>
16
17       <p><strong>Click on a name to go to that page.</strong></p>
18
19       <!-- create an unordered list -->
20       <ul>
21
22          <!-- add four list items -->
23          <li><a href = "http://www.deitel.com">Deitel</a></li>
24
25          <li><a href = "http://www.w3.org">W3C</a></li>
26
27          <li><a href = "http://www.yahoo.com">Yahoo!</a></li>
28
29          <li><a href = "http://www.cnn.com">CNN</a></li>
30       </ul>
31    </body>
32 </html>
```

Fig. 4.10 Unordered lists in XHTML (part 1 of 2).

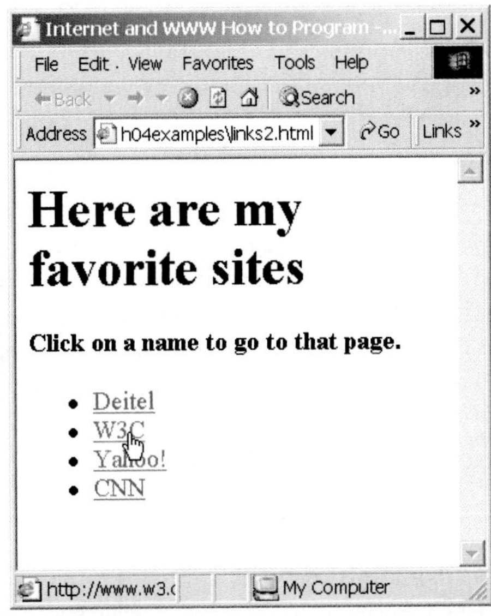

Fig. 4.10 Unordered lists in XHTML (part 2 of 2).

4.10 Nested and Ordered Lists

Lists may be nested to represent hierarchical relationships, as in an outline format. Figure 4.11 demonstrates nested lists and *ordered lists* (i.e., list that order their items by letter or number).

```
<?xml version = "1.0"?>
<!DOCTYPE html PUBLIC "-//W3C//DTD XHTML 1.0 Transitional//EN"
   "http://www.w3.org/TR/xhtml1/DTD/xhtml1-transitional.dtd">

<!-- Fig. 4.11: list.html              -->
<!-- Advanced Lists: nested and ordered -->

<html xmlns = "http://www.w3.org/1999/xhtml">
   <head>
      <title>Internet and WWW How to Program - Lists</title>
   </head>

   <body>

      <h1>The Best Features of the Internet</h1>

      <!-- create an unordered list -->
      <ul>
         <li>You can meet new people from countries around
            the world.</li>
```

Fig. 4.11 Nested and ordered lists in XHTML (part 1 of 3).

```
         <li>
            You have access to new media as it becomes public:

            <!-- this starts a nested list, which uses a -->
            <!-- modified bullet. The list ends when you -->
            <!-- close the <ul> tag.                     -->
            <ul>
               <li>New games</li>
               <li>
                  New applications

                  <!-- ordered nested list -->
                  <ol type = "I">
                     <li>For business</li>
                     <li>For pleasure</li>
                  </ol>
               </li>

               <li>Around the clock news</li>
               <li>Search engines</li>
               <li>Shopping</li>
               <li>
                  Programming

                  <!-- another nested ordered list -->
                  <ol type = "a">
                     <li>XML</li>
                     <li>Java</li>
                     <li>XHTML</li>
                     <li>Scripts</li>
                     <li>New languages</li>
                  </ol>

               </li>

            </ul> <!-- ends the nested list of line 27 -->
         </li>

         <li>Links</li>
         <li>Keeping in touch with old friends</li>
         <li>It is the technology of the future!</li>

      </ul>   <!-- ends the unordered list of line 18 -->

      <h1>My 3 Favorite <em>CEOs</em></h1>

      <!-- ol elements without a type attribute      -->
      <!-- have a numeric sequence type (i.e., 1, 2, ...) -->
      <ol>
         <li>Harvey Deitel</li>
         <li>Bill Gates</li>
         <li>Michael Dell</li>
      </ol>
```

Fig. 4.11 Nested and ordered lists in XHTML (part 2 of 3).

```
74
75       </body>
76    </html>
```

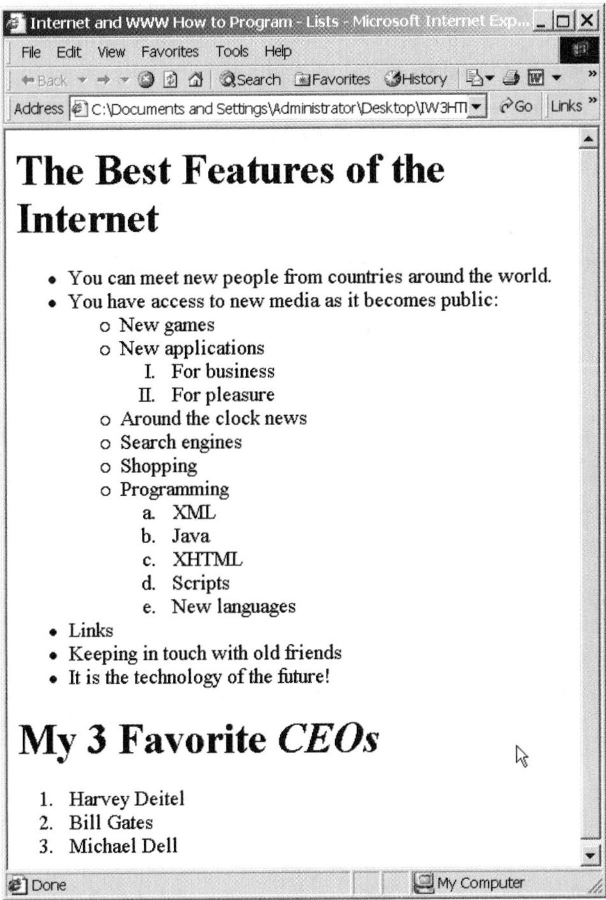

Fig. 4.11 Nested and ordered lists in XHTML (part 3 of 3).

The first ordered list begins on line 33. Attribute **`type`** specifies the *sequence type* (i.e., the set of numbers or letters used in the ordered list). In this case, setting **`type`** to **`"I"`** specifies upper-case roman numerals. Line 46 begins the second ordered list and sets attribute **`type`** to **`"a"`**, specifying lowercase letters for the list items. The last ordered list (lines 64–68) does not use attribute **`type`**. By default, the list's items are enumerated from one to three.

A Web browser indents each nested list to indicate a hierarchal relationship. By default, the items in the outermost unordered list (line 18) are preceded by discs. List items nested inside the unordered list of line 18 are preceded by *circles*. Although not demonstrated in this example, subsequent nested list items are preceded by *squares*. Unordered list items may be explicitly set to discs, circles or squares by setting the **`ul`** element's **`type`** attribute to **`"disc"`**, **`"circle"`** or **`"square"`**, respectively.

Note: XHTML is based on HTML (HyperText Markup Language)—a legacy technology of the World Wide Web Consortium (W3C). In HTML, it was common to specify the document's content, structure and formatting. Formatting might specify where the browser places an element in a Web page or the fonts and colors used to display an element. The so called *strict* form of XHTML allows only a document's content and structure to appear in a valid XHTML document, and not that document's formatting. Our first several examples used only the strict form of XHTML. In fact, the purpose of lines 2–3 in each of the examples before Fig. 4.11 was to indicate to the browser that each document conformed to the strict XHTML definition. This enables the browser to confirm that the document is valid. There are other XHTML document types as well. This particular example uses the XHTML *transitional* document type. This document type exists to enable XHTML document creators to use legacy HTML technologies in an XHTML document. In this example, the **`type`** attribute of the **`ol`** element (lines 33 and 46) is a legacy HTML technology. Changing lines 2–3 as shown in this example, enables us to demonstrate ordered lists with different numbering formats. Normally, such formatting is specified with style sheets (Chapter 6). Most examples in this book adhere to strict HTML form.

Testing and Debugging Tip 4.2

Most current browsers still attempt to render XHTML documents, even if they are invalid.

4.11 Internet and World Wide Web Resources

`www.w3.org/TR/xhtml1`
The *XHTML 1.0 Recommendation* contains XHTML 1.0 general information, compatibility issues, document type definition information, definitions, terminology and much more.

`www.xhtml.org`
XHTML.org provides XHTML development news and links to other XHTML resources, which include books and articles.

`www.w3schools.com/xhtml/default.asp`
The *XHTML School* provides XHTML quizzes and references. This page also contains links to XHTML syntax, validation and document type definitions.

`validator.w3.org`
This is the W3C XHTML validation service site.

`hotwired.lycos.com/webmonkey/00/50/index2a.html`
This site provides an article about XHTML. Key sections of the article overview XHTML and discuss tags, attributes and anchors.

`wdvl.com/Authoring/Languages/XML/XHTML`
The Web Developers Virtual Library provides an introduction to XHTML. This site also contains articles, examples and links to other technologies.

`www.w3.org/TR/1999/xhtml-modularization-19990406/DTD/doc`
The XHTML 1.0 DTD documentation site provides links to DTD documentation for the strict, transitional and frameset document type definitions.

SUMMARY

- XHTML (Extensible Hypertext Markup Language) is a markup language for creating Web pages.

- A key issue when using XHTML is the separation of the presentation of a document (i.e., the document's appearance when rendered by a browser) from the structure of the information in the document.
- In XHTML, text is marked up with elements, delimited by tags that are names contained in pairs of angle brackets. Some elements may contain additional markup called attributes, which provide additional information about the element.
- A machine that runs specialized piece of software called a Web server stores XHTML documents.
- XHTML documents that are syntactically correct are guaranteed to render properly. XHTML documents that contain syntax errors may not display properly.
- Validation services (e.g., **validator.w3.org**) ensure that an XHTML document is syntactically correct.
- Every XHTML document contains a start **<html>** tag and an end **</html>** tag.
- Comments in XHTML always begin with **<!--** and end with **-->**. The browser ignores all text inside a comment.
- Every XHTML document contains a **head** element, which generally contains information, such as a title, and a **body** element, which contains the page content. Information in the **head** element generally is not rendered in the display window but may be made available to the user through other means.
- The **title** element names a Web page. The title usually appears in the colored bar (called the title bar) at the top of the browser window and also appears as the text identifying a page when users add your page to their list of **Favorites** or **Bookmarks**.
- The body of an XHTML document is the area in which the document's content is placed. The content may include text and tags.
- All text placed between the **<p>** and **</p>** tags form one paragraph.
- XHTML provides six headers (**h1** through **h6**) for specifying the relative importance of information. Header element **h1** is considered the most significant header and is rendered in a larger font than the other five headers. Each successive header element (i.e., **h2**, **h3**, etc.) is rendered in a smaller font.
- Web browsers typically underline text hyperlinks and color them blue by default.
- The **<strong>** tag renders text in a bold font.
- Users can insert links with the **a** (anchor) element. The most important attribute for the **a** element is **href**, which specifies the resource (e.g., page, file, e-mail address, etc.) being linked.
- Anchors can link to an e-mail address using a **mailto** URL. When someone clicks this type of anchored link, most browsers launch the default e-mail program (e.g., Outlook Express) to initiate e-mail messages to the linked addresses.
- The **img** element's **src** attribute specifies an image's location. Optional attributes **width** and **height** specify the image width and height, respectively. Images are measured in pixels ("picture elements"), which represent dots of color on the screen. Every **img** element in a valid XHTML document must have an **alt** attribute, which contains text that is displayed if the client cannot render the image.
- The **alt** attribute makes Web pages more accessible to users with disabilities, especially those with vision impairments.
- Some XHTML elements are empty elements and contain only attributes and do not mark up text. Empty elements (e.g., **img**) must be terminated, either by using the forward slash character (**/**) or by explicitly writing an end tag.

- The **br** element causes most browsers to render a line break. Any markup or text following a **br** element is rendered on the next line.
- XHTML provides special characters or entity references (in the form **&**code**;**) for representing characters that cannot be marked up.
- Most browsers render a horizontal rule, indicated by the **<hr />** tag, as a horizontal line. The **hr** element also inserts a line break above and below the horizontal line.
- The unordered list element **ul** creates a list in which each item in the list begins with a bullet symbol (called a disc). Each entry in an unordered list is an **li** (list item) element. Most Web browsers render these elements with a line break and a bullet symbol at the beginning of the line.
- Lists may be nested to represent hierarchical data relationships.
- Attribute **type** specifies the sequence type (i.e., the set of numbers or letters used in the ordered list).

TERMINOLOGY

<!--…--> (XHTML comment)
a element (**<a>**…**</a>**)
alt attribute
& (**&** special character)
anchor
angle brackets (**< >**)
attribute
body element
br (line break) element
comments in XHTML
© (© special character)
disc
element
e-mail anchor
empty tag
Extensible Hypertext Markup Language (XHTML)
head element
header
header elements (**h1** through **h6**)
height attribute
hexadecimal code
<hr /> tag (horizontal rule)
href attribute
.htm (XHTML file-name extension)
<html> tag
.html (XHTML file-name extension)
hyperlink
image hyperlink
img element
level of nesting
<li> (list item) tag
linked document
mailto: URL
markup language
nested list
ol (ordered list) element
p (paragraph) element
special character
src attribute (**img**)
<strong> tag
sub element
subscript
superscript
syntax
tag
text editor
text editor
title element
type attribute
unordered-list element (**ul**)
valid document
Web page
width attribute
World Wide Web (WWW)
XHTML (Extensible Hypertext Markup Language)
XHTML comment
XHTML markup
XHTML tag
XML declaration
xmlns attribute

SELF-REVIEW EXERCISES

4.1 State whether the following are *true* or *false*. If *false*, explain why.

a) Attribute **type**, when used with an **ol** element, specifies a sequence type.

b) An ordered list cannot be nested inside an unordered list.
c) XHTML is an acronym for XML HTML.
d) Element **br** represents a line break.
e) Hyperlinks are marked up with **<link>** tags.

4.2 Fill in the blanks in each of the following:
a) The __________ element inserts a horizontal rule.
b) A superscript is marked up using element __________ and a subscript is marked up using element __________.
c) The least important header element is __________ and the most important header element is __________.
d) Element __________ marks up an unordered list.
e) Element __________ marks up a paragraph.

ANSWERS TO SELF-REVIEW EXERCISES

4.1 a) True. b) False. An ordered list can be nested inside an unordered list. c) False. XHTML is an acronym for Extensible HyperText Markup Language. d) True. e) False. A hyperlink is marked up with **<a>** tags.

4.2 a) **hr**. b) **sup**, **sub**. c) **h6**, **h1**. d) **ul**. e) **p**.

EXERCISES

4.3 Use XHTML to create a document that contains the to mark up the following text:

Internet and World Wide Web How to Program: Second Edition
Welcome to the world of Internet programming. We have provided topical coverage for many Internet-related topics.

Use **h1** for the title (the first line of text), **p** for text (the second and third lines of text) and **sub** for each world that begins with a capital letter. Insert a horizontal rule between the **h1** element and the **p** element. Open your new document in a Web browser to view the marked up document.

4.4 Why is the following markup invalid?

```
<p>Here is some text...
<hr />
<p>And some more text...</p>
```

4.5 Why is the following markup invalid?

```
<p>Here is some text...<br>
And some more text...</p>
```

4.6 An image named **deitel.gif** is 200 pixels wide and 150 pixels high. Use the **width** and **height** attributes of the **<img>** tag to (a) increase the size of the image by 100%; (b) increase the size of the image by 50%; and (c) change the width-to-height ratio to 2:1, keeping the **width** attained in part (a). Write separate XHTML statements for parts (a), (b) and (c).

4.7 Create a link to each of the following: (a) **index.html**, located in the **files** directory; (b) **index.html**, located in the **text** subdirectory of the **files** directory; (c) **index.html**, located in the **other** directory in your *parent directory* [*Hint*: **..** signifies parent directory.]; (d) A link to the President of the United States' e-mail address (**president@whitehouse.gov**); and (e) An **FTP** link to the file named **README** in the **pub** directory of **ftp.cdrom.com** [*Hint*: Use **ftp://**.].

4.8 Create an XHTML document that marks up your resume.

4.9 Create an XHTML document containing three ordered lists: ice cream, soft serve and frozen yogurt. Each ordered list should contain a nested, unordered list of your favorite flavors. Provide a minimum of three flavors in each unordered list.

4.10 Create an XHTML document that uses an image as an e-mail link. Use attribute **`alt`** to provide a description of the image and link.

4.11 Create an XHTML document that contains an ordered list of your favorite Web sites. Your page should contain the header "My Favorite Web Sites."

4.12 Create an XHTML document that contains links to all the examples presented in this chapter. [*Hint*: Place all the chapter examples in one directory].

4.13 Modify the XHTML document (**`picture.html`**) in Fig. 4.7 by removing all end tags. Validate this document using the W3C validation service. What happens? Next remove the **`alt`** attributes from the **`<img>`** tags and revalidate your document. What happens?

4.14 Identify each of the following as either an element or an attribute:

a) **`html`**
b) **`width`**
c) **`href`**
d) **`br`**
e) **`h3`**
f) **`a`**
g) **`src`**

4.15 State which of the following statements are *true* and which are *false*. If *false*, explain why.

a) A valid XHTML document can contain uppercase letters in element names.
b) Tags need not be closed in a valid XHTML document.
c) XHTML documents can have the file extension **`.htm`**.
d) Valid XHTML documents can contain tags that overlap.
e) **`&less;`** is the special character for the less-than (**`<`**) character.
f) In a valid XHTML document, **`<li>`** can be nested inside either **`<ol>`** or **`<ul>`** tags.

4.16 Fill in the blanks for each of the following:

a) XHTML comments begin with **`<!--`** and end with __________.
b) In XHTML, attribute values must be enclosed in __________.
c) __________ is the special character for an ampersand.
d) Element __________ can be used to bold text.

Introduction to XHTML: Part 2

Objectives

- To be able to create tables with rows and columns of data.
- To be able to control table formatting.
- To be able to create and use forms.
- To be able to create and use image maps to aid in Web-page navigation.
- To be able to make Web pages accessible to search engines using **`<meta>`** tags.
- To be able to use the **`frameset`** element to display multiple Web pages in a single browser window.

Yea, from the table of my memory
I'll wipe away all trivial fond records.
William Shakespeare

Outline

5.1 Introduction

In the previous chapter, we introduced XHTML. We built several complete Web pages featuring text, hyperlinks, images, horizontal rules and line breaks. In this chapter, we discuss more substantial XHTML features, including presentation of information in *tables* and *incorporating forms* for collecting information from a Web-page visitor. We also introduce *internal linking* and *image maps* for enhancing Web page navigation and *frames* for displaying multiple documents in the browser.

By the end of this chapter, you will be familiar with the most commonly used XHTML features and will be able to create more complex Web documents. In Chapter 6, we discuss how to make Web pages more visually appealing by manipulating fonts, colors and text.

5.2 Basic XHTML Tables

This section presents XHTML *tables*—a frequently used feature that organizes data into rows and columns. Our first example (Fig. 5.1) uses a table with six rows and two columns to display price information for fruit.

```
<?xml version = "1.0"?>
<!DOCTYPE html PUBLIC "-//W3C//DTD XHTML 1.0 Strict//EN"
   "http://www.w3.org/TR/xhtml1/DTD/xhtml1-strict.dtd">

<!-- Fig. 5.1: table1.html    -->
<!-- Creating a basic table   -->

<html xmlns = "http://www.w3.org/1999/xhtml">
   <head>
      <title>A simple XHTML table</title>
   </head>
```

Fig. 5.1 XHTML table (part 1 of 3).

```

   <body>

      <!-- the <table> tag opens a table -->
      <table border = "1" width = "40%"
         summary = "This table provides information about
            the price of fruit">

         <!-- the <caption> tag summarizes the table's    -->
         <!-- contents (this helps the visually impaired) -->
         <caption><strong>Price of Fruit</strong></caption>

         <!-- the <thead> is the first section of a table -->
         <!-- it formats the table header area            -->
         <thead>
            <tr>              <!-- <tr> inserts a table row -->
               <th>Fruit</th> <!-- insert a heading cell -->
               <th>Price</th>
            </tr>
         </thead>

         <!-- all table content is enclosed  -->
         <!-- within the <tbody>             -->
         <tbody>
            <tr>
               <td>Apple</td> <!-- insert a data cell -->
               <td>$0.25</td>
            </tr>

            <tr>
               <td>Orange</td>
               <td>$0.50</td>
            </tr>

            <tr>
               <td>Banana</td>
               <td>$1.00</td>
            </tr>

            <tr>
               <td>Pineapple</td>
               <td>$2.00</td>
            </tr>
         </tbody>

         <!-- the <tfoot> is the last section of a table -->
         <!-- it formats the table footer                -->
         <tfoot>
            <tr>
               <th>Total</th>
               <th>$3.75</th>
            </tr>
         </tfoot>
```

Fig. 5.1 XHTML table (part 2 of 3).

```
65
66          </table>
67
68       </body>
69    </html>
```

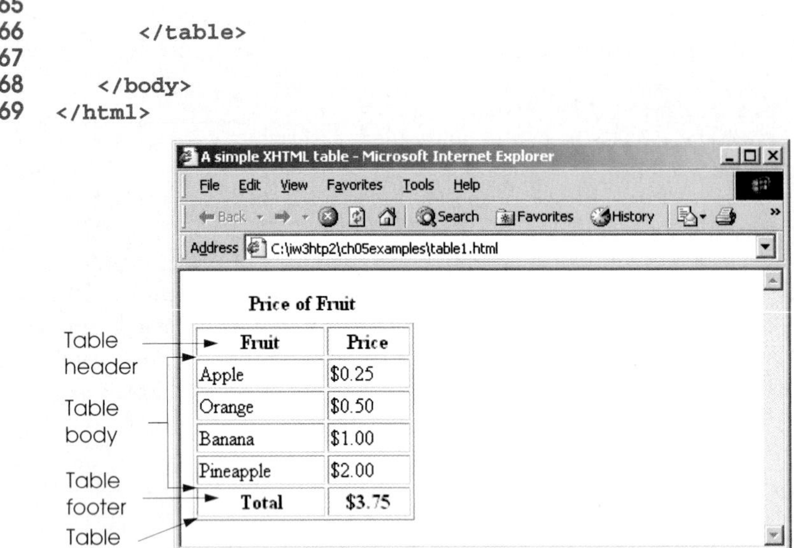

Fig. 5.1 XHTML table (part 3 of 3).

Tables are defined with the **`table`** element. Lines 16–18 specify the start tag for a table element that has several attributes. The ***`border`*** attribute specifies the table's border width in pixels. To create a table without a border, set **`border`** to **`"0"`**. This example assigns attribute **`width "40%"`** to set the table's width to 40 percent of the browser's width. A developer can also set attribute **`width`** to a specified number of pixels.

Testing and Debugging Tip 5.1

Try resizing the browser window to see how the width of the window affects the width of the table.

As its name implies, attribute ***`summary`*** (line 17) describes the table's contents. Speech devices use this attribute to make the table more accessible to users with visual impairments. The ***`caption`*** element (line 22) describes the table's content and helps text-based browsers interpret the table data. Text inside the **`<caption>`** tag is rendered above the table by most browsers. Attribute **`summary`** and element **`caption`** are two of many XHTML features that make Web pages more accessible to users with disabilities. We discuss accessibility programming in detail in Chapter 34, Accessibility.

A table has three distinct sections—*head*, *body* and *foot*. The head section (or *header cell*) is defined with a ***`thead`*** element (lines 26–31), which contains header information such as column names. Each ***`tr`*** element (lines 27–30) defines an individual *table row*. The columns in the head section are defined with **`th`** elements. Most browsers center and display text formatted by **`th`** (table header column) elements in bold. Table header elements are nested inside table row elements.

The body section, or *table body*, contains the table's primary data. The table body (lines 35–55) is defined in a **`tbody`** element. *Data cells* contain individual pieces of data and are defined with **`td`** (*table data*) elements.

The foot section (lines 59–64) is defined with a ***tfoot*** (table foot) element and represents a footer. Common text placed in the footer includes calculation results and footnotes. Like other sections, the foot section can contain table rows and each row can contain columns.

5.3 Intermediate XHTML Tables and Formatting

In the previous section, we explored the structure of a basic table. In Fig. 5.2, we enhance our discussion of tables by introducing elements and attributes that allow the document author to build more complex tables.

The table begins on line 17. Element ***colgroup*** (lines 22–27) groups and formats columns. The ***col*** element (line 26) specifies two attributes in this example. The ***align*** attribute determines the alignment of text in the column. The ***span*** attribute determines how many columns the ***col*** element formats. In this case, we set **align**'s value to **"right"** and **span**'s value to **"1"** to right-align text in the first column (the column containing the picture of the camel in the sample screen capture).

Table cells are sized to fit the data they contain. Document authors can create larger data cells by using attributes ***rowspan*** and ***colspan***. The values assigned to these attributes specify the number of rows or columns occupied by a cell. The **th** element at lines 36–39 uses the attribute **rowspan = "2"** to allow the cell containing the picture of the camel to use two vertically adjacent cells (thus the cell *spans* two rows). The **th** element at lines 42–45 uses the attribute **colspan = "4"** to widen the header cell (containing **Camelid comparison** and **Approximate as of 9/2002**) to span four cells.

```
1  <?xml version = "1.0"?>
2  <!DOCTYPE html PUBLIC "-//W3C//DTD XHTML 1.0 Strict//EN"
3     "http://www.w3.org/TR/xhtml1/DTD/xhtml1-strict.dtd">
4
5  <!-- Fig. 5.2: table2.html     -->
6  <!-- Intermediate table design -->
7
8  <html xmlns = "http://www.w3.org/1999/xhtml">
9     <head>
10       <title>Internet and WWW How to Program - Tables</title>
11    </head>
12
13    <body>
14
15       <h1>Table Example Page</h1>
16
17       <table border = "1">
18          <caption>Here is a more complex sample table.</caption>
19
20          <!-- <colgroup> and <col> tags are used to -->
21          <!-- format entire columns                 -->
22          <colgroup>
23
24             <!-- span attribute determines how many columns -->
25             <!-- the <col> tag affects                      -->
26             <col align = "right" span = "1" />
```

Fig. 5.2 Complex XHTML table (part 1 of 3).

```
         </colgroup>

         <thead>

            <!-- rowspans and colspans merge the specified    -->
            <!-- number of cells vertically or horizontally   -->
            <tr>

               <!-- merge two rows -->
               <th rowspan = "2">
                  <img src = "camel.gif" width = "205"
                     height = "167" alt = "Picture of a camel" />
               </th>

               <!-- merge four columns -->
               <th colspan = "4" valign = "top">
                  <h1>Camelid comparison</h1><br />
                  <p>Approximate as of 9/2002</p>
               </th>
            </tr>

            <tr valign = "bottom">
               <th># of Humps</th>
               <th>Indigenous region</th>
               <th>Spits?</th>
               <th>Produces Wool?</th>
            </tr>

         </thead>

         <tbody>

            <tr>
               <th>Camels (bactrian)</th>
               <td>2</td>
               <td>Africa/Asia</td>
               <td rowspan = "2">Llama</td>
               <td rowspan = "2">Llama</td>
            </tr>

            <tr>
               <th>Llamas</th>
               <td>1</td>
               <td>Andes Mountains</td>
            </tr>

         </tbody>

      </table>

   </body>
</html>
```

Fig. 5.2 Complex XHTML table (part 2 of 3).

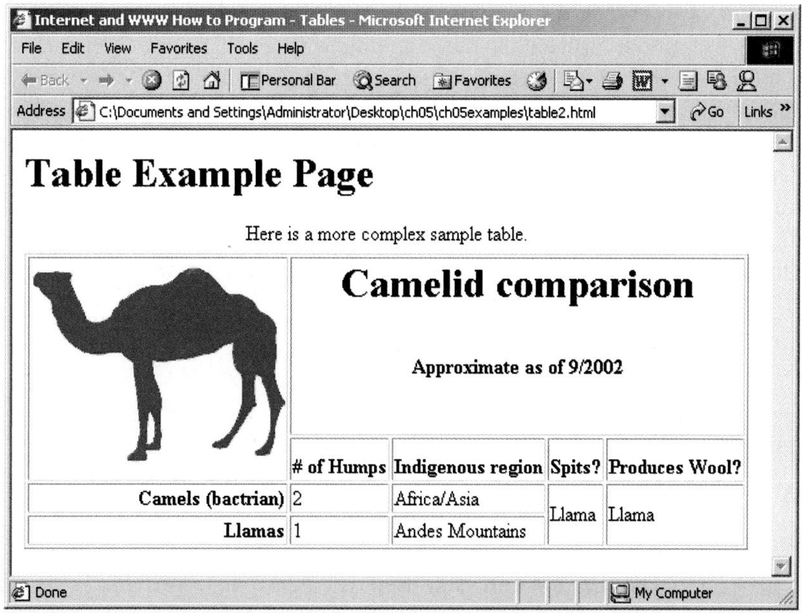

Fig. 5.2 Complex XHTML table (part 3 of 3).

Common Programming Error 5.1

When using **`colspan`** *and* **`rowspan`** *to adjust the size of table data cells, keep in mind that the modified cells will occupy more than one column or row. Other rows or columns of the table must compensate for the extra rows or columns spanned by individual cells. If you do not, the formatting of your table will be distorted and you may inadvertently create more columns and rows than you originally intended.*

Line 42 introduces attribute ***`valign`***, which aligns data vertically and may be assigned one of four values—**`"top"`** aligns data with the top of the cell, **`"middle"`** vertically centers data (the default for all data and header cells), **`"bottom"`** aligns data with the bottom of the cell and **`"baseline"`** ignores the fonts used for the row data and sets the bottom of all text in the row on a common *baseline* (i.e., the horizontal line to which each character in a word is aligned).

5.4 Basic XHTML Forms

When browsing Web sites, users often need to provide information such as e-mail addresses, search keywords and zip codes. XHTML provides a mechanism, called a *form*, for collecting such user information.

Data that users enter on a Web page normally is sent to a Web server that provides access to a site's resources (e.g., XHTML documents, images, etc.). These resources are either located on the same machine as the Web server or on a machine that the Web server can access through the network. When a browser requests a Web page or file that is located on a server, the server processes the request and returns the requested resource. A request contains the name and path of the desired resource and the method of communication (called a *protocol*). XHTML documents use the HyperText Transfer Protocol (HTTP).

Figure 5.3 sends the form data to the Web server which passes the form data to a *CGI* (*Common Gateway Interface*) script (i.e., a program) written in Perl, C or some other language. The script processes the data received from the Web server and typically returns information to the Web server. The Web server then sends the information in the form of an XHTML document to the Web browser. We discuss Web servers in Chapter 21. [*Note*: This example demonstrates client-side functionality. If the form is submitted (by clicking **Submit Your Entries**) an error occurs. In later chapters such as Perl and Python, we present the server-side programming necessary to process information entered into a form.]

```
<?xml version = "1.0"?>
<!DOCTYPE html PUBLIC "-//W3C//DTD XHTML 1.0 Strict//EN"
   "http://www.w3.org/TR/xhtml1/DTD/xhtml1-strict.dtd">

<!-- Fig. 5.3: form.html    -->
<!-- Form Design Example 1 -->

<html xmlns = "http://www.w3.org/1999/xhtml">
   <head>
      <title>Internet and WWW How to Program - Forms</title>
   </head>

   <body>

      <h1>Feedback Form</h1>

      <p>Please fill out this form to help
         us improve our site.</p>

      <!-- this tag starts the form, gives the    -->
      <!-- method of sending information and the -->
      <!-- location of form scripts              -->
      <form method = "post" action = "/cgi-bin/formmail">

         <p>
            <!-- hidden inputs contain non-visual -->
            <!-- information                      -->
            <input type = "hidden" name = "recipient"
               value = "deitel@deitel.com" />
            <input type = "hidden" name = "subject"
               value = "Feedback Form" />
            <input type = "hidden" name = "redirect"
               value = "main.html" />
         </p>

         <!-- <input type = "text"> inserts a text box -->
         <p><label>Name:
               <input name = "name" type = "text" size = "25"
                  maxlength = "30" />
            </label></p>
```

Fig. 5.3 Simple form with hidden fields and a text box (part 1 of 2).

```
41
42          <p>
43             <!-- input types "submit" and "reset" insert  -->
44             <!-- buttons for submitting and clearing the  -->
45             <!-- form's contents                          -->
46             <input type = "submit" value =
47                "Submit Your Entries" />
48             <input type = "reset" value =
49                "Clear Your Entries" />
50          </p>
51
52       </form>
53
54 </html>
```

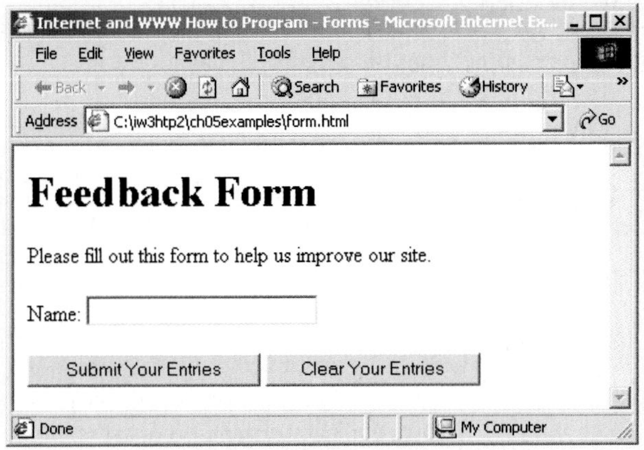

Fig. 5.3 Simple form with hidden fields and a text box (part 2 of 2).

Forms can contain visual and non-visual components. Visual components include clickable buttons and other graphical user interface components with which users interact. Non-visual components, called *hidden inputs*, store any data that the document author specifies, such as e-mail addresses and XHTML document file names that act as links. The form begins on line 23 with the **`form`** element. Attribute **`method`** specifies how the form's data is sent to the Web server.

Using **`method = "post"`** appends form data to the browser request, which contains the protocol (i.e., HTTP) and the requested resource's URL. Scripts located on the Web server's computer (or on a computer accessible through the network) can access the form data sent as part of the request. For example, a script may take the form information and update an electronic mailing list. The other possible value, **`method = "get"`** appends the form data directly to the end of the URL. For example, the URL **`/cgi-bin/formmail`** might have the form information **`name = bob`** appended to it.

The **`action`** attribute in the **`<form>`** tag specifies the URL of a script on the Web server; in this case, it specifies a script that e-mails form data to an address. Most Internet Service Providers (ISPs) have a script like this on their site; ask the Web site system administrator how to set up an XHTML document to use the script correctly.

Lines 28–33 define three ***input*** elements that specify data to provide to the script that processes the form (also called the *form handler*). These three **input** element have ***type*** attribute **"hidden"**, which allows the document author to send form data that is not entered by a user to a script.

The three hidden inputs are: an e-mail address to which the data will be sent, the e-mail's subject line and a URL where the browser will be redirected after submitting the form. Two other **input** attributes are ***name***, which identifies the **input** element, and ***value***, which provides the value that will be sent (or posted) to the Web server.

Good Programming Practice 5.1

*Place hidden **input** elements at the beginning of a form, immediately after the opening **<form>** tag. This placement allows document authors to locate hidden **input** elements quickly.*

We introduce another **type** of **input** in lines 38–39. The ***"text"*** **input** inserts a *text box* into the form. Users can type data in text boxes. The ***label*** element (lines 37–40) provides users with information about the **input** element's purpose.

Common Programming Error 5.2

*Forgetting to include a **label** element for each form element is a design error. Without these labels, users cannot determine the purpose of individual form elements.*

The **input** element's ***size*** attribute specifies the number of characters visible in the text box. Optional attribute ***maxlength*** limits the number of characters input into the text box. In this case, the user is not permitted to type more than **30** characters into the text box.

There are two types of **input** elements in lines 46–49. The ***"submit"*** **input** element is a button. When the user presses a **"submit"** button, the browser sends the data in the form to the Web server for processing. The ***value*** *attribute* sets the text displayed on the button (the default value is **Submit**). The ***"reset"*** **input** element allows a user to reset all **form** elements to their default values. The **value** attribute of the **"reset"** **input** element sets the text displayed on the button (the default value is **Reset**).

5.5 More Complex XHTML Forms

In the previous section, we introduced basic forms. In this section, we introduce elements and attributes for creating more complex forms. Figure 5.4 contains a form that solicits user feedback about a Web site.

The ***textarea*** element (lines 37–39) inserts a multiline text box, called a *text area*, into the form. The number of rows is specified with the ***rows*** *attribute* and the number of columns (i.e., characters) is specified with the ***cols*** *attribute*. In this example, the **textarea** is four rows high and 36 characters wide. To display default text in the text area, place the text between the **<textarea>** and **</textarea>** tags. Default text can be specified in other **input** types, such as text boxes, by using the **value** attribute.

```
1  <?xml version = "1.0"?>
2  <!DOCTYPE html PUBLIC "-//W3C//DTD XHTML 1.0 Strict//EN"
3     "http://www.w3.org/TR/xhtml1/DTD/xhtml1-strict.dtd">
4
```

Fig. 5.4 Form with textareas, password boxes and checkboxes (part 1 of 4).

```
<!-- Fig. 5.4: form2.html  -->
<!-- Form Design Example 2 -->

<html xmlns = "http://www.w3.org/1999/xhtml">
   <head>
      <title>Internet and WWW How to Program - Forms</title>
   </head>

   <body>

      <h1>Feedback Form</h1>

      <p>Please fill out this form to help
         us improve our site.</p>

      <form method = "post" action = "/cgi-bin/formmail">

         <p>
            <input type = "hidden" name = "recipient"
               value = "deitel@deitel.com" />
            <input type = "hidden" name = "subject"
               value = "Feedback Form" />
            <input type = "hidden" name = "redirect"
               value = "main.html" />
         </p>

         <p><label>Name:
            <input name = "name" type = "text" size = "25" />
         </label></p>

         <!-- <textarea> creates a multiline textbox -->
         <p><label>Comments:<br />
            <textarea name = "comments" rows = "4" cols = "36">
Enter your comments here.
            </textarea>
         </label></p>

         <!-- <input type = "password"> inserts a   -->
         <!-- textbox whose display is masked with  -->
         <!-- asterisk characters                   -->
         <p><label>E-mail Address:
            <input name = "email" type = "password"
               size = "25" />
         </label></p>

         <p>
            <strong>Things you liked:</strong><br />

            <label>Site design
            <input name = "thingsliked" type = "checkbox"
               value = "Design" /></label>

```

Fig. 5.4 Form with textareas, password boxes and checkboxes (part 2 of 4).

```
            <label>Links
            <input name = "thingsliked" type = "checkbox"
               value = "Links" /></label>

            <label>Ease of use
            <input name = "thingsliked" type = "checkbox"
               value = "Ease" /></label>

            <label>Images
            <input name = "thingsliked" type = "checkbox"
               value = "Images" /></label>

            <label>Source code
            <input name = "thingsliked" type = "checkbox"
               value = "Code" /></label>
         </p>

         <p>
            <input type = "submit" value =
               "Submit Your Entries" />
            <input type = "reset" value =
               "Clear Your Entries" />
         </p>

      </form>
</html>
```

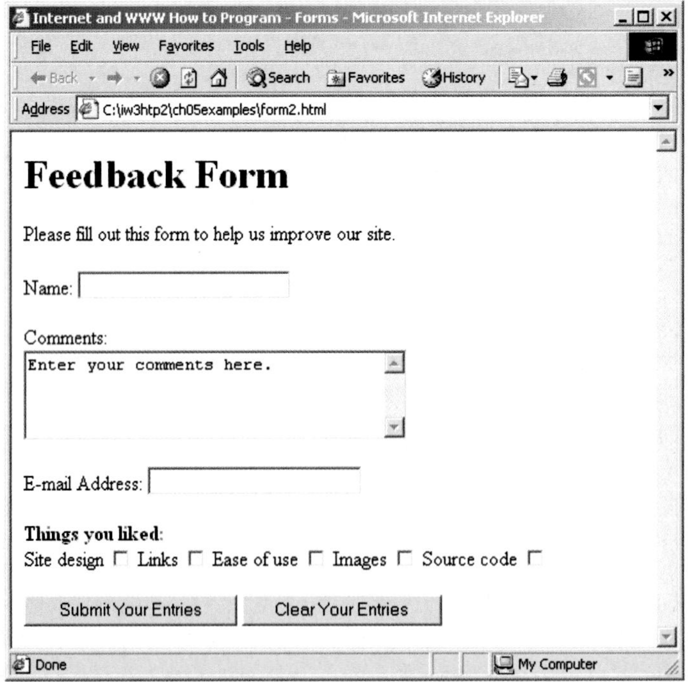

Fig. 5.4 Form with textareas, password boxes and checkboxes (part 3 of 4).

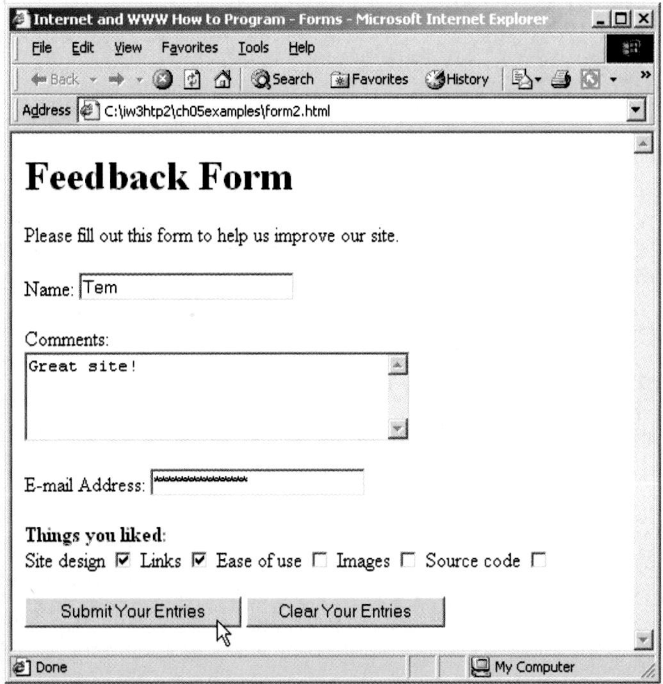

Fig. 5.4 Form with textareas, password boxes and checkboxes (part 4 of 4).

The **"password"** input in lines 46–47, inserts a password box with the specified **size**. A password box allows users to enter sensitive information, such as credit card numbers and passwords, by "masking" the information input with asterisks. The actual value input is sent to the Web server, not the asterisks that mask the input.

Lines 54–71 introduce the *checkbox* **form** element. Checkboxes enable users to select from a set of options. When a user selects a checkbox, a check mark appears in the check box. Otherwise, the checkbox remains empty. Each **"checkbox" input** creates a new checkbox. Checkboxes can be used individually or in groups. Checkboxes that belong to a group are assigned the same **name** (in this case, **"thingsliked"**).

Common Programming Error 5.3

*When your **form** has several checkboxes with the same **name**, you must make sure that they have different **value**s, or the scripts running on the Web server will not be able to distinguish between them.*

We continue our discussion of forms by presenting a third example that introduces several more form elements from which users can make selections (Fig. 5.5). In this example, we introduce two new **input** types. The first type is the *radio button* (lines 76–94) specified with type **"radio"**. Radio buttons are similar to checkboxes, except that only one radio button in a group of radio buttons may be selected at any time. All radio buttons in a group have the same **name** attributes and are distinguished by their different **value** attributes. The attribute-value pair **checked = "checked"** (line 77) indicates which radio button, if any, is selected initially. The **checked** attribute also applies to checkboxes.

```
<?xml version = "1.0"?>
<!DOCTYPE html PUBLIC "-//W3C//DTD XHTML 1.0 Strict//EN"
   "http://www.w3.org/TR/xhtml1/DTD/xhtml1-strict.dtd">

<!-- Fig. 5.5: form3.html  -->
<!-- Form Design Example 3 -->

<html xmlns = "http://www.w3.org/1999/xhtml">
   <head>
      <title>Internet and WWW How to Program - Forms</title>
   </head>

   <body>

      <h1>Feedback Form</h1>

      <p>Please fill out this form to help
         us improve our site.</p>

      <form method = "post" action = "/cgi-bin/formmail">

         <p>
            <input type = "hidden" name = "recipient"
               value = "deitel@deitel.com" />
            <input type = "hidden" name = "subject"
               value = "Feedback Form" />
            <input type = "hidden" name = "redirect"
               value = "main.html" />
         </p>

         <p><label>Name:
               <input name = "name" type = "text" size = "25" />
            </label></p>

         <p><label>Comments:<br />
               <textarea name = "comments" rows = "4"
                  cols = "36"></textarea>
            </label></p>

         <p><label>E-mail Address:
               <input name = "email" type = "password"
                  size = "25" /></label></p>

         <p>
            <strong>Things you liked:</strong><br />

            <label>Site design
               <input name = "thingsliked" type = "checkbox"
                  value = "Design" /></label>

            <label>Links
               <input name = "thingsliked" type = "checkbox"
                  value = "Links" /></label>
```

Fig. 5.5 Form including radio buttons and drop-down lists (part 1 of 4).

```
            <label>Ease of use
               <input name = "thingsliked" type = "checkbox"
                  value = "Ease" /></label>

            <label>Images
               <input name = "thingsliked" type = "checkbox"
                  value = "Images" /></label>

            <label>Source code
               <input name = "thingsliked" type = "checkbox"
                  value = "Code" /></label>
         </p>

         <!-- <input type = "radio" /> creates a radio     -->
         <!-- button. The difference between radio buttons -->
         <!-- and checkboxes is that only one radio button -->
         <!-- in a group can be selected.                  -->
         <p>
            <strong>How did you get to our site?:</strong><br />

            <label>Search engine
               <input name = "howtosite" type = "radio"
                  value = "search engine" checked = "checked" />
            </label>

            <label>Links from another site
               <input name = "howtosite" type = "radio"
                  value = "link" /></label>

            <label>Deitel.com Web site
               <input name = "howtosite" type = "radio"
                  value = "deitel.com" /></label>

            <label>Reference in a book
               <input name = "howtosite" type = "radio"
                  value = "book" /></label>

            <label>Other
               <input name = "howtosite" type = "radio"
                  value = "other" /></label>

         </p>

         <p>
            <label>Rate our site:

               <!-- the <select> tag presents a drop-down -->
               <!-- list with choices indicated by the    -->
               <!-- <option> tags                         -->
               <select name = "rating">
                  <option selected = "selected">Amazing</option>
                  <option>10</option>
```

Fig. 5.5 Form including radio buttons and drop-down lists (part 2 of 4).

```
                  <option>9</option>
                  <option>8</option>
                  <option>7</option>
                  <option>6</option>
                  <option>5</option>
                  <option>4</option>
                  <option>3</option>
                  <option>2</option>
                  <option>1</option>
                  <option>Awful</option>
               </select>

            </label>
         </p>

         <p>
            <input type = "submit" value =
               "Submit Your Entries" />
            <input type = "reset" value = "Clear Your Entries" />
         </p>

      </form>

   </body>
</html>
```

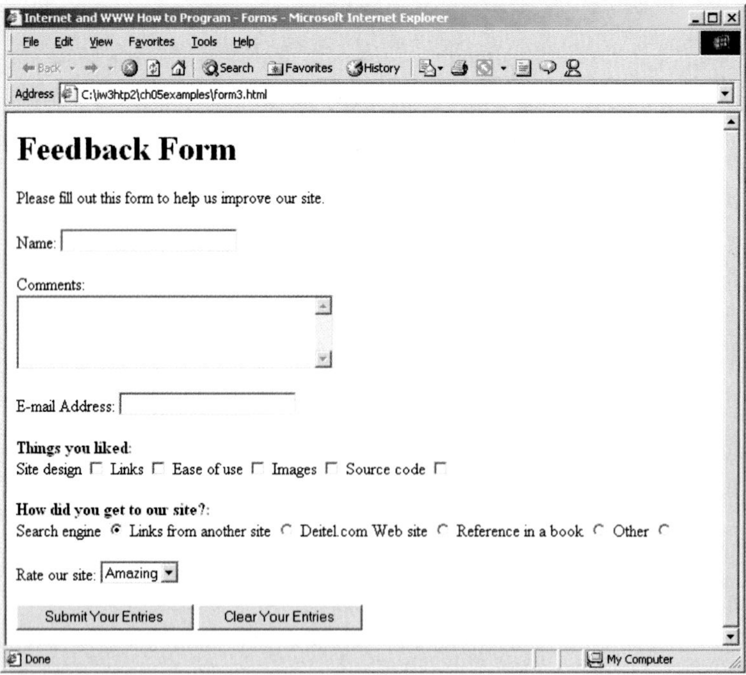

Fig. 5.5 Form including radio buttons and drop-down lists (part 3 of 4).

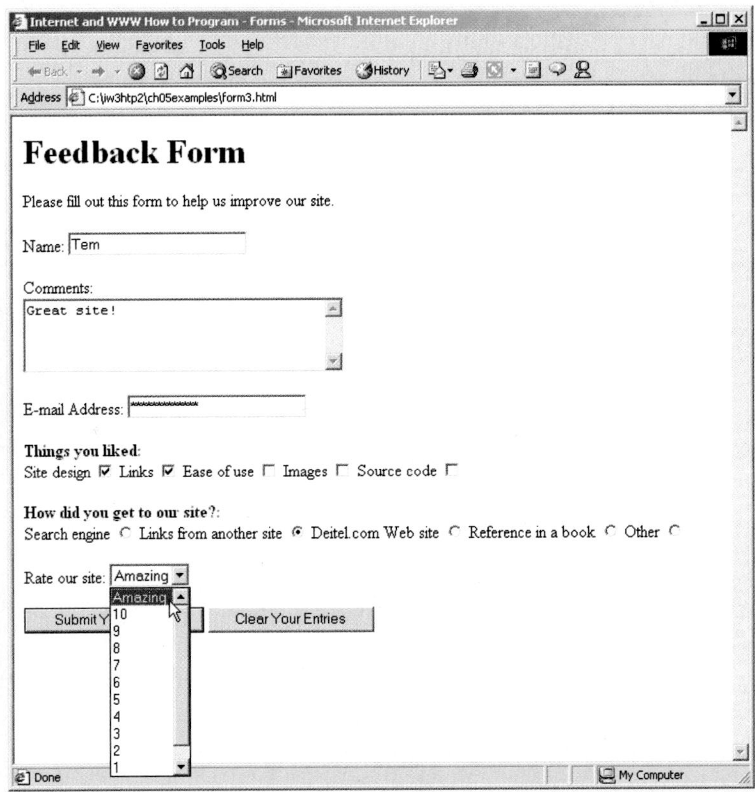

Fig. 5.5 Form including radio buttons and drop-down lists (part 4 of 4).

Common Programming Error 5.4

*When using a group of radio buttons in a form, forgetting to set the **`name`** attributes to the same name lets the user select all of the radio buttons at the same time, which is a logic error.*

The ***`select`*** element (lines 104–117) provides a drop-down list of items from which the user can select an item. The **`name`** attribute identifies the drop-down list. The ***`option`*** element (lines 105–116) adds items to the drop-down list. The **`option`** element's ***`selected`*** *attribute* specifies which item initially is displayed as the selected item in the **`select`** element.

5.6 Internal Linking

In Chapter 4, we discussed how to hyperlink one Web page to another. Figure 5.6 introduces *internal linking*—a mechanism that enables the user to jump between locations in the same document. Internal linking is useful for long documents that contain many sections. Clicking an internal link enables users to find a section without scrolling through the entire document.

```
<?xml version = "1.0"?>
<!DOCTYPE html PUBLIC "-//W3C//DTD XHTML 1.0 Strict//EN"
   "http://www.w3.org/TR/xhtml1/DTD/xhtml1-strict.dtd">

<!-- Fig. 5.6: links.html -->
<!-- Internal Linking     -->

<html xmlns = "http://www.w3.org/1999/xhtml">
   <head>
      <title>Internet and WWW How to Program - List</title>
   </head>

   <body>

      <!-- <a name = ".."></a> creates an internal hyperlink -->
      <p><a name = "features"></a></p>
      <h1>The Best Features of the Internet</h1>

      <!-- an internal link's address is "#linkname"         -->
      <p><a href = "#ceos">Go to <em>Favorite CEOs</em></a></p>

      <ul>
         <li>You can meet people from countries
            around the world.</li>

         <li>You have access to new media as it becomes public:
            <ul>
               <li>New games</li>
               <li>New applications
                  <ul>
                     <li>For Business</li>
                     <li>For Pleasure</li>
                  </ul>
               </li>

               <li>Around the clock news</li>
               <li>Search Engines</li>
               <li>Shopping</li>
               <li>Programming
                  <ul>
                     <li>XHTML</li>
                     <li>Java</li>
                     <li>Dynamic HTML</li>
                     <li>Scripts</li>
                     <li>New languages</li>
                  </ul>
               </li>
            </ul>
         </li>

         <li>Links</li>
         <li>Keeping in touch with old friends</li>
```

Fig. 5.6 Using internal hyperlinks to make pages more navigable (part 1 of 2).

```
            <li>It is the technology of the future!</li>
         </ul>

         <!-- named anchor -->
         <p><a name = "ceos"></a></p>
         <h1>My 3 Favorite <em>CEOs</em></h1>

         <p>

            <!-- internal hyperlink to features -->
            <a href = "#features">Go to <em>Favorite Features</em>
            </a></p>

         <ol>
            <li>Bill Gates</li>
            <li>Steve Jobs</li>
            <li>Michael Dell</li>
         </ol>

      </body>
   </html>
```

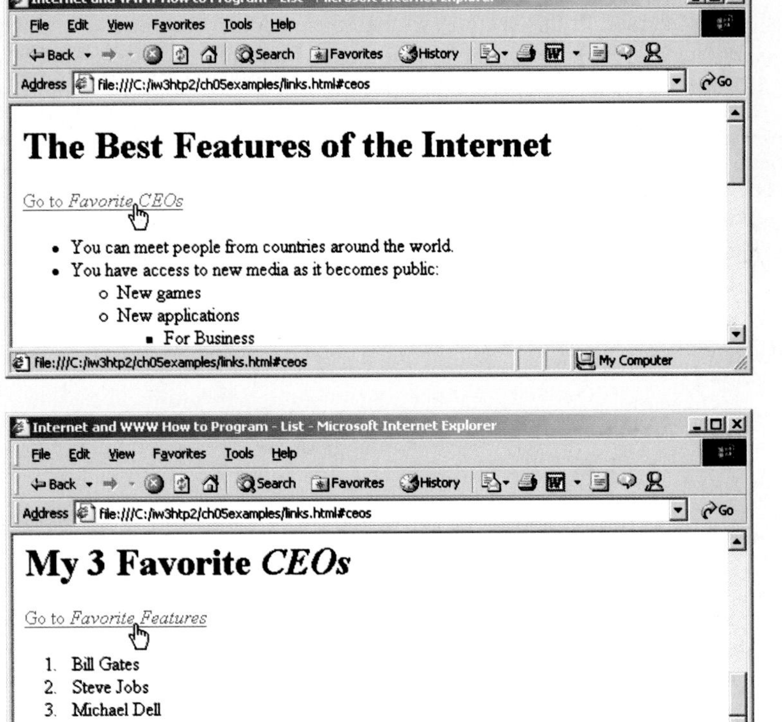

Fig. 5.6 Using internal hyperlinks to make pages more navigable (part 2 of 2).

Line 16 contains a *named anchor* (called **features**) for an internal hyperlink. To link to this type of anchor inside the same Web page, the href attribute of another anchor element includes the named anchor preceded with a pound sign (as in **#features**). Lines 63–64 contain a hyperlink with the anchor **features** as its target. Selecting this hyperlink in a Web browser scrolls the browser window to the **features** anchor at line 16.

Look-and-Feel Observation 5.1

Internal hyperlinks are useful in XHTML documents that contain large amounts of information. Internal links to various sections on the page makes it easier for users to navigate the page. They do not have to scroll to find a specific section.

Although not demonstrated in this example, a hyperlink can specify an internal link in another document by specifying the document name followed by a pound sign and the named anchor as in:

href = "*page.html#name*"

For example, to link to a named anchor called **booklist** in **books.html**, **href** is assigned **"books.html#booklist"**.

5.7 Creating and Using Image Maps

In Chapter 4, we demonstrated how images can be used as hyperlinks to link to other resources on the Internet. In this section, we introduce another technique for image linking called *image maps*, which designate certain areas of an image (called *hotspots*) as links. Figure 5.7 introduces image maps and hotspots.

```
<?xml version = "1.0" ?>
<!DOCTYPE html PUBLIC "-//W3C//DTD XHTML 1.0 Strict//EN"
   "http://www.w3.org/TR/xhtml1/DTD/xhtml1-strict.dtd">

<!-- Fig. 5.7: picture.html          -->
<!-- Creating and Using Image Maps -->

<html xmlns = "http://www.w3.org/1999/xhtml">
   <head>
      <title>
         Internet and WWW How to Program - Image Map
      </title>
   </head>

   <body>

      <p>

      <!-- the <map> tag defines an image map -->
      <map id = "picture">

         <!-- shape = "rect" indicates a rectangular    -->
         <!-- area, with coordinates for the upper-left -->
         <!-- and lower-right corners                   -->
```

Fig. 5.7 Image with links anchored to an image map (part 1 of 2).

```
25          <area href = "form.html" shape = "rect"
26             coords = "2,123,54,143"
27             alt = "Go to the feedback form" />
28          <area href = "contact.html" shape = "rect"
29             coords = "126,122,198,143"
30             alt = "Go to the contact page" />
31          <area href = "main.html" shape = "rect"
32             coords = "3,7,61,25" alt = "Go to the homepage" />
33          <area href = "links.html" shape = "rect"
34             coords = "168,5,197,25"
35             alt = "Go to the links page" />
36
37          <!-- value "poly" creates a hotspot in the shape -->
38          <!-- of a polygon, defined by coords             -->
39          <area shape = "poly" alt = "E-mail the Deitels"
40             coords = "162,25,154,39,158,54,169,51,183,39,161,26"
41             href = "mailto:deitel@deitel.com" />
42
43          <!-- shape = "circle" indicates a circular -->
44          <!-- area with the given center and radius -->
45          <area href = "mailto:deitel@deitel.com"
46             shape = "circle" coords = "100,36,33"
47             alt = "E-mail the Deitels" />
48       </map>
49
50       <!-- <img src =... usemap = "#id"> indicates that the -->
51       <!-- specified image map is used with this image     -->
52       <img src = "deitel.gif" width = "200" height = "144"
53          alt = "Deitel logo" usemap = "#picture" />
54       </p>
55    </body>
56 </html>
```

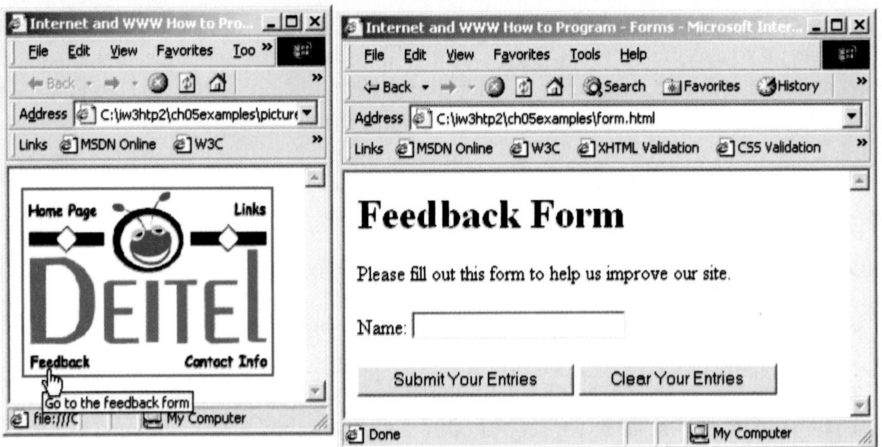

Fig. 5.7 Image with links anchored to an image map (part 2 of 2).

Lines 20–48 define an image maps by using a ***map*** element. Attribute ***id*** (line 20) identifies the image map. If **id** is omitted, the map cannot be referenced by an image. We discuss how to reference an image map momentarily. Hotspots are defined with **area** elements (as shown on lines 25–27). Attribute **href** (line 25) specifies the link's target (i.e., the resource to which to link). Attributes ***shape*** (line 25) and ***coords*** (line 26) specify the hotspot's shape and coordinates, respectively. Attribute **alt** (line 27) provides alternate text for the link.

Common Programming Error 5.5

Not specifying an **id** *attribute for a* **map** *element prevents an* **img** *element from using the* **map***'s* **area** *elements to define hotspots.*

The markup on lines 25–27 creates a *rectangular hotspot* (**shape = "rect"**) for the *coordinates* specified in the **coords** attribute. A coordinate pair consists of two numbers representing the location of a point on the *x*-axis and the *y*-axis, respectively. The *x*-axis extends horizontally and the *y*-axis extends vertically from the upper-left corner of the image. Every point on an image has a unique *x*-*y*-coordinate. For rectangular hotspots, the required coordinates are those of the upper-left and lower-right corners of the rectangle. In this case, the upper-left corner of the rectangle is located at 2 on the *x*-axis and 123 on the *y*-axis, annotated as *(2, 123)*. The lower-right corner of the rectangle is at *(54, 143)*. Coordinates are measured in pixels.

Common Programming Error 5.6

Overlapping coordinates of an image map cause the browser to render the first hotspot it encounters for the area.

The map **area** (lines 39–41) assigns the **shape** attribute ***"poly"*** to create a hotspot in the shape of a polygon using the coordinates in attribute **coords**. These coordinates represent each *vertex*, or corner, of the polygon. The browser connects these points with lines to form the hotspot's area.

The map **area** (lines 45–47) assigns the **shape** attribute ***"circle"*** to create a *circular hotspot*. In this case, the **coords** attribute specifies the circle's center coordinates and the circle's radius, in pixels.

To use an image map with an **img** element, the **img** element's ***usemap*** attribute is assigned the **id** of a **map**. Lines 52–53 reference the image map named **"picture"**. The image map is located within the same document so internal linking is used.

5.8 meta Elements

People use search engines to find useful Web sites. Search engines usually catalog sites by following links from page to page and saving identification and classification information for each page. One way that search engines catalog pages is by reading the content in each page's ***meta*** elements, which specify information about a document.

Two important attributes of the **meta** element are ***name***, which identifies the type of **meta** element and ***content***, which provides the information search engines use to catalog pages. Figure 5.8 introduces the **meta** element.

Lines 14–16 demonstrate a ***"keywords"*** **meta** element. The ***content*** attribute of such a **meta** element provides search engines with a list of words that describe a page. These words are compared with words in search requests. Thus, including **meta** elements and their **content** information can draw more viewers to your site.

```
1  <?xml version = "1.0"?>
2  <!DOCTYPE html PUBLIC "-//W3C//DTD XHTML 1.0 Strict//EN"
3     "http://www.w3.org/TR/xhtml1/DTD/xhtml1-strict.dtd">
4
5  <!-- Fig. 5.8: main.html -->
6  <!-- <meta> tag           -->
7
8  <html xmlns = "http://www.w3.org/1999/xhtml">
9     <head>
10       <title>Internet and WWW How to Program - Welcome</title>
11
12       <!-- <meta> tags provide search engines with -->
13       <!-- information used to catalog a site      -->
14       <meta name = "keywords" content = "Web page, design,
15          XHTML, tutorial, personal, help, index, form,
16          contact, feedback, list, links, frame, deitel" />
17
18       <meta name = "description" content = "This Web site will
19          help you learn the basics of XHTML and Web page design
20          through the use of interactive examples and
21          instruction." />
22
23    </head>
24
25    <body>
26
27       <h1>Welcome to Our Web Site!</h1>
28
29       <p>We have designed this site to teach about the wonders
30       of <strong><em>XHTML</em></strong>. <em>XHTML</em> is
31       better equipped than <em>HTML</em> to represent complex
32       data on the Internet. <em>XHTML</em> takes advantage of
33       XML's strict syntax to ensure well-formedness. Soon you
34       will know about many of the great new features of
35       <em>XHTML.</em></p>
36
37      <p>Have Fun With the Site!</p>
38
39    </body>
40 </html>
```

Fig. 5.8 Using **meta** to provide keywords and a description .

Lines 18–21 demonstrate a ***"description"*** **meta** element. The **content** attribute of such a **meta** element provides a three- to four-line description of a site, written in sentence form. Search engines also use this description to catalog your site and sometimes display this information as part of the search results.

Software Engineering Observation 5.1

meta *elements are not visible to users and must be placed inside the* ***head*** *section of your XHTML document. If* ***meta*** *elements are not placed in this section, they will not be read by search engines.*

5.9 `frameset` Element

All of the Web pages we have presented in this book have the ability to link to other pages, but can display only one page at a time. Figure 5.9 uses *frames*, which allow the browser to display more than one XHTML document simultaneously, to display the documents in Fig. 5.8 and Fig. 5.10.

Most of our prior examples adhered to the strict XHTML document type. This particular example uses the *frameset* document type—a special XHTML document type specifically for framesets. This new document type is specified in lines 2–3 and is required for documents that define framesets.

```
1  <?xml version = "1.0"?>
2  <!DOCTYPE html PUBLIC "-//W3C//DTD XHTML 1.0 Frameset//EN"
3     "http://www.w3.org/TR/xhtml1/DTD/xhtml1-frameset.dtd">
4
5  <!-- Fig. 5.9: index.html -->
6  <!-- XHTML Frames I       -->
7
8  <html xmlns = "http://www.w3.org/1999/xhtml">
9     <head>
10       <title>Internet and WWW How to Program - Main</title>
11       <meta name = "keywords" content = "Webpage, design,
12          XHTML, tutorial, personal, help, index, form,
13          contact, feedback, list, links, frame, deitel" />
14
15       <meta name = "description" content = "This Web site will
16          help you learn the basics of XHTML and Web page design
17          through the use of interactive examples
18          and instruction." />
19
20    </head>
21
22    <!-- the <frameset> tag sets the frame dimensions     -->
23    <frameset cols = "110,*">
24
25       <!-- frame elements specify which pages -->
26       <!-- are loaded into a given frame      -->
27       <frame name = "leftframe" src = "nav.html" />
28       <frame name = "main" src = "main.html" />
29
30       <noframes>
31          <p>This page uses frames, but your browser does not
32          support them.</p>
33
34          <p>Please, <a href = "nav.html">follow this link to
35          browse our site without frames</a>.</p>
36       </noframes>
37
38    </frameset>
39 </html>
```

Fig. 5.9 Web document containing two frames—navigation and content (part 1 of 2).

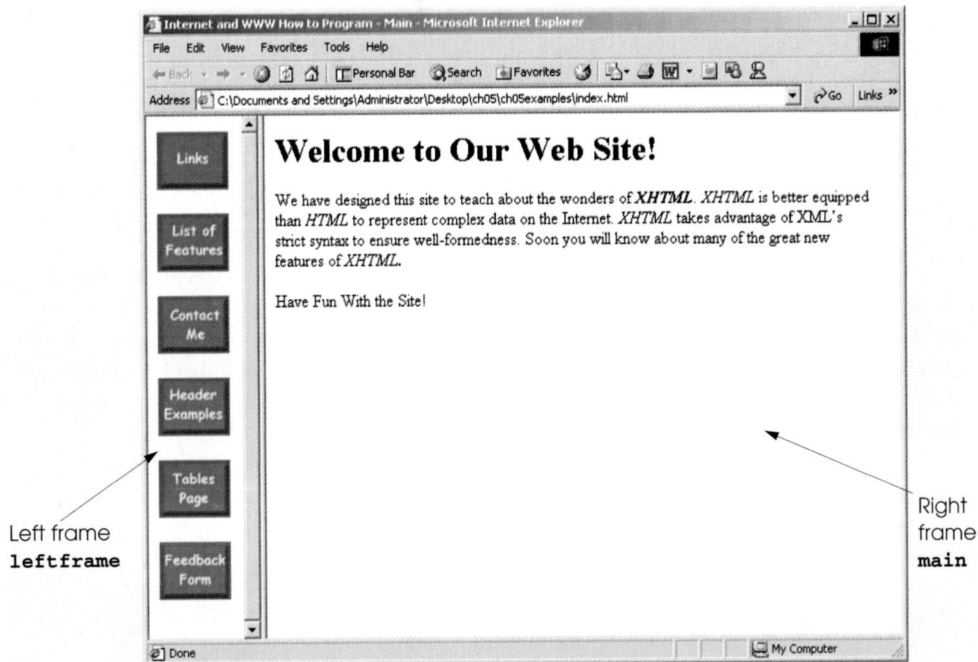

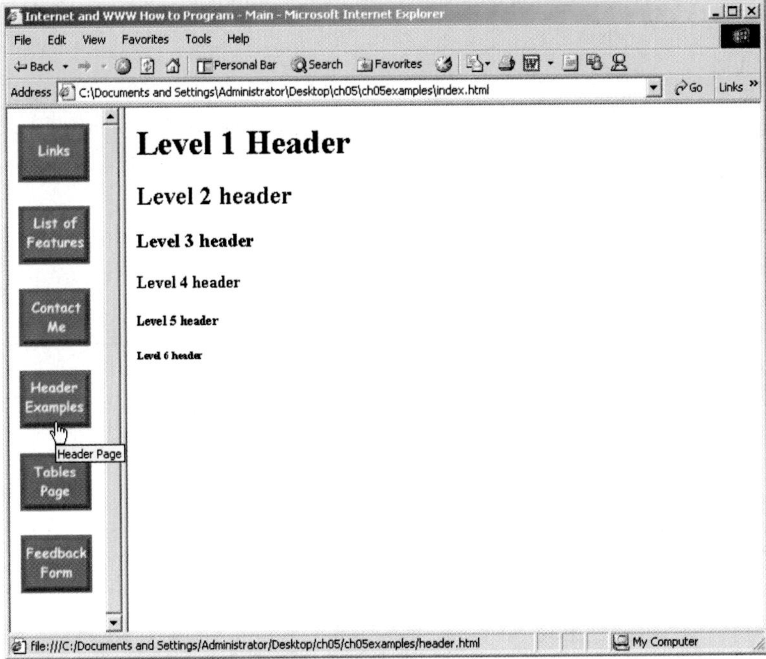

Fig. 5.9 Web document containing two frames—navigation and content (part 2 of 2).

A document that defines a frameset normally consists of an **html** element that contains a **head** element and a ***frameset*** element. The ***<frameset>*** tag (line 23) informs the browser that the page contains frames. Attribute ***cols*** specifies the frameset's column layout. The value of **cols** gives the width of each frame, either in pixels or as a percentage of the browser width. In this case, the attribute **cols = "110,*"** informs the browser that there are two vertical frames. The first frame extends **110** pixels from the left edge of the browser window and the second frame fills the remainder of the browser width (as indicated by the asterisk). Similarly, **frameset** attribute ***rows*** can be used to specify the number of rows and the size of each row in a frameset.

The documents that will be loaded into the **frameset** are specified with ***frame*** elements (lines 27–28 in this example). Attribute **src** specifies the URL of the page to display in the frame. Each frame has **name** and **src** attributes. The first frame (which covers **110** pixels on the left side of the **frameset**) is named **leftframe** and displays the page **nav.html** (Fig. 5.10). The second frame is named main and displays the page **main.html**.

Attribute **name** identifies a frame, enabling hyperlinks in a **frameset** to specify the ***target*** **frame** in which a linked document should display when the user clicks the link. For example

```
<a href = "links.html" target = "main">
```

loads **links.html** in the frame whose **name** is **"main"**.

Not all browsers support frames. XHTML provides the ***noframes*** element (lines 30–36) to enable XHTML document designers to specify alternate content for browsers that do not support frames.

Portability Tip 5.1

Some browsers do not support frames. Use the **noframes** *element inside a* **frameset** *to direct users to a nonframed version of your site.*

Fig. 5.10 is the Web page displayed in the left frame of Fig. 5.9. This XHTML document provides the navigation buttons that, when clicked, determine which document is displayed in the right frame.

```
<?xml version = "1.0"?>
<!DOCTYPE html PUBLIC "-//W3C//DTD XHTML 1.0 Transitional//EN"
    "http://www.w3.org/TR/xhtml1/DTD/xhtml1-transitional.dtd">

<!-- Fig. 5.10: nav.html             -->
<!-- Using images as link anchors -->

<html xmlns = "http://www.w3.org/1999/xhtml">

   <head>
      <title>Internet and WWW How to Program - Navigation Bar
      </title>
   </head>
```

Fig. 5.10 XHTML document displayed in the left frame of Fig. 5.9 (part 1 of 2).

```
14
15      <body>
16
17         <p>
18            <a href = "links.html" target = "main">
19               <img src = "buttons/links.jpg" width = "65"
20                  height = "50" alt = "Links Page" />
21            </a><br />
22
23            <a href = "list.html" target = "main">
24               <img src = "buttons/list.jpg" width = "65"
25                  height = "50" alt = "List Example Page" />
26            </a><br />
27
28            <a href = "contact.html" target = "main">
29               <img src = "buttons/contact.jpg" width = "65"
30                  height = "50" alt = "Contact Page" />
31            </a><br />
32
33            <a href = "header.html" target = "main">
34               <img src = "buttons/header.jpg" width = "65"
35                  height = "50" alt = "Header Page" />
36            </a><br />
37
38            <a href = "table1.html" target = "main">
39               <img src = "buttons/table.jpg" width = "65"
40                  height = "50" alt = "Table Page" />
41            </a><br />
42
43            <a href = "form.html" target = "main">
44               <img src = "buttons/form.jpg" width = "65"
45                  height = "50" alt = "Feedback Form" />
46            </a><br />
47         </p>
48
49      </body>
50   </html>
```

Fig. 5.10 XHTML document displayed in the left frame of Fig. 5.9 (part 2 of 2).

Line 27 (Fig. 5.9) displays the XHTML page in Fig. 5.10. Anchor attribute **`target`** (line 18 in Fig. 5.10) specifies that the linked documents are loaded in frame **`main`** (line 28 in Fig. 5.9). A **`target`** can be set to a number of preset values: **`"_blank"`** loads the page into a new browser window, **`"_self"`** loads the page into the frame in which the anchor element appears and **`"_top"`** loads the page into the full browser window (i.e., removes the **`frameset`**).

5.10 Nested `framesets`

You can use the **`frameset`** element to create more complex layouts in a Web page by nesting **`frameset`**s, as in Fig. 5.11. The nested **`frameset`** in this example displays the XHTML documents in Fig. 5.7, Fig. 5.8 and Fig. 5.10.

The outer frameset element (lines 23–41) defines two columns. The left frame extends over the first 110 pixels from the left edge of the browser and the right frame occupies the rest of the window's width. The **frame** element on line 24 specifies that the document **nav.html** (Fig. 5.10) will be displayed in the left column.

Lines 28–31 define a nested **frameset** element for the second column of the outer frameset. This **frameset** defines two rows. The first row extends 175 pixels from the top of the browser window, as indicated by **rows = "175,*"**. The second row occupies the remainder of the browser window's height. The **frame** element at line 29 specifies that the first row of the nested **frameset** will display **picture.html** (Fig. 5.7). The **frame** element at line 30 specifies that the second row of the nested **frameset** will display **main.html** (Fig. 5.9).

```
1   <?xml version = "1.0"?>
2   <!DOCTYPE html PUBLIC "-//W3C//DTD XHTML 1.0 Frameset//EN"
3      "http://www.w3.org/TR/xhtml1/DTD/xhtml1-frameset.dtd">
4
5   <!-- Fig. 5.11: index2.html -->
6   <!-- XHTML Frames II        -->
7
8   <html xmlns = "http://www.w3.org/1999/xhtml">
9      <head>
10        <title>Internet and WWW How to Program - Main</title>
11
12        <meta name = "keywords" content = "Webpage, design,
13           XHTML, tutorial, personal, help, index, form,
14           contact, feedback, list, links, frame, deitel" />
15
16        <meta name = "description" content = "This Web site will
17           help you learn the basics of XHTML and Web page design
18           through the use of interactive examples
19           and instruction." />
20
21     </head>
22
23     <frameset cols = "110,*">
24        <frame name = "leftframe" src = "nav.html" />
25
26        <!-- nested framesets are used to change the -->
27        <!-- formatting and layout of the frameset   -->
28        <frameset rows = "175,*">
29           <frame name = "picture" src = "picture.html" />
30           <frame name = "main" src = "main.html" />
31        </frameset>
32
33        <noframes>
34           <p>This page uses frames, but your browser does not
35           support them.</p>
36
37           <p>Please, <a href = "nav.html">follow this link to
38           browse our site without frames</a>.</p>
39        </noframes>
```

Fig. 5.11 Framed Web site with a nested frameset (part 1 of 2).

```

    </frameset>
</html>
```

Fig. 5.11 Framed Web site with a nested frameset (part 2 of 2).

Testing and Debugging Tip 5.2

When using nested **`frameset`** *elements, indent every level of* **`<frame>`** *tag. This practice makes the page clearer and easier to debug.*

In this chapter, we presented XHTML for marking up information in tables, creating forms for gathering user input, linking to sections within the same document, using **`<meta>`** tags and creating frames. In Chapter 6, we build upon the XHTML introduced in this chapter by discussing how to make Web pages more visually appealing with Cascading Style Sheets.

5.11 Internet and World Wide Web Resources

`courses.e-survey.net.au/xhtml/index.html`

The *Web Page Design - XHTML* site provides descriptions and examples for various XHTML features, such as links, tables, frames, forms, etc. Users can e-mail questions or comments to the Web Page Design support staff.

`www.vbxml.com/xhtml/articles/xhtml_tables`

The *VBXML.com* Web site contains a tutorial on creating XHTML tables.

`www.webreference.com/xml/reference/xhtml.html`

This Web page contains a list of the frequently used XHTML tags, such as header tags, table tags, frame tags and form tags. It also provides a description of each tag.

SUMMARY

- XHTML tables mark up tabular data and are one of the most frequently used features in XHTML.
- The **table** element defines an XHTML table. Attribute **border** specifies the table's border width, in pixels. Tables without borders set this attribute to **"0"**.
- Element **summary** summarizes the table's contents and is used by speech devices to make the table more accessible to users with visual impairments.
- Element **caption** describe's the table's content. The text inside the **<caption>** tag is rendered above the table in most browsers.
- A table can be split into three distinct sections: head (**thead**), body (**tbody**) and foot (**tfoot**). The head section contains information such as table titles and column headers. The table body contains the primary table data. The table foot contains information such as footnotes.
- Element **tr**, or table row, defines individual table rows. Element **th** defines a header cell. Text in **th** elements usually is centered and displayed in bold by most browsers. This element can be present in any section of the table.
- Data within a row are defined with **td**, or table data, elements.
- Element **colgroup** groups and formats columns. Each **col** element can format any number of columns (specified with the **span** attribute).
- The document author has the ability to merge data cells with the **rowspan** and **colspan** attributes. The values assigned to these attributes specify the number of rows or columns occupied by the cell. These attributes can be placed inside any data-cell tag.
- XHTML provides forms for collecting information from users. Forms contain visual components such as buttons that users click. Forms may also contain non-visual components, called hidden inputs, which are used to store any data, such as e-mail addresses and XHTML document file names used for linking.
- A form begins with the **form** element. Attribute **method** specifies how the form's data is sent to the Web server.
- The **"text"** input inserts a text box into the form. Text boxes allow the user to input data.
- The **input** element's **size** attribute specifies the number of characters visible in the **input** element. Optional attribute **maxlength** limits the number of characters input into a text box.
- The **"submit"** input submits the data entered in the form to the Web server for processing. Most Web browsers create a button that submits the form data when clicked. The **"reset"** input allows a user to reset all **form** elements to their default values.
- The **textarea** element inserts a multiline text box, called a text area, into a form. The number of rows in the text area is specified with the **rows** attribute and the number of columns (i.e., characters) is specified with the **cols** attribute.
- The **"password"** input inserts a password box into a form. A password box allows users to enter sensitive information, such as credit card numbers and passwords, by "masking" the information input with another character. Asterisks are the masking character used for password boxes. The actual value input is sent to the Web server, not the asterisks that mask the input.
- The checkbox input allows the user to make a selection. When the checkbox is selected, a check mark appears in the check box. Otherwise, the checkbox is empty. Checkboxes can be used individually and in groups. Checkboxes that are part of the same group have the same **name**.
- A radio button is similar in function and use to a checkbox, except that only one radio button in a group can be selected at any time. All radio buttons in a group have the same **name** attribute value and have different attribute **value**s.

- The **select** input provides a drop-down list of items. The **name** attribute identifies the drop-down list. The **option** element adds items to the drop-down list. The **selected** attribute, like the **checked** attribute for radio buttons and checkboxes, specifies which list item is displayed initially.
- Image maps designate certain sections of an image as links. These links are more properly called hotspots.
- Image maps are defined with **map** elements. Attribute **id** identifies the image map. Hotspots are defined with the **area** element. Attribute **href** specifies the link's target. Attributes **shape** and **coords** specify the hotspot's shape and coordinates, respectively, and **alt** provides alternate text.
- One way that search engines catalog pages is by reading the **meta** elements's contents. Two important attributes of the **meta** element are **name**, which identifies the type of **meta** element and ***content***, which provides information a search engine uses to catalog a page.
- Frames allow the browser to display more than one XHTML document simultaneously. The **frameset** element informs the browser that the page contains frames. Not all browsers support frames. XHTML provides the **noframes** element to specify alternate content for browsers that do not support frames.
- You can use the **frameset** element to create more complex layouts in a Web page by nesting **frameset**s.

TERMINOLOGY

action attribute
area element
border attribute
browser request
<caption> tag
checkbox
checked attribute
col element
colgroup element
cols attribute
colspan attribute
coords element
form
form element
frame element
frameset element
header cell
hidden input element
hotspot
href attribute
image map
img element
input element
internal hyperlink
internal linking
map element
maxlength attribute
meta element
method attribute
name attribute
navigational frame
nested **frameset** element
nested tag
noframes element
password box
"radio" (attribute value)
rows attribute (**textarea**)
rowspan attribute (**tr**)
selected attribute
size attribute (**input**)
table element
target = "_blank"
target = "_self"
target = "_top"
tbody element
td element
textarea
textarea element
tfoot (table foot) element
<thead>...</thead>
tr (table row) element
type attribute
usemap attribute
valign attribute (**th**)
value attribute
Web server
XHTML form
x-*y*-coordinate

SELF-REVIEW EXERCISES

5.1 State whether the following statements are *true* or *false*. If *false*, explain why.

a) The width of all data cells in a table must be the same.
b) Framesets can be nested.
c) You are limited to a maximum of 100 internal links per page.
d) All browsers can render **frameset**s.

5.2 Fill in the blanks in each of the following statements:

a) Assigning attribute **type** __________ in an **input** element inserts a button that, when clicked, clears the contents of the form.
b) The layout of a **frameset** is set by including the __________ attribute or the __________ attribute inside the **<frameset>** tag.
c) The __________ element marks up a table row.
d) __________ are used as masking characters in a password box.
e) The common shapes used in image maps are __________, __________ and __________.

5.3 Write XHTML markup to accomplish each of the following:

a) Insert a framed Web page, with the first frame extending 300 pixels across the page from the left side.
b) Insert a table with a border of 8.
c) Indicate alternate content to a **frameset**.
d) Insert an image map in a page using **deitel.gif** as an image and **map** with **name = "hello"** as the image map, and set the **alt** text to "**hello**".

ANSWERS TO SELF-REVIEW EXERCISES

5.1 a) False. You can specify the width of any column, either in pixels or as a percentage of the table width. b) True. c) False. You can have an unlimited number of internal links. d) False. Some browsers are unable to render a **frameset** and must therefore rely on the information that you include inside the **<noframes>**...**</noframes>** tags.

5.2 a) **"reset"**. b) **cols**, **rows**. c) **tr**. d) asterisks. e) **poly** (polygons), **circle**s, **rect** (rectangles).

5.3

a) `<frameset cols = "300,*">...</frameset>`
b) `<table border = "8">...</table>`
c) `<noframes>...</noframes>`
d) `<img src = "deitel.gif" alt = "hello" usemap = "#hello" />`

EXERCISES

5.4 Categorize each of the following as an element or an attribute:

a) **width**
b) **td**
c) **th**
d) **frame**
e) **name**
f) **select**
g) **type**

5.5 What will the **frameset** produced by the following code look like? Assume that the pages referenced are blank with white backgrounds and that the dimensions of the screen are 800 by 600. Sketch the layout, approximating the dimensions.

```
<frameset rows = "20%,*">
   <frame src = "hello.html" name = "hello" />
      <frameset cols = "150,*">
         <frame src = "nav.html" name = "nav" />
         <frame src = "deitel.html" name = "deitel" />
      </frameset>
</frameset>
```

5.6 Write the XHTML markup to create a frame with a table of contents on the left side of the window, and have each entry in the table of contents use internal linking to scroll down the document frame to the appropriate subsection.

5.7 Create XHTML markup that produces the table shown in Fig. 5.12. Use **<em>** and **<strong>** tags as necessary. The image (**camel.gif**) is included in the Chapter 5 examples directory on the CD-ROM that accompanies this book.

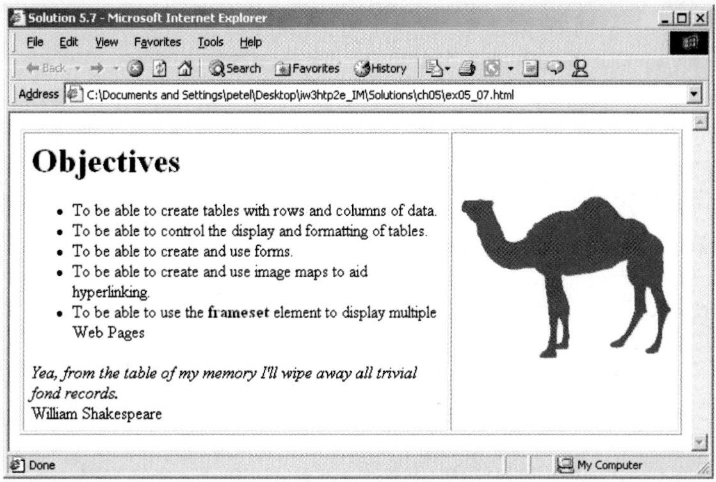

Fig. 5.12 XHTML table for Exercise 5.7.

5.8 Write an XHTML document that produces the table shown in Fig. 5.13.

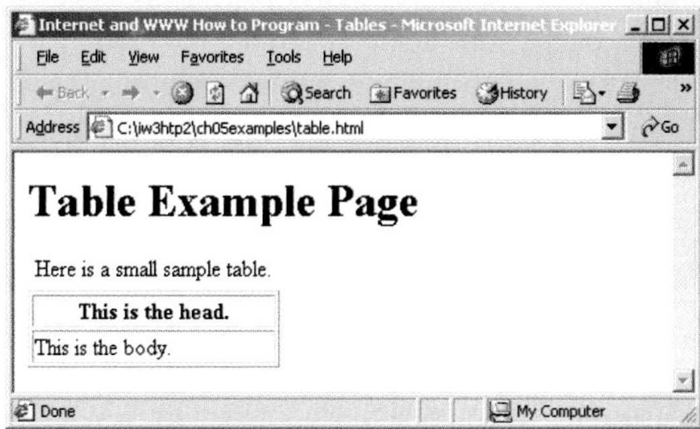

Fig. 5.13 XHTML table for Exercise 5.8.

5.9 A local university has asked you to create an XHTML document that allows potential students to provide feedback about their campus visit. Your XHTML document should contain a form with text boxes for a name, address and e-mail. Provide check boxes that allow prospective students to indicate what they liked most about the campus. These check boxes should include: students, location, campus, atmosphere, dorm rooms and sports. Also, provide radio buttons that ask the prospective student how they became interested in the university. Options should include: friends, television, Internet and other. In addition, provide a text area for additional comments, a submit button and a reset button.

5.10 Create an XHTML document titled "How to Get Good Grades." Use **`<meta>`** tags to include a series of keywords that describe your document.

5.11 Create an XHTML document that displays a tic-tac-toe table with player X winning. Use **`<h2>`** to mark up both Xs and Os. Center the letters in each cell horizontally. Title the game using an **`<h1>`** tag. This title should span all three columns. Set the table border to one.

6

Cascading Style Sheets™ (CSS)

Objectives

- To take control of the appearance of a Web site by creating style sheets.
- To use a style sheet to give all the pages of a Web site the same look and feel.
- To use the `class` attribute to apply styles.
- To specify the precise font, size, color and other properties of displayed text.
- To specify element backgrounds and colors.
- To understand the box model and how to control the margins, borders and padding.
- To use style sheets to separate presentation from content.

Fashions fade, style is eternal.
Yves Saint Laurent

A style does not go out of style as long as it adapts itself to its period. When there is an incompatibility between the style and a certain state of mind, it is never the style that triumphs.
Coco Chanel

How liberating to work in the margins, outside a central perception.
Don DeLillo

I've gradually risen from lower-class background to lower-class foreground.
Marvin Cohen

Outline

6.1 Introduction

In Chapters 4 and 5, we introduced the Extensible Markup Language (XHTML) for marking up information. In this chapter, we shift our focus from marking up information to formatting and presenting information using a W3C technology called *Cascading Style Sheets* (*CSS*) that allows document authors to specify the presentation of elements on a Web page (spacing, margins, etc.) separately from the structure of the document (section headers, body text, links, etc.). This *separation of structure from presentation* simplifies maintaining and modifying a document's layout.

6.2 Inline Styles

A Web developer can declare document styles in many ways. In this section, we present *inline styles* that declare an individual element's format using *attribute* **`style`**. Figure 6.1 applies inline styles to **`p`** elements to alter their font size and color.

```
<?xml version = "1.0"?>
<!DOCTYPE html PUBLIC "-//W3C//DTD XHTML 1.0 Strict//EN"
   "http://www.w3.org/TR/xhtml1/DTD/xhtml1-strict.dtd">

<!-- Fig. 6.1: inline.html -->
<!-- Using inline styles   -->

<html xmlns = "http://www.w3.org/1999/xhtml">
   <head>
      <title>Inline Styles</title>
   </head>

```

Fig. 6.1 Inline styles (part 1 of 2).

```
13      <body>
14
15         <p>This text does not have any style applied to it.</p>
16
17         <!-- The style attribute allows you to declare -->
18         <!-- inline styles. Separate multiple styles    -->
19         <!-- with a semicolon.                           -->
20         <p style = "font-size: 20pt">This text has the
21         <em>font-size</em> style applied to it, making it 20pt.
22         </p>
23
24         <p style = "font-size: 20pt; color: #0000ff">
25         This text has the <em>font-size</em> and
26         <em>color</em> styles applied to it, making it
27         20pt. and blue.</p>
28
29      </body>
30   </html>
```

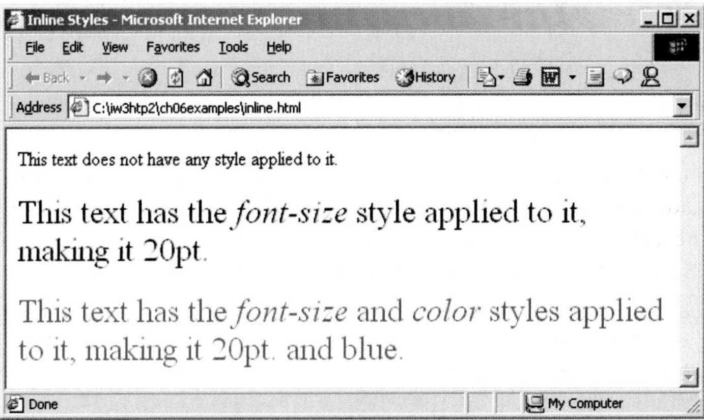

Fig. 6.1 Inline styles (part 2 of 2).

The first inline style declaration appears in line 20. Attribute **`style`** specifies the style for an element. Each *CSS property* (the ***`font-size`*** property in this case) is followed by a colon and a value. On line 20, we declare the **`p`** element to have 20-point text size. Line 21 uses element ***`em`*** to "emphasize" text, which most browsers do by making the font italic.

Line 24 specifies the two properties, **`font-size`** and ***`color`***, separated by a semicolon. In this line, we set the text's **`color`** to blue, using the hexadecimal code **`#0000ff`**. Color names may be used in place of hexadecimal codes, as we demonstrate in the next example. We provide a list of hexadecimal color codes and color names in Appendix E. [*Note*: Inline styles override any other styles applied using the techniques we discuss later in this chapter.]

6.3 Embedded Style Sheets

In this section, we present a second technique for using style sheets called *embedded style sheets*. Embedded style sheets enable a Web-page author to embed an entire CSS document in an XHTML document's **head** section. Figure 6.2 creates an embedded style sheet containing four styles.

```
<?xml version = "1.0"?>
<!DOCTYPE html PUBLIC "-//W3C//DTD XHTML 1.0 Strict//EN"
   "http://www.w3.org/TR/xhtml11/DTD/xhtml11-strict.dtd">

<!-- Fig. 6.2: declared.html                      -->
<!-- Declaring a style sheet in the header section. -->

<html xmlns = "http://www.w3.org/1999/xhtml">
   <head>
      <title>Style Sheets</title>

      <!-- this begins the style sheet section -->
      <style type = "text/css">

         em       { background-color: #8000ff;
                    color: white }

         h1       { font-family: arial, sans-serif }

         p        { font-size: 14pt }

         .special { color: blue }

      </style>
   </head>

   <body>

      <!-- this class attribute applies the .blue style -->
      <h1 class = "special">Deitel & Associates, Inc.</h1>

      <p>Deitel & Associates, Inc. is an internationally
      recognized corporate training and publishing organization
      specializing in programming languages, Internet/World
      Wide Web technology and object technology education.
      Deitel & Associates, Inc. is a member of the World Wide
      Web Consortium. The company provides courses on Java,
      C++, Visual Basic, C, Internet and World Wide Web
      programming, and Object Technology.</p>

      <h1>Clients</h1>
      <p class = "special"> The company's clients include many
      <em>Fortune 1000 companies</em>, government agencies,
      branches of the military and business organizations.
      Through its publishing partnership with Prentice Hall,
      Deitel & Associates, Inc. publishes leading-edge
      programming textbooks, professional books, interactive
      CD-ROM-based multimedia Cyber Classrooms, satellite
      courses and World Wide Web courses.</p>
```

Fig. 6.2 Declaring styles in the **head** of a document (part 1 of 2).

```
50
51       </body>
52    </html>
```

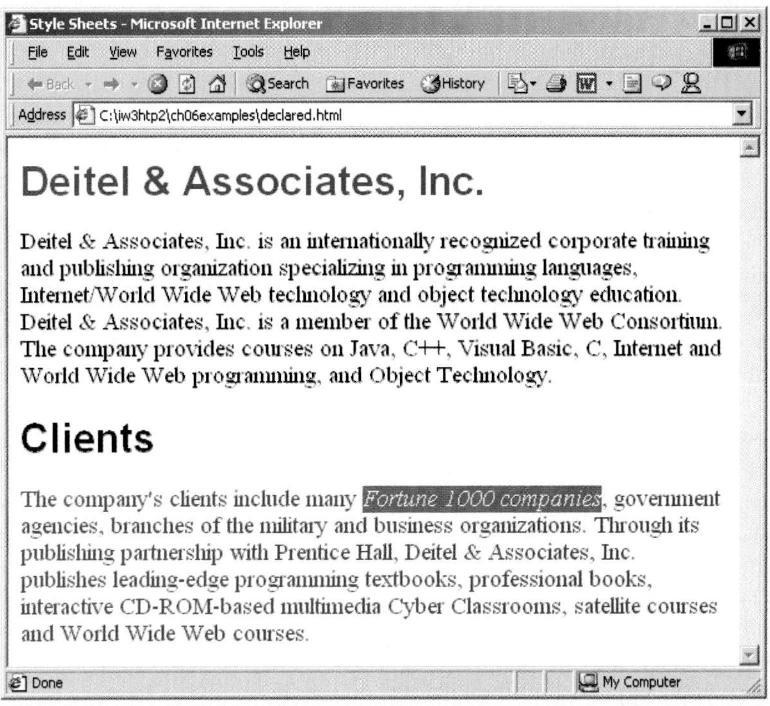

Fig. 6.2 Declaring styles in the **head** of a document (part 2 of 2).

The **style** element (lines 13–24) defines the embedded style sheet. Styles placed in the **head** apply to matching elements in the entire document, not just to a single element. The **type** attribute specifies the *Multipurpose Internet Mail Extension (MIME) type* that describes a file's content. CSS documents use the MIME type **text/css**. Other MIME types include **image/gif** (for GIF images) and **text/javascript** (for the JavaScript scripting language, which we discuss in Chapters 7–12).

The body of the style sheet (lines 15–22) declares the *CSS rules* for the style sheet. We declare rules for **em** (lines 15–16), **h1** (line 18) and **p** (line 20) elements. When the browser renders this document, it applies the properties defined in these rules to each element to which the rule applies. For example, the rule on lines 15–16 will be applied to all **em** elements. The body of each rule is enclosed in curly braces (**{** and **}**). We declare a *style class* named **special** in line 22. Class declarations are preceded with a period and are applied to elements only of that class. We discuss how to apply a style class momentarily.

CSS rules in embedded style sheets use the same syntax as inline styles; the property name is followed by a colon (**:**) and the value of that property. Multiple properties are separated by *semicolons* (**;**). In this example, the **color** property specifies the color of text in an element line and property ***background-color*** specifies the background color of the element.

The **font-family** property (line 18) specifies the name of the font to use. In this case, we use the **arial** font. The second value, **sans-serif**, is a *generic font family*. Not all users have the same fonts installed on their computers, so Web-page authors often specify a comma-separated list of fonts to use for a particular style. The browser attempts to use the fonts in the order they appear in the list. Many Web-page authors end a font list with a generic font family name in case the other fonts are not installed on the user's computer. In this example, if the **arial** font is not found on the system, the browser instead will display a generic **sans-serif** font such as **helvetica** or **verdana**. Other generic font families include **serif** (e.g., **times new roman**, **Georgia**), **cursive** (e.g., **script**), **fantasy** (e.g., **critter**) and **monospace** (e.g., **courier**, **fixedsys**).

The ***font-size*** *property* (line 20) specifies a 14-point font. Other possible measurements in addition to **pt** (point) are introduced later in the chapter. Relative values— ***xx-small***, ***x-small***, ***small***, ***smaller***, ***medium***, ***large***, ***larger***, ***x-large*** and ***xx-large*** also can be used. Generally, relative values for **font-size** are preferred over point sizes because an author does not know the specific measurements of the display for each client. For example, a user may wish to view a Web page on a handheld device with a small screen. Specifying an 18-point font size in a style sheet will prevent such a user from seeing more than one or two characters at a time. However, if a relative font size is specified, such as **large** or **larger**, the actual size will be determined by the browser that displays the font.

Line 30 uses attribute ***class*** in an **h1** element to apply a *style class*—in this case class **special** (declared as **.special** in the style sheet). When the browser renders the **h1** element, notice that the text appears on screen with both the properties of an **h1** element (**arial** or **sans-serif** font defined at line 18) and the properties of the **.special** style class applied (the color **blue** defined on line 22).

The **p** element and the **.special** class style are applied to the text in lines 42–49. All styles applied to an element (the *parent*, or *ancestor*, *element*) also apply to that element's nested elements (*descendant elements*). The **em** element *inherits* the style from the **p** element (namely, the 14-point font size in line 20), but retains its italic style. However, this property overrides the **color** property of the **special** class because the **em** element has its own **color** property. We discuss the rules for resolving these conflicts in the next section.

6.4 Conflicting Styles

Cascading style sheets are "cascading" because styles may be defined by a user, an author or a *user agent* (e.g., a Web browser). Styles defined by authors take precedence over styles defined by the user and styles defined by the user take precedence over styles defined by the user agent. Styles defined for parent and ancestor elements are also inherited by child and descendant elements. In this section, we discuss the rules for resolving conflicts between styles defined for elements and styles inherited from parent and ancestor elements.

Figure 6.2 presented an example of *inheritance* in which a child **em** element inherited the **font-size** property from its parent **p** element. However, in Fig. 6.2, the child **em** element had a **color** property that conflicted with (i.e., had a different value than) the **color** property of its parent **p** element. Properties defined for child and descendant elements have a greater *specificity* than properties defined for parent and ancestor elements. According to the W3C CSS Recommendation, conflicts are resolved in favor of properties with a higher specificity. In other words, the styles defined for the child (or descendant) are more specific than the styles for that child's parent (or ancestor) element; therefore, the child's styles take precedence. Figure 6.3 illustrates examples of inheritance and specificity.

```
<?xml version = "1.0"?>
<!DOCTYPE html PUBLIC "-//W3C//DTD XHTML 1.0 Strict//EN"
   "http://www.w3.org/TR/xhtml1/DTD/xhtml1-strict.dtd">

<!-- Fig 6.3: advanced.html      -->
<!-- More advanced style sheets -->

<html xmlns = "http://www.w3.org/1999/xhtml">
   <head>
      <title>More Styles</title>

      <style type = "text/css">

         a.nodec   { text-decoration: none }

         a:hover   { text-decoration: underline;
                     color: red;
                     background-color: #ccffcc }

         li em     { color: red;
                     font-weight: bold }

         ul        { margin-left: 75px }

         ul ul     { text-decoration: underline;
                     margin-left: 15px }

      </style>
   </head>

   <body>

      <h1>Shopping list for <em>Monday</em>:</h1>

      <ul>
         <li>Milk</li>
         <li>Bread
            <ul>
               <li>White bread</li>
               <li>Rye bread</li>
               <li>Whole wheat bread</li>
            </ul>
         </li>
         <li>Rice</li>
         <li>Potatoes</li>
         <li>Pizza <em>with mushrooms</em></li>
      </ul>

```

Fig. 6.3 Inheritance in style sheets (part 1 of 2).

```
49          <p><a class = "nodec" href = "http://www.food.com">
50          Go to the Grocery store</a></p>
51
52       </body>
53    </html>
```

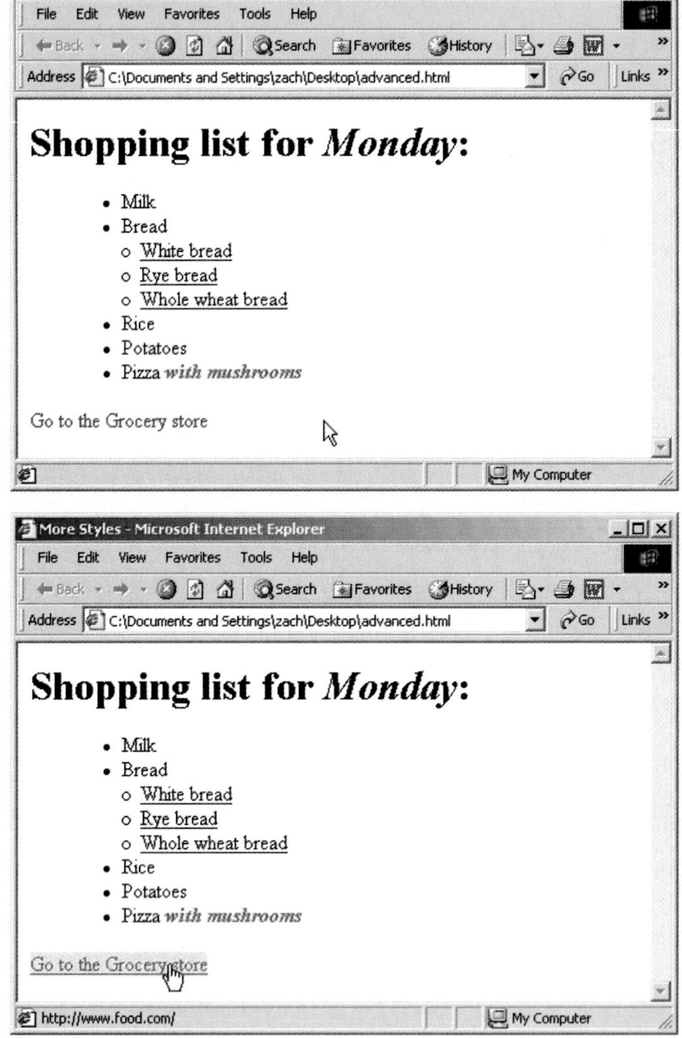

Fig. 6.3 Inheritance in style sheets (part 2 of 2).

Line 14 applies property **`text-decoration`** to all **`a`** elements whose **`class`** attribute is set to **`nodec`**. The **`text-decoration`** property applies *decorations* to text within an element. By default, browsers underline the text marked up with an **`a`** element. Here, we set the **`text-decoration`** property to **`none`** to indicate that the browser should not underline hyperlinks. Other possible values for **`text-decoration`** include ***`blink`***, ***`overline`***,

line-through and ***underline***. The **.nodec** appended to **a** is an extension of class styles; this style will apply only to **a** elements that specify **nodec** as their class.

Lines 16–18 specify a style for **hover**, which is a *pseudoclass*. Pseudoclasses give the author access to content not specifically declared in the document. The **hover** pseudoclass is activated dynamically when the user moves the mouse cursor over an element.

Portability Tip 6.1

To ensure that your style sheets work in various Web browsers, test your style sheets on all client Web browsers that will render documents using your styles.

Lines 20–21 declare a style for all **em** elements that are descendants of **li** elements. In the screen output of Fig. 6.3, notice that **Monday** (which line 33 contains in an **em** element) does not appear in bold red, because the **em** element is not in an **li** element. However, the **em** element containing **with mushrooms** (line 46) is in an **li** element; therefore, it is formatted in bold red.

The syntax for applying rules to multiple elements is similar. For example, to apply the rule in lines 20–21 to all **li** and **em** elements, you would separate the elements with commas, as follows:

```
li, em  { color: red;
          font-weight: bold }
```

Lines 25–26 specify that all nested lists (**ul** elements that are descendants of **ul** elements) be underlined and have a left-hand margin of 15 pixels. A pixel is a *relative-length measurement*—it varies in size, based on screen resolution. Other relative lengths are ***em*** (the so-called "*M*-height" of the font, which is usually set to the height of an uppercase *M*), ***ex*** (the so-called "*x*-height" of the font, which is usually set to the height of a lowercase *x*) and percentages (e.g., **margin-left: 10%**). To set an element to display text at 150% of its default text size, the author could use the syntax

```
font-size: 1.5em
```

Other units of measurement available in CSS are *absolute-length measurements*—i.e., units that do not vary in size based on the system. These units are ***in*** (inches), ***cm*** (centimeters), ***mm*** (millimeters), **pt** (points; 1 **pt**=1/72 **in**) and ***pc*** (picas—1 **pc** = 12 **pt**).

Good Programming Practice 6.1

Whenever possible, use relative-length measurements. If you use absolute-length measurements, your document may not be readable on some client browsers (e.g., wireless phones).

In Fig. 6.3, the entire list is indented because of the 75-pixel left-hand margin for top-level **ul** elements. However, the nested list is indented only 15 pixels more (not another 75 pixels) because the child **ul** element's **margin-left** property overrides the parent **ul** element's **margin-left** property.

6.5 Linking External Style Sheets

Style sheets are a convenient way to create a document with a uniform theme. With *external style sheets* (i.e., separate documents that contain only CSS rules), Web-page authors can provide a uniform look and feel to an entire Web site. Different pages on a site can all use the same style sheet. Then, when changes to the style are required, the Web-page author needs to modify only a single CSS file to make style changes across the entire Web site.

Figure 6.4 presents an external style sheet and Fig. 6.5 contains an XHTML document that references the style sheet.

```
/* Fig. 6.4: styles.css   */
/* An external stylesheet */

a       { text-decoration: none }

a:hover { text-decoration: underline;
          color: red;
          background-color: #ccffcc }

li em   { color: red;
          font-weight: bold;
          background-color: #ffffff }

ul      { margin-left: 2cm }

ul ul   { text-decoration: underline;
          margin-left: .5cm }
```

Fig. 6.4 External style sheet (**styles.css**).

```
<?xml version = "1.0"?>
<!DOCTYPE html PUBLIC "-//W3C//DTD XHTML 1.0 Strict//EN"
   "http://www.w3.org/TR/xhtml1/DTD/xhtml1-strict.dtd">

<!-- Fig. 6.5: external.html         -->
<!-- Linking external style sheets   -->

<html xmlns = "http://www.w3.org/1999/xhtml">
   <head>
      <title>Linking External Style Sheets</title>
      <link rel = "stylesheet" type = "text/css"
         href = "styles.css" />
   </head>

   <body>

      <h1>Shopping list for <em>Monday</em>:</h1>
      <ul>
         <li>Milk</li>
         <li>Bread
            <ul>
               <li>White bread</li>
               <li>Rye bread</li>
               <li>Whole wheat bread</li>
            </ul>
         </li>
         <li>Rice</li>
         <li>Potatoes</li>
```

Fig. 6.5 Linking an external style sheet (part 1 of 2).

```
29             <li>Pizza <em>with mushrooms</em></li>
30          </ul>
31
32          <p>
33          <a href = "http://www.food.com">Go to the Grocery store</a>
34          </p>
35
36       </body>
37    </html>
```

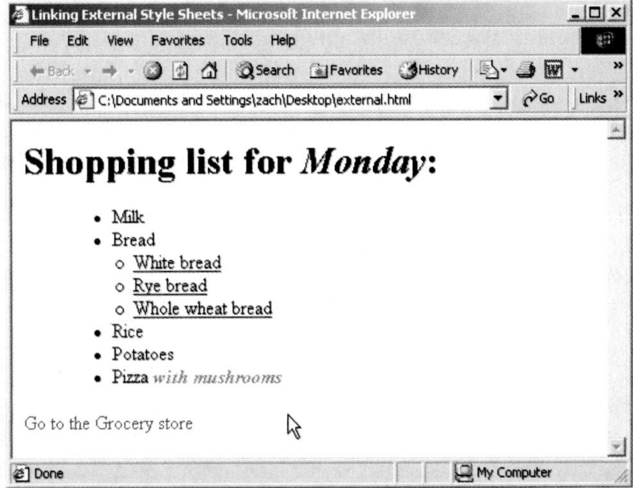

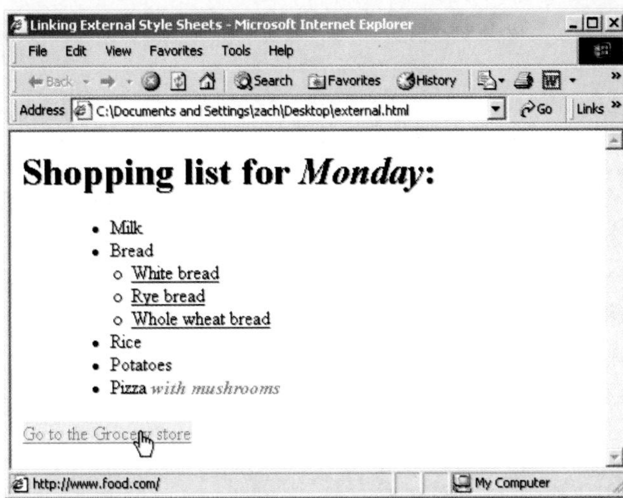

Fig. 6.5 Linking an external style sheet (part 2 of 2).

Lines 11–12 (Fig. 6.5) show a ***link*** *element*, which uses the ***rel*** *attribute* to specify a *relationship* between the current document and another document. In this case, we declare the linked document to be a ***stylesheet*** for this document. The **type** attribute specifies the MIME type as **`text/css`**. The **`href`** attribute provides the URL for the document containing the style sheet .

Software Engineering Observation 6.1

Style sheets are reusable. Creating them once and reusing them reduces programming effort.

Software Engineering Observation 6.2

The **`link`** *element can be placed only in the* **`head`** *element. The user can specify* **`next`** *and* **`previous`**, *which allow the user to link a whole series of documents. This feature allows browsers to print a large collection of related documents at once. (In Internet Explorer, select* ***Print all linked documents*** *in the* ***Print...*** *submenu of the* ***File*** *menu.)*

6.6 W3C CSS Validation Service

The W3C provides a validation service (**`jigsaw.w3.org/css-validator`**) that validates external CSS documents to ensure that they conform to the W3C CSS Recommendation. Like XHTML validation, CSS validation ensures that style sheets are syntactically correct. The validator provides the option of either entering the CSS document's URL, pasting the CSS document's contents into a text area or uploading a CSS document from disk. Figure 6.6 illustrates uploading a CSS document from a disk.

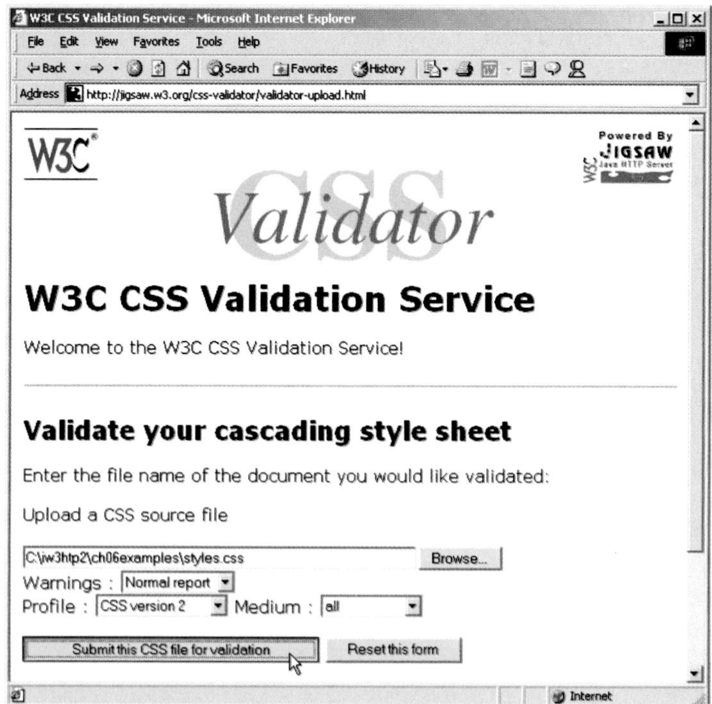

Fig. 6.6 Validating a CSS document. (Courtesy of World Wide Web Consortium (W3C).)

Figure 6.7 shows the results of validating **`styles.css`** (Fig. 6.4), using the file upload feature available at

`jigsaw.w3.org/css-validator/validator-upload.html`

To validate the document, click the **Browse** button to locate the file on your computer. After locating the file, click **Submit this CSS file for validation** to upload the file for validation. [*Note*: Like many W3C technologies, CSS is being developed in stages (or *versions*). The current version under development is Version 3.]

6.7 Positioning Elements

Prior to CSS, controlling the positioning of elements in an XHTML document was difficult—the browser determined positioning. CSS introduces the ***`position`*** property and a capability called *absolute positioning*, which provides authors greater control over how document elements are displayed. Figure 6.8 demonstrates absolute positioning.

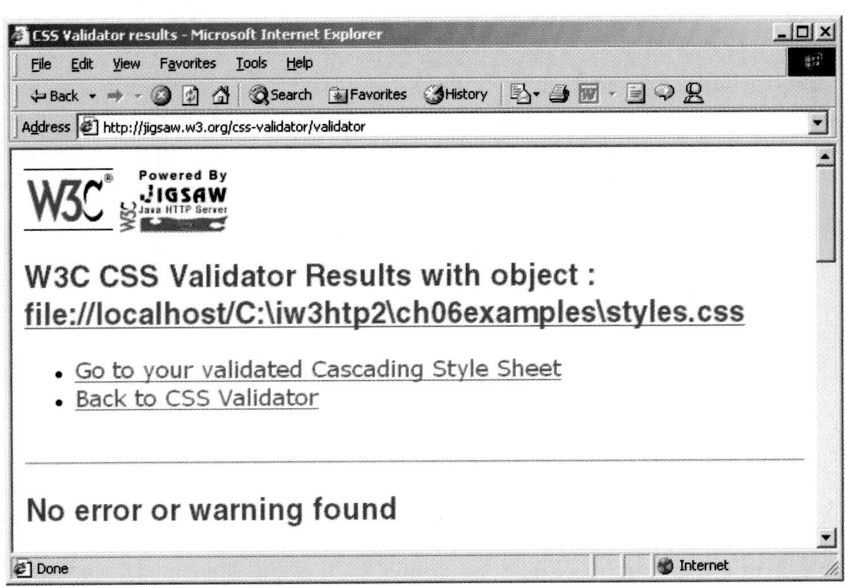

Fig. 6.7 CSS validation results. (Courtesy of World Wide Web Consortium (W3C).)

```
<?xml version = "1.0"?>
<!DOCTYPE html PUBLIC "-//W3C//DTD XHTML 1.0 Strict//EN"
   "http://www.w3.org/TR/xhtml1/DTD/xhtml1-strict.dtd">

<!-- Fig 6.8: positioning.html        -->
<!-- Absolute positioning of elements -->

<html xmlns = "http://www.w3.org/1999/xhtml">
```

Fig. 6.8 Positioning elements with CSS (part 1 of 2).

```
9       <head>
10         <title>Absolute Positioning</title>
11      </head>
12
13      <body>
14
15         <p><img src = "i.gif" style = "position: absolute;
16            top: 0px; left: 0px; z-index: 1"
17            alt = "First positioned image" /></p>
18         <p style = "position: absolute; top: 50px; left: 50px;
19            z-index: 3; font-size: 20pt;">Positioned Text</p>
20         <p><img src = "circle.gif" style = "position: absolute;
21            top: 25px; left: 100px; z-index: 2" alt =
22            "Second positioned image" /></p>
23
24      </body>
25   </html>
```

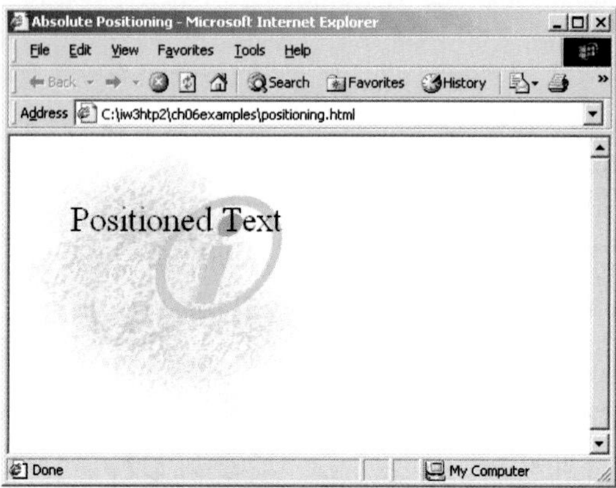

Fig. 6.8 Positioning elements with CSS (part 2 of 2).

Lines 15–17 position the first **img** element (**i.gif**) on the page. Specifying an element's **position** as ***absolute*** removes the element from the normal flow of elements on the page, instead positioning the element according to the distance from the **top**, **left**, **right** or **bottom** margins of its *containing block* (i.e., an element such as **body** or **p**). Here, we position the element to be **0** pixels away from both the **top** and **left** margins of the **body** element.

The ***z-index*** *attribute* allows you to layer overlapping elements properly. Elements that have higher **z-index** values are displayed in front of elements with lower **z-index** values. In this example, **i.gif** has the lowest **z-index** (**1**), so it displays in the background. The **img** element at lines 20–22 (**circle.gif**) has a **z-index** of **2**, so it displays in front of **i.gif**. The **p** element at lines 18–19 (**Positioned Text**) has a **z-index** of **3**, so it displays in front of the other two. If you do not specify a **z-index** or if elements have the same **z-index** value, the elements are placed from background to foreground in the order they are encountered in the document.

Absolute positioning is not the only way to specify page layout. Figure 6.9 demonstrates *relative positioning* in which elements are positioned relative to other elements.

Setting the **position** property to **relative**, as in class **super** (lines 21–22), lays out the element on the page and offsets the element by the specified **top**, **bottom**, **left** or **right** values. Unlike absolute positioning, relative positioning keeps elements in the general flow of elements on the page, so positioning is relative to other elements in the flow.

```
1  <?xml version = "1.0"?>
2  <!DOCTYPE html PUBLIC "-//W3C//DTD XHTML 1.0 Strict//EN"
3     "http://www.w3.org/TR/xhtml1/DTD/xhtml1-strict.dtd">
4
5  <!-- Fig. 6.9: positioning2.html         -->
6  <!-- Relative positioning of elements    -->
7
8  <html xmlns = "http://www.w3.org/1999/xhtml">
9     <head>
10       <title>Relative Positioning</title>
11
12       <style type = "text/css">
13
14          p           { font-size: 1.3em;
15                        font-family: verdana, arial, sans-serif }
16
17          span        { color: red;
18                        font-size: .6em;
19                        height: 1em }
20
21          .super      { position: relative;
22                        top: -1ex }
23
24          .sub        { position: relative;
25                        bottom: -1ex }
26
27          .shiftleft  { position: relative;
28                        left: -1ex }
29
30          .shiftright { position: relative;
31                        right: -1ex }
32
33       </style>
34    </head>
35
36    <body>
37
38       <p>The text at the end of this sentence
39       <span class = "super">is in superscript</span>.</p>
40
41       <p>The text at the end of this sentence
42       <span class = "sub">is in subscript</span>.</p>
43
44       <p>The text at the end of this sentence
45       <span class = "shiftleft">is shifted left</span>.</p>
46
```

Fig. 6.9 Relative positioning of elements (part 1 of 2).

```
47          <p>The text at the end of this sentence
48          <span class = "shiftright">is shifted right</span>.</p>
49
50       </body>
51    </html>
```

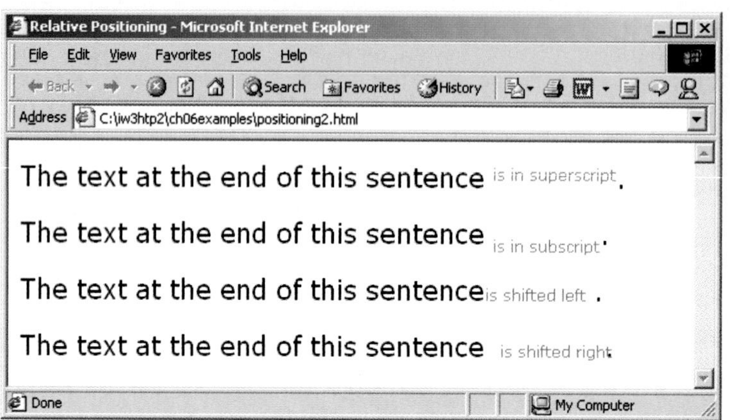

Fig. 6.9 Relative positioning of elements (part 2 of 2).

We introduce the ***span*** element in line 39. Element **span** is a *grouping element*—it does not apply any inherent formatting to its contents. Its primary purpose is to apply CSS rules or ***id*** *attributes* to a block of text. Element **span** is an *inline-level element*—it is displayed inline with other text and with no line breaks. Lines 17–19 define the CSS rule for **span**. A similar element is the ***div*** element, which also applies no inherent styles but is displayed on its own line, with margins above and below (a *block-level element*).

Common Programming Error 6.1

Because relative positioning keeps elements in the flow of text in your documents, be careful to avoid unintentionally overlapping text.

6.8 Backgrounds

CSS also provides control over the element backgrounds. In previous examples, we introduced the **background-color** property. CSS also can add background images to documents. Figure 6.10 add a corporate logo to the bottom-right corner of the document. This logo stays fixed in the corner, even when the user scrolls up or down the screen.

```
<?xml version = "1.0"?>
<!DOCTYPE html PUBLIC "-//W3C//DTD XHTML 1.0 Strict//EN"
   "http://www.w3.org/TR/xhtml1/DTD/xhtml1-strict.dtd">

<!-- Fig. 6.10: background.html                    -->
<!-- Adding background images and indentation -->

<html xmlns = "http://www.w3 .org/1999/xhtml">
```

Fig. 6.10 Adding a background image with CSS (part 1 of 2).

```
   <head>
      <title>Background Images</title>

      <style type = "text/css">

         body  { background-image: url(logo.gif);
                 background-position: bottom right;
                 background-repeat: no-repeat;
                 background-attachment: fixed; }

         p     { font-size: 18pt;
                 color: #aa5588;
                 text-indent: 1em;
                 font-family: arial, sans-serif; }

         .dark { font-weight: bold; }

      </style>
   </head>

   <body>

      <p>
      This example uses the background-image,
      background-position and background-attachment
      styles to place the <span class = "dark">Deitel
      & Associates, Inc.</span> logo in the bottom,
      right corner of the page. Notice how the logo
      stays in the proper position when you resize the
      browser window.
      </p>

   </body>
</html>
```

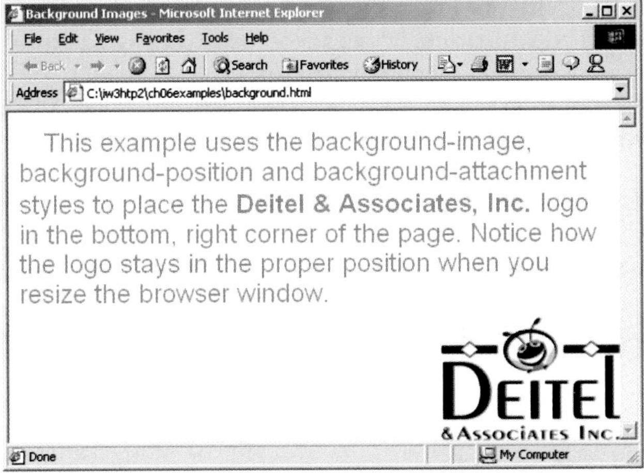

Fig. 6.10 Adding a background image with CSS (part 2 of 2).

The **background-image** *property* (line 14) specifies the image URL for the image **logo.gif** in the format **url(***fileLocation***)**. The Web-page author can set the **background-color** in case the image is not found.

The **background-position** *property* (line 15) places the image on the page. The keywords ***top***, ***bottom***, ***center***, ***left*** and ***right*** are used individually or in combination for vertical and horizontal positioning. Image can be positioned using lengths by specifying the horizontal length followed by the vertical length. For example, to position the image as vertically centered (positioned at 50% of the distance across the screen) and 30 pixels from the top, use

```
background-position: 50% 30px;
```

The **background-repeat** *property* (line 16) controls the *tiling* of the background image. Tiling places multiple copies of the image next to each other to fill the background. Here, we set the tiling to ***no-repeat*** to display only one copy of the background image. The **background-repeat** property can be set to ***repeat*** (the default) to tile the image vertically and horizontally, ***repeat-x*** to tile the image only horizontally or ***repeat-y*** to tile the image only vertically.

The final property setting, ***background-attachment: fixed*** (line 17), fixes the image in the position specified by **background-position**. Scrolling the browser window will not move the image from its position. The default value, ***scroll***, moves the image as the user scrolls through the document.

Line 21 indents the first line of text in the element by the specified amount, in this case **1em**. An author might use this property to create a Web page that reads more like a novel, in which the first line of every paragraph is indented.

Line 24 uses the ***font-weight*** *property* to specify the "boldness" of text. Possible values are ***bold***, ***normal*** (the default), ***bolder*** (bolder than **bold** text) and ***lighter*** (lighter than **normal** text). Boldness also can be specified with multiples of 100, from 100 to 900 (e.g., **100**, **200**, …, **900**). Text specified as **normal** is equivalent to **400**, and **bold** text is equivalent to **700**. However, many systems do not have fonts can scale this finely, so using the values from **100** to **900** might not display the desired effect.

Another CSS property that formats text is the ***font-style*** *property*, which allows the developer to set text to ***none***, ***italic*** or ***oblique*** (**oblique** will default to **italic** if the system does not support oblique text).

6.9 Element Dimensions

In addition to positioning elements, CSS rules can specify the actual dimensions of each page element. Figure 6.11 demonstrates how to set the dimensions of elements.

```
<?xml version = "1.0"?>
<!DOCTYPE html PUBLIC "-//W3C//DTD XHTML 1.0 Strict//EN"
   "http://www.w3.org/TR/xhtml1/DTD/xhtml1-strict.dtd">

<!-- Fig. 6.11: width.html                          -->
<!-- Setting box dimensions and aligning text       -->

```

Fig. 6.11 Setting box dimensions and aligning text (part 1 of 2).

```
<html xmlns = "http://www.w3.org/1999/xhtml">
   <head>
      <title>Box Dimensions</title>

      <style type = "text/css">

         div { background-color: #ffccff;
               margin-bottom: .5em }
      </style>

   </head>

   <body>

      <div style = "width: 20%">Here is some
      text that goes in a box which is
      set to stretch across twenty percent
      of the width of the screen.</div>

      <div style = "width: 80%; text-align: center">
      Here is some CENTERED text that goes in a box
      which is set to stretch across eighty percent of
      the width of the screen.</div>

      <div style = "width: 20%; height: 30%; overflow: scroll">
      This box is only twenty percent of
      the width and thirty percent of the height.
      What do we do if it overflows? Set the
      overflow property to scroll!</div>

   </body>
</html>
```

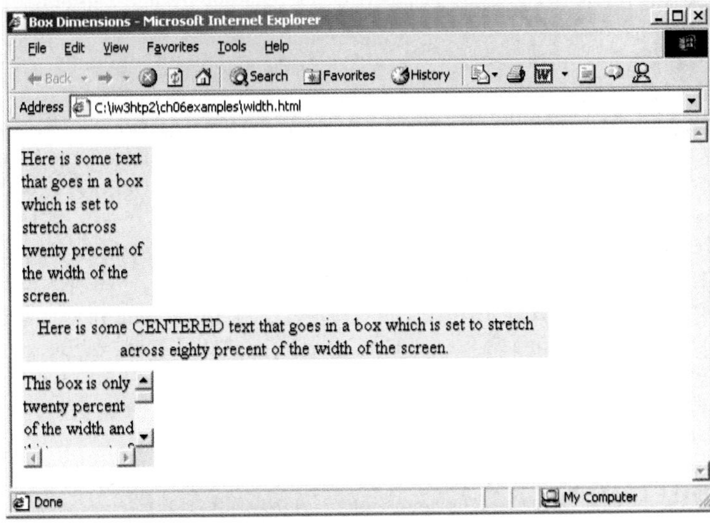

Fig. 6.11 Setting box dimensions and aligning text (part 2 of 2).

The inline style in line 22 illustrates how to set the ***width*** of an element on screen; here, we indicate that the **div** element should occupy 20% of the screen width. Most elements are left-aligned by default; however, this alignment can be altered to position the element elsewhere. The height of an element can be set similarly, using the ***height*** property. The **height** and **width** values also can be specified relative and absolute lengths. For example

```
width: 10em
```

sets the element's width to be equal to 10 times the font size. Line 27 sets text in the element to be ***center*** aligned; some other values for the **text-align** property are ***left*** and ***right***.

One problem with setting both dimensions of an element is that the content inside the element can exceed the set boundaries, in which case the element is simply made large enough for all the content to fit. However, in line 32, we set the ***overflow*** property to ***scroll***, a setting that adds scrollbars if the text overflows the boundaries.

6.10 Text Flow and the Box Model

A browser normally places text and elements on screen in the order in which they appear in the XHTML document. However, as we have seen with absolute positioning, it is possible to remove elements from the normal flow of text. *Floating* allows you to move an element to one side of the screen; other content in the document then flows around the floated element. In addition, each block-level element has a box drawn around it, known as the *box model*. The properties of this box can be adjusted to control the amount of padding inside the element and the margins outside the element (Fig. 6.12).

In addition to text, whole elements can be *floated* to the left or right of content. This means that any nearby text will wrap around the floated element. For example, in lines 30–32 we float a **div** element to the **right** side of the screen. As you can see from the sample screen capture, the text from lines 34–41 flows cleanly to the left and underneath the **div** element.

The second property on line 30, **margin**, specifies the distance between the edge of the element and any other element on the page. When the browser renders elements using the box model, the content of each element is surrounded by *padding*, a *border* and a *margin* (Fig. 6.13).

Margins for individual sides of an element can be specified by using ***margin-top***, ***margin-right***, ***margin-left*** and ***margin-bottom***.

Lines 43–45 specify a **div** element that floats at the right side of the content. Property ***padding*** for the **div** element is set to **.5em**. *Padding* is the distance between the content inside an element and the element's border. Like the **margin**, the **padding** can be set for each side of the box, with ***padding-top***, ***padding-right***, ***padding-left*** and ***padding-bottom***.

A portion of lines 54–55 show that you can interrupt the flow of text around a **float**ed element by setting the **clear** *property* to the same direction as that in which the element is **float**ed—**right** or **left**. Setting the ***clear*** property to ***all*** interrupts the flow on both sides of the document.

```
<?xml version = "1.0"?>
<!DOCTYPE html PUBLIC "-//W3C//DTD XHTML 1.0 Strict//EN"
   "http://www.w3.org/TR/xhtml1/DTD/xhtml1-strict.dtd">

<!-- Fig. 6.12: floating.html             -->
<!-- Floating elements and element boxes -->

<html xmlns = "http://www.w3.org/1999/xhtml">
   <head>
      <title>Flowing Text Around Floating Elements</title>

      <style type = "text/css">

         div { background-color: #ffccff;
               margin-bottom: .5em;
               font-size: 1.5em;
               width: 50% }

         p   { text-align: justify; }

      </style>

   </head>

   <body>

      <div style = "text-align: center">
         Deitel & Associates, Inc.</div>

      <div style = "float: right; margin: .5em;
         text-align: right">
         Corporate Training and Publishing</div>

      <p>Deitel & Associates, Inc. is an internationally
      recognized corporate training and publishing organization
      specializing in programming languages, Internet/World
      Wide Web technology and object technology education.
      Deitel & Associates, Inc. is a member of the World Wide
      Web Consortium. The company provides courses on Java,
      C++, Visual Basic, C, Internet and World Wide Web
      programming, and Object Technology.</p>

      <div style = "float: right; padding: .5em;
         text-align: right">
         Leading-edge Programming Textbooks</div>

      <p>The company's clients include many Fortune 1000
      companies, government agencies, branches of the military
      and business organizations. Through its publishing
      partnership with Prentice Hall, Deitel & Associates,
      Inc. publishes leading-edge programming textbooks,
      professional books, interactive CD-ROM-based multimedia
      Cyber Classrooms, satellite courses and World Wide Web
```

Fig. 6.12 Floating elements, aligning text and setting box dimensions (part 1 of 2).

```
         courses.<span style = "clear: right"> Here is some
         unflowing text. Here is some unflowing text.</span></p>

      </body>
   </html>
```

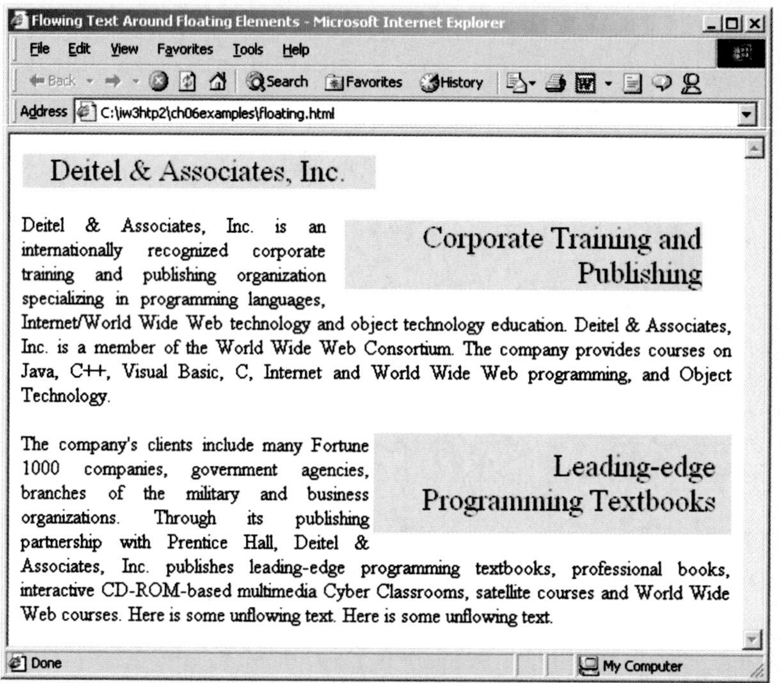

Fig. 6.12 Floating elements, aligning text and setting box dimensions (part 2 of 2).

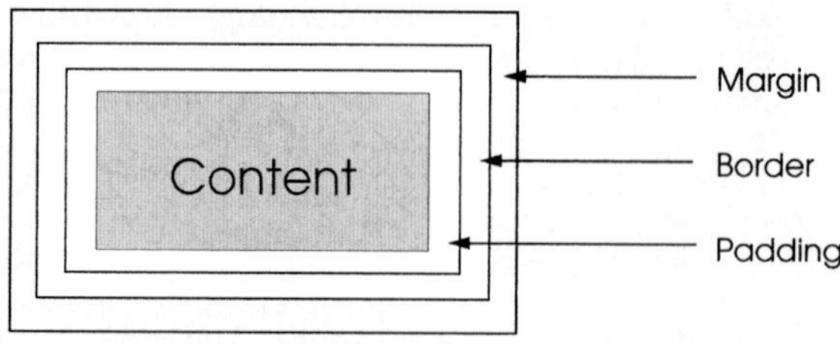

Fig. 6.13 Box model for block-level elements.

Another property of every block-level element on screen is the border, which lies between the padding space and the margin space and has numerous properties for adjusting its appearance as shown in Fig. 6.14.

```
<?xml version = "1.0"?>
<!DOCTYPE html PUBLIC "-//W3C//DTD XHTML 1.0 Strict//EN"
   "http://www.w3.org/TR/xhtml1/DTD/xhtml1-strict.dtd">

<!-- Fig. 6.14: borders.html        -->
<!-- Setting borders of an element -->

<html xmlns = "http://www.w3.org/1999/xhtml">
   <head>
      <title>Borders</title>

      <style type = "text/css">

         body    { background-color: #ccffcc }

         div     { text-align: center;
                   margin-bottom: 1em;
                   padding: .5em }

         .thick  { border-width: thick }

         .medium { border-width: medium }

         .thin   { border-width: thin }

         .groove { border-style: groove }

         .inset  { border-style: inset }

         .outset { border-style: outset }

         .red    { border-color: red }

         .blue   { border-color: blue }

      </style>
   </head>

   <body>

      <div class = "thick groove">This text has a border</div>
      <div class = "medium groove">This text has a border</div>
      <div class = "thin groove">This text has a border</div>

      <p class = "thin red inset">A thin red line...</p>
      <p class = "medium blue outset">
         And a thicker blue line</p>

   </body>
</html>
```

Fig. 6.14 Applying borders to elements (part 1 of 2).

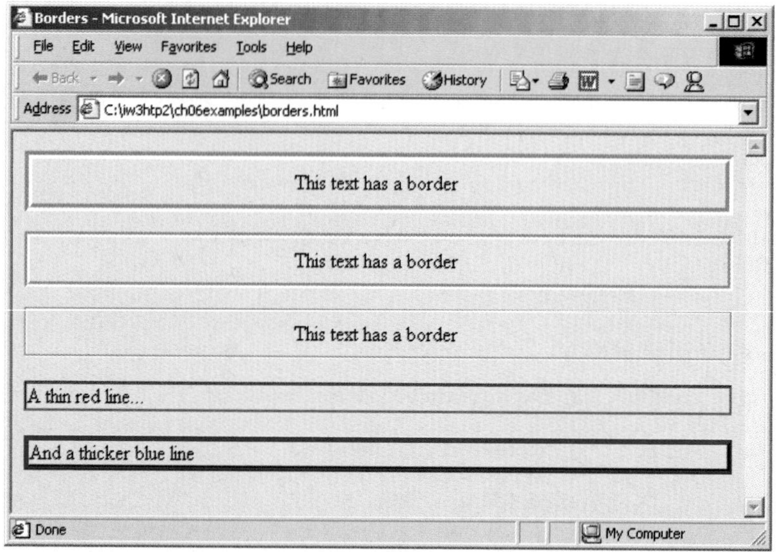

Fig. 6.14 Applying borders to elements (part 2 of 2).

In this example, we set three properties—**border-width**, **border-color** and **border-style**. The **border-width** property may be set to any of the CSS lengths or to the predefined values of ***thin***, ***medium*** or ***thick***. The **border-color** property sets the color. (This property has different meanings for different borders.)

As with **padding** and **margin**s, each of the border properties may be set for individual sides of the box (e.g., **border-top-style** or **border-left-color**). A developer can assign more than one class to an XHTML element by using the **class** attribute as shown in line 41.

The **border-style**s are ***none***, ***hidden***, ***dotted***, ***dashed***, ***solid***, ***double***, ***groove***, ***ridge***, ***inset*** and ***outset***. Borders ***groove*** and ***ridge*** have opposite effects, as do ***inset*** and ***outset***. Figure 6.15 illustrates these border styles.

```
<?xml version = "1.0"?>
<!DOCTYPE html PUBLIC "-//W3C//DTD XHTML 1.0 Strict//EN"
   "http://www.w3.org/TR/xhtml1/DTD/xhtml1-strict.dtd">

<!-- Fig. 6.15: borders2.html   -->
<!-- Various border-styles      -->

<html xmlns = "http://www.w3.org/1999/xhtml">
   <head>
      <title>Borders</title>

      <style type = "text/css">

         body    { background-color: #ccffcc }
```

Fig. 6.15 Various **border-style**s (part 1 of 2).

```

         div      { text-align: center;
                    margin-bottom: .3em;
                    width: 50%;
                    position: relative;
                    left: 25%;
                    padding: .3em }
      </style>
   </head>

   <body>

      <div style = "border-style: solid">Solid border</div>
      <div style = "border-style: double">Double border</div>
      <div style = "border-style: groove">Groove border</div>
      <div style = "border-style: ridge">Ridge border</div>
      <div style = "border-style: inset">Inset border</div>
      <div style = "border-style: outset">Outset border</div>

   </body>
</html>
```

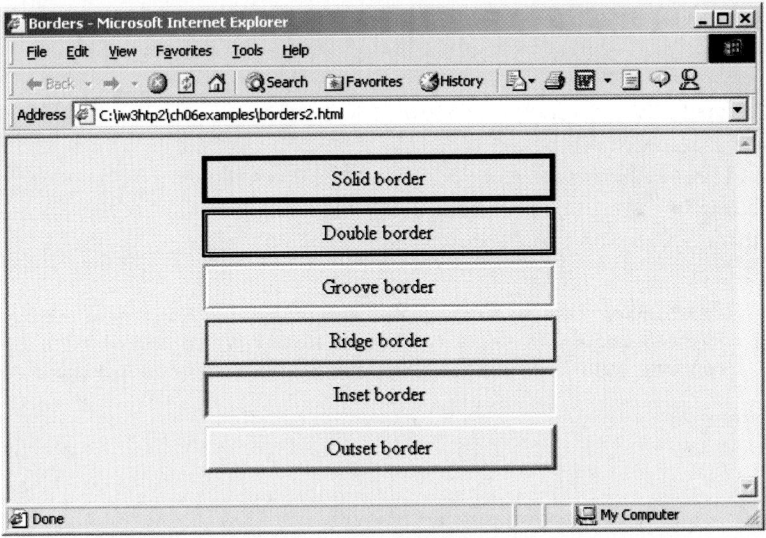

Fig. 6.15 Various **border-style**s (part 2 of 2).

6.11 User Style Sheets

Users can define their own *user style sheets* to format pages based on their preferences. For example, people with visual impairments may want to increase the page's text size. A Web-page author needs to be careful because they may inadvertently override user preferences with defined styles. This section discusses possible conflicts between *author styles* and *user styles*.

Figure 6.16 contains an author style. The **font-size** is set to **9pt** for all **<p>** tags that have class **note** applied to them.

User style sheets are external style sheets. Figure 6.17 shows a user style sheet that sets the **body**'s **font-size** to **20pt**, **color** to **yellow** and **background-color** to **#000080**.

User style sheets are not **link**ed to a document; rather, they are set in the browser's options. To add a user style sheet in Internet Explorer 5.5, select **Internet Options...**, located in the **Tools** menu. In the **Internet Options** dialog (Fig. 6.18) that appears, click **Accessibility...**, Check the **Format documents using my style sheet** check box and type the location of the user style sheet. Internet Explorer 5.5 applies the user style sheet to any document it loads.

```
<?xml version = "1.0"?>
<!DOCTYPE html PUBLIC "-//W3C//DTD XHTML 1.0 Strict//EN"
   "http://www.w3.org/TR/xhtml1/DTD/xhtml1-strict.dtd">

<!-- Fig. 6.16: user_absolute.html   -->
<!-- User styles                     -->

<html xmlns = "http://www.w3.org/1999/xhtml">
   <head>
      <title>User Styles</title>

      <style type = "text/css">

         .note { font-size: 9pt }

      </style>
   </head>

   <body>

      <p>Thanks for visiting my Web site. I hope you enjoy it.
      </p><p class = "note">Please Note: This site will be
      moving soon. Please check periodically for updates.</p>

   </body>
</html>
```

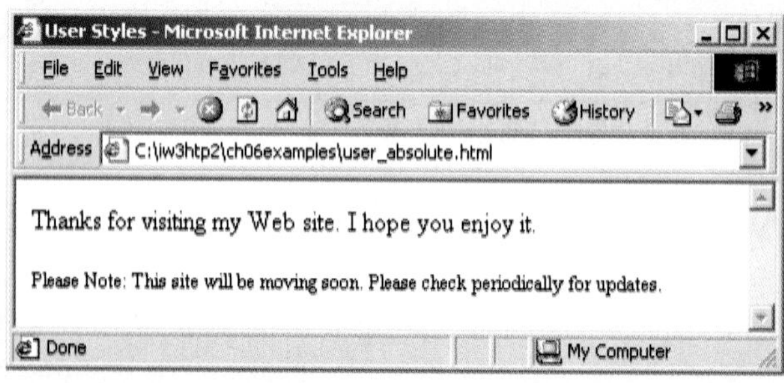

Fig. 6.16 Modifying text size with the **pt** measurement.

```
/* Fig. 6.17: userstyles.css */
/* A user stylesheet        */

body      { font-size: 20pt;
            color: yellow;
            background-color: #000080 }
```

Fig. 6.17 User style sheet.

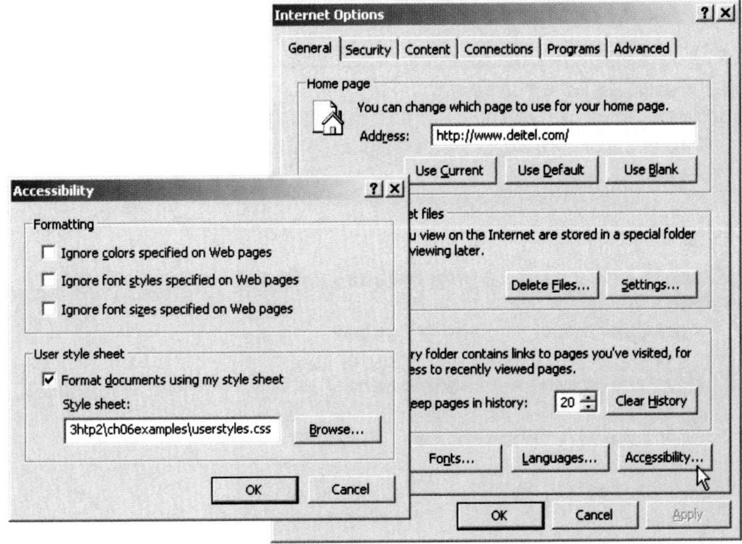

Fig. 6.18 Adding a user style sheet in Internet Explorer 5.5.

The Web page from Fig. 6.16 is displayed in Fig. 6.19, with the user style sheet from Fig. 6.17 applied.

Fig. 6.19 Web page with user styles applied.

In this example if users define their own **font-size** in a user style sheet, the author style has a higher precedence and overrides the user style. The **9pt** font specified in the author style sheet overrides the **20pt** font specified in the user style sheet. This small font may make pages difficult to read, especially for individuals with visual impairments. A developer can avoid this problem by using relative measurements (such as **em** or **ex**) instead of absolute measurements such as **pt**. Figure 6.20 changes the **font-size** property to use a relative measurement (line 14), which does not override the user style set in Fig. 6.17. Instead, the font size displayed is relative to that specified in the user style sheet. In this case, text enclosed in the **<p>** tag displays as **20pt** and **<p>** tags that have class **note** applied to them are displayed in **15pt** (**.75** times **20pt**).

```
1  <?xml version = "1.0"?>
2  <!DOCTYPE html PUBLIC "-//W3C//DTD XHTML 1.0 Strict//EN"
3     "http://www.w3.org/TR/xhtml1/DTD/xhtml1-strict.dtd">
4
5  <!-- Fig. 6.20: user_relative.html   -->
6  <!-- User styles                     -->
7
8  <html xmlns = "http://www.w3.org/1999/xhtml">
9     <head>
10       <title>User Styles</title>
11
12       <style type = "text/css">
13
14          .note { font-size: .75em }
15
16       </style>
17    </head>
18
19    <body>
20
21       <p>Thanks for visiting my Web site. I hope you enjoy it.
22       </p><p class = "note">Please Note: This site will be
23       moving soon. Please check periodically for updates.</p>
24
25    </body>
26 </html>
```

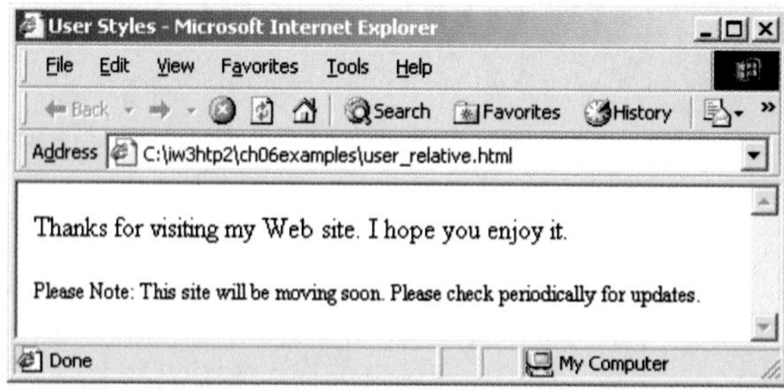

Fig. 6.20 Modifying text size with the **em** measurement.

Fig. 6.21 displays the Web page from Fig. 6.20 with the user style sheet from Fig. 6.16 applied. Notice that the second line of text displayed is larger than the same line of text in Fig. 6.19.

6.12 Internet and World Wide Web Resources

`www.w3.org/TR/REC-CSS2`
The W3C *Cascading Style Sheets, Level 2* specification contains a list of all the CSS properties. The specification also provides helpful examples detailing the use of many of the properties.

`www.webreview.com/style`
This site has several charts of CSS properties, including a list containing which browsers support what attributes and to what extent.

`tech.irt.org/articles/css.htm`
This site contains articles dealing with CSS.

`msdn.microsoft.com/workshop/author/css/site1014.asp`
This site contains samples of some CSS features.

`www.web-weaving.net`
This site contains many CSS articles.

SUMMARY

- The inline style allows a developer to declare a style for an individual element by using the **`style`** attribute in that element's opening XHTML tag.
- Each CSS property is followed by a colon and the value of the attribute.
- The **`color`** property sets text color. Color names and hexadecimal codes may be used as the value.
- Styles that are placed in the **`<style>`** tag apply to the entire document.
- **`style`** element attribute **`type`** specifies the MIME type (the specific encoding format) of the style sheet. Style sheets use **`text/css`**.
- Each rule body begins and ends with a curly brace (**`{`** and **`}`**).
- Style class declarations are preceded by a period and are applied to elements of that specific class.
- The CSS rules in a style sheet use the same format as inline styles: The property is followed by a colon (**`:`**) and the value of that property. Multiple properties are separated by semicolons (**`;`**).
- The **`background-color`** attribute specifies the background color of the element.

Fig. 6.21 Using relative measurements in author styles.

- The **font-family** attribute names a specific font that should be displayed. Generic font families allow authors to specify a type of font instead of a specific font, in case a browser does not support a specific font. The **font-size** property specifies the size used to render the font.
- The **class** attribute applies a style class to an element.
- Pseudoclasses provide the author access to content not specifically declared in the document. The **hover** pseudoclass is activated when the user moves the mouse cursor over an element.
- The **text-decoration** property applies decorations to text within an element, such as **underline**, **overline**, **line-through** and **blink**.
- To apply rules to multiple elements, separate the elements with commas in the style sheet.
- A pixel is a relative-length measurement: It varies in size based on screen resolution. Other relative lengths are **em**, **ex** and percentages.
- The other units of measurement available in CSS are absolute-length measurements—i.e., units that do not vary in size. These units can be **in** (inches), **cm** (centimeters), **mm** (millimeters), **pt** (points; 1 **pt**=1/72 **in**) and **pc** (picas; 1 **pc** = 12 **pt**).
- External linking can create a uniform look for a Web site; separate pages can all use the same styles. Modifying a single file makes changes to styles across an entire Web site.
- **link**'s **rel** attribute specifies a relationship between two documents.
- The CSS **position** property allows absolute positioning, which provides greater control over where on a page elements reside. Specifying an element's **position** as **absolute** removes it from the normal flow of elements on the page and positions it according to distance from the **top**, **left**, **right** or **bottom** margins of its parent element.
- The **z-index** property allows a developer to layer overlapping elements. Elements that have higher **z-index** values are displayed in front of elements with lower **z-index** values.
- Unlike absolute positioning, relative positioning keeps elements in the general flow on the page and offsets them by the specified **top**, **left**, **right** or **bottom** values.
- Property **background-image** specifies the URL of the image, in the format **url(***fileLocation***)**. The property **background-position** places the image on the page using the values **top**, **bottom**, **center**, **left** and **right** individually or in combination for vertical and horizontal positioning. You can also position by using lengths.
- The **background-repeat** property controls the tiling of the background image. Setting the tiling to **no-repeat** displays one copy of the background image on screen. The **background-repeat** property can be set to **repeat** (the default) to tile the image vertically and horizontally, to **repeat-x** to tile the image only horizontally or to **repeat-y** to tile the image only vertically.
- The property setting **background-attachment: fixed** fixes the image in the position specified by **background-position**. Scrolling the browser window will not move the image from its set position. The default value, **scroll**, moves the image as the user scrolls the window.
- The **text-indent** property indents the first line of text in the element by the specified amount.
- The **font-weight** property specifies the "boldness" of text. Values besides **bold** and **normal** (the default) are **bolder** (bolder than **bold** text) and **lighter** (lighter than **normal** text). The value also may be justified using multiples of 100, from 100 to 900 (i.e., **100**, **200**, ..., **900**). Text specified as **normal** is equivalent to **400**, and **bold** text is equivalent to **700**.
- The **font-style** property allows the developer to set text to **none**, **italic** or **oblique** (**oblique** will default to **italic** if the system does not have a separate font file for oblique text, which is normally the case).
- **span** is a generic grouping element; it does not apply any inherent formatting to its contents. Its main use is to apply styles or **id** attributes to a block of text. Element **span** is displayed inline (an

inline element) with other text and with no line breaks. A similar element is the **div** element, which also applies no inherent styles, but is displayed on a separate line, with margins above and below (a block-level element).

- The dimensions of elements on a page can be set with CSS by using the **height** and **width** properties.
- Text within an element can be **center**ed using **text-align**; other values for the **text-align** property are **left** and **right**.
- One problem with setting both dimensions of an element is that the content inside the element might sometimes exceed the set boundaries, in which case the element must be made large enough for all the content to fit. However, a developer can set the **overflow** property to **scroll**; this setting adds scroll bars if the text overflows the boundaries set for it.
- Browsers normally place text and elements on screen in the order in which they appear in the XHTML file. Elements can be removed from the normal flow of text. Floating allows you to move an element to one side of the screen; other content in the document will then flow around the floated element.
- Each block-level element has a box drawn around it, known as the box model. The properties of this box are easily adjusted.
- The **margin** property determines the distance between the element's edge and any outside text.
- CSS uses a box model to render elements on screen. The content of each element is surrounded by padding, a border and margins.
- Margins for individual sides of an element can be specified by using **margin-top**, **margin-right**, **margin-left** and **margin-bottom**.
- The padding is the distance between the content inside an element and the edge of the element. Padding can be set for each side of the box by using **padding-top**, **padding-right**, **padding-left** and **padding-bottom**.
- A developer can interrupt the flow of text around a **float**ed element by setting the **clear** property to the same direction in which the element is **float**ed—**right** or **left**. Setting the **clear** property to **all** interrupts the flow on both sides of the document.
- A property of every block-level element on screen is its border. The border lies between the padding space and the margin space and has numerous properties with which to adjust its appearance.
- The **border-width** property may be set to any of the CSS lengths or to the predefined values of **thin**, **medium** or **thick**.
- The **border-style**s available are **none**, **hidden**, **dotted**, **dashed**, **solid**, **double**, **groove**, **ridge**, **inset** and **outset**.
- The **border-color** property sets the color used for the border.
- The class attribute allows more than one class to be assigned to an XHTML element.

TERMINOLOGY

absolute positioning
absolute-length measurement
arial font
background
background-attachment
background-color
background-image
background-position
background-repeat
blink
block-level element
border
border-color
border-style
border-width
box model

Cascading Style Sheets (CSS)
class attribute
clear property value
cm (centimeter)
colon (**:**)
color
CSS rule
cursive generic font family
dashed border-style
dotted border-style
double border-style
em (size of font)
embedded style sheet
ex (*x*-height of font)
floated element
font-style property
generic font family
groove border style
hidden border style
href attribute
in (inch)
inline style
inline-level element
inset border-style
large relative font size
larger relative font size
left
line-through text decoration
link element
linking to an external style sheet
margin
margin-bottom property
margin-left property
margin-right property
margin-top property
medium relative border width
medium relative font size
mm (millimeter)
monospace
none border-style
outset border-style
overflow property
overline text decoration
padding
parent element
pc (pica)
pseudoclass
pt (point)
rel attribute (**link**)
relative positioning
relative-length measurement
repeat
ridge border-style
right
sans-serif generic font family
scroll
separation of structure from content
serif generic font family
small relative font size
smaller relative font size
solid border-style
span element
style
style attribute
style class
style in header section of the document
text flow
text/css MIME type
text-align
text-decoration property
text-indent
thick border width
thin border width
user style sheet
x-large relative font size
x-small relative font size
xx-large relative font size
xx-small relative font size
z-index

SELF-REVIEW EXERCISES

6.1 Assume that the size of the base font on a system is 12 points.
a) How big is 36-point font in **em**s?
b) How big is 8-point font in **em**s?
c) How big is 24-point font in picas?
d) How big is 12-point font in inches?
e) How big is 1-inch font in picas?

6.2 Fill in the blanks in the following statements:
a) Using the __________ element allows authors to use external style sheets in their pages.

b) To apply a CSS rule to more than one element at a time, separate the element names with a __________.
c) Pixels are a(n) __________ -length measurement unit.
d) The **hover** __________ is activated when the user moves the mouse cursor over the specified element.
e) Setting the **overflow** property to __________ provides a mechanism for containing inner content without compromising specified box dimensions.
f) While __________ is a generic inline element that applies no inherent formatting, __________ is a generic block-level element that applies no inherent formatting.
g) Setting the **background-repeat** property to __________ tiles the specified **background-image** only vertically.
h) If you **float** an element, you can stop the flowing text by using property __________.
i) The __________ property allows you to indent the first line of text in an element.
j) Three components of the box model are the __________, __________ and __________.

ANSWERS TO SELF-REVIEW EXERCISES

6.1 a) 3 **em**s. b) 0.75 **em**s. c) 2 picas. d) 1/6 inch. e) 6 picas.

6.2 a) **link**. b) comma. c) relative. d) pseudoclass. e) **scroll**. f) **span**, **div**. g) **y-repeat**. h) **clear**. i) **text-indent**. j) padding, border, margin.

EXERCISES

6.3 Write a CSS rule that makes all text 1.5 times larger than the base font of the system and colors the text red.

6.4 Write a CSS rule that removes the underline from all links inside list items (**li**) and shifts them left by 3 **em**s.

6.5 Write a CSS rule that places a background image halfway down the page, tiling it horizontally. The image should remain in place when the user scrolls up or down.

6.6 Write a CSS rule that gives all **h1** and **h2** elements a padding of 0.5 **em**s, a **groove**d border style and a margin of 0.5 **em**s.

6.7 Write a CSS rule that changes the color of all elements containing attribute **class = "greenMove"** to green and shifts them down 25 pixels and right 15 pixels.

6.8 Write an XHTML document that shows the results of a color survey. The document should contain a form with radio buttons that allows users to vote for their favorite color. One of the colors should be selected as a default. The document should also contain a table showing various colors and the corresponding percentage of votes for each color. (Each row should be displayed in the color to which it is referring.) Use attributes to format width, border and cell spacing for the table.

6.9 Add an embedded style sheet to the XHTML document of Fig. 4.5. This style sheet should contain a rule that displays **h1** elements in blue. In addition, create a rule that displays all links in blue without underlining them. When the mouse hovers over a link, change the link's background color to yellow.

6.10 Modify the style sheet of Fig. 6.4 by changing **a:hover** to **a:hver** and **margin-left** to **margin left**. Validate the style sheet using the CSS Validator. What happens?

7

JavaScript: Introduction to Scripting

Objectives

- To be able to write simple JavaScript programs.
- To be able to use input and output statements.
- To understand basic memory concepts.
- To be able to use arithmetic operators.
- To understand the precedence of arithmetic operators.
- To be able to write decision-making statements.
- To be able to use relational and equality operators.

Comment is free, but facts are sacred.
C. P. Scott

The creditor hath a better memory than the debtor.
James Howell

When faced with a decision, I always ask, "What would be the most fun?"
Peggy Walker

Equality, in a social sense, may be divided into that of condition and that of rights.
James Fenimore Cooper

Outline

7.1 Introduction

In the first six chapters, we introduced the Internet and World Wide Web, Internet Explorer 5.5, Adobe Photoshop Elements, XHTML and Cascading Style Sheets (CSS). In this chapter, we begin our introduction to the *JavaScript*[1] *scripting language*, which facilitates a disciplined approach to designing computer programs that enhance the functionality and appearance of Web pages.

In Chapters 7–12, we present a detailed discussion of JavaScript—the *de facto* client-side scripting language for Web-based applications. These chapters provide the programming foundation for both client-side scripting (Chapters 7–20) and server-side scripting (Chapters 25–31). Our treatment of JavaScript (Chapters 7–12) serves two purposes—it introduces client-side scripting, which makes Web pages more dynamic and interactive, and it provides the foundation for the more complex server-side scripting presented in Chapters 25–31.

We now introduce JavaScript programming and present examples that illustrate several important features of JavaScript. Each example is carefully analyzed one line at a time. In Chapters 8–9, we present a detailed treatment of *program development* and *program control* in JavaScript.

7.2 Simple Program: Printing a Line of Text in a Web Page

JavaScript uses notations that may appear strange to nonprogrammers. We begin by considering a simple *script* (or *program*) that displays the text "**`Welcome to JavaScript Programming!`**" in the body of an XHTML document. The Internet Explorer Web browser contains a *JavaScript interpreter*, which processes the commands written in JavaScript. The JavaScript code and its output are shown in Fig. 7.1.

---

1. Microsoft's version of JavaScript is called *JScript*. JavaScript was originally created by Netscape. Both Netscape and Microsoft have been instrumental in the standardization of JavaScript/JScript by the *ECMA* (*European Computer Manufacturer's Association*) as *ECMAScript*. For information on the current ECMAScript standard, visit **`www.ecma.ch/stand/ecma-262.htm`**. Throughout this book, we refer to JavaScript and JScript generically as JavaScript.

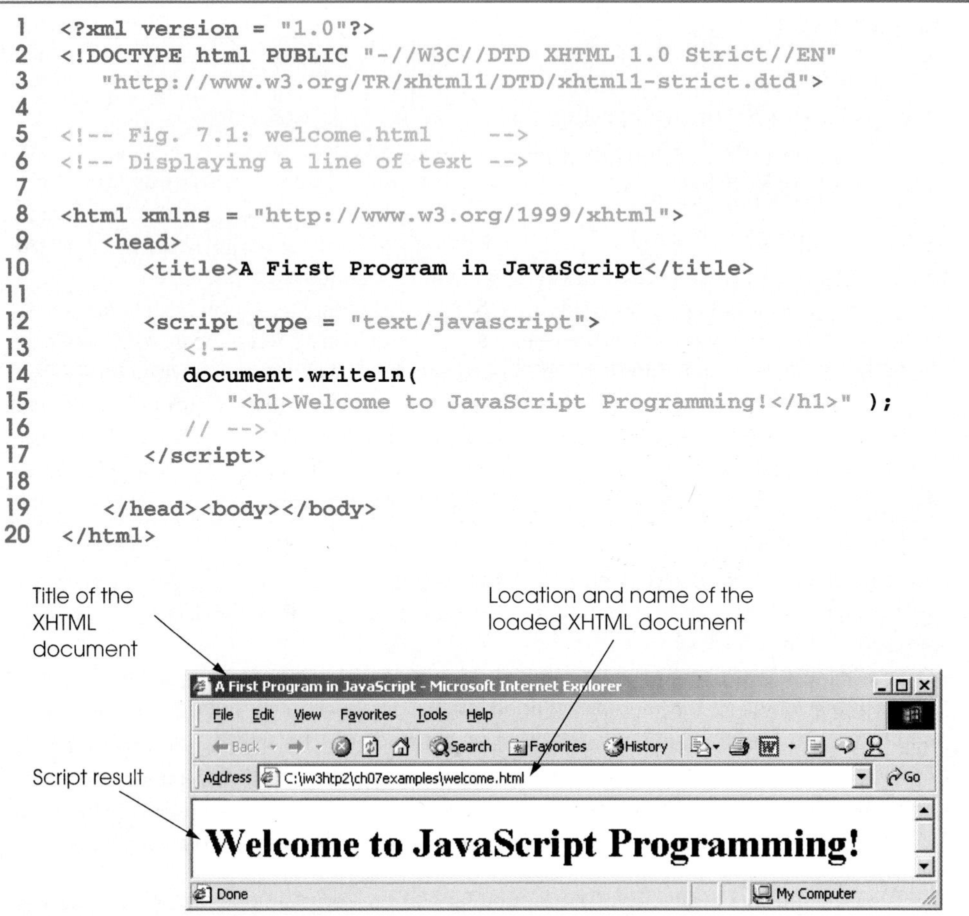

```
1  <?xml version = "1.0"?>
2  <!DOCTYPE html PUBLIC "-//W3C//DTD XHTML 1.0 Strict//EN"
3     "http://www.w3.org/TR/xhtml1/DTD/xhtml1-strict.dtd">
4
5  <!-- Fig. 7.1: welcome.html    -->
6  <!-- Displaying a line of text -->
7
8  <html xmlns = "http://www.w3.org/1999/xhtml">
9     <head>
10       <title>A First Program in JavaScript</title>
11
12       <script type = "text/javascript">
13          <!--
14          document.writeln(
15             "<h1>Welcome to JavaScript Programming!</h1>" );
16          // -->
17       </script>
18
19    </head><body></body>
20 </html>
```


Fig. 7.1 First program in JavaScript.

This program illustrates several important JavaScript features. We consider each line of the XHTML document and script in detail. We have given each XHTML document line numbers for the reader's convenience; those line numbers are not part of the XHTML document or of the JavaScript programs. Lines 14–15 do the "real work" of the script, namely displaying the phrase **`Welcome to JavaScript Programming!`** in the Web page. However, let us consider each line in order.

Line 9 indicates the beginning of the **`<head>`** section of the XHTML document. For the moment, the JavaScript code we write will appear in the **`<head>`** section. The browser interprets the contents of the **`<head>`** section first, so the JavaScript programs we write there will execute before the **`<body>`** of the XHTML document displays. In later chapters on JavaScript and in the chapters on dynamic HTML, we illustrate *inline scripting*, in which JavaScript code is written in the **`<body>`** of an XHTML document.

Line 11 is simply a blank line to separate the **`<script>`** tag at line 12 from the other XHTML elements. This effect helps the script stand out in the XHTML document and makes the document easier to read.

Good Programming Practice 7.1

Place a blank line before **`<script>`** *and after* **`</script>`** *to separate the script from the surrounding XHTML elements and to make the script stand out in the document.*

Line 12 uses the **`<script>`** tag to indicate to the browser that the text which follows is part of a script. The ***type*** *attribute* specifies the type of file as well as the *scripting language* used in the script—in this case, a **text** file written in **javascript**. Both Microsoft Internet Explorer and Netscape Communicator use JavaScript as the default scripting language. [*Note*: Even though Microsoft calls the language JScript, the **type** attribute specifies **javascript**, to adhere to the ECMAScript standard.]

Lines 14–15 instruct the browser's JavaScript interpreter to perform an *action*, namely to display in the Web page the *string* of characters contained between the *double quotation* (**"**) *marks*. A string is sometimes called a *character string*, a *message* or a *string literal*. We refer to characters between double quotation marks generically as strings. Individual whitespace characters between words in a string are not ignored by the browser. However, if consecutive spaces appear in a string, browsers condense those spaces to a single space. Also, in most cases, browsers ignore leading whitespace characters (i.e., whitespace at the beginning of a string).

Software Engineering Observation 7.1

Strings in JavaScript can also be enclosed in single quotation marks (**'** *).*

Lines 14–15 use the browser's ***document*** *object*, which represents the XHTML document the browser is currently displaying. The **document** object allows a script programmer to specify text to display in the XHTML document. The browser contains a complete set of objects that allow script programmers to access and manipulate every element of an XHTML document. In the next several chapters, we overview some of these objects. Chapters 13 through 18 provide in-depth coverage of many more objects that a script programmer can manipulate.

An object resides in the computer's memory and contains information used by the script. The term *object* normally implies that *attributes* (*data*) and *behaviors* (*methods*) are associated with the object. The object's methods use the attributes to provide useful services to the *client of the object* (i.e., the script that calls the methods). In lines 14–15, we call the **document** object's ***writeln*** *method* to write a line of XHTML markup in the XHTML document. The parentheses following the method name **writeln** contain the *arguments* that the method requires to perform its task (or its action). Method **writeln** instructs the browser to display the argument string. If the string contains XHTML elements, the browser interprets these elements and renders them on the screen. In this example, the browser displays the phrase **Welcome to JavaScript Programming!** as an **h1**-level XHTML head, because the phrase is enclosed in an **h1** element.

The code elements in lines 14–15, including **document.writeln**, its *argument* in the parentheses (the string) and the *semicolon* (**;**), together are called a *statement*. Every statement should end with a semicolon (also known as the *statement terminator*), although this practice is not required by JavaScript. Line 17 indicates the end of the script.

Good Programming Practice 7.2

Always include the semicolon at the end of a statement to terminate the statement. This notation clarifies where one statement ends and the next statement begins.

Common Programming Error 7.1

Forgetting the ending **</script>** *tag for a script may prevent the browser from interpreting the script properly and may prevent the XHTML document from loading properly.*

The **</head>** tag at line 19 indicates the end of the **<head>** section. Also on line 19, the tags **<body>** and **</body>** specify that this XHTML document has an empty body—no XHTML appears in the **body** element. Line 20 indicates the end of this XHTML document.

We are now ready to view our XHTML document in Internet Explorer. Open the XHTML document in Internet Explorer by double-clicking it. If the script contains no syntax errors, it should produce the output shown in Fig. 7.1.

Common Programming Error 7.2

JavaScript is case sensitive. Not using the proper uppercase and lowercase letters is a syntax error. *A syntax error occurs when the script interpreter cannot recognize a statement. The interpreter normally issues an error message to help the programmer locate and fix the incorrect statement. Syntax errors are violations of the rules of the programming language. The interpreter notifies you of a syntax error it attempts to execute the statement containing the error. The JavaScript interpreter in Internet Explorer reports all syntax errors by indicating in a separate popup window that a* "runtime error" *occurred (i.e., a problem occurred while the interpreter was running the script).*

Testing and Debugging Tip 7.1

When the interpreter reports a syntax error, the error may not be on the line indicated by the error message. First, check the line for which the error was reported. If that line does not contain errors, check the preceding several lines in the script.

Some older Web browsers do not support scripting. In such browsers, the actual text of a script often will display in the Web page. To prevent this from happening, many script programmers enclose the script code in an XHTML comment, so that browsers which do not support scripts ignore the script. The syntax used is as follows:

```
<script type = "text/javascript">
   <!--
   script code here
   // -->
</script>
```

When a browser that does not support scripts encounters the preceding code, it ignores the **<script>** and **</script>** tags and the script code in the XHTML comment. Browsers that do support scripting will interpret the JavaScript code as expected. [*Note*: Some browsers require the *JavaScript single-line comment* **//** (see Section 7.3 for an explanation) before the ending XHTML comment delimiter (**-->**) to interpret the script properly.]

Portability Tip 7.1

Some browsers do not support the **<script>**...**</script>** *tags. If your document is to be rendered with such browsers, the script code between these tags should be enclosed in an XHTML comment, so that the script text does not get displayed as part of the Web page.*

A script can display **Welcome to JavaScript Programming!** several ways. Figure 7.2 uses two JavaScript statements to produce one line of text in the XHTML document. This example also displays the text in a different color using the CSS **color** property.

```
1  <?xml version = "1.0"?>
2  <!DOCTYPE html PUBLIC "-//W3C//DTD XHTML 1.0 Strict//EN"
3     "http://www.w3.org/TR/xhtml1/DTD/xhtml1-strict.dtd">
4
5  <!-- Fig. 7.2: welcome2.html                     -->
6  <!-- Printing a Line with Multiple Statements -->
7
8  <html xmlns = "http://www.w3.org/1999/xhtml">
9     <head>
10       <title>Printing a Line with Multiple Statements</title>
11
12       <script type = "text/javascript">
13          <!--
14          document.write( "<h1 style = \"color: magenta\">" );
15          document.write( "Welcome to JavaScript " +
16             "Programming!</h1>" );
17          // -->
18       </script>
19
20    </head><body></body>
21 </html>
```

Fig. 7.2 Printing on one line with separate statements.

Most of this XHTML document is identical to Fig. 7.1, so we concentrate only on lines 14–16 of Fig. 7.2, which display one line of text in the XHTML document. The first statement uses **`document`** method ***`write`*** to display a string. Unlike **`writeln`**, **`write`** does not position the output cursor in the XHTML document at the beginning of the next line after writing its argument. [*Note*: The output cursor keeps track of where the next character appears in the XHTML document.] The next character written in the XHTML document appears immediately after the last character written with **`write`**. Thus, when line 16 executes, the first character written, "**`J`**," appears immediately after the last character displayed with **`write`** (the space character inside the right double quote on line 15). Each **`write`** or **`writeln`** statement resumes writing characters where the last **`write`** or **`writeln`** statement stopped writing characters. So, after a **`writeln`** statement, the next output appears on the next line. In effect, the two statements in lines 14–16 result in one line of XHTML text. Remember that statements in JavaScript are separated by semicolons (**`;`**). Therefore, lines 15–16 represent one statement. JavaScript allows large statements to be split over many lines. However, you cannot split a statement in the middle of a string.

Common Programming Error 7.3

Splitting a statement in the middle of a string is a syntax error.

Notice, however, that the two characters "****" and "**"**" are not displayed in the browser. The *backslash* (****) in a string is an *escape character*. It indicates that a "special" character is to be used in the string. When a backslash is encountered in a string of characters, the next character is combined with the backslash to form an *escape sequence*. The escape sequence **\"** is the *double-quote character*, which causes a double-quote character to be inserted into the string. We use this escape sequence to insert double-quotes around the attribute value for **style**. We discuss escape sequences in greater detail momentarily.

It is important to note that the preceding discussion has nothing to do with the actual rendering of the XHTML text. Remember that the browser does not create a new line of text unless the browser window is too narrow for the text being rendered, or unless the browser encounters an XHTML element that explicitly starts a new line—e.g., **
** to start a new line, **<p>** to start a new paragraph, etc.

Common Programming Error 7.4

Many people confuse the writing of XHTML text with the rendering of XHTML text. Writing XHTML text creates the XHTML that will be rendered by the browser for presentation to the user.

In the next example, we demonstrate that a single statement can cause the browser to display multiple lines through the use of line-break XHTML tags (**
) throughout the string of XHTML text in a **write or **writeln** method call. Figure 7.3 demonstrates the use of line-break XHTML tags. Lines 13–14 produce three separate lines of text when the browser renders the XHTML document.

```
 1  <?xml version = "1.0"?>
 2  <!DOCTYPE html PUBLIC "-//W3C//DTD XHTML 1.0 Strict//EN"
 3     "http://www.w3.org/TR/xhtml1/DTD/xhtml1-strict.dtd">
 4
 5  <!-- Fig. 7.3: welcome3.html    -->
 6  <!-- Printing Multiple Lines    -->
 7
 8  <html xmlns = "http://www.w3.org/1999/xhtml">
 9     <head><title>Printing Multiple Lines</title>
10
11        <script type = "text/javascript">
12           <!--
13           document.writeln( "<h1>Welcome to<br />JavaScript" +
14              "<br />Programming!</h1>" );
15           // -->
16        </script>
17
18     </head><body></body>
19  </html>
```

Fig. 7.3 Printing on multiple lines with a single statement (part 1 of 2).

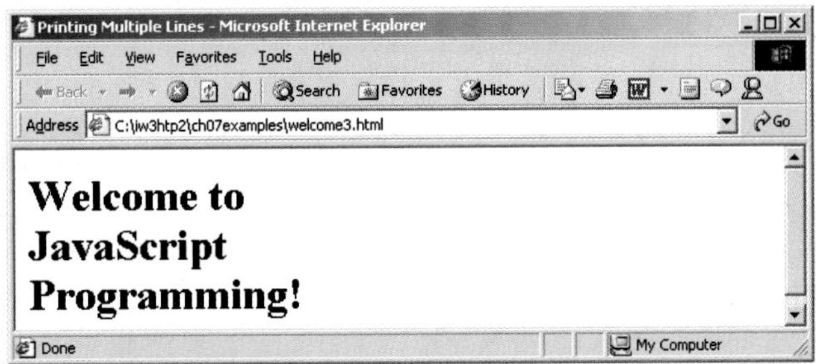

Fig. 7.3 Printing on multiple lines with a single statement (part 2 of 2).

The first several programs in this chapter display text in the XHTML document. Sometimes it is useful to display information in windows called *dialogs* (or *dialog boxes*) that "pop up" on the screen to grab the user's attention. Dialogs typically display important messages to users browsing the Web page. JavaScript allows you easily to display a dialog box containing a message. The program in Fig. 7.4 displays **`Welcome to JavaScript Programming!`** as three lines in a predefined dialog called an ***`alert`*** *dialog*.

Line 13 in the script uses the browser's ***`window`*** object to display an alert dialog. The argument to the **`window`** object's ***`alert`*** method is the string to display. Executing the preceding statement displays the dialog shown in the first window of Fig. 7.4. The *title bar* of the dialog contains the string **Microsoft Internet Explorer**, to indicate that the browser is presenting a message to the user. The dialog provides an **OK** button that allows the user to *dismiss* (i.e., *hide*) *the dialog* by clicking the button. To dismiss the dialog position the *mouse cursor* (also called the *mouse pointer*) over the **OK** button and click the mouse.

```
1  <?xml version = "1.0"?>
2  <!DOCTYPE html PUBLIC "-//W3C//DTD XHTML 1.0 Strict//EN"
3     "http://www.w3.org/TR/xhtml1/DTD/xhtml1-strict.dtd">
4
5  <!-- Fig. 7.4: welcome4.html                -->
6  <!-- Printing multiple lines in a dialog box -->
7
8  <html xmlns = "http://www.w3.org/1999/xhtml">
9     <head><title>Printing Multiple Lines in a Dialog Box</title>
10
11       <script type = "text/javascript">
12          <!--
13             window.alert( "Welcome to\nJavaScript\nProgramming!" );
14          // -->
15       </script>
16
17    </head>
18
19    <body>
20       <p>Click Refresh (or Reload) to run this script again.</p>
21    </body>
22 </html>
```

Fig. 7.4 Displaying multiple lines in a dialog (part 1 of 2).

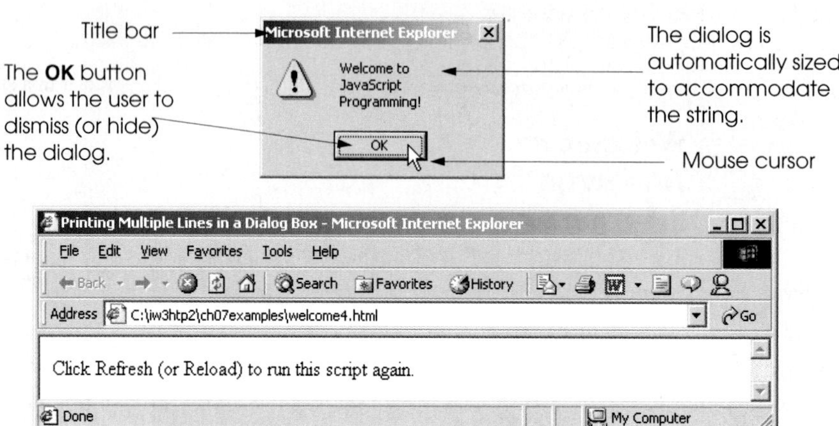

Fig. 7.4 Displaying multiple lines in a dialog (part 2 of 2).

Common Programming Error 7.5

Dialogs display plain text; they do not render XHTML. Therefore, specifying XHTML elements as part of a string to be displayed in a dialog results in the actual characters of the tags being displayed.

Note that the **`alert`** dialog contains three lines of plain text. Normally, a diaolg displays the characters in a string exactly as they appear between the double quotes. Notice, however, that the dialog does not display the two characters "**`\`**" and "**`n`**." The escape sequence **`\n`** is the *newline character*. In a dialog, the newline character causes the *cursor* (the current screen position indicator) to move to the beginning of the next line in the dialog. Some other common escape sequences are listed in Fig. 7.5. The **`\n`**, **`\t`** and **`\r`** escape sequences in the table do not affect XHTML rendering unless they are in a **`pre`** *element* (this element displays the text between its tags in a fixed-width font exactly as it is formatted between the tags, including leading whitespace characters and consecutive whitespace characters). The other escape sequences result in characters that will be displayed in plain text dialogs and in XHTML.

Escape sequence	Description
`\n`	Newline. Position the screen cursor at the beginning of the next line.
`\t`	Horizontal tab. Move the screen cursor to the next tab stop.
`\r`	Carriage return. Position the screen cursor to the beginning of the current line; do not advance to the next line. Any characters output after the carriage return overwrite the characters previously output on that line.
`\\`	Backslash. Used to represent a backslash character in a string.

Fig. 7.5 Some common escape sequences (part 1 of 2).

Escape sequence	Description
`\"`	Double quote. Used to represent a double quote character in a string contained in double quotes. For example, `window.alert( "\"in quotes\"" );` displays **`"in quotes"`** in an **`alert`** dialog.
`\'`	Single quote. Used to represent a single quote character in a string. For example, `window.alert( '\'in quotes\'' );` displays **`'in quotes'`** in an **`alert`** dialog.

Fig. 7.5 Some common escape sequences (part 2 of 2).

7.3 Another JavaScript Program: Adding Integers

Our next script inputs two *integers* (whole numbers, such as 7, –11, 0 and 31,914) typed by a user at the keyboard, computes the sum of the values and displays the result.

The script uses another predefined dialog box from the **`window`** object, one called a ***`prompt`*** *dialog*, that allows the user to input a value for use in the script. The program displays the results of the addition operation in the XHTML document. Figure 7.6 shows the script and some sample screen captures. [*Note*: In later JavaScript chapters, we will obtain input via GUI components in XHTML forms, as introduced in Chapter 5.]

```
<?xml version = "1.0"?>
<!DOCTYPE html PUBLIC "-//W3C//DTD XHTML 1.0 Strict//EN"
   "http://www.w3.org/TR/xhtml1/DTD/xhtml1-strict.dtd">

<!-- Fig. 7.6: Addition.html -->
<!-- Addition Program        -->

<html xmlns = "http://www.w3.org/1999/xhtml">
   <head>
      <title>An Addition Program</title>

      <script type = "text/javascript">
         <!--
         var firstNumber,    // first string entered by user
             secondNumber,   // second string entered by user
             number1,        // first number to add
             number2,        // second number to add
             sum;            // sum of number1 and number2

         // read in first number from user as a string
         firstNumber =
            window.prompt( "Enter first integer", "0" );
```

Fig. 7.6 Addition script "in action" (part 1 of 2).

```
23
24           // read in second number from user as a string
25           secondNumber =
26              window.prompt( "Enter second integer", "0" );
27
28           // convert numbers from strings to integers
29           number1 = parseInt( firstNumber );
30           number2 = parseInt( secondNumber );
31
32           // add the numbers
33           sum = number1 + number2;
34
35           // display the results
36           document.writeln( "<h1>The sum is " + sum + "</h1>" );
37           // -->
38        </script>
39
40     </head>
41     <body>
42        <p>Click Refresh (or Reload) to run the script again</p>
43     </body>
44  </html>
```

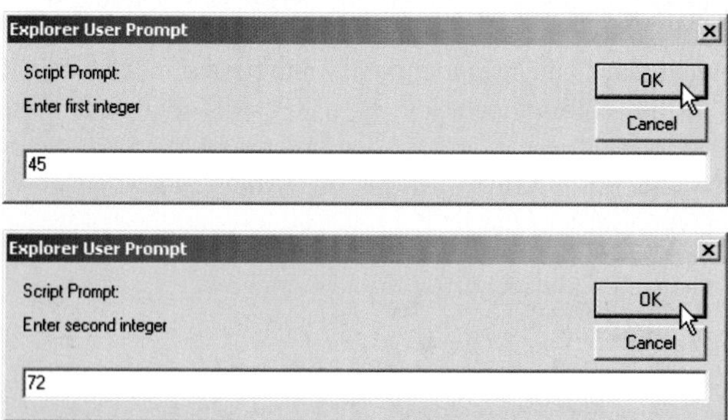

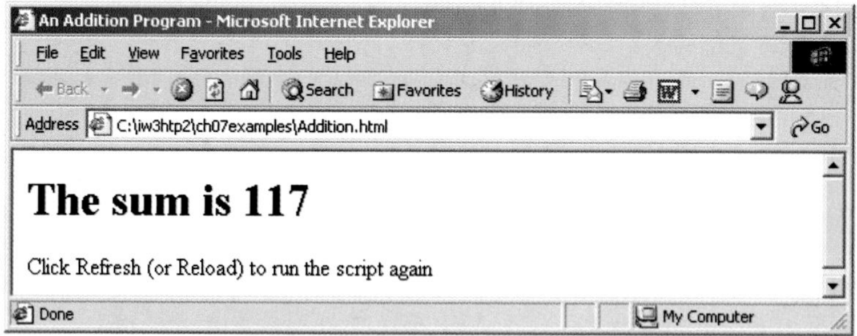

Fig. 7.6 Addition script "in action" (part 2 of 2).

Lines 14–18 are *declarations*. The keyword **var** at the beginning of the statement indicates that the words **firstNumber**, **secondNumber**, **number1**, **number2** and **sum** are the names of *variables*. A variable is a location in the computer's memory where a value can be stored for use by a program. All variables should be declared with a name in a **var** statement before they are used in a program. Although using **var** to declare variables is not required, we will see in Chapter 10, "JavaScript/JScript: Functions," that **var** sometimes ensures proper behavior of a script.

The name of a variable can be any valid *identifier*. An identifier is a series of characters consisting of letters, digits, underscores (_) and dollar signs (**$**) that does not begin with a digit and does not contain any spaces. Some valid identifiers are **Welcome**, **$value**, **_value**, **m_inputField1** and **button7**. The name **7button** is not a valid identifier, because it begins with a digit, and the name **input field** is not a valid identifier, because it contains a space. Remember that JavaScript is *case sensitive*—uppercase and lowercase letters are considered to be different characters, so **firstNumber**, **FiRsTnUmBeR** and **FIRSTNUMBER** are different identifiers.

Good Programming Practice 7.3

Choosing meaningful variable names helps a script to be "self-documenting" (i.e., easy to understand by simply reading the script, rather than having to read manuals or excessive comments).

Good Programming Practice 7.4

By convention, variable-name identifiers begin with a lowercase first letter. Every word in the name after the first word should begin with a capital first letter. For example, identifier **firstNumber** *has a capital* **N** *in its second word,* **Number**.

Common Programming Error 7.6

Splitting a statement in the middle of an identifier is normally a syntax error.

Declarations, like statements, end with a semicolon (**;**) and can be split over several lines (as shown in Fig. 7.6) with each variable in the declaration separated by a comma—known as a *comma-separated list* of variable names. Several variables may be declared either in one declaration or in multiple declarations. We could have written five declarations, one for each variable, but the single declaration we used in the program is more concise.

Programmers often indicate the purpose of each variable in the program by placing a JavaScript comment at the end of each line in the declaration. In lines 14–18, *single-line comments* that begin with the characters **//** state the purpose of each variable in the script. This form of comment is called a single-line comment because the comment terminates at the end of the line. A **//** comment can begin at any position in a line of JavaScript code and continues until the end of that line. Comments do not cause the browser to perform any action when the script is interpreted; rather, comments are ignored by the JavaScript interpreter.

Good Programming Practice 7.5

Some programmers prefer to declare each variable on a separate line. This format allows for easy insertion of a descriptive comment next to each declaration.

Another comment notation facilitates the writing of *multiple-line comments*. For example,

```
/* This is a multiple-line
   comment. It can be
   split over many lines. */
```

comments can be spread over several lines. Such comments begin with delimiter **/*** and end with delimiter ***/**. All text between the delimiters of the comment is ignored by the compiler.

Common Programming Error 7.7

Forgetting one of the delimiters of a multiple-line comment is a syntax error.

Common Programming Error 7.8

Nesting multiple-line comments (i.e., placing a multiple-line comment between the delimiters of another multiple-line comment) is a syntax error.

JavaScript adopted comments delimited with **/*** and ***/** from the C programming language and single-line comments delimited with **//** from the C++ programming language. JavaScript programmers generally prefer C++-style single-line comments over C-style comments. Throughout this book, we use C++-style single-line comments.

Line 20 is a single-line comment indicating the purpose of the statement in the next two lines. Lines 21–22 allow the user to enter a string representing the first of the two integers that will be added. The **window** object's ***prompt*** method displays the dialog in Fig. 7.7.

The first argument to **prompt** indicates to the user what to type in the text field. This message is called a *prompt* because it directs the user to take a specific action. The optional second argument is the default string to display in the text field; if the second argument is not supplied, the text field does not display a default value. The user types characters in the text field, then clicks the **OK** button to return the string to the program. [If you type, but nothing appears in the text field, position the mouse pointer in the text field and click the left mouse button to activate the text field.] Unfortunately, JavaScript does not provide a simple form of input that is analogous to writing a line of text with **document.write** and **document.writeln**. For this reason, we normally receive input from a user through a GUI component such as the **prompt** dialog, as in this program, or through an XHTML form GUI component, as we will see in later chapters.

Technically, the user can type anything in the text field of the **prompt** dialog. For this program, if the user either types a noninteger value or clicks the **Cancel** button, a runtime logic error will occur, and the sum of the two values will appear in the XHTML document as *NaN* (*not a number*). In Chapter 12, JavaScript: Objects, we discuss the **Number** object and its methods that can determine whether a value is not a number.

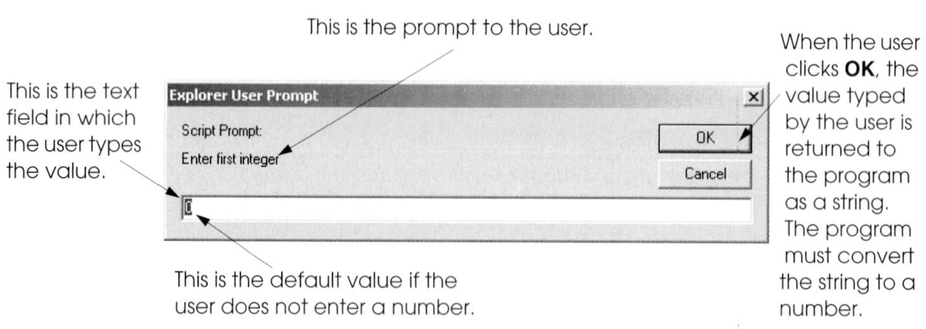

Fig. 7.7 Prompt dialog displayed by the **window** object's **prompt** method.

The statement at lines 21–22 gives the result of the call to the **window** object's **prompt** method (a string containing the characters typed by the user) to variable **firstNumber** by using the *assignment operator*, **=**. The statement is read as, **firstNumber** *gets* the value of **window.prompt("Enter first integer", "0")**. The **=** operator is called a *binary operator*, because it has two *operands*—**firstNumber** and the result of the expression **window.prompt("Enter first integer", "0")**. This entire statement is called an *assignment statement*, because it assigns a value to a variable. The expression to the right of the assignment operator always is evaluated first.

Lines 24 is a single-line comment that indicates the purpose of the statement in lines 25 and 26. The statement displays a **prompt** dialog in which the user types a string representing the second of the two integers to add.

Lines 29–30 convert the two strings input by the user to integer values that can be used in a calculation. Function ***parseInt*** converts its string argument to an integer. Line 29 assigns the integer that function **parseInt** returns to the variable **number1**. Any subsequent references to **number1** in the program use this same integer value. Line 30 assigns the integer that function **parseInt** returns to variable **number2**. Any subsequent references to **number2** in the program use this same integer value. [*Note*: We refer to **parseInt** as a *function* rather than a *method* because we do not precede the function call with an object name (such as **document** or **window**) and a dot operator (**.**). The term *method* implies that the function belongs to a particular object. For example, method **writeln** belongs to the **document** object and method **prompt** belongs to the **window** object.]

The assignment statement on line 33 calculates the sum of the variables **number1** and **number2** and assigns the result to variable **sum** by using the assignment operator, **=**. The statement is read as "**sum** *gets* the value of **number1 + number2**." Most calculations occur in assignment statements.

Good Programming Practice 7.6

Place spaces on either side of a binary operator. This format makes the operator stand out and makes the program more readable.

After line 33 performs the calculation, line 36 uses **document.writeln** to display the result of the addition. The expression from the preceding statement uses the operator **+** to "add" a string (the literal **"<h1>The sum is "**) and **sum** (the variable containing the integer result of the addition on line 33). JavaScript has a version of the **+** operator for *string concatenation* that enables a string and a value of another data type (including another string) to be concatenated. The result of this operation is a new (and normally longer) string. If we assume that **sum** contains the value **117**, the expression evaluates as follows: JavaScript determines that the two operands of the **+** operator (the string **"<h1>The sum is "** and the integer **sum**) are different types and that one of them is a string. Next, the statement converts the value of variable **sum** to a string and concatenates it with **"<h1>The sum is "**, which results in the string **"<h1>The sum is 117"**. Then, the statement concatenates the string **"</h1>"** to produce the string **"<h1>The sum is 117</h1>"**. The browser renders this string as part of the XHTML document. Note that the automatic conversion of integer **sum** occurs because it is concatenated with the string literal **"<h1>The sum is "**. Also note that the space between **is** and **117** is part of the string **"<h1>The sum is "**.

Common Programming Error 7.9

Confusing the **+** *operator used for string concatenation with the* **+** *operator used for addition can lead to strange results. For example, assuming that integer variable* **y** *has the value* **5***, the expression* **"y + 2 = " + y + 2** *results in the string* **"y + 2 = 52"***, not* **"y + 2 = 7"***, because first the value of* **y** *is concatenated with the string* **"y + 2 = "***, then the value* **2** *is concatenated with the new, larger string* **"y + 2 = 5"***. The expression* **"y + 2 = " + (y + 2)** *produces the desired result.*

After the browser interprets the **<head>** section of the XHTML document (which contains the JavaScript), it then interprets the **<body>** of the XHTML document (lines 41–43) and renders the XHTML. If you click your browser's **Refresh** (or **Reload**) button, the browser will reload the XHTML document, so that you can execute the script again and add two new integers. [*Note*: In some cases, it may be necessary to hold down the *Shift* key while clicking your browser's **Refresh** (or **Reload**) button, to ensure that the XHTML document reloads properly.]

7.4 Memory Concepts

Variable names such as **number1**, **number2** and **sum** actually correspond to *locations* in the computer's memory. Every variable has a *name*, a *type* and a *value*.

In the addition program in Fig. 7.6, when line 22 executes, the string **firstNumber** (previously entered by the user in a **prompt** dialog) is converted to an integer and placed into a memory location to which the name **number1** has been assigned by the interpreter. Suppose the user entered the string **45** as the value for **firstNumber**. The program converts **firstNumber** to an integer, and the computer places the integer value **45** into location **number1**, as shown in Fig. 7.8.

Whenever a value is placed in a memory location, the value replaces the previous value in that location. The previous value is lost.

When line 26 executes, suppose the user enters the string **72** as the value for **secondNumber**. The program converts **secondNumber** to an integer, the computer places that integer value, **72**, into location **number2** and the memory appears as shown in Fig. 7.9.

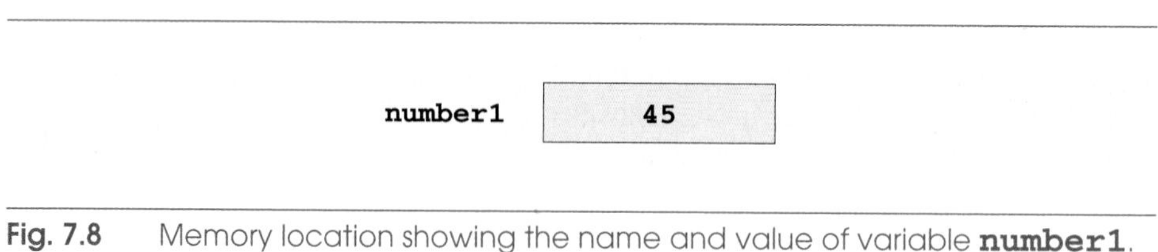

Fig. 7.8 Memory location showing the name and value of variable **number1**.

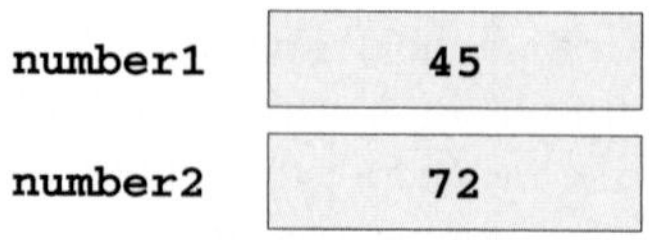

number1 45

number2 72

Fig. 7.9 Memory locations after values for variables **number1** and **number2** have been input.

Once the program has obtained values for **number1** and **number2**, it adds the values and places the sum into variable **sum**. The statement

```
sum = number1 + number2;
```

performs the addition and also replaces **sum**'s previous value. After **sum** is calculated, the memory appears as shown in Fig. 7.10. Note that the values of **number1** and **number2** appear exactly as they did before they were used in the calculation of **sum**. These values were used, but not destroyed, as the computer performed the calculation. When a value is read from a memory location, the process is *nondestructive.*

7.5 Arithmetic

Many scripts perform arithmetic calculations. Figure 7.11 summarizes the *arithmetic operators*. Note the use of various special symbols not used in algebra. The *asterisk* (*****) indicates multiplication; the *percent sign* (**%**) is the *modulus operator*, which is discussed shortly. The arithmetic operators in Fig. 7.11 are binary operators, because each operates on two operands. For example, the expression **sum + value** contains the binary operator **+** and the two operands **sum** and **value**.

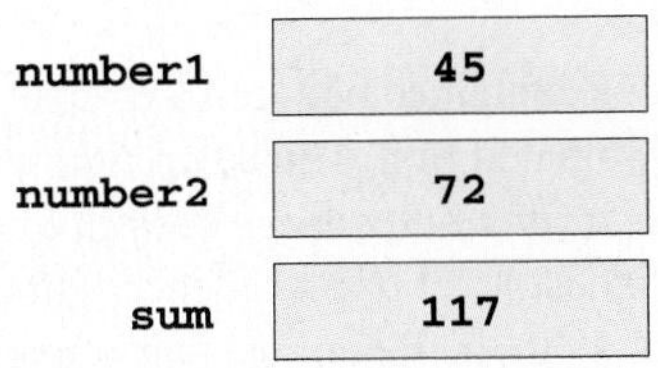

number1	45
number2	72
sum	117

Fig. 7.10 Memory locations after calculating the **sum** of **number1** and **number2**.

JavaScript operation	Arithmetic operator	Algebraic expression	JavaScript expression
Addition	+	$f+7$	`f + 7`
Subtraction	-	$p-c$	`p - c`
Multiplication	*	bm	`b * m`
Division	/	x / y or $\frac{x}{y}$ or $x \div y$	`x / y`
Modulus	%	$r \bmod s$	`r % s`

Fig. 7.11 Arithmetic operators.

JavaScript provides the modulus operator, **%**, which yields the remainder after division. The expression **x % y** yields the remainder after **x** is divided by **y**. Thus, **7.4 % 3.1** yields **1.2**, and **17 % 5** yields **2**. In later chapters, we consider many interesting applications of the modulus operator, such as determining whether one number is a multiple of another. There is no arithmetic operator for exponentiation in JavaScript. (Chapter 9 shows how to perform exponentiation in JavaScript.)

Arithmetic expressions in JavaScript must be written in *straight-line form* to facilitate entering programs into the computer. Thus, expressions such as "**a** divided by **b**" must be written as **a / b**, so that all constants, variables and operators appear in a straight line. The following algebraic notation is generally not acceptable to computers:

$$\frac{a}{b}$$

Parentheses are used in JavaScript expressions in the same manner as in algebraic expressions. For example, to multiply **a** times the quantity **b + c** we write:

```
a * ( b + c )
```

JavaScript applies the operators in arithmetic expressions in a precise sequence determined by the following *rules of operator precedence*, which are generally the same as those followed in algebra:

1. Operators in expressions contained between a left parenthesis and its corresponding right parenthesis are evaluated first. Thus, *parentheses may be used to force the order of evaluation to occur in any sequence desired by the programmer.* Parentheses are said to be at the highest level of precedence." In cases of *nested*, or *embedded*, parentheses, the operators in the innermost pair of parentheses are applied first.

2. Multiplication, division and modulus operations are applied next. If an expression contains several multiplication, division and modulus operations, operators are applied from left to right. Multiplication, division and modulus operations are said to have the same level of precedence.

3. Addition and subtraction operations are applied last. If an expression contains several addition and subtraction operations, operators are applied from left to right. Addition and subtraction operations have the same level of precedence.

The rules of operator precedence enable JavaScript to apply operators in the correct order. When we say that operators are applied from left to right, we are referring to the *associativity* of the operators—the order in which operators of equal priority are evaluated. We will see that some operators associate from right to left. Figure 7.12 summarizes these rules of operator precedence. The table in Fig. 7.12 will be expanded as additional JavaScript operators are introduced. A complete precedence chart is included in Appendix B.

Now, in light of the rules of operator precedence, let us consider several algebraic expressions. Each example lists an algebraic expression and the equivalent JavaScript expression.

Operator(s)	Operation(s)	Order of evaluation (precedence)
`( )`	Parentheses	Evaluated first. If the parentheses are nested, the expression in the innermost pair is evaluated first. If there are several pairs of parentheses on the same level (i.e., not nested), they are evaluated from left to right.
`*`, `/` or `%`	Multiplication Division Modulus	Evaluated second. If there are several such operations, they are evaluated from left to right.
`+` or `-`	Addition Subtraction	Evaluated last. If there are several such operations, they are evaluated from left to right.

Fig. 7.12 Precedence of arithmetic operators.

The following is an example of an arithmetic mean (average) of five terms:

Algebra: $m = \frac{a + b + c + d + e}{5}$

JavaScript: `m = ( a + b + c + d + e ) / 5;`

The parentheses are required, because division has higher precedence than that of addition. The entire quantity **(a + b + c + d + e)** is to be divided by **5**. If the parentheses are erroneously omitted, we obtain **a + b + c + d + e / 5**, which evaluates as

$$a + b + c + d + \frac{e}{5}$$

The following is an example of the equation of a straight line:

Algebra: $y = mx + b$

JavaScript: `y = m * x + b;`

No parentheses are required. The multiplication operator is applied first, because multiplication has a higher precedence than that of addition. The assignment occurs last, because it has a lower precedence than that of multiplication and division.

The following example contains modulus (**%**), multiplication, division, addition and subtraction operations:

Algebra: $z = pr\%q + w/x - y$

JavaScript:
```
z  =  p  *  r  %  q  +  w  /  x  -  y;
   6     1     2     4     3     5
```

The circled numbers under the statement indicate the order in which JavaScript applies the operators. The multiplication, modulus and division operations are evaluated first in left-to-right order (i.e., they associate from left to right), because they have higher precedence than that of addition and subtraction. The addition and subtraction operations are evaluated next. These operations are also applied from left to right.

Not all expressions with several pairs of parentheses contain nested parentheses. For example, the expression

```
a * ( b + c ) + c * ( d + e )
```

does not contain nested parentheses. Rather, these parentheses are on the same level.

To develop a better understanding of the rules of operator precedence, consider the evaluation of a second-degree polynomial ($y = ax^2 + bx + c$):

```
y = a * x * x + b * x + c;
```

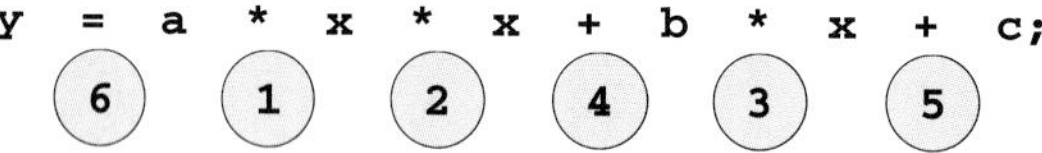

The circled numbers under the preceding statement indicate the order in which JavaScript applies the operators. There is no arithmetic operator for exponentiation in JavaScript; x^2 is represented as **`x * x`**.

Suppose that **`a`**, **`b`**, **`c`** and **`x`** are initialized as follows: **`a = 2`**, **`b = 3`**, **`c = 7`** and **`x = 5`**. Figure 7.13 illustrates the order in which the operators are applied in the preceding second-degree polynomial.

As in algebra, it is acceptable to place unnecessary parentheses in an expression to make the expression clearer. Such unnecessary parentheses are also called *redundant parentheses*. For example, the preceding assignment statement might be parenthesized as follows:

```
y = ( a * x * x ) + ( b * x ) + c;
```

Good Programming Practice 7.7

Using parentheses for complex arithmetic expressions, even when the parentheses are not necessary, can make the arithmetic expressions easier to read.

7.6 Decision Making: Equality and Relational Operators

This section introduces a version of JavaScript's **`if`** structure that allows a program to make a decision based on the truth or falsity of a *condition*. If the condition is met (i.e., the condition is *true*), the statement in the body of the **`if`** structure is executed. If the condition is not met (i.e., the condition is *false*), the statement in the body of the **`if`** structure is not executed. We will see an example shortly.

Conditions in **`if`** structures can be formed by using the *equality operators* and *relational operators* summarized in Fig. 7.14. The relational operators all have the same level of precedence and associate from left to right. The equality operators both have the same level of precedence, which is lower than the precedence of the relational operators. The equality operators also associate from left to right.

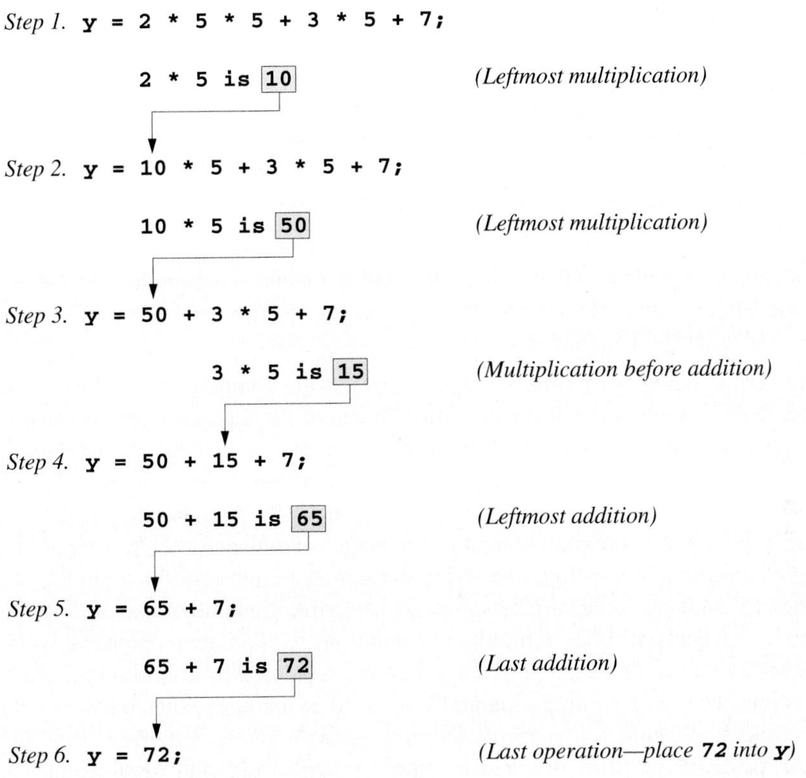

Fig. 7.13 Order in which a second-degree polynomial is evaluated.

Standard algebraic equality operator or relational operator	JavaScript equality or relational operator	Sample JavaScript condition	Meaning of JavaScript condition
Equality operators			
=	`==`	`x == y`	`x` is equal to `y`
≠	`!=`	`x != y`	`x` is not equal to `y`
Relational operators			
>	`>`	`x > y`	`x` is greater than `y`
<	`<`	`x < y`	`x` is less than `y`
≥	`>=`	`x >= y`	`x` is greater than or equal to `y`
≤	`<=`	`x <= y`	`x` is less than or equal to `y`

Fig. 7.14 Equality and relational operators.

Common Programming Error 7.10

It is a syntax error if the operators **==**, **!=**, **>=** *and* **<=** *contain spaces between their symbols, as in* **= =**, **! =**, **> =** *and* **< =**, *respectively.*

Common Programming Error 7.11

Reversing the operators **!=**, **>=** *and* **<=**, *as in* **=!**, **=>** *and* **=<**, *respectively, is a syntax error.*

Common Programming Error 7.12

Confusing the equality operator, **==**, *with the assignment operator,* **=**, *is a logic error. The equality operator should be read as "is equal to," and the assignment operator should be read as "gets" or "gets the value of." Some people prefer to read the equality operator as "double equals" or "equals equals."*

The script in Fig. 7.15 uses six **if** statements to compare two values input into **prompt** dialogs by the user. If the condition in any of the **if** statements is satisfied, the assignment statement associated with that **if** statement is executed. The user inputs two values through input dialogs. The program stores the values in the variables **first** and **second**, then converts the values to integers and stores them in variables **number1** and **number2**. Finally, the program compares the values and displays the results of the comparison in an information dialog. The script and sample outputs are shown in Fig. 7.15.

Lines 15–18 declare the variables used in the script. Remember that variables may be declared in one declaration or in multiple declarations. If more than one name is declared in a declaration (as in this example), the names are separated by commas (**,**). This list of names is referred to as a comma-separated list. Once again, notice the comment at the end of each line, indicating the purpose of each variable in the program. Line 21 uses **window.prompt** to allow the user to input the first value and to store the value in **first**.

Line 24 uses **window.prompt** to allow the user to input the second value and to store the value in **second**. Lines 27–28 conver the strings to integers and stores them in variables **number1** and **number2**. Line 30 outputs a line of XHTML text containing the **<h1>** head **Comparison Results**. Lines 31–32 output a line of XHTML text that indicates the start of a **<table>** that has a one-pixel border and is 100% of the browser window's width.

The **if** structure (lines 34–36) compares the values of variables **first** and **second** to test them for equality. If the values are equal, the statement on lines 35–36 outputs a line of XHTML text representing one row of an XHTML table (as indicated by the **<tr>** and **</tr>** tags). The text in the row contains the result of **first + " == " + second**. As in Fig. 7.6, the **+** operator is used in this expression to perform string concatenation. If the conditions are true in one or more of the **if** structures starting at lines 38, 42, 46, 50 and 54, the corresponding **document.writeln** statement(s) output(s) a line of XHTML text representing a row in the XHTML table.

Notice the indentation in the **if** statements throughout the program. Such indentation enhances program readability.

Good Programming Practice 7.8

Indent the statement in the body of an **if** *structure to make the body of the structure stand out and to enhance program readability.*

```
<?xml version = "1.0"?>
<!DOCTYPE html PUBLIC "-//W3C//DTD XHTML 1.0 Strict//EN"
   "http://www.w3.org/TR/xhtml1/DTD/xhtml1-strict.dtd">

<!-- Fig. 7.14: comparison.html                         -->
<!-- Using if statements, relational operators          -->
<!-- and equality operators                             -->

<html xmlns = "http://www.w3.org/1999/xhtml">
   <head>
      <title>Performing Comparisons</title>

      <script type = "text/javascript">
         <!--
         var first,   // first string entered by user
             second,  // second string entered by user
             number1,       // first number to compare
             number2;       // second number to compare

         // read first number from user as a string
         first = window.prompt( "Enter first integer:", "0" );

         // read second number from user as a string
         second = window.prompt( "Enter second integer:", "0" );

         // convert numbers from strings to integers
         number1 = parseInt( first );
         number2 = parseInt( second );

         document.writeln( "<h1>Comparison Results</h1>" );
         document.writeln(
            "<table border = \"1\" width = \"100%\">" );

         if ( number1 == number2 )
            document.writeln( "<tr><td>" + number1 + " == " +
               number2 + "</td></tr>" );

         if ( number1 != number2 )
            document.writeln( "<tr><td>" + number1 + " != " +
               number2 + "</td></TR>" );

         if ( number1 < number2 )
            document.writeln( "<tr><td>" + number1 + " < "  +
               number2 + "</td></tr>" );

         if ( number1 > number2 )
            document.writeln( "<tr><td>" + number1 + " > " +
               number2 + "</td></tr>" );

         if ( number1 <= number2 )
            document.writeln( "<tr><td>" + number1 + " <= " +
               number2 + "</td></tr>" );

```

Fig. 7.15 Using equality and relational operators (part 1 of 3).

```
         if ( number1 >= number2 )
            document.writeln( "<tr><td>" + number1 + " >= " +
               number2 + "</td></tr>" );

         // Display results
         document.writeln( "</table>" );
         // -->
      </script>

   </head>
   <body>
      <p>Click Refresh (or Reload) to run the script again</p>
   </body>
</html>
```

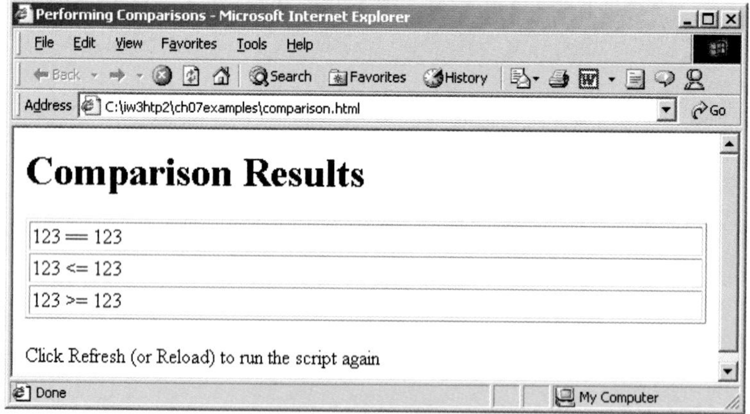

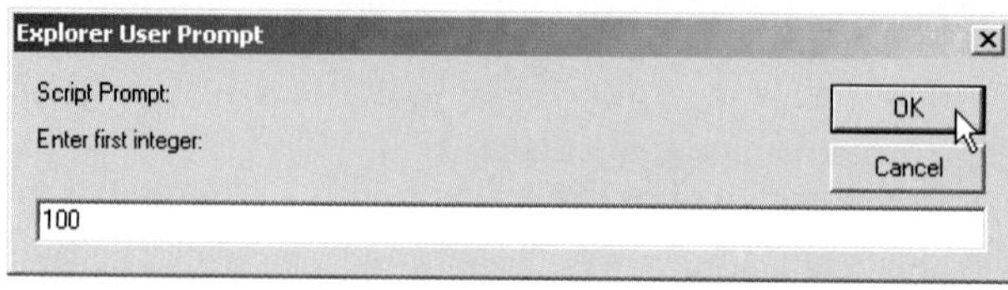

Fig. 7.15 Using equality and relational operators (part 2 of 3).

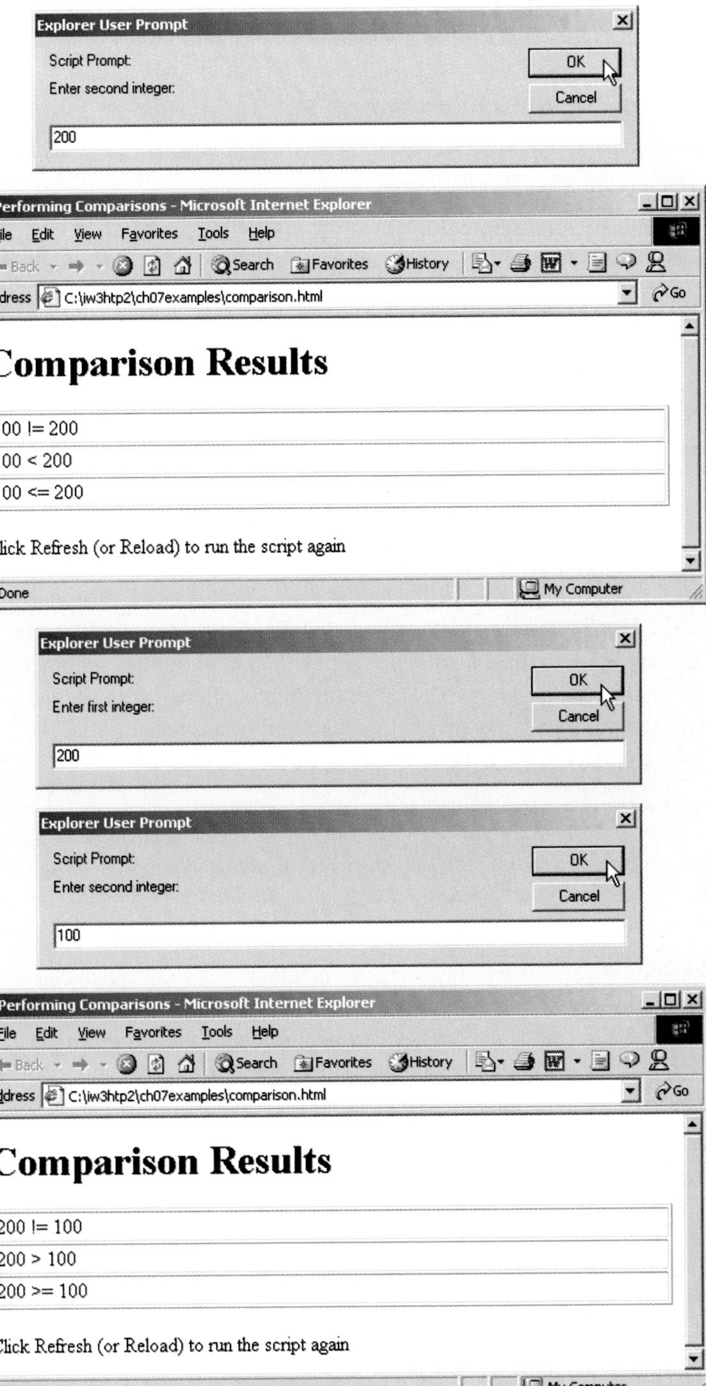

Fig. 7.15 Using equality and relational operators (part 3 of 3).

Good Programming Practice 7.9

Place only one statement per line in a program. This format enhances program readability.

Common Programming Error 7.13

Forgetting the left and right parentheses for the condition in an **if** *structure is a syntax error. The parentheses are required.*

Notice that there is no semicolon (**;**) at the end of the first line of each **if** structure. Such a semicolon would result in a logic error at execution time. For example,

```
if ( number1 == number2 ) ;
   document.writeln( "<tr><td>" + number1 + " == " +
      number2 + "</td></tr>" );
```

would actually be interpreted by JavaScript as

```
if ( number1 == number2 )
   ;

document.writeln( "<tr><td>" + number1 + " == " +
   number2 + "</td></tr>" );
```

where the semicolon on the line by itself—called the *empty statement*—is the statement to execute if the condition in the **if** structure is true. When the empty statement executes, no task is performed in the program. The program then continues with the assignment statement, which executes regardless of whether the condition is true or false.

Common Programming Error 7.14

Placing a semicolon immediately after the right parenthesis of the condition in an **if** *structure is normally a logic error. The semicolon would cause the body of the* **if** *structure to be empty, so the* **if** *structure itself would perform no action, regardless of whether its condition is true. Worse yet, the intended body statement of the* **if** *structure would now become a statement in sequence after the* **if** *structure and would always be executed.*

Notice the use of spacing in Fig. 7.15. Remember that whitespace characters, such as tabs, newlines and spaces, are normally ignored by the compiler. So, statements may be split over several lines and may be spaced according to the programmer's preferences without affecting the meaning of a program. However, it is incorrect to split identifiers and string literals. Ideally, statements should be kept small, but it is not always possible to do so.

Good Programming Practice 7.10

A lengthy statement may be spread over several lines. If a single statement must be split across lines, choose breaking points that make sense, such as after a comma in a comma-separated list or after an operator in a lengthy expression. If a statement is split across two or more lines, indent all subsequent lines.

The chart in Fig. 7.16 shows the precedence of the operators introduced in this chapter. The operators are shown from top to bottom in decreasing order of precedence. Notice that all of these operators, with the exception of the assignment operator, **=**, associate from left to right. Addition is left associative, so an expression like **x + y + z** is evaluated as if it had been written as **(x + y) + z**. The assignment operator, **=**, associates from right to left, so an expression like **x = y = 0** is evaluated as if it had been written as **x = (y = 0)**, which, as we will soon see, first assigns the value **0** to variable **y** and then assigns the result of that assignment, **0**, to **x**.

Good Programming Practice 7.11

Refer to the operator precedence chart when writing expressions containing many operators. Confirm that the operators in the expression are performed in the order in which you expect them to be performed. If you are uncertain about the order of evaluation in a complex expression, use parentheses to force the order, exactly as you would do in algebraic expressions. Be sure to observe that some operators, such as assignment (=), associate from right to left rather than from left to right.

We have introduced many important features of JavaScript, including how to display data, how to input data from the keyboard, how to perform calculations and how to make decisions. In Chapter 8, we build on the techniques of Chapter 7 as we introduce *structured programming*. You will become more familiar with indentation techniques. We will study how to specify and vary the order in which statements are executed; this order is called the *flow of control.*

7.7 JavaScript Internet and World Wide Web Resources

There are a tremendous number of resources for JavaScript programmers on the Internet and World Wide Web. This section lists a variety of JScript, JavaScript and ECMAScript resources available on the Internet and provides a brief description of each. Additional resources for these topics are presented in the subsequent chapters on JavaScript and in other chapters as necessary.

www.ecma.ch/ecma1/stand/ecma-262.htm
JScript is Microsoft's version of *JavaScript*—a scripting language that is standardized by the *ECMA (European Computer Manufacturer's Association)* as *ECMAScript*. This site is the home of the standard document for ECMAScript.

msdn.microsoft.com/scripting/default.htm
The *Microsoft Windows Script Technologies* page includes an overview of JScript, complete with tutorials, FAQs, demos, tools for downloading and newsgroups.

www.webteacher.com/javascript
Webteacher.com is an excellent source for tutorials that focus on teaching with detailed explanations and examples. This site is particularly useful for nonprogrammers.

Operators	Associativity	Type
`()`	left to right	parentheses
`*  /  %`	left to right	multiplicative
`+  -`	left to right	additive
`<  <=  >  >=`	left to right	relational
`==  !=`	left to right	equality
`=`	right to left	assignment

Fig. 7.16 Precedence and associativity of the operators discussed so far.

wsabstract.com
Website Abstraction is devoted to JavaScript and provides specialized tutorials and many free scripts. This site is good for beginners, as well as people with prior experience who are looking for help in a specific area of JavaScript.

www.webdeveloper.com/javascript
WebDeveloper.com provides tutorials, tools, and links to many free scripts.

SUMMARY

- The JavaScript language facilitates a disciplined approach to the design of computer programs that enhance Web pages.
- JScript is Microsoft's version of JavaScript—a scripting language that is standardized by the ECMA (European Computer Manufacturer's Association) as ECMAScript.
- The spacing displayed by a browser in a Web page is determined by the XHTML elements used to format the page.
- Often, JavaScripts appear in the **<head>** section of the XHTML document.
- The browser interprets the contents of the **<head>** section first.
- The **<script>** tag indicates to the browser that the text that follows is part of a script. Attribute **type** specifies the scripting language used in the script—such as **JavaScript**.
- A string of characters can be contained between double (**"**) or single (**'**) quotation marks.
- A string is sometimes called a character string, a message or a string literal.
- The browser's **document** object represents the XHTML document currently being displayed in the browser. The **document** object allows a script programmer to specify XHTML text to be displayed in the XHTML document.
- The browser contains a complete set of objects that allow script programmers to access and manipulate every element of an XHTML document.
- An object resides in the computer's memory and contains information used by the script. The term *object* normally implies that attributes (data) and behaviors (methods) are associated with the object. The object's methods use the attributes to provide useful services to the client of the object—the script that calls the methods.
- The **document** object's **writeln** method writes a line of XHTML text in the XHTML document.
- The parentheses following the name of a method contain the arguments that the method requires to perform its task (or its action).
- Using **writeln** to write a line of XHTML text into a **document** does not guarantee that a corresponding line of text will appear in the XHTML document. The text displayed is dependent on the contents of the string written, which is subsequently rendered by the browser. The browser will interpret the XHTML elements as it normally does to render the final text in the document.
- Every statement should end with a semicolon (also known as the statement terminator), although none is required by JavaScript.
- JavaScript is case sensitive. Not using the proper uppercase and lowercase letters is a syntax error.
- Sometimes it is useful to display information in windows called dialogs that "pop up" on the screen to grab the user's attention. Dialogs are typically used to display important messages to the user browsing the Web page. The browser's **window** object uses method **alert** to display an alert dialog. Method **alert** requires as its argument the string to be displayed.
- When a backslash is encountered in a string of characters, the next character is combined with the backslash to form an escape sequence. The escape sequence **\n** is the newline character. It causes the cursor in the XHTML document to move to the beginning of the next line in the dialog.

- The keyword **var** is used to declare the names of variables. A variable is a location in the computer's memory where a value can be stored for use by a program. Though you are not required to do so, you should declare all variables with a name in a **var** statement before they are used in a program.
- A variable name can be any valid identifier consisting of letters, digits, underscores (_) and dollar signs (**$**) that does not begin with a digit and does not contain any spaces.
- Declarations end with a semicolon (**;**) and can be split over several lines, with each variable in the declaration separated by a comma (forming a comma-separated list of variable names). Several variables may be declared in one declaration or in multiple declarations.
- Programmers often indicate the purpose of each variable in the program by placing a JavaScript comment at the end of each line in the declaration. A single-line comment begins with the characters **//** and terminates at the end of the line. Comments do not cause the browser to perform any action when the script is interpreted; rather, comments are ignored by the JavaScript interpreter.
- Multiple-line comments begin with delimiter **/*** and end with delimiter ***/**. All text between the delimiters of the comment is ignored by the compiler.
- The **window** object's **prompt** method displays a dialog into which the user can type a value. The first argument is a message (called a prompt) that directs the user to take a specific action. The optional second argument is the default string to display in the text field.
- A variable is assigned a value with an assignment statement, using the assignment operator, **=**. The **=** operator is called a binary operator, because it has two operands.
- Function **parseInt** converts its string argument to an integer.
- JavaScript has a version of the **+** operator for string concatenation that enables a string and a value of another data type (including another string) to be concatenated.
- Variable names correspond to locations in the computer's memory. Every variable has a name, a type, a size and a value.
- When a value is placed in a memory location, the value replaces the previous value in that location. When a value is read out of a memory location, the process is nondestructive.
- The arithmetic operators are binary operators, because they each operate on two operands.
- Operators in arithmetic expressions are applied in a precise sequence determined by the rules of operator precedence.
- Parentheses may be used to force the order of evaluation of operators to occur in any sequence desired by the programmer.
- When we say that operators are applied from left to right, we are referring to the associativity of the operators. Some operators associate from right to left.
- Java's **if** structure allows a program to make a decision based on the truth or falsity of a condition. If the condition is met (i.e., the condition is true), the statement in the body of the **if** structure is executed. If the condition is not met (i.e., the condition is false), the statement in the body of the **if** structure is not executed.
- Conditions in **if** structures can be formed by using the equality operators and relational operators.

TERMINOLOGY

\" double-quote escape sequence
\n newline escape sequence
<head> section of the XHTML document
<script></script>
addition operator (**+**)
alert dialog
alert method of the **window** object
argument to a method
arithmetic expressions in straight-line form
arithmetic operator

assignment operator (**=**)
assignment statement
attribute
automatic conversion
backslash (****) escape character
behavior
binary operator
blank line
case sensitive
character string
client of an object
comma-separated list
comment
condition
data
decision making
declaration
dialog
division operator (**/**)
document object
double quotation (**"**) marks
ECMA
ECMAScript
empty statement
equality operators
error message
escape sequence
European Computer Manufacturer's Association (ECMA)
false
identifier
if structure
inline scripting
integer
interpreter
JavaScript
JavaScript interpreter
JScript
location in the computer's memory
logic error
meaningful variable names
method
modulus operator (**%**)
multiple-line comment (**/*** and ***/**)
multiplication operator (*****)
name of a variable
object
operand
operator associativity
operator precedence
parentheses
parseInt function
perform an action
program
prompt
prompt dialog
prompt method of the **window** object
redundant parentheses
relational operators
remainder after division
rules of operator precedence
runtime error
script
scripting language
self-documenting
semicolon (**;**) statement terminator
single quotation (**'**) marks
single-line comment (**//**)
statement
string concatenation
string concatenation operator (**+**)
string literal
string of characters
subtraction operator (**-**)
syntax error
text field
true
type attribute of the **<script>** tag
type of a variable
value of a variable
var keyword
variable
violation of the language rules
whitespace characters
whole number
window object
write method of the **document** object
writeln method of the **document** object

SELF-REVIEW EXERCISES

7.1 Fill in the blanks in each of the following statements:

a) __________ begins a single-line comment.

b) Every statement should end with a __________.

c) The __________ structure is used to make decisions.
d) __________, __________, __________ and __________ are known as whitespace.
e) The __________ object displays alert dialogs and prompt dialogs.
f) __________ are reserved for use by JavaScript.
g) Methods __________ and __________ of the __________ object write XHTML text into an XHTML document.

7.2 State whether each of the following is *true* or *false*. If *false*, explain why.
a) Comments cause the computer to print the text after the **//** on the screen when the program is executed.
b) JavaScript considers the variables **number** and **NuMbEr** to be identical.
c) The modulus operator (**%**) can be used only with any numeric operands.
d) The arithmetic operators *****, **/**, **%**, **+** and **-** all have the same level of precedence.
e) Method **parseInt** converts an integer to a string.

7.3 Write JavaScript statements to accomplish each of the following tasks:
a) Declare variables **c**, **thisIsAVariable**, **q76354** and **number**.
b) Display a dialog asking the user to enter an integer. Show a default value of **0** in the text field.
c) Convert a string to an integer, and store the converted value in variable **age**. Assume that the string is stored in **stringValue**.
d) If the variable **number** is not equal to **7**, display **"The variable number is not equal to 7"** in a message dialog.
e) Output a line of XHTML text that will display the message **"This is a JavaScript program"** on one line in the XHTML document.
f) Output a line of XHTML text that will display the message **"This is a JavaScript program"** on two lines in the XHTML document. Use only one statement.

7.4 Identify and correct the errors in each of the following statements:
a)
```
if ( c < 7 );
   window.alert( "c is less than 7" );
```
b)
```
if ( c => 7 )
   window.alert( "c is equal to or greater than 7" );
```

7.5 Write a statement (or comment) to accomplish each of the following tasks:
a) State that a program will calculate the product of three integers.
b) Declare the variables **x**, **y**, **z** and **result**.
c) Declare the variables **xVal**, **yVal** and **zVal**.
d) Prompt the user to enter the first value, read the value from the user and store it in the variable **xVal**.
e) Prompt the user to enter the second value, read the value from the user and store it in the variable **yVal**.
f) Prompt the user to enter the third value, read the value from the user and store it in the variable **zVal**.
g) Convert **xVal** to an integer, and store the result in the variable **x**.
h) Convert **yVal** to an integer, and store the result in the variable **y**.
i) Convert **zVal** to an integer, and store the result in the variable **z**.
j) Compute the product of the three integers contained in variables **x**, **y** and **z**, and assign the result to the variable **result**.
k) Write a line of XHTML text containing the string **"The product is "** followed by the value of the variable **result**.

7.6 Using the statements you wrote in Exercise 7.5, write a complete program that calculates and prints the product of three integers.

ANSWERS TO SELF-REVIEW EXERCISES

7.1 a) `//`. b) Semicolon (`;`). c) `if`. d) Blank lines, space characters, newline characters and tab characters. e) `window`. f) Keywords. g) `write`, `writeln`, `document`.

7.2 a) False. Comments do not cause any action to be performed when the program is executed. They are used to document programs and improve their readability. b) False. JavaScript is case sensitive, so these variables are distinct. c) True. d) False. The operators `*`, `/` and `%` are on the same level of precedence, and the operators `+` and `-` are on a lower level of precedence. e) False. Function `parseInt` converts a string to an integer value.

7.3
a) `var c, thisIsAVariable, q76354, number;`
b) `value = window.prompt( "Enter an integer", "0" );`
c) `var age = parseInt( stringValue );`
d)
```
if ( number != 7 )
   window.alert( "The variable number is not equal to 7" );
```
e) `document.writeln( "This is a JavaScript program" );`
f)
```
document.writeln( "This is a<br />JavaScript program" );
```

7.4 a) Error: There should not be a semicolon after the right parenthesis of the condition in the `if` statement. Correction: Remove the semicolon after the right parenthesis. [*Note*: The result of this error is that the output statement is executed whether or not the condition in the `if` statement is true. The semicolon after the right parenthesis is considered an empty statement—a statement that does nothing.]
b) Error: The relational operator `=>` is incorrect.
Correction: Change `=>` to `>=`.

7.5
a) `// Calculate the product of three integers`
b) `var x, y, z, result;`
c) `var xVal, yVal, zVal;`
d) `xVal = window.prompt( "Enter first integer:", "0" );`
e) `yVal = window.prompt( "Enter second integer:", "0" );`
f) `zVal = window.prompt( "Enter third integer:", "0" );`
g) `x = parseInt( xVal );`
h) `y = parseInt( yVal );`
i) `z = parseInt( zVal );`
j) `result = x * y * z;`
k)
```
document.writeln(
   "<h1>The product is " + result + "</h1>" );
```

7.6 The program is as follows:

```
<?xml version = "1.0"?>
<!DOCTYPE html PUBLIC "-//W3C//DTD XHTML 1.0 Strict//EN"
   "http://www.w3.org/TR/xhtml1/DTD/xhtml1-strict.dtd">

<!-- Exercise 7.6: product.html -->

<html xmlns = "http://www.w3.org/1999/xhtml">
   <head>
      <title>Product of Three Integers</title>

      <script type = "text/javascript">
         <!--
         // Calculate the product of three integers
```

```
         var x, y, z, result;
         var xVal, yVal, zVal;

         xVal = window.prompt( "Enter first integer:", "0" );
         yVal = window.prompt( "Enter second integer:", "0" );
         zVal = window.prompt( "Enter third integer:", "0" );

         x = parseInt( xVal );
         y = parseInt( yVal );
         z = parseInt( zVal );

         result = x * y * z;
         document.writeln( "<h1>The product is " +
            result + "<h1>" );
         // -->
      </script>

   </head><body></body>
</html>
```

EXERCISES

7.7 Fill in the blanks in each of the following statements:

a) __________ are used to document a program and improve its readability.

b) A dialog capable of receiving input from the user is displayed with method __________ of object __________.

c) A JavaScript statement that makes a decision is __________.

d) Calculations are normally performed by __________ statements.

e) A dialog capable of showing a message to the user is displayed with method __________ of object __________.

7.8 Write JavaScript statements that accomplish each of the following tasks:

a) Display the message **"Enter two numbers"** using the **window** object.

b) Assign the product of variables **b** and **c** to variable **a**.

c) State that a program performs a sample payroll calculation [*Hint*: Use text that helps to document a program].

7.9 State whether each of the following is *true* or *false*. If *false*, explain why.

a) JavaScript operators are evaluated from left to right.

b) The following are all valid variable names: **_under_bar_**, **m928134**, **t5**, **j7**, **her_sales$**, **his_$account_total**, **a**, **b$**, **c**, **z**, **z2**.

c) A valid JavaScript arithmetic expression with no parentheses is evaluated from left to right.

d) The following are all invalid variable names: **3g**, **87**, **67h2**, **h22**, **2h**.

7.10 Fill in the blanks in each of the following statements:

a) What arithmetic operations have the same precedence as multiplication? __________.

b) When parentheses are nested, which set of parentheses is evaluated first in an arithmetic expression? __________.

c) A location in the computer's memory that may contain different values at various times throughout the execution of a program is called a __________.

7.11 What displays in the message dialog when each of the given JavaScript statements is performed? Assume that **x = 2** and **y = 3**.

a) `window.alert( "x = " + x );`
b) `window.alert( "The value of x + x is " + ( x + x ) );`
c) `window.alert( "x =" );`
d) `window.alert( ( x + y ) + " = " + ( y + x ) );`

7.12 Which of the following JavaScript statements contain variables whose values are destroyed (i.e., changed or replaced)?

a) `p = i + j + k + 7;`
b) `window.alert( "variables whose values are destroyed" );`
c) `window.alert( "a = 5" );`
d) `stringVal = window.prompt( "Enter string:" );`

7.13 Given $y = ax^3 + 7$, which of the following are correct statements for this equation?

a) `y = a * x * x * x + 7;`
b) `y = a * x * x * (x + 7);`
c) `y = (a * x) * x * (x + 7);`
d) `y = (a * x) * x * x + 7;`
e) `y = a * (x * x * x) + 7;`
f) `y = a * x * (x * x + 7);`

7.14 State the order of evaluation of the operators in each of the following JavaScript statements, and show the value of **`x`** after each statement is performed.

a) `x = 7 + 3 * 6 / 2 - 1;`
b) `x = 2 % 2 + 2 * 2 - 2 / 2;`
c) `x = ( 3 * 9 * ( 3 + ( 9 * 3 / ( 3 ) ) ) );`

7.15 Write a script that displays the numbers 1 to 4 on the same line, with each pair of adjacent numbers separated by one space. Write the program using the following methods:

a) Using one **`document.writeln`** statement.
b) Using four **`document.write`** statements.

7.16 Write a script that asks the user to enter two numbers, obtains the two numbers from the user and outputs XHTML text that displays the sum, product, difference and quotient of the two numbers. Use the techniques shown in Fig. 7.6.

7.17 Write a script that asks the user to enter two integers, obtains the numbers from the user and outputs XHTML text that displays the larger number followed by the words "**`is larger`**" in an information message dialog. If the numbers are equal, output XHTML text that displays the message "**`These numbers are equal`**." Use the techniques shown in Fig. 7.15.

7.18 Write a script that inputs three integers from the user and displays the sum, average, product, smallest and largest of the numbers in an **`alert`** dialog.

7.19 Write a script that inputs from the user the radius of a circle and outputs XHTML text that displays the circle's diameter, circumference and area. Use the constant value 3.14159 for π. Use the GUI techniques shown in Fig. 7.6. [*Note*: You may also use the predefined constant **`Math.PI`** for the value of π. This constant is more precise than the value 3.14159. The **`Math`** object is defined by JavaScript and provides many common mathematical capabilities.] Use the following formulas (r is the radius): $diameter = 2r$, $circumference = 2\pi r$, $area = \pi r^2$.

7.20 Write a script that outputs XHTML text that displays in the XHTML document an oval, an arrow and a diamond using asterisks (**`*`**), as follows [*Note*: Use the **`<pre>`** and **`</pre>`** tags to specify that the asterisks should be displayed using a fixed-width font]:

7.21 Modify the program you created in Exercise 7.20 to display the shapes without using the **<pre>** and **</pre>** tags. Does the program display the shapes exactly as in Exercise 7.20?

7.22 What does the following code print?

```
document.writeln( "*\n**\n***\n****\n*****" );
```

7.23 What does the following code print?

```
document.writeln( "*" );
document.writeln( "***" );
document.writeln( "*****" );
document.writeln( "****" );
document.writeln( "**" );
```

7.24 What does the following code print?

```
document.write( "*<br />" );
document.write( "***<br />" );
document.write( "*****<br />" );
document.write( "****<br />" );
document.writeln( "**" );
```

7.25 What does the following code print?

```
document.write( "*<br />" );
document.writeln( "***" );
document.writeln( "*****" );
document.write( "****<br />" );
document.writeln( "**" );
```

7.26 Write a script that reads five integers and determines and outputs XHTML text that displays the largest integer and the smallest integer in the group. Use only the programming techniques you learned in this chapter.

7.27 Write a script that reads an integer and determines and outputs XHTML text that displays whether it is odd or even. [*Hint*: Use the modulus operator. An even number is a multiple of 2. Any multiple of 2 leaves a remainder of zero when divided by 2.]

7.28 Write a script that reads in two integers and determines and outputs XHTML text that displays whether the first is a multiple of the second. [*Hint*: Use the modulus operator.]

7.29 Write a script that outputs XHTML text that displays in the XHTML document a checkerboard pattern, as follows:

7.30 Write a script that inputs five numbers and determines and outputs XHTML text that displays the number of negative numbers input, the number of positive numbers input and the number of zeros input.

7.31 Using only the programming techniques you learned in this chapter, write a script that calculates the squares and cubes of the numbers from 0 to 10 and outputs XHTML text that displays the resulting values in an XHTML table format, as follows:

number	square	cube
0	0	0
1	1	1
2	4	8
3	9	27
4	16	64
5	25	125
6	36	216
7	49	343
8	64	512
9	81	729
10	100	1000

[*Note*: This program does not require any input from the user.]

JavaScript: Control Structures 1

Objectives

- To understand basic problem-solving techniques.
- To be able to develop algorithms through the process of top-down, stepwise refinement.
- To be able to use the **`if`** and **`if/else`** selection structures to choose among alternative actions.
- To be able to use the **`while`** repetition structure to execute statements in a script repeatedly.
- To understand counter-controlled repetition and sentinel-controlled repetition.
- To be able to use the increment, decrement and assignment operators.

Let's all move one place on.
Lewis Carroll

The wheel is come full circle.
William Shakespeare, *King Lear*

How many apples fell on Newton's head before he took the hint!
Robert Frost, Comment

Outline

8.1 Introduction

Before writing a script to solve a problem, it is essential to have a thorough understanding of the problem and a carefully planned approach to solving the problem. When writing a script, it is equally essential to understand the types of building blocks that are available and to employ proven program-construction principles. In this chapter and in Chapter 9, we discuss these issues in our presentation of the theory and principles of structured programming. The techniques you learn here are applicable to most high-level languages, including JavaScript.

8.2 Algorithms

Any computing problem can be solved by executing a series of actions in a specific order. A *procedure* for solving a problem in terms of

1. the *actions* to be executed and
2. the *order* in which the actions are to be executed

is called an *algorithm*. The following example demonstrates that correctly specifying the order in which the actions are to execute is important.

Consider the "rise-and-shine algorithm" followed by one junior executive for getting out of bed and going to work: (1) Get out of bed, (2) take off pajamas, (3) take a shower, (4) get dressed, (5) eat breakfast, (6) carpool to work. This routine gets the executive to work well prepared to make critical decisions. Suppose, however, that the same steps are performed in a slightly different order: (1) Get out of bed, (2) take off pajamas, (3) get dressed, (4) take a shower, (5) eat breakfast, (6) carpool to work. In this case, our junior executive shows up for work soaking wet. Specifying the order in which statements are to be executed in a computer program is called *program control*. In this chapter and Chapter 9, we investigate the program-control capabilities of JavaScript.

8.3 Pseudocode

Pseudocode is an artificial and informal language that helps programmers develop algorithms. The pseudocode we present here is useful for developing algorithms that will be converted to structured portions of JavaScript programs. Pseudocode is similar to everyday English; it is convenient and user friendly, although it is not an actual computer programming language.

Software Engineering Observation 8.1

Pseudocode is often used to "think out" a program during the program design process. Then the pseudocode program is converted to a programming language such as JavaScript.

The style of pseudocode we present consists purely of characters, so programmers may conveniently type pseudocode in an editor program. The computer can produce a fresh printed copy of a pseudocode program on demand. Carefully prepared pseudocode may be converted easily to a corresponding JavaScript program. This process is done in many cases simply by replacing pseudocode statements with their JavaScript equivalents. In this chapter, we give several examples of pseudocode.

Pseudocode normally describes only executable statements—the actions that are performed when the program is converted from pseudocode to JavaScript and is run. Declarations are not executable statements. For example, the declaration

```
var value1;
```

instructs the JavaScript interpreter to reserve space in memory for the variable **value1**. This declaration does not cause any action—such as input, output or a calculation—to occur when the script executes. Some programmers choose to list variables and mention the purpose of each variable at the beginning of a pseudocode program.

8.4 Control Structures

Normally, statements in a program execute one after the other in the order in which they are written. This process is called *sequential execution.* Various JavaScript statements we will soon discuss enable the programmer to specify that the next statement to execute may be one other than the next one in sequence. This process is called *transfer of control.*

During the 1960s, it became clear that the indiscriminate use of transfers of control was the root of much difficulty experienced by software development groups. The finger of blame was pointed at the ***goto*** *statement*, which allows the programmer to specify a transfer of control to one of a wide range of possible destinations in a program. The notion of so-called *structured programming* became almost synonymous with "***goto*** elimination." JavaScript does not have a **goto** statement.

The research of Bohm and Jacopini[1] demonstrated that programs could be written without any **goto** statements. The challenge of the era for programmers was to shift their styles to "**goto**-less programming." It was not until the 1970s that programmers started taking structured programming seriously. The were been impressive, as software development groups reported reduced development times, more frequent on-time delivery of systems and more frequent within-budget completion of software projects. The key to these successes is that structured programs are clearer, easier to debug and modify and more likely to be bug free in the first place.

Bohm and Jacopini's work demonstrated that all programs could be written in terms of only three *control structures*, namely the *sequence structure*, the *selection structure* and the *repetition structure*. The sequence structure is built into JavaScript. Unless directed otherwise, the computer executes JavaScript statements one after the other in the order in which they are written (i.e., in sequence). The *flowchart* segment of Fig. 8.1 illustrates a typical sequence structure in which two calculations are performed in order.

A flowchart is a graphical representation of an algorithm or of a portion of an algorithm. Flowcharts are drawn using certain special-purpose symbols such as rectangles, diamonds, ovals and small circles; these symbols are connected by arrows called *flowlines*, which indicate the order in which the actions of the algorithm execute.

Like pseudocode, flowcharts often are useful for developing and representing algorithms, although pseudocode is strongly preferred by many programmers. Flowcharts show clearly how control structures operate; that is all we use them for in this text. The reader should carefully compare the pseudocode and flowchart representations of each control structure.

Consider the flowchart segment for the sequence structure on the left side of Fig. 8.1. We use the *rectangle symbol* (or *action symbol*) to indicate any type of action, including a calculation or an input/output operation. The flowlines in the figure indicate the order in which the actions are performed—the first action adds **grade** to **total**, then the second action adds **1** to **counter**. JavaScript allows us to have as many actions as we want in a sequence structure. As we will soon see, anywhere a single action may be placed, we may place several actions in sequence.

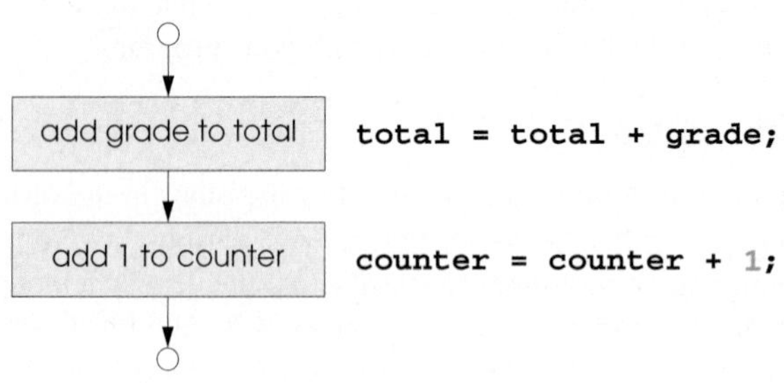

Fig. 8.1 Flowcharting JavaScript's sequence structure.

1. Bohm, C., and G. Jacopini, "Flow Diagrams, Turing Machines, and Languages with Only Two Formation Rules," *Communications of the ACM*, Vol. 9, No. 5, May 1966, pp. 336–371.

In a flowchart that represents a *complete* algorithm, an *oval symbol* containing the word "Begin" is the first symbol used; an oval symbol containing the word "End" indicates where the algorithm ends. In a flowchart that shows only a portion of an algorithm, as in Fig. 8.1, the oval symbols are omitted in favor of using *small circle symbols*, also called *connector symbols*.

Perhaps the most important flowcharting symbol is the *diamond symbol*, also called the *decision symbol*, which indicates that a decision is to be made. We discuss the diamond symbol in the next section.

JavaScript provides three types of selection structures; we discuss each in this chapter and in Chapter 9. The **`if`** selection structure performs (selects) an action if a condition is true or skips the action if the condition is false. The **`if/else`** selection structure performs an action if a condition is true and performs a different action if the condition is false. The **`switch`** selection structure (Chapter 9) performs one of many different actions, depending on the value of an expression.

The **`if`** structure is called a *single-selection structure*, because it selects or ignores a single action (or, as we will soon see, a single group of actions). The **`if/else`** structure is called a *double-selection structure*, because it selects between two different actions (or groups of actions). The **`switch`** structure is called a *multiple-selection structure*, because it selects among many different actions (or groups of actions).

JavaScript provides four repetition structure types, namely **`while`**, **`do/while`**, **`for`** and **`for/in`**. (**`do/while`** and **`for`** are covered in Chapter 9; **`for/in`** is covered in Chapter 11.) Each of the words **`if`**, **`else`**, **`switch`**, **`while`**, **`do`**, **`for`** and **`in`** is a JavaScript *keyword*. These words are reserved by the language to implement various features, such as JavaScript's control structures. Keywords cannot be used as identifiers (such as for variable names). A complete list of JavaScript keywords is shown in Fig. 8.2.

Common Programming Error 8.1

Using a keyword as an identifier is a syntax error.

JavaScript Keywords				
`break`	`case`	`continue`	`delete`	`do`
`else`	`false`	`for`	`function`	`if`
`in`	`new`	`null`	`return`	`switch`
`this`	`true`	`typeof`	`var`	`void`
`while`	`with`			
Keywords that are reserved, but not used by JavaScript				
`catch`	`class`	`const`	`debugger`	`default`
`enum`	`export`	`extends`	`finally`	`import`
`super`	`try`			

Fig. 8.2 JavaScript keywords.

As we have shown, JavaScript has only eight control structures: sequence, three types of selection and four types of repetition. Each program is formed by combining as many of each type of control structure as is appropriate for the algorithm the program implements. As with the sequence structure in Fig. 8.1, we will see that each control structure is flowcharted with two small circle symbols, one at the entry point to the control structure and one at the exit point.

Single-entry/single-exit control structures make it easy to build programs; the control structures are attached to one another by connecting the exit point of one control structure to the entry point of the next. This process is similar to the way in which a child stacks building blocks, so we call it *control-structure stacking*. We will learn that there is only one other way in which control structures may be connected—*control-structure nesting*. Thus, algorithms in JavaScript programs are constructed from only eight different types of control structures combined in only two ways.

8.5 `if` Selection Structure

A selection structure is used to choose among alternative courses of action in a program. For example, suppose that the passing grade on an examination is 60 (out of 100). Then the pseudocode statement

If student's grade is greater than or equal to 60
    Print "Passed"

determines if the condition "student's grade is greater than or equal to 60" is true or false. If the condition is true, then "Passed" is printed, and the next pseudocode statement in order is "performed" (remember that pseudocode is not a real programming language). If the condition is false, the print statement is ignored, and the next pseudocode statement in order is performed. Note that the second line of this selection structure is indented. Such indentation is optional, but it is highly recommended, because it emphasizes the inherent structure of structured programs. The JavaScript interpreter ignores whitespace characters—blanks, tabs and newlines used for indentation and vertical spacing. Programmers insert these whitespace characters to enhance program clarity.

Good Programming Practice 8.1

Consistently applying reasonable indentation conventions throughout your programs improves program readability. We suggest a fixed-size tab of about 1/4 inch or three spaces per indent.

The preceding pseudocode *If* statement can be written in JavaScript as

```
if ( studentGrade >= 60 )
   document.writeln( "Passed" );
```

Notice that the JavaScript code corresponds closely to the pseudocode. This similarity is the reason that pseudocode is a useful program development tool. The statement in the body of the **`if`** structure outputs the character string **`"Passed"`** in the XHTML document.

The flowchart in Fig. 8.3 illustrates the single-selection **`if`** structure. This flowchart contains what is perhaps the most important flowcharting symbol—the *diamond symbol* (or *decision symbol*), which indicates that a decision is to be made. The decision symbol contains an expression, such as a condition, that can be either ***`true`*** or ***`false`***. The decision symbol has two flowlines emerging from it. One indicates the path to follow in the program when the expression in the symbol is true; the other indicates the path to follow in the program when the expression is false. A decision can be made on any expression that evaluates to a value of JavaScript's boolean type (i.e., any expression that evaluates to **`true`** or **`false`**).

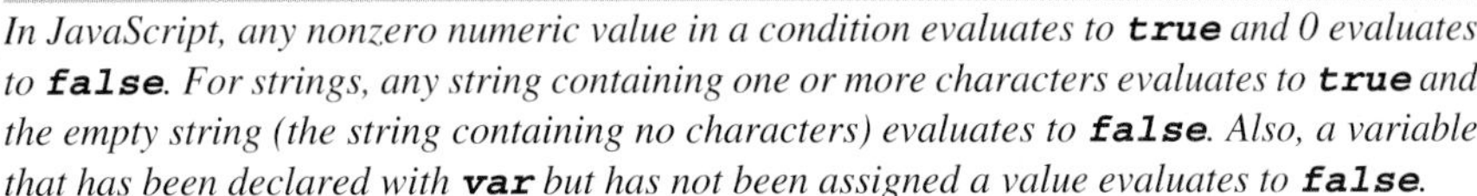

Software Engineering Observation 8.2

In JavaScript, any nonzero numeric value in a condition evaluates to **`true`** *and 0 evaluates to* **`false`**. *For strings, any string containing one or more characters evaluates to* **`true`** *and the empty string (the string containing no characters) evaluates to* **`false`**. *Also, a variable that has been declared with* **`var`** *but has not been assigned a value evaluates to* **`false`**.

Note that the **`if`** structure is a single-entry/single-exit structure. We will soon learn that the flowcharts for the remaining control structures also contain (besides small circle symbols and flowlines) only rectangle symbols, to indicate the actions to be performed, and diamond symbols, to indicate decisions to be made. This type of flowchart represents the *action/decision model of programming.*

We can envision eight bins, each containing only control structures of one of the eight types. These control structures are empty. Nothing is written in the rectangles or in the diamonds. The programmer's task, then, is to assemble a program from as many of each type of control structure as the algorithm demands, combining the control structures in only two possible ways (stacking or nesting), then filling in the actions and decisions in a manner appropriate for the algorithm. We will discuss the variety of ways in which actions and decisions may be written.

8.6 `if/else` Selection Structure

The **`if`** selection structure performs an indicated action only when the condition evaluates to **`true`**; otherwise, the action is skipped. The **`if/else`** selection structure allows the programmer to specify that a different action is to be performed when the condition is true than when the condition is false. For example, the pseudocode statement

If student's grade is greater than or equal to 60
Print "Passed"
Else
Print "Failed"

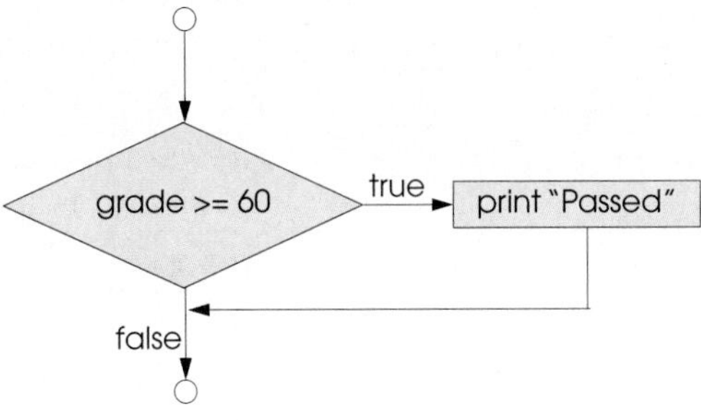

Fig. 8.3 Flowcharting the single-selection **`if`** structure.

prints *Passed* if the student's grade is greater than or equal to 60 and prints *Failed* if the student's grade is less than 60. In either case, after printing occurs, the next pseudocode statement in sequence (i.e., the next statement after the whole **if/else** structure) is performed. Note that the body of the *Else* part of the structure is also indented.

Good Programming Practice 8.2

*Indent both body statements of an **if/else** structure.*

The indentation convention you choose should be applied carefully throughout your programs (both in pseudocode and in JavaScript). It is difficult to read programs that do not use uniform spacing conventions.

The preceding pseudocode *If/Else* structure may be written in JavaScript as

```
if ( studentGrade >= 60 )
   document.writeln( "Passed" );
else
   document.writeln( "Failed" );
```

The flowchart in Fig. 8.4 nicely illustrates the flow of control in the **if/else** structure. Once again, note that the only symbols in the flowchart (besides small circles and arrows) are rectangles (for actions) and a diamond (for a decision). We continue to emphasize this action/decision model of computing. Imagine again a deep bin containing as many empty double-selection structures as might be needed to build a JavaScript algorithm. The programmer's job is to assemble the selection structures (by stacking and nesting) with other control structures required by the algorithm and to fill in the empty rectangles and empty diamonds with actions and decisions appropriate to the algorithm's implementation.

JavaScript provides an operator, called the *conditional operator* (**?:**), that is closely related to the **if/else** structure. The operator **?:** is JavaScript's only *ternary operator*—it takes three operands. The operands together with the **?:** form a *conditional expression.* The first operand is a boolean expression, the second is the value for the conditional expression if the condition evaluates to true and the third is the value for the conditional expression if the condition evaluates to false. For example, the statement

```
document.writeln(
   studentGrade >= 60 ? "Passed" : "Failed" );
```

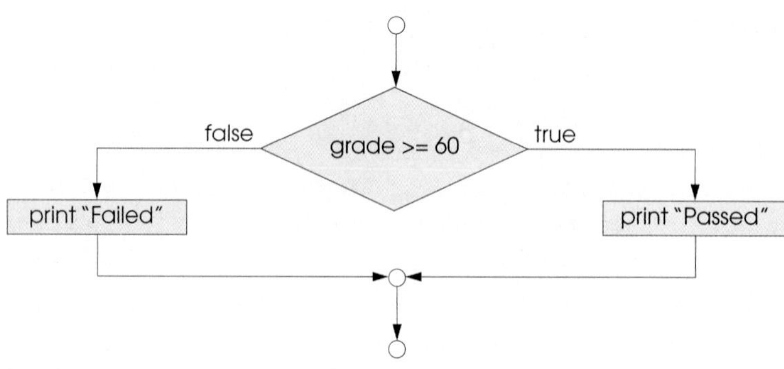

Fig. 8.4 Flowcharting the double-selection **if/else** structure.

contains a conditional expression that evaluates to the string **"Passed"** if the condition **studentGrade >= 60** is true and evaluates to the string **"Failed"** if the condition is false. Thus, this statement with the conditional operator performs essentially the same operation as the preceding **if/else** structure. The precedence of the conditional operator is low, so the entire conditional expression is normally placed in parentheses to ensure that it evaluates correctly.

*Nested **if/else** structures* test for multiple cases by placing **if/else** structures inside **if/else** structures. For example, the following pseudocode statement will print **A** for exam grades greater than or equal to 90, **B** for grades in the range 80 to 89, **C** for grades in the range 70 to 79, **D** for grades in the range 60 to 69 and **F** for all other grades:

```
If student's grade is greater than or equal to 90
     Print "A"
Else
     If student's grade is greater than or equal to 80
          Print "B"
     Else
          If student's grade is greater than or equal to 70
               Print "C"
          Else
               If student's grade is greater than or equal to 60
                    Print "D"
               Else
                    Print "F"
```

This pseudocode may be written in JavaScript as

```
if ( studentGrade >= 90 )
   document.writeln( "A" );
else
   if ( studentGrade >= 80 )
      document.writeln( "B" );
   else
      if ( studentGrade >= 70 )
         document.writeln( "C" );
      else
         if ( studentGrade >= 60 )
            document.writeln( "D" );
         else
            document.writeln( "F" );
```

If **studentGrade** is greater than or equal to 90, the first four conditions will be true, but only the **document.writeln** statement after the first test will execute. After that particular **document.writeln** executes, the **else** part of the outer **if/else** structure is skipped.

Good Programming Practice 8.3

If there are several levels of indentation, each level should be indented the same additional amount of space.

Most JavaScript programmers prefer to write the preceding **if** structure as

```
if ( grade >= 90 )
   document.writeln( "A" );
else if ( grade >= 80 )
   document.writeln( "B" );
else if ( grade >= 70 )
   document.writeln( "C" );
else if ( grade >= 60 )
   document.writeln( "D" );
else
   document.writeln( "F" );
```

The two forms are equivalent. The latter form is popular because it avoids the deep indentation of the code to the right. Such deep indentation often leaves little room on a line, forcing lines to be split and decreasing program readability.

It is important to note that the JavaScript interpreter always associates an **else** with the previous **if**, unless told to do otherwise by the placement of braces (**{}**). This situation is referred to as the *dangling-else problem*. For example,

```
if ( x > 5 )
   if ( y > 5 )
      document.writeln( "x and y are > 5" );
else
   document.writeln( "x is <= 5" );
```

appears to indicate with its indentation that if **x** is greater than **5**, the **if** structure in its body determines whether **y** is also greater than **5**. If so, the body of the nested **if** structure outputs the string **"x and y are > 5"**. Otherwise, it *appears* that if **x** is not greater than **5**, the **else** part of the **if/else** structure outputs the string **"x is <= 5"**.

Beware! The preceding nested **if** structure does not execute as it appears. The interpreter actually interprets the preceding structure as

```
if ( x > 5 )
   if ( y > 5 )
      document.writeln( "x and y are > 5" );
   else
      document.writeln( "x is <= 5" );
```

in which the body of the first **if** structure is a nested **if/else** structure. This structure tests whether **x** is greater than **5**. If so, execution continues by testing whether **y** is also greater than **5**. If the second condition is true, the proper string—**"x and y are > 5"**—is displayed. However, if the second condition is false, the string **"x is <= 5"** is displayed, even though we know that **x** is greater than **5**.

To force the preceding nested **if** structure to execute as it was intended originally, the structure must be written as follows:

```
if ( x > 5 ) {
   if ( y > 5 )
      document.writeln( "x and y are > 5" );
}
else
   document.writeln( "x is <= 5" );
```

The braces (**{}**) indicate to the interpreter that the second **if** structure is in the body of the first **if** structure and that the **else** is matched with the first **if** structure. In Exercises 8.21 and 8.22, you will investigate the dangling-else problem further.

The **if** selection structure expects only one statement in its body. To include several statements in the body of an **if**, enclose the statements in braces (**{** and **}**). A set of statements contained within a pair of braces is called a *compound statement* or a *block*.

Software Engineering Observation 8.3

A compound statement can be placed anywhere in a program that a single statement can be placed.

Software Engineering Observation 8.4

Unlike individual statements, a compound statement does not end with a semicolon. However, each statement within the braces of a compound statement should end with a semicolon.

The following example includes a compound statement in the **else** part of an **if/else** structure:

```
if ( grade >= 60 )
   document.writeln( "Passed" );
else {
   document.writeln( "Failed<br />" );
   document.writeln( "You must take this course again." );
}
```

In this case, if **grade** is less than 60, the program executes both statements in the body of the **else** and prints

```
Failed.
You must take this course again.
```

Notice the braces surrounding the two statements in the **else** clause. These braces are important. Without the braces, the statement

```
document.writeln( "You must take this course again." );
```

would be outside the body of the **else** part of the **if** and would execute regardless of whether the grade is less than 60.

Common Programming Error 8.2

Forgetting one or both of the braces that delimit a compound statement can lead to syntax errors or logic errors.

Syntax errors (such as when one brace in a compound statement is left out of the program) are caught by the interpreter when it attempts to interpret the code containing the syntax error. A *logic error* (such as the one caused when both braces in a compound statement are left out of the program) also has its effect at execution time. A *fatal logic error* causes a program to fail and terminate prematurely. A *nonfatal logic error* allows a program to continue executing, but the program produces incorrect results.

Software Engineering Observation 8.5

Just as a compound statement can be placed anywhere a single statement can be placed, it is also possible to have no statement at all (the empty statement) in such places. The empty statement is represented by placing a semicolon (`;`) where a statement would normally be.

Common Programming Error 8.3

Placing a semicolon after the condition in an `if` structure leads to a logic error in single-selection `if` structures and a syntax error in double-selection `if` structures (if the `if` part contains a nonempty body statement).

Good Programming Practice 8.4

Some programmers prefer to type the beginning and ending braces of compound statements before typing the individual statements within the braces. This procedure helps the programmers avoid omitting one or both of the braces.

8.7 `while` Repetition Structure

A *repetition structure* allows the programmer to specify that a script should repeat an action while some condition remains true. The pseudocode statement

While there are more items on my shopping list
  Purchase next item and cross it off my list

describes the repetition that occurs during a shopping trip. The condition "there are more items on my shopping list" may be true or false. If it is true, then the action "Purchase next item and cross it off my list" is performed. This action will be performed repeatedly while the condition remains true. The statement(s) contained in the *While* repetition structure constitute the body of the *While*. The body of the *While* structure may be a single statement or a compound statement. Eventually, the condition becomes false (i.e., when the last item on the shopping list has been purchased and crossed off the list). At this point, the repetition terminates, and the first pseudocode statement after the repetition structure executes.

Common Programming Error 8.4

Not providing in the body of a `while` structure an action that eventually causes the condition in the `while` structure to become false is a logic error. Normally, such a repetition structure will never terminate—an error called an "infinite loop." Browsers handle infinite loops differently. For example, Internet Explorer allows the user to terminate the script containing the infinite loop.

Common Programming Error 8.5

Remember that JavaScript is a case-sensitive language. Spelling the keyword `while` with an uppercase `W`, as in `While`, is a syntax error. All of JavaScript's reserved keywords, such as `while`, `if` and `else`, contain only lowercase letters.

As an example of a **`while`** structure, consider a program segment designed to find the first power of 2 larger than 1000. Variable **`product`** begins with the value 2. The structure is as follows:

```
var product = 2;

while ( product <= 1000 )
   product = 2 * product;
```

When the **while** structure finishes executing, **product** contains the result 1024. The flowchart in Fig. 8.5 illustrates the flow of control of the preceding **while** repetition structure. Once again, note that (besides small circles and arrows) the flowchart contains only a rectangle symbol and a diamond symbol.

When the script enters the **while** structure, **product** is 2. The script repeatedly multiplies variable **product** by 2, so **product** takes on the values 4, 8, 16, 32, 64, 128, 256, 512 and 1024 successively. When **product** becomes 1024, the condition **product <= 1000** in the **while** structure becomes **false**. This terminates the repetition, with 1024 as **product**'s final value. Execution continues with the next statement after the **while** structure. [*Note*: If a **while** structure's condition is initially **false**, the body statement(s) will never execute.]

The flowchart clearly shows the repetition. The flowline emerging from the rectangle wraps back to the decision, which the script tests each time through the loop until the decision eventually becomes false. At this point, the **while** structure exits, and control passes to the next statement in the program.

8.8 Formulating Algorithms: Case Study 1 (Counter-Controlled Repetition)

To illustrate how to develop algorithms, we solve several variations of a class-averaging problem. Consider the following problem statement:

> *A class of ten students took a quiz. The grades (integers in the range 0 to 100) for this quiz are available to you. Determine the class average on the quiz.*

The class average is equal to the sum of the grades divided by the number of students (10 in this case). The algorithm for solving this problem on a computer must input each of the grades, perform the averaging calculation and display the result.

Let us use pseudocode to list the actions to execute and specify the order in which the actions should execute. We use *counter-controlled repetition* to input the grades one at a time. This technique uses a variable called a *counter* to control the number of times a set of statements executes. In this example, repetition terminates when the counter exceeds 10. In this section, we present a pseudocode algorithm (Figure 8.6) and the corresponding program (Fig. 8.7). In the next section, we show how to develop pseudocode algorithms. Counter-controlled repetition often is called *definite repetition*, because the number of repetitions is known before the loop begins executing.

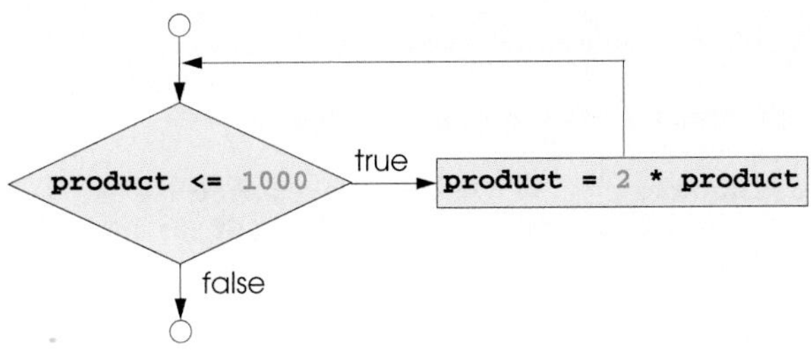

Fig. 8.5 Flowcharting the **while** repetition structure.

Set total to zero
Set grade counter to one

While grade counter is less than or equal to ten
    Input the next grade
    Add the grade into the total
    Add one to the grade counter

Set the class average to the total divided by ten
Print the class average

Fig. 8.6 Pseudocode algorithm that uses counter-controlled repetition to solve the class-average problem.

Note the references in the algorithm to a total and a counter. A *total* is a variable in which a script accumulates the sum of a series of values. A counter is a variable a script uses to count—in this case, to count the number of grades entered. Variables that store totals normally should be initialized to zero before they are used in a program.

Good Programming Practice 8.5

Variables to be used in calculations should be initialized before their use.

Lines 14–18 declare variables **total**, **gradeCounter**, **gradeValue**, **average** and **grade**. The variable **grade** will store the string the user types into the **prompt** dialog. The variable **gradeValue** will store the integer value of the **grade** the user enters in a **prompt** dialog.

```
1  <?xml version = "1.0"?>
2  <!DOCTYPE html PUBLIC "-//W3C//DTD XHTML 1.0 Strict//EN"
3     "http://www.w3.org/TR/xhtml1/DTD/xhtml1-strict.dtd">
4  
5  <!-- Fig. 8.7: average.html -->
6  <!-- Class Average Program  -->
7  
8  <html xmlns = "http://www.w3.org/1999/xhtml">
9     <head>
10       <title>Class Average Program</title>
11 
12       <script type = "text/javascript">
13          <!--
14          var total,          // sum of grades
15              gradeCounter,   // number of grades entered
16              gradeValue,     // grade value
17              average,        // average of all grades
18              grade;          // grade typed by user
19 
```

Fig. 8.7 Class-average program with counter-controlled repetition (part 1 of 2).

```
         // Initialization Phase
         total = 0;          // clear total
         gradeCounter = 1;   // prepare to loop

         // Processing Phase
         while ( gradeCounter <= 10 ) {  // loop 10 times

            // prompt for input and read grade from user
            grade = window.prompt( "Enter integer grade:", "0" );

            // convert grade from a string to an integer
            gradeValue = parseInt( grade );

            // add gradeValue to total
            total = total + gradeValue;

            // add 1 to gradeCounter
            gradeCounter = gradeCounter + 1;
         }

         // Termination Phase
         average = total / 10;  // calculate the average

         // display average of exam grades
         document.writeln(
            "<h1>Class average is " + average + "</h1>" );
         // -->
      </script>

   </head>
   <body>
      <p>Click Refresh (or Reload) to run the script again<p>
   </body>
</html>
```

Explorer User Prompt

Script Prompt:

Enter integer grade:

100

OK

Cancel

This dialog is displayed 10 times. User input is 100, 88, 93, 55, 68, 77, 83, 95, 73 and 62.

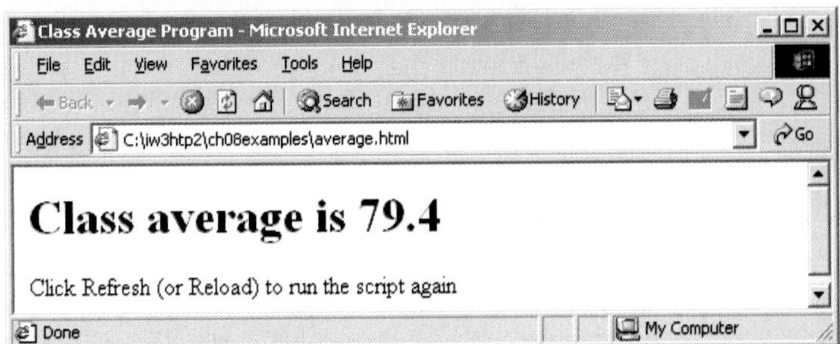

Fig. 8.7 Class-average program with counter-controlled repetition (part 2 of 2).

Lines 21–22 are assignment statements that initialize **total** to **0** and **gradeCounter** to **1**. Note that variables **total** and **gradeCounter** are initialized before they are used in a calculation. Uninitialized variables used in calculations result in logic errors and produce the value ***NaN*** (*not a number*).

Common Programming Error 8.6

Not initializing a variable that will be used in a calculation, results in a logic error. You must initialize the variable before it is used in a calculation.

Testing and Debugging Tip 8.1

Initialize variables that will be used in calculations to avoid subtle errors.

Line 25 indicates that the **while** structure continues iterating while the value of **gradeCounter** is less than or equal to 10. Line 28 corresponds to the pseudocode statement "*Input the next grade.*" The statement displays a **prompt** dialog with the prompt "**Enter integer grade:**" on the screen.

After the user enters the **grade**, line 31 converts it from a string to an integer. We must convert the string to an integer in this example; otherwise, the addition statement in line 34 will be a string concatenation statement rather than a numeric sum.

Next, the program updates the **total** with the new **gradeValue** entered by the user. Line 34 adds **gradeValue** to the previous value of **total** and assigns the result to **total**. This statement seems a bit strange, because it does not follow the rules of algebra. Keep in mind that JavaScript operator precedence evaluates the addition (**+**) operation before the assignment (**=**) operation. The value of the expression on the right side of the assignment operator always replaces the value of the variable on the left side of the assignment operator.

The program now is ready to increment the variable **gradeCounter** to indicate that a grade has been processed and to read the next grade from the user. Line 37 adds **1** to **gradeCounter**, so the condition in the **while** structure will eventually become **false** and terminate the loop. After this statement executes, the program continues by testing the condition in the **while** structure on line 25. If the condition is still true, the statements in lines 28–37 repeat. Otherwise the program continues execution with the first statement in sequence after the body of the loop (i.e., line 41).

Line 41 assigns the results of the average calculation to variable **average**. Lines 44–45 write a line of XHTML text in the document that displays the string **"Class average is "** followed by the value of variable **average** as an **<h1>** head in the browser.

After saving the XHTML document, execute the script in Internet Explorer by double clicking the XHTML document (from Windows Explorer). This script reads only integer values from the user. In the sample program execution in Fig. 8.7, the sum of the values entered (100, 88, 93, 55, 68, 77, 83, 95, 73 and 62) is 794. Although the script reads only integers, the averaging calculation in the program does not produce an integer. Rather, the calculation produces a *floating-point number* (i.e., a number containing a decimal point). The average of the 10 integers input by the user in this example is 79.4.

Software Engineering Observation 8.6

If the string passed to **parseInt** *contains a floating-point numeric value,* **parseInt** *simply truncates the floating-point part. For example, the string "27.95" results in the integer 27, and the string –123.45 results in the integer –123. If the string passed to* **parseInt** *is not a numeric value,* **parseInt** *returns* **NaN** *(not a number).*

JavaScript actually represents all numbers as floating-point numbers in memory. Floating-point numbers often develop through division, as shown in this example. When we divide 10 by 3, the result is 3.3333333…, with the sequence of 3s repeating infinitely. The computer allocates only a fixed amount of space to hold such a value, so the stored floating-point value can be only an approximation. Despite the fact that floating-point numbers are not always 100% precise, they have numerous applications. For example, when we speak of a "normal" body temperature of 98.6, we do not need to be precise to a large number of digits. When we view the temperature on a thermometer and read it as 98.6, it may actually be 98.5999473210643. The point here is that few applications require high-precision floating-point values, so calling this number simply 98.6 is fine for most applications.

Common Programming Error 8.7

Using floating-point numbers in a manner that assumes they are represented precisely can lead to incorrect results. Real numbers are represented only approximately by computers. For example, no fixed-size floating-point representation of π can ever be precise, because π is a transcendental number whose value cannot be expressed in a finite amount of space.

8.9 Formulating Algorithms with Top-Down, Stepwise Refinement: Case Study 2 (Sentinel-Controlled Repetition)

Let us generalize the class-average problem. Consider the following problem:

> *Develop a class-averaging program that will process an arbitrary number of grades each time the program is run.*

In the first class-average example, the number of grades (10) was known in advance. In this example, no indication is given of how many grades the user will enter. The program must process an arbitrary number of grades. How can the program determine when to stop the input of grades? How will it know when to calculate and display the class average?

One way to solve this problem is to use a special value called a *sentinel value* (also called a *signal value*, a *dummy value* or a *flag value*) to indicate the end of data entry. The user types in grades until all legitimate grades have been entered. Then the user types the sentinel value to indicate that the last grade has been entered. Sentinel-controlled repetition is often called *indefinite repetition*, because the number of repetitions is not known before the loop begins executing.

Clearly, the sentinel value must be chosen so that it cannot be confused with an acceptable input value. Because grades on a quiz are normally nonnegative integers from 0 to 100, –1 is an acceptable sentinel value for this problem. Thus, an execution of the class-average program might process a stream of inputs such as 95, 96, 75, 74, 89 and –1. The program would compute and print the class average for the grades 95, 96, 75, 74 and 89 (–1 is the sentinel value, so it should not enter into the average calculation).

Common Programming Error 8.8

Choosing a sentinel value that is also a legitimate data value results in a logic error and may prevent a sentinel-controlled loop from terminating properly.

We approach the class-average program with a technique called *top-down, stepwise refinement*, a technique that is essential to the development of well-structured algorithms. We begin with a pseudocode representation of the *top*:

> *Determine the class average for the quiz*

The top is a single statement that conveys the overall purpose of the program. As such, the top is, in effect, a complete representation of a program. Unfortunately, the top rarely conveys a sufficient amount of detail from which to write the JavaScript algorithm. So, we now begin the refinement process. We divide the top into a series of smaller tasks and list these tasks in the order in which they need to be performed, creating the following *first refinement*:

Initialize variables
Input, sum up and count the quiz grades
Calculate and print the class average

Here, only the sequence structure is used; the steps listed are to be executed in order, one after the other.

Software Engineering Observation 8.7

Each refinement, as well as the top itself, is a complete specification of the algorithm; only the level of detail varies.

To proceed to the next level of refinement (the *second refinement*), we commit to specific variables. We need a running total of the numbers, a count of how many numbers have been processed, a variable to receive the string representation of each grade as it is input, a variable to store the value of the grade after it is converted to an integer and a variable to hold the calculated average. The pseudocode statement

Initialize variables

may be refined as follows:

Initialize total to zero
Initialize gradeCounter to zero

Notice that only the variables *total* and *gradeCounter* are initialized before they are used; the variables *average*, *grade* and *gradeValue* (for the calculated average, the user input and the integer representation of the *grade*, respectively) need not be initialized, because their values are determined as they are calculated or input.

The pseudocode statement

Input, sum up and count the quiz grades

requires a repetition structure (a loop) that successively inputs each grade. We do not know in advance how many grades are to be processed, so we will use sentinel-controlled repetition. The user at the keyboard will enter legitimate grades, one at a time. After entering the last legitimate grade, the user will enter the sentinel value. The program will test for the sentinel value after the user enters each grade and will terminate the loop when the sentinel value is encountered. The second refinement of the preceding pseudocode statement is then

Input the first grade (possibly the sentinel)
While the user has not as yet entered the sentinel
    Add this grade into the running total
    Add one to the grade counter
    Input the next grade (possibly the sentinel)

Notice that in pseudocode, we do not use braces around the pseudocode that forms the body of the *While* structure. We simply indent the pseudocode under the *While*, to show that it belongs to the body of the *While*. Remember, pseudocode is only an informal program development aid.

The pseudocode statement

Calculate and print the class average

may be refined as follows:

If the counter is not equal to zero
Set the average to the total divided by the counter
Print the average
Else
Print "No grades were entered"

Notice that we are testing for the possibility of division by zero—a *logic error* that, if undetected, would cause the program to produce invalid output. The complete second refinement of the pseudocode algorithm for the class-average problem is shown in Fig. 8.8.

Testing and Debugging Tip 8.2

When performing division by an expression whose value could be zero, explicitly test for this case, and handle it appropriately in your program (such as by printing an error message) rather than allowing the division by zero to occur.

Good Programming Practice 8.6

Include completely blank lines in pseudocode programs to make the pseudocode more readable. The blank lines separate pseudocode control structures and separate the phases of the programs.

Software Engineering Observation 8.8

Many algorithms can be divided logically into three phases: an initialization phase that initializes the program variables, a processing phase that inputs data values and adjusts program variables accordingly and a termination phase that calculates and prints the results.

Initialize total to zero
Initialize gradeCounter to zero

Input the first grade (possibly the sentinel)
While the user has not as yet entered the sentinel
Add this grade into the running total
Add one to the grade counter
Input the next grade (possibly the sentinel)

If the counter is not equal to zero
Set the average to the total divided by the counter
Print the average
Else
Print "No grades were entered"

Fig. 8.8 Pseudocode algorithm that uses sentinel-controlled repetition to solve the class-average problem.

The pseudocode algorithm in Fig. 8.8 solves the more general class-averaging problem. This algorithm was developed after only two refinements. Sometimes more refinements are necessary.

Software Engineering Observation 8.9

The programmer terminates the top-down, stepwise refinement process after specifying the pseudocode algorithm in sufficient detail for the programmer to convert the pseudocode to a JavaScript program. Then, implementing the JavaScript program normally is straightforward.

Good Programming Practice 8.7

When converting a pseudocode program to JavaScript, keep the pseudocode in the JavaScript program as comments.

Software Engineering Observation 8.10

Experience has shown that the most difficult part of solving a problem on a computer is developing the algorithm for the solution. After specifying a correct algorithm, the process of producing a working JavaScript program from the algorithm normally is straightforward.

Software Engineering Observation 8.11

Many experienced programmers write programs without ever using program development tools like pseudocode. These programmers feel that their ultimate goal is to solve the problem on a computer and that writing pseudocode merely delays the production of final outputs. Although this approach may work for simple and familiar problems, it can lead to serious errors in large, complex projects.

Figure 8.9 shows the JavaScript program and a sample execution. Although each grade is an integer, the averaging calculation is likely to produce a number with a decimal point (a real number).

In this example, we see that control structures may be stacked on top of one another (in sequence) just as a child stacks building blocks. The **`while`** structure (lines 33–46) is followed immediately by an **`if/else`** structure (lines 49–57) in sequence. Much of the code in this program is identical to the code in Fig. 8.7, so we concentrate in this example on the new features.

```
1  <?xml version = "1.0"?>
2  <!DOCTYPE html PUBLIC "-//W3C//DTD XHTML 1.0 Strict//EN"
3     "http://www.w3.org/TR/xhtml1/DTD/xhtml1-strict.dtd">
4  
5  <!-- Fig. 8.9: Average2.html          -->
6  <!-- Sentinel-controlled Repetition -->
7  
8  <html xmlns = "http://www.w3.org/1999/xhtml">
9     <head>
10       <title>Class Average Program:
11          Sentinel-controlled Repetition</title>
12 
```

Fig. 8.9 Class-average program with sentinel-controlled repetition (part 1 of 3).

```
      <script type = "text/javascript">
         <!--
         var gradeCounter,  // number of grades entered
             gradeValue,    // grade value
             total,         // sum of grades
             average,       // average of all grades
             grade;         // grade typed by user

         // Initialization phase
         total = 0;         // clear total
         gradeCounter = 0;  // prepare to loop

         // Processing phase
         // prompt for input and read grade from user
         grade = window.prompt(
              "Enter Integer Grade, -1 to Quit:", "0" );

         // convert grade from a string to an integer
         gradeValue = parseInt( grade );

         while ( gradeValue != -1 ) {
            // add gradeValue to total
            total = total + gradeValue;

            // add 1 to gradeCounter
            gradeCounter = gradeCounter + 1;

            // prompt for input and read grade from user
            grade = window.prompt(
                 "Enter Integer Grade, -1 to Quit:", "0" );

            // convert grade from a string to an integer
            gradeValue = parseInt( grade );
         }

         // Termination phase
         if ( gradeCounter != 0 ) {
            average = total / gradeCounter;

            // display average of exam grades
            document.writeln(
               "<h1>Class average is " + average + "</h1>" );
         }
         else
            document.writeln( "<p>No grades were entered</p>" );
         // -->
      </script>
   </head>

   <body>
      <p>Click Refresh (or Reload) to run the script again</p>
   </body>
</html>
```

Fig. 8.9 Class-average program with sentinel-controlled repetition (part 2 of 3).

This dialog is displayed four times. User input is 97, 88, 72 and -1.

Fig. 8.9 Class-average program with sentinel-controlled repetition (part 3 of 3).

Line 23 initializes **gradeCounter** to **0**, because no grades have been entered yet. Remember that this program uses sentinel-controlled repetition. To keep an accurate record of the number of grades entered, the script increments **gradeCounter** only after processing a valid grade value.

Notice the difference in program logic for sentinel-controlled repetition as compared with the counter-controlled repetition in Fig. 8.7. In counter-controlled repetition, we read a value from the user during each iteration of the **while** structure's body for the specified number of iterations. In sentinel-controlled repetition, we read one value (lines 27–28) and convert it to an integer (line 31) before the program reaches the **while** structure. The script uses this value to determine whether the program's flow of control should enter the body of the **while** structure. If the **while** structure's condition is **false** (i.e., the user typed the sentinel as the first grade), the script ignores the body of the **while** structure (i.e., no grades were entered). If, on the other hand, the condition is **true**, the body begins execution and processes the value entered by the user (i.e., adds the value to the **total** at line 35). After processing the value, the script increments **gradeCounter** by 1 (line 38), inputs the next **grade** from the user (lines 41–42) and converts the **grade** to an integer (line 45), before the end of the **while** structure's body. When the script reaches the closing right brace (**}**) of the body at line 46, execution continues with the next test of the condition of the **while** structure (line 33), using the new value just entered by the user to determine whether the **while** structure's body should execute again. Notice that the next value always is input from the user immediately before the script evaluates the condition of the **while** structure. This order allows us to determine whether the value just entered by the user is the sentinel value *before* processing that value (i.e., adding it to the **total**). If the value entered is the sentinel value, the **while** structure terminates and the script does not add the value to the **total**.

Good Programming Practice 8.8

In a sentinel-controlled loop, the prompts requesting data entry should explicitly remind the user what the sentinel value is.

Notice the compound statement in the **while** loop in Fig 8.9. Without the braces, the last four statements in the body of the loop would fall outside of the loop, causing the computer to interpret the code incorrectly as follows:

```
while ( gradeValue != -1 )
   // add gradeValue to total
   total = total + gradeValue;

// add 1 to gradeCounter
gradeCounter = gradeCounter + 1;

// prompt for input and read grade from user
grade = window.prompt(
   "Enter Integer Grade, -1 to Quit:", "0" );

// convert grade from a string to an integer
gradeValue = parseInt( grade );
```

This interpretation would cause an infinite loop in the program if the user does not input the sentinel **-1** as the input value at lines 27–28 (i.e., before the **while** structure).

Common Programming Error 8.9

Omitting the curly braces that delineate a compound statement can lead to logic errors such as infinite loops.

8.10 Formulating Algorithms with Top-Down, Stepwise Refinement: Case Study 3 (Nested Control Structures)

Let us work through another complete problem. We will once again formulate the algorithm using pseudocode and top-down, stepwise refinement, and we will write a corresponding JavaScript program.

Consider the following problem statement:

A college offers a course that prepares students for the state licensing exam for real estate brokers. Last year, several of the students who completed this course took the licensing examination. Naturally, the college wants to know how well its students did on the exam. You have been asked to write a program to summarize the results. You have been given a list of these 10 students. Next to each name is written a 1 if the student passed the exam and a 2 if the student failed.

Your program should analyze the results of the exam as follows:

1. *Input each test result (i.e., a 1 or a 2). Display the message "Enter result" on the screen each time the program requests another test result.*
2. *Count the number of test results of each type.*
3. *Display a summary of the test results indicating the number of students who passed and the number of students who failed.*
4. *If more than 8 students passed the exam, print the message "Raise tuition."*

After reading the problem statement carefully, we make the following observations about the problem:

1. The program must process test results for 10 students. A counter-controlled loop will be used.

2. Each test result is a number—either a 1 or a 2. Each time the program reads a test result, the program must determine if the number is a 1 or a 2. We test for a 1 in our algorithm. If the number is not a 1, we assume that it is a 2. (An exercise at the end of the chapter considers the consequences of this assumption.)
3. Two counters are used to keep track of the exam results—one to count the number of students who passed the exam and one to count the number of students who failed the exam.

After the program processes all the results, it must decide if more than eight students passed the exam. Let us proceed with top-down, stepwise refinement. We begin with a pseudocode representation of the top:

Analyze exam results and decide if tuition should be raised

Once again, it is important to emphasize that the top is a complete representation of the program, but that several refinements are necessary before the pseudocode can be evolved naturally into a JavaScript program. Our first refinement is as follows:

Initialize variables
Input the ten exam grades and count passes and failures
Print a summary of the exam results and decide whether tuition should be raised

Here, too, even though we have a complete representation of the entire program, further refinement is necessary. We now commit to specific variables. Counters are needed to record the passes and failures, a counter will be used to control the looping process and a variable is needed to store the user input. The pseudocode statement

Initialize variables

may be refined as follows:

Initialize passes to zero
Initialize failures to zero
Initialize student to one

Notice that only the counters for the number of passes, the number of failures and the number of students are initialized. The pseudocode statement

Input the ten quiz grades and count passes and failures

requires a loop that successively inputs the result of each exam. Here, it is known in advance that there are precisely 10 exam results, so counter-controlled looping is appropriate. Inside the loop (i.e., *nested* within the loop), a double-selection structure will determine whether each exam result is a pass or a failure and will increment the appropriate counter accordingly. The refinement of the preceding pseudocode statement is then

```
While student counter is less than or equal to ten
    Input the next exam result

    If the student passed
        Add one to passes
    Else
        Add one to failures

    Add one to student counter
```

Notice the use of blank lines to set off the *If/Else* control structure to improve program readability. The pseudocode statement

Print a summary of the exam results and decide whether tuition should be raised

may be refined as follows:

Print the number of passes
Print the number of failures
If more than eight students passed
    Print "Raise tuition"

The complete second refinement appears in Fig. 8.10. Notice that blank lines are also used to set off the *While* structure for program readability.

This pseudocode now is refined sufficiently for conversion to JavaScript. The JavaScript program and two sample executions are shown in Fig. 8.11.

Lines 15–18 declare the variables used to process the examination results. Note that JavaScript allows variable initialization to be incorporated into declarations (**`passes`** is assigned **`0`**, **`failures`** is assigned **`0`** and **`student`** is assigned **`1`**). Some programs may require initialization at the beginning of each repetition; such initialization would normally occur in assignment statements.

The processing of the exam results occurs in the **`while`** structure at lines 21–31. Notice that the **`if/else`** structure at lines 25–28 in the loop tests only whether the exam result was 1; it assumes that all other exam results are 2. Normally, you should validate the values input by the user (i.e., determine whether the values are correct). In the exercises, we ask you to modify this example to validate the input values to ensure that they are either 1 or 2.

Initialize passes to zero
Initialize failures to zero
Initialize student to one

While student counter is less than or equal to ten
    Input the next exam result

    If the student passed
        Add one to passes
    Else
        Add one to failures

    Add one to student counter

Print the number of passes
Print the number of failures
If more than eight students passed
    Print "Raise tuition"

Fig. 8.10 Pseudocode for examination-results problem.

Good Programming Practice 8.9

When inputting values from the user, validate the input to ensure that it is correct. If an input value is incorrect, prompt the user to input the value again.

```
<?xml version = "1.0"?>
<!DOCTYPE html PUBLIC "-//W3C//DTD XHTML 1.0 Strict//EN"
   "http://www.w3.org/TR/xhtml1/DTD/xhtml1-strict.dtd">

<!-- Fig. 8.11: analysis.html -->
<!-- Analyzing Exam Results   -->

<html xmlns = "http://www.w3.org/1999/xhtml">
   <head>
      <title>Analysis of Examination Results</title>

      <script type = "text/javascript">
         <!--
         // initializing variables in declarations
         var passes = 0,       // number of passes
             failures = 0,     // number of failures
             student = 1,      // student counter
             result;           // one exam result

         // process 10 students; counter-controlled loop
         while ( student <= 10 ) {
            result = window.prompt(
               "Enter result (1=pass,2=fail)", "0" );

            if ( result == "1" )
               passes = passes + 1;
            else
               failures = failures + 1;

            student = student + 1;
         }

         // termination phase
         document.writeln( "<h1>Examination Results</h1>" );
         document.writeln(
            "Passed: " + passes + "<br />Failed: " + failures );

         if ( passes > 8 )
            document.writeln( "<br />Raise Tuition" );
         // -->
      </script>

   </head>
   <body>
      <p>Click Refresh (or Reload) to run the script again</p>
   </body>
</html>
```

Fig. 8.11 JavaScript program for examination-results problem (part 1 of 2).

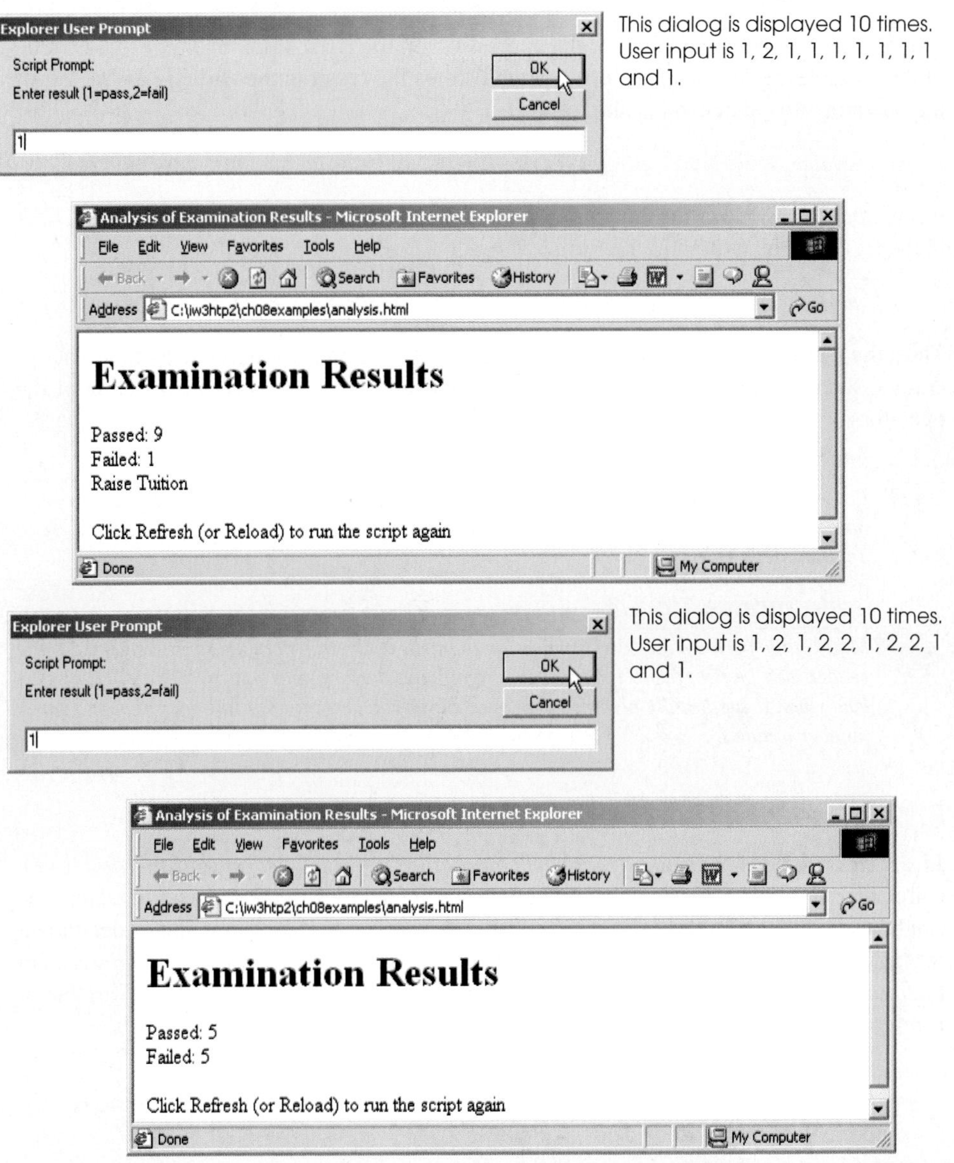

Fig. 8.11 JavaScript program for examination-results problem (part 2 of 2).

8.11 Assignment Operators

JavaScript provides several assignment operators for abbreviating assignment expressions. For example, the statement

```
c = c + 3;
```

can be abbreviated with the *addition assignment operator*, **+=**, as

```
c += 3;
```

The **+=** operator adds the value of the expression on the right of the operator to the value of the variable on the left of the operator and stores the result in the variable on the left of the operator. Any statement of the form

variable **=** *variable operator expression***;**

where *operator* is one of the binary operators **+**, **-**, *****, **/** or **%** (or others we will discuss later in the text), can be written in the form

*variable operator***=** *expression***;**

Thus, the assignment **c += 3** adds **3** to **c**. Figure 8.12 shows the arithmetic assignment operators, sample expressions using these operators and explanations of the meaning of the operators.

Performance Tip 8.1

Programmers can write programs that execute a bit faster when the abbreviated assignment operators are used, because the variable on the left side of the assignment does not have to be evaluated twice.

Performance Tip 8.2

Many of the performance tips we mention in this text result in nominal improvements, so the reader may be tempted to ignore them. Significant performance improvement often is realized when a supposedly nominal improvement is placed in a loop that may repeat a large number of times.

8.12 Increment and Decrement Operators

JavaScript provides the unary *increment operator* (**++**) and *decrement operator* (**--**), (summarized in Fig. 8.13). If a variable **c** is incremented by 1, the increment operator, **++**, can be used rather than the expression **c = c + 1** or **c += 1**. If an increment or decrement operator is placed before a variable, it is referred to as the *preincrement* or *predecrement operator*, respectively. If an increment or decrement operator is placed after a variable, it is referred to as the *postincrement* or *postdecrement operator*, respectively.

Assignment operator	Initial value of variable	Sample expression	Explanation	Assigns
`+=`	`c = 3`	`c += 7`	`c = c + 7`	**10** to **c**
`-=`	`d = 5`	`d -= 4`	`d = d - 4`	**1** to **d**
`*=`	`e = 4`	`e *= 5`	`e = e * 5`	**20** to **e**
`/=`	`f = 6`	`f /= 3`	`f = f / 3`	**2** to **f**
`%=`	`g = 12`	`g %= 9`	`g = g % 9`	**3** to **g**

Fig. 8.12 Arithmetic assignment operators.

Operator	Called	Sample expression	Explanation
`++`	preincrement	`++a`	Increment **a** by 1, then use the new value of **a** in the expression in which **a** resides.
`++`	postincrement	`a++`	Use the current value of **a** in the expression in which **a** resides, then increment **a** by 1.
`--`	predecrement	`--b`	Decrement **b** by 1, then use the new value of **b** in the expression in which **b** resides.
`--`	postdecrement	`b--`	Use the current value of **b** in the expression in which **b** resides, then decrement **b** by 1.

Fig. 8.13 Increment and decrement operators.

Preincrementing (or predecrementing) a variable causes the program to increment (decrement) the variable by 1, then use the new value of the variable in the expression in which it appears. Postincrementing (postdecrementing) the variable causes the program to use the current value of the variable in the expression in which it appears, then increment (decrement) the variable by 1.

The script in Fig. 8.14 demonstrates the difference between the preincrementing version and the postincrementing version of the **++** increment operator. Postincrementing the variable **c** causes it to be incremented after it is used in the **document.writeln** method call (line 20). Preincrementing the variable **c** causes it to be incremented before it is used in the **document.writeln** method call (line 27). The program displays the value of **c** before and after the **++** operator is used. The decrement operator (**--**) works similarly.

```
1  <?xml version = "1.0"?>
2  <!DOCTYPE html PUBLIC "-//W3C//DTD XHTML 1.0 Strict//EN"
3     "http://www.w3.org/TR/xhtml1/DTD/xhtml1-strict.dtd">
4
5  <!-- Fig. 8.14: increment.html              -->
6  <!-- Preincrementing and Postincrementing -->
7
8  <html xmlns = "http://www.w3.org/1999/xhtml">
9     <head>
10       <title>Preincrementing and Postincrementing</title>
11
12       <script type = "text/javascript">
13          <!--
14          var c;
15
16          c = 5;
17          document.writeln( "<h3>Postincrementing</h3>" );
18          document.writeln( c );           // print 5
19          // print 5 then increment
20          document.writeln( "<br />" + c++ );
21          document.writeln( "<br />" + c );    // print 6
22
```

Fig. 8.14 Differences between preincrementing and postincrementing (part 1 of 2).

```
            c = 5;
            document.writeln( "<h3>Preincrementing</h3>" );
            document.writeln( c );              // print 5
            // increment then print 6
            document.writeln( "<br />" + ++c );
            document.writeln( "<br />" + c );   // print 6
            // -->
         </script>

      </head><body></body>
   </html>
```

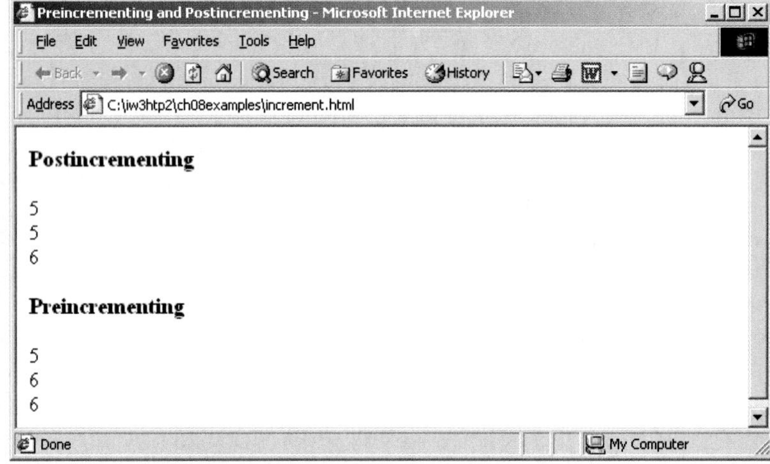

Fig. 8.14 Differences between preincrementing and postincrementing (part 2 of 2).

Good Programming Practice 8.10

For readability, unary operators should be placed next to their operands, with no intervening spaces.

The three assignment statements in Fig 8.11 (lines 26, 28 and 30, respectively),

```
passes = passes + 1;
failures = failures + 1;
student = student + 1;
```

can be written more concisely with assignment operators as

```
passes += 1;
failures += 1;
student += 1;
```

with preincrement operators as

```
++passes;
++failures;
++student;
```

or with postincrement operators as

```
passes++;
failures++;
student++;
```

It is important to note here that when incrementing or decrementing a variable in a statement by itself, the preincrement and postincrement forms have the same effect, and the predecrement and postdecrement forms have the same effect. It is only when a variable appears in the context of a larger expression that preincrementing the variable and postincrementing the variable have different effects. Predecrementing and postdecrementing behave similarly.

Common Programming Error 8.10

Attempting to use the increment or decrement operator on an expression other than an lvalue *is a syntax error. An* lvalue *is a variable or expression that can appear on the left side of an assignment operation. For example, writing* **`++(x + 1)`** *is a syntax error, because* **`(x + 1)`** *is not an* lvalue.

Figure 8.15 lists the precedence and associativity of the operators introduced up to this point. The operators are shown from top to bottom in decreasing order of precedence. The second column describes the associativity of the operators at each level of precedence. Notice that the conditional operator (**`?:`**), the unary operators increment (**`++`**) and decrement (**`--`**) and the assignment operators **`=`**, **`+=`**, **`-=`**, **`*=`**, **`/=`** and **`%=`** associate from right to left. All other operators in the operator precedence table (Fig. 8.15) associate from left to right. The third column names the groups of operators.

8.13 Note on Data Types

Unlike its predecessor languages C, C++ and Java, JavaScript does not require variables to have a type before they can be used in a program. A variable in JavaScript can contain a value of any data type, and in many situations, JavaScript automatically converts between values of different types for you. For this reason, JavaScript is referred to as a *loosely typed language*. When a variable is declared in JavaScript, but is not given a value, the variable has an *undefined* value. Attempting to use the value of such a variable is normally a logic error.

Operators	Associativity	Type
`()`	left to right	parentheses
`++ --`	right to left	unary
`* / %`	left to right	multiplicative
`+ -`	left to right	additive
`< <= > >=`	left to right	relational
`== !=`	left to right	equality
`?:`	right to left	conditional
`= += -= *= /= %=`	right to left	assignment

Fig. 8.15 Precedence and associativity of the operators discussed so far.

When variables are declared, they are not assigned default values, unless specified otherwise by the programmer. To indicate that a variable does not contain a value, you can assign the value **`null`** to the variable.

8.14 JavaScript Internet and World Wide Web Resources

There are a tremendous number of resources for JavaScript programmers on the Internet and World Wide Web. This section lists a few JavaScript and ECMAScript resources available on the Internet and provides a brief description of each. Additional resources for these topics are presented at the end of other JavaScript chapters as necessary.

`www.javascriptmall.com`
The *JavaScript Mall* provides free scripts, FAQs, tools for Web pages and a JavaScript tutorial.

`developer.netscape.com/tech/javascript`
This *JavaScript Reference* provides JavaScript documentation, FAQs, recommended books, newsgroups and much more.

SUMMARY

- Any computing problem can be solved by executing a series of actions in a specific order.
- A procedure for solving a problem in terms of the actions to execute and the order in which the actions are to execute is called an algorithm.
- Specifying the order in which statements are to be executed in a computer program is called program control.
- Pseudocode is an artificial and informal language that helps programmers develop algorithms.
- Carefully prepared pseudocode may be converted easily to a corresponding JavaScript program.
- Pseudocode normally describes only executable statements—the actions that are performed when the program is converted from pseudocode to JavaScript and executed.
- Normally, statements in a program execute one after the other, in the order in which they are written. This process is called sequential execution.
- Various JavaScript statements enable the programmer to specify that the next statement to be executed may be other than the next one in sequence. This process is called transfer of control.
- All programs can be written in terms of only three control structures, namely, the sequence structure, the selection structure and the repetition structure.
- A flowchart is a graphical representation of an algorithm or of a portion of an algorithm. Flowcharts are drawn using certain special-purpose symbols, such as rectangles, diamonds, ovals and small circles; these symbols are connected by arrows called flowlines, which indicate the order in which the actions of the algorithm execute.
- JavaScript provides three selection structures. The **`if`** structure either performs (selects) an action if a condition is true or skips the action if the condition is false. The **`if/else`** structure performs an action if a condition is true and performs a different action if the condition is false. The **`switch`** structure performs one of many different actions, depending on the value of an expression.
- JavaScript provides four repetition structures, namely, **`while`**, **`do/while`**, **`for`** and **`for/in`**.
- Keywords cannot be used as identifiers (such as for variable names).
- Single-entry/single-exit control structures make it easy to build programs. Control structures are attached to one another by connecting the exit point of one control structure to the entry point of the next. This procedure is called control-structure stacking. There is only one other way control structures may be connected: control-structure nesting.

- The JavaScript interpreter ignores whitespace characters: blanks, tabs and newlines used for indentation and vertical spacing. Programmers insert whitespace characters to enhance program clarity.
- A decision can be made on any expression that evaluates to a value of JavaScript's boolean type (i.e., any expression that evaluates to **true** or **false**).
- The indentation convention you choose should be carefully applied throughout your programs. It is difficult to read programs that do not use uniform spacing conventions.
- The conditional operator (**?:**) is closely related to the **if/else** structure. Operator **?:** is JavaScript's only ternary operator—it takes three operands. The operands together with the **?:** operator form a conditional expression. The first operand is a boolean expression, the second is the value for the conditional expression if the condition evaluates to true and the third is the value for the conditional expression if the condition evaluates to false.
- Nested **if/else** structures test for multiple cases by placing **if/else** structures inside other **if/else** structures.
- The JavaScript interpreter always associates an **else** with the previous **if**, unless told to do otherwise by the placement of braces (**{}**).
- The **if** selection structure expects only one statement in its body. To include several statements in the body of an **if** structure, enclose the statements in braces (**{** and **}**). A set of statements contained within a pair of braces is called a compound statement or a block.
- A logic error has its effect at execution time. A fatal logic error causes a program to fail and terminate prematurely. A nonfatal logic error allows a program to continue executing, but the program produces incorrect results.
- A repetition structure allows the programmer to specify that an action is to be repeated while some condition remains true.
- Counter-controlled repetition is often called definite repetition, because the number of repetitions is known before the loop begins executing.
- Uninitialized variables used in mathematical calculations result in logic errors and produce the value **NaN** (not a number).
- JavaScript represents all numbers as floating-point numbers in memory. Floating-point numbers often develop through division. The computer allocates only a fixed amount of space to hold such a value, so the stored floating-point value can only be an approximation.
- In sentinel-controlled repetition, a special value called a sentinel value (also called a signal value, a dummy value or a flag value) indicates the end of data entry. Sentinel-controlled repetition often is called indefinite repetition, because the number of repetitions is not known in advance.
- The sentinel value must be chosen so that it is not confused with an acceptable input value.
- Top-down, stepwise refinement is a technique that is essential to the development of well-structured algorithms. The top is a single statement that conveys the overall purpose of the program. As such, the top is, in effect, a complete representation of a program. The stepwise refinement process divides the top into a series of smaller tasks. The programmer terminates the top-down, stepwise refinement process when the pseudocode algorithm is specified in sufficient detail for the programmer to be able to convert the pseudocode to a JavaScript program.
- JavaScript provides the arithmetic assignment operators **+=**, **-=**, ***=**, **/=** and **%=**, which abbreviate certain common types of expressions.
- The increment operator, **++**, and the decrement operator, **--**, increment or decrement a variable by 1, respectively. If the operator is prefixed to the variable, the variable is incremented or decremented by 1, then used in its expression. If the operator is postfixed to the variable, the variable is used in its expression, then incremented or decremented by 1.

- JavaScript does not require variables to have a type before they can be used in a program. A variable in JavaScript can contain a value of any data type, and in many situations, JavaScript automatically converts between values of different types for you. For this reason, JavaScript is referred to as a loosely typed language.
- When a variable is declared in JavaScript, but is not given a value, that variable has an undefined value. Attempting to use the value of such a variable is normally a logic error.
- When variables are declared, they are not assigned default values, unless specified otherwise by the programmer. To indicate that a variable does not contain a value, you can assign the value **null** to the variable.

TERMINOLOGY

-- operator
?: operator
++ operator
action
action/decision model
algorithm
arithmetic assignment operators:
  +=, -=, *=, /= and %=
block
body of a loop
compound statement
conditional operator (?:)
control structure
counter-controlled repetition
decision
decrement operator (--)
definite repetition
double-selection structure
empty statement (;)
if selection structure
if/else selection structure
increment operator (++)
indefinite repetition
infinite loop
initialization
logic error
loop counter
loop-continuation condition
nested control structures
postdecrement operator
postincrement operator
predecrement operator
preincrement operator
pseudocode
repetition
repetition structure
selection
sentinel value
sequential execution
single-entry/single-exit control structure
single-selection structure
stacked control structure
structured programming
syntax error
top-down, stepwise refinement
unary operator
while repetition structure
whitespace character

SELF-REVIEW EXERCISES

8.1 State whether each of the following is *true* or *false*. If *false*, explain why.

a) All programs can be written in terms of three types of control structures: ________, ________ and ________.
b) The ________ selection structure is used to execute one action when a condition is true and another action when that condition is false.
c) Repetition of a set of instructions a specific number of times is called ________ repetition.
d) When it is not known in advance how many times a set of statements will be repeated, a ________ value can be used to terminate the repetition.

8.2 Write four JavaScript statements that each add 1 to variable **x**, which contains a number.

8.3 Write JavaScript statements to accomplish each of the following tasks:

a) Assign the sum of **x** and **y** to **z**, and increment the value of **x** by 1 after the calculation. Use only one statement.

b) Test whether the value of the variable **count** is greater than 10. If it is, print **"Count is greater than 10"**.

c) Decrement the variable **x** by 1, then subtract it from the variable **total**. Use only one statement.

d) Calculate the remainder after **q** is divided by **divisor**, and assign the result to **q**. Write this statement in two different ways.

8.4 Write a JavaScript statement to accomplish each of the following tasks:

a) Declare variables **sum** and **x**.

b) Assign **1** to variable **x**.

c) Assign **0** to variable **sum**.

d) Add variable **x** to variable **sum**, and assign the result to variable **sum**.

e) Print **"The sum is: "**, followed by the value of variable **sum**.

8.5 Combine the statements that you wrote in Exercise 8.4 into a JavaScript program that calculates and prints the sum of the integers from 1 to 10. Use the **while** structure to loop through the calculation and increment statements. The loop should terminate when the value of **x** becomes 11.

8.6 Determine the value of each variable after the calculation is performed. Assume that, when each statement begins executing, all variables have the integer value 5.

a) **product *= x++;**

b) **quotient /= ++x;**

8.7 Identify and correct the errors in each of the following segments of code:

a)
```
while ( c <= 5 ) {
   product *= c;
   ++c;
```

b)
```
if ( gender == 1 )
   document.writeln( "Woman" );
else;
   document.writeln( "Man" );
```

8.8 What is wrong with the following **while** repetition structure?

```
while ( z >= 0 )
  sum += z;
```

ANSWERS TO SELF-REVIEW EXERCISES

8.1 a) Sequence, selection and repetition. b) **if/else**. c) Counter-controlled (or definite). d) Sentinel, signal, flag or dummy.

8.2
```
x = x + 1;
x += 1;
++x;
x++;
```

8.3

a)
```
z = x++ + y;
```

b)
```
if ( count > 10 )
   document.writeln( "Count is greater than 10" );
```

c)
```
total -= --x;
```

d)
```
q %= divisor;
q = q % divisor;
```

8.4 a) `var sum, x;`
b) `x = 1;`
c) `sum = 0;`
d) `sum += x;` or `sum = sum + x;`
e) `document.writeln( "The sum is: " + sum );`

8.5 The solution is as follows:

```
<?xml version = "1.0"?>
<!DOCTYPE html PUBLIC "-//W3C//DTD XHTML 1.0 Transitional//EN"
   "http://www.w3.org/TR/xhtml1/DTD/xhtml1-transitional.dtd">

<!-- Exercise 8.5: sum.html -->

<html xmlns = "http://www.w3.org/1999/xhtml">
   <head><title>Sum the Integers from 1 to 10</title>

      <script type = "text/javascript">
         <!--
         var sum, x;

         x = 1;
         sum = 0;

         while ( x <= 10 ) {
            sum += x;
            ++x;
         }

         document.writeln( "The sum is: " + sum );
         // -->
      </script>

   </head><body></body>
</html>
```

8.6 a) `product = 25, x = 6;`
b) `quotient = 0.833333..., x = 6;`

8.7 a) Error: Missing the closing right brace of the **while** body.
Correction: Add closing right brace after the statement **++c;**.
b) Error: The semicolon after **else** results in a logic error. The second output statement will always be executed.
Correction: Remove the semicolon after **else**.

8.8 The value of the variable **z** is never changed in the body of the **while** structure. Therefore, if the loop-continuation condition **(z >= 0)** is true, an infinite loop is created. To prevent the creation of the infinite loop, **z** must be decremented so that it eventually becomes less than 0.

EXERCISES

8.9 Identify and correct the errors in each of the following segments of code. [*Note*: There may be more than one error in each piece of code]:

a)
```
if ( age >= 65 );
    document.writeln( "Age greater than or equal to 65" );
else
    document.writeln( "Age is less than 65 )";
```
b)
```
var x = 1, total;
while ( x <= 10 ) {
    total += x;
    ++x;
}
```
c)
```
While ( x <= 100 )
    total += x;
    ++x;
```
d)
```
while ( y > 0 ) {
    document.writeln( y );
    ++y;
```

8.10 What does the following program print?

```
<?xml version = "1.0"?>
<!DOCTYPE html PUBLIC "-//W3C//DTD XHTML 1.0 Transitional//EN"
   "http://www.w3.org/TR/xhtml1/DTD/xhtml1-transitional.dtd">

<html xmlns="http://www.w3.org/1999/xhtml">
   <head><title>Mystery Script</title>

      <script type = "text/javascript">
         <!--
         var y, x = 1, total = 0;

         while ( x <= 10 ) {
            y = x * x;
            document.writeln( y + "<br />" );
            total += y;
            ++x;
         }

         document.writeln( "<br />Total is " + total );
         // -->
      </script>

   </head><body></body>
</html>
```

For Exercises 8.11–8.14, perform each of the following steps:

a) Read the problem statement.
b) Formulate the algorithm using pseudocode and top-down, stepwise refinement.
c) Write a JavaScript program.
d) Test, debug and execute the JavaScript program.
e) Process three complete sets of data.

8.11 Drivers are concerned with the mileage obtained by their automobiles. One driver has kept track of several tankfuls of gasoline by recording the number of miles driven and the number of gallons used for each tankful. Develop a JavaScript program that will input the miles driven and gallons used (both as integers) for each tankful. The program should calculate and output XHTML text that displays the number of miles per gallon obtained for each tankful and prints the combined number of miles per gallon obtained for all tankfuls up to this point. Use **`prompt`** dialogs to obtain the data from the user.

8.12 Develop a JavaScript program that will determine whether a department-store customer has exceeded the credit limit on a charge account. For each customer, the following facts are available:

a) Account number
b) Balance at the beginning of the month
c) Total of all items charged by this customer this month
d) Total of all credits applied to this customer's account this month
e) Allowed credit limit

The program should input each of these facts from **`prompt`** dialogs as integers, calculate the new balance (= *beginning balance* + *charges* – *credits*), display the new balance and determine whether the new balance exceeds the customer's credit limit. For customers whose credit limit is exceeded, the program should output XHTML text that displays the message "Credit limit exceeded."

8.13 A large company pays its salespeople on a commission basis. The salespeople receive \$200 per week, plus 9% of their gross sales for that week. For example, a salesperson who sells \$5000 worth of merchandise in a week receives \$200 plus 9% of \$5000, or a total of \$650. You have been supplied with a list of items sold by each salesperson. The values of these items are as follows:

Item	Value
1	239.99
2	129.75
3	99.95
4	350.89

Develop a program that inputs one salesperson's items sold for last week, calculates the salesperson's earnings and outputs XHTML text that displays the salesperson's earnings.

8.14 Develop a JavaScript program that will determine the gross pay for each of three employees. The company pays "straight time" for the first 40 hours worked by each employee and pays "time and a half" for all hours worked in excess of 40 hours. You are given a list of the employees of the company, the number of hours each employee worked last week and the hourly rate of each employee. Your program should input this information for each employee, determine the employee's gross pay and output XHTML text that displays the employee's gross pay. Use **`prompt`** dialogs to input the data.

8.15 The process of finding the largest value (i.e., the maximum of a group of values) is used frequently in computer applications. For example, a program that determines the winner of a sales contest would input the number of units sold by each salesperson. The salesperson who sells the most units wins the contest. Write a pseudocode program and then a JavaScript program that inputs a series of 10 single-digit numbers as characters, determines the largest of the numbers and outputs XHTML text that displays the largest number. Your program should use three variables as follows:

a) **`counter`**: A counter to count to 10 (i.e., to keep track of how many numbers have been input and to determine when all 10 numbers have been processed);
b) **`number`**: The current digit input to the program;
c) **`largest`**: The largest number found so far.

8.16 Write a JavaScript program that uses looping to print the following table of values. Output the results in an XHTML table.

N	10*N	100*N	1000*N
1	10	100	1000
2	20	200	2000
3	30	300	3000
4	40	400	4000
5	50	500	5000

8.17 Using an approach similar to that in Exercise 8.15, find the *two* largest values among the 10 digits entered. [*Note*: You may input each number only once.]

8.18 Modify the program in Fig. 8.11 to validate its inputs. For every value input, if the value entered is other than 1 or 2, keep looping until the user enters a correct value.

8.19 What does the following program print?

```
<?xml version = "1.0"?>
<!DOCTYPE html PUBLIC "-//W3C//DTD XHTML 1.0 Transitional//EN"
   "http://www.w3.org/TR/xhtml1/DTD/xhtml1-transitional.dtd">

<html xmlns = "http://www.w3.org/1999/xhtml">
   <head><title>Mystery Script</title>

      <script type = "text/javascript">
         <!--
         var count = 1;

         while ( count <= 10 ) {
            document.writeln(
               count % 2 == 1 ? "****<br />" : "++++++++<br />" );
            ++count;
         }
         // -->
      </script>

   </head><body></body>
</html>
```

8.20 What does the following program print?

```
<?xml version = "1.0"?>
<!DOCTYPE html PUBLIC "-//W3C//DTD XHTML 1.0 Transitional//EN"
   "http://www.w3.org/TR/xhtml1/DTD/xhtml1-transitional.dtd">

<html xmlns = "http://www.w3.org/1999/xhtml">
   <head><title>Mystery Script</title>

      <script type = "text/javascript">
         <!--
         var row = 10, column;

```

```
         while ( row >= 1 ) {
            column = 1;

            while ( column <= 10 ) {
               document.write( row % 2 == 1 ? "<" : ">" );
               ++column;
            }

            --row;
            document.writeln( "<br />" );
         }
         // -->
      </script>

   </head><body></body>
</html>
```

8.21 *(Dangling-Else Problem)* Determine the output for each of the given segments of code when **x** is **9** and **y** is **11**, and when **x** is **11** and **y** is **9**. Note that the interpreter ignores the indentation in a JavaScript program. Also, the JavaScript interpreter always associates an **else** with the previous **if**, unless told to do otherwise by the placement of braces (**{}**). Because, on first glance, the programmer may not be sure which **if** an **else** matches, this situation is referred to as the "dangling-else" problem. We have eliminated the indentation from the given code to make the problem more challenging. [*Hint*: Apply indentation conventions you have learned.]

a)
```
if ( x < 10 )
if ( y > 10 )
document.writeln( "*****<br />" );
else
document.writeln( "#####<br />" );
document.writeln( "$$$$$<br />" );
```

b)
```
if ( x < 10 ) {
if ( y > 10 )
document.writeln( "*****<br />" );
}
else {
document.writeln( "#####<br />" );
document.writeln( "$$$$$<br />" );
}
```

8.22 *(Another Dangling-Else Problem)* Modify the given code to produce the output shown in each part of this problem. Use proper indentation techniques. You may not make any changes other than inserting braces and changing the indentation of the code. The interpreter ignores indentation in a JavaScript program. We have eliminated the indentation from the given code to make the problem more challenging. [*Note*: It is possible that no modification is necessary for some of the segments of code.]

```
if ( y == 8 )
if ( x == 5 )
document.writeln( "@@@@@<br />" );
else
document.writeln( "#####<br />" );
document.writeln( "$$$$$<br />" );
document.writeln( "&&&&&<br />" );
```

a) Assuming that **x = 5** and **y = 8**, the following output is produced:

```
@@@@@
$$$$$
&&&&&
```

b) Assuming that **x = 5** and **y = 8**, the following output is produced:

```
@@@@@
```

c) Assuming that **x = 5** and **y = 8**, the following output is produced:

```
@@@@@
&&&&&
```

d) Assuming that **x = 5** and **y = 7**, the following output is produced [*Note*: The last three output statements after the **else** statements are all part of a compound statement]:

```
#####
$$$$$
&&&&&
```

8.23 Write a script that reads in the size of the side of a square and outputs XHTML text that displays a hollow square of that size constructed of asterisks. Use a **prompt** dialog to read the size from the user. Your program should work for squares of all side sizes between 1 and 20.

8.24 A palindrome is a number or a text phrase that reads the same backward as forward. For example, each of the following five-digit integers is a palindrome: 12321, 55555, 45554 and 11611. Write a script that reads in a five-digit integer and determines whether it is a palindrome. If the number is not five digits long, output XHTML text that displays an **alert** dialog indicating the problem to the user. When the user dismisses the **alert** dialog, allow the user to enter a new value.

8.25 Write a script that outputs XHTML text that displays the following checkerboard pattern:

Your program may use only three output statements, one of the form

```
document.write( "* " );
```

one of the form

```
document.write( " " );
```

and one of the form

```
document.writeln( "<br />" );
```

[*Hint*: Repetition structures are required in this exercise.]

8.26 Write a script that outputs XHTML text that keeps displaying in the browser window the multiples of the integer 2, namely 2, 4, 8, 16, 32, 64, etc. Your loop should not terminate (i.e., you should create an infinite loop). What happens when you run this program?

8.27 A company wants to transmit data over the telephone, but it is concerned that its phones may be tapped. All of its data are transmitted as four-digit integers. It has asked you to write a program that will encrypt its data so that the data may be transmitted more securely. Your script should read a four-digit integer entered by the user in a **`prompt`** dialog and encrypt it as follows: Replace each digit by *(the sum of that digit plus 7) modulus 10*. Then swap the first digit with the third, and swap the second digit with the fourth. Then output XHTML text that displays the encrypted integer.

8.28 Write a program that inputs an encrypted four-digit integer (from Exercise 8.27) and decrypts it to form the original number.

JavaScript: Control Structures II

Objectives

- To be able to use the **for** and **do/while** repetition structures to execute statements in a program repeatedly.
- To understand multiple selection using the **switch** selection structure.
- To be able to use the **break** and **continue** program control statements.
- To be able to use the logical operators.

Who can control his fate?
William Shakespeare, *Othello*

The used key is always bright.
Benjamin Franklin

Outline

9.1 Introduction

Chapter 8 began our introduction to the types of building blocks that are available for problem solving and used those building blocks to employ proven program construction principles. In this chapter, we continue our presentation of the theory and principles of structured programming by introducing JavaScripts's remaining control structures (with the exception of **for/in**, which is presented in Chapter 11). As in Chapter 8, the JavaScript techniques you learn here are applicable to most high-level languages. In later chapters, we will see that the control structures we study in this chapter and Chapter 8 are helpful in manipulating objects.

9.2 Essentials of Counter-Controlled Repetition

Counter-controlled repetition requires:

1. The *name* of a control variable (or loop counter).
2. The *initial value* of the control variable.
3. The *increment* (or *decrement*) by which the control variable is modified each time through the loop (also known as *each iteration of the loop*).
4. The condition that tests for the *final value* of the control variable to determine whether looping should continue.

To see the four elements of counter-controlled repetition, consider the simple script shown in Fig. 9.1, which displays lines of XHTML text that illustrate the seven different font sizes supported by XHTML. The declaration in line 14 *names* the control variable (**counter**), reserves space for it in memory and sets it to an *initial value* of **1**. Declarations that include initialization are, in effect, executable statements.

```
<?xml version = "1.0"?>
<!DOCTYPE html PUBLIC "-//W3C//DTD XHTML 1.0 Strict//EN"
   "http://www.w3.org/TR/xhtml1/DTD/xhtml1-strict.dtd">

<!-- Fig. 9.1: WhileCounter.html   -->
<!-- Counter-Controlled Repetition -->

<html xmlns = "http://www.w3.org/1999/xhtml">
   <head>
      <title>Counter-Controlled Repetition</title>

      <script type = "text/javascript">
         <!--
         var counter = 1;            // initialization

         while ( counter <= 7 ) {    // repetition condition
            document.writeln( "<p style = \"font-size: " +
               counter + "ex\">XHTML font size " + counter +
               "ex</p>" );
            ++counter;               // increment
         }
         // -->
      </script>

   </head><body></body>
</html>
```

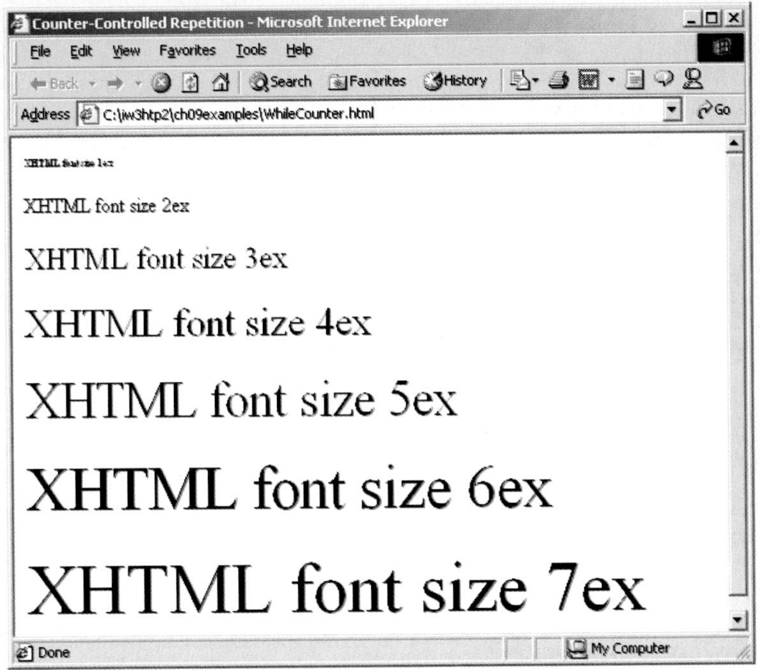

Fig. 9.1 Counter-controlled repetition.

The declaration and initialization of **counter** could also have been accomplished by the following declaration and statement:

```
var counter;                    // declare counter
counter = 1;                    // initialize counter to 1
```

The declaration is not executable, but the assignment statement is. We use both methods of initializing variables throughout the book.

Lines 17–19 in the **while** structure write a paragraph element consisting of the string "**XHTML font size**" concatenated with the control variable **counter**'s value, which represents the font size. An inline CSS **style** attribute sets the **font-size** property to the value of **counter** concatenated to **ex**. Notice the use of the escape sequence **\"**, which is placed around attribute **style**'s value. Because the double-quote character delimits the beginning and end of a string literal in JavaScript, it cannot be used in the contents of the string unless it is preceded by a **** to create the escape sequence **\"**. For example, if **counter** is 5, the preceding statement produces the markup

```
<p style = "font-size: 5ex">XHTML font size 5ex</p>
```

XHTML allows either single quotes (**'**) or double quotes (**"**) to be placed around the value specified for an attribute. JavaScript allows single quotes to be placed in a string literal, and XHTML allows single quotes to delimit an attribute value.

Common Programming Error 9.1

*Placing a double-quote (**"**) character inside a string literal that is delimited by double quotes causes a runtime error when the script is interpreted. To display a double-quote (**"**) character as part of a string literal, the double-quote (**"**) character must be preceded by a **** to form the escape sequence **\"**.*

Line 20 in the **while** structure *increments* the control variable by 1 for each iteration of the loop (i.e., each time the body of the loop is performed). The loop-continuation condition (line 16) in the **while** structure tests whether the value of the control variable is less than or equal to **7** (the *final value* for which the condition is **true**). Note that the body of this **while** structure executes even when the control variable is **7**. The loop terminates when the control variable exceeds **7** (i.e., **counter** becomes **8**).

Good Programming Practice 9.1

Use integer values to control the counting of loops.

Good Programming Practice 9.2

Indent the statements in the body of each control structure.

Good Programming Practice 9.3

Put a blank line before and after each major control structure, to make it stand out in the program.

Good Programming Practice 9.4

Too many levels of nesting can make a program difficult to understand. As a general rule, try to avoid using more than three levels of nesting.

Good Programming Practice 9.5

Vertical spacing above and below control structures and indentation of the bodies of control structures within the headers of the control structure, give programs a two-dimensional appearance that enhances readability.

9.3 `for` Repetition Structure

The **`for`** *repetition structure* handles all the details of counter-controlled repetition. Figure 9.2 illustrates the power of the **`for`** structure by reimplementing the script of Fig. 9.1.

When the **`for`** structure begins executing (line 17), the control variable **`counter`** is declared and is initialized to **`1`** (the first two elements of counter-controlled repetition are declaring the control variable's *name* and providing the control variable's *initial value*). Next, the loop-continuation condition, **`counter <= 7`**, is checked. The condition contains the *final value* (**`7`**) of the control variable. Because the initial value of **`counter`** is **`1`**, the condition is satisfied (i.e., **`true`**), so the body statement (lines 18–20) writes a paragraph element in the XHTML document. Then, variable **`counter`** is incremented in the expression **`++counter`** and the loop continues execution with the loop-continuation test. The control variable is now equal to **`2`**, so the final value is not exceeded and the program performs the body statement again (i.e., performs the next iteration of the loop). This process continues until the control variable **`counter`** becomes **`8`**, at which point the loop-continuation test fails and the repetition terminates.

```
1  <?xml version = "1.0"?>
2  <!DOCTYPE html PUBLIC "-//W3C//DTD XHTML 1.0 Strict//EN"
3     "http://www.w3.org/TR/xhtml1/DTD/xhtml1-strict.dtd">
4
5  <!-- Fig. 9.2: ForCounter.html                           -->
6  <!-- Counter-Controlled Repetition with for structure -->
7
8  <html xmlns = "http://www.w3.org/1999/xhtml">
9     <head>
10       <title>Counter-Controlled Repetition</title>
11
12       <script type = "text/javascript">
13          <!--
14          // Initialization, repetition condition and
15          // incrementing are all included in the for
16          // structure header.
17          for ( var counter = 1; counter <= 7; ++counter )
18             document.writeln( "<p style = \"font-size: " +
19                counter + "ex\">XHTML font size " + counter +
20                "ex</p>" );
21          // -->
22       </script>
23
24    </head><body></body>
25 </html>
```

Fig. 9.2 Counter-controlled repetition with the **`for`** structure (part 1 of 2).

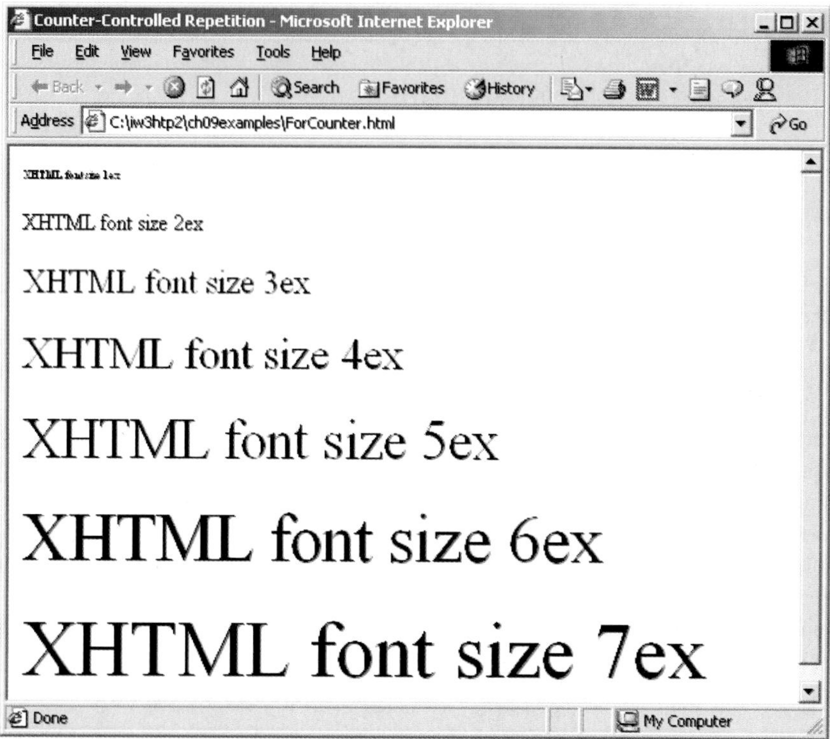

Fig. 9.2 Counter-controlled repetition with the **for** structure (part 2 of 2).

The program continues by performing the first statement after the **for** structure. (In this case, the script terminates, because the interpreter reaches the end of the script.)

Note that **counter** is declared inside the **for** structure in this example, but this practice is not required. Variable **counter** could have been declared before the **for** structure or not declared at all. Remember that JavaScript does not explicitly require variables to be declared before they are used. If a variable is used without being declared, the JavaScript interpreter creates the variable at the point of its first use in the script.

Figure 9.3 takes a closer look at the **for** structure of Fig. 9.2. The **for** structure's first line (including the keyword **for** and everything in parentheses after **for**) often is called the ***for*** *structure header*. Notice that the **for** structure "does it all"—it specifies each of the items needed for counter-controlled repetition with a control variable. If there is more than one statement in the body of the **for** structure, braces (**{** and **}**) are required to define the body of the loop.

Notice that Fig. 9.3 uses the loop-continuation condition **counter <= 7**. If the programmer incorrectly wrote **counter < 7**, the loop would execute only six times. This is an example of a common logic error called an *off-by-one error*.

Common Programming Error 9.2

Using an incorrect relational operator or using an incorrect final value of a loop counter in the condition of a **while**, **for** *or* **do/while** *structure can cause an off-by-one error or an infinite loop.*

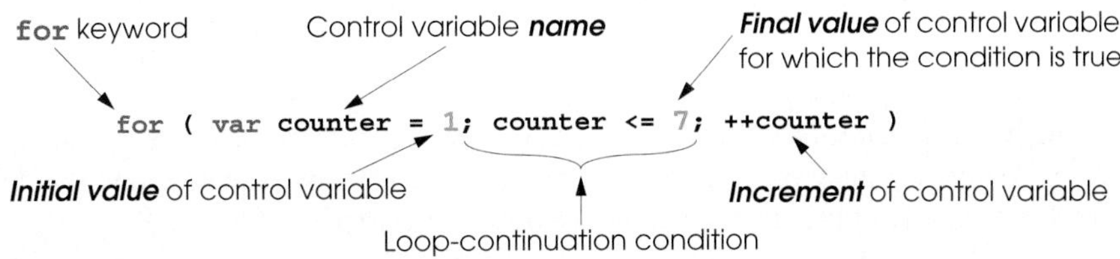

Fig. 9.3 Components of a typical **for** structure header.

Good Programming Practice 9.6

*Using the final value in the condition of a **while** or **for** structure and using the **<=** relational operator will help avoid off-by-one errors. For a loop used to print the values 1 to 10, for example, the loop-continuation condition should be **counter <= 10** rather than **counter < 10** (which is an off-by-one error) or **counter < 11** (which is correct). Many programmers prefer so-called zero-based counting, in which, to count 10 times through the loop, **counter** would be initialized to zero and the loop-continuation test would be **counter < 10**.*

The general format of the **for** structure is

```
for ( initialization; loopContinuationTest; increment )
    statement;
```

where the *initialization* expression names the loop's control variable and provides its initial value, *loopContinuationTest* is the expression that tests the loop-continuation condition (containing the final value of the control variable for which the condition is true) and *increment* is an expression that increments the control variable. The **for** structure can be represented by an equivalent **while** structure, with *initialization*, *loopContinuationTest* and *increment* placed as follows:

```
initialization;

while ( loopContinuationTest ) {
    statement;
    increment;
}
```

There is an exception to this rule that we will discuss in Section 9.7.

If the *initialization* expression in the **for** structure's header is the first definition of the control variable, the control variable can still be used after the **for** structure in the script. The part of a script in which a variable name can be used is known as the variable's *scope*. Scope is discussed in detail in Chapter 10, "JavaScript: Functions."

Good Programming Practice 9.7

*Place only expressions involving the control variable in the initialization and increment sections of a **for** structure. Manipulations of other variables should appear either before the loop (if they execute only once, like initialization statements) or in the loop body (if they execute once per iteration of the loop, like incrementing or decrementing statements).*

The three expressions in the **for** structure are optional. If *loopContinuationTest* is omitted, JavaScript assumes that the loop-continuation condition is **true**, thus creating an infinite loop. One might omit the *initialization* expression if the control variable is initialized elsewhere in the program before the loop. One might omit the *increment* expression if the increment is calculated by statements in the body of the **for** structure or if no increment is needed. The increment expression in the **for** structure acts like a stand-alone statement at the end of the body of the **for** structure. Therefore, the expressions

```
counter = counter + 1
counter += 1
++counter
counter++
```

are all equivalent in the incrementing portion of the **for** structure. Many programmers prefer the form **counter++**, because the incrementing of the control variable occurs after the body of the loop is executed. The postincrementing form therefore seems more natural. Because the variable being incremented in our example does not appear in an expression, preincrementing and postincrementing both have the same effect. The two semicolons in the **for** structure are required.

Common Programming Error 9.3

Using commas instead of the two required semicolons in the header of a **for** *structure is a syntax error.*

Common Programming Error 9.4

Placing a semicolon immediately to the right of the right parenthesis of the header of a **for** *structure makes the body of that* **for** *structure an empty statement. This code normally results in a logic error.*

The initialization, loop-continuation condition and increment portions of a **for** structure can contain arithmetic expressions. For example, assume that **x = 2** and **y = 10**. If **x** and **y** are not modified in the body of the loop, then the statement

```
for ( var j = x; j <= 4 * x * y; j += y / x )
```

is equivalent to the statement

```
for ( var j = 2; j <= 80; j += 5 )
```

The "increment" of a **for** structure may be negative, in which case it is really a decrement and the loop actually counts downward.

If the loop-continuation condition initially is **false**, the body of the **for** structure is not performed. Instead, execution proceeds with the statement following the **for** structure.

The control variable frequently is printed or used in calculations in the body of a **for** structure, but it does not have to be. It is common to use the control variable for controlling repetition while never mentioning it in the body of the **for** structure.

Testing and Debugging Tip 9.1

Although the value of the control variable can be changed in the body of a **for** *loop, avoid changing it, because doing so can lead to subtle errors.*

The **for** structure is flowcharted much like the **while** structure. For example, Fig. 9.4 shows the flowchart of the **for** structure

```
for ( var counter = 1; counter <= 7; ++counter )
   document.writeln( "<p style = \"font-size: " +
      counter + "ex\">XHTML font size " + counter +
      "ex</p>" );
```

This flowchart makes it clear that the initialization occurs only once and that incrementing occurs each time *after* the body statement executes. Note that, besides small circles and arrows, the flowchart contains only rectangle symbols and a diamond symbol.

9.4 Examples Using the for Structure

The examples in this section show methods of varying the control variable in a **for** structure. In each case, we write the appropriate **for** header. Note the change in the relational operator for loops that decrement the control variable.

Common Programming Error 9.5

Not using the proper relational operator in the loop-continuation condition of a loop that counts downward (such as using **i <= 1** *in a loop that counts down to 1) is usually a logic error that will yield incorrect results when the program runs.*

a) Vary the control variable from **1** to **100** in increments of **1**.

```
for ( var i = 1; i <= 100; ++i )
```

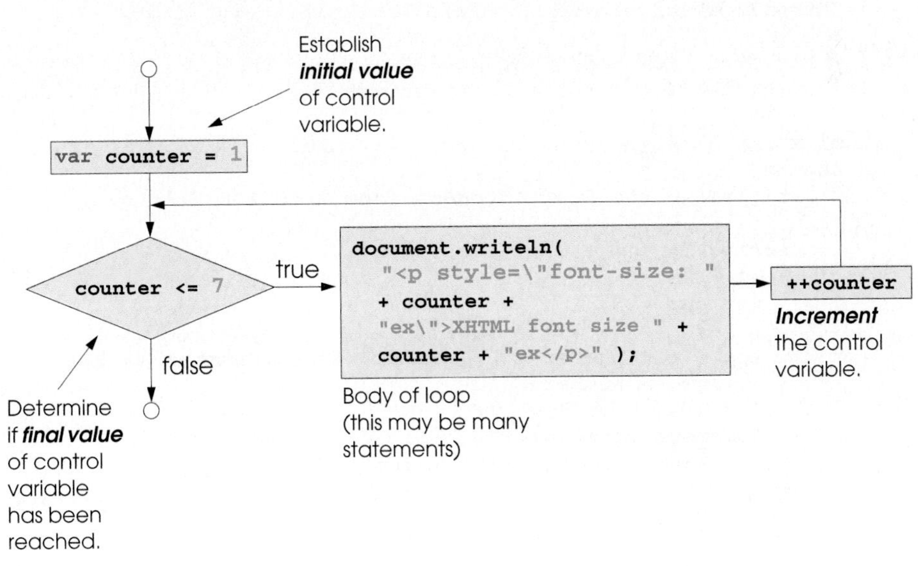

Fig. 9.4 Flowcharting a typical **for** repetition structure.

b) Vary the control variable from **100** to **1** in increments of **-1** (i.e., decrements of **1**).

```
for ( var i = 100; i >= 1; --i )
```

c) Vary the control variable from **7** to **77** in steps of **7**.

```
for ( var i = 7; i <= 77; i += 7 )
```

d) Vary the control variable from **20** to **2** in steps of **-2**.

```
for ( var i = 20; i >= 2; i -= 2 )
```

e) Vary the control variable over the following sequence of values: **2**, **5**, **8**, **11**, **14**, **17**, **20**.

```
for ( var j = 2; j <= 20; j += 3 )
```

f) Vary the control variable over the following sequence of values: **99**, **88**, **77**, **66**, **55**, **44**, **33**, **22**, **11**, **0**.

```
for ( var j = 99; j >= 0; j -= 11 )
```

The next two scripts demonstrate the **for** repetition structure. Figure 9.5 uses the **for** structure to sum the even integers from **2** to **100**. Notice that the increment expression adds **2** to the control variable **number** after the body executes during each iteration of the loop. The loop terminates when **number** has the value 102 (which is not added to the sum).

```
<?xml version = "1.0"?>
<!DOCTYPE html PUBLIC "-//W3C//DTD XHTML 1.0 Strict//EN"
   "http://www.w3.org/TR/xhtml1/DTD/xhtml1-strict.dtd">

<!-- Fig. 9.5: Sum.html                     -->
<!-- Using the for repetition structure -->

<html xmlns = "http://www.w3.org/1999/xhtml">
   <head>
      <title>Sum the Even Integers from 2 to 100</title>

      <script type = "text/javascript">
         <!--
         var sum = 0;

         for ( var number = 2; number <= 100; number += 2 )
            sum += number;

         document.writeln( "The sum of the even integers " +
            "from 2 to 100 is " + sum );
         // -->
      </script>

   </head><body></body>
</html>
```

Fig. 9.5 Summation with **for** (part 1 of 2).

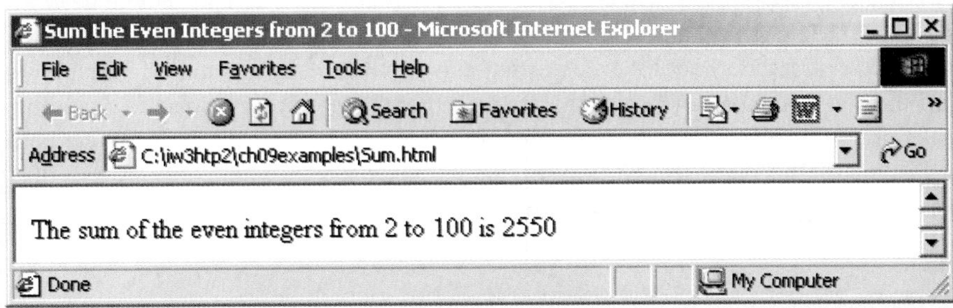

Fig. 9.5 Summation with **for** (part 2 of 2).

Note that the body of the **for** structure in Fig. 9.5 actually could be merged into the rightmost (increment) portion of the **for** header, by using a *comma* as follows:

```
for ( var number = 2; number <= 100;
      sum += number, number += 2)
   ;
```

Similarly, the initialization **sum = 0** could be merged into the initialization section of the **for** structure.

Good Programming Practice 9.8

Although statements preceding a **for** *and in the body of a* **for** *often can be merged into the* **for** *header, avoid doing so, because it makes the program more difficult to read.*

Good Programming Practice 9.9

For clarity, limit the size of control-structure headers to a single line, if possible.

The next example computes compound interest (compounded yearly) using the **for** structure. Consider the following problem statement:

> *A person invests $1000.00 in a savings account yielding 5% interest. Assuming that all interest is left on deposit, calculate and print the amount of money in the account at the end of each year for 10 years. Use the following formula to determine the amounts:*
>
> $a = p\,(1 + r)^{\,n}$
>
> *where*
>
> p is the original amount invested (i.e., the principal)
> r is the annual interest rate
> n is the number of years
> a is the amount on deposit at the end of the nth year.

This problem involves a loop that performs the indicated calculation for each of the 10 years the money remains on deposit. The solution is the script shown in Fig. 9.6.

Line 14 declares three variables and initializes **principal** to **1000.0** and **rate** to **.05**. Lines 16–24 write an XHTML **<table>** tag that has a **border** of **1** and a **width** of **100%** (the table uses the entire width of the browser window). After lines 16–17 write the initial attributes of the **table**, lines 18–19 write the **caption** that summarizes the table's content. Lines 20–21 create the table's header (**<thead>**), a row (**<tr>**) and a table heading (**<th>**) that **left align**s "**Year**." Lines 22fl24 create a table heading for "**Amount on deposit**" and write the closing **</tr>** and **</thead>** tags.

The **for** structure (line 26) executes its body 10 times, varying control variable **year** from 1 to 10 in increments of 1 (note that **year** represents *n* in the statement of the problem). JavaScript does not include an exponentiation operator. Instead, we use the ***Math*** object's ***pow*** method for this purpose. **Math.pow(x, y)** calculates the value of **x** raised to the **y**th power. Method **Math.pow** takes two numbers as arguments and returns the result.

Line 27 performs the calculation given in the problem statement

$$a = p(1 + r)^{n}$$

where *a* is **amount**, *p* is **principal**, *r* is **rate** and *n* is **year**.

```
1   <?xml version = "1.0"?>
2   <!DOCTYPE html PUBLIC "-//W3C//DTD XHTML 1.0 Strict//EN"
3      "http://www.w3.org/TR/xhtml1/DTD/xhtml1-strict.dtd">
4
5   <!-- Fig. 9.6: interest.html                -->
6   <!-- Using the for repetition structure -->
7
8   <html xmlns = "http://www.w3.org/1999/xhtml">
9      <head>
10        <title>Calculating Compound Interest</title>
11
12        <script type = "text/javascript">
13           <!--
14           var amount, principal = 1000.0, rate = .05;
15
16           document.writeln(
17              "<table border = \"1\" width = \"100%\">" );
18           document.writeln(
19              "<caption>Calculating Compound Interest</caption>" );
20           document.writeln(
21              "<thead><tr><th align = \"left\">Year</th>" );
22           document.writeln(
23              "<th align = \"left\">Amount on deposit</th>" );
24           document.writeln( "</tr></thead>" );
25
26           for ( var year = 1; year <= 10; ++year ) {
27              amount = principal * Math.pow( 1.0 + rate, year );
28              document.writeln( "<tbody><tr><td>" + year +
29                 "</td><td>" + Math.round( amount * 100 ) / 100 +
30                 "</td></tr>" );
31           }
32
33           document.writeln( "</tbody></table>" );
34           // -->
35        </script>
36
37     </head><body></body>
38  </html>
```

Fig. 9.6 Calculating compound interest with **for** (part 1 of 2).

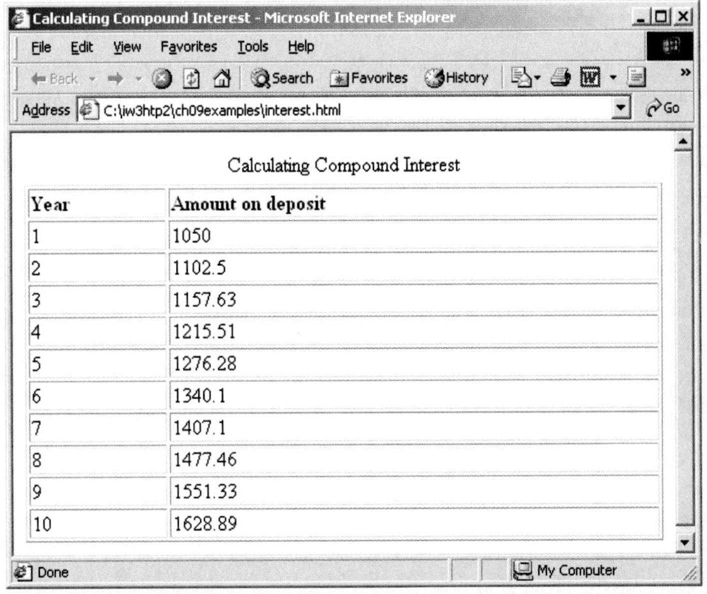

Fig. 9.6 Calculating compound interest with **for** (part 2 of 2).

Lines 28–30, write a line of XHTML markup that creates another row in the table. The first column is the current **year** value, and the second column is the result of the expression

```
Math.round( amount * 100 ) / 100
```

which multiplies the current value of **amount** by 100 to convert the value from dollars to cents, then uses the **Math** object's ***round*** method to round the value to the closest integer. The result is divided by 100, to produce a dollar value that has a maximum of two digits to the right of the decimal point. Unlike many other programming languages, JavaScript does not provide numeric-formatting capabilities that allow you to precisely control the display format of a number. When the loop terminates, line 33 writes the closing **</tbody>** and **</table>** tags.

Variables **amount**, **principal** and **rate** represent numbers in this script. Remember that JavaScript represents all numbers as floating-point numbers. This feature is convenient in this example, because we are dealing with fractional parts of dollars and need a type that allows decimal points in its values. Unfortunately, floating-point numbers can cause trouble. Here is a simple example of what can go wrong when using floating-point numbers to represent dollar amounts (assuming that dollar amounts are displayed with two digits to the right of the decimal point): Two dollar amounts stored in the machine could be 14.234 (which would normally be rounded to 14.23 for display purposes) and 18.673 (which would normally be rounded to 18.67 for display purposes). When these amounts are added, they produce the internal sum 32.907, which would normally be rounded to 32.91 for display purposes. Thus your printout could appear as

```
   14.23
 + 18.67
 -------
   32.91
```

but a person adding the individual numbers as printed would expect the sum to be 32.90! You have been warned!

9.5 **switch** Multiple-Selection Structure

Previously, we discussed the **if** single-selection structure and the **if/else** double-selection structure. Occasionally, an algorithm will contain a series of decisions in which a variable or expression is tested separately for each of the values it may assume, and different actions are taken for each value. JavaScript provides the **switch** multiple-selection structure to handle such decision making. The script in Fig. 9.7 demonstrates one of three different XHTML list formats determined by the value the user enters.

```
<?xml version = "1.0"?>
<!DOCTYPE html PUBLIC "-//W3C//DTD XHTML 1.0 Strict//EN"
   "http://www.w3.org/TR/xhtml1/DTD/xhtml1-strict.dtd">

<!-- Fig. 9.7: SwitchTest.html  -->
<!-- Using the switch structure -->

<html xmlns = "http://www.w3.org/1999/xhtml">
   <head>
      <title>Switching between XHTML List Formats</title>

      <script type = "text/javascript">
         <!--
         var choice,              // user's choice
             startTag,            // starting list item tag
             endTag,              // ending list item tag
             validInput = true,   // indicates if input is valid
             listType;            // list type as a string

         choice = window.prompt( "Select a list style:\n" +
            "1 (bullet), 2 (numbered), 3 (lettered)", "1" );

         switch ( choice ) {
            case "1":
               startTag = "<ul>";
               endTag = "</ul>";
               listType = "<h1>Bullet List</h1>";
               break;
            case "2":
               startTag = "<ol>";
               endTag = "</ol>";
               listType = "<h1>Ordered List: Numbered</h1>";
               break;
```

Fig. 9.7 Example using **switch** (part 1 of 3).

```
            case "3":
               startTag = "<ol type = \"A\">";
               endTag = "</ol>";
               listType = "<h1>Ordered List: Lettered</h1>";
               break;
            default:
               validInput = false;
         }

         if ( validInput == true ) {
            document.writeln( listType + startTag );

            for ( var i = 1; i <= 3; ++i )
               document.writeln( "<li>List item " + i + "</li>" );

            document.writeln( endTag );
         }
         else
            document.writeln( "Invalid choice: " + choice );
         // -->
      </script>

   </head>
   <body>
      <p>Click Refresh (or Reload) to run the script again</p>
   </body>
</html>
```

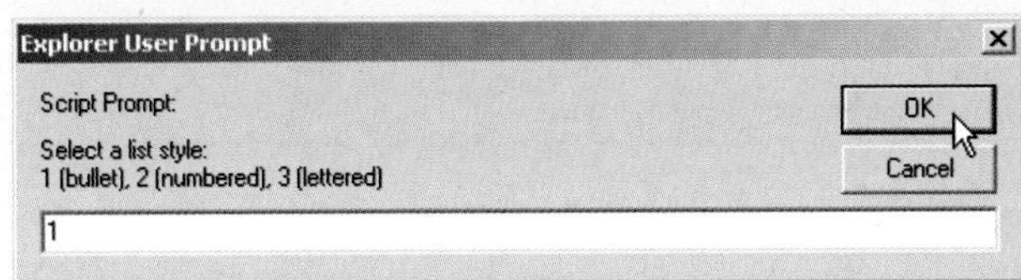

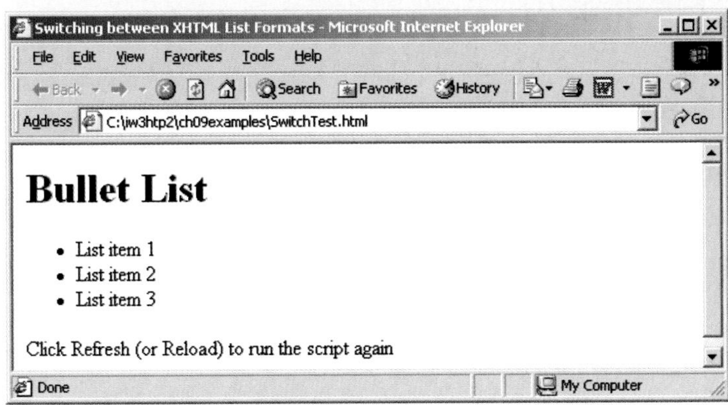

Fig. 9.7 Example using **switch** (part 2 of 3).

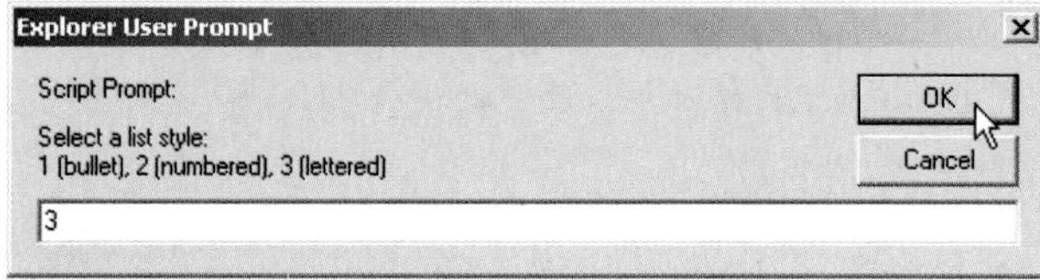

Fig. 9.7 Example using **`switch`** (part 3 of 3).

Line 14 in the script declares the variable **choice**. This variable will store the user's choice, which determines which type of XHTML list to display. Lines 15–16 declare variables **startTag** and **endTag**, which store the XHTML tags that indicate the XHTML list type the user chooses. Line 17 declares variable **validInput** and initializes it to **true**. The script uses this variable to determine whether the user made a valid choice (indicated by the value of **true**). If a choice is invalid, the script sets this variable's value to **false**. Line 18 declares variable **listType**, which stores a string indicating the XHTML list type. This string appears before the list in the XHTML document.

Lines 20–21 prompt the user to enter a **1** to display a bullet (unordered) list, a **2** to display a numbered (ordered) list and a **3** to display a lettered (ordered) list. Lines 23–41 define a **switch** structure that assigns to the variables **startTag**, **endTag** and **listType** values based on the value input by the user in the **prompt** dialog. The **switch** structure consists of a series of ***case*** *labels* and an optional ***default*** *case*.

When the flow of control reaches the **switch** structure, the script evaluates the *controlling expression* (**choice** in this example) in the parentheses following keyword **switch**. The value of this expression is compared with the value in each of the ***case*** *labels,* starting with the first **case** label. Assume that the user entered **2**. Remember that the value typed by the user in a **prompt** dialog is returned as a string. So, the string **2** is compared to the string in each **case** in the **switch** structure. If a match occurs (**case "2":**), the statements for that **case** execute. For the string **2** (lines 30–32) set **startTag** to **"<ol>"** to indicate an ordered list (such lists are numbered by default), set **endTag** to **"</ol>"** to indicate the end of an ordered list and set **listType** to **"<h1>Ordered List: Numbered</h1>"**. Line 33 exits the **switch** structure immediately. The **break** statement causes program control to proceed with the first statement after the **switch** structure. The **break** statement is used because the **case**s in a **switch** statement would otherwise run together. If **break** is not used anywhere in a **switch** structure, then each time a match occurs in the structure, the statements for all the remaining **case**s execute. If no match occurs between the controlling expression's value and a **case** label, the **default** case executes and sets variable **validInput** to **false**.

Next, the flow of control continues with the **if** structure at line 43, which tests variable **validInput** to determine whether its value is **true**. If so, lines 44–49 write the **listType**, the **startTag**, three list items (**<li>**) and the **endTag**. Otherwise, the script writes text in the XHTML document indicating that an invalid choice was made.

Each **case** can have multiple actions (statements). The **switch** structure is different from other structures in that braces are not required around multiple actions in a **case** of a **switch**. The general **switch** structure (i.e., using a **break** in each **case**) is flowcharted in Fig. 9.8. [*Note*: As an exercise, flowchart the general **switch** structure without **break** statements.]

The flowchart makes it clear that each **break** statement at the end of a **case** causes control to exit from the **switch** structure immediately. The **break** statement is not required for the last **case** in the **switch** structure (or the **default** case, when it appears last), because program control automatically continues with the next statement after the **switch** structure.

Common Programming Error 9.6

Forgetting a ***break*** *statement when one is needed in a* ***switch*** *structure is a logic error.*

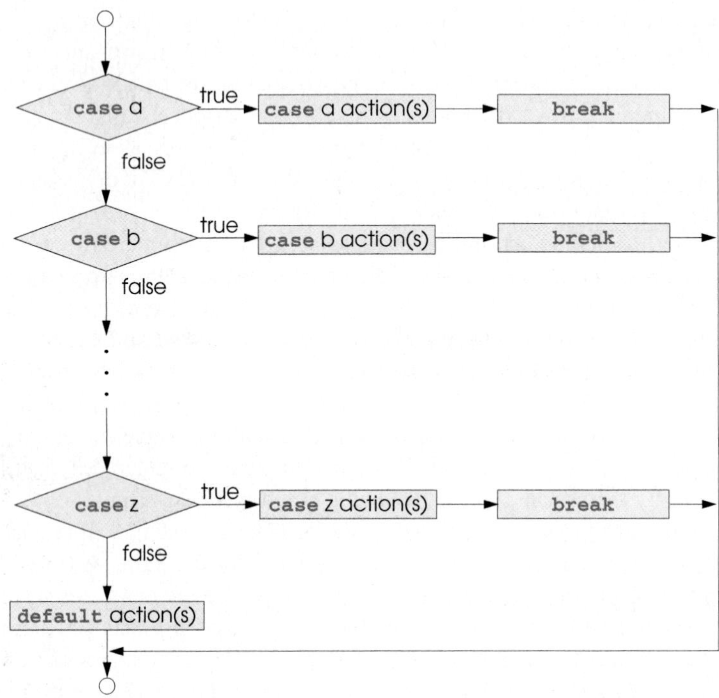

Fig. 9.8 **switch** multiple-selection structure.

Good Programming Practice 9.10

Provide a **default** *case in* **switch** *statements. Cases not explicitly tested in a* **switch** *statement without a* **default** *case are ignored. Including a* **default** *case focuses the programmer on processing exceptional conditions. However, there are situations in which no* **default** *processing is needed.*

Good Programming Practice 9.11

Although the **case** *clauses and the* **default** *case clause in a* **switch** *structure can occur in any order, it is a good programming practice to place the* **default** *clause last.*

Good Programming Practice 9.12

In a **switch** *structure, when the* **default** *clause is listed last, the* **break** *for that* **case** *statement is not required. Some programmers include this* **break** *for clarity and for symmetry with other* **case***s.*

Note that having several **case** labels listed together (such as **case 1: case 2:** with no statements between the cases) simply means that the same set of actions is to occur for each of the cases. Again, note that, besides small circles and arrows, the flowchart contains only rectangle symbols and diamond symbols.

9.6 **do/while** Repetition Structure

The **do/while** repetition structure is similar to the **while** structure. In the **while** structure, the loop-continuation test occurs at the beginning of the loop, before the body of the loop executes. The **do/while** structure tests the loop-continuation condition *after* the loop body executes; therefore, *the loop body always executes at least once.* When a **do/while** terminates, execution continues with the statement after the **while** clause. Note that it is not necessary to use braces in a **do/while** structure if there is only one statement in the body. However, the braces usually are included, to avoid confusion between the **while** and **do/while** structures. For example,

```
while ( condition )
```

normally is regarded as the header to a **while** structure. A **do/while** structure with no braces around a single-statement body appears as

```
do
   statement;
while ( condition );
```

which can be confusing. The last line—**while(** *condition* **);**—may be misinterpreted by the reader as a **while** structure containing an empty statement (the semicolon by itself). Thus, to avoid confusion, the **do/while** structure with one statement often is written as follows:

```
do {
   statement;
} while ( condition );
```

Good Programming Practice 9.13

Some programmers always include braces in a **do/while** *structure, even if the braces are not necessary. This procedure helps eliminate ambiguity between the* **while** *structure and the* **do/while** *structure containing one statement.*

Common Programming Error 9.7

Infinite loops are caused when the loop-continuation condition never becomes **false** *in a* **while***,* **for** *or* **do/while** *structure. To prevent this, make sure that there is not a semicolon immediately after the header of a* **while** *or* **for** *structure. In a counter-controlled loop, make sure that the control variable is incremented (or decremented) in the body of the loop. In a sentinel-controlled loop, make sure that the sentinel value is eventually input.*

The script in Fig. 9.9 uses a **do/while** structure to display each of the six different XHTML header types (**h1** through **h6**). Line 14 declares control variable **counter** and initializes it to **1**. Upon entering the **do/while** structure, lines 17–19 write a line of XHTML text in the document. The value of control variable **counter** is used both to create the starting and ending header tags (e.g., **<h1>** and **</h1>**) and to create the line of text to display (e.g., **This is an h1 level head**). Line 21 increments the **counter** before the loop-continuation test occurs at the bottom of the loop.

The **do/while** flowchart in Fig. 9.10 makes it clear that the loop-continuation test does not occur until the action executes at least once.

```
<?xml version = "1.0"?>
<!DOCTYPE html PUBLIC "-//W3C//DTD XHTML 1.0 Strict//EN"
   "http://www.w3.org/TR/xhtml1/DTD/xhtml1-strict.dtd">

<!-- Fig. 9.9: DoWhileTest.html   -->
<!-- Using the do/while structure -->

<html xmlns = "http://www.w3.org/1999/xhtml">
   <head>
      <title>Using the do/while Repetition Structure</title>

      <script type = "text/javascript">
         <!--
         var counter = 1;

         do {
            document.writeln( "<h" + counter + ">This is " +
               "an h" + counter + " level head" + "</h" +
               counter + ">" );

            ++counter;
         } while ( counter <= 6 );
         // -->
      </script>

   </head><body></body>
</html>
```

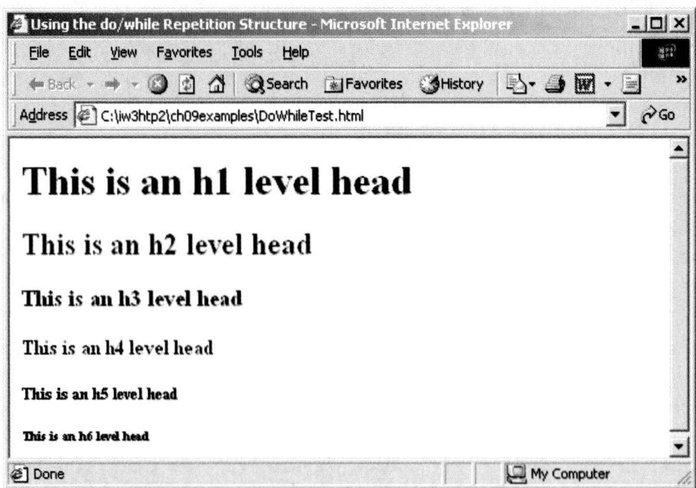

Fig. 9.9 Using the **do/while** repetition structure.

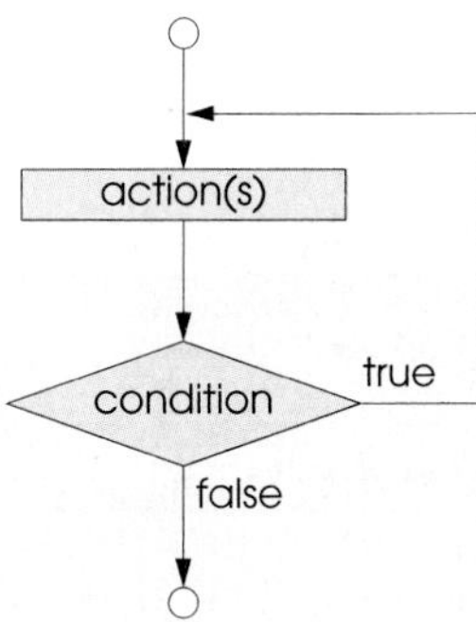

Fig. 9.10 Flowcharting the **do/while** repetition structure.

9.7 break and continue Statements

The ***break*** and ***continue*** statements alter the flow of control. The **break** statement, when executed in a **while**, **for**, **do/while** or **switch** structure, causes immediate exit from that structure. Execution continues with the first statement after the structure. Common uses of the **break** statement are to escape early from a loop or to skip the remainder of a **switch** structure (as in Fig. 9.7). Figure 9.11 demonstrates the **break** statement in a **for** repetition structure.

```
<?xml version = "1.0"?>
<!DOCTYPE html PUBLIC "-//W3C//DTD XHTML 1.0 Strict//EN"
   "http://www.w3.org/TR/xhtml1/DTD/xhtml1-strict.dtd">

<!-- Fig. 9.11: BreakTest.html    -->
<!-- Using the break statement    -->

<html xmlns = "http://www.w3.org/1999/xhtml">
   <head>
      <title>
         Using the break Statement in a for Structure
      </title>

      <script type = "text/javascript">
         <!--
         for ( var count = 1; count <= 10; ++count ) {
            if ( count == 5 )
               break;  // break loop only if count == 5

            document.writeln( "Count is: " + count + "<br />" );
         }

         document.writeln(
            "Broke out of loop at count = " + count );
         // -->
      </script>
```

Fig. 9.11 Using the **break** statement in a **for** structure (part 1 of 2).

```
27
28      </head><body></body>
29   </html>
```

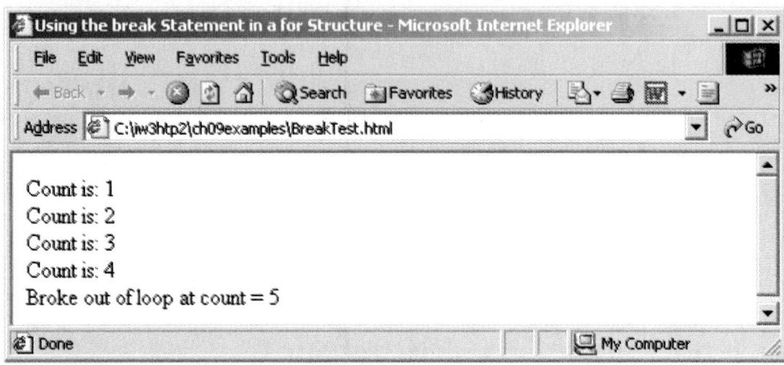

Fig. 9.11 Using the **break** statement in a **for** structure (part 2 of 2).

During each iteration of the **for** structure at lines 16–21, the script writes the value of **count** in the XHTML document. When the **if** structure at line 17 detects that **count** is **5**, the **break** at line 18 executes. This statement terminates the **for** structure, and the program proceeds to line 23 (the next statement in sequence immediately after the **for** structure), where the script writes the value of **count** when the loop terminated (i.e., **5**). The loop executes its body only four times.

The **continue** statement, when executed in a **while**, **for** or **do/while** structure, skips the remaining statements in the body of that structure and proceeds with the next iteration of the loop. In **while** and **do/while** structures, the loop-continuation test evaluates immediately after the **continue** statement executes. In **for** structures, the increment expression executes, then the loop-continuation test evaluates. This is the one case in which **for** and **while** differ. Improper placement of **continue** before the increment in a **while** may result in an infinite loop.

Figure 9.12 uses **continue** in a **for** structure to skip the **document.writeln** statement in line 21 when the **if** structure at line 17 determines that the value of **count** is **5**. When the **continue** statement executes, the script skips the remainder of the **for** structure's body. Program control continues with the increment of the **for** structure's control variable, followed by the loop-continuation test to determine whether the loop should continue executing.

Good Programming Practice 9.14

*Some programmers feel that **break** and **continue** violate structured programming. Because the effects of these statements can be achieved by structured programming techniques, these programmers do not use **break** and **continue**.*

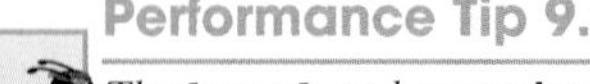

Performance Tip 9.1

*The **break** and **continue** statements, when used properly, perform faster than the corresponding structured techniques.*

```
<?xml version = "1.0"?>
<!DOCTYPE html PUBLIC "-//W3C//DTD XHTML 1.0 Strict//EN"
   "http://www.w3.org/TR/xhtml1/DTD/xhtml1-strict.dtd">

<!-- Fig. 9.12: ContinueTest.html  -->
<!-- Using the break statement     -->

<html xmlns = "http://www.w3.org/1999/xhtml">
   <head>
      <title>
         Using the continue Statement in a for Structure
      </title>

      <script type = "text/javascript">
         <!--
         for ( var count = 1; count <= 10; ++count ) {
            if ( count == 5 )
               continue;  // skip remaining code in loop
                          // only if count == 5

            document.writeln( "Count is: " + count + "<br />" );
         }

         document.writeln( "Used continue to skip printing 5" );
         // -->
      </script>

   </head><body></body>
</html>
```

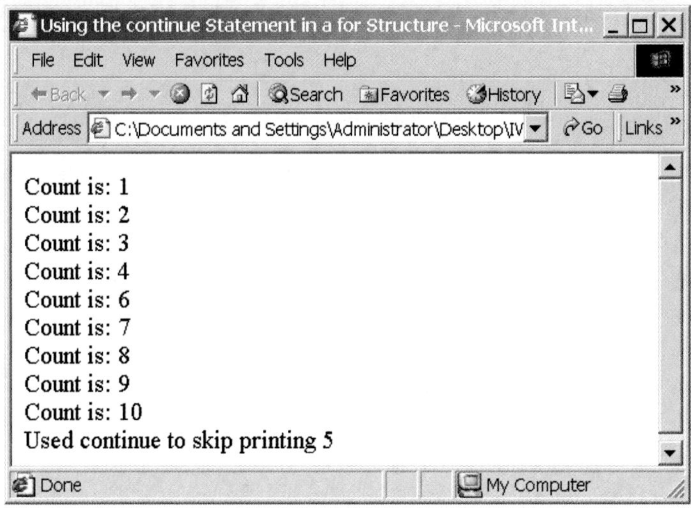

Fig. 9.12 Using the `continue` statement in a `for` structure .

Software Engineering Observation 9.1

There is a tension between achieving quality software engineering and achieving the best-performing software. Often, one of these goals is achieved at the expense of the other. For all but the most performance-intensive situations, the following "rule of thumb" should be followed: First make your code simple, readable and correct; then make it fast and small, but only if necessary.

9.8 Labeled `break` and `continue` Statements

The **`break`** statement can break out of an immediately enclosing **`while`**, **`for`**, **`do/while`** or **`switch`** structure. To break out of a nested set of structures, you can use the *labeled **`break`** statement.* This statement, when executed in a **`while`**, **`for`**, **`do/while`** or **`switch`** structure, causes immediate exit from that structure and any number of enclosing repetition structures; program execution resumes with the first statement after the enclosing *labeled statement* (a statement preceded by a label). The labeled statement can be a compound statement (a set of statements enclosed in curly braces, **`{}`**). Labeled **`break`** statements commonly are used to terminate nested looping structures containing **`while`**, **`for`**, **`do/while`** or **`switch`** structures. Figure 9.13 demonstrates the labeled **`break`** statement in a nested **`for`** structure.

```
<?xml version = "1.0"?>
<!DOCTYPE html PUBLIC "-//W3C//DTD XHTML 1.0 Strict//EN"
   "http://www.w3.org/TR/xhtml1/DTD/xhtml1-strict.dtd">

<!-- Fig. 9.13: BreakLabelTest.html            -->
<!-- Using the break statement with a Label -->

<html xmlns = "http://www.w3.org/1999/xhtml">
   <head>
      <title>Using the break Statement with a Label</title>

      <script type = "text/javascript">
         <!--
         stop: {   // labeled compound statement
            for ( var row = 1; row <= 10; ++row ) {
               for ( var column = 1; column <= 5 ; ++column ) {

                  if ( row == 5 )
                     break stop; // jump to end of stop block

                  document.write( "* " );
               }

               document.writeln( "<br />" );
            }

            // the following line is skipped
            document.writeln( "This line should not print" );
         }

```

Fig. 9.13 Using a labeled **`break`** statement in a nested **`for`** structure (part 1 of 2).

```
31            document.writeln( "End of script" );
32            // -->
33         </script>
34
35      </head><body></body>
36   </html>
```

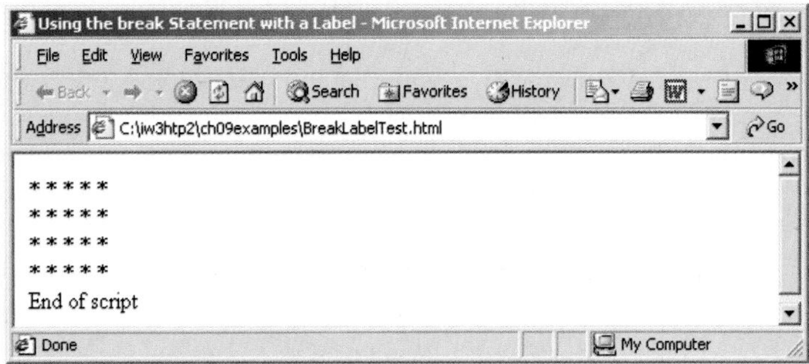

Fig. 9.13 Using a labeled **break** statement in a nested **for** structure (part 2 of 2).

The labeled compound statement (lines 14–29) begins with a *label* (an identifier followed by a colon). Here, we use the label "**stop:**." The compound statement is enclosed between the braces at the end of line 14 and in line 29, and includes both the nested **for** structure starting at line 15 and the **document.writeln** statement in line 28. When the **if** structure in line 18 detects that **row** is equal to **5**, the statement in line 19 executes. This statement terminates both the **for** structure at line 16 and its enclosing **for** structure at line 15, and the program proceeds to the statement in line 31 (the first statement in sequence after the labeled compound statement). The inner **for** structure executes its body only four times. Notice that the **document.writeln** statement in line 28 never executes, because it is included in the labeled compound statement and the outer **for** structure never completes.

The **continue** statement proceeds with the next iteration (repetition) of the immediately enclosing **while**, **for** or **do/while** structure. The *labeled* ***continue*** *statement*, when executed in a repetition structure (**while**, **for** or **do/while**), skips the remaining statements in that structure's body and any number of enclosing repetition structures, then proceeds with the next iteration of the enclosing *labeled repetition structure* (a repetition structure preceded by a label). In labeled **while** and **do/while** structures, the loop-continuation test evaluates immediately after the **continue** statement executes. In a labeled **for** structure, the increment expression executes, then the loop-continuation test evaluates. Figure 9.14 uses the labeled **continue** statement in a nested **for** structure to cause execution to continue with the next iteration of the outer **for** structure.

The labeled **for** structure (lines 14–26) starts with the **nextRow** label in line 14. When the **if** structure at line 20 in the inner **for** structure detects that **column** is greater than **row**, line 21 executes and program control continues with the increment of the control variable of the outer **for** loop. Even though the inner **for** structure counts from 1 to 10, the number of ***** characters output on a row never exceeds the value of **row**.

```
<?xml version = "1.0"?>
<!DOCTYPE html PUBLIC "-//W3C//DTD XHTML 1.0 Strict//EN"
   "http://www.w3.org/TR/xhtml1/DTD/xhtml1-strict.dtd">

<!-- Fig. 9.14: ContinueLabelTest.html -->
<!-- Using the continue statement      -->

<html xmlns = "http://www.w3.org/1999/xhtml">
   <head>
      <title>Using the continue Statement with a Label</title>

      <script type = "text/javascript">
         <!--
         nextRow:   // target label of continue statement
            for ( var row = 1; row <= 5; ++row ) {
               document.writeln( "<br />" );

               for ( var column = 1; column <= 10; ++column ) {

                  if ( column > row )
                     continue nextRow; // next iteration of
                                       // labeled loop

                  document.write( "* " );
               }
            }
         // -->
      </script>

   </head><body></body>
</html>
```

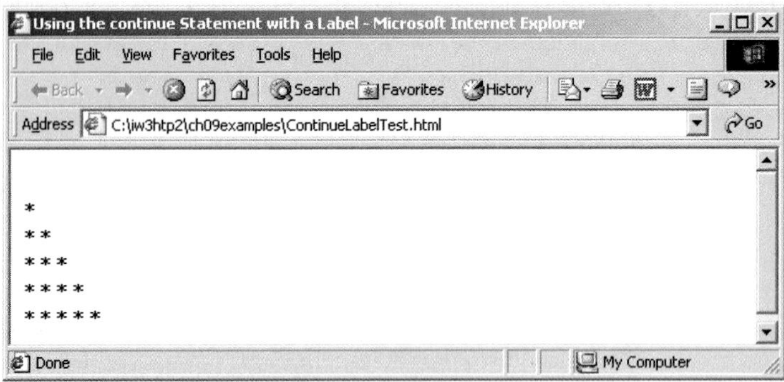

Fig. 9.14 Using a labeled **continue** statement in a nested **for** structure .

9.9 Logical Operators

So far, we have studied only such *simple conditions* as **count <= 10**, **total > 1000** and **number != sentinelValue**. These conditions were expressed in terms of the relational operators **>**, **<**, **>=** and **<=** and in terms of the equality operators **==** and **!=**. Each decision tested one condition. To test multiple conditions in the process of making a decision, we performed these tests in separate statements or in nested **if** or **if/else** structures.

JavaScript provides *logical operators* that can be used to form more complex conditions by combining simple conditions. The logical operators are **&&** (*logical AND*), **||** (*logical OR*) and **!** (*logical NOT*, also called *logical negation*). We consider examples of each of these operators.

Suppose that, at some point in a program, we wish to ensure that two conditions are *both* **true** before we choose a certain path of execution. In this case, we can use the logical **&&** operator as follows:

```
if ( gender == 1 && age >= 65 )
   ++seniorFemales;
```

This **if** statement contains two simple conditions. The condition **gender == 1** might be evaluated to determine, for example, whether a person is a female. The condition **age >= 65** is evaluated to determine whether a person is a senior citizen. The two simple conditions are evaluated first, because the precedences of **==** and **>=** are both higher than the precedence of **&&**. The **if** statement then considers the combined condition

```
gender == 1 && age >= 65
```

This condition is **true** *if and only if* both of the simple conditions are **true**. Finally, if this combined condition is indeed **true**, the count of **seniorFemales** is incremented by **1**. If either or both of the simple conditions are **false**, the program skips the incrementing and proceeds to the statement following the **if** structure. The preceding combined condition can be made more readable by adding redundant parentheses:

```
( gender == 1 ) && ( age >= 65 )
```

The table in Fig. 9.15 summarizes the **&&** operator. The table shows all four possible combinations of **false** and **true** values for *expression1* and *expression2*. Such tables are often called *truth tables*. JavaScript evaluates to **false** or **true** all expressions that include relational operators, equality operators and/or logical operators.

Now let us consider the **||** (logical OR) operator. Suppose we wish to ensure that either *or* both of two conditions are **true** before we choose a certain path of execution. In this case, we use the **||** operator as in the following program segment:

```
if ( semesterAverage >= 90 || finalExam >= 90 )
   document.writeln( "Student grade is A" );
```

expression1	expression2	expression1 && expression2
false	false	false
false	true	false
true	false	false
true	true	true

Fig. 9.15 Truth table for the **&&** (logical AND) operator.

This statement also contains two simple conditions. The condition **semesterAverage >= 90** is evaluated to determine whether the student deserves an "A" in the course because of a solid performance throughout the semester. The condition **finalExam >= 90** is evaluated to determine whether the student deserves an "A" in the course because of an outstanding performance on the final exam. The **if** statement then considers the combined condition

```
semesterAverage >= 90 || finalExam >= 90
```

and awards the student an "A" if either or both of the simple conditions are **true**. Note that the message "**Student grade is A**" is *not* printed only when both of the simple conditions are **false**. Figure 9.16 is a truth table for the logical OR operator (**||**).

The **&&** operator has a higher precedence than the **||** operator. Both operators associate from left to right. An expression containing **&&** or **||** operators is evaluated only until truth or falsity is known. Thus, evaluation of the expression

```
gender == 1 && age >= 65
```

will stop immediately if **gender** is not equal to **1** (i.e., the entire expression is **false**) and continues if **gender** is equal to **1** (i.e., the entire expression could still be **true** if the condition **age >= 65** is **true**). This performance feature for evaluation of logical AND and logical OR expressions is called *short-circuit evaluation.*

JavaScript provides the **!** (logical negation) operator to enable a programmer to "reverse" the meaning of a condition (i.e., a **true** value becomes **false**, and a **false** value becomes **true**). Unlike the logical operators **&&** and **||**, which combine two conditions (i.e., they are binary operators), the logical negation operator has only a single condition as an operand (i.e., it is a unary operator). The logical negation operator is placed before a condition to choose a path of execution if the original condition (without the logical negation operator) is **false**, such as in the following program segment:

```
if ( ! ( grade == sentinelValue ) )
   document.writeln( "The next grade is " + grade );
```

The parentheses around the condition **grade == sentinelValue** are needed, because the logical negation operator has a higher precedence than does the equality operator. Figure 9.17 is a truth table for the logical negation operator.

expression1	expression2	expression1 || expression2
false	false	false
false	true	true
true	false	true
true	true	true

Fig. 9.16 Truth table for the || (logical OR) operator.

expression	! expression
`false`	`true`
`true`	`false`

Fig. 9.17 Truth table for operator **!** (logical negation).

In most cases, the programmer can avoid using logical negation by expressing the condition differently with an appropriate relational or equality operator. For example, the preceding statement may also be written as follows:

```
if ( grade != sentinelValue )
   document.writeln( "The next grade is " + grade );
```

This flexibility can help a programmer express a condition in a more convenient manner.

The script in Fig. 9.18 demonstrates all of the logical operators by producing their truth tables. The script produces an XHTML table containing the results.

In the output of Fig. 9.18, the strings "false" and "true" indicate **false** and **true** for the operands in each condition. The result of the condition is shown as **true** or **false**. Note that when you add a boolean value to a string, JavaScript automatically adds the string "false" or "true," depending on the boolean value. Lines 14–42 build an XHTML table containing the results.

An interesting feature of JavaScript is that most non-boolean values can be converted by JavaScript into a boolean **true** or **false** value. Nonzero numeric values are considered to be **true**. The numeric value zero is considered to be **false**. Any string that contains characters is considered to be **true**. The empty string (i.e., the string containing no characters) is considered to be **false**. The value **null** and variables that have been declared but not initialized are considered to be **false**. All objects (such as the browser's **document** and **window** objects and JavaScript's **Math** object) are considered to be **true**.

```
1  <?xml version = "1.0"?>
2  <!DOCTYPE html PUBLIC "-//W3C//DTD XHTML 1.0 Strict//EN"
3     "http://www.w3.org/TR/xhtml1/DTD/xhtml1-strict.dtd">
4
5  <!-- Fig. 9.18: LogicalOperators.html   -->
6  <!-- Demonstrating Logical Operators     -->
7
8  <html xmlns = "http://www.w3.org/1999/xhtml">
9     <head>
10       <title>Demonstrating the Logical Operators</title>
11
12       <script type = "text/javascript">
13          <!--
14          document.writeln(
15             "<table border = \"1\" width = \"100%\">" );
16
```

Fig. 9.18 Demonstrating the logical operators (part 1 of 2).

```
            document.writeln(
               "<caption>Demonstrating Logical " +
               "Operators</caption>" );

            document.writeln(
               "<tr><td width = \"25%\">Logical AND (&&)</td>" +
               "<td>false && false: " + ( false && false ) +
               "<br />false && true: " + ( false && true ) +
               "<br />true && false: " + ( true && false ) +
               "<br />true && true: " + ( true && true ) +
               "</td>" );

            document.writeln(
               "<tr><td width = \"25%\">Logical OR (||)</td>" +
               "<td>false || false: " + ( false || false ) +
               "<br />false || true: " + ( false || true ) +
               "<br />true || false: " + ( true || false ) +
               "<br />true || true: " + ( true || true ) +
               "</td>" );

            document.writeln(
               "<tr><td width = \"25%\">Logical NOT (!)</td>" +
               "<td>!false: " + ( !false ) +
               "<br />!true: " + ( !true ) + "</td>" );

            document.writeln( "</table>" );
            // -->
         </script>

      </head><body></body>
   </html>
```

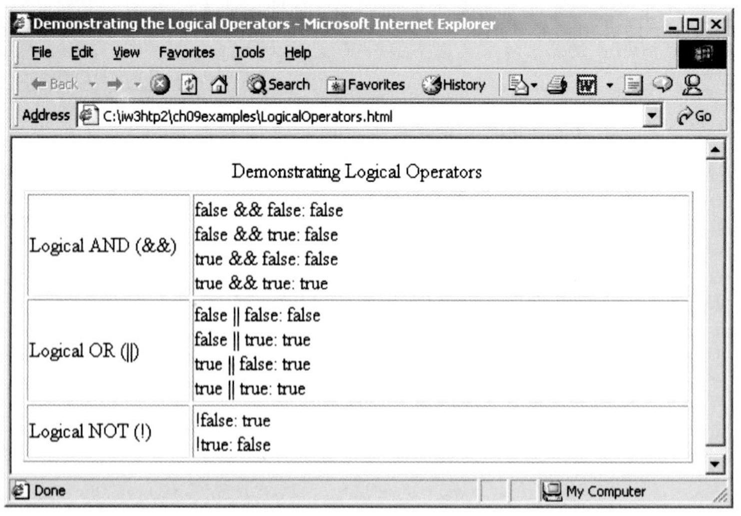

Fig. 9.18 Demonstrating the logical operators (part 2 of 2).

Figure 9.19 shows the precedence and associativity of the JavaScript operators introduced up to this point. The operators are shown from top to bottom in decreasing order of precedence.

9.10 Summary of Structured Programming

Just as architects design buildings by employing the collective wisdom of their profession, so should programmers design programs. Our field is younger than architecture is, and our collective wisdom is considerably sparser. We have learned that structured programming produces programs that are easier than unstructured programs to understand and hence are easier to test, debug, modify and even prove correct in a mathematical sense.

Figure 9.20 summarizes JavaScript's control structures. Small circles are used in the figure to indicate the single entry point and the single exit point of each structure. Connecting individual flowchart symbols arbitrarily can lead to unstructured programs. Therefore, the programming profession has chosen to combine flowchart symbols to form a limited set of control structures and to build structured programs by properly combining control structures in two simple ways.

For simplicity, only single-entry/single-exit control structures are used—that is, there is only one way to enter and only one way to exit each control structure. Connecting control structures in sequence to form structured programs is simple: The exit point of one control structure is connected to the entry point of the next control structure (i.e., the control structures are simply placed one after another in a program). We have called this process *control structure stacking*. The rules for forming structured programs also allow for control structures to be nested.

Figure 9.21 shows the rules for forming properly structured programs. The rules assume that the rectangle flowchart symbol may be used to indicate any action, including input/output.

Operators	Associativity	Type
`()`	left to right	parentheses
`++ -- !`	right to left	unary
`* / %`	left to right	multiplicative
`+ -`	left to right	additive
`< <= > >=`	left to right	relational
`== !=`	left to right	equality
`&&`	left to right	logical AND
`||`	left to right	logical OR
`?:`	right to left	conditional
`= += -= *= /= %=`	right to left	assignment

Fig. 9.19 Precedence and associativity of the operators discussed so far.

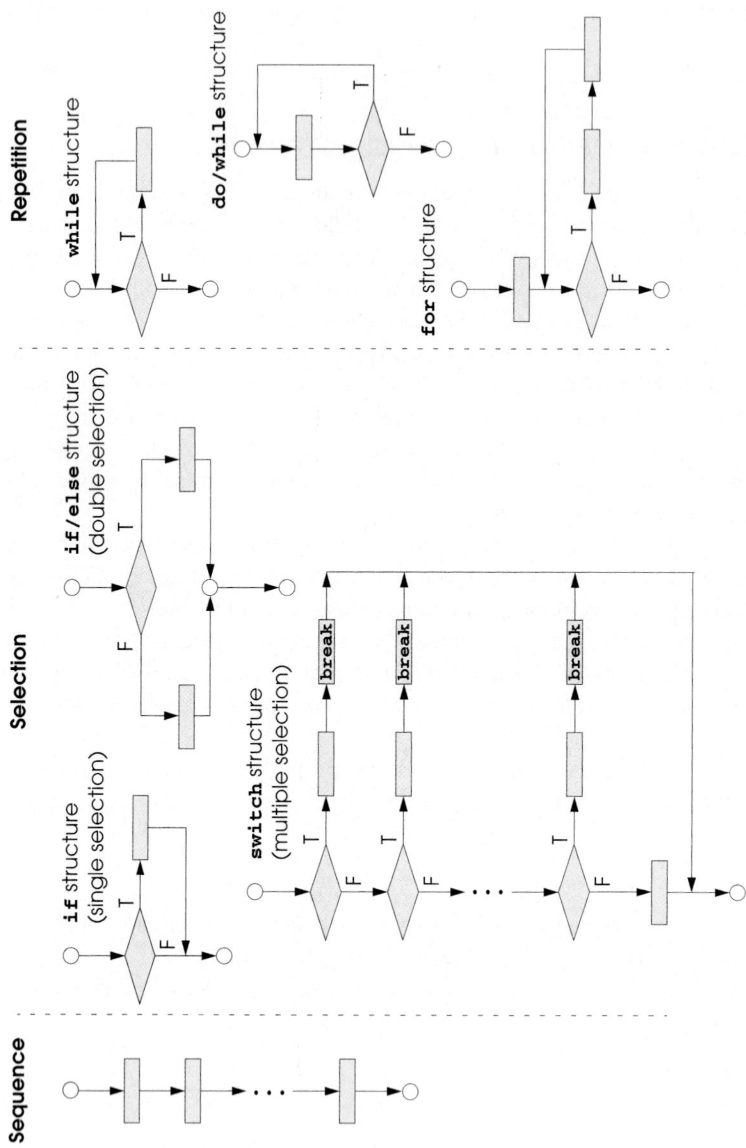

Fig. 9.20 JavaScript's single-entry/single-exit sequence, selection and repetition structures.

Applying the rules of Fig. 9.21 always results in a structured flowchart with a neat, building-block-like appearance. For example, repeatedly applying rule 2 to the simplest flowchart (Fig. 9.22) results in a structured flowchart containing many rectangles in sequence (Fig. 9.23). Notice that rule 2 generates a stack of control structures; so, let us call rule 2 the *stacking rule*.

Rules for Forming Structured Programs

1) Begin with the "simplest flowchart" (Fig. 9.22).
2) Any rectangle (action) can be replaced by two rectangles (actions) in sequence.
3) Any rectangle (action) can be replaced by any control structure (sequence, **`if`**, **`if/else`**, **`switch`**, **`while`**, **`do/while`** or **`for`**).
4) Rules 2 and 3 may be applied as often as you like and in any order.

Fig. 9.21 Rules for forming structured programs.

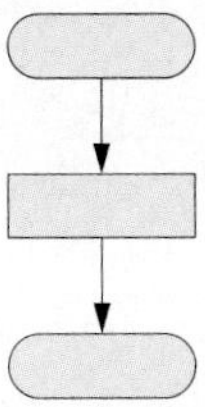

Fig. 9.22 Simplest flowchart.

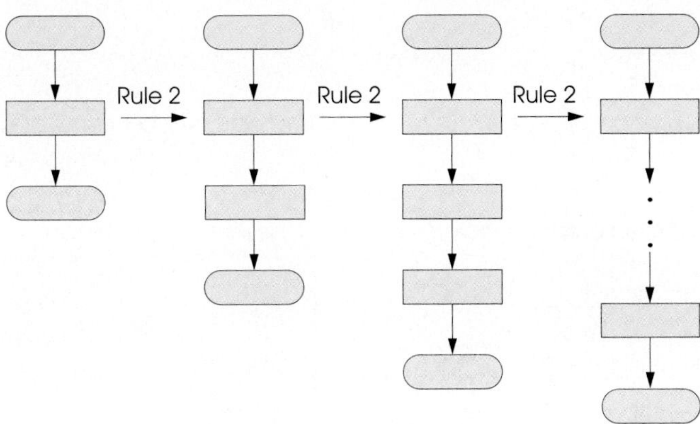

Fig. 9.23 Repeatedly applying rule 2 of Fig. 9.21 to the simplest flowchart.

Rule 3 is called the *nesting rule*. Repeatedly applying rule 3 to the simplest flowchart results in a flowchart with neatly nested control structures. For example, in Fig. 9.24, the rectangle in the simplest flowchart is first replaced with a double-selection (**`if/else`**) structure. Then rule 3 is applied again to both of the rectangles in the double-selection structure, by replacing each of these rectangles with double-selection structures. The dashed box around each of the double-selection structures represents the rectangle in the original simplest flowchart that was replaced.

Rule 4 generates larger, more involved and more deeply nested structures. The flowcharts that emerge from applying the rules in Fig. 9.21 constitute the set of all possible structured flowcharts and hence the set of all possible structured programs.

The beauty of the structured approach is that we use only seven simple single-entry/single-exit pieces and that we assemble them in only two simple ways. Figure 9.25 shows the kinds of stacked building blocks that emerge from applying rule 2 and the kinds of nested building blocks that emerge from applying rule 3. The figure also shows the kind of overlapped building blocks that cannot appear in structured flowcharts (because of the elimination of the **goto** statement).

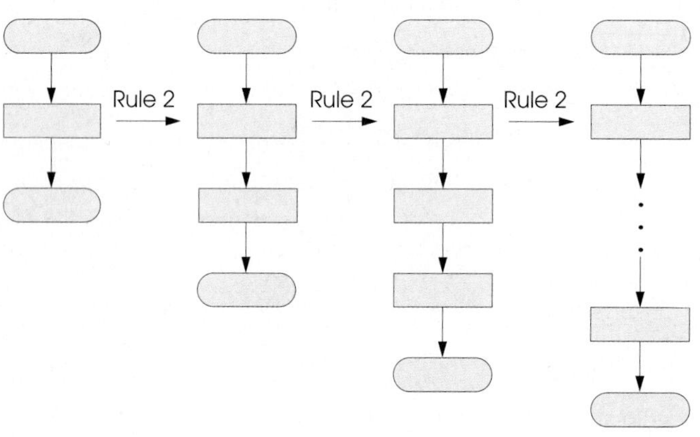

Fig. 9.24 Applying rule 3 of Fig. 9.21 to the simplest flowchart.

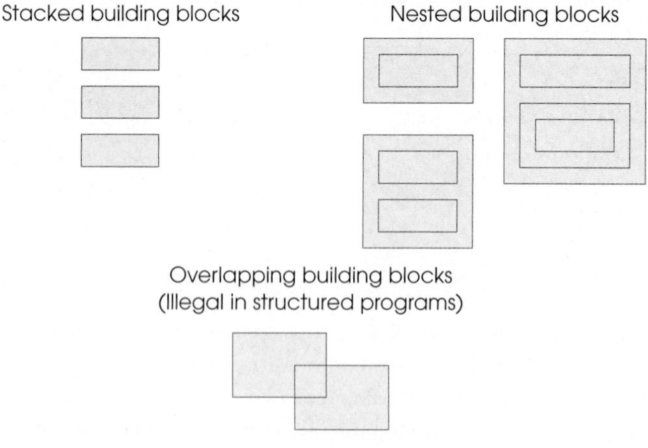

Fig. 9.25 Stacked, nested and overlapped building blocks.

If the rules in Fig. 9.21 are followed, an unstructured flowchart (such as that in Fig. 9.26) cannot be created. If you are uncertain about whether a particular flowchart is structured, apply the rules of Fig. 9.21 in reverse to try to reduce the flowchart to the simplest flowchart. If the flowchart is reducible to the simplest flowchart, the original flowchart is structured; otherwise, it is not.

Structured programming promotes simplicity. Bohm and Jacopini have given us the result that only three forms of control are needed:

- sequence
- selection
- repetition

Sequence is trivial. Selection is implemented in one of three ways:

- `if` structure (single selection)
- `if/else` structure (double selection)
- `switch` structure (multiple selection)

In fact, it is straightforward to prove that the **`if`** structure is sufficient to provide any form of selection; everything that can be done with the **`if/else`** structure and the **`switch`** structure can be implemented by combining **`if`** structures (although perhaps not as smoothly).

Repetition is implemented in one of four ways:

- `while` structure
- `do/while` structure
- `for` structure
- `for/in` structure (discussed in Chapter 11)

It is straightforward to prove that the **`while`** structure is sufficient to provide any form of repetition. Everything that can be done with the **`do/while`** structure and the **`for`** structure can be done with the **`while`** structure (although perhaps not as elegantly).

Combining these results illustrates that any form of control ever needed in a JavaScript program can be expressed in terms of:

- sequence
- `if` structure (selection)
- `while` structure (repetition)

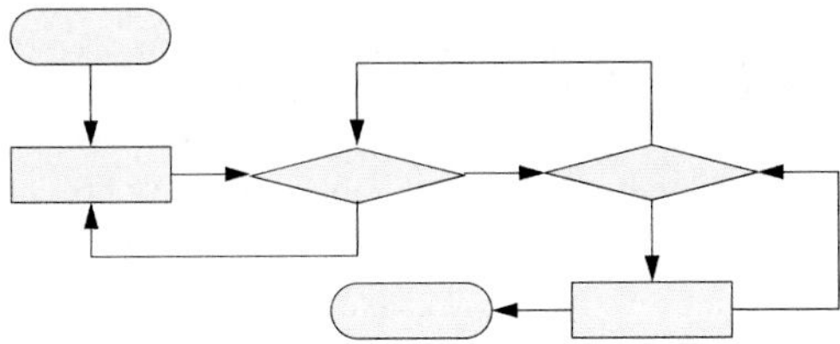

Fig. 9.26 Unstructured flowchart.

These control structures can be combined in only two ways—stacking and nesting. Indeed, structured programming promotes simplicity.

In this chapter, we have discussed composition of programs from control structures containing actions and decisions. In Chapter 10, we introduce another program-structuring unit, called the *function*. We will learn to compose large programs by combining functions that are composed of control structures. We will also discuss how functions promote software reusability.

SUMMARY

- Counter-controlled repetition requires the name of a control variable (or loop counter), the initial value of the control variable, the increment (or decrement) by which the control variable is modified each time through the loop (also known as *each iteration of the loop*) and the condition that tests for the final value of the control variable to determine whether looping should continue.
- The double-quote character cannot be used in the contents of the string unless it is preceded by a `\`, to create the escape sequence `\"`.
- The **`for`** repetition structure handles all the details of counter-controlled repetition.
- JavaScript does not require variables to be declared before they are used. If a variable is used without being declared, the JavaScript interpreter creates the variable at the point of its first use in the script.
- The **`for`** structure's first line (including the keyword **`for`** and everything in parentheses after **`for`**) is often called the **`for`** structure.
- Braces (**`{`** and **`}`**) are required to define the body of a **`for`** loop with multiple statements in its body.
- The general format of the header for the **`for`** structure is

```
for ( initialization; loopContinuationTest; increment )
    statement;
```

  where the *initialization* expression names the loop's control variable and provides its initial value, the *loopContinuationTest* expression is the loop-continuation condition and *increment* is an expression that increments the control variable.
- In most cases, the **`for`** structure can be represented by an equivalent **`while`** structure, with *initialization*, *loopContinuationTest* and *increment* placed as follows:

```
initialization;

while ( loopContinuationTest ) {
    statement;
    increment;
}
```

- The three expressions in the **`for`** structure are optional. If *loopContinuationTest* is omitted, the loop-continuation condition is **`true`**, thus creating an infinite loop. Omit the *initialization* expression if the control variable is initialized in the program before the loop. Omit the *increment* expression if the increment is calculated in the body of the **`for`** struccture or if no increment is needed.
- The increment expression in a **`for`** structure acts like a stand-alone statement at the end of the **`for`** structure's body.
- The initialization, loop-continuation condition and increment portions of a **`for`** structure can contain arithmetic expressions.

- The "increment" of a **for** structure may be negative, in which case it is really a decrement and the loop actually counts downward.
- If the loop-continuation condition is initially **false**, the body of the **for** structure is not performed.
- JavaScript does not include an exponentiation operator. The **Math** object's **pow** method calculates the value of **x** raised to the **y**th power and returns the result.
- The **Math** object's **round** method rounds its argument to the closest integer.
- The **switch** multiple-selection structure handles a series of decisions in which a variable or expression is tested separately for each of the values it may assume, and different actions are taken, depending on the value.
- The **switch** structure consists of a series of **case** labels and an optional **default** case. When the flow of control reaches the **switch** structure, the controlling expression in the parentheses following keyword **switch** is evaluated. The value of this expression is compared with the value in each of the **case** labels, starting with the first **case** label. If a match occurs, the statements for that **case** are executed. If no match occurs between the controlling expression's value and the value in a **case** label, the statements in the **default** case execute.
- Each **case** can have multiple actions (statements). The **switch** structure is different from other structures in that braces are not required around multiple actions in a **case** of a **switch**.
- The **break** statement at the end of a **case** causes control to immediately exit the **switch** structcure. The **break** statement is not required for the last **case** (or the **default** case when it appears last), because program control automatically continues with the next statement after the **switch** structure.
- Listing several **case** labels together means that the same action is to occur for each of the cases.
- The **do/while** structure tests the loop-continuation condition after the body of the loop is performed; therefore, the body of the loop is always executed at least once.
- Braces are not necessary in the **do/while** structure if there is only one statement in the body. The braces are usually included to avoid confusion between the **while** and **do/while** structures.
- The **break** statement, when executed in a **while**, **for**, **do/while** or **switch** structure, causes immediate exit from that structure.
- The **continue** statement, when executed in a **while**, **for** or **do/while** structure, skips the remaining statements in the body of that structure and proceeds with the next iteration of the loop.
- The labeled **break** statement, when executed in a **while**, **for**, **do/while** or **switch** structure, causes immediate exit from that structure and any number of enclosing repetition structures; program execution resumes with the first statement after the enclosing labeled (compound) statement.
- The labeled **continue** statement, when executed in a repetition structure (**while**, **for** or **do/while**), skips the remaining statements in that structure's body and in any number of enclosing repetition structures and proceeds with the next iteration of the enclosing labeled loop.
- JavaScript provides logical operators **&&** (logical AND), **||** (logical OR) and **!** (logical NOT), which may be used to form more complex conditions by combining simple conditions.
- A logical AND (**&&**) condition is **true** if and only if both of its operands are **true**. A logical OR (**||**) condition is **true** if either or both of its operands are **true**.
- An expression containing **&&** or **||** operators is evaluated only until truth or falsity is known. This performance feature is called *short-circuit evaluation*.
- The unary logical negation (**!**) operator reverses the meaning of a condition.
- JavaScript uses only single-entry/single-exit control structures—that is, there is only one way to enter and only one way to exit each control structure.

- Structured programming promotes simplicity. Any form of control ever needed in a program can be expressed in terms of the sequence structure, the **if** structure (selection) or the **while** structure (repetition). These control structures can be combined in only two ways—stacking and nesting.
- Selection is implemented in one of three ways: the **if** structure (single selection), the **if/else** structure (double selection) or the **switch** structure (multiple selection).
- Repetition is implemented in one of four ways: the **while** structure, the **do/while** structure, the **for** structure or the **for/in** structure.

TERMINOLOGY

! operator
&& operator
|| operator
break
case label
continue
counter-controlled repetition
default case in **switch**
definite repetition
do/**while** repetition structure
for repetition structure
infinite loop
labeled **break** statement
labeled compound statement
labeled **continue** statement
labeled repetition structure
logical AND (**&&**)
logical negation (**!**)
logical operators
logical OR (||)
loop-continuation condition
multiple selection
nested control structures
off-by-one error
repetition structures
scroll box
scrollbar
short-circuit evaluation
single-entry/single-exit control structures
stacked control structures
switch selection structure
while repetition structure

SELF-REVIEW EXERCISES

9.1 State whether each of the following is *true* or *false*. If *false*, explain why.

a) The **default** case is required in the **switch** selection structure.
b) The **break** statement is required in the default case of a **switch** selection structure.
c) The expression **(x > y && a < b)** is true if either **x > y** is true or **a < b** is true.
d) An expression containing the || operator is true if either or both of its operands is true.

9.2 Write a JavaScript statement or a set of statements to accomplish each of the following tasks:

a) Sum the odd integers between 1 and 99. Use a **for** structure. Assume that the variables **sum** and **count** have been declared.
b) Calculate the value of **2.5** raised to the power of **3**. Use the **pow** method.
c) Print the integers from 1 to 20 by using a **while** loop and the counter variable **x**. Assume that the variable **x** has been declared, but not initialized. Print only five integers per line. [*Hint*: Use the calculation **x % 5**. When the value of this expression is **0**, use **document.write("<br />")** to output a line break in the XHTML document.]
d) Repeat Exercise 9.2 (c), but using a **for** structure.

9.3 Find the error in each of the following code segments, and explain how to correct it:

a)
```
x = 1;
while ( x <= 10 );
   x++;
}
```

b)
```
for ( y = .1; y != 1.0; y += .1 )
   document.write( y + " " );
```

c)
```
switch ( n ) {
   case 1:
      document.writeln( "The number is 1" );
   case 2:
      document.writeln( "The number is 2" );
      break;
   default:
      document.writeln( "The number is not 1 or 2" );
      break;
}
```

d) The following code should print the values from1 to 10:

```
n = 1;
while ( n < 10 )
   document.writeln( n++ );
```

ANSWERS TO SELF-REVIEW EXERCISES

9.1 a) False. The **default** case is optional. If no default action is needed, then there is no need for a **default** case. b) False. The **break** statement is used to exit the **switch** structure. The **break** statement is not required for the last case in a **switch** structure. c) False. Both of the relational expressions must be true in order for the entire expression to be true when using the **&&** operator. d) True.

9.2 a)
```
sum = 0;
for ( count = 1; count <= 99; count += 2 )
    sum += count;
```

b) `Math.pow( 2.5, 3 )`

c)
```
x = 1;
while ( x <= 20 ) {
   document.write( x + " " );
   if ( x % 5 == 0 )
      document.write( "<br />" );
   ++x;
}
```

d)
```
for ( x = 1; x <= 20; x++ ) {
   document.write( x + " " );

   if ( x % 5 == 0 )
      document.write( "<br />" );
}
```

or

```
for ( x = 1; x <= 20; x++ )

   if ( x % 5 == 0 )
      document.write( x + "<br />" );
   else
      document.write( x + " " );
```

9.3 a) Error: The semicolon after the **while** header causes an infinite loop, and there is a missing left brace. Correction: Replace the semicolon by a **{**, or remove both the **;** and the **}**.

b) Error: Using a floating-point number to control a **for** repetition structure may not work, because floating-point numbers are represented approximately by most computers.
Correction: Use an integer, and perform the proper calculation to get the values you desire:

```
for ( y = 1; y != 10; y++ )
   document.writeln( y / 10 );
```

c) Error: Missing **break** statement in the statements for the first **case**.
Correction: Add a **break** statement at the end of the statements for the first **case**. Note that this missing ststement is not necessarily an error if the programmer wants the statement of **case 2:** to execute every time the **case 1:** statement executes.

d) Error: Improper relational operator used in the **while** repetition-continuation condition.
Correction: Use **<=** rather than **<**, or change **10** to **11**.

EXERCISES

9.4 Find the error in each of the following segemnts of code. [*Note*: There may be more than one error]:

a)
```
For ( x = 100, x >= 1, x++ )
   document.writeln( x );
```

b) The following code should print whether integer **value** is odd or even:

```
switch ( value % 2 ) {
   case 0:
      document.writeln( "Even integer" );
   case 1:
      document.writeln( "Odd integer" );
}
```

c) The following code should output the odd integers from 19 to 1:

```
for ( x = 19; x >= 1; x += 2 )
   document.writeln( x );
```

d) The following code should output the even integers from 2 to 100:

```
counter = 2;
do {
   document.writeln( counter );
   counter += 2;
} While ( counter < 100 );
```

9.5 What does the following script do?

```
<?xml version = "1.0"?>
<!DOCTYPE html PUBLIC "-//W3C//DTD XHTML 1.0 Strict//EN"
   "http://www.w3.org/TR/xhtml1/DTD/xhtml1-strict.dtd">

<html xmlns = "http://www.w3.org/1999/xhtml">
   <head><title>Mystery</title>
      <script type = "text/javascript">
         <!--
         for ( var i = 1; i <= 10; i++ ) {

            for ( var j = 1; j <= 5; j++ )
               document.writeln( "@" );

            document.writeln( "<br />" );
         }
```

```
            // -->
        </script>

    </head><body></body>
</html>
```

9.6 Write a script that finds the smallest of several integers. Assume that the first value read specifies the number of values to be input from the user.

9.7 Write a script that calculates the product of the odd integers from 1 to 15 and then outputs XHTML text that displays the results.

9.8 Modify the compound-interest program of Fig. 9.6 to repeat its steps for interest rates of 5, 6, 7, 8, 9 and 10%. Use a **for** loop to vary the interest rate.

9.9 Write a script that outputs XHTML to display the given patterns separately, one below the other. Use **for** loops to generate the patterns. All asterisks (*****) should be printed by a single statement of the form **document.write("*");** (this causes the asterisks to print side by side). A statement of the form **document.writeln("<br />");** can be used to position to the next line. A statement of the form **document.write(" ");** can be used to display a space (needed for the last two patterns). There should be no other output statements in the program. [*Hint*: The last two patterns require that each line begin with an appropriate number of blanks. You may need to use the XHTML **<pre></pre>** tags.]

9.10 One interesting application of computers is the drawing of graphs and bar charts (sometimes called *histograms*). Write a script that reads five numbers between 1 and 30. For each number read, output XHTML text that displays a line containing that number of adjacent asterisks. For example, if your program reads the number 7, it should output XHTML text that displays ***********.

9.11 *("The Twelve Days of Christmas" Song)* Write a script that uses repetition and **switch** structures to print the song "The Twelve Days of Christmas." One **switch** structure should be used to print the day (i.e., "First," "Second," etc.). A separate **switch** structure should be used to print the remainder of each verse. You can find the words at the site

www.santas.net/twelvedaysofchristmas.htm

9.12 A mail-order house sells five different products whose retail prices are as follows: product 1, $2.98; product 2, $4.50; product 3, $9.98; product 4, $4.49; and product 5, $6.87. Write a script that reads a series of pairs of numbers as follows:

a) Product number
b) Quantity sold for one day

Your program should use a **switch** structure to help determine the retail price for each product and should calculate and output XHTML that displays the total retail value of all products sold last week.

Use a **prompt** dialog to obtain the product number from the user. Use a sentinel-controlled loop to determine when the program should stop looping and display the final results.

9.13 Assume that **i = 1**, **j = 2**, **k = 3** and **m = 2**. What does each of the given statements print? Are the parentheses necessary in each case?

a) `document.writeln( i == 1 );`
b) `document.writeln( j == 3 );`
c) `document.writeln( i >= 1 && j < 4 );`
d) `document.writeln( m <= 99 && k < m );`
e) `document.writeln( j >= i || k == m );`
f) `document.writeln( k + m < j | 3 - j >= k );`
g) `document.writeln( !( k > m ) );`

9.14 Modify Exercise 9.9 to combine your code from the four separate triangles of asterisks into a single script that prints all four patterns side by side, making clever use of nested **for** loops.

```
*           **********  **********           *
**          *********    *********          **
***         ********      ********         ***
****        *******        *******        ****
*****       ******          ******       *****
******      *****            *****      ******
*******     ****              ****     *******
********    ***                ***    ********
*********   **                  **   *********
**********  *                    *  **********
```

9.15 *(De Morgan's Laws)* In this chapter, wehave discussed the logical operators **&&**, **||** and **!**. De Morgan's Laws can sometimes make it more convenient for us to express a logical expression. These laws state that the expression **!(***condition1* **&&** *condition2***)** is logically equivalent to the expression **(!***condition1* **||** **!***condition2***)**. Also, the expression **!(***condition1* **||** *condition2***)** is logically equivalent to the expression **(!***condition1* **&&** **!***condition2***)**. Use De Morgan's Laws to write equivalent expressions for each of the following, and then write a program to show that the original expression and the new expression are equivalent in each case:

a) `!( x < 5 ) && !( y >= 7 )`
b) `!( a == b ) || !( g != 5 )`
c) `!( ( x <= 8 ) && ( y > 4 ) )`
d) `!( ( i > 4 ) || ( j <= 6 ) )`

9.16 Write a script that prints the following diamond shape:

```
    *
   ***
  *****
 *******
*********
 *******
  *****
   ***
    *
```

You may use output statements that print a single asterisk (*), a single space or a single newline character. Maximize your use of repetition (with nested **for** structures), and minimize the number of output statements.

9.17 Modify the program you wrote in Exercise 9.16 to read an odd number in the range 1 to 19. This number specifies the number of rows in the diamond. Your program should then display a diamond of the appropriate size.

9.18 A criticism of the **break** statement and the **continue** statement is that each is unstructured. Actually, **break** statements and **continue** statements can always be replaced by structured statements, although coding the replacement can be awkward. Describe in general how you would remove any **break** statement from a loop in a program and replace that statement with some structured equivalent. [*Hint*: The **break** statement "jumps out of" a loop from the body of that loop. The other way to leave is by failing the loop-continuation test. Consider using in the loop-continuation test a second test that indicates "early exit because of a 'break' condition."] Use the technique you developed here to remove the **break** statement from the program of Fig. 9.11.

9.19 What does the following script do?

```
<?xml version = "1.0"?>
<!DOCTYPE html PUBLIC "-//W3C//DTD XHTML 1.0 Strict//EN"
   "http://www.w3.org/TR/xhtml1/DTD/xhtml1-strict.dtd">

<html xmlns = "http://www.w3.org/1999/xhtml">
   <head><title>Mystery</title>
      <script type = "text/javascript">
         <!--
         for ( var i = 1; i <= 5; i++ ) {
            for ( var j = 1; j <= 3; j++ ) {
               for ( var k = 1; k <= 4; k++ )
                  document.write( "*" );
               document.writeln( "<br />" );
            }
            document.writeln( "<br />" );
         }
         // -->
      </script>

   </head><body></body>
</html>
```

9.20 Describe in general how you would remove any **continue** statement from a loop in a program and replace that statement with some structured equivalent. Use the technique you develop to remove the **continue** statement from the program of Fig. 9.12.

9.21 Given the following **switch** structure:

```
switch ( k ) {
   case 1:
      break;
   case 2:
   case 3:
      ++k;
      break;
```

```
      case 4:
         --k;
         break;
      default:
         k *= 3;
}

x = k;
```

what values are assigned to **x** when **k** has values of 1, 2, 3, 4 and 10.

10

JavaScript: Functions

Objectives

- To understand how to construct programs modularly from small pieces called functions.
- To be able to create new functions.
- To understand the mechanisms used to pass information between functions.
- To introduce simulation techniques that use random-number generation.
- To understand how the visibility of identifiers is limited to specific regions of programs.

Form ever follows function.
Louis Henri Sullivan

E pluribus unum.
(One composed of many.)
Virgil

O! call back yesterday, bid time return.
William Shakespeare, *Richard II*

Call me Ishmael.
Herman Melville, *Moby Dick*

When you call me that, smile.
Owen Wister

Outline

10.1 Introduction

Most computer programs that solve real-world problems are much larger than the programs presented in the first few chapters of this book. Experience has shown that the best way to develop and maintain a large program is to construct it from small, simple pieces, or *modules*. This technique is called *divide and conquer*. This chapter describes many key features of JavaScript that facilitate the design, implementation, operation and maintenance of large scripts.

10.2 Program Modules in JavaScript

Modules in JavaScript are called *functions*. JavaScript programs are written by combining new functions that the programmer writes with "prepackaged" functions and objects available in JavaScript. The prepackaged functions that belong to JavaScript objects (such as **`Math.pow`** and **`Math.round`**, introduced previously) are often called *methods*. The term method implies that the function belongs to a particular object; however, the terms function and method can be used interchangeably. We will refer to functions that belong to a particular JavaScript object as methods; all others are referred to as functions.

JavaScript provides several objects that have a rich collection of methods for performing common mathematical calculations, string manipulations, date and time manipulations, and manipulations of collections of data called **`Array`**s. These objects make the programmer's job easier, because they provide many of the capabilities programmers need. Some common predefined objects of JavaScript and their methods are discussed in Chapter 11, "JavaScript: Arrays" and Chapter 12, "JavaScript: Objects."

Good Programming Practice 10.1

Familiarize yourself with the rich collection of objects and methods provided by JavaScript.

Software Engineering Observation 10.1

Avoid reinventing the wheel. If possible, use JavaScript objects, methods and functions instead of writing new functions. This practice reduces script development time and helps prevent the introduction of new errors.

Portability Tip 10.1

Using the methods built into JavaScript objects helps make scripts more portable.

Performance Tip 10.1

Do not try to rewrite existing methods of JavaScript objects to make them more efficient. You usually will not be able to increase the performance of the methods.

The programmer can write functions to define specific tasks that may be used at many points in a script. These functions are referred to as *programmer-defined functions.* The actual statements defining the function are written only once and are hidden from other functions.

A function is *invoked* (i.e., made to perform its designated task) by a *function call.* The function call specifies the function name and provides information (as *arguments*) that the called function needs to perform its task. A common analogy for this structure is the hierarchical form of management. A boss (the *calling function*, or *caller*) asks a worker (the *called function*) to perform a task and *return* (i.e., report back) the results when the task is done. The boss function does not know *how* the worker function performs its designated tasks. The worker may call other worker functions, and the boss will be unaware of this situation. We will soon see how this "hiding" of implementation details promotes good software engineering. Figure 10.1 shows the **boss** function communicating with several worker functions in a hierarchical manner. Note that **worker1** acts as a "boss" function to **worker4** and **worker5**. Relationships among functions may be other than the hierarchical structure shown in this figure.

Functions (and methods) are invoked by writing the name of the function (or method), followed by a left parenthesis, followed by the argument(s) of the function (or method), if any, followed by a right parenthesis. For example, a programmer desiring to convert a string stored in variable **inputValue** to a floating-point number and add it to variable **total**, might write

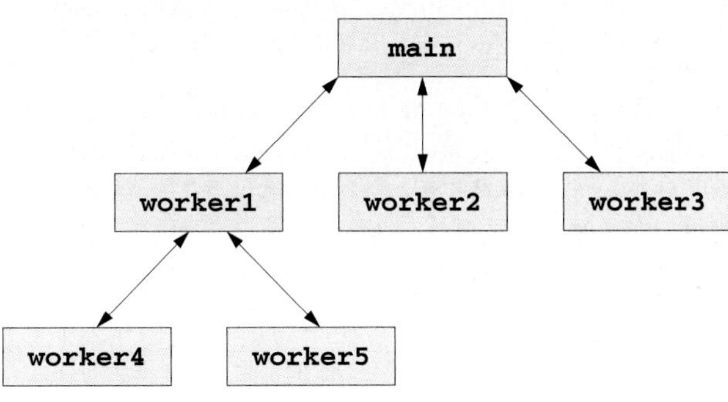

Fig. 10.1 Hierarchical boss-function/worker-function relationship.

```
total += parseFloat( inputValue );
```

When this statement executes, JavaScript function ***parseFloat*** converts the string contained in the parentheses (stored in variable **inputValue** in this case) to a floating-point value and adds value to **total**. The variable **inputValue** is the argument of the **parseFloat** function. Function **parseFloat** takes a string representation of a floating-point number as an argument and returns the corresponding floating-point numeric value.

Function (and method) arguments may be constants, variables or expressions. If **s1 = "22.3"** and **s2 = "45"**, then the statement

```
total += parseFloat( s1 + s2 );
```

evaluates the expression **s1 + s2**, concatenates the strings **s1** and **s2** (resulting in the string **"22.345"**), converts the result into a floating-point number and adds the floating-point number to variable **total**.

10.3 Programmer-Defined Functions

Functions allow the programmer to modularize a program. All variables declared in function definitions are *local variables*—i.e., they are known only in the function in which they are defined. Most functions have a list of *parameters* that provide the means for communicating information between functions via function calls. A function's parameters are also considered to be local variables. When a function is called, the arguments in the function call are assigned to the corresponding parameters in the function definition.

There are several motivations for modularizing a program with functions. The divide-and-conquer approach makes program development more manageable. Another motivation is *software reusability* (i.e., using existing functions as building blocks to create new programs). With good function naming and definition, programs can be created from standardized functions rather than being built by using customized code. For example, we did not have to define how to convert strings to integers and floating-point numbers—JavaScript already provides function **parseInt** to convert a string to an integer and function **parseFloat** to convert a string to a floating-point number. A third motivation is to avoid repeating code in a program. Packaging code as a function allows that code to be executed from several locations in a program by calling the function.

Software Engineering Observation 10.2

Each function should perform a single, well-defined task, and the name of the function should express that task effectively. This promotes software reusability.

Software Engineering Observation 10.3

If you cannot choose a concise name that expresses the function's task, it is possible that your function is performing too many diverse tasks. Usually, it is best to break such a function into several smaller functions.

10.4 Function Definitions

Each script we have presented thus far in the text has consisted of a series of statements and control structures in sequence. These scripts have been executed as the browser loads the Web page and evaluates the **<head>** section of the page. We now consider how programmers write their own customized functions and call them in a script.

Consider a script (Fig. 10.2) that uses a function **square** to calculate the squares of the integers from 1 to 10. [*Note*: We continue to show many examples in which the **body** element of the XHTML document is empty and the document is created directly by a JavaScript. In later chapters, we show many examples in which JavaScripts interact with the elements in the **body** of a document.]

The **for** structure in lines 18–20 outputs XHTML that displays the results of squaring the integers from 1 to 10. Each iteration of the loop calculates the **square** of the current value of control variable **x** and outputs the result by writing a line in the XHTML document. Function **square** is *invoked*, or *called*, on line 20 with the expression **square(x)**. When program control reaches this expression, the program calls function **square** (defined at lines 26–29). The **()** represent the *function-call operator*, which has high precedence. At this point, the program makes a copy of the value of **x** (the argument) and program control transfers to the first line of function **square**. Function **square** receives the copy of the value of **x** and stores it in the parameter **y**. Then **square** calculates **y * y**. The result is passed back to the point in line 20 where **square** was invoked. Lines 19–20 concatenate **"The square of "**, the value of **x**, **" is "**, the value returned by function **square** and a **
** tag and write that line of text in the XHTML document. This process is repeated 10 times.

```
1  <?xml version = "1.0"?>
2  <!DOCTYPE html PUBLIC "-//W3C//DTD XHTML 1.0 Strict//EN"
3     "http://www.w3.org/TR/xhtml1/DTD/xhtml1-strict.dtd">
4
5  <!-- Fig. 10.2: SquareInt.html -->
6  <!-- Square function           -->
7
8  <html xmlns = "http://www.w3.org/1999/xhtml">
9     <head>
10       <title>A Programmer-Defined square Function</title>
11
12       <script type = "text/javascript">
13          <!--
14          document.writeln(
15             "<h1>Square the numbers from 1 to 10</h1>" );
16
17          // square the numbers from 1 to 10
18          for ( var x = 1; x <= 10; ++x )
19             document.writeln( "The square of " + x + " is " +
20                square( x ) + "<br />" );
21
22          // The following square function's body is executed
23          // only when the function is explicitly called.
24
25          // square function definition
26          function square( y )
27          {
28             return y * y;
29          }
30          // -->
31       </script>
```

Fig. 10.2 Using programmer-defined function **square** (part 1 of 2).

```
32
33      </head><body></body>
34   </html>
```

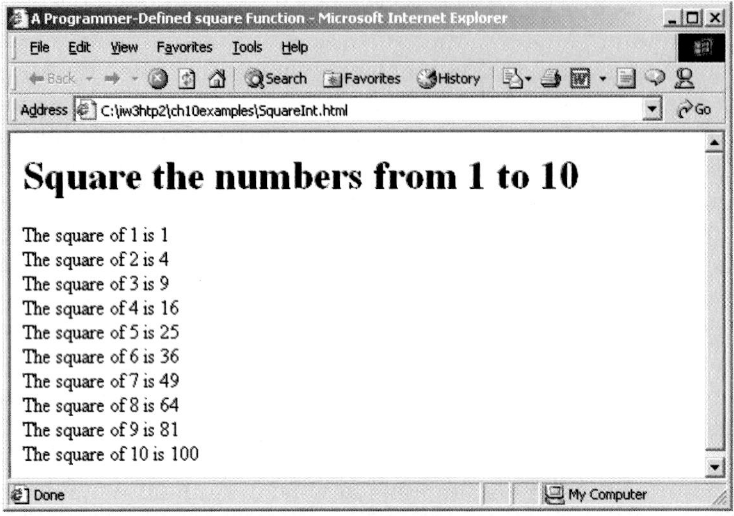

Fig. 10.2 Using programmer-defined function **square** (part 2 of 2).

The definition of function **square** (lines 26–29) shows that **square** expects a single parameter **y**. Function **square** uses this name in its body to manipulate the value passed to **square** from line 20. The ***return*** *statement* in **square** passes the result of the calculation **y * y** back to the calling function. Note that JavaScript keyword **var** is not used to declare variables in the parameter list of a function.

Common Programming Error 10.1

Using the JavaScript **var** *keyword to declare a variable in a function parameter list results in a JavaScript runtime error.*

In this example, function **square** follows the rest of the script. When the **for** structure terminates, JavaScript will not continue to flow sequentially into function **square**. A function must be called explicitly for the code in its body to execute. Thus, when the **for** structure terminates in this example, the script terminates.

Good Programming Practice 10.2

Place a blank line between function definitions to separate the functions and enhance program readability.

Software Engineering Observation 10.4

Statements that are enclosed in the body of a function definition are not executed by the JavaScript interpreter unless the function is invoked explicitly.

The format of a function definition is

```
function function-name( parameter-list )
{
    declarations and statements
}
```

The *function-name* is any valid identifier. The *parameter-list* is a comma-separated list containing the names of the parameters received by the function when it is called (remember that the arguments in the function call are assigned to the corresponding parameter in the function definition). There should be one argument in the function call for each parameter in the function definition. If a function does not receive any values, the *parameter-list* is empty (i.e., the function name is followed by an empty set of parentheses).

The *declarations* and *statements* within braces form the *function body*. The function body is also referred to as a *block*. A block is a compound statement that includes declarations. The terms block and compound statement often are used interchangeably.

Common Programming Error 10.2

Forgetting to return a value from a function that is supposed to return a value is a logic error.

Common Programming Error 10.3

Placing a semicolon after the right parenthesis enclosing the parameter list of a function definition results in a JavaScript runtime error.

Common Programming Error 10.4

Redefining a function parameter as a local variable in the function is a logic error.

Common Programming Error 10.5

Passing to a function an argument that is not compatible with the corresponding parameter's expected type is a logic error and may result in a JavaScript runtime error.

Good Programming Practice 10.3

Although it is not incorrect to do so, do not use the same name for an argument passed to a function and the corresponding parameter in the function definition. Using different names avoids ambiguity.

Good Programming Practice 10.4

Choosing meaningful function names and meaningful parameter names makes programs more readable and helps avoid excessive use of comments.

Software Engineering Observation 10.5

A function should usually be no longer than one printed page. Better yet, a function should usually be no longer than half a printed page. Regardless of how long a function is, it should perform one task well. Small functions promote software reusability.

Software Engineering Observation 10.6

Scripts should be written as collections of small functions. This practice makes programs easier to write, debug, maintain and modify.

Software Engineering Observation 10.7

A function requiring a large number of parameters may be performing too many tasks. Consider dividing the function into smaller functions that perform the separate tasks. The function header should fit on one line, if possible.

Software Engineering Observation 10.8

Modularizing programs in a neat, hierarchical manner promotes good software engineering— sometimes, however, at the expense of performance.

Performance Tip 10.2

A heavily modularized program—as compared with a monolithic (i.e., one-piece) program without functions—makes potentially large numbers of function calls, which consume execution time and space on a computer's processor(s). But monolithic programs are difficult to program, test, debug, maintain and evolve. So modularize your programs judiciously, always keeping in mind the delicate balance between performance and good software engineering.

Testing and Debugging Tip 10.1

Small functions are easier to test, debug and understand than large ones.

There are three ways to return control to the point at which a function was invoked. If the function does not return a result, control returns when the program reaches the function-ending right brace or by executing the statement

```
return;
```

If the function does return a result, the statement

```
return expression;
```

returns the value of *expression* to the caller. When a **`return`** statement is executed, control returns immediately to the point at which the function was invoked.

The script in our next example (Fig. 10.3) uses a programmer-defined function called **`maximum`** to determine and return the largest of three floating-point values.

```
<?xml version = "1.0"?>
<!DOCTYPE html PUBLIC "-//W3C//DTD XHTML 1.0 Strict//EN"
   "http://www.w3.org/TR/xhtml1/DTD/xhtml1-strict.dtd">

<!-- Fig. 10.3: maximum.html -->
<!-- Maximum function        -->

<html xmlns = "http://www.w3.org/1999/xhtml">
   <head>
      <title>Finding the Maximum of Three Values</title>

      <script type = "text/javascript">
         <!--
         var input1 =
            window.prompt( "Enter first number", "0" );
```

Fig. 10.3 Programmer-defined **`maximum`** function (part 1 of 3).

```
         var input2 =
            window.prompt( "Enter second number", "0" );
         var input3 =
            window.prompt( "Enter third number", "0" );

         var value1 = parseFloat( input1 );
         var value2 = parseFloat( input2 );
         var value3 = parseFloat( input3 );

         var maxValue = maximum( value1, value2, value3 );

         document.writeln( "First number: " + value1 +
            "<br />Second number: " + value2 +
            "<br />Third number: " + value3 +
            "<br />Maximum is: " + maxValue );

         // maximum method definition (called from line 25)
         function maximum( x, y, z )
         {
            return Math.max( x, Math.max( y, z ) );
         }
         // -->
      </script>

   </head>
   <body>
      <p>Click Refresh (or Reload) to run the script again</p>
   </body>
</html>
```

Fig. 10.3 Programmer-defined `maximum` function (part 2 of 3).

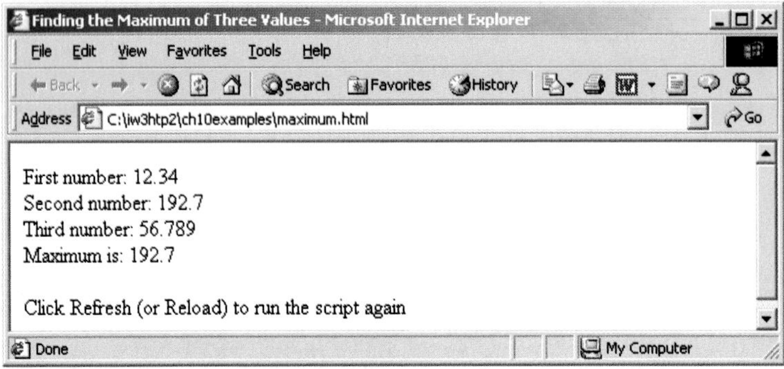

Fig. 10.3 Programmer-defined **maximum** function (part 3 of 3).

The three floating-point values are input by the user via **prompt** dialogs (lines 14–19). Lines 21–23 use function **parseFloat** to convert the strings input by the user to floating-point values. The statement in line 25 passes the three floating-point values to function **maximum** (defined at lines 33–36), which determines the largest floating-point value. This value is returned to line 25 by the **return** statement in function **maximum**. The value returned is assigned to variable **maxValue**. Lines 27–30 concatenate and display the three floating-point values input by the user and the **maxValue**.

Notice the implementation of the function **maximum** (lines 33–36). The first line indicates that the function's name is **maximum** and that the function takes three parameters (**x**, **y** and **z**) to accomplish its task. Also, the body of the function contains the statement which returns the largest of the three floating-point values, using two calls to the **Math** object's **max** method. First, method **Math.max** is invoked with the values of variables **y** and **z** to determine the larger of the two values. Next, the value of variable **x** and the result of the first call to **Math.max** are passed to method **Math.max**. Finally, the result of the second call to **Math.max** is returned to the point at which **maximum** was invoked (i.e., line 25). Note once again that the script terminates before sequentially reaching the definition of function **maximum**. The statement in the body of function **maximum** executes only when the function is invoked from line 25.

10.5 Random-Number Generation

We now take a brief and, it is hoped, entertaining diversion into a popular programming application, namely simulation and game playing. In this section and the next section, we will develop a nicely structured game-playing program that includes multiple functions. The program uses most of the control structures we have studied thus far.

There is something in the air of a gambling casino that invigorates people, from the high-rollers at the plush mahogany-and-felt craps tables to the quarter poppers at the one-armed bandits. It is the *element of chance*, the possibility that luck will convert a pocketful of money into a mountain of wealth. The element of chance can be introduced through the **Math** object's ***random*** method. (Remember, we are calling **random** a method because it belongs to the **Math** object.)

Consider the following statement:

```
var randomValue = Math.random();
```

Method **random** generates a floating-point value from 0.0 up to, but not including, 1.0. If **random** truly produces values at random, then every value from 0.0 up to, but not including, 1.0 has an equal *chance* (or *probability*) of being chosen each time **random** is called.

The range of values produced directly by **random** often is different than what is needed in a specific application. For example, a program that simulates coin tossing might require only 0 for "heads" and 1 for "tails." A program that simulates rolling a six-sided die would require random integers in the range from 1 to 6. A program that randomly predicts the next type of spaceship, out of four possibilities, that will fly across the horizon in a video game might require random integers in the range 0–3 or 1–4.

To demonstrate method **random**, let us develop a program (Fig. 10.4) that simulates 20 rolls of a six-sided die and displays the value of each roll. We use the multiplication operator (*****) with **random** as follows:

```
Math.floor( 1 + Math.random() * 6 )
```

First, the preceding expression multiplies the result of a call to **Math.random()** by 6 to produce a number in the range 0.0 up to, but not including, 6.0. This is called *scaling* the range of the random numbers. The number 6 is called the *scaling factor*. Next, we add 1 to the result to *shift* the range of numbers to produce a number in the range 1.0 up to, but not including, 7.0. Finally, we use method ***Math.floor*** to *round* the result down to the closest integer value in the range 1 to 6. **Math** method **floor** rounds its floating-point number argument to the closest integer not greater than the argument's value—e.g., 1.75 is rounded to 1, and –1.25 is rounded to –2. Figure 10.4 confirms that the results are in the range 1 to 6.

```
<?xml version = "1.0"?>
<!DOCTYPE html PUBLIC "-//W3C//DTD XHTML 1.0 Strict//EN"
   "http://www.w3.org/TR/xhtml1/DTD/xhtml1-strict.dtd">

<!-- Fig. 10.4: RandomInt.html          -->
<!-- Demonstrating the Random method -->

<html xmlns = "http://www.w3.org/1999/xhtml">
   <head>
      <title>Shifted and Scaled Random Integers</title>

      <script type = "text/javascript">
         <!--
         var value;

         document.writeln(
            "<table border = \"1\" width = \"50%\">" );
         document.writeln(
            "<caption>Random Numbers</caption><tr>" );

```

Fig. 10.4 Shifted and scaled random integers (part 1 of 2).

```
         for ( var i = 1; i <= 20; i++ ) {
            value = Math.floor( 1 + Math.random() * 6 );
            document.writeln( "<td>" + value + "</td>" );

            // write end and start <tr> tags when
            // i is a multiple of 5 and not 20
            if ( i % 5 == 0 && i != 20 )
               document.writeln( "</tr><tr>" );
         }

         document.writeln( "</tr></table>" );
         // -->
      </script>

   </head>
   <body>
      <p>Click Refresh (or Reload) to run the script again</p>
   </body>
</html>
```

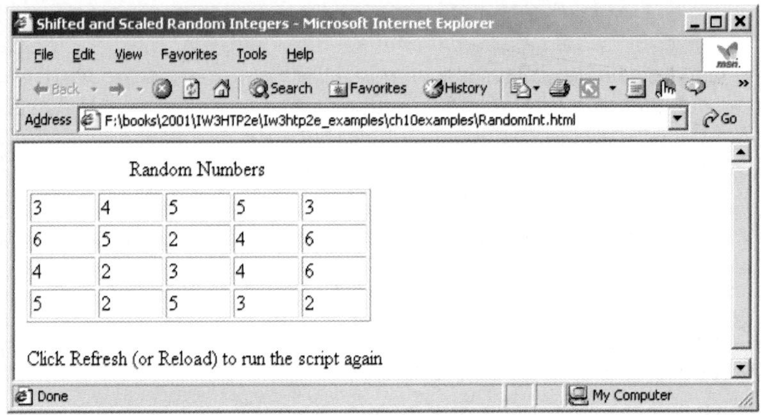

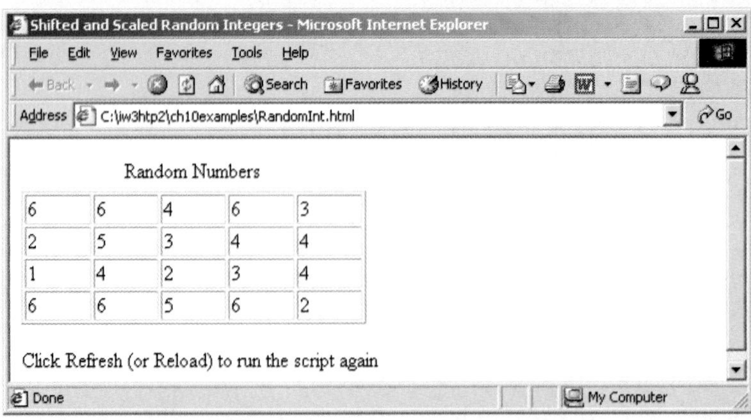

Fig. 10.4 Shifted and scaled random integers (part 2 of 2).

To show that these numbers occur with approximately equal likelihood, let us simulate 6000 rolls of a die with the program in Fig. 10.5. Each integer from 1 to 6 should appear approximately 1000 times. Use your browser's **Refresh** (or **Reload**) button to execute the script again.

As the output of the program shows, we used **Math** method **random** to simulate the rolling of a six-sided die scaling and shifting. Note that we used nested control structures to determine the number of times each side of the six-sided die occurred. The **for** loop in lines 19–42 iterates 6000 times. During each iteration of the loop, line 20 produces a value from 1 to 6. The nested **switch** structure in lines 22–41 uses the **face** value that was randomly chosen as its controlling expression. Based on the value of **face**, the program increments one of the six counter variables during each iteration of the loop. Note that no **default** case is provided in this **switch** structure, because the statement in line 20 only produces only the values 1, 2, 3, 4, 5 and 6. In this example, the **default** case would never execute. After we study **Array**s in Chapter 11, we will discuss how to replace the entire **switch** structure in this program with a single-line statement.

Run the program several times, and observe the results. Notice that the program produces different random numbers each time the script executes, so the results should vary.

The values returned by **random** are always in the range

```
0.0 ≤ Math.random() < 1.0
```

Previously, we demonstrated the statement

```
face = Math.floor( 1 + Math.random() * 6 );
```

which simulates the rolling of a six-sided die, which always assigns an integer (at random) to variable **face**, in the range $1 \le$ **face** ≤ 6. Note that the width of this range (i.e., the number of consecutive integers in the range) is 6, and the starting number in the range is 1. Referring to the preceding statement, we see that the width of the range is determined by the number used to scale **random** with the multiplication operator (6 in the preceding statement) and that the starting number of the range is equal to the number (1 in the preceding statement) added to **Math.random() * 6**. We can generalize this result as

```
face = Math.floor( a + Math.random() * b );
```

where **a** is the *shifting value* (which is equal to the first number in the desired range of consecutive integers) and **b** is the *scaling factor* (which is equal to the width of the desired range of consecutive integers). In the exercises at the end of this chapter, we will see that it is possible to choose integers at random from sets of values other than ranges of consecutive integers.

```
1  <?xml version = "1.0"?>
2  <!DOCTYPE html PUBLIC "-//W3C//DTD XHTML 1.0 Strict//EN"
3     "http://www.w3.org/TR/xhtml1/DTD/xhtml1-strict.dtd">
4
5  <!-- Fig. 10.5: RollDie.html -->
6  <!-- Rolling a Six-Sided Die -->
7
8  <html xmlns = "http://www.w3.org/1999/xhtml">
```

Fig. 10.5 Rolling a six-sided die 6000 times (part 1 of 3).

```
   <head>
      <title>Roll a Six-Sided Die 6000 Times</title>

      <script type = "text/javascript">
         <!--
         var frequency1 = 0, frequency2 = 0,
             frequency3 = 0, frequency4 = 0,
             frequency5 = 0, frequency6 = 0, face;

         // summarize results
         for ( var roll = 1; roll <= 6000; ++roll ) {
            face = Math.floor( 1 + Math.random() * 6 );

            switch ( face ) {
               case 1:
                  ++frequency1;
                  break;
               case 2:
                  ++frequency2;
                  break;
               case 3:
                  ++frequency3;
                  break;
               case 4:
                  ++frequency4;
                  break;
               case 5:
                  ++frequency5;
                  break;
               case 6:
                  ++frequency6;
                  break;
            }
         }

         document.writeln( "<table border = \"1\"" +
            "width = \"50%\">" );
         document.writeln( "<thead><th>Face</th>" +
            "<th>Frequency<th></thead>" );
         document.writeln( "<tbody><tr><td>1</td><td>" +
            frequency1 + "</td></tr>" );
         document.writeln( "<tr><td>2</td><td>" + frequency2 +
            "</td></tr>" );
         document.writeln( "<tr><td>3</td><td>" + frequency3 +
            "</td></tr>" );
         document.writeln( "<tr><td>4</td><td>" + frequency4 +
            "</td></tr>" );
         document.writeln( "<tr><td>5</td><td>" + frequency5 +
            "</td></tr>" );
         document.writeln( "<tr><td>6</td><td>" + frequency6 +
            "</td></tr></tbody></table>" );
         // -->
      </script>
```

Fig. 10.5 Rolling a six-sided die 6000 times (part 2 of 3).

```
   </head>
   <body>
      <p>Click Refresh (or Reload) to run the script again</p>
   </body>
</html>
```

Roll a Six-Sided Die 6000 Times - Microsoft Internet Explorer

Face	Frequency
1	986
2	993
3	985
4	984
5	1059
6	993

Click Refresh (or Reload) to run the script again

Roll a Six-Sided Die 6000 Times - Microsoft Internet Explorer

Face	Frequency
1	1009
2	1010
3	997
4	1010
5	1007
6	967

Click Refresh (or Reload) to run the script again

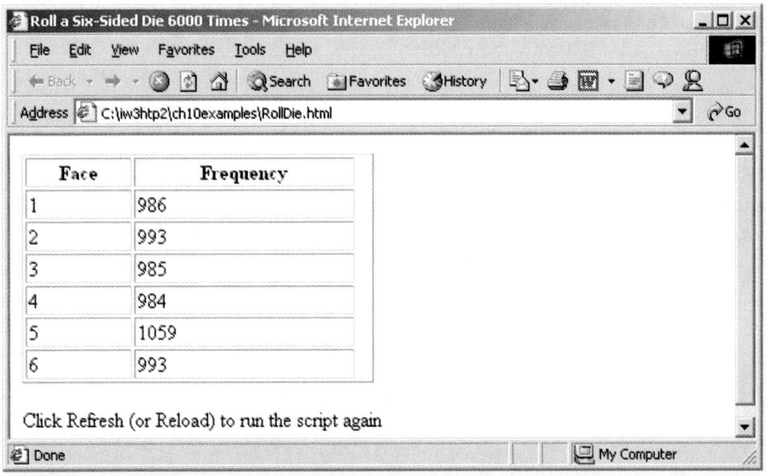

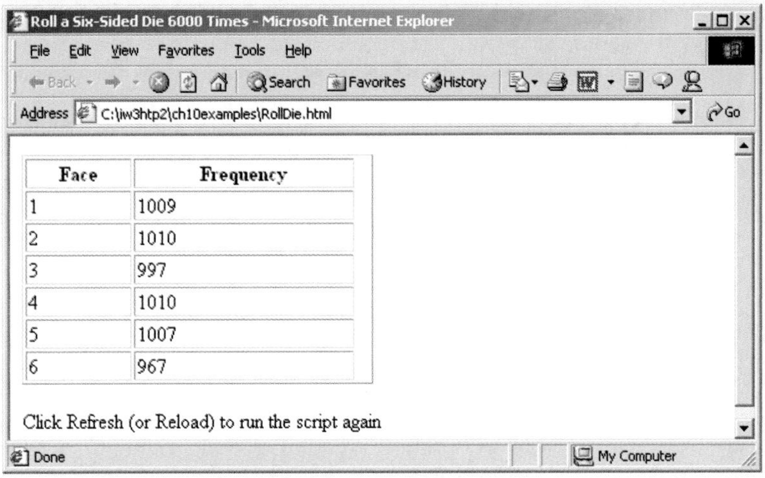

Fig. 10.5 Rolling a six-sided die 6000 times (part 3 of 3).

10.6 Example: Game of Chance

One of the most popular games of chance is a dice game known as "craps," which is played in casinos and back alleys throughout the world. The rules of the game are straightforward:

> *A player rolls two dice. Each die has six faces. These faces contain 1, 2, 3, 4, 5 and 6 spots, respectively. After the dice have come to rest, the sum of the spots on the two upward faces is calculated. If the sum is 7 or 11 on the first throw, the player wins. If the sum is 2, 3 or 12 on the first throw (called "craps"), the player loses (i.e., the "house" wins). If the sum is 4, 5,*

6, 8, 9 or 10 on the first throw, that sum becomes the player's "point." To win, you must continue rolling the dice until you "make your point" (i.e., roll your point value). The player loses by rolling a 7 before making the point.

The script in Fig. 10.6 simulates the game of craps.

```
<?xml version = "1.0"?>
<!DOCTYPE html PUBLIC "-//W3C//DTD XHTML 1.0 Transitional//EN"
   "http://www.w3.org/TR/xhtml1/DTD/xhtml1-transitional.dtd">

<!-- Fig. 10.6: Craps.html -->
<!-- Craps Program         -->

<html xmlns = "http://www.w3.org/1999/xhtml">
   <head>
      <title>Program that Simulates the Game of Craps</title>

      <script type = "text/javascript">
         <!--
         // variables used to test the state of the game
         var WON = 0, LOST = 1, CONTINUE_ROLLING = 2;

         // other variables used in program
         var firstRoll = true,            // true if first roll
             sumOfDice = 0,               // sum of the dice
             myPoint = 0, // point if no win/loss on first roll
             gameStatus = CONTINUE_ROLLING; // game not over yet

         // process one roll of the dice
         function play()
         {
            if ( firstRoll ) {          // first roll of the dice
               sumOfDice = rollDice();

               switch ( sumOfDice ) {
                  case 7: case 11:          // win on first roll
                     gameStatus = WON;
                     // clear point field
                     document.craps.point.value = "";
                     break;
                  case 2: case 3: case 12: // lose on first roll
                     gameStatus = LOST;
                     // clear point field
                     document.craps.point.value = "";
                     break;
                  default:                    // remember point
                     gameStatus = CONTINUE_ROLLING;
                     myPoint = sumOfDice;
                     document.craps.point.value = myPoint;
                     firstRoll = false;
               }
            }
```

Fig. 10.6 Program to simulate the game of craps (part 1 of 5).

```
               else {
                  sumOfDice = rollDice();

                  if ( sumOfDice == myPoint ) // win by making point
                     gameStatus = WON;
                  else
                     if ( sumOfDice == 7 )    // lose by rolling 7
                        gameStatus = LOST;
               }

               if ( gameStatus == CONTINUE_ROLLING )
                  window.status = "Roll again";
               else {
                  if ( gameStatus == WON )
                     window.status = "Player wins. " +
                        "Click Roll Dice to play again.";
                  else
                     window.status = "Player loses. " +
                        "Click Roll Dice to play again.";

                  firstRoll = true;
               }
            }

            // roll the dice
            function rollDice()
            {
               var die1, die2, workSum;

               die1 = Math.floor( 1 + Math.random() * 6 );
               die2 = Math.floor( 1 + Math.random() * 6 );
               workSum = die1 + die2;

               document.craps.firstDie.value = die1;
               document.craps.secondDie.value = die2;
               document.craps.sum.value = workSum;

               return workSum;
            }
            // -->
         </script>

      </head>
      <body>
         <form name = "craps" action = "">
            <table border = "1">
            <caption>Craps</caption>
            <tr><td>Die 1</td>
                <td><input name = "firstDie" type = "text" />
                </td></tr>
            <tr><td>Die 2</td>
                <td><input name = "secondDie" type = "text" />
                </td></tr>
```

Fig. 10.6 Program to simulate the game of craps (part 2 of 5).

```
            <tr><td>Sum</td>
               <td><input name = "sum" type = "text" />
               </td></tr>
            <tr><td>Point</td>
               <td><input name = "point" type = "text" />
               </td></tr>
            <tr><td><input type = "button" value = "Roll Dice"
               onclick = "play()" /></td></tr>
            </table>
         </form>
      </body>
   </html>
```

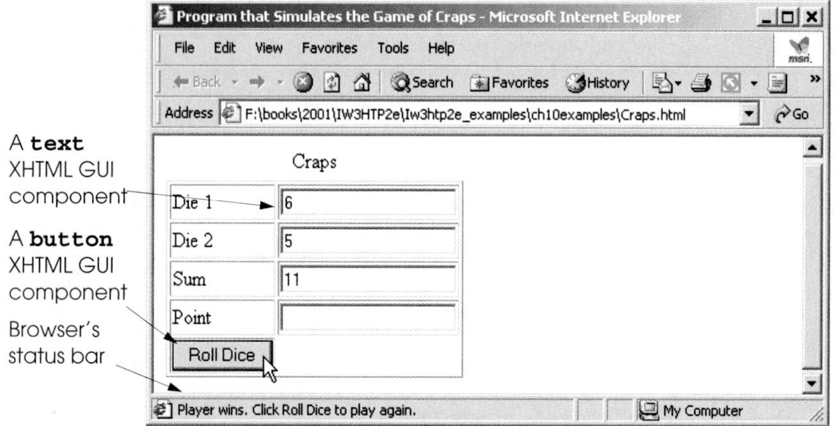

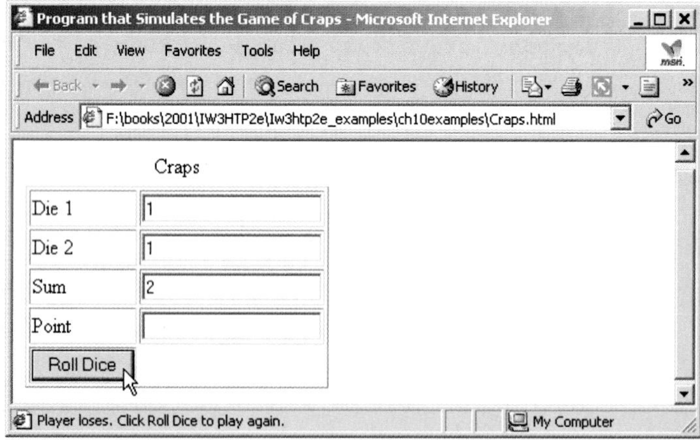

Fig. 10.6 Program to simulate the game of craps (part 3 of 5).

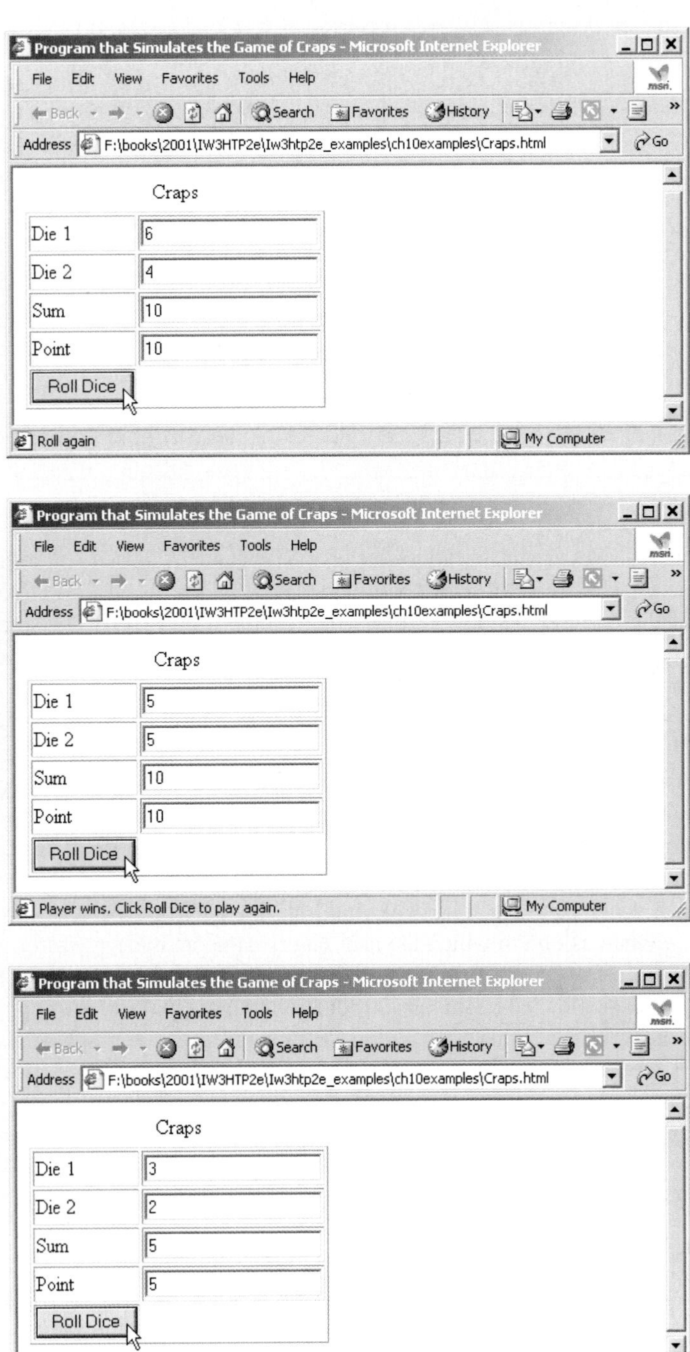

Fig. 10.6 Program to simulate the game of craps (part 4 of 5).

Fig. 10.6 Program to simulate the game of craps (part 5 of 5).

Notice that the player must roll two dice on the first and all subsequent rolls. When you execute the script, click the **Roll Dice** button to play the game. The *status bar* in the lower-left corner of the browser window displays the results of each roll. The screen captures show four separate executions of the script (a win and a loss on the first roll, and a win and a loss after the first roll).

Until now, all user interactions with scripts have been through either a **prompt** dialog (into which the user types an input value for the program) or an **alert** dialog (in which a message is displayed to the user, and the user can click **OK** to dismiss the dialog). Although these dialogs are valid ways to receive input from a user and to display messages in a JavaScript program, they are fairly limited in their capabilities—i.e., a **prompt** dialog can obtain only one value at a time from the user and a message dialog can display only one message.

It is much more common to receive multiple inputs from the user at once via an XHTML *form* (such as one in which the user enters name and address information) or to display many pieces of data at once (such as the values of the dice, the sum of the dice and the point in this example). To begin our introduction to more elaborate user interfaces, this program uses an XHTML form (discussed in Chapter 5) and a new graphical user interface concept: GUI *event handling*. This example is our first in which the JavaScript executes in response to the user's interaction with a GUI component in an XHTML form. This interaction causes an *event*. Scripts often are used to respond to events.

Before we discuss the script code, we first discuss the **<body>** section (lines 90–110) of the XHTML document. The GUI components in this section are used extensively in the script.

Line 91 begins the definition of an XHTML **<form>** with its ***name*** attribute set to **craps**. The **name** attribute **craps** enables script code to refer to the elements of the form. This attribute helps a script distinguish between multiple forms in the same XHTML document. Similarly, the **name** attribute is specified for each GUI component in the form, so that the script code can refer to each GUI component individually. Valid XHTML code requires that every **form** contain an **action** attribute. This form does not post its information to a Web server, so the empty string, **""**, is used.

In this example, we have decided to place the form's GUI components in an XHTML **<table>**, so line 92 begins the definition of the XHTML table and indicates that it has a **1**-pixel border.

Lines 94–96 define the first row of the table. The column on the left contains the text **Die 1**, and the column on the right contains the text field named **firstDie**. Lines 97–99 define the second row of the table. The column on the left contains the text **Die 2**, and the column on the right contains the text field named **secondDie**.

Lines 100–102 define the third row of the table. The column on the left contains the text **Sum**, and the column on the right contains the text field named **sum**.

Lines 103–105 define the fourth row of the table. The column on the left contains the text **Point**, and the column on the right contains the text field named **point**.

Lines 106–107 define the last row of the table. The column on the left contains the button **Roll Dice**. The button's ***onclick*** attribute indicates the action to take when the user of the XHTML document clicks the **Roll Dice** button. In this example, clicking the button causes a call to function **play**.

This style of programming is known as *event-driven programming*—the user interacts with a GUI component, the script is notified of the event and the script processes the event. The user's interaction with the GUI "drives" the program. The clicking of the button is known as the *event*. The function that is called when an event occurs is known as an *event-handling function* or *event handler*. When a GUI event occurs in a form, the browser *automatically calls* the specified event-handling function. Before any event can be processed, each GUI component must know which event-handling function will be called when a particular event occurs. Most XHTML GUI components have several different event types. The event model is discussed in detail in Chapter 14, Dynamic HTML: Event Model. By specifying **onclick = "play()"** for the **Roll Dice** button, we enable the browser to *listen for events* (button-click events in particular). This *registers the event handler* for the GUI component. (We also like to call the line on which it occurs the *start listening line*, because the browser is now listening for button-click events from the button.) If no event handler is specified for the **Roll Dice** button, the script will not respond when the user presses the button. Lines 108–109 end the **<table>** and **<form>** tags, respectively.

The game is reasonably involved. The player may win or lose on the first roll, or may win or lose on any roll. Line 15 creates variables that define the three game states—game won, game lost or continue rolling the dice. Unlike many other programming languages, JavaScript does not provide a mechanism to define a *constant variable* (i.e., a variable whose value cannot be modified). For this reason, we used all capital letters for these variable names, to indicate that we do not intend to modify their values and to make them stand out in the code.

Good Programming Practice 10.5

Use only uppercase letters (with underscores between words) in the names of variables that should be used as constants. This format makes these variables stand out in a program.

Good Programming Practice 10.6

Use meaningfully named variables rather than constants (such as 2) to make programs more readable.

Lines 18–21 declare several variables that are used throughout the script. Variable **firstRoll** indicates whether the next roll of the dice is the first roll in the current game.

Variable **sumOfDice** maintains the sum of the dice from the last roll. Variable **myPoint** stores the "point" if the player does not win or lose on the first roll. Variable **gameStatus** keeps track of the current state of the game (**WON**, **LOST** or **CONTINUE_ROLLING**).

We define a function **rollDice** (line 72) to roll the dice and to compute and display their sum. Function **rollDice** is defined once, but is called from two places in the program (lines 27 and 48). Function **rollDice** takes no arguments, so it has an empty parameter list. Function **rollDice** returns the sum of the two dice.

The user clicks the **Roll Dice** button to roll the dice. This action invokes function **play** (line 24) of the script. Function **play** checks the variable **firstRoll** (line 26) to determine whether it is **true** or **false**. If it is **true**, the roll is the first roll of the game. Line 27 calls **rollDice** (defined at line 72), which picks two random values from 1 to 6, displays the value of the first die, the value of the second die and the sum of the dice in the first three text fields and returns the sum of the dice. (We discuss function **rollDice** in detail shortly.) After the first roll has taken place, the nested **switch** structure at line 29 determines whether the game is won or lost, or whether the game should continue with another roll. After the first roll, if the game is not over, **sumOfDice** is saved in **myPoint** and displayed in the text field **point** in the XHTML form. Notice how the text field's value is changed at lines 33, 38 and 43. The expression

```
craps.point.value
```

accesses the ***value*** property of the text field **point**. The **value** property specifies the text to display in the text field. To access this property, we specify the name of the form (**craps**) that contains the text field, followed by a *dot operator* (**.**), followed by the name of the text field we would like to manipulate. The dot operator is also known as the *field-access operator* or the *member-access operator*. The preceding expression uses the dot operator to access the **point** member of the **craps** form. Similarly, the second member-access operator accesses the **value** member (or property) of the **point** text field. Actually, we will see in the chapters on dynamic HTML that every element of an XHTML document is accessable in a manner similar to that shown here.

The program proceeds to the nested **if/else** structure at line 57, which sets the **window** object's **status** property (**window.status** in lines 58, 61 and 64) to

```
Roll again.
```

if **gameStatus** is equal to **CONTINUE**, to

```
Player wins. Click Roll Dice to play again.
```

if **gameStatus** is equal to **WON** and to

```
Player loses. Click Roll Dice to play again.
```

if **gameStatus** is equal to **LOST**. The **window** object's **status** property displays the string assigned to it in the status bar of the browser. If the game was won or lost, line 67 sets **firstRoll** to **true** to indicate that the next roll of the dice begins the next game.

The program then waits for the user to click the button **Roll Dice** again. Each time the user clicks **Roll Dice**, the program calls function **play**, which, in turn, calls the **rollDice** function to produce a new value for **sumOfDice**. If **sumOfDice** matches **myPoint**, **gameStatus** is set to **WON**, the **if/else** structure at line 57 executes and the game is complete. If **sum** is equal to **7**, **gameStatus** is set to **LOST**, the **if/else** structure at line 57 executes and the game is complete. Clicking the **Roll Dice** button starts a new game. The program updates the four text fields in the XHTML form with the new values of the dice and the sum on each roll, and updates the text field **point** each time a new game begins.

Function **rollDice** (line 72) defines its own local variables **die1**, **die2** and **workSum** at line 74. These variables are defined inside the body of **rollDice**, so they are known only in that function. If these three variable names are used elsewhere in the program, they will be entirely separate variables in memory. Lines 76–77 pick two random values in the range 1 to 6 and assign them to variables **die1** and **die2**, respectively. Lines 80–82 assign the values of **die1**, **die2** and **workSum** to the corresponding text fields in the XHTML form **craps**. Note that the integer values are converted automatically to strings when they are assigned to each text field's **value** property. Line 84 returns the value of **workSum** for use in function **play**.

Software Engineering Observation 10.9

Variables that are defined inside the body of a function are known only in that function. If the same variable names are used elsewhere in the program, they will be entirely separate variables in memory.

Note the interesting use of the various program control mechanisms we have discussed. The craps program uses two functions—**play** and **rollDice**—and the **switch**, **if/else** and nested **if** structures. Note also the use of multiple **case** labels in the **switch** structure to execute the same statements (lines 30 and 35). In the exercises at the end of this chapter, we investigate various interesting characteristics of the game of craps.

Testing and Debugging Tip 10.2

Initializing variables when they are declared in functions helps the programmer avoid incorrect results and interpreter messages warning of uninitialized data.

10.7 Duration of Identifiers

Chapters 7 through 9 have used identifiers for variable names. The attributes of variables include name, value and data type (such as string, number or boolean). We also use identifiers as names for user-defined functions. Actually, each identifier in a program has other attributes, including *duration* and *scope* (discussed in Section 10.8).

An identifier's *duration* (also called its *lifetime*) is the period during which the identifier exists in memory. Some identifiers exist briefly, some are repeatedly created and destroyed and others exist for the entire execution of a script.

Identifiers that represent local variables in a function (i.e., parameters and variables declared in the function body) have *automatic duration*. Automatic-duration variables are created *automatic*ally when program control enters the function in which they are declared; they exist while the function in which they are declared is active; and they are *automatic*ally destroyed when the function in which they are declared is exited. For the remainder of the text, we will refer to variables of automatic duration as local variables.

Software Engineering Observation 10.10

Automatic duration is a means of conserving memory, because automatic-duration variables are created when program control enters the function in which they are declared and are destroyed when the function in which they are declared is exited.

Software Engineering Observation 10.11

Automatic duration is an example of the principle of least privilege. *This principle states that each component of a system should have sufficient rights and privileges to accomplish its designated task, but no additional rights or privileges. This feature helps prevent accidental and/or malicious errors from occurring in systems. Why have variables stored in memory and accessible when they are not needed?*

JavaScript also has identifiers of *static duration*. Such identifiers are typically defined in the **<head>** of the XHTML document and exist from the point at which the **<head>** of the XHTML document is interpreted until the browsing session terminates (i.e., the browser is closed by the user). Even though static-duration variables exist after the **<head>** section of the document is interpreted, they cannot necessarily be used throughout the script. Duration and *scope* (where a name can be used) are separate issues, as shown in Section 10.8. Static-duration variables are globally accessible to the script—i.e., every function in the script can potentially use the variables. For the remainder of the text, we refer to variables of static duration as *global variables*, or *script-level variables*.

10.8 Scope Rules

The *scope* of an identifier for a variable or function is the portion of the program in which the identifier can be referenced. A local variable declared in a function can be used only in that function. The types of scope for an identifier are *global scope* and *function* (or *local*) *scope*.

Identifiers declared inside a function have *function* (or *local*) *scope*. Function scope begins with the opening left brace (**{**) of the function in which the identifier is declared and ends at the terminating right brace (**}**) of the function. Local variables of a function have function scope; so do function parameters, which are also local variables of the function. If a local variable in a function has the same name as a global variable, the global variable is "hidden" from the body of the function.

Good Programming Practice 10.7

Avoid local-variable names that hide global variable names. This can be accomplished by avoiding the use of duplicate identifiers in a script.

The script in Fig. 10.7 demonstrates scoping issues in JavaScript with global variables and local variables. This example also demonstrates the event ***onload***, which calls an event handler when the **<body>** of the XHTML document is completely loaded into the browser window.

Global variable **x** (line 14) is declared and initialized to 1. This global variable is hidden in any block (or function) that declares a variable named **x**. Function **start** (line 16) declares a local variable **x** (line 18) and initializes it to **5**. This variable is output in a line of XHTML text to show that the global variable **x** is hidden in **start**. The script defines two other functions—**functionA** and **functionB**—that each take no arguments and return nothing. Each function is called twice from function **start**.

Function **functionA** defines local variable **x** (line 33) and initializes it to **25**. When **functionA** is called, the variable is output in a line of XHTML text to show that the global variable **x** is hidden in **functionA**; then the variable is incremented and output in a line of XHTML text again before the function is exited. Each time this function is called, local variable **x** is re-created and initialized to **25**.

```
<?xml version = "1.0"?>
<!DOCTYPE html PUBLIC "-//W3C//DTD XHTML 1.0 Strict//EN"
   "http://www.w3.org/TR/xhtml1/DTD/xhtml1-strict.dtd">

<!-- Fig. 10.7: scoping.html    -->
<!-- Local and Global Variables -->

<html xmlns = "http://www.w3.org/1999/xhtml">
   <head>
      <title>A Scoping Example</title>

      <script type = "text/javascript">
         <!--
         var x = 1;       // global variable

         function start()
         {
            var x = 5;   // variable local to function start

            document.writeln( "local x in start is " + x );

            functionA(); // functionA has local x
            functionB(); // functionB uses global variable x
            functionA(); // functionA reinitializes local x
            functionB(); // global variable x retains its value

            document.writeln(
               "<p>local x in start is " + x + "</p>" );
         }

         function functionA()
         {
            var x = 25;  // initialized each time
                         // functionA is called

            document.writeln( "<p>local x in functionA is " +
                              x + " after entering functionA" );
            ++x;
            document.writeln( "<br />local x in functionA is " +
               x + " before exiting functionA" + "</p>" );
         }

         function functionB()
         {
            document.writeln( "<p>global variable x is " + x +
               " on entering functionB" );
            x *= 10;
            document.writeln( "<br />global variable x is " +
               x + " on exiting functionB"  + "</p>" );
         }
         // -->
      </script>

```

Fig. 10.7 Scoping example (part 1 of 2).

```
    </head>
    <body onload = "start()"></body>
</html>
```

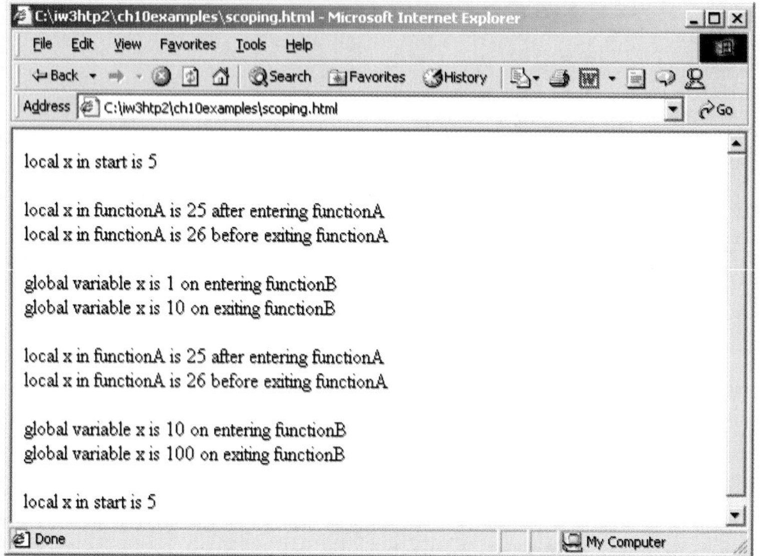

Fig. 10.7 Scoping example (part 2 of 2).

Function **functionB** does not declare any variables. Therefore, when it refers to variable **x**, the global variable **x** is used. When **functionB** is called, the global variable is output in a line of XHTML text, multiplied by **10** and output in a line of XHTML text again before the function is exited. The next time function **functionB** is called, the global variable has its modified value, **10**. Finally, the program outputs local variable **x** in **start** in a line of XHTML text again, to show that none of the function calls modified the value of **x** in **start**, because the functions all referred to variables in other scopes.

10.9 JavaScript Global Functions

JavaScript provides seven functions that are available globally in a JavaScript. We have already used two of these functions—**parseInt** and **parseFloat**. The global functions are summarized in Fig. 10.8.

Actually, the global functions in Fig. 10.8 are all part of JavaScript's ***Global** object*. The **Global** object contains all the global variables in the script, all the user-defined functions in the script and all the listed functions in Fig. 10.8. Because global functions and user-defined functions are part of the **Global** object, some JavaScript programmers refer to these functions as *methods*. We will use the term *method* only when referring to a function that is called for a particular object (such as **Math.random()**). As a JavaScript programmer, you do not need to use the **Global** object directly; JavaScript uses it for you.

Global function	Description
escape	This function takes a string argument and returns a string in which all spaces, punctuation, accent characters and any other character that is not in the ASCII character set (see Appendix C, ASCII Character Set) are encoded in a hexadecimal format (see the Number Systems appendix) that can be represented on all platforms.
eval	This function takes a string argument representing JavaScript code to execute. The JavaScript interpreter evaluates the code and executes it when the **eval** function is called. This function allows JavaScript code to be stored as strings and executed dynamically.
isFinite	This function takes a numeric argument and returns **true** if the value of the argument is not **NaN**, **Number.POSITIVE_INFINITY** or **Number.NEGATIVE_INFINITY**; otherwise, the function returns **false**.
isNaN	This function takes a numeric argument and returns **true** if the value of the argument is not a number; otherwise, the function returns **false**. The function is commonly used with the return value of **parseInt** or **parseFloat** to determine whether the result is a proper numeric value.
parseFloat	This function takes a string argument and attempts to convert the beginning of the string into a floating-point value. If the conversion is unsuccessful, the function returns **NaN**; otherwise, it returns the converted value (e.g., **parseFloat("abc123.45")** returns **NaN**, and **parseFloat("123.45abc")** returns the value **123.45**).
parseInt	This function takes a string argument and attempts to convert the beginning of the string into an integer value. If the conversion is unsuccessful, the function returns **NaN**; otherwise, it returns the converted value (e.g., **parseInt("abc123")** returns **NaN**, and **parseInt("123abc")** returns the integer value **123**). This function takes an optional second argument, from 2 to 36, specifying the *radix* (or *base*) of the number. Base 2 indicates that the first argument string is in *binary* format, base 8 indicates that the first argument string is in *octal* format and base 16 indicates that the first argument string is in *hexadecimal* format. See see the "Number Systems" appendix for more information on binary, octal and hexadecimal numbers.
unescape	This function takes a string as its argument and returns a string in which all characters previously encoded with **escape** are decoded.

Fig. 10.8 **JavaScript** global functions.

10.10 Recursion

The programs we have discussed thus far are generally structured as functions that call one another in a disciplined, hierarchical manner. For some problems, however, it is useful to have functions call themselves. A *recursive function* is a function that calls itself, either directly, or indirectly through another function. Recursion is an important topic discussed at length in upper-level computer science courses. In this section and the next, simple examples of recursion are presented. This book contains an extensive treatment of recursion. Figure 10.13 (at the end of Section 10.12) summarizes the recursion examples and exercises in the book.

We consider recursion conceptually first; then we examine several programs containing recursive functions. Recursive problem-solving approaches have a number of elements in common. A recursive function is called to solve a problem. The function actually knows how to solve only the simplest case(s), or *base case(s)*. If the function is called with a base case, the function returns a result. If the function is called with a more complex problem, the function divides the problem into two conceptual pieces: A piece that the function knows how to process (the base case) and a piece that the function does not know how to process. To make recursion feasible, the latter piece must resemble the original problem, but be a slightly simpler or slightly smaller version of the original problem. Because this new problem looks like the original problem, the function invokes (calls) a fresh copy of itself to go to work on the smaller problem; this invocation is referred to as a *recursive call*, or the *recursion step*. The recursion step also normally includes the keyword **`return`**, because its result will be combined with the portion of the problem the function knew how to solve to form a result that will be passed back to the original caller.

The recursion step executes while the original call to the function is still open (i.e., it has not finished executing). The recursion step can result in many more recursive calls, as the function divides each new subproblem into two conceptual pieces. For the recursion eventually to terminate, each time the function calls itself with a slightly simpler version of the original problem, the sequence of smaller and smaller problems must converge on the base case. At that point, the function recognizes the base case, returns a result to the previous copy of the function and a sequence of returns ensues up the line until the original function call eventually returns the final result to the caller. This process sounds exotic when compared with the conventional problem solving we have performed to this point. As an example of these concepts at work, let us write a recursive program to perform a popular mathematical calculation.

The factorial of a nonnegative integer n, written $n!$ (and pronounced "n factorial"), is the product

$$n \cdot (n - 1) \cdot (n - 2) \cdot \ldots \cdot 1$$

where $1!$ is equal to 1 and $0!$ is defined to be 1. For example, $5!$ is the product $5 \cdot 4 \cdot 3 \cdot 2 \cdot 1$, which is equal to 120.

The factorial of an integer (**`number`** in the following example) greater than or equal to zero, can be calculated *iteratively* (nonrecursively) using a **`for`** structure as follows:

```
var factorial = 1;

for ( var counter = number; counter >= 1; --counter )
   factorial *= counter;
```

A recursive definition of the factorial function is arrived at by observing the following relationship:

$$n! = n \cdot (n - 1)!$$

For example, *5!* is clearly equal to 5 * *4!*, as is shown by the following equations:

$$5! = 5 \cdot 4 \cdot 3 \cdot 2 \cdot 1$$
$$5! = 5 \cdot (4 \cdot 3 \cdot 2 \cdot 1)$$
$$5! = 5 \cdot (4!)$$

The evaluation of *5!* would proceed as shown in Fig. 10.9. Figure 10.9 (a) shows how the succession of recursive calls proceeds until *1!* is evaluated to be 1, which terminates the recursion. Figure 10.9 (b) shows the values returned from each recursive call to its caller until the final value is calculated and returned.

Figure 10.10 uses recursion to calculate and print the factorials of the integers 0 to 10. The recursive function **`factorial`** first tests (line 25) to see if a terminating condition is **`true`** (i.e., if **`number`** less than or equal to 1). If **`number`** is indeed less than or equal to 1, **`factorial`** returns 1, no further recursion is necessary and the function returns. If **`number`** is greater than 1, line 28 expresses the problem as the product of **`number`** and a recursive call to **`factorial`** evaluating the factorial of **`number - 1`**. Note that **`factorial( number - 1 )`** is a slightly simpler problem than the original calculation, **`factorial( number )`**.

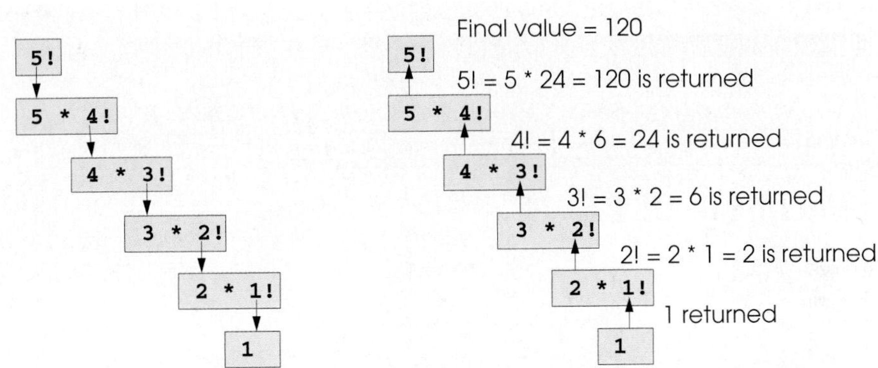

Fig. 10.9 Recursive evaluation of *5!*.

```
1   <?xml version = "1.0"?>
2   <!DOCTYPE html PUBLIC "-//W3C//DTD XHTML 1.0 Strict//EN"
3      "http://www.w3.org/TR/xhtml1/DTD/xhtml1-strict.dtd">
4   <!-- Fig. 10.10: FactorialTest.html -->
5   <!-- Recursive factorial example    -->
6
7   <html xmlns = "http://www.w3.org/1999/xhtml">
8      <head>
9         <title>Recursive Factorial Function</title>
10
```

Fig. 10.10 Calculating factorials with a recursive function (part 1 of 2).

```
11        <script language = "javascript">
12           document.writeln( "<h1>Factorials of 1 to 10</h1>" );
13           document.writeln(
14              "<table border = '1' width = '100%'>" );
15
16           for ( var i = 0; i <= 10; i++ )
17              document.writeln( "<tr><td>" + i + "!</td><td>" +
18                       factorial( i ) + "</td></tr>" );
19
20           document.writeln( "</table>" );
21
22           // Recursive definition of function factorial
23           function factorial( number )
24           {
25              if ( number <= 1 )  // base case
26                 return 1;
27              else
28                 return number * factorial( number - 1 );
29           }
30        </script>
31     </head><body></body>
32  </html>
```

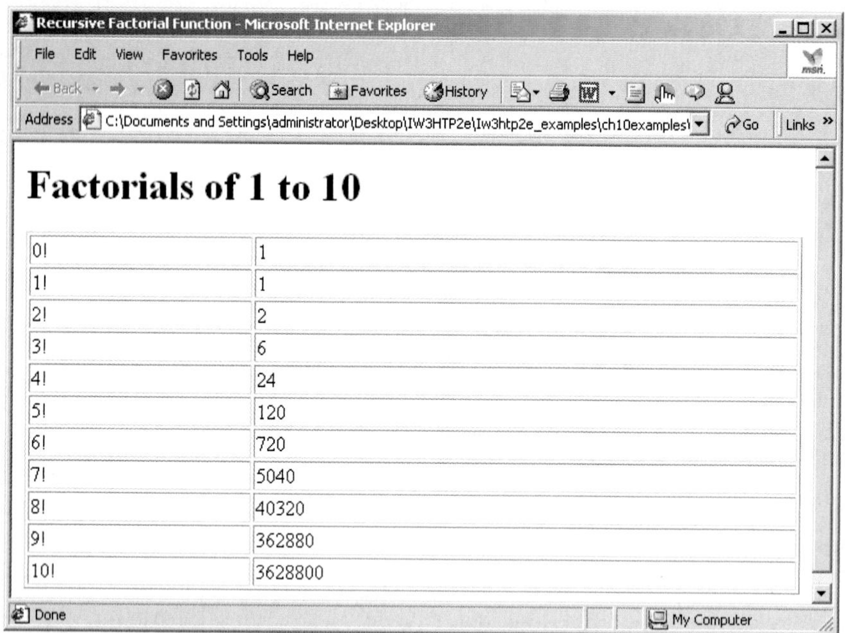

Fig. 10.10 Calculating factorials with a recursive function (part 2 of 2).

Function **factorial** (line 23) receives as its argument the value for which to calculate the factorial. As can be seen in the screen capture in Fig. 10.10, factorial values become large quickly. Because JavaScript uses floating-point numeric representations, we are able to calculate factorials of larger numbers.

Common Programming Error 10.6

Forgetting to return a value from a recursive function when one is needed results in a logic error.

Common Programming Error 10.7

Either omitting the base case or writing the recursion step incorrectly so that it does not converge on the base case will cause infinite recursion, eventually exhausting memory. This situation is analogous to the problem of an infinite loop in an iterative (nonrecursive) solution.

Testing and Debugging Tip 10.3

Internet Explorer displays a message when a script takes an unusually long time to execute. This information allows the user of the Web page to recover from a script that contains an infinite loop or infinite recursion.

10.11 Example Using Recursion: Fibonacci Series

The Fibonacci series

0, 1, 1, 2, 3, 5, 8, 13, 21, …

begins with 0 and 1 and has the property that each subsequent Fibonacci number is the sum of the previous two Fibonacci numbers.

The series occurs in nature and, in particular, describes a form of spiral. The ratio of successive Fibonacci numbers converges on a constant value of 1.618…. This number, too, repeatedly occurs in nature and has been called the *golden ratio* or the *golden mean.* Humans tend to find the golden mean aesthetically pleasing. Architects often design windows, rooms and buildings whose length and width are in the ratio of the golden mean. Postcards are often designed with a golden mean length/width ratio.

The Fibonacci series may be defined recursively as follows:

$$fibonacci(0) = 0$$
$$fibonacci(1) = 1$$
$$fibonacci(n) = fibonacci(n-1) + fibonacci(n-2)$$

Note that there are two base cases for the Fibonacci calculation: *fibonacci(0)* is defined to be 0, and *fibonacci(1)* is defined to be 1. The script of Fig. 10.11 calculates the ith Fibonacci number recursively, using function **`fibonacci`**. Lines 36–45 define an XHTML form (**`myForm`**) consisting of two text fields and a button. The user enters an integer in the first text field (**`number`**), indicating the ith Fibonacci number to calculate, and clicks the **Calculate** button. When the event occurs, function **`getFibonacciValue`** (defined at line 14) executes in response to the user-interface event and calls recursive function **`fibonacci`** (defined at line 25) to calculate the specified Fibonacci number. Notice that Fibonacci numbers tend to become large quickly. In Fig. 10.11, the screen captures show the results of calculating several Fibonacci numbers.

The event handling in this example is similar to the event handling of the **`Craps`** script in Fig. 10.6. Lines 40–41 define the form's button and define **`getFibonacciValue`** as the event handler for the button's **`onclick`** event. When **`getFibonacciValue`** is called, it converts from a string to an integer the value the user typed into the number text field (lines 16–17). Then, the value is displayed in the browser's status bar (lines 18–19). Next, the value is passed to function **`fibonacci`** (line 20), and the result is displayed in the text field **result** (line 20). Finally, a message is displayed in the browser's status bar, indicating that the call to function **fibonacci** is complete (line 21).

The call to **fibonacci** (line 20) from **getFibonacciValue** is not a recursive call, but all subsequent calls to **fibonacci** are recursive. Each time **fibonacci** is invoked, it immediately tests for the base case—**n** equal to 0 or 1. If this condition is true, **n** is returned (*fibonacci(0)* is 0, and *fibonacci(1)* is 1). Interestingly, if **n** is greater than 1, the recursion step generates *two* recursive calls, each of which is for a slightly simpler problem than the original call to **fibonacci**. Figure 10.12 shows how function **fibonacci** evaluates **fibonacci(3)**; we abbreviate **fibonacci** as **f** to make the figure more readable.

```
1  <?xml version = "1.0"?>
2  <!DOCTYPE html PUBLIC "-//W3C//DTD XHTML 1.0 Transitional//EN"
3     "http://www.w3.org/TR/xhtml1/DTD/xhtml1-transitional.dtd">
4  <!-- Fig. 10.11: FibonacciTest.html -->
5  <!-- Recursive Fibonacci example    -->
6
7  <html xmlns = "http://www.w3.org/1999/xhtml">
8     <head>
9        <title>Recursive Fibonacci Function</title>
10
11       <script language = "javascript">
12
13          // Event handler for button XHTML component in myForm
14          function getFibonacciValue()
15          {
16             var value = parseInt(
17                document.myForm.number.value );
18             window.status =
19                "Calculating Fibonacci number for " + value;
20             document.myForm.result.value = fibonacci( value );
21             window.status = "Done calculating Fibonacci number";
22          }
23
24          // Recursive definition of function fibonacci
25          function fibonacci( n )
26          {
27             if ( n == 0 || n == 1 )  // base case
28                return n;
29             else
30                return fibonacci( n - 1 ) + fibonacci( n - 2 );
31          }
32       </script>
33    </head>
34
35    <body>
36       <form name = "myForm">
37          <table border = "1">
38             <tr><td>Enter an integer</td>
39             <td><input name = "number" type = "text"></td>
```

Fig. 10.11 Recursively generating Fibonacci numbers (part 1 of 2).

```
            <td><input type = "button" value = "Calculate"
               onclick = "getFibonacciValue()"</tr>
            <tr><td>Fibonacci value</td>
            <td><input name = "result" type = "text"></td></tr>
         </table>
      </form></body>
</html>
```

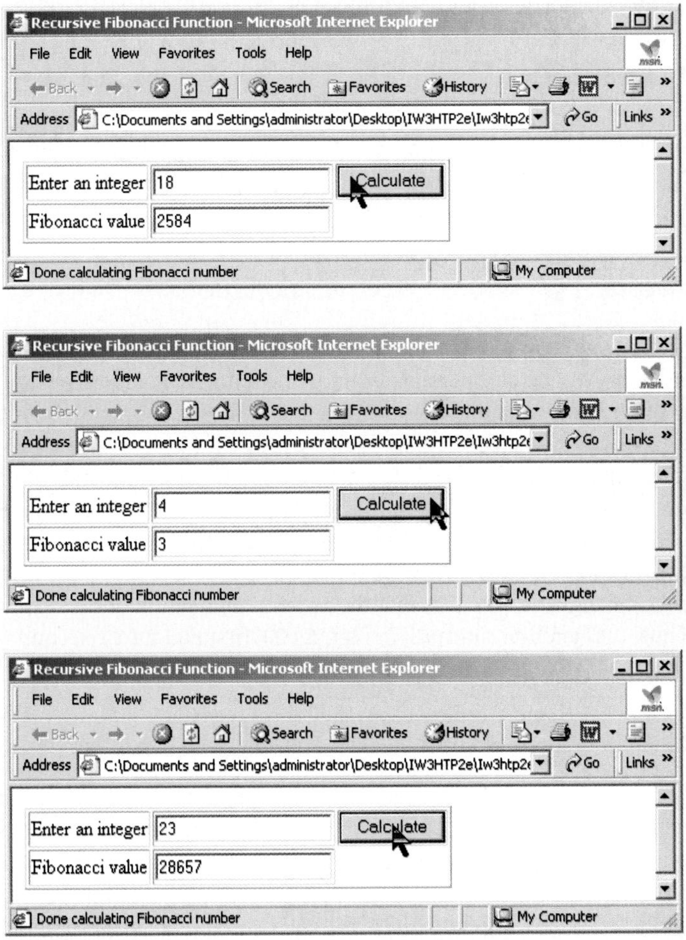

Fig. 10.11 Recursively generating Fibonacci numbers (part 2 of 2).

This figure raises some interesting issues about the order in which JavaScript interpreters will evaluate the operands of operators. This issue is different than the order in which operators are applied to their operands, namely the order dictated by the rules of operator precedence. From Fig. 10.12, it appears that while evaluating **`f(3)`**, two recursive calls will be made, namely **`f(2)`** and **`f(1)`**. But in what order will these calls be made? Most programmers assume that the operands will be evaluated from left to right. In JavaScript, this assumption is true.

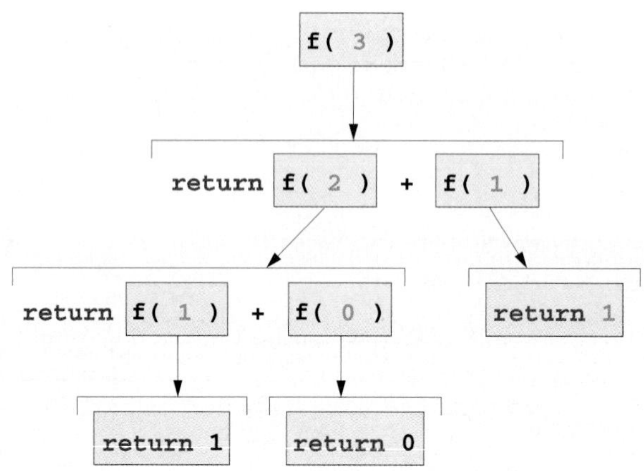

Fig. 10.12 Set of recursive calls to function **fibonacci**.

The C and C++ languages (on which many of JavaScript's features are based) do not specify the order in which the operands of most operators (including **+**) are evaluated. Therefore, the programmer can make no assumption in those languages about the order in which these calls execute. The calls could, in fact execute **f(2)** first and **f(1)** second, or the calls could execute in the reverse order: **f(1)** first and **f(2)** second. In this program and in most other programs, it turns out that the final result would be the same. But in some programs, the evaluation of an operand may have *side effects* that could affect the final result of the expression.

The JavaScript language specifies that the order of evaluation of the operands is from left to right. Thus, the function calls are, in fact, **f(2)** first and **f(1)** second.

Good Programming Practice 10.8

Do not write expressions that depend on the order of evaluation of the operands of an operator. This often results in programs that are difficult to read, debug, modify and maintain.

A word of caution is in order about recursive programs like the one we use here to generate Fibonacci numbers. Each invocation of the **fibonacci** function that does not match one of the base cases (i.e., 0 or 1) results in two more recursive calls to the **fibonacci** function. This set of calling rapidly gets out of hand. Calculating the Fibonacci value of 20 using the program in Fig. 10.11 requires 21,891 calls to the **fibonacci** function; calculating the Fibonacci value of 30 requires 2,692,537 calls to the **fibonacci** function.

As you try to calculate larger Fibonacci values, you will notice that each consecutive Fibonacci number you ask the script to calculate results in a substantial increase in calculation time and number of calls to the **fibonacci** function. For example, the Fibonacci value of 31 requires 4,356,617 calls, and the Fibonacci value of 32 requires 7,049,155 calls. As you can see, the number of calls to **fibonacci** is increasing quickly—1,664,080 additional calls between Fibonacci values of 30 and 31, and 2,692,538 additional calls between Fibonacci values of 31 and 32. This difference in the number of calls made between Fibonacci values of 31 and 32 is more than 1.5 times the difference between Fibonacci values of 30 and 31. Problems of this nature humble even the world's most powerful computers! Computer scientists study, in the field of complexity theory, how hard algorithms have to work to do their jobs. Complexity issues are discussed in detail in the upper level computer science curriculum course generally called "Algorithms."

Performance Tip 10.3

Avoid Fibonacci-style recursive programs, which result in an exponential "explosion" of calls.

10.12 Recursion vs. Iteration

In the previous sections, we studied two functions that can easily be implemented either recursively or iteratively. In this section, we compare the two approaches and discuss why the programmer might choose one approach over the other in a particular situation.

Both iteration and recursion are based on a control structure: Iteration uses a repetition structure (such as **`for`**, **`while`** or **`do/while`**); recursion uses a selection structure (such as **`if`**, **`if/else`** or **`switch`**). Both iteration and recursion involve repetition: Iteration explicitly uses a repetition structure; recursion achieves repetition through repeated function calls. Iteration and recursion each involve a termination test: Iteration terminates when the loop-continuation condition fails; recursion terminates when a base case is recognized. Iteration with counter-controlled repetition and recursion both gradually approach termination: Iteration keeps modifying a counter until the counter assumes a value that makes the loop-continuation condition fail; recursion keeps producing simpler versions of the original problem until the base case is reached. Both iteration and recursion can occur infinitely: An infinite loop occurs with iteration if the loop-continuation test never becomes false; infinite recursion occurs if the recursion step does not reduce the problem each time via a sequence that converges on the base case, or if the base case is incorrect.

Recursion has many negatives. It repeatedly invokes the mechanism and, consequently, the overhead of function calls. This effect can be expensive in terms of both processor time and memory space. Each recursive call causes another copy of the function (actually, only the function's variables) to be created; this effect can consume a considerable amount of memory. Iteration, on the other hand, normally occurs within a function, so the overhead of repeated function calls and extra memory assignment is omitted. So why choose recursion?

Software Engineering Observation 10.12

Any problem that can be solved recursively can also be solved iteratively (nonrecursively). A recursive approach is normally chosen in preference to an iterative approach when the recursive approach more naturally mirrors the problem and results in a program that is easier to understand and debug. Another reason to choose a recursive solution is that an iterative solution may not be apparent.

Performance Tip 10.4

Avoid using recursion in performance-oriented situations. Recursive calls take time and consume additional memory.

Common Programming Error 10.8

Accidentally having a nonrecursive function call itself, either directly, or indirectly through another function, can cause infinite recursion.

Most programming textbooks introduce recursion much later than we have done here. We feel that recursion is a sufficiently rich and complex topic that it is better to introduce it earlier and spread examples of it over the remainder of the JavaScript chapters. Figure 10.13 summarizes the recursion examples and exercises in the text.

Let us reconsider some observations we make repeatedly throughout the book. Good software engineering is important. High performance is often important. Unfortunately, these goals are often at odds with one another. Good software engineering is key to making more manageable the task of developing larger and more complex software systems. High performance in these systems is key to realizing the systems of the future, which will place ever greater computing demands on hardware. Where do functions fit in here?

Software Engineering Observation 10.13

Modularizing programs in a neat, hierarchical manner promotes good software engineering, sometimes at the expense of performance.

Performance Tip 10.5

A heavily modularized program—as compared with a monolithic (i.e., one-piece) program without functions—makes potentially large numbers of function calls, which consume execution time and space on a computer's processor(s). But monolithic programs are difficult to program, test, debug, maintain and evolve. So modularize your programs judiciously, always keeping in mind the delicate balance between performance and good software engineering.

Chapter	Recursion examples and exercises
10	Factorial function Greatest common divisor Sum of two integers Multiply two integers Raising an integer to an integer power Towers of Hanoi Visualizing recursion
11	Sum the elements of an array Print an array Print an array backward Check if a string is a palindrome Minimum value in an array Selection sort Eight Queens Linear search Binary search Quicksort Maze traversal
12	Printing a string input at the keyboard backward

Fig. 10.13 Summary of recursion examples and exercises in the text.

10.13 JavaScript Internet and World Wide Web Resources

rummelplatz.uni-mannheim.de/~skoch/js/tutorial.htm
Voodoo's Introduction to JavaScript teaches how to program in JavaScript.

www.stars.com/Authoring/JavaScript/Tutorial/functions.html
This site provides a tutorial on JavaScript functions.

www.w3schools.com/js/js_functions.asp
This URL provides an introduction to JavaScript functions.

SUMMARY

- Experience has shown that the best way to develop and maintain a large program is to construct it from small, simple pieces, or modules. This technique is called *divide and conquer*.
- Modules in JavaScript are called *functions*. JavaScript programs are written by combining new functions that the programmer writes with "prepackaged" functions and objects available in JavaScript.
- The "prepackaged" functions that belong to JavaScript objects are often called *methods*. The term *method* implies that the function belongs to a particular object.
- The programmer can write programmer-defined functions to define specific tasks that may be used at many points in a script. The actual statements defining the function are written only once and are hidden from other functions.
- A function is invoked by a function call. The function call specifies the function name and provides information (as arguments) that the called function needs to do its task.
- Functions allow the programmer to modularize a program.
- All variables declared in function definitions are local variables—they are known only in the function in which they are defined.
- Most functions have parameters that provide the means for communicating information between functions via function calls. A function's parameters are also considered to be local variables.
- The divide-and-conquer approach to program development makes program development more manageable.
- Using existing functions as building blocks with which to create new programs promotes software reusability. With good function naming and definition, programs can be created from standardized functions rather than be built by using customized code.
- The `()` represent the *function-call operator*.
- The **`return`** *statement* passes the result of a function call back to the calling function.
- The format of a function definition is

```
function function-name( parameter-list )
{
    declarations and statements
}
```

  The *function-name* is any valid identifier. The *parameter-list* is a comma-separated list containing the names of the parameters received by the function when it is called. There should be one argument in the function call for each parameter in the function definition. If a function does not receive any values, the *parameter-list* is empty (i.e., the function name is followed by an empty set of parentheses).

- The declarations and statements within braces form the function body. The function body is also referred to as a *block*. A block is a compound statement that includes declarations. Variables can be declared in any block, and blocks can be nested.
- There are three ways to return control to the point at which a function was invoked. If the function does not return a result, control is returned when the function-ending right brace is reached or by executing the statement

```
return;
```

- If the function does return a result, the statement

```
return expression;
```

  returns the value of *expression* to the caller. When a **return** statement is executed, control returns immediately to the point at which the function was invoked.
- The **Math** object **max** method determines the larger of its two argument values.
- The **Math** object **random** method generates numeric values from 0.0 up to, but not including, 1.0.
- **Math** method **floor** rounds its floating-point number argument to the closest integer not greater than its argument's value.
- The values produced directly by **random** are always in the range

```
0.0 ≤ Math.random() < 1.0
```

- We can generalize picking a random number from a range of values by writing

```
value = Math.floor( a + Math.random() * b );
```

  where **a** is the shifting value (the first number in the desired range of consecutive integers) and **b** is the scaling factor (the width of the desired range of consecutive integers).
- Graphical-user-interface event handling enables JavaScript code to execute in response to the user's interaction with a GUI component in an XHTML form. This interaction causes an event. Scripts are often used to respond to events.
- Specifying the **name** attribute of an XHTML **<form>** enables script code to refer to the elements of the form. This attribute helps a script distinguish between multiple forms in the same XHTML document. Similarly, the **name** attribute is specified for each GUI component in the form, so the script code can individually refer to each GUI component.
- An XHTML button's attribute **onclick** indicates the action to take when the user clicks the button.
- When the user interacts with a GUI component, the script is notified of the event and processes the event. The user's interaction with the GUI "drives" the program. This style of programming is known as event-driven programming.
- The clicking of the button (or any other GUI interaction) is known as the event. The function that is called when an event occurs is known as an event-handling function, or event handler. When a GUI event occurs in a form, the browser automatically calls the specified event-handling function.
- The **value** property specifies the text to display in an XHTML text-field GUI component.
- The dot operator (**.**) is known as the *field-access operator*, or the *member-access operator*.
- Each identifier in a program has many attributes, including duration and scope.
- An identifier's duration, or lifetime, is the period during which the identifier exists in memory.
- Identifiers that represent local variables in a function have automatic duration. Automatic-duration variables are created when program control enters the function in which they are declared; they

exist while the function in which they are declared is active; and they are destroyed when the function in which they are declared is exited.

- Identifiers of static duration are typically defined in the **<head>** section of the XHTML document and exist from the point at which the **<head>** section of the XHTML document is interpreted until the browsing session terminates.
- Variables of static duration are normally called global variables, or script-level variables.
- The scope of an identifier for a variable or function is the portion of the program in which the identifier can be referenced. The scopes for an identifier are global scope and function (or local) scope.
- Event **onload** calls an event handler when the **<body>** of the XHTML document is loaded into the browser.
- Identifiers declared inside a function have function (or local) scope. Function scope begins with the opening left brace (**{**) of the function in which the identifier is declared and ends at the terminating right brace (**}**) of the function. Local variables of a function have function scope, as do function parameters, which are also local variables of the function.
- If a local variable in a function has the same name as a global variable, the global variable is "hidden" from the body of the function.
- Function **escape** takes a string argument and returns a string in which all spaces, punctuation, accent characters and any other character that is not in the ASCII character set are encoded in a hexadecimal format that can be represented on all platforms.
- Function **eval** takes a string argument representing JavaScript code to execute. The JavaScript interpreter evaluates the code and executes it when the **eval** function is called.
- Function **isFinite** takes a numeric argument and returns **true** if the value of the argument is not **NaN**, **Number.POSITIVE_INFINITY** or **Number.NEGATIVE_INFINITY**; otherwise, the function returns **false**.
- Function **isNaN** takes a numeric argument and returns **true** if the value of the argument is not a number; otherwise, the function returns **false**.
- Function **parseFloat** takes a string argument and attempts to convert the beginning of the string into a floating-point value. If the conversion is not successful, the function returns **NaN**; otherwise, it returns the converted value.
- Function **parseInt** takes a string argument and attempts to convert the beginning of the string into an integer value. If the conversion is not successful, the function returns **NaN**; otherwise, it returns the converted value. This function takes an optional second argument between 2 and 36 specifying the *radix* (or *base*) of the number.
- Function **unescape** takes a string as its argument and returns a string in which all characters that were previously encoded with **escape** are decoded.
- JavaScript's global functions are all part of the **Global** object, which also contains all the global variables in the script and all the user-defined functions in the script.
- A recursive function is a function that calls itself, either directly or indirectly.
- If a recursive function is called with a base case, the function returns a result. If the function is called with a more complex problem, the function divides the problem into two or more conceptual pieces: A piece that the function knows how to do, and a slightly smaller version of the original problem. Because this new problem looks like the original problem, the function launches a recursive call to work on the smaller problem.
- For recursion to terminate, each time the recursive function calls itself with a slightly simpler version of the original problem, the sequence of smaller and smaller problems must converge on the base case. When the function recognizes the base case, the result is returned to the previous func-

tion call, and a sequence of returns ensues all the way up the line until the original call of the function eventually returns the final result.

- Both iteration and recursion are based on a control structure: Iteration uses a repetition structure; recursion uses a selection structure.
- Both iteration and recursion involve repetition: Iteration explicitly uses a repetition structure; recursion achieves repetition through repeated function calls.
- Iteration and recursion each involve a termination test: Iteration terminates when the loop-continuation condition fails; recursion terminates when a base case is recognized.
- Iteration and recursion can occur infinitely: An infinite loop occurs with iteration if the loop-continuation test never becomes false; infinite recursion occurs if the recursion step does not reduce the problem in a manner that converges on the base case.
- Recursion repeatedly invokes the mechanism and, consequently, the overhead of function calls. This effect can be expensive in term of both processor time and memory space.

TERMINOLOGY

argument in a function call
automatic duration
automatic variable
base case
block
call a function
called function
caller
calling function
compound statement
converge on the base case
copy of a value
divide and conquer
dot operator (**.**)
duration
escape function
eval function
event
event handler
event-driven programming
field-access operator (**.**)
floor method of the **Math** object
function
function argument
function body
function call
function definition
function keyword
function name
function parameter
function scope
function-call operator **()**
Global object
global scope
global variable
invoke a function
isFinite function
isNaN function
lifetime
local scope
local variable
max method of the **Math** object
member-access operator (**.**)
method
modularize a program
module
name attribute of an XHTML **<form>**
onclick
onload
parameter in a function definition
parseFloat function
parseInt function
programmer-defined function
random method of the **Math** object
random-number generation
recursion
recursive function
recursive step
respond to an event
return statement
scaling
scaling factor
scope
script-level variable
shifting
shifting value

script-level variable
shifting
shifting value
side effect
signature
simulation
software engineering
software reusability
static duration
unescape function
value property of an XHTML text field

SELF-REVIEW EXERCISES

10.1 Fill in the blanks in each of the following statements:

a) Program modules in JavaScript are called __________.
b) A function is invoked with a __________.
c) A variable known only within the function in which it is defined is called a __________.
d) The __________ statement in a called function can be used to pass the value of an expression back to the calling function.
e) The keyword __________ indicates the beginning of a function definition.

10.2 For the given program, state the scope (either global scope or function scope) of each of the following elements:

a) The variable **x**.
b) The variable **y**.
c) The function **cube**.
d) The function **output**.

```
<?xml version = "1.0"?>
<!DOCTYPE html PUBLIC "-//W3C//DTD XHTML 1.0 Transitional//EN"
   "http://www.w3.org/TR/xhtml1/DTD/xhtml1-transitional.dtd">

<!-- Exercise 10.2: scoping.html -->

<html xmlns = "http://www.w3.org/1999/xhtml">
   <head>
      <title>Scoping</title>

      <script type = "text/javascript">
         <!--
         var x;

         function output()
         {
            for ( var x = 1; x <= 10; x++ )
               document.writeln( cube( x ) + "<br />" );
         }

         function cube( y )
         {
            return y * y * y;
         }
         // -->
   </script>

   </head><body onload = "output()"></body>
</html>
```

10.3 Fill in the blanks in each of the following statements:

a) Programmer-defined functions, global variables and JavaScript's global functions are all part of the ________ object.
b) Function ________ determines if its argument is or is not a number.
c) Function ________ takes a string argument and returns a string in which all spaces, punctuation, accent characters and any other character that is not in the ASCII character set are encoded in a hexadecimal format.
d) Function ________ takes a string argument representing JavaScript code to execute.
e) Function ________ takes a string as its argument and returns a string in which all characters that were previously encoded with **escape** are decoded.

10.4 Fill in the blanks in each of the following statements:

a) The ________ of an identifier is the portion of the program in which the identifier can be used.
b) The three ways to return control from a called function to a caller are ________, ________ and ________.
c) The ________ function is used to produce random numbers.
d) Variables declared in a block or in a function's parameter list are of ________ duration.

10.5 Locate the error in each of the following program segments, and explain how to correct the error:

a)
```
method g() {
   document.writeln( "Inside method g" );
}
```
b)
```
// This function should return the sum of its arguments
function sum( x, y ) {
   var result;
   result = x + y;
}
```
c)
```
function f( a ); {
   document.writeln( a );
}
```

10.6 Write a complete JavaScript program to prompt the user for the radius of a sphere, and call function **sphereVolume** to calculate and display the volume of that sphere. Use the statement

```
volume = ( 4.0 / 3.0 ) * Math.PI * Math.pow( radius, 3 );
```

to calculate the volume. The user should input the radius through an XHTML text field in a **<form>** and clicks an XHTML button to initiate the calculation.

ANSWERS TO SELF-REVIEW EXERCISES

10.1 a) functions. b) function call. c) local variable. d) **return**. e) **function**.

10.2 a) Global scope. b) Function scope. c) Global scope. d) Global scope.

10.3 a) **Global**. b) **isNaN**. c) **escape**. d) **eval**. e) **unescape**.

10.4 a) scope. b) **return;** or **return** *expression***;** or encountering the closing right brace of a function. c) **Math.random**. e) automatic.

10.5 a) Error: **method** is not the keyword used to begin a function definition.
Correction: Change **method** to **function**.

b) Error: The function is supposed to return a value, but does not.
Correction: Delete variable **result**, and either place the statement

return x + y;

in the function or add the following statement at the end of the function body:

return result;

c) Error: The semicolon after the right parenthesis that encloses the parameter list.
Correction: Delete the semicolon after the right parenthesis of the parameter list.

10.6 The following solution calculates the volume of a sphere using the radius entered by the user.

```
<?xml version = "1.0"?>
<!DOCTYPE html PUBLIC "-//W3C//DTD XHTML 1.0 Transitional//EN"
   "http://www.w3.org/TR/xhtml1/DTD/xhtml1-transitional.dtd">

<!-- Exercise 10.6: volume.html -->

<html xmlns = "http://www.w3.org/1999/xhtml">
   <head>
      <title>Calculating Sphere Volumes</title>

      <script type = "text/javascript">
         <!--
         function displayVolume()
         {
            var radius = parseFloat( myForm.radiusField.value );
            window.status = "Volume is " + sphereVolume( radius );
         }

         function sphereVolume( r )
         {
            return ( 4.0 / 3.0 ) * Math.PI * Math.pow( r, 3 );
         }
         // -->
      </script>

   </head>

   <body>
      <form name = "myForm" action = "">
         Enter radius of sphere<br />
         <input name = "radiusField" type = "text" />
         <input name = "calculate" type = "button" value =
            "Calculate" onclick = "displayVolume()" />
      </form>
   </body>
</html>
```

EXERCISES

10.7 Write a script that uses a function **circleArea** to prompt the user for the radius of a circle and to calculate and print the area of that circle.

10.8 A parking garage charges a $2.00 minimum fee to park for up to three hours. The garage charges an additional $0.50 per hour for each hour *or part thereof* in excess of three hours. The maximum charge for any given 24-hour period is $10.00. Assume that no car parks for longer than 24 hours at a time. Write a script that calculates and displays the parking charges for each customer who parked a car in this garage yesterday. You should input from the user the hours parked for each customer. The program should display the charge for the current customer and should calculate and display the running total of yesterday's receipts. The program should use the function **calculateCharges** to determine the charge for each customer. Use the techniques described in Self-Review Exercise 10.6 to obtain the input from the user.

10.9 Write function **distance** that calculates the distance between two points ($x1$, $y1$) and ($x2$, $y2$). All numbers and return values should be floating-point values. Incorporate this function into a script that enables the user to enter the coordinates of the points through an XHTML form.

10.10 Answer each of the following questions:

a) What does it mean to choose numbers "at random"?
b) Why is the **Math.random** function useful for simulating games of chance?
c) Why is it often necessary to scale and/or shift the values produced by **Math.random**?
d) Why is computerized simulation of real-world situations a useful technique?

10.11 Write statements that assign random integers to the variable n in the following ranges:

a) $1 \le n \le 2$
b) $1 \le n \le 100$
c) $0 \le n \le 9$
d) $1000 \le n \le 1112$
e) $-1 \le n \le 1$
f) $-3 \le n \le 11$

10.12 For each of the following sets of integers, write a single statement that will print a number at random from the set:

a) 2, 4, 6, 8, 10.
b) 3, 5, 7, 9, 11.
c) 6, 10, 14, 18, 22.

10.13 Write a function **integerPower(base, exponent)** that returns the value of

$$base^{exponent}$$

For example, **integerPower(3, 4) = 3 * 3 * 3 * 3**. Assume that **exponent** is a positive, nonzero integer and **base** is an integer. Function **integerPower** should use a **for** or **while** structure to control the calculation. Do not use any math library functions. Incorporate this function into a script that reads integer values from an XHTML form for **base** and **exponent** and performs the calculation with the **integerPower** function. The XHTML form should consist of two text fields and a button to initiate the calculation. The user should interact with the program by typing numbers in both text fields and then clicking the button.

10.14 Write a function **multiple** that determines, for a pair of integers, whether the second integer is a multiple of the first. The function should take two integer arguments and return **true** if the second is a multiple of the first, and **false** otherwise. Incorporate this function into a script that inputs a series of pairs of integers (one pair at a time, using **JTextFields**). The XHTML form should consist of two text fields and a button to initiate the calculation. The user should interact with the program by typing numbers in both text fields, and then clicking the button.

10.15 Write a script that inputs integers (one at a time) and passes them one at a time to function **isEven**, which uses the modulus operator to determine if an integer is even. The function should take an integer argument and return **true** if the integer is even and **false** otherwise. Use sentinel-controlled looping and a **prompt** dialog.

10.16 Write a function **squareOfAsterisks** that displays a solid square of asterisks whose side is specified in integer parameter **side**. For example, if **side** is **4**, the function displays

Incorporate this function into a script that reads an integer value for **side** from the user at the keyboard and performs the drawing with the **squareOfAsterisks** function.

10.17 Modify the function created in Exercise 10.16 to form the square out of whatever character is contained in parameter **fillCharacter**. Thus, if **side** is **5** and **fillCharacter** is "**#**", the function should print

```
#####
#####
#####
#####
#####
```

10.18 Write program segments that accomplish each of the following tasks:

a) Calculate the integer part of the quotient when integer **a** is divided by integer **b**.
b) Calculate the integer remainder when integer **a** is divided by integer **b**.
c) Use the program pieces developed in parts (a) and (b) to write a function **displayDigits** that receives an integer between **1** and **99999** and prints it as a series of digits, each pair of which is separated by two spaces. For example, the integer **4562** should be printed as

```
4  5  6  2.
```

d) Incorporate the function developed in part (c) into a script that inputs an integer from a **prompt** dialog and invokes **displayDigits** by passing to the function the integer entered.

10.19 Implement the following functions:

a) Function **celsius** returns the Celsius equivalent of a Fahrenheit temperature, using the calculation

```
C = 5.0 / 9.0 * ( F - 32 );
```

b) Function **fahrenheit** returns the Fahrenheit equivalent of a Celsius temperature, using the calculation

```
F = 9.0 / 5.0 * C + 32;
```

c) Use these functions to write a script that enables the user to enter either a Fahrenheit or a Celsius temperature and displays the Celsius or Fahrenheit equivalent, respectively.

Your XHTML document should contain two buttons—one to initiate the conversion from Fahrenheit to Celsius and one to initiate the conversion from Celsius to Fahrenheit.

10.20 Write a function **minimum3** that returns the smallest of three floating-point numbers. Use the **Math.min** function to implement **minimum3**. Incorporate the function into a script that reads three values from the user and determines the smallest value. Display the result in the status bar.

10.21 An integer number is said to be a *perfect number* if its factors, including 1 (but not the number itself), sum to the number. For example, 6 is a perfect number, because 6 = 1 + 2 + 3. Write a function **perfect** that determines whether parameter **number** is a perfect number. Use this function in a script that determines and displays all the perfect numbers between 1 and 1000. Print the factors of each perfect number to confirm that the number is indeed perfect. Challenge the computing power of your computer by testing numbers much larger than 1000. Display the results in a **<textarea>**.

10.22 An integer is said to be *prime* if it is divisible by only 1 and itself. For example, 2, 3, 5 and 7 are prime, but 4, 6, 8 and 9 are not.

a) Write a function that determines whether a number is prime.
b) Use this function in a script that determines and prints all the prime numbers between 1 and 10,000. How many of these 10,000 numbers do you really have to test before being sure that you have found all the primes? Display the results in a **<textarea>**.
c) Initially, you might think that $n/2$ is the upper limit for which you must test to see whether a number is prime, but you only need go as high as the square root of n. Why? Rewrite the program, and run it both ways. Estimate the performance improvement.

10.23 Write a function that takes an integer value and returns the number with its digits reversed. For example, given the number 7631, the function should return 1367. Incorporate the function into a script that reads a value from the user. Display the result of the function in the status bar.

10.24 The *greatest common divisor* (*GCD*) of two integers is the largest integer that evenly divides each of the two numbers. Write a function **gcd** that returns the greatest common divisor of two integers. Incorporate the function into a script that reads two values from the user. Display the result of the function in the browser's status bar.

10.25 Write a function **qualityPoints** that inputs a student's average and returns 4 if the student's average is 90–100, 3 if the average is 80–89, 2 if the average is 70–79, 1 if the average is 60–69 and 0 if the average is lower than 60. Incorporate the function into a script that reads a value from the user. Display the result of the function in the browser's status bar.

10.26 Write a script that simulates coin tossing. Let the program toss the coin each time the user clicks the "**Toss**" button. Count the number of times each side of the coin appears. Display the results. The program should call a separate function **flip** that takes no arguments and returns **false** for tails and **true** for heads. [*Note*: If the program realistically simulates the coin tossing, each side of the coin should appear approximately half the time.]

10.27 Computers are playing an increasing role in education. Write a program that will help an elementary school student learn multiplication. Use **Math.random** to produce two positive one-digit integers. It should then display a question such as

```
How much is 6 times 7?
```

The student then types the answer into a text field. Your program checks the student's answer. If it is correct, display the string **"Very good!"** in the browser's status bar, and generate a new question. If the answer is wrong, display the string **"No. Please try again."** in the browser's status bar, and let the student try the same question again repeatedly until the student finally gets it right. A separate function should be used to generate each new question. This function should be called once when the script begins execution and each time the user answers the question correctly.

10.28 The use of computers in education is referred to as *computer-assisted instruction* (CAI). One problem that develops in CAI environments is student fatigue. This problem can be eliminated by varying the computer's dialogue to hold the student's attention. Modify the program of Exercise 10.27 print one of a variety of comments for each correct answer and each incorrect answer. The set of responses for correct answers is as follows:

```
Very good!
Excellent!
Nice work!
Keep up the good work!
```

The set of responses for incorrect answers is as follows:

```
No. Please try again.
Wrong. Try once more.
Don't give up!
No. Keep trying.
```

Use random-number generation to choose a number from 1 to 4 that will be used to select an appropriate response to each answer. Use a **switch** structure to issue the responses.

10.29 More sophisticated computer-aided instruction systems monitor the student's performance over a period of time. The decision to begin a new topic is often based on the student's success with previous topics. Modify the program of Exercise 10.28 to count the number of correct and incorrect responses typed by the student. After the student answers 10 questions, your program should calculate the percentage of correct responses. If the percentage is lower than 75%, print **Please ask your instructor for extra help**, and reset the program so another student can try it.

10.30 Write a script that plays a "guess the number" game as follows: Your program chooses the number to be guessed by selecting a random integer in the range 1 to 1000. The script displays the prompt **Guess a number between 1 and 1000** next to a text field. The player types a first guess into the text field and clicks a button to submit the guess to the script. If the player's guess is incorrect, your program should display **Too high. Try again.** or **Too low. Try again.** in the browser's status bar to help the player "zero in" on the correct answer and should clear the text field so the user can enter the next guess. When the user enters the correct answer, display **Congratulations. You guessed the number!** in the status bar, and clear the text field so the user can play again. [*Note*: The guessing technique employed in this problem is similar to a *binary search*.]

10.31 Modify the program of Exercise 10.30 to count the number of guesses the player makes. If the number is 10 or fewer, display **Either you know the secret or you got lucky!** If the player guesses the number in 10 tries, display **Ahah! You know the secret!** If the player makes more than 10 guesses, display **You should be able to do better!** Why should it take no more than 10 guesses? Well, with each "good guess," the player should be able to eliminate half of the numbers. Now show why any number 1 to 1000 can be guessed in 10 or fewer tries.

10.32 Exercises 10.27 through 10.29 developed a computer-assisted instruction program to teach an elementary school student multiplication. This exercise suggests enhancements to that program.

a) Modify the program to allow the user to enter a grade-level capability. A grade level of 1 means to use only single-digit numbers in the problems, a grade level of 2 means to use numbers as large as two digits, etc.
b) Modify the program to allow the user to pick the type of arithmetic problems he or she wishes to study. An option of 1 means addition problems only, 2 means subtraction problems only, 3 means multiplication problems only, 4 means division problems only and 5 means to intermix randomly problems of all these types.

10.33 Modify the craps program of Fig. 10.6 to allow wagering. Initialize variable **bankBalance** to 1000 dollars. Prompt the player to enter a **wager**. Check that the **wager** is less than or equal to

bankBalance and, if not, have the user reenter **wager** until a valid **wager** is entered. After a valid **wager** is entered, run one game of craps. If the player wins, increase **bankBalance** by **wager**, and print the new **bankBalance**. If the player loses, decrease **bankBalance** by **wager**, print the new **bankBalance**, check if **bankBalance** has become zero and, if so, print the message **Sorry. You busted!** As the game progresses, print various messages to create some "chatter," such as **Oh, you're going for broke, huh?** or **Aw c'mon, take a chance!** or **You're up big. Now's the time to cash in your chips!**. Implement the "chatter" as a separate function that randomly chooses the string to display.

10.34 Write a recursive function **power(base, exponent)** that, when invoked, returns

$$base^{exponent}$$

for example, **power(3, 4) = 3 * 3 * 3 * 3**. Assume that **exponent** is an integer greater than or equal to 1. (*Hint:* The recursion step would use the relationship

$$base^{exponent} = base \cdot base^{exponent - 1}$$

and the terminating condition occurs when **exponent** is equal to **1**, because

$$base^1 = base$$

Incorporate this function into a script that enables the user to enter the **base** and **exponent**.)

10.35 *(Towers of Hanoi)* Every budding computer scientist must grapple with certain classic problems, and the Towers of Hanoi (see Fig. 10.14) is one of the most famous. Legend has it that in a temple in the Far East, priests are attempting to move a stack of disks from one peg to another. The initial stack has 64 disks threaded onto one peg and arranged from bottom to top by decreasing size. The priests are attempting to move the stack from this peg to a second peg, under the constraints that exactly one disk is moved at a time and at no time may a larger disk be placed above a smaller disk. A third peg is available for temporarily holding disks. Supposedly, the world will end when the priests complete their task, so there is little incentive for us to facilitate their efforts.

Fig. 10.14 Towers of Hanoi for the case with four disks.

Let us assume that the priests are attempting to move the disks from peg 1 to peg 3. We wish to develop an algorithm that will print the precise sequence of peg-to-peg disk transfers.

If we were to approach this problem with conventional functions, we would rapidly find ourselves hopelessly knotted up in managing the disks. Instead, if we attack the problem with recursion in mind, it immediately becomes tractable. Moving n disks can be viewed in terms of moving only $n - 1$ disks (and hence the recursion) as follows:

a) Move $n - 1$ disks from peg 1 to peg 2, using peg 3 as a temporary holding area.
b) Move the last disk (the largest) from peg 1 to peg 3.
c) Move the $n - 1$ disks from peg 2 to peg 3, using peg 1 as a temporary holding area.

The process ends when the last task involves moving $n = 1$ disk (i.e., the base case). This task is accomplished simply by moving the disk, without the need for a temporary holding area.

Write a script to solve the Towers of Hanoi problem. Allow the user to enter the number of disks in a text field. Use a recursive **`tower`** function with four parameters:

a) The number of disks to be moved
b) The peg on which the disks are initially threaded
c) The peg to which the stack of disks is to be moved
d) The peg to be used as a temporary holding area

Your program should display in a **`<textarea>`** the precise instructions it will take to move the disks from the starting peg to the destination peg. For example, to move a stack of three disks from peg 1 to peg 3, your program should display the following series of moves:

1 → 3 (This notation means to move one disk from peg 1 to peg 3.)
1 → 2
3 → 2
1 → 3
2 → 1
2 → 3
1 → 3

10.36 Any program that can be implemented recursively can be implemented iteratively, although sometimes with more difficulty and less clarity. Try writing an iterative version of the Towers of Hanoi. If you succeed, compare your iterative version with the recursive version you developed in Exercise 10.35. Investigate issues of performance, clarity and your ability to demonstrate the correctness of the programs.

10.37 *(Visualizing Recursion)* It is interesting to watch recursion "in action." Modify the factorial function of Fig. 10.10 to display its local variable and recursive-call parameter. For each recursive call, display the outputs on a separate line and add a level of indentation. Do your utmost to make the outputs clear, interesting and meaningful. Your goal here is to design and implement an output format that helps a person understand recursion better. You may want to add such display capabilities to the many other recursion examples and exercises throughout the text.

10.38 The greatest common divisor of integers **`x`** and **`y`** is the largest integer that evenly divides into both **`x`** and **`y`**. Write a recursive function **`gcd`** that returns the greatest common divisor of **`x`** and **`y`**. The **`gcd`** of **`x`** and **`y`** is defined recursively as follows: If **`y`** is equal to **`0`**, then **`gcd( x, y )`** is **`x`**; otherwise, **`gcd( x, y )`** is **`gcd( y, x % y )`**, where **`%`** is the modulus operator. Use this function to replace the one you wrote in the script of Exercise 10.24.

10.39 What does the following function do?

```
// Parameter b must be a positive
// integer to prevent infinite recursion
```

```
function mystery( a, b )
{
   if ( b == 1 )
      return a;
   else
      return a + mystery( a, b - 1 );
}
```

10.40 After you determine what the program of Exercise 10.39 does, modify the function to operate properly after removing the restriction of the second argument being nonnegative. Also, incorporate the function into a script that enables the user to enter two integers, and test the function.

10.41 Find the error in the following recursive function, and explain how to correct it:

```
function sum( n )
{
   if ( n == 0 )
      return 0;
   else
      return n + sum( n );
}
```

11

JavaScript: Arrays

Objectives

- To introduce the array data structure.
- To understand the use of arrays to store, sort and search lists and tables of values.
- To understand how to declare an array, initialize an array and refer to individual elements of an array.
- To be able to pass arrays to functions.
- To be able to search and sort an array.
- To be able to declare and manipulate multiple-subscript arrays.

With sobs and tears he sorted out
Those of the largest size …
Lewis Carroll

Attempt the end, and never stand to doubt;
Nothing's so hard, but search will find it out.
Robert Herrick

Now go, write it before them in a table,
and note it in a book.
Isaiah 30:8

'Tis in my memory lock'd,
And you yourself shall keep the key of it.
William Shakespeare

Outline

11.1 Introduction

This chapter serves as an introduction to the important topic of data structures. *Arrays* are data structures consisting of related data items (sometimes called *collections* of data items). JavaScript arrays are "dynamic" entities, in that they can change size after they are created. Many of the techniques demonstrated in this chapter are used frequently in the chapters on Dynamic HTML, as we introduce the collections that allow a script programmer to manipulate every element of an XHTML document dynamically.

11.2 Arrays

An array is a group of memory locations that all have the same name and normally are of the same type (although this attribute is not required). To refer to a particular location or element in the array, we specify the name of the array and the *position number* of the particular element in the array.

Figure 11.1 shows an array of integer values named **c**. This array contains 12 *elements*. Any one of these elements may be referred to by giving the name of the array followed by the position number of the particular element in square brackets (**[]**). The first element in every array is the *zeroth element*. Thus, the first element of array **c** is referred to as **c[0]**, the second element of array **c** is referred to as **c[1]**, the seventh element of array **c** is referred to as **c[6]** and, in general, the *i*th element of array **c** is referred to as **c[i-1]**. Array names follow the same conventions as do other identifiers.

The position number in square brackets is called a *subscript* (or an *index*). A subscript must be an integer or an integer expression. If a program uses an expression as a subscript, then the expression is evaluated to determine the value of the subscript. For example, if we assume that variable **a** is equal to **5** and that variable **b** is equal to **6**, then the statement

```
c[ a + b ] += 2;
```

adds **2** to array element **c[11]**. Note that a subscripted array name is an *lvalue*—it can be used on the left side of an assignment to place a new value into an array element.

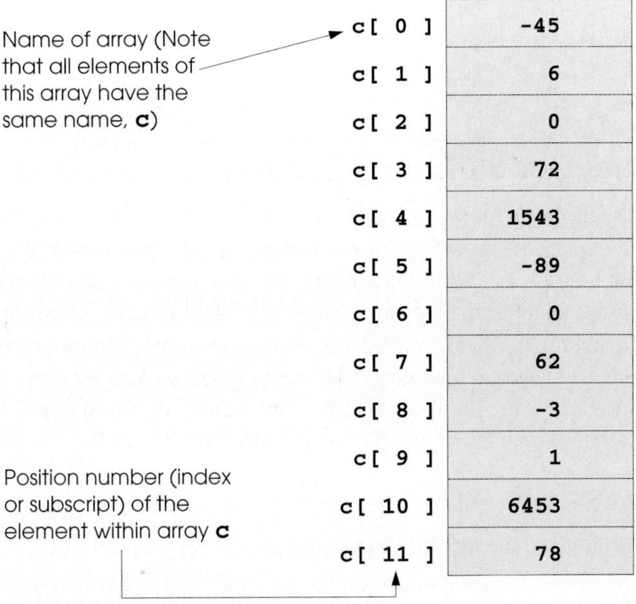

Fig. 11.1 A 12-element array.

Let us examine array **c** in Fig. 11.1 more closely. The array's *name* is **c**. The *length* of array **c** is 12 and is determined by the following expression:

```
c.length
```

Every array in JavaScript *knows* its own length. The array's 12 elements are referred to as **c[0]**, **c[1]**, **c[2]**, …, **c[11]**. The *value* of **c[0]** is **-45**, the value of **c[1]** is **6**, the value of **c[2]** is **0**, the value of **c[7]** is **62** and the value of **c[11]** is **78**. To calculate the sum of the values contained in the first three elements of array **c** and store the result in variable **sum**, we would write

```
sum = c[ 0 ] + c[ 1 ] + c[ 2 ];
```

To divide the value of the seventh element of array **c** by **2** and assign the result to the variable **x**, we would write

```
x = c[ 6 ] / 2;
```

Common Programming Error 11.1

It is important to note the difference between the "seventh element of the array" and "array element seven." Because array subscripts begin at 0, the "seventh element of the array" has a subscript of 6, while "array element seven" has a subscript of 7 and is actually the eighth element of the array. This confusion is a source of "off-by-one" errors.

The brackets that enclose the array subscript are a JavaScript operator. Brackets have the same level of precedence as do parentheses. The chart in Fig. 11.2 shows the precedence and associativity of the operators introduced to this point in the text. They are shown from top to bottom in decreasing order of precedence, alongside their associativity and type.

11.3 Declaring and Allocating Arrays

Arrays occupy space in memory. Actually, an array in JavaScript is an **`Array`** *object*. The programmer uses *operator* **`new`** to allocate dynamically the number of elements required by each array. Operator **`new`** creates an object as the program executes by obtaining enough memory to store an object of the type specified to the right of **`new`**. The process of creating new objects is also known as *creating an instance*, or *instantiating an object,* and operator **`new`** is known as the *dynamic memory allocation operator*. **`Array`** objects are allocated with **`new`** because arrays are considered to be objects, and all objects must be created with **`new`**. To allocate 12 elements for integer array **`c`**, use the statement

```
var c = new Array( 12 );
```

The preceding statement can also be performed in two steps as follows:

```
var c;                    // declares the array
c = new Array( 12 );      // allocates the array
```

When arrays are allocated, the elements are not initialized.

Common Programming Error 11.2

Assuming that the elements of an array are initialized when the array is allocated may result in logic errors.

Operators	Associativity	Type
`() [] .`	left to right	highest
`++ -- !`	right to left	unary
`* / %`	left to right	multiplicative
`+ -`	left to right	additive
`< <= > >=`	left to right	relational
`== !=`	left to right	equality
`&&`	left to right	logical AND
`||`	left to right	logical OR
`?:`	right to left	conditional
`= += -= *= /= %=`	right to left	assignment

Fig. 11.2 Precedence and associativity of the operators discussed so far.

Memory may be reserved for several arrays by using a single declaration. The following declaration reserves 100 elements for array **b** and 27 elements for array **x**:

```
var b = new Array( 100 ), x = new Array( 27 );
```

11.4 Examples Using Arrays

The script of Fig. 11.3 uses operator **new** to allocate an **Array** of five elements and an empty array. The script demonstrates initializing an **Array** of existing elements and also shows that an **Array** can grow dynamically to accommodate new elements. The **Array**'s values are displayed in XHTML tables. [*Note*: Many of the scripts in this chapter are executed in response to the **<body>**'s **onload** event.]

```
<?xml version = "1.0"?>
<!DOCTYPE html PUBLIC "-//W3C//DTD XHTML 1.0 Strict//EN"
   "http://www.w3.org/TR/xhtml1/DTD/xhtml1-strict.dtd">

<!-- Fig. 11.3: InitArray.html -->
<!-- Initializing an Array     -->

<html xmlns = "http://www.w3.org/1999/xhtml">
   <head>
      <title>Initializing an Array</title>

      <script type = "text/javascript">
         <!--
         // this function is called when the <body> element's
         // onload event occurs
         function initializeArrays()
         {
            var n1 = new Array( 5 );    // allocate 5-element Array
            var n2 = new Array();       // allocate empty Array

            // assign values to each element of Array n1
            for ( var i = 0; i < n1.length; ++i )
               n1[ i ] = i;

            // create and initialize five-elements in Array n2
            for ( i = 0; i < 5; ++i )
               n2[ i ] = i;

            outputArray( "Array n1 contains", n1 );
            outputArray( "Array n2 contains", n2 );
         }

         // output "header" followed by a two-column table
         // containing subscripts and elements of "theArray"
         function outputArray( header, theArray )
         {
            document.writeln( "<h2>" + header + "</h2>" );
            document.writeln( "<table border = \"1\" width =" +
               "\"100%\">" );
```

Fig. 11.3 Initializing the elements of an array (part 1 of 2).

```
40
41             document.writeln( "<thead><th width = \"100\"" +
42                "align = \"left\">Subscript</th>" +
43                "<th align = \"left\">Value</th></thead><tbody>" );
44
45             for ( var i = 0; i < theArray.length; i++ )
46                document.writeln( "<tr><td>" + i + "</td><td>" +
47                   theArray[ i ] + "</td></tr>" );
48
49             document.writeln( "</tbody></table>" );
50          }
51          // -->
52       </script>
53
54    </head><body onload = "initializeArrays()"></body>
55 </html>
```

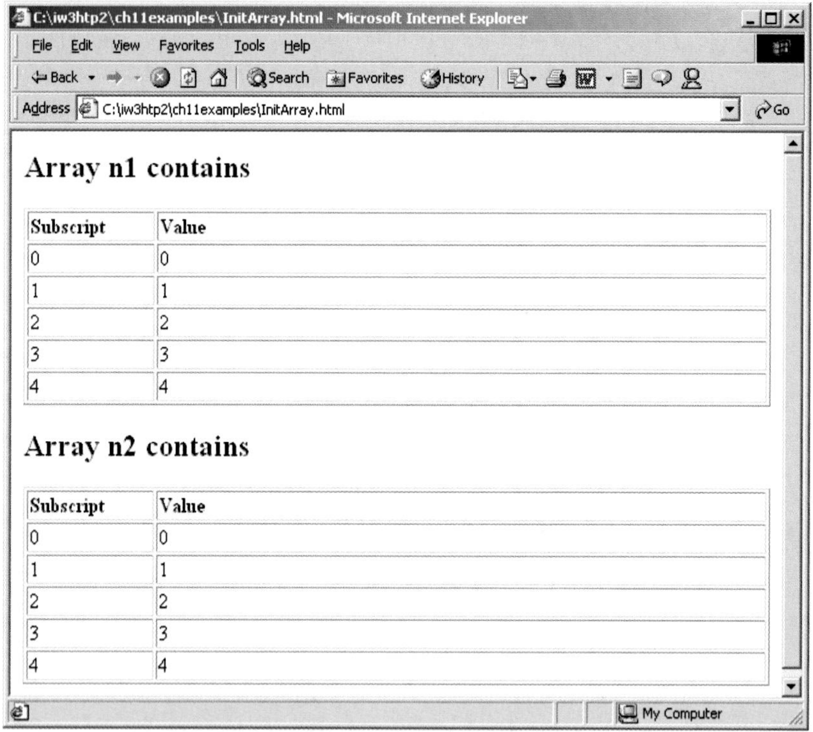

Fig. 11.3 Initializing the elements of an array (part 2 of 2).

Function **`initializeArrays`** (defined at lines 16–31) is called by the browser as the event handler for the **`<body>`**'s **`onload`** event. Line 18 creates **`Array n1`** as an array of five elements. Line 19 creates **`Array n2`** as an empty array.

Lines 22–23 use a **`for`** structure to initialize the elements of **`n1`** to their subscript numbers (0 to 4). Note the use of zero-based counting (remember, array subscripts start at 0), so the loop can access every element of the array. Also, note the use of the expression

n1.length in the condition for the **for** structure to determine the length of the array. In this example, the length of the array is 5, so the loop continues executing as long as the value of control variable **i** is less than **5**. For a five-element array, the subscript values are 0 through 4, so using the less than operator, **<**, guarantees that the loop does not attempt to access an element beyond the end of the array.

Lines 26–27 use a **for** structure to add five elements to the **Array n2** and initialize each element to its subscript number (0 to 4). Note that **Array n2** grows dynamically to accommodate the values assigned to each element of the array.

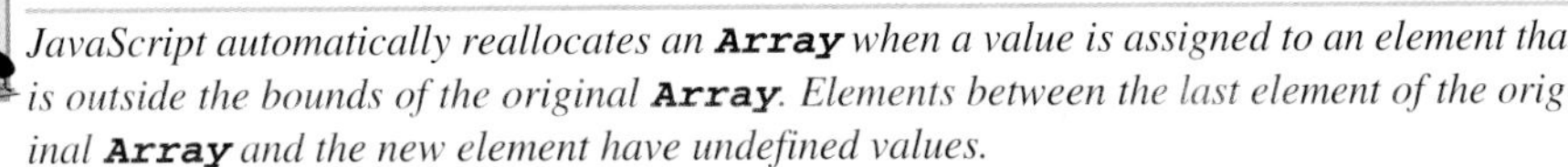

Software Engineering Observation 11.1

JavaScript automatically reallocates an **Array** *when a value is assigned to an element that is outside the bounds of the original* **Array**. *Elements between the last element of the original* **Array** *and the new element have undefined values.*

Lines 29–30 invoke function **outputArray** (defined at lines 35–51) to display the contents of each array in XHTML tables. Function **outputArray** receives two arguments: A string to be output before the XHTML table that displays the contents of the array and the array to output. Lines 37–44 output the header string and begin the definition of the XHTML table with two columns: **Subscript** and **Value**. Lines 46–48 use a **for** structure to output XHTML text that defines each row of the table. Once again, note the use of zero-based counting, so the loop can access every element of the array. Line 50 terminates the definition of the XHTML table.

Common Programming Error 11.3

Referring to an element outside the **Array** *bounds is normally a logic error.*

Testing and Debugging Tip 11.1

When using subscripts to loop through an **Array**, *the subscript should never go below 0 and should always be less than the number of elements in the* **Array** *(i.e., one less than the size of the* **Array**). *Make sure that the loop-terminating condition prevents the access of elements outside this range.*

If the values of an **Array**'s elements are known in advance, the elements of the **Array** can be allocated and initialized in the declaration of the array. There are two ways in which the initial values can be specified. The statement

```
var n = [ 10, 20, 30, 40, 50 ];
```

uses a comma-separated *initializer list* enclosed in square brackets (**[** and **]**) to create a five-element **Array** with subscripts of **0**, **1**, **2**, **3** and **4**. The array size is determined by the number of values in the initializer list. Note that the preceding declaration does not require the **new** operator to create the **Array** object—this functionality is provided by the interpreter when it encounters an array declaration that includes an initializer list. The statement

```
var n = new Array( 10, 20, 30, 40, 50 );
```

also creates a five-element array with subscripts of **0**, **1**, **2**, **3** and **4**. In this case, the initial values of the array elements are specified as arguments in the parentheses following **new Array**. The size of the array is determined by the number of values in parentheses. It is also possible to reserve a space in an **Array** for a value to be specified later by using a comma as a *place holder* in the initializer list. For example, the statement

```
var n = [ 10, 20, , 40, 50 ];
```

creates a five-element array with no value specified for the third element (**`n[ 2 ]`**).

The script of Fig. 11.4 creates three **`Array`** objects to demonstrate initializing arrays with initializer lists and displays each array in an XHTML table using the same function **`outputArray`** discussed in Fig. 11.3. Notice that when **`Array integers2`** is displayed in the Web page, the elements with subscripts 1 and 2 (the second and third elements of the array) appear in the Web page as **`undefined`**. These elements are the two elements of the array for which we did not supply values in the declaration in line 21 in the script.

```
1   <?xml version = "1.0"?>
2   <!DOCTYPE html PUBLIC "-//W3C//DTD XHTML 1.0 Strict//EN"
3      "http://www.w3.org/TR/xhtml1/DTD/xhtml1-strict.dtd">
4   
5   <!-- Fig. 11.4: InitArray2.html                  -->
6   <!-- Initializing an Array with a Declaration -->
7   
8   <html xmlns = "http://www.w3.org/1999/xhtml">
9      <head>
10        <title>Initializing an Array with a Declaration</title>
11  
12        <script type = "text/javascript">
13           <!--
14           function start()
15           {
16              // Initializer list specifies number of elements and
17              // value for each element.
18              var colors = new Array( "cyan", "magenta",
19                 "yellow", "black" );
20              var integers1 = [ 2, 4, 6, 8 ];
21              var integers2 = [ 2, , , 8 ];
22  
23              outputArray( "Array colors contains", colors );
24              outputArray( "Array integers1 contains", integers1 );
25              outputArray( "Array integers2 contains", integers2 );
26           }
27  
28           // output "header" followed by a two-column table
29           // containing subscripts and elements of "theArray"
30           function outputArray( header, theArray )
31           {
32              document.writeln( "<h2>" + header + "</h2>" );
33              document.writeln( "<table border = \"1\"" +
34                 "width = \"100%\">" );
35              document.writeln( "<thead><th width = \"100\" " +
36                 "align = \"left\">Subscript</th>" +
37                "<th align = \"left\">Value</th></thead><tbody>" );
38  
39              for ( var i = 0; i < theArray.length; i++ )
40                 document.writeln( "<tr><td>" + i + "</td><td>" +
41                    theArray[ i ] + "</td></tr>" );
42  
```

Fig. 11.4 Initializing the elements of an array (part 1 of 2).

```
            document.writeln( "</tbody></table>" );
         }
         // -->
      </script>

   </head><body onload = "start()"></body>
</html>
```

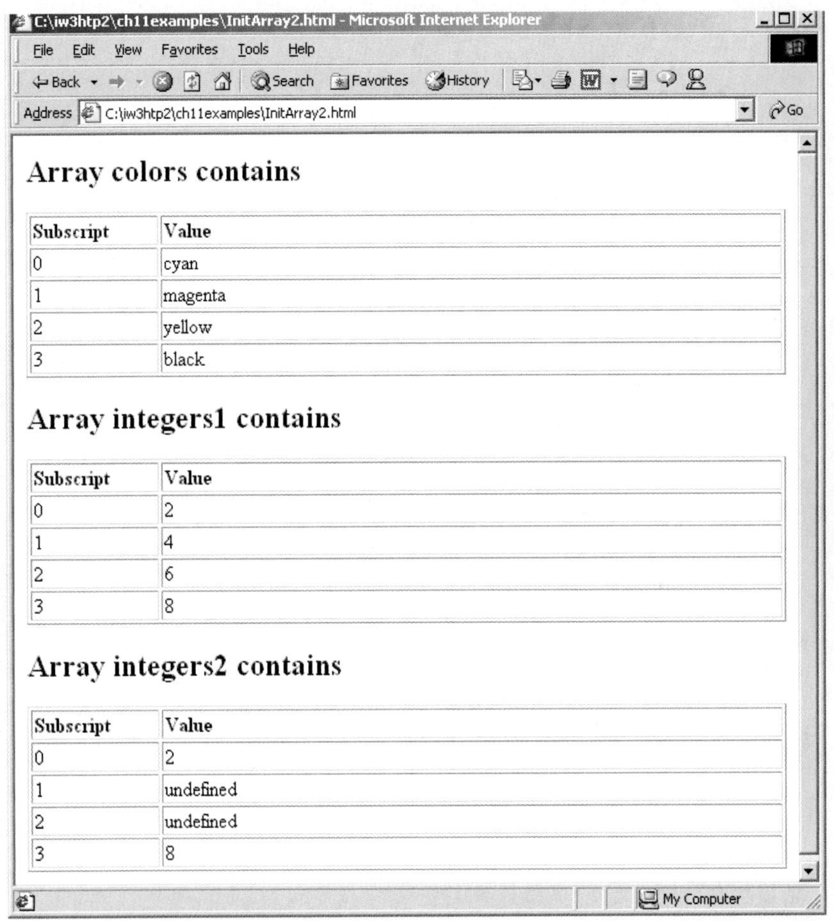

Fig. 11.4 Initializing the elements of an array (part 2 of 2).

The script of Fig. 11.5 sums the values contained in the 10-element integer array called **theArray**, which is declared, allocated and initialized in line 16 in function **start**. When the Web page loads, the script calls function **start** in response to the **<body>**'s **onload** event. The statement in line 20 in the body of the first **for** loop does the totaling. It is important to remember that the values being supplied as initializers for array **the-Array** normally would be read into the program. For example, in a script, the user could enter the values through an XHTML form.

```
1  <?xml version = "1.0"?>
2  <!DOCTYPE html PUBLIC "-//W3C//DTD XHTML 1.0 Strict//EN"
3     "http://www.w3.org/TR/xhtml1/DTD/xhtml1-strict.dtd">
4
5  <!-- Fig. 11.5: SumArray.html      -->
6  <!-- Summing Elements of an Array -->
7
8  <html xmlns = "http://www.w3.org/1999/xhtml">
9     <head>
10       <title>Sum the Elements of an Array</title>
11
12       <script type = "text/javascript">
13          <!--
14          function start()
15          {
16             var theArray = [ 1, 2, 3, 4, 5, 6, 7, 8, 9, 10 ];
17             var total1 = 0, total2 = 0;
18
19             for ( var i = 0; i < theArray.length; i++ )
20                total1 += theArray[ i ];
21
22            document.writeln( "Total using subscripts: " + total1 );
23
24             for ( var element in theArray )
25                total2 += theArray[ element ];
26
27             document.writeln( "<br />Total using for/in: " +
28                total2 );
29          }
30          // -->
31       </script>
32
33    </head><body onload = "start()"></body>
34 </html>
```

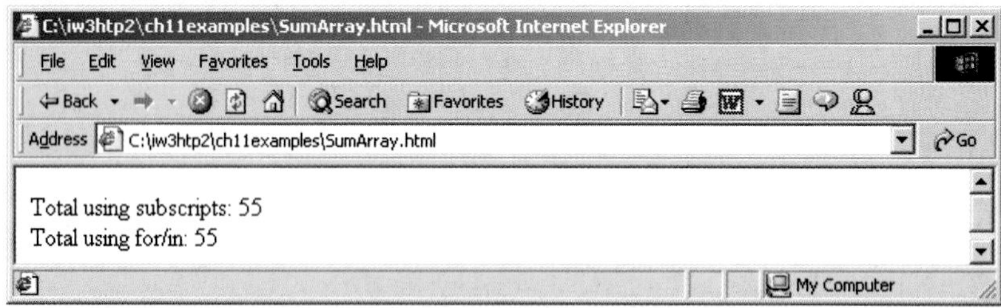

Fig. 11.5 Computing the sum of the elements of an array.

In this example, we introduce JavaScript's ***for/in*** control structure, which enables a script to perform a task ***for*** *each element* ***in*** *an array* (or, as we will see in the chapters on Dynamic HTML, for each element in a collection). This process is also known as *iterating over the elements of an array*. Lines 24–25 show the syntax of a **for/in** structure. Inside the parentheses, we declare the **element** variable used to select each element in the object to the right of keyword **in** (**theArray** in this case). In the preceding **for/in** structure, JavaScript automatically determines the number of elements in the array. As the JavaScript interpreter iterates over **theArray**'s elements, variable **element** is assigned a value that can be used as a subscript for **theArray**. In the case of an **Array**, the value assigned is a subscript in the range from 0 up to, but not including, **theArray.length**. Each value is added to **total2** to produce the sum of the elements in the array.

Testing and Debugging Tip 11.2

When iterating over all the elements of an **Array***, use a* **for/in** *control structure to ensure that you manipulate only the existing elements of the* **Array***.*

In Chapter 10, we indicated that there is a more elegant way to implement the dice-rolling program of Fig. 10.5. The program rolled a single six-sided die 6000 times and used a **switch** structure to total the number of times each value was rolled. An array version of this script is shown in Fig. 11.6. The **switch** structure in lines 22–41 of Fig. 10.5 is replaced by line 19 of this program. This line uses the random **face** value as the subscript for the array **frequency** to determine which element should to increment during each iteration of the loop. Because the random-number calculation on line 18 produces numbers from 1 to 6 (the values for a six-sided die), the **frequency** array must be large enough to allow subscript values of 1 to 6. The smallest number of elements required for an array to have these subscript values is seven elements (subscript values from 0 to 6). In this program, we ignore element 0 of array **frequency**. Also, lines 28–30 of this program replace lines 48–59 in Fig. 10.5. Because we can loop through array **frequency** to help product the output, we do not have to enumerate each XHTML table row, as we did in Fig. 10.5.

```
1  <?xml version = "1.0"?>
2  <!DOCTYPE html PUBLIC "-//W3C//DTD XHTML 1.0 Strict//EN"
3     "http://www.w3.org/TR/xhtml1/DTD/xhtml1-strict.dtd">
4
5  <!-- Fig. 11.6: RollDie.html           -->
6  <!-- Roll a Six-Sided Die 6000 Times -->
7
8  <html xmlns = "http://www.w3.org/1999/xhtml">
9     <head>
10       <title>Roll a Six-Sided Die 6000 Times</title>
11
12       <script type = "text/javascript">
13          <!--
14          var face, frequency = [ , 0, 0, 0, 0, 0, 0 ];
15
16          // summarize results
17          for ( var roll = 1; roll <= 6000; ++roll ) {
18             face = Math.floor( 1 + Math.random() * 6 );
19             ++frequency[ face ];
20          }
21
22          document.writeln( "<table border = \"1\""  +
23             "width = \"100%\">" );
24          document.writeln( "<thead><th width = \"100\"" +
25             " align = \"left\">Face<th align = \"left\">" +
26             "Frequency</th></thead></tbody>" );
```

Fig. 11.6 Dice-rolling program using arrays instead of a **switch** (part 1 of 2).

```

         for ( face = 1; face < frequency.length; ++face )
            document.writeln( "<tr><td>" + face + "</td><td>" +
               frequency[ face ] + "</td></tr>" );

         document.writeln( "</tbody></table>" );
         // -->
      </script>

   </head>
   <body>
      <p>Click Refresh (or Reload) to run the script again</p>
   </body>
</html>
```

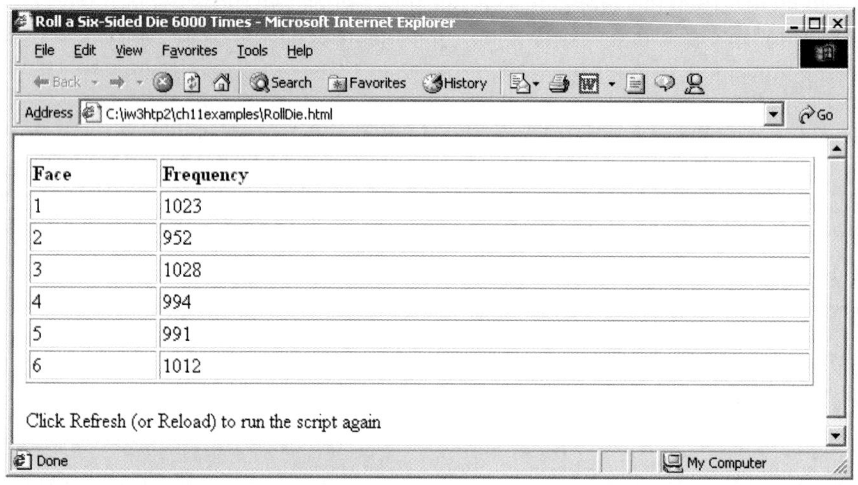

Fig. 11.6 Dice-rolling program using arrays instead of a **switch** (part 2 of 2).

11.5 References and Reference Parameters

Two ways to pass arguments to functions (or methods) in many programming languages are *call-by-value* and *call-by-reference* (also called *pass-by-value* and *pass-by-reference*). When an argument is passed to a function using call-by-value, a *copy* of the argument's value is made and is passed to the called function. In JavaScript, numbers and boolean values are passed to functions by value.

Testing and Debugging Tip 11.3

With call-by-value, changes to the called function's copy do not affect the original variable's value in the calling function. This prevents the accidental side effects that so greatly hinder the development of correct and reliable software systems.

With call-by-reference, the caller gives the called function direct access to the caller's data and to modify those data if the called function so chooses. This procedure is accomplished by passing to the called function the actual *location in memory* (also called the *address*) where the data resides. Call-by-reference can improve performance, because it can eliminate the overhead of copying large amounts of data, but it can weaken security, because the called function can access the caller's data. In JavaScript, all objects and **Array**s are passed to functions by reference.

Software Engineering Observation 11.2

Unlike some other languages, JavaScript does not allow the programmer to choose whether to pass each argument by value or by reference. Numbers and boolean values are passed by value. Objects are not passed to functions; rather, references to objects are passed to functions. When a function receives a reference to an object, the function can manipulate the object directly.

Software Engineering Observation 11.3

When returning information from a function via a **return** *statement, numbers and boolean values are always returned by value (i.e., a copy is returned), and objects are always returned by reference (i.e., a reference to the object is returned).*

To pass a reference to an object into a function, simply specify in the function call the reference name. Normally, the reference name is the identifier that the program uses to manipulate the object. Mentioning the reference by its parameter name in the body of the called function actually refers to the original object in memory, and the original object can be accessed directly by the called function.

Arrays are objects in JavaScript, so **Array**s are passed to functions call-by-reference—a called function can access the elements of the caller's original **Array**s. The name of an array actually is a reference to an object that contains the array elements and the **length** variable, which indicates the number of elements in the array. In the next section, we demonstrate call-by-value and call-by-reference, using arrays.

Performance Tip 11.1

Passing arrays by reference makes sense for performance reasons. If arrays were passed by value, a copy of each element would be passed. For large, frequently passed arrays, this procedure would waste time and would consume considerable storage for the array copies.

11.6 Passing Arrays to Functions

To pass an array argument to a function, specify the name of the array (a reference to the array) without brackets. For example, if array **hourlyTemperatures** has been declared as

```
var hourlyTemperatures = new Array( 24 );
```

then the function call

```
modifyArray( hourlyTemperatures );
```

passes array **hourlyTemperatures** to function **modifyArray**. In JavaScript, every array object "knows" its own size (via the **length** attribute). Thus, when we pass an array object into a function, we do not pass the size of the array separately as an argument. In fact, Fig. 11.3 illustrated this concept when we passed **Array**s **n1** and **n2** to function **outputArray** to display each **Array**'s contents.

Although entire arrays are passed by using call-by-reference, *individual numeric and boolean array elements are passed by call-by-value exactly as simple numeric and boolean variables are passed* (the objects referred to by individual elements of an **Array** of objects are still passed by call-by-reference). Such simple single pieces of data are called *scalars*, or *scalar quantities*. To pass an array element to a function, use the subscripted name of the element as an argument in the function call.

For a function to receive an **Array** through a function call, the function's parameter list must specify a parameter that will refer to the **Array** in the body of the function. Unlike other programming languages, JavaScript does not provide a special syntax for this purpose. JavaScript simply requires that the identifier for the **Array** be specified in the parameter list. For example, the function header for function **modifyArray** might be written as

```
function modifyArray( b )
```

indicating that **modifyArray** expects to receive a parameter named **b** (the argument supplied in the calling function must be an **Array**). Because arrays are passed by reference, when the called function uses the array name **b**, it refers to the actual array in the caller (array **hourlyTemperatures** in the preceding call).

Software Engineering Observation 11.4

JavaScript does not check the number of arguments or types of arguments that are passed to a function. It is possible to pass any number of values to a function. JavaScript will attempt to perform conversions when the values are used.

The script of Fig. 11.7 demonstrates the difference between passing an entire array and passing an array element. [*Note*: Function **start** (defined at lines 15–37) is called in response to the **<body>**'s **onload** event.]

The statement in lines 21–22 invokes function **outputArray** to display the contents of array **a** before it is modified. Function **outputArray** (defined at line 40) receives a string to output and the array to output. The statement in lines 42–43 uses **Array** method **join** to create a string containing all the elements in **theArray**. Method **join** takes as its argument a string containing the *separator* that should be used to separate the elements of the array in the string that is returned. If the argument is not specified, the empty string is used as the separator.

Line 24 invokes function **modifyArray** and passes it array **a**. The **modifyArray** function multiplies each element by 2. To illustrate that array **a**'s elements were modified, the statement in lines 26–27 invokes function **outputArray** again to display the contents of array **a** after it is modified. As the screen capture shows, the elements of **a** are indeed modified by **modifyArray**.

```
1  <?xml version = "1.0"?>
2  <!DOCTYPE html PUBLIC "-//W3C//DTD XHTML 1.0 Strict//EN"
3     "http://www.w3.org/TR/xhtml1/DTD/xhtml1-strict.dtd">
4
5  <!-- Fig. 11.7: PassArray.html -->
6  <!-- Passing Arrays            -->
7
8  <html xmlns = "http://www.w3.org/1999/xhtml">
9     <head>
10       <title>Passing Arrays and Individual Array
11             Elements to Functions</title>
```

Fig. 11.7 Passing arrays and individual array elements to functions (part 1 of 3).

```

      <script type = "text/javascript">
         <!--
         function start()
         {
            var a = [ 1, 2, 3, 4, 5 ];

            document.writeln( "<h2>Effects of passing entire " +
               "array call-by-reference</h2>" );
            outputArray(
               "The values of the original array are: ", a );

            modifyArray( a );  // array a passed call-by-reference

            outputArray(
               "The values of the modified array are: ", a );

            document.writeln( "<h2>Effects of passing array " +
               "element call-by-value</h2>" +
               "a[3] before modifyElement: " + a[ 3 ] );

            modifyElement( a[ 3 ] );

            document.writeln(
               "<br />a[3] after modifyElement: " + a[ 3 ] );
         }

         // outputs "header" followed by the contents of "theArray"
         function outputArray( header, theArray )
         {
            document.writeln(
               header + theArray.join( " " ) + "<br />" );
         }

         // function that modifies the elements of an array
         function modifyArray( theArray )
         {
            for ( var j in theArray )
               theArray[ j ] *= 2;
        }

         // function that attempts to modify the value passed
         function modifyElement( e )
         {
            e *= 2;
           document.writeln( "<br />value in modifyElement: " + e );
         }
         // -->
      </script>

   </head><body onload = "start()"></body>
</html>
```

Fig. 11.7 Passing arrays and individual array elements to functions (part 2 of 3).

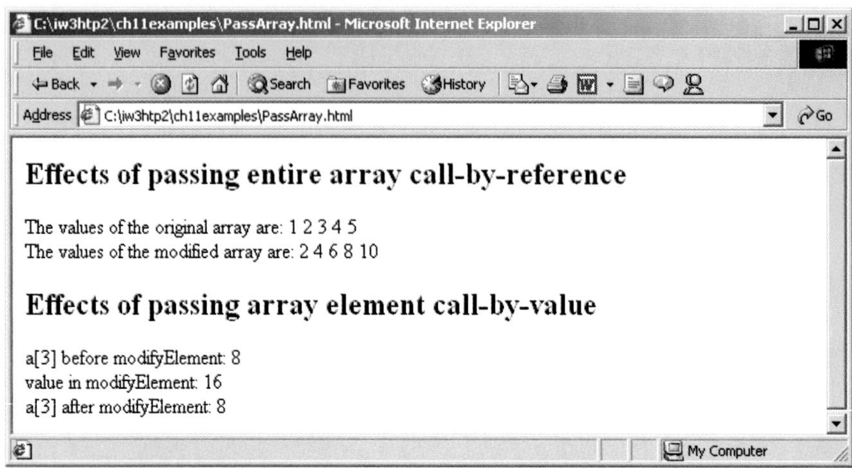

Fig. 11.7 Passing arrays and individual array elements to functions (part 3 of 3).

To show the value of **`a[ 3 ]`** before the call to **`modifyElement`**, lines 29–31 output the value of **`a[ 3 ]`** (as well as other information). Line 33 invokes **`modifyElement`** and passes **`a[ 3 ]`**. Remember that **`a[ 3 ]`** actually is one integer value in the array **`a`**. Also, remember that numeric values and boolean values always are passed to functions call-by-value. Therefore, a copy of **`a[ 3 ]`** is passed. Function **`modifyElement`** multiplies its argument by 2 and stores the result in its parameter **`e`**. The parameter of function **`modifyElement`** is a local variable in that function, so when the function terminates, the local variable is destroyed. Thus, when control is returned to **`start`**, the unmodified value of **`a[ 3 ]`** is displayed by the statement in lines 35–36.

11.7 Sorting Arrays

Sorting data (placing the data into some particular order, such as ascending or descending) is one of the most important computing functions. A bank sorts all checks by account number, so that it can prepare individual bank statements at the end of each month. Telephone companies sort their lists of accounts by last name and, within that, by first name, to make it easy to find phone numbers. Virtually every organization must sort some data—in many cases, massive amounts of data. Sorting data is an intriguing problem that has attracted some of the most intense research efforts in the field of computer science.

The **`Array`** object in JavaScript has a built-in method ***`sort`*** for sorting arrays. Figure 11.8 demonstrates the **`Array`** object's **`sort`** method.

```
<?xml version = "1.0"?>
<!DOCTYPE html PUBLIC "-//W3C//DTD XHTML 1.0 Strict//EN"
   "http://www.w3.org/TR/xhtml1/DTD/xhtml1-strict.dtd">

<!-- Fig. 11.8: sort.html -->
<!-- Sorting an Array     -->
```

Fig. 11.8 Sorting an array with **`sort`** (part 1 of 2).

```
<html xmlns = "http://www.w3.org/1999/xhtml">
   <head>
      <title>Sorting an Array with Array Method sort</title>

      <script type = "text/javascript">
         <!--
         function start()
         {
            var a = [ 10, 1, 9, 2, 8, 3, 7, 4, 6, 5 ];

            document.writeln( "<h1>Sorting an Array</h1>" );
            outputArray( "Data items in original order: ", a );
            a.sort( compareIntegers );  // sort the array
            outputArray( "Data items in ascending order: ", a );
         }

         // outputs "header" followed by the contents of "theArray"
         function outputArray( header, theArray )
         {
            document.writeln( "<p>" + header +
               theArray.join( " " ) + "</p>" );
         }

         // comparison function for use with sort
         function compareIntegers( value1, value2 )
         {
            return parseInt( value1 ) - parseInt( value2 );
         }
         // -->
      </script>

   </head><body onload = "start()"></body>
</html>
```

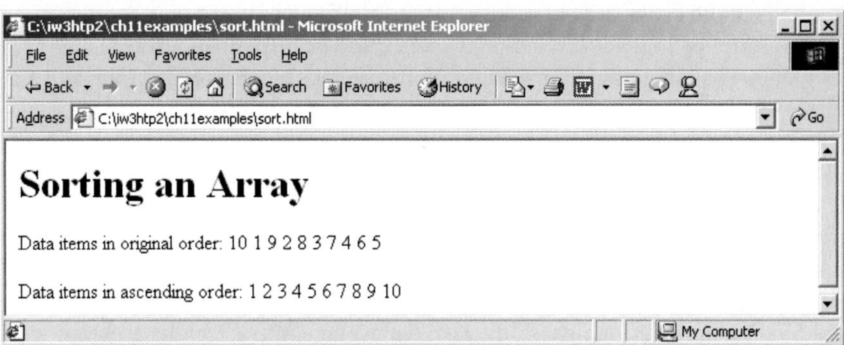

Fig. 11.8 Sorting an array with **sort** (part 2 of 2).

By default, **Array** method **sort** (with no arguments) uses string comparisons to determine the sorting order of the **Array** elements. The strings are compared by the ASCII values of their characters. [*Note*: String comparison is discussed in more detail in

Chapter 12, JavaScript: Objects.] In this example, we would like once again to sort an array of integers.

Method **sort** takes as its optional argument the name of a function (called the *comparator function*) that compares its two arguments and returns one of the following:

- a negative value if the first argument is less than the second argument
- zero if the arguments are equal, or
- a positive value if the first argument is greater than the second argument

This example uses function **compareIntegers** (defined at lines 32–35) as the comparator function for method **sort**. It calculates the difference between the integer values of its two arguments (function **parseInt** ensures that the arguments are handled properly as integers). If the first argument is less than the second argument, the difference will be a negative value. If the arguments are equal, the difference will be zero. If the first argument is greater than the second argument, the difference will be a positive value.

Line 20 invokes **Array** object **a**'s **sort** method and passes function **compareIntegers** as an argument. In JavaScript, functions are considered to be data and can be assigned to variables and passed to functions like any other data. Here, method **sort** receives function **compareIntegers** as an argument, then uses the function to compare elements of the **Array a** to determine their sorting order.

Software Engineering Observation 11.5

Functions in JavaScript are considered to be data. Therefore, functions can be assigned to variables, stored in **Array***s and passed to functions as other data types can.*

11.8 Searching Arrays: Linear Search and Binary Search

Often, a programmer will be working with large amounts of data stored in arrays. It may be necessary to determine whether an array contains a value that matches a certain *key value.* The process of locating a particular element value in an array is called *searching.* In this section we discuss two searching techniques—the simple *linear search* technique (Fig. 11.9) and the more efficient *binary search* (Fig. 11.10) technique.

In the script of Fig. 11.9, function **linearSearch** (defined at lines 38–45) uses a **for** structure containing an **if** structure to compare each element of an array with a *search key* (lines 40–42). If the search key is found, the function returns the subscript value (line 42) of the element to indicate the exact position of the search key in the array. [*Note*: The loop in the **linearSearch** function terminates, and the function returns control to the caller as soon as the **return** statement in its body executes.] If the search key is not found, the function returns a value of **-1**. The function returns the value **-1** because it is not a valid subscript number.

If the array being searched is not in any particular order, it is just as likely that the value will be found in the first element as the last. On average, therefore, the program will have to compare the search key with half the elements of the array.

The program contains a 100-element array (defined at line 14) filled with the even integers from 0 to 198. The user types the search key in a text field (defined in the XHTML form in lines 52–60) and clicks the **Search** button to start the search. [*Note*: The array is passed to **linearSearch** even though the array is a global variable. This step occurs because an array is normally passed to a function for searching.]

```
<?xml version = "1.0"?>
<!DOCTYPE html PUBLIC "-//W3C//DTD XHTML 1.0 Strict//EN"
   "http://www.w3.org/TR/xhtml1/DTD/xhtml1-strict.dtd">

<!-- Fig. 11.9: LinearSearch.html -->
<!-- Linear Search of an Array    -->

<html xmlns = "http://www.w3.org/1999/xhtml">
   <head>
      <title>Linear Search of an Array</title>

      <script type = "text/javascript">
         <!--
         var a = new Array( 100 );  // create an Array

         // fill Array with even integer values from 0 to 198
         for ( var i = 0; i < a.length; ++i )
            a[ i ] = 2 * i;

         // function called when "Search" button is pressed
         function buttonPressed()
         {
            var searchKey = searchForm.inputVal.value;

            // Array a is passed to linearSearch even though it
            // is a global variable. Normally an array will
            // be passed to a method for searching.
           var element = linearSearch( a, parseInt( searchKey ) );

            if ( element != -1 )
               searchForm.result.value =
                  "Found value in element " + element;
            else
               searchForm.result.value = "Value not found";
         }

         // Search "theArray" for the specified "key" value
         function linearSearch( theArray, key )
         {
            for ( var n = 0; n < theArray.length; ++n )
               if ( theArray[ n ] == key )
                  return n;

            return -1;
         }
         // -->
      </script>

   </head>

   <body>
      <form name = "searchForm" action  = "">
         <p>Enter integer search key<br />
```

Fig. 11.9 Linear search of an array (part 1 of 2).

```
            <input name = "inputVal" type = "text" />
            <input name = "search" type = "button" value = "Search"
                   onclick = "buttonPressed()" /><br /></p>

            <p>Result<br />
            <input name = "result" type = "text" size = "30" /></p>
         </form>
      </body>
   </html>
```

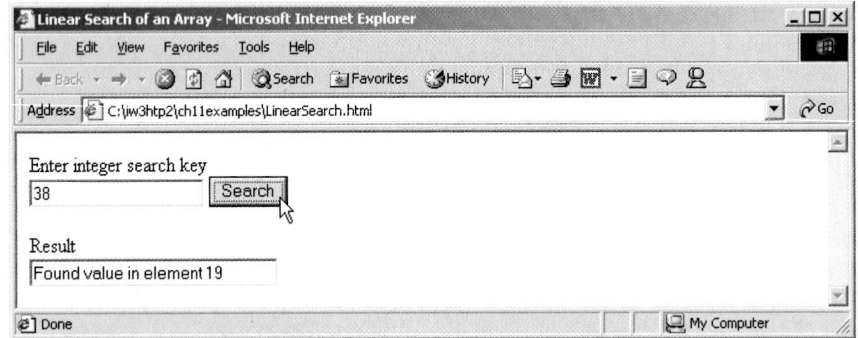

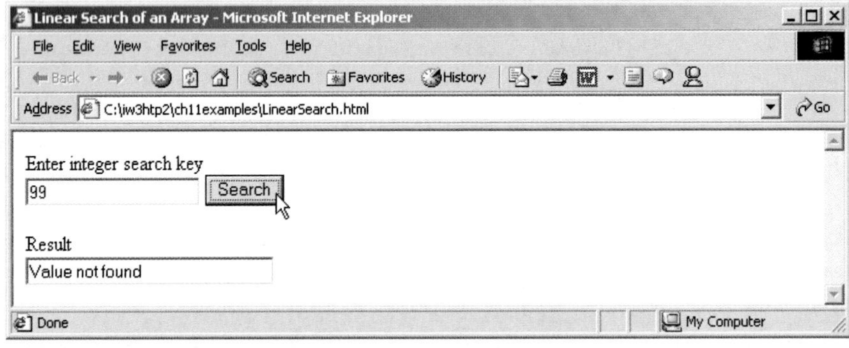

Fig. 11.9 Linear search of an array (part 2 of 2).

After each comparison, the binary search algorithm eliminates half of the elements in the array being searched. The algorithm locates the middle array element and compares it to the search key. If they are equal, the search key has been found and the subscript of that element is returned. Otherwise, the problem is reduced to searching half of the array. If the search key is less than the middle array element, the first half of the array is searched; otherwise, the second half of the array is searched. If the search key is not the middle element in the specified subarray (piece of the original array), the algorithm is repeated on one quarter of the original array. The search continues until the search key is equal to the middle element of a subarray or until the subarray consists of one element that is not equal to the search key (i.e., the search key is not found).

In a worst-case scenario, searching an array of 1024 elements will take only 10 comparisons using a binary search. Repeatedly dividing 1024 by 2 (because after each comparison we are able to eliminate half of the array) yields the values 512, 256, 128, 64, 32, 16, 8, 4, 2 and 1. The number 1024 (2^{10}) is divided by 2 only ten times to get the value 1. Dividing by 2 is equivalent to one comparison in the binary search algorithm. An array of 1,048,576 (2^{20}) elements takes a maximum of 20 comparisons to find the key. An array of one billion elements takes a maximum of 30 comparisons to find the key. When searching a sorted array, this is a tremendous increase in performance over the linear search that required comparing the search key to an average of half the elements in the array. For a one-billion-element array, this is a difference between an average of 500 million comparisons and a maximum of 30 comparisons! The maximum number of comparisons needed for the binary search of any sorted array is the exponent of the first power of 2 greater than the number of elements in the array.

Figure 11.10 presents the iterative version of function **binarySearch** (lines 42–66). Function **binarySearch** is called from function **buttonPressed**—the event handler for the **Search** button in the XHTML form. Function **binarySearch** receives two arguments—an array called **theArray** (the array to search) and **key** (the search key). The array is passed to **binarySearch**, even though the array is global variable. Once again, this is done because an array is normally passed to a function for searching. If **key** matches the **middle** element of a subarray, **middle** (the subscript of the current element) is returned, to indicate that the value was found and the search is complete. If **key** does not match the **middle** element of a subarray, the **low** subscript or the **high** subscript (both declared in the function) is adjusted, so that a smaller subarray can be searched. If **key** is less than the middle element, the **high** subscript is set to **middle - 1** and the search is continued on the elements from **low** to **middle - 1**. If **key** is greater than the middle element, the **low** subscript is set to **middle + 1** and the search is continued on the elements from **middle + 1** to **high**. These comparisons are performed by the nested **if/else** structure at lines 57–62.

```
1   <?xml version = "1.0"?>
2   <!DOCTYPE html PUBLIC "-//W3C//DTD XHTML 1.0 Transitional//EN"
3      "http://www.w3.org/TR/xhtml1/DTD/xhtml1-transitional.dtd">
4
5   <!-- Fig. 11.10 : BinarySearch.html -->
6   <!-- binary search                  -->
7
8   <html xmlns = "http://www.w3.org/1999/xhtml">
9      <head>
10        <title>Binary Search</title>
11
12        <script type = "text/javascript">
13           <!--
14           var a = new Array( 15 );
15
```

Fig. 11.10 Using a binary search (part 1 of 4).

```
         for ( var i = 0; i < a.length; ++i )
            a[ i ] = 2 * i;

         // function called when "Search" button is pressed
         function buttonPressed()
         {
            var searchKey = searchForm.inputVal.value;

            searchForm.result.value =
               "Portions of array searched\n";

            // Array a is passed to binarySearch even though it
            // is a global variable. This is done because
            // normally an array is passed to a method
            // for searching.
            var element =
               binarySearch( a, parseInt( searchKey ) );

            if ( element != -1 )
               searchForm.result.value +=
                  "\nFound value in element " + element;
            else
               searchForm.result.value += "\nValue not found";
         }

         // Binary search
         function binarySearch( theArray, key )
         {
            var low = 0;                     // low subscript
            var high = theArray.length - 1; // high subscript
            var middle;                      // middle subscript

            while ( low <= high ) {
               middle = ( low + high ) / 2;

               // The following line is used to display the
               // part of theArray currently being manipulated
               // during each iteration of the binary
               // search loop.
               buildOutput( theArray, low, middle, high );

               if ( key == theArray[ middle ] )  // match
                  return middle;
               else if ( key < theArray[ middle ] )
                  high = middle - 1; // search low end of array
               else
                  low = middle + 1; // search high end of array
            }

            return -1;   // searchKey not found
         }

```

Fig. 11.10 Using a binary search (part 2 of 4).

```
         // Build one row of output showing the current
         // part of the array being processed.
         function buildOutput( theArray, low, mid, high )
         {
            for ( var i = 0; i < theArray.length; i++ ) {
               if ( i < low || i > high )
                  searchForm.result.value += "    ";
               // mark middle element in output
               else if ( i == mid )
                  searchForm.result.value += a[ i ] +
                     ( theArray[ i ] < 10 ? "*  " : "* " );
               else
                  searchForm.result.value += a[ i ] +
                     ( theArray[ i ] < 10 ? "   " : "  " );
            }

            searchForm.result.value += "\n";
         }
         // -->
      </script>
   </head>

   <body>
      <form name = "searchForm" action = "">
         <p>Enter integer search key<br />
         <input name = "inputVal" type = "text" />
         <input name = "search" type = "button" value =
            "Search" onclick = "buttonPressed()" /><br /></p>
         <p>Result<br />
         <textarea name = "result" rows = "7" cols = "60">
         </textarea></p>
      </form>
   </body>
</html>
```

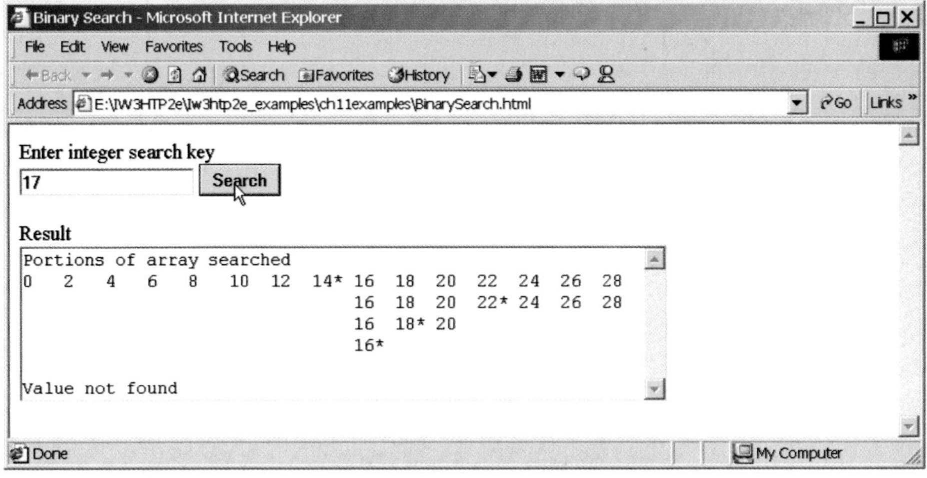

Fig. 11.10 Using a binary search (part 3 of 4).

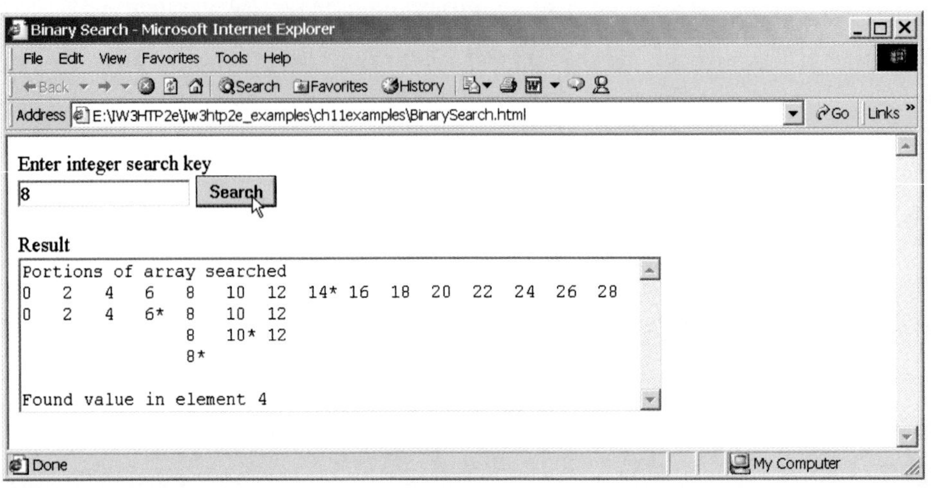

Fig. 11.10 Using a binary search (part 4 of 4).

11.9 Multiple-Subscripted Arrays

Multiple-subscripted arrays with two subscripts often are used to represent *tables* of values consisting of information arranged in *rows* and *columns*. To identify a particular table element, we must specify the two subscripts; by convention, the first identifies the element's row, and the second identifies the element's column. Arrays that require two subscripts to identify a particular element are called *double-subscripted arrays* (also called *two-dimensional arrays*). Note that multiple-subscripted arrays can have more than two subscripts. JavaScript does not support multiple-subscripted arrays directly, but does allow the programmer to specify single-subscripted arrays whose elements are also single-subscripted arrays, thus achieving the same effect. Figure 11.11 illustrates a double-subscripted array **a**, that contains three rows and four columns (i.e., a three-by-four array). In general, an array with *m* rows and *n* columns is called an *m-by-n array*.

Every element in array **a** is identified in Fig. 11.11 by an element name of the form **a[i][j]**; **a** is the name of the array, and **i** and **j** are the subscripts that uniquely identify the row and column, respectively, of each element in **a**. Notice that the names of the elements in the first row all have a first subscript of **0**; the names of the elements in the fourth column all have a second subscript of **3**.

Multiple-subscripted arrays can be initialized in declarations like a single-subscripted array. Array **b** with two rows and two columns could be declared and initialized with the statement

```
var b = [ [ 1, 2 ], [ 3, 4 ] ];
```

The values are grouped by row in square brackets. So, **1** and **2** initialize **b[0][0]** and **b[0][1]**, and **3** and **4** initialize **b[1][0]** and **b[1][1]**. The interpreter determines the number of rows by counting the number of sub-initializer lists (represented by sets of square brackets) in the main initializer list. The interpreter determines the number of columns in each row by counting the number of initializer values in the sub-initializer list for that row.

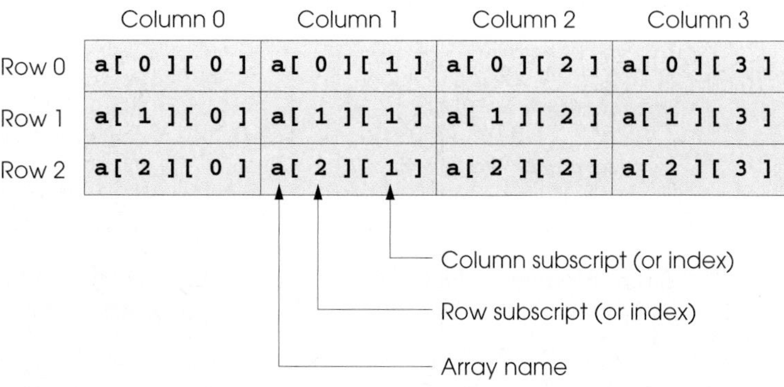

Fig. 11.11 Double-subscripted array with three rows and four columns.

Multiple-subscripted arrays are maintained as arrays of arrays. The declaration

```
var b = [ [ 1, 2 ], [ 3, 4, 5 ] ];
```

creates array **b** with row **0** containing two elements (**1** and **2**) and row **1** containing three elements (**3**, **4** and **5**).

A multiple-subscripted array in which each row has a different number of columns can be allocated dynamically as follows:

```
var b;
b = new Array( 2 );       // allocate rows
b[ 0 ] = new Array( 5 ); // allocate columns for row 0
b[ 1 ] = new Array( 3 ); // allocate columns for row 1
```

The preceding code creates a two-dimensional array with two rows. Row **0** has five columns, and row **1** has three columns.

Figure 11.12 initializes double-subscripted arrays in declarations and uses nested **for/in** loops to *traverse the arrays* (i.e., manipulate every element of the array).

```
<?xml version = "1.0"?>
<!DOCTYPE html PUBLIC "-//W3C//DTD XHTML 1.0 Strict//EN"
   "http://www.w3.org/TR/xhtml1/DTD/xhtml1-strict.dtd">

<!-- Fig. 11.12: InitArray3.html            -->
<!-- Initializing Multidimensional Arrays -->

<html xmlns = "http://www.w3.org/1999/xhtml">
   <head>
      <title>Initializing Multidimensional Arrays</title>

```

Fig. 11.12 Initializing multidimensional arrays (part 1 of 2).

```
      <script type = "text/javascript">
         <!--
         function start()
         {
            var array1 = [ [ 1, 2, 3 ],     // first row
                           [ 4, 5, 6 ] ];   // second row
            var array2 = [ [ 1, 2 ],        // first row
                           [ 3 ],           // second row
                           [ 4, 5, 6 ] ];   // third row

            outputArray( "Values in array1 by row", array1 );
            outputArray( "Values in array2 by row", array2 );
         }

         function outputArray( header, theArray )
         {
            document.writeln( "<h2>" + header + "</h2><tt>" );

            for ( var i in theArray ) {

               for ( var j in theArray[ i ] )
                  document.write( theArray[ i ][ j ] + " " );

               document.writeln( "<br />" );
            }

            document.writeln( "</tt>" );
         }
         // -->
      </script>

   </head><body onload = "start()"></body>
</html>
```

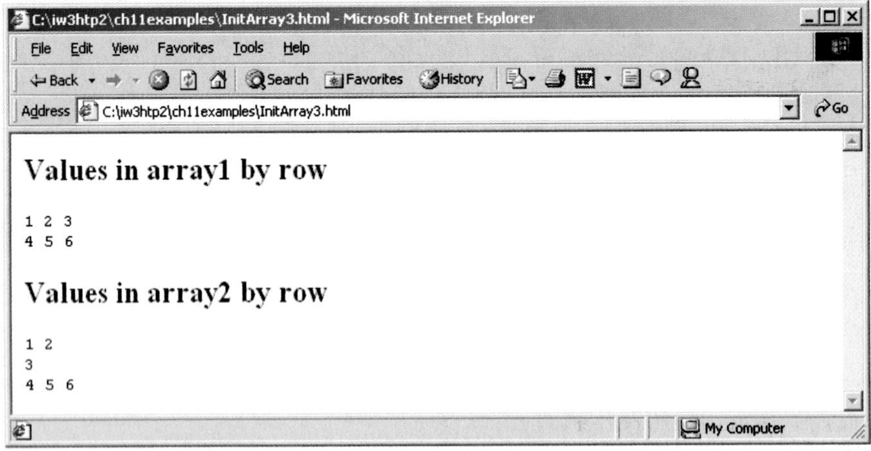

Fig. 11.12 Initializing multidimensional arrays (part 2 of 2).

The program declares two arrays in function **start** (which is called in response to the **<body>**'s **onload** event). The declaration of **array1** (lines 16–17) provides six initializers in two sublists. The first sublist initializes the first row of the array to the values 1, 2 and 3; the second sublist initializes the second row of the array to the values 4, 5 and 6. The declaration of **array2** (lines 18–20) provides six initializers in three sublists. The sublist for the first row explicitly initializes the first row to have two elements, with values 1 and 2, respectively. The sublist for the second row initializes the second row to have one element, with value 3. The sublist for the third row initializes the third row to the values 4, 5 and 6.

Function **start** calls function **outputArray** from lines 22–23 to display each array's elements in the Web page. Function **outputArray** (lines 26–39) receives two arguments—a string **header** to output before the array and the array to output (called **theArray**). Note the use of a nested **for/in** structure to output the rows of each double-subscripted array. The outer **for/in** structure iterates over the rows of the array. The inner **for/in** structure iterates over the columns of the current row being processed. The nested **for/in** structure in this example could have been written with **for** structures as follows:

```
for ( var i = 0; i < theArray.length; ++i ) {

   for ( var j = 0; j < theArray[ i ].length; ++j )
      document.write( theArray[ i ][ j ] + " " );

   document.writeln( "<br />" );
}
```

In the outer **for** structure, the expression **theArray.length** determines the number of rows in the array. In the inner **for** structure, the expression **theArray[i].length** determines the number of columns in each row of the array. This condition enables the loop to determine, for each row, the exact number of columns.

Many common array manipulations use **for** or **for/in** repetition structures. For example, the following **for** structure sets all the elements in the third row of array **a** in Fig. 11.11 to zero:

```
for ( var col = 0; col < a[ 2 ].length; ++col )
   a[ 2 ][ col ] = 0;
```

We specified the *third* row; therefore, we know that the first subscript is always **2** (**0** is the first row and **1** is the second row). The **for** loop varies only the second subscript (i.e., the column subscript). The preceding **for** structure is equivalent to the assignment statements

```
a[ 2 ][ 0 ] = 0;
a[ 2 ][ 1 ] = 0;
a[ 2 ][ 2 ] = 0;
a[ 2 ][ 3 ] = 0;
```

The following **for/in** structure is also equivalent to the preceding **for** structure:

```
for ( var col in a[ 2 ] )
   a[ 2 ][ col ] = 0;
```

The following nested **for** structure determines the total of all the elements in array **a**:

```
var total = 0;

for ( var row = 0; row < a.length; ++row )

   for ( var col = 0; col < a[ row ].length; ++col )
      total += a[ row ][ col ];
```

The **for** structure totals the elements of the array, one row at a time. The outer **for** structure begins by setting the **row** subscript to **0**, so the elements of the first row may be totaled by the inner **for** structure. The outer **for** structure then increments **row** to **1**, so the elements of the second row can be totaled. Then, the outer **for** structure increments **row** to **2**, so the elements of the third row can be totaled. The result can be displayed when the nested **for** structure terminates. The preceding **for** structure is equivalent to the following **for/in** structure:

```
var total = 0;

for ( var row in a )

   for ( var col in a[ row ] )
      total += a[ row ][ col ];
```

11.10 JavaScript Internet and World Wide Web Resources

alwaysfreewebtools.com/docs/Jscript/option5.htm#arrays
This site discusses JavaScript arrays.

hotwired.lycos.com/webmonkey/98/04/index1a_page8.html?tw=programming
Thau's JavaScript Tutorial introduces JavaScript arrays.

SUMMARY

- Arrays are data structures consisting of related data items (sometimes called collections).
- Arrays are "dynamic" entities, in that they can change size after they are created.
- An array is a group of memory locations that all have the same name and are normally of the same type (although this attribute is not required).
- To refer to a particular location or element in the array, specify the name of the array and the position number of the particular element in the array.
- The first element in every array is the zeroth element.
- The length of an array is determined by *arrayName*.**length**.
- An array in JavaScript is an **Array** object. Operator **new** is used to dynamically allocate the number of elements required by an array. Operator **new** creates an object as the program executes, by obtaining enough memory to store an object of the type specified to the right of **new**.
- The process of creating new objects is also known as creating an instance, or instantiating an object, and operator **new** is known as the dynamic memory allocation operator.
- An array can be initialized with a comma-separated initializer list enclosed in square brackets (**[** and **]**). The array size is determined by the number of values in the initializer list. When using an initializer list in an array declaration, the **new** operator is not required to create the **Array** object—this operator is provided by the interpreter.
- It is possible to reserve a space in an **Array** for a value to be specified later, by using a comma as a place holder in the initializer list.

- JavaScript's **for/in** control structure enables a script to perform a task **for** each element **in** an array. This process is also known as *iterating over the elements of an array*.
- The basic syntax of a **for/in** structure is

```
for ( var element in arrayName )
   statement
```

  where **element** is the name of the variable to which the **for/in** structure assigns a subscript number and **arrayName** is the array over which to iterate.
- When a value is assigned to an element of an **Array** that is outside the current bounds of the **Array**, JavaScript allocates more memory so the **Array** contains the appropriate number of elements. The new elements of the array are not initialized.
- Two ways to pass arguments to functions (or methods) in many programming languages are call-by-value and call-by-reference (also called pass-by-value and pass-by-reference).
- When an argument is passed to a function by using call-by-value, a copy of the argument's value is made and passed to the called function. Numbers and boolean values are passed by value.
- With call-by-reference, the caller gives the called function the ability to access directly the caller's data and to modify those data. This procedure is accomplished by passing to the called function the location or address in memory where the data reside. All objects and **Array**s are passed by reference.
- To pass a reference to an object into a function, specify in the function call the name of the reference. The name of the reference is the identifier that is used to manipulate the object in the program.
- The name of an array is actually a reference to an object that contains the elements of the array and the **length** variable, which indicates the number of elements in the array.
- Placing data into some particular order, such as ascending or descending, is called sorting the data.
- The **Array** object in JavaScript has a built-in method, **sort**, for sorting arrays. By default, **Array** method **sort** uses string comparisons to determine the sorting order of the elements of the **Array**.
- Method **sort** takes as its optional argument the comparator function, which compares its two arguments and returns a negative value if the first argument is less than the second argument, zero if the arguments are equal or a positive value if the first argument is greater than the second argument.
- The process of locating a particular element value (the key value) in an array is called searching.
- A linear search compares each element of an array with a search key. If the search key is found, the linear search normally returns the subscript for the element, to indicate the exact position of the search key in the array. If the search key is not found, the linear search normally returns **-1**.
- If the array being searched with a linear search is not in any particular order, it is just as likely that the value will be found in the first element as the last. On average, the program has to compare the search key with half the elements of the array.
- If an array is sorted, the binary search technique can be used to locate a search key. The binary search algorithm eliminates half of the elements in the array being searched after each comparison. The algorithm locates the middle array element and compares it to the search key. If they are equal, the search key has been found and the subscript of that element is returned. Otherwise, the problem is reduced to searching half of the array. If the search key is less than the middle array element, the first half of the array is searched; otherwise, the second half of the array is searched.
- The maximum number of comparisons needed for the binary search of any sorted array is the exponent of the first power of 2 greater than the number of elements in the array.

- Multiple-subscripted arrays with two subscripts are often used to represent tables of values consisting of information arranged in rows and columns. Two subscripts identify a particular table element; the first identifies the element's row, and the second identifies the element's column.
- Arrays requiring two subscripts to identify a particular element are called double-subscripted arrays (or two-dimensional arrays). Multiple-subscripted arrays can have more than two subscripts.
- JavaScript does not support multiple-subscripted arrays directly, but does allow single-subscripted arrays whose elements are also single-subscripted arrays, thus achieving the same effect.
- In general, an array with *m* rows and *n* columns is called an *m*-by-*n* array.
- Multiple-subscripted arrays can be initialized with initializer lists. The compiler determines the number of rows by counting the number of sub-initializer lists (represented by sets of square brackets) in the main initializer list. The compiler determines the number of columns in each row by counting the number of initializer values in the sub-initializer list for that row.

TERMINOLOGY

a[i]
a[i][j]
array
array initializer list
Array object
binary search
bounds of an array
call by reference
call by value
column subscript
comma-separated initializer list
comparator function
creating an instance
data structure
declare an array
double-subscripted array
dynamic memory allocation operator (**new**)
element of an array
for/in repetition structure
index of an element
initialize an array
initializer
initializer list
instantiating an object
iterating over an array's elements
join method
length of an **Array**
linear search of an array
location in an array
lvalue
m-by-*n* array
multiple-subscripted array
name of an array
off-by-one error
pass by reference
pass by value
passing arrays to functions
place holder in an initializer list (**,**)
position number of an element
reserve a space in an **Array**
row subscript
search key
searching an array
single-subscripted array
sort method of the **Array** object
sorting an array
square brackets **[]**
subscript
table of values
tabular format
value of an element
zeroth element

SELF-REVIEW EXERCISES

11.1 Fill in the blanks in each of the following statements:

a) Lists and tables of values can be stored in __________.
b) The elements of an array are related by the fact that they have the same __________ and normally the same __________.
c) The number used to refer to a particular element of an array is called its __________.
d) The process of placing the elements of an array in order is called __________ the array.

e) Determining whether an array contains a certain key value is called ________ the array.
f) An array that uses two subscripts is referred to as a ________ array.

11.2 State whether each of the following is *true* or *false*. If *false*, explain why.
a) An array can store many different types of values.
b) An array subscript should normally be a floating-point value.
c) An individual array element that is passed to a function and modified in that function will contain the modified value when the called function completes execution.

11.3 Write JavaScript statements (regarding array **fractions**) to accomplish each of the following tasks:
a) Declare an array with 10 elements, and initialize the elements of the array to **0**.
b) Name the fourth element of the array.
c) Refer to array element 4.
d) Assign the value **1.667** to array element 9.
e) Assign the value **3.333** to the seventh element of the array.
f) Sum all the elements of the array, using a **for/in** repetition structure. Define variable **x** as a control variable for the loop.

11.4 Write JavaScript statements (regarding array **table**) to accomplish each of the following tasks:
a) Declare and create the array with 3 rows and 3 columns.
b) Display the number of elements.
c) Use a **for/in** repetition structure to initialize each element of the array to the sum of its subscripts. Assume that the variables **x** and **y** are declared as control variables.

11.5 Find the error(s) in each of the following program segments, and correct the errors.
a) Assume that `var b = new Array( 10 );`
```
for ( var i = 0; i <= b.length; ++i )
   b[ i ] = 1;
```
b) Assume that `var a = [ [ 1, 2 ], [ 3, 4 ] ];`
```
   a[ 1, 1 ] = 5;
```

ANSWERS TO SELF-REVIEW EXERCISES

11.1 a) Arrays. b) Name, type. c) Subscript. d) Sorting. e) Searching. f) Double-subscripted.

11.2 a) True. b). False. An array subscript must be an integer or an integer expression. c) False. Individual primitive-data-type elements are passed call-by-value. If a reference to an array is passed, then modifications to the elements of the array are reflected in the original element of the array. Also, an individual element of an object type passed to a function is passed with call-by-reference, and changes to the object will be reflected in the original array element.

11.3 a) `var fractions = [ 0, 0, 0, 0, 0, 0, 0, 0, 0, 0 ];`
b) `fractions[ 3 ]`
c) `fractions[ 4 ]`
d) `fractions[ 9 ] = 1.667;`
e) `fractions[ 6 ] = 3.333;`
f)
```
var total = 0;
for ( var x in fractions )
   total += fractions[ x ];
```

11.4 a)
```
var table = new Array( new Array( 3 ), new Array( 3 ),
   new Array( 3 ) );
```

b) `document.write( "total: " + ( table.length * table[ i ].length * table[ i ][ j ].length ) );`.

c)
```
for ( var x in table )
   for ( var y in table[ x ] )
      table[ x ][ y ] = x + y;
```

11.5 a) Error: Referencing an array element outside the bounds of the array (**b[10]**). [*Note*: This error is actually a logic error, not a syntax error.] Correction: Change the **<=** operator to **<**. b) Error: The array subscripting is done incorrectly. Correction: Change the statement to **a[1][1] = 5;**.

EXERCISES

11.6 Fill in the blanks in each of the following statements:

a) JavaScript stores lists of values in ________.

b) The names of the four elements of array an **p** are ________, ________, ________ and ________.

c) The process of placing the elements of an array into either ascending or descending order is called ________.

d) In a double-subscripted array, the first subscript identifies the ________ of an element, and the second subscript identifies the ________ of an element.

e) An *m*-by-*n* array contains ________ rows, ________ columns and ________ elements.

f) The name of the element in row 3 and column 5 of array **d** is ________.

g) The name of the element in the third row and fifth column of array **d** is ________.

11.7 State whether each of the following is *true* or *false*. If *false*, explain why.

a) To refer to a particular location or element within an array, we specify the name of the array and the value of the particular element.

b) An array declaration reserves space for the array.

c) To indicate that 100 locations should be reserved for integer array **p**, the programmer should write the declaration

```
p[ 100 ];
```

d) A JavaScript program that initializes the elements of a 15-element array to zero must contain at least one **for** statement.

e) A JavaScript program that totals the elements of a double-subscripted array must contain nested **for** statements.

11.8 Write JavaScript statements to accomplish each of the following tasks:

a) Display the value of the seventh element of array **f**.

b) Initialize each of the five elements of single-subscripted array **g** to **8**.

c) Total the elements of array **c**, which contains 100 numeric elements.

d) Copy 11-element array **a** into the first portion of array **b**, which contains 34 elements.

e) Determine and print the smallest and largest values contained in 99-element floating-point array **w**.

11.9 Consider a two-by-three array **t** that will store integers.

a) Write a statement that declares and creates array **t**.

b) How many rows does **t** have?

c) How many columns does **t** have?

d) How many elements does **t** have?

e) Write the names of all the elements in the second row of **t**.

f) Write the names of all the elements in the third column of **t**.

g) Write a single statement that sets the element of **t** in row 1 and column 2 to zero.

h) Write a series of statements that initializes each element of **t** to zero. Do not use a repetition structure.

i) Write a nested **for** structure that initializes each element of **t** to zero.
j) Write a series of statements that determines and prints the smallest value in array **t**.
k) Write a statement that displays the elements of the first row of **t**.
l) Write a statement that totals the elements of the fourth column of **t**.
m) Write a series of statements that prints the array **t** in neat, tabular format. List the column subscripts as headings across the top, and list the row subscripts at the left of each row.

11.10 Use a single-subscripted array to solve the following problem: A company pays its salespeople on a commission basis. The salespeople receive $200 per week plus 9% of their gross sales for that week. For example, a salesperson who grosses $5000 in sales in a week receives $200 plus 9% of $5000, or a total of $650. Write a script (using an array of counters) that obtains the gross sales for each employee through an XHTML form and determines how many of the salespeople earned salaries in each of the following ranges (assume that each salesperson's salary is truncated to an integer amount):

a) $200-$299
b) $300-$399
c) $400-$499
d) $500-$599
e) $600-$699
f) $700-$799
g) $800-$899
h) $900-$999
i) $1000 and over

11.11 Write statements that perform the following operations for a single-subscripted array:
a) Set the 10 elements of array **counts** to zeros.
b) Add 1 to each of the 15 elements of array **bonus**.
c) Display the five values of array **bestScores**, separated by spaces.

11.12 Use a single-subscripted array to solve the following problem: Read in 20 numbers, each of which is between 10 and 100, inclusive. As each number is read, print it only if it is not a duplicate of a number that has already been read. Provide for the "worst case," in which all 20 numbers are different. Use the smallest possible array to solve this problem.

11.13 Label the elements of three-by-five double-subscripted array **sales** to indicate the order in which they are set to zero by the following program segment:

```
for ( var row in sales )
   for ( var col in sales[ row ] )
      sales[ row ][ col ] = 0;
```

11.14 Write a script to simulate the rolling of two dice. The script should use **Math.random** to roll the first die and should use **Math.random** again to roll the second die. The sum of the two values should then be calculated. [*Note*: Because each die can show an integer value from 1 to 6, the sum of the values will vary from 2 to 12, with 7 being the most frequent sum and 2 and 12 being the least frequent sums. Figure 11.13 shows the 36 possible combinations of the two dice. Your program should roll the dice 36,000 times. Use a single-subscripted array to tally the numbers of times each possible sum appears. Display the results in an XHTML table. Also, determine whether the totals are reasonable (e.g., there are six ways to roll a 7, so approximately one sixth of all the rolls should be 7).]

11.15 Write a script that runs 1000 games of craps and answers the following questions:
a) How many games are won on the first roll, second roll, ..., twentieth roll and after the twentieth roll?
b) How many games are lost on the first roll, second roll, ..., twentieth roll and after the twentieth roll?

	1	2	3	4	5	6
1	2	3	4	5	6	7
2	3	4	5	6	7	8
3	4	5	6	7	8	9
4	5	6	7	8	9	10
5	6	7	8	9	10	11
6	7	8	9	10	11	12

Fig. 11.13 Thirty-six possible outcomes of rolling two dice.

c) What are the chances of winning at craps? [*Note*: You should discover that craps is one of the fairest casino games. What do you suppose this means?]

d) What is the average length of a game of craps?

e) Do the chances of winning improve with the length of the game?

11.16 *(Airline Reservations System)* A small airline has just purchased a computer for its new automated reservations system. You have been asked to program the new system. You are to write a program to assign seats on each flight of the airline's only plane (capacity: 10 seats).

Your program should display the following menu of alternatives: **`Please type 1 for "First Class"`** and **`Please type 2 for "Economy"`**. If the person types **`1`**, your program should assign a seat in the first-class section (seats 1–5). If the person types **`2`**, your program should assign a seat in the economy section (seats 6–10). Your program should print a boarding pass indicating the person's seat number and whether it is in the first-class or economy section of the plane.

Use a single-subscripted array to represent the seating chart of the plane. Initialize all the elements of the array to **`0`** to indicate that all seats are empty. As each seat is assigned, set the corresponding elements of the array to **`1`** to indicate that the seat is no longer available.

Your program should, of course, never assign a seat that has already been assigned. When the first-class section is full, your program should ask the person if it is acceptable to be placed in the economy section (and vice versa). If yes, then make the appropriate seat assignment. If no, then print the message **`"Next flight leaves in 3 hours."`**

11.17 Use a double-subscripted array to solve the following problem: A company has four salespeople (1 to 4) who sell five different products (1 to 5). Once a day, each salesperson passes in a slip for each different type of product actually sold. Each slip contains

1. the salesperson number,
2. the product number, and
3. the total dollar value of that product sold that day.

Thus, each salesperson passes in between zero and five sales slips per day. Assume that the information from all of the slips for last month is available. Write a script that will read all this information for last month's sales and summarize the total sales by salesperson by product. All totals should be stored in the double-subscripted array **`sales`**. After processing all the information for last month, display the results in an XHTML table format, with each of the columns representing a particular salesperson and each of the rows representing a particular product. Cross-total each row to get the total sales of each product for last month; cross-total each column to get the total sales by salesperson for last month. Your tabular printout should include these cross-totals to the right of the totaled rows and to the bottom of the totaled columns.

11.18 *(Turtle Graphics)* The Logo language, which is popular among young computer users, made the concept of *turtle graphics* famous. Imagine a mechanical turtle that walks around the room under the control of a JavaScript program. The turtle holds a pen in one of two positions, up or down. While the pen is down, the turtle traces out shapes as it moves; while the pen is up, the turtle moves about freely without writing anything. In this problem, you will simulate the operation of the turtle and create a computerized sketchpad as well.

Use a 20-by-20 array **`floor`** that is initialized to zeros. Read commands from an array that contains them. Keep track of the current position of the turtle at all times and of whether the pen is currently up or down. Assume that the turtle always starts at position (0,0) of the floor, with its pen up. The set of turtle commands your script must process are as follows:

Command	Meaning
1	Pen up
2	Pen down
3	Turn right
4	Turn left
5,10	Move forward 10 spaces (or a number other than 10)
6	Print the 20-by-20 array
9	End of data (sentinel)

Suppose that the turtle is somewhere near the center of the floor. The following "program" would draw and print a 12-by-12 square, and then leave the pen in the up position:

```
2
5,12
3
5,12
3
5,12
3
5,12
1
6
9
```

As the turtle moves with the pen down, set the appropriate elements of array **`floor`** to **`1`**s. When the **`6`** command (print) is given, display an asterisk or some other character of your choosing wherever there is a **`1`** in the array. Wherever there is a zero, display a blank. Write a script to implement the turtle graphics capabilities discussed here. Write several turtle graphics programs to draw interesting shapes. Add other commands to increase the power of your turtle graphics language.

11.19 *(The Sieve of Eratosthenes)* A prime integer is an integer that is evenly divisible by only itself and 1. The Sieve of Eratosthenes is an algorithm for finding prime numbers. It operates as follows:

a) Create an array with all elements initialized to 1 (true). Array elements with prime subscripts will remain as 1. All other array elements will eventually be set to zero.
b) Starting with array subscript 2 (subscript 1 must be prime), every time an array element is found whose value is 1, loop through the remainder of the array and set to zero every

element whose subscript is a multiple of the subscript for the element with value 1. For array subscript 2, all elements beyond 2 in the array that are multiples of 2 will be set to zero (subscripts 4, 6, 8, 10, etc.); for array subscript 3, all elements beyond 3 in the array that are multiples of 3 will be set to zero (subscripts 6, 9, 12, 15, etc.); and so on.

When this process is complete, the array elements that are still set to 1 indicate that the subscript is a prime number. These subscripts can then be printed. Write a script that uses an array of 1000 elements to determine and print the prime numbers between 1 and 999. Ignore element 0 of the array.

11.20 *Simulation: The Tortoise and the Hare)* In this problem, you will re-create one of the truly great moments in history, namely the classic race of the tortoise and the hare. You will use random-number generation to develop a simulation of this memorable event.

Our contenders begin the race at "square 1" of 70 squares. Each square represents a possible position along the race course. The finish line is at square 70. The first contender to reach or pass square 70 is rewarded with a pail of fresh carrots and lettuce. The course weaves its way up the side of a slippery mountain, so occasionally the contenders lose ground.

There is a clock that ticks once per second. With each tick of the clock, your script should adjust the position of the animals according to the following rules:

Animal	Move type	Percentage of the time	Actual move
Tortoise	Fast plod	50%	3 squares to the right
	Slip	20%	6 squares to the left
	Slow plod	30%	1 square to the right
Hare	Sleep	20%	No move at all
	Big hop	20%	9 squares to the right
	Big slip	10%	12 squares to the left
	Small hop	30%	1 square to the right
	Small slip	20%	2 squares to the left

Use variables to keep track of the positions of the animals (i.e., position numbers are 1–70). Start each animal at position 1 (i.e., the "starting gate"). If an animal slips left before square 1, move the animal back to square 1.

Generate the percentages in the preceding table by producing a random integer i in the range $1 \le i \le 10$. For the tortoise, perform a "fast plod" when $1 \le i \le 5$, a "slip" when $6 \le i \le 7$ and a "slow plod" when $8 \le i \le 10$. Use a similar technique to move the hare.

Begin the race by printing

```
BANG !!!!!
AND THEY'RE OFF !!!!!
```

Then, for each tick of the clock (i.e., each repetition of a loop), print a 70-position line showing the letter **T** in the position of the tortoise and the letter **H** in the position of the hare. Occasionally, the contenders will land on the same square. In this case, the tortoise bites the hare, and your script should print **OUCH!!!** beginning at that position. All print positions other than the **T**, the **H** or the **OUCH!!!** (in case of a tie) should be blank.

After each line is printed, test whether either animal has reached or passed square 70. If so, print the winner, and terminate the simulation. If the tortoise wins, print **TORTOISE WINS!!!**

YAY!!! If the hare wins, print **Hare wins. Yuch.** If both animals win on the same tick of the clock, you may want to favor the turtle (the "underdog"), or you may want to print **It's a tie**. If neither animal wins, perform the loop again to simulate the next tick of the clock. When you are ready to run your script, assemble a group of fans to watch the race. You'll be amazed at how involved your audience gets!

Later in the book, we introduce a number of Dynamic HTML capabilities, such as graphics, images, animation and sound. As you study those features, you might enjoy enhancing your tortoise-and-hare contest simulation.

12

JavaScript: Objects

Objectives

- To understand object-based programming terminology and concepts.
- To understand encapsulation and data hiding.
- To appreciate the value of object orientation.
- To be able to use the **`Math`** object.
- To be able to use the **`String`** object.
- To be able to use the **`Date`** object.
- To be able to use the **`Boolean`** and **`Number`** objects.

My object all sublime
I shall achieve in time.
W. S. Gilbert

Is it a world to hide virtues in?
William Shakespeare, *Twelfth Night*

Good as it is to inherit a library, it is better to collect one.
Augustine Birrell

A philosopher of imposing stature doesn't think in a vacuum. Even his most abstract ideas are, to some extent, conditioned by what is or is not known in the time when he lives.
Alfred North Whitehead

Outline

12.1 Introduction

Most JavaScript programs demonstrated to this point illustrate basic computer programming concepts. These programs provide you with the foundation you need to build powerful and complex scripts as part of your Web pages. As you proceed beyond this chapter, you will use JavaScript to manipulate every element of an XHTML document from a script.

This chapter presents a more formal treatment of *objects*. The chapter overviews—and serves as a reference for—several of JavaScript's built-in objects and demonstrates many of their capabilities. In the chapters on Dynamic HTML that follow this chapter, you will be introduced to many objects provided by the browser that enable scripts to interact with the different elements of an XHTML document.

12.2 Thinking About Objects

Now we begin our introduction to objects. We will see that objects are a natural way of thinking about the world and of writing scripts that manipulate XHTML documents.

In Chapters 7 through 11, we used built-in JavaScript objects—**`Math`** and **`Array`**—and we used objects provided by the Web browser—**`document`** and **`window`**—to perform tasks in our scripts. JavaScript uses objects to perform many tasks, so JavaScript is referred to as an *object-based programming language.* As we have seen, JavaScript also uses constructs from the "conventional" structured programming methodology supported by many other programming languages. The first six JavaScript chapters concentrated on these "conventional" parts of JavaScript, as they are important components of all JavaScript programs.

This section introduces the basic concepts (i.e., "object think") and terminology (i.e., "object speak") of object-based programming, so we can properly refer to the object-based concepts as we encounter them in the remainder of the text.

Let us start by introducing some of the key terminology of object orientation. Look around you in the real world. Everywhere you look you see them—objects! People, animals, plants, cars, planes, buildings, computers and the like. Humans think in terms of objects. We have the marvelous ability of *abstraction,* which enables us to view screen images as objects such as people, planes, trees and mountains rather than as individual dots of color (called *pixels,* for "picture elements"). We can, if we wish, think in terms of beaches rather than grains of sand, forests rather than trees and houses rather than bricks.

We might be inclined to divide objects into two categories—animate objects and inanimate objects. Animate objects are "alive" in some sense. They move around and do things. Inanimate objects, like towels, seem not to do much at all. They just kind of "sit around." All these objects, however, do have some things in common. They all have *attributes,* such as size, shape, color, weight and the like; and they all exhibit *behaviors*—for example, a ball rolls, bounces, inflates and deflates; a baby cries, sleeps, crawls, walks and blinks; a car accelerates, decelerates, brakes and turns; a towel absorbs water.

Humans learn about objects by studying their attributes and observing their behaviors. Different objects can have similar attributes and can exhibit similar behaviors. Comparisons can be made, for example, between babies and adults and between humans and chimpanzees. Cars, trucks, little red wagons and skateboards have much in common.

Objects *encapsulate* data (attributes) and methods (behavior); the data and methods of an object are tied together intimately. Objects have the property of *information hiding.* Programs communicate with objects through well-defined *interfaces.* Normally, implementation details of objects are hidden within the objects themselves.

Most people reading this book probably drive (or have driven) an automobile—a perfect example of an object. Surely it is possible to drive an automobile effectively without knowing the details of how engines, transmissions and exhaust systems work internally. Millions of human years of research and development have been performed for automobiles and have resulted in extremely complex objects containing thousands of parts (attributes). All of this complexity is hidden (encapsulated) from the driver. The driver only sees the friendly user interface of behaviors that enable the driver to make the car go faster by pressing the gas pedal, go slower by pressing the brake pedal, turn left or right by turning the steering wheel, go forward or backward by selecting the gear and turn on and off by turning the key in the ignition.

Like the designers of an automobile, the designers of World Wide Web browsers have defined a set of objects that encapsulate the elements of an XHTML document and expose to a JavaScript programmer attributes and behaviors that enable a JavaScript program to interact with (or script) the elements (objects) in an XHTML document. The browser's **`window`** object provides attributes and behaviors that enable a script to manipulate a browser window. When a string is assigned to the **`window`** object's **`status`** property (attribute), that string is displayed in the status bar of the browser window. The **`window`** object's **`alert`** method (behavior) allows the programmer to display a message in a separate window. We will soon see that the browser's **`document`** object contains attributes and behaviors that provide access to every element of an XHTML document. Similarly, JavaScript provides objects that encapsulate various capabilities in a script. For example, the

JavaScript **Array** object provides attributes and behaviors that enable a script to manipulate a collection of data. The **Array** object's **length** property (attribute) contains the number of elements in the **Array**. The **Array** object's **sort** method (behavior) orders the elements of the **Array**.

Indeed, with object technology, we will build most future software by combining "standardized, interchangeable parts" called objects. These parts allow programmers to create new programs without having to "reinvent the wheel." Objects will allow programmers to speed and enhance the quality of future software development efforts.

12.3 Math Object

The **Math** object's methods allow the programmer to perform many common mathematical calculations. As shown previously, an object's methods are called by writing the name of the object followed by a dot operator (**.**) and the name of the method. In parentheses following the method name is the argument (or a comma-separated list of arguments) to the method. For example, a programmer desiring to calculate and display the square root of **900.0** might write

```
document.writeln( Math.sqrt( 900.0 ) );
```

When this statement executes, it calls method **Math.sqrt** to calculate the square root of the number contained in the parentheses (**900.0**). The number **900.0** is the argument of the **Math.sqrt** method. The preceding statement would display **30.0**. Invoking the **sqrt** method of the **Math** object is also referred to as *sending the* ***sqrt*** *message to* ***Math*** *object*. Similarly, invoking the **writeln** method of the **document** object is also referred to as *sending the* ***writeln*** *message to the* ***document*** *object*. Some **Math** object methods are summarized in Fig. 12.1.

Method	Description	Example
abs(x)	absolute value of **x**	**abs(7.2)** is **7.2** **abs(0.0)** is **0.0** **abs(-5.6)** is **5.6**
ceil(x)	rounds **x** to the smallest integer not less than **x**	**ceil(9.2)** is **10.0** **ceil(-9.8)** is **-9.0**
cos(x)	trigonometric cosine of **x** (**x** in radians)	**cos(0.0)** is **1.0**
exp(x)	exponential method e^x	**exp(1.0)** is **2.71828** **exp(2.0)** is **7.38906**
floor(x)	rounds **x** to the largest integer not greater than **x**	**floor(9.2)** is **9.0** **floor(-9.8)** is **-10.0**
log(x)	natural logarithm of **x** (base *e*)	**log(2.718282)** is **1.0** **log(7.389056)** is **2.0**

Fig. 12.1 Commonly used **Math** object methods (part 1 of 2).

Method	Description	Example
`max( x, y )`	larger value of **`x`** and **`y`**	`max( 2.3, 12.7 )` is `12.7` `max( -2.3, -12.7 )` is `-2.3`
`min( x, y )`	smaller value of **`x`** and **`y`**	`min( 2.3, 12.7 )` is `2.3` `min( -2.3, -12.7 )` is `-12.7`
`pow( x, y )`	**`x`** raised to power **`y`** (x^y)	`pow( 2.0, 7.0 )` is `128.0` `pow( 9.0, .5 )` is `3.0`
`round( x )`	rounds **`x`** to the closest integer	`round( 9.75 )` is `10` `round( 9.25 )` is `9`
`sin( x )`	trigonometric sine of **`x`** (**`x`** in radians)	`sin( 0.0 )` is `0.0`
`sqrt( x )`	square root of **`x`**	`sqrt( 900.0 )` is `30.0` `sqrt( 9.0 )` is `3.0`
`tan( x )`	trigonometric tangent of **`x`** (**`x`** in radians)	`tan( 0.0 )` is `0.0`

Fig. 12.1 Commonly used **`Math`** object methods (part 2 of 2).

Common Programming Error 12.1

*Forgetting to invoke a **`Math`** method by preceding the method name with the object name **`Math`** and a dot operator (**`.`**) is an error.*

Software Engineering Observation 12.1

The primary difference between invoking a function and invoking a method is that a function does not require an object name and a dot operator to call the function.

The **`Math`** object also defines several commonly used mathematical constants, summarized in Fig. 12.2. [*Note*: By convention, the names of these constants are written in all uppercase letters.]

Good Programming Practice 12.1

*Use the mathematical constants of the **`Math`** object rather than explicitly typing the numeric value of the constant.*

Constant	Description	Value
`Math.E`	Euler's constant.	Approximately 2.718.
`Math.LN2`	Natural logarithm of 2.	Approximately 0.693.
`Math.LN10`	Natural logarithm of 10.	Approximately 2.302.
`Math.LOG2E`	Base 2 logarithm of Euler's constant.	Approximately 1.442.
`Math.LOG10E`	Base 10 logarithm of Euler's constant.	Approximately 0.434.

Fig. 12.2 Properties of the **`Math`** object (part 1 of 2).

Constant	Description	Value
`Math.PI`	π—the ratio of a circle's circumference to its diameter.	Approximately 3.141592653589793.
`Math.SQRT1_2`	Square root of 0.5.	Approximately 0.707.
`Math.SQRT2`	Square root of 2.0.	Approximately 1.414.

Fig. 12.2 Properties of the **`Math`** object (part 2 of 2).

12.4 `String` Object

In this section, we introduce JavaScript's string- and character-processing capabilities. The techniques discussed here are appropriate for processing names, addresses, credit card information, etc.

12.4.1 Fundamentals of Characters and Strings

Characters are the fundamental building blocks of JavaScript programs. Every program is composed of a sequence of characters that—when grouped together meaningfully—is interpreted by the computer as a series of instructions used to accomplish a task.

A string is a series of characters treated as a single unit. A string may include letters, digits and various *special characters,* such as **+**, **-**, *****, **/**, **$** and others. JavaScript supports the set of characters called *Unicode*® that represents a large portion of the world's commercially viable languages. (We discuss Unicode in detail in Appendix G.) A string is an object of type **`String`**. *String literals* or *string constants* (often called *anonymous* ***`String`*** *objects*) are written as a sequence of characters in double quotation marks or single quotation marks as follows:

```
"John Q. Doe"                  (a name)
'9999 Main Street'             (a street address)
"Waltham, Massachusetts"       (a city and state)
'(201) 555-1212'               (a telephone number)
```

A **`String`** may be assigned to a variable in a declaration. The declaration

```
var color = "blue";
```

initializes variable **`color`** with the **`String`** object containing the string **`"blue"`**. **`String`**s can be compared with the relational operators (**<**, **<=**, **>** and **>=**) and the equality operators (**==** and **!=**).

12.4.2 Methods of the `String` Object

The **`String`** object encapsulates the attributes and behaviors of a string of characters. The **`String`** object provides many methods (behaviors) for selecting characters from a string, combining strings (called *concatenation*), obtaining substrings of a string, searching for substrings within a string, tokenizing a string and converting strings to all uppercase or lowercase letters. The **`String`** object also provides several methods that generate XHTML tags. Figure 12.3 summarizes many **String** methods. Figures 12.4–12.7 demonstrate some of these methods.

Method	Description
charAt(*index* **)**	Returns a string containing the character at the specified *index*. If there is no character at that *index*, **charAt** returns an empty string. The first character is located at *index* 0.
charCodeAt(*index* **)**	Returns the Unicode value of the character at the specified *index*. If there is no character at that *index*, **charCodeAt** returns **NaN**.
concat(*string* **)**	Concatenates its argument to the end of the string that invokes the method. The string invoking this method is not modified; rather a new **String** is returned. This method is the same as adding two strings with the string concatenation operator **+** (e.g., **s1.concat(s2)** is the same as **s1 + s2**).
fromCharCode(*value1*, *value2*, ...**)**	Converts a list of Unicode values into a string containing the corresponding characters.
indexOf(*substring*, *index* **)**	Searches for the first occurrence of *substring* starting from position *index* in the string that invokes the method. The method returns the starting index of *substring* in the source string or –1 if *substring* is not found. If the *index* argument is not provided, the method begins searching from index 0 in the source string.
lastIndexOf(*substring*, *index* **)**	Searches for the last occurrence of *substring* starting from position *index* and searching toward the beginning of the string that invokes the method. The method returns the starting index of *substring* in the source string or –1 if *substring* is not found. If the *index* argument is not provided, the method begins searching from end of the source string.
slice(*start*, *end* **)**	Returns a string containing the portion of the string from index *start* through index *end*. If the *end* index is not specified, the method returns a string from the *start* index to the end of the source string. A negative *end* index specifies an offset from the end of the string starting from a position one past the end of the last character (so, –1 indicates the last character position in the string).
split(*string* **)**	Splits the source string into an array of strings (tokens) where its *string* argument specifies the delimiter (i.e., the characters that indicate the end of each token in the source string).
substr(*start*, *length* **)**	Returns a string containing *length* characters starting from index *start* in the source string. If *length* is not specified, a string containing characters from *start* to the end of the source string is returned.
substring(*start*, *end* **)**	Returns a string containing the characters from index *start* up to but not including index *end* in the source string.
toLowerCase()	Returns a string in which all uppercase letters are converted to lowercase letters. Non-letter characters are not changed.

Fig. 12.3 Some methods of the **String** object (part 1 of 2).

Method	Description
`toUpperCase()`	Returns a string in which all lowercase letters are converted to uppercase letters. Non-letter characters are not changed.
`toString()`	Returns the same string as the source string.
`valueOf()`	Returns the same string as the source string.
Methods that generate XHTML tags	
`anchor(` *name* **`)`**	Wraps the source string in an anchor element (`<a></a>`) with *name* as the anchor name.
`blink()`	Wraps the source string in a `<blink></blink>` element.
`fixed()`	Wraps the source string in a `<tt></tt>` element.
`link(` *url* **`)`**	Wraps the source string in an anchor element (`<a></a>`) with *url* as the hyperlink location.
`strike()`	Wraps the source string in a `<strike></strike>` element.
`sub()`	Wraps the source string in a `<sub></sub>` element.
`sup()`	Wraps the source string in a `<sup></sup>` element.

Fig. 12.3 Some methods of the **`String`** object (part 2 of 2).

12.4.3 Character Processing Methods

The script of Fig. 12.4 demonstrates some of the **`String`** object's character processing methods, including ***`charAt`*** (returns the character at a specific position), ***`charCodeAt`*** (returns the Unicode value of the character at a specific position), ***`fromCharCode`*** (returns a string created from a series of Unicode values), ***`toLowerCase`*** (returns the lowercase version of a string) and ***`toUpperCase`*** (returns the uppercase version of a string).

```
<?xml version = "1.0"?>
<!DOCTYPE html PUBLIC "-//W3C//DTD XHTML 1.0 Strict//EN"
   "http://www.w3.org/TR/xhtml1/DTD/xhtml1-strict.dtd">

<!-- Fig. 12.4: CharacterProcessing.html -->
<!-- Character Processing Methods       -->

<html xmlns = "http://www.w3.org/1999/xhtml">
   <head>
      <title>Character Processing Methods</title>

      <script type = "text/javascript">
         <!--
         var s = "ZEBRA";
         var s2 = "AbCdEfG";

```

Fig. 12.4 String methods **`charAt`**, **`charCodeAt`**, **`fromCharCode`**, **`toLowercase`** and **`toUpperCase`** (part 1 of 2).

```
17            document.writeln( "<p>Character at index 0 in '" +
18               s + "' is " + s.charAt( 0 ) );
19            document.writeln( "<br />Character code at index 0 in '"
20               + s + "' is " + s.charCodeAt( 0 ) + "</p>" );
21
22            document.writeln( "<p>'" +
23               String.fromCharCode( 87, 79, 82, 68 ) +
24               "' contains character codes 87, 79, 82 and 68</p>" )
25
26            document.writeln( "<p>'" + s2 + "' in lowercase is '" +
27               s2.toLowerCase() + "'" );
28            document.writeln( "<br />'" + s2 + "' in uppercase is '"
29               + s2.toUpperCase() + "'</p>" );
30            // -->
31         </script>
32
33      </head><body></body>
34   </html>
```

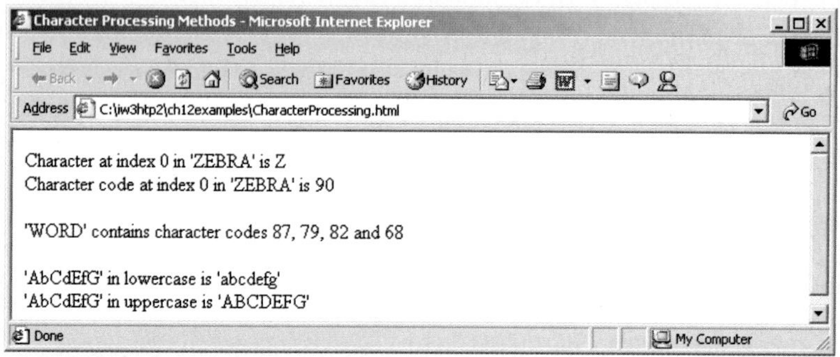

Fig. 12.4 String methods **charAt**, **charCodeAt**, **fromCharCode**, **toLowercase** and **toUpperCase** (part 2 of 2).

Lines 17–18 display the first character in **String s** (**"ZEBRA"**) using **String** method **charAt**. Method ***charAt*** returns a string containing the character at the specified index (**0** in this example). Indices for the characters in a string start at 0 (the first character) and go up to (but not including) the string's **length** (i.e., if the string contains five characters, the indices are 0 through 4). If the index is outside the bounds of the string, the method returns an empty string.

Lines 19–20 display the character code for the first character in **String s** (**"ZEBRA"**) by calling **String** method ***charCodeAt***. Method **charCodeAt** returns the Unicode value of the character at the specified index (**0** in this example). If the index is outside the bounds of the string, the method returns **NaN**.

String method ***fromCharCode*** receives as its argument a comma-separated list of Unicode values and builds a string containing the character representation of those Unicode values. Lines 22–24 display the string "**WORD**," which consists of the character codes 87, 79, 82 and 68. Notice that the **String** object calls method **fromCharCode**, rather than a specific **String** variable. Appendix C, ASCII Character Set, contains the character codes ASCII character set—a subset of the Unicode character set (Appendix G) that contains only Western characters.

The statements at lines 26–27 and 28–29 use **String** methods ***toLowerCase*** and ***toUpperCase*** to display versions of **String s2** (**"AbCdEfG"**) in all lowercase letters and all uppercase letters, respectively.

12.4.4 Searching Methods

Often it is useful to search for a character or a sequence of characters in a string. For example, if you are creating your own word processor, you may want to provide a capability for searching through the document. The script of Fig. 12.5 demonstrates the **String** object methods ***indexOf*** and ***lastIndexOf*** that search for a specified substring in a string. All the searches in this example are performed on the global string **letters** (initialized at line 16 with **"abcdefghijklmnopqrstuvwxyzabcdefghijklm"** in the script).

The user types a substring in the XHTML form **searchForm**'s **inputVal** text field and presses **search** (with the label **Search** on the screen) to search for the substring in **letters**. Clicking the **Search** button calls function **buttonPressed** (defined at lines 18–29) to respond to the **onclick** event and to perform the searches. The results of each search are displayed in the appropriate text field of **searchForm**.

Lines 20–21 use **String** method **indexOf** to determine the location of the first occurrence in string **letters** of the string **searchForm.inputVal.value** (i.e., the string the user typed in the **inputVal** text field). If the substring is found, the index at which the first occurrence of the substring begins is returned; otherwise, –1 is returned.

Lines 22–23 use **String** method **lastIndexOf** to determine the location of the last occurrence in **letters** of the string in text field **inputVal**. If the substring is found, the index at which the last occurrence of the substring begins is returned; otherwise, –1 is returned.

```
1   <?xml version = "1.0"?>
2   <!DOCTYPE html PUBLIC "-//W3C//DTD XHTML 1.0 Strict//EN"
3      "http://www.w3.org/TR/xhtml1/DTD/xhtml1-strict.dtd">
4
5   <!-- Fig. 12.5: SearchingStrings.html -->
6   <!-- Searching Strings                 -->
7
8   <html xmlns = "http://www.w3.org/1999/xhtml">
9      <head>
10        <title>
11           Searching Strings with indexOf and lastIndexOf
12        </title>
13
14        <script type = "text/javascript">
15           <!--
16           var letters = "abcdefghijklmnopqrstuvwxyzabcdefghijklm";
17
18           function buttonPressed()
19           {
20              searchForm.first.value =
21                 letters.indexOf( searchForm.inputVal.value );
```

Fig. 12.5 Searching **String**s with **indexOf** and **lastIndexOf** (part 1 of 3).

```
               searchForm.last.value =
                  letters.lastIndexOf( searchForm.inputVal.value );
               searchForm.first12.value =
                  letters.indexOf( searchForm.inputVal.value, 12 );
               searchForm.last12.value =
                  letters.lastIndexOf(
                     searchForm.inputVal.value, 12 );
            }
            // -->
         </script>

      </head>
      <body>
         <form name = "searchForm" action = "">
            <h1>The string to search is:<br />
                abcdefghijklmnopqrstuvwxyzabcdefghijklm</h1>
            <p>Enter substring to search for
            <input name = "inputVal" type = "text" />
            <input name = "search" type = "button" value = "Search"
                   onclick = "buttonPressed()" /><br /></p>

            <p>First occurrence located at index
            <input name = "first" type = "text" size = "5" />
            <br />Last occurrence located at index
            <input name = "last" type = "text" size = "5" />
            <br />First occurrence from index 12 located at index
            <input name = "first12" type = "text" size = "5" />
            <br />Last occurrence from index 12 located at index
            <input name = "last12" type = "text" size = "5" /></p>
         </form>
      </body>
   </html>
```

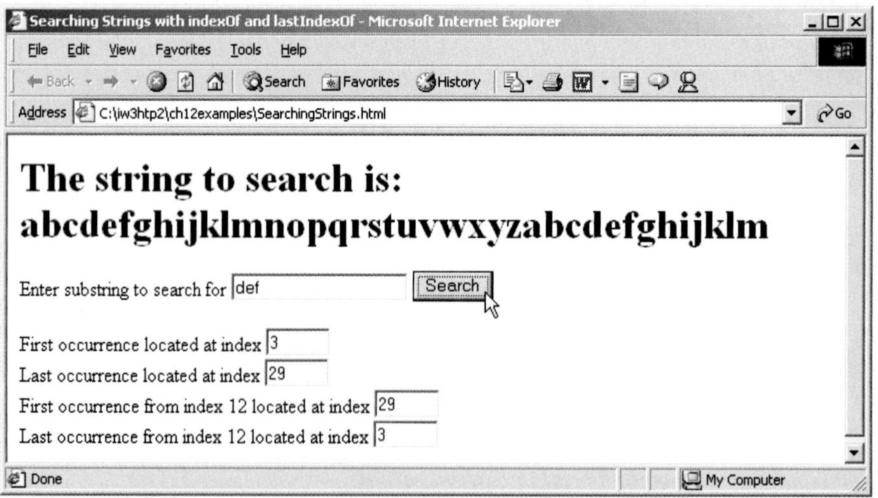

Fig. 12.5 Searching **String**s with **indexOf** and **lastIndexOf** (part 2 of 3).

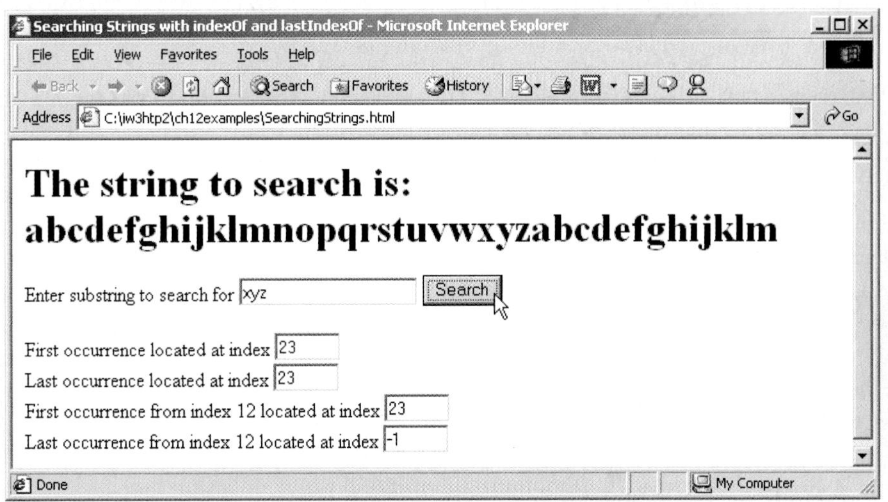

Fig. 12.5 Searching **String**s with **indexOf** and **lastIndexOf** (part 3 of 3).

Lines 24–25 use **String** method **indexOf** to determine the location of the first occurrence in string **letters** of the string in the **inputVal** text field, starting from index **12** in **letters**. If the substring is found, the index at which the first occurrence of the substring (starting from index **12**) begins is returned; otherwise, –1 is returned.

Lines 26–28 use **String** method **lastIndexOf** to determine the location of the last occurrence in **letters** of the string in the **inputVal** text field starting from index **12** in **letters**. If the substring is found, the index at which the first occurrence of the substring (starting from index **12**) begins is returned; otherwise, –1 is returned.

***String** methods **indexOf** or **lastIndexOf**, with their optional second argument (the starting index from which to search), are particularly useful for continuing a search through a large amount of text.*

12.4.5 Splitting Strings and Obtaining Substrings

When you read a sentence, your mind breaks the sentence into individual words, or *tokens,* each of which conveys meaning to you. The process of breaking a string into tokens is called *tokenization*. Interpreters also perform tokenization. They break up statements into such individual pieces as keywords, identifiers, operators and other elements of a programming language. Figure 12.6 demonstrates **String** method ***split*** that breaks a string into its component tokens. Tokens are separated from one another by *delimiters*, typically white-space characters such as blank, tab, newline and carriage return. Other characters may also be used as delimiters to separate tokens.The XHTML document displays a form containing a text field where the user types a sentence to tokenize. The results of the tokenization process are displayed in an XHTML **textarea** GUI component. The script also demonstrates **String** method ***substring*** which returns a portion of a string.

The user types a sentence into form **myForm**'s **inputVal** text field and presses button **splitButton** (labeled **Split** on the screen) to tokenize the string. Function

splitButtonPressed (defined at lines 14–21) handles **splitButton**'s **onclick** event.

Line 16 calls **String** method **split** to tokenize **myForm.inputVal.value**, which contains the string the user entered. The argument to method **split** is the *delimiter string*—the string that determines the end of each token in the original string. In this example, the space character delimits the tokens. The delimiter string can contain multiple characters that should be used as delimiters. Method **split** returns an array of strings containing the tokens. Line 17 uses **Array** method **join** to combine the strings in array **strings** and separate each string with a newline character (**\n**). The resulting string is assigned to the **value** property of the XHTML form's **output** GUI component (an XHTML **textarea**).

```
1  <?xml version = "1.0"?>
2  <!DOCTYPE html PUBLIC "-//W3C//DTD XHTML 1.0 Strict//EN"
3     "http://www.w3.org/TR/xhtml1/DTD/xhtml1-strict.dtd">
4
5  <!-- Fig. 12.6: SplitAndSubString.html -->
6  <!-- String Method split and substring -->
7
8  <html xmlns = "http://www.w3.org/1999/xhtml">
9     <head>
10       <title>String Method split and substring</title>
11
12       <script type = "text/javascript">
13          <!--
14          function splitButtonPressed()
15          {
16             var strings = myForm.inputVal.value.split( " " );
17             myForm.output.value = strings.join( "\n" );
18
19             myForm.outputSubstring.value =
20                myForm.inputVal.value.substring( 0, 10 );
21          }
22          // -->
23       </script>
24    </head>
25
26    <body>
27       <form name = "myForm" action = "">
28          <p>Enter a sentence to split into words<br />
29          <input name = "inputVal" type = "text" size = "40" />
30          <input name = "splitButton" type = "button" value =
31                "Split" onclick = "splitButtonPressed()" /></p>
32
33          <p>The sentence split into words is<br />
34          <textarea name = "output" rows = "8" cols = "34">
35          </textarea></p>
36
37          <p>The first 10 characters of the input string are
38          <input name = "outputSubstring" type = "text"
39                size = "15" /></p>
```

Fig. 12.6 Using **String** method **split** and **Array** method **join** (part 1 of 2).

```
40          </form>
41       </body>
42    </html>
```

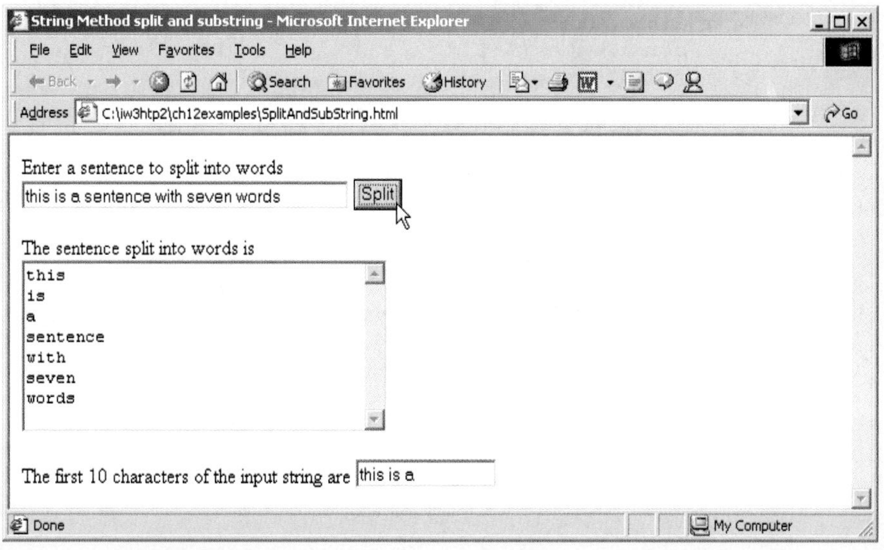

Fig. 12.6 Using **String** method **split** and **Array** method **join** (part 2 of 2).

Lines 19–20 use **String** method **substring** to obtain a string containing the first 10 characters of the string the user entered in text field **inputVal**. The method returns the substring from the *starting index* (**0** in this example) up to but not including the *ending index* (**10** in this example). If the ending index is greater than the length of the string, the substring returned includes the characters from the starting index to the end of the original string.

12.4.6 XHTML Markup Methods

The script of Fig. 12.7 demonstrates the **String** object's methods that generate XHTML markup tags. When a **String** object invokes a markup method, the method wraps the **String**'s contents in the appropriate XHTML tag. These methods are particularly useful for generating XHTML dynamically during script processing. [*Note*: Internet Explorer ignores the **blink** element.]

```
<?xml version = "1.0"?>
<!DOCTYPE html PUBLIC "-//W3C//DTD XHTML 1.0 Strict//EN"
   "http://www.w3.org/TR/xhtml1/DTD/xhtml1-strict.dtd">

<!-- Fig. 12.7: MarkupMethods.html              -->
<!-- XHTML markup methods of the String object -->

<html xmlns = "http://www.w3.org/1999/xhtml">
   <head>
```

Fig. 12.7 XHTML markup methods of the **String** object (part 1 of 2).

```
10        <title>XHTML Markup Methods of the String Object</title>
11
12        <script type = "text/javascript">
13           <!--
14           var anchorText = "This is an anchor",
15               blinkText = "This is blinking text",
16               fixedText = "This is monospaced text",
17               linkText = "Click here to go to anchorText",
18               strikeText = "This is strike out text",
19               subText = "subscript",
20               supText = "superscript";
21
22           document.writeln( anchorText.anchor( "top" ) );
23           document.writeln( "<br />" + blinkText.blink() );
24           document.writeln( "<br />" + fixedText.fixed() );
25           document.writeln( "<br />" + strikeText.strike() );
26           document.writeln(
27              "<br />This is text with a " + subText.sub() );
28           document.writeln(
29              "<br />This is text with a " + supText.sup() );
30           document.writeln(
31              "<br />" + linkText.link( "#top" ) );
32           // -->
33        </script>
34
35     </head><body></body>
36  </html>
```

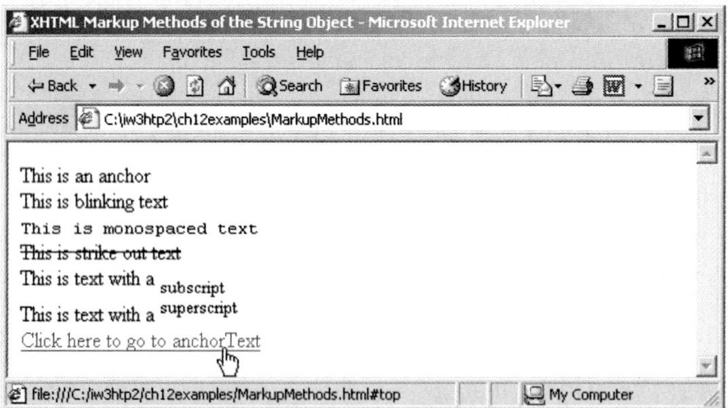

Fig. 12.7 XHTML markup methods of the **String** object (part 2 of 2).

Lines 14–20 define the strings that call each of the XHTML markup methods of the **String** object. Line 22 uses **String** method ***anchor*** to format the string in variable **anchorText** (**"This is an anchor"**) as

```
<a name = "top">This is an anchor</a>
```

The **name** of the anchor is the argument to the method. This anchor will be used later in the example as the target of a hyperlink.

Line 23 calls **String** method ***blink*** to make the string blink in the Web page by formatting the string in variable **blinkText** (**"This is blinking text"**) as

```
<blink>This is blinking text</blink>
```

Line 24 uses **String** method ***fixed*** to display text in a fixed-width font by formatting the string in variable **fixedText** (**"This is monospaced text"**) as

```
<tt>This is monospaced text</tt>
```

Line 25 uses **String** method ***strike*** to display text with a line through it by formatting the string in variable **strikeText** (**"This is strike out text"**) as

```
<strike>This is strike out text</strike>
```

Lines 26–27 use **String** method ***sub*** to display subscript text by formatting the string in variable **subText** (**"subscript"**) as

```
<sub>subscript</sub>
```

Notice that the resulting line in the XHTML document displays the word **subscript** smaller than the rest of the line and slightly below the line. Lines 28–29 call **String** method ***sup*** to display superscript text by formatting the string in variable **supText** (**"superscript"**) as

```
<sup>superscript</sup>
```

Notice that the resulting line in the XHTML document displays the word **superscript** smaller than the rest of the line and slightly above the line.

Lines 30–31use **String** method ***link*** to create a hyperlink by formatting the string in variable **linkText** (**"Click here to go to anchorText"**) as

```
<a href = "#top">Click here to go to anchorText</a>
```

The target of the hyperlink (**#top** in this example) is the argument to the method and can be any URL. In this example, the hyperlink target is the anchor created at line 22. If you make your browser window short and scroll to the bottom of the Web page, then click this link, the browser will reposition to the top of the Web page.

12.5 Date Object

JavaScript's ***Date*** object provides methods for date and time manipulations. Date and time processing can be performed based on the computer's *local time zone* or based on World Time Standard's *Universal Coordinated Time (UTC)*—formerly called *Greenwich Mean Time (GMT)*. Most methods of the **Date** object have a local time zone and a UTC version. The methods of the **Date** object are summarized in Fig. 12.8.

Method	Description
getDate() **getUTCDate()**	Returns a number from 1 to 31 representing the day of the month in local time or UTC, respectively.

Fig. 12.8 Methods of the **Date** object (part 1 of 3).

Method	Description
`getDay()` `getUTCDay()`	Returns a number from 0 (Sunday) to 6 (Saturday) representing the day of the week in local time or UTC, respectively.
`getFullYear()` `getUTCFullYear()`	Returns the year as a four-digit number in local time or UTC, respectively.
`getHours()` `getUTCHours()`	Returns a number from 0 to 23 representing hours since midnight in local time or UTC, respectively.
`getMilliseconds()` `getUTCMilliSeconds()`	Returns a number from 0 to 999 representing the number of milliseconds in local time or UTC, respectively. The time is stored in hours, minutes, seconds and milliseconds.
`getMinutes()` `getUTCMinutes()`	Returns a number from 0 to 59 representing the minutes for the time in local time or UTC, respectively.
`getMonth()` `getUTCMonth()`	Returns a number from 0 (January) to 11 (December) representing the month in local time or UTC, respectively.
`getSeconds()` `getUTCSeconds()`	Returns a number from 0 to 59 representing the seconds for the time in local time or UTC, respectively.
`getTime()`	Returns the number of milliseconds between January 1, 1970 and the time in the **Date** object.
`getTimezoneOffset()`	Returns the difference in minutes between the current time on the local computer and UTC—previously known as Greenwich Mean Time (GMT).
setDate(*val* **)** **setUTCDate(** *val* **)**	Sets the day of the month (1 to 31) in local time or UTC, respectively.
setFullYear(*y*, *m*, *d* **)** **setUTCFullYear(** *y*, *m*, *d* **)**	Sets the year in local time or UTC, respectively. The second and third arguments representing the month and the date are optional. If an optional argument is not specified, the current value in the **Date** object is used.
setHours(*h*, *m*, *s*, *ms* **)** **setUTCHours(** *h*, *m*, *s*, *ms* **)**	Sets the hour in local time or UTC, respectively. The second, third and fourth arguments representing the minutes, seconds and milliseconds are optional. If an optional argument is not specified, the current value in the **Date** object is used.
setMilliSeconds(*ms* **)** **setUTCMilliseconds(** *ms* **)**	Sets the number of milliseconds in local time or UTC, respectively.
setMinutes(*m*, *s*, *ms* **)** **setUTCMinutes(** *m*, *s*, *ms* **)**	Sets the minute in local time or UTC, respectively. The second and third arguments representing the seconds and milliseconds are optional. If an optional argument is not specified, the current value in the **Date** object is used.
setMonth(*m*, *d* **)** **setUTCMonth(** *m*, *d* **)**	Sets the month in local time or UTC, respectively. The second argument representing the date is optional. If the optional argument is not specified, the current date value in the **Date** object is used.

Fig. 12.8 Methods of the **Date** object (part 2 of 3).

Method	Description
setSeconds(*s*, *ms* **)** **setUTCSeconds(** *s*, *ms* **)**	Sets the second in local time or UTC, respectively. The second argument representing the milliseconds is optional. If this argument is not specified, the current millisecond value in the **Date** object is used.
setTime(*ms* **)**	Sets the time based on its argument—the number of elapsed milliseconds since January 1, 1970.
toLocaleString()	Returns a string representation of the date and time in a form specific to the computer's locale. For example, September 13, 2001 at 3:42:22 PM is represented as *09/13/01 15:47:22* in the United States and *13/09/01 15:47:22* in Europe.
toUTCString()	Returns a string representation of the date and time in the form: *19 Sep 2001 15:47:22 UTC*
toString()	Returns a string representation of the date and time in a form specific to the locale of the computer (*Mon Sep 19 15:47:22 EDT 2001* in the United States).
valueOf()	The time in number of milliseconds since midnight, January 1, 1970.

Fig. 12.8 Methods of the **Date** object (part 3 of 3).

The script of Fig. 12.9 demonstrates many of the local time zone methods in Fig. 12.8. Line 14 creates a new **Date** object. The **new** operator allocates the memory for the **Date** object. The empty parentheses indicate a call to the **Date** object's *constructor* with no arguments. A constructor is an initializer method for an object. Constructors are called automatically when an object is allocated with **new**. The **Date** constructor with no arguments initializes the local computer's **Date** object with the current date and time.

Software Engineering Observation 12.3

When an object is allocated with **new***, the object's constructor is called automatically to initialize the object before it is used in the program.*

Lines 18–21 demonstrate the methods **toString**, **toLocaleString**, **toUTCString** and **valueOf**. Notice that method **valueOf** returns a large integer value representing the total number of milliseconds between midnight, January 1, 1970 and the date and time stored in **Date** object **current**.

Lines 25–35 demonstrate the **Date** object's *get* methods for the local time zone. Notice that method **getFullYear** returns the year as a four-digit number. Also, notice that method **getTimeZoneOffset** returns the difference in minutes between the local time zone and UTC time (a difference of four hours at the time of the sample execution).

```
1  <?xml version = "1.0"?>
2  <!DOCTYPE html PUBLIC "-//W3C//DTD XHTML 1.0 Strict//EN"
3     "http://www.w3.org/TR/xhtml1/DTD/xhtml1-strict.dtd">
```

Fig. 12.9 Demonstrating date and time methods of the **Date** object (part 1 of 3).

```

<!-- Fig. 12.9: DateTime.html -->
<!-- Date and Time Methods    -->

<html xmlns = "http://www.w3.org/1999/xhtml">
   <head>
      <title>Date and Time Methods</title>

      <script type = "text/javascript">
         <!--
         var current = new Date();

         document.writeln(
            "<h1>String representations and valueOf</h1>" );
         document.writeln( "toString: " + current.toString() +
            "<br />toLocaleString: " + current.toLocaleString() +
            "<br />toUTCString: " + current.toUTCString() +
            "<br />valueOf: " + current.valueOf() );

         document.writeln(
            "<h1>Get methods for local time zone</h1>" );
         document.writeln( "getDate: " + current.getDate() +
            "<br />getDay: " + current.getDay() +
            "<br />getMonth: " + current.getMonth() +
            "<br />getFullYear: " + current.getFullYear() +
            "<br />getTime: " + current.getTime() +
            "<br />getHours: " + current.getHours() +
            "<br />getMinutes: " + current.getMinutes() +
            "<br />getSeconds: " + current.getSeconds() +
            "<br />getMilliseconds: " +
            current.getMilliseconds() +
            "<br />getTimezoneOffset: " +
            current.getTimezoneOffset() );

         document.writeln(
            "<h1>Specifying arguments for a new Date</h1>" );
         var anotherDate = new Date( 2001, 2, 18, 1, 5, 0, 0 );
         document.writeln( "Date: " + anotherDate );

         document.writeln(
            "<h1>Set methods for local time zone</h1>" );
         anotherDate.setDate( 31 );
         anotherDate.setMonth( 11 );
         anotherDate.setFullYear( 2001 );
         anotherDate.setHours( 23 );
         anotherDate.setMinutes( 59 );
         anotherDate.setSeconds( 59 );
         document.writeln( "Modified date: " + anotherDate );
         // -->
      </script>

   </head><body></body>
</html>
```

Fig. 12.9 Demonstrating date and time methods of the **Date** object (part 2 of 3).

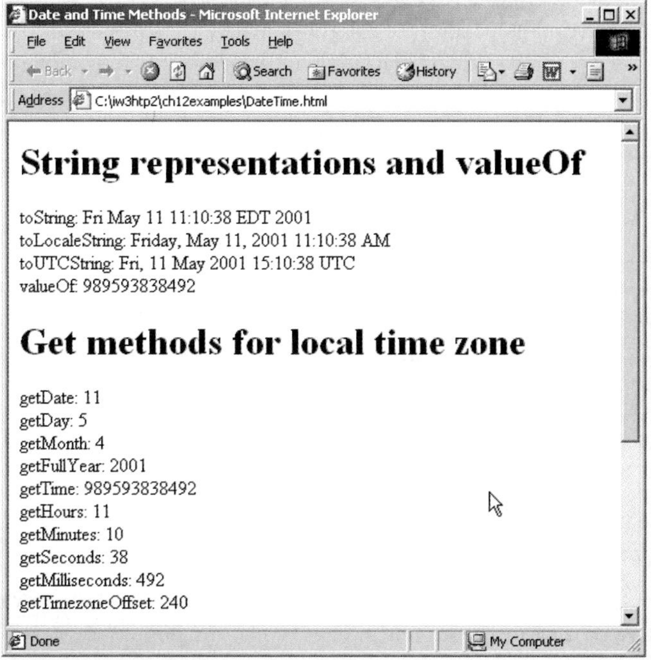

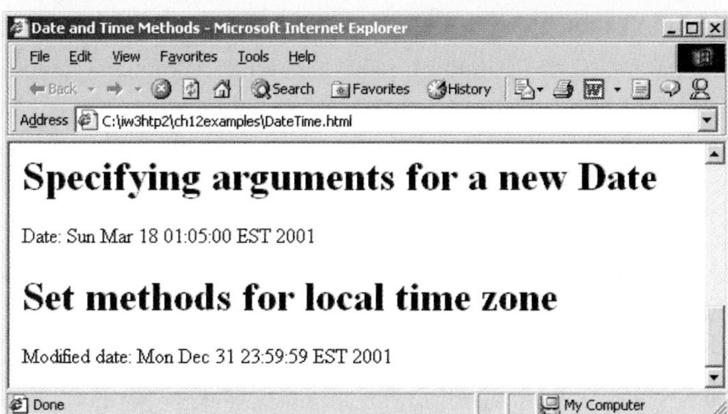

Fig. 12.9 Demonstrating date and time methods of the **`Date`** object (part 3 of 3).

Line 39 demonstrates creating a new **`Date`** object and supplying arguments to the **`Date`** constructor for *year*, *month*, *date*, *hours*, *minutes*, *seconds* and *milliseconds*. Note that the *hours*, *minutes*, *seconds* and *milliseconds* arguments are all optional. If any one of these arguments is not specified, a zero is supplied in its place. For the *hours*, *minutes* and *seconds* arguments, if the argument to the right of any of these arguments is specified, that argument must also be specified (e.g., if the *minutes* argument is specified, the *hours* argument must be specified; if the *milliseconds* argument is specified, all the arguments must be specified).

Lines 44–49 demonstrate the **Date** object *set* methods for the local time zone. **Date** objects represent the month internally as an integer from 0 to 11. These values are off-by-one from what you might expect (i.e., 1 for January, 2 for February, ..., and 12 for December). When creating a **Date** object, you must specify 0 to indicate January, 1 to indicate February, ..., and 11 to indicate December.

Common Programming Error 12.2

Assuming months are represented as numbers from 1 to 12 leads to off-by-one errors when you are processing ***Date****s.*

The **Date** object provides two other methods that can be called without creating a new **Date** object—***Date.parse*** and ***Date.UTC***. Method **Date.parse** receives as its argument a string representing a date and time, and returns the number of milliseconds between midnight, January 1, 1970 and the specified date and time. This value can be converted to a **Date** object with the statement

```
var theDate = new Date( numberOfMilliseconds );
```

which passes to the **Date** constructor the number of milliseconds since midnight, January 1, 1970 for the **Date** object.

Method **parse** converts the string using the following rules:

- Short dates can be specified in the form **MM-DD-YY**, **MM-DD-YYYY**, **MM/DD/YY** or **MM/DD/YYYY**. The month and day are not required to be two digits.
- Long dates that specify the complete month name (e.g., "January"), date and year can specify the month, date and year in any order.
- Text in parentheses within the string is treated as a comment and ignored. Commas and whitespace characters are treated as delimiters.
- All month and day names must have at least two characters. The names are not required to be unique. If the names are identical, the name is resolved as the last match (e.g., "Ju" represents "July" rather than "June").
- If the name of the day of the week is supplied, it is ignored.
- All standard time zones (e.g., EST for Eastern Standard Time), Universal Coordinated Time (UTC) and Greenwich Mean Time (GMT) are recognized.
- When specifying hours, minutes and seconds, separate each by colons.
- When using 24-hour clock format, "PM" should not be used for times after 12 noon.

Date method **UTC** returns the number of milliseconds between midnight, January 1, 1970 and the date and time specified as its arguments. The arguments to the **UTC** method include the required *year*, *month* and *date*, and the optional *hours*, *minutes*, *seconds* and *milliseconds*. If any of the *hours*, *minutes*, *seconds* or *milliseconds* arguments is not specified, a zero is supplied in its place. For the *hours*, *minutes* and *seconds* arguments, if the argument to the right of any of these arguments in the argument list is specified, that argument must also be specified (e.g., if the *minutes* argument is specified, the *hours* argument must be specified; if the *milliseconds* argument is specified, all the arguments must be specified). As with the result of **Date.parse**, the result of **Date.UTC** can be converted to a **Date** object by creating a new **Date** object with the result of **Date.UTC** as its argument.

12.6 Boolean and Number Objects

JavaScript provides the **Boolean** and **Number** objects as object *wrappers* for boolean **true/false** values and numbers, respectively. These wrappers define methods and properties useful in manipulating boolean values and numbers.

When a JavaScript program requires boolean value, JavaScript automatically creates a **Boolean** object to store the value. JavaScript programmers can create **Boolean** objects explicitly with the statement

```
var b = new Boolean( booleanValue );
```

The constructor argument *booleanValue* specifies whether the value of the **Boolean** object should be **true** or **false**. If *booleanValue* is **false**, **0**, **null**, **Number.NaN** or the empty string (**""**), or if no argument is supplied, the new **Boolean** object contains **false**. Otherwise, the new **Boolean** object contains **true**. Figure 12.10 summarizes the methods of the **Boolean** object.

Method	Description
toString()	Returns the string "true" if the value of the **Boolean** object is true; otherwise, returns the string "false."
valueOf()	Returns the value **true** if the **Boolean** object is **true**; otherwise, returns **false**.

Fig. 12.10 Methods of the **Boolean** object.

JavaScript automatically creates **Number** objects to store numeric values in a JavaScript program. JavaScript programmers can create a **Number** object with the statement

```
var n = new Number( numericValue );
```

The constructor argument *numericValue* is the number to store in the object. Although you can explicitly create **Number** objects, normally the JavaScript interpreter creates them as needed. Figure 12.11 summarizes the methods and properties of the **Number** object.

Method or Property	Description
toString(*radix* **)**	Returns the string representation of the number. The optional *radix* argument (a number from 2 to 36) specifies the number's base. For example, radix 2 results in the binary representation of the number, 8 results in the octal representation, 10 results in the decimal representation and 16 results in the hexadecimal representation. See Appendix D "Number Systems" for a review of the binary, octal, decimal and hexadecimal number systems.

Fig. 12.11 Methods and properties of the **Number** object.

Method or Property	Description
valueOf()	Returns the numeric value.
Number.MAX_VALUE	This property represents the largest value that can be stored in a JavaScript program—approximately 1.79E+308
Number.MIN_VALUE	This property represents the smallest value that can be stored in a JavaScript program—approximately 2.22E–308
Number.NaN	This property represents *not a number*—a value returned from arithmetic expressions that do not result in a number (e.g., the expression **parseInt("hello")** cannot convert the string **"hello"** into a number, so **parseInt** would return **Number.NaN**). To determine whether a value is **NaN**, test the result with function **isNaN** which returns **true** if the value is **NaN**; otherwise, it returns **false**.
Number.NEGATIVE_INFINITY	This property represents a value less than **-Number.MAX_VALUE**.
Number.POSITIVE_INFINITY	This property represents a value greater than **Number.MAX_VALUE**.

Fig. 12.11 Methods and properties of the **Number** object.

12.7 JavaScript Internet and World Wide Web Resources

www.javascript.com
JavaScript.com provides JavaScript tips and articles.

www.iboost.com/build/programming/js/tutorial/885.htm
This page provides a tutorial on JavaScript objects.

www.cs.uidaho.edu/~acm/javascript/jsdoc
This site provides a list of JavaScript language features and a short reference section that includes objects.

www.javascriptsearch.com
This site provides a variety of JavaScript examples.

www.a1javascripts.com
This site provides JavaScript examples, links, tutorials and tools.

SUMMARY

- Objects are a natural way of thinking about the world.
- Because JavaScript uses objects to perform many tasks, JavaScript is commonly referred to as an object-based programming language.
- Humans think in terms of objects. We have the marvelous ability of abstraction, which enables us to view screen images as objects such as people, planes, trees and mountains rather than as individual dots of color (called pixels for "picture elements"). All objects have attributes and exhibit behaviors. Humans learn about objects by studying their attributes and observing their behaviors.
- Objects encapsulate data (attributes) and methods (behavior).

- Objects have the property of information hiding.
- Programs communicate with objects by using well-defined interfaces.
- World Wide Web browsers have a set of objects that encapsulate the elements of an XHTML document and expose to a JavaScript programmer attributes and behaviors that enable a JavaScript program to interact with (or script) the elements (i.e., objects) in an XHTML document.
- **Math** object methods allow programmers to perform many common mathematical calculations.
- An object's methods are called by writing the name of the object followed by a dot operator (**.**) and the name of the method. In parentheses following the method name is the argument (or a comma-separated list of arguments) to the method.
- Invoking (or calling) a method of an object is called "sending a message to the object."
- Characters are the fundamental building blocks of JavaScript programs. Every program is composed of a sequence of characters that—when grouped together meaningfully—is interpreted by the computer as a series of instructions used to accomplish a task.
- A string is a series of characters treated as a single unit.
- A string may include letters, digits and various special characters, such as **+**, **-**, *****, **/**, **$** and others.
- String literals or string constants (often called anonymous **String** objects) are written as a sequence of characters in double quotation marks or single quotation marks.
- String method **charAt** returns the character at a specific index in a string. Indices for the characters in a string start at 0 (the first character) and go up to (but not including) the string's **length** (i.e., if the string contains five characters, the indices are 0 through 4). If the index is outside the bounds of the string, the method returns an empty string.
- **String** method **charCodeAt** returns the Unicode value of the character at a specific index in a string. If the index is outside the bounds of the string, the method returns **NaN**. **String** method **fromCharCode** creates a string from a list of Unicode values.
- **String** method **toLowerCase** returns the lowercase version of a string. **String** method **toUpperCase** returns the uppercase version of a string.
- **String** method **indexOf** determines the location of the first occurrence of its argument in the string used to call the method. If the substring is found, the index at which the first occurrence of the substring begins is returned; otherwise, **-1** is returned. This method receives an optional second argument specifying the index from which to begin the search.
- **String** method **lastIndexOf** determines the location of the last occurrence of its argument in the string used to call the method. If the substring is found, the index at which the first occurrence of the substring begins is returned; otherwise, **-1** is returned. This method receives an optional second argument specifying the index from which to begin the search.
- The process of breaking a string into tokens is called tokenization. Tokens are separated from one another by delimiters, typically white-space characters such as blank, tab, newline and carriage return. Other characters may also be used as delimiters to separate tokens.
- **String** method **split** breaks a string into its component tokens. The argument to method **split** is the delimiter string—the string that determines the end of each token in the original string. Method **split** returns an array of strings containing the tokens.
- **String** method **substring** returns the substring from the starting index (its first argument) up to but not including the ending index (its second argument). If the ending index is greater than the length of the string, the substring returned includes the characters from the starting index to the end of the original string.
- **String** method **anchor** wraps the string that calls the method in XHTML element **<a></a>** with the **name** of the anchor supplied as the argument to the method.

- **String** method **blink** makes a string blink in a Web page by wrapping the string that calls the method in a **<blink></blink>** XHTML element.
- **String** method **fixed** displays text in a fixed-width font by wrapping the string that calls the method in a **<tt></tt>** XHTML element.
- **String** method **strike** displays struck-out text (i.e., text with a line through it) by wrapping the string that calls the method in a **<strike></strike>** XHTML element.
- **String** method **sub** displays subscript text by wrapping the string that calls the method in a **** XHTML element.
- **String** method **sup** displays superscript text by wrapping the string that calls the method in a **** XHTML element.
- **String** method **link** creates a hyperlink by wrapping the string that calls the method in XHTML element **<a></a>**. The target of the hyperlink (i.e, value of the **href** property) is the argument to the method and can be any URL.
- JavaScript's **Date** object provides methods for date and time manipulations.
- Date and time processing can be performed based on the computer's local time zone or based on World Time Standard's Universal Coordinated Time (UTC)—formerly called Greenwich Mean Time (GMT).
- Most methods of the **Date** object have a local time zone and a UTC version.
- **Date** method **parse** receives as its argument a string representing a date and time and returns the number of milliseconds between midnight, January 1, 1970 and the specified date and time.
- **Date** method **UTC** returns the number of milliseconds between midnight, January 1, 1970 and the date and time specified as its arguments. The arguments to the **UTC** method include the required year, month and date, and the optional hours, minutes, seconds and milliseconds. If any of the hours, minutes, seconds or milliseconds arguments is not specified, a zero is supplied in its place. For the hours, minutes and seconds arguments, if the argument to the right of any of these arguments is specified, that argument must also be specified (e.g., if the minutes argument is specified, the hours argument must be specified; if the milliseconds argument is specified, all the arguments must be specified).
- JavaScript provides the **Boolean** and **Number** objects as object wrappers for boolean **true**/**false** values and numbers, respectively.
- When a boolean value is required in a JavaScript program, JavaScript automatically creates a **Boolean** object to store the value.
- JavaScript programmers can create **Boolean** objects explicitly with the statement

```
var b = new Boolean( booleanValue );
```

- The argument *booleanValue* specifies whether the value of the **Boolean** object should be **true** or **false**. If *booleanValue* is **false**, **0**, **null**, **Number.NaN** or the empty string (**""**), or if no argument is supplied, the new **Boolean** object contains **false**. Otherwise, the new **Boolean** object contains **true**.
- JavaScript automatically creates **Number** objects to store numeric values in a JavaScript program.
- JavaScript programmers can create a **Number** object with the statement

```
var n = new Number( numericValue );
```

- The argument *numericValue* is the number to store in the object. Although you can explicitly create **Number** objects, normally they are created when needed by the JavaScript interpreter.

TERMINOLOGY

abs method of **Math**
abstraction
anchor method of **String**
anonymous **String** object
attribute
behavior
blink method of **String**
Boolean object
bounds of the string
ceil method of **Math**
character
charAt method of **String**
charCodeAt method of **String**
concat method of **String**
cos method of **Math**
date
Date object
delimiters
double quotation marks
E property of **Math**
empty string
encapsulation
ending index
exp method of **Math**
fixed method of **String**
floor method of **Math**
fromCharCode method of **String**
getDate method of **Date**
getDay method of **Date**
getFullYear method of **Date**
getHours method of **Date**
getMilliseconds method of **Date**
getMinutes method of **Date**
getMonth method of **Date**
getSeconds method of **Date**
getTime method of **Date**
getTimezoneOffset method of **Date**
getUTCDate method of **Date**
getUTCDay method of **Date**
getUTCFullYear method of **Date**
getUTCHours method of **Date**
getUTCMilliSeconds method of **Date**
getUTCMinutes method of **Date**
getUTCMonth method of **Date**
getUTCSeconds method of **Date**
Greenwich Mean Time (GMT)
hiding
index in a string
indexOf method of **String**
information hiding
lastIndexOf method of **String**
link method of **String**
LN10 property of **Math**
LN2 property of **Math**
local time zone
log method of **Math**
LOG10E property of **Math**
LOG2E property of **Math**
Math object
max method of **Math**
MAX_SIZE property of **Number**
min method of **Math**
MIN_SIZE property of **Number**
NaN property of **Number**
NEGATIVE_INFINITY property of **Number**
Number object
object
object wrapper
object-based programming language
parse method of **Date**
PI property of **Math**
POSITIVE_INFINITY property of **Number**
pow method of **Math**
round method of **Math**
search a string
sending a message to an object
setDate method of **Date**
setFullYear method of **Date**
setHours method of **Date**
setMilliSeconds method of **Date**
setMinutes method of **Date**
setMonth method of **Date**
setSeconds method of **Date**
setTime method of **Date**
setUTCDate method of **Date**
setUTCFullYear method of **Date**
setUTCHours method of **Date**
setUTCMilliseconds method of **Date**
setUTCMinutes method of **Date**
setUTCMonth method of **Date**
setUTCSeconds method of **Date**
sin method of **Math**
single quotation marks
slice method of **String**
special characters
split method of **String**
sqrt method of **Math**
SQRT1_2 property of **Math**

SQRT2 property of **Math**
starting index
strike method of **String**
string
string constant
string literal
sub method of **String**
substr method of **String**
substring
substring method of **String**
sup method of **String**
sup method of **String**
tan method of **Math**
time
token
tokenization
toLocaleString method of **Date**
toLowerCase method of **String**
toString method of **Date**
toString method of **String**
toUpperCase method of **String**
toUTCString method of **Date**
Unicode
Universal Coordinated Time (UTC)
UTC method of **Date**
valueOf method of **Boolean**
valueOf method of **Date**
valueOf method of **Number**
valueOf method of **String**
well-defined interfaces
wrap in XHTML tags

SELF-REVIEW EXERCISES

12.1 Fill in the blanks in each of the following statements:

a) Because JavaScript uses objects to perform many tasks, JavaScript is commonly referred to as an __________.
b) All objects have __________ and exhibit __________.
c) The methods of the __________ object allow programmers to perform many common mathematical calculations.
d) Invoking (or calling) a method of an object is referred to as __________.
e) String literals or string constants are written as a sequence of characters in __________ or __________.
f) Indices for the characters in a string start at __________.
g) **String** methods __________ and __________ search for the first and last occurrence of a substring in a **String**, respectively.
h) The process of breaking a string into tokens is called __________.
i) **String** method __________ formats a **String** as a hyperlink.
j) Date and time processing can be performed based on the __________ or based on World Time Standard's __________.
k) **Date** method __________ receives as its argument a string representing a date and time, and returns the number of milliseconds between midnight, January 1, 1970 and the specified date and time.

ANSWERS TO SELF-REVIEW EXERCISES

12.1 a) object-based programming language. b) attributes, behaviors. c) **Math**. d) sending a message to the object. e) double quotation marks, single quotation marks. f) 0. g) **indexOf**, **lastIndexOf**. h) tokenization. i) **link**. j) computer's local time zone, Universal Coordinated Time (UTC). k) **parse**.

EXERCISES

12.2 Write a script that tests whether the examples of the **Math** method calls shown in Fig. 12.1 actually produce the indicated results.

12.3 Write a script that tests as many of the **Math** library functions in Fig. 12.1 as you can. Exercise each of these functions by having your program display tables of return values for a diversity of argument values in an XHTML **textarea**.

12.4 **Math** method **floor** may be used to round a number to a specific decimal place. For example, the statement

```
y = Math.floor( x * 10 + .5 ) / 10;
```

rounds **x** to the tenths position (the first position to the right of the decimal point). The statement

```
y = Math.floor( x * 100 + .5 ) / 100;
```

rounds **x** to the hundredths position (i.e., the second position to the right of the decimal point). Write a script that defines four functions to round a number **x** in various ways:

a) **roundToInteger(number)**
b) **roundToTenths(number)**
c) **roundToHundredths(number)**
d) **roundToThousandths(number)**

For each value read, your program should display the original value, the number rounded to the nearest integer, the number rounded to the nearest tenth, the number rounded to the nearest hundredth and the number rounded to the nearest thousandth.

12.5 Modify the solution to Exercise 12.4 to use **Math** method **round** instead of method **floor**.

12.6 Write a script that uses relational and equality operators to compare two **String**s input by the user through an XHTML form. Output in an XHTML **textarea** whether the first string is less than, equal to or greater than the second.

12.7 Write a script that uses random number generation to create sentences. Use four arrays of strings called **article**, **noun**, **verb** and **preposition**. Create a sentence by selecting a word at random from each array in the following order: **article**, **noun**, **verb**, **preposition**, **article** and **noun**. As each word is picked, concatenate it to the previous words in the sentence. The words should be separated by spaces. When the final sentence is output, it should start with a capital letter and end with a period. The program should generate 20 sentences and output them to an XHTML **textarea**.

The arrays should be filled as follows: the **article** array should contain the articles **"the"**, **"a"**, **"one"**, **"some"** and **"any"**; the **noun** array should contain the nouns **"boy"**, **"girl"**, **"dog"**, **"town"** and **"car"**; the **verb** array should contain the verbs **"drove"**, **"jumped"**, **"ran"**, **"walked"** and **"skipped"**; the **preposition** array should contain the prepositions **"to"**, **"from"**, **"over"**, **"under"** and **"on"**.

After the preceding script is written, modify the script to produce a short story consisting of several of these sentences.

12.8 *(Limericks)* A limerick is a humorous five-line verse in which the first and second lines rhyme with the fifth, and the third line rhymes with the fourth. Using techniques similar to those developed in Exercise 12.7, write a script that produces random limericks. Polishing this program to produce good limericks is a challenging problem, but the result will be worth the effort!

12.9 *(Pig Latin)* Write a script that encodes English language phrases into pig Latin. Pig Latin is a form of coded language often used for amusement. Many variations exist in the methods used to form pig Latin phrases. For simplicity, use the following algorithm:

To form a pig Latin phrase from an English language phrase, tokenize the phrase into an array of words using **String** method **split**. To translate each English word into a pig Latin word, place the first letter of the English word at the end of the word and add the letters "**ay**." Thus the word "**jump**" becomes "**umpjay**," the word "**the**" becomes "**hetay**" and the word "**computer**" becomes "**omputercay**." Blanks between words remain as blanks. Assume the following: The English phrase consists of words separated by blanks, there are no punctuation marks and all words have two or more letters. Function **printLatinWord** should display each word. Each token (i.e., word in the sentence) is passed to method **printLatinWord** to print the pig Latin word. Enable the user to input the sentence through an XHTML form. Keep a running display of all the converted sentences in an XHTML **textarea**.

12.10 Write a script that inputs a telephone number as a string in the form **(555) 555-5555**. The script should use **String** method **split** to extract the area code as a token, the first three digits of the phone number as a token and the last four digits of the phone number as a token. Display the area code in one text field and the seven-digit phone number in another text field.

12.11 Write a script that inputs a line of text, tokenizes the line with **String** method **split** and outputs the tokens in reverse order.

12.12 Write a script that inputs text from an XHTML form and outputs the text in uppercase and lowercase letters.

12.13 Write a script that inputs several lines of text and a search character and uses **String** method **indexOf** to determine the number of occurrences of the character in the text.

12.14 Write a script based on the program of Exercise 12.13 that inputs several lines of text and uses **String** method **indexOf** to determine the total number of occurrences of each letter of the alphabet in the text. Uppercase and lowercase letters should be counted together. Store the totals for each letter in an array, and print the values in tabular format in an XHTML **textarea** after the totals have been determined.

12.15 Write a script that reads a series of strings and outputs in an XHTML **textarea** only those strings beginning with the letter "**b**."

12.16 Write a script that reads a series of strings and outputs in an XHTML **textarea** only those strings ending with the letters "**ED**."

12.17 Write a script that inputs an integer code for a character and displays the corresponding character.

12.18 Modify your solution to Exercise 12.17 so that it generates all possible three-digit codes in the range 000 to 255 and attempts to display the corresponding characters. Display the results in an XHTML **textarea**.

12.19 Write your own version of the **String** method **indexOf** and use it in a script.

12.20 Write your own version of the **String** method **lastIndexOf** and use it in a script.

12.21 Write a program that reads a five-letter word from the user and produces all possible three-letter words that can be derived from the letters of the five-letter word. For example, the three-letter words produced from the word "bathe" include the commonly used words "ate," "bat," "bet," "tab," "hat," "the" and "tea." Output the results in an XHTML **textarea**.

12.22 *(Printing Dates in Various Formats)* Dates are printed in several common formats. Write a script that reads a date from an XHTML form and creates a **Date** object in which to store that date. Then, use the various methods of the **Date** object that convert **Date**s into strings to display the date in several formats.

SPECIAL SECTION: ADVANCED STRING MANIPULATION EXERCISES

The preceding exercises are keyed to the text and designed to test the reader's understanding of fundamental string manipulation concepts. This section includes a collection of intermediate and advanced string manipulation exercises. The reader should find these problems challenging, yet entertaining. The problems vary considerably in difficulty. Some require an hour or two of program writing and implementation. Others are useful for lab assignments that might require two or three weeks of study and implementation. Some are challenging term projects.

12.23 *(Text Analysis)* The availability of computers with string manipulation capabilities has resulted in some rather interesting approaches to analyzing the writings of great authors. Much attention has been focused on whether William Shakespeare ever lived. Some scholars believe there is substantial evidence indicating that Christopher Marlowe or other authors actually penned the masterpieces attributed to Shakespeare. Researchers have used computers to find similarities in the writings of these two authors. This exercise examines three methods for analyzing texts with a computer.

a) Write a script that reads several lines of text from the keyboard and prints a table indicating the number of occurrences of each letter of the alphabet in the text. For example, the phrase

```
To be, or not to be: that is the question:
```

contains one "a," two "b's," no "c's," etc.

b) Write a script that reads several lines of text and prints a table indicating the number of one-letter words, two-letter words, three-letter words, etc. appearing in the text. For example, the phrase

```
Whether 'tis nobler in the mind to suffer
```

contains

Word length	Occurrences
1	0
2	2
3	1
4	2 (including 'tis)
5	0
6	2
7	1

c) Write a script that reads several lines of text and prints a table indicating the number of occurrences of each different word in the text. The first version of your program should include the words in the table in the same order in which they appear in the text. For example, the lines

```
To be, or not to be: that is the question:
Whether 'tis nobler in the mind to suffer
```

contain the words "to" three times, the word "be" two times, the word "or" once, etc. A more interesting (and useful) printout should then be attempted in which the words are sorted alphabetically.

12.24 *(Check Protection)* Computers are frequently employed in check-writing systems such as payroll and accounts payable applications. Many strange stories circulate regarding weekly paychecks being printed (by mistake) for amounts in excess of $1 million. Incorrect amounts are printed by computerized check-writing systems because of human error and/or machine failure. Systems designers build controls into their systems to prevent such erroneous checks from being issued.

Another serious problem is the intentional alteration of a check amount by someone who intends to cash a check fraudulently. To prevent a dollar amount from being altered, most computerized check-writing systems employ a technique called *check protection.*

Checks designed for imprinting by computer contain a fixed number of spaces in which the computer may print an amount. Suppose a paycheck contains eight blank spaces in which the computer is supposed to print the amount of a weekly paycheck. If the amount is large, then all eight of those spaces will be filled, for example:

```
1,230.60 (check amount)
--------
12345678 (position numbers)
```

On the other hand, if the amount is less than $1000, then several of the spaces would ordinarily be left blank. For example,

```
   99.87
--------
12345678
```

contains three blank spaces. If a check is printed with blank spaces, it is easier for someone to alter the amount of the check. To prevent a check from being altered, many check-writing systems insert *leading asterisks* to protect the amount as follows:

```
***99.87
--------
12345678
```

Write a script that inputs a dollar amount to be printed on a check, and then prints the amount in check-protected format with leading asterisks if necessary. Assume that nine spaces are available for printing the amount.

12.25 *(Writing the Word Equivalent of a Check Amount)* Continuing the discussion of the previous exercise, we reiterate the importance of designing check-writing systems to prevent alteration of check amounts. One common security method requires that the check amount be written both in numbers and "spelled out" in words as well. Even if someone is able to alter the numerical amount of the check, it is extremely difficult to change the amount in words.

Many computerized check-writing systems do not print the amount of the check in words. Perhaps the main reason for this omission is the fact that most high-level languages used in commercial applications do not contain adequate string manipulation features. Another reason is that the logic for writing word equivalents of check amounts is somewhat involved.

Write a script that inputs a numeric check amount and writes the word equivalent of the amount. For example, the amount 112.43 should be written as

```
ONE HUNDRED TWELVE and 43/100
```

12.26 *(Morse Code)* Perhaps the most famous of all coding schemes is the Morse code, developed by Samuel Morse in 1832 for use with the telegraph system. The Morse code assigns a series of dots and dashes to each letter of the alphabet, each digit and a few special characters (such as period, comma, colon and semicolon). In sound-oriented systems, the dot represents a short sound and the dash represents a long sound. Other representations of dots and dashes are used with light-oriented systems and signal-flag systems.

Separation between words is indicated by a space, or, quite simply, by the absence of a dot or dash. In a sound-oriented system, a space is indicated by a short period of time during which no sound is transmitted. The international version of the Morse code appears in Fig. 12.12.

Write a script that reads an English language phrase and encodes the phrase into Morse code. Also write a program that reads a phrase in Morse code and converts the phrase into the English language equivalent. Use one blank between each Morse-coded letter and three blanks between each Morse-coded word.

12.27 *(Metric Conversion Program)* Write a script that will assist the user with metric conversions. Your program should allow the user to specify the names of the units as strings (i.e., centimeters, liters, grams, etc. for the metric system and inches, quarts, pounds, etc. for the English system) and should respond to simple questions such as

```
"How many inches are in 2 meters?"
"How many liters are in 10 quarts?"
```

Your program should recognize invalid conversions. For example, the question

```
"How many feet in 5 kilograms?"
```

is not a meaningful question because **`"feet"`** is a unit of length while **`"kilograms"`** is a unit of mass.

Character	Code	Character	Code
A	.-	T	-
B	-...	U	..-
C	-.-.	V	...-
D	-..	W	.--
E	.	X	-..-
F	..-.	Y	-.--
G	--.	Z	--..
H	....		
I	..	Digits	
J	.---	1	.----
K	-.-	2	..---
L	.-..	3	...--
M	--	4	....-
N	-.	5	.....
O	---	6	-....
P	.--.	7	--...
Q	--.-	8	---..
R	.-.	9	----.
S	...	0	-----

Fig. 12.12 Letters of the alphabet as expressed in international Morse code.

SPECIAL SECTION: CHALLENGING STRING MANIPULATION PROJECTS

12.28 *(Project: A Spelling Checker)* Many popular word processing software packages have built-in spell checkers.

In this project, you are asked to develop your own spell-checker utility. We make suggestions to help get you started. You should then consider adding more capabilities. Use a computerized dictionary (if you have access to one) as a source of words.

Why do we type so many words with incorrect spellings? In some cases, it is because we simply do not know the correct spelling, so we make a "best guess." In some cases, it is because we transpose two letters (e.g., "defualt" instead of "default"). Sometimes we double-type a letter accidentally (e.g., "hanndy" instead of "handy"). Sometimes we type a nearby key instead of the one we intended (e.g., "biryhday" instead of "birthday"). And so on.

Design and implement a spell-checker application in JavaScript. Your program should maintain an array **`wordList`** of strings. Enable the user to enter these strings.

Your program should ask a user to enter a word. The program should then look up that word in the **`wordList`** array. If the word is present in the array, your program should print "**`Word is spelled correctly`**."

If the word is not present in the array, your program should print "**`word is not spelled correctly`**." Then your program should try to locate other words in **`wordList`** that might be the word the user intended to type. For example, you can try all possible single transpositions of adjacent letters to discover that the word "default" is a direct match to a word in **`wordList`**. Of course, this implies that your program will check all other single transpositions, such as "edfault," "dfeault," "deafult," "defalut" and "defautl." When you find a new word that matches one in **`wordList`**, print that word in a message, such as "**`Did you mean "default?"`**."

Implement other tests, such as replacing each double letter with a single letter and any other tests you can develop to improve the value of your spell checker.

12.29 *(Project: Crossword Puzzle Generator)* Most people have worked a crossword puzzle, but few have ever attempted to generate one. Generating a crossword puzzle is suggested here as a string manipulation project requiring substantial sophistication and effort.

There are many issues the programmer must resolve to get even the simplest crossword puzzle generator program working. For example, how does one represent the grid of a crossword puzzle inside the computer? Should one use a series of strings, or should double-subscripted arrays be used?

The programmer needs a source of words (i.e., a computerized dictionary) that can be directly referenced by the program. In what form should these words be stored to facilitate the complex manipulations required by the program?

The really ambitious reader will want to generate the "clues" portion of the puzzle, in which the brief hints for each "across" word and each "down" word are printed for the puzzle worker. Merely printing a version of the blank puzzle itself is not a simple problem.

13

Dynamic HTML: Object Model and Collections

Objectives

- To use the Dynamic HTML Object Model and scripting to create dynamic Web pages.
- To understand the Dynamic HTML object hierarchy.
- To use the **`all`** and **`children`** collections to enumerate all of the XHTML elements of a Web page.
- To use dynamic styles and dynamic positioning.
- To use the **`frames`** collection to access objects in a separate frame on your Web page.
- To use the **`navigator`** object to determine which browser is being used to access your page.

Absolute freedom of navigation upon the seas...
Woodrow Wilson

Our children may learn about heroes of the past. Our task is to make ourselves architects of the future.
Jomo Mzee Kenyatta

The complex is made over into the simple, the hypothetical into the dogmatic, and the relative into an absolute.
Walter Lippmann

The thing that impresses me most about America is the way parents obey their children.
Duke of Windsor

The test of greatness is the page of history.
William Hazlitt

Outline

13.1 Introduction[1]

In this chapter we introduce the Dynamic HTML object model. The object model allows Web authors to control the presentation of their pages and gives them access to all elements on their Web page. The whole Web page—elements, forms, frames, tables, etc.—is represented in an object hierarchy. Using scripting, an author is able to retrieve and modify any properties or attributes of the Web page dynamically.

This chapter begins by examining several of the objects available in the object hierarchy. Toward the end of the chapter there is a diagram of the extensive object hierarchy, with explanations of the various objects and properties and links to Web sites with further information on the topic.

Software Engineering Observation 13.1

With Dynamic HTML, XHTML elements can be treated as objects and attributes of these elements can be treated as properties of those objects. Then, objects identified with an **`id`** *attribute can be scripted with languages like JavaScript and VBScript (Chapter 24) to achieve dynamic effects.*

13.2 Object Referencing

The simplest way to reference an element is by using the element's **`id`** attribute. The element is represented as an object, and its various XHTML attributes become properties that can be manipulated by scripting. Figure 13.1 uses this method to read the **`innerText`** *property* of a **`p`** element.

1. Microsoft Dynamic HTML (discussed in Chapters 13–18) and Netscape Dynamic HTML are incompatible. In this book, we focus on Microsoft Dynamic HTML. We have tested all of the Dynamic HTML examples in Microsoft Internet Explorer 5.5 and Netscape® Communicator® 6. All of these examples execute in Microsoft Internet Explorer; most do not execute in Netscape Communicator 6. We have posted the testing results at **`www.deitel.com`**. The material we present in Chapter 19, Macromedia® Flash,™ executes properly in both of the latest Microsoft and Netscape browsers and enables you to achieve many of the effects of Dynamic HTML.

```
1  <?xml version = "1.0"?>
2  <!DOCTYPE html PUBLIC "-//W3C//DTD XHTML 1.0 Strict//EN"
3     "http://www.w3.org/TR/xhtml1/DTD/xhtml1-strict.dtd">
4
5  <!-- Fig. 13.1: reference.html  -->
6  <!-- Object Model Introduction -->
7
8  <html xmlns = "http://www.w3.org/1999/xhtml">
9     <head>
10       <title>Object Model</title>
11
12       <script type = "text/javascript">
13          <!--
14          function start()
15          {
16             alert( pText.innerText );
17             pText.innerText = "Thanks for coming.";
18          }
19          // -->
20       </script>
21
22    </head>
23
24    <body onload = "start()">
25       <p id = "pText">Welcome to our Web page!</p>
26    </body>
27 </html>
```

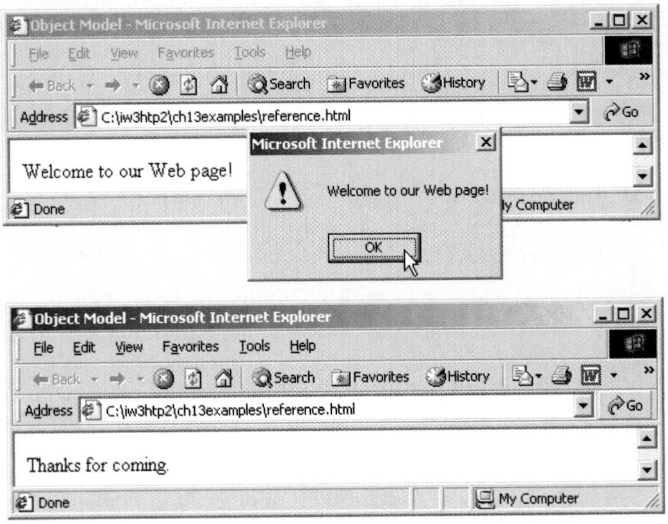

Fig. 13.1 Object referencing with the Dynamic HTML Object Model .

Line 24 uses the ***onload*** *event* to call the JavaScript **start** function when document loading completes. (Events are covered in depth in the next chapter.) Function **start** displays an **alert** box containing the value of **pText.innerText**. The object **pText** refers to the **p** element whose **id** is set to **pText** (line 25). The **innerText** property of the object refers to the text contained in that element (**Welcome to our Web page!**). Line 17 of function **start** sets the **innerText** property of **pText** to a different value. Changing the text displayed on screen in this manner is an example of a Dynamic HTML capability called *dynamic content*.

13.3 Collections all and children

Included in the Dynamic HTML Object Model is the notion of *collections*, which basically are arrays of related objects on a page. There are several special collections in the object model (several collections are listed in Fig. 13.10 and Fig. 13.11 at the end of this chapter). The Dynamic HTML Object Model includes a special collection, **all**. The **all** *collection* is a collection of all the XHTML elements in a document, in the order in which they appear. This provides an easy way of referring to any specific element, especially if it does not have an **id**. The script in Fig. 13.2 iterates through the **all** collection and displays the list of XHTML elements on the page by writing to the **innerHTML** *property* of a **p** element.

```
<?xml version = "1.0"?>
<!DOCTYPE html PUBLIC "-//W3C//DTD XHTML 1.0 Strict//EN"
   "http://www.w3.org/TR/xhtml1/DTD/xhtml1-strict.dtd">

<!-- Fig 13.2: all.html        -->
<!-- Using the all collection -->

<html xmlns = "http://www.w3.org/1999/xhtml">
   <head>
      <title>Object Model</title>

      <script type = "text/javascript">
         <!--
         var elements = "";

         function start()
         {
           for ( var loop = 0; loop < document.all.length; ++loop )
              elements += "<br />" + document.all[ loop ].tagName;

            pText.innerHTML += elements;
            alert( elements );
         }
         // -->
      </script>
   </head>

   <body onload = "start()">
      <p id = "pText">Elements on this Web page:</p>
   </body>
</html>
```

Fig. 13.2 Looping through the **all** collection (part 1 of 2).

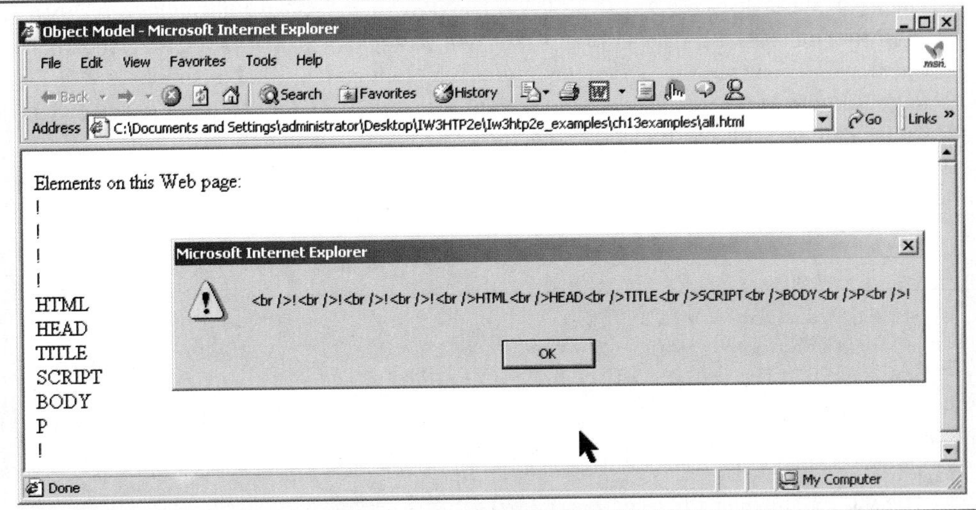

Fig. 13.2 Looping through the **all** collection (part 2 of 2).

Lines 18–19 in function **start** loop through the elements of the **all** collection and display each element's name. The **all** collection is a property of the **document** object (discussed in more detail later in this chapter). The **length** *property* of the **all** collection (and other collections) specifies the number of elements in the collection. For each element in the collection, we append to **elements** the name of the XHTML element (determined with the **tagName** *property*). When the loop terminates, we write the names of the elements to **pText.innerHTML**—the **innerHTML** *property* is similar to the **innerText** property, but it can include XHTML formatting. Note that line 1, lines 2–3 and all the comment elements are represented with a **tagName** property of **!** in the document.

When we use the **document.all** collection, we refer to all the XHTML elements in the document. However, every element has its own **all** collection, consisting of all the elements contained within that element. For example, the **body** element's **all** collection contains the **p** element in line 28.

A collection similar to the **all** collection is the **children** collection, which for a specific element contains that element's child elements. For example, an **html** element has only two children—the **head** element and the **body** element. Figure 13.3 uses the **children** collection to walk through all the elements in the document. When you look at the script in this XHTML document, do you notice anything different about this script's use of functions compared to the uses of functions in our prior scripts? The difference is that function **child** (defined at line 16) calls itself at line 25 in the program. This is a programming technique called *recursion*, which is an alternative problem-solving approach to looping and iteration. Recursion was introduced in Chapter 10.

Function **child** uses recursion to view all the elements on the page—it starts at the level of the **html** element (**document.all[4]** on line 38) and begins walking through all the children of that element. If it encounters an element that has its own children (line 24), it recursively calls the **child** function, passing the object of the new element through which the function should loop. As that loop finishes, the loop which called it proceeds to the next element in its own array of **children**. We use the **tagName** property to gather the names of the tags we encounter while looping through the document, and we place them in the string **elements**. The script adds **ul** and **li** tags to display the element in a hierarchical manner on the page. When the original call to function **child** completes, line 39 changes the **outerHTML** property of the **p** element **myDisplay** to string **elements**. Property **outerHTML** is similar to property **innerHTML** we introduced in the previous example, but it includes the enclosing XHTML tags (tags **<p id = "myDisplay">** and **</p>** in this case) as well as the content inside them.

```
1  <?xml version = "1.0"?>
2  <!DOCTYPE html PUBLIC "-//W3C//DTD XHTML 1.0 Strict//EN"
3     "http://www.w3.org/TR/xhtml1/DTD/xhtml1-strict.dtd">
4  
5  <!-- Fig 13.3: children.html -->
6  <!-- The children collection -->
7  
8  <html xmlns = "http://www.w3.org/1999/xhtml">
9     <head>
10       <title>Object Model</title>
11 
12       <script type = "text/javascript">
13          <!--
14          var elements = "<ul>";
15 
16          function child( object )
17          {
18             var loop = 0;
19 
20             elements += "<li>" + object.tagName + "<ul>";
21 
22             for ( loop = 0; loop < object.children.length; loop++ )
23             {
24                if ( object.children[ loop ].children.length )
25                   child( object.children[ loop ] );
26                else
27                   elements += "<li>" +
28                               object.children[ loop ].tagName +
29                               "</li>";
30             }
31 
32             elements += " </ul> ";
33          }
34          // -->
35       </script>
36    </head>
37 
38    <body onload = "child( document.all[ 4 ] );
39                    myDisplay.outerHTML += elements;">
40 
41       <p>Welcome to our <strong>Web</strong> page!</p>
42 
```

Fig. 13.3 Navigating the object hierarchy by using collection **children** (part 1 of 2).

```
         <p id = "myDisplay">
            Elements on this Web page:
         </p>

      </body>
   </html>
```

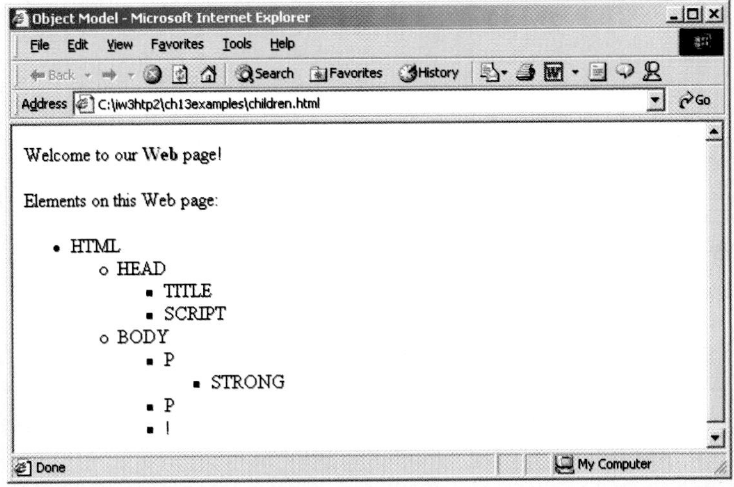

Fig. 13.3 Navigating the object hierarchy by using collection **children** (part 2 of 2).

13.4 Dynamic Styles

An element's style can be changed dynamically. Often such a change is made in response to user events, which are discussed in the next chapter. Figure 13.4 is a simple example of changing styles in response to user input.

Function **start**, in lines 14–20 **prompt**s the user to enter a color name, then sets the background color to that value. We refer to the background color as **document.body.style.backgroundColor**—the **body** property of the **document** object refers to the **body** element. We then use the **style** object (a property of most XHTML elements) to set the **background-color** CSS property. (This is referred to as **backgroundColor** in JavaScript, to avoid confusion with the subtraction (**-**) operator. This naming convention is consistent for most of the CSS properties. For example, **borderWidth** correlates to the **border-width** CSS property, and **fontFamily** correlates to the **font-family** CSS property).

```
1  <?xml version = "1.0"?>
2  <!DOCTYPE html PUBLIC "-//W3C//DTD XHTML 1.0 Strict//EN"
3     "http://www.w3.org/TR/xhtml1/DTD/xhtml1-strict.dtd">
4
5  <!-- Fig. 13.4: dynamicstyle.html -->
6  <!-- Dynamic Styles               -->
```

Fig. 13.4 Dynamic styles (part 1 of 2).

```

<html xmlns = "http://www.w3.org/1999/xhtml">
   <head>
      <title>Object Model</title>

      <script type = "text/javascript">
         <!--
         function start()
         {
            var inputColor = prompt(
               "Enter a color name for the " +
               "background of this page", "" );
            document.body.style.backgroundColor = inputColor;
         }
         // -->
      </script>
   </head>

   <body onload = "start()">
      <p>Welcome to our Web site!</p>
   </body>
</html>
```

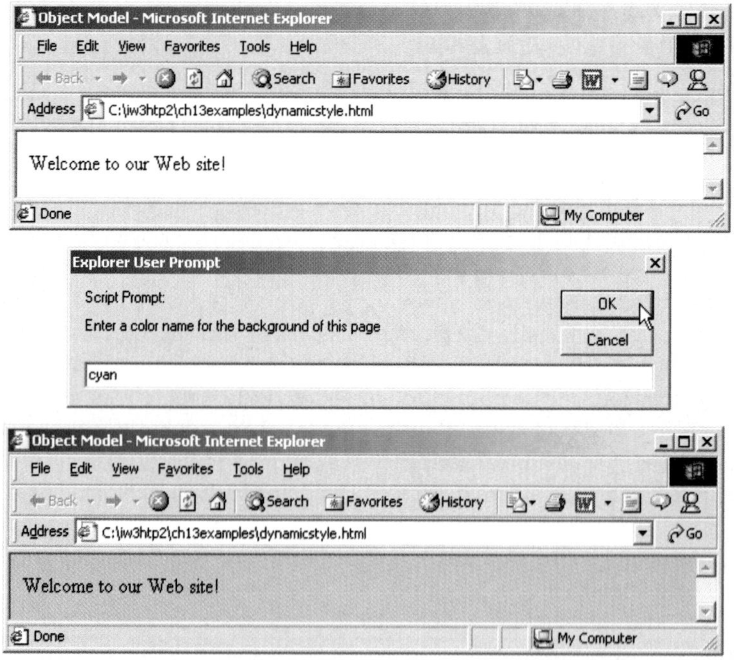

Fig. 13.4 Dynamic styles (part 2 of 2).

The Dynamic HTML object model also allows you to change the **`class`** attribute of an element—instead of changing many individual styles at a time, you can have preset style classes for easily altering element styles. Figure 13.5 prompts the user to enter the name of a style class, and then changes the screen text to that style.

```
<?xml version = "1.0"?>
<!DOCTYPE html PUBLIC "-//W3C//DTD XHTML 1.0 Strict//EN"
   "http://www.w3.org/TR/xhtml1/DTD/xhtml1-strict.dtd">

<!-- Fig. 13.5: dynamicstyle2.html -->
<!-- More Dynamic Styles          -->

<html xmlns = "http://www.w3.org/1999/xhtml">
   <head>
      <title>Object Model</title>

      <style type = "text/css">

         .bigText   { font-size: 3em;
                      font-weight: bold }

         .smallText { font-size: .75em }

      </style>

      <script type = "text/javascript">
         <!--
         function start()
         {
            var inputClass = prompt(
               "Enter a className for the text "  +
               "(bigText or smallText)", "" );
            pText.className = inputClass;
         }
         // -->
      </script>
   </head>

   <body onload = "start()">
      <p id = "pText">Welcome to our Web site!</p>
   </body>
</html>
```

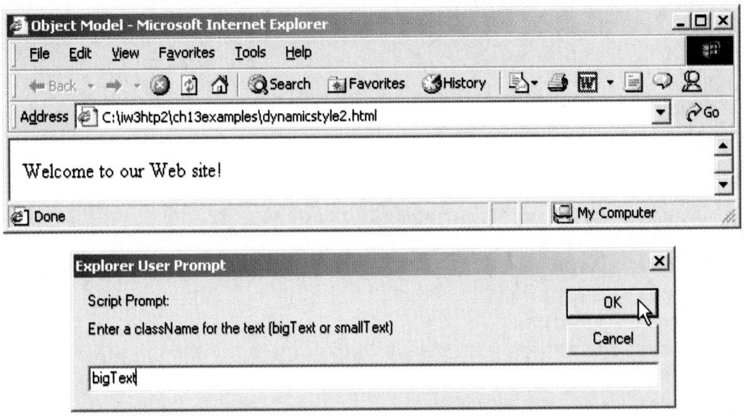

Fig. 13.5 Dynamic styles in action (part 1 of 2).

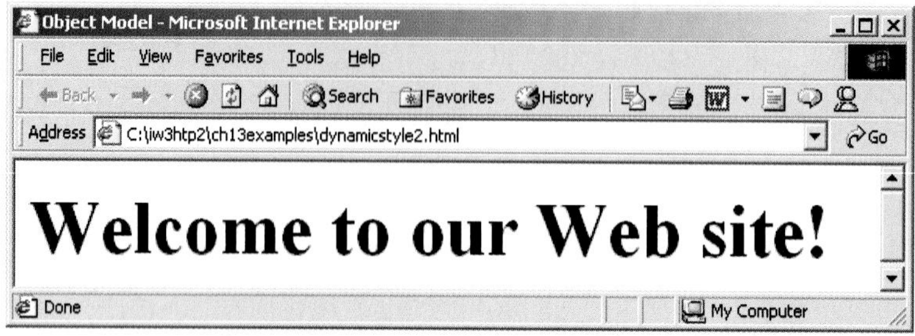

Fig. 13.5 Dynamic styles in action (part 2 of 2).

As in the previous example, we prompt the user for information—in this case, we ask for the name of a style class to apply, either **`bigText`** or **`smallText`**. Once we have this information, we then use the **`className`** property to change the style class of **`pText`**.

13.5 Dynamic Positioning

Another important feature of Dynamic HTML is *dynamic positioning*, by means of which XHTML elements can be positioned with scripting. This is done by declaring an element's CSS **`position`** property to be either **`absolute`** or **`relative`**, and then moving the element by manipulating any of the **`top`**, **`left`**, **`right`** or **`bottom`** CSS properties.

The example of Fig. 13.6 demonstrates dynamic positioning, dynamic styles and dynamic content—we vary the position of the element on the page by accessing its CSS **`left`** attribute, we use scripting to vary the **`color`**, **`fontFamily`** and **`fontSize`** attributes, and we use the element's **`innerHTML`** property to alter the content of the element.

```
<?xml version = "1.0"?>
<!DOCTYPE html PUBLIC "-//W3C//DTD XHTML 1.0 Strict//EN"
   "http://www.w3.org/TR/xhtml1/DTD/xhtml1-strict.dtd">

<!-- Fig. 13.6: dynamicposition.html -->
<!-- Dynamic Positioning              -->

<html xmlns = "http://www.w3.org/1999/xhtml">
   <head>
      <title>Dynamic Positioning</title>

      <script type = "text/javascript">
         <!--
         var speed = 5;
         var count = 10;
         var direction = 1;
         var firstLine = "Text growing";
         var fontStyle = [ "serif", "sans-serif", "monospace" ];
         var fontStylecount = 0;
```

Fig. 13.6 Dynamic positioning (part 1 of 3).

```

         function start()
         {
            window.setInterval( "run()", 100 );
         }

         function run()
         {
            count += speed;

            if ( ( count % 200 ) == 0 ) {
               speed *= -1;
               direction = !direction;

               pText.style.color =
                  ( speed < 0 ) ? "red" : "blue" ;
               firstLine =
                 ( speed < 0 ) ? "Text shrinking" : "Text growing";
               pText.style.fontFamily =
                  fontStyle[ ++fontStylecount % 3 ];
            }

            pText.style.fontSize = count / 3;
            pText.style.left = count;
            pText.innerHTML = firstLine + "<br /> Font size: " +
                              count + "px";
         }
         // -->
      </script>
   </head>

   <body onload = "start()">
      <p id = "pText" style = "position: absolute; left: 0;
                              font-family: serif; color: blue">
      Welcome!</p>
   </body>
</html>
```

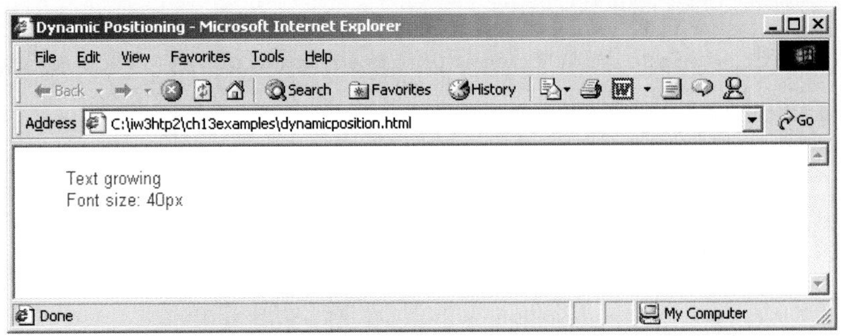

Fig. 13.6 Dynamic positioning (part 2 of 3).

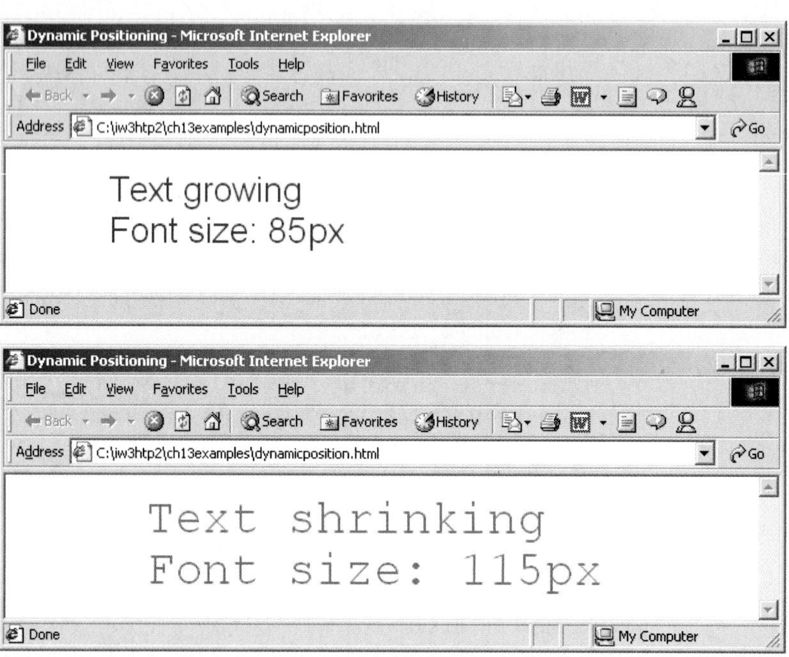

Fig. 13.6 Dynamic positioning (part 3 of 3).

To continuously update the **`p`** element's content, in line 23 we use a new function, ***`setInterval`***. This function takes two parameters—a function name, and how often to *run* that function (in this case, every **`100`** milliseconds). A similar JavaScript function is **`setTimeout`**, which takes the same parameters but instead waits the specified amount of time before calling the named function only once. There are also JavaScript functions for stopping either of these two timers—the **`clearTimeout`** and **`clearInterval`** functions. To stop a specific timer, the parameter you pass to either of these functions should be the value that the corresponding set time function returned. For example, if you started a **`setTimeout`** timer with

```
timer1 = window.setTimeout( "timedFunction()", 2000 );
```

you could then stop the timer by calling

```
window.clearTimeout( timer1 );
```

which would stop the timer before it fired.

13.6 Using the `frames` Collection

One problem that you might run into while developing applications is communication between frames. The referencing we have used certainly allows for access to objects and

XHTML elements on the same page, but what if those elements and objects are in different frames? Figure 13.7 and Fig. 13.8 solve this problem by using the **frames** collection.

```
<?xml version = "1.0"?>
<!DOCTYPE html PUBLIC "-//W3C//DTD XHTML 1.0 Frameset//EN"
   "http://www.w3.org/TR/xhtml1/DTD/xhtml1-frameset.dtd">

<!-- Fig. 13.7: index.html        -->
<!-- Using the frames collection -->

<html xmlns = "http://www.w3.org/1999/xhtml">
   <head>
      <title>Frames collection</title>
   </head>

   <frameset rows = "100, *">
      <frame src = "top.html" name = "upper" />
      <frame src = "" name = "lower" />
   </frameset>

</html>
```

Fig. 13.7 **frameset** file for cross-frame scripting.

```
<?xml version = "1.0"?>
<!DOCTYPE html PUBLIC "-//W3C//DTD XHTML 1.0 Strict//EN"
   "http://www.w3.org/TR/xhtml1/DTD/xhtml1-strict.dtd">

<!-- Fig. 13.8: top.html     -->
<!-- Cross-frame scripting -->

<html xmlns = "http://www.w3.org/1999/xhtml">
   <head>
      <title>The frames collection</title>

      <script type = "text/javascript">
         <!--
         function start()
         {
            var text = prompt( "What is your name?", "" );
            parent.frames( "lower" ).document.write(
               "<h1>Hello, " +  text + "</h1>" );
         }
         // -->
      </script>
   </head>

   <body onload = "start()">
      <h1>Cross-frame scripting!</h1>
   </body>
</html>
```

Fig. 13.8 Accessing other frames.

Fig. 13.8 Accessing other frames.

Lines 17–18 (Fig. 13.8) apply changes to the lower frame. To reference the lower frame, we first reference the **`parent`** frame of the current frame, then use the **`frames`** collection. We use a new notation here—**`frames( "lower" )`**—to refer to the element in the frames collection with an **`id`** or **`name`** of lower. The **`<frame>`** tag for the lower frame appears second in the XHTML file, so the frame is second in the **`frames`** collection. We then use the familiar **`document.write`** method in that frame to update it with the user input from our **`prompt`** on line 17.

13.7 `navigator` Object

One of the most appealing aspects of the Internet is its diversity. Unfortunately, because of this diversity, sometimes standards are compromised. Each of the two most popular browsers currently on the market, Netscape's Communicator and Microsoft's Internet Explorer, has many features that give the Web author great control over the browser, but many of their features are incompatible. Each, however, supports the **`navigator`** object, which contains information about the Web browser that is viewing the page. This allows Web authors to determine which browser the user has—this is especially important when the page uses browser-specific features, because it allows the author to redirect users to pages that their browsers can display properly. Figure 13.9 demonstrates how to determine the type of browser that requests the document **navigator.html**.

```
<?xml version = "1.0"?>
<!DOCTYPE html PUBLIC "-//W3C//DTD XHTML 1.0 Strict//EN"
   "http://www.w3.org/TR/xhtml1/DTD/xhtml1-strict.dtd">

<!-- Fig 13.9: navigator.html    -->
<!-- Using the navigator object -->

<html xmlns = "http://www.w3.org/1999/xhtml">
   <head>
      <title>The navigator Object</title>

      <script type = "text/javascript">
         <!--
         function start()
         {
            if (navigator.appName=="Microsoft Internet Explorer")
            {
               if ( navigator.appVersion.substring( 1, 0 ) >= "4" )
                  document.location = "newIEversion.html";
               else
                  document.location = "oldIEversion.html";
            }
            else
               document.location = "NSversion.html";
         }
         // -->
      </script>
   </head>

   <body onload = "start()">
      <p>Redirecting your browser to the appropriate page,
      please wait...</p>
   </body>
</html>
```

Fig. 13.9 Using the **navigator** object to redirect users (part 1 of 2).

Fig. 13.9 Using the **navigator** object to redirect users (part 2 of 2).

When the page loads, the **onload** event calls function **start**, which checks the value of the property **navigator.appName**. This property of the **navigator** object contains the name of the browser application (for IE, this property is "**Microsoft Internet Explorer**"; for Netscape, it is "**Netscape**"). If the browser viewing this page is not Internet Explorer, in line 24 we redirect the browser to the document "**NSversion.html**" by assigning the document name to property **document.location**—the URL of the document being viewed. When a script assigns **document.location** a new URL, the browser immediately switches Web pages.

Line 18 checks the version of the browser with the **navigator.appVersion** property. The value of **appVersion** is not a simple integer, however—it is a string containing other information, such as the Operating System of the user's computer. Therefore, the script uses method **substring** to retrieve the first character of the string, which is the actual version number. If the version number is **4** or greater, we redirect to **newIEversion.html**. Otherwise, we redirect the browser to **oldIEversion.html**.

As we see here, the **navigator** object is crucial in providing browser-specific pages so that as many users as possible can view your site properly.

Portability Tip 13.1

Always make provisions for other browsers if you are using a browser-specific technology or feature on your Web page.

13.8 Summary of the DHTML Object Model

As you have seen in the preceding sections, the objects and collections supported by Internet Explorer allow the script programmer tremendous flexibility in manipulating the elements of a Web page. We have shown how to access the objects in a page, how to navigate the objects in a collection, how to change element styles dynamically and how to change the position of elements dynamically.

The Dynamic HTML object model provided by Internet Explorer allows a script programmer to access every element in an XHTML document. Literally every element in a document is represented by a separate object. The diagram in Fig. 13.10 shows many of the important objects and collections supported in Internet Explorer. The table of Fig. 13.11 provides a brief description of each object and collection in the diagram of Fig. 13.10. For a comprehensive listing of all objects and collections supported by Internet Explorer, browse the Microsoft *DHTML, HTML and CSS* Web site,

msdn.microsoft.com/workshop/c-frame.htm#/workshop/author/default.asp

This site provides detailed information on HTML, Dynamic HTML and Cascading Style Sheets technologies. The *DHTML References* section of this site provides detailed descriptions of every object, event and collection used in DHTML. For each object, all the properties, methods and collections supported by that object are discussed. For each collection, all the properties and methods supported by that collection are discussed.

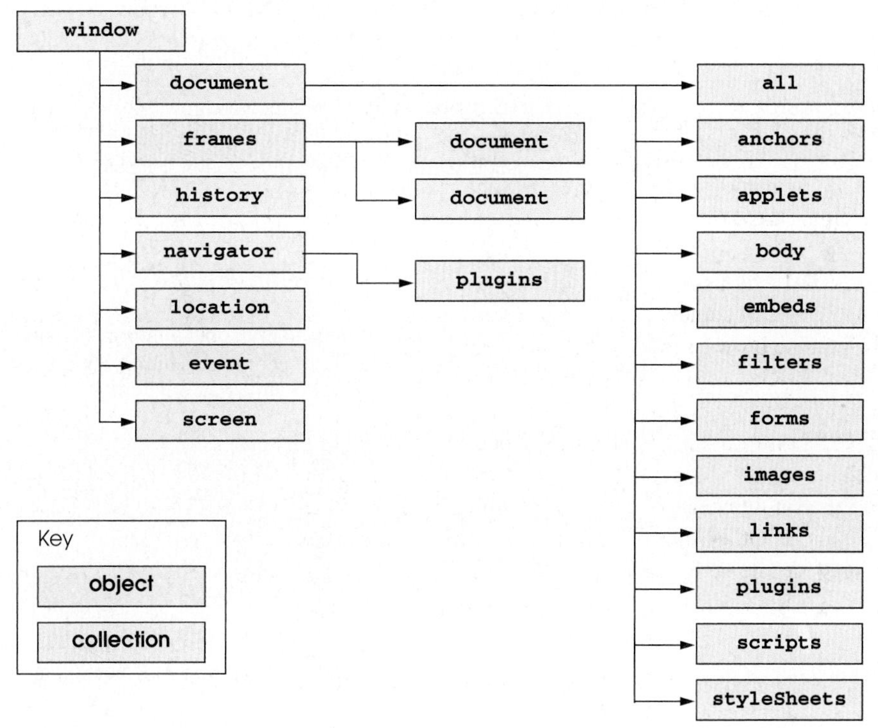

Fig. 13.10 DHTML Object Model.

Object or collection	Description
Objects	
window	This object represents the browser window and provides access to the **document** object contained in the **window**. If the **window** contains frames, a separate **window** object is created automatically for each frame, to provide access to the **document** rendered in that frame. Frames are considered to be subwindows in the browser.

Fig. 13.11 Objects in the Internet Explorer 5.5 object model (part 1 of 3).

Object or collection	Description
document	This object represents the XHTML document rendered in a **window**. The **document** object provides access to every element in the XHTML document and allows dynamic modification of the XHTML document.
body	This object provides access to the **body** element of an XHTML document.
history	This object keeps track of the sites visited by the browser user. The object provides a script programmer with the ability to move forward and backward through the visited sites, but for security reasons does not allow the actual site URLs to be manipulated.
navigator	This object contains information about the Web browser, such as the name of the browser, the version of the browser, the operating system on which the browser is running and other information that can help a script writer customize the user's browsing experience.
location	This object contains the URL of the rendered document. When this object is set to a new URL, the browser immediately switches (navigates) to the new location.
event	This object can be used in an event handler to obtain information about the event that occurred (e.g., the mouse coordinates during a mouse event).
screen	The object contains information about the computer screen for the computer on which the browser is running. Information such as the width and height of the screen in pixels can be used to determine the size at which elements should be rendered in a Web page.
Collections	
all	Many objects have an **all** collection that provides access to every element contained in the object. For example, the **body** object's **all** collection provides access to every element in the **body** element of an XHTML document.
anchors	This collection contains all anchor elements (**a**) that have a **name** or **id** attribute. The elements appear in the collection in the order they were defined in the XHTML document.
applets	This collection contains all the **applet** elements in the XHTML document. Currently, the most common **applet** elements are Java™ applets.
embeds	This collection contains all the **embed** elements in the XHTML document.
forms	This collection contains all the **form** elements in the XHTML document. The elements appear in the collection in the order they were defined in the XHTML document.
frames	This collection contains **window** objects that represent each frame in the browser window. Each frame is treated as its own subwindow.

Fig. 13.11 Objects in the Internet Explorer 5.5 object model (part 2 of 3).

Object or collection	Description
images	This collection contains all the **img** elements in the XHTML document. The elements appear in the collection in the order they were defined in the XHTML document.
links	This collection contains all the anchor elements (**a**) with an **href** property. This collection also contains all the **area** elements that represent links in an image map.
plugins	Like the **embeds** collection, this collection contains all the **embed** elements in the XHTML document.
scripts	This collection contains all the **script** elements in the XHTML document.
styleSheets	This collection contains **styleSheet** objects that represent each **style** element in the XHTML document and each style sheet included in the XHTML document via **link**.

Fig. 13.11 Objects in the Internet Explorer 5.5 object model (part 3 of 3).

SUMMARY

- The Dynamic HTML object model gives Web authors great control over the presentation of their pages by giving them access to all elements on their Web page. The whole Web page—elements, forms, frames, tables, etc.—is represented in an object hierarchy. Using scripting, an author is able to retrieve and modify any properties or attributes of the Web page dynamically.
- The simplest way to reference an element is by its **id** attribute. The element is represented as an object, and its various XHTML attributes become properties that can be manipulated by scripting.
- The **innerText** property of the object refers to the text contained in that element
- Changing the text displayed on screen is a Dynamic HTML ability called dynamic content.
- Collections are basically arrays of related objects on a page. There are several special collections in the object model.
- The **all** collection contains all the XHTML elements in a document.
- The **length** property of the a collection specifies the size of the collection.
- Property **innerHTML** is similar to property **innerText**, but it can include XHTML formatting.
- Every element has its own **all** collection consisting of all the elements contained in that element.
- The **children** collection of an element contains only that element's direct child elements. For example, an **html** element has only two children: the **head** element and the **body** element.
- The **tagName** property contains the name of the tags we encounter while looping through the document, to place them in the string **elements**.
- The **outerHTML** property is similar to the **innerHTML** property, but it includes the enclosing XHTML tags as well as the content inside them.
- The **className** property of an element is used to change that element's style class.
- An important feature of Dynamic HTML is dynamic positioning, in which XHTML elements can be positioned with scripting. This is done by declaring an element's CSS **position** property to be either **absolute** or **relative**, and then moving the element by manipulating any of the **top**, **left**, **right** or **bottom** CSS properties.

- Function **setInterval** takes two parameters—a function name and how often to call it.
- Function **setTimeout** takes the same parameters as **setInterval**, but instead waits the specified amount of time before calling the named function only once.
- There are also JavaScript functions for stopping the **setTimeout** and **setInterval** timers—the **clearTimeout** and **clearInterval** functions. To stop a specific timer, the parameter you pass to either of these functions should be the value that the corresponding *set time* function returned.
- The **frames** collections contains all the frames in a document.
- The **navigator** object contains information about the Web browser that is viewing the page. This allows Web authors to determine which browser the user has.
- The **navigator.appName** property contains the name of the application—IE, this property is "**Microsoft Internet Explorer**", for Netscape it is "**Netscape**".
- The version of the browser is accessible through the **navigator.appVersion** property. The value of **appVersion** is not a simple integer, however—it is a string containing other information, such as the current Operating System. The **navigator** object is crucial in providing browser-specific pages so that as many users as possible can view your site properly.

TERMINOLOGY

all
all collection of an element
background-color CSS property
base case
body property of **document** object
bottom CSS property
children collection
className property
clearInterval JavaScript function
clearTimeout JavaScript function
collection
document object
document.all.length
dynamic content
Dynamic HTML Object Model
dynamic positioning
dynamic style
fontSize property
id attribute
innerHTML property
innerText property
iteration
JavaScript
left CSS property
length property of a collection
loop through a collection
object referencing
onload event
outerHTML property
position: absolute
position: relative
prompt dialog
reference an object
right CSS property
setInterval JavaScript function
setTimeout JavaScript function
style object
tagName property
top CSS property
window.setInterval
window.setTimeout

SELF-REVIEW EXERCISES

13.1 State whether each of the following is *true* or *false*. If *false*, explain why.

a) An XHTML element may be referred to in JavaScript by its **id** attribute.
b) Only the **document** object has an **all** collection.
c) An element's tag is accessed with the **tagName** property.
d) You can change an element's style class dynamically with the **style** property.
e) The **frames** collection contains all the frames on a page.
f) The **setTimeout** method calls a function repeatedly at a set time interval.
g) The **browser** object is often used to determine which Web browser is viewing the page.

h) The browser may be sent to a new URL by setting the **document.url** property.
i) Collection **links** contains all links in a document with specified **name** or **id** attributes.

13.2 Fill in the blanks for each of the following statements.
a) The ________ property refers to the text inside an element.
b) The ________ property refers to the text inside an element, including XHTML tags.
c) The ________ property refers to the text and XHTML inside an element *and* the enclosing XHTML tags.
d) The ________ property contains the length of a collection.
e) An element's CSS **position** property must be set to ________ or ________ in order to reposition it dynamically.
f) The ________ property contains the name of the browser viewing the Web page.
g) The ________ property contains the version of the browser viewing the Web page.
h) The ________ collection contains all **img** elements on a page.
i) The ________ object contains information about the sites that a user previously visited.
j) CSS properties may be accessed using the ________ object.

ANSWERS TO SELF-REVIEW EXERCISES

13.1 a) True. b) False. All elements have an **all** collection. c) True. d) False; this is done with the **className** property. e) True. f) False; the **setInterval** method does this. g) False; the navigator object does this. h) False; use the **document.location** object to send the browser to a different URL. i) False; the **anchors** collection contains all links in a document.

13.2 a) **innerText**. b) **innerHTML**. c) **outerHTML**. d) **length**. e) **absolute**, **relative**. f) **navigator.appName**. g) **navigator.appVersion**. h) **images**. i) **history**. j) **style**.

EXERCISES

13.3 Modify Fig.13.9 to display a greeting to the user which contains the name and version of their browser.

13.4 Use the **screen** object to get the size of the user's screen, then use this information to place an image (using dynamic positioning) in the middle of the page.

13.5 Write a script that loops through the elements in a page and places enclosing **<strong>**...**</strong>** tags around all text inside all **p** elements.

13.6 Write a script that prints out the length of all collections on a page.

13.7 Create a Web page in which users are allowed to select their favorite layout and formatting through the use of the **className** property.

13.8 *(15 Puzzle)* Write a Web page that enables the user to play the game of 15. There is a 4-by-4 board (implemented as an XHTML table) for a total of 16 slots. One of the slots is empty. The other slots are occupied by 15 tiles, randomly numbered from 1 through 15. Any tile next to the currently empty slot can be moved into the currently empty slot by clicking on the tile. Your program should create the board with the tiles out of order. The user's goal is to arrange the tiles into sequential order row by row. Using the DHTML object model and the **onclick** event, write a script that allows the user swap the positions of the open position and an adjacent tile. [*Hint*: The **onclick** event should be specified for each table cell.]

13.9 Modify your solution to Exercise 13.8 to determine when the game is over, then prompt the user to determine whether to play again. If so, scramble the numbers.

13.10 Modify your solution to Exercise 13.9 to use an image that is split into 16 equally sized pieces. Discard one of the pieces and randomly place the other 15 pieces in the XHTML table.

14

Dynamic HTML: Event Model

Objectives

- To understand the notion of events, event handlers and event bubbling.
- To be able to create event handlers that respond to mouse and keyboard events.
- To be able to use the event object to be made aware of, and ultimately, respond to user actions.
- To understand how to recognize and respond to the most popular events.

The wisest prophets make sure of the event first.
Horace Walpole

Do you think I can listen all day to such stuff?
Lewis Carroll

The user should feel in control of the computer; not the other way around. This is achieved in applications that embody three qualities: responsiveness, permissiveness, and consistency.
Inside Macintosh, Volume 1
Apple Computer, Inc., 1985

We are responsible for actions performed in response to circumstances for which we are not responsible.
Allan Massie

Outline

14.1 Introduction

We have seen that XHTML pages can be controlled via scripting. Dynamic HTML with the *event model* exists so that scripts can respond to user interactions and change the page accordingly. This makes Web applications more responsive and user-friendly and can reduce server load—a concern we will learn more about in Chapters 25–31.

With the event model, scripts can respond to a user who is moving the mouse, scrolling up or down the screen or entering keystrokes. Content becomes more dynamic while interfaces become more intuitive.

In this chapter, we discuss how to use the event model to respond to user actions. We give examples of event handling for 10 of the most common and useful events, which range from mouse capture to error handling to form processing. For example, we use the **`onreset`** event to prompt a user to confirm that they want to reset a form. Included at the end of the chapter is a table of all DHTML events.

14.2 Event `onclick`

One of the most common events is **`onclick`**. When the user clicks the mouse, the **`onclick`** event *fires*. With JavaScript, we are able to respond to **`onclick`** and other events. Figure 14.1 is an example of simple event handling for the **`onclick`** event.

The script beginning on lines 15–16 introduces a new notation. The **`for`** attribute of the **`script`** element specifies another element's **`id`** attribute. In this case, **`para`** represents the **`p`** element in line 26. When the event specified in the **`event`** attribute occurs for the element specified in the **`for`** attribute, the statements in the script execute. Line 26 sets the **`id`** for the **`p`** element to **`para`**. Attribute **`id`** specifies a unique identifier for an XHTML element. When the **`onclick`** event for this element is *fired*, the script in lines 15–20 executes.

Another way to handle events is with inline scripting. Lines 29–30 specify the event as an XHTML attribute. This syntax associates the script directly with the **`input`** element. Inline scripting like this often is used to pass a value associated with the clicked element, to an event handler.

```
1  <?xml version = "1.0"?>
2  <!DOCTYPE html PUBLIC "-//W3C//DTD XHTML 1.0 Transitional//EN"
3     "http://www.w3.org/TR/xhtml1/DTD/xhtml1-transitional.dtd">
4
5  <!-- Fig 14.1: onclick.html                 -->
6  <!-- Demonstrating the onclick event -->
7
8  <html xmlns = "http://www.w3.org/1999/xhtml">
9     <head>
10       <title>DHTML Event Model - onclick</title>
11
12       <!-- The for attribute declares the script for -->
13       <!-- a certain element, and the event for a     -->
14       <!-- certain event.                              -->
15       <script type = "text/javascript" for = "para"
16          event = "onclick">
17          <!--
18          alert( "Hi there" );
19          // -->
20       </script>
21    </head>
22
23    <body>
24
25       <!-- The id attribute gives a unique identifier -->
26       <p id = "para">Click on this text!</p>
27
28       <!-- You can specify event handlers inline -->
29       <input type = "button" value = "Click Me!"
30          onclick = "alert( 'Hi again' )" />
31
32    </body>
33 </html>
```

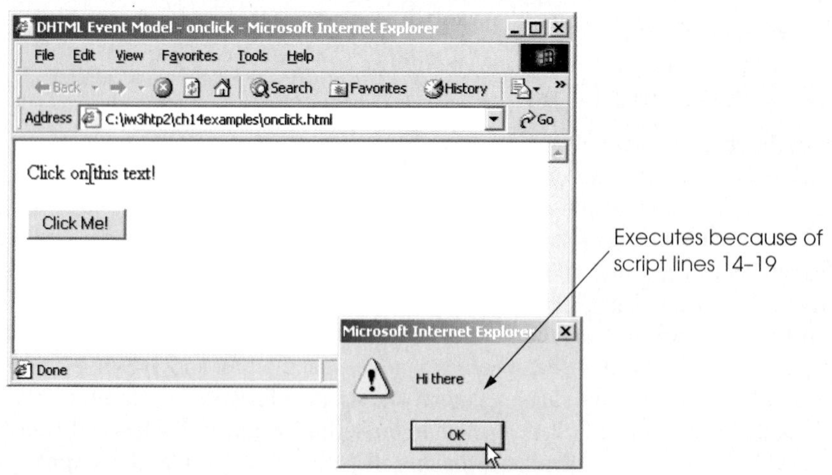

Fig. 14.1 Triggering an **onclick** event (part 1 of 2).

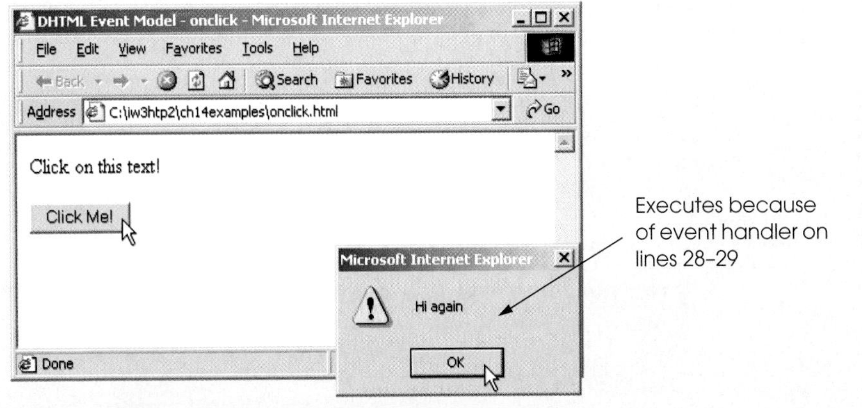

Fig. 14.1 Triggering an **onclick** event (part 2 of 2).

14.3 Event onload

The **onload** event fires whenever an element finishes loading successfully. Frequently, this event is used in the **body** element to initiate a script after the page loads into the client. Figure 14.2 uses the **onload** event for this purpose. The script called by the **onload** event, updates a timer that indicates how many seconds have elapsed since the document has been loaded.

```
<?xml version = "1.0"?>
<!DOCTYPE html PUBLIC "-//W3C//DTD XHTML 1.0 Strict//EN"
   "http://www.w3.org/TR/xhtml1/DTD/xhtml1-strict.dtd">

<!-- Fig. 14.2: onload.html         -->
<!-- Demonstrating the onload event -->

<html xmlns = "http://www.w3.org/1999/xhtml">
   <head>
      <title>DHTML Event Model - onload</title>
      <script type = "text/javascript">
         <!--
         var seconds = 0;

         function startTimer() {
            // 1000 milliseconds = 1 second
            window.setInterval( "updateTime()", 1000 );
         }

         function updateTime() {
            seconds++;
            soFar.innerText = seconds;
         }
         // -->
```

Fig. 14.2 Demonstrating the **onload** event (part 1 of 2).

```
25         </script>
26      </head>
27
28      <body onload = "startTimer()">
29
30         <p>Seconds you have spent viewing this page so far:
31         <a id = "soFar"><strong>0</strong></a></p>
32
33      </body>
34   </html>
```

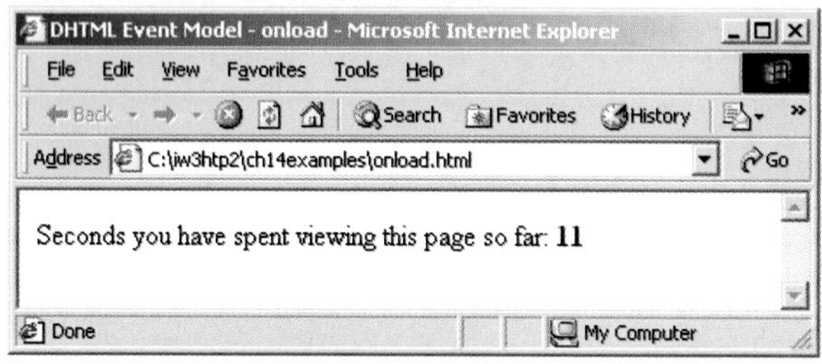

Fig. 14.2 Demonstrating the **onload** event (part 2 of 2).

Our reference to the **onload** event occurs in line 28. After the **body** section loads, the browser triggers the **onload** event. This calls function **startTimer**, which in turn uses method **window.setInterval** to specify that function **updateTime** should be called every **1000** milliseconds. Other uses of the **onload** event are to open a popup window once your page has loaded, or to trigger a script when an image or applet loads.

14.4 Error Handling with onerror

The Web is a dynamic medium. Sometimes scripts refer to objects that existed at a specified location when the script was written, but the location changes at a later time, rendering your scripts invalid. The error dialog presented by browsers in such cases can be confusing to the user. To prevent this dialog box from displaying and to handle errors more elegantly, scripts can use the **onerror** event to execute specialized error-handling code. Figure 14.3 uses the **onerror** event to launch a script that writes error messages to the status bar of the browser. [*Note*: This program works correctly if "Script debugging" is disabled in Internet Explorer. In the **Tools** menu's **Internet Options** dialog, click the **Advanced** tab, and select **Disable script debugging** under **Browsing**.]

```
<?xml version = "1.0"?>
<!DOCTYPE html PUBLIC "-//W3C//DTD XHTML 1.0 Transitional//EN"
   "http://www.w3.org/TR/xhtml1/DTD/xhtml1-transitional.dtd">

<!-- Fig 14.3: onerror.html             -->
<!-- Demonstrating the onerror event  -->

<html xmlns = "http://www.w3.org/1999/xhtml">
```

Fig. 14.3 Handling script errors by handling an **onerror** event (part 1 of 2).

```
9      <head>
10        <title>DHTML Event Model - onerror</title>
11        <script type = "text/javascript">
12           <!--
13           // Specify that if an onerror event is triggered
14           // in the window function handleError should execute
15           window.onerror = handleError;
16
17           function doThis() {
18              alrrt( "hi" ); // alert misspelled, creates an error
19           }
20
21           // The ONERROR event passes three values to the
22           // function: the name of the error, the url of
23           // the file, and the line number.
24           function handleError( errType, errURL, errLineNum )
25           {
26              // Writes to the status bar at the
27              // bottom of the window.
28              window.status = "Error: " + errType + " on line " +
29                 errLineNum;
30
31              // Returning a value of true cancels the
32              // browser's reaction.
33              return true;
34           }
35           // -->
36        </script>
37     </head>
38
39     <body>
40
41        <input id = "mybutton" type = "button" value = "Click Me!"
42           onclick = "doThis()" />
43
44     </body>
45  </html>
```

Custom error output

Fig. 14.3 Handling script errors by handling an **onerror** event (part 2 of 2).

Line 15 indicates that function **handleError** should execute when an **onerror** event occurs in the **window** object. The misspelled function name (**alrrt**) in line 18 intentionally creates an error; the code in line 15 then calls function **handleError**.

The function definition (lines 24–34) accepts three parameters from the **onerror** event, which is one of the few events that passes parameters to an event handler. The parameters are the type of error that occurred, the URL of the file that had the error and the line number on which the error occurred.

Lines 28–29 use the parameters passed to the function by **onerror** to write information about the scripting error to the status bar at the bottom of the browser window (Fig. 14.3). You can use this technique to provide error messages that are more user friendly.

Line 33 returns **true** to the event handler to indicate that the error has been handled. This prevents the browser's default response (the dialog we wish to circumvent). Returning **false** indicates that the error has not been handled and causes the default response to occur. Chances are that, if you are using an advanced feature of JavaScript, there will be some browsers that cannot view your site properly. In these cases, error handling is particularly useful. If a browser triggers an **onerror** event, your Web page can provide a custom message to the user such as "Your browser does not support some features on this site. It may not render correctly."

Software Engineering Observation 14.1

Use error handling on your Web site to prevent incompatible browsers from complaining about scripts they cannot process.

14.5 Tracking the Mouse with Event onmousemove

Event **onmousemove** fires repeatedly whenever the user moves the mouse over the Web page. Figure 14.4 uses this event to update a coordinate display that gives the position of the mouse in the coordinate system of the object containing the mouse cursor.

```
<?xml version = "1.0"?>
<!DOCTYPE html PUBLIC "-//W3C//DTD XHTML 1.0 Transitional//EN"
   "http://www.w3.org/TR/xhtml1/DTD/xhtml1-transitional.dtd">

<!-- Fig. 14.4: onmousemove.html              -->
<!-- Demonstrating the onmousemove event      -->

<html xmlns = "http://www.w3.org/1999/xhtml">
   <head>
      <title>DHTML Event Model - onmousemove event</title>
      <script type = "text/javascript">
         <!--
         function updateMouseCoordinates()
         {
            coordinates.innerText = event.srcElement.tagName +
               " (" + event.offsetX + ", " + event.offsetY + ")";
         }
         // -->
      </script>
   </head>

   <body style = "back-groundcolor: wheat"
      onmousemove = "updateMouseCoordinates()">
```

Fig. 14.4 Demonstrating the **onmousemove** event (part 1 of 2).

```
24
25          <span id = "coordinates">(0, 0)</span><br />
26          <img src = "deitel.gif" style = "position: absolute;
27             top: 100; left: 100" alt = "Deitel" />
28
29       </body>
30    </html>
```

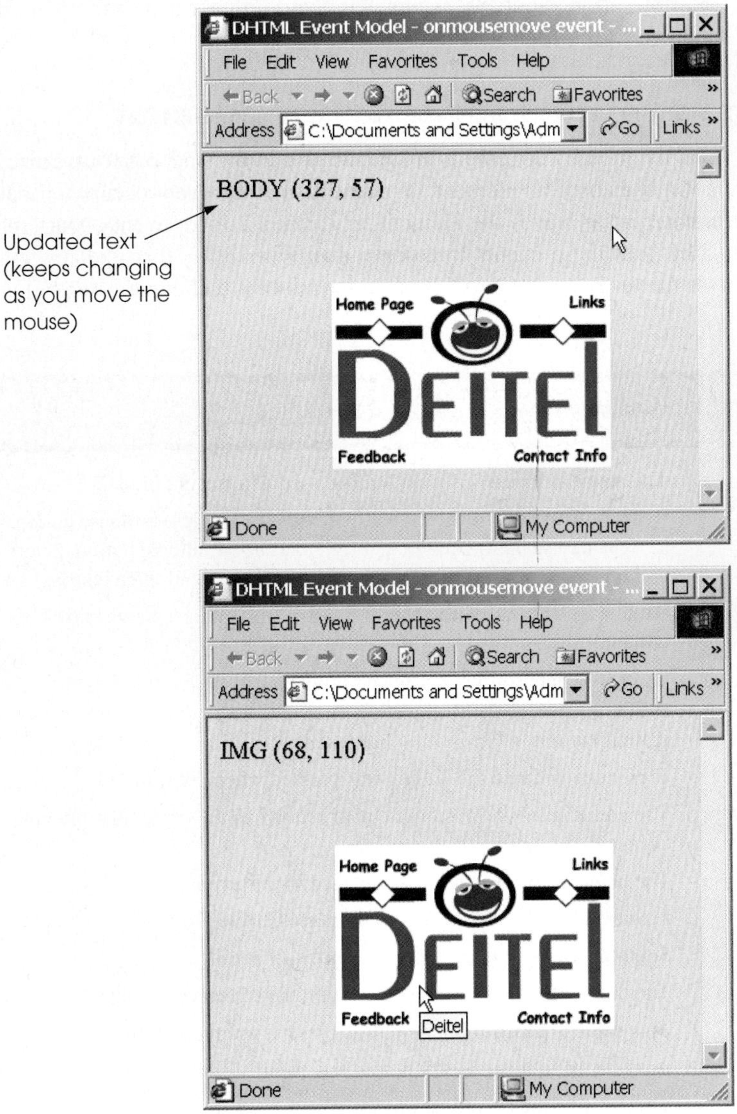

Updated text (keeps changing as you move the mouse)

Fig. 14.4 Demonstrating the **`onmousemove`** event (part 2 of 2).

Our event handling in this example occurs in lines 15–16. The **`event`** object (line 15) contains information about the triggered event. Property **`srcElement`** references the element that triggered the event. The script uses **tagName** to retrieve the element's name and display the name in the **innerText** (line 15) of the **span** called **coordinates** (line 25).

The ***offsetX*** and ***offsetY*** properties of the **event** object give the location of the mouse cursor relative to the top-left corner of the object on which the event was triggered. Notice that when you move the cursor over the image, the coordinate display changes to the image's coordinate system. This is because the **onmousemove** event occurs over the image. Figure 14.5 lists several other **event** object properties. The properties of the **event** object contain information about any events that occur on your page and are used to create Web pages that are truly dynamic and responsive to the user.

14.6 Rollovers with onmouseover and onmouseout

Two more events fired by mouse movement are **onmouseover** and **onmouseout**. When the mouse cursor moves over an element, an **onmouseover** event occurs for that element. When the mouse cursor leaves the element, an **onmouseout** event occurs for that element. Figure 14.6 uses these events to achieve a *rollover effect* that updates text when the mouse cursor moves over that text. We also introduce a technique for creating rollover images.

Property of event	Description
altkey	This value is **true** if *Alt* key was pressed when event fired.
button	Returns which mouse button was pressed by user (1: left-mouse button, 2: right-mouse button, 3: left and right buttons, 4: middle button, 5: left and middle buttons, 6: right and middle buttons, 7: all three buttons).
cancelBubble	Set to **false** to prevent this event from bubbling (see Section 14.9, "Event Bubbling").
clientX / clientY	The coordinates of the mouse cursor inside the client area (i.e., the active area where the Web page is displayed, excluding scrollbars, navigation buttons, etc.).
ctrlKey	This value is **true** if *Ctrl* key was pressed when event fired.
offsetX / offsetY	The coordinates of the mouse cursor relative to the object that fired the event.
propertyName	The name of the property that changed in this event.
recordset	A reference to a data field's recordset (see Chapter 16, "Data Binding").
returnValue	Set to **false** to cancel the default browser action.
screenX / screenY	The coordinates of the mouse cursor on the screen coordinate system.
shiftKey	This value is **true** if *Shift* key was pressed when event fired.
srcElement	A reference to the object that fired the event.
type	The name of the event that fired.
x / y	The coordinates of the mouse cursor relative to this element's parent element.

Fig. 14.5 Some **event** object properties.

To create a rollover effect for the image in the table caption, lines 15–18 create two new JavaScript **Image** objects—**captionImage1** and **captionImage2**. Image **captionImage2** displays when the mouse hovers over the image. Image **captionImage1** displays when the mouse is outside the image. The script sets the **src** properties of each **Image** in lines 16 and 18. Creating **Image** objects pre-loads the images, so the browser does not need to download the rollover image the first time the script indicates to display the image. If the image is large or the connection is slow, this causes a noticeable delay in the image update.

Lines 22–25 in the **mOver** function handle the **onmouseover** event for the image by setting its **src** attribute (**event.srcElement.src**) to the **src** property of the appropriate **Image** object (**captionImage2.src**). The same task occurs with **captionImage1** in the **mOut** function (lines 36–39).

```
1  <?xml version = "1.0"?>
2  <!DOCTYPE html PUBLIC "-//W3C//DTD XHTML 1.0 Strict//EN"
3     "http://www.w3.org/TR/xhtml1/DTD/xhtml1-strict.dtd">
4
5  <!-- Fig 14.6: onmouseoverout.html      -->
6  <!-- Events onmouseover and onmouseout -->
7
8  <html xmlns = "http://www.w3.org/1999/xhtml">
9     <head>
10       <title>
11          DHTML Event Model - onmouseover and onmouseout
12       </title>
13       <script type = "text/javascript">
14          <!--
15          captionImage1 = new Image();
16          captionImage1.src = "caption1.gif";
17          captionImage2 = new Image();
18          captionImage2.src = "caption2.gif";
19
20          function mOver()
21          {
22             if ( event.srcElement.id == "tableCaption" ) {
23                event.srcElement.src = captionImage2.src;
24                return;
25             }
26
27             // If the element which triggered onmouseover has
28             // an id, change its color to its id.
29             if ( event.srcElement.id )
30                 event.srcElement.style.color =
31                    event.srcElement.id;
32          }
33
34          function mOut()
35          {
36            if ( event.srcElement.id == "tableCaption" ) {
37               event.srcElement.src = captionImage1.src;
38               return;
39            }
```

Fig. 14.6 Events **onmouseover** and **onmouseout** (part 1 of 4).

```

         // If it has an id, change the text inside to the
         // text of the id.
         if ( event.srcElement.id )
            event.srcElement.innerText = event.srcElement.id;
      }

      document.onmouseover = mOver;
      document.onmouseout = mOut;
      // -->
   </script>
</head>

<body style = "background-color: wheat">

   <h1>Guess the Hex Code's Actual Color</h1>

   <p>Can you tell a color from its hexadecimal RGB code
   value? Look at the hex code, guess the color. To see
   what color it corresponds to, move the mouse over the
   hex code. Moving the mouse out will display the color
   name.</p>

   <table style = "width: 50%; border-style: groove;
      text-align: center; font-family: monospace;
      font-weight: bold">

      <caption>
         <img src = "caption1.gif" id = "tableCaption"
            alt = "Table Caption" />
      </caption>

      <tr>
         <td><a id = "Black">#000000</a></td>
         <td><a id = "Blue">#0000FF</a></td>
         <td><a id = "Magenta">#FF00FF</a></td>
         <td><a id = "Gray">#808080</a></td>
      </tr>
      <tr>
         <td><a id = "Green">#008000</a></td>
         <td><a id = "Lime">#00FF00</a></td>
         <td><a id = "Maroon">#800000</a></td>
         <td><a id = "Navy">#000080</a></td>
      </tr>
      <tr>
         <td><a id = "Olive">#808000</a></td>
         <td><a id = "Purple">#800080</a></td>
         <td><a id = "Red">#FF0000</a></td>
         <td><a id = "Silver">#C0C0C0</a></td>
      </tr>
      <tr>
         <td><a id = "Cyan">#00FFFF</a></td>
         <td><a id = "Teal">#008080</a></td>
```

Fig. 14.6 Events **onmouseover** and **onmouseout** (part 2 of 4).

```
               <td><a id = "Yellow">#FFFF00</a></td>
               <td><a id = "White">#FFFFFF</a></td>
            </tr>
         </table>

      </body>
   </html>
```

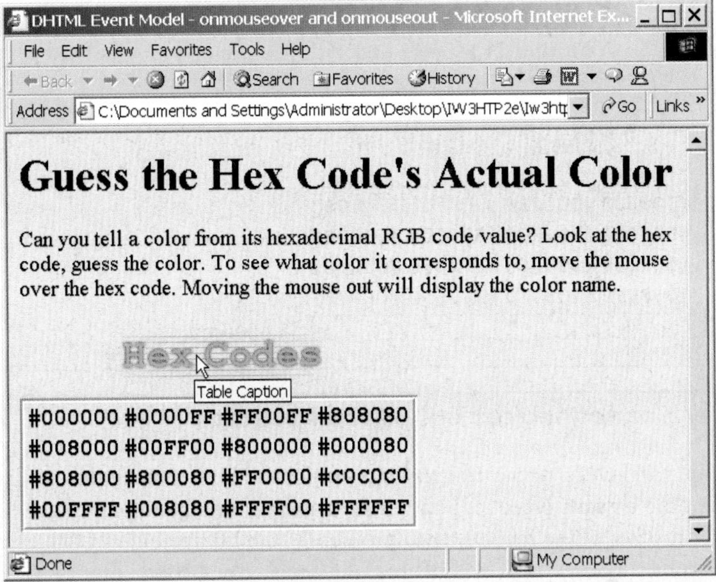

Fig. 14.6 Events **onmouseover** and **onmouseout** (part 3 of 4).

Fig. 14.6 Events **onmouseover** and **onmouseout** (part 4 of 4).

The script handles the **onmouseover** event for the table cells in lines 29–31. As mentioned earlier, the **event** object contains information about the triggered event. In particular, the **id** property of the **srcElement** object is the **id** attribute of that element. This code tests if an **id** is specified, and, if it is, the code changes the color of the element to match the color name in the **id**. As you can see in the code for the table (lines 63–96), each **id** is one of the 16 basic XHTML colors.

Lines 43–44 handle the **onmouseout** event by changing the text in the table cell the cursor just left to match the color that it represents.

14.7 Form Processing with onfocus and onblur

The **onfocus** and **onblur** events are particularly useful when dealing with form elements that allow user input (Fig. 14.7).

```
<?xml version = "1.0"?>
<!DOCTYPE html PUBLIC "-//W3C//DTD XHTML 1.0 Transitional//EN"
   "http://www.w3.org/TR/xhtml1/DTD/xhtml1-transitional.dtd">

<!-- Fig. 14.7: onfocusblur.html                        -->
<!-- Demonstrating the onfocus and onblur events    -->

<html xmlns = "http://www.w3.org/1999/xhtml">
   <head>
      <title>DHTML Event Model - onfocus and onblur</title>
      <script type = "text/javascript">
```

Fig. 14.7 Events **onfocus** and **onblur** (part 1 of 3).

```
         <!--
         var helpArray =
            [ "Enter your name in this input box.",
              "Enter your email address in this input box, " +
              "in the format user@domain.",
              "Check this box if you liked our site.",
              "In this box, enter any comments you would " +
              "like us to read.",
              "This button submits the form to the " +
              "server-side script",
              "This button clears the form",
              "This textarea provides context-sensitive " +
              "help. Click on any input field or use the TAB " +
              "key to get more information about the " +
              "input field." ];

         function helpText( messageNum )
         {
            myForm.helpBox.value = helpArray[ messageNum ];
         }
         // -->
      </script>
   </head>

   <body>

      <form id = "myForm" action = "">
      Name: <input type = "text" name = "name"
         onfocus = "helpText(0)" onblur = "helpText(6)" /><br />
      Email: <input type = "text" name = "email"
         onfocus = "helpText(1)" onblur = "helpText(6)" /><br />
      Click here if you like this site
      <input type = "checkbox" name = "like" onfocus =
         "helpText(2)" onblur = "helpText(6)" /><br /><hr />

      Any comments?<br />
      <textarea name = "comments" rows = "5" cols = "45"
         onfocus = "helpText(3)" onblur = "helpText(6)">
      </textarea><br />
      <input type = "submit" value = "Submit" onfocus =
         "helpText(4)" onblur = "helpText(6)" />
      <input type = "reset" value = "Reset" onfocus =
         "helpText(5)" onblur = "helpText(6)" />

      <textarea name = "helpBox" style = "position: absolute;
         right: 0; top: 0" rows = "4" cols = "45">
      This textarea provides context-sensitive help. Click on
      any input field or use the Tab key to get more information
      about the input field.</textarea>
      </form>

   </body>
</html>
```

Fig. 14.7 Events **onfocus** and **onblur** (part 2 of 3).

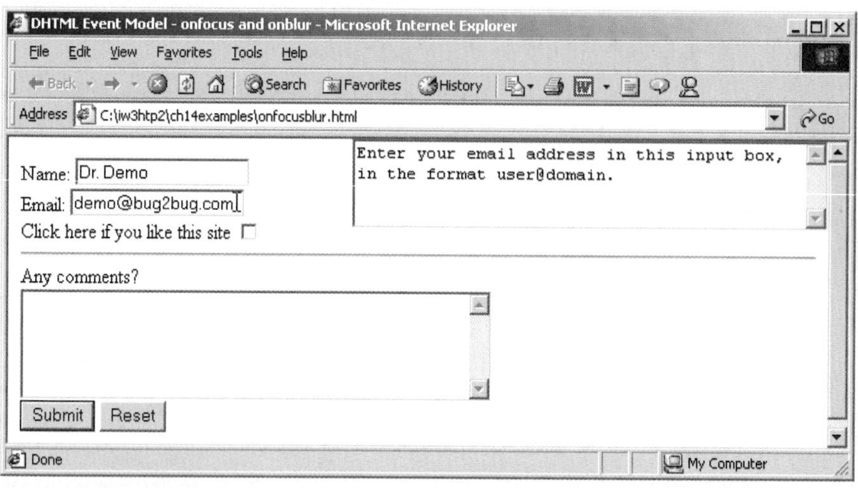

Fig. 14.7 Events **onfocus** and **onblur** (part 3 of 3).

The **onfocus** event fires when an element gains focus (i.e., when the user clicks a form field or when the user uses the *Tab* key to move between form elements) and **onblur** fires when an element loses focus, which occurs when another control gains the focus. In line 30, the script changes the text inside the text box in the upper-right corner based on the **messageNum** passed to **helpText**. The elements of the form, for example on lines 39–40 each pass a different value to the **helpText** function when they gain focus and the **onfocus** event is fired. When elements lose focus, they all pass the value **6** to **helpText** so that **helpBox** can display the default message, "**This textarea provides context-sensitive help. Click on any**..."

14.8 More Form Processing with onsubmit and onreset

Two more useful events for processing forms are **onsubmit** and **onreset**. These events fire when a form is submitted or reset, respectively (Fig. 14.8).

```
<?xml version = "1.0"?>
<!DOCTYPE html PUBLIC "-//W3C//DTD XHTML 1.0 Transitional//EN"
   "http://www.w3.org/TR/xhtml1/DTD/xhtml1-transitional.dtd">

<!-- Fig 14.8: onsubmitreset.html                      -->
<!-- Demonstrating the onsubmit and onreset events -->

<html xmlns = "http://www.w3.org/1999/xhtml">
   <head>
      <title>
         DHTML Event Model - onsubmit and onreset events
      </title>
      <script type = "text/javascript">
```

Fig. 14.8 Events **onsubmit** and **onreset** (part 1 of 3).

```
         <!--
         var helpArray =
            [ "Enter your name in this input box.",
              "Enter your email address in this input box, " +
              "in the format user@domain.",
              "Check this box if you liked our site.",
              "In this box, enter any comments you would " +
              "like us to read.",
              "This button submits the form to the " +
              "server-side script",
              "This button clears the form",
              "This textarea provides context-sensitive " +
              "help. Click on any input field or use the Tab " +
              "key to get more information about " +
              "the input field." ];

         function helpText( messageNum )
         {
            myForm.helpBox.value = helpArray[ messageNum ];
         }

         function formSubmit() {
            window.event.returnValue = false;

            if ( confirm ( "Are you sure you want to submit?" ) )
               window.event.returnValue = true;
         }

         function formReset() {
            window.event.returnValue = false;

            if ( confirm( "Are you sure you want to reset?" ) )
               window.event.returnValue = true;
         }
         // -->
      </script>
   </head>

   <body>

      <form id = "myForm" onsubmit = "formSubmit()"
         onreset = "formReset()" action = "">
      Name: <input type = "text" name = "name"
         onfocus =  "helpText(0)" onblur = "helpText(6)" /><br />
      Email: <input type = "text" name = "email"
         onfocus = "helpText(1)" onblur = "helpText(6)" /><br />
      Click here if you like this site
      <input type = "checkbox" name = "like" onfocus =
         "helpText(2)" onblur = "helpText(6)" /><hr />

      Any comments?<br />
      <textarea name = "comments" rows = "5" cols = "45"
         onfocus = "helpText(3)" onblur = "helpText(6)">
```

Fig. 14.8 Events **onsubmit** and **onreset** (part 2 of 3).

```
67          </textarea><br />
68          <input type = "submit" value = "Submit" onfocus =
69            "helpText(4)"  onblur = "helpText(6)" />
70          <input type = "reset" value = "Reset" onfocus =
71             "helpText(5)" onblur = "helpText(6)" />
72
73          <textarea name = "helpBox" style = "position: absolute;
74             right:0; top: 0" rows = "4" cols = "45">
75          This textarea provides context-sensitive help. Click on
76          any input field or use the Tab key to get more
77          information about the input field.</textarea>
78          </form>
79
80       </body>
81    </html>
```

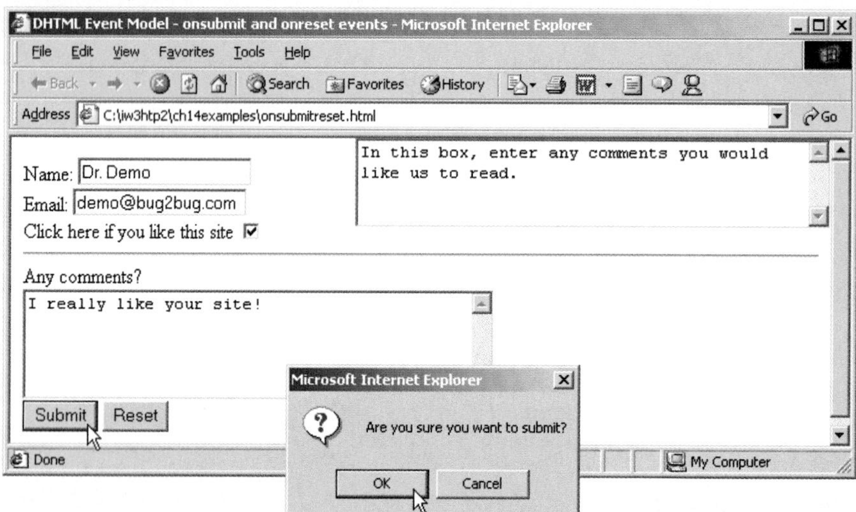

Fig. 14.8 Events **onsubmit** and **onreset** (part 3 of 3).

Line 36 sets the **returnValue** property to **false** and cancels the default action of the event on the element, which in this case is for the browser to submit the form. Line 38 pops up a dialog asking the user a question. If the user clicks **OK**, function **confirm** returns **true**. If the user clicks **Cancel**, **confirm** returns **false**. Using this information, line 39 sets the **returnValue** back to **true**, because the user has confirmed that the form should indeed be submitted.

14.9 Event Bubbling

Event bubbling, a crucial part of the event model, is the process whereby events fired in child elements also "bubble" up to their parent elements for handling. If you intend to handle an event in a child element, you might need to cancel the bubbling of that event in that child element's event-handling code by using the **cancelBubble** property of the **event** object, as shown in Fig. 14.9.

```
<?xml version = "1.0"?>
<!DOCTYPE html PUBLIC "-//W3C//DTD XHTML 1.0 Strict//EN"
   "http://www.w3.org/TR/xhtml1/DTD/xhtml1-strict.dtd">

<!-- Fig 14.9: bubbling.html  -->
<!-- Disabling event bubbling -->

<html xmlns = "http://www.w3.org/1999/xhtml">
   <head>
      <title>DHTML Event Model - Event Bubbling</title>

      <script type = "text/javascript">
         <!--
         function documentClick()
         {
            alert( "You clicked in the document" );
         }

         function paragraphClick( value )
         {
            alert( "You clicked the text" );

            if ( value )
               event.cancelBubble = true;
         }

         document.onclick = documentClick;
         // -->
      </script>
   </head>

   <body>

      <p onclick = "paragraphClick( false )">Click here!</p>
      <p onclick = "paragraphClick( true )">Click here, too!</p>
   </body>
</html>
```

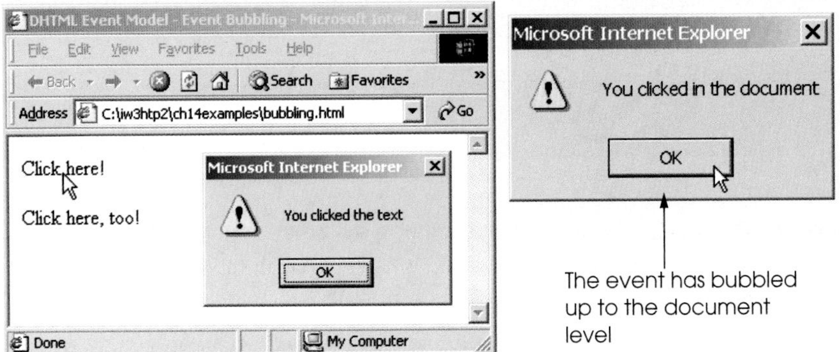

Fig. 14.9 Event bubbling (part 1 of 2).

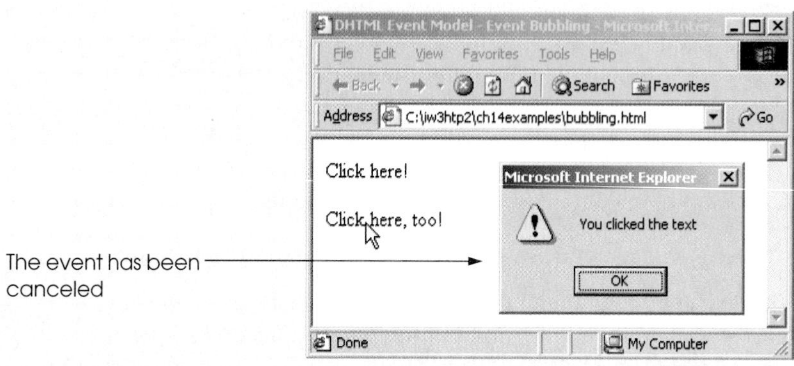

Fig. 14.9 Event bubbling (part 2 of 2).

Common Programming Error 14.1

Forgetting to cancel event bubbling when necessary may cause unexpected results in your scripts.

Clicking the first **p** element (line 34) triggers the statement

```
onclick = "paragraphClick( false )"
```

then triggers the statement (in line 27)

```
document.onclick = documentClick;
```

because the **onclick** event has bubbled up to the document level. This is probably not the desired result. However, clicking the second **p** element (line 35) passes a value of **true** to function **paragraphClick**, so that the **if** statement on line 23 executes line 24 which disables the event bubbling for this event by setting the **cancelBubble** property of the **event** object to **true**.

14.10 More DHTML Events

The events we covered in this chapter are among the most common in use. The remaining DHTML events and their descriptions are listed in Fig. 14.10.

Event	Description
Clipboard events	
onbeforecut	Fires before a selection is cut to the clipboard.
onbeforecopy	Fires before a selection is copied to the clipboard.
onbeforepaste	Fires before a selection is pasted from the clipboard.
oncopy	Fires when a selection is copied to the clipboard.

Fig. 14.10 Dynamic HTML events (part 1 of 3).

Event	Description
oncut	Fires when a selection is cut to the clipboard.
onabort	Fires if image transfer has been interrupted by user.
onpaste	Fires when a selection is pasted from the clipboard.
Data binding events	
onafterupdate	Fires immediately after a databound object has been updated.
onbeforeupdate	Fires before a data source is updated.
oncellchange	Fires when a data source has changed.
ondataavailable	Fires when new data from a data source become available.
ondatasetchanged	Fires when content at a data source has changed.
ondatasetcomplete	Fires when transfer of data from the data source has completed.
onerrorupdate	Fires if an error occurs while updating a data field.
onrowenter	Fires when a new row of data from the data source is available.
onrowexit	Fires when a row of data from the data source has just finished.
onrowsdelete	Fires when a row of data from the data source is deleted.
onrowsinserted	Fires when a row of data from the data source is inserted.
Keyboard Events	
onhelp	Fires when the user initiates help (i.e., by pressing the *F1* key).
onkeydown	Fires when the user pushes down a key.
onkeypress	Fires when the user presses a key.
onkeyup	Fires when the user ends a key press.
marquee events	
onbounce	Fires when a scrolling **marquee** bounces back in the other direction.
onfinish	Fires when a **marquee** finishes its scrolling.
onstart	Fires when a **marquee** begins a new loop.
Mouse events	
oncontextmenu	Fires when the context menu is shown (right-click).
ondblclick	Fires when the mouse is double-clicked.
ondrag	Fires during a mouse drag.
ondragend	Fires when a mouse drag ends.
ondragenter	Fires when something is dragged onto an area.
ondragleave	Fires when something is dragged out of an area.

Fig. 14.10 Dynamic HTML events (part 2 of 3).

Event	Description
ondragover	Fires when a drag is held over an area.
ondragstart	Fires when a mouse drag begins.
ondrop	Fires when a mouse button is released over a valid target during a drag.
onmousedown	Fires when a mouse button is pressed down.
onmouseup	Fires when a mouse button is released.
Miscellaneous Events	
onafterprint	Fires immediately after the document prints.
onbeforeeditfocus	Fires before an element gains focus for editing.
onbeforeprint	Fires before a document is printed.
onbeforeunload	Fires before a document is unloaded (i.e., the window was closed or a link was clicked).
onchange	Fires when a new choice is made in a **select** element, or when a text input is changed and the element loses focus.
onfilterchange	Fires when a filter changes properties or finishes a transition (see Chapter 15, Filters and Transitions).
onlosecapture	Fires when the **releaseCapture** method is invoked.
onpropertychange	Fires when the property of an object is changed.
onreadystatechange	Fires when the **readyState** property of an element changes.
onreset	Fires when a form resets (i.e., the user clicks an **<input type = "reset">**).
onresize	Fires when the size of an object changes (i.e., the user resizes a window or frame).
onscroll	Fires when a window or frame is scrolled.
onselect	Fires when a text selection begins (applies to **input** or **textarea**).
onselectstart	Fires when the object is selected.
onstop	Fires when the user stops loading the object.
onunload	Fires when a page is about to unload.

Fig. 14.10 Dynamic HTML events (part 3 of 3).

SUMMARY

- The event model allows scripts to respond to user actions and change a page accordingly. This makes Web applications responsive and user-friendly and can lessen server load greatly.
- With the event model, scripts can respond to a user moving the mouse, scrolling up or down the screen or entering keystrokes. Content becomes more dynamic, and interfaces become more intuitive.
- One of the most common events is **onclick**. When the user clicks the mouse, **onclick** fires.

- The **for** attribute of the **script** element specifies an element by its **id** attribute. When the event specified in the **event** attribute occurs for the element with **id** specified in the **for** attribute, the designated script runs.
- Specifying an event as an XHTML attribute allows you to insert script directly into your XHTML. Inline scripting is usually used to pass a value (to a event handler) based on the element that was clicked.
- The **onload** event fires whenever an element finishes loading successfully and is often used in the **body** element to initiate scripts as soon as the page has been loaded into the client.
- You can use the **onerror** event to write error-handling code.
- The syntax **window.onerror** = *functionName* specifies that *functionName* runs if the **onerror** event is triggered in the **window** object.
- Event handlers can accept three parameters from the **onerror** event (one of the few events that passes parameters to an event handler). The **onerror** event passes the type of error that occurred, the URL of the file that had the error and the line number on which the error occurred.
- Returning **true** in an error handler prevents the browser from displaying an error dialog.
- Writing a function to ignore other script errors is not a good idea—try writing scripts that adjust or stop their actions if an error in loading the page has been detected.
- Event **onmousemove** fires constantly whenever the mouse is in motion.
- The **event** object contains much information about the triggered event.
- Property **srcElement** of the **event** object is a pointer to the element that triggered the event. The **offsetX** and **offsetY** properties of the **event** object give the location of the cursor relative to the top-left corner of the object on which the event was triggered.
- Notice that when you move the mouse cursor over an element like an image, the **offsetX** and **offsetY** properties change to that element's coordinate system. This is because it is now the element over which the **onmousemove** is being triggered.
- Whenever the mouse cursor moves over an element, it fires event **onmouseover** for that element. Once the mouse cursor leaves the element, an **onmouseout** event is fired.
- The **id** property of the **srcElement** object is the **id** attribute of that element.
- Events **onfocus** and **onblur** fire when an element gains or loses focus, respectively.
- The events **onsubmit** and **onreset** fire when a form is submitted or reset, respectively.
- The code **window.event.returnValue = false** cancels the default browser action.
- Event bubbling, a crucial part of the event model, is the process whereby events fired in child elements also "bubble" up to their parent elements for handling. If you intend to handle an event in a child element, you might need to cancel the bubbling of that event in that child element's event-handling code by using the **cancelBubble** property of the **event** object.

TERMINOLOGY

altKey property of **event** object
button property of **event** object
cancelBubble property of **event** object
clientX property of **event** object
clientY property of **event** object
confirm method of **window** object
ctrlKey property of **event** object
Dynamic HTML event model
event attribute of **script** element
event bubbling
event handler
event model
event object (property of the **window** object)
events in DHTML
fire an event
for attribute of **script** element

innerText property of an XHTML element
keyboard events
mouse events
offsetX property of **event** object
offsetY property of **event** object
onafterprint event
onafterupdate event
onbeforecopy event
onbeforecut event
onbeforeeditfocus event
onbeforepaste event
onbeforeprint event
onbeforeunload event
onbeforeupdate event
onblur event
onbounce event
oncellchange event
onchange event
onclick event
oncontextmenu event
oncopy event
oncut event
ondataavailable event
ondatasetchanged event
ondatasetcomplete event
ondblclick event
ondrag event
ondragend event
ondragenter event
ondragleave event
ondragover event
ondragstart event
ondrop event
onerrorupdate event
onfinish event
onfocus event
onhelp event
onkeydown event
onkeypress event
onkeyup event
onload event
onlosecapture event
onmousedown event
onmousemove event
onmouseout event
onmouseover event
onmouseup event
onpaste event
onpropertychange event
onreadystatechange event
onreset event
onresize event
onrowexit event
onrowsdelete event
onrowsinserted event
onscroll event
onselect event
onselectstart event
onstart event
onstop event
onsubmit event
onunload event
position of the mouse cursor
propertyName property of **event** object
returnValue property of **event**
screenX property of event
screenY property of event
setInterval method of **window** object
shiftkey property of **event**
srcElement property of **event**
status bar at bottom of a window
status property of **window** object
Tab key to switch between fields on a form
tagName property of **event** object
trigger an event
type property of event
x property of **event** object
y property of **event** object

SELF-REVIEW EXERCISES

14.1 Fill in the blanks in each of the following statements:

a) The state of three special keys can be retrieved by using the **event** object. These keys are __________, __________ and __________.
b) If a child element does not handle an event, __________ lets the event rise through the object hierarchy.
d) Using the __________ property of the **script** element allows you to specify to which element the script applies.
e) The __________ property of the **event** object specifies whether to continue bubbling the current event.

f) Setting **window.returnValue** to __________ cancels the default browser action for the event.

g) In an event handler, the reference for the **id** of an element that fired an event is __________.

h) Three events that fire when the user clicks the mouse are __________, __________ and __________.

14.2 State whether each of the following is *true* or *false*. If the statement is *false*, explain why.

a) The **onload** event fires whenever an element starts loading successfully.

b) The **onclick** even fires directly when the user clicks the mouse.

c) It is generally a good idea to include a function in your document that will ignore other script errors.

d) When using the rollover effect with images, it is a good programming practice to create image objects that preload the desired images.

e) Returning **true** in an error handler prevents the browser from displaying an error dialog.

ANSWERS TO SELF-REVIEW EXERCISES

14.1 a) *Ctrl, Alt* and *Shift*. b) event bubbling. c) **for**. d) **returnValue**. e) **false**. f) **event.srcElement.id**. g) **onclick**, **onmousedown**, **onmouseup**.

14.2 a) False. The ***onload*** event fires whenever an element *finishes* loading successfully. b) True. c) False. it is not a good idea to write a function that ignores other script errors, instead, you should try writing a script that adjusts or stops the actions if an error has occurred when loading a page. d) True. e) True.

EXERCISES

14.3 Write an error handler that changes the **alt** text of an image to "Error Loading" if the image loading is not completed.

14.4 You have a server-side script that cannot handle any ampersands (**&**) in the form data. Write a function that converts all ampersands in a form field to "and" when the field loses focus (**onblur**).

14.5 Write a function that responds to a click anywhere on the page by displaying an **alert** dialog. Display the event name if the user held *Shift* during the mouse click. Display the element name that triggered the event if the user held *Ctrl* during the mouse click.

14.6 Use CSS absolute positioning, **onmousemove** and **event.x**/**event.y** to have a sentence of text follow the mouse as the user moves the mouse over the Web page. Disable this feature if the user double-clicks (**ondblclick**).

14.7 Modify Exercise 14.5 to have an image follow the mouse as the user moves the mouse over the Web page.

14.8 Add two elements to Fig. 14.9 that users can click. Use the **deitel.gif** image file as the first element. When the user clicks the image, display an **alert** dialog box with the text "you clicked the image." For the second element, create a one-row table containing a text string. Set the table border to one. When the user clicks the table element, display an **alert** dialog box containing "you clicked the table." In the two accompanying functions, set each event object to **true**.

15

Dynamic HTML: Filters and Transitions

Objectives

- To use filters to achieve special effects.
- To combine filters to achieve an even greater variety of special effects.
- To be able to create animated visual transitions between Web pages.
- To be able to modify filters dynamically, using DHTML.

...as through a filter, before the clear product emerges.
F. Scott Fitzgerald

There is strong shadow where there is much light.
Johann Wolfgang von Goethe

When all things are equal, translucence in writing is more effective than transparency, just as glow is more revealing than glare.
James Thurber

...one should disdain the superficial and let the true beauty of one's soul shine through.
Fran Lebowitz

Modernity exists in the form of a desire to wipe out whatever came earlier, in the hope of reaching at least a point that could be called a true present, a point of origin that marks a new departure.
Paul de Man

Outline

15.1 Introduction

Just a few years ago it was not realistic to offer the kinds of dramatic visual effects you will see in this chapter, because desktop computer processing power was insufficient. Today, with powerful processors, these visual effects are realizable without delays. Just as you expect to see dramatic visual effects on TV weather reports, Web users appreciate visual effects when browsing Web pages.

In the past, achieving these kinds of effects, if you could get them at all, demanded frequent trips back and forth to the server. With the consequent delays, the beauty of the effects was lost.

Performance Tip 15.1

With Dynamic HTML, many visual effects are implemented directly in the client-side browser (Internet Explorer 5.5 for this book), so no server-side processing delays are incurred. The DHTML code that initiates these effects is generally quite small and is coded directly into the XHTML Web page.

You will be able to achieve a great variety of effects, such as transitioning between pages with *random dissolves* and *horizontal and vertical blinds* effects similar to those you find in slide presentation software packages. You can convert colored images to gray in response to user actions; this could be used, for example, to indicate that some option is not currently selectable. You can make letters *glow* for emphasis. You can create *drop shadows* to give text a three-dimensional appearance.

In this chapter, we discuss both *filters* and *transitions*. Applying filters to text and images causes changes that are persistent. Transitions are temporary; applying a transition allows you to transfer from one page to another with a pleasant visual effect such as a random dissolve. Filters and transitions do not add content to your pages—rather, they present existing content in an engaging manner to capture the user's attention.

Each of the visual effects achievable with filters and transitions is programmable, so these effects can be adjusted dynamically by programs that respond to user-initiated events, such as mouse clicks and keystrokes. Filters and transitions are so easy to use that virtually any Web page designer or programmer can incorporate these effects with minimal effort.

Look-and-Feel Observation 15.1

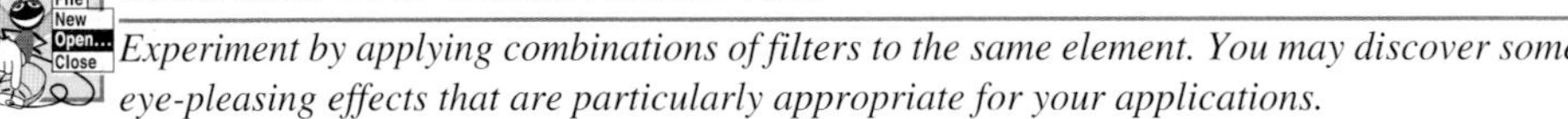

Experiment by applying combinations of filters to the same element. You may discover some eye-pleasing effects that are particularly appropriate for your applications.

Part of the beauty of DHTML filters and transitions is that they are built right into Internet Explorer. You do not need to spend time working with sophisticated graphics packages, preparing images that will be downloaded (slowly) from servers. When Internet Explorer renders your page, it applies all the special effects and does this while running on the client computer, without lengthy waits for files to download from the server.

Look-and-Feel Observation 15.2

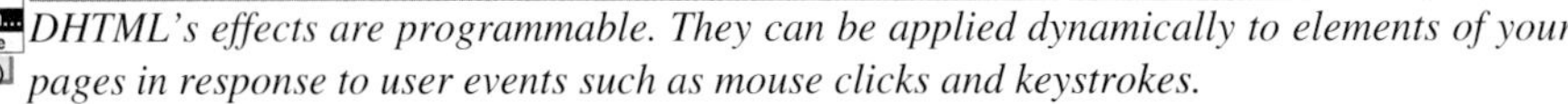

DHTML's effects are programmable. They can be applied dynamically to elements of your pages in response to user events such as mouse clicks and keystrokes.

Filters and transitions are specified with the *CSS* **`filter`** *property*. They give you the same kind of graphics capabilities you get through presentation software like Microsoft's PowerPoint®. You can have new pages or portions of pages fade in and fade out. You can have a page randomly dissolve into the next page. You can make portions of the page transparent or semitransparent so that you can see what is behind them. You can make elements glow for emphasis. You can blur text or an image to give it the illusion of motion. You can create drop shadows on elements to give them a three-dimensional effect. You can even combine effects to generate a greater variety of effects.

Software Engineering Observation 15.1

Filters and transitions can be applied to block-level elements such as **`div`** *or* **`p`**, *but can be applied only to inline-level elements such as* **`strong`** *or* **`em`** *if the element has its* **`height`** *or* **`width`** *CSS properties set.*

Portability Tip 15.1

Filters and transitions are Microsoft technologies available only in Windows-based versions of Internet Explorer 5.5. Do not use these capabilities if you are writing for other browsers. If you are writing for an audience with a diversity of browsers and you use DHTML filters and transitions, you should also make alternate provisions.

15.2 Flip Filters: `flipv` and `fliph`

The ***`flipv`*** and ***`fliph`*** *filters* mirror text or images vertically and horizontally, respectively. Figure 15.1 demonstrates these effects, using both filters to flip text.

Line 32 applies a filter using the **style** attribute. The value of the **filter** property is the name of the filter. In this case, the filter is **fliph**, which flips the affected object horizontally.

Line 38 applies more than one filter at once by specifying multiple filters separated by spaces as values of the **filter** attribute. In this case, the **flipv** filter is also applied, which vertically flips the object to which the filter is applied.

```
1  <?xml version = "1.0"?>
2  <!DOCTYPE html PUBLIC "-//W3C//DTD XHTML 1.0 Strict//EN"
3     "http://www.w3.org/TR/xhtml1/DTD/xhtml1-strict.dtd">
4
5  <!-- Fig. 15.1: flip.html    -->
6  <!-- Using the flip filters -->
7
8  <html xmlns = "http://www.w3.org/1999/xhtml">
9     <head>
10       <title>The flip filter</title>
11
12       <style type = "text/css">
13          body  { background-color: #CCFFCC }
14
15          table { font-size: 3em;
16                  font-family: Arial, sans-serif;
17                  background-color: #FFCCCC;
18                  border-style: ridge ;
19                  border-collapse: collapse }
20
21          td    { border-style: groove;
22                  padding: 1ex }
23       </style>
24    </head>
25
26    <body>
27
28       <table>
29
30          <tr>
31             <!-- Filters are applied in style declarations -->
32             <td style = "filter: fliph">Text</td>
33             <td>Text</td>
34          </tr>
35
36          <tr>
37             <!-- More than one filter can be applied at once -->
38             <td style = "filter: flipv fliph">Text</td>
39             <td style = "filter: flipv">Text</td>
40          </tr>
41
42       </table>
43
44    </body>
45 </html>
```

Fig. 15.1 Using the **flip** filter (part 1 of 2).

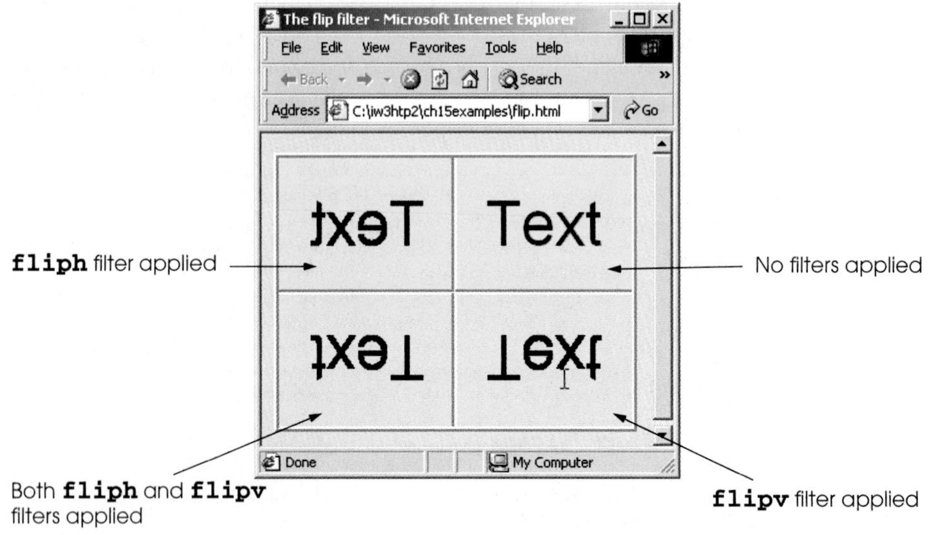

Fig. 15.1 Using the **flip** filter (part 2 of 2).

15.3 Transparency with the chroma Filter

The ***chroma*** *filter* applies *transparency effects* dynamically, without using a graphics editor to hard-code transparency into the image. Figure 15.2 alters the transparency of an image, using object model scripting based on a user selection from a **select** element.

```
<?xml version = "1.0"?>
<!DOCTYPE html PUBLIC "-//W3C//DTD XHTML 1.0 Transitional//EN"
   "http://www.w3.org/TR/xhtml1/DTD/xhtml1-transitional.dtd">

<!-- Fig 15.2: chroma.html                              -->
<!-- Applying transparency using the chroma filter   -->

<html xmlns = "http://www.w3.org/1999/xhtml">
   <head>
      <title>Chroma Filter</title>

      <script type = "text/javascript">
         <!--
         function changecolor( theColor )
         {
            if ( theColor ) {
               // if the user selected a color, parse the
               // value to hex and set the filter color.
               chromaImg.filters( "chroma" ).color = theColor;
               chromaImg.filters( "chroma" ).enabled = true;
            }
```

Fig. 15.2 Changing values of the **chroma** filter (part 1 of 2).

```
            else // if the user selected "None",
               // disable the filter.
               chromaImg.filters( "chroma" ).enabled = false;
         }
         // -->
      </script>
   </head>

   <body>

      <h1>Chroma Filter:</h1>

      <img id = "chromaImg" src = "trans.gif" style =
         "position: absolute; filter: chroma"  alt =
         "Transparent Image" />

      <form action = "">
         <!-- The onchange event fires when -->
         <!-- a selection is changed        -->
         <select onchange = "changecolor( this.value )">
            <option value = "">None</option>
            <option value = "#00FFFF">Cyan</option>
            <option value = "#FFFF00">Yellow</option>
            <option value = "#FF00FF">Magenta</option>
            <option value = "#000000" selected = "selected">
               Black</option>
         </select>
      </form>

   </body>
</html>
```

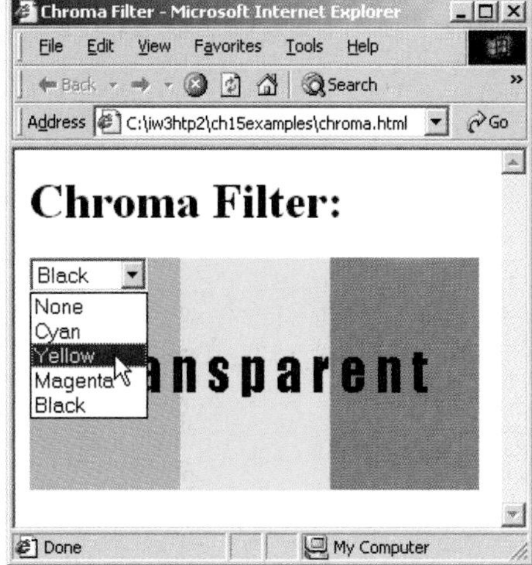

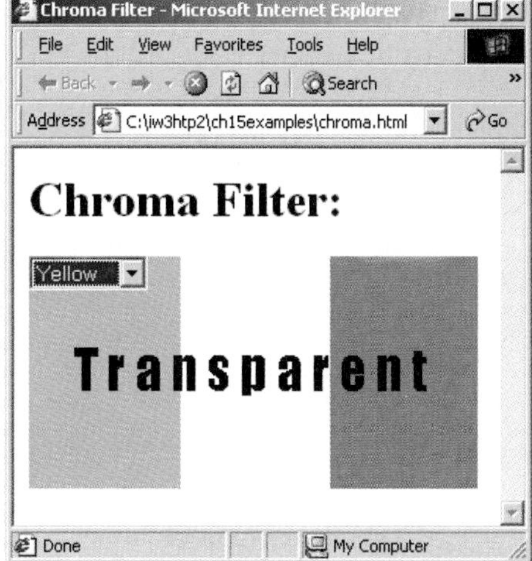

Fig. 15.2 Changing values of the **chroma** filter (part 2 of 2).

Lines 19 sets the filter properties dynamically using JavaScript. In this case, the value of the **select** drop-down list (lines 41–48) is a string containing the color value. This value is passed as an argument to function **changecolor**.

Line 20 turns on the filter. Each filter has a property named **enabled**. If this property is set to **true**, the filter is applied. If it is set to **false**, the filter is not applied. Line 24 indicates that, if the user selected **None** (line 43) from the drop-down list, the filter is disabled.

Line 41 introduces a new event, ***onchange***. This event fires whenever the **value** of a form field changes. In this example, an **onchange** event occurs when the user makes a new selection in the **colorSelect** drop-down list. The expression **this.value** represents the currently selected value in the **select** GUI component.

15.4 Creating Image masks

Applying the **mask** *filter* to an image allows you to create an *image mask*, in which the background of an element is a solid color and the foreground of an element is transparent to the image or color behind it. Figure 15.3 adds the **mask** filter to an **h1** element which overlaps an image. The foreground of that **h1** element (the text inside it) is transparent, so you can see the background image through the letters in the foreground.

Line 21 sets the color parameter for the **mask** filter. Parameters always are specified in the format *param* = *value*.

```
1  <?xml version = "1.0"?>
2  <!DOCTYPE html PUBLIC "-//W3C//DTD XHTML 1.0 Transitional//EN"
3     "http://www.w3.org/TR/xhtml1/DTD/xhtml1-transitional.dtd">
4
5  <!-- Fig 15.3: mask.html          -->
6  <!-- Placing a mask over an image -->
7
8  <html xmlns = "http://www.w3.org/1999/xhtml">
9     <head>
10       <title>Mask Filter</title>
11    </head>
12
13    <body>
14
15       <h1>Mask Filter</h1>
16
17       <!-- Filter parameters are specified in parentheses, -->
18       <!-- in the form param1 = value1, param2 = value2,   -->
19       <!-- etc.                                             -->
20       <div style = "position: absolute; top: 125; left: 20;
21          filter: mask( color = #CCFFFF )">
22       <h1 style = "font-family: Courier, monospace">
23       AaBbCcDdEeFfGgHhIiJj<br />
24       KkLlMmNnOoPpQqRrSsTt
25       </h1>
26       </div>
```

Fig. 15.3 Using the **mask** filter (part 1 of 2).

```

      <img src = "gradient.gif" width = "400" height = "200"
         alt = "Image with Gradient Effect" />
   </body>
</html>
```

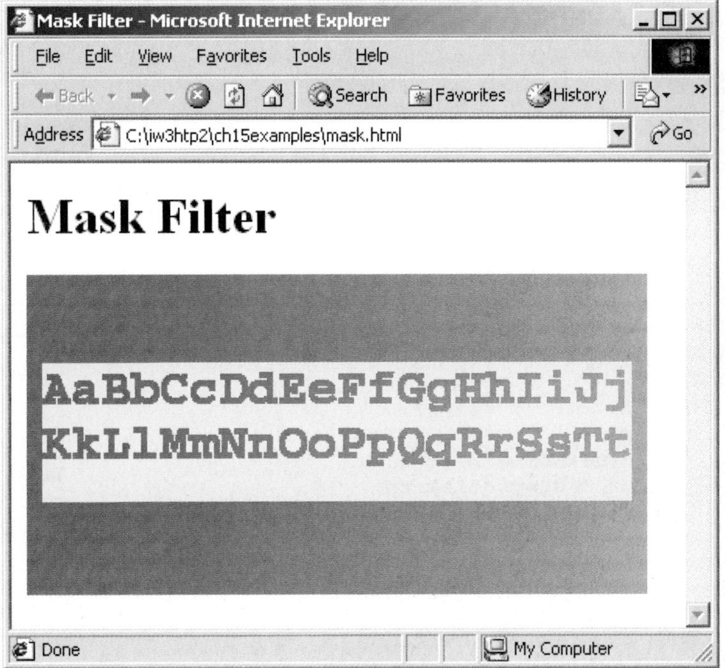

Fig. 15.3 Using the **`mask`** filter (part 2 of 2).

15.5 Miscellaneous Image Filters: `invert`, `gray` and `xray`

The three image filters discussed in this section apply simple image effects to images or text. The ***`invert`*** *filter* applies a *negative image effect*—dark areas become light and light areas become dark. The ***`gray`*** *filter* applies a *grayscale image effect*, in which all color is stripped from the image and all that remains is brightness data. The ***`xray`*** *filter* applies an x-ray effect, which basically is an inversion of the grayscale effect. Figure 15.4 demonstrates applying these filters, alone and in combination, to a simple image. Each of our filters in lines 26–41 applies a separate image effect to **hc.jpg**.

```
1  <?xml version = "1.0"?>
2  <!DOCTYPE html PUBLIC "-//W3C//DTD XHTML 1.0 Strict//EN"
3     "http://www.w3.org/TR/xhtml1/DTD/xhtml1-strict.dtd">
4
5  <!-- Fig 15.4: misc.html                                    -->
6  <!-- Image filters to invert, grayscale or xray an image -->
7
8  <html xmlns = "http://www.w3.org/1999/xhtml">
9     <head>
10       <title>Misc. Image filters</title>
11
12       <style type = "text/css">
13          .cap { font-weight: bold;
14                 background-color: #DDDDAA;
15                 text-align: center }
16       </style>
17    </head>
18
19    <body>
20       <table class = "cap">
21          <tr>
22             <td>Normal</td>
23             <td>Grayscale</td>
24          </tr>
25          <tr>
26             <td><img src = "hc.jpg" alt =
27                   "normal scenic view" /></td>
28             <td><img src = "hc.jpg" style = "filter: gray"
29                   alt = "gray scenic view"/>
30             </td>
31          </tr>
32          <tr>
33             <td>Xray</td>
34             <td>Invert</td>
35          </tr>
36          <tr>
37             <td><img src = "hc.jpg" style = "filter: xray"
38                   alt = "xray scenic view"/>
39             </td>
40             <td><img src = "hc.jpg" style = "filter: invert"
41                alt = "inverted scenic view"/>
42             </td>
43          </tr>
44       </table>
45
46    </body>
47 </html>
```

Fig. 15.4 Filters **invert**, **gray** and **xray** (part 1 of 2).

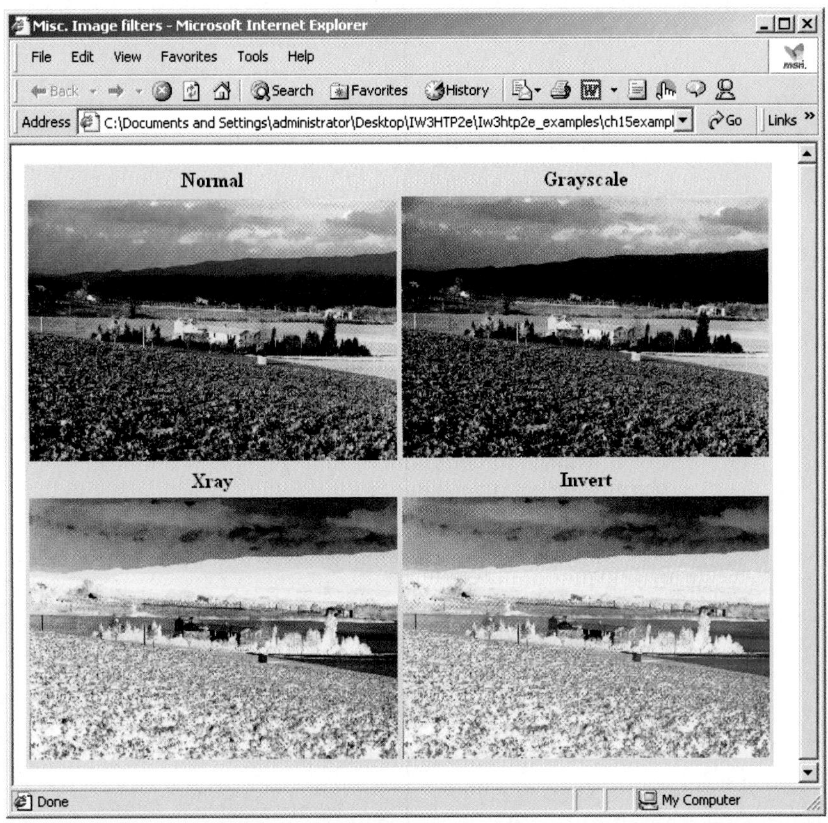

Fig. 15.4 Filters **invert**, **gray** and **xray** (part 2 of 2).

Look-and-Feel Observation 15.3

A good use of the **invert** *filter is to signify that something has just been clicked or selected.*

15.6 Adding shadows to Text

A simple filter that adds depth to your text is the ***shadow*** *filter*. This filter creates a shadowing effect that gives your text a three-dimensional appearance (Fig. 15.5).

```
<?xml version = "1.0"?>
<!DOCTYPE html PUBLIC "-//W3C//DTD XHTML 1.0 Strict//EN"
   "http://www.w3.org/TR/xhtml1/DTD/xhtml1-strict.dtd">

<!-- Fig 15.5: shadow.html      -->
<!-- Applying the shadow filter -->

<html xmlns = "http://www.w3.org/1999/xhtml">
```

Fig. 15.5 Applying a **shadow** filter to text (part 1 of 2).

```
   <head>
      <title>Shadow Filter</title>

      <script type = "text/javascript">
         <!--
         var shadowDirection = 0;

         function start()
         {
            window.setInterval( "runDemo()", 500 );
         }

         function runDemo()
         {
            shadowText.innerText =
               "Shadow Direction: " + shadowDirection % 360;
            shadowText.filters( "shadow" ).direction =
               ( shadowDirection % 360 );
            shadowDirection += 45;
         }
         // -->
      </script>
   </head>

   <body onload = "start()">

      <h1 id = "shadowText" style = "position: absolute; top: 25;
         left: 25; padding: 10; filter: shadow( direction = 0,
         color = red )">Shadow Direction: 0</h1>
   </body>
</html>
```

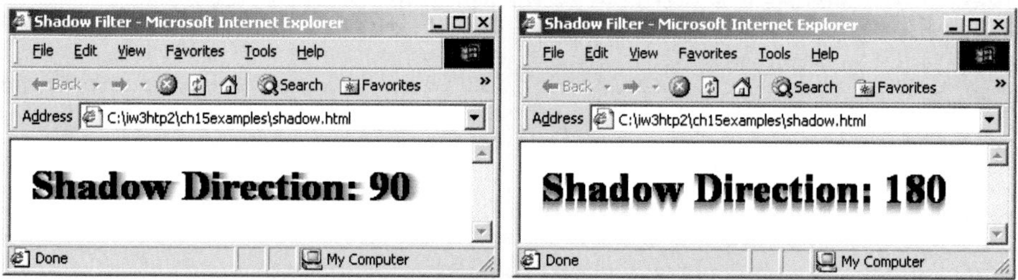

Fig. 15.5 Applying a **shadow** filter to text (part 2 of 2).

Lines 35–37 apply the **shadow** filter to text. Property **direction** of the **shadow** filter determines in which direction the shadow effect is applied—this can be set to one of eight directions expressed in angular notation: **0** (up), **45** (above-right), **90** (right), **135** (below-right), **180** (below), **225** (below-left), **270** (left) and **315** (above-left). Property **color** specifies the color of the shadow that is applied to the text. Lines 23–27 in function **runDemo**, cycle through the **direction** property values, from **0** to **315**, and update property **innerText** of the **h1** element (**shadowText**) to match the current shadow direction.

Note that we apply a **padding** CSS style to the **h1** element. Otherwise, the shadow effect is partially cut off by the border of the element. Increasing the **padding** provides greater distance between the text and the border of the element, allowing the full effect to be displayed.

Software Engineering Observation 15.2

Some filters may be cut off by element borders—make sure to increase the padding in that element if this happens.

15.7 Creating Gradients with alpha

In Chapter 3, we saw a brief example of the gradient effect, which is a gradual progression from a starting color to a target color. Internet Explorer 5.5 allows you to create the same effect dynamically using the ***alpha** filter* (Fig. 15.6). The **alpha** filter also is used for transparency effects not achievable with the **chroma** filter.

Lines 26–29 apply the **alpha** filter to a **div** element containing an image. The **style** property of the filter determines in what style the opacity is applied; a value of 0 applies *uniform opacity*, a value of 1 applies a *linear gradient*, a value of 2 applies a *circular gradient* and a value of 3 applies a *rectangular gradient*.

The **opacity** and **finishopacity** properties are both percentages that determine at what percent opacity the specified gradient starts and finishes, respectively. Additional attributes are **startX**, **startY**, **finishX** and **finishY**. These specify at what *x-y* coordinates the gradient starts and finishes in that element.

```
1  <?xml version = "1.0"?>
2  <!DOCTYPE html PUBLIC "-//W3C//DTD XHTML 1.0 Strict//EN"
3     "http://www.w3.org/TR/xhtml1/DTD/xhtml1-strict.dtd">
4
5  <!-- Fig 15.6: alpha.html                     -->
6  <!-- Applying the alpha filter to an image -->
7
8  <html xmlns = "http://www.w3.org/1999/xhtml">
9     <head>
10       <title>Alpha Filter</title>
11    <script type = "text/javascript">
12       <!--
13       function run()
14       {
15          pic.filters( "alpha" ).opacity = opacityButton.value;
16          pic.filters( "alpha" ).finishopacity =
17             opacityButton2.value;
```

Fig. 15.6 Applying the **alpha** filter (part 1 of 3).

```
            pic.filters( "alpha" ).style = styleSelect.value;
         }
         // -->
      </script>
      </head>

      <body>

         <div id = "pic"
            style = "position: absolute; left:0; top: 0;
                     filter: alpha( style = 2, opacity = 100,
                     finishopacity = 0 )">
            <img src = "flag.gif" alt = "Flag" />
         </div>

         <table style = "position: absolute; top: 250; left: 0;
            background-color: #CCFFCC" border = "1">

            <tr>
               <td>Opacity (0-100):</td>
               <td><input type = "text" id = "opacityButton"
                  size = "3" maxlength = "3" value = "100" /></td>
            </tr>

            <tr>
              <td>FinishOpacity (0-100):</td>
               <td><input type = "text" id = "opacityButton2"
                  size = "3" maxlength = "3" value = "0" /></td>
            </tr>

            <tr>
               <td>Style:</td>
               <td><select id = "styleSelect">
                  <option value = "1">Linear</option>
                  <option value = "2" selected = "selected">
                     Circular</option>
                  <option value = "3">Rectangular</option>
                  </select></td>
            </tr>

            <tr>
               <td align = "center" colspan = "2">
                  <input type = "button" value = "Apply"
                     onclick = "run()" />
               </td>
            </tr>
         </table>

      </body>
   </html>
```

Fig. 15.6 Applying the **alpha** filter (part 2 of 3).

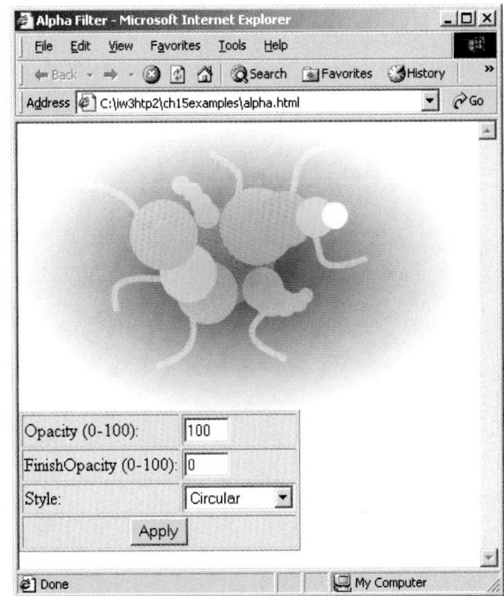

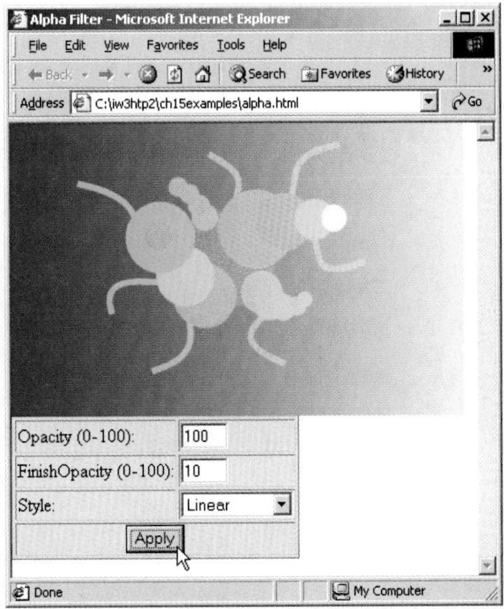

Fig. 15.6 Applying the **`alpha`** filter (part 3 of 3).

15.8 Making Text `glow`

The ***`glow`** filter* adds an aura of color around text. The color and strength can both be specified as demonstrated in Fig. 15.7.

```
<?xml version = "1.0"?>
<!DOCTYPE html PUBLIC "-//W3C//DTD XHTML 1.0 Transitional//EN"
   "http://www.w3.org/TR/xhtml1/DTD/xhtml1-transitional.dtd">

<!-- Fig 15.7: glow.html      -->
<!-- Applying the glow filter -->

<html xmlns = "http://www.w3.org/1999/xhtml">
   <head>
      <title>Glow Filter</title>
      <script type = "text/javascript">
         <!--
         var strengthIndex = 1;
         var counter = 1;
         var upDown = true;
```

Fig. 15.7 Applying changes to the **`glow`** filter (part 1 of 3).

```
         var colorArray = [ "FF0000", "FFFF00", "00FF00",
                           "00FFFF", "0000FF", "FF00FF" ];
         function apply()
         {
            glowSpan.filters( "glow" ).color =
               parseInt( glowColor.value, 16 );
            glowSpan.filters( "glow" ).strength =
               glowStrength.value;
         }

         function startdemo()
         {
            window.setInterval( "rundemo()", 150 );
         }

         function rundemo()
         {
            if ( upDown ) {
               glowSpan.filters( "glow" ).strength =
                  strengthIndex++;
            }
            else {
               glowSpan.filters( "glow" ).strength =
                  strengthIndex--;
            }

            if ( strengthIndex == 1 ) {
               upDown = !upDown;
               counter++;
               glowSpan.filters( "glow" ).color =
                  parseInt( colorArray[ counter % 6 ], 16 );
            }

            if ( strengthIndex == 10 ) {
               upDown = !upDown;
            }
         }
         // -->
      </script>
   </head>

   <body style = "background-color: #00AAAA">
      <h1>Glow Filter:</h1>

      <span id = "glowSpan" style = "position: absolute;
         left: 200;top: 100; padding: 5; filter: glow(
         color = red, strength = 5 ); font-size: 2em">
         Glowing Text
      </span>

      <table border = "1" style = "background-color: #CCFFCC">
         <tr>
            <td>Color (Hex)</td>
```

Fig. 15.7 Applying changes to the **glow** filter (part 2 of 3).

```
69                <td><input id = "glowColor" type = "text" size = "6"
70                   maxlength = "6" value = "FF0000" /></td>
71             </tr>
72             <tr>
73                <td>Strength (1-255)</td>
74                <td><input id = "glowStrength" type = "text"
75                      size = "3" maxlength = "3" value = "5" />
76                </td>
77             </tr>
78             <tr>
79                <td colspan = "2">
80                   <input type = "button" value = "Apply"
81                      onclick = "apply()" />
82                   <input type = "button" value = "Run Demo"
83                      onclick = "startdemo()" /></td>
84             </tr>
85          </table>
86 
87       </body>
88    </html>
```

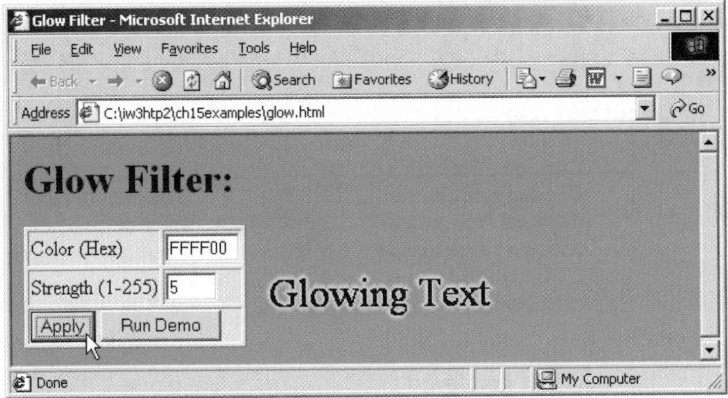

Fig. 15.7 Applying changes to the **glow** filter (part 3 of 3).

Lines 16–17 establish an array of color values to cycle through in the demo. Lines 45–46 change the **color** attribute of the **glow** filter based on **counter**, which is incremented (line 44) every time the value of **strengthIndex** becomes 1. As in the example with the **chroma** filter, we use the **parseInt** function to assign a proper hexadecimal value (taken from the **colorArray** we declared in lines 16–17) to the **color** property.

Lines 33–40 increment or decrement the **strength** property of the **glow** filter based on the value of **upDown**, which is toggled in the **if** structures at lines 42 and 49 when **strengthIndex** reaches either 1 or 10.

Clicking the **Run Demo** button starts a cycle that oscillates the filter **strength**, cycling through the colors in **colorArray** after every loop.

Common Programming Error 15.1

*When the **glow** filter is set to a large **strength**, the effect is often cut off by the borders of the element. Add CSS **padding** to prevent this.*

15.9 Creating Motion with **blur**

The ***blur*** *filter* creates an illusion of motion by blurring text or images in a certain direction. As we see in Fig. 15.8, the **blur** filter can be applied in any of eight directions, and its strength can vary.

```
<?xml version = "1.0"?>
<!DOCTYPE html PUBLIC "-//W3C//DTD XHTML 1.0 Transitional//EN"
   "http://www.w3.org/TR/xhtml1/DTD/xhtml1-transitional.dtd">

<!-- Fig 15.8: blur.html -->
<!-- The blur filter    -->

<html xmlns = "http://www.w3.org/1999/xhtml">
   <head>
      <title>Blur Filter</title>
      <script type = "text/javascript">
         <!--
         var strengthIndex = 1;
         var blurDirection = 0;
         var upDown = 0;
         var timer;

         function reBlur()
         {
            blurImage.filters( "blur" ).direction =
               document.forms( "myForm" ).Direction.value;
            blurImage.filters( "blur" ).strength =
               document.forms( "myForm" ).Strength.value;
            blurImage.filters( "blur" ).add =
               document.forms( "myForm" ).AddBox.checked;
         }

         function startDemo()
         {
            timer = window.setInterval( "runDemo()", 5 );
         }

         function runDemo( )
         {
            document.forms( "myForm" ).Strength.value =
               strengthIndex;
            document.forms( "myForm" ).Direction.value =
               ( blurDirection % 360 );

            if ( strengthIndex == 35 || strengthIndex == 0 )
               upDown = !upDown;

            blurImage.filters( "blur" ).strength =
               ( upDown ? strengthIndex++ : strengthIndex-- );

```

Fig. 15.8 Using the **blur** filter (part 1 of 3).

```
            if ( strengthIndex == 0 )
               blurImage.filters( "blur" ).direction =
                  ( ( blurDirection += 45 ) % 360 );
         }
         // -->
      </script>
   </head>

   <body>
      <form name = "myForm" action = "">

      <table border = "1" style = "background-color: #CCFFCC">
      <caption>Blur filter controls</caption>

         <tr>
            <td>Direction:</td>
            <td><select name = "Direction">
               <option value = "0">above</option>
               <option value = "45">above-right</option>
               <option value = "90">right</option>
               <option value = "135">below-right</option>
               <option value = "180">below</option>
               <option value = "225">below-left</option>
               <option value = "270">left</option>
               <option value = "315">above-left</option>
            </select></td>
         </tr>

         <tr>
            <td>Strength:</td>
            <td><input name = "Strength" size = "3" type = "text"
               maxlength = "3" value = "0" /></td>
         </tr>

         <tr>
            <td>Add original?</td>
            <td><input type = "checkbox" name = "AddBox" /></td>
         </tr>

         <tr>
            <td align = "center" colspan = "2">
               <input type = "button" value = "Apply"
                  onclick = "reBlur();" /></td>
         </tr>

         <tr>
            <td colspan = "2">
            <input type = "button" value = "Start demo"
              onclick = "startDemo();" />
            <input type = "button" value = "Stop demo"
              onclick = "window.clearInterval( timer );" /></td>
         </tr>

```

Fig. 15.8 Using the **blur** filter (part 2 of 3).

```
      </table>
      </form>

      <div id = "blurImage" style = "position: absolute;
         top: 0; left: 300; padding: 0; filter: blur(
         add = 0, direction = 0, strength = 0 );
         background-color: white;">
         <img align = "middle" src = "shapes.gif"
            alt = "Shapes" />
      </div>

   </body>
</html>
```

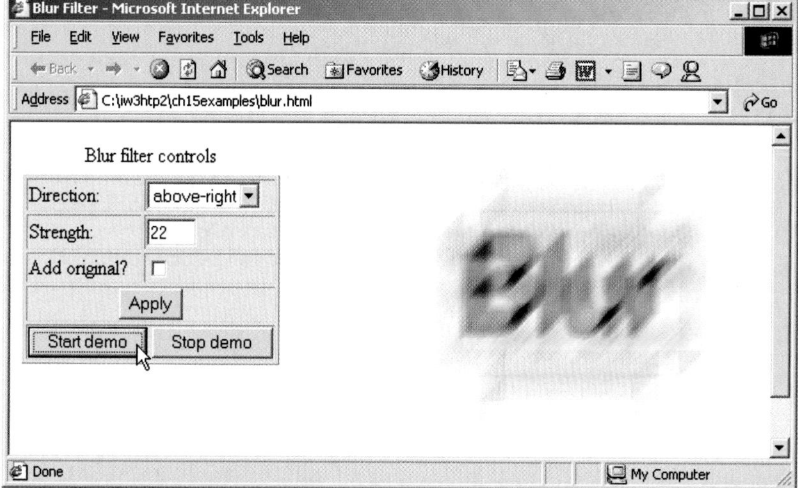

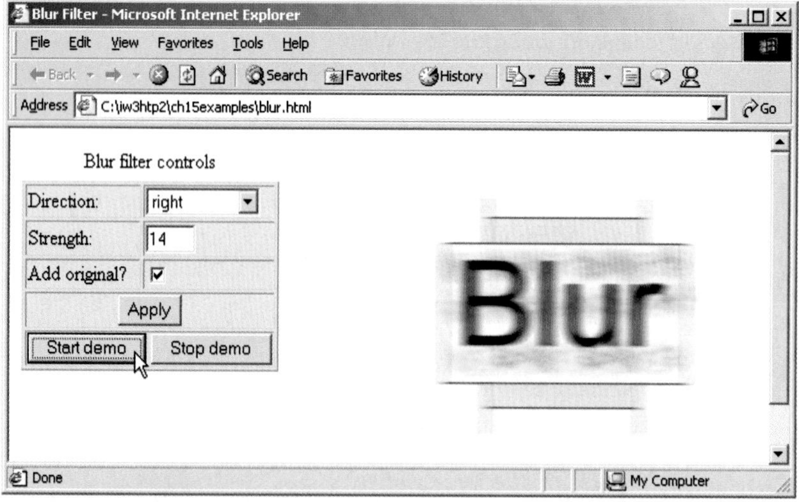

Fig. 15.8 Using the **blur** filter (part 3 of 3).

The three properties of the **blur** filter are ***add***, ***direction*** and ***strength***. The **add** property, when set to **true**, adds a copy of the original image over the blurred image, creating a more subtle blurring effect; Fig. 15.8 demonstrates the contrast between setting this to **true** or **false**.

The **direction** property determines in which direction the **blur** filter is applied. This is expressed in angular form (as we saw in Fig. 15.5 with the **shadow** filter). The **strength** property determines how strong the blurring effect is.

Lines 24–25 assign to the **add** property of the **blur** filter the boolean **checked** property of the **Add** checkbox—if the box was checked, the value is **true**.

Lines 47–48 increment the **direction** property whenever the **strength** of the **blur** filter is 0 (i.e., whenever an iteration has completed). The value assigned to the **direction** property cycles through all the multiples of 45 between 0 and 360.

15.10 Using the wave Filter

The ***wave*** *filter* allows you to apply *sine-wave distortions* to text and images on your Web pages (Fig. 15.9). The **wave** filter, as seen in lines 35–36, has many properties. The **add** property, like the **blur** filter, adds a copy of the text or image underneath the filtered effect. The **add** property is useful only when applying the **wave** filter to images.

```
1  <?xml version = "1.0"?>
2  <!DOCTYPE html PUBLIC "-//W3C//DTD XHTML 1.0 Transitional//EN"
3     "http://www.w3.org/TR/xhtml1/DTD/xhtml1-transitional.dtd">
4
5  <!-- Fig 15.9: wave.html      -->
6  <!-- Applying the wave filter -->
7
8  <html xmlns = "http://www.w3.org/1999/xhtml">
9     <head>
10       <title>Wave Filter</title>
11
12       <script type = "text/javascript">
13          <!--
14          var wavePhase = 0;
15
16          function start()
17          {
18             window.setInterval( "wave()", 5 );
19          }
20
21          function wave()
22          {
23             wavePhase++;
24             flag.filters( "wave" ).phase = wavePhase;
25          }
26          // -->
27       </script>
28    </head>
29
```

Fig. 15.9 Adding a **wave** filter to text (part 1 of 2).

```
   <body onload = "start();">

      <span id = "flag"
         style = "align: center; position: absolute;
         left: 30; padding: 15;
         filter: wave(add = 0, freq = 1, phase = 0,
            strength = 10); font-size: 2em">
      Here is some waaaavy text
      </span>

   </body>
</html>
```

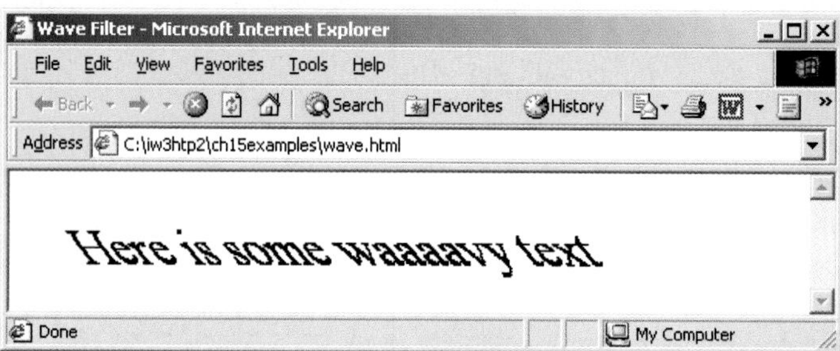

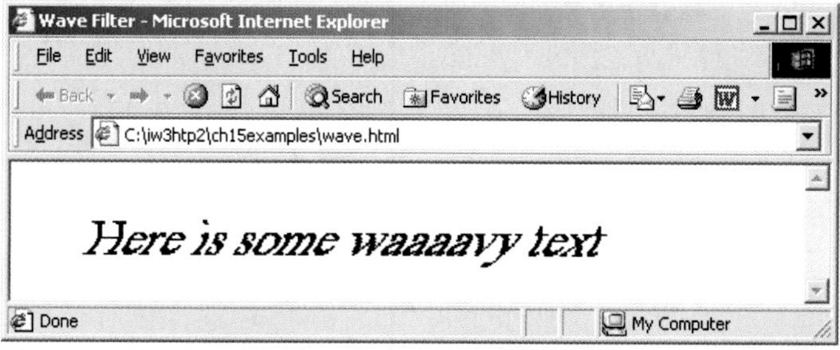

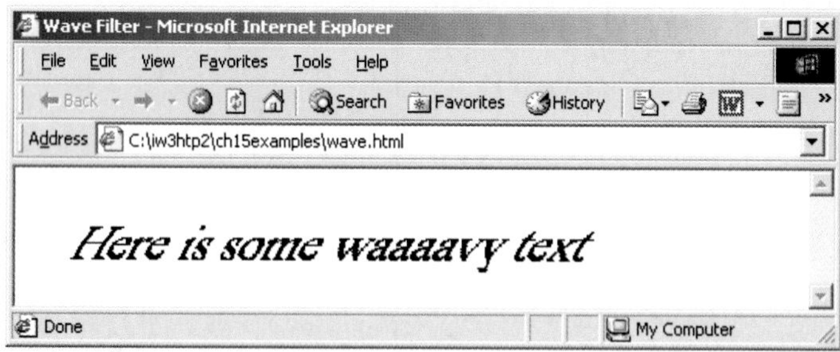

Fig. 15.9 Adding a **wave** filter to text (part 2 of 2).

Performance Tip 15.2

Applying the **wave** *filter to images is processor intensive—if your viewers have inadequate processor power, your pages may act sluggishly on their systems.*

The **freq** property determines the *frequency of the wave* applied—i.e., how many complete sine waves are applied in the affected area. Increasing this property creates a more pronounced wave effect, but makes the text harder to read.

The **phase** property indicates the *phase shift of the wave*. Increasing this property does not modify any physical attributes of the wave, but merely shifts it in space. This property is useful for creating a gentle waving effect, as we do in this example. The last property, **strength**, is the amplitude of the sine wave that is applied. In the script, lines 23–24, increment the **phase** shift of the wave in every call to the **wave** function.

15.11 Advanced Filters: dropShadow and light

Two filters that apply advanced image processing effects are the ***dropShadow*** and ***light*** *filters*. The **dropShadow** filter, as you can probably tell, applies an effect similar to the drop shadow we applied to our images with Photoshop Elements in Chapter 3—it creates a blacked-out version of the image, and places it behind the image, offset by a specified number of pixels.

The **light** filter is the most powerful and advanced filter available in Internet Explorer 5.5. It allows you to simulate the effect of a light source shining on your page. With scripting, this filter can be used with dazzling results. Fig. 15.10 combines these two filters to create an interesting effect.

```
<?xml version = "1.0"?>
<!DOCTYPE html PUBLIC "-//W3C//DTD XHTML 1.0 Transitional//EN"
   "http://www.w3.org/TR/xhtml1/DTD/xhtml1-transitional.dtd">

<!-- Fig. 15.10: dropshadow.html                              -->
<!-- Using the light filter with the dropshadow filter        -->

<html xmlns = "http://www.w3.org/1999/xhtml">
   <head>
      <title>DHTML dropShadow and light Filters</title>

      <script type = "text/javascript">
         <!--
         function setlight( )
         {
            dsImg.filters( "light" ).addPoint( 150, 150,
               125, 255, 255, 255, 100 );
         }

         function run()
         {
            eX = event.offsetX;
            eY = event.offsetY;

            xCoordinate = Math.round(
               eX-event.srcElement.width / 2, 0 );
            yCoordinate = Math.round(
               eY-event.srcElement.height / 2, 0 );
```

Fig. 15.10 Applying **light** filter with a **dropShadow** (part 1 of 2).

```
29
30                 dsImg.filters( "dropShadow" ).offx =
31                    xCoordinate / -3;
32                 dsImg.filters( "dropShadow" ).offy =
33                    yCoordinate / -3;
34
35                 dsImg.filters( "light" ).moveLight(
36                    0, eX, eY, 125, 1 );
37              }
38              // -->
39           </script>
40        </head>
41
42        <body onload = "setlight()" style = "background-color: green">
43
44           <img id = "dsImg" src = "circle.gif"
45              style = "top: 100; left: 100; filter: dropShadow(
46              offx = 0, offy = 0, color = black ) light()"
47              onmousemove = "run()" alt = "Circle Image" />
48
49        </body>
50     </html>
```

Fig. 15.10 Applying **light** filter with a **dropShadow** (part 2 of 2).

Let us begin by examining the **dropShadow** filter. In lines 44–47, we apply the **dropShadow** filter to our image. The **offx** and **offy** properties determine by how many pixels the drop shadow is offset. The **color** property specifies the color of the drop shadow. Note that we also declare the **light** filter in line 46, although we do not give it any initial parameters—all the parameters and methods of the **light** filter are set by scripting. Lines 16–17 call the **addPoint** method of the **light** filter. This adds a *point light source*—a source of light which emanates from a single point and radiates in all directions. The first two parameters (**150, 150**) set the *x-y* coordinates at which to add the point source. In this case we place the source at the center of the image, which is 300-by-300 pixels. The next parameter (**125**) sets the *height* of the point source. This simulates how far above the surface the light is situated. Small values create a small but high-intensity circle of light on the image, while large values cast a circle of light which is darker, but spreads over a greater distance. The next three parameters (**255**, **255**, **255**) specify the RGB value of the light, in decimal. In this case we set the light to a color of white (**#FFFFFF**). The last value (**100**), is a strength percentage—we set our light in this case to radiate with 100% strength.

This point light source creates a pleasant lighting effect, but it is static. We can use scripting to animate the light source in response to user actions. We use the **onmousemove** event (line 47) to have the light source follow the mouse cursor as the user moves it over the image. Lines 22–36 of the **run** function animate both the **dropshadow** and **light** filters in response to user actions. First we set the variables **xCoord** and **yCoord** to the distance between the current cursor position (**eX** and **eY**, which were set to **event.offsetX** and **event.offsetY** on lines 22–23) and the middle of the image (**event.srcElement.width / 2** or **event.srcElement.height / 2**). In the next lines of code, we set the **offx** and **offy** properties of the **dropShadow** filter relative to the current *x-y* coordinates of the image. We divide by a certain amount to create an effect of height (shadows cast by objects far from light sources only move a small amount when the light source moves by a larger amount).

We then call the **moveLight** method to update the position of the light source as well. The first parameter (**0**) is the index of the light source on the page. Multiple light sources have index numbers assigned to them in the order in which they are added. The next two parameters (**event.offsetX**, **event.offsetY**) specify the *x-y* coordinates to which we should move the light source. We use the **offsetX** and **offsetY** properties of the **event** object to move the light source to the current mouse cursor position over the image. The next parameter (**125**) specifies the height to which we move the light source. In this case, we keep the light source as the same level it was when we declared it. The last parameter (**1**) indicates that the values we are using are absolute. To move the light source by relative amounts instead, use a value of **0** for the last parameter of the **moveLight** function.

As you can see, combining the **dropShadow** and **light** filters creates a stunning effect that responds to user actions. The point source is not the only type of light source available for the light filter. Figure 15.11 demonstrates the use of a *cone light source* for illuminating an image.

```
<?xml version = "1.0"?>
<!DOCTYPE html PUBLIC "-//W3C//DTD XHTML 1.0 Transitional//EN"
   "http://www.w3.org/TR/xhtml1/DTD/xhtml1-transitional.dtd">

<!-- Fig 15.11: conelight.html         -->
<!-- Automating the cone light source -->

<html xmlns = "http://www.w3.org/1999/xhtml">
   <head><title>Cone lighting</title>

```

Fig. 15.11 Dynamic cone source lighting (part 1 of 3).

```
   <script type = "text/javascript">
      var upDown = true;
      var counter = 0;
      var moveRate = -2;

      function setLight()
      {
         marquee.filters( "light" ).addCone( 0, marquee.height,
            8, marquee.width / 2, 30, 255, 150, 255, 50, 15 );
         marquee.filters( "light" ).addCone( marquee.width,
            marquee.height, 8, 200, 30, 150, 255, 255, 50, 15 );
         marquee.filters( "light" ).addCone( marquee.width / 2,
            marquee.height, 4, 200, 100, 255, 255, 150, 50, 50 );

         window.setInterval( "display()", 100 );
      }

      function display()
      {
         counter++;

         if ( ( counter % 30 ) == 0 )
            upDown = !upDown;

         if ( ( counter % 10 ) == 0 )
            moveRate *= -1;

         if ( upDown ) {
            marquee.filters( "light" ).moveLight(
               0, -1, -1, 3, 0 );
            marquee.filters( "light" ).moveLight(
               1, 1, -1, 3, 0 );
            marquee.filters( "light" ).moveLight(
               2, moveRate, 0, 3, 0);
         }
         else {
            marquee.filters( "light" ).moveLight(
               0, 1, 1, 3, 0 );
            marquee.filters( "light" ).moveLight(
               1, -1, 1, 3, 0 );
            marquee.filters( "light" ).moveLight(
               2, moveRate, 0, 3, 0) ;
         }
      }
   </script>
   </head>
   <body style = "background-color: #000000"
      onload = "setLight()">

      <img id = "marquee" src = "marquee.gif"
         style = "filter: light; position: absolute; left: 25;
         top: 25" alt = "Deitel movie marquee" />

```

Fig. 15.11 Dynamic cone source lighting (part 2 of 3).

```
64     </body>
65  </html>
```

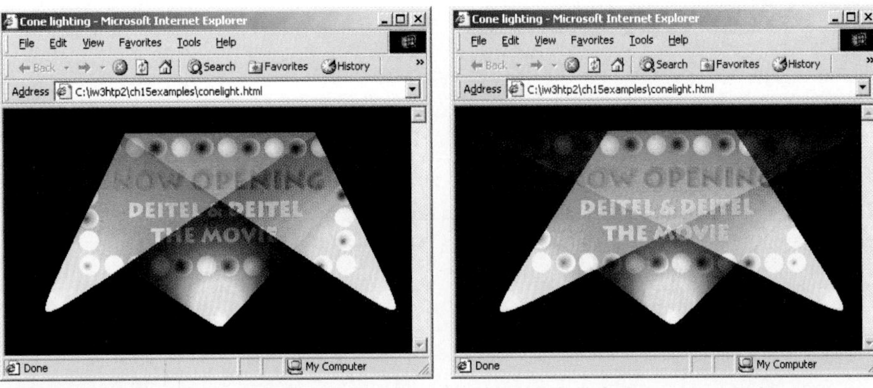

Fig. 15.11 Dynamic cone source lighting (part 3 of 3).

Lines 18–19 add our first cone light source, using the **`addCone`** method. The parameters of this method are similar to the **`addPoint`** method. The first two parameters specify the *x*-*y* coordinates of the light source, and the third parameter specifies the simulated height above the page at which the light should be placed. The next two parameters (**`marquee.width / 2`**, **`30`**) are new—they specify the *x*-*y* coordinates at which the cone source is targeted. The next three parameters (**`255`**, **`150`**, **`255`**) specify the RGB value of the light which is cast, just as we did in the **`addPoint`** method. The next parameter (**`50`**) specifies the strength of the cone source, in a percentage (also equivalent to the strength parameter in the **`addPoint`** method). The last value (**`15`**) specifies the *spread* of the light source, in degrees (this can be set in the range **`0`**–**`90`**). In this case we set the spread of the cone to **`15`** degrees, illuminating a relatively narrow area.

In lines 39–40, we use the **`moveLight`** method once again. When used on cone sources, the **`moveLight`** method moves the target of the light. In this case we set the last parameter to **`0`** to move the light by a relative amount, not an absolute amount, as we did in Fig 15.10.

15.12 Transitions I: Filter `blendTrans`

The transitions included with Internet Explorer 5.5 give the author control of many scriptable PowerPoint type effects. Transitions are set as values of the **`filter`** CSS property, just as regular filters are. We then use scripting to begin the transition. Figure 15.12 is a simple example of the ***`blendTrans`*** *transition*, which creates a smooth fade-in/fade-out effect.

```
<?xml version = "1.0"?>
<!DOCTYPE html PUBLIC "-//W3C//DTD XHTML 1.0 Strict//EN"
   "http://www.w3.org/TR/xhtml1/DTD/xhtml1-strict.dtd">

<!-- Fig 15.12: blendtrans.html -->
<!-- Blend transition           -->
```

Fig. 15.12 Using the **`blendTrans`** transition (part 1 of 2).

```
7
8  <html xmlns = "http://www.w3.org/1999/xhtml">
9     <head>
10       <title>Using blendTrans</title>
11
12       <script type = "text/javascript">
13          <!--
14          function blendOut()
15          {
16             textInput.filters( "blendTrans" ).apply();
17             textInput.style.visibility = "hidden";
18             textInput.filters( "blendTrans" ).play();
19          }
20          // -->
21       </script>
22    </head>
23
24    <body>
25
26       <div id = "textInput" onclick = "blendOut()" style =
27          "width: 300; filter: blendTrans( duration = 3 )">
28          <h1>Some fading text</h1>
29       </div>
30
31    </body>
32 </html>
```

Fig. 15.12 Using the **blendTrans** transition (part 2 of 2).

Lines 26–27 set the **filter** to **blendTrans** and the **duration** parameter to **3**. This determines how long the transition takes. In lines 16–18, we invoke two methods of **blendTrans**. The **apply** method (line 16) initializes the transition for the affected element. Once this is done, we set the **visibility** of the element to **hidden**—this takes effect when we invoke method **play** in line 18.

Figure 15.13 is a more complex example of the **blendTrans** transition. We use this to transition between two separate images.

```
<?xml version = "1.0"?>
<!DOCTYPE html PUBLIC "-//W3C//DTD XHTML 1.0 Transitional//EN"
   "http://www.w3.org/TR/xhtml1/DTD/xhtml1-transitional.dtd">
```

Fig. 15.13 Blending between images with **blendTrans** (part 1 of 3).

```
<!-- Fig 15.13: blendtrans2.html -->
<!-- Blend Transition            -->

<html xmlns = "http://www.w3.org/1999/xhtml">
   <head>
      <title>Blend Transition II</title>

      <script type = "text/javascript">
         <!--
         var whichImage = true;

         function blend()
         {
            if ( whichImage ) {
               image1.filters( "blendTrans" ).apply();
               image1.style.visibility = "hidden";
               image1.filters( "blendTrans" ).play();
            }
            else {
               image2.filters( "blendTrans" ).apply();
               image2.style.visibility = "hidden";
               image2.filters( "blendTrans" ).play();
            }
         }

         function reBlend( fromImage )
         {
            if ( fromImage ) {
               image1.style.zIndex -= 2;
               image1.style.visibility = "visible";
            }
            else {
               image1.style.zIndex += 2;
               image2.style.visibility = "visible";
            }

            whichImage = !whichImage;
            blend();
         }
         // -->
      </script>
   </head>

   <body style = "color: darkblue; background-color: lightblue"
         onload = "blend()">

      <h1>Blend Transition Demo</h1>

      <img id = "image2" src = "cool12.jpg"
      onfilterchange = "reBlend( false )"
      style = "position: absolute; left: 50; top: 50;
      width: 300; filter: blendTrans( duration = 4 );
```

Fig. 15.13 Blending between images with **blendTrans** (part 2 of 3).

```
         z-index: 1" alt = "First Transition Image"  />

      <img id = "image1" src = "cool8.jpg"
         onfilterchange = "reBlend( true )"
         style = "position: absolute; left: 50; top: 50;
         width: 300; filter: blendTrans( duration = 4 );
         z-index: 2" alt = "Second Transition Image"  />

   </body>
</html>
```

Fig. 15.13 Blending between images with **`blendTrans`** (part 3 of 3).

We begin by placing two overlapping images on the page, with **id**s **image1** and **image2** (lines 53–63). The **body** tag's **onload** event (line 49) calls function **blend** as the **body** loads. The **blend** function checks the value of the **whichImage** variable, and, because it is set to **true**, begins a fade transition on **image1**. Because there are two images in the same place, when **image1** fades out, it appears that **image2** fades in to replace it. When the transition is complete, **image1**'s **onfilterchange** event (line 60) fires. This calls function **reBlend**, which in lines 33–34 changes the **zIndex** (the JavaScript version of the **z-index** CSS property) of **image1** so that it is now below **image2**. Once this is done, the image is made visible again. The function then toggles the **whichImage** property, and calls function **blend** so that the whole process starts again, now transitioning from **image2** back to **image1**.

15.13 Transitions II: Filter revealTrans

The ***revealTrans*** *filter* allows you to transition by using professional-style transitions, from *box out* to *random dissolve*. Figure 15.14 cycles through all 24 of these, transitioning from one image to another.

```
<?xml version = "1.0"?>
<!DOCTYPE html PUBLIC "-//W3C//DTD XHTML 1.0 Transitional//EN"
   "http://www.w3.org/TR/xhtml1/DTD/xhtml1-transitional.dtd">

<!-- Fig. 15.14: revealtrans.html     -->
<!-- Cycling through 24 transitions -->

<html xmlns = "http://www.w3.org/1999/xhtml">
   <head>
      <title>24 DHTML Transitions</title>

   <script type = "text/javascript">
      <!--
      var transitionName =
        ["Box In", "Box Out",
         "Circle In", "Circle Out",
         "Wipe Up", "Wipe Down", "Wipe Right", "Wipe Left",
         "Vertical Blinds", "Horizontal Blinds",
         "Checkerboard Across", "Checkerboard Down",
         "Random Dissolve",
         "Split Vertical In", "Split Vertical Out",
         "Split Horizontal In", "Split Horizontal Out",
         "Strips Left Down", "Strips Left Up",
         "Strips Right Down", "Strips Right Up",
         "Random Bars Horizontal", "Random Bars Vertical",
         "Random" ];

      var counter = 0;
      var whichImage = true;

```

Fig. 15.14 Transitions using **revealTrans** (part 1 of 4).

```
      function blend()
      {
         if ( whichImage ) {
            image1.filters( "revealTrans" ).apply();
            image1.style.visibility = "hidden";
            image1.filters( "revealTrans" ).play();
         }
         else {
            image2.filters( "revealTrans" ).apply();
            image2.style.visibility = "hidden";
            image2.filters( "revealTrans" ).play();
         }
      }

      function reBlend( fromImage )
      {
         counter++;

         if ( fromImage ) {
            image1.style.zIndex -= 2;
            image1.style.visibility = "visible";
            image2.filters( "revealTrans" ).transition =
               counter % 24;
         }
         else {
            image1.style.zIndex += 2;
            image2.style.visibility = "visible";
            image1.filters( "revealTrans" ).transition =
               counter % 24;
         }

         whichImage = !whichImage;
         blend();
         transitionDisplay.innerHTML = "Transition " +
            counter % 24 + ": " + transitionName[ counter % 24 ];
      }
      // -->
   </script>
   </head>

   <body style = "color: white; background-color: lightcoral"
         onload = "blend()">

      <img id = "image2" src = "icontext.gif"
           style = "position: absolute; left: 10; top: 10;
           width: 300; z-index:1; visibility: visible;
           filter: revealTrans( duration = 2, transition = 0 )"
           onfilterchange = "reBlend( false )" alt =
           "Programming Tips" />

      <img id = "image1" src = "icons2.gif"
           style = "position: absolute; left: 10; top: 10;
           width: 300; z-index:1; visibility: visible;
```

Fig. 15.14 Transitions using **revealTrans** (part 2 of 4).

```
            filter: revealTrans( duration = 2, transition = 0 )"
            onfilterchange = "reBlend( true )" alt = "Icons" />

         <div id = "transitionDisplay" style = "position: absolute;
            top: 70; left: 80">Transition 0: Box In</div>

      </body>
   </html>
```

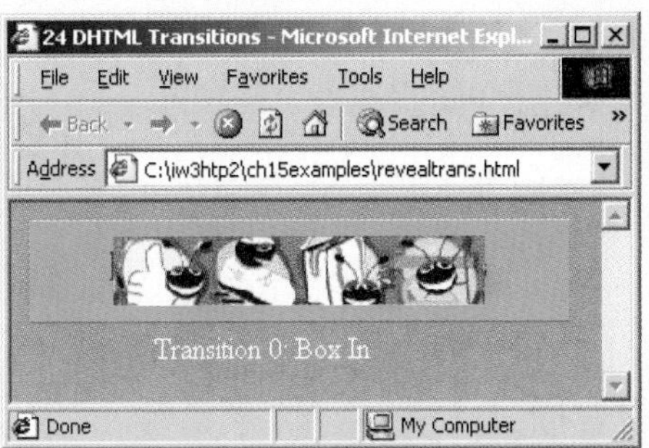

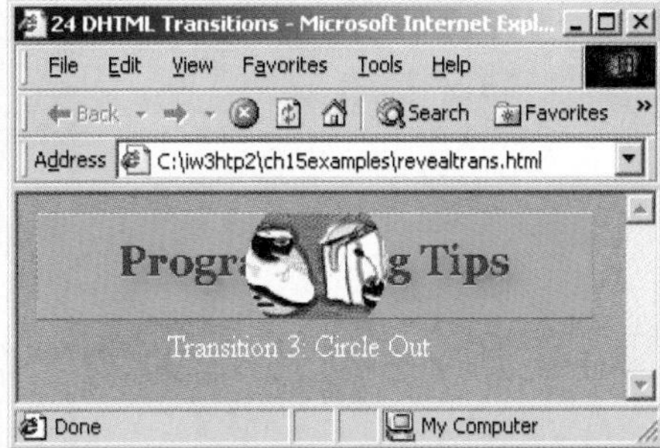

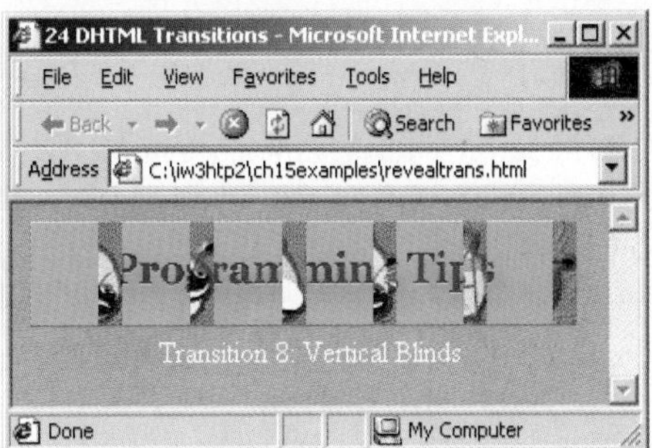

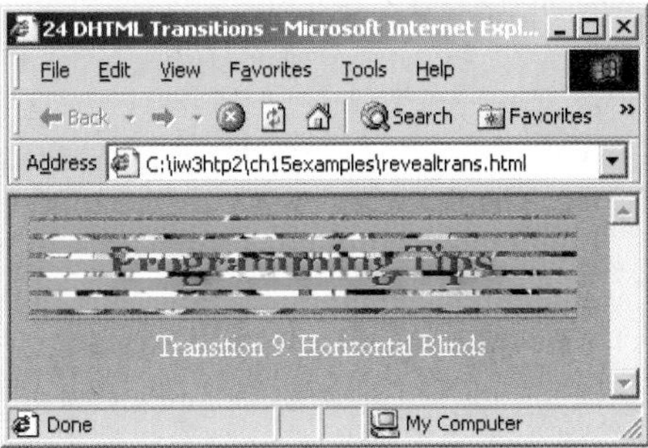

Fig. 15.14 Transitions using **`revealTrans`** (part 3 of 4).

Fig. 15.14 Transitions using **`revealTrans`** (part 4 of 4).

The script in this example is almost the same as the script in the **`blendTrans`** example. In lines 52–53, we set the **`transition`** property of the image, which determines what visual transition is used here. There are 24 different visual transitions (their names are listed in the **`transitionName`** array) for updating the **`div`** element **`transitionDisplay`**.

SUMMARY

- Applying filters to text and images causes changes that are persistent.
- Transitions are temporary phenomena; applying a transition allows you to transfer from one page to another with a pleasant visual effect, such as a random dissolve.
- Filters and transitions do not add content to your pages—rather, they present existing content in an engaging manner to help hold the user's attention.
- Each of the visual effects achievable with filters and transitions is programmable, so these effects can be adjusted dynamically by programs that respond to user-initiated events like mouse clicks and keystrokes.
- When Internet Explorer renders your page, it applies all the special effects and does this while running on the client computer without lengthy waits for files to download from the server.
- The **`flipv`** and **`fliph`** filters mirror text or images vertically and horizontally, respectively.
- Filters are applied in the **`style`** attribute. The **`filter`** property's value is the name of the filter.
- More than one filter can be applied at once. Enter multiple filters as values of the **`filter`** attribute, separated by spaces.
- The **`chroma`** filter applies transparency effects dynamically, without using a graphics editor to hard-code transparency into the image.

- Use the **parseInt** function to convert a string to a hexadecimal integer for setting the **color** property of the **chroma** filter. The second parameter of **parseInt** specifies the base of the integer.
- Each filter has a property named **enabled**. If this property is set to **true**, the filter is applied. If it is set to **false**, the filter is not applied.
- The **onchange** event fires whenever the **value** of a form field changes.
- Applying the **mask** filter to an image allows you to create an image mask, in which the background of an element is a solid color and the foreground of an element is transparent to the image or color behind it.
- Parameters for filters are always specified in the format *param* = *value*.
- The **invert** filter applies a negative image effect—dark areas become light, and light areas become dark.
- The **gray** filter applies a grayscale image effect, in which all color is stripped from the image and all that remains is brightness data.
- The **xray** filter applies an x-ray effect which is basically just an inversion of the grayscale effect.
- A simple filter that adds depth to your text is the **shadow** filter. This filter creates a shadowing effect that gives your text a three-dimensional look. The **direction** property of the **shadow** filter determines in which direction the shadow effect will be applied—this can be set to any of eight directions, expressed in angular notation: **0** (up), **45** (above-right), **90** (right), **135** (below-right), **180** (below), **225** (below-left), **270** (left) and **315** (above-left). The **color** property of the **shadow** filter specifies the color of the shadow that is applied to the text.
- Internet Explorer 5.5 allows you to create gradient effects dynamically, using the **alpha** filter. The **style** property of the filter determines in what style the opacity is applied; a value of **0** applies uniform opacity, a value of **1** applies a linear gradient, a value of **2** applies a circular gradient and a value of **3** applies a rectangular gradient. The **opacity** and **finishopacity** properties are both percentages determining at what percent opacity the specified gradient will start and finish, respectively. Additional attributes are **startX**, **startY**, **finishX** and **finishY**. These allow you to specify at what *x*-*y* coordinates the gradient starts and finishes in that element.
- The **glow** filter allows you to add an aura of color around your text. The **color** and **strength** can both be specified.
- The **blur** filter creates an illusion of motion by blurring text or images in a certain direction. The **blur** filter can be applied in any of eight directions, and its strength can vary. The **add** property, when set to **true**, adds a copy of the original image over the blurred image, creating a more subtle blurring effect. The **direction** property determines in which direction the **blur** filter will be applied. This is expressed in angular form (as with the **shadow** filter). The **strength** property determines how strong the blurring effect is.
- The **wave** filter allows you to apply sine-wave distortions to text and images on your Web pages.
- The **add** property, as in the case of the **blur** filter, adds a copy of the text or image, but underneath the filtered effect. The **add** property is useful when applying the **wave** filter to images. The **freq** property determines the frequency of the wave applied—i.e., how many complete sine waves are applied in the affected area. Increasing this property would create a more pronounced wave effect, but makes the text harder to read. The **phase** property indicates the phase shift of the wave. Increasing this property does not modify any physical attributes of the wave, but merely shifts it in space. This property is useful for creating a gentle waving effect, as we do in this example. The last property, **strength**, is the amplitude of the sine wave that is applied.
- Two filters that apply advanced image processing effects are the **dropShadow** and **light** filters. The **dropShadow** filter applies an effect similar to the drop shadow we applied to our im-

ages in Chapter 3—it creates a blacked-out version of the image, and places it behind the image, offset by a specified number of pixels.

- The **light** filter is the most powerful and advanced filter available in Internet Explorer 5.5. It allows you to simulate the effect of a light source shining on your page.
- The **offx** and **offy** properties of the **dropShadow** filter determine by how many pixels the drop shadow offsets. The **color** property specifies the color of the drop shadow.
- All the parameters and methods of the light **filter** are done by scripting. The **addPoint** method adds a point light source—a source of light which emanates from a single point and radiates in all directions. The first two parameters set the *x-y* coordinates at which to add the point source. The next parameter sets the height of the point source.This simulates how far above the surface the light is situated. Small values create a small but high-intensity circle of light on the image, while large values cast a circle of light which is darker, but spreads over a greater distance. The next three parameters specify the RGB value of the light, in decimal.The last parameter is a strength percentage.
- The **moveLight** method updates the position of the light source. The first parameter is the index of the light source on the page. Multiple light sources have index numbers assigned to them in the order they are added. The next two parameters specify the *x-y* coordinates to which we should move the light source. The next parameter specifies the height to which we move the light source. Setting the last parameter to **1** indicates that the values we are using are absolute. To move your light source by relative amounts instead, use a value of **0** for the last parameter of the **moveLight** function.
- The parameters of the **addCone** method are similar to the **addPoint** method. The first two parameters specify the *x-y* coordinates of the light source, and the third parameter specifies the simulated height above the page at which the light should be placed. The next two parameters specify the *x-y* coordinates at which the cone source is targeted. The next three parameters specify the RGB value of the light which is cast, just as in the **addPoint** method. The next parameter specifies the strength of the cone source, in a percentage. The last value specifies the spread of the light source, in degrees (this can be set in the range **0-90**).
- The transitions included with Internet Explorer 5.5 give the author control of scriptable PowerPoint type effects. Transitions are set as values of the **filter** CSS property, just as regular filters are.
- The **duration** parameter of **blendTrans** determines how long the transition will take.
- The **apply** method initializes the transition for the affected element. The **play** method then begins the transition.
- The **revealTrans** filter allows you to transition using professional-style transitions, from Box Out to Random Dissolve. The **transition** property determines what visual transition is used. There are 24 different visual transitions.

TERMINOLOGY

add property of **blur** filter
add property of **wave** filter
addCone method of **light** filter
addPoint method of **light** filter
alpha filter
blendTrans filter
blur filter
chroma filter
circular gradient
color property of **chroma** filter
color property of **dropshadow** filter
color property of **glow** filter
color property of **shadow** filter
combining filters
cone light source
CSS **filter** property
direction property of **blur** filter
direction property of **shadow** filter
dropShadow filter
duration of **blendTrans** filter

enabled property of each filter
fade-in/fade-out effect
filter
filter property with **style** attribute
filter **strength**
filter:alpha
filter:blur
filter:chroma
filter:dropshadow
filter:fliph
filter:flipv
filter:glow
filter:gray
filter:invert
filter:light
filter:mask
filter:shadow
filter:wave
filter:xray
finishopacity property of **alpha** filter
finishx property of **alpha** filter
finishy property of **alpha** filter
flipH filter
flipV filter
freq property of **wave** filter
glow filter
gradient
gray filter
grayscale image effect
height of light source
horizontal blinds transition
illusion of motion by blurring
image mask
invert filter
light filter
linear opacity
mask filter
moveLight property of **light** filter
negative image effect with **invert** filter
offx property of **dropshadow** filter
offy property of **dropshadow** filter
opacity property of **alpha** filter
padding (CSS)
phase property of **wave** filter
phase shift of a wave
point light source
radial opacity
random dissolve transition
rectangular opacity
revealTrans filter
shadow filter
sine-wave distortions
spread of cone light source
startx property of **alpha** filter
starty property of **alpha** filter
strength property of **blur** filter
strength property of **glow** filter
strength property of **wave** filter
style property of **alpha** filter
three-dimensional effect with **shadow** filter
transition effects
transparency effects
uniform opacity
vertical blinds transition
visibility
visual filters
wave filter
xray filter

SELF-REVIEW EXERCISES

15.1 State whether the following are *true* or *false*. If *false*, explain why.

a) You can determine the strength of the **shadow** filter.
b) The **flip** filter flips text horizontally.
c) The **mask** filter makes the foreground of an element transparent.
d) The **freq** property of the wave filter determines how many sine waves are applied to that element.
e) Increasing the margin of an element prevents the **glow** filter from being clipped by the element's border.
f) The **apply** method begins a transition.
g) The **invert** filter creates a negative image effect.
h) The **add** property adds a duplicate image below the affected image.

15.2 Fill in the blanks in the following statements:

a) You must use the __________ function to pass a value to the **color** property.

b) The last parameter of the **moveLight** method determines whether the move is __________ or __________.

c) The amplitude of the **wave** filter is controlled by the __________ property.

d) There are __________ **directions** in which the **blur** filter can be applied.

e) There are two coordinate pairs in the parameters of the **addCone** method: the __________ and the __________.

f) There are __________ different transition styles for the **revealTrans** transition.

g) The two properties of the **dropShadow** filter that specify the offset of the shadow are __________ and __________.

h) The four styles of opacity are __________, __________, __________ and __________.

i) The __________ filter creates a grayscale version of the effected image.

ANSWERS TO SELF-REVIEW EXERCISES

15.1 a) False; there is no **strength** property for the **shadow** filter. b) False; the **flipH** filter flips text horizontally. c) True. d) True. e) False; increasing the padding of an element prevents clipping. f) False; the **play** method begins a transition. g) True. h) True.

15.2 a) **parseInt**. b) relative, absolute. c) **strength**. d) eight. e) source, target. f) 24. g) **offx**, **offy**. h) uniform, linear, circular, rectangular. i) **gray**.

EXERCISES

15.3 Create a Web page that applies the **invert** filter to an image if the user moves the mouse over the image.

15.4 Create a Web page that applies the **glow** filter to a hyperlink if the user moves the mouse over the link.

15.5 Write a script that **blur**s images and slowly unblurs them when they are finished loading into the browser (use event **onload** for the image).

15.6 Write a script that creates a cone **light** filter that tracks mouse movements across the page.

15.7 Write a script that uses the **blendTrans** filter to transition into an image after the image fully loads (use event **onload** for the image).

15.8 Write a script that changes the attributes of an **alpha** filter every 20 seconds (see **setInterval** in Chapter 13). Change both the color and the style of the **alpha** filter every time.

15.9 *(Slide Show)* Use the **revealTrans** filter to present your own slide show in a Web page. On each transition, display a new image.

15.10 *(Image Selector)* Design a Web page that allows the user to choose from a series of images and allows the user to view the image in color and in grayscale.

16

Dynamic HTML: Data Binding with Tabular Data Control

Objectives

- To understand Dynamic HTML's notion of data binding and how to bind data to XHTML elements.
- To be able to sort and filter data directly on the client without involving the server.
- To be able to bind a **`table`** and other XHTML elements to data source objects (DSOs).
- To be able to filter data to select only records appropriate for a particular application.
- To be able to navigate backward and forward through a database with the **`Move`** methods.

Let's look at the record.
Alfred Emanuel Smith

It is a capital mistake to theorize before one has data.
Sir Arthur Conan Doyle

The more the data banks record about each one of us, the less we exist.
Marshall McLuhan

Poor fellow, he suffers from files.
Aneurin Bevan

Outline

16.1 Introduction

This is one of the most important chapters for people who will build substantial, real-world, Web-based applications. Businesses and organizations thrive on data. Dynamic HTML helps Web application developers produce more responsive data-intensive applications.

Performance Tip 16.1

Prior to Dynamic HTML, the kinds of data manipulations we discuss in this chapter had to be done on the server, increasing the server load and the network load and resulting in choppy application responsiveness. With Dynamic HTML, these manipulations, such as sorting and filtering data, can now be done directly on the client without involving the server and the network.

With *data binding*, data need no longer reside exclusively on the server. The data can be maintained on the client and in a manner that distinguishes that data from the XHTML markup on the page. Typically, data are sent to the client and then all subsequent manipulations take place on that data directly on the client, thus eliminating server activity and network delays.

Performance Tip 16.2

With Dynamic HTML (rather than server-based database processing) it is more likely that a larger amount of data will be sent to the client on the first request. This initial downloading of the data by Internet Explorer is performed in a manner that enables processing to begin immediately on the portion of the data that has arrived.

Also, with the kind of data-binding technology we discuss in this chapter, changes to data made on the client do not propagate back to the server. This is not a problem for a great many popular applications. If you do need to access the database directly and have the changes that you make on the client actually update the original database, you can use techniques we demonstrate in Chapters 25–31.

Once the data is available on the client, the data can then be sorted and filtered in various ways. We present examples of each of these operations.

To bind external data to XHTML elements, Internet Explorer employs software capable of connecting the browser to live data sources. These are known as *Data Source*

Objects (DSOs). There are several DSOs available in IE5.5—in this chapter we discuss the most popular DSO—the *Tabular Data Control (TDC)*.

Software Engineering Observation 16.1

Data-bound properties can be modified with Dynamic HTML even after the browser renders the page.

16.2 Simple Data Binding

The Tabular Data Control (TDC) is an ActiveX control that is added to a page with the **object** element. Data are stored in a separate file (Fig. 16.1) and not embedded into the XHTML document. Figure 16.2 demonstrates a simple use of data binding with the TDC to update the contents of a **span** element (the data file used by this example is listed in Fig. 16.1).

```
@ColorName@|@ColorHexRGBValue@
@aqua@|@#00FFFF@
@black@|@#000000@
@blue@|@#0000FF@
@fuchsia@|@#FF00FF@
@gray@|@#808080@
@green@|@#008000@
@lime@|@#00FF00@
@maroon@|@#800000@
@navy@|@#000080@
@olive@|@#808000@
@purple@|@#800080@
@red@|@#FF0000@
@silver@|@#C0C0C0@
@teal@|@#008080@
@yellow@|@#FFFF00@
@white@|@#FFFFFF@
```

Fig. 16.1 XHTML color table data (**HTMLStandardColors.txt**).

```
<?xml version = "1.0"?>
<!DOCTYPE html PUBLIC "-//W3C//DTD XHTML 1.0 Strict//EN"
   "http://www.w3.org/TR/xhtml1/DTD/xhtml1-strict.dtd">

<!-- Fig 16.2: introdatabind.html                       -->
<!-- Simple data binding and recordset manipulation -->

<html xmlns = "http://www.w3.org/1999/xhtml">
   <head>
      <title>Intro to Data Binding</title>

      <!-- This object element inserts an ActiveX control -->
      <!-- for handling and parsing our data. The PARAM    -->
      <!-- tags give the control starting parameters       -->
      <!-- such as URL.                                    -->
      <object id = "Colors"
         classid = "CLSID:333C7BC4-460F-11D0-BC04-0080C7055A83">
```

Fig. 16.2 Simple data binding (part 1 of 4).

```
         <param name = "DataURL" value =
            "HTMLStandardColors.txt" />
         <param name = "UseHeader" value = "TRUE" />
         <param name = "TextQualifier" value = "@" />
         <param name = "FieldDelim" value = "|" />
      </object>

      <script type = "text/javascript">
         <!--
         var recordSet = Colors.recordset;

         function reNumber()
         {
            if ( !recordSet.EOF )
               recordNumber.innerText =
                  recordSet.absolutePosition;
            else
               recordNumber.innerText = " ";
         }

         function forward()
         {
            recordSet.MoveNext();

            if ( recordSet.EOF )
               recordSet.MoveFirst();

            colorSample.style.backgroundColor =
               colorRGB.innerText;
            reNumber();
         }
         // -->
      </script>
   </head>

   <body onload = "reNumber()" onclick = "forward()">

      <h1>XHTML Color Table</h1>
      <h3>Click to move forward in the recordset.</h3>

      <p><strong>Color Name: </strong>
      <span id = "colorId" style = "font-family: monospace"
         datasrc = "#Colors" datafld = "ColorName"></span><br />

      <strong>Color RGB Value: </strong>
      <span id = "colorRGB" style = "font-family: monospace"
         datasrc = "#Colors" datafld = "ColorHexRGBValue">
      </span><br />

      Currently viewing record number
      <span id = "recordNumber" style = "font-weight: 900">
      </span><br />

```

Fig. 16.2 Simple data binding (part 2 of 4).

```
         <span id = "colorSample" style = "background-color: aqua;
            color: 888888; font-size: 30pt">Color Sample
         </span></p>

      </body>
   </html>
```

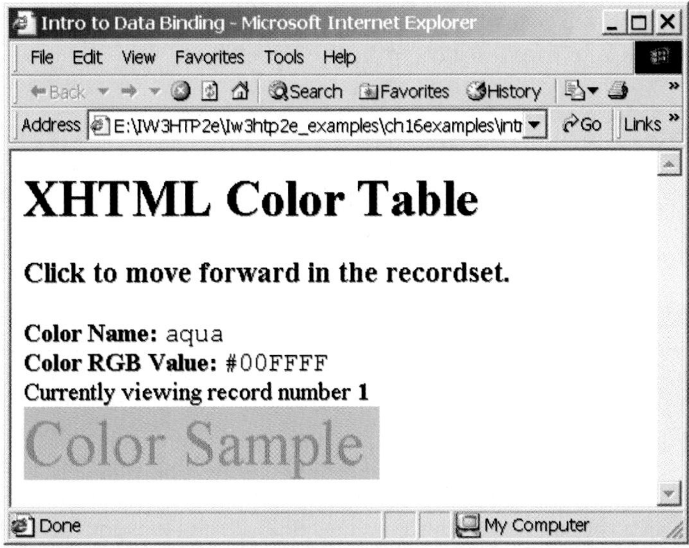

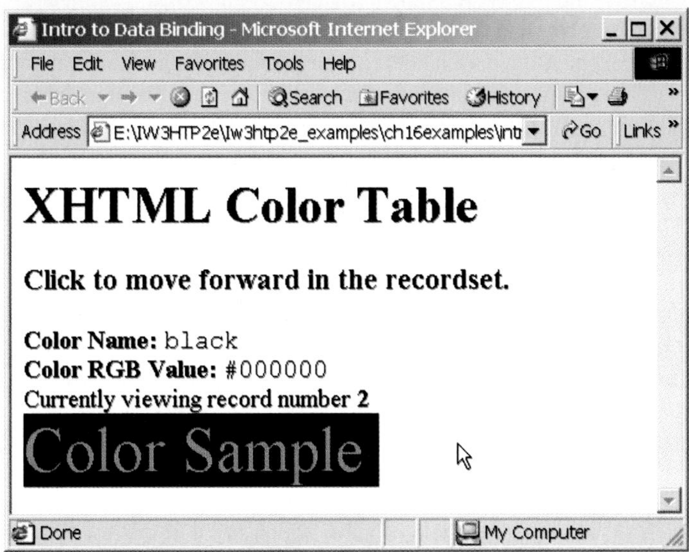

Fig. 16.2 Simple data binding (part 3 of 4).

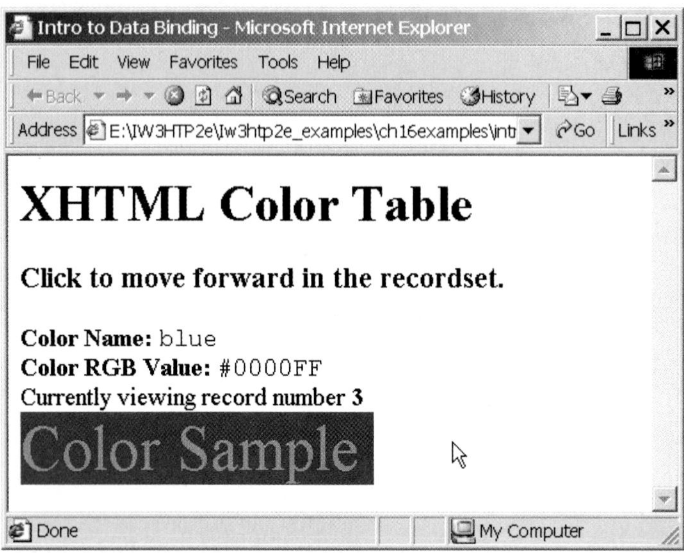

Fig. 16.2 Simple data binding (part 4 of 4).

Line 1 of Fig. 16.1 begins our data file with a *header row*. This row specifies the names of the columns below (**`ColorName`** and **`ColorHexRGBValue`**). Data in each field is enclosed in *text qualifiers* (**`@`**) and each field is separated with a *field delimiter* (|).

The **`object`** element (lines 16–23 in Fig. 16.2) here inserts the Tabular Data Control—one of the Microsoft ActiveX controls built into Internet Explorer 5.5. Attribute **`classid`** specifies the ActiveX control to add to the Web page—here we use the **`classid`** of the Tabular Data Control.

The **`param`** tag specifies parameters for the object in the **`object`** element. Attribute **`name`** is the parameter name and attribute **`value`** is the value. Parameter **`DataURL`** is the URL of the data source (**`HTMLStandardColors.txt`**). Parameter **`UseHeader`**, when set to **`true`**, specifies that the first line of our data file has a header row.

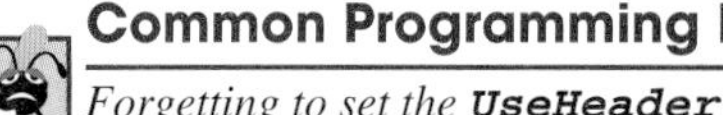

Common Programming Error 16.1

Forgetting to set the **`UseHeader`** *parameter to* **`true`** *when you have a header row in your data source is an error that can cause problems in referencing columns.*

The third parameter, **`TextQualifier`**, sets the *text qualifier* of our data (in this case to **`@`**). A text qualifier is the character placed on both ends of the field data. The fourth parameter, **`FieldDelim`**, sets the field delimiter of our data (in this case to |). The field is the character delimiting separate data fields.

Lines 59–60 bind the data to a **`span`** element. The **`datasrc`** attribute refers to the **`id`** of the TDC object (**`Colors`**, in this case) preceded with a hash mark (**`#`**), and the **`datafld`** attribute specifies the name of the field to bind it to (**`ColorName`**, in this case). This places the data contained in the first *record* (i.e., row) of the **`ColorName`** column into the **`span`** element.

So far, we only have a static display of data. We can update it dynamically with some simple scripting. Line 27 assigns the **`recordset`** property of the **`Colors`** object (our

TDC **object** element) to the variable **recordSet**. A *recordset* is simply a set of data—in our case, it is the data from our **HTMLStandardColors.txt** data source. To move the recordset to a different row in the data source, line 41 calls the **MoveNext** ***method*** of the **recordSet** object. This moves the current recordset forward by one row, automatically updating the **span** to which we bound our data. Note that line 40 determines if the boolean **EOF** property of the **recordSet** is **false**. If **false**, it indicates that the end of the data source has been reached. If **EOF** is **true**, line 43 calls the **MoveFirst** method to move to the first recordset in the file.

Common Programming Error 16.2

Trying to use the **MoveNext** *or* **MovePrevious** *methods past the boundaries of the data source is a JavaScript error.*

16.3 Moving a Recordset

Most applications will probably need more functionality than simply moving forward. Figure 16.3 demonstrates creating a user interface for navigating the data source of Fig. 16.1.

The **switch** on lines 31–64 evaluates the value passed to **move**. The two new functions we use are ***MoveLast*** and ***MovePrevious***, which move to the last recordset and the previous recordset, respectively. Line 41 tests if the recordset is pointing to the beginning of the file (**BOF**), so that we can redirect it.

Common Programming Error 16.3

Calling **MovePrevious** *when a recordset points to the first record in a data file is an error.*

```
1  <?xml version = "1.0"?>
2  <!DOCTYPE html PUBLIC "-//W3C//DTD XHTML 1.0 Transitional//EN"
3     "http://www.w3.org/TR/xhtml1/DTD/xhtml1-transitional.dtd">
4
5  <!-- Fig 16.3: moving.html       -->
6  <!-- Moving through a recordset -->
7
8  <html xmlns = "http://www.w3.org/1999/xhtml">
9     <head>
10       <title>Dynamic Recordset Viewing</title>
11       <object id = "Colors"
12          classid = "CLSID:333C7BC4-460F-11D0-BC04-0080C7055A83">
13          <param name = "DataURL" value =
14             "HTMLStandardColors.txt" />
15          <param name = "UseHeader" value = "TRUE" />
16          <param name = "TextQualifier" value = "@" />
17          <param name = "FieldDelim" value = "|" />
18       </object>
19
20       <script type = "text/javascript">
21          <!--
22          var recordSet = Colors.recordset;
23
```

Fig. 16.3 Moving through a recordset using JavaScript (part 1 of 4).

```
         function update()
         {
            h1Title.style.color = colorRGB.innerText;
         }

         function move( whereTo )
         {
            switch ( whereTo ) {

               case "first":
                  recordSet.MoveFirst();
                  update();
                  break;

               // If recordset is at beginning, move to end.
               case "previous":

                  recordSet.MovePrevious();

                  if ( recordSet.BOF )
                     recordSet.MoveLast();

                  update();
                  break;

               // If recordset is at end, move to beginning.
               case "next":

                  recordSet.MoveNext();

                  if ( recordSet.EOF )
                     recordSet.MoveFirst();

                  update();
                  break;

               case "last":
                  recordSet.MoveLast();
                  update();
                  break;
            }
         }
         // -->
      </script>

      <style type = "text/css">
        input { background-color: khaki;
                color: green;
                font-weight: bold }
      </style>
   </head>

   <body style = "background-color: darkkhaki">
```

Fig. 16.3 Moving through a recordset using JavaScript (part 2 of 4).

```

      <h1 style = "color: black" id = "h1Title">
         XHTML Color Table</h1>
      <span style = "position: absolute; left: 200; width: 270;
         border-style: groove; text-align: center;
         background-color: cornsilk; padding: 10">
      <strong>Color Name: </strong>
      <span id = "colorName" style = "font-family: monospace"
         datasrc = "#Colors" datafld = "ColorName">ABC</span>
      <br />

      <strong>Color RGB Value: </strong>
      <span id = "colorRGB" style = "font-family: monospace"
         datasrc = "#Colors" datafld = "ColorHexRGBValue">ABC
      </span><br />

      <input type = "button" value = "First"
         onclick = "move( 'first' );" />

      <input type = "button" value = "Previous"
         onclick = "move( 'previous' );" />

      <input type = "button" value = "Next"
         onclick = "move( 'next' );" />

      <input type = "button" value = "Last"
         onclick = "move( 'last' );" />
      </span>

   </body>
</html>
```

Fig. 16.3 Moving through a recordset using JavaScript (part 3 of 4).

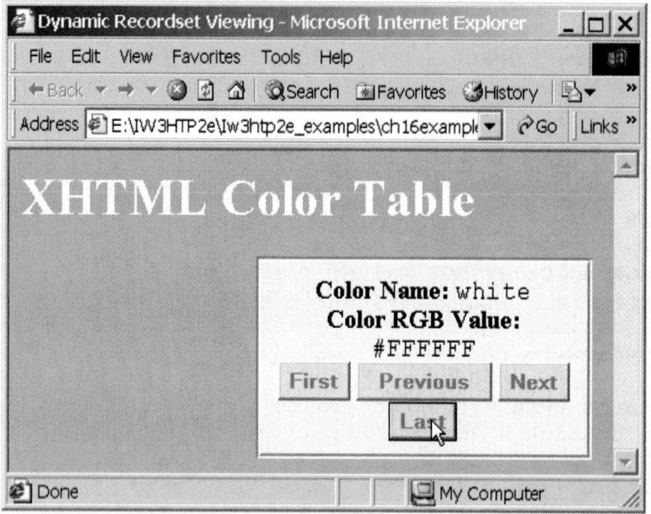

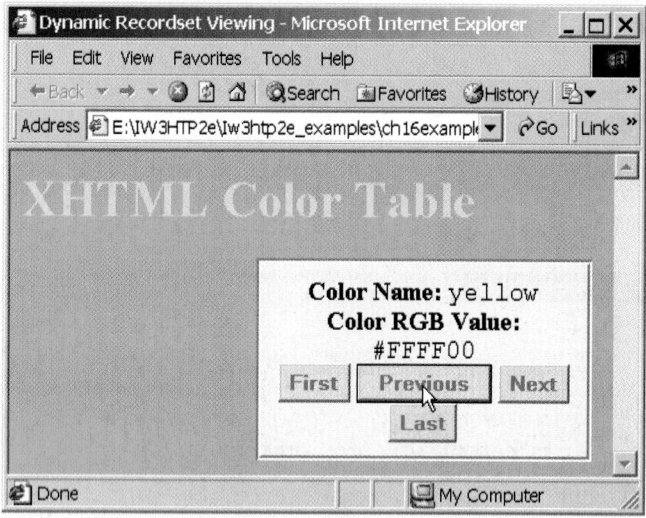

Fig. 16.3 Moving through a recordset using JavaScript (part 4 of 4).

16.4 Binding to an `img`

Many different types of XHTML elements can be bound to data sources. One of the more interesting elements in which to bind data is the **`img`** element. Figure 16.4 lists a data source that contains image file names. Figure 16.5 binds an **`img`** element to the data source shown in Fig. 16.4.

```
image
numbers/0.gif
numbers/1.gif
numbers/2.gif
numbers/3.gif
numbers/4.gif
numbers/5.gif
numbers/6.gif
numbers/7.gif
numbers/8.gif
numbers/9.gif
```

Fig. 16.4 **images.txt** data source file for Fig. 16.5.

```
<?xml version = "1.0"?>
<!DOCTYPE html PUBLIC "-//W3C//DTD XHTML 1.0 Transitional//EN"
   "http://www.w3.org/TR/xhtml1/DTD/xhtml1-transitional.dtd">

<!-- Fig. 16.5: bindimg.html  -->
<!-- Binding data to an image -->

<html xmlns = "http://www.w3.org/1999/xhtml">
   <head>
      <title>Binding to a img</title>

      <object id = "Images"
         classid = "CLSID:333C7BC4-460F-11D0-BC04-0080C7055A83">
         <param name = "DataURL" value = "images.txt" />
         <param name = "UseHeader" value = "True" />
      </object>

      <script type = "text/javascript">
         <!--
         recordSet = Images.recordset;

         function move( whereTo )
         {
            switch( whereTo ) {

               case "first":
                  recordSet.MoveFirst();
                  break;

               case "previous":

                  recordSet.MovePrevious();

                  if ( recordSet.BOF )
                     recordSet.MoveLast();

                  break;

```

Fig. 16.5 Binding data to an **img** element (part 1 of 2).

```
               case "next":

                  recordSet.MoveNext();

                  if ( recordSet.EOF )
                     recordSet.MoveFirst();

                  break;

               case "last":
                  recordSet.MoveLast();
                  break;
            }
         }
         // -->
      </script>
   </head>

   <body>

      <img datasrc = "#Images" datafld = "image" alt = "Image"
          style = "position: relative; left: 45px" /><br />

      <input type = "button" value = "First"
        onclick = "move( 'first' );" />

      <input type = "button" value = "Previous"
         onclick = "move( 'previous' );" />

      <input type = "button" value = "Next"
         onclick = "move( 'next' );" />

      <input type = "button" value = "Last"
         onclick = "move( 'last' );" />

   </body>
</html>
```

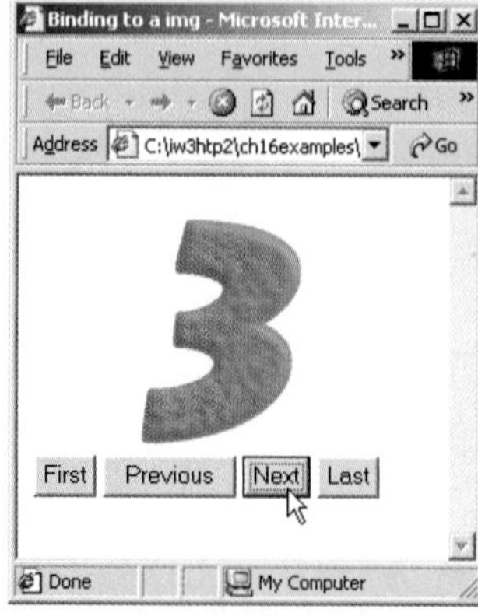

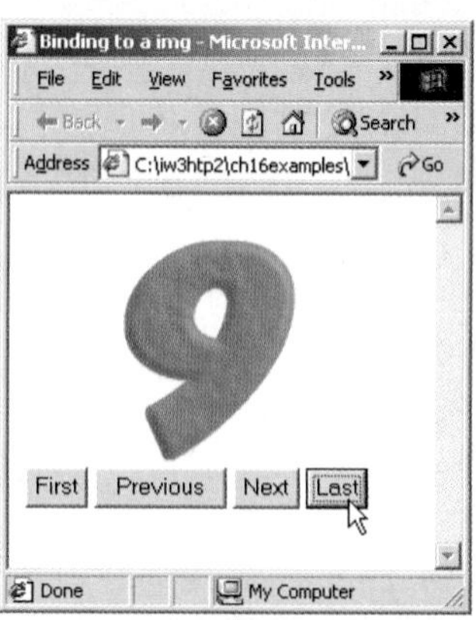

Fig. 16.5 Binding data to an **img** element (part 2 of 2).

Lines 59–60 bind the data source to an **`img`** element. When binding to an **`img`** element, changing the recordset updates the **`src`** attribute of the image. Clicking any of the navigation buttons changes the image displayed on screen.

16.5 Binding to a `table`

Binding data to a **`table`** element is perhaps the most important feature of data binding. This is done somewhat differently from the data binding we have seen. Figure 16.6 binds to a **`table`** element the data in Fig. 16.1.

```
<?xml version = "1.0"?>
<!DOCTYPE html PUBLIC "-//W3C//DTD XHTML 1.0 Strict//EN"
   "http://www.w3.org/TR/xhtml1/DTD/xhtml1-strict.dtd">

<!-- Fig. 16.6: tablebind.html      -->
<!-- Using Data Binding with tables -->

<html xmlns = "http://www.w3.org/1999/xhtml">
   <head>
      <title>Data Binding and Tables</title>
      <object id = "Colors"
         classid = "CLSID:333C7BC4-460F-11D0-BC04-0080C7055A83">
         <param name = "DataURL" value =
            "HTMLStandardColors.txt" />
         <param name = "UseHeader" value = "TRUE" />
         <param name = "TextQualifier" value = "@" />
         <param name = "FieldDelim" value = "|" />
      </object>
   </head>

   <body style = "background-color: darkseagreen">

      <h1>Binding Data to a <code>table</code></h1>

      <table datasrc = "#Colors" style = "border-style: ridge;
         border-color: darkseagreen;
         background-color: lightcyan">

         <thead>
         <tr style = "background-color: mediumslateblue">
            <th>Color Name</th>
            <th>Color RGB Value</th>
         </tr>
         </thead>

         <tbody>
            <tr style = "background-color: lightsteelblue">
               <td><span datafld = "ColorName"></span></td>
               <td><span datafld = "ColorHexRGBValue"
                  style = "font-family: monospace"></span></td>
            </tr>
         </tbody>
```

Fig. 16.6 Binding data to a **`table`** element (part 1 of 2).

```
43
44          </table>
45
46       </body>
47    </html>
```

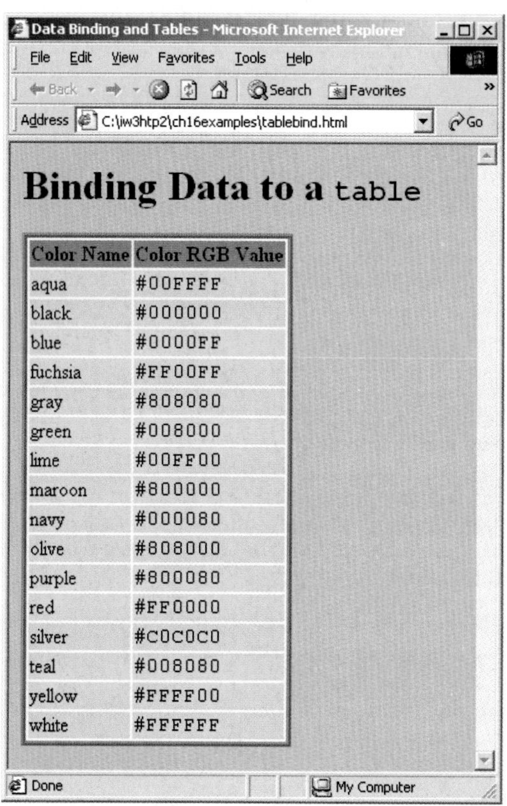

Fig. 16.6 Binding data to a **table** element (part 2 of 2).

Lines 25–27 begin binding the table by adding the **datasrc** attribute to the opening **table** tag. We complete the data binding in lines 38–40 by adding the **datafld** attribute to **span** tags that reside in the table cells. Note that in the file we only have one row of table cells—Internet Explorer iterates through the data file, and creates a table row for each record it finds.

16.6 Sorting table Data

If you are manipulating a large data source, your client will probably need some way to sort the data. This is accomplished with the **Sort** property of the TDC (Fig. 16.7).

```
<?xml version = "1.0"?>
<!DOCTYPE html PUBLIC "-//W3C//DTD XHTML 1.0 Strict//EN"
   "http://www.w3.org/TR/xhtml1/DTD/xhtml1-strict.dtd">

<!-- Fig 16.7: sorting.html -->
<!-- Sorting table data     -->

<html xmlns = "http://www.w3.org/1999/xhtml">
   <head>
      <title>Data Binding and Tables</title>
      <object id = "Colors"
         classid = "CLSID:333C7BC4-460F-11D0-BC04-0080C7055A83">
         <param name = "DataURL" value =
            "HTMLStandardColors.txt" />
         <param name = "UseHeader" value = "TRUE" />
         <param name = "TextQualifier" value = "@" />
         <param name = "FieldDelim" value = "|" />
      </object>
   </head>

   <body style = "background-color: darkseagreen">

      <h1>Sorting Data</h1>

      <table datasrc = "#Colors" style = "border-style: ridge;
         border-color: darkseagreen;
         background-color: lightcyan">
         <caption>
         Sort by:

         <select onchange = "Colors.Sort = this.value;
            Colors.Reset();">
            <option value = "ColorName">Color Name (Ascending)
               </option>
            <option value = "-ColorName">Color Name (Descending)
               </option>
            <option value = "ColorHexRGBValue">Color RGB Value
               (Ascending)</option>
            <option value = "-ColorHexRGBValue">Color RGB Value
               (Descending)</option>
         </select>
         </caption>

         <thead>
         <tr style = "background-color: mediumslateblue">
            <th>Color Name</th>
            <th>Color RGB Value</th>
         </tr>
         </thead>

         <tbody>
         <tr style = "background-color: lightsteelblue">
            <td><span datafld = "ColorName"></span></td>
```

Fig. 16.7 Sorting data in a **table** (part 1 of 2).

```
54                  <td><span datafld = "ColorHexRGBValue"
55                     style = "font-family: monospace"></span></td>
56               </tr>
57               </tbody>
58
59            </table>
60
61         </body>
62      </html>
```

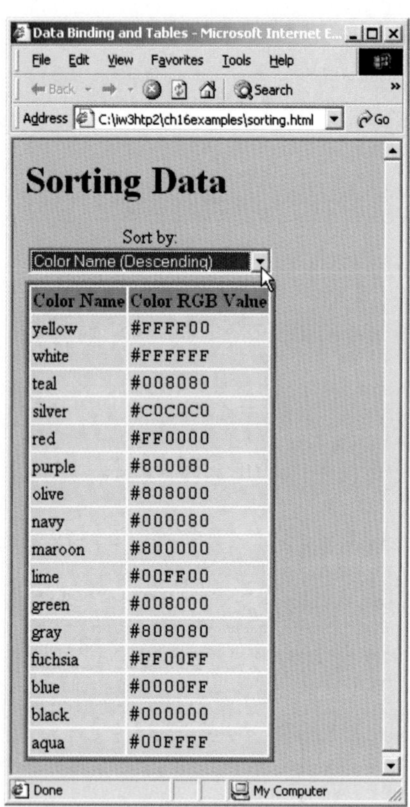

Fig. 16.7 Sorting data in a **table** (part 2 of 2).

Lines 31–32 sort our data by specifying the column by which to sort in the **Sort** property of the TDC. This example sets property **Sort** to the value of the selected **option** tag (**this.value**) when the **onchange** event is fired. JavaScript keyword **this** refers to the element in which the statement resides (i.e., the **select** element). Therefore, the **value** property refers to the currently selected **option** tag. After setting the **Sort** property, we invoke the **Reset** method of the TDC to display our data in its new sort order.

Lines 33–36 set the **value** attributes of the **option** tags to the column names in our data file. By default, a column is sorted in ascending order. To sort in descending order, the column name is preceded with a minus sign (**-**).

16.7 Advanced Sorting and Filtering

The TDC can sort data containing multiple columns (Fig. 16.8). Combined with *filtering* (i.e., selecting data that meets a specific criteria), this provides a powerful means of data rendering (Fig. 16.9).

```
@Title:String@|@Authors:String@|@Copyright:String@|
@Edition:String@|@Type:String@
@C How to Program@|@Deitel,Deitel@|@1992@|@1@|@BK@
@C How to Program@|@Deitel,Deitel@|@1994@|@2@|@BK@
@C++ How to Program@|@Deitel,Deitel@|@1994@|@1@|@BK@
@C++ How to Program@|@Deitel,Deitel@|@1998@|@2@|@BK@
@Java How to Program@|@Deitel,Deitel@|@1997@|@1@|@BK@
@Java How to Program@|@Deitel,Deitel@|@1998@|@2@|@BK@
@Java How to Program@|@Deitel,Deitel@|@2000@|@3@|@BK@
@Visual Basic 6 How to Program@|@Deitel,Deitel,Nieto@|@1999@|
@1@|@BK@
@Internet and World Wide Web How to Program@|@Deitel,Deitel@|
@2000@|@1@|@BK@
@The Complete C++ Training Course@|@Deitel,Deitel@|@1996@|
@1@|@BKMMCD@
@The Complete C++ Training Course@|@Deitel,Deitel@|@1998@|
@2@|@BKMMCD@
@The Complete Java Training Course@|@Deitel,Deitel@|@1997@|
@1@|@BKMMCD@
@The Complete Java Training Course@|@Deitel,Deitel@|@1998@|
@2@|@BKMMCD@
@The Complete Java Training Course@|@Deitel,Deitel@|@2000@|
@3@|@BKMMCD@
@The Complete Visual Basic 6 Training Course@|
@Deitel,Deitel,Nieto@|@1999@|@1@|@BKMMCD@
@The Complete Internet and World Wide Web Programming Training Course@|@Deitel,Deitel@|@2000@|@1@|@BKMMCD@
```

Fig. 16.8 **DBPublications.txt** data file for Fig. 16.9.

```
<?xml version = "1.0"?>
<!DOCTYPE html PUBLIC "-//W3C//DTD XHTML 1.0 Strict//EN"
   "http://www.w3.org/TR/xhtml1/DTD/xhtml1-strict.dtd">

<!-- Fig 16.9: advancedsort.html -->
<!-- Sorting and filtering data  -->

<html xmlns = "http://www.w3.org/1999/xhtml">
   <head>
      <title>Data Binding - Sorting and Filtering</title>

```

Fig. 16.9 Advanced sorting and filtering (part 1 of 7).

```
      <object id = "Publications"
         classid = "CLSID:333C7BC4-460F-11D0-BC04-0080C7055A83">
         <param name = "DataURL" value = "DBPublications.txt" />
         <param name = "UseHeader" value = "TRUE" />
         <param name = "TextQualifier" value = "@" />
         <param name = "FieldDelim" value = "|" />
         <param name = "Sort" value = "+Title" />
      </object>

      <style type = "text/css">

         a       { font-size: 9pt;
                   text-decoration: underline;
                   cursor: hand;
                   color: blue }

         caption { cursor: hand; }

         span    { cursor: hand; }

      </style>

      <script type = "text/javascript">
         <!--
         var sortOrder;

         function reSort( column, order )
         {
            if ( order )
               sortOrder = "";
            else
               sortOrder = "-";

            if ( event.ctrlKey ) {
               Publications.Sort += "; " + sortOrder + column;
               Publications.Reset();
            }
            else {
               Publications.Sort = sortOrder + column;
               Publications.Reset();
            }

            spanSort.innerText = "Current sort: " +
               Publications.Sort;
         }

         function filter( filterText, filterColumn )
         {
            Publications.Filter = filterColumn + "=" +
               filterText;
            Publications.Reset();
```

Fig. 16.9 Advanced sorting and filtering (part 2 of 7).

```
            spanFilter.innerText =
               "Current filter: " + Publications.Filter;
         }

         function clearAll()
         {
            Publications.Sort = " ";
            spanSort.innerText = "Current sort: None";
            Publications.Filter = " ";
            spanFilter.innerText = "Current filter: None";
            Publications.Reset();
         }
         // -->
      </script>
   </head>

   <body>
      <h1>Advanced Sorting</h1>
      <p>Click the link next to a column head to sort by that
      column. To sort by more than one column at a time, hold
      down Ctrl while you click another sorting link. Click
      any cell to filter by the data of that cell. To clear
      filters and sorts, click the green caption bar.</p>

      <table datasrc = "#Publications" border = "1"
         cellspacing = "0" cellpadding = "2" style =
         "background-color: papayawhip;">

         <caption style = "background-color: lightgreen;
            padding: 5" onclick = "clearAll()">
            <span id = "spanFilter" style = "font-weight: bold;
               background-color: lavender">Current filter: None
               </span>
            <span id = "spanSort" style = "font-weight: bold;
               background-color: khaki">Current sort: None</span>
         </caption>

         <thead>
         <tr>
            <th>Title <br />
               (<a onclick = "reSort( 'Title', true )">
                  Ascending</a>
               <a onclick = "reSort( 'Title', false )">
                  Descending</a>)
            </th>

            <th>Authors <br />
               (<a onclick = "reSort( 'Authors', true )">
                  Ascending</a>
               <a onclick = "reSort( 'Authors', false )">
                  Descending</a>)
            </th>
```

Fig. 16.9 Advanced sorting and filtering (part 3 of 7).

```

               <th>Copyright <br />
                  (<a onclick = "reSort( 'Copyright', true )">
                     Ascending</a>
                  <a onclick = "reSort( 'Copyright', false )">
                     Descending</a>)
               </th>

               <th>Edition <br />
                  (<a onclick = "reSort( 'Edition', true )">
                     Ascending</a>
                  <a onclick = "reSort( 'Edition', false )">
                     Descending</a>)
               </th>

               <th>Type <br />
                  (<a onclick = "reSort( 'Type', true )">
                     Ascending</a>
                  <a onclick = "reSort( 'Type', false )">
                     Descending</a>)
               </th>
            </tr>
            </thead>

            <tr>
               <td><span datafld = "Title" onclick =
                  "filter( this.innerText, 'Title' )"></span>
               </td>

               <td><span datafld = "Authors" onclick =
                  "filter( this.innerText, 'Authors')"></span>
               </td>

               <td><span datafld = "Copyright" onclick =
                  "filter( this.innerText, 'Copyright' )"></span>
               </td>

               <td><span datafld = "Edition" onclick =
                  "filter( this.innerText, 'Edition' )"></span>
               </td>

               <td><span datafld = "Type" onclick =
                  "filter( this.innerText, 'Type' )"></span>
               </td>

            </tr>

         </table>

      </body>
   </html>
```

Fig. 16.9 Advanced sorting and filtering (part 4 of 7).

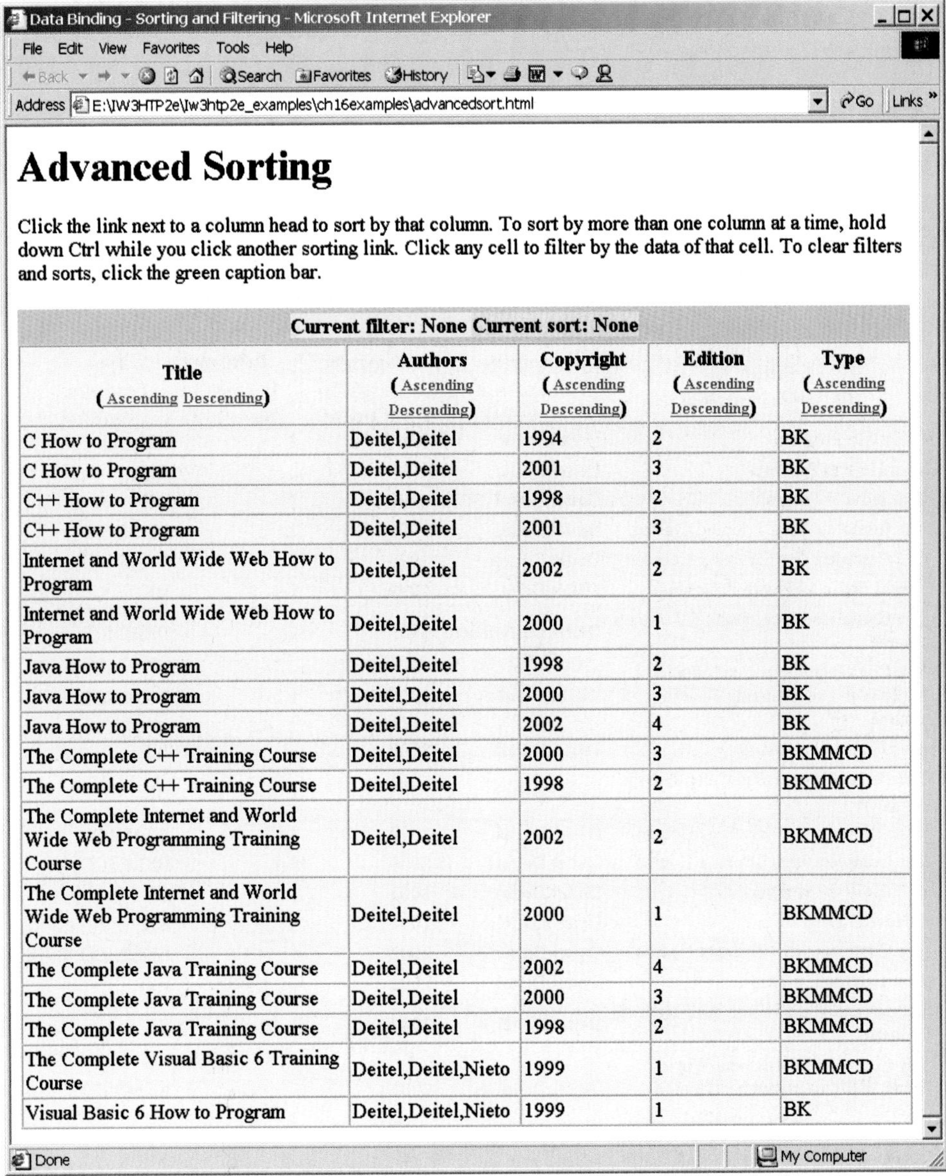

Advanced Sorting

Click the link next to a column head to sort by that column. To sort by more than one column at a time, hold down Ctrl while you click another sorting link. Click any cell to filter by the data of that cell. To clear filters and sorts, click the green caption bar.

Current filter: None Current sort: None

Title (Ascending Descending)	Authors (Ascending Descending)	Copyright (Ascending Descending)	Edition (Ascending Descending)	Type (Ascending Descending)
C How to Program	Deitel,Deitel	1994	2	BK
C How to Program	Deitel,Deitel	2001	3	BK
C++ How to Program	Deitel,Deitel	1998	2	BK
C++ How to Program	Deitel,Deitel	2001	3	BK
Internet and World Wide Web How to Program	Deitel,Deitel	2002	2	BK
Internet and World Wide Web How to Program	Deitel,Deitel	2000	1	BK
Java How to Program	Deitel,Deitel	1998	2	BK
Java How to Program	Deitel,Deitel	2000	3	BK
Java How to Program	Deitel,Deitel	2002	4	BK
The Complete C++ Training Course	Deitel,Deitel	2000	3	BKMMCD
The Complete C++ Training Course	Deitel,Deitel	1998	2	BKMMCD
The Complete Internet and World Wide Web Programming Training Course	Deitel,Deitel	2002	2	BKMMCD
The Complete Internet and World Wide Web Programming Training Course	Deitel,Deitel	2000	1	BKMMCD
The Complete Java Training Course	Deitel,Deitel	2002	4	BKMMCD
The Complete Java Training Course	Deitel,Deitel	2000	3	BKMMCD
The Complete Java Training Course	Deitel,Deitel	1998	2	BKMMCD
The Complete Visual Basic 6 Training Course	Deitel,Deitel,Nieto	1999	1	BKMMCD
Visual Basic 6 How to Program	Deitel,Deitel,Nieto	1999	1	BK

Fig. 16.9 Advanced sorting and filtering (part 5 of 7).

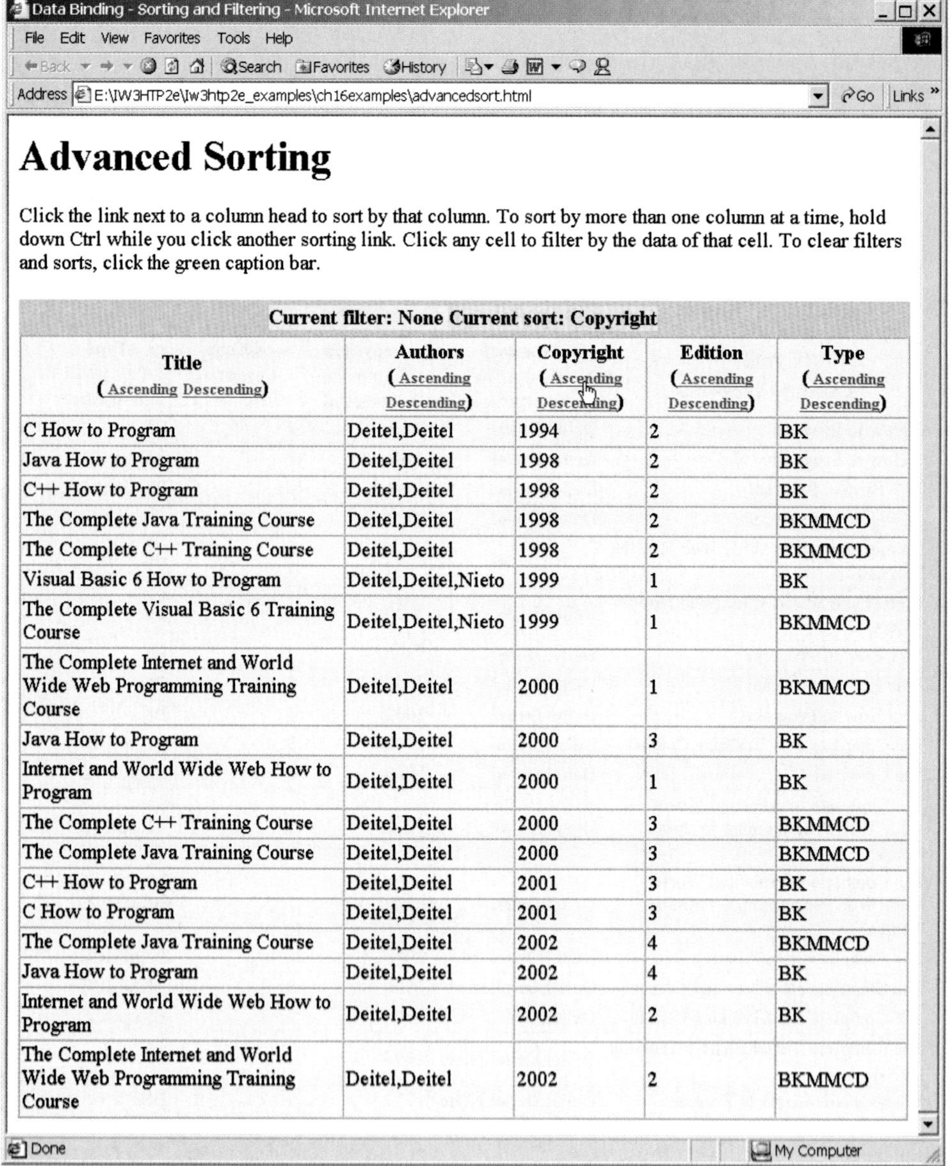

Title (Ascending Descending)	Authors (Ascending Descending)	Copyright (Ascending Descending)	Edition (Ascending Descending)	Type (Ascending Descending)
C How to Program	Deitel,Deitel	1994	2	BK
Java How to Program	Deitel,Deitel	1998	2	BK
C++ How to Program	Deitel,Deitel	1998	2	BK
The Complete Java Training Course	Deitel,Deitel	1998	2	BKMMCD
The Complete C++ Training Course	Deitel,Deitel	1998	2	BKMMCD
Visual Basic 6 How to Program	Deitel,Deitel,Nieto	1999	1	BK
The Complete Visual Basic 6 Training Course	Deitel,Deitel,Nieto	1999	1	BKMMCD
The Complete Internet and World Wide Web Programming Training Course	Deitel,Deitel	2000	1	BKMMCD
Java How to Program	Deitel,Deitel	2000	3	BK
Internet and World Wide Web How to Program	Deitel,Deitel	2000	1	BK
The Complete C++ Training Course	Deitel,Deitel	2000	3	BKMMCD
The Complete Java Training Course	Deitel,Deitel	2000	3	BKMMCD
C++ How to Program	Deitel,Deitel	2001	3	BK
C How to Program	Deitel,Deitel	2001	3	BK
The Complete Java Training Course	Deitel,Deitel	2002	4	BKMMCD
Java How to Program	Deitel,Deitel	2002	4	BK
Internet and World Wide Web How to Program	Deitel,Deitel	2002	2	BK
The Complete Internet and World Wide Web Programming Training Course	Deitel,Deitel	2002	2	BKMMCD

Fig. 16.9 Advanced sorting and filtering (part 6 of 7).

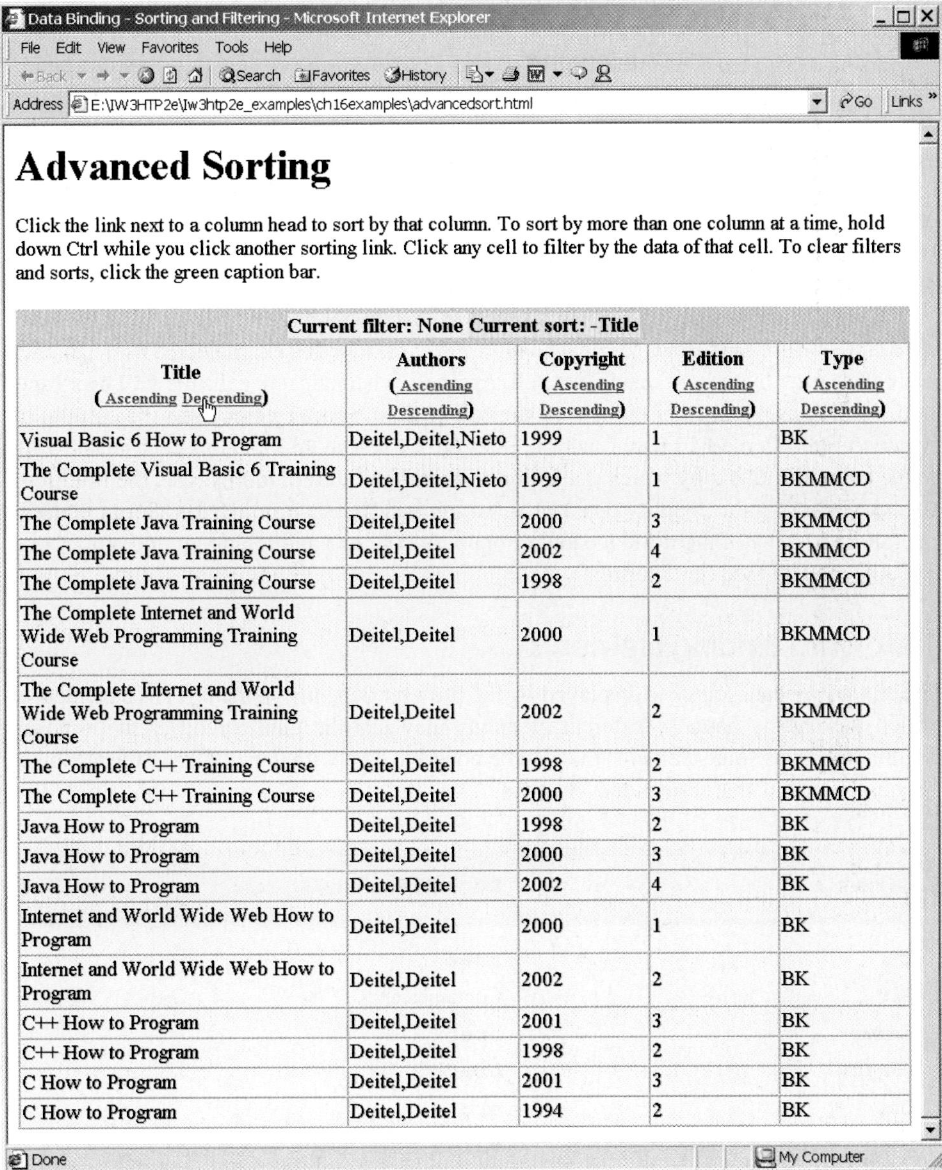

Current filter: None Current sort: -Title				
Title (Ascending Descending)	Authors (Ascending Descending)	Copyright (Ascending Descending)	Edition (Ascending Descending)	Type (Ascending Descending)
Visual Basic 6 How to Program	Deitel,Deitel,Nieto	1999	1	BK
The Complete Visual Basic 6 Training Course	Deitel,Deitel,Nieto	1999	1	BKMMCD
The Complete Java Training Course	Deitel,Deitel	2000	3	BKMMCD
The Complete Java Training Course	Deitel,Deitel	2002	4	BKMMCD
The Complete Java Training Course	Deitel,Deitel	1998	2	BKMMCD
The Complete Internet and World Wide Web Programming Training Course	Deitel,Deitel	2000	1	BKMMCD
The Complete Internet and World Wide Web Programming Training Course	Deitel,Deitel	2002	2	BKMMCD
The Complete C++ Training Course	Deitel,Deitel	1998	2	BKMMCD
The Complete C++ Training Course	Deitel,Deitel	2000	3	BKMMCD
Java How to Program	Deitel,Deitel	1998	2	BK
Java How to Program	Deitel,Deitel	2000	3	BK
Java How to Program	Deitel,Deitel	2002	4	BK
Internet and World Wide Web How to Program	Deitel,Deitel	2000	1	BK
Internet and World Wide Web How to Program	Deitel,Deitel	2002	2	BK
C++ How to Program	Deitel,Deitel	2001	3	BK
C++ How to Program	Deitel,Deitel	1998	2	BK
C How to Program	Deitel,Deitel	2001	3	BK
C How to Program	Deitel,Deitel	1994	2	BK

Fig. 16.9 Advanced sorting and filtering (part 7 of 7).

Line 18 sets the **Sort** property of the TDC using a **param** tag instead of scripting. This provides the initial sorting order (in this case, alphabetically by **Title**). Line 30 introduces the **cursor** CSS attribute, which specifies what the mouse cursor looks like when hovering over an object. In this case we set the property to **hand** (the same hand that appears when you move your cursor over a link). This lets the user know that a **span** is clickable when the cursor is moved over it.

When a user clicks the **Ascending** or **Descending** links in any of the column heads, the table resorts by that column. To do this, each column head has an associated **onclick** event that calls the **reSort** function, passing the name of the column to sort and a boolean value that specifies the sort order (**true** for ascending, **false** for descending).

The user can sort by multiple columns by holding *Ctrl* while clicking a link. Line 45 checks the boolean value **event.ctrlKey**, which returns **true** if *Ctrl* was pressed when the event was triggered. If the user did press *Ctrl*, line 46 adds another sort criterion to property **Sort**, separated from the first with a semicolon (**"; "**).

The **Filter** property filters out all records that do not have a cell matching the specified text. We use the format *ColumnName* = *FilterText*. In this example, the user can click any cell to filter by the text inside that cell. Any cell, when clicked, calls the **filter** function, passing as parameters the text of the cell (**this.innerText**) and the column by which to filter. In the **filter** function, lines 60–61 set the **Filter** property of the TDC to the column and text by which that column should be filtered. In this case, the filter tests for equality using the equality operator **=** (which is different from the JavaScript equality operator **==**). Any of the normal equality operators (**=**, **<>**) and relational operators (**>**, **<**, **>=**, **<=**) may be used for filtering.

16.8 Data Binding Elements

Exactly how a data source is displayed by the browser depends on the XHTML element to which the data is bound—different elements may use the data for different purposes. Figure 16.10 lists some elements that can be bound to data with the TDC, and the attributes of those elements that reflect data changes.

Element	Bindable Property/Attribute
a	**href**
div	Contained text
frame	**href**
iframe	**href**
img	**src**
input type = "button"	**value** (button text)
input type = "checkbox"	**checked** (use a boolean value in the data)
input type = "hidden"	**value**
input type = "password"	**value**

Fig. 16.10 XHTML elements that allow data binding.

Element	Bindable Property/Attribute
input type = "radio"	**checked** (use a boolean value in the data)
input type = "text"	**value**
marquee	Contained text
param	**value**
select	Selected **option**
span	Contained text
table	Cell elements (see Section 16.6)
textarea	Contained text (**value**)

Fig. 16.10 XHTML elements that allow data binding.

16.9 Internet and World Wide Web Resources

www.microsoft.com/data
The Microsoft *Universal Data Access Technologies* Web site provides information about Microsoft database access strategies and data source objects.

www.msdn.microsoft.com/resources/schurmandhtml.asp
This Web site for the Microsoft Press book for *Dynamic HTML in Action, Second Edition* (by Eric M. Schurman and William J. Pardi) provides information about Dynamic HTML and Microsoft database access.

SUMMARY

- With data binding, data need no longer reside exclusively on the server. The data can be maintained on the client and in a manner that distinguishes that data from the XHTML code on the page.
- Once the data is available on the client, the Web application designer can provide various functionality, especially the ability to sort and filter the data in various ways.
- The Tabular Data Control (TDC) is an ActiveX control that can be added to the page with an **object** tag.
- When a Web page is loaded with data-bound elements, the client retrieves the data from the data source specified by the TDC. The data is then formatted for display on the Web page and remains accessible on the client.
- A header row in a data source specifies the names of the columns. The data in each field can be encapsulated in text qualifiers and the fields are separated with a field delimiter.
- An **object** tag inserts an ActiveX Tabular Data Control. The **classid** attribute specifies the ActiveX control identifier.
- The **param** tag specifies parameters for the object in the **object** tag. The **name** attribute is the parameter name, and the **value** attribute is the value. The **DataURL** parameter is the URL of the data source. The **UseHeader** parameter specifies that the first line of the data file have a header row when set to **true**. The **TextQualifier** parameter sets the text qualifier of our data. The **FieldDelim** parameter sets the field delimiter of our data.
- The **datasrc** attribute refers to the **id** of the TDC object, and the **datafld** attribute specifies the name of the field to which it is bound.

- A recordset is simply a set of data—in our case, it is the current row of data from the data source.
- The **MoveNext** method moves the current recordset forward by one row, automatically updating the **bound** element.
- The **EOF** property indicates whether the recordset has reached the end of the data source.
- The **MoveFirst** method moves the recordset to the first row in the file.
- The **BOF** property indicates whether the recordset points to the first row of the data source.
- When binding to an **img** element, changing the recordset updates the **src** attribute of the image.
- To bind to a table, add the **datasrc** attribute to the opening **table** tag. Then add the **datafld** attribute to **span** tags that reside in the table cells. Internet Explorer iterates through the data file, and creates a table row for each row it finds.
- The **Sort** property of the ActiveX control determines by what column the data is sorted. Once the **Sort** property is set, call the **Reset** method to display the data in its new sort order. By default, a column will be sorted in ascending order—to sort in descending order, the column name is preceded with a minus sign (**-**).
- Setting the **Sort** property of the TDC using a **param** tag instead of scripting is useful for providing an initial sorting order.
- The **cursor** CSS attribute specifies what the mouse cursor will look like when hovering over an object. The value **hand** makes the mouse appear as the same hand that appears when you move your cursor over a link.
- The boolean value **event.ctrlKey** returns **true** if *Ctrl* was held down when the event was triggered.
- An additional sort criterion can be added to the **Sort** property, separated from the first with a semicolon.
- The **Filter** property allows you to filter out all records that do not have a cell that matches the text you specify.
- Any of the normal equality operators (**=**, **<>**) and relational operators (**>**, **<**, **>=**, **<=**) can be used for filtering.

TERMINOLOGY

ActiveX control
ascending sort order
binding
BOF (beginning-of-file) property of **recordset**
bound elements
classid property
column in a database
current record of a **recordset**
data binding
data source
data source object (DSO)
database
data-bound elements
datafld attribute
datasrc attribute
DataURL property of Tabular Data Control
descending sort order
DSO (data source object)
EOF (end-of-file) property of **recordset**
field delimiter
field of a record
FieldDelim property of Tabular Data Control
filter data
Filter property of Tabular Data Control
header row
minus sign (**-**) for descending sort order
Move methods
MoveFirst method of **recordset**
MoveLast method of **recordset**
MoveNext method of **recordset**
MovePrevious method of **recordset**
multicolumn sort
record
recordset

sort in ascending order
sort in descending order
`Sort` property of Tabular Data Control
Tabular Data Control (**`CLSID:333C7BC4-460F-11D0-BC04-0080C7055A83`**)
Tabular Data Control (TDC) DSO of IE5.5
text qualifier
`TextQualifer` property of TDC
`UseHeader` property of Tabular Data Control

SELF-REVIEW EXERCISES

16.1 State whether each of the following is *true* or *false*. If *false*, explain why.

a) A TDC recordset is one row of data.
b) You can bind any XHTML element to data sources.
c) The **`classid`** attribute for the TDC never changes.
d) **`span`** elements display bound data as inner text.
e) **`img`** elements display bound data as **`alt`** text.
f) You separate multiple sort criteria of the **`Sort`** property with a comma (**`,`**).
g) The equality operator (**`=`**) is the only operator that can be used in filtering data.
h) Calling **`MoveNext`** when **`EOF`** is true will move the recordset to the first row of data.
i) Calling **`MoveLast`** when **`EOF`** is true causes an error.

16.2 Fill in the blank for each of the following statements:

a) When binding data to a table, the __________ attribute is placed in the opening **`<table>`** tag and the __________ attribute is placed inside the table cells.
b) The TDC is an __________ control.
c) To sort in descending order, precede the sort criterion with a __________.
d) To display data with recently applied sorting, call the __________ method.
e) The __________ parameter specifies that the data source has a header row.
f) A __________ encapsulates text in a data source and a __________ separates fields in a data source.
g) The __________ CSS property changes the appearance of the mouse cursor.

ANSWERS TO SELF-REVIEW EXERCISES

16.1 a) True. b) False; only some XHTML elements may be bound to data. c) True. d) True. e) False; data bound to **`img`** elements affects the **`src`** attribute of that **`img`**. f) False; you separate them with a semicolon (**`;`**). g) False; any of the equality operators or relational operators can be used. h) False; this causes an error. i) False; the recordset moves to the last row of data.

16.2 a) **`datasrc`**, **`datafld`**. b) ActiveX. c) minus sign, (**`-`**). d) **`Reset`**. e) **`UseHeader`**. f) text qualifier, field delimiter. g) **`cursor`**.

EXERCISES

16.3 Create a data source file with two columns: one for URLs, and one for URL descriptions. Bind the first column to an **`a`** element on a page and the second to a **`span`** element contained within the **`a`** element.

16.4 Bind the data source file you created in Exercise 16.3 to a **`table`** to create a table of clickable links.

16.5 Add a drop-down **`select`** list to Fig. 16.9 that allows you to choose the binary operator used for filter matching, from any of **`=`**, **`>`**, **`<`**, **`>=`** or **`<=`**.

16.6 Create a data source with a set of name/password pairs. Bind these fields to an **input type = "text"** and **input type = "password"** and provide navigation buttons to allow the user to move throughout the data source.

16.7 Apply the transitions you learned in Chapter 15 to Fig. 16.5 to create a virtual slide show.

16.8 Modify the table binding example in Fig. 16.6 to store between 5 and 10 of your friends' names and phone numbers. Change the text file's name to **friends.txt**. The left column should be titled "Friends" and the right column should be titled "Phone Numbers."

17

Dynamic HTML: Structured Graphics ActiveX Control

Objectives

- To be able to use the Structured Graphics Control to create various shapes.
- To understand the Structured Graphics Control methods for modifying lines and borders.
- To understand the Structured Graphics Control methods for modifying colors and fill styles.
- To be able to enable event capturing for the Structured Graphics Control.
- To be able to import external lists of methods into the Structured Graphics Control.
- To be able to scale, rotate and translate shapes in the Structured Graphics Control.

One picture is worth ten thousand words.
Chinese proverb

Treat nature in terms of the cylinder, the sphere, the cone, all in perspective.
Paul Cezanne

Nothing ever becomes real till it is experienced—even a proverb is no proverb to you till your life has illustrated it.
John Keats

Capture its reality in paint!
Paul Cezanne

Outline

17.1 Introduction

Although high-quality content is what visitors to your site are usually looking for, it may not be enough to hold their attention and keep them coming back. Eye-catching graphics may help. This chapter explores the *Structured Graphics* ActiveX Control included with Internet Explorer 5.5.

The Structured Graphics Control, like the Tabular Data Control we discussed in the previous chapter, is an ActiveX control that you can add to your page with an **object** element. Like the TDC, the Structured Graphics Control is easily accessible through scripting. Unlike the TDC, the Structured Graphics Control is meant primarily for visual presentations, not for displaying data and content.

The Structured Graphics Control is a Web interface for the widely used *DirectAnimation* subset of Microsoft's *DirectX* software, used in many high-end video games and graphical applications. To explore the Structured Graphics Control and DirectAnimation further, visit Microsoft's DirectAnimation reference site at

www.microsoft.com/directx/dxm/help/da/default.htm

17.2 Shape Primitives

The Structured Graphics Control allows you to create simple shapes by using methods that can be called via scripting or through **param** tags inside **object** elements. Figure 17.1 demonstrates most of the shapes included in the Structured Graphics Control.

Lines 15–17 insert the Structured Graphics ActiveX Control. We give it an **id** of **shapes** for reference purposes. Note that this **id** is a different **classid** than that of the Tabular Data Control, introduced in Chapter 16.

The first **param** tag in lines 19–20 calls the ***SetLineColor*** *method* of the Structured Graphics Control. The **name** attribute determines the order in which the function is called.

Common Programming Error 17.1

Forgetting to assign successive line numbers (i.e., **name = "Line0001"**, **name = "Line0002"**, *etc.) to method calls prevents the intended methods from being called.*

```
<?xml version = "1.0"?>
<!DOCTYPE html PUBLIC "-//W3C//DTD XHTML 1.0 Transitional//EN"
   "http://www.w3.org/TR/xhtml1/DTD/xhtml1-transitional.dtd">

<!-- Fig 17.1: shapes.html  -->
<!-- Creating simple shapes -->

<html xmlns = "http://www.w3.org/1999/xhtml">
   <head>
      <title>Structured Graphics - Shapes</title>
   </head>

   <body>

      <object id = "shapes" style = "background-color: #CCCCFF;
         width: 500; height: 400"
         classid = "CLSID:369303C2-D7AC-11d0-89D5-00A0C90833E6">

         <param name = "Line0001"
            value = "SetLineColor( 0, 0, 0 )" />
         <param name = "Line0002"
            value = "SetLineStyle( 1, 1 )" />
         <param name = "Line0003"
            value = "SetFillColor( 0, 255, 255 )" />
         <param name = "Line0004"
            value = "SetFillStyle( 1 )" />

         <param name = "Line0005"
            value = "Oval( 0, -175, 25, 50, 45 )" />
         <param name = "Line0006"
            value = "Arc( -200, -125, 100, 100, 45, 135, 0 )" />
         <param name = "Line0007"
            value = "Pie( 100, -100, 150, 150, 90, 120, 0 )" />
         <param name = "Line0008"
            value = "Polygon(5, 0, 0, 10, 20, 0, -30,
                              -10, -10, -10, 25)" />
         <param name = "Line0009"
            value = "Rect( -185, 0, 60, 30, 25 )" />
         <param name = "Line0010"
            value = "RoundRect( 200, 100, 35, 60, 10, 10, 25 )" />

      <param name = "Line0011"
         value = "SetFont( 'Arial', 65, 400, 0, 0, 0 )" />
      <param name = "Line0012"
         value = "Text( 'Shapes', -200, 200 , -35 )" />

         <param name = "Line0013"
               value = "SetLineStyle( 2,1 )" />
         <param name = "Line0014"
            value = "PolyLine( 5, 100, 0, 120, 175, -150, -50,
                               -75, -75, 75, -75)" />
      </object>

```

Fig. 17.1 Creating shapes with the Structured Graphics ActiveX Control (part 1 of 2).

```
54      </body>
55   </html>
```

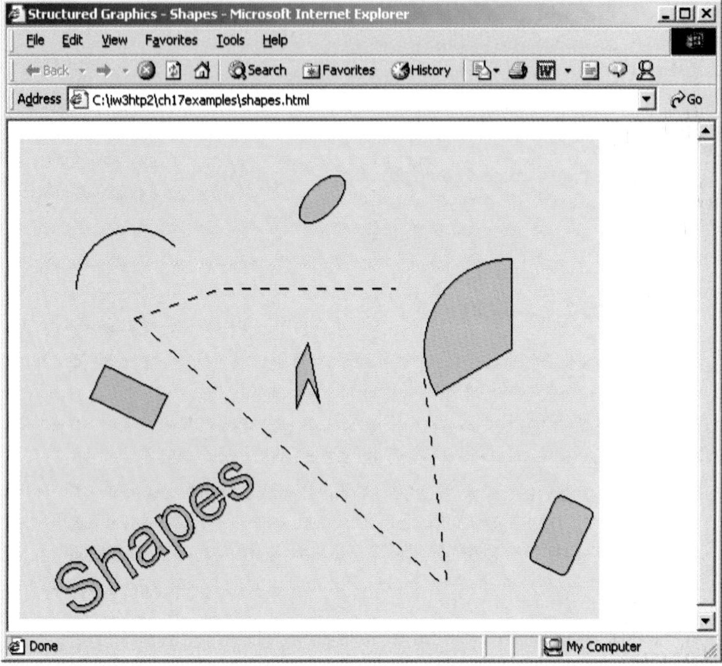

Fig. 17.1 Creating shapes with the Structured Graphics ActiveX Control (part 2 of 2).

The order of calls must be **`Line0001`**, **`Line0002`**, **`Line0003`**, and so on. Method **`SetLineColor`** sets the color of lines and borders of shapes. It takes an RGB triplet in decimal notation as its three parameters—in this case, we set the line color to black (**`0, 0, 0`**).

Lines 21–22 call method **`SetLineStyle`**. Its two parameters set the *line style* and *line width*, respectively. Line-style value **`1`** creates a solid line (the default), **`0`** does not draw any lines or borders and **`2`** creates a dashed line. The line width is specified in pixels. In order to create a dashed line with the **`SetLineStyle`** method, you must set the line width to **`1`**.

Method **`SetFillColor`** (lines 23–24) sets the foreground color with which to fill shapes. Like method **`SetLineColor`**, it takes a decimal RGB triplet as its parameters. We set the foreground color to cyan (**`0`**, **`255`**, **`255`**). The **`SetFillStyle`** method (lines 25–26) determines the style in which a shape is filled with color; a value of **`1`**, as we set it here, fills shapes with the solid color we declared with the method **`SetFillColor`**. There are 14 possible fill styles, some of which we demonstrate later in this chapter. Figure 17.2 lists all the possible fill styles available with the Structured Graphics Control.

Lines 28–29 create a shape, using the ***`Oval`*** *method*. The first two parameters, (**`0, -175`**), specify *x–y* coordinates at which to place the oval. All shapes in the Structured Graphics Control effectively have a surrounding box—that is, when you place the image at a certain *x–y* position, it is the upper left corner of that box which is placed at that position. It is important to note that inside the control, the point (**`0, 0`**) (also known as the *origin*) is at the *center* of the control, not at the upper left corner.

Number	Fill Style
`0`	None
`1`	Solid fill
`2`	None
`3`	Horizontal lines
`4`	Vertical lines
`5`	Diagonal lines
`6`	Diagonal lines
`7`	Cross-hatch
`8`	Diagonal cross-hatch
`9`	Horizontal Gradient
`10`	Vertical Gradient
`11`	Circular Gradient
`12`	Line Gradient
`13`	Rectangular Gradient
`14`	Shaped Gradient

Fig. 17.2 Fill styles available for the **`SetFillStyle`** method.

The next two parameters, (**`25, 50`**), specify the height and width of the oval, respectively. The last parameter (**`45`**) specifies the clockwise rotation of the oval relative to the *x*-axis, expressed in degrees.

Lines 30–31 create another shape, an *arc*. The **`Arc`** method takes seven parameters: The *x*–*y* coordinates of the arc; the height and width of the box that the arc encloses; the starting angle of the arc, in degrees, the size of the arc relative to the starting angle, also in degrees, and the rotation of the arc. The **`Pie`** method (lines 32–33) takes the same parameters as does the **`Arc`** method, but it fills the arc with the color of the foreground, thus creating a *pie* shape.

Lines 34–36 create a *polygon*, using the **`Polygon`** method. The first parameter specifies the number of vertices in the polygon; each successive pair of parameters specifies the *x*–*y* coordinates of the next vertex of the polygon. The last point of the polygon is automatically connected to the first, to close the polygon.

Lines 37–38 create a *rectangle*, using the **`Rect`** method. Here, the first two parameters specify the coordinates, the next two specify height and width, respectively, and the last parameter specifies rotation, in degrees.

Lines 39–40 add a *rounded rectangle*. The **`RoundRect`** method is almost identical to the **`Rect`** method, but it adds two new parameters, which specify the width and height, respectively, of the rounded arc at the corners of the rectangle—in this case, 10 pixels wide and 10 pixels high (**`10, 10`**).

Lines 42–45 add text to our Structured Graphics Control, using methods, **`SetFont`** and **`Text`**. The **`SetFont`** method sets the font style to use when we use the **`Text`** method to place text. Here, we instruct **`SetFont`** to use a font face of **`Arial`** that is **`65`** points high, has a boldness of **400** (this attribute is similar to the CSS **font-weight** property, with values ranging from 100 to 700) and is neither italic (**0**), underline (**0**) nor strikethrough (**0**). Then, we use the **Text** method to place the text (**Shapes**) on the screen, positioned at (**-200**, **200**), with a rotation of **-35** degrees.

In lines 47–50, we use the **PolyLine** method to draw a line with multiple line segments. Before we draw the line, we call the **SetLineStyle** method again to override the settings we gave it before; in this case, we set the line style to dashed, with a width of **1** pixel (**2**, **1**). The **PolyLine** method itself operates much like the **Polygon** method—the first parameter declares the number of points in the line, and each successive pair declares the *x*–*y* coordinates of the next vertex.

17.3 Moving Shapes with Translate

The Structured Graphics Control provides several scriptable methods that allow you to move and transform shapes on the screen. Figure 17.3 provides an example of use of the **Translate** function to move an oval.

```
<?xml version = "1.0"?>
<!DOCTYPE html PUBLIC "-//W3C//DTD XHTML 1.0 Transitional//EN"
   "http://www.w3.org/TR/xhtml1/DTD/xhtml1-transitional.dtd">

<!-- Fig. 17.3: bounce.html                -->
<!-- Textures and the Translate method -->

<html xmlns = "http://www.w3.org/1999/xhtml">
   <head>
      <title>Structured Graphics - Translate</title>

      <script type = "text/javascript">
         <!--
         var x = 15;
         var y = 15;
         var upDown = -1;
         var leftRight = 1;

         function start()
         {
            window.setInterval( "run()", 50 );
         }

         function run()
         {
            // if the ball hits the top or bottom side...
            if ( y == -100 || y == 50 )
               upDown *= -1;

            // if the ball hits the left or right side...
            if ( x == -150 || x == 100 )
               leftRight *= -1;

```

Fig. 17.3 Methods **SetTextureFill** and **Translate** (part 1 of 2).

```
34             // Move the ball and increment our counters
35             ball.Translate( leftRight * 5, upDown * 5, 0 );
36             y += upDown * 5;
37             x += leftRight * 5;
38          }
39          // -->
40       </script>
41    </head>
42 
43    <body onload = "start()">
44 
45       <object id = "ball" style = "background-color: ffffff;
46          width: 300; height: 200; border-style: groove;
47          position: absolute;"
48          classid = "CLSID:369303C2-D7AC-11d0-89D5-00A0C90833E6">
49 
50          <param name = "Line0001" value = "SetLineStyle( 0 )" />
51          <param name = "Line0002"
52             value = "SetTextureFill( 0, 0, 'ball.gif', 0 )" />
53          <param name = "Line0003"
54             value = "Oval( 15, 15, 50, 50 )" />
55       </object>
56 
57    </body>
58 </html>
```

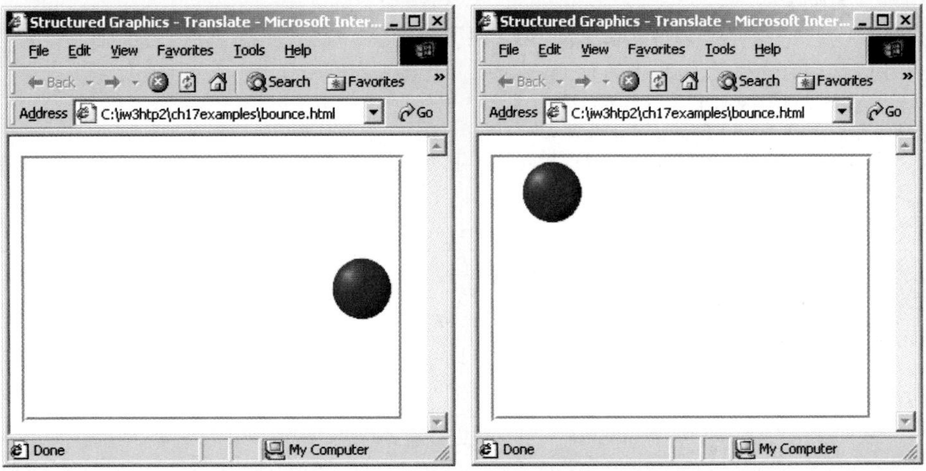

Fig. 17.3 Methods **SetTextureFill** and **Translate** (part 2 of 2).

In this example, we create a ball that bounces around inside the Structured Graphics Control box. Instead of the **SetFillColor** method, we use the **SetTextureFill** method (line 52) to fill the oval we create with a *texture*. A texture is a picture that is placed on the surface of a polygon. The first two parameters, (**0, 0**), specify the *x–y* coordinates inside the shape at which the texture begins. The next parameter (**'ball.gif'**) specifies the location of the texture to use, and the last parameter (**0**) specifies that the texture should be stretched to fit inside the shape. A last parameter of **1** would instead tile the texture as many times as necessary inside the shape.

Now that the shape is in place, we use the **Translate** method to *translate* the shape—that is, to move the shape in coordinate space without deforming it. In every call to function **run**, we determine whether the ball has reached the edge of the box (lines 27 and 31); if this is the case, we reverse the ball's direction, to simulate a bounce. Then, in line 35, we call the **Translate** function, passing it three parameters, which determine the relative distance to move the **ball** along the *x*-, *y*- and *z*-axes, respectively. (The z- axis is the third-demensional coordinate axis.)

17.4 Rotation

Another useful method for moving shapes is **Rotate**, which can rotate shapes in three-dimensional space. Figure 17.4 demonstrates use of the **Rotate** method, along with some new fill style effects.

```
<?xml version = "1.0"?>
<!DOCTYPE html PUBLIC "-//W3C//DTD XHTML 1.0 Transitional//EN"
   "http://www.w3.org/TR/xhtml1/DTD/xhtml1-transitional.dtd">

<!-- Fig. 17.4: gradient.html  -->
<!-- Gradients and rotation    -->

<html xmlns = "http://www.w3.org/1999/xhtml">
   <head>
      <title>Structured Graphics - Gradients</title>

      <script type = "text/javascript">
         <!--
         var speed = 5;
         var counter = 180;

         function start()
         {
            window.setInterval( "run()", 100 );
         }

         function run()
         {
            counter += speed;

            // accelerate half the time...
            if ( ( counter % 360 ) > 180 )
               speed *= ( 5 / 4 );

            // decelerate the other half.
            if ( ( counter % 360 ) < 180 )
               speed /= ( 5 / 4 );

            pies.Rotate( 0, 0, speed );
         }
```

Fig. 17.4 Using gradients and **Rotate** (part 1 of 2).

```
         // -->
      </script>

   </head>

   <body onload = "start()">

      <object id = "pies" style = "background-color:blue;
         width: 300; height: 200;"
         classid = "CLSID:369303C2-D7AC-11d0-89D5-00A0C90833E6">

         <param name = "Line0001"
            value = "SetFillColor( 255, 0, 0, 0, 0, 0 )" />
         <param name = "Line0002"
            value = "SetFillStyle( 13 )" />
         <param name = "Line0003"
            value = "Pie( -75, -75, 150, 150, 90, 120, 300 )" />

         <param name = "Line0004"
            value = "SetFillStyle( 9 )" />
         <param name = "Line0005"
            value = "Pie( -75, -75, 150, 150, 90, 120, 180 )" />

         <param name = "Line0006"
            value = "SetFillStyle( 11 )" />
         <param name = "Line0007"
            value = "Pie( -75, -75, 150, 150, 90, 120, 60 )" />
      </object>

   </body>
</html>
```

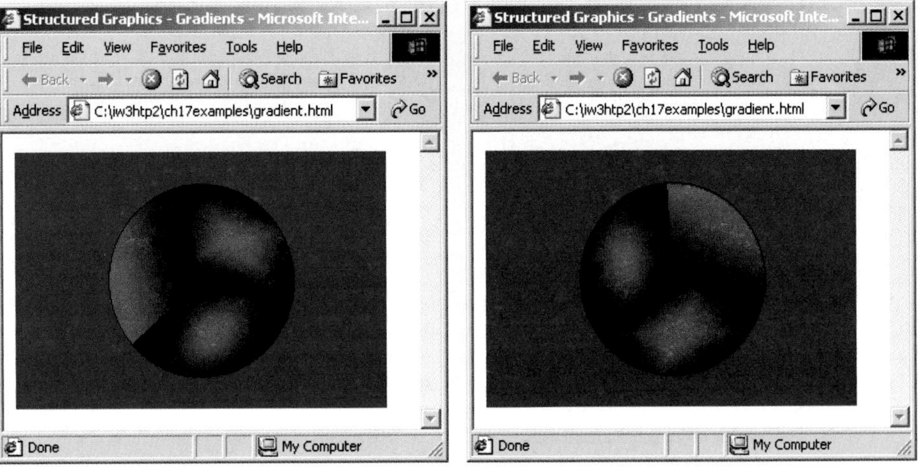

Fig. 17.4 Using gradients and **Rotate** (part 2 of 2).

In this example, we create three pie shapes that we place together to form a circle. Line 34 calls function **Rotate** to rotate the circle around the *z*-axis. (As with the **Translate** method, the three parameters of the **Rotate** function specify rotation in the *x*-, *y*- and *z*-coordinate planes, respectively.) Lines 26–32 in the JavaScript code provide a mechanism for varying the speed of rotation about the *z* axis.

The gradient fills are set with the **SetFillStyle** method (lines 50, 55 and 60). A parameter of **9** for **SetFillStyle** fills the shape with a linear gradient from the foreground color to the background color. The background color is specified with the method **SetFillColor** in lines 47–48 by adding a second RGB triplet; here, we set the foreground color to white (**255, 255, 255**) and the background color to black (**0,0,0**). The two other parameters we use for **SetFillStyle**, **11** and **13**, fill the pies with circular and rectangular gradients, respectively.

17.5 Mouse Events and External Source Files

To provide interaction with the user, the Structured Graphics Control can process the Dynamic HTML events **onmouseup**, **onmousedown**, **onmousemove**, **onmouseover**, **onmouseout**, **onclick** and **ondblclick** (see Chapter 14). By default, the Structured Graphics Control does not capture these mouse events, because doing so takes a small amount of processing power. The **MouseEventsEnabled** property allows you to turn on capturing for these events. In Fig. 17.5, we use mouse events to trigger another feature of the Structured Graphics Control, one that allows you to keep a set of method calls in a separate source file (Fig. 17.6) and invoke them by calling the **SourceURL** method.

We toggle the mouse-event capturing in line 59 by setting the **MouseEventsEnabled** property to a value of **1** (true) to enable event capturing.

Lines 12–17 designate a script for the **onclick** event of our Structured Graphics Control object. This event sets property **SourceURL** to **newoval.txt** (Fig. 17.6)—the new drawing instructions. Each command is on a separate line, consisting of only the method call and its parameters.

```
1  <?xml version = "1.0"?>
2  <!DOCTYPE html PUBLIC "-//W3C//DTD XHTML 1.0 Transitional//EN"
3     "http://www.w3.org/TR/xhtml1/DTD/xhtml1-transitional.dtd">
4
5  <!-- Fig. 17.5: bounce2.html              -->
6  <!-- SourceURL and MouseEventsEnabled -->
7
8  <html xmlns = "http://www.w3.org/1999/xhtml">
9     <head>
10       <title>Structured Graphics - Shapes</title>
11
```

Fig. 17.5 Using **SourceURL** and **MouseEventsEnabled** (part 1 of 3).

```
      <script for = "ball" event = "onclick" type =
         "text/javascript">
            <!--
            ball.SourceURL = "newoval.txt";
            // -->
      </script>

      <script type = "text/javascript">
         <!--
         var x = 20;
         var y = 20;
         var upDown = -1;
         var leftRight = 1;

         function start()
         {
            window.setInterval( "run()", 50 );
         }

         function run()
         {
            if ( y == -100 || y == 50 )
               upDown *= -1;

            if ( x == -150 || x == 100 )
               leftRight *= -1;

            ball.Translate( leftRight * 5, upDown * 5, 0 );
            y += upDown * 5;
            x += leftRight *5;
         }
         // -->
      </script>
   </head>

   <body onload = "start()">

      <object id = "ball"
         style = "width: 300; height: 200; border-style: groove;
         position: absolute; top: 10; left: 10;"
         classid = "clsid:369303C2-D7AC-11d0-89D5-00A0C90833E6">

         <param name = "Line0001" value = "SetLineStyle(0)" />
         <param name = "Line0002"
            value = "SetTextureFill( 0, 0, 'ball.gif', 0 )" />
         <param name = "Line0003"
            value = "Oval( 20, 20, 50, 50 )" />
         <param name = "MouseEventsEnabled" value = "1" />
      </object>

   </body>
</html>
```

Fig. 17.5 Using **SourceURL** and **MouseEventsEnabled** (part 2 of 3).

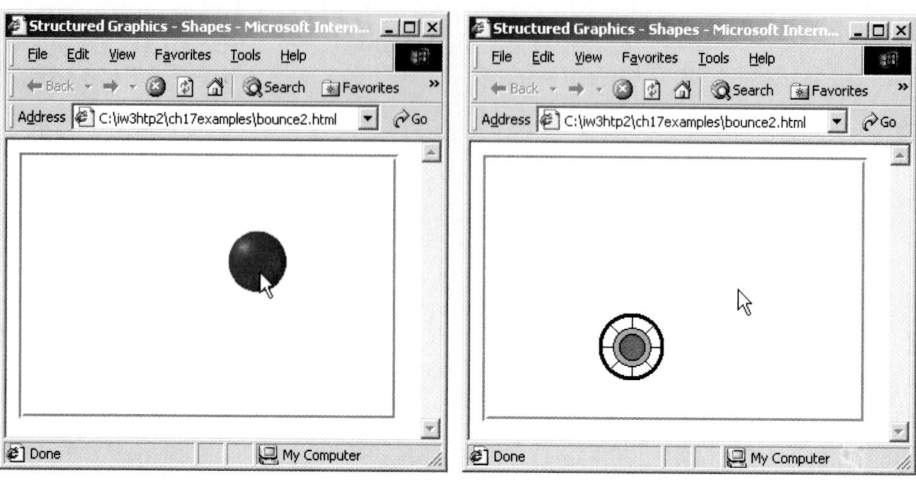

Fig. 17.5 Using **SourceURL** and **MouseEventsEnabled** (part 3 of 3).

```
SetLineStyle( 1, 3 )
SetFillStyle( 1 )
Oval( 20, 20, 50, 50, 0 )

SetLineStyle( 1, 1 )
PolyLine( 2, 45, 20, 45, 70, 0 )
PolyLine( 2, 45, 20, 45, 70, 90 )
PolyLine( 2, 45, 20, 45, 70, 45 )
PolyLine( 2, 45, 20, 45, 70, 135 )

SetFillColor( 0, 255, 0 )
Oval( 30, 30, 30, 30, 0 )
SetFillColor( 255 ,0, 0 )
Oval( 35, 35, 20, 20, 0 )
```

Fig. 17.6 External source file **newoval.txt** for Fig. 17.5.

17.6 Scaling

The third type of shape transformation that the Structured Graphics Control provides is *scaling*, which modifies the size of an object while retaining its position and shape. Figure 17.7 provides an example of scaling, using the **Scale** method.

In this example, we use two separate controls—the first (lines 55–90) for our rotating foreground, and the second (lines 92–101) for the oval in the background. We position these objects over each other by using the **position** and **z-index** CSS attribute. We then use the five buttons to the side of the Structured Graphics Controls to control rotation and scaling of the upper layer. In line 27, the **Scale** method scales object **drawing** uniformly in the three dimensions, based on the variable **scale**.

```
<?xml version = "1.0"?>
<!DOCTYPE html PUBLIC "-//W3C//DTD XHTML 1.0 Transitional//EN"
   "http://www.w3.org/TR/xhtml1/DTD/xhtml1-transitional.dtd">

<!-- Fig. 17.7: scaling.html -->
<!-- Scaling a shape          -->

<html xmlns = "http://www.w3.org/1999/xhtml">
   <head>
      <title>Structured Graphics - Scaling</title>

      <script type = "text/javascript">
         <!--
         var speedX = 0;
         var speedY = 0;
         var speedZ = 0;
         var scale = 1;

         function start()
         {
            window.setInterval( "run()", 100 );
         }

         function run()
         {
            drawing.Rotate( speedX, speedY, speedZ );
            drawing.Scale( scale, scale, scale );
         }

         function rotate( axis )
         {
            axis = ( axis ? 0 : 5 );
         }
         // -->
      </script>

   </head>

   <body onload = "start()">

      <div style = "position: absolute; top: 25; left: 220">
      <input type = "button" value = "Rotate-X"
         onclick = "speedX = ( speedX ? 0 : 5 )" /><br />
      <input type = "button" value = "Rotate-Y"
         onclick = "speedY = ( speedY ? 0 : 5 )" /><br />
      <input type = "button" value = "Rotate-Z"
         onclick = "speedZ = ( speedZ ? 0 : 5 )" /><br />
      <br />
      <input type = "button" value = "Scale Up"
         onclick = "scale = ( scale * 10 / 9 )" /><br />
      <input type = "button" value = "Scale Down"
         onclick = "scale = ( scale * 9 / 10 )" />
      </div>
```

Fig. 17.7 Rotating a shape in three dimensions and scaling up and down (part 1 of 3).

```
         <object id = "drawing" style = " position: absolute;
            z-index: 2; width: 200; height: 300;"
            classid = "CLSID:369303C2-D7AC-11d0-89D5-00A0C90833E6">

           <param name = "Line0001" value = "SetFillColor( 0,0,0 )" />
            <param name = "Line0002" value = "SetFillStyle( 0 )" />
            <param name = "Line0003" value = "SetLineStyle( 1, 3 )" />

            <param name = "Line0004"
                  value = "Oval( -25, -100, 50, 50, 0 )" />

            <param name = "Line0005"
               value = "PolyLine(2, 0, -50, 0, 50 )" />

            <param name = "Line0006"
               value = "PolyLine( 3, -30, -25, 0, -15, 30, -25 )" />

            <param name = "Line0007"
               value = "PolyLine( 3, -15, 90, 0, 50, 15, 90 )" />

            <param name = "Line0008"
               value = "SetFillColor ( 255, 0, 0 )" />
            <param name = "Line0009"
               value = "Oval( -15, -85, 7, 7, 0 )" />
            <param name = "Line0010"
               value = "Oval( 5, -85, 7, 7, 0 )" />

            <param name = "Line0011"
               value = "SetLineStyle( 1, 2 )" />
            <param name = "Line0012"
               value = "SetLineColor( 255, 0, 0 )" />
            <param name = "Line0013"
               value = "SetFont( 'Courier', 25, 200, 0, 0, 0 )" />
            <param name = "Line0014"
               value = "Text( 'Hello', -35, -115 , 0 )" />
         </object>

         <object id = "background" style = " position:absolute;
            z-index: 1; width: 200; height: 300;
            background-color: none" classid =
            "CLSID:369303C2-D7AC-11d0-89D5-00A0C90833E6">

            <param name = "Line0001"
               value = "SetFillColor( 38, 250, 38 )" />
            <param name = "Line0002"
               value = "Oval( -75, -125, 150, 250, 0 )" />
         </object>
      </body>
   </html>
```

Fig. 17.7 Rotating a shape in three dimensions and scaling up and down (part 2 of 3).

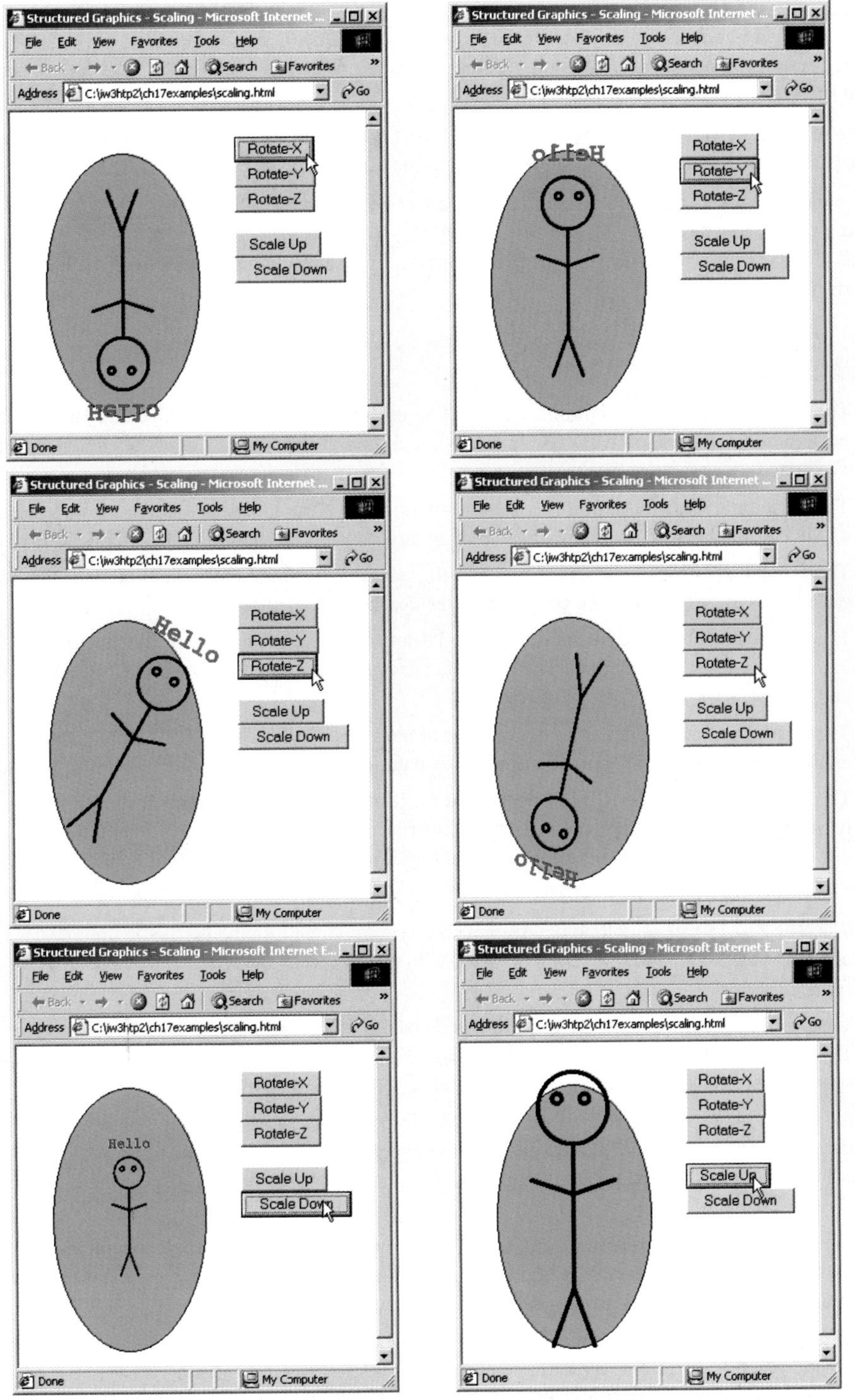

Fig. 17.7 Rotating a shape in three dimensions and scaling up and down (part 3 of 3).

17.7 Internet and World Wide Web Resources

`dec26.ncat.edu/~esterlin/c600s01/Notes/Ch19.pdf`

This document discusses the Structured Graphics ActiveX Control's methods. Translating, rotating and scaling objects are also discussed.

`obelix.dawsoncollege.qc.ca/~c811c02/project/dhtmltutorial.html`

This Web site contains an animation created with the Structured Graphics ActiveX Control.

`www.microsoft.com/windows/ie/press/whitepaper/iwhite/white003.htm#E12E9`

This technical document describes ActiveX controls. It also discusses how ActiveX technology and ActiveX scripting work.

SUMMARY

- The Structured Graphics Control is an ActiveX control that you can add with an **`object`** tag. The Structured Graphics Control is easily accessible through scripts and is used for creating dynamic Web pages.
- The Structured Graphics Control is a Web interface for the widely used DirectAnimation subset of Microsoft's DirectX software, used in many high-end games and graphical applications.
- The Structured Graphics control allows you to create simple shapes by using functions that can be called via scripting or through **`param`** tags inside **`object`** elements.
- The **`name`** attribute of the **`param`** tag method determines the order in which the function specified in the **`value`** attribute is called. The order of calls must be **`Line0001`**, **`Line0002`**, **`Line0003`**, and so on.
- The **`SetLineColor`** function sets the color of lines and borders of shapes that are drawn. It takes an RGB triplet in decimal notation as its three parameters.
- The two parameters of the **`SetLineStyle`** function set the line style and line width, respectively. A value of **`1`** for line style creates a solid line (the default). A value of **`0`** does not draw any lines or borders, and a value of **`2`** creates a dashed line. The line width is specified in pixels.
- The **`SetFillColor`** method sets the foreground color with which to fill shapes.
- The **`SetFillStyle`** method determines the style in which a shape is filled with color; a value of **`1`** fills shapes with the solid color declared with the **`SetFillColor`** method. There are 14 possible fill styles.
- The first two parameters of the **`Oval`** method specify *x–y* coordinates at which to place the oval. The next two parameters specify the height and width of the oval, respectively. The last parameter specifies the clockwise rotation of the oval relative to the *x*-axis, expressed in degrees.
- All shapes in the Structured Graphics control effectively have a surrounding box; when you place the image at a certain *x–y* coordinate, it is the upper left corner of that box that is placed at that coordinate. Inside the control, the point (**`0, 0`**) (also known as the origin) is at the center of the control, not at the upper left corner.
- The **`Arc`** method takes seven parameters: The *x–y* coordinates of the arc; the height and width of the box in which the arc is enclosed; the starting angle of the arc, in degrees; the size of the arc relative to the starting angle, also in degrees, and the rotation of the arc.
- The **`Pie`** method takes the same parameters as the **`Arc`** method, but it fills in the arc with the foreground color, thus creating a pie shape.
- The first parameter of method **`Polygon`** specifies the number of vertices in the polygon; each successive pair of numbers specifies the *x–y* coordinates of the next vertex in the polygon.

- The **Rect** method creates a rectangle. The first two parameters specify the coordinates, the next two specify height and width, respectively, and the last parameter specifies rotation, in degrees.
- The **RoundRect** method is almost identical to the **Rect** method, but it adds two new parameters, which specify the height and width, respectively, of the rounded arcs at the corners of the rectangle.
- The **SetFont** method sets the font style to use when placing text with the **Text** method.
- The **PolyLine** method draws a line with multiple segments. The **PolyLine** method functions much like the **Polygon** method—the first parameter declares the number of points in the line, and each successive pair declares the *x–y* coordinates of another vertex.
- The **SetTextureFill** method fills a shape with a texture. A texture is a picture that is placed on the surface of a polygon. The first two parameters specify the *x–y* coordinates inside the shape of which the texture begins. The next parameter specifies the location of the texture to use. A last parameter of **0** specifies that the texture should be stretched to fit inside the shape. A last parameter of **1** would instead tile the texture as many times as necessary inside the shape.
- The **Translate** method moves a shape in coordinate space without deforming it. Its three parameters determine the relative distance to move along the *x*-, *y*- and *z*-axes, respectively. (The *z*-axis is the third-dimensional coordinate axis.)
- The **Rotate** method rotates shapes in three-dimensional space. The three parameters of the **Rotate** function specify rotation in the x-, y- and z-coordinate planes, respectively.
- A parameter of **9** for **SetFillStyle** fills the shape with a linear gradient from the foreground color to the background color.
- A background color can be specified with the **SetFillColor** method by adding a second RGB triplet to the parameters.
- Two other parameters for **SetFillStyle**, **11** and **13**, fill shapes with circular and rectangular gradients, respectively.
- To provide interaction with the user, the Structured Graphics Control can process the Dynamic HTML mouse events **onmouseup**, **onmousedown**, **onmousemove**, **onmouseover**, **onmouseout**, **onclick** and **ondblclick**.
- By default, the Structured Graphics Control does not capture mouse events, because doing so takes a small amount of processing power.
- The Structure Graphics Control allows you to keep a set of method calls in a separate source file and to invoke those methods by calling the **SourceURL** function.
- Turn event capturing on by calling the **MouseEventsEnabled** method with a **value** of **1** (true).
- Each command in a file targeted by **SourceURL** is on a separate line and consists of only the method call and its parameters.

TERMINOLOGY

arc
Arc method
DirectAnimation
DirectX
line style
line width
Line0001, (**Line0002**, etc.)
mouse events
object tag
onclick event
ondblclick event
onmousedown event
onmousemove event
onmouseout event
onmouseover event
onmouseup event
origin name
oval

Oval method
param tag
pie
Pie method
polygon
Polygon method
PolyLine method
Rect method
rectangle
Rotate method
rounded rectangle
RoundRect method
Scale method
SetFillColor method
SetFillStyle method
SetFont method
SetLineColor method
SetLineStyle method
SetTextureFill method
SourceURL method
Structured Graphics Control
Text method
texture
translate
Translate method

SELF-REVIEW EXERCISES

17.1 Fill in the blanks in each of the following statements:

a) The Structured Graphics Control is a subset of Microsoft's __________ software package.
b) The Structured Graphics Control captures only __________-related events.
c) The __________ method allows you to draw a multisegmented line.
d) There are __________ different styles for the **SetFillStyle** method.
e) The __________ method allows you to import external lists of commands.
f) A __________ is an image that is placed on the surface of a polygon.
g) The __________ method moves shapes in the Structured Graphics Control without distorting or rotating them.
h) To place text with the **Text** method, the __________ method must first be called to set the properties of the text to be placed.

17.2 State whether each of the following is *true* or *false*. If *false*, explain why.

a) By default, event capturing is turned on for the Structured Graphics Control.
b) The **SetLineColor** and **SetLineStyle** methods also apply to shape borders.
c) The **Pie** method has the same parameters as does the **Arc** method.
d) Calling **SetFillStyle** with an argument of **1** fills shapes with a solid color.
e) The dotted-line style may be used at any line width.
f) The **SetFillTexture** method specifies whether the texture is tiled or stretched.

ANSWERS TO SELF-REVIEW EXERCISES

17.1 a) DirectX. b) mouse. c) **PolyLine**. d) 15. e) **SourceURL**. f) texture. g) **Translate**. h) **SetFont**.

17.2 a) False. It is off by default. b) True. c) True. d) True. e) False. It may be used only with lines that are one pixel wide. f) True.

EXERCISES

17.3 Modify Fig. 17.5 to do the following:

a) Speed up when the ball is clicked;
b) change the ball's shape when it hits a wall;
c) have the ball stop if the user moves the mouse cursor over the ball, and resume moving if the user moves the mouse cursor off the ball.

17.4 Use the Structured Graphics Control to create several ovals in different sizes, shapes, locations, colors and fill styles.

17.5 Use the primitive shapes to create simple pictures of a person, a car, a house, a bicycle and a dog.

17.6 Look up the **`Spline`** method mentioned in the documentation at the URL provided in Section 17.1, and use it to create a figure-eight shape.

17.7 Draw a series of eight concentric circles, each separation being 10 pixels wide.

17.8 Draw four triangles of different sizes. Each triangle should be filled with a different color (or fill style).

17.9 Create a Web page that uses JavaScript and the Structured Graphics Control to create an interactive hangman game.

17.10 Use the Structured Graphics Control to draw a cube.

17.11 Modify Exercise 17.10 to rotate the cube continuously.

17.12 Modify Exercise 17.10 to rotate the cube in response to the user moving the mouse. The cube should rotate in the direction in which the user drags the mouse. [*Hint*: Use the **`onmousedown`** event to determine when the user begins a drag, and use the **`onmouseup`** event to determine when the drag operation terminates.]

17.13 Modify Exercise 17.12 to determine the speed at which the cube rotates, by calculating the distance between two consecutive **`onmousemove`** events.

18

Dynamic HTML: Path, Sequencer and Sprite ActiveX Controls

Objectives

- To be able to use the DirectAnimation multimedia ActiveX controls, including the Path, Sequencer and Sprite controls.
- To be able to add animation to Web pages with the DirectAnimation ActiveX controls.
- To use the Path Control to specify the path along which an animated Web page element moves.
- To use the Sequencer Control to control the timing and synchronization of actions on a Web page.
- To use the Sprite Control to create animated images for a Web page.

There is a natural hootchy-kootchy motion to a goldfish.
Walt Disney

Isn't life a series of images that change as they repeat themselves?
Andy Warhol

Between the motion and the act falls the shadow.
Thomas Stearns Eliot, *The Hollow Men*

Grass grows, birds fly, waves pound the sand.
Muhammad Ali

Outline

18.1 Introduction

In this chapter, we discuss the remaining three DirectAnimation ActiveX controls available for use with Internet Explorer 5.5: The *Path Control*, the *Sequencer Control* and the *Sprite Control*. Each one of these controls allows a Web page designer to add certain multimedia effects to Web pages. When used with one another, with the Structured Graphics Control we discussed in the previous chapter and with other Dynamic HTML effects, they help create stunning visual presentations for your content.

Performance Tip 18.1

Multimedia is performance intensive. Internet bandwidth and processor speed are still precious resources. Multimedia-based Web applications must be carefully designed to use resources wisely, or they may perform poorly.

18.2 DirectAnimation Path Control

The *DirectAnimation Path Control* allows you to control the position of elements on your page. This mechanism is more advanced than dynamic CSS positioning, because it allows you to define paths that the targeted elements follow. This capacity to define paths gives you the ability to create professional presentations, especially when integrated with other Dynamic HTML features such as filters and transitions. Figure 18.1 uses the Path Control to create a short linear path for an **h1** element.

```
<?xml version = "1.0"?>
<!DOCTYPE html PUBLIC "-//W3C//DTD XHTML 1.0 Transitional//EN"
        "http://www.w3.org/TR/xhtml1/DTD/xhtml1-transitional.dtd">

<!-- Fig. 18.1: path1.html        -->
<!-- Introducing the path control -->

<html xmlns = "http://www.w3.org/1999/xhtml">
   <head>
      <title>Path control</title>
```

Fig. 18.1 Demonstrating the DirectAnimation Path Control (part 1 of 2).

```
11      </head>
12
13      <body style = "background-color: wheat">
14
15         <h1 id = "headerText" style = "position: absolute">
16         Path animation:</h1>
17
18         <object id = "oval"
19            classid = "CLSID:D7A7D7C3-D47F-11D0-89D3-00A0C90833E6">
20            <param name = "AutoStart" value = "1" />
21            <param name = "Repeat" value = "-1" />
22            <param name = "Duration" value = "2" />
23            <param name = "Bounce" value = "1" />
24            <param name = "Shape"
25               value = "PolyLine( 2, 0, 0, 200, 50 )" />
26            <param name = "Target" value = "headerText" />
27         </object>
28
29      </body>
30   </html>
```

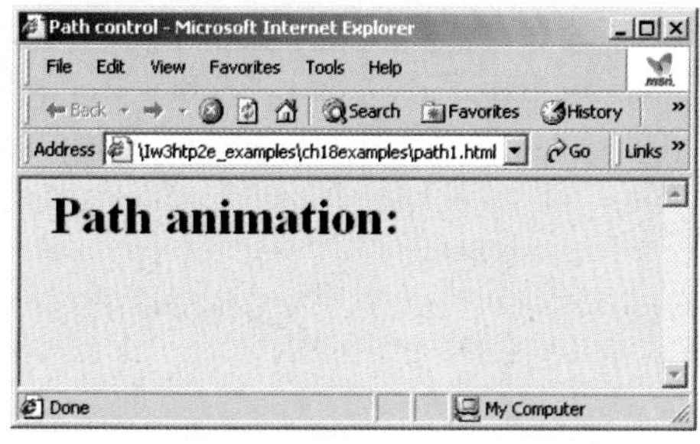

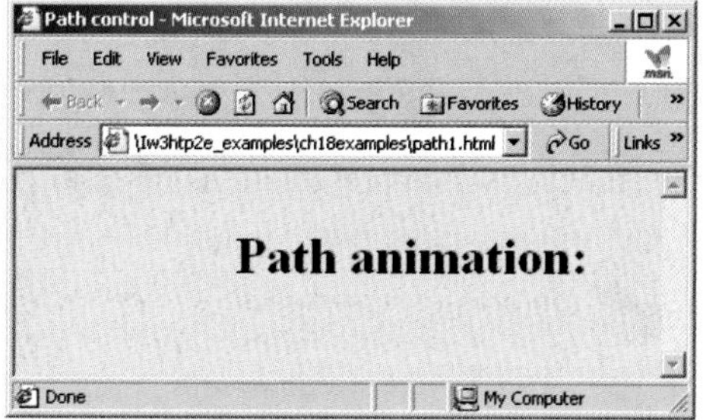

Fig. 18.1 Demonstrating the DirectAnimation Path Control (part 2 of 2).

Lines 18–27 use the **`object`** element to place the Path Control on the page. The **`classid`** attribute identifies the DirectAnimation Path Control. The **`param`** tags in the **`object`** element specify certain properties of the control. Setting **`AutoStart`** to a non-zero value (**`1`** in this case) starts the element along the path as soon as the page loads (setting a zero value would prevent it from starting, in which case a script would have to call the **`Play`** method to start the path). The **`Repeat`** method specifies how many times the path is traversed; setting the value to **`-1`**, as we do here, specifies that the path should loop continuously. The **`Duration`** parameter specifies the amount of time that it takes to traverse the path, in seconds.

Parameter **`Bounce`**, when set to **`1`**, reverses the element's direction on the path when it reaches the end. Setting the value to **`0`** would instead return the element to the beginning of the path when the path has been traversed. The **`Shape`** parameter is what actually determines the path of the element; as we saw with the Structured Graphics Control, the **`PolyLine`** value creates a path with multiple line segments. In this case, we declare a path with **`2`** points, located at (**`0, 0`**) and (**`200, 50`**). Finally, the **`Target`** parameter specifies the **`id`** of the element that is targeted by the path control. Line 15 sets the CSS attribute **`position`** to **`absolute`**; this setting allows the Path Control to move the element around the screen. Otherwise, the element is stationary, locked in the position determined by the browser when the page loads.

18.3 Multiple Path Controls

The Path Control also allows you to set paths for multiple objects present on your page. To set paths for multiple objects, you must add a separate **object** tag for each object you wish to control. Figure 18.2 creates **PolyLine** paths for seven separate objects that create a splash screen effect.

```
<?xml version = "1.0"?>
<!DOCTYPE html PUBLIC "-//W3C//DTD XHTML 1.0 Transitional//EN"
     "http://www.w3.org/TR/xhtml1/DTD/xhtml1-transitional.dtd">

<!-- Fig. 18.2: path2.html       -->
<!-- Controlling multiple paths -->

<html xmlns = "http://www.w3.org/1999/xhtml">
   <head>
      <title>Path Control - Multiple paths</title>

      <style type = "text/css">

         span { position: absolute;
                font-family: sans-serif;
                font-size: 2em;
                font-weight: bold;
                filter: shadow( direction = 225 );
                padding: 9px;
              }

      </style>
   </head>

   <body style = "background-color: lavender">

      <img src = "icons2.gif"
         style = "position: absolute; left: 30; top: 110" />

      <span id = "titleTxt"
          style = "left: 500; top: 500; color: white">
        Multimedia Cyber Classroom<br />
        Programming Tip Icons</span>

      <span id = "CPEspan"
          style = "left: 75; top: 500; color: red">
        Common Programming Errors</span>

      <span id = "GPPspan"
          style = "left: 275; top: 500; color: orange">
        Good Programming Practices</span>
```

Fig. 18.2 Controlling multiple elements with the Path Control (part 1 of 4).

```

      <span id = "PERFspan"
            style = "left: 475; top: 500; color: yellow">
         Performance Tips</span>

      <span id = "PORTspan"
            style = "left: 100; top: -50; color: green">
         Portability Tips</span>

      <span id = "SEOspan"
            style = "left: 300; top: -50; color: blue">
         Software Engineering Observations</span>

      <span id = "TDTspan"
            style = "left: 500; top: -50; color: violet">
         Testing and Debugging Tips</span>

      <object id = "CyberPath"
         classid = "CLSID:D7A7D7C3-D47F-11D0-89D3-00A0C90833E6">
         <param name = "Target" value = "titleTxt" />
         <param name = "Duration" value = "10" />
         <param name = "Shape"
            value = "PolyLine( 2, 500, 500, 100, 10 )" />
         <param name = "AutoStart" value = "1" />
      </object>

      <object id = "CPEPath"
         classid = "CLSID:D7A7D7C3-D47F-11D0-89D3-00A0C90833E6">
         <param name = "Target" value = "CPEspan" />
         <param name = "Duration" value = "4" />
         <param name = "Shape"
            value = "PolyLine( 3, 75, 500, 300, 170, 35, 175 )" />
         <param name = "AutoStart" value = "1" />
      </object>

      <object id = "GPPPath"
         classid = "CLSID:D7A7D7C3-D47F-11D0-89D3-00A0C90833E6">
         <param name = "Target" value = "GPPspan" />
         <param name = "Duration" value = "5" />
         <param name = "Shape" value =
            "PolyLine( 3, 275, 500, 300, 340, 85, 205 )" />
         <param name = "AutoStart" value = "1" />
      </object>

      <object id = "PERFPath"
         classid = "CLSID:D7A7D7C3-D47F-11D0-89D3-00A0C90833E6">
         <param name = "Target" value = "PERFspan" />
         <param name = "Duration" value = "6" />
         <param name = "Shape" value =
            "PolyLine( 3, 475, 500, 300, 340, 140, 235 )" />
         <param name = "AutoStart" value = "1" />
      </object>

```

Fig. 18.2 Controlling multiple elements with the Path Control (part 2 of 4).

```
      <object id = "PORTPath"
         classid = "CLSID:D7A7D7C3-D47F-11D0-89D3-00A0C90833E6">
         <param name = "Target" value = "PORTspan" />
         <param name = "Duration" value = "7" />
         <param name = "Shape" value =
            "PolyLine( 3, 600, -50, 300, 340, 200, 265 )" />
         <param name = "AutoStart" value = "1" />
      </object>

      <object id = "SEOPath"
         classid = "CLSID:D7A7D7C3-D47F-11D0-89D3-00A0C90833E6">
         <param name = "Target" value = "SEOspan" />
         <param name = "Duration" value = "8" />
         <param name = "Shape" value =
            "PolyLine( 3, 300, -50, 300, 340, 260, 295 )" />
         <param name = "AutoStart" value = "1" />
      </object>

      <object id = "TDTPath"
         classid = "CLSID:D7A7D7C3-D47F-11D0-89D3-00A0C90833E6">
         <param name = "Target" value = "TDTspan" />
         <param name = "Duration" value = "9" />
         <param name = "Shape" value =
            "PolyLine( 3, 500, -50, 300, 340, 310, 325 )" />
         <param name = "AutoStart" value = "1" />
      </object>
   </body>
</html>
```

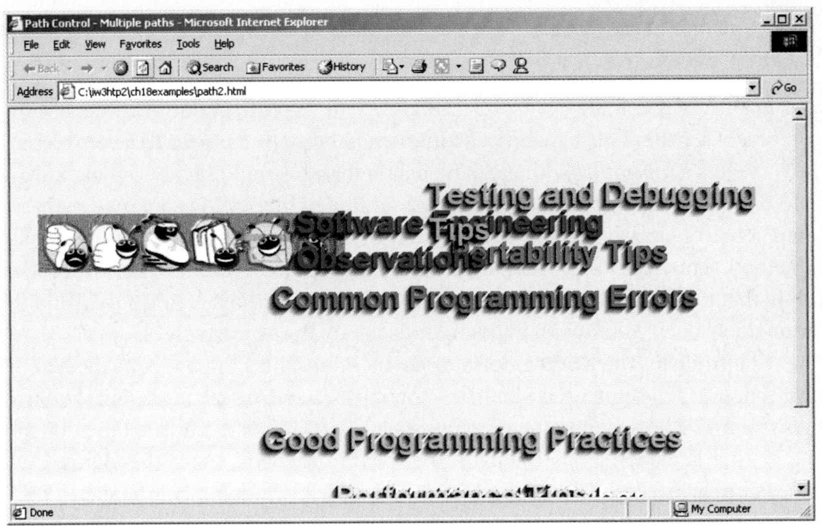

Fig. 18.2 Controlling multiple elements with the Path Control (part 3 of 4).

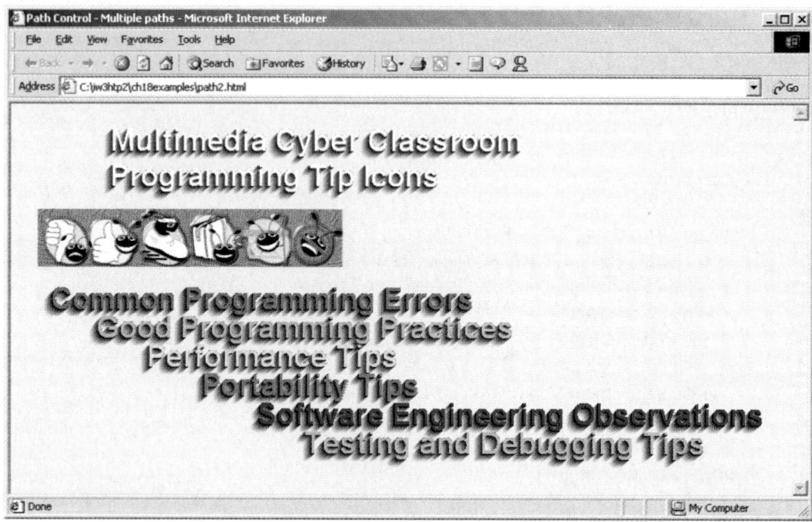

Fig. 18.2 Controlling multiple elements with the Path Control (part 4 of 4).

Each **`object`** element in our program controls a separate **`span`** element. As the page loads, these elements move separately into place, creating a visually pleasing effect. Note that because we did not specify the **`z-index`** properties, the **`z-index`** of elements that overlap each other is determined by their order of declaration in the XHTML source: elements declared later in the XHTML file are displayed above elements declared earlier.

18.4 Time Markers for Path Control

A useful feature of the Path Control is the ability to execute certain actions at any point along an object's path. This capability is implemented with the **`AddTimeMarker`** method, which creates a *time marker* that can be handled with simple JavaScript event handling. Figure 18.3 has two separate time markers for an image that follows an *oval* path.

Lines 39–40 place the image with the **`id`** of **`largebug`** on an oval path, using the **`Oval`** method. This method is similar to the **`Oval`** method from the Structured Graphics Control, in that the first two parameters specify the *x*–*y* coordinates of the oval and the next two parameters specify the width and height of the oval, respectively.

Line 42 introduces the **`AddTimeMarker`** method. The **`1`** appended to the **`AddTimeMarker`** function is a sequential identifier—much as **`Line0001`** is used in the Structured Graphics Control. The first parameter in the **`value`** attribute determines the point at which our time marker is placed along the path, specified in seconds; when this point is reached, event **`onmarker`** is fired. The second parameter gives an identifying name to the event, which is later passed on to the event handler for the **`onmarker`** function. The last parameter specifies whether to fire the **`onmarker`** event every time the object's path loops past the time marker (as we do here by setting the parameter to **`0`**) or to fire the event just the first time that the time marker is passed (by setting the parameter to **`1`**).

```
<?xml version = "1.0"?>
<!DOCTYPE html PUBLIC "-//W3C//DTD XHTML 1.0 Transitional//EN"
      "http://www.w3.org/TR/xhtml1/DTD/xhtml1-transitional.dtd">

<!-- Fig 18.3: path3.html       -->
<!-- Oval paths and time markers -->

<html xmlns = "http://www.w3.org/1999/xhtml">
   <head>
      <title>Path control - Advanced Paths</title>

      <script type = "text/javascript" for = "oval"
         event = "onmarker ( marker )">
         <!--
         if ( marker == "mark1" )
            pole.style.zIndex +=  2;

         if ( marker == "mark2" )
            pole.style.zIndex -=  2;
         // -->
      </script>
   </head>

   <body style = "background-color: #9C00FF">

      <img id = "pole" src = "pole.gif" style =
         "position: absolute; left: 350; top: 80;
         z-index: 3; height: 300" />

      <img id = "largebug" src = "animatedbug_large.gif"
           style = "position: absolute; z-index: 4" />

      <object id = "oval"
         classid = "CLSID:D7A7D7C3-D47F-11D0-89D3-00A0C90833E6">
         <param name = "AutoStart" value = "-1" />
         <param name = "Repeat" value = "-1" />
         <param name = "Relative" value = "1" />
         <param name = "Duration" value = "8" />
         <param name = "Shape"
            value = "Oval( 100, 80, 300, 60 )" />
         <param name = "Target" value = "largebug" />
         <param name = "AddTimeMarker1" value = "2, mark1, 0" />
         <param name = "AddTimeMarker2" value = "6, mark2, 0" />
      </object>

      <object id = "swarmPath"
         classid = "CLSID:D7A7D7C3-D47F-11D0-89D3-00A0C90833E6">
         <param name = "AutoStart" value = "-1" />
         <param name = "Repeat" value = "-1" />
         <param name = "Relative" value = "1" />
         <param name = "Duration" value = "15" />
```

Fig. 18.3 Adding time markers for script interaction (part 1 of 3).

```
            <param name = "Shape"
               value = "Polygon(6, 0, 0, 400, 300, 450, 50, 320,
                              300, 150, 180, 50, 250 )" />
            <param name = "Target" value = "swarm" />
         </object>

         <span id = "swarm" style =
            "position:absolute; top: 0; left: 0; z-index: 1">

         <img src = "animatedbug_small.gif"
            style = "position:absolute; top: 25; left: -30" />
         <img src = "animatedbug_small.gif"
            style = "position:absolute; top: 0; left: 0" />
         <img src = "animatedbug_small.gif"
            style = "position:absolute; top: 15; left: 70" />
         <img src = "animatedbug_small.gif"
            style = "position:absolute; top: 30; left: 5" />
         <img src = "animatedbug_small.gif"
            style = "position: absolute; top: 10; left: 30" />
         <img src = "animatedbug_small.gif"
            style = "position: absolute; top: 40; left: 40" />
         <img src = "animatedbug_small.gif"
            style = "position: absolute; top: 65; left: 15" />

         </span>
      </body>
   </html>
```

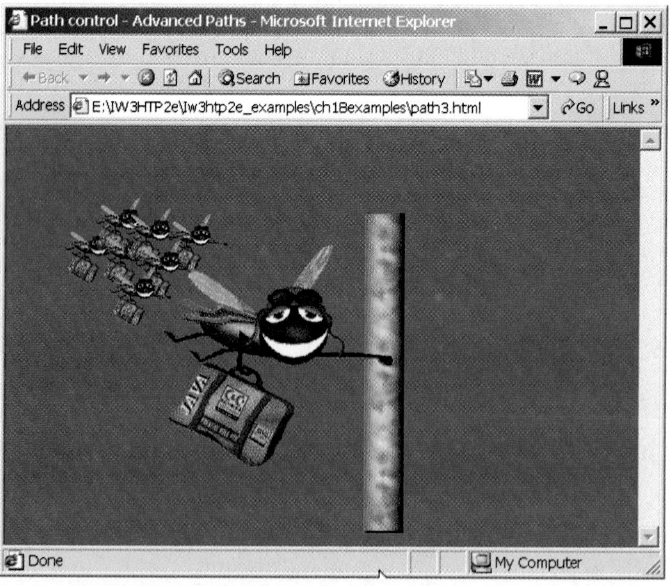

Fig. 18.3 Adding time markers for script interaction (part 2 of 3).

Fig. 18.3 Adding time markers for script interaction (part 3 of 3).

Lines 12–21create an event handler for the **onmarker** event. The parameter that the **onmarker** event receives (defined here as **marker** in line 13) identifies the marker that fired the event. The **if** control structures that follow change the **zIndex** attribute of element **pole** to correspond to the time marker in our Path Control that actually fired the event. These events fire when the large image is at the leftmost and rightmost extremes of its oval path, creating the appearance that the bee image is flying alternately behind and in front of the image of the pole.

18.5 DirectAnimation Sequencer Control

Thus far, we have been using the JavaScript function **window.setInterval** to control timed events on our Web pages. The Sequencer Control provides a simpler interface for calling functions or performing actions, at time intervals that you can set easily. Figure 18.4 uses the Sequencer Control to display four lines of text sequentially; when the fourth line of text has been displayed, the Sequencer Control then starts that fourth line on a **PolyLine** path, using the **Play** method of the Path Control.

Lines 66–68 add the Sequencer Control to our Web page. Notice that we do not include any **param** tags inside the **object** element; here, we set all the parameters for the Sequencer Control via scripting.

Lines 19–28 use a JavaScript event handler for the ***oninit*** *event* that fires when the sequencer loads. The **Item** object creates a grouping of events using a common name (in this case, **showThem**). The **at** method of the **Item** object takes two parameters: How many seconds to wait, and what action to perform when that period of time has expired. In this case, we call the **show** function for specific lines in the text at two, four, six and seven seconds after the **oninit** event fires, and we call the **runPath** function after eight seconds have elapsed. We then use the **runPath** function to initiate a Path Control by scripting. Line 44 calls the Path Control's **Play** method to start the targeted element (**line4**) along the path.

```
1  <?xml version = "1.0"?>
2  <!DOCTYPE html PUBLIC "-//W3C//DTD XHTML 1.0 Strict//EN"
3     "http://www.w3.org/TR/xhtml1/DTD/xhtml1-strict.dtd">
4
5  <!-- Fig. 18.4: sequencer.html -->
6  <!-- Sequencer Control          -->
7
8  <html xmlns = "http://www.w3.org/1999/xhtml">
9     <head>
10       <title>Sequencer Control</title>
11       <style type = "text/css">
12
13          div { font-size: 2em;
14                color: white;
15                font-weight: bold }
16
17       </style>
18
19       <script type = "text/javascript" for = "sequencer"
20          event = "oninit">
21          <!--
22          sequencer.Item( "showThem" ).at( 2.0, "show( line1 )" );
23          sequencer.Item( "showThem" ).at( 4.0, "show( line2 )" );
24          sequencer.Item( "showThem" ).at( 6.0, "show( line3 )" );
25          sequencer.Item( "showThem" ).at( 7.0, "show( line4 )" );
26          sequencer.Item( "showThem" ).at( 8.0, "runPath()" );
27          // -->
28       </script>
29
30       <script type = "text/javascript">
31          <!--
32          function show( object )
33          {
34             object.style.visibility = "visible";
35          }
36
37          function start()
38          {
39             sequencer.Item( "showThem" ).Play();
40          }
41
42          function runPath()
43          {
44             pathControl.Play();
45          }
46          // -->
47       </script>
48    </head>
```

Fig. 18.4 Using the DirectAnimation Sequencer Control (part 1 of 3).

```

   <body style = "background-color: limegreen" onload = "start()">

      <div id = "line1" style = "position: absolute; left: 50;
         top: 10; visibility: hidden">
         Sequencer DirectAnimation</div>

      <div id = "line2" style = "position: absolute; left: 70;
         top: 60; visibility: hidden">ActiveX Control</div>

      <div id = "line3" style = "position: absolute; left: 90;
         top: 110; visibility: hidden">
         Controls time intervals</div>

      <div id = "line4" style = "position: absolute; left: 110;
         top:160; visibility: hidden">For dynamic effects</div>

      <object id = "sequencer" classid =
         "CLSID:B0A6BAE2-AAF0-11d0-A152-00A0C908DB96">
      </object>

      <object id = "pathControl"
         classid = "CLSID:D7A7D7C3-D47F-11D0-89D3-00A0C90833E6">
         <param name = "AutoStart" value = "0" />
         <param name = "Repeat" value = "1" />
         <param name = "Relative" value = "1" />
         <param name = "Duration" value = "2" />
         <param name = "Shape" value =
            "PolyLine( 2, 0, 0, 250, 0 )" />
         <param name = "Target" value = "line4" />
      </object>

   </body>
</html>
```

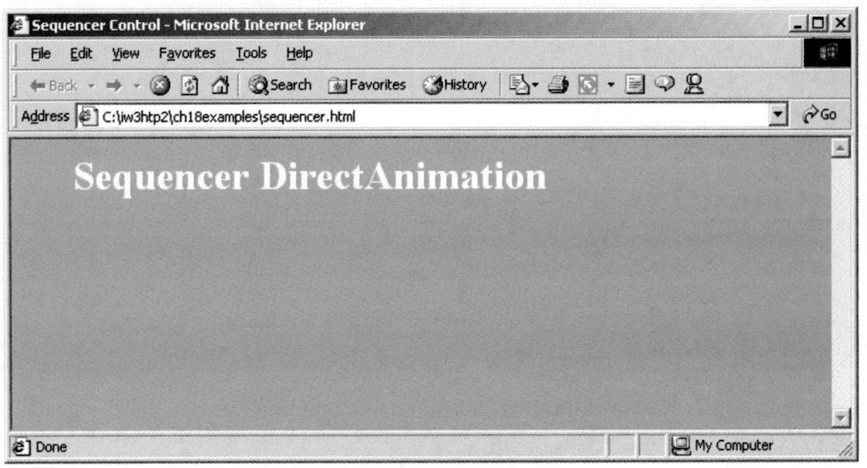

Fig. 18.4 Using the DirectAnimation Sequencer Control (part 2 of 3).

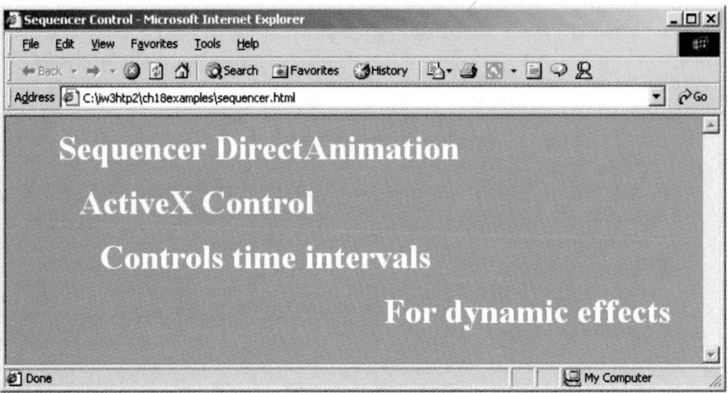

Fig. 18.4 Using the DirectAnimation Sequencer Control (part 3 of 3).

18.6 DirectAnimation Sprite Control

The images we have been using thus far have all been static. Some standards exist for standardized animation (the most common of which is an *animated GIF*), but none provides the dynamic control over animation that the Sprite Control provides. It allows you to control the rate of playback for images or even for individual *frames*. An animation is composed of many individual frames that create the illusion of motion. Figure 18.5 shows the image frames animated in Fig. 18.6.

Fig. 18.5 Source image for Sprite Control (**`walking.gif`**).

```
1  <?xml version = "1.0"?>
2  <!DOCTYPE html PUBLIC "-//W3C//DTD XHTML 1.0 Transitional//EN"
3     "http://www.w3.org/TR/xhtml1/DTD/xhtml1-transitional.dtd">
4
5  <!-- Fig 18.6: sprite.html -->
6  <!-- Sprite Control        -->
7
8  <html xmlns = "http://www.w3.org/1999/xhtml">
9     <head>
10       <title>Sprite Control</title>
11    </head>
12
13    <body>
14
15       <object id = "walking" style = "width: 150; height: 250"
16          classid  = "CLSID:FD179533-D86E-11d0-89D6-00A0C90833E6">
17          <param name = "Repeat" value = "-1" />
18          <param name = "NumFrames" value = "5" />
19          <param name = "NumFramesAcross" value = "3" />
20          <param name = "NumFramesDown" value = "2" />
21          <param name = "SourceURL" value = "walking.gif" />
22          <param name = "AutoStart" value = "-1" />
23       </object>
24
25    </body>
26 </html>
```

Fig. 18.6 Simple animation with the Sprite Control.

The **`object`** tag (lines 15–23) inserts the Sprite Control into a Web page. CSS properties **`width`** and **`height`** specify the image width and height, respectively. Setting the **`Repeat`** attribute to a nonzero **`value`** (**`-1`**) loops the animation continuously. The next attribute, **`NumFrames`**, specifies how many frames are present in the animation source image (Fig. 18.5). The next two attributes—**`NumFramesAcross`** and **`NumFrames-`**

Down—specify how many rows and columns of frames there are in the animation file. The **SourceURL** property gives a path to the file containing all the frames of the animation, and setting the **AutoStart** property to a nonzero **value** starts the animation automatically when the page loads.

What distinguishes the Sprite Control from other animation formats is that it can do much more than simply loop through frames repeatedly; it can, through Dynamic HTML, respond to user actions, as we demonstrate in Fig. 18.7.

```
<?xml version = "1.0"?>
<!DOCTYPE html PUBLIC "-//W3C//DTD XHTML 1.0 Transitional//EN"
   "http://www.w3.org/TR/xhtml1/DTD/xhtml1-transitional.dtd">

<!-- Fig. 18.7: sprite2.html     -->
<!-- Events with Sprite Control -->

<html xmlns = "http://www.w3.org/1999/xhtml">
   <head>
      <title>Sprite Control</title>

      <script type = "text/javascript" for = "bounce"
         event = "onmouseover">
         <!--
         bounce.Stop();
         bounce.PlayRate = -3;
         bounce.Play();
         // -->
      </script>

      <script type = "text/javascript" for = "bounce"
         event = "onmouseout">
         <!--
         bounce.Stop();
         bounce.PlayRate = 1;
         bounce.Play();
         // -->
      </script>
   </head>

   <body>

      <h1>Sprite Control</h1>

      <object id = "bounce" style =
         "width:75; height:75" classid  =
         "CLSID:FD179533-D86E-11d0-89D6-00A0C90833E6">
         <param name = "Repeat" value = "-1" />
         <param name = "PlayRate" value = "1" />
         <param name = "NumFrames" value = "22" />
         <param name = "NumFramesAcross" value = "4" />
         <param name = "NumFramesDown" value = "6" />
         <param name = "SourceURL" value = "bounce.jpg" />
```

Fig. 18.7 Responding to mouse events with the Sprite Control (part 1 of 2).

```
44            <param name = "MouseEventsEnabled" value = "True" />
45            <param name = "AutoStart" value = "-1" />
46         </object>
47
48      </body>
49   </html>
```

Fig. 18.7 Responding to mouse events with the Sprite Control (part 2 of 2).

This example introduces several new aspects of the Sprite Control. The **PlayRate** method controls the rate at which frames are displayed; **1** is the default value. Method **MouseEventsEnabled**, as with the Structured Graphics Control, allows the object to capture certain mouse events.

In lines 12–19 and 21–28, we provide event handlers for the events **onmouseover** and **onmouseout**, respectively. When the user moves the mouse over the Sprite Control, the event handler calls the **Stop** method, which stops the animation in place, and sets the **PlayRate** method to **-3**. The **PlayRate** method is writable only at runtime or when the animation is stopped. This action plays the animation in reverse at three times the normal speed. The script then calls the **Play** function to restart the animation. The **onmouseout** event handler sets the **PlayRate** back to the default of **1** when the user moves the mouse cursor off the animation.

18.7 Animated GIFs

Although the Sprite Control is useful for adding animation to Web pages, it is a proprietary format specific to Internet Explorer. The most popular method of creating animated graphics is a format known as *animated GIF*. As with the Sprite Control, animated GIFs are composed frames. Each frame contains a GIF image. However, unlike the images used with Sprite Control, GIF images must be inserted into animated GIFs by using graphics applications such as Adobe's PhotoShop Elements (see Chapter 3). Figure 18.8 shows the file **animatedbug_large.gif** loaded into PhotoShop Elements.

Each frame of a GIF animation is a separate image that, when shown in a particular sequence, gives the effect of motion. PhotoShop Elements combines the separate images into one image file by using layers, which allow the image's author to maintain separate images that are linked together.

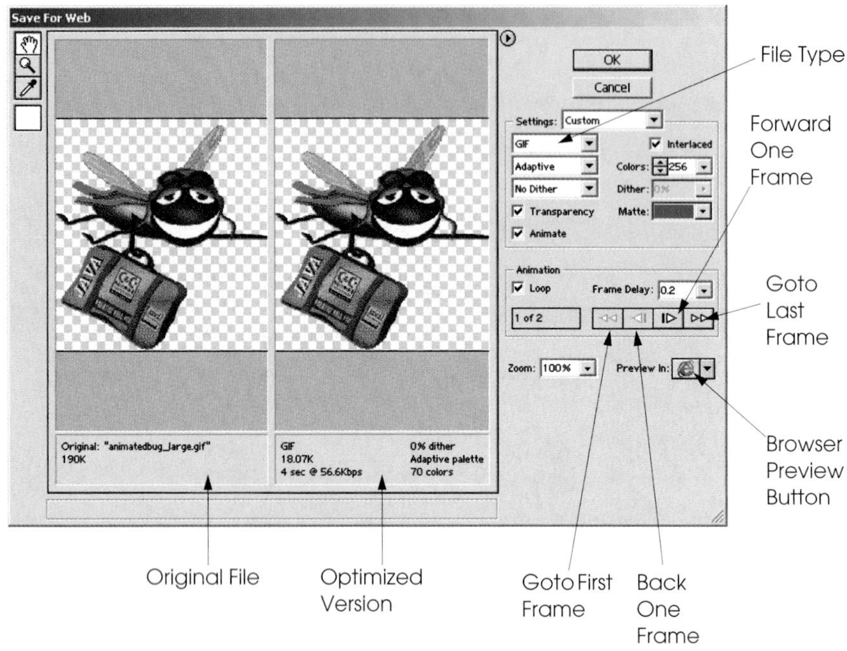

Fig. 18.8 Viewing an animated GIF in Photoshop® Elements. (Adobe and Photoshop are either registered trademarks or trademarks of Adobe Systems Incorporated in the United States and/or other countries.)

The animation effect is created from the **Save for Web** feature, located under the **File** menu in PhotoShop Elements. The **Save for Web** dialog is where the image's author determines the best file format and range of colors to use for an image.

Set the file type to GIF, and make sure that the **Animate** checkbox is checked (otherwise, the animation options remain inactive). The primary animation option is the ***Frame Delay*** (the amount of time that elapses before the image is switched). The ***Loop*** option, when checked, animates the GIF. Clicking the arrow buttons causes the animation to move forward and backward.

Animated GIFs can have transparent (i.e., "see-through") backgrounds. PhotoShop Elements uses a checkerboard pattern to represent transparency. This option is enabled by clicking the ***Transparency*** checkbox in the **Save for Web** dialog.

The GIF animation may be previewed in a Web browser before saving the file. Clicking the browser preview button in the **Save for Web** dialog opens the default Web browser. Photoshop Elements creates a temporary document with the GIF animation embedded into it. Return to the **Save for Web** dialog by closing the browser window. Save the image as an animated GIF.

Performance Tip 18.2

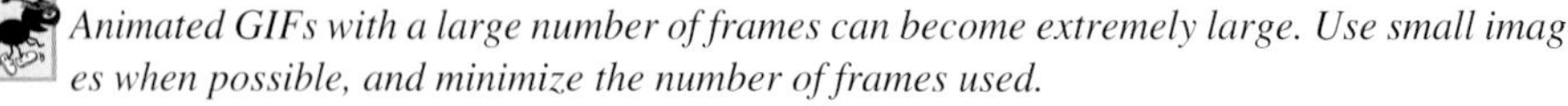

Animated GIFs with a large number of frames can become extremely large. Use small images when possible, and minimize the number of frames used.

18.8 Internet and World Wide Web Resources

www.dhtmlzone.com/articles/iemmcontrols.html
This Dynamic HTML Zone article introduces Internet Explorer's ActiveX controls related to multimedia. In particular, the article discusses the Transition and the Structured Graphics controls.

www.dhtmlzone.com/articles/ie4cont/ie4controls.html
This Dynamic HTML Zone article discusses Internet Explorer multimedia controls. The article includes sections on the Sequencer, the Sprite, the Structured Graphics and the Path Controls. Each section includes an example, the code and a description of the example.

hotwired.lycos.com/webmonkey/97/52/index0a.html?tw=authoring
This WebMonkey tutorial discusses several Active X controls, which include the Sprite, Structured Graphics and Path Controls. The tutorial includes links to articles related to Dynamic HTML.

SUMMARY

- The DirectAnimation Path Control allows you to control the positions of elements on your page.
- Setting **AutoStart** to a nonzero value starts the element along a path as soon as the page loads. Setting a zero value prevents it from starting automatically, in which case a script would have to call the **Play** method to start the path. The **Repeat** method determines how many times the path will be traversed; setting the value to **-1** specifies that the path should loop continuously.
- The **Duration** method specifies the amount of time that it takes to traverse the path, in seconds. The **Bounce** method, when set to **1**, reverses the element's direction on the path when it reaches the end. Setting the value to **0** returns the element to the beginning of the path when the path has been traversed.
- The **PolyLine** method creates a path with multiple line segments.
- The **Target** method specifies the **id** of the element that is targeted by the Path Control.
- Setting the CSS attribute **position** to **absolute** allows the Path Control to move an element around the screen. Otherwise, the element would be static, locked in the position determined by the browser when the page loads.
- The Path Control also allows you to set paths for multiple objects present on your page. To set paths for multiple objects, you must add a separate **object** tag for each object you wish to control.
- The **z-index** of elements that overlap is determined by their order of declaration in the XHTML source (elements declared later in the XHTML file are displayed above elements declared earlier).
- A useful feature of the Path Control is the ability to execute certain actions at any point along an object's path. This capability is implemented with the **AddTimeMarker** method, which creates a time marker that can be handled with simple JavaScript event handling.
- The number appended to the **AddTimeMarker** function is a sequential identifier, much as **Line0001** is used in the Structured Graphics Control. The first parameter in the **value** attribute determines the point at which our time marker is placed along the path, specified in seconds; when this point is reached, the **onmarker** event is fired. The second parameter gives an identifying name to the event, which is later passed on to the event handler for the **onmarker** event. The last parameter specifies whether to fire the **onmarker** event every time the object's path loops past the time marker (by setting the parameter to **0**) or to fire the event just the first time that the time marker is passed (by setting the parameter to **1**).
- The parameter received by the **onmarker** event identifies which marker fired the event.
- The Sequencer Control provides a simpler interface for calling functions or performing actions at time intervals that you can set easily.

- The **oninit** event fires when the Sequencer Control has loaded.
- The **Item** object of the Sequencer Control creates a grouping of events using a common name.
- The **at** method of the **Item** object takes two parameters: How many seconds to wait, and what action to perform when that period of time has expired.
- The **Play** method of the Path Control starts the targeted element along the path.
- The Sprite Control allows you to display animated images composed of individual frames.
- The **object** tag inserts the Sprite Control. The **height** and **width** CSS properties are needed to display the image correctly; they should be equal to the size of one frame in your file. Setting attribute **Repeat** to a nonzero **value** loops the animation indefinitely. **NumFrames** specifies how many frames are present in the animation source image. Attributes **NumFramesAcross** and **NumFramesDown** specify how many rows and columns of frames there are in the animation file, respectively. Property **SourceURL** gives a path to the file containing the frames of the animation. Setting property **AutoStart** to a nonzero **value** starts the animation automatically when the page loads.
- Sprite Control method **PlayRate** controls the rate at which frames are displayed (**1** is the default value). The **MouseEventsEnabled** method, as with the Structured Graphics Control, allows the object to capture certain mouse events. The **Stop** method stops the animation in place. Method **PlayRate** is writable only at runtime or when the animation is stopped.
- The most popular method of creating animated graphics is a format known as animated GIF. As with the Sprite Control, animated GIFs are composed frames in the GIF image format. GIF images must be inserted into animated GIF files by using graphics applications such as Adobe PhotoShop Elements.

TERMINOLOGY

AddTimeMarker method
animated GIF
at method of **Item** object
AutoStart
Bounce method
classid
Duration method
Item object of the Sequencer Control
MouseEventsEnabled
NumFrames
NumFramesAcross
NumFramesDown
oninit event
onmarker event
Oval method
Path Control
Play method
PlayRate method of the Sprite Control
PolyLine method
position: absolute
Relative method
Repeat attribute
Repeat method
Sequencer Control
Shape method
SourceURL
splash screen effect
Sprite Control
Stop method
Target method
time marker
visibility: hidden
window.setInterval
z-index

SELF-REVIEW EXERCISES

18.1 State whether each of the following is *true* or *false*. If *false*, explain why.

a) The **z-index** of elements in which the **z-index** property is not declared specifically is determined by the order of their appearance in the XHTML document.

b) The parameters for the Path Control **PolyLine** method are the same as those for the Structured Graphics Control **PolyLine**.

c) A time marker will fire the **onmarker** event only once.
d) You can control multiple paths with a single Path Control **object**.
e) The **oninit** event fires when the Sequencer Control has finished loading.
f) The **PlayRate** method of the Sprite Control is always writable.
g) All ActiveX controls use the same **classid** attribute.

18.2 Fill in the blanks in each of the following statements:
a) The _________ Control allows you to perform scripted actions on your Web page at timed intervals.
b) The _________ Control allows you to place animated images on your Web page.
c) The _________ Control can move elements around your page dynamically.
d) The _________ method is used to create a time marker for the Path Control.
e) An element's CSS **position** property must be set to _________ for the Path Control to target that object successfully.
f) The _________ method determines the number of iterations for which the Path Control continues on a certain path.

ANSWERS TO SELF-REVIEW EXERCISES

18.1 a) True. b) True. c) False; the number of time it is fired depends on the last parameter of the **AddTimeMarker** method, and it may be set to fire every time the time marker is reached. d) False; multiple controls are needed if you want to control multiple paths. e) True. f) False; it is writable only at runtime or when the animation is stopped. g) False; each uses a unique **classid**.

18.2 a) Sequencer. b) Sprite. c) Path. d) **AddTimeMarker**. e) **absolute**. f) **Repeat**.

EXERCISES

18.3 Use the Path Control to have the logo on your Web page follow an **Oval** path around the page.

18.4 Use the Path Control to simulate the motion of text inside a **marquee** tag.

18.5 Modify Exercise 18.4 by adding time markers that change the color of the text with every loop.

18.6 Use the Sequencer Control to create a slideshow of images.

18.7 Use Photoshop Elements to create a sprite that simulates a rotating planet. Modify Fig. 18.3 so that the sprite, animated with the Sprite control, rotates around a larger planet in the center of the page.

18.8 Create your own animated GIF with Photoshop Elements.

19

Macromedia® Flash™: Building Interactive Animations

Objectives

- To learn Flash 5 multimedia development.
- To learn Flash animation techniques.
- To learn ActionScript, the Flash programming language.
- To create an animation that preloads objects into a Flash movie.
- To add sound to Flash movies.
- To embed a Flash movie into a Web page.

A flash and where previously the brain held a dead fact, the soul grasps a living truth! At moments we are all artists.
Arnold Bennett

All the world's a stage and all the men and women merely players; they have their exits and their entrances; and one man in his time plays many parts…
William Shakespeare

Science and technology and the various forms of art, all unite humanity in a single and interconnected system.
Zhores Aleksandrovich Medvedev

Music hath charms to soothe a savage breast, To soften rocks, or bend a knotted oak.
William Congreve

The true art of memory is the art of attention.
Samuel Johnson

Outline

19.1 Introduction

Macromedia Flash 5 is an application that developers use to produce interactive, animated *movies*. Flash can be used to create Web-based banner advertisements, interactive Web sites and Web-based applications with stunning graphics and multimedia effects. An advantage Flash has over other multimedia development applications is that Flash has provides for drawing graphics, generating animation and adding sound and video. Flash movies can be embedded in Web pages, placed on CD-ROMs as independent applications or converted into standalone, executable programs.

Another advantage of using Flash to produce interactive content is that Flash includes tools for writing its scripting language, *ActionScript*. ActionScript, which is similar to JavaScript, is the enabling technology for Flash interactivity.

To play Flash movies, the *Flash Player plug-in* must be installed in a Web browser. This plug-in has several versions, the most recent of which is version 5. In addition to the full Flash application, Netscape Communicator versions 4.02 and higher and Microsoft Internet Explorer versions 4 and higher include the Flash Player plug-in. Other products with which the plug-in is bundled include Microsoft Windows® 98, NT, Me and 2000, AOL 5.0 and higher and various Macintosh software products. According to Macromedia's statistics, 96 percent of Web users (approximately 334 million) can view Flash movies with the Flash Player 4 plug-in. Of those users, 51 percent never had to download the plug-in because it was bundled with software that they already owned.[1] The plug-in can be downloaded from **www.macromedia.com/downloads**. There are ways to detect if a user does not have the appropriate plug-in to view Flash content. Macromedia provides a tool called the Flash Deployment Kit which contains files that work together to detect whether a suitable version of Macromedia Flash Player is installed in a user's Web browser. This kit, which is available at Macromedia's Web site, may be downloaded from

www.macromedia.com/support/flash/player/
flash_deployment_readme

This chapter provides an introduction to the construction of Flash movies, including the creation of interactive buttons, the addition of sound to movies, the creation of special graphic effects and the integration of ActionScript in movies. Other Deitel & Associates, Inc. Flash publications are currently under development. Visit **www.deitel.com** for more information.

It is necessary to install Flash 5 on a computer before proceeding with this chapter. A 30-day trial version of Flash 5 can be downloaded for free from Macromedia's Web site:

www.macromedia.com/software/flash/trial

Follow Macromedia's detailed installation instructions. The Flash 5 system requirements are available at

www.macromedia.com/software/flash/productinfo/systemreqs

[*Note*: Do not change the computer clock settings after installing Flash. Doing so causes the 30-day trial to expire, immediately disabling the program. Reinstalling Flash will not reactivate the program.]

19.2 Flash™ Movie Development

Once the program is installed, begin by opening Flash 5. Flash creates a new file called **Movie1** when the program opens. Figure 19.1 shows the Flash development environment.

The largest element in the development environment is the movie *stage*. The stage is the white area in which a developer places graphic elements during movie development. Directly above the stage is the movie *timeline*. The timeline represents a time period over which a movie runs. Timelines are divided into increments called *frames*, which are represented by gray and white rectangles. Each frame depicts a moment in time during the movie, into which the developer can insert movie elements.

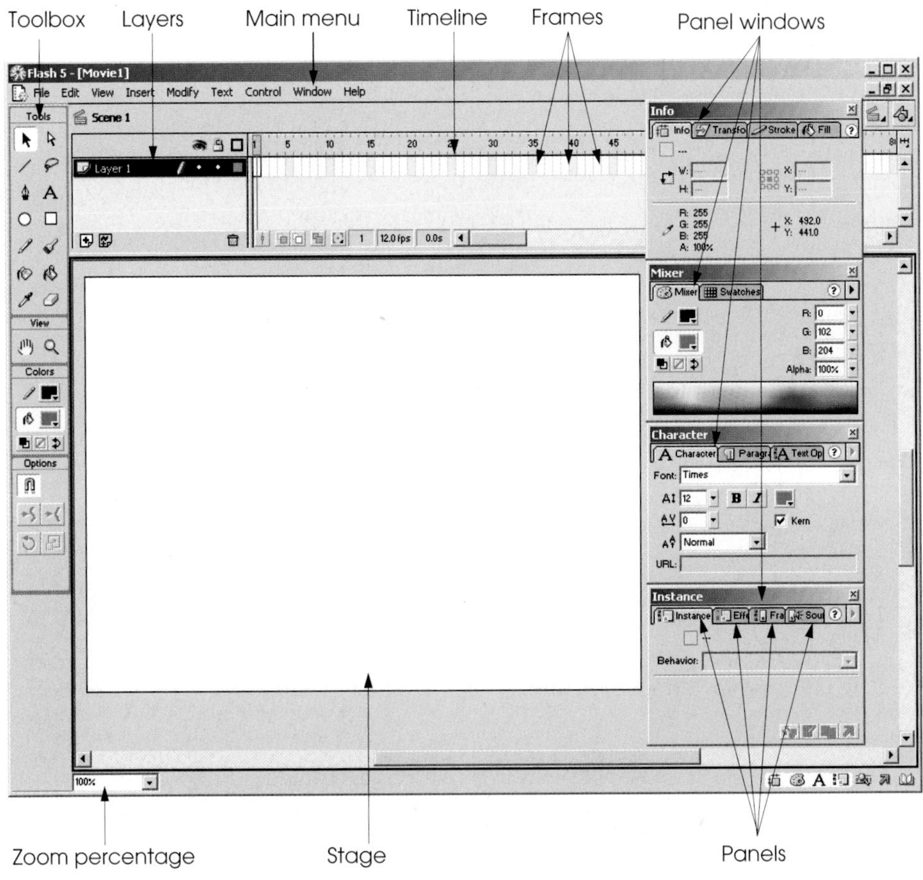

Fig. 19.1 Flash 5 development environment.

The development environment contains several windows that provide options and tools for the creation of Flash movies. Many of these tools are located in the *toolbox*, the vertical window located along the left side of the development environment. The toolbox is divided into four sections, each containing tools and functions that help the developer create Flash movies (Fig. 19.2). The ***Tools*** section contains tools that select, add and remove graphics from Flash movies. The ***View*** section contains the two tools that modify the appearance of the stage. The ***Colors*** section provides colors for shapes, lines and filled areas. The last section, ***Options***, contains settings for the *active tool* (i.e., the tool that is highlighted and is in use). A developer can make a tool behave differently by selecting a new mode with the tool options.

Application windows called *panels* organize frequently used movie options (Fig. 19.3). Panel options modify the size, shape, color, alignment and effects added to a movie's graphic elements. Panels may be placed anywhere in the development environment by clicking and dragging them with the mouse.

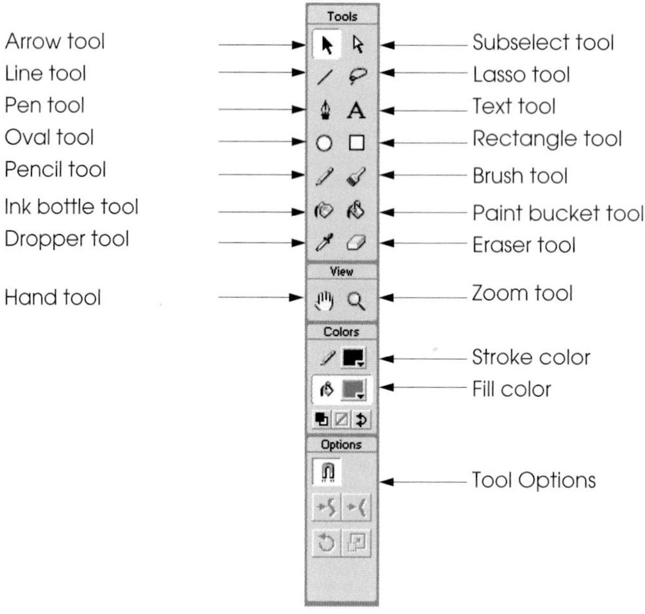

Fig. 19.2 Flash 5 Toolbox.

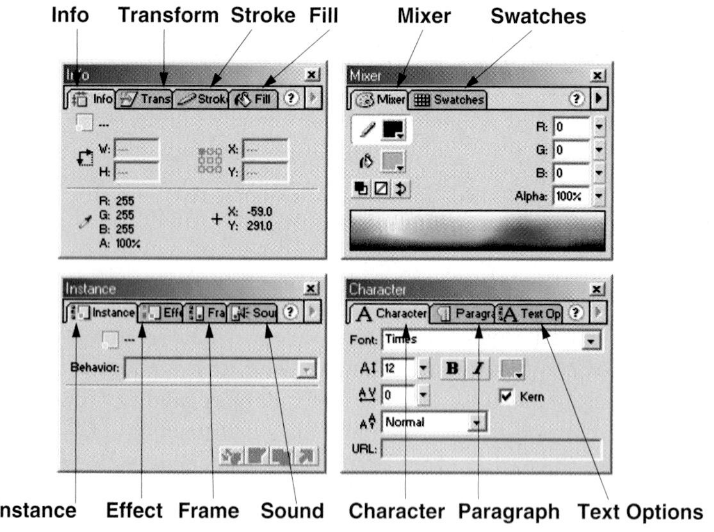

Fig. 19.3 Flash 5 panels.

Although the **Info**, **Mixer**, **Instance** and **Character** panels appear by default, a developer can access different panels by clicking the panel window tabs. Click a panel tab and drag it out of its panel window to create a new window for only that panel. Developers can save customized panel layouts by selecting **Save Panel Layout...** from the **Window** menu to save the panel arrangement. Select **Panel Sets** from the **Window** menu to load a saved panel layout or to restore the default panel layout. [*Note*: Pressing the *Tab* key temporarily hides all panels. Pressing *Tab* again displays them. This shortcut is helpful in managing the editing area of the screen.]

19.3 Learning Flash with Hands-on Examples

The best way to learn Flash is to create complete Flash movies. The first example demonstrates how to create an executable program by building an interactive, animated button. The addition of a basic script causes the button to produce a random string each time. The following steps describe how to create a Flash movie file and customize the movie settings. Open a new Flash movie by selecting **New** from the **File** menu. Next, choose **Save As...** from the **File** menu and save the movie as **`CeoAssistant.fla`**. The ***`.fla`*** file extension is a Flash-specific extension for editable movies.

Good Programming Practice 19.1

Save each project with a meaningful name in its own folder. Saving early and often is important for any work that you do. Creating a new folder for each movie helps keep projects organized.

Right click the stage to open a menu containing different movie options. Select **Movie Properties...** to display the **Movie Properties** dialog (this dialog also can be accessed through the **Modify** menu under **Movie...**). Settings such as the ***Frame Rate***, ***Dimensions*** and ***Background Color*** are established in this dialog (Fig. 19.4).

Frame Rate is the speed at which movie frames display. A higher frame rate causes more frames to be displayed in a given unit of time (the standard measurement is seconds) and creates a faster movie. The **Frame Rate** for Flash movies on the Web is generally between 5 and 15 frames per second (**fps**). For this example set the **Frame Rate** to **10** frames per second.

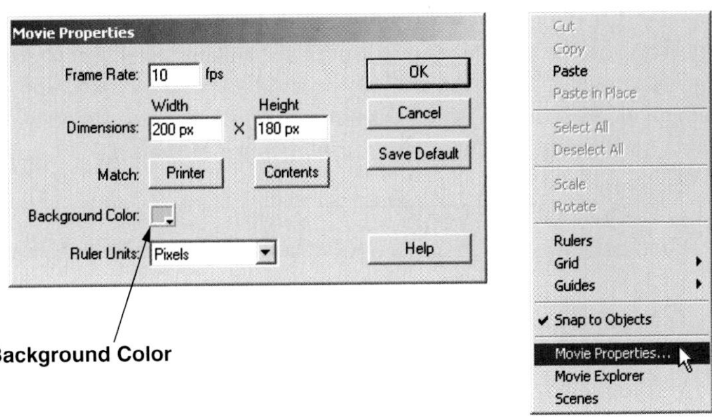

Fig. 19.4 Flash 5 **Movie Properties** dialog.

Performance Tip 19.1

Greater **frame rates** *increase the amount of information to be processed, thus increasing the file size.*

The ***Background Color*** is the stage color. Click the **Background Color** box (called a *swatch*) to select the background color. A new dialog opens presenting a Web-safe palette. Web-safe palettes and color selection are discussed in detail in Chapter 3, Photoshop® Elements. Notice that the mouse pointer has changed into an eyedropper. This eyedropper indicates that the developer may select a color. Choose a light blue color with the color selection eyedropper (Fig. 19.5).

The box in the upper left corner of the dialog displays the new background color. The *hexadecimal notation* for the selected color is beside this box. The hexadecimal notation is the color code that a Web browser uses to render color. Hexadecimal notation is discussed in detail in Appendix D, Number Systems.

Dimensions define the size of the movie as it displays on the screen. For this example, set the movie width to **200** pixels and the movie height to **180** pixels. Click **OK** to apply the changes in the movie settings.

Software Engineering Observation 19.1

The number of pixels per unit measure is called the resolution. The resolution of a Flash movie is always equal to the resolution of the monitor on which the movie displayed.

Software Engineering Observation 19.2

A movie's contents are not resized by changing the size of the movie stage.

With the new dimensions setting, the stage appears smaller. Select the *zoom* tool from the toolbox and click the stage once to enlarge it to 200% of its display size. Editing a movie with small dimensions is easier when the stage is enlarged. Press the *Alt* key while clicking the zoom tool to reduce the size of the work area. Select the hand tool from the toolbox, and drag the stage to the center of the editing area. The hand tool may be accessed at any time by holding down the *spacebar* key.

19.3.1 Creating a Shape With the Oval Tool

Graphics are created using the variety of editing tools and options Flash provides. Flash has an advantage over other graphic applications because it creates shapes using *vectors*. Vectors are mathematical equations which Flash uses to define size, shape and color. Some graphic applications create *raster graphics* or *bitmapped graphics*.

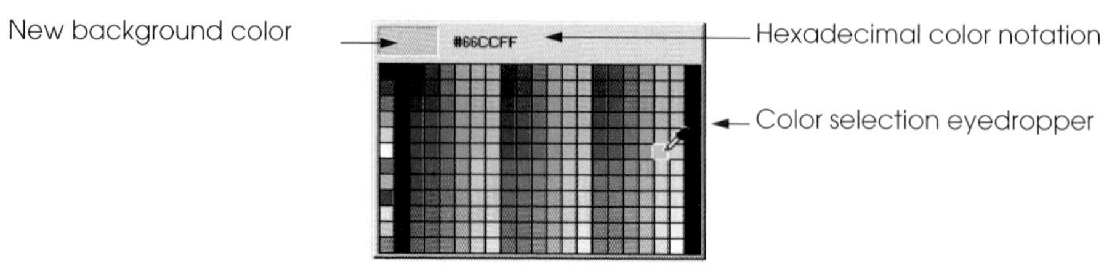

Fig. 19.5 Selecting a background color.

When vector graphics are saved, they are stored using these equations. Raster graphics are defined by areas of colored *pixels*—the unit of measurement for most computer monitors. Raster graphics typically have larger file sizes because the computer saves the information for every pixel. Vector and raster graphics also differ in their portability. Vector graphics can be resized without losing clarity whereas raster graphics lose clarity as they are enlarged or reduced. Chapter 3, Photoshop® Elements provides a detailed discussion of vector and raster graphics.

The next step is to create the interactive button out of a circular shape. A developer creates shapes by clicking and dragging with the shape tools. Select the *oval* tool from the toolbox to specify the button area. Every shape has a *stroke color* and a *fill color*. The stroke color is the color of a shape's outline and the fill color is the color that fills the shape. Click the swatches in the toolbar to set the fill color to red and the stroke color to black by selecting the colors from the Web-safe palette or by entering their hexadecimal values (Fig 19.6).

Clicking the default colors button resets the stroke color to black and the fill color to white. A shape can be created without a fill or stroke color by selecting the no stroke or fill option while either the stroke or fill swatch is selected. Selecting the swap stroke and fill colors option switches the stroke and fill colors.

Create the oval anywhere on the stage by clicking and dragging with the oval tool while pressing the *Shift* key. The *Shift* key *constrains* the oval's proportions to have equal height and width (i.e., a circle). The same technique creates a square with the rectangle tool or draws a straight line with the pencil tool. Drag the mouse until the circle is approximately the size of a dime, then release the mouse button.

Notice that when the shape was drawn, a dot appeared in frame 1, the first frame of the timeline. This dot signifies a *keyframe* (Fig. 19.7). Keyframes indicate points of change in a timeline. Whenever a shape is drawn in an empty frame, a keyframe is created. Adding keyframes is discussed later in this chapter.

The shape's fill and stroke may be edited individually. Click the red area with the *arrow* tool (black arrow) to select the circle fill. A grid of white dots appears over an object when it is selected (Fig. 19.8). Click the black stroke around the circle while pressing the *Shift* key to add to this selection. A developer also can make multiple selections by clicking and dragging with the arrow tool to draw a selection box around specific items.

A shape's size can be modified with the **Info** panel while the shape is selected (Fig. 19.9). Open the **Info** panel by clicking its panel tab or by selecting **Info** from the **Panels** submenu of the **Window** menu. The **Panels** submenu provides options to open every Flash panel.

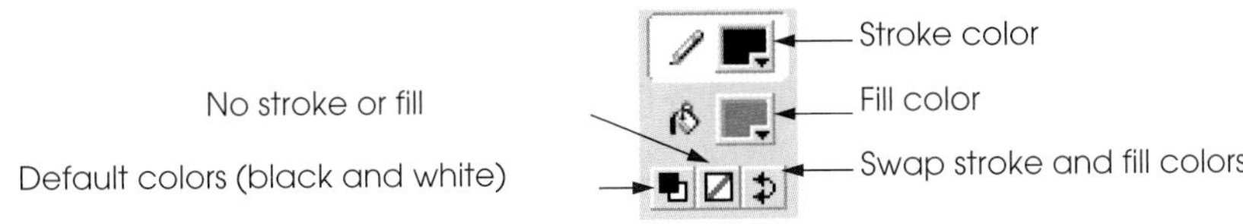

Fig. 19.6 Setting the fill and stroke colors.

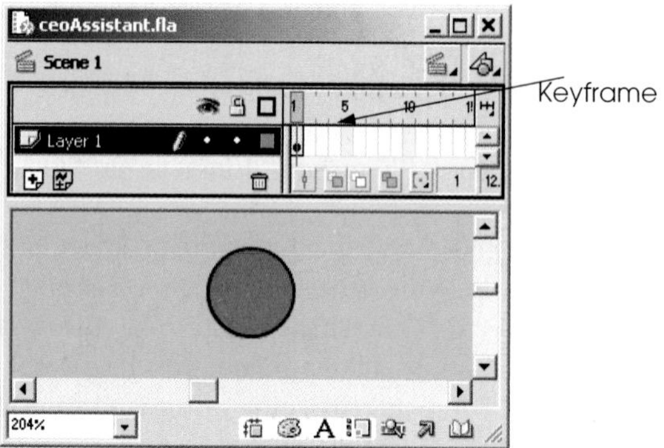

Fig. 19.7 Keyframe added to the timeline.

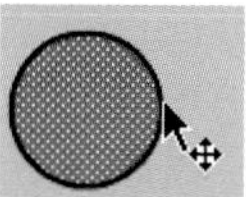

Fig. 19.8 Making multiple selections with the arrow tool.

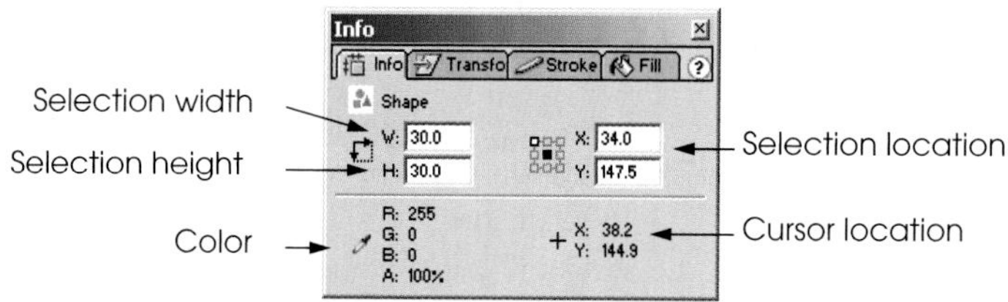

Fig. 19.9 Modifying the size of a shape with the **Info** panel.

Set the width and height of the circle by typing **30** into the **W:** text field and **30** into the **H:** text field. Entering an equal height and width maintains a *constrained aspect ratio* while enlarging the circle. A constrained aspect ratio maintains an object's proportions as it is resized. Press *Enter* to apply these values.

The next step is to modify the shape's color. Click outside the circle with the arrow tool to deselect the circle. Now, select only the red fill with the arrow tool. Click the fill swatch in the toolbox, and change the fill color to red *radial gradient* fill. The gradient fills are located at the bottom of the color palette (Fig. 19.10).

Gradient fills are gradual progressions of color. Flash provides four radial gradients and three linear gradients, although a developer also can create and edit gradients with the **Fill** panel. The circle should now have a red radial gradient fill with a black stroke surrounding it.

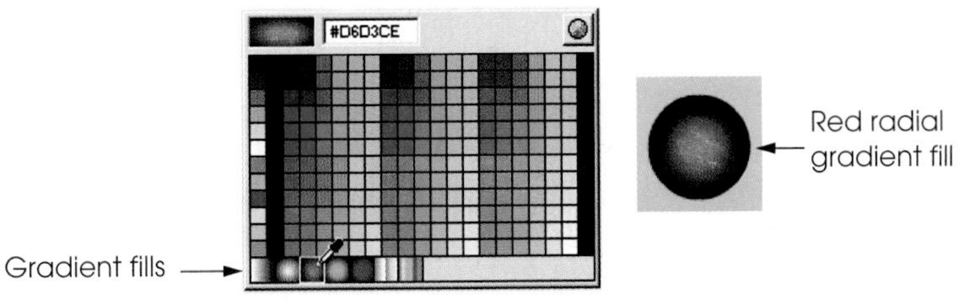

Fig. 19.10 Choosing a gradient fill.

19.3.2 Adding Text to a Button

Button titles communicate the button function to the user. The easiest way to create a title is with the *text* tool. This tool is used to add text to Flash movies. Create a button title by selecting the text tool and left clicking in the center of the button and typing **GO** in capital letters. Select the text with the text tool. Once text is selected, a developer can change the font, text size and font color with the Character panel (Fig. 19.11). Select a sans-serif font, such as **Arial** or **Verdana**, from the **Font** drop-down list.

Look-and-Feel Observation 19.1

Sans-serif fonts, such as Arial, Helvetica and Verdana are easier to read on a computer monitor, and therefore ensure better usability.

Set the font size to **14** pt either by typing the size into the font height field or by pressing the arrow button next to the font height field revealing the *size selection slider*. The size selection slider is a vertical slider that, when moved, changes the font size. Set the font weight to bold by clicking the bold button. Finally, change the font color by clicking the text color swatch and selecting white from the palette.

If the text did not appear in the correct location drag the text to the center of the button with the arrow tool. The button is almost finished and should now look similar to Fig. 19.12.

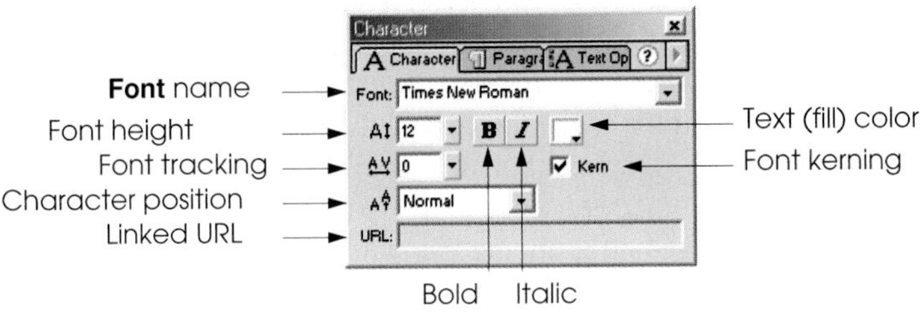

Fig. 19.11 Setting the font face, size, weight and color with the **Character** panel.

Fig. 19.12 Adding text to the button.

19.3.3 Converting a Shape into a Symbol

A Flash movie consists of a *parent movie* and *symbols*. The parent movie, sometimes called a *scene*, is the entire movie including all graphics and symbols. The parent movie may contain several symbols, which are reusable movie elements, such as *graphics*, *buttons* and *movie clips*. A parent movie timeline can contain numerous symbols, each with its own timeline and properties. A Flash movie also may have several *instances* of a particular symbol (i.e., the same symbol appears several times). A developer can edit symbols separately from the parent movie by using the symbol's *editing stage*. This editing stage is separate from the parent movie stage and only contains one symbol.

For this example, we must convert the button into a button symbol so that it can be made interactive. On the parent stage, the button consists of text, color fill and stroke. These items are combined and treated as one object when converted into a symbol. Use the arrow tool to drag a *selection box* around the button, selecting the button fill, the button stroke and the text all at one time (Fig. 19.13).

Select **Convert to Symbol...** from the **Insert** menu or use the shortcut *F8* on the keyboard. This opens the **Symbol Properties** dialog, in which a developer sets a new symbol's properties (Fig. 19.14).

Every symbol in a Flash movie must have a unique name. It is a good idea to name symbols by their contents or function, making them easier to reuse. Enter the name **go button** into the **Name** field of the **Symbol Properties** dialog. The *symbol behavior* determines what function a symbol has in a movie.

The behavior of a *movie clip symbol* is similar so that of the parent movie and ideal for recurring animations. *Graphic symbols* are ideal for static images and basic animations. *Button symbols* are objects that perform button actions such as *rollovers* and hyperlinking. A rollover is an action that changes the appearance of a button when the mouse passes over it. For this example, select **Button** as the type of symbol and click **OK**. The button should have a blue box surrounding it with a crosshairs in the center indicating that it is a symbol. Use the arrow tool to drag the button to the lower-right corner of the stage.

The **Library** panel stores every symbol in a movie, and is accessed through the **Window** menu or by the shortcut *Ctrl+L* (Fig. 19.15). Multiple instances of a symbol can be placed in a movie by dragging and dropping the symbol from the **Library** panel onto the stage.

Good Programming Practice 19.2

Proper symbol use can drastically reduce file size, thereby allowing faster downloads.

Fig. 19.13 Selecting an object with the arrow tool.

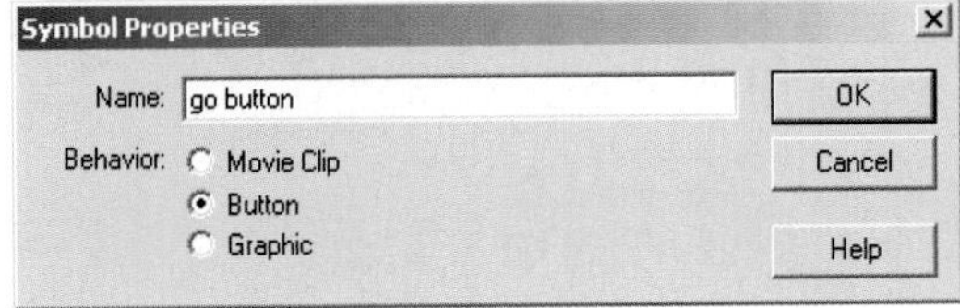

Fig. 19.14 Creating a new symbol with the **Symbol Properties** dialog.

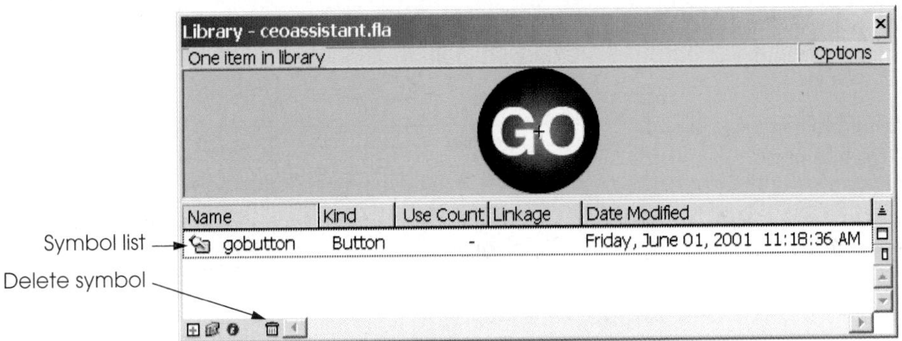

Fig. 19.15 **Library** panel.

The ***Movie Explorer*** displays the movie structure and is accessed by right clicking the stage and selecting **Movie Explorer...** from the resulting menu or by selecting **Movie Explorer** from the **Window** menu (Fig. 19.16). The **Movie Explorer** dialog illustrates the relationship between the parent movie, **Scene 1**, and its symbols.

19.3.4 Editing Button Symbols

The next step is to make the button symbol interactive. The different components of a button symbol, such as its fill and type, may be edited in the *editing stage*. The developer may access a symbol's editing stage by double clicking the symbol in the parent movie or by pressing the edit symbols button and selecting the symbol name (Fig. 19.17). The separate pieces that make up the button (i.e., the text, the color fill and the stroke) can all be changed in the editing stage. A button symbol's timeline contains four frames, one for each of the *button states* (*up*, *over* and *down*) and one for the *hit* area.

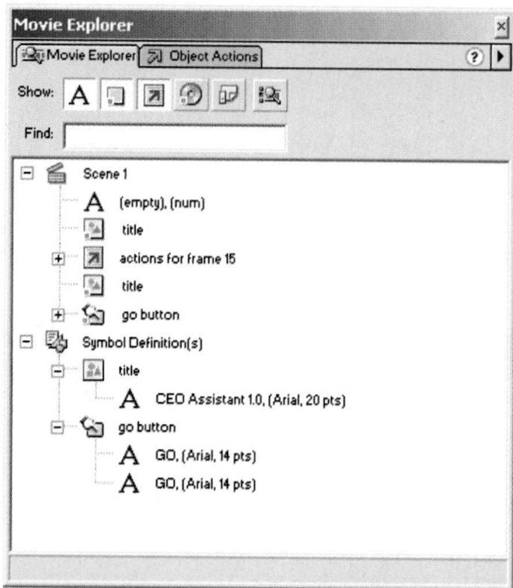

Fig. 19.16 **Movie Explorer** for **`ceoassist.fla`**.

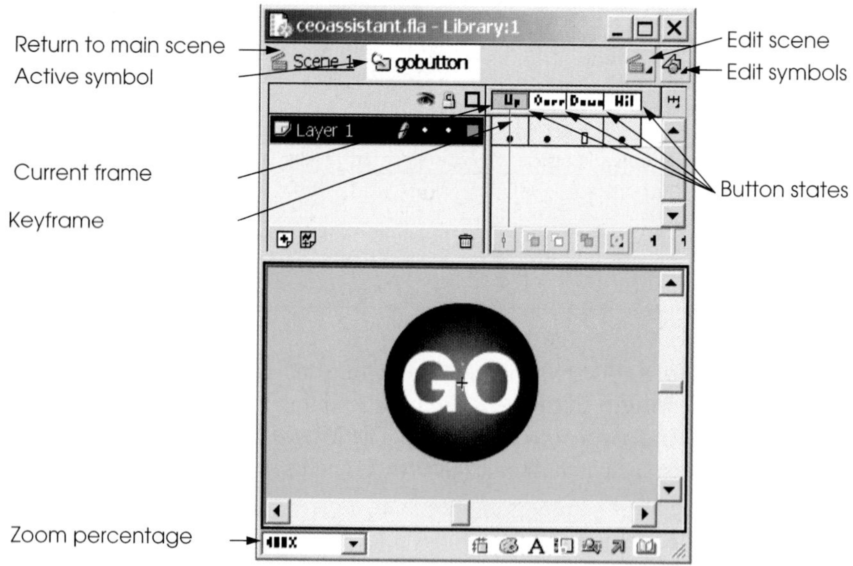

Fig. 19.17 Modifying button states with a button's editing stage.

The *up state* is the default state before the user presses the button or rolls over it with the mouse. The *over state* activates when the user rolls over the button with the mouse. The *down* state of the button occurs when a user presses a button, and the *hit state* defines the active area of the button.

By default, buttons only have the up state activated when they are created. The developer may activate other states by adding *keyframes* to the other frames. Keyframes, discussed in the next section, determine how a button reacts when it is rolled over or clicked with the mouse.

19.3.5 Adding Keyframes

Keyframes determine different points of change in a Flash movie and appear as gray with a black dot in the timeline. By adding keyframes to a button symbol's timeline, the developer can control how the button reacts to user input. The following step shows how to create a button rollover. A rollover is added by inserting a keyframe in the button's **Over** frame, then changing the button's appearance in that frame. Right click the **Over** frame and select **Insert Keyframe** from the resulting menu or press *F6* (Fig. 19.18).

Select the **Over** frame and click outside the button area with the move tool to deselect the button's components. Change the color of the button in the over state from red gradient fill to green gradient fill by reselecting only the fill portion of the button with the arrow tool. Click the fill color swatch in the toolbox, and select the green gradient fill to change the color of the button in the over state. Changing the color of the button in the over state does not affect the color of the button in the up state. Now the button will change from red to green when the user rolls over the button with the mouse.

19.3.6 Adding Sound to a Button

The next step is to add a sound effect that plays when a user clicks the button. Several button sounds are available free for download from sites such as Flashkit (**`www.flashkit.com`**) and Muinar (**`www.sounds.muinar.com`**). Flash imports sounds in the *WAV* (Windows), *AIFF* (Macintosh), or *MP3* formats. For this example, we downloaded the *cash register* sound in WAV format from

```
www.flashkit.com/soundfx/Industrial_Commercial/Cash
```

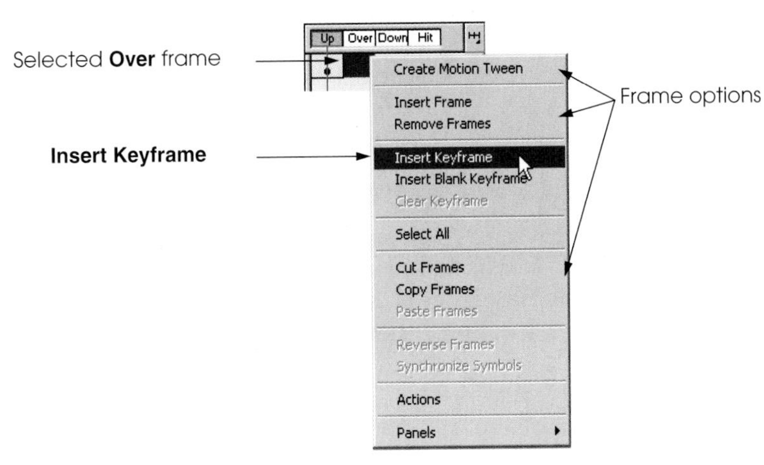

Fig. 19.18 Inserting a keyframe.

Click the **Download** link to download the sound from this site. This link opens a new Web page from which the user chooses the sound format. Choose **WAV** as the file format by clicking the **WAV** link. This link begins the download process. Select **Save to Disk** in the **File Download** dialog and save the file to the same folder as **`CeoAssistant.fla`**. Downloaded sound files usually are compressed as *ZIP archive* files. An archiving program such as *WinZip* can extract the sound file from the archive. WinZip is available as a trial download from **`www.winzip.com`**. Once WinZip is installed on a computer, extract a ZIP file by right clicking the file name in Windows Explorer and selecting **Extract To Folder** from the resulting menu. This menu item extracts the sound file and saves it in the same folder as the ZIP archive. The WinZip Web site also provides detailed instructions on how to use WinZip to compress and extract files.

Once the sound file is extracted, it can be imported into Flash. Import the sound into Flash by choosing **Import** from the **File** menu. Select **All Formats** in the **Files of Type** field of the **Import** dialog so that all available files are displayed. Select the sound file and press the **Open** button. This imports the sound file and places it in the movie's library, making it available to use in the movie.

A developer can add sound to a movie by placing the sound clip in a keyframe or over a series of frames. For this example, we are going to add the sound to the button's down state so that the sound plays when the user presses the button. Select the button's **Down** frame and press *F6* to add a keyframe.

The **Sound** panel selects sounds from the Library and defines their properties before adding them to the movie. Open the **Sound** panel either by selecting **Sound** from the **Panels** submenu of the **Window** menu or by clicking the **Sound** panel tab in the **Instance** panel window.

Choose a sound file name from the **Sound** drop-down list to add sound to the button. This list contains only sounds that have been added to the movie library. Make sure the **Sync** field is set to **Event** so that when the user clicks the button, the sound plays. If the **Down** frame has a blue wave or line through it, the sound effect as been added to the button (Fig. 19.19).

The next step is to optimize the sound for the Web. Double click the sound icon in the **Library** panel to open the **Sound Properties** dialog (Fig. 19.20). The settings in this dialog change the way that the sound is saved in the final movie. Different settings are optimal for different sounds and different audiences. For this example, set the ***Compression*** type to **Raw**. Raw compression uses no sound compression, making it ideal for short sound clips. If the sound clip is long, choose ***APDCM*** (*Adaptive Differential Pulse Code Modulation*) as the compression type because this setting reduces file size. When a developer changes the **Compression** type from default, the ***Sample Rate*** and ***Preprocessing*** options appear in the dialog.

The **Sample Rate** of a sound clip is the sound's frequency, which controls the sound playback quality. Set the **Sample Rate** to **11** or **22kHz** to lower the size of the sound file while maintaining sound clarity. The **Preprocessing** option converts stereo to mono sound. For low-quality sounds, it is a good idea to select this option because it reduces the audio file size. Press **OK** to apply these settings.

The sound clip is now optimized for use on the Web. Return to the parent movie by pressing the **Edit Scene** button and selecting **Scene 1** or by clicking **Scene 1** at the top of the movie window.

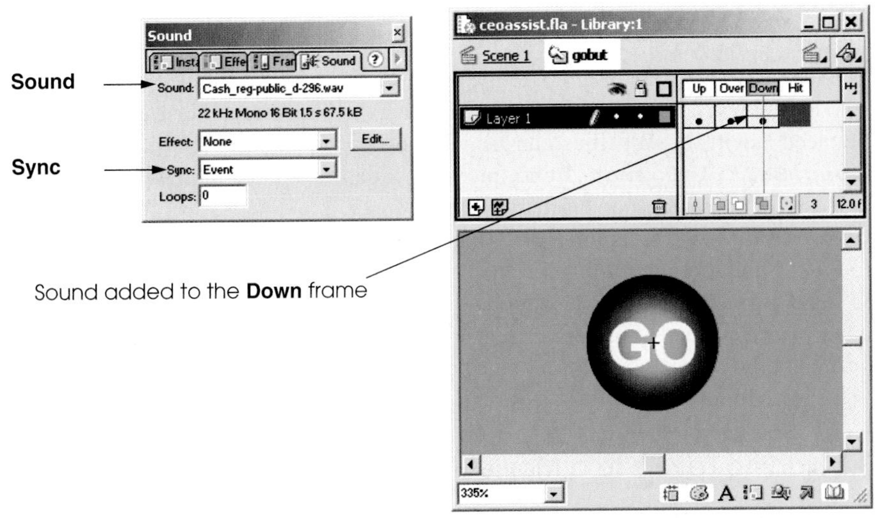

Fig. 19.19 Adding sound to a button.

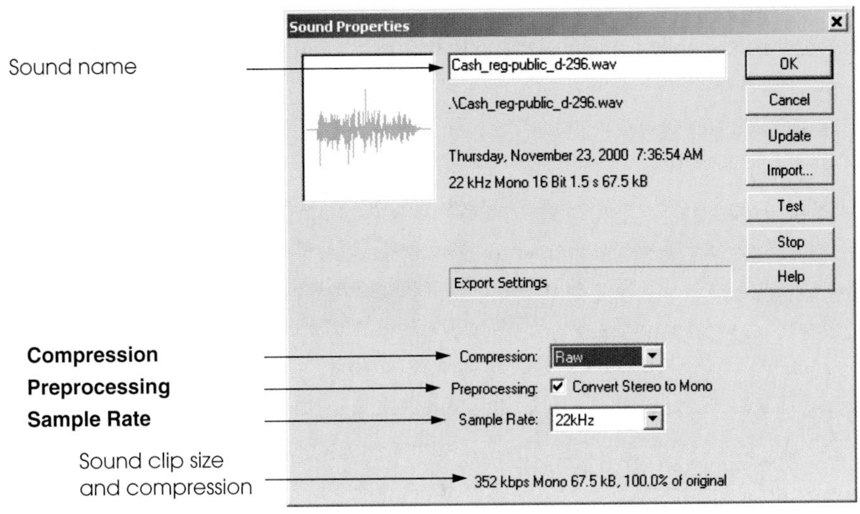

Fig. 19.20 Optimizing sound for wireless devices with the **Sound Properties** dialog.

Performance Tip 19.2

A sample rate of 11kHz or more is good for voice audio. Music should have a sample rate of 22kHz or higher to maintain sound quality.

19.3.7 Verifying Changes with Test Movie

It is a good idea to make sure that movie components function correctly before proceeding further with development. Movies can be viewed in their *published state* with the Flash Player. The published state of a movie is how it would appear if viewed over the Web or with the Flash Player. Published Flash movies have the Shockwave Flash extension **`.swf`** (pronounced "swiff"). SWF files can be viewed but not edited. The site **`www.open-swf.org/SWFfileformat.html`** provides a description of the SWF specification. Other Flash file extensions are discussed in Section 19.4.

Select **Test Movie** from the **Control** menu to *export* the movie into the Flash Player (*Ctrl+Enter* is the shortcut for this action). A new window opens with the movie in its published state. Move the cursor over the **GO** button to view the color change, then click the button to play the sound (Fig. 19.21). Close the test window to return to the stage. If the button's color did not change, return to the button's editing stage to make sure that the correct steps were followed.

19.3.8 Adding Layers to a Movie

The next step in this example is to create the movie's title animation. It is a good idea for a developer to create a new *layer* for new movie items. Layers organize different movie elements so that they can be edited separately, making composing complex movies easier. A movie can be composed of many layers, each having its own attributes and effects. Layers make composing complex movies easier. Each element of a movie can be animated and edited independently if kept in its own layer.

Before creating a new title layer, double click **Layer 1** next to the timeline. Rename the layer by entering the name **Button** into the name field (Fig. 19.22).

Fig. 19.21 **GO** button in its up and over states.

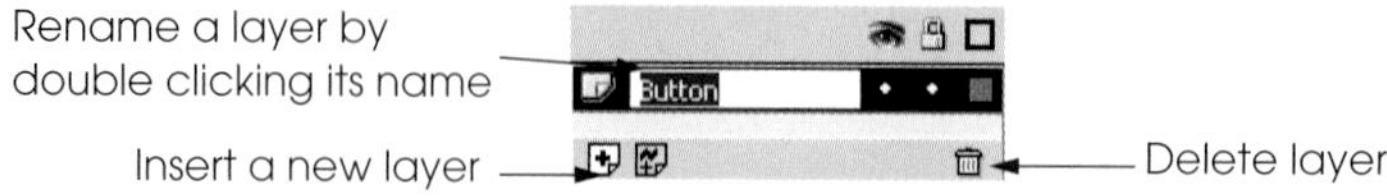

Fig. 19.22 Renaming a layer.

Create a new layer for the title animation by clicking the **Insert Layer** button or by selecting **Insert Layer** from the **Insert** menu. The **Insert Layer** button places a layer named **Layer 2** above the selected layer. Change the name of **Layer 2** to **Title**. Activate the new layer by clicking its name.

Good Programming Practice 19.3

Always give movie layers descriptive names. Descriptive names are especially helpful when working with many layers.

Select the type tool to create the title text. Use the **Character** panel to set the font face to Arial, the font color to navy blue (hexadecimal value **#000099**) and the font size to 20 pt. Open the **Paragraph** panel, which is found in the same panel window as the **Character** panel (Fig. 19.23). Set the text alignment to center by clicking the center justify button.

Click with the type tool in the center of the stage towards the top and type the title **CEO Assistant 1.0** (Fig. 19.24). The text may appear to have jagged edges, which can be remedied by selecting **Antialias Text** from the **View** menu. *Anti-aliasing* smooths edges on scalable fonts and other graphics by blending the color of the edge pixels with the color of the background on which the text is placed. Chapter 3, Photoshop® Elements provides a detailed discussion of anti-aliasing.

After applying anti-aliasing, select the arrow tool. A blue box should appear around the text, indicating that it is a *grouped object*. This text is a grouped object because each letter is a part of a text string and cannot be edited independently. Text can be ungrouped or regrouped for color editing, shape modification or animation. However, once text has been ungrouped, it may not be edited with the text tool.

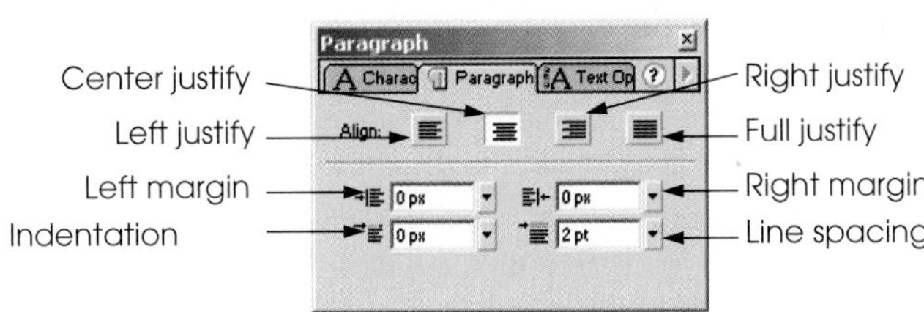

Fig. 19.23 Setting text alignment with the **Paragraph** panel.

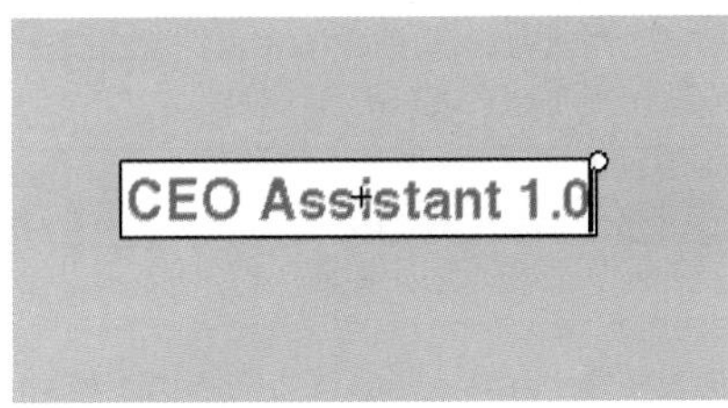

Fig. 19.24 Creating a title with the text tool.

19.3.9 Animating Text with Tweening

Animations in Flash are created by inserting keyframes into the timeline. Each keyframe represents a significant change in the position or appearance of the animated object.

A developer may use several methods to animate objects in Flash. One method is to create a series of successive keyframes in the timeline. Modifying the animated object in each keyframe creates an animation as the movie plays. Another method is to insert a keyframe later in the timeline representing the final position and change in the object, then create a *tween* between the two keyframes. Tweening is an automated process in which Flash creates all the intermediate steps of the animation between two keyframes.

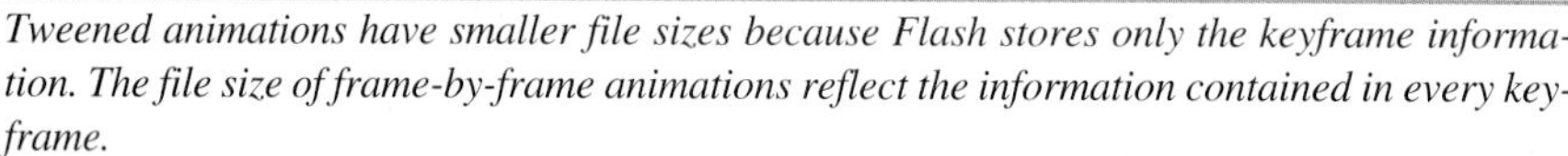

Performance Tip 19.3

Tweened animations have smaller file sizes because Flash stores only the keyframe information. The file size of frame-by-frame animations reflect the information contained in every keyframe.

Flash provides two methods to tween objects. The first, *shape tweening* morphs an object from one shape to another shape. For instance, the word "star" could morph into the shape of a star. Only ungrouped objects can have shape tweens applied to them. Shape tweening cannot be applied to symbols or grouped objects. The second type of tween, *motion,* moves objects around the stage. Motion tweening can be applied to symbols or grouped objects.

At this point in the movie development, only frame 1 is occupied in each layer. Keyframes must be designated in the timeline before adding the motion tween. Click frame 15 in the **Title** layer and press *F6* to add a new keyframe. All the intermediate frames in the timeline should turn gray, indicating that they are active (Fig. 19.25). Each active frame contains the same image as the first and last frames until the motion tween is added.

The button disappears from the movie because there are no active frames for the button layer after the first frame. Before the movie is completed, we will move the button to frame 15 of its layer so that it appears once the animation stops.

Select frame 1 of the **Title** layer to change the title position at the beginning of the animation. Select the title with the arrow tool and drag it to the upper left corner, just off the stage. When the motion tween is added, the title will move onto the stage. Change the width and height of the title to **1** with the **Info** panel. After adding the motion tween, the size of the text grows from a small size in the first frame to full size in the final frame. Add the motion tween by right clicking frame 1 in the **Title** layer. Then select **Create Motion Tween**. Tweens also can be added with the **Frame** panel. Frames 2–14 should turn blue, with an arrow pointing from the keyframe in frame 1 to the keyframe in frame 15 (Fig. 19.26).

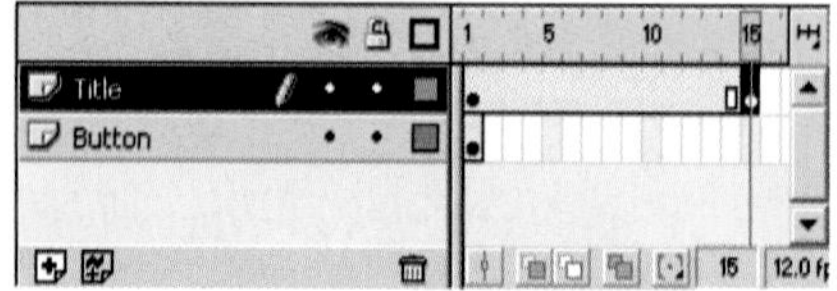

Fig. 19.25 Adding a keyframe to create an animation.

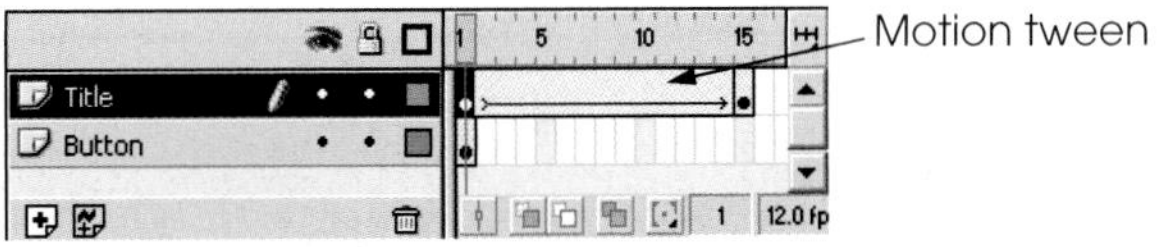

Fig. 19.26 Creating a motion tween.

Test the movie with the Flash Player by pressing *Ctrl+Enter* to view the new animation. Notice that the animation continues to loop—all Flash movies loop by default. Adding ActionScript to the last frame in the movie stops the movie from looping. For this example, right click frame 15 of the **Title** layer, and select **Action** from the menu. Actions are added to symbols and frames using the **Frame Actions** dialog (Fig. 19.27).

Any actions added to a particular frame appear in the ActionScript window. Press the **Basic Actions** button in the actions menu to reveal the list of basic actions. Double click the **Stop** action. The new action appears in the scripting window. Please note that the **Movie Explorer** may be accessed from this dialog by clicking the **Movie Explorer** tab at the top of the window. The **Movie Explorer**, as discussed in Section 19.3.3, contains the symbol hierarchy as well as frame and symbol actions.

Close the **Frame Actions** dialog to return to the movie. The small letter **a** in frame 15 of the **Title** layer indicates the new action. Test the movie again in the Flash Player. The animation should play only once.

The next step is to move the button to frame 15 so that it appears at the end of the movie. Hover the mouse pointer over the first frame in **Button** layer until the cursor turns into a hand. The hand indicates that the active frame can be moved by dragging and dropping it. Click and drag frame 1 to frame 15 of the **Button** layer (Fig. 19.28). Test the movie again with the Flash Player. The button should now appear at the end of the movie.

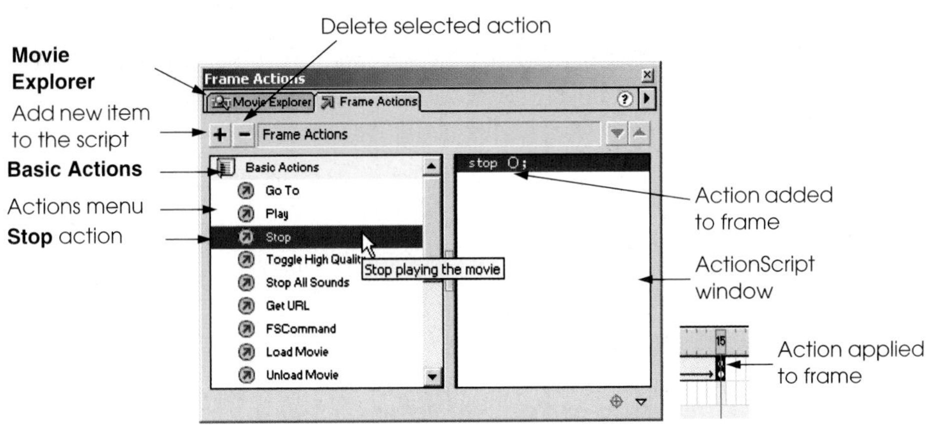

Fig. 19.27 Adding ActionScript to a frame with the **Frame Actions** dialog.

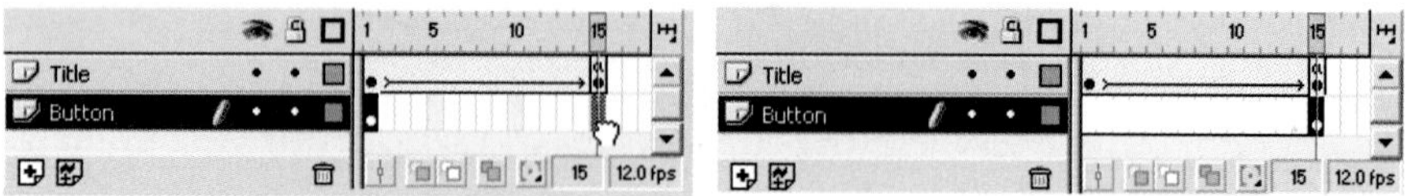

Fig. 19.28 Moving a keyframe.

19.3.10 Adding a Text Field

The last component to the movie is the *text field*, which contains a string that changes every time the user presses the button. A variable name is given to the text field so that the ActionScript can control its contents. This ActionScript is added to the button.

Create a new layer named **Advice** for the new text field. Set the text font to **Courier New**, **12 pt**, bold in the **Character** panel. Click the **Text Options** tab in the **Character** panel to open the **Text Options** panel (Fig. 19.29).

This panel presents several options for creating text fields. The top field, *text type*, contains the different types of text fields. ***Static Text***, the default setting for this panel, is used for text that is unchanging. The second option, ***Dynamic Text***, is text that can be changed or determined by outside variables. When a developer selects this text type, new options appear below this field. The line type specifies the text field size to either a single line or multiple lines of text. The variable field allows the developer to give the text field a variable name. By incorporating this variable into a script, the developer can control the text box contents. For example, if the text field variable name is **`newText`**, the developer could write a script setting **`newText`** equal to a string or a function output. The third text type, ***Input Text***, creates a text field in which the movie viewer can input their own text.

For this example, select **Dynamic Text** as the text type. Set the line type to **Single Line** and enter **`advicefield`** as the **Variable** name. This variable will be incorporated into a script later in this example. Make sure that the **Border/BG** box is unchecked so the text field will not have a border or background color.

Create the text field using the text tool by clicking and dragging with the mouse (Fig. 19.30). Place the text field directly below the title. The developer can alter text field by clicking it with the move tool and dragging the *anchor* that appears in the lower-right corner.

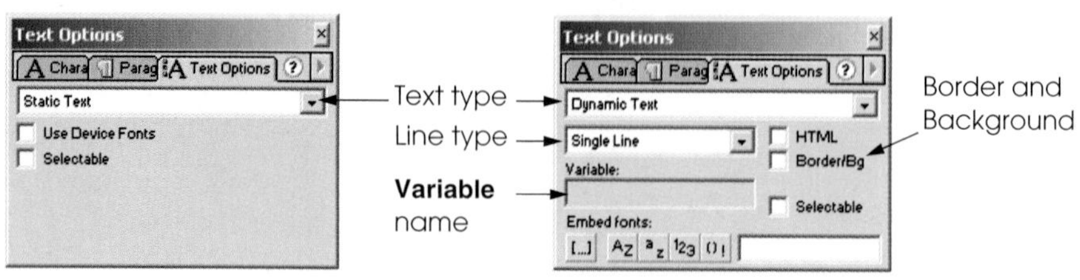

Fig. 19.29 Creating a dynamic text field with the **Text Options** panel.

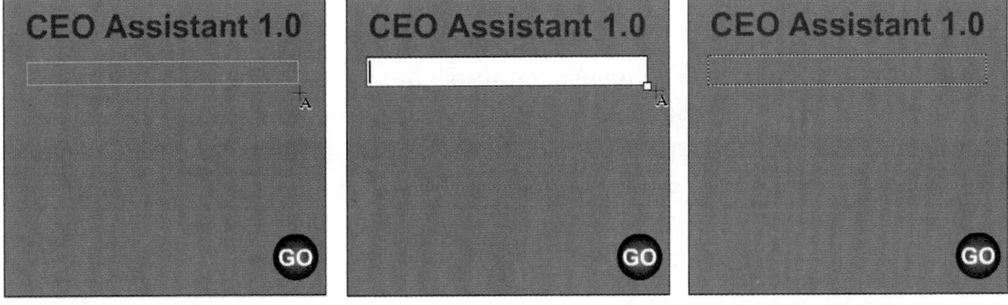

Fig. 19.30 Creating a text field.

19.3.11 Adding ActionScript

All movie objects are in place, so **`CEO Assistant 1.0`** is almost complete. The final step is to add ActionScript to the button, enabling the script to change the contents of the text field every time a user clicks the button. Our script calls a built-in Flash function to generate a random number. This random number corresponds to a message in a list of possible messages to display. [*Note*: The ActionScript in this chapter has been formatted to conform with the code layout conventions of this book. The Flash application produces code that its formatted differently.]

Make sure that you are working in frame 15 of the **Button** layer. Right-click the **GO** button on the stage and select **Actions** from the resulting menu to open the **Object Actions** dialog. The **Object Actions** dialog provides the same options as the **Frame Actions** dialog, except that the actions are specific to objects and not frames.

We want the action to occur when the user clicks the button. To achieve this, press the add action button, labeled **+**. Select **Actions** from the pop-up menu, then select **on** from the fly-out sub-menu. The ActionScript window contains the code

```
on ( release ) {
}
```

`Release` is the default event for the **`on`** function. Change **`release`** to **`press`** by unchecking the box labeled **Release** and checking the box labeled **Press** in the **Events** section below the ActionScript window (Fig. 19.31). The available options in this section change depending on the selected action.

The **`on ( press )`** action specifies that an action is performed when the user presses the mouse button. The next step is to add the code to define the result of the press event. Add another action by pressing the **+** button and selecting **Actions**. Select **set variable**, changing the code to

```
on ( press ) {
<not set yet> = "";
}
```

When this line is added, the code options change below the ActionScript window. There should be two new fields, one titled **Variable** and the other titled **Value**. Create a new variable named **`randomNumber`** by typing the name into the **Variable** field. Check the **Expression** box next to the **Value** field to set the value of variable **randomNumber** equal to an expression.

The expression assigned to **randomNumber** is a function that chooses a random number from 0–4. The generated number corresponds to a text string that displays in the text field created earlier. To enter the function, click inside the **Value** field. Then press the **+** button and select **Functions** from the list. Choose **random** as the type of function. Replace the word **number** in the **Value** text field with **5** to set the argument for function **random**. The code should now read:

```
on ( press ) {
   randomNumber = random ( 5 );
}
```

Common Programming Error 19.1

ActionScript is case sensitive. Be aware of the case when entering arguments or variable names.

Each time a user presses the button, the value of the variable **randomNumber** is set to a new random number between zero and four. This random number determines the text string that appears in the text field. An **if/else** statement sets the text field's value according to the value of **randomNumber**. Be sure that the line **randomNumber = random (5);** is highlighted, and select **If** from the **Actions** list four times. Your code should now appear as follows:

```
on ( press ) {
   randomNumber = random( 5 );
   if ( <not set yet> ) {
   }
}
```

Nested **if** statements cause different text to appear in the **advicefield** text field, depending on the value of the variable **randomNumber** in the **if** condition. In the text box labeled **Condition**, type the statement

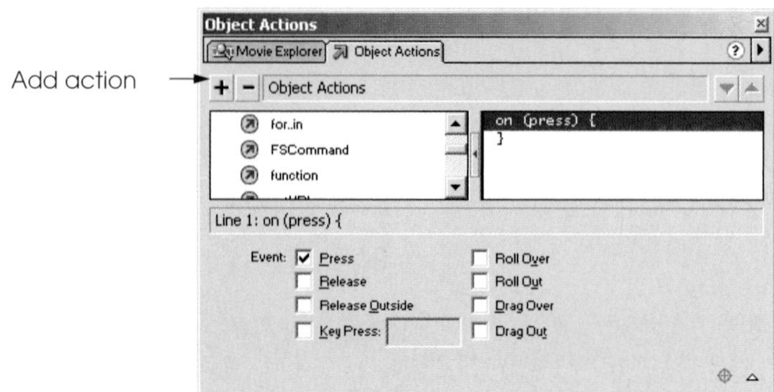

Fig. 19.31 Adding an action to a button with the **Object Actions** dialog.

```
randomNumber == 0
```

This causes an action to be performed only if **randomNumber** is equal to zero.

Common Programming Error 19.2

When testing equality, use the **==** *operator. The* **=** *operator modifies the value of the variable; it does not test equality.*

Highlight the **if** statement and add four **else if** statements by selecting **else if** from the **Actions** list. Five equality tests are needed to perform five (from 0 to 4) different actions. The code should appear as follows:

```
on ( press ) {
    randomNumber = random ( 5 );

    if ( randomNumber == 0 ) {
    } else if ( <not set yet> ) {
    } else if ( <not set yet> ) {
    } else if ( <not set yet> ) {
    } else if ( <not set yet> ) {
    }
}
```

Click the top **else if** in the code window and set the condition to

```
randomNumber == 1
```

This condition determines which action the **random** function performs when **randomNumber** is set to **1**. Repeat this process for each of the **else if** statements, increasing the value of **randomNumber** by one each time:

```
on ( press ) {
    randomNumber = random ( 5 )

    if ( randomNumber == 0 ) {
    } else if ( randomNumber == 1 ) {
    } else if ( randomNumber == 2 ) {
    } else if ( randomNumber == 3 ) {
    } else if ( randomNumber == 4 ) {
    }
}
```

For these numbers to produce text in the text field, actions must be added to each statement. Highlight the original statement code—**If (randomNumber == 0)**—and select **set variable** from the **Actions** list. The name of the text field is important for this statement. The text field in this example is named **advicefield**, so set value of the **Variable** attribute to **advicefield**. Verify that the **Expression** checkbox next to the **Value** field is unchecked, identifying the field's contents as a string. Now enter the string **Hire Someone!** into the **Value** field. Each time **randomNumber** is set to zero, the **advicefield** text field will read **Hire Someone!**. Highlight each **else if** statement and add the **setVariable** function to each. Give the variable **advicefield** a new string value for each **else if** statement. The code should now resemble the following, though the advice may vary:

```
on ( press ) {
   randomNumber = random ( 5 )

   if ( randomNumber == 0 ) {
      advice = "Hire Someone!";
   } else if ( randomNumber == 1 ) {
      advice = "Buy a Yacht!";
   } else if ( randomNumber == 2 ) {
      advice = "Buy Stock!";
   } else if ( randomNumber == 3 ) {
      advice = "Go Golfing!";
   } else {
      advice = "Hold A Meeting!";
   }
}
```

If you feel ambitious, increase the number of **advice** statements by making the argument for the **random** function larger and adding more **else if** statements. Close the **Object Actions** window to continue.

Congratulations! You have now completed building **CEO Assistant 1.0**. After testing the movie with the Flash Player, return to the main window and save the file.

19.4 Creating a Projector (.exe) File With Publish

Flash movies must be published for users to view them outside the program. This section discusses the more common methods of publishing Flash movies. The Flash **Publish** function is similar to the **Export** command in other programs; however, it has more advanced features. For this example, we want to publish in two formats, Flash and *Windows Projector*. Publishing as a **Windows Projector** generates a standard Windows executable file. Select **Publish Settings...** from the **File** menu, opening the **Publish Settings** dialog.

Select the **Flash** and **Windows Projector** checkboxes and uncheck all others. Then click the **Flash** tab at the top of the dialog. This section of the dialog allows the developer to choose the Flash settings. Flash movies may be published in a different Flash version to enable support by older Flash players. It is important to note that some Flash 5 ActionScript is not supported by older players, so choose a version with care. Click **OK** to enable the new publishing settings. Publish the movie in both formats by selecting **Publish** from the **File** menu. When the publish function is complete, the directory in which you saved the movie will have two new files (Fig. 19.32).

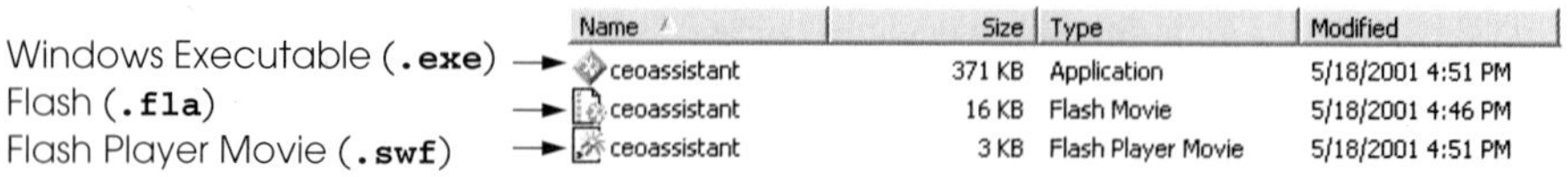

	Name	Size	Type	Modified
Windows Executable (**.exe**) →	ceoassistant	371 KB	Application	5/18/2001 4:51 PM
Flash (**.fla**) →	ceoassistant	16 KB	Flash Movie	5/18/2001 4:46 PM
Flash Player Movie (**.swf**) →	ceoassistant	3 KB	Flash Player Movie	5/18/2001 4:51 PM

Fig. 19.32 Published Flash files.

As we see in the **ceoassistant** example, Flash is a feature-rich program. We have only begun to use Flash to its full potential. ActionScript can create sophisticated programs and interactive movies. It also enables Flash to interact with Active Server Pages (Chapters 25–26), CGI (Chapter 27) and JavaScript (Chapters 7–12), making it a program that integrates smoothly into a Web environment.

19.5 Manually Embedding a Flash Movie in a Web Page

One of the most important aspects of Web development is ensuring browser compatibility. Flash movies have the same appearance in any browser with the Flash Player plug-in. By embedding a Flash SWF file into an XHTML Web document, Web browsers can display Flash content. However, to ensure that a Flash movie is visible in both Microsoft Internet Explorer and Netscape Communicator, two different tags must be placed in the Web document to embed the Flash movie. Like video and audio, Flash movies are added to a Web site with the **<object>** and **<embed>** tags. The **<object>** tag allows the movie to be viewed with Internet Explorer, and **<embed>** makes the movie viewable in Netscape. Figure 19.33 is an example of source code to embed a Flash movie in a Web document so it displays in both Internet Explorer and Netscape Communicator.

```
<?xml version = "1.0"?>
<!DOCTYPE html PUBLIC "-//W3C//DTD XHTML 1.0 Transitional//EN"
   "http://www.w3.org/TR/xhtml1/DTD/xhtml1-transitional.dtd">

<!-- Fig. 19.33: ceoassist.html                -->
<!-- Embedding a Flash movie into a Web site -->

<html xmlns = "http://www.w3.org/1999/xhtml">

   <head>
      <title>Adding Flash to your Web site</title>
   </head>

   <body>

      <!-- the following object tag tells the      -->
      <!-- Microsoft Internet Explorer browser to -->
      <!-- play the Flash movie and where to find -->
      <!-- the Flash Player plug-in if it is not  -->
      <!-- installed                               -->

      <object classid =
         "clsid:D27CDB6E-AE6D-11cf-96B8-444554000"
         codebase = "http://active.macromedia.com/flash5/cabs
         /swflash.cab#version=5,0,0,0">
         <param name = "Movie" value = "ceoassist.swf" />

         <!-- the following embed tag tells the Netscape -->
         <!-- Navigator browser to play the Flash movie  -->
         <!-- and where to find the Flash Player plug-in -->
         <!-- if it is not installed                     -->
```

Fig. 19.33 Embedding a Flash Movie into a Web site (part 1 of 2).

```
32
33             <embed src = "ceoassist.swf" plug-inspage =
34              "http://www.macromedia.com/shockwave/download/
35              index.cgi?P1_Prod_Version=ShockwaveFlash">
36             </embed>
37
38             <noembed>
39                This Web site contains the CEO Assistant 1.0
40                Flash movie. You must have the Flash Player
41                plug-in to view the Flash movie.
42             </noembed>
43
44          </object>
45
46       </body>
47    </html>
```

Fig. 19.33 Embedding a Flash Movie into a Web site (part 2 of 2).

The **<object>** tag in Fig. 19.33 has several attributes. For a developer to properly embed the movie, the **classid** and **codebase** attributes must appear exactly as shown. The **codebase** attribute prompts users to download the plug-in if they do not have it. It is also important to place the **<embed>** tag inside the **<object>** tag. Microsoft Internet Explorer ignores tags placed inside the **<object>** tag. Netscape reads only the **<embed>** tag; it ignores the **<object>** information. The **<noembed>** tag in lines 38–42 provides alternative content for those without the Flash Player. Any XHTML elements can be placed within the **<noembed>** section of the site.

Common Programming Error 19.3

It is a good idea to save SWF files and their corresponding XHTML pages in the same file directory, to reduce the number of lost files.

Good Programming Practice 19.4

It is not necessary to transfer the **.fla** *version of your Flash movie to a Web server unless you want other users to be able to download the editable version of the movie.*

19.6 Creating Special Effects with Flash

The following sections introduce a variety of special effects using more advanced Flash capabilities. By completing the previous example, you should understand basic movie development. The next sections cover many additional topics, from importing bitmaps to creating animations that preload Web pages.

19.6.1 Importing and Manipulating Bitmaps

Some of the examples in this chapter require importing bitmap images and other media into a Flash movie. The importing process is similar for all types of media, including images, sound and video. The following example shows how to import an image into a Flash movie.

Begin by opening a new movie in Flash. The image we are going to import is located on the CD-ROM included with this book. Once the CD-ROM is loaded, return to Flash and select **Import...** from the **File** menu. Open the Chapter 19 Examples directory. Finally, open the folder labeled **images** and select **bug.bmp**. Click **OK** to continue. A bug image should appear on the stage. The **Library** panel stores imported images. Developers can convert imported images into editable shapes by selecting the image and pressing *Ctrl+B* or by choosing **Break Apart** from the **Modify** menu. Once an imported image is broken apart, it may be shape tweened or edited with *editing tools* such as the *lasso*, *paint bucket*, *eraser* and *paintbrush*. The editing tools apply changes to a shape and are found in the toolbox.

Clicking and dragging to draw with the *lasso tool* selects areas of shapes. The color of a selected area may be changed or moved. Click and drag with the lasso tool to draw the boundaries of the selection. As with the button in the last example, when a developer selects a shape area, a mesh of white dots covers the selection. Once an area is selected, its color may be changed by selecting a new fill color with the fill swatch, or by clicking the selection with the paint bucket tool. The lasso tool has different options (located in the **Options** section of the toolbox) including *magic wand* and *polygonal lasso*. The magic wand option changes the lasso tool into the magic wand tool, which selects areas of similar colors. The polygonal lasso selects straight-edged areas. Clicking selection corners draws a straight selection boundary between the corners.

The *eraser tool* shape areas by clicking and dragging the tool across an area. A developer can change the eraser size using the tool options. Other options include settings which make the tool erase only fills or strokes.

The *paintbrush tool* applies color in the same way that the eraser removes color. The paintbrush color is selected with the fill swatch. The paintbrush tool options include *painting behind*, which sets the tool to only paint in areas void of color information; *paint selection*, which paints only areas that have been selected; and *paint inside*, which paints inside a line boundary.

Each of these tools can create original graphics. Experiment with the different tools to change the shape and color of the imported bug graphic.

19.6.2 Create an Advertisement Banner with Masking

Masking hides portions of layers, much like stenciling. A *masking layer* hides objects in the layers beneath it, revealing only the areas that can be seen through the shape of the mask. Items drawn on a masking layer define the mask's shape and cannot be seen in the final movie. The next example, which builds a Web site banner, shows how to use masking to add animation and color effects to text.

Portability Tip 19.1

When building Flash movies, try to use the smallest possible file size and Web-safe colors, ensuring that most people can view the movie regardless of bandwidth, processor speed or monitor resolution.

Open a new movie and set the size of the movie to **470** pixels wide by **60** pixels high. Create three new layers named **top**, **middle** and **bottom** according to their positions in the layer hierarchy. These names helps track the masked layer and the visible layers. The **top** layer contains the mask, the **middle** layer becomes the masked animation and the **bottom** layer contains an imported bitmapped logo. Import the graphic **bug_apple.bmp** (found on the CD-ROM in the **Images** folder of the Chapter 19 examples directory) into the first frame of the **top** layer, using the method described in the previous section. This image will appear too large to fit in the stage area. Select the image with the arrow tool and align it with the upper left corner of the stage. Then select the move tool's *scale* option, found in the **Options** section of the toolbox (Fig. 19.34).

The scale option is used to resize an image. When this option is selected, *anchors* appear around the corners and sides of the image. Click and drag an anchor to resize the image in any direction. Hold down the *Shift* key while clicking and dragging the lower right anchor upwards, until the image fits on the stage. Holding down the *Shift* key while dragging a corner anchor ensures that the image is resized proportionately.

Use the text tool to add text to frame 1 of the **top** layer. Use Verdana, 28 pt bold as the font. Type in the banner text, making sure that the text fits inside the banner and use the arrow tool to position the text next to the image. This text becomes the object which masks an animation.

The text must be converted into a shape before creating the mask. Click the text field with the arrow tool to ensure that it is active and select **Break Apart** from the **Modify** menu. Breaking apart text converts the letters into shapes that cannot be edited with the text tool.

Copy the contents of the **top** layer to the **bottom** layer before creating the mask, so that when the mask is added, the text remains visible. Right click frame 1 of the **top** layer and select **Copy Frames** from the resulting menu. Paste the contents of the **top** layer into frame 1 of the **bottom** layer by right clicking frame 1 and selecting **Paste Frames** from the menu. This shortcut pastes the frame's contents in the exact position as the original frame. Delete the extra copy of the bug image by selecting the bug image in the **top** layer with the arrow tool and pressing the *Delete* key.

The next step is to create the animated graphic that the type in the **top** layer masks. Click in the first frame of the **middle** layer and use the oval tool to draw an oval that is taller than the text (it does not have to fit inside the banner area). Set the oval stroke to *no color* by clicking the stroke swatch and selecting the **no color** option (Fig. 19.35). Set the fill color to rainbow gradient.

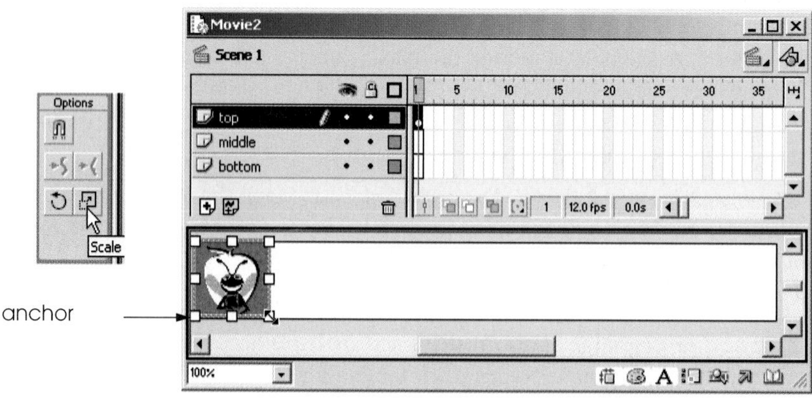

Fig. 19.34 Resizing an image with the move tool scale option.

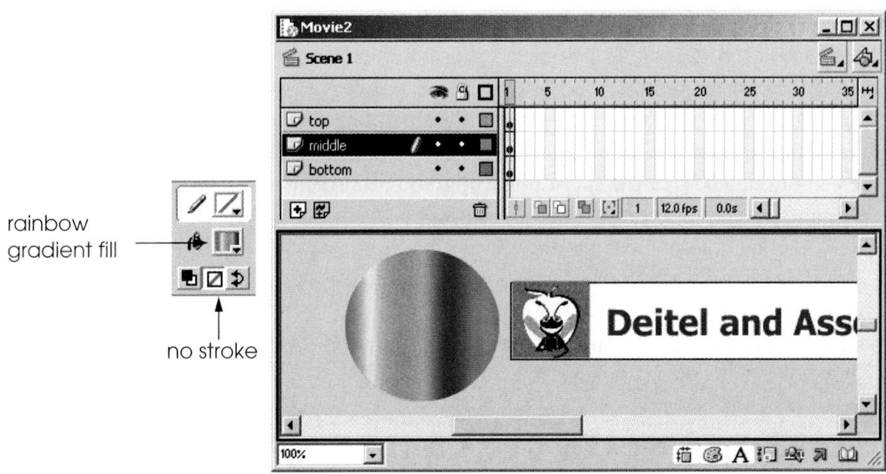

Fig. 19.35 Creating the `Circle` graphic.

Select the circle by clicking it with the arrow tool and convert the circle to a symbol by pressing *F8*. Name the symbol **oval** and set the behavior to **Graphic**. When the banner is complete, the oval will move across the stage; however, it will be visible only through the text mask in the **top** layer. Move the circle just outside the left edge of the stage, indicating the point at which the circle begins its animation. Create a keyframe in frame 20 of the **middle** layer and another in frame 40. These keyframes indicate the different locations of the **oval** symbol during the animation. Click frame 20 and move the circle just outside the right side of the banner to indicate the animation's next key position. Do not move the position of the **oval** graphic in frame 40 because the circle returns to its original position. Create the first part of the animation by right clicking frame 1 of the **middle** layer and choosing **Create Motion Tween** from the menu. Repeat this step for frame 20 of the **middle** layer, making the **oval** symbol move from left to right and back. Add keyframes to frame 40 of both the **top** and **bottom** layers so that the other movie elements appear throughout the movie.

Now that all supporting movie elements are in place, the next step is the application of the masking effect. This is accomplished by right clicking the **top** layer and selecting **Mask** from the resulting menu (Fig. 19.36). The addition of a mask to the **top** layer masks only the items in the layer directly beneath it (**middle** layer), causing the bug logo in the **bottom** layer to be visible while obscuring the animation in the **middle** layer.

Now that the movie is complete, test it with the Flash Player. The rainbow oval is visible through the text as it animates from left to right. The text in the bottom layer is visible in the portions not containing the rainbow (Fig. 19.37).

19.6.3 Adding Online Help to Forms

In this section, we build on Flash techniques introduced earlier in this chapter, including tweening, masking, the importation of bitmapped images and the writing of ActionScript. We apply these various techniques to the creation of an online form that offers interactive help. The interactive help consists of animations that appear when a user presses buttons located next to the form fields. Each button contains a script that triggers an animation, and each animation provides the user with information regarding the form field that corresponds to the button pressed.

Each animation is a movie clip symbol that is placed in a separate frame and layer of the parent movie. The addition of a **`stop`** action to frame 1 pauses the movie until the user presses a button. The **`press`** event makes the movie skip ahead in the timeline so that the corresponding animation plays.

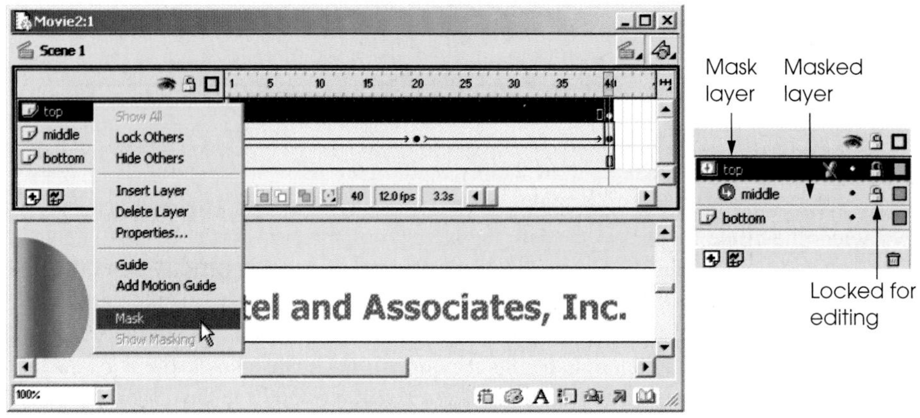

Fig. 19.36 Creating a mask layer.

Fig. 19.37 Completed banner.

Begin by creating a new movie, using default movie size settings. The first layer contains the site name, form title and the form captions. Change the name of **Layer 1** to **text**. Add a `stop` action to frame 1 of the text layer. Create the site name as static text in the **text** layer using a large, bold font, and place the title at the top of the page. Next, place the form name **Registration Form** beneath the site name, using the same font, but in a smaller size in a different color. The final text elements added to this layer are the form captions. Create the captions as one text box with three lines by pressing *Enter* after each caption. Name these captions `Name:`, `Member #:` and `Password:`. Adjust the *line spacing* (the amount of space between lines of text) with the **Paragraph** panel. Change the form field caption line spacing to `22` and set the text alignment to right justify (Fig. 19.38).

This example does not involve the creation of actual form fields, but rather graphic representations of form fields in an actual Web page. The first step in the production of these form fields is to create a new layer named **form**. In the **form** layer, draw a rectangle that is roughly the same height as the caption text. The **Round Rectangle Radius** option, found in the **Options** section of the toolbox, can be employed to round the corners of the rectangle; in this example, the corner radius should be set to `5` (Fig. 19.39). Feel free to experiment with other shapes and colors.

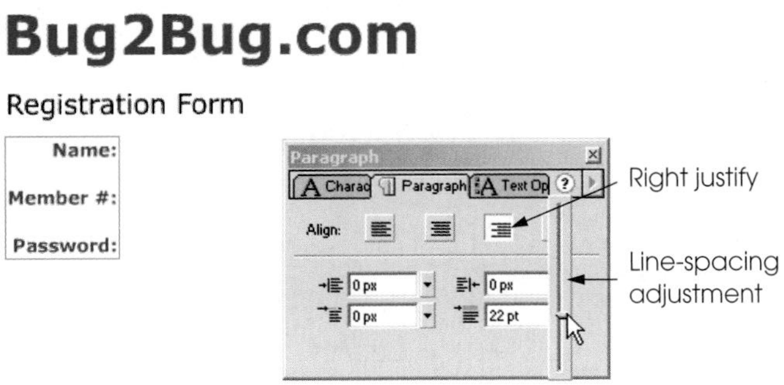

Fig. 19.38 Adjusting the line spacing with the **Paragraph** panel.

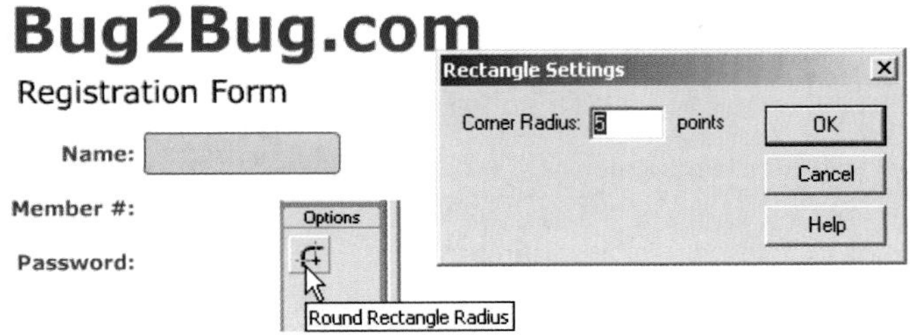

Fig. 19.39 Creating a rectangle with rounded corners.

The next step is to convert the rectangle into a symbol to that it may be reused in the movie. Select the rectangle fill and stroke with the arrow tool and press *F8* to convert the selection to a symbol. Set the symbol behavior to **Graphic** and name the symbol **form field**. This symbol should be positioned next to the **Name:** caption. When the symbol is in place, open the **Library** panel by pressing *Ctrl+L, s*elect the **form** layer and drag two copies of the **form field** symbol from the **Library** onto the stage. This will create two new instances. Use the arrow tool to align the fields with their corresponding captions. At this point, the movie should resemble Fig. 19.40.

Now that the form fields are in place, we can create the help associated with each field. Add a new layer to the movie, and call it **buttons**. Create a small button in frame 1 of the **buttons** layer next to the **Name** field. When the button is complete, select all the button's pieces with the arrow tool, and press *F8* to convert the shape into a button symbol named **helpButton**. Drag two more copies of the **helpButton** symbol from the **Library** panel onto the stage next to each of the form fields.

These buttons trigger animations that provide information about their corresponding form fields. A script is added to each button, which causes the *playhead* to jump to a particular frame when a user presses the button. The playhead is a counter that detects the movie's frame position during the play cycle. Right click the **helpButton** symbol associated with the **name** field and select **Actions** from the menu, opening the **Object Actions** dialog. Add the `on` action to the button, leaving the event for the action as `release`. Click the new script line so that it is highlighted blue and add a `goto` action. This action causes the movie playhead to skip to a particular frame based on the button `release` event. Uncheck the box at the bottom of the scripting window titled **Go to and Play**. This changes the action to `gotoAndStop`. Enter **2** into the **Frame** field. The script should now read

```
on ( release ) {
   gotoAndStop( 2 );
}
```

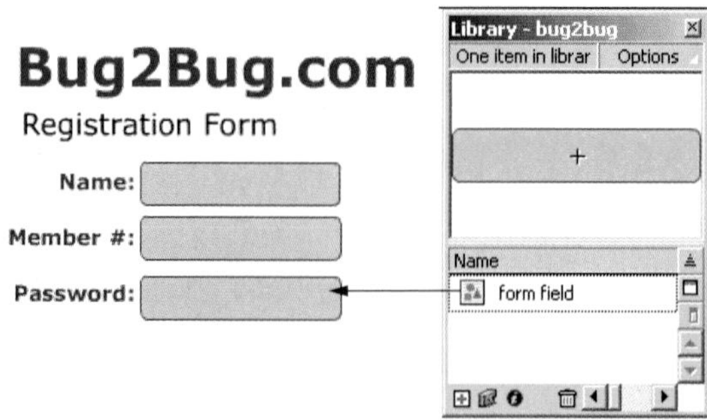

Fig. 19.40 Creating multiple instances of a symbol with the **Library** panel.

This script causes the playhead to advance to frame 2 and stop when a user presses the button. Add the same actions to the buttons associated with the **member#** field and the **password** field, changing the frame numbers to 3 and 4 respectively. All three buttons now have actions that point to frames 2, 3 and 4, even though these frames have not been activated. When activated, these frames will contain the interactive help animations.

To facilitate smooth navigation through the movie, each of the buttons' animations is created as a movie clip symbol that is inserted into the parent movie at the correct frame. For instance, the animation associated with the **Password** field is placed in frame 4 so that when the button is pressed, the **goto** action skips to the frame containing the correct animation.)

The movie clip should be created as a *new symbol* so that it can be edited without affecting the parent movie. Select **New Symbol...** from the **Insert** menu (or use the shortcut *Ctrl+F8*), name the symbol **nameWindow** and set the behavior to **Movie Clip**. When creating a new symbol, press **OK** to open that symbol's stage and timeline.

The next step is to create the interactive help animation. Begin by changing the name of **Layer 1** to **Background**. This animation contains text that describes the form field. Before adding the text, we are going to create a small background animation behind the text. Draw a dark blue rectangle with no border. This rectangle can be of any size because we will customize its proportions with the **Info** panel. Select the rectangle with the arrow tool and then open the **Info** panel. Set the **w** field in the **Info** panel to **230** and the **h** field to **120**, to define the rectangle's size. Next click the center dot on the **Registration Selection** in the **Info** panel and set both the **x** and **y** fields to **0.0** (Fig. 19.41). The registration selection and the *x*- and *y*-coordinates align the rectangle with the stage center (indicated by the crosshairs).

Now that the rectangle is correctly positioned we can begin to create the animation. Add keyframes to frames 5 and 10 of the **background** layer. Use the **Info** panel to change the size of the rectangle in frame 5, setting its height to **5.0**. Next right click frame 5 and select **Copy Frames**. Then right click frame 1 and select **Paste Frames**. While in frame 1, change the width of the rectangle to 5.

The animation is created by applying shape tweening to frames 1 and 5. Recall that shape tweening morphs one shape into another. The shape tween causes the dot in frame 1 to grow into a line by frame 5 and then into a rectangle in frame 10. Select frame 1 and apply the shape tween by selecting **Shape** from the **Tweening** drop-down list in the **Frame** panel. Shape tweens appear green in the timeline (Fig. 19.42). Follow the same procedure for frame 5.

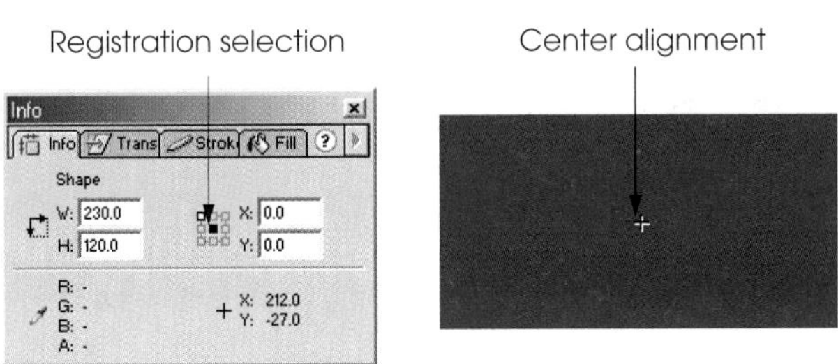

Fig. 19.41 Centering an image on the stage with the **Info** panel.

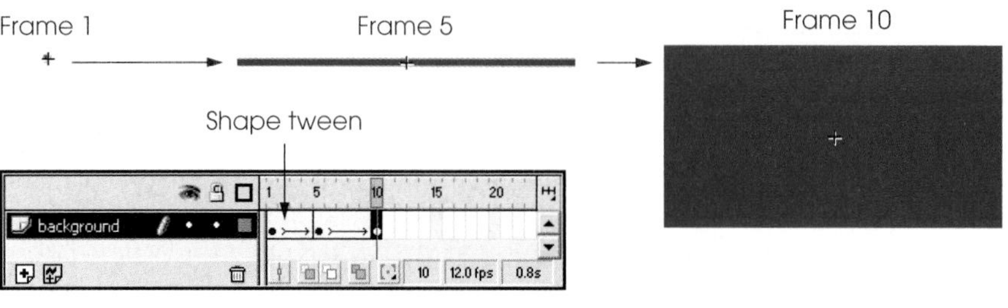

Fig. 19.42 Creating a shape tween.

Now that this portion of the animation is complete, it may be tested on the stage by pressing *Enter*. The animation should portray the dot from frame 1 growing into a line by frame 5 and subsequently into a rectangle by frame 10.

The next step is to add a mock form field to this animation which demonstrates what the user would type in the actual field. Add two new layers above the **background** layer, named **field** and **text**. The **field** layer contains a mock form and the **text** layer contains the help information.

First we will create a similar animation to the growing rectangle for the mock form field. Add a keyframe to frame 10 in both the **field** and **text** layers. When a keyframe is added to an empty layer, the keyframe in the timeline appears blank (with no dot). When a developer adds contents to the frame, a dot will appear in the keyframe.

Fortunately we have a form field already created as a symbol. Select frame 10 of the **field** layer, and drag the **form field** symbol from the **Library** panel onto the stage, placing the form field symbol within the current movie clip. Symbols may be embedded in one another; however, they cannot be placed within themselves (i.e., an instance of the **form field** symbol cannot be dragged onto the **form field** symbol editing stage). Align the **form field** symbol with the upper-left corner of the background rectangle, as shown in Fig. 19.43.

Next, determine the end of this movie clip by adding keyframes to the **background** and **field** layers in frame 40. Also add keyframes to frames 20 and 25 of the **field** layer. These keyframes define intermediate points in the animation. Refer to Fig. 19.44 for correct keyframe position.

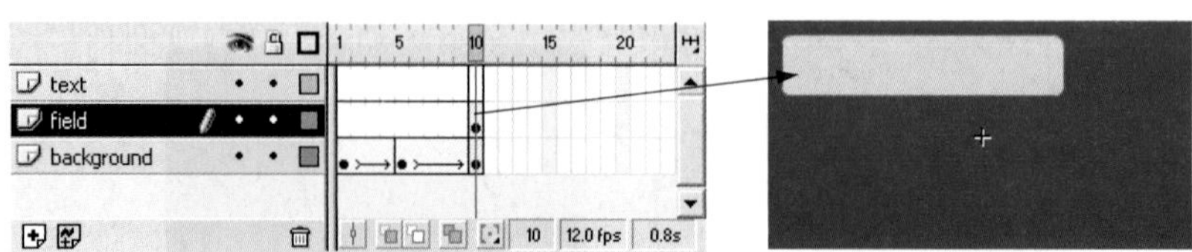

Fig. 19.43 Adding the **field** symbol to the **nameWindow** movie clip.

The next step in creating the animation is to make the **form field** symbol grow in size. Select frame 20 of the **field** layer, which contains only the **form field** symbol. Next open the **Transform** panel. The **Transform** panel, like the **Info** panel, can be used to change an object's size. Check the ***Constrain*** checkbox to constrain the object's proportions as it is resized. Selecting this option causes the ***scale factor*** to be equal in both the height and width fields. The **scale factor** measures the change in proportion. Set the scale factor for the width and height to **150%**, and press *Enter* to apply the changes. Repeat the previous step for frame 10 of the **field** layer, but scale the **form field** symbol down to **0%**.

The symbol's animation is created by adding a motion tween. The addition of the tween to **field** layer frames 10 and 20 will cause the form field symbol to grow from 0 percent of the original size to 150 percent, then to 100 percent. Figure 19.44 illustrates this portion of the animation.

It is necessary to add text to the movie clip which conveys to the user the purpose of the corresponding text field. Text appears over the **form field** symbol as an example to the user. The text that appears below the **form field** symbol directs the user as to what should be typed in the text field.

The next step is to add the description text. First insert a keyframe in frame 25 of the **text** layer. Then use the text tool with Arial, 14 pt font with the font color set to white, to type information for the **Name** field, indicating the purpose of the field in the help window. For instance, our example gives the following directions for the **Name** field: **Enter your name in this field. First name, Last name**. Align this text with the left side of the rectangle. Next, add a keyframe to frame 40 of this layer, causing the text to appear throughout the animation.

The next step is to duplicate this movie clip so that it may be customized and reused for the other two help buttons animations. Open the **Library** panel and right click the **nameWindow** movie clip. Select **Duplicate** from the menu, and name the new clip **passwordWindow**. Repeat this step once more and name the third clip **memberWindow** (Fig. 19.45).

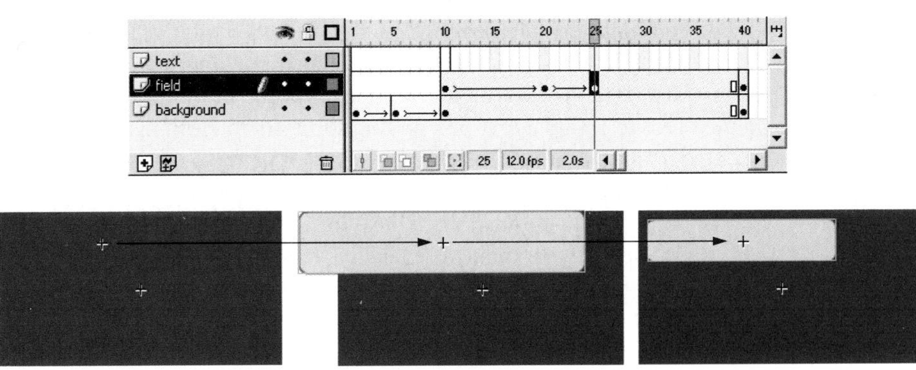

Fig. 19.44 Creating an animation with the **form field** symbol.

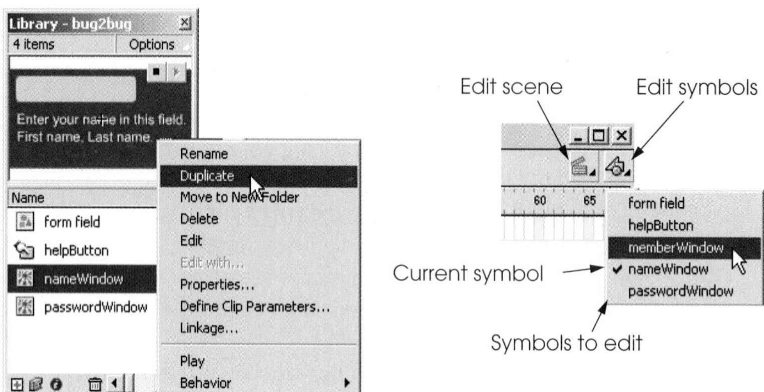

Fig. 19.45 Duplicating movie clip symbols with the **Library** panel.

It is necessary to customize the duplicated movie clips so their text reflects the corresponding form fields. To begin, open the **memberWindow** editing stage by pressing the edit symbols button, which is found in the upper right corner of the movie window, and selecting **memberWindow** from the list of available symbols (Fig. 19.45). Select frame 25 of the **text** layer and change the directions with the text tool so that the box contains the directions for the **member #** form field. Copy the text in frame 25 by selecting it with the text tool and using the shortcut *Ctrl+C*. This shortcut copies the selected text to the *clipboard*, an area of the computer's temporary memory in which text and graphics can be stored for immediate reuse. Click frame 40 of the **text** layer which contains the old text. Highlight the old text with the text tool and use the shortcut *Ctrl+V* to paste the copied text into this frame. Repeat these steps for the **passwordWindow** movie clip so that each clip contains the necessary information to help the user to fill out the form. Please note that changing a symbol's function or appearance with its editing stage updates that symbol in the parent movie.

The following steps further customize the help boxes for each form field. Open the **nameMovie** symbol's editing stage by pressing the edit symbols button. Add a new layer to this symbol called **typedText** above **text** layer. This layer contains an animation that simulates the typing of text into the form field. Insert a keyframe in frame 25. Select this frame and use the text tool to create a text box on top of the **form field** symbol. Set the text box type to **Static** using the **Text Options** panel and type the name **John Doe** in the text box.

The following frame-by-frame animation creates the appearance of the name being typed into the field. Add a keyframe to frame 40 to indicate the end of the animation. Then add new keyframes to frames 26–31. Each keyframe contains a new letter being typed in the sequence, so when the playhead advances, new letters appear. Select the **Jon Doe** text in frame 25 and delete everything except the first **J** with the text tool. Next, select frame 26 and delete all of the characters except the **J** and the **o**. This step must be repeated for all subsequent keyframes up to frame 31, each keyframe containing one more letter than the last (Fig. 19.46). Frame 31 should show the entire name. When this process is complete, press *Enter* to preview the frame-by-frame typing animation.

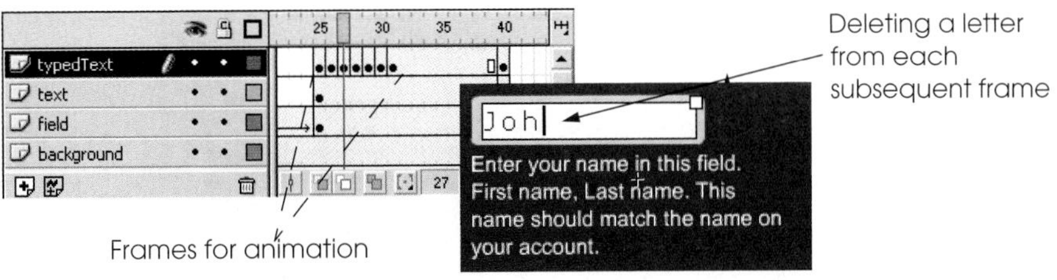

Fig. 19.46 Creating a frame-by-frame animation.

Create the same type of animation for both the **passwordWindow** and the **memberWindow** movie clips, using suitable words. For example, we use asterisks for the **passwordWindow** movie clip and six numbers for the **memberWindow** movie clip. Add a **`Stop`** action to frame 40 of all three movie clips so that the animations play only once.

The movie clips are now ready to be added to the parent movie. Click the edit scene button next to the edit symbol button, and select **Scene 1** to return to the parent movie (Fig. 19.45). Before inserting the movie clips, add the following layers to the timeline: **nameMovie**, **memberMovie** and **passwordMovie**, one for each of the movie clips. Add a keyframe in frame 2 of every layer, including the **form**, **text** and **helpButtons** layers.

Now we will place the movie clips in the correct position in the parent movie. Select frame 2 of the **nameMovie** layer. Recall that the ActionScript for each help button contains the script

```
on ( release ) {
   gotoAndStop( frame# );
}
```

in which **`frame#`** is **`2`**, **`3`** or **`4`**, depending on the button. This script causes the playhead to skip to the specified frame and stop. The placement of the movie clips in the correct frames, causes the playhead to skip to the desired frame, play the animation and stop. This effect is created by selecting frame 2 of the **nameMovie** layer and dragging the **nameWindow** movie clip onto the stage. Align the movie clip with the button next to the **Name** field, placing it halfway between the button and the right edge of the stage.

The previous step is repeated twice for the other two movie clips so that they appear in the correct frames. Add a keyframe to frame 3 of the **memberMovie** layer and drag the **memberWindow** movie clip onto the stage. Position this clip in the same manner as the previous clip. Repeat this step for the **passwordWindow** movie clip dragging it into frame 4 of the **passwordMovie** layer.

When all of the movie clips are placed, the parent movie is almost complete. Finish the movie by adding keyframes to frame 4 of the **form**, **text** and **buttons** layers, ensuring that the fields, field names, buttons and titles appear after a help button is pressed.

The movie is now complete. Press *Ctrl+Enter* to preview it with the Flash Player. If the triggered animations do not appear in the correct locations, return to the parent movie and adjust their position. The final movie is displayed in Fig. 19.47.

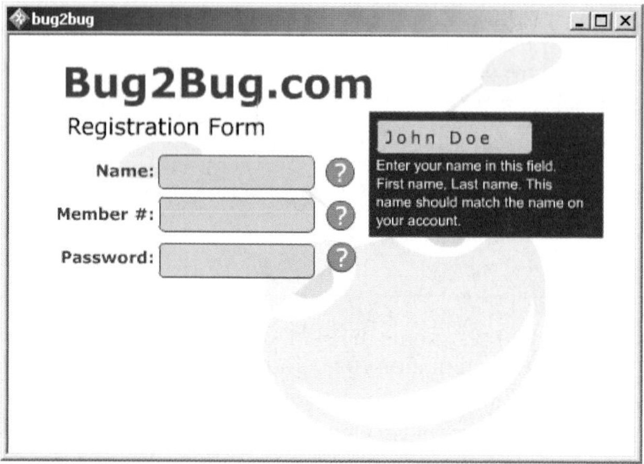

Fig. 19.47 **Bug2Bug.com** help form.

In our example, we have added a picture beneath the text layer. Movies can be enhanced in many ways, such as by changing colors and fonts or by adding pictures. Our movie (**bug2bug.fla**) can be found in the Chapter 19 examples directory on the CD-ROM that accompanies this book. If you want to use our symbols to recreate the movie, select **Open as Library...** from the **File** menu and open **bug2bug.fla**. The option **Open as Library...** allows a developer to reuse symbols from another movie.

19.7 Creating a Web-Site Introduction

Flash is becoming an important tool for e-Businesses. Many organizations use Flash to create Web-site introductions, product demos and Web applications. Others use Flash to build games and interactive entertainment in an effort to attract new visitors. However, these types of applications can take a long time to load, causing visitors—especially those with slow connections—to leave the site. One way to alleviate this problem is to provide visitors with a Flash animation introduction that draws and keeps their attention. Flash animations are ideal for amusing visitors while conveying information as the rest of a page downloads "behind the scenes."

Several methods are used to create animation preloaders. The following example explains the creation of an animation preloader that uses ActionScript to pause the movie at a particular frame until all the movie elements have loaded.

To start building the animation preloader, open a new movie, maintaining the default size and color settings. The first step involves the construction of the movie pieces that will be loaded later in the process. Create three new layers, one for each of the loaded objects. Place a keyframe in frame 2 of each of the new layers. Rename **Layer 2** to **C++**, **Layer 3** to **IW3** and **Layer 4** to **Java**. Because **Layer 1** contains the introductory animation, rename this layer **animation**.

The pre-loaded objects we use in this example are animated movie clip symbols. Create the first symbol by clicking frame 2 of the **C++** layer and creating a new movie clip symbol named **cbook**. When the symbol's editing stage opens, import the image **`chtp.gif`** (found in the **`images`** folder in the Chapter 19 examples directory). Place a keyframe in frame 20 of **Layer 1** and add a **`stop`** action to this frame. The type of animation in this example is produced with the motion tween *rotate* option, which causes an object to spin on its axis. Create a motion tween in frame 1 with the **Frame** panel, setting the ***Rotate*** option to **CCW** (counter-clockwise) and the ***Times*** field to **5** (Fig. 19.48). This setting causes the image **`chtp.gif`** to spin five times counter-clockwise over a period of 20 frames.

After returning to the parent movie, drag and drop a copy of the **cbook** symbol onto the stage in frame 2 of the **C++** layer. Move this symbol to the left side of the stage.

Build a similar movie clip for the **Java** and **IW3** layers, using the file **`java.gif`** and **`iw3.gif`** to create the symbols. Name the symbol for the **Java** layer **jbook** and the **IW3** symbol **ibook** to identify the symbols with their contents. Place the **jbook** symbol in frame 2 of the **Java** layer, positioning it in the center of the stage. Insert the **ibook** symbol in frame 2 of the **IW3** layer and position it to the right of the **jbook** symbol. Make sure to leave some space between these symbols so that when they spin, they will not overlap (Fig. 19.49).

Now that the preloading objects have been placed, it is time to create the preloading animation. By placing the preloading animation in the frame preceding the frame that contains the objects, we can use ActionScript to pause the movie until the objects have loaded. Begin by inserting a keyframe in frame 1 of the **animation** layer. Select this frame and create another new movie-clip symbol named **loader**. Use the text tool with a medium sized sans-serif font and place the word **Loading** in the center of the symbol's editing stage. This title indicates to the user that objects are loading. Insert a keyframe into frame 14 and rename this layer **load**.

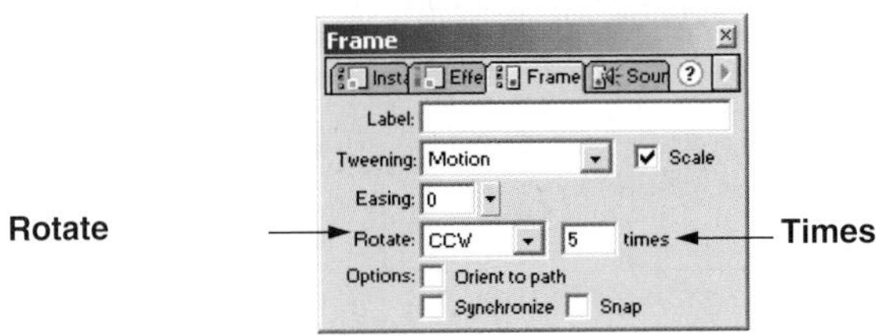

Fig. 19.48 Creating a rotating object with the motion tween **Rotate** option.

Fig. 19.49 Inserted movie clips.

Create a new layer called **orb** to contain the animation. Draw a circle about the size of a quarter above the word **Loading**. Give the circle a green radial gradient fill by selecting the radial gradient swatch for the fill color. The colors of this gradient can be edited with the **Fill** panel (Fig. 19.50).

The block furthest to the left indicates the innermost color of the radial gradient, whereas the block furthest to the right indicates the outermost color of the radial gradient. Click the green block to reveal the *gradient color* swatch. Click the swatch and select a medium blue as the inner color of the gradient. Then click the black, outer color box and change the outer color to white. Changing the gradient's outer color to the background color causes the gradient blend gradually into the background.

The rate of progression in a gradient can be changed by sliding the inner or outer color boxes. Slide the inner color box to the right so that the gradient contains more blue than white. Intermediate colors may be added to the gradient range by clicking beneath the bar, next to one of the existing color boxes. Click to the left of the blue, inner color box to add a new color box (Fig. 19.51). Slide the new color box to the left and change its color to dark blue. Any color may be removed from a gradient by clicking and dragging it downward off the gradient range.

Insert keyframes into frame 7 and 14 of the **orb** layer. Then select the circle in frame 7 with the arrow tool. Open the **Fill** panel and change the colors of the gradient to different shades of green, maintaining white as the outer color. By adding shape tweens to frames 1 and 7, the circle's colors gradually shift between blues and greens. The animation is now complete and may be previewed by pressing *Enter*.

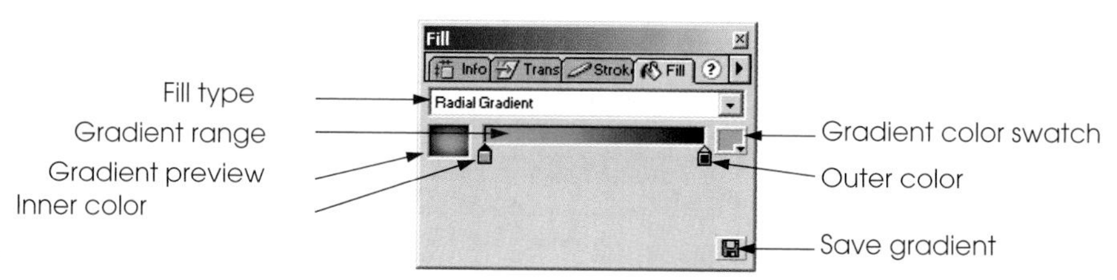

Fig. 19.50 Changing gradient colors with the **Fill** panel.

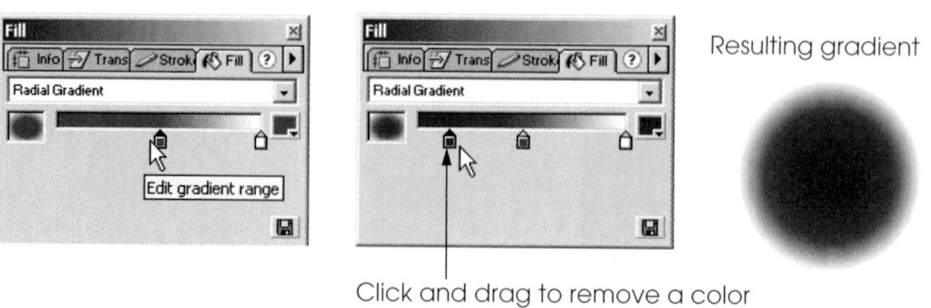

Fig. 19.51 Adding an intermediate color to a gradient.

Before inserting the movie clip into the parent movie, we are going to create a *hypertext linked button* that will enable the user to skip over the animations to the final destination. Add a new layer called **link** to the **loader** symbol with keyframes in frames 1 and 14. Using the text tool, place the words **skip directly to Deitel Web site** below **Loading** in a smaller font size. Select the words with the arrow tool, and convert them into a button symbol named **skip**. The conversion of the text into a button simulates a text hyperlink created with XHTML. Double click the words to open the **skip** button's editing stage. For this example, we are going to edit only the hit state. When a button is created from a shape, the button's hit area is, by default, the area of the shape. It is important to change the hit state of a button created from text so that it includes the spaces between the letters; otherwise, the link will work only when the user hovers over one letter's area. Place a keyframe in the hit state. Use the rectangle tool to draw the hit area of the button, covering the entire length and height of the text. This rectangle is not visible in the final movie, because it defines only the hit area (Fig. 19.52).

The button is activated by giving it an action that links it to another Web page. After returning to the **loader** movie clip editing stage, right click the **skip** button to open the **Actions** dialog. Add an **on** action to the button and set the event to **release.** When this line of script is highlighted in the dialog, add the action **getURL**, which creates a hyperlink which directs the user to a new page or site. The code now reads

```
on ( release ) {
   getURL ( "" );
}
```

The URL is defined in the lower part of the **Actions** dialog. Enter **http://www.deitel.com** into the **URL** field and choose **_blank** from the list in the **Window** field. These parameters cause a new browser window displaying the Deitel Web site when the user presses the button. The code now reads

```
on ( release ) {
   getURL ( "http://www.deitel.com", "_blank" );
}
```

Return to the parent movie by clicking **Scene 1** directly above the timeline, next to the name of the current symbol. Drag and drop a copy of the **Loading** movie clip from the **Library** panel into frame 1 of the **animation** layer, centering it on the stage.

Now, the process is nearly complete. Right click the **Loading** movie clip and open the **Actions** dialog. The following actions direct the movie clip to play until all of the parent movie's objects are loaded. Select **onClipEvent** as the first action and set its event to **enterFrame**. The **onClipEvent** action responds to particular events that occur when the movie is played with the Flash Player. The **enterFrame** event specifies the position of the movie's playhead when the movie is playing. The code now reads:

```
onClipEvent ( enterFrame ) {
}
```

The next action added to this sequence is an **if** statement. The **if** statement conditions determine what the current frame position and how many frames are *loaded.* Flash movies load frame by frame. Frames that contain complex images take longer to load. If the number of frames loaded is greater than two (remember frame 2 contains the objects to be loaded), then the movie moves to frame 3 and continues to play. If the number of frames loaded is less than 2, then the current movie clip continues to play. Add the **if** statement by highlighting the first line of code and selecting **if** from the list of actions. The condition for an **if** statement is blank by default. Flash has several built-in properties that can be added to a conditional statement. Press the **+** button, then select **Properties**. Select **_framesloaded** as the property. The **_framesloaded** property determines the number of frames that have been loaded in a movie. Use **>** as the operator and **2** as the comparative value to determine if the number of frames loaded is greater than two. Add another condition to the **if** statement by adding the **&&** operator. The second condition determines whether the number of frames loaded is equal to the number of the current frame. The code that performs this is **_framesloaded == _currentframe**. The **_currentframe** property is found in the same place as the **_framesloaded** property. The code now reads

```
onClipEvent ( enterFrame ) {
   if ( _framesloaded > 2 && _framesloaded == _current frame)
}
```

Highlight this line of code and add a **goto** action. Leave the action set to **gotoAndPlay**. Choose **Scene 1** from the list in the **Scene** field, directing the program to the parent movie. Then, set the **Frame** field to **2** so that, when the previous statement is true, the movie will begin playing the loaded images. The final script for this movie clip reads

```
onClipEvent ( enterFrame ) {
   if ( _framesloaded > 2 && _framesloaded == _current frame)
   {gotoAndPlay ("Scene 1", 2);}
}
```

Create one more layer in the parent movie and title the layer **title**. Add a keyframe to frame 2 of this layer, and use the text tool to create a title for the rotating text books. Below the title, create another text hyperlink button to the Deitel Web site. The simplest way to do this is to duplicate the existing **skip** button and modify the text. Right click the **skip** symbol in the **Library** panel and select **Duplicate**. Rename the new button **visit** by right clicking **skip copy** in the **Library** panel and selecting **Rename**. Place the **visit** symbol in frame 2 of the **title** layer. Double click the **visit** button and edit the text to say **Visit the Deitel Web site**.

The final step is to add a **stop** action to frame 2 of the title layer to prevent the movie from repeating. Once the **stop** action is added, the movie is complete. Test the movie with the Flash Player (Fig. 19.53). If the player appears to skip the introductory animation, it is because the objects have already been loaded. However, it is possible to reload the movie and play the animation by pressing *Ctrl+Enter*.

Fig. 19.52 Defining the hit area of a button.

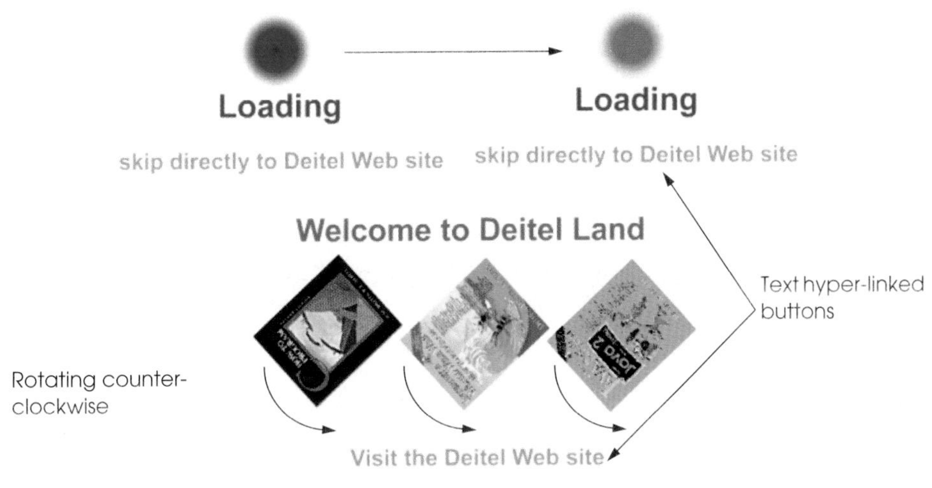

Fig. 19.53 Creating an animation to preload images.

19.8 ActionScript

Figure 19.54 lists common Flash ActionScript functions. By attaching these functions to frames and symbols, you can build some fairly complex Flash movies.

Action	Description
`goto`	Jump to a frame or scene in another part of the movie.
`play`	Start a movie at certain points at which the movie may have been stopped.
`stop`	Stop a movie.
`toggleHighQuality`	Turn anti-aliasing on and off. By turning it off, the movie is able to play faster, but renders with rough edges.
`stopAllSounds`	Stop the soundtrack without affecting the movie.
`getURL`	Load a URL into a new or existing browser window.
`FSCommand`	Insert JavaScript or other scripting languages into a Flash movie.
`loadMovie/ unloadMovie`	Load an SWF into the Flash Player from the current movie. Can also load another movie into the current movie.
`ifFrameLoaded`	Check whether certain frames have been loaded.

Fig. 19.54 Additional ActionScript functions (part 1 of 2).

Action	Description
`onClipEvent`	Assigns actions to a movie clip based on specific events. The events include **`load`**, **`unLoad`**, **`enterFrame`**, **`Mouse up`**, **`Mouse down`**, **`key up`**, **`key down`** and **`data`**.
`on`	Assign actions such as **`Press`**, **`Release`** and **`RollOver`** to a button.
`if`	Set up condition statements that run only when that condition is true.
`while/do while`	Run a collection of statements while a condition statement is true.
`call`	Give multiple buttons or frames the same action.
`setProperty`	Change the attributes of a movie clip while the movie plays.
`setVariable`	Assign a value to a variable within a Flash movie.
`duplicate/ removeMovieClip`	Dynamically add or remove a movie clip to or from a movie.
`start/stopDrag`	Move a movie clip while the movie is running.
`trace`	Display programming notes or variable values while testing a movie.
`//` (comment)	Keep track of personal notes in a frame or action for future reference.

Fig. 19.54 Additional ActionScript functions (part 2 of 2).

19.9 Internet and World Wide Web Resources

`www.macromedia.com`
Macromedia specializes in tools for creating multimedia-rich Web sites. Free 30-day trial versions of its multimedia authoring tools are available at this site.

`www.actionscripts.org`
This site is an online community that offers Flash tutorials for all levels. The community also provides free sounds, fonts and open source code for Flash developers. Their forums provide open discussions about Flash topics between developers.

`www.flashkit.com`
This site is geared towards Flash developers and enthusiasts. They have several forums covering various Flash topics.

`www.moock.org`
This site provides helpful information on ActionScript and links to other ActionScript resources. This site also offers professional Flash production tips and sample **`.fla`** files which may be downloaded for learning purposes.

`www.virtual-fx.net`
This site offers tutorials, news, discussion boards and other resources for Flash developers. The tutorials on this site are some of the most helpful on the Web.

`www.openswf.org`
This site provides discussion about SWF tools and open source SWF creation links to SWF resources.

`www.webmonkey.com/multimedia/shockwave_flash`
WebMonkey offers information on many facets of Web design and development including Flash and Shockwave.

www.shockwave.com
The *Shockwave* Web site contains a variety of Web-based games, cartoons and music. The site was created with Macromedia authoring tools.

www.deitel.com
The Deitel Web site provides information about our latest publications. Check our site for updates on new uses of Flash technology and announcements about our upcoming Flash publications.

SUMMARY

- Macromedia Flash 5 is an application for creating interactive, animated movies.
- Flash movies may be embedded in Web pages, placed on CD-ROMs as independent applications or converted into standalone, executable programs.
- Web users need the Flash Player plug-in to view Flash movies.
- When the program first opens, Flash creates a new file called **Movie1**, by default.
- The tools are located in the vertical window (called the toolbox) along the left side of the development environment.
- Panels modify the attributes for symbols, tools and shapes.
- The **.fla** file extension is a Flash specific extension for editable movies.
- The **Movie Properties** dialog sets properties such as the **Frame Rate**, **Dimensions** and **Background Color**.
- The **Frame Rate** of a movie is a movie's speed.
- The **Dimensions** define the size of the movie as it appears on the screen.
- The **Background Color** is the color of the movie background and is selected by clicking the background color box (called a swatch).
- Every movie in Flash is composed as a grid of dots called pixels, each storing color information based on its location.
- Shapes are created by clicking and dragging with the shape tools. Every shape is created with a stroke (border) and a fill. A shape's fill and stroke may be edited individually.
- Gradient fills are gradual progressions of color.
- Use the text tool in conjunction with the **Character** panel to create text.
- The arrow tool selects and moves objects.
- Symbols are the reusable elements of a Flash movies, such as graphics, buttons and movie clips, that make the movies interactive.
- Flash movies consist of a parent movie and symbols. The parent movie is the main movie.
- Editing stages for symbols are separate from the parent movie and may be accessed separately.
- The timeline for the parent movie may contain several symbols, each of which has its own timelines and properties.
- A Flash movie may have several instances of a particular symbol, meaning that the same symbol may appear several times.
- Every symbol in a Flash movie must have a unique name. The symbol behavior determines how a symbol performs in a movie.
- The **Library** panel stores every symbol in the movie. Multiple instances of a certain symbol can be placed in a movie by dragging and dropping a symbol from the **Library** panel on to the stage.
- The timeline for a button symbol contains four frames, one for each of the button's states (up, over and down) and one for the hit area.

- Keyframes indicate points of change in an object.
- Movies can be viewed in their published state with the Flash Player. Published Flash movies have the file extension **`.swf`**, which stands for Shockwave file.
- Shockwave files are read-only, meaning that they can be viewed but not edited.
- A movie can be composed of many layers, each having its own attributes and effects. Tweening is a process in which Flash creates all the intermediate steps of the animation between two keyframes.
- Shape tweening morphs an object from one shape to another. Shape tweening cannot be performed on symbols or grouped objects, only ungrouped objects.
- Motion tweening moves objects on the stage and can only be performed on symbols or grouped objects.
- ActionScript, the programming language of Flash, is similar to JavaScript.
- The **Text Type** determines a text field's interaction.
- A text field is created with the text tool by clicking and dragging with the mouse.
- Imported images are graphic symbols and can be accessed from the **Library** panel.
- Editable shapes may be shape tweened or edited with editing tools.
- When the scale option is selected, anchors appear around the corners and sides of the image which when clicked and dragged, resize an image.
- Breaking apart text converts the letters into shapes, causing them to be uneditable with the text tool.
- Adding a mask to a layer masks the items in the layer directly beneath it.
- Interactive help forms may be created with Flash.
- The **Go to and Play** action causes the movie to advance to a particular frame and play.
- Shape tweens appear green in the timeline.
- Frame-by-frame animations are created as a succession of keyframes.
- Preloading animations use ActionScript to pause the movie at a particular frame until all of the elements of the movie have loaded.
- The **Rotate** option for motion tweening spins a object on its axis in a particular direction over the length of the animation.
- The rate of progression in a gradient may be changed by sliding the inner or outer color boxes in the **Fill** panel.
- Converting text into a button simulates a text hyperlink created with XHTML.
- The **`getURL`** action creates a hyperlink directing the user to a new page or site.

TERMINOLOGY

ActionScript
active tool
arrow tool
Background Color
break apart
button state
button symbol
Character panel
constrained proportions
convert to symbol
Copy Frames
dynamic text
editing stage
`embed` tag
eraser tool
event
export to Flash Player
expression
file size
fill color
Flash Player plug-in
frame

Frame Rate
function
`getURL`
`goto`
gradient
graphic symbol
grouped object
hand tool
`If/Else`
Import
insert layer
instance
keyframe
layer
Library panel
masking
motion tween
movie
movie clip symbol
Movie Explorer
Movie Properties dialog
`noembed` tag
object tag
oval tool
parent movie
Paste Frames
playhead
Publish
`random`
rectangle tool
scale option
scene
shape tween
stage
`stop`
symbol
Test Movie
text field
text tool
timeline
tweening
zoom tool

SELF-REVIEW EXERCISES

19.1 Fill in the blanks in each of the following statements:

a) Macromedia Flash's _________ feature draws the in-between frames of an animation.
b) Graphics, buttons and movie clips are all types of _________.
c) The two types of tweening in Macromedia Flash are _________ tweening and _________ tweening.
d) Macromedia Flash's scripting language is called _________.
e) The area in which the movie is created is called the _________.
f) Holding down the *Shift* key while drawing with the oval tool draws a perfect _________.
g) "Morphing" one shape into another over a period of time requires _________.
h) Every shape in Flash is created with a _________ and a _________.
i) The _________ feature provides help when drawing by aligning items with each other and with the scene grid.
j) _________ tell Flash how a shape or symbol should look at the beginning and end of an animation.

19.2 State whether each of the following is *true* or *false*. If *false*, explain why.

a) A Macromedia Flash button's hit state is entered when the button is clicked.
b) To draw a straight line in Flash, hold down the *Shift* key while drawing with the pencil tool.
c) Motion tweening moves objects on the stage.
d) The more frames that you give to an animation, the slower it is.
e) Setting the argument of Flash's `random` function to 5 tells the function to generate a number between 1 and 5, inclusive.
f) The maximum number of layers allowed in a movie is ten.
g) Flash does not provide for text larger then 72 pt.
h) Flash can shape-tween only one shape per layer.
i) When a new layer is created, it is placed above the selected layer.

j) The lasso tool selects objects by drawing free-hand or straight-edge selection areas.

ANSWERS TO SELF-REVIEW EXERCISES

19.1 a) Tweening. b) symbols. c) shape, motion. d) ActionScript. e) stage. f) circle. g) shape tweening. h) fill, stroke. i) snap. j) Keyframes.

19.2 a) False. The down state is when the button is clicked. b) True. c) True. d) True. e) False. Setting the argument of Flash's **random** function to 5 tells the function to generate a number between 0 and 4, inclusive. f) False. Flash allows an unlimited number of layers for each movie. g) False. Although 72 pt is the highest you can select from the drop-down menu, you can enter up to 999 with the keyboard. h) False. Flash can tween as many shapes as there are on a layer. The effect is usually better when the shapes are placed on their own layers. i) True. j) True.

EXERCISES

19.3 Using the combination of one movie clip symbol and one button symbol to create a navigation bar that contains four buttons, make the buttons trigger an animation (contained in the movie clip) when the user rolls over the buttons with the mouse. Link the four buttons to **www.nasa.gov**, **www.w3c.org**, **www.flashkit.com**, and **www.cnn.com**.

19.4 Download and import five WAV files from **www.coolarchive.com**. Create five buttons, each activating a different sound when it is pressed.

19.5 Create an animated mask, which acts as a spotlight on an image. Import the file **arches.jpg** from the **images** folder in the Chapter 19 examples directory. Change the background color of the movie to black. Animate the mask in the layer above to create a spotlight effect.

19.6 Create a text "morph" animation using a shape tween. Make the text that appears in the first frame of the animation change into a shape in the last frame. Make the text and the shape different colors.

19.7 Give a brief description of the following terms:
- a) playhead.
- b) symbol.
- c) Flash Player plug-in.
- d) tweening.
- e) ActionScript.
- f) **Frame Rate**.
- g) **Library** panel.
- h) masking.

19.8 Describe what the following file extensions are used for related to Flash movie development.
- a) **.fla**.
- b) **.swf**.
- c) **.exe**.
- d) **.html**.

WORKS CITED

The notation <**www.domain-name.com**> indicates that the citation is for information found at that Web site.

1. <**www.macromedia.com**>

20

Extensible Markup Language (XML)

Objectives

- To understand XML.
- To be able to mark up data using XML.
- To become familiar with the types of markup languages created with XML.
- To understand the relationships among DTDs, Schemas and XML.
- To understand the fundamentals of DOM-based and SAX-based parsing.
- To understand the concept of an XML namespace.
- To be able to create simple XSL documents.

Knowing trees, I understand the meaning of patience.
Knowing grass, I can appreciate persistence.
Hal Borland

Like everything metaphysical, the harmony between thought and reality is to be found in the grammar of the language.
Ludwig Wittgenstein

Outline

20.1 Introduction

The *World Wide Web Consortium's* (*W3C's*) *XML Working Group* developed XML (*Extensible Markup Language*), which is related to *Standard Generalized Markup Language* (*SGML*), in 1996. XML is a widely supported *open technology* (i.e., nonproprietary technology) for data exchange.

XML documents contain only data, not formatting instructions, so applications that process XML documents must decide how to display the document's data. For example, a PDA (personal digital assistant) may render an XML document differently than a wireless phone or desktop computer would render that document.

XML permits document authors to create markup for virtually any type of information. This extensibility enables document authors to create entirely new markup languages for describing specific types of data, including mathematical formulas, chemical molecular structures, music, recipes, etc. Some XML-based markup languages include XHTML (Chapters 4 and 5), MathML (for mathematics), VoiceXML™ (for speech), SMIL™ (the Synchronous Multimedia Integration Language—for multimedia presentations), CML (Chemical Markup Language—for chemistry) and XBRL (Extensible Business Reporting Language—for financial data exchange).

XML elements describe the data contained in those elements, so XML-processing programs can search, sort, manipulate and render XML documents using technologies such as the *Extensible Stylesheet Language* (*XSL*), which we discuss later in this chapter.

XML documents are highly portable. Viewing or modifying an XML document—which typically ends with the **`.xml`** filename extension—does not require special software. Any text editor that supports ASCII/Unicode characters can open XML documents for viewing and editing. One important characteristic of XML is that it is both human readable and machine readable.

Processing an XML document requires a software program called an *XML parser* (or an *XML processor*). Most XML parsers are available at no charge and for a variety of programming languages (such as Java™, Python, C++, etc.). Parsers check an XML document's syntax and enable software programs to process marked-up data. XML parsers can support the *Document Object Model* (*DOM*) or the *Simple API for XML* (*SAX*).

DOM-based parsers build tree structures containing XML document data in memory. DOM-based parsers enable software programs to manipulate data in an XML document. SAX-based parsers process XML documents and generate events when the parser encounters tags, text, comments, etc. These events contain data from the XML document. Software programs can "listen" for these events to obtain data from the XML document. Several Independent Software Vendors (ISVs) have developed XML parsers, which can be found at **`www.xml.com/xml/pub/Guide/XML_Parsers`**. In Sections 20.6 and 20.8 we discuss DOM and SAX, respectively.

An XML document optionally can reference a document that defines that XML document's structure. This document is either a *Document Type Definition* (*DTD*) or a *schema*. When an XML document references a DTD or schema, some parsers (called *validating parsers)* can read the DTD/schema and check that the XML document follows the structure that the DTD/schema defines. If the XML document conforms to the DTD/schema (i.e., the document has the appropriate structure), the XML document is *valid*. Parsers that cannot check for document conformity against DTDs/schemas are *nonvalidating parsers*. If an XML parser (validating or non-validating) can process an XML document successfully, that XML document is *well formed* (i.e., it is syntactically correct). By definition, a valid XML document also is well-formed. We discuss DTDs and schemas in Section 20.4.

20.2 Structuring Data

In this section and throughout this chapter, we create our own XML markup. With XML, a document author can create elements that describe data precisely. Tags delimit the start and end of each element.

Common Programming Error 20.1

XML is case sensitive. Using the wrong case for an XML tag is a syntax error.

Common Programming Error 20.2

In an XML document, each start tag must have a matching end tag.

Common Programming Error 20.3

Not enclosing attribute values in either double quotes (**`""`** *) or single quotes (* **`''`** *) is an error.*

In Fig. 20.1, we mark up a simple news article using XML tags. We begin with the optional *XML declaration* on line 1. Value **`version`** indicates the XML version to which the document conforms. The current XML standard is version **`1.0`**. The World Wide Web Consortium may release new versions as XML evolves to meet the requirements of many fields.

Good Programming Practice 20.1

Always include an XML declaration.

Common Programming Error 20.4

Placing whitespace characters before the XML declaration is an error.

Comments (lines 3–4) in XML use the same syntax as XHTML. Every XML document must contain exactly one *root element*, which contains every other element. In Fig. 20.1, **`article`** (line 6) is the root element. The lines that precede the root element are the XML *prolog*. XML element and attribute names can be of any length and may contain letters, digits, underscores, hyphens and periods. However, XML names must begin with either a letter or an underscore.

Common Programming Error 20.5

Using either a space or a tab in an XML element or attribute name is an error.

Good Programming Practice 20.2

XML element and attribute names should be meaningful and human readable. For example, use **`<address>`** *instead of* **`<adr>`**.

```
1  <?xml version = "1.0"?>
2
3  <!-- Fig. 20.1: article.xml      -->
4  <!-- Article structured with XML -->
5
6  <article>
7
8     <title>Simple XML</title>
9
10    <date>September 19, 2001</date>
11
12    <author>
13       <firstName>Tem</firstName>
14       <lastName>Nieto</lastName>
15    </author>
16
17    <summary>XML is pretty easy.</summary>
18
19    <content>Once you have mastered XHTML, XML is easily
20       learned. You must remember that XML is not for
21       displaying information but for managing information.
22    </content>
23
24 </article>
```

Fig. 20.1 News article marked up with XML.

Common Programming Error 20.6

Attempting to create more than one root element is an error.

Element **title** (line 8) contains text that describes the article's title. Similarly, **date** (line 10), **summary** (line 17) and **content** (line 19) each contain text that describes the date, summary and content of the document, respectively.

Any element (such as **article** and **author**) that contains other elements is a *container element.* Elements inside a container element are *child elements* (or *children*) of that container element.

Note that the XML document of Fig. 20.1 does not contain formatting information for the letter. This is because XML is a technology only for structuring data. Formatting and displaying data from an XML document is application specific. For example, when Internet Explorer 5.5 (IE5.5) loads an XML document, IE5.5's parser *msxml* parses and displays the document. Figure 20.2 shows **article.xml** (Fig. 20.1) displayed in IE5.5. Notice that what IE5.5 displays is virtually identical to the listing of Fig. 20.1—because, again, an XML document does not contain formatting information. We will discuss how to format data in an XML document when we study the Extensible Stylesheet Language (XSL) later in this chapter.

Notice the minus sign (**–**) and plus sign (**+**) in Fig. 20.2. IE5.5 places these symbols next to all container elements. A minus sign indicates that IE5.5 is displaying that container element's child elements. Clicking the minus sign next to an element causes IE5.5 to hide that container element's children and replaces the minus sign with a plus sign. Clicking the plus sign next to an element causes IE5.5 to display that container element's children and replaces the plus sign with a minus sign.

Now that we have seen a simple XML document, let us examine a slightly more complex XML document that marks up a business letter (Fig. 20.3). As with the previous example, we begin the document with the XML declaration on line 1. This explicitly states the XML **version** to which the document conforms.

Line 6 specifies that this XML document references a *document type definition* (*DTD*). DTDs define the grammatical rules for an XML document. An XML document does not require a DTD, but validating XML parsers can use a DTD to ensure that an XML document has the proper structure. The DTD reference (line 6) contains three items: the name of the root element (**letter**) that the DTD specifies, the keyword ***SYSTEM*** (which denotes an *external DTD*—a DTD declared in a separate file), and the DTD's name and location (i.e., **letter.dtd** in the current directory). DTD documents typically end with the ***.dtd*** extension. We discuss DTDs and **letter.dtd** in detail in Section 20.4.

The output of Fig. 20.3 shows the results of validating the document using Microsoft's *XML Validator*. Several tools (many of which are free) exist that check a document's conformity to DTDs and schemas (discussed in Section 20.4). Visit **www.w3.org/XML/Schema.html** for a list of validating tools. Microsoft's XML Validator is available free of charge from **msdn.microsoft.com/downloads/samples/Internet/xml/xml_validator/sample.asp**.

Common Programming Error 20.7

Overlapping XML tags is a syntax error. For example, **<x><y>hello</x><y>** *is illegal.*

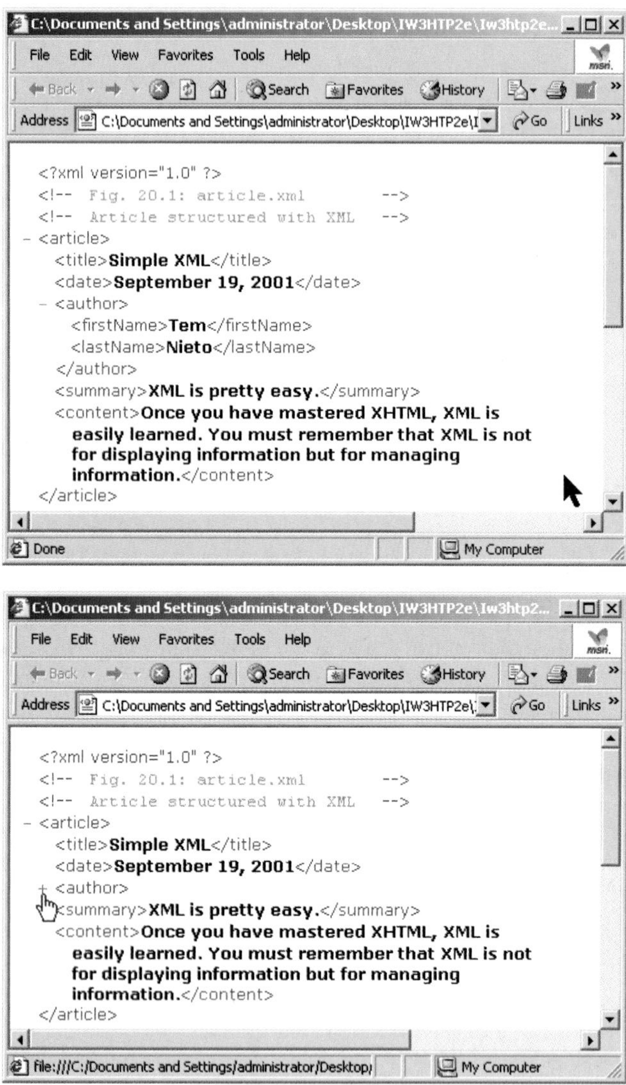

Fig. 20.2 IE5.5 displaying **article.xml**.

Root element **letter** contains child elements **contact**, **salutation**, **paragraph**, **closing** and **signature**. The first **contact** element (lines 10–19) has attribute **type** with value **from**, which indicates that this **contact** element identifies the letter's sender. The second **contact** element (lines 21–30) has attribute **type** with value **to**, which indicates that this **contact** element identifies the letter's recipient. A **contact** element stores the contact's name, address and phone number. Element **salutation** (line 32) marks up the letter's salutation. A **paragraph** element (lines 34–38) marks up the letter's body. Elements **closing** (line 39) and **signature** (line 40) mark up the closing sentence and the author's signature, respectively.

Line 18 introduces *empty element* **flag**, which does not contain any text. Empty element **flag** indicates contact's gender. This attribute allows us to address the recipient correctly either as Mr. (if **gender** is "**M**") or Ms. (if **gender** is "**F**"). Document authors can close an empty element either by placing a slash at the end of the element (as shown on line 18) or by writing a closing tag explicitly, as in

```
<flag gender = "F"></flag>
```

Common Programming Error 20.8

Not terminating an empty element with a closing tag or a forward slash (**/** *) is a syntax error.*

```
1   <?xml version = "1.0"?>
2
3   <!-- Fig. 20.3: letter.xml                   -->
4   <!-- Business letter formatted with XML     -->
5
6   <!DOCTYPE letter SYSTEM "letter.dtd">
7
8   <letter>
9
10     <contact type = "from">
11        <name>John Doe</name>
12        <address1>123 Main St.</address1>
13        <address2></address2>
14        <city>Anytown</city>
15        <state>Anystate</state>
16        <zip>12345</zip>
17        <phone>555-1234</phone>
18        <flag gender = "M"/>
19     </contact>
20
21     <contact type = "to">
22        <name>Joe Schmoe</name>
23        <address1>Box 12345</address1>
24        <address2>15 Any Ave.</address2>
25        <city>Othertown</city>
26        <state>Otherstate</state>
27        <zip>67890</zip>
28        <phone>555-4321</phone>
29        <flag gender = "M"/>
30     </contact>
31
32     <salutation>Dear Sir:</salutation>
33
34     <paragraph>It is our privilege to inform you about our new
35        database managed with XML. This new system allows
36        you to reduce the load of your inventory list server by
37        having the client machine perform the work of sorting
38        and filtering the data.</paragraph>
```

Fig. 20.3 Business letter marked up as XML (part 1 of 2).

```
      <closing>Sincerely</closing>
      <signature>Mr. Doe</signature>

   </letter>
```

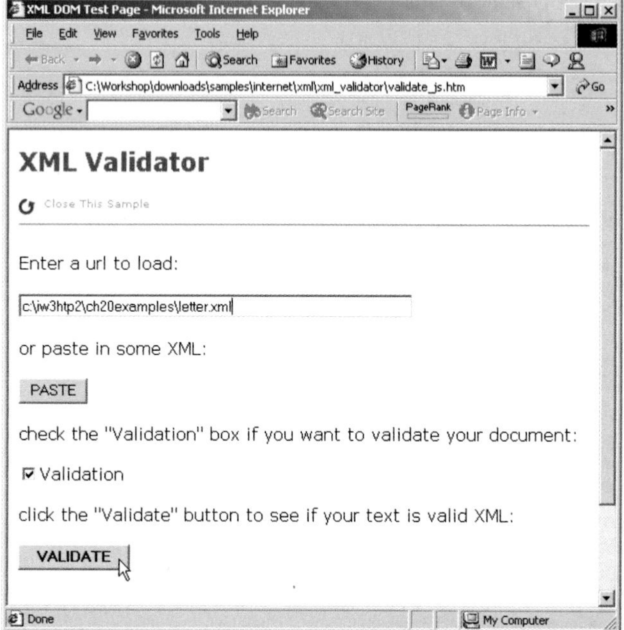

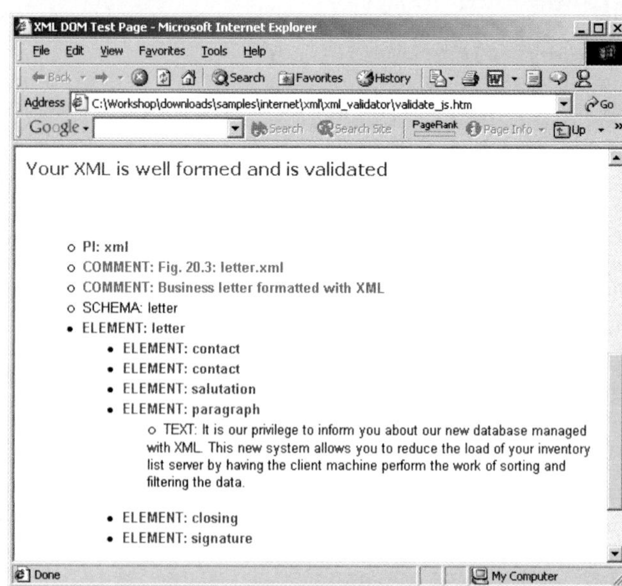

Fig. 20.3 Business letter marked up as XML (part 2 of 2).

20.3 XML Namespaces

XML allows document authors to create custom elements. This can result in *naming collisions* (i.e., multiple different elements that each have the same name) among elements in an XML document. For example, we may use the element **book** to mark up data about a Deitel publication. A stamp collector may use an element **book** to mark up data about a book of stamps. Using both of these elements in the same document would create a naming collision, making it difficult to determine which kind of data each element contained.

Namespaces provide a means for document authors to prevent collisions. For example,

```
<subject>Math</subject>
```

and

```
<subject>Thrombosis</subject>
```

use element **subject** to mark up a piece of data. However, in the first case the subject is something one studies in school, whereas in the second case the subject is in the field of medicine. Namespaces can differentiate these two **subject** elements. For example

```
<school:subject>Math</school:subject>
```

and

```
<medical:subject>Thrombosis</medical:subject>
```

Both **school** and **medical** are *namespace prefixes*. A document author prepends a namespace prefix to an element or attribute name to specify the namespace for that element or attribute. Each namespace prefix has a corresponding *uniform resource identifier* (*URI*) that uniquely identifies the namespace. A URI is simply a series of characters for differentiating names. For example, the string **urn:deitel:book** could be a URI for a namespace that contains elements and attributes related to Deitel & Associates, Inc. publications. Document authors can create their own namespace prefixes using virtually any name, except the reserved namespace **xml**.

Common Programming Error 20.9

Attempting to create a namespace prefix **xml** *in any mixture of case is an error.*

Figure 20.4 demonstrates namespaces. In this document, namespaces differentiate two distinct **file** elements.

```
<?xml version = "1.0"?>

<!-- Fig. 20.4 : namespace.xml -->
<!-- Demonstrating Namespaces  -->

<text:directory xmlns:text = "urn:deitel:textInfo"
   xmlns:image = "urn:deitel:imageInfo">

```

Fig. 20.4 Listing for **namespace.xml** (part 1 of 2).

```
9        <text:file filename = "book.xml">
10          <text:description>A book list</text:description>
11       </text:file>
12
13       <image:file filename = "funny.jpg">
14          <image:description>A funny picture</image:description>
15          <image:size width = "200" height = "100"/>
16       </image:file>
17
18    </text:directory>
```

Fig. 20.4 Listing for **namespace.xml** (part 2 of 2).

Software Engineering Observation 20.1

Attributes do not require namespace prefixes, because each attribute has a corresponding element that specifies the namespace prefix.

Lines 6–7 use the XML namespace keyword ***xmlns*** to create two namespace prefixes—**text** and **image**—and assign URIs to those namespace prefixes.

Document authors must provide a unique URI to ensure that a namespace is unique. Here, we use **urn:deitel:textInfo** and **urn:deitel:imageInfo** as URIs for the **text** and **image** namespace prefixes, respectively. Document authors commonly use *Universal Resource Locators* (*URLs*) for URIs, because the domain names (e.g., **deitel.com**) in URLs must be unique. For example, lines 6–7 could have used the namespace URIs

```
<text:directory xmlns:text =
   "http://www.deitel.com/xmlns-text"
   xmlns:image = "http://www.deitel.com/xmlns-image">
```

where URLs related to the Deitel & Associates, Inc. Web site (**www.deitel.com**) serve as URIs for the **text** and **image** namespace prefixes. The parser does not visit these URLs, nor do these URLs represent actual Web pages. These URLs simply represent unique series of characters for differentiating names.

Lines 9–11 use the namespace prefix **text** for elements **file** and **description**. Notice that the end tags also specify the namespace prefix **text**. Lines 13–16 apply namespace prefix **image** to elements **file**, **description** and **size**.

To eliminate the need to place namespace prefixes in each element, document authors may specify a *default namespace* for an element and that element's children. Figure 20.5 demonstrates using a default namespace (**urn:deitel:textInfo**) for element **directory**.

```
<?xml version = "1.0"?>

<!-- Fig. 20.5 : defaultnamespace.xml -->
<!-- Using Default Namespaces         -->

```

Fig. 20.5 Using default namespaces (part 1 of 2).

```
6  <directory xmlns = "urn:deitel:textInfo"
7     xmlns:image = "urn:deitel:imageInfo">
8
9     <file filename = "book.xml">
10       <description>A book list</description>
11    </file>
12
13    <image:file filename = "funny.jpg">
14       <image:description>A funny picture</image:description>
15       <image:size width = "200" height = "100"/>
16    </image:file>
17
18 </directory>
```

Fig. 20.5 Using default namespaces (part 2 of 2).

We declare a default namespace by using keyword **xmlns** and by specifying the namespace URI (line 6). Once this default namespace is in place, the element that declared the default namespace and that element's children do not need namespace prefixes to be part of the default namespace. Any element that does specify a namespace prefix is not part of the default namespace. Element **file** (lines 9–11) is in the **urn:deitel:textInfo** namespace, which is the default namespace. Compare this to Fig. 20.4, where we prefixed the **file** and **description** elements with the namespace prefix **text** (lines 9–11).

Element **file** (lines 13–16) uses the namespace prefix **image** to indicate that this element is in the **urn:deitel:imageInfo** namespace, not the default namespace.

XML-based languages such as XML Schema (Section 20.4.2), Extensible Stylesheet Language (Section 20.9), BizTalk (Section 20.10) and SOAP (Section 20.11) often use namespaces.

20.4 Document Type Definitions (DTDs) and Schemas

In this section, we discuss two types of documents for specifying XML document structure: Document Type Definitions (DTDs) and schemas. In Section 20.4.1, we present DTDs and in Section 20.4.2 we present schemas.

Software Engineering Observation 20.2

Because XML documents can have many different structures, an application cannot tell if a particular document it receives is complete, missing data or ordered properly. DTDs and Schemas solve this problem by providing an extensible means of describing XML document structure. Applications can use DTDs or schemas to perform validity checks on XML documents.

20.4.1 Document Type Definitions

In Fig. 20.3, we presented a simple business letter marked up with XML. The DTD of Fig 20.6 specifies the business letter's list of element types, attributes and their relationships to one another. A DTD enables an XML parser to verify whether an XML document is *valid* (i.e., its elements contain the proper attributes, are in the proper sequence, etc.). A DTD expresses the set of rules for document structure using an *EBNF* (*Extended Backus-Naur Form*) *grammar*—not XML syntax. Line 6 of Fig. 20.3 references this DTD.

```
1  <!-- Fig. 20.4: letter.dtd        -->
2  <!-- DTD document for letter.xml -->
3
4  <!ELEMENT letter ( contact+, salutation, paragraph+,
5     closing, signature )>
6
7  <!ELEMENT contact ( name, address1, address2, city, state,
8     zip, phone, flag )>
9  <!ATTLIST contact type CDATA #IMPLIED>
10
11 <!ELEMENT name ( #PCDATA )>
12 <!ELEMENT address1 ( #PCDATA )>
13 <!ELEMENT address2 ( #PCDATA )>
14 <!ELEMENT city ( #PCDATA )>
15 <!ELEMENT state ( #PCDATA )>
16 <!ELEMENT zip ( #PCDATA )>
17 <!ELEMENT phone ( #PCDATA )>
18 <!ELEMENT flag EMPTY>
19 <!ATTLIST flag gender (M | F) "M">
20
21 <!ELEMENT salutation ( #PCDATA )>
22 <!ELEMENT closing ( #PCDATA )>
23 <!ELEMENT paragraph ( #PCDATA )>
24 <!ELEMENT signature ( #PCDATA )>
```

Fig. 20.6 Business letter DTD.

Line 4's ***ELEMENT*** *element type declaration* defines the rules for element **letter**. In this case, **letter** contains one or more **contact** elements, one **salutation** element, one or more **paragraph** elements, one **closing** element and one **signature** element, in that sequence. The *plus sign* (**+**) *occurrence indicator* specifies that the DTD allows one or more occurrences of an element. Other occurrence indicators include the *asterisk* (*****), which indicates an optional element that can occur any number of times and the *question mark* (**?**), which indicates an optional element that can occur at most once. If an element does not have an occurrence indicator, the DTD allows exactly one occurrence.

The **contact** element definition (line 7) specifies that element **contact** contains child elements **name**, **address1**, **address2**, **city**, **state**, **zip**, **phone** and **flag**—in that order. The DTD requires exactly one occurrence of each element.

Line 9 uses the ***ATTLIST*** *element type declaration* to define an attribute (i.e., **type**) for the **contact** element. Keyword ***#IMPLIED*** specifies that if the parser finds a **contact** element without a **type** attribute, the parser can choose an arbitrary value for the attribute or ignore the attribute and the document will be valid. The XML document also is valid if a **contact** element does not have a **type** attribute. Other types of default values include ***#REQUIRED*** and ***#FIXED***. Keyword **#REQUIRED** specifies that the attribute must be present in the element, and keyword **#FIXED** specifies that the attribute (if present) must have the given fixed value. For example,

```
<!ATTLIST address zip #FIXED "01757">
```

indicates that attribute **zip** must have the value **01757** for the document to be valid. If the attribute is not present, the parser, by default, uses the fixed value that the **ATTLIST** declaration specifies. Flag ***CDATA*** specifies that attribute **type** contains *character data*, which indicates that the parser will not process the data, but will pass the data to the application without modification.

DTD syntax does not provide any mechanism for describing an element's (or attribute's) data type. For example, a DTD cannot specify that a particular element or attribute can contain only integer data.

Flag ***#PCDATA*** (line 11) specifies that the element can contain *parsed character data* (i.e., text). Parsable character data should not contain markup characters, such as less than (**<**), greater than (**>**) and ampersand (**&**). The document author should replace any markup character with its corresponding entity (i.e., **<**, **>** or **&**).

Line 18 creates an empty element named **flag**. Keyword ***EMPTY*** specifies that the element does not contain any data. Attributes commonly contain data that the empty element describes (e.g., the **gender** attribute of empty **element** flag).

Common Programming Error 20.10

If a document references a DTD and that document contains any element or attribute that the DTD does not define, the document is invalid.

Common Programming Error 20.11

Using markup characters (e.g., **<**, **>** *and* **&**) *in attribute values is an error. Attribute values can contain ampersands (***&***) only for inserting entities (e.g.,* **<**).

20.4.2 W3C XML Schema Documents

In this section, we introduce *schemas* for validating XML documents. Many developers in the XML community believe DTDs are not flexible enough to meet today's programming needs. For example, programs cannot manipulate DTDs (e.g., search, transform into different representations such as XHTML, etc.) in the same manner as XML documents because DTDs are not themselves XML documents. These and other limitations have led to the development of schemas.

Unlike DTDs, schemas do not use EBNF grammar. Instead, schemas use XML syntax and are actually XML documents that programs can manipulate like other XML documents. Like DTDs, schemas require validating parsers. In the near future, schemas likely will replace DTDs as the primary means of describing XML document structure.

In this section, we focus on *XML Schema*—the schema vocabulary that the W3C created. XML Schema is a *Recommendation* (i.e., a stable release suitable for use in industry). For the latest on W3C XML Schema, visit **www.w3.org/XML/Schema**. [*Note*: Because XML Schema became a Recommendation at the time of this writing, few validating parsers exist. Now that XML Schema is a recommendation, parser support should follow quickly.]

A DTD describes an XML document's structure, not the content of that document's elements. For example,

```
<quantity>5</quantity>
```

contains character data. If the document that contains element **quantity** references a DTD, an XML parser can validate the document to confirm that this element indeed does contains **PCDATA** content, but the parser cannot validate that the content is numeric; DTDs do not provide such capability. So, unfortunately, the parser also considers markup such as

```
<quantity>hello</quantity>
```

to be valid. The application that uses the XML document that contains this markup would need to test that the data in element **quantity** is numeric and take appropriate action if it is not.

Software Engineering Observation 20.4

XML Schema defines a DTD to which schemas must conform. Validating parsers include this DTD for validating schemas.

Software Engineering Observation 20.5

Many organizations and individuals are creating DTDs and schemas for a broad range of applications (e.g., financial transactions, medical prescriptions, etc.). These collections—called repositories*—often are available free for download from the Web (e.g.,* ***www.dtd.com****).*

XML Schema enables schema authors to specify that element **quantity**'s data must be numeric. When a parser validates the XML document against this schema, the parser can determine that **5** conforms and that **hello** does not. An XML document that conforms to a schema document is *schema valid* and a document that does not conform is invalid.

Software Engineering Observation 20.6

Because schemas are XML documents that reference DTDs, schemas themselves must be valid.

Figure 20.7 shows a schema-valid XML document named **book.xml** and Fig. 20.8 shows the XML Schema document (**book.xsd**) that defines the structure for **book.xml**. Although schema authors can use virtually any filename extension, schemas commonly use the ***.xsd*** extension. [*Note*: At the time of this writing, XML Schema was a new W3C Recommendation, so there were few validators available. We used Oracle's Java-based XML Schema validator to produce the output shown. Please visit **www.deitel.com**, for updates on XML Schema and available validator software.]

```
<?xml version = "1.0"?>
<!-- Fig. 20.7 : book.xml        -->
<!-- Book list marked up as XML -->

<deitel:books xmlns:deitel = "http://www.deitel.com/booklist">
   <book>
      <title>XML How to Program</title>
   </book>
   <book>
      <title>C How to Program</title>
   </book>
   <book>
      <title>Java How to Program</title>
   </book>
```

Fig. 20.7 Schema-valid XML document (part 1 of 2).

```
      <book>
         <title>C++ How to Program</title>
      </book>
      <book>
         <title>Perl How to Program</title>
      </book>
   </deitel:books>
```

```
java -classpath .;..\lib\xmlparserv2.jar;..\lib\xschema.jar
XSDSetSchema book.xsd book.xml
The input file <book.xml> parsed without errors
```

Fig. 20.7 Schema-valid XML document (part 2 of 2).

```
1  <?xml version = "1.0"?>
2
3  <!-- Fig. 20.8 : book.xsd              -->
4  <!-- Simple W3C XML Schema document -->
5
6  <xsd:schema xmlns:xsd = "http://www.w3.org/2000/10/XMLSchema"
7     xmlns:deitel = "http://www.deitel.com/booklist"
8     targetNamespace = "http://www.deitel.com/booklist">
9
10    <xsd:element name = "books" type = "deitel:BooksType"/>
11
12    <xsd:complexType name = "BooksType">
13       <xsd:element name = "book" type = "deitel:BookType"
14          minOccurs = "1" maxOccurs = "unbounded"/>
15    </xsd:complexType>
16
17    <xsd:complexType name = "BookType">
18       <xsd:element name = "title" type = "xsd:string"/>
19    </xsd:complexType>
20
21 </xsd:schema>
```

Fig. 20.8 XML Schema document for **books.xml**.

XML Schema uses the namespace URI ***http://www.w3.org/2000/10/XMLSchema*** and *namespace prefix* ***xsd*** (line 6 in Fig. 20.8). Root element ***schema*** contains elements that define the XML document structure. Line 7 binds the URI **http://www.deitel.com/booklist** to namespace prefix **deitel**. Line 8 specifies the ***targetNamespace***, which is the namespace for elements and attributes that this schema defines.

In XML Schema, element ***element*** (line 10) defines an element to be included in the XML document structure. Attributes ***name*** and ***type*** specify the **element**'s name and data type, respectively. In this case, the name of the element is **books** and the data type is **deitel:BooksType**. Any element (e.g., **books**) that contains attributes or child elements must define a *complex type*, which defines each attribute and child element. Type **deitel:BooksType** (lines 12–15) is an example of a complex type. We prefix **Book-**

sType with **deitel**, because this is a complex type that we have created, not an existing XML Schema complex type.

Lines 12–15 use element ***complexType*** to define an element type that has a child element named **book**. Because **book** contains a child element, its type must be a complex type (e.g., **BookType**). Attribute ***minOccurs*** specifies that **books** must contain a minimum of one **book** element. Attribute ***maxOccurs***, with value ***unbounded*** (line 14) specifies that **books** may have any number of **book** child elements.

Lines 17–19 define the **complexType BookType**. Line 18 defines element **title** with **type** ***xsd:string***. When an element has a *simple type* such as **xsd:string**, it is prohibited from containing attributes and child elements. XML Schema provides a large number of data types such as ***xsd:date*** for dates, ***xsd:int*** for integers, ***xsd:double*** for floating-point numbers and ***xsd:time*** for time.

Good Programming Practice 20.3

By convention, W3C XML Schema authors use namespace prefix **xsd** *when referring to the URI* ***www.w3.org/2000/10/XMLSchema***.

20.5 XML Vocabularies

XML allows authors to create their own tags to describe data precisely. People and organizations in various fields of study have created many different kinds of XML for structuring data. Some of these markup languages are: *MathML* (*Mathematical Markup Language*), *Scalable Vector Graphics* (*SVG*), *Wireless Markup Language* (*WML*), *Extensible Business Reporting Language* (*XBRL*), *Extensible User Interface Language* (*XUL*) and *Product Data Markup Language* (*PDML*). Two other examples of XML vocabularies are W3C XML Schema and the Extensible Stylesheet Language (XSL), which we discuss in Sections 20.4 and 20.9, respectively. The following subsections describe MathML, XBRL and other custom markup languages.

20.5.1 MathML™

Until recently, computers typically have required specialized software packages such as TeX and LaTeX for displaying complex mathematical expressions. This section introduces MathML, which the W3C developed for describing mathematical notations and expressions. One application that can parse and render MathML is the W3C's *Amaya*™ browser/editor, which can be downloaded at no charge from

www.w3.org/Amaya/User/BinDist.html

This Web page contains download links for the Windows 95/98/NT/2000, Linux® and Solaris™ platforms. Amaya documentation and installation notes also are available at the W3C Web site.

MathML markup describes mathematical expressions for display. Figure 20.9 uses MathML to mark up a simple expression.

We embed the MathML content into an XHTML file by using a **math** element with the default namespace **http://www.w3.org/1998/Math/MathML** (line 14). The ***mrow*** *element* (line 16) is a container element for expressions that contains more than one element. In this case, the **mrow** element contains five children. The ***mn*** *element* (line 17) marks up a number. The ***mo*** *element* (line 18) marks up an operator (e.g., +). Using this markup, we define the expression: 2+3=5, which a software program that supports MathML could display.

Let us now consider using MathML to mark up an algebraic equation that uses exponents and arithmetic operators (Fig. 20.10).

```
1  <?xml version="1.0"?>
2  <!DOCTYPE html PUBLIC "-//W3C//DTD XHTML 1.0 Transitional//EN"
3     "http://www.w3.org/TR/xhtml1/DTD/xhtml1-transitional.dtd">
4
5  <!-- Fig. 20.9: mathml1.html -->
6  <!-- Simple MathML           -->
7
8  <html xmlns="http://www.w3.org/1999/xhtml">
9
10    <head><title>Simple MathML Example</title></head>
11
12    <body>
13
14       <math xmlns = "http://www.w3.org/1998/Math/MathML">
15
16          <mrow>
17             <mn>2</mn>
18             <mo>+</mo>
19             <mn>3</mn>
20             <mo>=</mo>
21             <mn>5</mn>
22          </mrow>
23
24       </math>
25
26    </body>
27 </html>
```

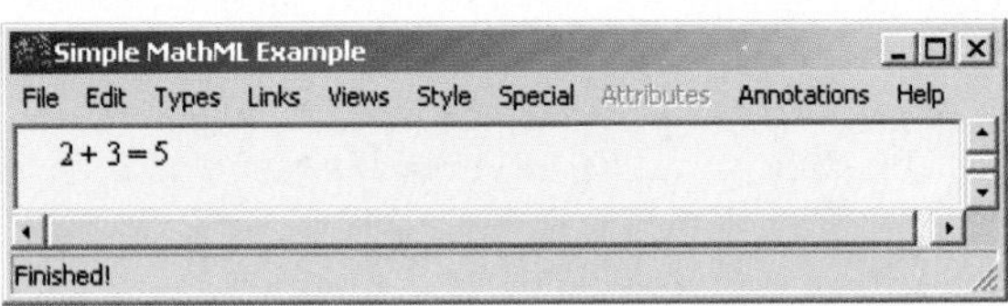

Fig. 20.9 Expression marked up with MathML. (Courtesy of World Wide Web Consortium (W3C).)

```
<?xml version="1.0"?>
<!DOCTYPE html PUBLIC "-//W3C//DTD XHTML 1.0 Transitional//EN"
   "http://www.w3.org/TR/xhtml1/DTD/xhtml1-transitional.dtd">
```

Fig. 20.10 Algebraic equation marked up with MathML (part 1 of 2). (Courtesy of World Wide Web Consortium (W3C).)

```
4   <!-- Fig. 20.10: mathml2.html -->
5   <!-- Simple MathML               -->
6
7   <html xmlns="http://www.w3.org/1999/xhtml">
8
9      <head><title>Algebraic MathML Example</title></head>
10
11     <body>
12
13        <math xmlns = "http://www.w3.org/1998/Math/MathML">
14           <mrow>
15
16              <mrow>
17                 <mn>3</mn>
18                 <mo>&InvisibleTimes;</mo>
19
20                 <msup>
21                    <mi>x</mi>
22                    <mn>2</mn>
23                 </msup>
24
25              </mrow>
26
27              <mo>+</mo>
28              <mi>x</mi>
29              <mo>-</mo>
30
31              <mfrac>
32                 <mn>2</mn>
33                 <mi>x</mi>
34              </mfrac>
35
36              <mo>=</mo>
37              <mn>0</mn>
38
39           </mrow>
40        </math>
41
42     </body>
43  </html>
```

Fig. 20.10 Algebraic equation marked up with MathML (part 2 of 2). (Courtesy of World Wide Web Consortium (W3C).)

Element **mrow** behaves like parentheses, which allows the document author to group related elements properly. Line 18 uses entity reference ***⁢*** to indicate a multiplication operation without a *symbolic representation* (i.e., the multiplication symbol does not appear between the **3** and **x**). For exponentiation, line 20 uses the ***msup*** element, which represents a superscript. This **msup** element has two children: the expression to be superscripted (i.e., the base) and the superscript (i.e., the exponent). Correspondingly, the ***msub*** element represents a subscript. To display variables such as **x**, line 21 uses *identifier element* ***mi***.

To display a fraction, line 31 uses element ***mfrac***. Lines 32–33 specify the numerator and the denominator for the fraction. If either the numerator or the denominator contains more than one element, it must appear in an **mrow** element.

Figure 20.11 marks up a calculus expression that contains an integral symbol and a square-root symbol.

```
<?xml version="1.0"?>
<!DOCTYPE html PUBLIC "-//W3C//DTD XHTML 1.0 Transitional//EN"
   "http://www.w3.org/TR/xhtml1/DTD/xhtml1-transitional.dtd">
<!-- Fig. 20.11 mathml3.html       -->
<!-- Calculus example using MathML -->

<html xmlns="http://www.w3.org/1999/xhtml">

   <head><title>Calculus MathML Example</title></head>

   <body>

      <math xmlns = "http://www.w3.org/1998/Math/MathML">
         <mrow>
            <msubsup>

               <mo>&Integral;</mo>
               <mn>0</mn>

               <mrow>
                  <mn>1</mn>
                  <mo>-</mo>
                  <mi>y</mi>
               </mrow>

            </msubsup>

            <msqrt>
               <mrow>

                  <mn>4</mn>
                  <mo>&InvisibleTimes;</mo>

                  <msup>
                     <mi>x</mi>
                     <mn>2</mn>
                  </msup>

```

Fig. 20.11 Calculus expression marked up with MathML (part 1 of 2). (Courtesy of World Wide Web Consortium (W3C).)

```
39                      <mo>+</mo>
40                      <mi>y</mi>
41
42                   </mrow>
43                </msqrt>
44
45                <mo>&delta;</mo>
46                <mi>x</mi>
47             </mrow>
48          </math>
49       </body>
50    </html>
```

Fig. 20.11 Calculus expression marked up with MathML (part 2 of 2). (Courtesy of World Wide Web Consortium (W3C).)

The *entity* **`∫`** (line 17) represents the integral symbol, while the **`msubsup`** element (line 15) specifies the superscript and subscript. Element **`mo`** marks up the integral operator. Element **`msubsup`** requires three child elements: an operator (e.g., the integral entity), the subscript expression (line 18) and the superscript expression (lines 20–24). Element **`mn`** (line 18) marks up the number (i.e., **`0`**) that represents the subscript. Element **`mrow`** marks up the expression (i.e., **`1-y`**) that specifies the superscript expression

Element **`msqrt`** (lines 28–43) represents a square root expression. Line 29 uses element **`mrow`** to group the expression contained in the square root. Line 45 introduces entity **`δ`** for representing a delta symbol. Delta is an operator, so line 45 places this entity in element **`mo`**. To see other operations and symbols in MathML, visit **`www.w3.org/Math`**.

20.5.2 Chemical Markup Language (CML)

Chemical Markup Language (*CML*) is an XML vocabulary for representing molecular and chemical information. Many previous methods for storing this type of information (e.g., special file types) inhibited document reuse. CML takes advantage of XML's portability to enable document authors to use and reuse molecular information without corrupting important data in the process. Although many of our readers will not know the chemistry required to understand the example in this section fully, we feel that CML so beautifully illustrates the purpose of XML that we chose to include the example for the readers who wish to see XML "at its best." Document authors can edit and view CML using the *Jumbo browser*, which is available at **`www.xml-cml.org`**. [*Note*: At the time of this writing, Jumbo did not allow users to load documents for rendering. For illustration purposes, we have created the image shown in Fig. 20.12.] Fig. 20.12 shows an ammonia molecule marked up in CML.

```
1  <?jumbo:namespace ns = "http://www.xml-cml.org"
2     prefix = "C" java = "jumbo.cmlxml.*Node" ?>
3
4  <!-- Fig. 20.12 : ammonia.xml -->
5  <!-- Structure of ammonia     -->
6
7  <C:molecule id = "Ammonia">
8
9     <C:atomArray builtin = "elsym">
10       N H H H
11    </C:atomArray>
12
13    <C:atomArray builtin = "x2" type = "float">
14       1.5 0.0 1.5 3.0
15    </C:atomArray>
16
17    <C:atomArray builtin = "y2" type = "float">
18       1.5 1.5 0.0 1.5
19    </C:atomArray>
20
21    <C:bondArray builtin = "atid1">
22       1 1 1
23    </C:bondArray>
24
25    <C:bondArray builtin = "atid2">
26       2 3 4
27    </C:bondArray>
28
29    <C:bondArray builtin = "order" type = "integer">
30       1 1 1
31    </C:bondArray>
32
33 </C:molecule>
```

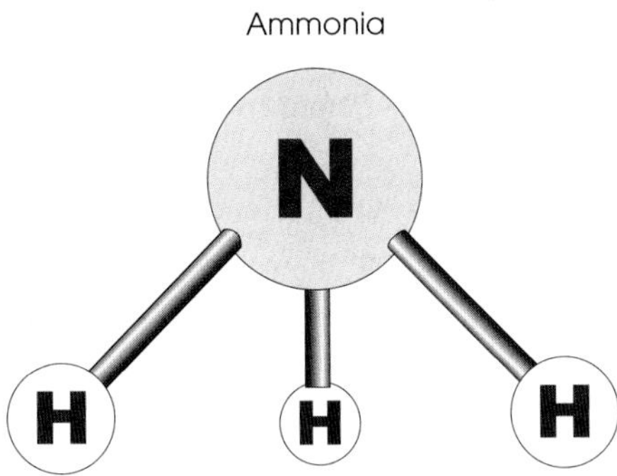

Fig. 20.12 CML markup for ammonia molecule .

Lines 1–2 contain a *processing instruction* (*PI*), which is application-specific information embedded in an XML document. The characters **<?** and **?>** delimit a processing instruction. The processing instruction of lines 1–2 provides application-specific information to the Jumbo CML browser. Processing instructions consist of a *PI target* (e.g.,

jumbo:namespace) and a *PI value* (e.g., **ns = "http://www.xml-cml.org" prefix = "C" java = "jumbo.cmlxml.*Node"**).

Portability Tip 20.1

Processing instructions allow document authors to embed application-specific information in an XML document, without affecting that document's portability.

Line 7 defines an ammonia molecule using element **molecule**. Attribute **id** identifies this molecule as **Ammonia**. Lines 9–11 use element **atomArray** and attribute **builtin** to specify the molecule's atoms. Ammonia contains one nitrogen atom and three hydrogen atoms.

Lines 13–15 show element **atomArray** with attribute **builtin** assigned the value **x2** and **type float**. This specifies that the element contains a list of floating-point numbers, each of which indicates the *x*-coordinate of an atom. The first value (**1.5**) is the *x*-coordinate of the first atom (nitrogen), the second value (**0.0**) is the *x*-coordinate of the second atom (the first hydrogen atom) and so forth.

Lines 17–19 show element **atomArray** with attribute **builtin** assigned the value **y2** and **type float**. This specifies that the element contains a list of *y*-coordinate values. The first value (**1.5**) is the *y*-coordinate of the first atom (nitrogen), the second value (**1.5**) is the *y*-coordinate of the second atom (the first hydrogen atom) and so forth.

Lines 21–23 show element **bondArray** with attribute **builtin** assigned the value **atid1**. Element **bondArray** defines the bonds between atoms. This element has a **builtin** value of **atid1**, so the values this element specifies compose the first atom in a pair of atoms. We are defining three bonds, so we specify three values. For each value we specify the first atom in the **atomArray**, the nitrogen atom.

Lines 25–27 show element **bondArray** with attribute **builtin** assigned the value **atid2**. The values of this element compose the second atom in a pair of atoms and denote the three hydrogen atoms.

Lines 29–31 show element **bondArray** with the attribute **builtin** assigned the value **order** and **type integer**. The values of this element are integers that represent the number of bonds between the pairs of atoms. Thus, the bond between the nitrogen atom and the first hydrogen is a single bond, the bond between the nitrogen atom and the second hydrogen atom is a single bond, and the bond between the nitrogen atom and the third hydrogen atom is a single bond.

20.5.3 Other Markup Languages

Literally hundreds of markup languages derive from XML. Everyday developers find new uses for XML. In Fig. 20.13, we summarize some of these markup languages.

20.6 Document Object Model (DOM)

Although an XML document is a text file, retrieving data from the document using traditional sequential-file access techniques is neither practical nor efficient, especially for adding and removing elements dynamically. As mentioned earlier, when a DOM parser successfully parses an XML document, the parser creates a tree structure in memory that contains the document's data. Figure 20.14 shows the tree structure for the document **article.xml** discussed in Fig. 20.1. This hierarchical tree structure is a *Document Object Model* (*DOM*) *tree*. Each name (e.g., **article**, **date**, **firstName**, etc.) represents a *node*. A node that contains other nodes (called *child nodes* or *children*) is called a *parent node* (e.g., **author**). A parent node can have many children, but a child node can have only one parent node. Nodes that are peers (e.g., **firstName** and **lastName**) are called *sibling nodes*. A node's *descendent nodes* include that node's children, its children's children and so on. A node's *ancestor nodes* include that node's parent, its parent's parent and so on.

The DOM has a single *root node*, which contains all other nodes in the document. For example, the root node for **article.xml** (Fig. 20.1) contains a node for the XML declaration (line 1), two nodes for the comments (lines 3–4) and a node for the root element (line 6).

Each node is an object that has properties, methods and events. Properties associated with a node include names, values, child nodes, etc. Methods enable programs to create, delete and append nodes, load XML documents, etc. The XML parser exposes these methods as a programmatic library—called an *Application Programming Interface* (*API*).

20.7 DOM Methods

To introduce document manipulation with the XML Document Object Model, we provide a simple scripting example that uses JavaScript and Microsoft's msxml parser. This example takes an XML document (Fig. 20.1) that marks up an article and uses the DOM API to display the document's element names and values. Figure 20.15 lists the JavaScript code that manipulates this XML document and displays its content in an XHTML page.

Markup Language	Description
VoiceXML™	The VoiceXML forum founded by AT&T, IBM, Lucent and Motorola developed VoiceXML. It provides interactive voice communication between humans and computers through a telephone, PDA (Personal Digital Assistant) or desktop computer. IBM's VoiceXML SDK can process VoiceXML documents. Visit **www.voicexml.org** for more information on VoiceXML. We introduce VoiceXML in Chapter 34, Accessibility.
Synchronous Multimedia Integration Language (SMIL™)	SMIL is an XML vocabulary for multimedia presentations. The W3C was the primary developer of SMIL, with contributions from other companies. Visit **www.w3.org/AudioVideo** for more on SMIL. We introduce SMIL in Chapter 33, Multimedia.
Research Information Exchange Markup Language (RIXML)	RIXML, which a consortium of brokerage firms developed, marks up investment data. Visit **www.rixml.org** for more information on RIXML.
ComicsML	A language developed by Jason MacIntosh for marking up comics. Visit **www.jmac.org/projects/comics_ml** for more information on ComicsML.

Fig. 20.13 Various markup languages derived from XML (part 1 of 2).

Markup Language	Description
Geography Markup Language (GML)	The OpenGIS developed the Geography Markup Language to describe geographic information. Visit **www.opengis.org** for more information on GML.
Extensible User Interface Language (XUL)	The Mozilla project created the Extensible User Interface Language for describing graphical user interfaces in a platform-independent way. For more information visit: **www.mozilla.org/xpfe/language-Spec.html**

Fig. 20.13 Various markup languages derived from XML (part 2 of 2).

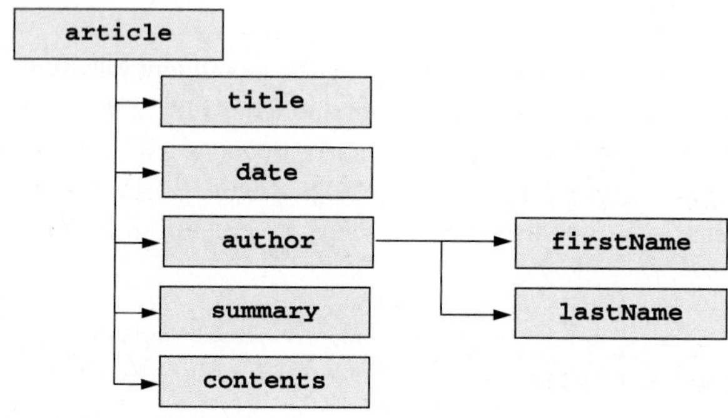

Fig. 20.14 Tree structure for **article.xml**.

```
<?xml version="1.0"?>
<!DOCTYPE html PUBLIC "-//W3C//DTD XHTML 1.0 Transitional//EN"
   "http://www.w3.org/TR/xhtml1/DTD/xhtml1-transitional.dtd">
<html xmlns="http://www.w3.org/1999/xhtml">

<!-- Fig. 20.15 : DOMExample.html -->
<!-- DOM with JavaScript          -->

   <head>
      <title>A DOM Example</title>
   </head>

   <body>
```

Fig. 20.15 Traversing **article.xml** with JavaScript (part 1 of 3).

```

   <script type = "text/javascript" language = "JavaScript">
      <!--
      var xmlDocument = new ActiveXObject( "Microsoft.XMLDOM" );

      xmlDocument.load( "article.xml" );

      // get the root element
      var element = xmlDocument.documentElement;

      document.writeln(
         "<p>Here is the root node of the document: " +
         "<strong>" + element.nodeName + "</strong>" +
         "<br />The following are its child elements:" +
         "</p><ul>" );

      // traverse all child nodes of root element
      for ( var i = 0; i < element.childNodes.length; i++ ) {
         var curNode = element.childNodes.item( i );

         // print node name of each child element
         document.writeln( "<li><strong>" + curNode.nodeName
            + "</strong></li>" );
      }

      document.writeln( "</ul>" );

      // get the first child node of root element
      var currentNode = element.firstChild;

      document.writeln( "<p>The first child of root node is: " +
         "<strong>" + currentNode.nodeName + "</strong>" +
         "<br />whose next sibling is:" );

      // get the next sibling of first child
      var nextSib = currentNode.nextSibling;

      document.writeln( "<strong>" + nextSib.nodeName +
         "</strong>.<br />Value of <strong>" +
         nextSib.nodeName + "</strong> element is: " );

      var value = nextSib.firstChild;

      // print the text value of the sibling
      document.writeln( "<em>" + value.nodeValue + "</em>" +
         "<br />Parent node of <strong>" + nextSib.nodeName +
         "</strong> is: <strong>" +
         nextSib.parentNode.nodeName + "</strong>.</p>" );
         -->
   </script>

   </body>
</html>
```

Fig. 20.15 Traversing **article.xml** with JavaScript (part 2 of 3).

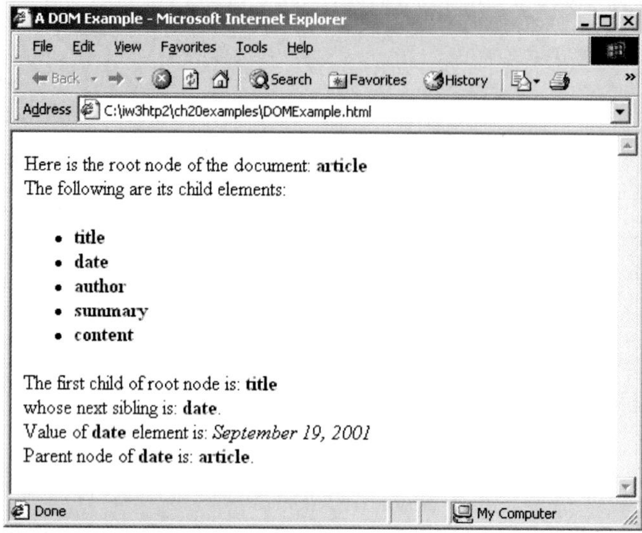

Fig. 20.15 Traversing **article.xml** with JavaScript (part 3 of 3).

Line 17 instantiates (i.e., creates) a Microsoft XML Document Object Model object and assigns it to reference **xmlDocument**. This object represents an XML document DOM tree and provides methods for manipulating its data. The statement creates the object, which does not yet refer to any specific XML document.

Line 19 calls method ***load*** to load **article.xml** (Fig. 20.1) into memory. The msxml parser parses the XML document and stores the document in memory as a tree structure.

Line 22 assigns the root element node (i.e., **article**) to variable **element**. Property ***documentElement*** corresponds to the root element in the document (e.g., **article**), which is important because this element is the reference point for retrieving all other nodes in the document.

Line 26 places the name of the root element in XHTML element **strong** and writes this string to the browser for rendering. Property ***nodeName*** corresponds to the name of an element, attribute, etc. In this particular case, **element** refers to the root node named **article**.

Line 31 iterates through the root node's children using property ***childNodes***. Property ***length*** returns the number of children in the root element.

Calling method ***item*** accesses individual child nodes. Each node has an integer index (starting at zero) based on the order in which the node occurs in the XML document. For example, in Fig. 20.1, **title** has index **0**, **date** has index **1**, etc. Line 32 calls method **item** to obtain the child node at index **i**. Line 32 assigns this node to reference **curNode**.

Line 42 retrieves the root node's first child node (i.e., **title**) using property ***firstChild***. The expression on line 42 is a more concise alternative to

```
var currentNode = element.childNodes.item( 0 );
```

Elements **title**, **date**, **author**, **summary** and **content** are all sibling nodes. Property ***nextSibling*** returns a node's next sibling. Line 49 assigns **currentNode**'s (i.e., **title**'s) next sibling node (i.e., **date**) to reference **nextSib**.

In addition to elements and attributes, text (e.g., **Simple XML** in line 8 of Fig. 20.1) also is a node. Line 55 assigns **nextSib**'s (i.e., **date**'s) first child node to **value**. In this case, the first child node is a text node. On line 58, method ***nodeValue*** retrieves the value of this text node. A text node's value is simply the text that the node contains. Element nodes have a value of ***null*** (i.e., the absence of a value). Line 61 retrieves and displays **nextSib**'s (i.e., **date**'s) parent node (i.e., **article**). Property ***parentNode*** returns a node's parent node.

The following tables list key DOM methods. The primary DOM interfaces are ***Node*** (which represents any node in the tree), ***NodeList*** (which represents an ordered set of nodes), ***NamedNodeMap*** (which represents an unordered set of nodes), ***Document*** (which represents the document), ***Element*** (which represents an element node), ***Attr*** (which represents an attribute node), ***Text*** (which represents a text node) and ***Comment*** (which represents a comment node). Figures 20.16–20.22 describe some methods of these objects.

Method	Description
getNodeType	Returns an integer representing the node type.
getNodeName	Returns the name of the node. If the node does not have a name, a string consisting of **#** followed by the type of the node is returned.
getNodeValue	Returns a string or null depending on the node type.
getParentNode	Returns the parent node.
getChildNodes	Returns a **NodeList** (Fig. 20.17) with all the children of the node.
getFirstChild	Returns the first child in the **NodeList**.
getLastChild	Returns the last child in the **NodeList**.
getPreviousSibling	Returns the node preceding this node, or null.
getNextSibling	Returns the node following this node, or null.
getAttributes	Returns a **NamedNodeMap** (Fig. 20.18) containing the attributes for this node.
insertBefore	Inserts the node passed as the first argument before the existing node passed as the second argument. If the new node is already in the tree, it is removed before insertion. The same behavior is true for other methods that add nodes.
replaceChild	Replaces the second argument node with the first argument node.
removeChild	Removes the child node passed to it.
appendChild	Appends the node passed to it to the list of child nodes.

Fig. 20.16 Some **Node** object methods (part 1 of 2).

Method	Description
`getElementsByTagName`	Returns a **`NodeList`** of all nodes in the subtree with the name specified as the first argument ordered as they would be encountered in a preorder traversal. An optional second argument specifies either the direct child nodes (`0`) or any descendant (`1`).
`getChildAtIndex`	Returns the child node at the specified index in the child list.
`addText`	Appends the string passed to it to the last **`Node`** if it is a **`Text`** node, otherwise creates a new **`Text`** node for the string and adds it to the end of the child list.
`isAncestor`	Returns **`true`** if the node passed is a parent of the node, or is the node itself.

Fig. 20.16 Some **`Node`** object methods (part 2 of 2).

Method	Description
`item`	Passed an index number, returns the element node at that index. Indices range from 0 to *length – 1*.
`getLength`	Returns the total number of nodes in the list.

Fig. 20.17 Some **`NodeList`** methods.

Method	Description
`getNamedItem`	Returns either a node in the **`NamedNodeMap`** with the specified name or null.
`setNamedItem`	Stores a node passed to it in the **`NamedNodeMap`**. Two nodes with the same name cannot be stored in the same **`NamedNodeMap`**.
`removeNamedItem`	Removes a specified node from the **`NamedNodeMap`**.
`getLength`	Returns the total number of nodes in the **`NamedNodeMap`**.
`getValues`	Returns a **`NodeList`** containing all nodes in the **`NamedNodeMap`**.

Fig. 20.18 Some **`NamedNodeMap`** methods.

Method	Description
`getDocumentElement`	Returns the root node of the document.

Fig. 20.19 Some **`Document`** methods (part 1 of 2).

Method	Description
`createElement`	Creates and returns an element node with the specified tag name.
`createAttribute`	Creates and returns an attribute node with the specified name and value.
`createTextNode`	Creates and returns a text node that contains the specified text.
`createComment`	Creates a comment to hold the specified text.

Fig. 20.19 Some **`Document`** methods (part 2 of 2).

Method	Description
`getTagName`	Returns the name of the element.
`setTagName`	Changes the name of the element to the specified name.
`getAttribute`	Returns the value of the specified attribute.
`setAttribute`	Changes the value of the attribute passed as the first argument to the value passed as the second argument.
`removeAttribute`	Removes the specified attribute.
`getAttributeNode`	Returns the specified attribute node.
`setAttributeNode`	Adds a new attribute node with the specified name.

Fig. 20.20 Some **`Element`** methods.

Method	Description
`getValue`	Returns the specified attribute's value.
`setValue`	Changes the value of the attribute to the specified value.
`getName`	Returns the name of the attribute.

Fig. 20.21 Some **`Attr`** methods.

Method	Description
`getData`	Returns the data contained tin the node (text or comment).
`setData`	Sets the node's data.
`getLength`	Returns the number of characters contained in the node.

Fig. 20.22 Some **`Text`** and **`Comment`** methods.

20.8 Simple API for XML (SAX)

Members of the *XML-DEV mailing list* developed the Simple API for XML (SAX), which they released in May, 1998. SAX is an alternate method for parsing XML documents that uses an *event-based model—SAX-based parsers* generate notifications called *events* as the parser parses the document. Software programs can "listen" for these events to retrieve particular data from the document. For example, a program that builds mailing lists might read name and address information from an XML document that contains much more than just mailing address information (e.g., birthdays, phone numbers, email addresses, etc.). Such a program could use a SAX parser to parse the document, and might listen only for events that contain name and address information. If this program used a DOM parser, the parser would load every element and attribute into memory, and the program would have to traverse the DOM tree to locate the relevant address information.

SAX and DOM provide dramatically different APIs for accessing XML document information; each API has advantages and disadvantages. DOM is a tree-based model that stores the document's data in a hierarchy of nodes. Programs can access data quickly, because all the document's data is in memory. DOM also provides facilities for adding or removing nodes, which enables programs to modify XML documents easily.

SAX-based parsers invoke *listener methods* when the parser encounters markup. With this event-based model, the SAX-based parser does not create a tree structure to store the XML document's data—instead, the parser passes data to the application from the XML document as the parser finds that data. This results in greater performance and less memory overhead than with DOM-based parsers. In fact, many DOM parsers use SAX parsers "under the hood" to retrieve data from a document for building the DOM tree in memory. Many programmers find it easier to traverse and manipulate XML documents using the DOM tree structure. As a result, programs typically use SAX parsers for reading XML documents that the program will not modify. SAX-based parsers are available for a variety of programming languages such as Java, Python, C++, etc.

Performance Tip 20.1

SAX-based parsing often is more efficient than DOM-based parsing when processing large XML documents, because SAX-based parsers do not load entire XML documents into memory at once.

Performance Tip 20.2

SAX-based parsing is an efficient means of parsing documents that only need parsing once.

Performance Tip 20.3

DOM-based parsing often is more efficient than SAX-based parsing when a program must retrieve specific information from the document quickly.

Performance Tip 20.4

Programs that must conserve memory commonly use SAX-based parsers.

Software Engineering Observation 20.7

Members of the XML-DEV mailing list developed SAX independently of the W3C, although SAX has wide industry support. DOM is the official W3C recommendation.

20.9 Extensible Stylesheet Language (XSL)[1]

Extensible Stylesheet Language (*XSL*) documents specify how programs should render XML document data. The relationship between XML and XSL is similar to the relationship between XHTML and Cascading Style Sheets (CSS), although XSL is much more powerful than CSS. Document authors also can use CSS to specify formatting information for XML documents. A subset of XSL— *XSL Transformations* (*XSLT*)—provides elements that define rules for transforming data from one XML document to produce a different XML document (e.g., XHTML). By convention, XSL documents have the filename extension **.xsl**.

Software Engineering Observation 20.8

XSL enables document authors to separate data presentation from data description.

Transforming an XML document using XSLT involves two tree structures: the *source tree* (i.e., the XML document to transform) and the *result tree* (i.e., the XML document to create).

Figure 20.23 lists an XML document that marks up various sports. The output shows the results of the transformation rendered in Internet Explorer 5.5. We discuss the specific XSL document that performs the transformation in Fig. 20.24.

```
<?xml version = "1.0"?>
<?xml:stylesheet type = "text/xsl" href = "games.xsl"?>

<!-- Fig. 20.23 : games.xml -->
<!-- Sports Database        -->

<sports>

   <game id = "783">
      <name>Cricket</name>

      <paragraph>
         More popular among commonwealth nations.
      </paragraph>
   </game>

   <game id = "239">
      <name>Baseball</name>

      <paragraph>
         More popular in America.
      </paragraph>
   </game>

```

Fig. 20.23 XML document containing a list of sports (part 1 of 2).

1. The examples in this section require msxml 3.0 or higher to run. For more information on downloading and installing msxml 3.0, visit **www.deitel.com**.

```
25      <game id = "418">
26         <name>Soccer (Football)</name>
27
28         <paragraph>
29            Most popular sport in the world.
30         </paragraph>
31      </game>
32
33   </sports>
```

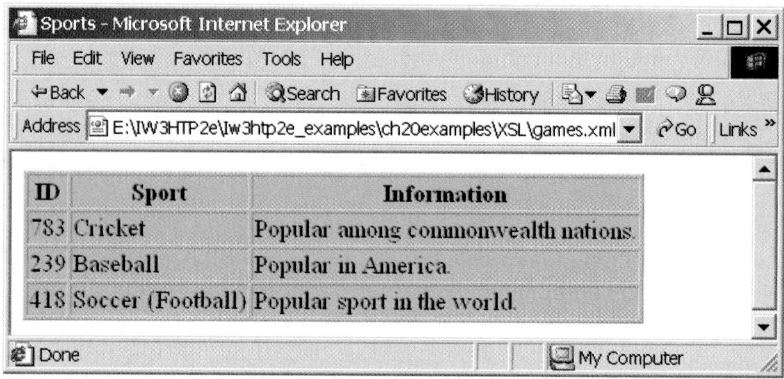

Fig. 20.23 XML document containing a list of sports (part 2 of 2).

Line 2 is a processing instruction that references the XSL stylesheet **games.xsl**. Value ***type*** specifies that **games.xsl** is a **text/xsl** file. Internet Explorer uses this processing instruction to determine the XSL transformation to apply to the XML document.

Figure 20.24 shows an XSLT document for transforming the XML document of Fig. 20.23 into an XHTML document.

```
<?xml version = "1.0"?>

<!-- Fig. 20.24 : elements.xsl         -->
<!-- A simple XSLT transformation      -->

<!-- reference XSL stylesheet URI      -->
<xsl:stylesheet version = "1.0"
   xmlns:xsl = "http://www.w3.org/1999/XSL/Transform">

   <xsl:output method = "html" omit-xml-declaration = "no"
      doctype-system =
         "http://www.w3.org/TR/xhtml1/DTD/xhtml1-strict.dtd"
      doctype-public = "-//W3C//DTD XHTML 1.0 Strict//EN"/>

<xsl:template match = "/">

```

Fig. 20.24 Using XSLT to create elements and attributes (part 1 of 2).

```
17    <html xmlns="http://www.w3.org/1999/xhtml">
18
19       <head>
20          <title>Sports</title>
21       </head>
22
23       <body>
24
25          <table border = "1" bgcolor = "cyan">
26
27          <thead>
28
29             <tr>
30                <th>ID</th>
31                <th>Sport</th>
32                <th>Information</th>
33             </tr>
34
35          </thead>
36
37           <!-- insert each name and paragraph element value  -->
38           <!-- into a table row.                            -->
39           <xsl:for-each select = "sports/game">
40
41              <tr>
42                 <td><xsl:value-of select = "@id"/></td>
43                 <td><xsl:value-of select = "name"/></td>
44                 <td><xsl:value-of select = "paragraph"/></td>
45              </tr>
46
47           </xsl:for-each>
48
49           </table>
50
51        </body>
52
53    </html>
54
55  </xsl:template>
56
57  </xsl:stylesheet>
```

Fig. 20.24 Using XSLT to create elements and attributes (part 2 of 2).

Lines 7–8 are the ***stylesheet*** start tag—which begins the XSL stylesheet. Line 8 binds namespace prefix ***xsl*** to the URI **http://www.w3.org/1999/XSL/Transform**, which uniquely identifies the XSL namespace.

Lines 10–13 use element ***xsl:output*** to write an XHTML document type declaration to the result tree. Attribute ***omit-xml-declaration*** specifies whether the transformation should write the XML declaration to the result tree. Attributes ***doctype-system*** and ***doctype-public*** specify the DTD system and public values for the resulting document, respectively.

XSLT documents consist of *templates*. Each template describes how to transform a particular node from the source tree into the result tree. Line 15 uses the ***match*** attribute to select the *document root* (i.e., the conceptual part of the document that contains the root element and everything above it) of the source document (i.e., **game.xml**). In Fig. 20.23, the child nodes of the document root are the processing instruction node (line 2), the two comment nodes (lines 4–5) and the **sports** element node (line 7).

The msxml processor writes lines 17–35 (Fig. 20.24) to the result tree exactly as those lines appear in the XSLT document. Line 39 uses element ***xsl:for-each*** to iterate through the source XML document and search for **game** elements. The **xsl:for-each** element is similar to JavaScript's **for/in** repetition structure. Attribute ***select*** specifies the node (called the *context node*) on which the **xsl:for-each** operates. The forward slash between **sports** and **game** indicates that **game** is a child node of **sports**. When the msxml processor encounters a **game** element, msxml processes the elements on lines 41–45 and places those elements in the result tree.

Line 42 uses element ***value-of*** to retrieve attribute **id**'s value and place it in a **td** element in the result tree. The symbol ***@*** specifies that **id** is an attribute node. Lines 43–44 also place the **name** and **paragraph** element values in **td** elements and insert those elements in the result tree.

Figure 20.25 presents an XML document (**sorting.xml**) that marks up information about a book. Line 6 references the XSL stylesheet **sorting.xsl** (Fig. 20.26).

```
1  <?xml version = "1.0"?>
2
3  <!-- Fig. 20.25 : sorting.xml             -->
4  <!-- Usage of elements and attributes -->
5
6  <?xml:stylesheet type = "text/xsl" href = "sorting.xsl"?>
7
8  <book isbn = "999-99999-9-X">
9     <title>Deitel&apos;s XML Primer</title>
10
11    <author>
12       <firstName>Paul</firstName>
13       <lastName>Deitel</lastName>
14    </author>
15
16    <chapters>
17       <frontMatter>
18          <preface pages = "2"/>
19          <contents pages = "5"/>
20          <illustrations pages = "4"/>
21       </frontMatter>
22
23       <chapter number = "3" pages = "44">
24          Advanced XML</chapter>
25       <chapter number = "2" pages = "35">
26          Intermediate XML</chapter>
27       <appendix number = "B" pages = "26">
28          Parsers and Tools</appendix>
```

Fig. 20.25 XML document containing book information.

```
      <appendix number = "A" pages = "7">
         Entities</appendix>
      <chapter number = "1" pages = "28">
         XML Fundamentals</chapter>
   </chapters>

   <media type = "CD"/>
</book>
```

Fig. 20.25 XML document containing book information.

Figure 20.26 presents an XSL document (**sorting.xsl**) that transforms **sorting.xml** (Fig. 20.25) to XHTML. Line 17 specifies that the msxml processor should apply **xsl:template**s to the document root's children. Line 21 specifies a template that matches element **book**.

Lines 23–24 create the title for the XHTML document. We use the book ISBN from attribute **isbn** and the contents of element **title** to create the title string (**ISBN 999-99999-9-X - Deitel's XML Primer**).

Lines 30–31 create a header element that displays the book's author. The context node is **book**, so the expression **author/lastName** selects the author's last name, and the expression **author/firstName** selects the author's first name.

```
1  <?xml version = "1.0"?>
2
3  <!-- Fig. 20.26 : sorting.xsl                        -->
4  <!-- Transformation of Book information into XHTML -->
5
6  <xsl:stylesheet version = "1.0"
7     xmlns:xsl = "http://www.w3.org/1999/XSL/Transform">
8
9     <xsl:output method = "html" omit-xml-declaration = "no"
10       doctype-system =
11          "http://www.w3.org/TR/xhtml1/DTD/xhtml1-strict.dtd"
12       doctype-public = "-//W3C//DTD XHTML 1.0 Strict//EN"/>
13
14    <xsl:template match = "/">
15
16       <html xmlns = "http://www.w3.org/1999/xhtml">
17          <xsl:apply-templates/>
18       </html>
19    </xsl:template>
20
21    <xsl:template match = "book">
22       <head>
23          <title>ISBN <xsl:value-of select = "@isbn"/> -
24             <xsl:value-of select = "title"/></title>
25       </head>
26
27       <body>
28          <h1><xsl:value-of select = "title"/></h1>
```

Fig. 20.26 XSL document that transforms **sort.xml** into XHTML (part 1 of 3).

```

            <h2>by <xsl:value-of select = "author/lastName"/>,
               <xsl:value-of select = "author/firstName"/></h2>

            <table border = "1">
               <xsl:for-each select = "chapters/frontMatter/*">
                  <tr>
                     <td align = "right">
                        <xsl:value-of select = "name()"/>
                     </td>

                     <td>
                        ( <xsl:value-of select = "@pages"/> pages )
                     </td>
                  </tr>
               </xsl:for-each>

               <xsl:for-each select = "chapters/chapter">
                  <xsl:sort select = "@number" data-type = "number"
                       order = "ascending"/>
                  <tr>
                     <td align = "right">
                        Chapter <xsl:value-of select = "@number"/>
                     </td>

                     <td>
                        ( <xsl:value-of select = "@pages"/> pages )
                     </td>
                  </tr>
               </xsl:for-each>

               <xsl:for-each select = "chapters/appendix">
                  <xsl:sort select = "@number" data-type = "text"
                       order = "ascending"/>
                  <tr>
                     <td align = "right">
                        Appendix <xsl:value-of select = "@number"/>
                     </td>

                     <td>
                        ( <xsl:value-of select = "@pages"/> pages )
                     </td>
                  </tr>
               </xsl:for-each>
            </table>

            <br />Pages:
               <xsl:variable name = "pagecount"
                  select = "sum(chapters//*/@pages)"/>
               <xsl:value-of select = "$pagecount"/>
            <br />Media Type: <xsl:value-of select = "media/@type"/>
         </body>
      </xsl:template>
```

Fig. 20.26 XSL document that transforms **sort.xml** into XHTML (part 2 of 3).

```
82
83 </xsl:stylesheet>
```

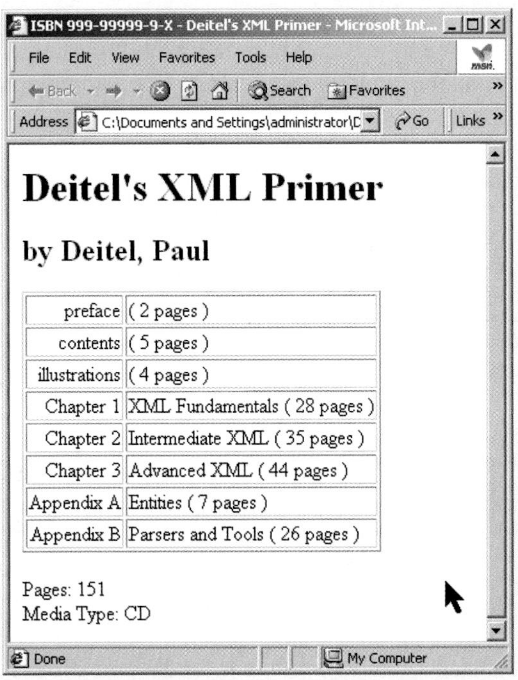

Fig. 20.26 XSL document that transforms **sort.xml** into XHTML (part 3 of 3).

Performance Tip 20.5

Using Internet Explorer 5.5 to process XSL documents conserves server resources.

Line 34 selects each element (indicated by an asterisk) that is a child of **front-Matter**. Line 37 calls *node-set function* ***name*** to retrieve the current node's element name (e.g., **preface**). The current node is the context node specified in the **xsl:for-each** element (line 34).

Lines 47–48 use *element* ***xsl:sort*** to sort **chapter**s by number in ascending order. Attribute **select** selects the value of attribute **number** in context node **chapter**. Attribute ***data-type*** specifies a numeric sort and attribute ***order*** specifies **ascending** order. Attribute **data-type** also accepts the value ***text*** (line 61) and attribute **order** also accepts the value ***descending***.

Lines 76–78 use an *XSL variable* to store the value of the book's page count and output the page count to the result tree. Attribute **name** specifies the variable's name and attribute **select** assigns a value to the variable. Function ***sum*** totals the values for all **page** attribute values. The two slashes between **chapters** and ***** indicate a *recursive descent*—the msxml processor will search all descendant nodes of **chapters** for elements that contain an attribute named **pages**.

20.10 Microsoft BizTalk™

Increasingly, organizations are using the Internet to exchange data. Sending data between organizations is difficult, because organizations use different platforms, applications and data specifications. XML simplifies sharing data among businesses. However, businesses need an easy method for transmitting and translating XML documents with partners, suppliers, etc. Microsoft developed *BizTalk* for managing and facilitating business transactions using XML.

BizTalk consists of three parts: The BizTalk Server, the BizTalk Framework and the BizTalk Schema Library. The *BizTalk Server* (*BTS*) parses and translates all inbound and outbound messages (or documents) going to and from a business. The *BizTalk Framework* is a schema for structuring those messages. The *BizTalk Schema Library* is a collection of Framework schemas. Businesses can design their own schema or choose one from the BizTalk Schema Library. Figure 20.27 summarizes BizTalk terminology.

Figure 20.28 is an example of a BizTalk message for a product offer from a retail company. The message schema (lines 15–46) for this example is for Microsoft online shopping. We use this schema for a fictitious company named ExComp.

BizTalk	Description
Framework	A specification that defines message formats.
Schema library	A repository of Framework XML schemas.
Server	An application that helps vendors convert their messages to BizTalk format. For more information visit: **www.microsoft.com/biztalkserver**.
JumpStart Kit	A set of tools for developing BizTalk applications.

Fig. 20.27 BizTalk Terminologies.

```
1  <?xml version = "1.0"?>
2  <BizTalk
3   xmlns = "urn:schemas-biztalk-org:BizTalk/biztalk-0.81.xml">
4
5  <!-- Fig. 20.28: BizTalkexample.xml -->
6  <!-- BizTalk example               -->
7  <Route>
8     <From locationID = "8888888" locationType = "DUNS"
9           handle = "23" />
10
11    <To locationID = "454545445" locationType = "DUNS"
12          handle = "45" />
13 </Route>
14
15 <Body>
16  <Offers xmlns =
17  "x-schema:http://schemas.biztalk.org/eshop_msn_com/t7ntoqnq.xml">
```

Fig. 20.28 BizTalk markup using an offer schema (part 1 of 2).

```
18       <Offer>
19          <Model>12-a-3411d</Model>
20          <Manufacturer>ExComp, Inc.</Manufacturer>
21          <ManufacturerModel>DCS-48403</ManufacturerModel>
22          <MerchantCategory>Clothes | Sports wear</MerchantCategory>
23          <MSNClassId></MSNClassId>
24          <StartDate>2000-06-05 T13:12:00</StartDate>
25          <EndDate>2000-12-05T13:12:00</EndDate>
26          <RegularPrice>89.99</RegularPrice>
27          <CurrentPrice>25.99</CurrentPrice>
28          <DisplayPrice value = "3" />
29          <InStock value = "15" />
30          <ReferenceImageURL>
31             http://www.Example.com/clothes/index.jpg
32          </ReferenceImageURL>
33          <OfferName>Clearance sale</OfferName>
34          <OfferDescription>This is a clearance sale</OfferDescription>
35          <PromotionalText>Free Shipping</PromotionalText>
36          <Comments>Clothes that you would love to wear.</Comments>
37          <IconType value = "BuyNow" />
38          <ActionURL>http://www.example.com/action.htm</ActionURL>
39          <AgeGroup1 value = "Infant" />
40          <AgeGroup2 value = "Adult" />
41          <Occasion1 value = "Birthday" />
42          <Occasion2 value = "Anniversary" />
43          <Occasion3 value = "Christmas" />
44        </Offer>
45       </Offers>
46    </Body>
47    </BizTalk>
```

Fig. 20.28 BizTalk markup using an offer schema (part 2 of 2).

All Biztalk documents have root element ***BizTalk***. Line 3 defines a default namespace for the BizTalk framework elements. Element ***Route*** contains the routing information, which is mandatory for all BizTalk documents. Element **Route** also contains elements ***To*** and ***From***. Element **To** specifies the document's destination and element **From** specifies the document's source. This makes it easier for the receiving application to communicate with the sender. Attributes ***locationType*** and ***locationID*** specify the type of business sending or receiving the information and a business identity (the unique identifier for a business) for the source and destination organizations. Attribute ***handle*** provides information to routing applications that manipulate the document.

Element ***Body*** contains the actual message, whose schema the businesses define. It contains the ***Offers*** element. Lines 16–17 specify the default namespace for the **Offers**. Each offer is marked up using an ***Offer*** element which contains elements that describe the offer. For additional information on BizTalk, visit **www.biztalk.com**.

20.11 Simple Object Access Protocol (SOAP)

Many applications use the Internet to transfer data. Some of these applications run on clients with little processing power, so these applications invoke methods on other machines to process data. Many of these applications use proprietary data specifications and protocols, which makes communication with other applications difficult. The majority of these applications also reside behind network firewalls, which often restrict data communication to and from the application. The. IBM, Lotus Development Corporation, Microsoft, DevelopMentor and Userland Software developed the *Simple Object Access Protocol* (*SOAP*) to address these problems. SOAP is an XML-based protocol that allows applications to communicate easily over the Internet using XML documents called *SOAP messages*.

A SOAP message contains an *envelope*, which is a structure that describes a method call. A SOAP message's body contains either a *request* or a *response*. A request message's body contains a *Remote Procedure Call* (*RPC*), which is a request for another machine to run a task. The RPC specifies the method to be invoked and any parameters the method takes. The application sends the SOAP message via an HTTP POST. A SOAP-response message is an HTTP response document that contains the results from the method call (e.g., return values, error messages, etc.). For more information on SOAP, visit **msdn.microsoft.com/xml/general/soaptemplate.asp**.

20.12 Internet and World Wide Web Resources

www.w3.org/xml

The W3C (World Wide Web Consortium) works to develop common protocols to ensure interoperability on the Web. Their XML page includes information about upcoming events, publications, software and discussion groups. Visit this site to read about the latest developments in XML.

www.xml.org

xml.org is a reference for XML, DTDs, schemas and namespaces.

www.w3.org/style/XSL

Provides information on XSL, including what is new in XSL, learning XSL, XSL-enabled tools, XSL specification, FAQs, XSL history, etc.

www.w3.org/TR

W3C technical reports and publications page. Contains links to working drafts, proposed recommendations, recommendations, etc.

xml.apache.org

The Apache XML Web site provides many resources related to XML, which include tools and downloads.

www.xmlbooks.com

Contains a list of recommended XML books by Charles Goldfarb—one of the original designers of GML (General Markup Language) from which SGML was derived.

www.xmlsoftware.com

The site contains links for downloading XML-related software. Downloads include XML browsers, conversion tools, database systems, DTD editors, XML editors, etc.

www.xml-zone.com

The Development Exchange XML Zone is a complete resource for XML information. This site includes FAQ, news, articles, links to other XML sites and newsgroups.

wdvl.internet.com/Authoring/Languages/XML

Web Developer's Virtual Library XML site includes tutorials, FAQ, the latest news and extensive links to XML sites and software downloads.

www.xml.com
Visit **XML.com** for the latest news and information about XML, conference listings, links to XML Web resources organized by topic, tools and more.

msdn.microsoft.com/xml/default.asp
The MSDN Online XML Development Center features articles on XML, Ask the Experts chat sessions, samples and demos, newsgroups and other helpful information.

www.oasis-open.org/cover/xml.html
The SGML/XML Web Page is an extensive resource that includes links to FAQs, online resources, industry initiatives, demos, conferences and tutorials.

www.gca.org/whats_xml/default.htm
The GCA site has an XML glossary, list of books, brief descriptions of the draft standards for XML and links to online drafts.

www.xmlinfo.com
XMLINFO is a resource site with tutorials, a list of recommended books, documentation, discussion forums and more.

xdev.datachannel.com
The title of this site is xDev: The Definitive Site for Serious XML Developers. This Web site includes several short tutorials with code examples, toolkits, downloads and a reference library.

www.ibm.com/developer/xml
The IBM XML Zone site is a great resource for developers. You will find news, tools, a library, case studies, events and information about standards.

developer.netscape.com/tech/xml/index.html
The XML and Metadata Developer Central site has demos, technical notes and news articles related to XML.

www.projectcool.com/developer/xmlz
The Project Cool Developer Zone site includes several tutorials covering introductory through advanced XML.

www.poet.com/products/cms/xml_library/xml_lib.html
POET XML Resource Library includes links to white papers, tools, news, publications and Web links.

www.ucc.ie/xml
This site is a detailed XML FAQ with responses to some popular questions. Submit your own questions through the site.

www.xml-cml.org
This site is a resource for the Chemical Markup Language (CML). It includes a FAQ list, documentation, software and XML links.

www.textuality.com/xml
Contains FAQ and the Lark nonvalidating XML parser.

www.zvon.org
Provides an XML tutorial.

SUMMARY

- XML is a widely-supported, open technology (i.e., nonproprietary technology) for data exchange.
- XML permits document authors to create their own markup for virtually any type of information. This extensibility enables document authors to create entirely new markup languages to describe

specific types of data, including mathematical formulas, chemical molecular structures, music and recipes.

- XML documents are highly portable. Opening an XML document does not require special software—any text editor that supports ASCII/Unicode characters will suffice. One important characteristic of XML is that it is both human readable and machine readable.
- Processing an XML document—which typically ends in the **.xml** extension—requires a software program called an XML parser (or an XML processor). Parsers check an XML document's syntax and can support the Document Object Model (DOM) or the Simple API for XML (SAX) API.
- DOM-based parsers build a tree structure containing the XML document's data in memory. This allows programs to manipulate the document's data. SAX-based parsers process the document and generate events as the parser encounters tags, text, comments, etc. These events contain data from the XML document.
- An XML document can reference an optional document that defines the XML document's structure. This optional document can be either a Document Type Definition (DTD) or a schema.
- If the XML document conforms to its DTD or schema, then the XML document is valid. Parsers that cannot check for document conformity against the DTD/Schema are nonvalidating parsers. If an XML parser (validating or nonvalidating) can process an XML document that does not have a DTD/Schema successfully, the XML document is well formed (i.e., it is syntactically correct). By definition, a valid XML document also is a well-formed document.
- The **ATTLIST** element type declaration in a DTD defines an attribute. Keyword **#IMPLIED** specifies that if the parser finds an element without the attribute, the parser can choose an arbitrary value or to ignore the attribute. Keyword **#REQUIRED** specifies that the attribute must be in the document, and keyword **#FIXED** specifies that the attribute must have the given fixed value. Flag **CDATA** specifies that an attribute contains a string that the parser should not process as markup. Keyword **EMPTY** specifies that the element does not contain any text.
- Flag **#PCDATA** specifies that the element can store parsed character data (i.e., text). Parsable character data should not contain markup. Document authors should replace the characters less than (**<**), greater than (**>**) and ampersand (**&**) with their corresponding entities (i.e., **<**, **>** and **&**).
- Schemas do not use the Extended Backus-Naur Form (EBNF) grammar. Instead, schemas use XML syntax and are XML documents that programs can manipulate (e.g., add elements, remove elements, etc.) like any other XML document.
- In XML Schema, element **element** defines an element. Attributes **name** and **type** specify the **element**'s name and data type, respectively. Any element that contains attributes or child elements must define a type—called a complex type—that defines each attribute and child element.
- Attribute **minOccurs** specifies the minimum number of occurrences for an element. Attribute **maxOccurs** specifies the maximum number of occurrences for an element.
- When an element is a simple type, such as **xsd:string**, that element cannot contain attributes and child elements.
- XML allows document authors to create their own tags, so naming collisions (i.e., different elements that have the same name) can occur. Namespaces enable document authors to prevent collisions among elements in an XML document.
- Namespace prefixes prepended to element and attribute names specify the namespace in which the element or attribute can be found. Each namespace prefix has a corresponding uniform resource identifier (URI) that uniquely identifies the namespace. By definition, a URI is a series of characters that differentiates names. Document authors can create their own namespace prefixes. Document authors can use virtually any namespace prefix, except the reserved namespace prefix **xml**.

- To eliminate the need to place a namespace prefix in each element, authors may specify a default namespace for an element and all of its child elements.
- MathML markup describes mathematical expressions.
- Chemical Markup Language (CML) marks up molecular and chemical information.
- The characters **<?** and **?>** delimit processing instructions (PIs), which are application-specific information embedded in an XML document. A processing instruction consists of a PI target and a PI value.
- A DOM tree has a single root node that contains all other nodes in the document. Each node is an object that has properties, methods and events. Properties associated with a node provide access to the node's name, value, child nodes, etc. Methods allow developers to create, delete and append nodes, load XML documents, etc. The XML parser exposes these methods and properties as a programmatic library—called an Application Programming Interface (API).
- A node that contains other nodes (called child nodes) is a parent node. Nodes that are peers are sibling nodes. A node's descendent nodes include that node's children, its children's children and so on. A node's ancestor nodes include that node's parent, its parent's parent and so on.
- SAX is an alternate method for parsing XML documents that uses an event-based model—SAX-based parsers generate notifications called events as the parser parses the document. Software programs can "listen" for these events to retrieve particular data from the document.
- Extensible Stylesheet Language (XSL) documents specify how programs should render an XML document data. A subset of XSL—XSL Transformations (XSLT)—provides elements that define rules for transforming data from one XML document to produce another XML document (e.g., XHTML).
- Transforming an XML document using XSLT involves two tree structures: the source tree (i.e., the XML document being transformed) and the result tree (i.e., the XML document to create).
- BizTalk consists of three parts: The BizTalk Server, the BizTalk Framework and the BizTalk Schema Library. The BizTalk Server (BTS) parses and translates all inbound and outbound messages (or documents) going to and from a business. The BizTalk Framework is a schema for structuring those messages. The BizTalk Schema Library is a collection of Framework schemas. Businesses can design their own schema or choose one from the BizTalk Schema Library.
- The Simple Object Access Protocol (SOAP) is an XML-based protocol that allows applications to communicate easily over the Internet using XML documents called SOAP messages. A SOAP message contains an envelope—a structure for describing a method call. A SOAP message's body contains either a request or a response.

TERMINOLOGY

#IMPLIED flag
#PCDATA flag
.xml file extension
.xsd extension
.xsl extension
addText method
ancestor node
appendChild method
asterisk (*****) occurrence indicator
atomArray element
ATTLIST element
attribute node
BizTalk Framework
BizTalk Schema Library
BizTalk Server (BTS)
CDATA flag
child node
childNodes property
complexType element
container element
context node
createAttribute method

createComment method
createElement method
createTextNode method
data-type attribute
default namespace
descendent node
doctype-public attribute
doctype-system attribute
document reuse
document root
Document Type Definition (DTD)
DOM (Document Object Model)
DOM API (Application Programming Interface)
DOM-based XML parser
EBNF (Extended Backus-Naur Form) grammar
ELEMENT element
element type declaration
empty element
EMPTY keyword
event
Extensible Stylesheet Language (XSL)
external DTD
firstChild property
foreach repetition structure
forward slash
getAttribute method
getAttributes method
getChildAtIndex method
getChildNodes method
getData method
getDocumentElement method
getElementsByTagName method
getFirstChild method
getLastChild method
getLength method
getName method
getNamedItem method
getNextSibling method
getNodeName method
getNodeType
getNodeValue
getParentNode
getPreviousSibling
getTagName method
getValue method
getValues method
Independent Software Vendor (ISV)
insertBefore method
invalid document
isAncestor
isbn attribute
item method (**childNodes**)
language attribute (**script**)
length property
load method (**xmlDocument**)
match attribute
maxOccurs attribute
minOccurs attribute
mn element
molecule element
mrow element
msqrt element
msub element
msubsup element
msxml parser
name attribute
name node-set function
namespace prefix
nextSibling property
node
nodeName property
node-set function
nodeValue property
nonvalidating XML parser
null
occurrence indicator
order attribute
parent node
parentNode property
parsed character data
parser
PI (processing instruction)
PI target
PI value
plus sign (**+**) occurrence indicator
processing instruction
prolog
question mark (**?**) occurrence indicator
recursive descent
removeAttribute method
removeChild method
removeNamedItem method
replaceChild method
request message (SOAP)
response message (SOAP)
result tree
root element
root node
SAX (Simple API for XML)
SAX-based parser

schema element
schema valid
select attribute
setAttribute method
setAttributeNode method
setData method
setNamedItem method
setTagName method
setValue method
sibling node
simple type
single-quote character (**'**)
SOAP (Simple Object Access Protocol)
source tree
stylesheet element
sum function
SYSTEM flag
targetNamespace attribute
TeX software package
text node
tree-based model
type attribute
unbounded value
validating XML parser
well-formed document
XML (Extensible Markup Language)
XML declaration
xml namespace
XML node
XML parser
XML processor
XML root
XML Schema
XML Validator
XML **version**
xmlns keyword
XSL (Extensible Stylesheet Language)
XSL Transformations (XSLT)
XSL variable
xsl:apply-templates
xsl:for-each element
xsl:output
xsl:sort
xsl:value-of element

SELF-REVIEW EXERCISES

20.1 Which of the following are valid XML element names?
a) **yearBorn**
b) **year.Born**
c) **year Born**
d) **year-Born1**
e) **2_year_born**
f) **--year/born**
g) **year*born**
h) **.year_born**
i) **_year_born_**
j) **y_e-a_r-b_o-r_n**

20.2 State whether the following are *true* or *false*. If *false*, explain why.
a) XML is a technology for creating markup languages.
b) Forward and backward slashes (**/** and ****) delimit XML markup text.
c) All XML start tags must have corresponding end tags.
d) Parsers check an XML document's syntax and may support the Document Object Model or the Simple API for XML.
e) URIs are strings that identify resources such as files, images, services, electronic mailboxes and more.
f) When creating new XML tags, document authors must use the set of XML tags that the W3C provides.
b) The pound character (**#**), the dollar sign (**$**), ampersand (**&**), greater-than (**>**) and less-than (**<**) are examples of XML reserved characters.

20.3 Fill in the blanks for each of the following statements:
a) MathML element _________ defines a mathematical operator.

b) __________ help avoid naming collisions.
c) __________ embed application-specific information into an XML document.
d) __________ is Microsoft's XML parser.
e) XSL element __________ inserts a **DOCTYPE** in the result tree.
f) XML Schema documents have root element __________.
g) Element __________ marks up the **∫** MathML symbol.
h) __________ defines element attributes in a DTD.
i) XSL element __________ is the root element in an XSL document.
j) XSL element __________ selects specific XML elements using repetition.

20.4 State which of the following statements are *true* and which are *false*. If *false*, explain why.
a) XML is not case sensitive.
b) An XML document may contain only one root element.
c) XML displays information.
d) A DTD/Schema defines the style of an XML document.
e) Element **xsl:for-each** is similar to JavaScript's **for/in** structure.
f) MathML is an XML vocabulary.
g) XSL is an acronym for XML Stylesheet Language.
h) The **<!ELEMENT list (item*)>** defines element **list** as containing one or more **item** elements.
b) XML documents must have the **.xml** extension.

20.5 Find the error(s) in each of the following and explain how to correct it (them).
a)
```
<job>
   <title>Manager</title>
   <task number = "42">
</job>
```
b)
```
<mfrac>
   <mi>x</mi>
   <mo>+</mo>
   <mn>4</mn>
   <mi>y</mi>
</mfrac>
```
c)
```
<company name = "Deitel & Associates, Inc." />
```

20.6 In Fig. 20.1 we subdivided the **author** element into more detailed pieces. How would you subdivide the **date** element?

20.7 What is the **#PCDATA** flag used for?

20.8 Write a processing instruction that includes the stylesheet **wap.xsl**.

ANSWERS TO SELF-REVIEW EXERCISES

20.1 a, b, d, i, j.

20.2 a) True. b) False. In an XML document, markup text is delimited by angle brackets (**<** and **>**) with a forward slash being used in the end tag. c) True. d) True. e) True. f) False. When creating new tags, document authors may use any valid name except the reserved word **xml** (also **XML**, **Xml**, etc.). g) False. XML reserved characters include the ampersand (**&**), the left-angle bracket (**<**) and the right-angle bracket (**>**) but not **#** and **$**.

20.3 a) **mo**. b) namespaces. c) processing instructions. d) msxml. e) **xsl:output**. f) **schema**. g) **mo**. h) **!ATTLIST**. i) **xsl:stylesheet**. j) **xsl:for-each**.

20.4 a) False. XML is case sensitive. b) True. c) False. XML is used to organize material in a structured manner. d) False. A DTD/schema defines the structure of an XML document. e) True. f) True. g) False. XSL is an acronym for Extensible Stylesheet Language. h) False. **(item*)** defines a **list** element containing any number of optional **item** elements. i) False. An XML document can have any extension.

20.5 a) The closing **/** in the empty element is missing:

```
<task number = "42"/>
```

b) **<mrow>** tag is needed to contain $x + 2$.

c) A character entity needs to be used to represent the ampersand:

```
<company name = "Deitel &amp; Associates, Inc." />
```

20.6

```
<date>
<month>September</month>
<day>19</day>
<year>2001</year>
</date>
```

20.7 Flag **#PCDATA** denotes that parsed character data is contained in the element.

20.8

```
<?xsl:stylesheet type = "text/xsl" href = "wap.xsl"?>
```

EXERCISES

20.9 Create an XML document that marks up the nutrition facts for a package of Grandma Deitel's Cookies. A package of Grandma Deitel's Cookies has a serving size of 1 package and the following nutritional value per serving: 260 calories, 100 fat calories, 11 grams of fat, 2 grams of saturated fat, 5 milligrams of cholesterol, 210 milligrams of sodium, 36 grams of total carbohydrates, 2 grams of fiber, 15 grams of sugar and 5 grams of protein. Load the XML document in Internet Explorer 5.5. [*Hint*: Your markup should contain elements that describe the product name, serving size/amount, calories, sodium, cholesterol, protein, etc. Mark up each nutrition fact/ingredient listed above.]

20.10 Write an XSL stylesheet for your solution to Exercise 20.9 that displays the nutritional facts in an XHTML table.

20.11 Write a DTD for Fig 20.1.

20.12 Using Amaya and MathML, generate the following mathematical expressions:

a) $\int_{-\frac{1}{2}}^{0} 5y\delta x$

b) $y = 2x - b^3 - 6cy^{kx} + 9$

c) $x = \sqrt{(2y^{-3})} - 8y + \frac{\sqrt{y}}{3}$

20.13 Write an XML document that marks up the following information in Fig. 20.29.

20.14 Write a DTD for the XML document in Exercise 20.13.

20.15 Modify your solution to Exercise 20.13 to qualify each person with a namespace prefix corresponding to their job. Your solution should not have the job as either an element or attribute.

20.16 Write an XSLT document that transforms the XML document of Exercise 20.13 into an XHTML sorted list.

20.17 Modify Fig. 20.26 (**sorting.xsl**) to sort by page number, rather than by chapter number.

20.18 Write the DTD for Fig. 20.28.

Name	Job	Department	Cubicle
Joe	Programmer	Engineering	5E
Erin	Designer	Marketing	9M
Melissa	Designer	Human Resources	8H
Craig	Administrator	Engineering	4E
Eileen	Project Coordinator	Marketing	3M
Danielle	Programmer	Engineering	12E
Frank	Salesperson	Marketing	17M
Corinne	Programmer	Technical Support	19T

Fig. 20.29 Data for Exercise 20.13.

20.19 Write JavaScript code that uses the DOM to replace every job description (from Exercise 20.13) that matches "Programmer" with "Developer."

21

Web Servers (IIS, PWS and Apache)

Objectives

- To understand a Web server's functionality.
- To introduce client-side scripting and server-side scripting.
- To introduce Microsoft Internet Information Services (IIS), Microsoft Personal Web Server (PWS) and Apache Web Server.
- To learn how to request documents from a Web server.

In fact, a fundamental interdependence exists between the personal right to liberty and the personal right to property.
Potter Stewart

Stop abusing my verses, or publish some of your own.
Marcus Valerius Martialis

There are three difficulties in authorship: to write anything worth the publishing, to find honest men to publish it, and to get sensible men to read it.
Charles Caleb Colton

When your Daemon is in charge, do not try to think consciously. Drift, wait and obey.
Rudyard Kipling

Outline

21.1 Introduction

In this chapter, we discuss specialized software—called a *Web server*—that responds to client (e.g., Web browser) requests by providing resources (e.g., XHTML documents). For example, when users enter a *Uniform Resource Locator* (*URL*) address, such as **`www.deitel.com`**, into a Web browser, they are requesting a specific document from a Web server. The Web server maps the URL to a file on the server (or to a file on the server's network) and returns the requested document to the client. During this interaction, the Web server and the client communicate using the platform-independent *HyperText Transfer Protocol* (*HTTP*), a protocol for transferring requests and files over the Internet (i.e., between Web servers and Web browsers).

Our Web-server discussion introduces *Microsoft Internet Information Services* (*IIS*), *Microsoft Personal Web Server* (*PWS*) and the open source *Apache Web Server*. Sections 21.6, 21.7 and 21.8 discuss IIS, PWS and Apache, respectively. Figure 21.1 overviews these Web servers.

For illustration purposes, we use Internet Explorer to request various documents—XHTML, Active Server Pages (ASP), Perl, Python and PHP. We discuss the specifics of ASP (Chapter 25), Perl (Chapter 27), Python (Chapter 28) and PHP (Chapter 29). This chapter concentrates on the steps for requesting documents from a Web server.

	IIS	PWS	Apache
Company	Microsoft Corporation	Microsoft Corporation	Apache Software Foundation
Version	5.0	4.0	1.3.20
Released	2/17/00	12/4/97	5/21/01
Platforms	Windows 2000	Windows 95/98/ Millennium Edition (Me)/NT	UNIX, Windows NT/2000, experimentally supports Windows 95/98
Brief description	The most popular Web server for Windows 2000.	A basic Web server for publishing personal Web pages.	Currently the most popular Web server.
Price	Included with Windows 2000.	Freeware. Packaged with Microsoft IIS in NT 4.0 Option Pack. Also included in Windows 98.	Freeware.

Fig. 21.1 Web servers discussed in this chapter.

21.2 HTTP Request Types

The two most common *HTTP request types* (also known as *request methods*) are *get* and *post*. These request types retrieve and send client form data to a Web server. A *get* request sends form content as part of the URL (e.g., **www.searchsomething.com/search?query=userquery**) and retrieves the appropriate resource from the Web server. In this request, the information following the **?** (**query=userquery**) indicates the user-specified input. For example, if the user performs a search on "Massachusetts," the last part of the URL would be **?query=Massachusetts**. A *get* request limits the **userquery** to 1024 characters. If **userquery** exceeds this limit, the *post* request is used. Also, the *post* request updates the contents of a Web server (e.g., posting a new message to a forum).

Software Engineering Observation 21.1

The data sent in a post *request is not part of the URL and cannot be seen by the user. Forms that contain many fields are submitted most often by a* post *request. Sensitive form fields, such as passwords, usually are sent using this request type.*

An HTTP request often posts data to a *server-side form handler* that processes the data. For example, when a user participates in a Web-based survey, the Web server receives the information specified in the XHTML form as part of the request.

Browsers often *cache* (save on a local disk) Web pages for quick reloading, to reduce the amount of data that the browser needs to download. However, browsers typically do not cache the server's response to a *post* request, because the next *post* request may not contain the same information. For example, several users participating in a Web-based survey may request the same Web page. Each user's response changes the overall results of the survey, thus the data on the Web server is changed.

On the other hand, Web browsers cache the server's responses to a *get* request. With a Web-based search engine, a *get* request normally supplies the search engine with the information specified in the XHTML form. The search engine then performs the search and returns the results as a Web page. These pages are cached in the event that the user performs the same search again.

21.3 System Architecture

A Web server is part of a *multi-tier application*, sometimes referred to as an *n*-tier application. Multi-tier applications divide functionality into separate tiers (i.e., logical groupings of functionality). Tiers can be located on the same computer or on separate computers. Figure 21.2 presents the basic structure of a three-tier application.

The *information tier* (also called the *data tier* or the *bottom tier*) maintains data for the application. This tier typically stores data in a *relational database management system (RDBMS)*. We discuss RDBMS in further detail in Chapter 22, Database: SQL, MySQL, DBI and ADO. For example, a retail store may have a database for product information, such as descriptions, prices and quantities in stock. The same database also may contain customer information, such as user names, billing addresses and credit-card numbers.

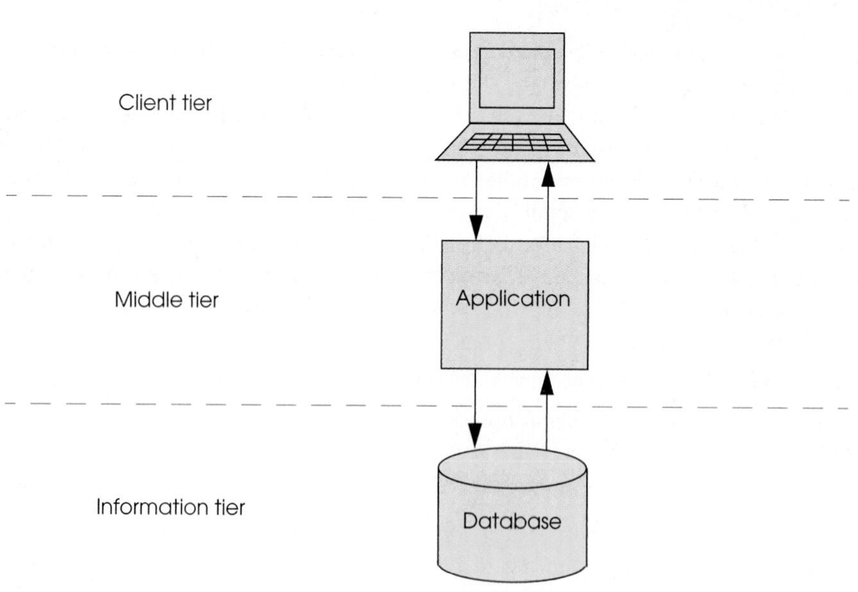

Fig. 21.2 Three-tier application model.

The *middle tier* implements *business logic* and *presentation logic* to control interactions between application clients and application data. The middle tier acts as an intermediary between data in the information tier and the application clients. The middle-tier *controller logic* processes client requests from the top tier (e.g., a request to view a product catalog) and retrieves data from the database. The middle-tier presentation logic then processes data from the information tier and presents the content to the client.

Business logic in the middle tier enforces *business rules* and ensures that data are reliable before updating the database or presenting data to a user. Business rules dictate how clients can and cannot access application data and how applications process data.

The middle tier also implements the application's presentation logic. Web applications typically present information to clients as XHTML documents (older applications present information as HTML). XHTML is discussed in Chapter 4, Introduction to XHTML: Part 1 and Chapter 5, Introduction to XHTML: Part 2. Many Web applications present information to wireless clients as Wireless Markup Language (WML) documents. We discuss WML in further detail in Chapter 23, Wireless Internet and m-Business.

The *client tier*, or *top tier*, is the application's user interface. Users interact directly with the application through the user interface. The client interacts with the middle tier to make requests and to retrieve data from the information tier. The client then displays the data retrieved from the middle tier to the user.

21.4 Client-Side Scripting versus Server-Side Scripting

In earlier chapters, we focused on client-side scripting with JavaScript. *Client-side scripting* validates user input, accesses the browser and enhances Web pages with ActiveX® controls, Dynamic HTML and *Java applets* (i.e., client-side Java programs that execute in a browser). Client-side *validation* reduces the number of requests that need to be passed to the server. Interactivity allows users to make decisions, click buttons, play games, etc.—making a Web site experience more interesting. ActiveX controls, Dynamic HTML and Java applets enhance a Web page's functionality. Client-side scripts can access the browser, use features specific to that browser and manipulate browser documents.

Client-side scripting does have limitations, such as browser dependency; the browser or *scripting host* must support the scripting language. Another limitation is that client-side scripts are viewable (e.g., by using the **View** menu's **Source** command in Internet Explorer) to the client. Some Web developers do not advocate this because users potentially can view proprietary scripting code. Sensitive information, such as passwords, should not be stored or validated on the client.

Software Engineering Observation 21.2

JavaScript is the most popular client-side scripting language and is supported by both Microsoft Internet Explorer and Netscape Communicator.

Performance Tip 21.1

To conserve server resources and minimize Internet traffic and delays, perform as much processing as possible on the client side.

Programmers have greater flexibility when using *server-side scripts*. Scripts executed on the server usually generate custom responses for clients. For example, a client might connect to an airline's Web server and request a list of all flights from Boston to San Antonio between September 19th and November 5th. The server queries the database, dynamically generates XHTML content containing the flight list and sends the XHTML to the client. This technology allows clients to obtain the most current flight information from the database by connecting to an airline's Web server.

Server-side scripting languages have a wider range of programmatic capabilities than their client-side equivalents. For example, server-side scripts can access the server's file directory structure, whereas client-side scripts cannot access the client's file directory.

Server-side scripts also have access to server-side software that extends server functionality. These pieces of software are called *ActiveX components* for Microsoft Web servers and *modules* for Apache Web servers. Components and modules range from programming language support to counting the number of Web page *hits*. We discuss some of these components and modules in Chapters 25–33.

Software Engineering Observation 21.3

Server-side scripts are not visible to the client; only XHTML (plus any client-side) scripts are visible to the client.

21.5 Accessing Web Servers

To request documents from Web servers, users must know the machine names (called *host names*) on which Web server software resides. Users can request documents from *local Web servers* (i.e, ones residing on users' machines) or *remote Web servers* (i.e., ones residing on different machines).

Local Web servers can be accessed in two ways: through the machine name or through ***localhost***—a host name that references the local machine. We use **localhost** in this book. To determine the machine name in Windows 98, right-click **Network Neighborhood**, and select **Properties** from the context menu to display the **Network** dialog. In the **Network** dialog, click the **Identification** tab. The computer name displays in the **Computer name:** field. Click **Cancel** to close the **Network** dialog. In Windows 2000, right click **My Network Places** and select **Properties** from the context menu to display the **Network and Dialup Connections** explorer. In the explorer, click **Network Identification**. The **Full Computer Name:** field in the **System Properties** window displays the computer name.

To request a document from a remote Web server in Windows 98, double click **Network Neighborhood**, which lists all the machine names in the network. From this list, select the name of the machine running the remote Web server. In Windows 2000, double click **My Network Places**, and double click **Computers Near Me**. This, too, lists all the machine names in the network. From this list, select the name of the machine running the remote Web server.

A *domain name* (e.g., **deitel** or **yahoo**) and an *Internet Protocol (IP) address* also can request documents. A domain name represents a group of hosts on the Internet; it combines with a host name (i.e, **www**—World Wide Web) and a *top-level domain (TLD)* to form a *fully qualified host name*, which provides a user-friendly way to identify a site on the Internet. In a fully qualified host name, the TLD often describes the type of organization that owns the domain name. For example, the **com** TLD usually refers to a commercial business, whereas the **org** TLD usually refers to a non-profit organization. In addition, each country has its own TLD, such as **cn** for China, **et** for Ethiopia, **om** for Oman and **us** for the United States.

Each fully qualified host name is assigned a unique address called an *IP address*, which is much like the street address of a house. Just as people use street addresses to locate houses or businesses in a city, computers use IP addresses to locate other computers on the Internet. The *domain name server (DNS)*, a computer that maintains a database of host names and their corresponding IP addresses, translates the fully qualified host name to an IP address. The translation operation is referred to as a *DNS lookup*. For example, to access the Deitel Web site, type either **www.deitel.com** or **207.60.134.230** into a Web browser. The DNS translates **www.deitel.com** into the IP address of the Deitel Web server (i.e., **207.60.134.230**). The IP address of **localhost** is always **127.0.0.1**.

21.6 Microsoft Internet Information Services (IIS)[1]

Microsoft Internet Information Services (IIS) 5.0 is an enterprise-level Web server that is included with Windows 2000. Installing IIS on a machine allows that computer to serve documents. For instructions on how to install IIS, visit **www.deitel.com**.

After installation, start IIS by opening the **Control Panel**, double clicking the **Administrative Tools** icon and double clicking the **Internet Services Manager** icon. This opens the *Internet Services Manager* dialog (Fig. 21.3)—the administration program for IIS. Place the documents that will be requested from IIS either in the *default directory* (i.e., **C:\Inetpub\Wwwroot**) or in a *virtual directory*. A virtual directory is an alias for an existing directory that resides on the local machine (e.g., **C:**) or on the network.

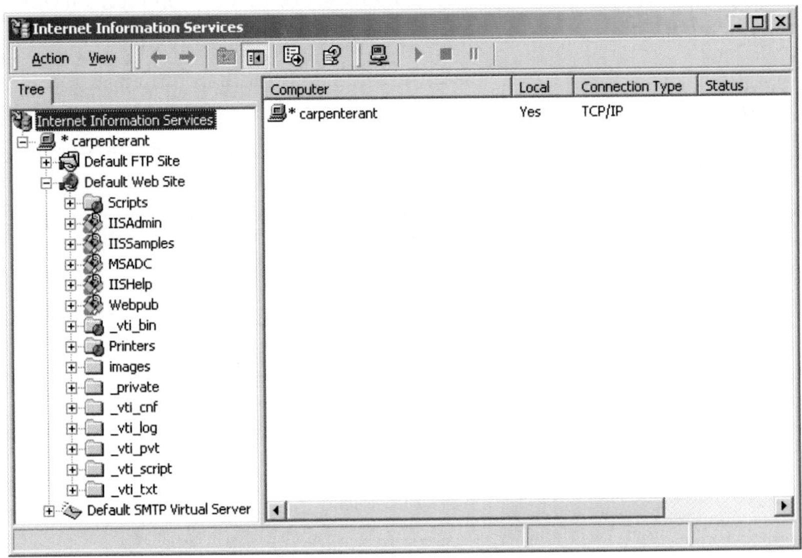

Fig. 21.3 Internet Services Manager dialog of **Internet Information Services**.

1. This section applies to Windows 2000 users.

In the Internet Services Manager dialog, the left pane contains the Web server's directory structure. The name of the machine running IIS (e.g., **carpenterant**) is listed under **Internet Information Services**. Clicking the **+** symbol to the left of the machine name displays **Default FTP Site**, **Default Web Site** and **Default SMTP Virtual Server**.

The **Default FTP Site** is a *File Transfer Protocol (FTP)* site; the **Default Web Site** is an HTTP site. Although FTP and HTTP permit transferring documents between a computer and a Web server, FTP provides a faster and more persistent connection between the client and the Web server than HTTP. HTTP is used most frequently to request documents from Web servers. The **Default SMTP Virtual Server** allows for the creation of a *Simple Mail Transfer Protocol (SMTP)* server, which sends and receives *electronic mail (e-mail)*.

Expand the **Default Web Site** directory by clicking the **+** to the left of it. In this directory we will create a virtual directory for the HTTP Web site. The **Default Web Site** subdirectories are virtual directories. Most Web documents are placed in the Web server's **Webpub** (Web publishing) directory. For this example, we create our virtual directory in the **Webpub** virtual directory. To create a virtual directory within this directory, right-click **Webpub**, select **New** and then **Virtual Directory**. This starts the **Virtual Directory Creation Wizard** (Fig. 21.4), which guides users through the virtual directory creation process.

To begin, click **Next** in the **Virtual Directory Creation Wizard** welcome dialog. In the **Virtual Directory Alias** dialog (Fig. 21.5), enter a name for the virtual directory and click **Next**. We use the name **Chapter21Test**, although the virtual directory may have any name provided that the name does not conflict with an existing virtual directory name.

In the **Web Site Content Directory** dialog (Fig. 21.6), enter the path for the directory containing the documents that clients will view. We created a directory named `C:\Chapter21Examples` that serves our documents, although any existing directory would be appropriate. If necessary, select the **Browse** button to navigate to the desired directory. Click **Next**.

Fig. 21.4 **Virtual Directory Creation Wizard** welcome dialog.

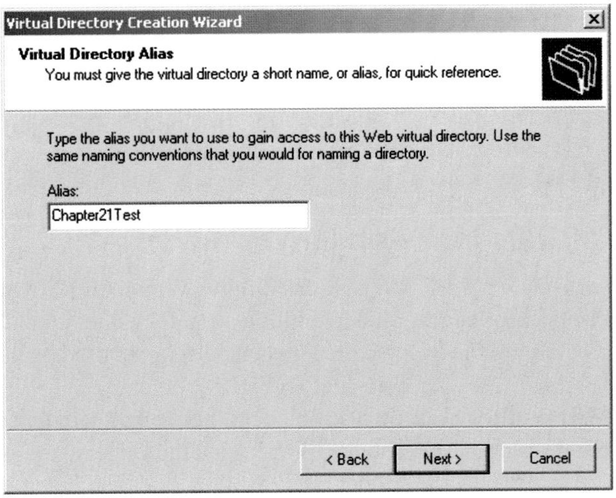

Fig. 21.5 **Virtual Directory Alias** dialog of **Virtual Directory Creation Wizard**.

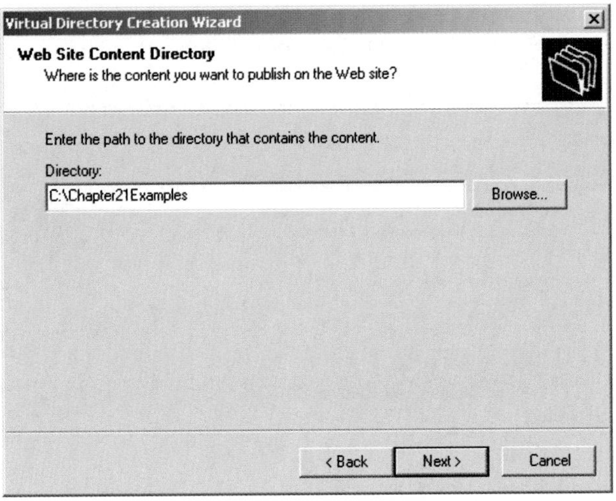

Fig. 21.6 **Web Site Content Directory** dialog of **Virtual Directory Creation Wizard**.

The **Access Permissions** dialog (Fig. 21.7) presents the virtual directory *security level* choices. Choose the access level appropriate for a Web document. The ***Read*** option allows users to read and download files located within the directory. The ***Run scripts (such as ASP)*** option allows scripts to run in the directory. The ***Execute (such as ISAPI applications or CGI)*** option allows applications to run in the directory. The ***Write*** option allows a Web page to accept user input (e.g., users enter their credit-card number to order a book). The ***Browse*** option allows users to navigate from one Web document to another through hyperlinks. By default, **Read** and **Run scripts** are enabled. Click **Next**.

Click **Finish** to complete the creation of the virtual directory and exit the **Virtual Directory Creation Wizard**. The newly created virtual directory, **Chapter21Test**, is now located under the **Webpub** virtual directory. To stop IIS, right click **Default Web Site** (or **Default FTP Site** or **Default SMTP Virtual Server**) and select **Stop**.

21.7 Microsoft Personal Web Server (PWS)[2]

Microsoft Personal Web Server (PWS) is a scaled-down version of IIS for a personal computer (PC). PWS is ideal for educational institutions, small businesses and individuals because PWS does not require the PC on which it is installed to be used exclusively as a Web server.

To install PWS, visit **`www.microsoft.com/msdownload/ntoptionpack/askwiz.asp`**. For instructions on installing PWS, visit the Deitel & Associates, Inc. Web site at **`www.deitel.com`**.

After installation, start PWS by opening the **Control Panel**. Double click the **Administration Tools** icon and double click the **Personal Web Manager** icon. To serve documents using PWS, place the files that will be requested in the default directory (i.e., **`C:\Inetpub\Wwwroot`**) or in a *virtual directory*. A virtual directory is an alias for an existing directory that resides on the local machine (e.g., **`C:\`**) or on the network. Figure 21.8 shows the **Personal Web Manager** dialog.

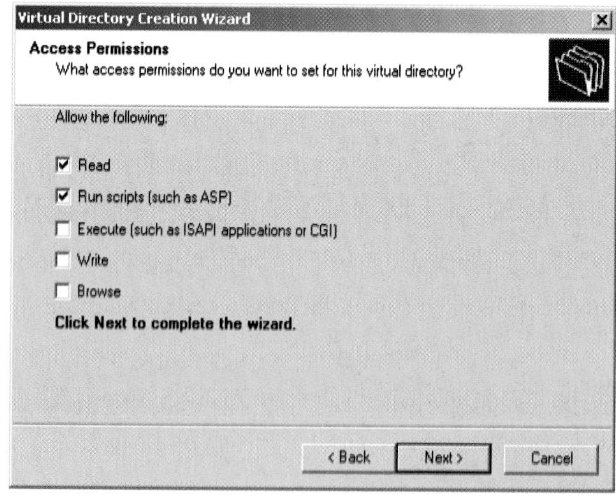

Fig. 21.7 **Access Permissions** dialog of **Virtual Directory Creation Wizard**.

2. This section applies to Windows 95/98/Me users.

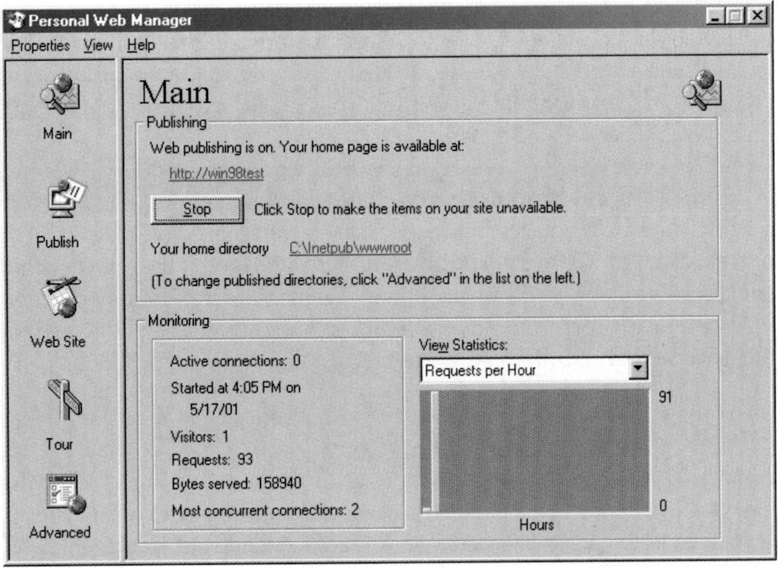

Fig. 21.8 **Personal Web Manager** dialog.

On the **Main** screen, double click the **Advanced** icon at the bottom of the left pane. In the screen that appears, click the **Add** button. In the **Directory** field of the **Edit Directory** dialog (Fig. 21.9), enter the directory path that contains the documents available to clients. We created a directory named `C:\Chapter21Examples` to serve our documents. You may choose any existing directory. If necessary, select the **Browse** button to navigate to the directory. In the **Alias** field, provide the virtual directory name (e.g., `Chapter21Test`). Next, select the security level of the virtual directory. The **Read** option allows users to read and download files residing in the virtual directory. The **Execute** option allows an application to run in the directory. The **Scripts** option allows scripts to run in the directory. By default, **Read** and **Scripts** are enabled. When finished, click **OK** to create the directory. To stop PWS, select the `Stop` button from the `Personal Web Manager` dialog.

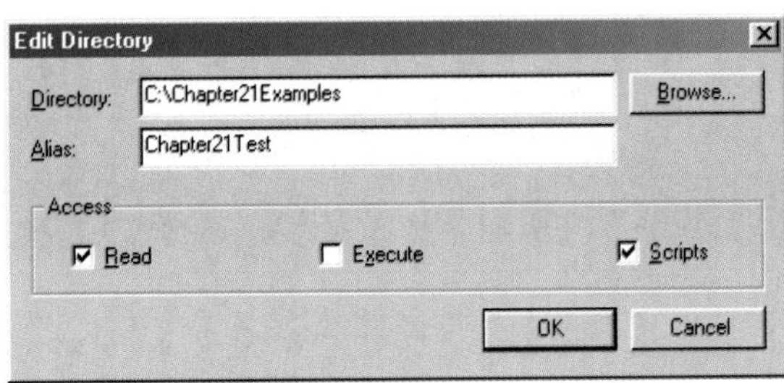

Fig. 21.9 Creating a virtual directory in PWS in **Edit Directory**.

21.8 Apache Web Server[3]

The Apache Web server, maintained by the Apache Software Foundation, is currently the most popular Web server because of its stability, efficiency and portability. It is an open source product (i.e., software that can be freely obtained and customized) that runs on UNIX, Linux and Windows platforms.

To install the Apache Web server, visit **www.apache.org**. *For instructions on installing Apache, visit* **www.deitel.com**. After installing the Apache Web server, start the application to serve Web pages. From the **Start** menu, successively select **Programs**, **Apache httpd Server**, **Control Apache Server** and **Start**. If the server starts successfully, a command-prompt window opens stating that the service is starting (Fig. 21.10). To stop the Apache Web server, from the **Start** menu, successively select **Programs**, **Apache httpd Server**, **Control Apache Server** and **Stop**.

21.9 Requesting Documents

This section demonstrates how to request five different documents—XHTML, Active Server Pages (ASP), Perl, Python and PHP. We discuss serving these documents using IIS, PWS and Apache Web server. We start with XHTML documents. [*Note*: This section discusses how to serve documents using a Web server; we discuss how to *create* ASP, Perl, Python and PHP documents in Chapters 25, 27, 28 and 29, respectively. To render ASP, Perl, Python and PHP documents, the respective programming languages must be installed on your computer. Visit the Deitel & Associates, Inc. Web site (**www.deitel.com**) to obtain installation instructions for these various programming languages.]

21.9.1 XHTML

This section shows how to request an XHTML document from the IIS, PWS and Apache Web servers. If you are using IIS or PWS, copy **test.html** from the Chapter 21 examples directory on the CD-ROM accompanying this book into **C:\Chapter21Examples** (or to the directory you created in Sections 21.6 or 21.7). We copy the XHTML document into the directory that references our virtual directory (**Chapter21Test**). [*Note*: A file cannot be copied directly to a virtual directory.] To request the document from IIS, launch Internet Explorer and enter the XHTML document's location in the **Address** field (i.e., **http://localhost/Webpub/Chapter21Test/test.html**). Figure 21.11 displays the result of requesting **test.html**.

Fig. 21.10 Starting the Apache Web server. (Courtesy of The Apache Software Foundation)

3. This section applies to Windows NT/2000, Unix and Linux users.

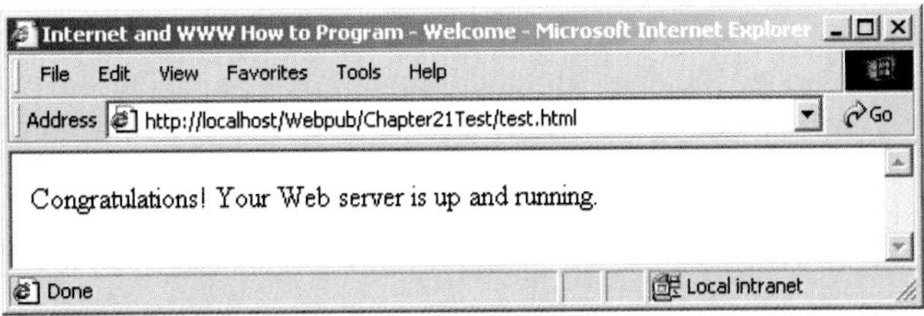

Fig. 21.11 Requesting **test.html** from IIS.

To request **test.html** from PWS, launch Internet Explorer and enter the XHTML document's location in the **Address** field (i.e., **http://localhost/Chapter21Test/*test.html***). Figure 21.12 displays the result of requesting **test.html**.

In the Apache Web server, XHTML documents need to be saved in the ***htdocs*** default directory. On a Windows platform, the **htdocs** directory resides in **C:\Program Files\Apache Group\Apache**; on a Linux platform, the **htdocs** directory resides in the **/usr/local/httpd** directory. Copy the **test.html** document from the Chapter 21 examples directory on the CD-ROM into the **htdocs** directory; all XHTML files need to reside in this directory. To request the document, launch Internet Explorer (or your UNIX/Linux equivalent browser) and enter the XHTML document's location in the **Address** field (i.e., **http://localhost/test.html**). Figure 21.13 shows the result of requesting **test.html**. [*Note*: In Apache, **localhost** refers to the default directory, **htdocs**, so we do not enter the directory name in the **Address** field.]

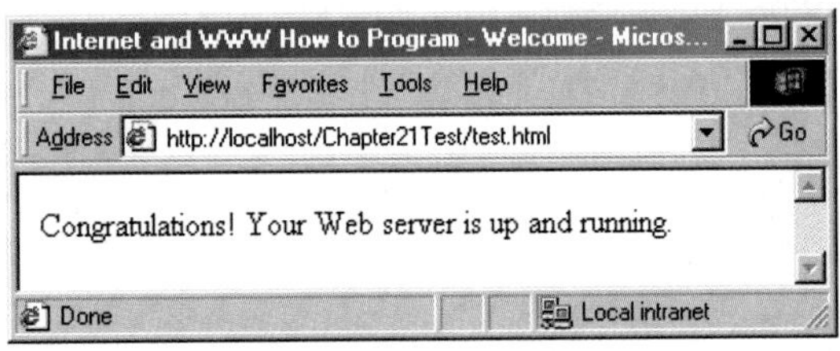

Fig. 21.12 Requesting **test.html** from PWS.

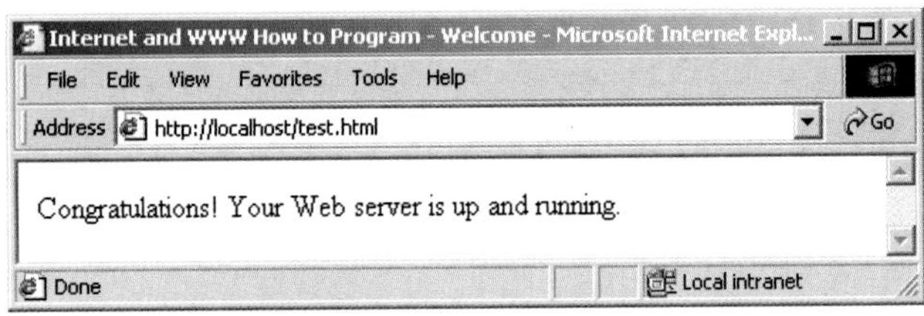

Fig. 21.13 Requesting **test.html** from Apache.

21.9.2 ASP

In addition to XHTML documents, IIS and PWS can serve Active Server Pages (ASP) documents. Currently, the Apache Web server does not provide support for ASP.

To request an ASP document, copy the **test.asp** file from the Chapter 21 examples directory on the CD-ROM into **C:\Chapter21Examples** (or the directory created in Sections 21.6 or 21.7). We copy the ASP document into the directory that references our virtual directory (**Chapter21Test**). To request the document from IIS, launch Internet Explorer and enter the ASP document's location in the **Address** field (i.e., **http://localhost/Webpub/Chapter21Test/test.asp**). Figure 21.14 displays the result of requesting **test.asp**.

To request **test.asp** from PWS, launch Internet Explorer and enter the ASP document's location in the **Address** field (i.e., **http://localhost/Chapter21Test/test.asp**). Figure 21.15 displays the result of requesting **test.asp**.

21.9.3 Perl

IIS, PWS and Apache Web servers can request Perl documents. To request a Perl document, copy the file **test.pl** from the Chapter 21 examples directory on the CD-ROM to **C:\Chapter21Examples** (or the directory you created in Sections 21.6 or 21.7). We copy the Perl document into the directory that references our virtual directory (**Chapter21Test**). To request the document from IIS, launch Internet Explorer and enter the Perl document's location in the **Address** field (i.e., **http://localhost/Webpub/Chapter21Test/test.pl**). Figure 21.16 displays the result of requesting **test.pl**.

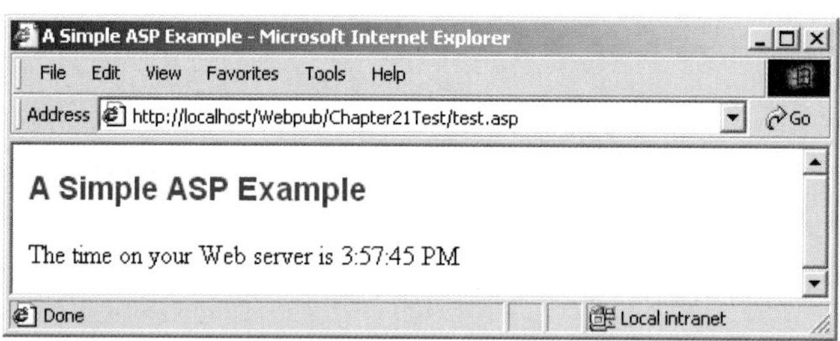

Fig. 21.14 Requesting **test.asp** from IIS.

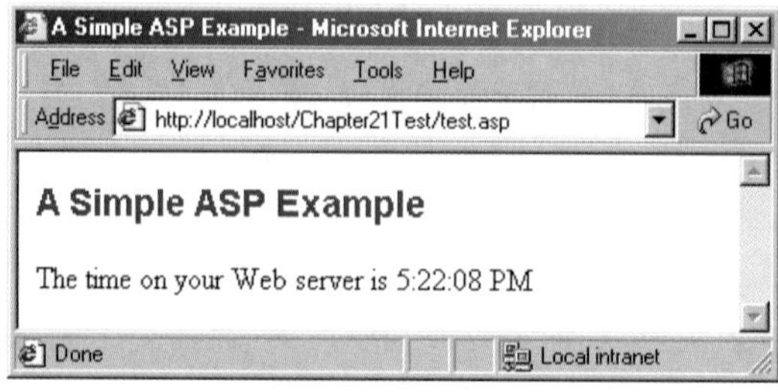

Fig. 21.15 Requesting **test.asp** from PWS.

Fig. 21.16 Requesting **test.pl** from IIS.

To request **test.pl** from PWS, launch Internet Explorer and enter the Perl document's location in the **Address** field (i.e., **http://localhost/Chapter21Test/test.pl**). Figure 21.17 displays the result of requesting **test.pl**.

To request Perl documents on the Apache Web server, copy the **test.pl** file from the Chapter 21 examples directory on the CD-ROM to the ***cgi-bin*** directory. On a Windows platform, the **cgi-bin** directory resides in **C:\Program Files\Apache Group\Apache**; on a Linux platform, it resides in the **/usr/local/httpd** directory. All Perl documents must reside in the **cgi-bin** directory, because certain environment variables have been registered that recognize the document. To request the document, launch Internet Explorer (or your UNIX/Linux equivalent browser) and enter the Perl document's location in the **Address** field (i.e., **http://localhost/cgi-bin/test.pl**). Figure 21.18 displays the result of requesting **test.pl**.

21.9.4 Python

IIS, PWS and Apache Web servers can request Python documents. To request a Python document, copy the file **test.py** from the Chapter 21 examples directory on the CD-ROM to **C:\Chapter21Examples** (or the directory you created in Sections 21.6 or 21.7). We copy the Python document into the directory that references our virtual directory (**Chapter21Test**). To request the document from IIS, launch Internet Explorer and enter the Python document's location in the **Address** field (i.e., **http://localhost/Webpub/Chapter21Test/test.py**). Figure 21.19 displays the result of requesting **test.py**.

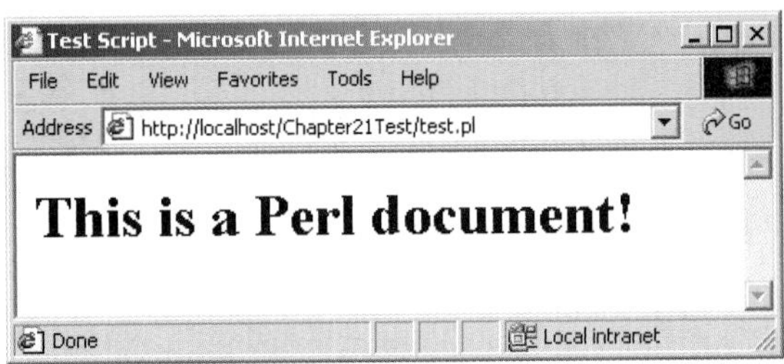

Fig. 21.17 Requesting **test.pl** from PWS.

Fig. 21.18 Requesting **test.pl** from Apache.

Fig. 21.19 Requesting **test.py** from IIS.

To request **test.py** from PWS, launch Internet Explorer and enter the Python document's location in the **Address** field (i.e., **http://localhost/Chapter21Test/test.py**). Figure 21.20 displays the result of requesting **test.py**.

To request Python documents on the Apache Web server, copy the file **test.py** from the Chapter 21 examples directory on the CD-ROM to the **cgi-bin** directory. On a Windows platform, the **cgi-bin** directory resides in **C:\Program Files\Apache Group\Apache**; on a Linux platform, it resides in the **/usr/local/httpd** directory. All Python documents must reside in the **cgi-bin** directory, because certain environment variables have been registered that recognize the document. To request the document, launch Internet Explorer (or the UNIX/Linux equivalent browser) and enter the Python document's location in the **Address** field (i.e., **http://localhost/cgi-bin/test.py**). Figure 21.21 displays the result of requesting **test.py**.

Fig. 21.20 Requesting **test.py** from PWS.

Fig. 21.21 Requesting **`test.py`** from Apache.

21.9.5 PHP

IIS, PWS and Apache Web servers can request PHP documents. To request a PHP document, copy the file **`test.php`** from the Chapter 21 examples directory on the CD-ROM into **`C:\Chapter21Examples`** (or the directory you created in Sections 21.6 or 21.7). We copy the PHP document into the directory that references our virtual directory (**`Chapter21Test`**). [*Note*: A file cannot be copied directly to a virtual directory.] To request the document from IIS, launch Internet Explorer and enter the PHP document's location in the **Address** field (i.e., **`http://localhost/Webpub/Chapter21Test/test.php`**). Figure 21.22 displays the result of requesting **`test.php`**.

To request **`test.php`** from PWS, launch Internet Explorer and enter the PHP document's location in the **Address** field (i.e., **`http://localhost/Chapter21Test/test.php`**). Figure 21.23 displays the result of requesting **`test.php`**.

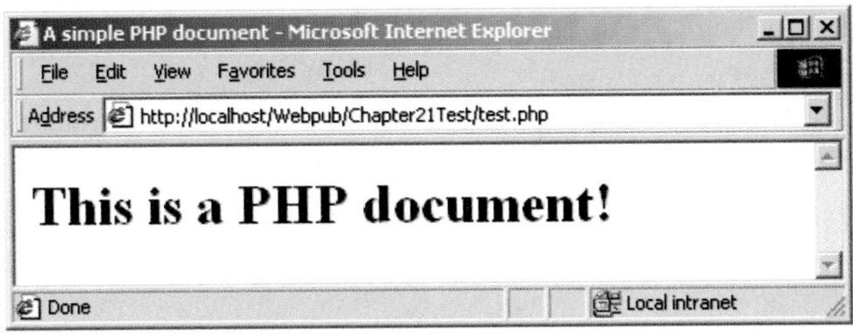

Fig. 21.22 Requesting **`test.php`** from IIS.

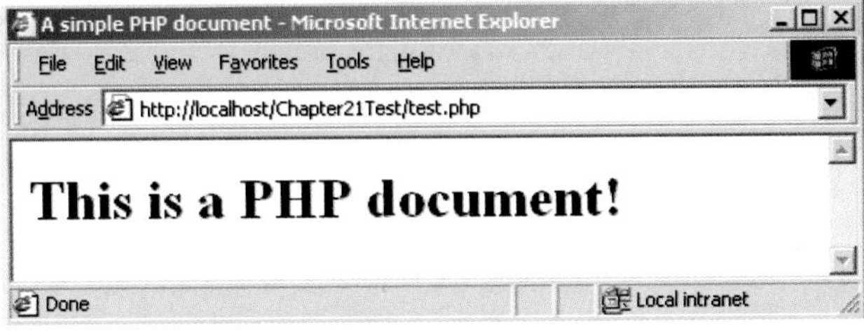

Fig. 21.23 Requesting **`test.php`** from PWS.

To request PHP documents on the Apache Web server, copy the file **`test.php`** from the Chapter 21 examples directory on the CD-ROM to the **`htdocs`** directory. On a Windows platform, the **`htdocs`** directory resides in **`C:\Program Files\Apache Group\Apache`**; on a Linux platform, it resides in the **`/usr/local/httpd`** directory. Save PHP documents in the **`htdocs`** directory. To request the document, launch Internet Explorer (or a UNIX/Linux equivalent browser) and enter the PHP document's location in the **Address** field (i.e., **`http://localhost/test.php`**). Figure 21.24 displays the result of requesting **`test.php`**.

21.10 Internet and World Wide Web Resources

This section lists several URLs for downloading Web servers, Option Packs, etc.

`www.microsoft.com/msdownload/ntoptionpack/askwiz.asp`
Visit this site to download the Windows NT 4.0 Option Pack, which can be installed on Windows 95/2000/NT.

`www.w3.org/Protocols`
The World Wide Web Consortium (W3C) Web site contains information on the HTTP specification. The site contains links to news, mailing lists and published articles.

`www.apache.org/`
The Apache Software Foundation was created to protect the use of Apache software products. This is the product home page for the Apache Web server.

`www.apacheweek.com/`
The online magazine Apache Week contains articles about Apache jobs, product reviews and other information concerning Apache software.

`linuxtoday.com/stories/18780.html`
This site contains an article discussing the widespread use of the Apache Web server. It contains links to other articles that discuss Apache.

`g-lea.tamu.edu/Getstart.htm`
Users can download Microsoft PWS from this Web site and receive help installing and configuring PWS.

`www.iisanswers.com`
The *IIS Answers* Web site provides links to articles that discuss IIS topics. The articles cover issues from installation to security.

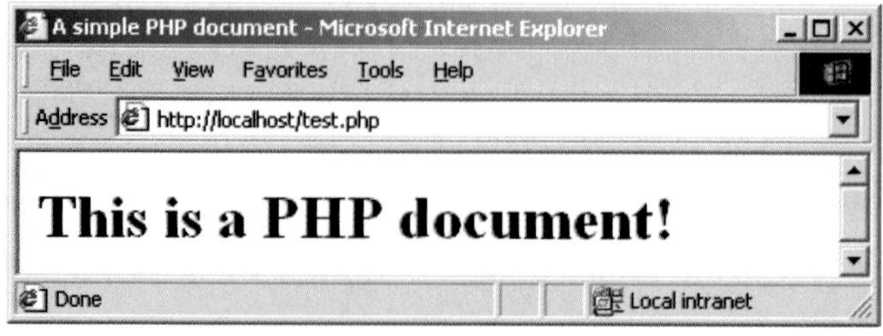

Fig. 21.24 Requesting **`test.php`** from Apache.

`www.iisadministrator.com`
The *IIS Administrator* Web site is a technical newsletter that provides tips and techniques for maintaining IIS.

`www.alphasierra.com/iisdev`
The *IIS Development* Web site provides information on how to publish ASP documents using IIS. The site contains links to various ASP components, code and resources.

`dynamicnet.net/support/fp/perlwithPWS.htm`
The *Dynamic Net* Web site provides instructions for executing Perl scripts on PWS.

`msdn.microsoft.com/library/officedev/office97/settinguppersonal-webserver.htm`
This Web page lists the installation requirements of PWS, explains how to install PWS and discusses how to request ASP documents using PWS.

`www.studiodeluxe.net/pws`
This Web site is dedicated to PWS. It contains links to installation instructions, publishing applications (Perl, Miva, PHP, etc.) and FAQs.

SUMMARY

- Web servers respond to client requests by providing resources, such as XHTML documents.
- Web servers and clients communicate with each other via the platform-independent HyperText Transfer Protocol (HTTP).
- The most common HTTP request types are *get* and *post*; these requests send client form data to a Web server.
- The *get* request sends form content as part of the URL; the *post* request attaches form contents to the end of an HTTP request. The data sent in a *post* request are not part of the URL and cannot be seen by the user.
- Browsers often cache Web pages for quick reloading. However, browsers typically do not cache the server's response to a *post* request, because the information may have changed.
- A Web server is part of a multi-tier application—sometimes referred to as an *n*-tier application. A multi-tier application divides functionality into separate tiers. The three-tier application contains an information tier, a middle tier and a client tier.
- The information tier maintains data for the application in a database.
- The middle tier implements business logic and presentation logic to control interactions between application clients and application data. A Web server is a middle-tier application.
- The client tier is the application's user interface. The client interacts with the middle tier to make requests and to retrieve data from the information tier. The client then displays data retrieved from the middle tier to the user.
- Client-side scripting often is used for validation, interactivity, accessing the browser and enhancing a Web page with ActiveX controls, Dynamic HTML and Java applets.
- Client-side scripting has some limitations—such as browser dependency, where the browser must support the scripting language.
- Microsoft Internet Information Services (IIS) is an enterprise-level Web server.
- Microsoft Personal Web Server (PWS) is a scaled-down version of the IIS.
- The Apache Web server, developed by the Apache Group, is the most popular Web server in use today. It runs on Windows and non-Windows platforms.
- A virtual directory is an alias for an existing directory on a local machine.

- In its default configuration, Apache only supports Perl and Python documents stored in the **cgi-bin** directory, whereas XHTML and PHP documents are stored in the **htdocs** directory (also the default directory in Apache).
- The Apache Web server does not serve ASP documents. ASP is a Microsoft-specific technology, so use IIS and PWS to serve such documents.

TERMINOLOGY

ActiveX control
ActiveX server component
Apache Web server
bottom tier
Browse access
business logic
business rule
cache
cgi-bin directory
client tier
client-side scripting
controller logic
data tier
DNS lookup
domain name
domain name server (DNS)
Execute access
File Transfer Protocol (FTP)
fully qualified host name
get (HTTP request)
host name
htdocs directory
HTTP request type
HyperText Transfer Protocol (HTTP)
information tier
Internet Information Services (IIS)
Internet Protocol (IP) address
Java applet
local Web server
localhost
middle tier
module
multi-tier application
n-tier application
open source
Personal Web Server (PWS)
post (HTTP request)
presentation logic
RDBMS
Read access
remote Web server
request method
request type
Run scripts (such as ASP) access
scripting host
security level
server-side form handler
server-side script
Simple Mail Transfer Protocol (SMTP)
top tier
top-level domain (TLD)
Uniform Resource Locator (URL)
validation
virtual directory
Web server
Web server
Wireless Markup Language (WML)
Write access

SELF-REVIEW EXERCISES

21.1 State whether each of the following is *true* or *false*. If *false*, explain why.

a) Web servers and clients communicate with each other through the platform-independent HTTP.
b) Web servers often cache the most popular Web pages for quick reloading.
c) The information tier implements business logic to control the type of information that is presented to a particular client.
d) Client-side scripts can access the browser, use features specific to that browser and manipulate browser documents.
e) Internet Information Services (IIS) is a scaled-down version of Personal Web Server (PWS) that is intended for universities and small businesses.
f) A virtual directory is an alias for an existing directory on a remote machine.

g) The Apache Web server is said to be platform-independent because it runs on various operating systems, such as Unix, Linux and Windows.
h) In Apache, Perl and PHP, documents are stored in the **cgi-bin** directory.
i) IIS, PWS and Apache can request ASP, Perl, Python and PHP documents.

21.2 Fill in the blanks in each of the following statements:
a) The two most common HTTP request types are ________ and ________.
b) Browsers often________ Web pages for quick reloading.
c) In a three-tier application, a Web server is typically part of the ________ tier.
d) Client-side validation reduces the number of requests passed to the ________.
e) The most popular client-side scripting language is ________.
f) A ________ translates a fully qualified host name to an IP address.
g) In a Web address, ________ is a host name that references the local computer.
h) A ________ directory references an existing directory on a local machine.
i) The ________ Web Server is intended for educational institutions and small businesses.
j) In the Apache Web server, Python documents are stored in the ________ directory.

ANSWERS TO SELF-REVIEW EXERCISES

21.1 a.) True. b) False. Web browsers often cache Web pages for quick reloading. c) False. The middle tier implements business logic and presentation logic to control interactions between application clients and application data. d) True. e) False. Personal Web Server (PWS) is a scaled-down version of Internet Information Services (IIS) that is intended for universities and small businesses. f) False. A virtual directory is an alias for an existing directory on the local machine. g) True. h) False. In Apache, Perl and Python, documents are stored in the **cgi-bin** directory. PHP documents are stored in the **htdocs** directory. i) False. IIS, PWS and Apache can request XHTML, Perl, Python and PHP documents. The Apache Web server does not serve ASP documents.

21.2 a) *get*, *post*. b) cache. c) middle. d) server. e) JavaScript. f) domain name server (DNS). g) **localhost**. h) virtual. i) Personal. j) **cgi-bin**.

EXERCISES

21.3 Define the following terms:
a) HTTP.
b) Multi-tier application.
c) Request method.

21.4 Define the following terms:
a) Top-level domain (TLD).
b) Virtual directory.
c) Web server.

21.5 In a three-tier application, explain how the middle tier (e.g., Web server) interacts with the client tier (e.g., Web browser).

21.6 Explain the difference between the *get* request type and the *post* request type. When is it ideal to use the *post* request type?

21.7 Explain how to determine the machine names of remote Web servers (in your local network).

21.8 Given that you have a document, **sample.php**, in the **C:\Exercises\Webservers** directory, explain how to request the document using
a) IIS.
b) PWS.
c) Apache.

22

Database: SQL, MySQL, DBI and ADO

Objectives

- To understand the relational database model.
- To be able to write database queries using the Structured Query Language (SQL).
- To understand the MySQL database server.
- To learn various database interfaces.
- To understand Microsoft's ActiveX Data Object (ADO) Technology.

Now go, write it before them in a table, and note it in a book, that it may be for the time to come for ever and ever.
The Holy Bible: The Old Testament

True art selects and paraphrases, but seldom gives a verbatim translation.
Thomas Bailey Aldrich

Get your facts first, and then you can distort them as much as you please.
Mark Twain

I like two kinds of men: domestic and foreign.
Mae West

Outline

22.1 Introduction

A *database* is an integrated collection of data. Many companies maintain databases to organize employee information, such as names, addresses and phone numbers. Many strategies exist for organizing data to facilitate access and manipulation. A *database management system* (*DBMS*) provides mechanisms for storing and organizing data in a manner consistent with the database's format. Database management systems allow users to access and store data without addressing the internal representation of databases.

Relational databases—composed of data that correspond to one another—are the most popular database systems in use. Almost all relational database systems use a language called *Structured Query Language* (*SQL*—pronounced as its individual letters or as "sequel") to create *queries* (i.e., requests information that satisfy given criteria) and manipulate data. Some popular enterprise-level relational database systems include Oracle, Microsoft SQL Server, MySQL, Sybase, DB2 and Informix.

In this chapter, we present basic SQL queries that manipulate a database containing several of our books. We introduce MySQL—a robust and scalable relational database management system—and present various *database interfaces* that interact with MySQL. We also discuss a Microsoft technology—*ActiveX Data Objects (ADO)*—that provides access to database contents and to data sources.

22.2 Relational Database Model

The *relational database model* is a logical representation of data that allows users to consider the relationships between the data separate from the physical structure of the data. A relational database consists of *tables*. Figure 22.1 illustrates a sample table named **`Employee`** that might be in a personnel system. The table illustrates the attributes of employees and how those attributes relate to specific employees. A table row is called a *record*, and a table column is called a *field*. This table consists of six records and five fields.

In the **`Employee`** table, the **`Number`** field of each record is the *primary key* for referencing data. A primary key is a field (or a set of fields) that contains unique data that cannot be duplicated in other records. Each record has a unique value in the primary key field to identify the record. Examples of primary fields include social security numbers and employee ID numbers.

Multiple records within a table are normally unique because of the primary key field. However, the remaining fields can contain duplicate values. For example, three records in the **`Employee`** table's **`Department`** field contain number 413. The records of Fig. 22.1 are *ordered* by primary key. In this case, the records are in increasing order—we also could use decreasing order.

Often, database users are interested in different data and different data relationships. Some users want only certain subsets of the table columns. To obtain table subsets, we use SQL statements to specify the data to *select* from the table. SQL provides a complete set of keywords that enable programmers to define complex queries. The results of a query are commonly called *result sets* (or *record sets*). For example, we might select data from the table in Fig. 22.1 to create a new result set that provides the geographic location of several departments. Figure 22.2 shows this result set. We discuss SQL queries in Section 22.4, Structured Query Language.

	`Number`	**`Name`**	**`Department`**	**`Salary`**	**`Location`**
	23603	Jones	413	1100	New Jersey
	24568	Kerwin	413	2000	New Jersey
Row/Record	34589	Larson	642	1800	Los Angeles
	35761	Myers	611	1400	Orlando
	47132	Neumann	413	9000	New Jersey
	78321	Stephens	611	8500	Orlando
	Primary key		Column/Field		

Fig. 22.1 Relational database structure.

Department	**Location**
413	New Jersey
611	Orlando
642	Los Angeles

Fig. 22.2 Result set formed by selecting data from a table.

Software Engineering Observation 22.1

Tables in a database normally have primary keys.

22.3 Relational Database Overview

In this section, we overview Structured Query Language (SQL) in the context of a sample database we created, **Books.mdb**. The Chapter 22 examples directory on the CD-ROM that accompanies this book contains the database. Before we discuss SQL, we overview the tables of this Microsoft Access database.

The database consists of four tables—**Authors**, **Publishers**, **AuthorISBN** and **Titles**. [*Note*: The figures containing the descriptions of the columns and the figures showing the contents of the tables display the primary key field for each table in italics.]

Figure 22.3 describes the **Authors** table, which consists of four fields that maintain each author's unique ID number, first name, last name and the author's year of birth. Figure 22.4 shows the data from the **Authors** table. Notice that the last record in the table contains a *null value* (i.e., the record contains no value) for the **YearBorn** field. This field, in addition to **FirstName** and **LastName**, is not a primary key field and therefore can contain null values.

Field	Description
AuthorID	An integer representing the author's ID number in the database. This field is the primary key field for this table.
FirstName	A string representing the author's first name.
LastName	A string representing the author's last name.
YearBorn	A string representing the author's year of birth.

Fig. 22.3 **Authors** table from **Books.mdb**.

AuthorID	**FirstName**	**LastName**	**YearBorn**
1	Harvey	Deitel	1946

Fig. 22.4 Data from the **Authors** table of **Books.mdb** (part 1 of 2).

AuthorID	FirstName	LastName	YearBorn
2	Paul	Deitel	1968
3	Tem	Nieto	1969
4	Kate	Steinbuhler	

Fig. 22.4 Data from the **Authors** table of **Books.mdb** (part 2 of 2).

Figure 22.5 describes the **Publishers** table, which consists of two fields representing each publisher's unique ID and name. Figure 22.6 shows the data from the **Publishers** table of the **Books.mdb** database.

Figure 22.7 describes the **Titles** table, which consists of six fields that maintain general information about each book in the database. These fields include the ISBN number, title, edition number, year published, a description of the book and the publisher's ID number. Figure 22.8 shows a portion of the data from the **Titles** table. [*Note*: We did not have space for the **Description** field of the **Titles** table in Fig. 22.8.]

Field	Description
PublisherID	An integer representing the publisher's ID number in the database. This is the primary key field for this table.
PublisherName	A string representing the abbreviated name for the publisher.

Fig. 22.5 **Publishers** table from **Books.mdb**.

PublisherID	PublisherName
1	Prentice Hall
2	Prentice Hall PTR

Fig. 22.6 Data from the **Publishers** table of **Books.mdb**.

Field	Description
ISBN	A string representing the ISBN number of the book.
Title	A string representing the title of the book.
EditionNumber	A string representing the edition number of the book.

Fig. 22.7 **Titles** table from **Books.mdb** (part 1 of 2).

Field	Description
`YearPublished`	A string representing the publication year.
`Description`	A string representing the description of the book.
`PublisherID`	An integer representing the publisher's ID number. This value must correspond to an ID number in the **`Publishers`** table.

Fig. 22.7 **`Titles`** table from **`Books.mdb`** (part 2 of 2).

`ISBN`	**`Title`**	**`Edition Number`**	**`Year Published`**	**`Publisher ID`**
0-13-012507-5	Java How to Program	3	1999	1
0-13-013249-7	Getting Started with Visual C++ 6 with an Introduction to MFC	1	1999	1
0-13-016143-8	Internet and World Wide Web How to Program	1	1999	1
0-13-020522-2	Visual Basic 6 How to Program Instructor's Manual with Solution Disk	1	1999	1
0-13-028417-3	XML How to Program	1	2001	1
0-13-089571-1	C++ How to Program	3	2001	1
0-13-089572-5	C How to Program	3	2001	1
0-13-271974-6	Java Multimedia Cyber Class-room	1	1996	2
0-13-456955-5	Visual Basic 6 How to Program	1	1998	1
0-13-899394-7	Java How to Program	2	1997	1

Fig. 22.8 Portion of the data from the **`Titles`** table of **`Books.mdb`**.

Figure 22.9 describes the **`AuthorISBN`** table, which consists of two fields that maintain each book's ISBN number and the corresponding author ID number for that book. This table links the names of the authors with their respective book titles. Figure 22.10 shows a portion of the data from the **`AuthorISBN`** table.

Figure 22.11 illustrates the relationships among the tables in the **`Books.mdb`** database. We created this diagram in Microsoft Access when we designed the database. A bold field name in a table is that table's primary key. Every record must have a value in the primary key field, and the value must be unique, according to the *Rule of Entity Integrity*.

Common Programming Error 22.1

Not providing a value for a primary key field in every record breaks the Rule of Entity Integrity and causes the DBMS to report an error.

Field	Description
ISBN	A string representing the ISBN number for a book. The ISBN number in this field also must appear in the **Titles** table.
AuthorID	An integer representing the author's ID number, which allows the database to connect each book to a specific author. The ID number in this field must also appear in the **Authors** table.

Fig. 22.9 **AuthorISBN** table from **Books.mdb**.

ISBN	**AuthorID**
0-13-010671-2	1
0-13-010671-2	2
0-13-012507-5	1
0-13-013249-7	2
0-13-016143-8	2
0-13-020522-2	3
0-13-032364-0	2
0-13-032364-0	4
0-13-082928-5	3

Fig. 22.10 Portion of the data from the **AuthorISBN** table of **Books.mdb**.

The lines between the tables represent relationships. Consider the line between the **Publishers** and **Titles** tables. On the **Publishers** end of the line there is a **1** and on the **Titles** end there is an *infinity symbol* (∞), to indicate a *one-to-many relationship* between the two tables. A single publisher in the **Publishers** table can have many books in the **Titles** table. The relationship line links the **PublisherID** field in the **Publishers** table to the **PublisherID** field in the **Titles** table.

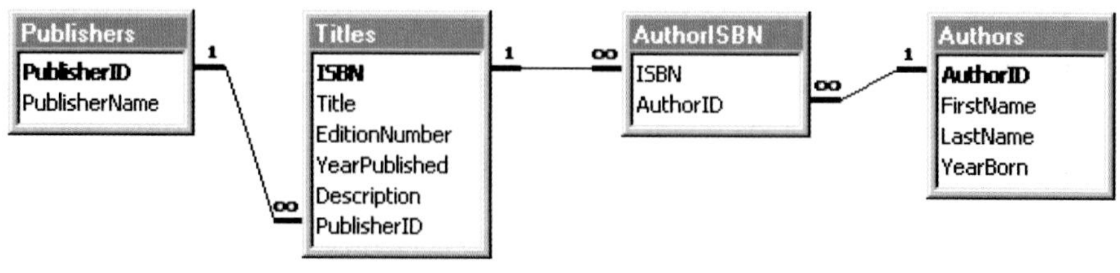

Fig. 22.11 Table relationships in **Books.mdb**.

Common Programming Error 22.2

Providing duplicate values for the primary key field in multiple records causes the DBMS to report an error.

The **PublisherID** field in the **Titles** table is a *foreign key*—a field which references the primary key field in another table. Foreign keys (sometimes called *constraints*) are specified when creating a table, and they help maintain the *Rule of Referential Integrity*—every foreign key field value must appear in another table's primary key field. For example, **PublisherID** in the **Titles** table is a foreign key to **PublisherID** in the **Publishers** table. Foreign keys enable information from multiple tables to be *joined* for analysis purposes. The line between the tables represents the link between the foreign key in one table and the primary key in another table. To maintain referential integrity, Microsoft Access ensures that every record in the **Titles** table refers to a record in the **Publishers** table (this was configured when we first created the database in Access).

The line between the **AuthorISBN** and **Authors** tables indicates that for each author in the **Authors** table there can be an infinite number of ISBNs for books written by that author in the **AuthorISBN** table. The **AuthorID** field in the **AuthorISBN** table is a foreign key of the **AuthorID** field (the primary key) of the **Authors** table. The **AuthorISBN** table links information in the **Titles** and **Authors** tables.

Finally, the line between the **Titles** and **AuthorISBN** tables indicates a one-to-many relationship—a title can be written by any number of authors.

22.4 Structured Query Language

In this section we provide an overview of Structured Query Language (SQL) in the context of the **Books.mdb** sample database. The SQL queries discussed here will appear again in the examples later in the chapter.

The next several subsections discuss some SQL keywords (Fig. 22.12) in the context of complete SQL queries. For more information on SQL, refer to Section 22.8, Internet and World Wide Web Resources.

SQL keyword	Description
`SELECT`	Select (retrieve) fields from one or more tables.
`FROM`	Tables from which to get fields. Required in every `SELECT`.
`WHERE`	Criteria for selection that determine the rows to be retrieved.
`GROUP BY`	Criteria for grouping records.
`ORDER BY`	Criteria for ordering (sorting) records.
`INSERT INTO`	Insert values into one or more tables. Some databases do not require the SQL keyword `INTO`.
`UPDATE`	Update existing data in one or more tables.
`DELETE FROM`	Delete data from a specified table.

Fig. 22.12 Some SQL query keywords.

22.4.1 Basic SELECT Query

Let us consider several SQL queries that extract information from the **Books.mdb** database. A typical SQL query selects information from one or more tables in a database by using the ***SELECT*** *command*. The simplest form of a **SELECT** query is

```
SELECT * FROM TableName
```

The *asterisk* (*****) indicates that the query selects all rows and columns (fields) from *TableName*, which specifies a table in the database. For example, to select the contents of the **Authors** table (i.e., all the data in Fig. 22.4), use the query

```
SELECT * FROM Authors
```

To select specific fields from a table, replace the asterisk (*****) with a comma-separated list of field names. For example, to select only the fields **AuthorID** and **LastName** for all rows in the **Authors** table, use the query

```
SELECT AuthorID, LastName FROM Authors
```

The preceding query returns the data shown in Fig. 22.13.

Common Programming Error 22.3

When performing ***SELECT*** *queries using the asterisk (********) do not assume that the query always returns the fields in the same order in the result set.*

Software Engineering Observation 22.2

To ensure that fields are returned in the same order, specify the field names in the desired order.

Performance Tip 22.1

An application receiving a result set can process the result set more efficiently if the field names are specified. This technique retrieves only the necessary fields and processes the fields by column number, which is more efficient than processing fields by field name.

Common Programming Error 22.4

SQL field names cannot contain blank spaces. Combine a field name containing spaces with an underscore (_). For example, the field name ***First Name*** *is incorrect; instead, this field name must appear as* ***First_Name****.*

AuthorID	LastName
1	Deitel
2	Deitel
3	Nieto
4	Steinbuhler

Fig. 22.13 **AuthorID** and **LastName** from the **Authors** table.

Good Programming Practice 22.1

For readability, it is best to create queries using multiple lines and indentation.

22.4.2 WHERE Clause

Many queries locate records in a database according to certain *selection criteria*. For example, a user may wish to query all books published after 1995. To specify the selection criteria for the query, SQL uses the optional ***WHERE** clause* in a **SELECT** query. The query selects only those records that match the selection criteria defined by the **WHERE** clause. The basic form of a **SELECT** query containing a selection criteria is

```
SELECT fieldName1, fieldName2, … FROM TableName WHERE criteria
```

For example, to select all fields from the **Authors** table in which the author's **YearBorn** is greater than **1960**, use the query

```
SELECT AuthorID, FirstName, LastName, YearBorn
   FROM Authors
   WHERE YearBorn > 1960
```

Our database contains only four authors in the **Authors** table. Two of the authors have listed dates of birth after **1960**, so Fig. 22.14 shows the two records that the preceding query selects.

Performance Tip 22.2

Using selection criteria improves performance by searching for a portion of the data, which is easier and faster than working with the entire set of data stored in the database.

The **WHERE** clause condition may contain the operators **<**, **>**, **<=**, **>=**, **=**, **<>** and **LIKE**. Operator **LIKE** performs *pattern matching* with wildcard characters *asterisk* (*****) and *question mark* (**?**). Pattern matching allows SQL to search for a particular character or a string of characters. An asterisk character (*****) indicates that the string can have zero or more characters at the asterisk character's position in the pattern. For example, the following query locates the records of all the authors whose last names start with the letter **D**:

```
SELECT AuthorID, FirstName, LastName, YearBorn
   FROM Authors
   WHERE LastName LIKE 'D*'
```

Figure 22.15 shows that the preceding query selects the two records because two of the four authors in the database have last names starting with the letter **D** (followed by zero or more characters). The ***** in the **WHERE** clause's **LIKE** pattern indicates that any number of characters can follow the letter **D** in the **LastName** field. Notice that the pattern string is surrounded by single-quote characters.

Portability Tip 22.1

Refer to the database system documentation to determine if SQL on your system is case sensitive (i.e., all uppercase letters, all lowercase letters or some combination of the two) and to determine the syntax for SQL keywords.

AuthorID	FirstName	LastName	YearBorn
2	Paul	Deitel	1968
3	Tem	Nieto	1969

Fig. 22.14 Authors from the **Authors** table born after **1960**.

AuthorID	FirstName	LastName	YearBorn
1	Harvey	Deitel	1946
2	Paul	Deitel	1968

Fig. 22.15 Authors from the **Authors** table whose last names start with **D**.

Portability Tip 22.2

Not all database systems support the **LIKE** *operator, so read the database system's documentation carefully.*

Good Programming Practice 22.2

To emphasize SQL keywords in a query, capitalize the keywords on systems that are case insensitive.

Good Programming Practice 22.3

In database systems that support uppercase and lowercase letters for table and field names, use an uppercase first letter for every word in a table name or field name (e.g., **LastName***). This makes SQL statements more readable.*

A question mark (**?**) indicates that a single character can occupy the question mark's position in the pattern string. For example, the following query locates the records of all the authors whose last names start with any character (specified with **?**) followed by the letter **i**, followed by any number of additional characters (specified with *****):

```
SELECT AuthorID, FirstName, LastName, YearBorn
   FROM Authors
   WHERE LastName LIKE '?i*'
```

The preceding query produces the result in Fig. 22.16 because only one author's last name has the letter **i** as its second letter.

Portability Tip 22.3

*Most databases use the underscore (_) and the percent (***%***) characters in place of* **?** *and* ***** *in a* **LIKE** *expression.*

A query can specify a range of characters that occupy one position in the pattern string. A range of characters can be specified as follows:

[*startValue-endValue***]**

in which *startValue* is the first character in the range and *endValue* is the last character in the range. For example, the following query locates the records of all the authors whose last names start with any letter (specified with the **?**), followed by any letter in the range **a** to **i** (specified with **[a-i]**), followed by any number of characters (specified with *****):

```
SELECT AuthorID, FirstName, LastName, YearBorn
   FROM Authors
   WHERE LastName LIKE '?[a-i]*'
```

The preceding query selects three records from the **Authors** table (Fig. 22.4) because "Harvey Deitel," "Paul Deitel" and "Tem Nieto" have last names that contain a second letter in the range **a** to **i**.

22.4.3 GROUP BY Clause

In certain situations, it is necessary to group a result set by a particular column. To group a result set, use the optional ***GROUP BY** clause*. The simplest form of a **GROUP BY** clause is

```
SELECT fieldName1, COUNT(*) FROM TableName
GROUP BY fieldName
```

where the **GROUP BY** clause groups the result set by a specified *fieldName*. The ***COUNT*** keyword returns the number of records that the query selects. For example, to obtain the number of ISBN values associated with an author, group the ISBNs by the author's ID number using the query

```
SELECT AuthorID, COUNT(*) AS Count
   FROM AuthorISBN
   GROUP BY AuthorID
```

Figure 22.17 shows the results of the preceding query.

AuthorID	FirstName	LastName	YearBorn
3	Tem	Nieto	1969

Fig. 22.16 Authors from the **Authors** table whose last names contain **i** as the second letter.

AuthorID	Count
1	28
2	28
3	11
4	1

Fig. 22.17 Number of ISBN values associated with each author.

In this particular query, the **COUNT(*) AS Count** clause assigns the name **Count** to the column that contains the value of the total count. If we do not use the **AS Count** clause, the database generates its own field name. In the current database, **AuthorID** 1 and 2 ("Harvey Deitel" and "Paul Deitel," respectively) each have 28 ISBN values associated with their names. **AuthorID** 3 ("Tem Nieto") has 11 ISBN values associated with his name and **AuthorID** 4 ("Kate Steinbuhler") has one ISBN value associated with her name. [*Note*: In the **COUNT** function, a *fieldName* can be substituted in place of the asterisk (*).]

A query can combine the **WHERE** and **GROUP BY** clauses. The query

```
SELECT AuthorID, COUNT(*) AS Count
   FROM AuthorISBN
   WHERE AuthorID <= 3
   GROUP BY AuthorID
```

selects all records from the **AuthorISBN** table in which **AuthorID** is less than or equal to **3** and groups the results by **AuthorID** (Fig. 22.18).

22.4.4 ORDER BY Clause

In certain situations, it is necessary to sort the result set by a given criteria. For example, we may want to organize our data in ascending order by last name. The result set also can be sorted in descending order. The optional ***ORDER BY** clause* sorts data. The simplest forms of an **ORDER BY** clause are

```
SELECT fieldName1, fieldName2, ... FROM TableName ORDER BY fieldName ASC
SELECT fieldName1, fieldName2, ... FROM TableName ORDER BY fieldName
DESC
```

in which **ASC** specifies ascending (lowest to highest) order, **DESC** specifies descending (highest to lowest) order and *fieldName* represents the field (the column of the table) that the query uses for sorting purposes.

For example, to obtain the list of authors in ascending order by last name (Fig. 22.19), use the query

```
SELECT AuthorID, FirstName, LastName, YearBorn
   FROM Authors
   ORDER BY LastName ASC
```

The default sorting order is ascending, so the **ASC** keyword is optional.

AuthorID	Count
1	28
2	28
3	11

Fig. 22.18 Combining **WHERE** and **GROUP BY** to retrieve the number of ISBN values associated with each author.

AuthorID	FirstName	LastName	YearBorn
1	Harvey	Deitel	1946
2	Paul	Deitel	1968
3	Tem	Nieto	1969
4	Kate	Steinbuhler	

Fig. 22.19 Authors from the **Authors** table in ascending order by **LastName**.

To obtain the same list of authors in descending order by last name (Fig. 22.20), use the query

```
SELECT AuthorID, FirstName, LastName, YearBorn
   FROM Authors
   ORDER BY LastName DESC
```

The **ORDER BY** can also order multiple fields using the form

```
ORDER BY fieldName1 SortingOrder, fieldName2 SortingOrder, ...
```

in which *SortingOrder* is either **ASC** or **DESC**. Note that the *SortingOrder* does not have to be identical for each field. The query

```
SELECT AuthorID, FirstName, LastName, YearBorn
   FROM Authors
   ORDER BY LastName, FirstName
```

sorts authors in ascending order by last name, then by first name (Fig. 22.21). In the set of selected records, the query sorts the records for authors with the same last name in ascending order by their first names.

Users can combine the **WHERE** and **ORDER BY** clauses in one query. The query

```
SELECT ISBN, Title, EditionNumber,
       YearPublished, PublisherID
   FROM Titles
   WHERE Title LIKE '*How to Program'
   ORDER BY Title ASC
```

selects records from the **Titles** table that have a **Title** ending in "**How to Program**" and sorts them in ascending order by **Title**. A portion of the query results is shown in Fig. 22.22 (we did not have space to show the **Description** field of the **Titles** table in Fig. 22.22).

22.4.5 Merging Data from Multiple Tables

A user performing a query often needs to merge information spread over multiple tables. Merging data is referred to as *joining* the tables and is achieved using a comma-separated list of tables in the **FROM** clause of a **SELECT** query. This operation merges records from two or more tables and extracts values common to both tables with the **WHERE** clause. The simplest form of this query is

```
SELECT fieldName1, fieldName2, ...
   FROM TableName1, TableName2
   HERE TableName1.fieldName = TableName2.fieldName
```

AuthorID	FirstName	LastName	YearBorn
4	Kate	Steinbuhler	
3	Tem	Nieto	1969
1	Harvey	Deitel	1946
2	Paul	Deitel	1968

Fig. 22.20 Authors from the **Authors** table in descending order by **LastName**.

AuthorID	FirstName	LastName	YearBorn
1	Harvey	Deitel	1946
2	Paul	Deitel	1968
3	Tem	Nieto	1969
4	Kate	Steinbuhler	

Fig. 22.21 Authors from the **Authors** table in ascending order by **LastName** and by **FirstName**.

ISBN	Title	EditionNumber	Year Published	Publisher ID
0-13-089572-5	C How to Program	3	2001	1
0-13-089571-7	C++ How to Program	3	2001	1
0-13-528910-6	C++ How to Program	2	1997	1
0-13-028419-X	e-Business and e-Commerce How to Program	1	2001	1
0-13-016143-8	Internet and World Wide Web How to Program	1	1999	1
0-13-012507-5	Java How to Program	3	1999	1
0-13-028418-1	Perl How to Program	1	2001	1
0-13-456955-5	Visual Basic 6 How to Program	1	1998	1
0-13-028417-3	XML How to Program	1	2001	1

Fig. 22.22 Portion of the books from the **Titles** table whose titles end with **How to Program**, sorted in ascending order by **Title**.

The **WHERE** clause of the query specifies the fields to be compared from each table. These fields normally represent the primary key in one table and the corresponding foreign key in the other table. For example, the following query produces a list of authors and the ISBN numbers of the books that each author wrote:

```
SELECT FirstName, LastName, ISBN
   FROM Authors, AuthorISBN
      WHERE Authors.AuthorID = AuthorISBN.AuthorID
   ORDER BY LastName, FirstName
```

The query merges the **FirstName** and **LastName** fields from the **Authors** table with the **ISBN** field from the **AuthorISBN** table. The query then sorts the results in ascending order by **LastName** and **FirstName**. The query syntax *TableName*.*fieldName* in the **WHERE** clause—called a *fully qualified name*—specifies the fields that should be compared to join the tables. Fields with the same name in both tables require the "*TableName*." syntax. Fully qualified names that include the database name can perform cross-database queries. Figure 22.23 shows the results of the preceding query.

Software Engineering Observation 22.3

If an SQL statement uses fields with the same name from multiple tables, the field name must be fully qualified with its table name and a dot operator (.), as in **Authors.AuthorID**.

Common Programming Error 22.5

When performing a query on two or more tables that contain identical field names, it is necessary to include fully qualified names. Not doing so results in an error.

FirstName	LastName	ISBN
Harvey	Deitel	0-13-226119-7
Harvey	Deitel	0-13-016143-8
Harvey	Deitel	0-13-085609-6
Harvey	Deitel	0-13-013249-7
Harvey	Deitel	0-13-899394-7
Paul	Deitel	0-13-899394-7
Paul	Deitel	0-13-226119-7
Paul	Deitel	0-13-118043-6
Paul	Deitel	0-13-028418-1
Paul	Deitel	0-13-083055-0
Tem	Nieto	0-13-016143-8
Tem	Nieto	0-13-456955-5
Tem	Nieto	0-13-020522-2

Fig. 22.23 Portion of the result set containing authors and ISBN numbers sorted in ascending order by **LastName** and **FirstName** (part 1 of 2).

FirstName	LastName	ISBN
Tem	Nieto	0-13-904947-9
Tem	Nieto	0-13-028419-X
Kate	Steinbuhler	0-13-0323-64-0

Fig. 22.23 Portion of the result set containing authors and ISBN numbers sorted in ascending order by **LastName** and **FirstName** (part 2 of 2).

22.4.6 Inserting a Record

Users can insert data into a table (e.g., add a new record) with an ***INSERT INTO*** operation. The simplest form for an **INSERT INTO** statement is

```
INSERT INTO TableName ( fieldName1, fieldName2, ..., fieldNameN )
   VALUES ( value1, value2, ..., valueN )
```

where *TableName* is the table into which the record will be inserted. The *TableName* is followed by a comma-separated list of field names in parentheses. This list is not required if the **INSERT INTO** operation specifies a value for every column of the table definition in the proper order (the first value corresponds to the first column, the second value corresponds to the second column, and so on).

The SQL keyword **VALUES** and a comma-separated list of values in parentheses follow the list of field names. The values specified should correspond in order and type to the field names specified after the table name (i.e., for the **Authors** table, *fieldName1* corresponds to the **FirstName** field, so *value1* should be a string in single quotes, representing a first name). The **INSERT INTO** statement

```
INSERT INTO Authors ( FirstName, LastName, YearBorn )
   VALUES ( 'Sue', 'Smith', 1960 )
```

inserts a record into the **Authors** table. The statement indicates that values will be inserted for the **FirstName**, **LastName** and **YearBorn** fields. The corresponding values to insert are **'Sue'**, **'Smith'** and **1960**. [*Note*: We do not specify an **AuthorID** in this example, because the **AuthorID** field is set up in the Microsoft Access database as an *auto-numbered* field. Every new record added to this table will automatically be assigned a unique **AuthorID**, which is the next value in the auto-numbered sequence (i.e., 1, 2, 3, etc.). In this case, Sue Smith would be assigned **AuthorID** number 5.] Figure 22.24 shows the **Authors** table after the **INSERT INTO** operation.

AuthorID	FirstName	LastName	YearBorn
1	Harvey	Deitel	1946

Fig. 22.24 **Authors** table after an **INSERT INTO** operation to add a record (part 1 of 2).

AuthorID	FirstName	LastName	YearBorn
2	Paul	Deitel	1968
3	Tem	Nieto	1969
4	Kate	Steinbuhler	
5	Sue	Smith	1960

Fig. 22.24 **`Authors`** table after an **`INSERT INTO`** operation to add a record (part 2 of 2).

Good Programming Practice 22.4

*To avoid data corruption or data mismatch, list field names in an **`INSERT INTO`** operation. If the inserted values do not correspond to the fields, incorrect data may be inserted into the wrong columns (data corruption), or field definitions may not correspond (data mismatch). For example, inserting a numeric value in a field that can only contain string literals produces data mismatch. This situation is less severe because most databases give notification of the error.*

Common Programming Error 22.6

*The single quote (**`'`**) character is used as a delimiter for strings inserted in the database. Therefore, to insert a name containing quotes (such as O'Malley) into a database, the name must have two single quotes in the position where the quote character appears in the name (e.g.,* **`'O''Malley'`**).

22.4.7 Updating a Record

An ***`UPDATE`*** operation modifies data in a table (e.g., updates a record). The simplest form for an **`UPDATE`** statement is

```
UPDATE TableName
   SET fieldName1 = value1, fieldName2 = value2, …, fieldNameN = valueN
   WHERE criteria
```

where *TableName* specifies the table that will be updated. The ***`SET`*** keyword and a comma-separated list of paired field names and values in the format *fieldName* **`=`** *value* follow the *TableName*. The **`WHERE`** clause specifies the criteria that determines which record(s) to update. The **`UPDATE`** statement

```
UPDATE Authors
   SET YearBorn = '1969'
   WHERE LastName = 'Deitel' AND FirstName = 'Paul'
```

updates a record in the **`Authors`** table. The statement assigns the value **`1969`** to the **`YearBorn`** field for the record in which **`LastName`** equals **`Deitel`** and **`FirstName`** equals **`Paul`**. The **`AND`** keyword indicates that all components of the selection criteria must be satisfied. If we know the **`AuthorID`** for "Paul Deitel" (possibly because we searched for the record previously), we can simplify the **`WHERE`** clause as follows:

```
WHERE AuthorID = 2
```

Figure 22.25 shows the **`Authors`** table after the **`UPDATE`** operation.

AuthorID	**FirstName**	**LastName**	**YearBorn**
1	Harvey	Deitel	1946
2	Paul	Deitel	1969
3	Tem	Nieto	1969
4	Kate	Steinbuhler	
5	Sue	Smith	1960

Fig. 22.25 **Authors** table after an **UPDATE** operation to modify a record.

22.4.8 DELETE FROM Statement

An SQL ***DELETE*** statement removes data from a table. A simple form of the **DELETE** statement is

```
DELETE FROM TableName WHERE criteria
```

where *TableName* specifies the table from which to delete a record. The **WHERE** clause specifies the criteria that determines which record to delete. The **DELETE** statement

```
DELETE FROM Authors
   WHERE LastName = 'Smith' AND FirstName = 'Sue'
```

deletes the record for Sue Smith from the **Authors** table. If we know the **AuthorID** in advance of the **DELETE** operation, we can simplify the **WHERE** clause as follows:

```
WHERE AuthorID = 5
```

Figure 22.26 shows the **Authors** table after the **DELETE** operation.

22.4.9 TitleAuthor Query from Books.mdb

The **Books.mdb** database contains one predefined query (**TitleAuthor**) that produces a table containing the book title, ISBN number, author's first name, author's last name, book's year published and publisher's name for each book in the database. For books with multiple authors, the query produces a separate composite record for each author.

AuthorID	**FirstName**	**LastName**	**YearBorn**
1	Harvey	Deitel	1946
2	Paul	Deitel	1969
3	Tem	Nieto	1969
4	Kate	Steinbuhler	

Fig. 22.26 Table **Authors** after a **DELETE** operation to remove a record.

Figure 22.27 shows the **TitleAuthor** query, and Fig. 22.28 shows a portion of the query results.

Good Programming Practice 22.5

Fully qualify the names of the fields used in an SQL query to ensure that the query references fields from the proper tables.

Software Engineering Observation 22.4

Many database programs that automatically generate SQL statements use fully-qualified field names for every field reference.

For the purpose of this query, we fully qualify each field name with its table name (e.g., **Titles.ISBN**). The query of Fig. 22.27 has several parts. Lines 1–3 indicate the fields that the query selects and their order in the result set from left to right. This query selects **Title** and **ISBN** fields from the **Titles** table, **FirstName** and **LastName** fields from the **Authors** table, **YearPublished** field from the **Titles** table and **PublisherName** field from the **Publishers** table.

```
1  SELECT Titles.Title, Titles.ISBN, Authors.FirstName,
2         Authors.LastName, Titles.YearPublished,
3         Publishers.PublisherName
4     FROM Publishers, Titles, Authors, AuthorISBN
5          WHERE Publishers.PublisherID = Titles.PublisherID
6                AND Authors.AuthorID = AuthorISBN.AuthorID
7                AND Titles.ISBN = AuthorISBN.ISBN
8     ORDER BY Titles.Title
```

Fig. 22.27 **TitleAuthor** query from the **Books.mdb** database.

Title	ISBN	First Name	Last Name	Year Published	Publisher Name
C How to Program	0-13-226119-7	Paul	Deitel	1994	Prentice Hall
C How to Program	0-13-089572-5	Harvey	Deitel	2001	Prentice Hall
C++ How to Program	0-13-089571-7	Paul	Deitel	2001	Prentice Hall
e-Business and e-Commerce for Managers	0-13-032364-0	Kate	Steinbuhler	2001	Prentice Hall
e-Business and e-Commerce How to Program	0-13-028419-X	Harvey	Deitel	2001	Prentice Hall
Internet and World Wide Web How to Program	0-13-016143-8	Paul	Deitel	1999	Prentice Hall

Fig. 22.28 Portion of the query results from the **TitleAuthor** query (part 1 of 2).

Title	ISBN	First Name	Last Name	Year Published	Publisher Name
Java How to Program	0-13-899394-7	Paul	Deitel	1997	Prentice Hall
Perl How to Program	0-13-028418-1	Tem	Nieto	2001	Prentice Hall
Visual Basic 6 How to Program	0-13-456955-5	Tem	Nieto	1998	Prentice Hall
XML How to Program	0-13-028417-3	Harvey	Deitel	2001	Prentice Hall
XML How to Program	0-13-028417-3	Paul	Deitel	2001	Prentice Hall

Fig. 22.28 Portion of the query results from the **TitleAuthor** query (part 2 of 2).

Line 4 of the query

```
FROM Publishers, Titles, Authors, AuthorISBN
```

uses a comma-separated list of table names in the **FROM** clause to merge data from each of these tables.

Line 5 of the query

```
WHERE Publishers.PublisherID = Titles.PublisherID
```

joins the **Publishers** table and the **Titles** table, provided that the **PublisherID** number in the **Publishers** table matches the **PublisherID** number in the **Titles** table. The temporary result set from this operation contains all the information about each book and its publisher.

Line 6 of the query

```
AND Authors.AuthorID = AuthorISBN.AuthorID
```

joins the tables **Authors** and **AuthorISBN** on the condition that the **AuthorID** field in the **Authors** table matches the **AuthorID** field from the **AuthorISBN** table. Remember that the **AuthorISBN** table may have multiple entries for an **ISBN** number if the book has more than one author.

Line 7 of the query

```
AND Titles.ISBN = AuthorISBN.ISBN
```

combines the two preceding result sets on the condition that the **ISBN** field in the **Titles** table matches the **ISBN** field in the **AuthorISBN** table. These operations result in a temporary table from which the appropriate fields are selected for the query results. Finally, line 8 of the query

```
ORDER BY Titles.Title
```

indicates that all rows should be sorted by their titles in ascending order (the default).

22.5 MySQL

In 1994, TcX, a Swedish consulting firm, needed a fast and flexible way to access their tables. Unable to find a database server that could accomplish the required task adequately, Michael Widenius, the principal developer at TcX, decided to create his own database server. The resulting product was called *MySQL* (pronounced "My Ess Que Ell"), a robust and scalable relational database management system (RDBMS).

MySQL is a multiuser, multithreaded (i.e., allows multiple simultaneous connections) RDBMS server that uses SQL to interact with and manipulate data. [*Note*: The Deitel & Associates, Inc. Web site (**`www.deitel.com`**) provides step-by-step instructions for installing MySQL and helpful MySQL commands for creating, populating and deleting tables.]

The MySQL Manual (**`www.mysql.com/doc`**) lists numerous features that characterize MySQL. A few important features include:

1. Multithreading capabilities that enable the database to perform multiple tasks concurrently, allowing the server to process client requests efficiently.
2. Support for various programming languages (C, C++, Java, Python, Perl, PHP, etc.). We demonstrate how to access a MySQL database in Chapters 27, 28 and 29.
3. Implementations of MySQL are available for Windows, Linux and Unix.
4. Full support of functions and operators within the **`SELECT`** and **`WHERE`** clauses of an SQL query that allow users to manipulate data.
5. The ability to access tables from different databases by using a single query, increasing the efficiency of retrieving accurate and necessary information.
6. The ability to handle large databases (e.g., tens of thousands of tables with millions of rows).

For these reasons, MySQL is becoming the database of choice for many businesses, universities and individuals. MySQL's rising popularity benefits from the open source software movement. The term *open source* refers to software that can be freely obtained and customized to fulfill corporate, educational or personal requirements. [*Note*: Under certain situations, a commercial license is required for MySQL.]

22.6 Introduction to DBI

Databases have become a crucial part of *distributed applications*—programs that divide work across multiple computer systems. For instance, one computer might be responsible for managing a Web site and another for a database management system. A distributed application uses both computers to retrieve a result set from a database and display those results on another computer—typically called a client.

Relational databases (e.g., MySQL, Microsoft Access, Oracle, etc.) have many different implementations. A software program, called a *driver*, helps programs access a database. Each database implementation requires its own driver and each driver can have a different syntax. To simplify the use of multiple databases, an *interface* provides uniform access to all database systems. Various programming languages provide programmatic libraries (called *database interfaces*) for accessing relational databases. This section provides a brief overview of database interfaces for Perl (Chapter 27), Python (Chapter 28) and PHP (Chapter 29). Each chapter demonstrates the manipulation of MySQL databases.

22.6.1 Perl Database Interface

The Perl *Database Interface* (*DBI*) enables users to access relational databases from Perl programs. Database vendors create drivers that can receive interactions through DBI and process those interactions in a database-specific manner. DBI is database independent, so it allows for easy migration from one DBMS to another. DBI is the most widely used interface available for database connectivity in Perl.

DBI uses object-oriented interfaces, known as *handles*. Figure 22.29 describes three different handle types—*driver handles*, *database handles* and *statement handles*. A driver handle creates any number of database handles and a database handle creates any number of statement handles.

22.6.2 Python DB-API

In Python, the database interface is referred to as *DB-API* (database application programming interface). The DB-API, which consists of **`Connection`** *data objects* and **`Cursor`** *data objects*, is portable (i.e., requires little modification of the source code) across several databases. **`Connection`** data objects access the database through four methods: **`close`**, **`commit`**, **`rollback`** and **`cursor`**. Figure 22.30 describes these methods.

Data Object Handles	Description
Driver Handles	Encapsulates the driver for the database; rarely used in a Perl script.
Database Handles	Encapsulates a specific connection to a database; can send SQL statements to a database.
Statement Handles	Encapsulates specific SQL statements and the results returned from them.

Fig. 22.29 Data object handles for Perl DBI.

Connection Data Objects	Description
`close`	Closes the connection to the database.
`commit`	Commits (saves) a transaction (i.e., interaction with a database through SQL keywords and commands).
`rollback`	Exits a pending transaction without saving changes. Returns the user to the beginning of the transaction.
`cursor`	Returns a new **`Cursor`** object or the current connection.

Fig. 22.30 **`Connection`** data objects for Python DB-API.

The **cursor** method invokes the **Cursor** data objects, which manipulate and retrieve data. Figure 22.31 lists some of the methods and attributes that constitute **Cursor** data objects.

22.6.3 PHP dbx module

In PHP, an XHTML-embedded scripting language, the database interface is referred to as a ***dbx** module*. The **dbx** module consists of seven functions that interface to database modules rather than to the database. Currently, the **dbx** module supports MySQL, PostgreSQL and ODBC databases. The seven **dbx** functions are listed in Fig. 22.32.

22.7 ActiveX Data Objects (ADO)

The architecture of Microsoft *Universal Data Access* (*UDA*) can support high-performance data access to relational data sources, non-relational data sources and mainframe/legacy data sources. The UDA architecture (Fig. 22.33) consists of three primary components. The *OLE DB* is the core of the UDA architecture that provides low-level access to any data source. The *Open Database Connectivity* (*ODBC*) is a C programming-language library that uses SQL to access data. *ActiveX Data Objects* (*ADO*) are simple object models (Fig. 22.34) that provide uniform access to any data source by interacting with OLE DB. [*Note*: OLE DB implements a minimum set of data access services for ADO.]

Cursor Data Objects	Description
rowcount	Returns the number of rows retrieved by the last execute method call.
close	Closes the **Cursor** object.
execute(*operation* **)**	Executes a database query or command. Return values not defined.
executemany(*operation*, *parameters* **)**	Executes a database query or command against a set of parameters. Return values not defined.
fetchone	Returns the next row of a query result.
fetchmany(*size* **)**	Returns a set of rows—defined in the parameter—for a query result set.
fetchall	Returns all the rows of a query result set.

Fig. 22.31 Some **Cursor** data objects for Python-API.

dbx functions	Description
dbx_close	Closes an open connection/database.

Fig. 22.32 Data objects for PHP **dbx** modules (part 1 of 2).

dbx functions	Description
`dbx_connect`	Opens a connection/database.
`dbx_error`	Reports any error messages from the last function call in the module.
`dbx_query`	Executes a query and returns the results.
`dbx_sort`	Sorts a result by a custom sort function.
`dbx_cmp_asc`	Compares two rows and sorts them in ascending order.
`dbx_cmp_desc`	Compares two rows and sorts them in descending order.

Fig. 22.32 Data objects for PHP **dbx** modules (part 2 of 2).

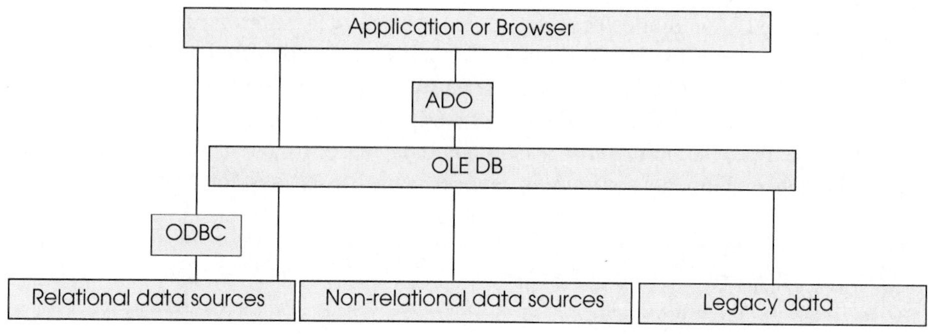

Fig. 22.33 Microsoft's UDA architecture.

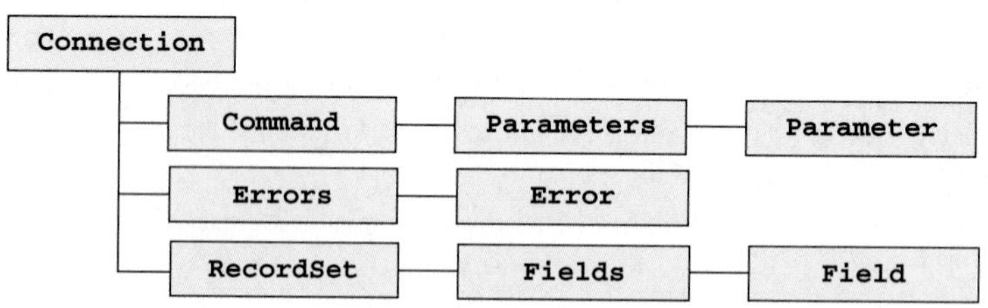

Fig. 22.34 Portion of the ADO object model.

More specifically, the *ADO object model* provides objects and *collections* (i.e., containers that hold one or more objects of a specific type). Figure 22.35 briefly describes some ADO objects and collections. In Chapter 25, Active Server Pages, we show live-code™ examples using ADO and VBScript to access a database.

Object/Collection	Description
`Connection` object	Connects to the *data source*.
`Command` object	Contains the query that interacts with the database (the data source) to manipulate data.
`Parameter` object	Contains information needed by a **`Command`** object to query the data source.
`Parameters` collection	Contains one or more **`Parameter`** objects.
`Error` object	Created when an error occurs while accessing data.
`Errors` collection	Contains one or more **`Error`** objects.
`Recordset` object	Contains zero or more records that match the database query. Collectively, this group of records is called a *recordset*.
`Field` object	Contains the value (and other attributes) of one data source field.
`Fields` collection	Contains one or more **`Field`** objects.
`Property` object	Contains a characteristic of an ADO object.
`Properties` collection	Contains one or more **`Property`** objects.
`Record` object	Contains a single row of a **`Recordset`**.
`Stream` object	Contains a stream of binary data.

Fig. 22.35 Some ADO object and collection types.

22.8 Internet and World Wide Web Resources

Many database-related resources are available on the Internet and World Wide Web. This section lists a variety of databases resources for SQL, MySQL, ADO and ODBC. This section also provides a brief description of each database resource.

`www.sql.org`
The **`sql.org`** site is an online resource that provides a tutorial on the SQL programming language. It offers links to news groups, discussion forums, free software and various database vendors.

`www.mysql.com`
The MySQL site is maintained by *MySQL AB*, a company that promotes and provides the MySQL database. The site contains product information on the MySQL database, downloads, MySQL news and future development plans.

`msdn.microsoft.com/workshop/c-frame.htm#/workshop/database/default.asp`
This is the *Microsoft Developer Network (MSDN) Online Web Workshop* on Data Access and Databases. This page is an excellent starting point for information from Microsoft on databases. The information focuses on ADO, ODBC, OLE DB, SQL, data binding and the Tabular Data Control.

`www.microsoft.com/sql`
The *Microsoft SQL Server 2000 Web Site* contains product information, technical support, SQL news and tips on using the SQL Server to solve business problems.

www.microsoft.com/sql/downloads/default.htm
This page offers tools for *Microsoft's SQL Server.*

www.postgresql.org
The *PostgreSQL* site discusses the history of the PostgreSQL database server. It contains HTTP and FTP mirror sites, technical support, a mailing list and a download page for this open source database.

www.interbase.com
This site discusses *InterBase*, an open source database server developed by *Borland*. The site provides product downloads, technical support, InterBase news and certification programs.

www.maverick-dbms.org
This site discusses the open source database product, *MaVerick*. From this site, you can download the product, register for a mailing list and read recent articles pertaining to MaVerick.

www.devshed.com
The *Developer Shed* Web site provides numerous resources on open source products, such as MySQL, Perl, Python and PHP. It also provides news, discussion forums and tutorials for server-side and client-side technologies.

www.cql.com
The *CQL++* site provides information on the CQL++ open source database product and offers the product for download.

leap.sourceforge.net
LEAP is an open source RDBMS, commonly used by students and teachers as an educational tool. The site contains a mailing list, forum, downloads and LEAP news.

www.voicenet.com/~gray/Home.html
This is the site for the *SQSH* database, which is an SQL shell for UNIX and Windows platforms. You can download the latest version of the product from this site.

www.deja.com
Deja.com is a newsgroup search engine that indexes the Microsoft newsgroup servers (e.g., **msnews.microsoft.com**) and other public newsgroup servers. Typing error messages into the search engine may help find information about how to solve a variety of programming problems.

msdn.microsoft.com/library/devprods/vs6/vstudio/mdac200/mdac3sc7.htm
The *Microsoft Data Access Components (MDAC) SDK Overview* site offers references to ADO, ODBC and other database-related technologies.

w3.one.net/~jhoffman/sqltut.htm
This is a tutorial that teaches data manipulation using standard SQL. The tutorial contains explanations of SQL statements with code examples.

www.w3schools.com/sql
The *SQL School* Web site provides a tutorial on basic to advanced SQL commands. The site contains a short quiz that reinforces SQL concepts.

clubs.yahoo.com/clubs/structuredquerylanguage
The *Yahoo SQL Club* is an online forum with a chat room, a message board, SQL news and links to SQL information sites.

www.sqlmag.com
SQL Server Magazine is an excellent SQL resource for those who subscribe. Subscribers receive monthly issues filled with articles on SQL design and information on current developments involving SQL. Certain articles are available for free at the Web site.

SUMMARY

- Database systems provide file-processing capabilities but organize data in a manner to facilitate sophisticated queries.
- The most popular style of database system on personal computers is the relational database.
- Structured Query Language (SQL) performs relational database queries.
- A database is an integrated collection of centrally controlled data.
- A database management system (DBMS) controls the storage and retrieval of data in a database.
- A distributed database is a database that is spread throughout a network's computer systems.
- A relational database is composed of tables that can be manipulated as result sets.
- A table row is called a record or a row.
- Each table column represents a different field.
- Select data from the table (**SELECT** in SQL) to create subsets. Table data can be combined with join operations.
- A table's primary key uniquely identifies each record in the table. Every record must have a value in the primary key field—Rule of Entity Integrity—and the value must be unique.
- A foreign key is a field in a table for which every entry has a unique value in another table and in which the field in the other table is the primary key. The foreign key helps maintain the Rule of Referential Integrity—every value in a foreign key field must appear in another table's primary key field. Foreign keys enable information from multiple tables to be joined and presented to the user.
- A typical SQL query "selects" information from one or more tables in a database. Such selections are performed by **SELECT** queries. The simplest form of a **SELECT** query is

  ```
  SELECT * FROM TableName
  ```

  in which the asterisk (*****) indicates that all fields from *TableName* should be selected. *TableName* specifies the table in the database from which the fields will be selected. To select specific fields from a table, replace the asterisk (*****) with a comma-separated list of the field names to select.
- SQL uses the optional **WHERE** clause to specify the selection criteria for the query. The simplest **SELECT** query with selection criteria is

  ```
  SELECT * FROM TableName WHERE criteria
  ```

  The condition in the **WHERE** clause can contain operators **<**, **>**, **<=**, **>=**, **=**, **<>** and **LIKE**. Operator **LIKE** matches a string using the wildcard characters asterisk (*****) and question mark (**?**).
- The results of a query can be grouped according to category using the optional **GROUP BY** clause. The simplest form of a **GROUP BY** clause is

  ```
  SELECT *, COUNT(*) FROM TableName GROUP BY field
  ```

  in which **COUNT** returns the number of records selected by the query, and *field* represents the field that is used for grouping purposes.
- Query results can be arranged in ascending or descending order using the optional **ORDER BY** clause. The simplest form of an **ORDER BY** clause is

  ```
  SELECT * FROM TableName ORDER BY field ASC
  SELECT * FROM TableName ORDER BY field DESC
  ```

in which **ASC** specifies ascending (lowest to highest) order, **DESC** specifies descending (highest to lowest) order and *field* represents the field used for sorting purposes.

- Multiple fields can order data with an **ORDER BY** clause in the form

```
ORDER BY field1 SortingOrder, field2 SortingOrder, ...
```

in which *SortingOrder* is either **ASC** or **DESC**.

- The **WHERE**, **GROUP BY** and **ORDER BY** clauses can be combined in one query.
- The query syntax *TableName.fieldName* distinguishes between fields with the same name that reside in different tables.
- The basic form of an **INSERT INTO** SQL statement is

```
INSERT INTO TableName ( fieldName1, fieldName2, ... )
   VALUES ( 'value1', 'value2', ... )
```

where *TableName* is the table in which the data will be inserted. Each field name to be updated is specified in a comma-separated list in parentheses. The value for each field is specified after the SQL keyword **VALUES** in another comma-separated list in parentheses.

- A basic **UPDATE** SQL statement has the form

```
UPDATE TableName
   SET fieldName1 = value1, fieldName2 = value2, ...
   WHERE criteria
```

in which *TableName* is the table to update. The individual fields to update are specified (followed by an equal sign and a new value in single quotes) after the SQL **SET** keyword, and the **WHERE** clause determines a single record to update.

- A record(s) can be permanently deleted from an existing table by using the **DELETE FROM** statement. The simplest form on a **DELETE FROM** command is

```
DELETE FROM TableName WHERE criteria
```

in which *TableName* is the table that contains the record to be deleted, and the **WHERE** clause determines the record to be deleted.

- *MySQL* is a scalable, robust and enterprise-level relational database management system (RDBMS). It provides multithreading capabilities, supports a variety of programming languages and handles large databases. MySQL is not a true open source product.
- Most databases are distributed applications, which are programs that divide work among multiple computer systems.
- Database interfaces are programmatic libraries that allow various programming languages to access and interact with a database.
- In Perl, the database interface is referred to as DBI. *The DBI objects are known as* handles. The three different handle types are driver handles, database handles and statement handles.
- The Python database interface is referred to as DB-API (database application programming interface). It uses **Connection** data objects and **Cursor** data objects to access the database.
- The PHP database interface is referred to as a **dbx** module. The **dbx** module consists of seven functions that interface to the database modules, not to the database.
- Microsoft Universal Data Access (UDA) is an architecture designed for high-performance data access to both relational data sources, non-relational data sources and mainframe/legacy data sourc-

es. The UDA architecture is comprised of three primary components: OLE DB—the core of the UDA architecture that provides uniform access to any data source; Open Database Connectivity (ODBC)—a C programming language library that uses SQL to access data; and ActiveX Data Objects (ADO)—a simple object model that exposes the capabilities of OLE DB.

- The ADO object model provides objects and collections. A collection is a container that holds one or more objects of a specific type.
- ADO provides the **Connection** object for connecting to a data source, the **Command** object for querying a data source, the **Parameter** object for providing additional information a **Command** object needs, the **Error** object for debugging, the **RecordSet** object for storing one or more records and the **Field** object for accessing a field.
- ADO provides collections **Parameters**, **Errors** and **Fields**.

TERMINOLOGY

***** SQL wildcard character
? SQL wildcard character
ActiveX Data Objects (ADO)
ASC
close
collection
Command object in ADO
commit
Connection data object
Connection object in ADO
COUNT function
Cursor data object
data binding
database
database handle
database interface (DBI)
database management system (DBMS)
DB-API
dbx module
dbx_close
dbx_cmp_asc
dbx_cmp_desc
dbx_connect
dbx_error
dbx_query
dbx_sort
DELETE FROM keyword
DESC
distributed application
driver handle
Error object
execute(*operation* **)**
executemany(*operation*, *parameters* **)**
fetchall
fetchmany(*size* **)**
fetchone
field
Field object in ADO
foreign key
FROM SQL keyword
fully qualified name
GROUP BY keyword
handle
INNER JOIN keyword
INSERT INTO keyword
LIKE operator
MySQL
Open Database Connectivity (ODBC)
ORDER BY keyword
Parameter object in ADO
primary key
record
record set
Recordset object in ADO
relational database management system (RDBMS)
result set
rollback
rowcount
Rule of Entity Integrity
Rule of Referential Integrity
SELECT keyword
SET keyword
statement handle
Structured Query Language (SQL)
Tabular Data Control (TDC)
TcX
UDA architecture
Universal Data Access (UDA)
UPDATE keyword
WHERE keyword
wildcard character

SELF-REVIEW EXERCISES

22.1 Fill in the blanks in each of the following statements:

a) The most popular database query language is ________.

b) A/An ________ is a field in a table for which every entry has a unique value in another table and where the field in the other table is the primary key for that table.

c) SQL keyword ________ is followed by the selection criteria that specify the records to select in a query.

d) A/An ________ is an integrated collection of centrally controlled data.

e) The Python interface is referred to as ________ and is composed of ________ and ________ data objects.

22.2 State whether the following are *true* or *false*. If *false*, explain why.

a) The foreign key uniquely identifies each record in a table.

b) A distributed application divides tasks across multiple computer systems.

c) A table in a database consists of rows and records.

d) In PHP, the **dbx** module interfaces directly to the database.

e) MySQL is a non-portable database that can be used only on the Windows platform.

ANSWERS TO SELF-REVIEW EXERCISES

22.1 a) SQL. b) foreign key. c) **WHERE**. d) database. e) DB-API, **Connection**, **Cursor**.

22.2 a) False. The primary key uniquely identifies each record in a table. b) True. c) False. A table in a database consists of rows (records) and columns (fields). d) False. In PHP, the dbx module consists of seven modules that interface to the database modules, not to the database itself. e) False. MySQL is a portable database that can execute on many platforms, including Windows, UNIX and Linux. Moreover, it can execute with various programming languages, such as C, C++ and Java.

EXERCISES

22.3 Define the following terms:

a) Database handle.

b) Fully qualified name.

c) Open source.

d) Rule of Referential Integrity.

e) Universal Data Access (UDA).

22.4 Define the following SQL keywords:

a) **ASC**.

b) **COUNT**.

c) **INSERT INTO**.

d) **LIKE**.

e) **UPDATE**.

22.5 Write SQL queries for the **Books.mdb** database (discussed in Section 22.3) that perform each of the following tasks:

a) Select all authors from the **Authors** table.

b) Select all publishers from the **Publishers** table.

c) Select a specific author and list all books for that author. Include the title, year and ISBN number. Order the information alphabetically by title.

d) Select a specific publisher and list all books published by that publisher. Include the title, year and ISBN number. Order the information alphabetically by title.

22.6 Write SQL queries for the **Books.mdb** database (discussed in Section 23.3) that perform each of the following tasks:

a) Add a new author to the **Authors** table.

b) Add a new title for an author (remember that the book must have an entry in the **AuthorISBN** table). Be sure to specify the publisher of the title.

c) Add a new publisher.

22.7 Fill in the blanks in each of the following statements:

a) MySQL is a robust and scalable __________.

b) The __________ module consists of seven functions that interface to the database module.

c) ADO is an acronym for __________.

d) ADO provides objects and __________.

e) ADO object __________ represents the connection to the data source.

22.8 Correct each of the following SQL queries that refer to the **Books.mdb** database.

a) `SELECT yearborn FROM Author WHERE Authorid = 3.`

b) `SELECT ISBN, Title FROM Titles GROUP BY Title DESC.`

c)
```
INSERT INTO Authors (AuthorID, FirstName, LastName, YearBorn)
  VALUES ("2", "Jane", "Doe").
```

d)
```
SELECT AuthorID, Titles.Title, Titles.YearPublished,
  Titles.ISBN
  FROM Titles, Authors, AuthorISBN
  WHERE AuthorISBN.ISBN = Titles.ISBN AND (AuthorID = 1)
  ORDER BY Titles.Title.
```

e)
```
UPDATE Publishers WITH PublisherID = 4
WHERE PublisherName =
  'Prentice Hall'.
```

23

Wireless Internet and m-Business

Objectives

- To provide an overview of wireless technologies and applications.
- To explore location-identification technologies.
- To introduce wireless marketing techniques and mobile payment options.
- To examine various wireless standards, platforms and programming languages.
- To introduce the Wireless Markup Language (WML).
- To explore the use of WML elements in creating Wireless Application Protocol (WAP) applications.
- To understand the relationship between WML and WMLScript.
- To review aspects of writing simple WMLScript programs.

A wise skepticism is the first attribute of a good critic.
James Russell Lowell (1819–1891)

How absolute the knave is! we must speak by the card, or equivocation will undo us.
William Shakespeare (1564–1616)

The chief merit of language is clearness, and we know that nothing detracts so much from this as do unfamiliar terms.
Galen (129–199)

Outline

23.1 Introduction

Wireless technology has developed into one of today's hottest topics because of its ability to bring the power of communications and the Internet into the hands of users worldwide. The introduction of wireless communications affects many aspects of society, including business management and operations, employee productivity, consumer purchasing behavior, marketing strategies and personal communications. As the popularity of wireless services grows, manufacturers are enabling wireless devices with an increasing array of features and capabilities. For example, many personal digital assistants (PDAs) now operate as cell phones, and vice versa.

In this chapter, we explore elements of the wireless Internet and mobile business. We present information regarding wireless marketing, wireless payment options and security and privacy issues. We also introduce wireless programming languages and techniques.

Although we begin our programming discussion with an examination of the *Wireless Application Protocol* (*WAP*) and *Wireless Markup Language* (*WML*), the chapter covers various programming languages and wireless platforms. These include *Java 2 Micro Edition* (*J2ME*), *Binary Run-Time Environment for Wireless* (BREW), *i-mode and Bluetooth™ wireless technology*.

In this chapter, we introduce WML wireless programming techniques and examine the use of WML in developing content. WML identifies the elements of a document so that a *wireless browser*, such as the *Openwave™ Mobile Browser*, can render the document on the small display screen of a wireless device. We begin with WML because the language provides an excellent foundation in the structuring of data using markup. The chapter first examines WML elements and attributes. Later, we explore the use of the *WMLScript scripting language* to write programs that enhance the functionality of WAP applications; WMLScript enables the creation of highly appealing and powerful wireless content. We introduce elements of WMLScript programming and present examples that illustrate important features of the language. The chapter also provides an overview of several of WMLScript's built-in objects and demonstrates their capabilities.

We discuss the basics of creating *applications* that use WML and WMLScript in accordance with the Wireless Application Protocol (WAP). WAP is an established standard for accessing information and displaying the information on a wireless device. The chapter presents many simple WAP applications. Further information about WAP can be found at the WAP Forum Web site, **`www.wapforum.org`**. In addition, we offer in-depth treatments of these and other topics pertaining to wireless communications in our book *Wireless Internet and Mobile Business How To Program.*

23.2 M-Business

M-business, or mobile business, defined as e-business enabled by wireless communications, is one of the newest frontiers in electronic communications. While still in its initial stages, m-business promises rapid growth. This will be fueled by m-business' ability to reach users effectively and allow them instant access to business-critical information and communications capabilities at any time, from almost anywhere.

Wireless access benefits businesses, employers, employees and consumers. For employers and employees, wireless access provides the ability to communicate, access corporate databases, manage administrative tasks (such as answer e-mail and schedule meetings) and enhance customer relations. In addition, wireless communications enables the streamlining of product shipment and tracking. Furthermore, both employees and consumers can manage responsibilities and complete tasks during idle time—waiting for a bus, or standing in line at a bank.

23.3 Identifying User Location

Location-identification technologies allow businesses and individuals to determine wireless users' locations to within yards. Some of the most impressive m-business applications are location-based services, or applications that are supported by location-identification technologies. Location-based services can be used to improve wireless marketing, customer relationship management (CRM) and business-to-consumer (B2C) and business-to-employee (B2E) applications. For instance, if a business knows that a customer is near one of its stores or offices, the business could send notification of a sale or promotion to the user's hand-held device. Emergency services and wireless accessibility also can be improved through the adoption of location-identification technologies. *In this section, we introduce location-based services and their enabling technologies. We also examine the E911 Act, a government mandate that requires all cell phones to host location-identification technologies.*

Location-based services are made possible by relationships among cellular service providers, cellular networks and mobile-device users. Many leading wireless companies have developed their own methods of determining a user's location. Some considerations that affect these methods are bandwidth availability, communication speed and *multipath errors* (errors resulting from signals reflecting off objects like buildings and mountains).

23.3.1 E911 A\ct

The *E911 Act* (the "E" stands for "Enhanced"), put forth by the Federal Trade Commission (FTC) in 1996 and signed into law in 1999, is designed to standardize and enhance 911 service across mobile devices. Its goal is to improve emergency response time to 911 calls made by cell-phone users. In addition, the *Disabilities Issues Task Force* of the FCC is making efforts to ensure that hearing- and speech-impaired people have access to 911 service through mobile devices. Although the E911 Act will improve the efficiency of emergency services, it raises concerns about wireless users' privacy. Privacy issues in relation to wireless communications are discussed in Section 23.6.

The first phase of the E911 Act requires all wireless services companies to provide *Automatic Number Information (ANI)*, or the phone numbers of cell phones calling in 911 emergencies. Carriers (such as AT&T, Verizon or Cingular) must also provide the locations of the *cell sites* (a cell site identifies the coverage area of a tower that receives and transmits cell-phone signals) receiving the 911 calls. Emergency technicians can use this information to determine users' locations, although only to within the range of the nearest tower. The second phase of the bill mandates that all mobile-phone carriers provide Automatic Location Identification (ALI) of a caller to within 125 meters, 67 percent of the time.

There are several benefits to the E911 Act. In many emergency situations, drivers do not know their exact locations. Information provided by the new technology can help emergency response teams accurately locate callers, improve response times and reduce the consequences of injuries. In addition, if a call breaks up or the operator cannot understand the caller, emergency personnel can obtain the information necessary to find and assist the caller.[1]

23.3.2 Location-Identification Technologies

Location-identification technologies enable businesses to provide wireless users with location-based services. For example, when a user asks for directions to the nearest coffee shop, the wireless carrier can use *triangulation* to determine the location of the user's wireless device. Triangulation is a popular technique employed by many location-identification technologies. A user's location is determined by analyzing the angles of cell-phone signals from (at least) two fixed points a known distance apart. This information is presented to the *content provider* (the business offering the location-based service) in the form of a *geocode* (the latitude and longitude of the user's location). The geocode is then translated into a map or step-by-step navigational instructions with the help of a mapping service and this information is passed to the user. Figure 23.1 outlines various location-identification technologies and their accuracy levels.

23.4 Wireless Marketing, Advertising and Promotions

Wireless communications, the Internet and the World Wide Web provide marketers with new tools for the development and delivery of marketing campaigns. Wireless technologies in particular have greatly enhanced the ability of organizations to target consumers and provide timely, relevant content. In this section, we discuss marketing via wireless devices and the delivery of wireless promotions and advertising. We also introduce aspects of customer relationship management via wireless communications.

E-marketing and m-marketing should be used in conjunction with traditional marketing to create an effective corporate marketing strategy. This strategy should focus on attracting new customers and bringing them back repeatedly. Because wireless marketing requires the alteration of traditional marketing strategies to meet the demands of wireless devices and consumers, marketers should develop wireless sites and campaigns separately from, but in parallel with, online initiatives. E-marketing is discussed in Chapter 32, e-Business & e-Commerce.

Wireless marketing can be classified as a *push strategy*, a *pull strategy* or a combination of both.[2] A *pull strategy* assumes that users will request that specific information be sent to their wireless devices in real time. By contrast, a *push strategy* is enacted when an organization delivers marketing messages to wireless devices at a time deemed appropriate by the company, rather than in real time. Regardless of which strategy is used, wireless marketing should be permission-based, also known as *opt-in*. *Permission-based marketing* protects customers' privacy and provides a well-defined target market, increasing campaign response rates and productivity. By allowing users to control the number and type of messages that they receive, marketers can improve customer satisfaction and campaign results. In addition, an opt-in policy can decrease the costs associated with wireless campaigns, because marketing material is delivered only to consumers who have expressed interest in the company and its products or services.

Successful implementation of wireless advertising requires that the content provider, advertiser and carrier establish a system that delivers ads to consumers at the right location and at the right time. When combined with location-identification technologies and location-based services, wireless advertising offers the benefit of highly targeted information delivery. For example, an individual who receives an e-coupon from a nearby fast-food restaurant is far more likely to respond to the ad than is a consumer 50 miles away who is sent a coupon for the same restaurant. The ability to provide location-specific advertisements increases the value of the advertisements, as companies are willing to pay more for ads to which many customers respond.

Although wireless communications provide many benefits, they also create new obstacles for advertisers. Security issues arise, because content delivered over the wireless Internet may be vulnerable at certain points during transmission. Security is discussed in detail in Chapter 32, e-Business & e-Commerce. Marketers must ensure that messages appear in the intended format. Limited technology and multiple protocols cause content to be displayed differently on various receiving devices. In addition, cell-phone reception is poor in some areas, and service can disconnect while customers are ordering or inquiring about a product or service.[3]

Technology	Degree of Accuracy
Cell of Origin (COO)	Least accurate. User could be anywhere in tower's range. Meets only Phase I of E911 Act.
Angle of Arrival (AOA)	Fairly accurate. User is within the overlap of two towers' cell sites. Used primarily in rural areas where there are fewer towers. Complies with Phase II of E911.
Time Difference of Arrival (TDOA)	Accurate. User's location is determined by triangulating from three locations. Complies with Phase II of E911. Most effective when towers are close together.
Enhanced Observed Time Difference (E-OTD)	Accurate. User's location is determined by triangulating from three locations. Complies with Phase II of E911.
Location Pattern Matching	Accurate. User's location is determined by analyzing multipath interference in a given area, making the method more effective for locating a device in an urban area.
Global Positioning Systems (GPS)	Highly accurate. Satellites determine a user's location anywhere on earth. However, GPS is not as effective when the user is indoors.

Fig. 23.1 Location-identification technologies.

Wireless advertising is further hindered by the lack of wireless-advertising standards and the complex value chain that exists in the wireless-advertising industry. Traditionally, advertisers work with publishers, who deliver advertisements to consumers through various media. When advertisements are distributed to wireless devices, a wireless carrier is added to this chain, as publishers must go through carriers to reach consumers. It is usually the *carrier* that captures users' geographic locations. Carriers have the potential to control the type and amount of wireless advertising that reaches their subscribers. It can be difficult to convince carriers to allow advertising through their services because the carriers do not want to annoy their customers.

To reach wireless customers, advertisers must either develop an in-house solution or use a wireless ad-serving network to deliver ads. A *publisher* or *publisher network* (i.e., a site or group of sites that carry wireless content and wireless advertisements) must also be selected. Advertisers should evaluate carriers' and publishers' wireless-transmission protocols; a device that operates on one standard may not be able to receive an advertisement designed for a different standard, and advertisers should work with carriers and publishers to minimize such problems. For example, sometimes graphics are more effective than text in a wireless advertisement, because graphics can display a font smaller than those supported by the device. Using a graphic, the advertiser may be able to send more text than is possible in a text-formatted ad. However, marketers must be aware that some wireless devices cannot display graphics.[4]

Short Message Service (*SMS*), a service that delivers text messages of up to 160 alphanumeric characters, is one option for delivering wireless advertisements. When marketers send SMS messages, the length, creativity and interactivity of the message are limited because the message cannot contain graphics. However, text messages take far less time to load than do rich multimedia and graphics-packed messages.[5] SMS can also be used to send mobile alerts, which provide customers with valuable news and product updates.[6]

m-Fact 23.1

Over one billion messages are sent through SMS in Europe per month.[7]

Alternatively, companies can send promotions to customers by distributing e-coupons to users' wireless devices. For example, wireless promotions delivered to automobile drivers and passengers can alert them to nearby shopping malls, gas stations and restaurants that are offering special deals. However, some users might find this kind of advertising intrusive. A wireless promotional strategy can enable opt-in users to indicate the type and amount of promotional information they wish to receive, as well as allowing them to select the time of day that the coupons will be sent.

Wireless communications also can be used to improve customer relationship management (CRM). *CRM* focuses on providing and maintaining quality service for customers by effectively communicating and delivering products, services, information and solutions. By using wireless devices, customers can receive timely and relevant information on demand, and companies can interact more efficiently with their sales and field forces.

Sales-force automation assists companies with aspects of the sales process, including the maintenance and discovery of leads and the management of contacts. Sales-force automation can lighten the administrative load on the sales force, allowing salespeople to focus on important details and leads that can increase revenue. Furthermore, information about products and customers can be accessed in real time, providing salespeople with current company and client information.[8]

A sales force's ability to access information almost anywhere at any time improves its level of overall production. For example, imagine that a salesperson is at a professional hockey game with a potential client. The prospective client asks the salesperson a question that must be answered before the sale can be made. Using a cell phone or PDA, the salesperson can access information at that moment and close the sale. Without the wireless Internet and enabled devices, the salesperson would have had to call the office or find a wired Internet connection—which is not easy to do at a sporting event.

23.5 Wireless Payment Options

Secure electronic funds transfer and positive user transaction experiences are crucial to the success of e-commerce and m-commerce. Businesses that offer domestic and international products and services must ensure that *m-payments* (payments made via wireless devices) will be received securely and that the transactions are valid.

The variety of wireless devices, the lack of m-payment *interoperability* and the immaturity of the m-payment industry have led to inconsistent user experiences. Interoperability, the ability for transactions to be performed using any software or device, is a major hurdle for the m-payment market. Organizations such as *Global Mobile Commerce Interoperability Group* (*GMCIG*) and *Mobile Electronic Transactions* (*MeT*) *Group* support standards that enhance interoperability.

Traditionally, banks and credit-card companies process payments. Currently, *micropayments*, or payments under $10, are the most popular m-payment application. This creates problems, because banks and credit-card companies cannot process micropayments profitably. Often, the cost to financial institutions of processing small payments is more than the actual payment amount. Mobile-phone operators are best suited to handle micropayments because the phone bills that they produce are composed almost exclusively of small charges. However, mobile operators are not equipped to assume the financial risk associated with payment processing for services other than theirs, and consumers may not trust a mobile operator to act as a financial institution.[9]

To address this issue until m-payments are used for larger purchases, banks and wireless operators have begun to form partnerships. Through such affiliations, wireless operators can offer their users a convenient billing system for m-payments, while banks provide experience in payment processing and financial risk management. Another alternative is for banks to become *Mobile Virtual Network Operators* (*MVNO*). MVNOs purchase bandwidth capacity from mobile carriers and resell it under their brand name, coupled with value-added services.[10]

M-wallets are the most common form of transaction software offered by the developing m-payments market. M-wallets, like e-wallets, allow users to store billing and shipping information. Users can recall this information and enter it with one click while shopping from a mobile device. Data entry on wireless devices can be time-consuming, because most devices have small keypads on which multiple keys must be pressed to display a correct letter. By enabling one-click shopping, m-wallet software simplifies the ordering process and adds convenience to m-business transactions. In addition, companies are integrating new technologies into m-wallet software. For example, Qpass' *TalkWallet*™ uses speech-recognition and voice-authentication technologies to enable cell-phone users to make purchases by speaking into their phones. Such applications eliminate the need for keypad data entry.[11]

23.6 Privacy and the Wireless Internet

As we discuss in Chapter 32, the Internet presents many new consumer privacy issues. When people communicate through wireless devices, privacy is further threatened; transmissions can be intercepted, and users can be located with a high degree of accuracy. Wireless location-tracking will offer access to information about users' activities, including where they go, when they go and the length of their stay. Over time, a compilation of this data could contribute to a substantial profile of a user's habits.

Currently, the accepted protocol for collecting a user's information is called an *opt-in* policy—i.e., the user agrees to the collection of his or her personal information in exchange for receiving targeted content. In some cases, a business installs a *double opt-in* policy. Double opt-in policies require the user to request information and then to confirm that request by replying to a follow-up e-mail. In theory, this practice provides greater protection of privacy. An *opt-out* policy enables an organization to send marketing information to consumers until individual users request to be removed from the mailing list.

When an opt-in policy is used, consumers should request and expect the information that they receive from advertisers. Companies that wish to collect personal information must inform consumers as to how their information will be managed. The complicated legalese of privacy policies could be difficult to display effectively on small interfaces, making the wireless Internet more susceptible to privacy violations. For example, if a company has partners or affiliates, location information might be shared with and used by these companies. As a result, consumers could find themselves bombarded with unsolicited e-mail—while they are in their cars, at the movie theater or enjoying an evening out. In addition, although the Federal Communications Commission (FCC) has guidelines outlining a telecommunications carrier's responsibilities for protecting a user's privacy, marketers and vendors are not subject to the same guidelines.[12] Third-party vendors, in most cases, will have their own privacy policies.

To date, there is no legislation that monitors the use and misuse of location-identification technology. Industry leaders and government agencies fear that such legislation could slow the development of wireless technology. Even if the government perceives a need for regulation, there are many ways to approach privacy legislation; one "comprehensive" privacy law could target some issues, but miss others. Personal information collected from wireless users, for example, can be of a different nature than that collected from wired users.

To address privacy concerns, the *Cellular Telecommunications and Internet Association (CTIA)* has presented guidelines for protecting consumer privacy. These include: (1) Companies should alert consumers when their locations are being identified, (2) Opt-in should be the standard, meaning that companies should inform users of the services that they will receive in exchange for personal information and allow users to make educated decisions, (3) Consumers should be able to access their own information and (4) The same protections should be offered to all consumers, regardless of carrier or device.[13]

23.7 International Wireless Communications

Wireless communications and related technologies are driving forces behind the global economy. The United States does not dominate the world's wireless communications market; in fact, researchers estimate that the United States is up to two years behind the forefront of wireless technology.[14] Although more Americans subscribe to cell-phone service than do citizens of any other country, the U.S. *market penetration* (i.e., the percentage of the population using the service) is lower than that in 10 of the top 20 wireless markets. Competing wireless standards and the availability of inexpensive wireline phone service have slowed the adoption of wireless technology in the United States. As a result, the percentage of Europeans who own cell phones is nearly twice that of Americans.

The popularity of certain wireless applications differs greatly from country to country. For example, European consumers have embraced text-messaging services, whereas Americans often limit cell-phone use to voice applications. In addition, the United States has an extensive wireline telecommunications infrastructure that delivers relatively inexpensive telephone service and Internet access. Many other parts of the world do not have the same level of infrastructure, making telephone and Internet service costly and difficult to access. Some developing regions are turning to wireless infrastructure solutions by implementing *wireless local access*, as well as wireline networks.[15] Wireless local access refers to the establishment of wireless networks that serve as primary telephone and Internet connections.

Next to voice service, *messaging* is the most popular cell-phone application in the global market. Messaging refers to the transmission of brief text messages to the display of another cell phone. According to the *Global System for Mobile Communications (GSM)*

Association, an organization that supports the extensive GSM cell-phone system, 15 billion Short Message Service (SMS) text messages were sent over GSM wireless networks during December 2000. SMS is used to send short, e-mail-like messages, as well as to alert subscribers to new e-mails, faxes or voice messages. Carriers worldwide are launching SMS Web portals that offer m-commerce applications, corporate services, sports, financial news and weather-based information services. In addition, individuals are creating innovative uses for SMS services; televised award ceremonies poll audiences via SMS, and some religions use SMS to send reminders regarding prayer time.[16]

23.8 Wireless-Communications Technologies

The proliferation of wireless consumer devices, such as personal digital assistants (PDAs), digital cell phones and two-way pagers is increasing the demand for m-business and m-commerce. Wireless devices enabled with Internet access allow users to manage their personal and professional lives while away from their desktop computers. By using PDAs, such as the *Palm*™ handheld computer and the *Pocket PC*, as well as digital cell phones and laptop computers, users can buy airline tickets and groceries, trade stocks and check their e-mail from remote locations.[17]

Wireless communications technologies are categorized and identified by generation. These include first generation (1G), second generation (2G), two-and-a half generation (2.5G), third generation (3G) and even fourth generation (4G). The analog cell phone is an example of a first-generation technology. As wireless communications evolved from analog to digital transmission, first-generation technologies gave way to second-generation technologies. Second-generation technology, which offers transmission speeds of up to 9.6Kbps, is the current standard for the United States. Today, service providers are developing the next generation—third generation (3G)—of transmission technologies, which promises speeds far greater than those of standard dial-up connections.

The 2.5-generation technologies represent an intermediate step between second-generation and third-generation technologies. These technologies rely on networks that use *packet-switching* technologies (information is divided into packets when it is sent and then reassembled at the receiving end). Many countries, with the exception of Japan and parts of Europe, do not have the spectrum available or the networks to support 3G technologies. Even in Japan and Europe, 3G technologies are not expected to be widely available until 2003 or even 2005. The services are not expected to be released in the United States until 2006.

3G technology enables increased data speeds, larger network capacity and transmission support of multiple data types, including streaming audio, video, multimedia, voice and data. Japan's NTT DoCoMo leads the world in the development of third-generation technologies with the anticipated release of *Wideband Code Division Multiple Access* (*W-CDMA*). NTT DoCoMo is also the developer of *i-mode*, the most popular wireless Internet service, which boasts over 25 million subscribers.[18] Using a compact version of HTML called *cHTML*, i-mode offers voice services combined with text messaging, animated graphics and Web browsing.

In the wireless world, there are many programming platforms and technologies. The Wireless Application Protocol (WAP) and Wireless Markup Language (WML) are the most commonly used technologies for wireless communications in the United States; they also are popular in parts of Europe and Asia. In the following sections, we demonstrate how to build wireless applications that use WAP/WML.

23.9 WAP and WML

One of the most important aspects of wireless communications is standardization. In 1997, the Wireless Application Protocol (WAP) was developed by dominant cell-phone manufacturers Nokia, Ericsson, Motorola and others to facilitate the introduction and standardization of wireless Internet access.[19] WAP is a set of communications protocols that are designed to enable wireless devices to access the Internet. WAP applications can be used on Palm OS, Windows CE, Mac OS and Java 2 Micro Edition devices.[20]

Although WAP communications involve many components, we focus on three—a *WAP-enabled mobile device*, a *WAP gateway* and a *Web server*. When a user of a WAP-enabled device requests information from the Internet, the device sends the request to a WAP gateway. WAP gateways serve as links between mobile devices and the Internet. WAP gateways are designed to convert Web content from WML to HTTP, which is the standard protocol used to transfer and view information in Web transactions. The WAP gateway communicates with the Web server (i.e., the server that has a connection to the Internet). The Web server processes the mobile-device request by searching through existing databases and information resources, such as Web pages. The Web server then transmits the requested information back to the WAP gateway, using HTTP. The gateway translates the information into WML and sends it to the mobile device for use.[21]

The Wireless Markup Language (WML), which is based on XML, is the markup language used to create Web content delivered to wireless handheld devices. *WML tags* are the markup commands that specify how a Web page should be formatted for viewing on a wireless device. *Microbrowsers*, browsers designed with limited bandwidth and memory requirements, can access the Web via the wireless Internet. WAP supports WML to deliver the content.

A WML document is called a *deck*; each contains one or more pages, called *cards*. Cards are renderable units of WML documents useful for WAP clients (a WAP client being any WAP-enabled device) that generally use the devices with limited screen sizes. Each card can contain both text content and navigational controls to facilitate user interaction. Though only one card can be viewed at a time, navigation between cards is rapid, because the entire deck is stored by the microbrowser.[22]

Although WAP and WML provide many advantages, they also have many opponents. Those who favor WAP technology see it as a short-term solution for the delivery of wireless Internet access. WAP opponents cite various disadvantages that are associated with the protocol, including possible security breaches, limited bandwidth and unreliability.

The limited bandwidth capabilities of WAP-enabled devices cause a host of problems. Not only are WAP-enabled devices unable to handle the transmission of multimedia, but they can also become overloaded during peak hours, the busiest hours of the day for conducting wireless communications.[23] This limitation causes business-to-business (B2B) and business-to-consumer (B2C) application developers to anticipate the release of faster 3G technologies and a new WAP specification that supports increased functionality.

When learning about mobile communications, it is vital to understand the process by which mobile devices connect to and interact with the Internet, because this process is organized differently for each protocol and programming language. However, no protocol currently existing allows a wireless device to communicate directly with the Internet. Each system (i.e., WAP and WML, i-mode and Java and J2ME) employs its own method of sending and receiving information to and from the Internet.

23.10 Phone Simulator and Setup Instructions

Several free browsers are available for the development and testing of WAP applications. Openwave and Nokia® are the two most popular WAP browsers. The Openwave Software Development Kit is available at

`developer.openwave.com/download/license_41.html`

and the Nokia Wireless Toolkit is available at

`forum.nokia.com/main/1,6668,1_1,00.html`

The Openwave Simulator is part of Openwave's *Software Development Kit (SDK)*, a group of tools for wireless developers. The Openwave Simulator replicates the behavior of the Openwave browser that is used on actual wireless devices. Openwave's *UP.SDK Getting Started Guide*, which facilitates the installation and use of the SDK, is available at **`developer.openwave.com/htmldoc/41/getstart`**.

In this chapter, we use the Openwave UP.Simulator. To install the Openwave UP.SDK on a machine running Windows 2000, perform the following steps: [*Note*: More detailed installation instructions are available on the Deitel & Associates, Inc., Web site, **`www.deitel.com`**.]

1. Go to the Openwave Web site, and click the **Download** button.
2. Check the **Save this program to disk** option, and click **OK**.
3. Select a name and location for the file, and click **OK**.
4. Once the document is complete, click **Open** to begin the installation process.
5. When the **Welcome** screen of the installation program appears, click **Next**.
6. Read the license agreement, and click **Yes**.
7. Read the **SCREENSHOTS AND IMAGE USE AGREEMENT**, and click **Yes**.
8. Read the text of the **Safe Country Verification** dialog, and check the **Yes** box before clicking **Next**.
9. Choose a destination folder in which to install the Openwave browser by clicking the **Browse** button, or select the default folder (recommended). Click **Next** to continue.
10. Specify the name of the folder to appear in the **Start** menu, and click **Next**.
11. Setup is now complete. To view the **`README`** file and launch the Openwave browser (UP.Simulator), check each respective option. Click **Finish**.

To simulate WAP applications by using the Openwave and Nokia browsers, WAP documents must be requested from a Web server (see Chapter 21), such as *Apache* or *Internet Information Services (IIS)*. Visit the **Downloads and Resources** page on our Web site (**`www.deitel.com`**) to access Web server installation and configuration instructions. The following instructions cover the configuration of the Internet Information Services Web server. Apache configuration instructions can be found at our Web site.

In IIS, copy the files from the Chapter 23 examples directory on the CD-ROM that accompanies this book to **`C:\Inetpub\wwwroot`**. Alternatively, these files can be placed in a directory referenced by a virtual directory. We discuss the creation of virtual directories in detail in Chapter 21, Web Servers.

To configure IIS to respond to requests for WAP documents, perform the following:

1. Right click the Windows task bar, click **Properties** and select the **Advanced** tab. Under **Start Menu Settings**, select **Display Administrative Tools**, and click **OK**.
2. Click the **Start** button on the Windows task bar and select **Programs**, then **Administrative Tools**, then **Internet Services Manager**.
3. In the **Internet Information Services** dialog, double click the computer name, or click the plus sign next to the computer icon to expand the list.
4. Right click **Default Web Site**, and select **Properties**.
5. Click the **HTTP Headers** tab, and select the **File Types...** button, which is located within the **(MIME): Map Frame Settings** box.
6. Click the **New Type** button.
7. In the **Associate Extension** text box, type **wml**. In the **Content type {MIME}** text box, type **text/vnd.wap.wml**. This allows the server to map WML documents to the **.wml** file extension.
8. Click **OK**.
9. Click the **New Type** button.
10. In the **Associate Extension** text box, type **wmls**. In the **Content type (MIME):** text box, type **text/vnd.wap.wmlscript**. This allows the server to map WMLScript files to the **.wmls** file extension.
11. Click **OK**.

To request a document, it is necessary to launch the Openwave Simulator. This is achieved by typing **localhost/***fileName***.wml**, in the Openwave Simulator's **Go** field and pressing *Enter*. For example, to request our first WML document (Fig, 23.2), type **localhost/fig23_2.wml**. If the document is located in a **wwwroot** subdirectory or in a virtual directory, the folder name or virtual directory name must precede the document's file name (e.g., **localhost/***folderName***/***fileName***.wml**).

23.11 Creating WML Documents

In this section, we begin to create WAP applications by marking up information using WML. Figure 23.2 presents a WML document that displays a welcome message. The screen shot of the Openwave Simulator displays the WML document. The **Phone Information** window below the simulator displays the status of the simulator. If an error occurs during the rendering of the document, the error is listed in this window.

Like XHTML, WML is an *XML vocabulary* (i.e., a markup language that is created using XML). Line 1 is the optional XML declaration that specifies the **version** of XML to which this document's syntax adheres. Lines 2–3 specify the Document Type Definition (DTD) to which the document conforms. The root element for every WML document is ***wml***.

```
<?xml version = "1.0"?>
<!DOCTYPE wml PUBLIC "-//WAPFORUM//DTD WML 1.2//EN"
   "http://www.wapforum.org/DTD/wml12.dtd">

<!-- Fig. 23.2: fig23_2.wml -->
<!-- Simple WML Page          -->

<wml>
   <card id = "index" title = "WML Title">
      <p>
         Welcome to wireless programming!
      </p>
   </card>
</wml>
```

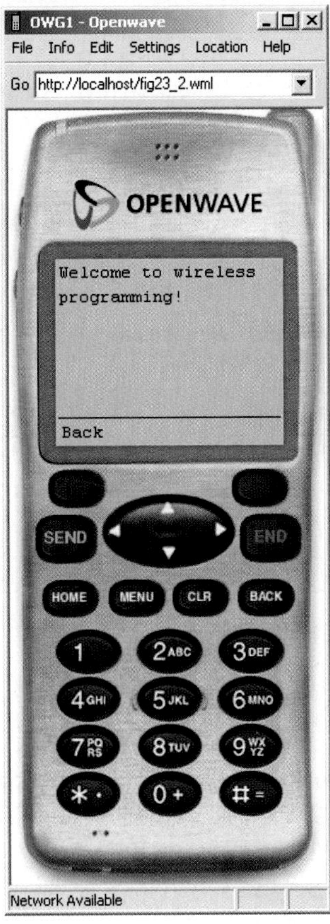

Fig. 23.2 Simple WML document (part 1 of 2). (Image of UP.SDK courtesy of Openwave Systems Inc. Openwave, the Openwave logo, and UP.SDK are trademarks of Openwave Systems Inc. All rights reserved.)

```
Phone Information
                <http://updev.phone.com/dev/wml/devhome4.wml>
              >

HTTP GET Request: http://updev.phone.com/dev/wml/devhome4.wml
Checking for URL 'updev.phone.com/dev/wml/devhome4.wml' in Whitelist
        not found

---------------- DATA SIZE ------------------------
Uncompiled data from HTTP is 1109 bytes.
...found Content-Type: text/vnd.wap.wml.
Compiled WAP binary is 527 bytes.
---------------------------------------------------
cache miss: <http://localhost/fig23_2.wml>
net request: <http://localhost/fig23_2.wml>

HTTP GET Request: http://localhost/fig23_2.wml
Checking for URL 'localhost/fig23_2.wml' in Whitelist
        not found

---------------- DATA SIZE ------------------------
Uncompiled data from HTTP is 1492 bytes.
...found Content-Type: text/vnd.wap.wml.
Compiled WAP binary is 168 bytes.
---------------------------------------------------
```

Fig. 23.2 Simple WML document (part 2 of 2). (Image of UP.SDK courtesy of Openwave Systems Inc. Openwave, the Openwave logo, and UP.SDK are trademarks of Openwave Systems Inc. All rights reserved.)

Line 9 contains the opening **`card`** *element*. The **`card`** element has two important attributes: ***`id`***, which uniquely identifies the card, and **`title`**, which displays a title at the top of most browser windows. The Openwave browser does not display **`card`** **`title`**s.

Common Programming Error 23.1

WML element and attribute names are case sensitive and must be written in lowercase. Writing a WML tag in uppercase is a syntax error.

Common Programming Error 23.2

Every WML document requires a minimum of one **`card`** *element, which contains information (e.g., text, images or links). Failure to include this element is a syntax error.*

Good Programming Practice 23.1

A wireless device's display is often small, so keep **`card`** **`title`***s concise.*

Portability Tip 23.1

Some browsers do not display the value of the **`title`** *attribute.*

All text in a WML document is placed between **`<p>`** tags that are nested within **`<card>`** tags. Although the text occupies only one line in the document, the screen capture in Fig. 23.2 shows the text as displayed on two lines. When a line of text exceeds the width of the display, the Openwave browser wraps the text onto the next line.

Portability Tip 23.2

Not all browsers wrap text onto the next line of the display window. In some cases, long lines of text run off the right side of the screen. Many devices do not support horizontal scrolling; therefore, the text cannot be read. Always test WAP applications on devices on which these applications are likely to run.

Figure 23.2 also includes a screen capture of the ***Phone Information*** window. This window alerts the developer to any errors that occur during the testing of WML and WMLScript documents. For example, if we had left out the closing **`card`** element (line 13 of Fig. 23.2), the Openwave Simulator would display the error message, "**`Compile Error. See Info Window for Details.`**" in the display window. Figure 23.3 shows a screen capture of the **Phone Information** window detailing the specifics of the error. Wireless devices do not contain this window.

The section labeled **WML Errors** lists each error, along with an accompanying line number. Below the list of errors, the window lists the WML code. Note that in this example, the closing card element is missing.

One of WML's most important capabilities is its ability to create hyperlinks between WML documents on the Web. Both text and images can be used as links to other decks. Figure 23.4 creates both internal links (i.e., links to locations inside the same document) and external links (i.e., links to locations in separate documents), by using *local icons*, or small images stored in the wireless device's memory. Figure 23.5 is a WML document which contains two cards. Figure 23.4 provides an external link to each card. These icons are part of the browser and do not have to be downloaded with the **`card`**. The Openwave browser supports over 175 different local icons, including such images as symbols, clouds, cell phones, cars and footballs. The WML Language Reference documentation that is included with the SDK download contains a complete list of local icons supported by the Openwave browser.

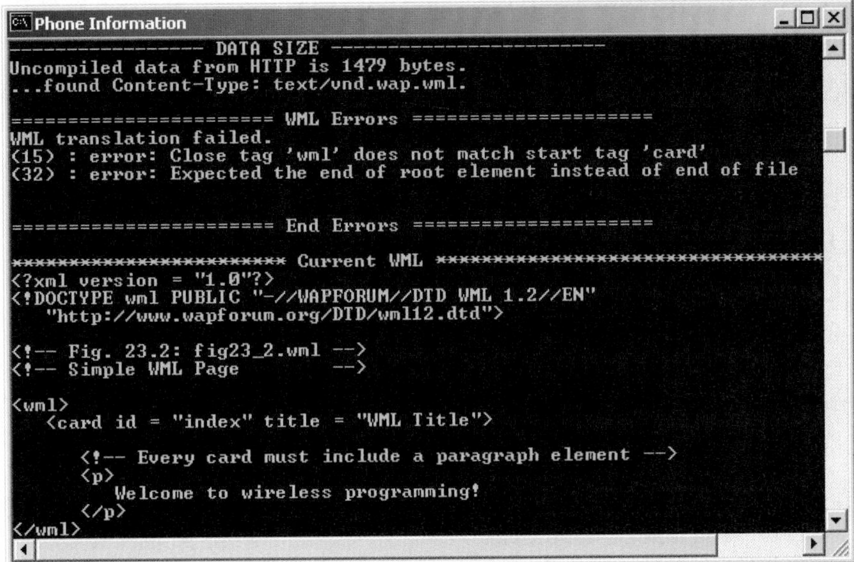

Fig. 23.3 **Phone Information** window showing an error in the deck.

As in XHTML, WML links are marked up with the **a** (*anchor*) *element*. In line 14 (Fig. 23.4), the **href** attribute is assigned a card name in the current deck, preceded by a pound sign (**#**). This creates an *internal link* to a **card** that is inside the document's deck. External linking to **card**s in other WML decks is specified by assigning to **href** the external document's name, followed by a **#** and **card** name (i.e., **href = "***page***.wml#***cardname***"**). Line 26 links to **card4** in **fig23_5.wml** (Fig. 23.5). If the card name is not specified, the first card in the deck is displayed.

```
1  <?xml version = "1.0"?>
2  <!DOCTYPE wml PUBLIC "-//WAPFORUM//DTD WML 1.2//EN"
3     "http://www.wapforum.org/DTD/wml12.dtd">
4
5  <!-- Fig. 23.4: fig23_4.wml -->
6  <!-- Using local icons      -->
7
8  <wml>
9     <card id = "index" title = "Icons">
10       <p>
11          Local Icons<br />
12
13          <!-- link to the second card -->
14          <a href = "#card2">
15
16             <!-- insert the local icon -->
17             <img src = "" alt = "Link" localsrc = "link" />
18          </a>Link<br />
19
20          <!-- link to the third card -->
21          <a href = "#card3">
22             <img src = "" alt = "Wrench" localsrc = "wrench" />
23          </a>Wrench<br />
24
25          <!--link to an external card-->
26          <a href = "fig23_5.wml#card4">
27             <img src = "" alt = "Football" localsrc = "football" />
28          </a>Football<br />
29
30          <a href = "fig23_5.wml#card5">
31             <img src = "" alt = "Boat" localsrc = "boat" />
32          </a>Boat
33       </p>
34    </card>
35
36    <card id = "card2" title = "Icons">
37       <p>
38          You chose the link!
39       </p>
40    </card>
41
```

Fig. 23.4 Using local icons as links (part 1 of 2).

```
      <card id = "card3" title = "Wrench Link">
         <p>
            You chose the wrench!
         </p>
      </card>
   </wml>
```

Fig. 23.4 Using local icons as links (part 2 of 2).

Two types of images can be used as links—*imported images* and local icons. Imported images must be downloaded or created using software programs such as Paint Shop Pro (included on the CD at the back of this book), PhotoShop Elements (discussed in Chapter 3) or Paint. Imported images are referenced using the **img** element's **src** attribute. Before an image can be rendered by the Openwave browser, it must be converted to *wireless bitmap (**wbmp**) format* by using a conversion program such as Pic2WBMP, which can be downloaded for free from **www.gingco.de/wap**.

Performance Tip 23.1

Large images can take a long time to download. Some wireless Internet billing plans charge by the amount of data downloaded; others charge by the amount of time spent using the service. In either case, the downloading of large images can result in additional wireless- access charges for users. Using local icons instead of imported images minimizes download time.

Local icons are included as part of the Openwave browser and are referenced via the **img** element's ***localsrc*** attribute. Although the ***height*** and ***width*** of an image can be specified in pixels, the size of an image is limited to the device's display area.

Portability Tip 23.3

Currently, only a small number of wireless devices can display color.

Portability Tip 23.4

*Some wireless browsers do not provide local icons. If the icon specified by the **localsrc** attribute is not supported by the browser, the image specified by the **src** attribute is used. If neither image can be displayed, then the value of the **alt** attribute is displayed.*

Every **img** element requires an **alt** attribute that contains a short text description of the image. The **alt** attribute is used when an image cannot be displayed.

Common Programming Error 23.3

*Omitting the **alt** attribute is a syntax error.*

```
<?xml version = "1.0"?>
<!DOCTYPE wml PUBLIC "-//WAPFORUM//DTD WML 1.2//EN"
   "http://www.wapforum.org/DTD/wml12.dtd">

```

Fig. 23.5 Linking to an external card (part 1 of 2). (Image of UP.SDK courtesy Openwave Systems Inc. Openwave, the Openwave logo, and UP.SDK are trademarks of Openwave Systems Inc. All rights reserved.)

```
<!-- Fig. 23.5: fig23_5.wml       -->
<!-- Linking to an external card -->

<wml>
   <card id = "card4" title = "Football Link">
      <p>
         You chose the football!
      </p>
   </card>

   <card id = "card5" title = "Boat Link">
      <p>
         You chose the boat!
      </p>
   </card>
</wml>
```

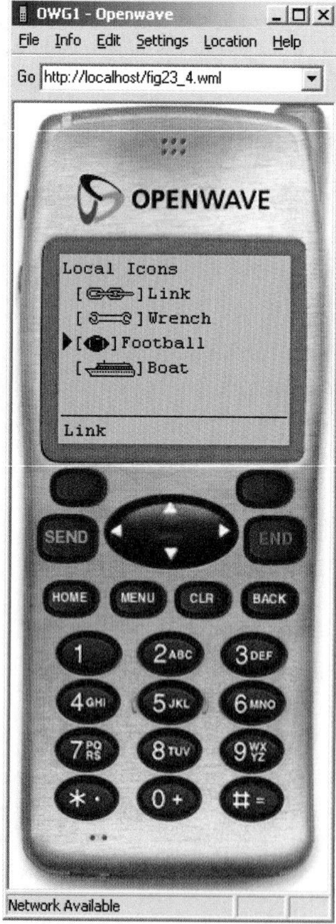

Fig. 23.5 Linking to an external card (part 2 of 2). (Image of UP.SDK courtesy Openwave Systems Inc. Openwave, the Openwave logo, and UP.SDK are trademarks of Openwave Systems Inc. All rights reserved.)

Lines 14–18 (Fig. 23.4) contain an image hyperlink. By nesting the **<img>** tag in an **<a>** tag, the image becomes a hyperlink. In this case, we provide an internal link to **card2** (line 14).

The **src** attribute of the **img** element in line 17 is empty because the image is specified in the **localsrc** attribute, and we do not provide an alternate image to display if the browser does not support the local icon. The **src** attribute is also a required attribute of the **img** element, but can be left blank. The **link** local icon is specified in the **localsrc** attribute.

23.12 WMLScript Programming

We now begin our introduction to the WMLScript scripting language. WMLScript facilitates a disciplined approach to the designing of programs that enhance the functionality of WML documents. The relationship between WML and WMLScript is similar to that between XHTML and JavaScript. However, one key difference is that WMLScript is placed in a separate document and cannot be embedded inside a WML document.

Common Programming Error 23.4

WMLScript is case sensitive. Failure to use the proper case is a syntax error.

Software Engineering Observation 23.1

The Openwave browser caches each deck loaded from the server. The cache is an area of a device in which the browser saves Web pages to facilitate the rapid retrieval of the pages in the future. The Openwave browser looks for a document in the device's cache before going to the Web to access the document. When developing applications, be sure to clear the cache every time a page is changed by selecting **Clear Cache** *from the* **Edit** *menu in the simulator.*

Our first WMLScript example provides the text "**Welcome to WMLScript Programming!**" to a WML document. Openwave's browser contains a *WMLScript interpreter* for the execution of WMLScript commands. Our first script is shown in Fig. 23.6; the associated WML document and output are shown in Fig. 23.7.

Common Programming Error 23.5

Placing any WMLScript code outside a function definition is an error.

```
// Fig. 23.6: welcomeDoc.wmls
// Writing a line of text

extern function welcome()
{
   // creating a browser variable and assigning it a value
   WMLBrowser.setVar( "welcome",
      "Welcome to WMLScript programming!" );

   // refresh the display window
   WMLBrowser.refresh();
}
```

Fig. 23.6 WMLScript listing for **welcomeDoc.wmls**.

Lines 4–12 define function **welcome**. Keyword **extern** denotes that the function is externally accessible to other WML and WMLScript documents. The omission of this keyword restricts the function's visibility (or scope) to the WMLScript file in which it is defined. Functions that do not use **extern** are called *utility* or *helper* functions. These functions often contain logic that is specific to the WMLScript file. Other external documents cannot not call these functions directly.

WMLScript provides objects for performing common mathematical calculations, string manipulations, browser manipulations and other functions. These objects offer many basic capabilities that programmers need. WMLScript provides the ***WMLBrowser*** object for interacting with the browser. We call the **WMLBrowser** object's ***setVar*** *method* (lines 7–8) to create a *browser variable named* **welcome** *and to assign it a string. Browser variables are global variables; they reside in the browser's memory and are accessible to any WML or WMLScript document residing in the browser's memory.*

Common Programming Error 23.6

Failure to terminate a WMLScript statement with a semicolon is an error.

Line 11 calls the **WMLBrowser** object's ***refresh*** method to update (or refresh) the values of all browser variables. This allows the WML document that calls function **welcome** to use the browser variable's new value. In this instance, invoking the **refresh** method refreshes the browser, updating **welcome**'s value. If the variable is not refreshed, browser variable **welcome** will display an empty string when it is dereferenced in the WML document (line 19 of Fig. 23.7).

Common Programming Error 23.7

If a browser variable is created in a WMLScript document and control goes back to the card that referenced the function, the browser must be refreshed using the **refresh** *method. If this is not done, the value of the variable will not be updated and displayed.*

The WML document in Fig. 23.7 invokes function **welcome** in **welcomeDoc.wmls** (Fig. 23.6). The result of function **welcome** is displayed by the WML document.

```
1  <?xml version = "1.0"?>
2  <!DOCTYPE wml PUBLIC "-//WAPFORUM//DTD WML 1.2//EN"
3     "http://www.wapforum.org/DTD/wml12.dtd">
4
5  <!-- Fig. 23.7: fig23_7.wml  -->
6  <!-- Printing a line of text -->
7
8  <wml>
9     <card id = "Line" title = "Line">
10
11       <onevent type = "onenterforward">
12
13          <!-- call function welcome -->
14          <go href = "welcomeDoc.wmls#welcome()" />
```

Fig. 23.7 WML document that calls function **welcome** (part 1 of 2). (Image of UP.SDK courtesy Openwave Systems Inc. Openwave, the Openwave logo, and UP.SDK are trademarks of Openwave Systems Inc. All rights reserved.)

```
15
16         </onevent>
17
18         <p>
19            $welcome <!-- dereference browser variable welcome -->
20         </p>
21      </card>
22   </wml>
```

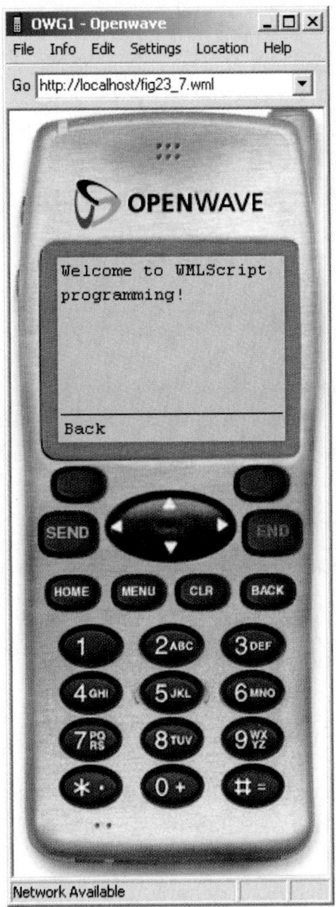

Fig. 23.7 WML document that calls function **welcome** (part 2 of 2). (Image of UP.SDK courtesy Openwave Systems Inc. Openwave, the Openwave logo, and UP.SDK are trademarks of Openwave Systems Inc. All rights reserved.)

Lines 11–16 contain the ***onevent*** element that invokes WMLScript function **welcome**. The **onevent** element is an *event element* that executes a *task element*, such as the **go** element (line 14), which is wrapped in its tags. Task elements such as **go**, **refresh** and **prev** perform certain actions when executed. A complete list of task elements can be found at **www.w3schools.com/wap/wml_reference.asp**. Attribute **type** is set to **"onenterforward"**. This executes the task element **go** when the **card** is loaded.

Function **welcome** in **welcomeDoc.wmls** is invoked in line 14 by assigning to attribute **href** the WMLScript document name followed by a **#** sign and the function name (Fig. 23.6). WMLScript documents have the **.wmls** file extension and are referenced from within a WML document.

Good Programming Practice 23.2

*If the value of the **href** attribute does not include the name of the function, the first function declared using keyword **extern** is executed. Always include the function name when calling a WMLScript file.*

Common Programming Error 23.8

Failure to enclose link addresses in quotes is a syntax error.

Common Programming Error 23.9

*When referencing a function from an **href** attribute's value, failure to precede a function name with a pound sign (**#**) is a runtime error.*

Common Programming Error 23.10

*When referencing a function from an **href** attribute's value, failure to follow the function name with a set of parentheses is a logic error.*

Lines 18–20 mark up browser variable **welcome**'s value with **<p>** tags. The insertion of the *dollar sign* (**$**) before the variable name retrieves the browser variable's value from the device's memory.

Common Programming Error 23.11

Browsers that do not support scripting cannot interpret WMLScript instructions. The browser renders only the WML document.

Sometimes it is useful to display important messages, such as those that inform users that required form fields have been left blank, in windows called *dialogs*. Function **displayDialog** (Fig. 23.8) displays text in an *alert dialog*. This function is called from within the WML document shown in Fig. 23.9.

The **Dialogs** object contains methods for the displaying of messages on clients devices. Line 6 (Fig. 23.8) calls **Dialogs** method **alert**, which displays an alert dialog (Fig. 23.9). The string passed to this method is displayed to the user. The dialog output displays three lines of text. As each newline character (**\n**) is rendered, subsequent text is displayed on the next line.

```
1  // Fig. 23.8: dialogPrompt.wmls
2  // Printing multiple lines in a dialog
3
4  extern function displayDialog()
5  {
6     Dialogs.alert( "Welcome to\nWMLScript\nProgramming!" );
7  }
```

Fig. 23.8 WMLScript listing for **dialogPrompt.wmls**.

Figure 23.9 is the WML document that invokes function **displayDialog**. Most browsers contain one or more *soft keys* that allow users to select options. Soft keys are the physical buttons on a wireless device that enable a user to navigate between documents. By default, the alert dialog labels the left soft key **OK**. When the user presses the soft key, the dialog is closed (or dismissed). After the dialog is closed, any remaining WML markup is rendered.

In our next example, we explore WMLScript functions in greater detail. Figure 23.10 calls a programmer-defined function, **count**, to obtain a number from the user, convert the number to an integer and pass that value to a second programmer-defined function, **square**. This function returns the square of the integer.

Lines 7–8 call **Dialogs** method ***prompt*** to obtain a number from the user. The first argument passed to method **prompt** is the prompt message that is displayed to the user. The second argument specifies a default value for which we provide an empty string value. The default value is displayed in the input field when the dialog opens. If a default value is supplied, the user would have to delete this value to enter information. Method **prompt** creates a soft key labeled **alpha**, which limits the information that users can enter to letters typed via the device's keypad. Variable **inputNumber** stores the string input by the user. In line 12, we call **Lang** object method **parseInt** to convert **inputNumber**'s value from a string to an integer. Object **Lang** provides methods for conversion between data types and for the performing of mathematical calculations.

There are two ways to declare variables in WMLScript: Method **setVar** and keyword **var**. Method **setVar** declares a browser variable that can be accessed by both WML and WMLScript documents, and keyword **var** declares a *local variable* (i.e., a variable that can be accessed only in the function in which it is declared).

```
<?xml version = "1.0"?>
<!DOCTYPE wml PUBLIC "-//WAPFORUM//DTD WML 1.2//EN"
   "http://www.wapforum.org/DTD/wml12.dtd">

<!-- Fig. 23.9: fig23_9.wml -->
<!-- Using dialogs          -->

<wml>
   <card id = "Dialog" title = "Dialog">

      <!-- event element to execute go element -->
      <onevent type = "onenterforward">

         <!-- call function displayDialog -->
         <!-- in dialogPrompt.wmls        -->
         <go href = "dialogPrompt.wmls#displayDialog()" />

      </onevent>

   </card>
</wml>
```

Fig. 23.9 Displaying multiple lines in a dialog (part 1 of 2). (Image of UP.SDK courtesy Openwave Systems Inc. Openwave, the Openwave logo, and UP.SDK are trademarks of Openwave Systems Inc. All rights reserved.)

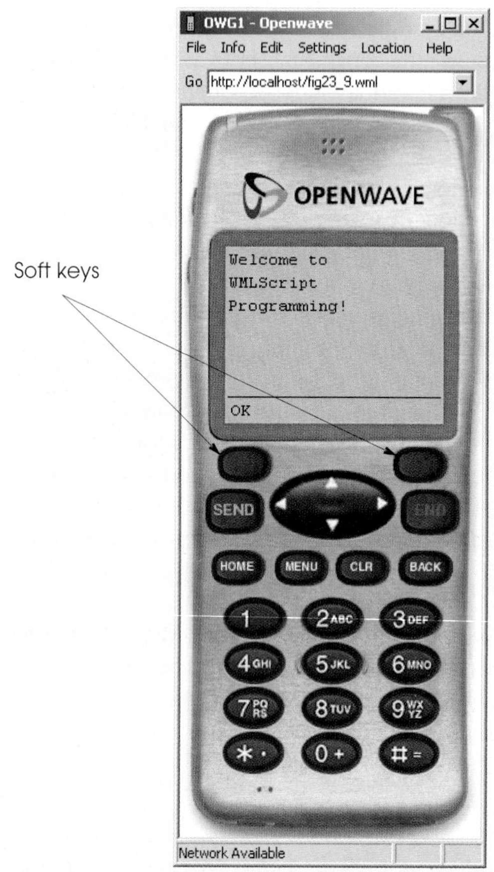

Fig. 23.9 Displaying multiple lines in a dialog (part 2 of 2). (Image of UP.SDK courtesy Openwave Systems Inc. Openwave, the Openwave logo, and UP.SDK are trademarks of Openwave Systems Inc. All rights reserved.)

```
// Fig. 23.10: squareNumbers.wmls
// Programmer-defined functions

extern function count()
{
   // prompt the user for a number
   var inputNumber = Dialogs.prompt(
      "Enter a number to be squared", "" );

   // convert the number to an integer and pass
   // the number to function square
   var numberSquared = square( Lang.parseInt( inputNumber ) );

```

Fig. 23.10 Using programmer-defined functions to square a number (part 1 of 2).

```
14      var outputSquare = inputNumber + " squared is " +
15          numberSquared;
16
17      // set the string to a browser variable and
18      // redirect the client to the card named result
19      WMLBrowser.setVar( "result1", outputSquare );
20      WMLBrowser.go( "#result" );
21  }
22
23  function square( y )
24  {
25      return y * y;
26  }
```

Fig. 23.10 Using programmer-defined functions to square a number (part 2 of 2).

Function **square** (line 23) calculates the square of a number and **return**s the result to function **count**. The scope of function **square** is restricted to **squareNumbers.wmls**, because keyword **extern** has been omitted from the definition. Lines 14–15 concatenate **inputNumber**'s value, the string **" squared is "** and the value of variable **numberSquared**. The result is then stored in variable **outputSquare**. Line 19 calls the **WMLBrowser** method **setVar** to create a new browser variable named **result1**, which is assigned the value of **outputSquare**. Line 20 calls **WMLBrowser** method **go** to load **card result** into the browser.

Common Programming Error 23.12

The placing of a semicolon after the right parenthesis in a function definition is a runtime error.

Common Programming Error 23.13

The failure to return a value from a function that is expected to do so is a logic error.

Figure 23.11 lists the WML document that contains the call to function **count** (Fig. 23.10). The document contains two **card**s. The first **card** programs a soft key (lines 12–14), that, when pressed, invokes function **count**.

Element ***do*** (lines 12–14) programs a soft key for a wireless device. Attribute ***label*** defines the text that appears above the soft key on the display screen. Attribute ***type*** assigns an action to the soft key. When a device has two soft keys, the **"accept"** value programs the left soft keys and the **"options"** value programs the right soft key.

When a soft key is pressed, the **go** element's action is executed. Line 13 contains the **go** element that calls function **count** in **squareNumber.wmls**. After the number is squared, the browser displays **card result**. Lines 24–26 program a soft key that displays the previous **card**, which asks the user to enter the number to be squared. Element ***prev*** is a task element that displays the previous **card**.

In the previous examples, we used the **WMLBrowser** object for creating browser variables. In Fig. 23.12, **WMLBrowser** method ***getVar*** is called to retrieve a variable's value from a WML document.

Line 6 calls method **getVar** to obtain the value of browser variable **username**. This value is then assigned to local variable **x**. Figure 23.13 shows the WML document that defines browser variable **username**. Line 21 creates an *input box* for user input. The **input** element's ***name*** attribute identifies the **input** box. An input box's **name** becomes a browser variable once it is posted. The value of variable **username** is retrieved on line 6 of Fig. 23.12 and is assigned to variable **x**. We then call **WMLBrowser** method **go** to display **card2** (Fig. 23.13). Lines 30–32 create a soft key that allows the user to return to the previous **card** to enter a new name. Line 35 displays the value of browser variable **result**.

23.13 String Object Methods

Characters are the fundamental building blocks of WMLScript programs. Every program is composed of a sequence of characters that, when grouped together meaningfully, are interpreted by the wireless device as a series of instructions used to accomplish a task.

The ***String*** object provides methods for selecting characters, obtaining substrings and searching for substrings within a string. A complete list of **String** object methods is available at

www.wirelessdevnet.com/channels/
coderef.phtml?catid=5&subid=5.

Figure 23.14 demonstrates some of these methods.

```
<?xml version = "1.0"?>
<!DOCTYPE wml PUBLIC "-//WAPFORUM//DTD WML 1.2//EN"
   "http://www.wapforum.org/DTD/wml12.dtd">

<!-- Fig. 23.11: fig23_11.wml -->
<!-- Squaring numbers         -->

<wml>
   <card id = "index" title = "Number Squared">

      <!-- soft key to invoke function count -->
      <do type = "accept" label = "OK">
         <go href = "squareNumbers.wmls#count()" />
      </do>

      <p>
         Press OK to square a number.
      </p>
   </card>

   <card id = "result" title = "Results">

      <!-- soft key that returns the user to the previous card -->
      <do type = "accept" label = "Home">
         <prev />
      </do>
```

Fig. 23.11 Squaring a number by using programmer-defined functions (part 1 of 2). (Image of UP.SDK courtesy Openwave Systems Inc. Openwave, the Openwave logo, and UP.SDK are trademarks of Openwave Systems Inc. All rights reserved.)

```

      <p>
         $result1
      </p>
   </card>
</wml>
```

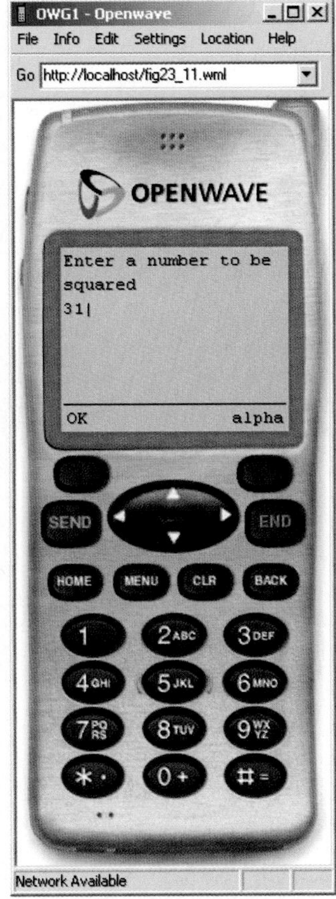

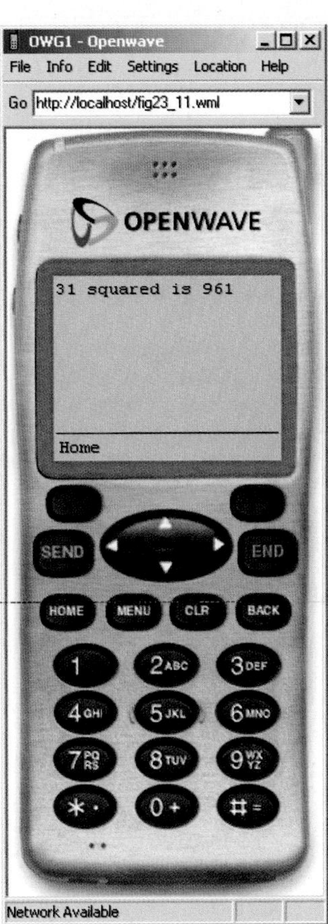

Fig. 23.11 Squaring a number by using programmer-defined functions (part 2 of 2). (Image of UP.SDK courtesy Openwave Systems Inc. Openwave, the Openwave logo, and UP.SDK are trademarks of Openwave Systems Inc. All rights reserved.)

```
// Fig. 23.12: getVariable.wmls
// Using the WMLBrowser object's getVar method

```

Fig. 23.12 Using the **`WMLBrowser`** object's **`getVar`** method (part 1 of 2).

```
extern function getName()
{
   var x = WMLBrowser.getVar( "username" );
   var y = x + ", thanks for visiting!";

   WMLBrowser.setVar( "result", y );
   WMLBrowser.go( "#card2" );
}
```

Fig. 23.12 Using the **WMLBrowser** object's **getVar** method (part 2 of 2).

```
<?xml version = "1.0"?>
<!DOCTYPE wml PUBLIC "-//WAPFORUM//DTD WML 1.2//EN"
   "http://www.wapforum.org/DTD/wml12.dtd">

<!-- Fig. 23.13: getVar.wml                          -->
<!-- Using the WMLBrowser object's getVar method -->

<wml>
   <card id = "index" title = "getVar">
      <do type = "accept" label = "Run">

         <!-- call function getName -->
         <go href = "getVariable.wmls#getName()" />

      </do>

      <p>
         Enter your name:<br />

         <!-- create input box for user input -->
         <input name = "username" value = "" />

      </p>
   </card>

   <card id = "card2" title = "getVar">

      <!-- create a soft key to return the client -->
      <!-- to the previous card                   -->
      <do type = "accept" label = "Back">
         <prev />
      </do>

      <p>
         $result <!-- dereference browser variable result -->
      </p>
   </card>
</wml>
```

Fig. 23.13 Setting and displaying a variable using WMLScript (part 1 of 2). (Image of UP.SDK courtesy Openwave Systems Inc. Openwave, the Openwave logo, and UP.SDK are trademarks of Openwave Systems Inc. All rights reserved.)

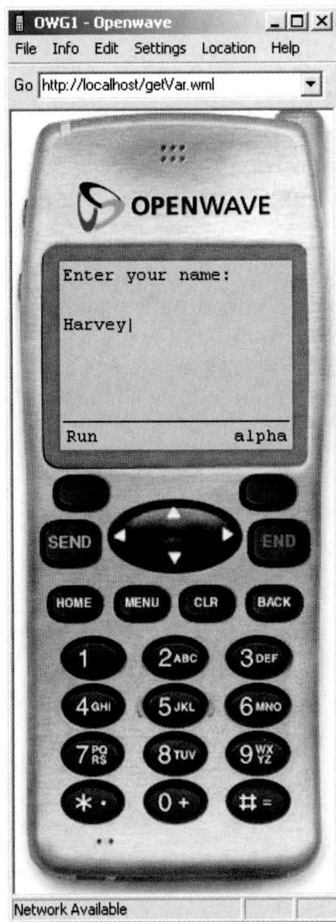

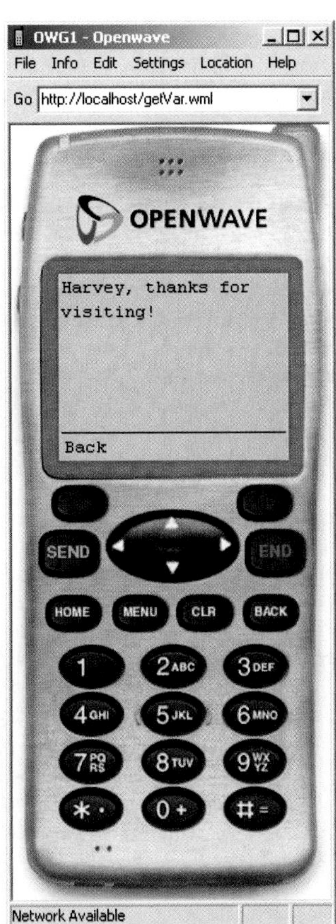

Fig. 23.13 Setting and displaying a variable using WMLScript (part 2 of 2). (Image of UP.SDK courtesy Openwave Systems Inc. Openwave, the Openwave logo, and UP.SDK are trademarks of Openwave Systems Inc. All rights reserved.)

The example begins with the value of variable **`string1`** set to an empty string (**`""`**). Through the course of the example, we call **`String`** object methods to change the string **`"Wireless Web"`** to the string **`"Deitel Book"`**.

```
// Fig. 23.14: functionSet.wmls
// Demonstrating String object methods

extern function stringMethods()
{
   var string1 = "";
   var empty;

```

Fig. 23.14 Demonstrating String object methods (part 1 of 2).

```
   // test if string1 is empty
   if ( String.isEmpty( string1 ) )
      empty = "string1 is empty";
   else
      empty = "string1 is not empty";

   WMLBrowser.setVar( "emptyString1", empty );

   // format the string to have 12 spaces between
   // "Wireless" and "Web"
   string1 = String.format( "Wireless%15s", "Web" );

   WMLBrowser.setVar( "formatString1", string1 );

   // squeeze the string until one space is left
   string1 = String.squeeze( string1 );

   WMLBrowser.setVar( "squeezeString1", string1 );

   // use method element to count the elements in string1
   // use the toString method to convert the integer to
   // a string
   var count = String.toString( String.elements( string1, " ") );

   WMLBrowser.setVar( "elementsString1", count );

   // find string starting at index 8 and ending with a space
   var string1Element = String.elementAt( string1, 8, " " );

   WMLBrowser.setVar( "elementAtString1", string1Element );

   // get the length of string1
   var length = String.length( string1 );

   // insert "Book" at the end of string1
   string1 = String.insertAt( string1, "Book", length, " " );

   WMLBrowser.setVar( "insertAtString1", string1 );

   // replace "Web" with "Deitel" where "Web" has an
   // index of 1
   string1 = String.replaceAt( string1, "Deitel", 1, " " );

   WMLBrowser.setVar( "replaceAtString1", string1 );

   // remove "Wireless" from string1
   string1 = String.removeAt( string1, 0, " " );

   WMLBrowser.setVar( "removeAtString1", string1 );
   WMLBrowser.go( "#card2" );
}
```

Fig. 23.14 Demonstrating String object methods (part 2 of 2).

In line 6, we declare variable **string1** and assign it to an empty string. Line 10 determines if the value of **string1** is empty. If the condition in line 10 evaluates to **true**, variable **empty** is assigned the string **"string1 is empty"**; otherwise, **empty** is assigned the string **"string1 is not empty"**. Line 15 calls **WMLBrowser** method **setVar** to declare browser variable **emptystring1**, setting its value to that of variable **empty**. We assign each value to a different browser variable throughout the script so that the results in Fig. 23.15 are displayed.

In line 19, we assign to **string1** the strings **"Wireless"** and **"Web"**. By calling method **format**, we place 12 spaces (indicated by **%15s**) between the two strings. Although the notation **%15s** creates 15 space characters, three are occupied by the string **"Web"**, leaving only 12 spaces between the two strings. The Openwave browser automatically wraps the line (Fig. 23.15) because it is too long to display on a single line. The value of **string1** becomes

```
"Wireless            Web"
```

Line 24 calls **String** method ***squeeze*** to combine all consecutive whitespace characters in **string1** into a single whitespace character. Variable **string1** now becomes

```
"Wireless Web"
```

Line 31 calls **String** method ***elements*** to return the number of words in the string, separated by a space character. Method **toString** converts the integer value returned by **elements** to a string. This method is useful if a value must be concatenated to another string.

In line 36, we call method ***elementAt*** to return a substring of **string1** from index **8** to the first space encountered. Indices point to individual characters in a string, beginning at **0**. In this case, the string returned is

```
"Web"
```

In line 41, we call method **length** to retrieve the number of characters in **string1**. This value is assigned to variable **length**. In line 44, we call method ***insertAt*** to insert the string **"Book"** into the end of **string1**, separated by a space. The value of **string1** becomes

```
"Wireless Web Book"
```

Line 50 calls **String** method ***replaceAt*** to return a new string in which the string **"Deitel"** replaces everything from the first space to the second space in **string1**. After the **replaceAt** method is invoked, the value of **string1** becomes

```
"Wireless Deitel Book"
```

Line 55 calls method **removeAt** to remove characters in **string1** from index **0** to the first occurrence of a space. When invoked, method **removeAt** removes the string **"Wireless"**. The value of **string1** becomes

```
"Deitel Book"
```

The WML document in Fig 23.15 calls function **stringMethods** in Fig. 23.14 and displays the results.

```
<?xml version = "1.0"?>
<!DOCTYPE wml PUBLIC "-//WAPFORUM//DTD WML 1.2//EN"
   "http://www.wapforum.org/DTD/wml12.dtd">

<!-- Fig. 23.15: stringMisc.wml                       -->
<!-- WML document that references stringMisc.wmls -->

<wml>

   <card id = "index" title = "strings">
      <do type = "accept" label = "Run">

         <!-- call function stringMethods in functionSet.wmls -->
         <go href = "functionSet.wmls#stringMethods()" />

      </do>

      <p>
         Click Run to execute the script.
      </p>
   </card>

   <card id  ="card2" title = "strings">
      <do type = "accept" label = "Run">

         <!-- redirect the user to the next card to -->
         <!-- display further results              -->
         <go href = "#card3" />

      </do>

      <p>
         isEmpty method:<br />

         <!-- dereference browser variable emptyString1 -->
         $emptyString1

      </p>
   </card>

   <card id = "card3" title = "strings">
      <do type = "accept" label = "Run">

         <!-- redirect the user to the next card to -->
         <!-- display further results              -->
         <go href = "#card4" />
```

Fig. 23.15 WML document that references **stringMisc.wmls**. (part 1 of 5). (Image of UP.SDK courtesy Openwave Systems Inc. Openwave, the Openwave logo, and UP.SDK are trademarks of Openwave Systems Inc. All rights reserved.)

```

      </do>

      <p>
         String.format method:<br />

         <!-- dereference browser variable formatString1 -->
         $formatString1
      </p>
   </card>

   <card id = "card4" title = "strings">
      <do type = "accept" label = "Run">

         <!-- redirect the user to the next card to -->
         <!-- display further results             -->
         <go href = "#card5" />
      </do>

      <p>
         String.squeeze method:<br />

         <!-- dereference browser variable squeezeString1 -->
         $squeezeString1
      </p>

   </card>

   <card id = "card5" title = "strings">
      <do type = "accept" label = "Run">

         <!-- redirect the user to the next card to -->
         <!-- display further results             -->
         <go href = "#card6" />
      </do>

      <p>
         String.elements method:<br />

         <!-- dereference browser variable elementsString1 -->
         $elementsString1
      </p>
   </card>

   <card id = "card6" title = "strings">
      <do type = "accept" label = "Run">

         <!-- redirect the user to the next card to -->
         <!-- display further results             -->
         <go href = "#card7" />
```

Fig. 23.15 WML document that references **stringMisc.wmls**. (part 2 of 5). (Image of UP.SDK courtesy Openwave Systems Inc. Openwave, the Openwave logo, and UP.SDK are trademarks of Openwave Systems Inc. All rights reserved.)

```
      </do>

      <p>
         String.elementAt method:<br />

         <!-- dereference browser variable elementAtString1 -->
         $elementAtString1
      </p>
   </card>

   <card id = "card7" title = "strings">
      <do type = "accept" label = "Run">

         <!-- redirect the user to the next card to -->
         <!-- display further results              -->
         <go href = "#card8" />
      </do>

      <p>
         String.insertAt method:<br />

         <!-- dereference browser variable insertAtString1 -->
         $insertAtString1
      </p>
   </card>

   <card id = "card8" title = "strings">
      <do type = "accept" label = "Run">

         <!-- redirect the user to the next card to -->
         <!-- display further results              -->
         <go href = "#card9" />
      </do>

      <p>
         String.replaceAt method:<br />

         <!-- dereference browser variable replaceAtString1 -->
         $replaceAtString1
      </p>
   </card>

   <card id = "card9" title = "strings">
      <do type = "accept" label = "Home">

         <!-- redirect the user to the first card -->
         <go href = "#index" />
      </do>

      <p>
```

Fig. 23.15 WML document that references **stringMisc.wmls**. (part 3 of 5). (Image of UP.SDK courtesy Openwave Systems Inc. Openwave, the Openwave logo, and UP.SDK are trademarks of Openwave Systems Inc. All rights reserved.)

```
            String.removeAt method:<br />

            <!-- dereference browser variable removeAtString1 -->
            $removeAtString1
         </p>
      </card>
</wml>
```

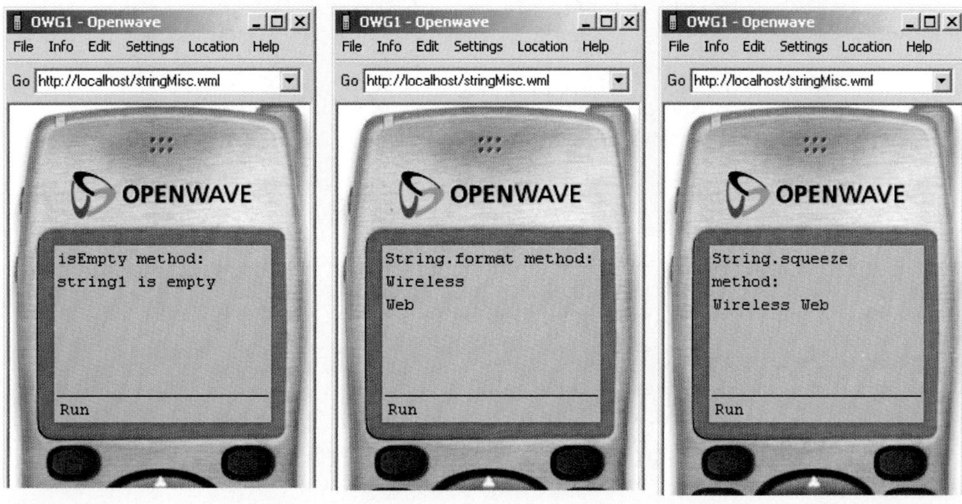

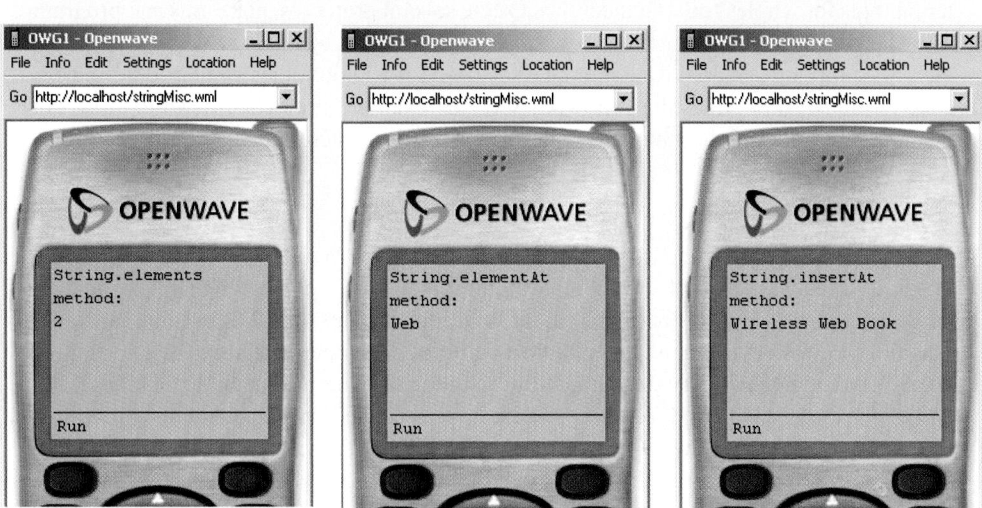

Fig. 23.15 WML document that references **`stringMisc.wmls`**. (part 4 of 5). (Image of UP.SDK courtesy Openwave Systems Inc. Openwave, the Openwave logo, and UP.SDK are trademarks of Openwave Systems Inc. All rights reserved.)

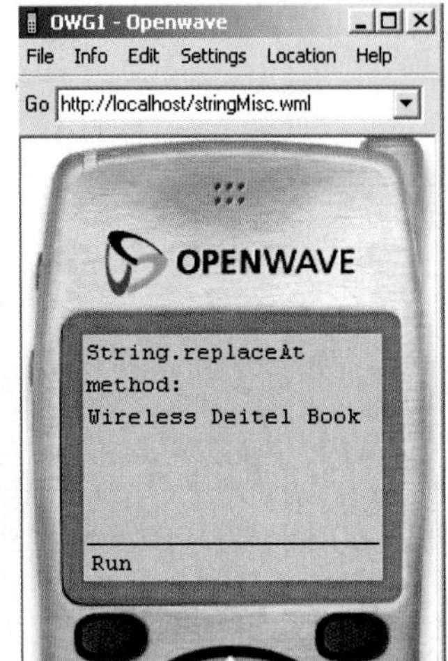

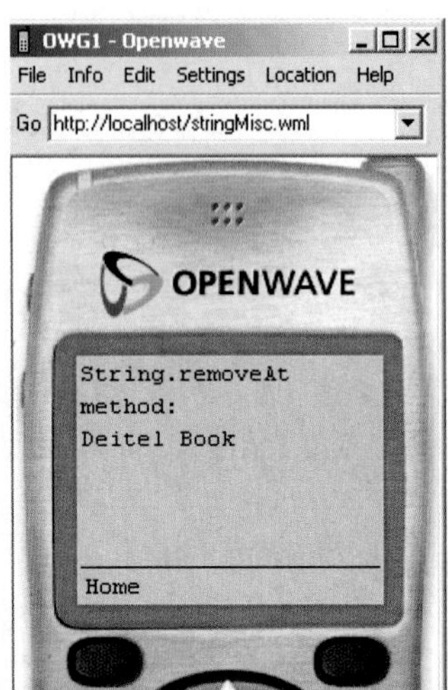

Fig. 23.15 WML document that references **stringMisc.wmls**. (part 5 of 5). (Image of UP.SDK courtesy Openwave Systems Inc. Openwave, the Openwave logo, and UP.SDK are trademarks of Openwave Systems Inc. All rights reserved.)

23.14 Wireless Protocols, Platforms and Programming Languages

Programming languages, platforms and protocols are pivotal development and implementation tools for wireless communications. Often, several protocols, platforms and programming languages are used simultaneously in a single wireless technology development. The lack of a unifying standard results in incompatibilities and obstacles similar to those associated with WAP/WML. The following sections examine protocols, programming languages, their uses and their unique contributions to wireless communications.

23.14.1 WAP 2.0

WAP 2.0, scheduled for release in 2001, is a revision of the Wireless Application Protocol. WAP 2.0 specifies XHTML Basic, a subset of XHTML, to replace WML as the markup language used by wireless devices to render Web content. This new W3C Recommendation benefits wireless device manufacturers, Web content developers and users. Manufacturers will have a de facto industry standard, allowing them to develop compatible mobile devices and applications. Content developers will be able to create Web pages for such platforms as diverse as mobile phones, PDAs, pagers, WebTV and desktop computers. In addition, wireless device users acquire access to a wider selection of content that is easier to navigate.

WAP 2.0 will likely include WML extensions that allow programmers to embed WML within the XHTML Basic markup. Features, such as soft keys that are not supported by XHTML Basic will be implemented using WML. In addition, the new protocol is also expected to include specifications for color, animation and such multimedia features as MP3 audio and MPEG video streaming.

23.14.2 Handheld Devices Markup Languages (HDML)

The *Handheld Devices Markup Language* (*HDML*) was one of the first markup languages used to deliver content handheld devices. HDML was originally developed in 1996 by a company called Unwired Planet, now known as Openwave (**www.openwave.com**).[24]

HDML is similar to *Hypertext Markup Language* (*HTML*), which is used to design and format Web pages. However, HTML is not effective for use on devices with limited screen sizes and viewing capabilities. Although HDML was implemented in millions of devices when it was first introduced, it has been replaced with other emerging standards that support 2.5G and 3G technologies. HDML eventually evolved into WML.[25]

In Japan and parts of Europe, consumer wireless devices function using WAP and no longer support HDML. However, some CDMA-based phones in the United States and Canada still support both WML and HDML.[26] The conversion of HDML to WML code is not difficult, and Openwave (HDML's creator) is currently working to replace HDML with WML.

23.14.3 Compact HTML (cHTML) and i-mode

NTT DoCoMo and its popular i-mode service employ *Compact Hypertext Markup Language* (*cHTML*) to format Web pages. cHTML a subset of HTML that is designed for mobile devices, uses a limited set of HTML tags and attributes. With the exception of i-mode phones and devices, cHTML is not widely used. However, in the future, cHTML could merge with a form of WAP or XHTML Basic.

Previous sections of this chapter described the process by which WAP and WML communicate with the Internet. using specific protocols and markup tags. Although the i-mode service functions similarly, there are a few notable differences. When a user requests information from the Internet via an i-mode phone, the request is sent directly to Web servers at NTT DoCoMo, which send the desired information back to the user. NTT DoCoMo maintains over 30,000 pages of content designed specifically for the i-mode service, and this information is stored on the company's own servers.

23.14.4 Java and Java 2 Micro Edition (J2ME)

Java is one of the most popular programming languages in the software-development industry. Sun Microsystems created Java to facilitate the development of Internet and Web-based applications that can run consistently on any operating system without requiring alteration. Sun coined the term, "write once, run anywhere™" to describe this feature.

Over the past few years, Java has matured into the Java 2 platform, which provides an even higher level of consistency among different systems. Java 2 has evolved into three platforms:

1. Java 2 Standard Edition (J2SE™), which enables developers to create standalone programs and client-side applications,
2. Java 2 Enterprise Edition (J2EE™), which enables developers to create powerful enterprise systems for the management of entire businesses, and
3. Java 2 Micro Edition (J2ME™), which enables developers to create applications targeted to consumer devices.

Java 2 Micro Edition is the newest option for Java programming. This platform enables developers to write applications for such consumer devices as set-top boxes, web terminals and embedded systems. However, much of J2ME's popularity is attributed to the fact that developers can write applications for wireless devices. J2ME excels in assisting the development of applications for devices with limited resources (i.e., limited screen size, memory, power and bandwidth). J2ME also offers programmers tools to create user interfaces, connect to networks (to send and receive data) and save various program information (such as phone numbers and e-mail addresses). For more information on J2ME, visit **www.java.sun.com/j2me**.

23.14.5 Binary Run-Time Environment for Wireless (BREW)

The market for wireless devices, especially cell phones, is exploding. Great demand exists for cell phones to support more functions; however, there are problems adapting applications on the devices' varying runtime environments. One possible solution is for manufacturers to improve the hardware of mobile devices, enabling devices to support a larger number of applications. However, the costs associated with hardware improvements are extremely high. To provide additional functionality relatively inexpensively, Qualcomm has developed Binary Runtime Environment for Wireless (BREW). This new application platform was introduced in May 2001.[27]

BREW is a layer of code that works with Qualcomm chips and other cell-phone operating systems that allow cell phones to run application programs written using BREW development kits. Applications developed with the BREW standard development kit are platform-independent, allowing them to run on devices with varying runtime environments. The simplicity of application development using BREW allows manufacturers to reduce costs and shorten development timetables. In addition, the platform enables software developers to create applications, including navigation assistance, instant messaging, e-mail, e-wallets, games and personal information management, that are be accessible through a variety of wireless devices.[28]

23.14.6 Bluetooth Wireless Technology

Bluetooth wireless technology enables low-power, short-range wireless communications between computers, PDAs, cell phones and other devices. This technology has the potential to reduce and even eliminate the need for wires in offices, homes, cars and elsewhere.

Bluetooth wireless technology communicates by using radio frequencies to create a *personal area network* (*PAN*) of connected devices, also called a *piconet*. Bluetooth technology supports *point-to-point* communication, through which a Bluetooth-enabled device, such as a wireless phone, sends a signal to one other device, as well as *point-to-multipoint* communications, that connects one device to up to seven others. One Bluetooth device can recognize and connect to any other Bluetooth-enabled device within a 30 feet radius. For example, imagine that an employee uses a PDA to schedule a meeting with another user in the network. When both users return to their desktop computers, the information stored on their PDAs can be transferred to the users' desktop computer calendars by using Bluetooth wireless technology instead of user commands. This eliminates the need for users to perform a manual synchronization process later to update devices.

More than 2,200 companies are members of the Bluetooth Special Interest Group (SIG) (**www.bluetooth.com**). The SIG pools the patents of member companies and provides a free intellectual property license to member companies as long as the members submit products to qualification testing before sending their Bluetooth products to market.[29]

23.15 Internet and World Wide Web Resources

Wireless-Application Solution Providers/Enterprise Solutions

www.xcellenet.com
RemoteWare and *Afaria* allow organizations to manage communications among smartphones, PDAs, pagers, cell phones, kiosks and point-of-sale devices.

www.infowave.com
Infowave builds wireless applications for businesses-to-employee communications. The *Wireless Business Engine*® allows employees to access e-mail accounts, the corporate intranet, schedules, contact lists and other information.

www.terion.com
This end-to-end solutions provider offers two-way messaging and other technologies designed for the shipping and transportation industries.

Location-Based Service Providers

www.trueposition.com
TruePosition® uses TDOA technology to provide location-based services. TruePosition specializes in E911 applications.

www.ericsson.com
GSM phones can be located by using the Ericsson Mobile Positioning System. Ericsson has developed a wide variety of wireless location solutions.

Location-Based Technology News and Information

www.lbszone.com
This site provides links to news regarding location-based services and leading location-based service providers.

www.lbsz.com
This portal provides extensive links to news and information regarding location-based services.

Location-Based Services Standards and Legislation

www.locationforum.org
The Location Interoperability Forum (LIF) is dedicated to developing standards for location-identifying technologies.

www.fcc.gov/e911
This Web site was established by the FCC to provide information regarding the E911 Act.

www.fcc.gov/Bureaus/Wireless/Public_Notices/2000/da002099.html
This Web site was established by the FCC to provide details about the automatic location-identification specifications of the E911 Act.

Wireless Marketing and Advertising

www.mobliss.com
Mobliss develops wireless marketing solutions and focuses on targeting and tracking campaigns, including games, contests, sweepstakes and location-based promotions.

www.digitalimpact.com
Digital Impact designs and implements direct permission-based marketing campaigns. The company tracks and analyzes campaign results and delivers marketing through online and wireless channels.

www.advertising.com
This company provides marketing solutions for the Web, e-mail and wireless platforms. Ads are served for PDAs, on wireless Internet sites and through SMS.

WAP, WML and WMLScript

www.wapforum.org
This Web site contains information regarding WAP's history and its present status. The WAP Forum's goal is to establish wireless device interoperablility. This site is a good place to find the latest information about WAP, WML and WMLScript.

www.wirelessdevnet.com/channels/wap/training/wml.html
This document provides an introductory tutorial on building WAP applications using WML.

www.wirelessdevnet.com/channels/refview.phtml?cat=wmltags
This site is an online WML reference. It lists WML elements and attributes. Examples of WML markup are also provided.

www.wirelessdevnet.com/channels/wap/training/wml.html
This site provides a WML tutorial for beginners.

SUMMARY

- Wireless technology has developed into one of today's hottest topics.
- The wireless medium affects business management and operations, employee productivity, consumer purchasing behavior, marketing strategies and personal communications.
- M-business is defined as e-business enabled by wireless communications.
- Businesses and individuals can determine wireless users' locations within yards by using location-based services.
- The E911 Act is designed to standardize and enhance 911 service across mobile devices. Phase one of the E911 Act requires all wireless cellular carriers to provide Automatic Number Information (ANI), or the phone numbers of cell phones calling in 911 emergencies. The carriers must also provide the locations of the cell sites (a cell site identifies a particular tower's area of coverage) receiving the 911 calls.
- Phase two E911 bill mandates that all mobile-phone carriers provide Automatic Location Identification (ALI) of a caller within 125 meters, 67 percent of the time.
- Triangulation determines a user's location by analyzing the angles from (at least) two fixed points a known distance apart.
- A geocode is the latitude and longitude of the user's location.
- A pull strategy assumes that people will request that specific information be sent to their wireless devices in real time. A push strategy is enacted when marketing messages requested by the recipient are not delivered to wireless devices in real time.

- Permission-based marketing helps guard customer privacy. It also increases campaign response rates and productivity, because the target market is better defined.
- Limited technology and a variety of protocols cause marketing content to be displayed differently on various receiving devices.
- The carrier determines the type and amount of wireless advertising that reach its subscribers.
- To reach wireless customers, advertisers must either develop an in-house solution or use a wireless ad-serving network to deliver ads.
- A publisher or publisher network is a site or group of sites that carry wireless content and wireless advertisements.
- Wireless advertisements can be delivered by using Short Message Service (SMS), a service that transmits text messages of 160 alphanumeric characters or less.
- Sales-force automation assists companies in the sales process, including the maintenance and discovery of leads and the management of contacts and other sales-force activities.
- The variety of wireless devices, the lack of m-payment interoperability and the immaturity of the m-payment industry have created inconsistent user experiences in relation to m-payment applications.
- Interoperability is the ability for transactions to be performed using any software or device.
- Mobile transactions are well-suited for micropayments, which are payments under $10.
- Some banks are becoming Mobile Virtual Network Operators (MVNO). MVNOs purchase bandwidth capacity from mobile carriers and resell it under their brand names, coupled with value-added services.
- M-wallets allow a user to store billing and shipping information that the user can recall with one click while shopping from a mobile device.
- The accepted protocol for collecting user information is called an opt-in policy—the user requests targeted information. An opt-out policy allows organizations to send information to consumers until users request to be taken off the mailing lists.
- The Cellular Telecommunications and Internet Association (CTIA) has presented guidelines for protecting consumer privacy.
- Market penetration refers to the percent of the population using a marketed service.
- Messaging is the ability to send brief text messages to the display of another cell phone.
- Wireless communications technologies are identified by generations. These include first (1G), second (2G), two and a half (2.5G), third (3G) and even fourth generation (4G).
- The 2.5-generation technologies include networks that use packet-switching technologies (information is divided into packets when it is sent and reassembled at the receiving end; this provides faster transmission speeds).
- 3G technologies allow for increased data speeds, larger network capacity and transmission support of multiple data types, including streaming audio, video, multimedia, voice and data.
- WAP is a set of communication protocols designed to enable wireless devices to access the Internet.
- The Wireless Markup Language (WML) is the markup language used to create Web content delivered to wireless handheld devices.
- WML documents are divided into renderable units called cards.
- Each WML document consists of one or more cards, which are organized in a deck.

- Every WML document requires a **card** element, which contains information (such as text, images and links).
- The **card** element has two important attributes: **id**, which identifies the card, and **title**, which displays a title at the top of most browser windows.
- All text in a WML document is placed between **<p>** tags.
- Links are marked up with the **a** (anchor) element.
- There are two types of images that can be used as links: Imported images and local icons. A local icon is a small image stored in the wireless device's memory.
- Local icons are referenced using the **localsrc** attribute of the **img** element. Attribute **src** specifies the location and file name of an imported image.
- Every **img** element requires an **alt** attribute that contains a short description of the image.
- The WMLScript scripting language facilitates a disciplined approach to the designing of programs that enhance the functionality of WML documents. WMLScript documents are saved with the **.wmls** file extension. WMLScript files must be referenced from within a WML document.
- Keyword **extern** denotes that the function is accessible externally to other WML and WMLScript documents. Omitting this keyword restricts the function to the WMLScript file in which it is defined, and the function cannot be called from other documents.
- There are two ways to declare variables in WMLScript: **setVar**, and **var**. Method **setVar** declares a browser variable that is accessible from other WML documents; keyword **var** declares a local variable that can be accessed only in the WMLScript document in which it is declared.
- The **onevent** element is an event element that executes the task element enclosed in its tags.
- The **go** element is a task element that causes an action to be performed by the browser.
- The dollar sign (**$**) preceding the variable name retrieves the variable's value from the device's memory.
- The **Dialogs** object contains methods for the displaying of messages to the client.
- Soft keys are the physical buttons on the device immediately below the display screen.
- **Lang** object's **parseInt** method converts a number to an integer.
- The **do** element programs the soft keys for a wireless device. Most devices have two soft keys. The **label** attribute of the **do** element defines the soft key's label, which appears on the display screen. When a device has two soft keys, the **accept** value programs the left soft key, and the **options** value programs the right soft key.
- When a soft key is pressed, the action of the **go** element is performed.
- The **prev** element is a task element that displays the previous card.
- The **WMLBrowser** object's methods allow the WMLScript document to communicate with its associated WML document. This object is used to get variable values, to set variable values and to navigate between WML documents and **cards**.
- The **WMLBrowser** object is often used to set browser variables. Browser variables are necessary to provide access to the variable in other documents. The variable is referenced by preceding the identifier with a dollar sign (**$**identifier).
- The value of the input box is referenced by the **input** element's **name** attribute.
- The **String** object encapsulates the characteristics and behaviors of a string of characters. The **String** object provides methods for selecting characters from a string, concatenating strings, obtaining substrings of a string and searching for substrings within a string.

- The Handheld Devices Markup Language (HDML) is similar to Hypertext Markup Language (HTML), which is used to design and format Web pages.
- NTT DoCoMo's i-mode service has become the most popular wireless service in Japan. It offers voice service, combined with access to text-messaging, animated graphics and Web browsing.
- Java is one of the most popular programming languages in the software-development industry. Sun Microsystems created Java to facilitate the development of Internet and Web- based applications that can run consistently on any operating system without requiring alteration.
- XHTML Basic is a markup language for identifying the elements of a page so that a browser can render that Web page on a mobile device.
- Binary Run-Time Environment for Wireless (BREW) is a new software applications platform that enables software developers to create applications that are accessible through a variety of wireless devices.
- Bluetooth wireless technology, which is based on radio frequency technology (radio frequency uses radio signals to communicate), is used in the development of Wireless Personal Area Networks (WPANs).
- Bluetooth wireless technology supports point-to-point transmission (occurs when a Bluetooth-enabled device, such as a cell phone, sends a signal to one other point, which can be a single machine or device, such as a computer in an office) and point-to-multipoint (communication between one device and up to six others) connections.
- Bluetooth wireless technology eliminates the need for cables and wires and does not have line-of-sight limitations.

TERMINOLOGY

a element
alert dialog
Apache Web server
automatic location identification (ALI)
automatic number information (ANI)
Bluetooth wireless technology
BREW (Binary Runtime Environment for Wireless)
browser variable
card element
carrier
cell site
Cellular Telecommunications and Internet Association (CTIA)
circuit-switching network
compact HTML (cHTML)
connected device configuration (CDC)
connected limited device configuration (CLDC)
deck
dialog
Disabilities Issues Task Force
double opt-in policy
elements method
empty string (**""**)
frequency hopping spread spectrum (FHSS)
geocode
getVar method
Global Mobile Commerce Interoperability Group (GMCIG)
Handheld Devices Markup Language (HDML)
height attribute
hide a dialog
href attribute (**go**)
IIS (Internet Information Services)
i-mode
input box
interoperability
isEmpty method
Java
Java 2 micro edition (J2ME)
keyword **extern**
length method
market penetration
mathematical calculation
m-business
messaging
method
microbrowser

micropayment
MID profile (MIDP)
Mobile Electronic Transactions (MeT)
Mobile Virtual Network Operator (MVNO)
m-payment
multipath error
m-wallet
Nokia browser
open technology
Openwave browser
opt-in policy
opt-out policy
p (paragraph) element
packet-switching technology
Palm
permission-based marketing
Pocket PC
point-to-multipoint transmission
point-to-point transmission
pound sign (**#**)
prev element
programmer-defined function **square**
proxy server
publisher network
pull strategy
push strategy
radio frequency
refresh method
removeAt method
replace method
replaceAt method
sales-force automation
setVar method
short message service (SMS)
squeeze method
src attribute (**img**)
String object
substr method
substrings of a string
title element
toString method
triangulation
var keyword
WAP application
WAP Forum
WAP gateway
WAP-enabled mobile device
width attribute
Wireless Application Protocol (WAP)
wireless browser
wireless local access
WML (Wireless Markup Language)
WMLBrowser object
WMLScript

SELF-REVIEW EXERCISES

23.1 State whether each of the following is *true* or *false*. If *false*, explain why.
a) M-business is business performed over wireline networks.
b) A geocode is the latitude and longitude of a user's location and can be determined through triangulation.
c) Marketing content is displayed identically on all receiving devices.
d) The accepted protocol for collecting user information is an opt-out policy.
e) The **String** object's methods allow programmers to perform many common string-manipulation techniques.

23.2 Fill in the blanks in each of the following statements.
a) __________ determines a user's location by analyzing the angles from at least two fixed points a known distance apart.
b) The __________, or wireless service provider, decides the type and amount of wireless advertising that reach its subscribers.
c) __________ generation technologies include networks that use packet-switching technologies.
d) NTT DoCoMo's __________ service offers voice service, along with access to text messaging, animated graphics and Web browsing.
e) Keyword __________ begins a function definition for a function that is accessible to other WML and WMLScript documents.

23.3 State whether the following are *true* or *false*. If *false*, explain why.
a) WML is a markup language derived from HTML
b) A hyperlink is created by marking up text with **<hyperlink>** tags.
c) A browser variable can be accessed by any WML or WMLScript document in memory.
d) WMLScript commands are embedded directly into WML documents.
e) The **Lang** object provides methods that allow WMLScript document to communicate with the associated WML document.

23.4 Fill in the blanks in each of the following statements:
a) Each WML document consists of one or more **cards**, which are organized into a __________.
b) __________ is the root element in a WML document.
c) All text in a WML document is placed between __________ tags.
d) Keyword __________ declares a local variable.
e) WMLScript files have the __________ extension.
f) Local icons are referenced by attribute __________.
g) Images have the __________ extension.

23.5 Fill in the blanks in each of the following statements:
a) Method __________ combines all consecutive whitespace characters in a string into a single whitespace character.
b) Indices for the characters in a string start at __________.
c) The __________ value for the **type** attribute programs the right soft key.
d) Preceding a browser variable name with a __________ retrieves the variable's value.
e) The __________ value for the **type** attribute programs the left soft key.
f) In WMLScript, concatenation is performed with the __________ operator.

23.6 Identify each of the following as an element or an attribute:
a) **wml**.
b) **localsrc**.
c) **card**.
d) **onevent**.
e) **label**.

ANSWERS TO SELF-REVIEW EXERCISES

23.1 a) False. M-business is e-business enabled by wireless communications. E-business is performed over wireline networks. b) True. c) False. Limited technology and multiple protocols cause marketing content to be displayed differently on different devices. d) False. The accepted protocol for collecting user information is an opt-in policy, in which the user requests the targeted information. An opt-out policy allows organizations to send information to consumers until the users request to be taken off the mailing lists.

23.2 a) Triangulation. b) carrier. c) 2.5. d) i-mode.

23.3 a) False. WML is derived from XML. b) False. A hyperlink is created by marking up text with **<a>** tags. c) True. d) False. WMLScript commands are placed in external files. e) False. The **Lang** object provides methods for data-type conversions and mathematical calculations. f) True.

23.4 a) deck. b) **wml**. c) **<p>**. d) **var**. e) **.wmls**. f) **localsrc**. g) **.wbmp**. h) **extern**.

23.5 a) **squeeze**. b) 0. c) **"options"**. d) **$**. e) **"accept"**. f) plus (**+**).

23.6 a) Element. b) Attribute. c) Element. d) Element. e) Attribute.

EXERCISES

23.7 State whether each of the following is *true* or *false*;. If *false*, explain why.

a) A wireless user's location can be determined within yards by using location-based services.

b) The E911 Act guides the implementation of Internet technology in ambulance and police headquarters.

c) A publisher is a site that carriers wireless content and wireless advertisements.

d) Interoperability refers to the ability of wireline and wireless devices to communicate with one another.

23.8 Fill in the blanks in each of the following statements:

a) A __________ assumes that people will request that specific information be sent to their wireless devices in real time.

b) __________ marketing increases campaign response rates and productivity, because is better defined.

c) __________ is a set of communication protocols designed to enable wireless devices to access the Internet.

d) The markup language used to create Web content that is delivered to wireless handheld devices is __________.

23.9 Define the following:

a) WML.

b) Bluetooth wireless technology.

c) Short Message Service (SMS).

d) Automatic Number Information (ANI).

23.10 (*Class discussion*) In Fig. 23.1, we outline various location-identification technologies. Divide the class into two groups and have each group research three of the technologies in the table. Research can be conducted online or through various other media, such as magazines, articles and journals. Teams should create a list of pros and cons for each technology, focusing on each technology's cost, accuracy and ability to protect users' privacy. After data has been gathered, the class should present each technology in detail.

23.11 Search the Web for information regarding third-generation (3G) wireless technology. Visit such sites as **www.3gnewsroom.com**, **www.nokia.com** and **www.ericsson.com/org**. Use information gathered from these sites and other sources to answer to the following question: What advancements are expected for future wireless technologies and protocols?

23.12 Identify and correct the error in each of the following segments.

a)

```
<deck>
   <card>
   <p>
      This is the first card.
   </card>
   </p>
</deck>
```

b)

```
<WML>
   <card id = "card1" title = "Beginning">card!</card>
</WML>
```

23.13 Use the search engine found at **wap.fast.no/html** to find three sites that provide weather information. Create a WML document that links to each of these sites.

23.14 Use WML and WMLScript to display the following sentence (including line breaks) in a WML document:

```
Programming with
WMLScript is
easy!
```

23.15 Write a WMLScript document that inputs integers (one at a time) and passes them (one at a time) to function **isEven**, which determines whether an integer is even. The modulus operator (**%**) in WMLScript determines whether an integer remainder exists after division. For example, the expression **x % y** yields the integer remainder after **x** is divided by **y**. All even numbers have a remainder of 0 when divided by 2. The function should take an integer argument and return **true** if the integer is even, **false** otherwise.

23.16 Write a WML document that passes two numbers input by a user to a function that calls a second function to add the numbers, returning the result to the first function. Display the results in a WML document.

23.17 Write a WMLScript document that reads in a user's first and last name as separate inputs. Use **String** object's **charAt** method (**www.wirelessdevnet.com/channels/coderef.phtml?catid=5&subid=5**) to retrieve the first letter of each name and display them in a WML document.

WORKS CITED

The notation <**www.domain-name.com**> indicates that the citation is for information found at that Web site.

1. S. A. Pignone, "When Cell Phones Save Lives," *NEAR* Volume 1 Issue 2: 11-14.

2. "First-to-Wireless™," WindWire, Inc. 27 December 2000: 2.

3. E. Newborne, "Look Ma! No Ads!," *Inside* 6 February 2001: 81.

4. T. Bair, "True Tales of Mobile Advertising: The Need for Standards," Wireless Advertising Conference Atlanta, Georgia May 20-23.

5. K. Bayne, "Wireless Devices: The New Marketing Frontier," *e-Business Advisor* December 2000:12.

6. D. Callaghan, "Marketers Targeting Mobile Buyers," *eWeek* 26 February 2001: 35.

7. J. O'Brien, "M-Commerce Off to a Slow Start," *Computer Shopper* February 2001: 62.

8. D. Drucker, "The Web: Hardly Death Of A Salesman," *InternetWeek* 25 October 1999: 73.

9. "MeT Threatened by Mobile SET Payments?" 7 March 2001 <**www.epaynews.com/archives/index.cgi?keywords=MeT&optional=&subject=&location=&ref=keyword&f=view&id=983973203212120150 50&block=2**>.

10. J. Blau "Carriers, Banks Partner for Payments," *m-business* April 2001: 37.

11. "Say. Buy It!: Nuance and Qpass Team to Offer Voice-Driven Commerce Services to Wireless Carriers with the Qpass TalkWallet™," Qpass Press Release 20 March 2001.

12. C. Nobel and D. Callaghan, "Wireless Services Hit Snags," *eWeek* 18 December 2000: 15.

13. M. Hamblen, "Ensuring Portable Privacy," *Computerworld* 11 December 2000: 50.

14. J. Daitch, R. Kamath, R. Kapoor, A. Nemiccolo, J. Sahni, S. Varma, "Wireless Applications for Business," Kellogg TechVenture 2000 Anthology **<www.intel.com/eBusiness/pdf/busstrat/hi004618.pdf>**.

15. "Wireless Facts," CWTA **<www.cwta.ca/industry_guide/facts.php3>**.

16. M. Smith, "More Than 200 Billion GSM Text Messages Forecast for Full Year 2001," GSM World **<www.gsmworld.com/news/press_2001/press_releases_4.html>** 12 February 2001.

17. B. Issberner, "How 'Context Switch Radios' Will Streamline with Personal Area Networks," *Wireless Integration* **<wi.pennwellnet.com/home/articles>** 1 March 2000.

18. **<www.nttdocomo.com/imode>**

19. T. Hughes, "The Web Unwired," *Global Technology Business* December 1999: 33.

20. Fixing WAP's Security Flaw," *m-business* January 2001: 92.

21. **<www.wapuseek.com/wapfaqs.cfm#4>**.

22. **<www.wapuseek.com>**.

23. S. Phan, "Who Needs a PC?" *Business 2.0* 14 November 2000: 54.

24. T. Hyland, "Handheld Devices Markup Language FAQ," **<www.w3.org/TR/NOTE-Submission-HDML-FAQ.html>**.

25. C. Biggs, "HDML or WML?," **<www.allnetdevices.com/developer/tutorials/2000/06/09/hdml_or.html>**.

26. C. Biggs, "HDML or WML?," **<www.allnetdevices.com/developer/tutorials/2000/06/09/hdml_or.html>**.

27. **<www.qualcomm.com/cda/brew>**.

28. P. Tam, "Qualcomm Strives for Wireless Standard," *The Wall Street Journal* 31 January 2001: B6.

29. **<www.bluetooth.com>**.

24

VBScript

Objectives

- To become familiar with the VBScript language.
- To use VBScript keywords, operators and functions to write client-side scripts.
- To be able to write **`Sub`** and **`Function`** procedures.
- To use VBScript arrays and regular expressions.
- To be able to write VBScript abstract data types called **`Class`**es.
- To be able to create objects from **`Class`**es.
- To be able to write **`Property Let`**, **`Property Get`** and **`Property Set`** procedures.

When they call the roll in the Senate, the senators do not know whether to answer "present" or "not guilty."
Theodore Roosevelt

While I nodded, nearly napping,
suddenly there came a tapping,
As of someone gently rapping, rapping at my chamber door.
Edgar Allan Poe

Basic research is what I am doing when I don't know what I am doing.
Wernher von Braun

A problem is a chance for you to do your best.
Duke Ellington

Everything comes to him who hustles while he waits.
Thomas Alva Edison

Outline

24.1 Introduction

Visual Basic Script (*VBScript*) is a subset of Microsoft Visual Basic® used in World Wide Web XHTML documents to enhance the functionality of a Web page displayed in a Web browser. Microsoft's Internet Explorer Web browser contains a *VBScript scripting engine* (i.e., an interpreter) that executes VBScript code. In this chapter, we introduce client-side VBScript for use in XHTML documents. Because JavaScript has become the de facto client-side scripting language in industry, you are not likely to use client-side VBScript.

Earlier in the text we used JavaScript to introduce fundamental computer programming concepts in the context of XHTML documents and the World Wide Web. In this chapter, we overview VBScript, which provides capabilities similar to those of JavaScript. The material presented in this chapter is valuable for two reasons. First, company Intranets tend to standardize on a particular Web browser, and, if that browser is Internet Explorer, the VBScript techniques introduced in this chapter can readily be used on the client side to enhance XHTML documents. Second, VBScript is particularly valuable when used with Microsoft Web servers to create *Active Server Pages* (*ASP*)—a technology that allows a server-side script to create dynamic content that is sent to the client's browser. Although other scripting languages can be used, VBScript is the de facto language for ASP. You will learn about ASP in Chapters 25 and 26.

24.2 Operators

VBScript is a case-insensitive language that provides arithmetic operators, logical operators, concatenation operators, comparison operators and relational operators. VBScript's arithmetic operators (Fig. 24.1) are similar to the JavaScript arithmetic operators. Two major differences are the *division operator*, \, which returns an integer result and the *exponentiation operator*, ^, which raises a value to a power. [*Note*: the precedence of operators is different in JavaScript. See Section 24.9 for a list of VBScript operators and their precedences.]

VBScript operation	Arithmetic operator	Algebraic expression	VBScript expression
Addition	`+`	$x + y$	`x + y`
Subtraction	`-`	$z - 8$	`z - 8`
Multiplication	`*`	yb	`y * b`
Division (floating-point)	`/`	$v \div u$ or $\frac{v}{u}$	`v / u`
Division (integer)	`\`	none	`v \ u`
Exponentiation	`^`	q^p	`q ^ p`
Negation	`-`	$-e$	`-e`
Modulus	`Mod`	$q \bmod r$	`q Mod r`

Fig. 24.1 Arithmetic operators.

Figure 24.2 lists VBScript's comparison operators. Only the symbols for the equality operator and the inequality operator are different in JavaScript. In VBScript, these comparison operators may also be used to compare strings.

The VBScript logical operators are ***And*** (logical AND), ***Or*** (logical OR), ***Not*** (logical negation), ***Imp*** (logical implication), ***Xor*** (exclusive OR) and ***Eqv*** (logical equivalence). Figure 24.3 shows truth tables for these logical operators. *Note*: Despite the mixture of case in keywords, functions, etc., VBScript is not case-sensitive—uppercase and lowercase letters are treated the same, except, as we will see, in *character string constants* (also called *character string literals*).

Performance Tip 24.1

VBScript logical operators do not use "short-circuit" evaluation. Both conditions are always evaluated.

Standard algebraic equality operator or relational operator	VBScript comparison operator	Example of VBScript condition	Meaning of VBScript condition
$=$	`=`	`d = g`	**d** is equal to **g**
$\neq$	`<>`	`s <> r`	**s** is not equal to **r**
$>$	`>`	`y > x`	**y** is greater than **x**
$<$	`<`	`p < m`	**p** is less than **m**
$\geq$	`>=`	`c >= z`	**c** is greater than or equal to **z**
$\leq$	`<=`	`m <= s`	**m** is less than or equal to **s**

Fig. 24.2 Comparison operators.

Truth tables for VBScript Logical Operators

Logical And:
```
True And True = True
True And False = False
False And True = False
False And False = False
```

Logical Or:
```
True Or True = True
True Or False = True
False Or True = True
False Or False = False
```

Logical Imp:
```
True Imp True = True
True Imp False = False
False Imp True = True
False Imp False = True
```

Logical Eqv:
```
True Eqv True = True
True Eqv False = False
False Eqv True = False
False Eqv False = True
```

Logical Xor:
```
True Xor True = False
True Xor False = True
False Xor True = True
False Xor False = False
```

Logical Not:
```
Not True = False
Not False = True
```

Fig. 24.3 Truth tables for VBScript logical operators.

VBScript provides the *plus sign*, +, and *ampersand*, **&**, operators for string concatenation as follows:

```
s1 = "Pro"
s2 = "gram"
s3 = s1 & s2
```

or

```
s3 = s1 + s2
```

The ampersand is more formally called the *string concatenation operator*. The above statements would concatenate (or append) **s2** to the right of **s1** to create an entirely new string, **s3**, containing **"Program"**.

If both operands of the concatenation operator are strings, these two operators can be used interchangeably; however, if the **+** operator is used in an expression consisting of varying data types, there can be a problem. For example, consider the statement

```
s1 = "hello" + 22
```

VBScript first tries to convert the string **"hello"** to a number, then add **22** to it. The string **"hello"** cannot be converted to a number, so a type mismatch error occurs at run time. For this reason, the **&** operator should be used for string concatenation.

Testing and Debugging Tip 24.1

Always use the ampersand (&) operator for string concatenation.

24.3 Data Types and Control Structures

VBScript has only one data type—*variant*—that is capable of storing different types of data (e.g., strings, integers, floating-point numbers etc.). The data types (or *variant subtypes*) a variant stores are listed in Fig. 24.4. VBScript interprets a variant in a manner that is suitable to the type of data it contains. For example, if a variant contains numeric information, it will be treated as a number; if it contains string information, it will be treated as a string.

Software Engineering Observation 24.1

Because all variables are of type variant, the programmer does not specify a data type when declaring a variable in VBScript.

Variable names cannot be keywords and must begin with a letter. The maximum length of a variable name is 255 characters containing only letters, digits (0–9) and underscores. Variables can be declared simply by using their name in the VBScript code. The statement **`Option Explicit`** can be used to force all variables to be declared before they are used.

Common Programming Error 24.1

Attempting to declare a variable name that does not begin with a letter is an error.

Testing and Debugging Tip 24.2

Forcing all variables to be declared, by using **`Option Explicit`**, *can help eliminate various kinds of subtle errors.*

Common Programming Error 24.2

If a variable name is misspelled (when not using **`Option Explicit`**), *a new variable is declared, usually resulting in an error.*

Subtype	Range/Description
Boolean	**`True`** or **`False`**
Byte	Integer in the range `0` to `255`
Currency	`-922337203685477.5808` to `922337203685477.5807`
Date/Time	1 January 100 to 31 December 9999 / 0:00:00 to 23:59:59.
Double	`-1.79769313486232E308` to `-4.94065645841247E-324` (negative) `4.94065645841247E-324` to `1.79769313486232E308` (positive)
Empty	Uninitialized. This value is `0` for numeric types (e.g., double), **`False`** for booleans and the *empty string* (i.e., `""`) for strings.
Integer	`-32768` to `32767`
Long	`-2147483648` to `2147483647`
Object	Any object type.
Single	`-3.402823E38` to `-1.401298E-45` (negative) `1.401298E-45` to `3.402823E38` (positive)
String	`0` to `~2000000000` characters.

Fig. 24.4 Some VBScript variant subtypes.

VBScript provides control structures (Fig. 24.5) for controlling program execution. Many of the control structures provide the same capabilities as their JavaScript counterparts. Syntactically, every VBScript control structure ends with one or more keywords (e.g., **`End If`**, **`Loop`**, etc.). Keywords delimit a control structure's body—not curly braces (i.e., **`{}`**, as in JavaScript).

The **`If/Then/End If`** and **`If/Then/Else/End If`** control structures behave identically to their JavaScript counterparts. VBScript's multiple selection version of **`If/Then/Else/End If`** uses a different syntax from JavaScript's version because it includes keyword ***`ElseIf`*** (Fig. 24.6).

Notice that VBScript does not use a statement terminator like the semicolon (**`;`**) in JavaScript. Unlike in JavaScript, placing parentheses around conditions in VBScript is optional. A condition evaluates to **`True`** if the variant subtype is boolean **`True`** or if the variant subtype is considered non-zero. A condition evaluates to **`False`** if the variant subtype is boolean **`False`** or if the variant subtype is considered to be 0.

VBScript's ***`Select Case/End Select`*** structure provides all the functionality of JavaScript's **`switch`** structure, and more (Fig. 24.7).

JavaScript Control Structure	VBScript Control Structure Equivalent
sequence	sequence
`if`	`If/Then/End If`
`if/else`	`If/Then/Else/End If`
`while`	`While/Wend` or `Do While/Loop`
`for`	`For/Next`
`do/while`	`Do/Loop While`
`switch`	`Select Case/End Select`
none	`Do Until/Loop`
none	`Do/Loop Until`

Fig. 24.5 Comparing VBScript control structures to JavaScript control structures.

JavaScript

```
if ( s == t )
   u = s + t;
else if ( s > t )
   u = r;
else
   u = n;
```

VBScript

```
If s = t Then
   u = s + t
ElseIf s > t Then
   u = r
Else
   u = n
End If
```

Fig. 24.6 Comparing JavaScript's **`if`** structure to VBScript's **`If`** structure.

JavaScript

```
switch ( x ) {
   case 1:
      alert("1");
      break;
    case 2:
      alert("2");
      break;
   default:
      alert("?");
}
```

VBScript

```
Select Case x
   Case 1
      Call MsgBox("1")
   Case 2
      Call MsgBox("2")
   Case Else
      Call MsgBox("?")
End Select
```

Fig. 24.7 Comparing JavaScript's **switch** with VBScript's **Select Case**.

Common Programming Error 24.3

*Writing an **If** control structure that does not contain keyword **Then** is an error.*

Notice that the **Select Case/End Select** structure does not require the use of a statement like **break**. One **Case** cannot accidentally run into another. The VBScript **Select Case/End Select** structure is equivalent to VBScript's **If/Then/Else/End If** multiple selection structure. The only difference is syntax. Any variant subtype can be used with the **Select Case/End Select** structure.

VBScript's ***While/Wend*** repetition structure and ***Do While/Loop*** behave identically to JavaScript's **while** repetition structure. VBScript's ***Do/Loop While*** structure behaves identically to JavaScript's **do/while** repetition structure.

VBScript contains two additional repetition structures, ***Do Until/Loop*** and ***Do/Loop Until***, that do not have direct JavaScript equivalents. Figure 24.8 shows the closest comparison between VBScript's **Do Until/Loop** structure and JavaScript's **while** structure. The **Do Until/Loop** structure loops until its condition becomes **True**. In this example, the loop terminates when **x** becomes 10. We used the condition **! (x == 10)** in JavaScript here, so both control structures have a test to determine whether **x** is **10**. The JavaScript **while** structure loops while **x** is not equal to 10 (i.e., until **x** becomes 10).

Figure 24.9 shows the closest comparison between VBScript's **Do/Loop Until** structure and JavaScript's **do/while** structure. The **Do/Loop Until** structure loops until its condition becomes **True**. In this example, the loop terminates when **x** becomes 10. Once again, we used the condition **! (x == 10)** in JavaScript here so both control structures have a test to determine if **x** is **10**. The JavaScript **do/while** structure loops while **x** is not equal to 10 (i.e., until **x** becomes 10).

Notice that these **Do Until** repetition structures iterate until the condition becomes **True**. VBScript ***For*** repetition structure behaves differently from JavaScript's **for** repetition structure. Consider the side-by-side comparison in Fig. 24.10.

Unlike JavaScript's **for** repetition structures condition, VBScript's **For** repetition structure's condition cannot be changed during the loop's iteration. In the JavaScript **for/** VBScript **For** loop side-by-side code comparison, the JavaScript **for** loop would iterate exactly two times, because the condition is evaluated on each iteration. The VBScript **For** loop would iterate exactly eight times because the condition is fixed as **1 To 8**—even though the value of **x** is changing in the body. VBScript **For** loops may also use the optional **Step** keyword to indicate an increment or decrement. By default, **For** loops increment in units of 1. Figure 24.11 shows a **For** loop that begins at **2** and counts to **20** in **Step**s of **2**.

JavaScript

```
while ( !( x == 10 ) )
   ++x;
```

VBScript

```
Do Until x = 10
   x = x + 1
Loop
```

Fig. 24.8 Comparing JavaScript's **while** to VBScript's **Do Until**.

JavaScript

```
do {
   ++x;
} while ( !( x == 10 ) );
```

VBScript

```
Do
   x = x + 1
Loop Until x = 10
```

Fig. 24.9 Comparing JavaScript's **do/while** to VBScript's **Do Loop/Until**.

JavaScript

```
x = 8;
for ( y = 1; y < x; y++ )
   x /= 2;
```

VBScript

```
x = 8
For y = 1 To x
   x = x \ 2
Next
```

Fig. 24.10 Comparing JavaScript's **for** to VBScript's **For**.

```
' VBScript
For y = 2 To 20 Step 2
   Call MsgBox( "y = " & y )
Next
```

Fig. 24.11 Using keyword **Step** in VBScript's **For** repetition structure.

Common Programming Error 24.4

Attempting to use a relational operator in a **For/Next** *loop (e.g.,* **For x = 1 < 10**) *is an error.*

The ***Exit Do*** statement, when executed in a **Do While/Loop**, **Do/Loop While**, **Do Until/Loop** or **Do/Loop Until**, causes immediate exit from that structure. The fact that a **Do While/Loop** may contain **Exit Do** is the only difference, other than syntax, between **Do While/Loop** and **While/Wend**. Statement ***Exit For*** causes immediate exit from the **For/Next** structure. With **Exit Do** and **Exit For**, program execution continues with the first statement after the exited repetition structure.

Common Programming Error 24.5

Attempting to use **Exit Do** *or* **Exit For** *to exit a* **While/Wend** *repetition structure is an error.*

Common Programming Error 24.6

Attempting to place the name of a **For** *repetition structures's control variable after* **Next** *is an error.*

24.4 VBScript Functions

VBScript provides several predefined functions, many of which are summarized in this section. We overview variant functions, math functions, functions for interacting with the user, formatting functions and functions for obtaining information about the interpreter.

Figure 24.12 summarizes several functions that allow the programmer to determine which subtype is currently stored in a variant. VBScript provides function ***IsEmpty*** to determine if the variant has ever been initialized by the programmer. If **IsEmpty** returns **True** the variant has not been initialized by the programmer.

VBScript math functions allow the programmer to perform common mathematical calculations. Figure 24.13 summarizes some VBScript math functions. Note that trigonometric functions such as **Cos**, **Sin**, etc. take arguments expressed in radians. To convert from degrees to radians use the formula: $radians = degrees \times \pi / 180$.

Function	Variant subtype returned	Description
IsArray	Boolean	Returns **True** if the variant subtype is an array and **False** otherwise.
IsDate	Boolean	Returns **True** if the variant subtype is a date or time and **False** otherwise.
IsEmpty	Boolean	Returns **True** if the variant subtype is **Empty** (i.e., has not been explicitly initialized by the programmer) and **False** otherwise.
IsNumeric	Boolean	Returns **True** if the variant subtype is numeric and **False** otherwise.
IsObject	Boolean	Returns **True** if the variant subtype is an object and **False** otherwise.

Fig. 24.12 Some variant functions (part 1 of 2).

Function	Variant subtype returned	Description
TypeName	String	Returns a string that provides subtype information. Some strings returned are "Byte", "Integer", "Long", "Single", "Double", "Date", "Currency", "String", "Boolean" and "Empty".
VarType	Integer	Returns a value indicating the subtype (e.g., 0 for **Empty**, 2 for integer, 3 for long, 4 for single, 5 for double, 6 for currency, 7 for date/time, 8 for string, 9 for object, etc.).

Fig. 24.12 Some variant functions (part 2 of 2).

Function	Description	Example
Abs(x)	Absolute value of **x**	**Abs(-7)** is 7 **Abs(0)** is 0 **Abs(76)** is 76
Atn(x)	Trigonometric arctangent of **x** (in radians)	**Atn(1)*4** is 3.14159265358979
Cos(x)	Trigonometric cosine of **x** (in radians)	**Cos(0)** is 1
Exp(x)	Exponential function e^x	**Exp(1.0)** is 2.71828 **Exp(2.0)** is 7.38906
Int(x)	Returns the whole-number part of **x**. **Int** rounds to the next smallest number.	**Int(-5.3)** is -6 **Int(0.893)** is 0 **Int(76.45)** is 76
Fix(x)	Returns the whole-number part of **x** [*Note*: **Fix** and **Int** are different. When **x** is negative, **Int** rounds to the next smallest number, while **Fix** rounds to the next-largest number.]	**Fix(-5.3)** is -5 **Fix(0.893)** is 0 **Fix(76.45)** is 76
Log(x)	Natural logarithm of **x** (base *e*)	**Log(2.718282)** is 1.0 **Log(7.389056)** is 2.0
Rnd()	Returns a pseudo-random floating-point number in the range 0 ≤ **Rnd** < 1. Call function ***Randomize*** once before calling **Rnd** to get a different sequence of random numbers each time the program is run.	**Call Randomize** **...** **z = Rnd()**
Round(x, y)	Rounds **x** to **y** decimal places. If **y** is omitted, **x** is returned as an integer.	**Round(4.844)** is 5 **Round(5.7839, 2)** is 5.78

Fig. 24.13 VBScript math functions (part 1 of 2).

Function	Description	Example

`Sgn(x)`	Sign of **x**	`Sgn(-1988)` is `-1`
		`Sgn(0)` is `0`
		`Sgn(3.3)` is `1`

`Sin(x)`	Trigonometric sine of **x** (in radians)	`Sin(0)` is `0`
`Sqr(x)`	Square root of **x**	`Sqr(900.0)` is `30.0` `Sqr(9.0)` is `3.0`
`Tan(x)`	Trigonometric tangent of **x** (in radians)	`Tan(0)` is `0`

Fig. 24.13 VBScript math functions (part 2 of 2).

VBScript provides formatting functions for currency values, dates, times, numbers and percentages. Figure 24.14 summarizes these formatting functions.

Although they are not discussed in this chapter, VBScript provides many functions for manipulating dates and times. Manipulations include adding dates, subtracting dates, parsing dates, etc. Consult the VBScript documentation for a list of these functions.

Function	Description
`FormatCurrency`	Returns a string formatted according to the local machine's currency **Regional Settings** (in the **Control Panel**). For example, the call `FormatCurrency("-1234.789")` returns `"($1,234.79)"` and the call `FormatCurrency(123456.789)` returns `"$123,456.79"`. Note the rounding to the right of the decimal place.
`FormatDateTime`	Returns a string formatted according to the local machine's date/time **Regional Settings** (in the **Control Panel**). For example, the call `FormatDateTime(Now, vbLongDate)` returns the current date in the format `"Wednesday, September 01, 1999"` and the call `FormatDateTime(Now, vbShortTime)` returns the current time in the format `"17:26"`. Function ***Now*** returns the local machine's time and date. Constant `vbLongDate` indicates that the day of the week, month, day and year is displayed. Constant `vbShortTime` indicates that the time is displayed in 24-hour format. Consult the VBScript documentation for additional constants that specify other date and time formats.
`FormatNumber`	Returns a string formatted according to the number **Regional Settings** (in the **Control Panel**) on the local machine. For example, the call `FormatNumber("3472435")` returns `"3,472,435.00"` and the call `FormatNumber(-123456.789)` returns `"-123,456.79"`. Note the rounding to the right of the decimal place.
`FormatPercent`	Returns a string formatted as a percentage. For example the call `FormatPercent(".789")` returns `"78.90%"` and the call `FormatPercent(0.45)` returns `"45.00%"`.

Fig. 24.14 Some VBScript formatting functions.

VBScript also provides functions for getting information about the scripting engine (i.e., the VBScript interpreter). These functions are ***ScriptEngine*** (which returns "**JScript**", "**VBScript**" or "**VBA**"), ***ScriptEngineBuildVersion*** (which returns the current *build version*—i.e., the identification number for the current release), ***ScriptEngineMajorVersion*** (which returns the major version number for the script engine) and ***ScriptEngineMinorVersion*** (which returns the minor release number). For example, the expression

```
ScriptEngine() & ", " & ScriptEngineBuildVersion() & ", " _
& ScriptEngineMajorVersion() & ", " & _
ScriptEngineMinorVersion()
```

evaluates to **"VBScript, 5207, 5, 5"** (where the numbers are the build version, major version and minor version of the script engine at the time of this writing).

Testing and Debugging Tip 24.3

*VBScript functions **ScriptEngine**, **ScriptEngineBuildVersion**, **ScriptEngineMajorVersion** and **ScriptEngineMinorVersion** are useful if you are experiencing difficulty with the scripting engine and need to report information about the scripting engine to Microsoft.*

Portability Tip 24.1

*VBScript functions **ScriptEngine**, **ScriptEngineBuildVersion**, **ScriptEngineMajorVersion** and **ScriptEngineMinorVersion** can be used to determine whether the browser's script engine version is different from the script engine version you used to develop the page. Older script engines do not support the latest VBScript features.*

VBScript provides two functions, ***InputBox*** and ***MsgBox***, for interacting with the user. Function **InputBox** displays a dialog in which the user can input data. For example, the statement

```
intValue = InputBox( "Enter an integer", "Input Box", , _
                     1000, 1000 )
```

displays an *input dialog* (Fig. 24.15) containing the prompt (**"Enter an integer"**) and the caption (**"Input Box"**) at position (*1000, 1000*) on the screen. VBScript coordinates are measured in units of *twips* (1440 twips equal 1 inch). Position (*1000, 1000*) is relative to the upper-left corner of the screen, which is position (*0, 0*). On the screen, *x* coordinates increase from left to right and *y* coordinates increase from top to bottom.

VBScript functions often take *optional arguments* (i.e., arguments that programmers can pass if they wish or that can be omitted). Notice, in the preceding call to **InputBox**, the consecutive commas (between **"Input Box"** and **1000**)—these indicate that an optional argument is being omitted. In this particular case, the optional argument corresponds to the initial value displayed in the input dialog—a feature we do not wish to use in this particular call to **InputBox**. Before using a VBScript function, check the VBScript documentation

msdn.microsoft.com/scripting/default.htm?/scripting/vbscript

to determine whether the function allows for optional arguments.

The *underscore character*, _, is VBScript's *line-continuation character*. A statement cannot extend beyond the current line without using this character. A statement may use as many line-continuation characters as necessary.

Common Programming Error 24.7

Splitting a statement over several lines without the line-continuation character is an error.

Common Programming Error 24.8

Placing anything, including comments, after a line-continuation character is an error.

When called, function **MsgBox** displays a *message dialog* (a sample is shown in Fig. 24.15). For example, the statement

```
Call MsgBox( "VBScript is fun!", , "Results" )
```

displays a message dialog containing **"VBScript is fun!"** with **"Results"** in the title bar. Although not used here, the optional argument allows the programmer to customize the **MsgBox**'s buttons (e.g., **OK**, **Yes**, etc.) and icon (e.g., question mark, exclamation point, etc.)—see the VBScript documentation for more information on these features. The preceding statement could also have been written as

```
MsgBox "VBScript is fun!", , "Results"
```

which behaves identically to the version of the statement that explicitly uses **Call**. In VBScript, function calls that wrap arguments in parentheses must be preceded with keyword ***Call***—unless the function call is assigning a value to a variable, as in

```
a = Abs( z )
```

We prefer the more formal syntax that uses **Call** and parentheses to clearly indicate a function call.

24.5 VBScript Example Programs

In this section, we present several complete VBScript "live-code" programs and show the screen inputs and outputs produced as the programs execute. The XHTML document of Fig. 24.15 includes VBScript code that enables users to click a button to display an input dialog in which they can type an integer to be added into a running total. When the input dialog's **OK** button is clicked, a message dialog is displayed with a message indicating the number that was entered and the total of all the numbers entered so far.

```
<?xml version = "1.0"?>
<!DOCTYPE html PUBLIC "-//W3C//DTD XHTML 1.0 Transitional//EN"
   "http://www.w3.org/TR/xhtml1/DTD/xhtml1-transitional.dtd">

<!--Fig. 24.15: addition.html -->
<!--Adding Integers           -->
```

Fig. 24.15 Adding integers on a Web page using VBScript (part 1 of 3).

```
<html xmlns = "http://www.w3.org/1999/xhtml">
   <head>
      <title>Our first VBScript</title>

      <script type = "text/vbscript">
         <!--
         Option Explicit
         Dim intTotal

         Sub cmdAdd_OnClick()
            Dim intValue

            intValue = InputBox(_
               "Enter an integer", "Input Box", , 1000, 1000)
            intTotal = CInt( intTotal ) + CInt( intValue )
            Call MsgBox("You entered " & intValue & _
               "; total so far is " & intTotal, , "Results")
         End Sub
         -->
      </script>
   </head>

   <body>
      Click the button to add an integer to the total.
      <hr />
      <form action = "">
      <input name = "cmdAdd" type = "button"
             value = "Click Here to Add to the Total" />
      </form>
   </body>
</html>
```

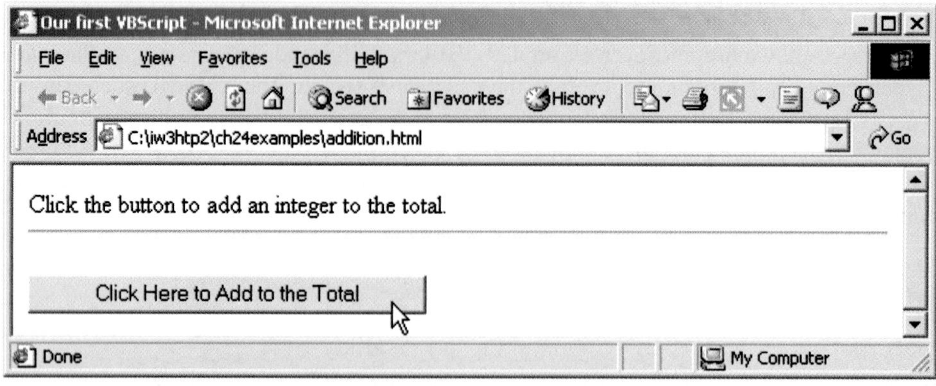

Fig. 24.15 Adding integers on a Web page using VBScript (part 2 of 3).

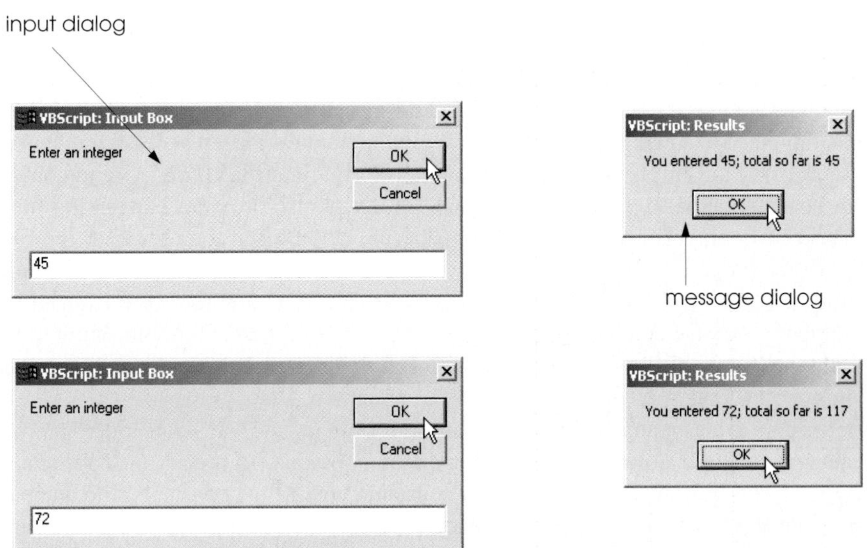

Fig. 24.15 Adding integers on a Web page using VBScript (part 3 of 3).

On Line 12, the XHTML tag **`script`** sets the **`type`** attribute to ***`vbscript`***. This tag tells the browser to use its built-in VBScript interpreter to interpret the script code. Notice the XHTML comment tags on lines 13 and 26 which appear to "comment out" the VBScript code.

If the browser understands VBScript, these XHTML comments are ignored, and the VBScript is interpreted. If the browser does not understand VBScript, the XHTML comment prevents the VBScript code from being displayed as text.

Portability Tip 24.2

Always place client-side VBScript code inside XHTML comments to prevent the code from being displayed as text in browsers that do not understand VBScript.

Line 14 uses the **`Option Explicit`** statement to force all variables in the VBScript code to be declared. Statement **`Option Explicit`**, if present, must be the first statement in the VBScript code. Line 15 declares variant variable **`intTotal`**, which is visible to all procedures within the script. Variables declared outside of procedures are called *script variables*.

Common Programming Error 24.9

Placing VBScript code before the **`Option Explicit`** *statement is an error.*

Lines 17–25 define a *procedure* (i.e., VBScript's equivalent of a function in JavaScript) called **`OnClick`** for the **`cmdAdd`** button. VBScript procedures that do not return a value begin with the keyword ***`Sub`*** (line 17) and end with the keywords ***`End Sub`*** (line 25). We will discuss VBScript procedures that return values later in this chapter. Line 18 declares the *local variable* **`intValue`**. Variables declared within a VBScript procedure are visible only within that procedure's body. Procedures that perform event handling (such as the **cmdAdd_OnClick** procedure in lines 17–25) are more properly called *event procedures*.

Line 20 calls the function **InputBox** to display an input dialog. The value entered into the input dialog is assigned to the **intValue** variable and is treated by VBScript as a string subtype. When using variants, conversion functions are often necessary to ensure that you are using the proper type. Line 22 calls VBScript function ***CInt*** twice to convert from the string subtype to the integer subtype. VBScript also provides conversion functions ***CBool*** for converting to the boolean subtype, ***CByte*** for converting to the byte subtype, ***CCur*** for converting to the currency subtype, ***CDate*** for converting to the date/time subtype, ***CDbl*** for converting to the double subtype, ***CLng*** for converting to the long subtype, ***CSng*** for converting to the single subtype and ***CStr*** for converting to the string subtype. Lines 23–24 display a message dialog indicating the last value input and the running total.

VBScript provides many predefined constants for use in your VBScript code. The constant categories include color constants, comparison constants (to specify how values are compared), date/time constants, date format constants, drive type constants, file attribute constants, file I/O constants, **MsgBox** constants, special folder constants, string constants, **VarType** constants (to help determine the type stored in a variable) and miscellaneous other constants. VBScript constants usually begin with the prefix ***vb***. For a list of VBScript constants, see the VBScript documentation. You can also create your own constants by using keyword ***Const***, as in

```
Const PI = 3.14159
```

Figure 24.16 provides another VBScript example. The XHTML form provides a **select** component, to allow the user to select a Web site from a list of sites. When the selection is made, the new Web site is displayed in the browser. Lines 34–39 specify a VBScript. In such code, the **<script>** tag's **for** attribute indicates the XHTML component on which the script operates (**SiteSelector**), the **event** attribute indicates the event to which the script responds (**OnChange**, which occurs when the user makes a selection) and the **type** attribute specifies the scripting language (**VBScript**).

```
1  <?xml version = "1.0"?>
2  <!DOCTYPE html PUBLIC "-//W3C//DTD XHTML 1.0 Transitional//EN"
3     "http://www.w3.org/TR/xhtml1/DTD/xhtml1-transitional.dtd">
4
5  <!-- Fig. 24.16: site.html -->
6  <!-- Displaying a Web site -->
7
8  <html xmlns = "http://www.w3.org/1999/xhtml">
9     <head>
10       <title>Select a site to browse</title>
11    </head>
12
```

Fig. 24.16 Using VBScript code to respond to an event (part 1 of 3). (Courtesy of Prentice Hall, Inc.)

```
   <body>
      Select a site to browse<p>
      <hr />
      <form action = "">
      <select name = "SiteSelector" size = "1">

         <option value = "http://www.deitel.com">
            Deitel & Associates, Inc.
         </option>

         <option value = "http://www.prenhall.com">
            Prentice Hall
         </option>

         <option value = "http://www.phptr.com/phptrinteractive">
            Prentice Hall Interactive
         </option>

      </select>

      <!-- VBScript code -->
      <script for = "SiteSelector" event = "onchange"
         type = "text/vbscript">
         <!--
        Document.Location = Document.Forms( 0 ).SiteSelector.Value
         -->
      </script>
      </form></p>
   </body>
</html>
```

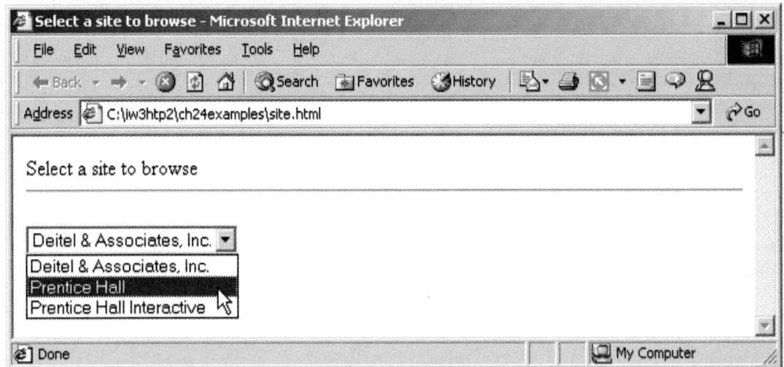

Fig. 24.16 Using VBScript code to respond to an event (part 2 of 3). (Courtesy of Prentice Hall, Inc.)

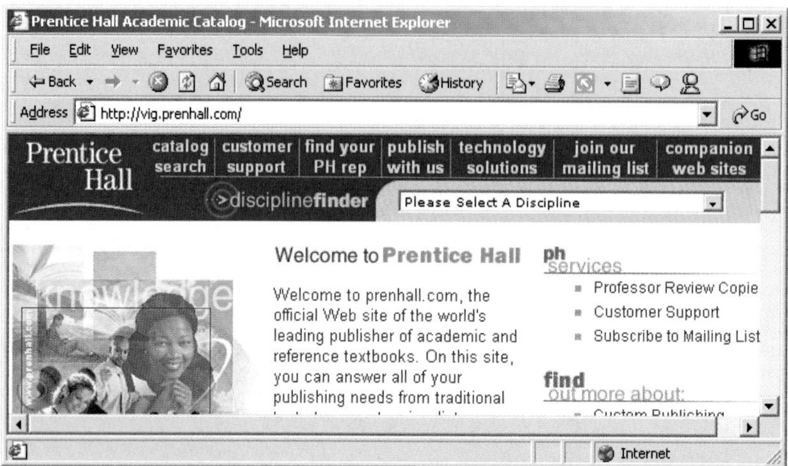

Fig. 24.16 Using VBScript code to respond to an event (part 3 of 3). (Courtesy of Prentice Hall, Inc.)

Line 37 causes the browser to change to the selected location. This line uses Internet Explorer's **Document** object to change the location. The **Document** object's ***Location*** *property* specifies the URL of the page to display. The expression **SiteSelector.Value** gets the **value** of the selected **option** in the **select**. When the assignment is performed, Internet Explorer automatically loads and displays the Web page for the selected location.

Fig. 24.17 uses programmer-defined procedures: **Minimum**, to determine the smallest of three numbers; and **OddEven**, to determine whether the smallest number is odd or even.

```
<?xml version = "1.0"?>
<!DOCTYPE html PUBLIC "-//W3C//DTD XHTML 1.0 Transitional//EN"
   "http://www.w3.org/TR/xhtml1/DTD/xhtml1-transitional.dtd">

<!--Fig. 24.17: minimum.html -->
<!-- VBScript Procedures     -->

<html xmlns = "http://www.w3.org/1999/xhtml">
   <head>
      <title>Using VBScript Procedures</title>

      <script type = "text/vbscript">
         <!--
         Option Explicit

         ' Find the minimum value. Assume that first value is
         ' the smallest.
```

Fig. 24.17 Program that determines the smallest of three numbers (part 1 of 3).

```
         Function Minimum( min, a, b )

            If a < min Then
               min = a
            End If

            If b < min Then
               min = b
            End If

            Minimum = min      ' Return value
         End Function

         Sub OddEven( n )
            If n Mod 2 = 0 Then
               Call MsgBox( n & " is the smallest and is even" )
            Else
               Call MsgBox( n & " is the smallest and is odd" )
            End If
         End Sub

         Sub cmdButton_OnClick()
            Dim number1, number2, number3, smallest

            ' Convert each input to Long subtype
            number1 = CLng( Document.Forms( 0 ).txtBox1.Value )
            number2 = CLng( Document.Forms( 0 ).txtBox2.Value )
            number3 = CLng( Document.Forms( 0 ).txtBox3.Value )

            smallest = Minimum( number1, number2, number3 )
            Call OddEven( smallest )
         End Sub
         -->
      </script>
   </head>

   <body>
      <form action = ""> Enter a number
         <input type = "text" name = "txtBox1" size = "5"
            value = "0" />
            <p>Enter a number
         <input type = "text" name = "txtBox2" size = "5"
            value = "0" /></p>
            <p>Enter a number
         <input type = "text" name = "txtBox3" size = "5"
            value = "0" /></p>
         <p><input type = "button" name = "cmdButton"
            value = "Enter" /></p>

      </form>
   </body>
</html>
```

Fig. 24.17 Program that determines the smallest of three numbers (part 2 of 3).

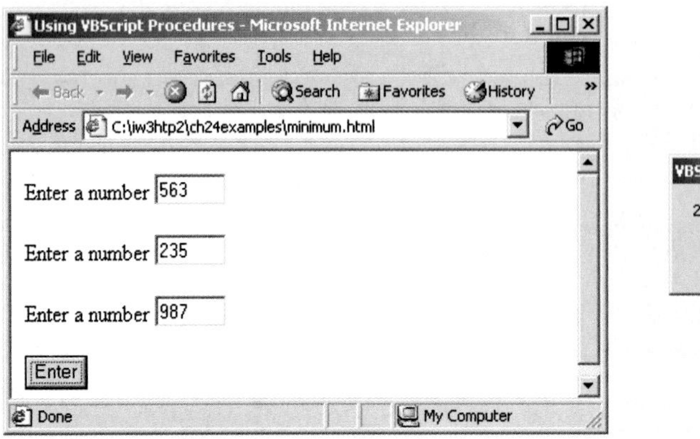

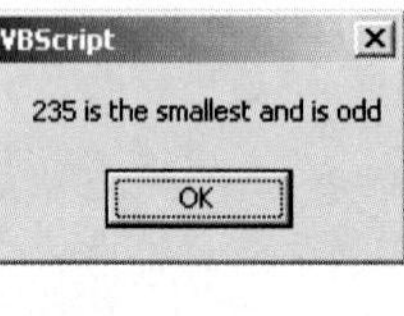

Fig. 24.17 Program that determines the smallest of three numbers (part 3 of 3).

Lines 16–17 are VBScript single-line comments. VBScript code is commented by either using a single quote (**'**) or the keyword ***Rem*** (for *remark*) before the comment. [*Note*: Keyword **Rem** can be used only at the beginning of a line of VBScript code.]

Good Programming Practice 24.1

VBScript programmers use the single-quote character for comments. The use of **Rem** *is considered archaic.*

Lines 18–29 define the programmer-defined procedure **Minimum**. VBScript procedures that return a value are delimited with the keywords ***Function*** (line 18) and ***End Function*** (line 29). This procedure determines the smallest of its three arguments by using **If/Then/Else** structures. A value is returned from a **Function** procedure by assigning a value to the **Function** procedure name (line 28). A **Function** procedure can return only one value.

Procedure **OddEven** (lines 31–37) takes one argument and displays a message dialog indicating the smallest value and whether or not it is odd or even. The modulus operator **Mod** is used to determine whether the number is odd or even. Because the data stored in the variant variable can be viewed as a number, VBScript performs any conversions between subtypes implicitly before performing the modulus operation. The advantage of placing these procedures in the **head** is that other VBScripts can call them.

Lines 39–49 define an event procedure for handling **cmdButton**'s **OnClick** event. The statement in line 47 calls **Minimum**, passing **number1**, **number2** and **number3** as arguments. Parameters **min**, **a** and **b** are declared in **Minimum** to receive the values of **number1**, **number2** and **number3**, respectively. Procedure **OddEven** is passed the smallest number, on line 48.

Common Programming Error 24.10

Declaring a variable in a procedure body with the same name as a parameter variable is an error.

One last word about procedures—VBScript provides statements **Exit Sub** and **Exit Function** for exiting **Sub** procedures and **Function** procedures, respectively. Control is returned to the caller and the next statement in sequence after the call is executed.

24.6 Arrays

Arrays are data structures consisting of related data items of the same type. A *fixed-size array*'s size does not change during program execution; a *dynamic array*'s size can change during execution. A dynamic array is also called a *redimmable array* (short for a "re-dimensionable" array). Individual array elements are referred to by giving the array name followed by the element position number in parentheses, **()**. The first array element is at position zero.

The position number contained within parentheses is more formally called an *index*. An index must be in the range 0 to 2,147,483,648 (any floating-point number is rounded to the nearest whole number).

The declaration

```
Dim numbers( 2 )
```

instructs the interpreter to reserve three elements for array **numbers**. The value **2** defines the *upper bound* (i.e., the highest valid index) of **numbers**. The *lower bound* (the lowest valid index) of **numbers** is **0**. When an upper bound is specified in the declaration, a fixed-size array is created.

Common Programming Error 24.11

Attempting to access an index that is less than the lower bound or greater than the upper bound is an error.

The programmer can explicitly initialize the array with assignment statements. For example, the lines

```
numbers(0) = 77
numbers(1) = 68
numbers(2) = 55
```

initialize **numbers**. Repetition statements can also be used to initialize arrays. For example, the statements

```
Dim h( 11 ), x, i
i = 0
For x = 0 To 30 Step 3
   h(i) = CInt( x )
   i = CInt( i ) + 1
Next
```

initializes the elements of **h** to the values 0, 3, 6, 9, …, 30.

The program in Fig. 24.18 declares, initializes and prints three arrays. Two of the arrays are fixed-size arrays and one of the arrays is a dynamic array. The program introduces function ***UBound***, which returns the upper bound (i.e., the highest-numbered index). [*Note*: VBScript does provide function ***LBound*** for determining the lowest-numbered index. However, the current version of VBScript does not permit the lowest-numbered index to be non-zero.]

Testing and Debugging Tip 24.4

Array upper bounds can vary. Use function ***UBound*** *to ensure that each index is in range (i.e., within the bounds of the array).*

```
<?xml version = "1.0"?>
<!DOCTYPE html PUBLIC "-//W3C//DTD XHTML 1.0 Transitional//EN"
   "http://www.w3.org/TR/xhtml1/DTD/xhtml1-transitional.dtd">

<!--Fig. 24.18: arrays.html -->
<!--VBScript Arrays         -->

<html xmlns = "http://www.w3.org/1999/xhtml">
   <head>
      <title>Using VBScript Arrays</title>

      <script type = "text/vbscript">
         <!--
         Option Explicit

         Public Sub DisplayArray( x, s )
            Dim j

            Document.Write( s & ": " )
            For j = 0 To UBound( x )
               Document.Write( x( j ) & " " )
            Next

            Document.Write( "<br />" )
         End Sub

         Dim fixedSize( 3 ), fixedArray, dynamic(), k

         ReDim dynamic( 3 )  ' Dynamically size array
         fixedArray = Array( "A", "B", "C" )

         ' Populate arrays with values
         For k = 0 to UBound( fixedSize )
            fixedSize( k ) = 50 - k
            dynamic( k ) = Chr( 75 + k )
         Next

         ' Display contents of arrays
         Call DisplayArray( fixedSize, "fixedSize" )
         Call DisplayArray( fixedArray, "fixedArray" )
         Call DisplayArray( dynamic, "dynamic" )

         ' Resize dynamic, preserve current values
         ReDim Preserve dynamic( 5 )
         dynamic( 3 ) = 3.343
         dynamic( 4 ) = 77.37443

         Call DisplayArray( dynamic, _
                            "dynamic after ReDim Preserve" )
         -->
      </script>
   </head><body></body>
</html>
```

Fig. 24.18 Using VBScript arrays (part 1 of 2).

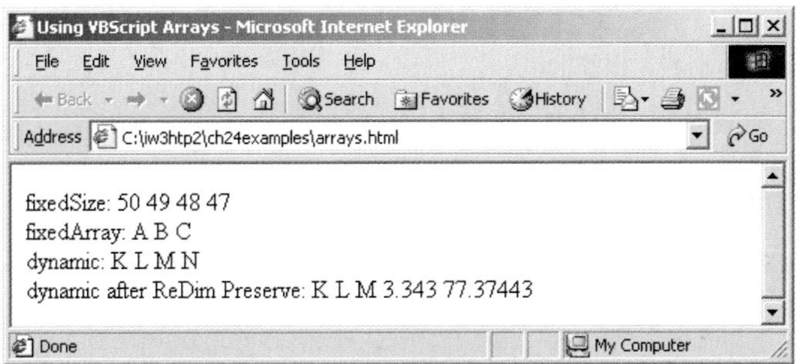

Fig. 24.18 Using VBScript arrays (part 2 of 2).

Lines 16–25 define **`Sub`** procedure **`DisplayArray`**. VBScript procedures are ***`Public`*** by default; therefore, they are accessible to scripts on other Web pages. Keyword **`Public`** can be used explicitly to indicate that a procedure is public. A procedure can be marked as ***`Private`*** to indicate that the procedure can be called only from the XHTML document in which it is defined.

Procedure **`DisplayArray`** receives arguments **`x`** and **`s`** and declares local variable **`j`**. Parameter **`x`** receives an array and parameter **`s`** receives a string. The **`For`** header (line 20) calls function **`UBound`** to get the upper bound of **`x`**. The **`Document`** object's **`Write`** method is used to print each element of **`x`**.

Line 27 declares a four element fixed-sized array named **`fixedSize`** (the value in parentheses indicates the highest index in the array, and the array has a starting index of 0), variants **`fixedArray`** and **`k`**, and dynamic array **`dynamic`**.

Statement ***`ReDim`*** (line 29) allocates memory for array **`dynamic`** (four elements, in this example). All dynamic array memory must be allocated via **`ReDim`**. Dynamic arrays are more flexible than fixed-sized arrays, because they can be resized anytime by using **`ReDim`**, to accommodate new data.

Performance Tip 24.2

Dynamic arrays allow the programmer to manage memory more efficiently than do fixed-size arrays.

Performance Tip 24.3

Resizing dynamic arrays consumes processor time and can slow a program's execution speed.

Common Programming Error 24.12

Attempting to use **`ReDim`** *on a fixed-size array is an error.*

Line 30 creates an array containing three elements and assigns it to **`fixedArray`**. VBScript function ***`Array`*** takes any number of arguments and returns an array containing those arguments. Lines 39–41 pass the three arrays and three strings to **`DisplayArray`**. Line 44 reallocates **`dynamic`**'s memory to 5 elements. When keyword ***`Preserve`*** is used with **`ReDim`**, VBScript maintains the current values in the array; otherwise, all values in the array are lost when the **`ReDim`** operation occurs.

Common Programming Error 24.13

Using **ReDim** *without* **Preserve** *and assuming that the array still contains previous values is a logic error.*

Testing and Debugging Tip 24.5

Failure to **Preserve** *array data can result in unexpected loss of data at run time. Always double check every array* **ReDim** *to determine whether* **Preserve** *is needed.*

If **ReDim Preserve** creates a larger array, every element in the original array is preserved. If **ReDim Preserve** creates a smaller array, every element up to (and including) the new upper bound is preserved (e.g., if there were 10 elements in the original array and the new array contains five elements, the first five elements of the original array are preserved). Lines 45–46 assign values to the new elements. Procedure **DisplayArray** is called to display array **dynamic**.

Arrays can have multiple dimensions. VBScript supports at least 60 array dimensions, but most programmers will need to use only two- or three-dimensional arrays.

Common Programming Error 24.14

Referencing a two-dimensional array element **u(x, y)** *incorrectly as* **u(x)(y)** *is an error.*

A multidimensional array is declared much like a one-dimensional array. For example, consider the following declarations

```
Dim b(2, 2), tripleArray(100, 8, 15)
```

which declares **b** as a two-dimensional array and **tripleArray** as a three-dimensional array. Functions **UBound** and **LBound** can also be used with multidimensional arrays. When calling **UBound** or **LBound**, the dimension is passed as the second argument. Array dimensions always begin at one. If a dimension is not provided, the default dimension 1 is used. For example, the **For** header

```
For x = 0 To UBound(tripleArray, 3)
```

would increment **x** from the third dimension's lower bound, **0**, to the third dimension's upper bound, **15**.

Multidimensional arrays can also be created dynamically. Consider the declaration

```
Dim threeD()
```

which declares a dynamic array **threeD**. The number of dimensions is not set until the first time **ReDim** is used. Once the number of dimensions is set, the number of dimensions cannot be changed by **ReDim** (e.g., if the array is a two-dimensional array, it cannot become a three-dimensional array). The statement

```
ReDim threeD(11, 8, 1)
```

allocates memory for **threeD** and sets the number of dimensions at 3.

Common Programming Error 24.15

Attempting to change the total number of array dimensions using **ReDim** *is an error.*

Common Programming Error 24.16

Attempting to change the upper bound for any dimension except the last dimension in a dynamic-multidimensional array (when using **ReDim Preserve***) is an error.*

Memory allocated for dynamic arrays can be *deallocated* (*released*) at run-time using the keyword ***Erase***. A dynamic array that has been deallocated must be redimensioned with **ReDim** before it can be used again. **Erase** can also be used with fixed-sized arrays to initialize all the array elements to the empty string. For example, the statement

```
Erase mDynamic
```

releases **mDynamic**'s memory.

Common Programming Error 24.17

Accessing a dynamic array that has been deallocated is an error.

24.7 String Manipulation

One of VBScript's most powerful features is its string-manipulation functions, some of which are summarized in Fig. 24.19. For a complete list consult the VBScript documentation. VBScript strings are case sensitive. The first character in a string has index 1 (as opposed to arrays which begin at index 0). [*Note*: Almost all VBScript string-manipulation functions do not modify their string argument(s); rather, they return new strings containing the results. Most VBScript string-manipulation functions take optional arguments.]

Function	Description
Asc	Returns the ASCII numeric value of a character. For example, **Asc("x")** returns **120**.
Chr	Returns the character representation for an ASCII value. For example the call **Chr(120)** returns "**x**." The argument passed must be in the range 0 to 255 inclusive, otherwise an error occurs.
InStr	Searches a string (i.e., the first argument) for a substring (i.e., the second argument). Searching is performed from left to right. If the substring is found, the index of the found substring in the search string is returned. For example, the call **Instr("sparrow", "arrow")** returns **3** and the call **Instr("japan", "wax")** returns **0**.
Len	Returns the number of characters in a string. For example, the call **Len("hello")** returns **5**.
LCase	Returns a lowercase string. For example, the call **LCase("HELLO@97[")** returns "**hello@97[**."
UCase	Returns an uppercase string. For example, the call **UCase("hello@97[")** returns "**HELLO@97[**."

Fig. 24.19 Some string-manipulation functions (part 1 of 3).

Function	Description
`Left`	Returns a string containing characters from the left side of a string argument. For example, the call `Left("Web",2)` returns "**We**."
`Mid`	Function **`Mid`** returns a string containing a range of characters from a string. For example, the call `Mid("abcd",2,3)` returns "**bcd**."
`Right`	Returns a string containing characters from the right side of a string argument. For example, the call `Right("Web",2)` returns "**eb**."
`Space`	Returns a string of spaces. For example, the call `Space(4)` returns a string containing four spaces.
`StrComp`	Compares two strings for equality. Returns `1` if the first string is greater than the second string, returns `-1` if the first string is less than the second string and returns `0` if the strings are equivalent. The default is a binary comparison (i.e., case-sensitive). An optional third argument of `vbTextCompare` indicates a case-insensitive comparison. For example the call `StrComp("bcd", "BCD")` returns `1`, the call `StrComp("BCD", "bcd")` returns `-1`, the call `StrComp("bcd", "bcd")` returns `0` and the call `StrComp("bcd", "BCD", vbTextCompare)` returns `0`.
`String`	Returns a string containing a repeated character. For example, the call `String(4,"u")` returns "**uuuu**."
`Trim`	Returns a string that does not contain leading or trailing space characters. For example the call `Trim("  hi   ")` returns "**hi**."
`LTrim`	Returns a string that does not contain any leading space characters. For example, the call `LTrim("   yes")` returns "**yes**."
`RTrim`	Returns a string that does not contain any trailing space characters. For example, the call `RTrim("no  ")` returns "**no**".
`Filter`	Returns an array of strings containing the result of the **`Filter`** operation. For example, the call `Filter(Array("A","S","D","F","G","D"),"D")` returns a two-element array containing `"D"` and `"D"`, and the call `Filter(Array("A","S","D","F","G","D"),"D",False)` returns an array containing `"A"`, `"S"`, `"F"` and `"G"`.
`Join`	Returns a string containing the concatenation of array elements separated by a delimiter. For example, the call `Join(Array("one","two","three"))` returns "**one two three**." The default delimiter is a space which can be changed by passing a delimiter string for the second argument. For example, the call `Join(Array("one","two","three"),"$^")` returns "**one^two^three**."
`Replace`	Returns a string containing the results of a **`Replace`** operation. Function **`Replace`** requires three string arguments: the string where characters will be replaced, the substring to search for and the replacement string. For example, `Replace("It's Sunday and the sun is out","sun","moon")` returns "**It's Sunday and the moon is out**." Note the case-sensitive replacement.

Fig. 24.19 Some string-manipulation functions (part 2 of 3).

Function	Description
Split	Returns an array containing substrings. The default delimiter for **Split** is a space character. For example, the call **Split("I met a traveller")** returns an array containing elements "I", "met", "a" and "traveller" and **Split("red,white,and blue", ",")** returns an array containing elements "red", "white" and "and blue". The optional second argument changes the delimiter.
StrReverse	Returns a string in reverse order. For example, the call **StrReverse("deer")** returns "**reed**."
InStrRev	Searches a string (i.e., the first argument) for a substring (i.e., the second argument). Searching is performed from right to left. If the substring is found, the index of the found substring in the search string is returned. For example, the call **InstrRev("sparrow","arrow")** returns 3, the call **InstrRev("japan","wax")** returns 0 and the call **InstrRev("to be or not to be","to be")** returns 14.

Fig. 24.19 Some string-manipulation functions (part 3 of 3).

We now present a VBScript program (Fig. 24.20) that converts a line of text into its pig Latin equivalent. Pig Latin is a form of coded language often used for amusement. Many variations exist in the methods used to form pig Latin phrases. For simplicity, we use the following algorithm:

> *To form a pig Latin phrase from an English language phrase, the translation proceeds one word at a time. To translate an English word into a pig Latin word, place the first letter of the English word (if it is not a vowel) at the end of the English word and add the letters "***ay***." If the first letter of the English word is a vowel place it at the end of the word and add "***y***." Thus, the word "***jump***" becomes "***umpjay***," the word "***the***" becomes "***hetay***," and the word "***ace***" becomes "***ceay***." Blanks between words remain as blanks. Make the following assumptions: the English phrase consists of words separated by blanks, there are no punctuation marks and all words have two or more letters.*

Lines 16–42 define the **Function** procedure **TranslateToPigLatin** which translates the string input by the user from English to pig Latin. Line 22 calls function **Split** to extract each word in the sentence. By default, **Split** uses spaces as delimiters. The condition in line 26 calls functions **InStr**, **LCase** and **Left** to determine whether the first letter of a word is a vowel. Function **Left** is called to retrieve the first letter in **words(k)**—which is then converted to lowercase using **LCase**. Function **InStr** is called to search the string **"aeiou"** for the string returned by **LCase**. The starting index in every string is **1**, and this is where **Instr** begins searching.

```
1  <?xml version = "1.0"?>
2  <!DOCTYPE html PUBLIC "-//W3C//DTD XHTML 1.0 Transitional//EN"
3     "http://www.w3.org/TR/xhtml1/DTD/xhtml1-transitional.dtd">
4
```

Fig. 24.20 Using VBScript string-processing functions (part 1 of 3).

```
<!--Fig. 24.20: piglatin.html  -->
<!-- VBScript String Functions -->

<html xmlns = "http://www.w3.org/1999/xhtml">
   <head>
      <title>Using VBScript String Functions</title>

      <script type = "text/vbscript">
         <!--
         Option Explicit

         Public Function TranslateToPigLatin( englishPhrase )
            Dim words       ' Stores each individual word
            Dim k, suffix

            ' Get each word and store in words the
            ' default delimiter for Split is a space
            words = Split( englishPhrase )

            For k = 0 To UBound( words )
               ' Check if first letter is a vowel
               If InStr( 1, "aeiou", _
                     LCase( Left( words( k ), 1 ) ) ) Then
                  suffix = "y"
               Else
                  suffix = "ay"
               End If

               ' Convert the word to pig Latin
               words( k ) = Right( words( k ), _
                             Len( words( k ) ) - 1 ) & _
                            Left( words( k ), 1 ) & suffix
            Next

            ' Return translated phrase, each word
            ' is separated by spaces
            TranslateToPigLatin = Join( words )
         End Function

         Sub cmdButton_OnClick()
            Dim phrase

            phrase = Document.Forms( 0 ).txtInput.Value

            Document.forms( 0 ).txtPigLatin.Value = _
               TranslateToPigLatin( phrase )
         End Sub
         -->
      </script>
   </head>

   <body>
      <form action = ""> Enter a sentence
```

Fig. 24.20 Using VBScript string-processing functions (part 2 of 3).

```
58            <input type = "text" name = "txtInput" size = "50" />
59            <p>Pig Latin
60            <input type = "text" name = "txtPigLatin" size = "70" />
61            </p><p>
62            <input type = "button" name = "cmdButton"
63               value = "Translate" /></p>
64         </form>
65      </body>
66   </html>
```

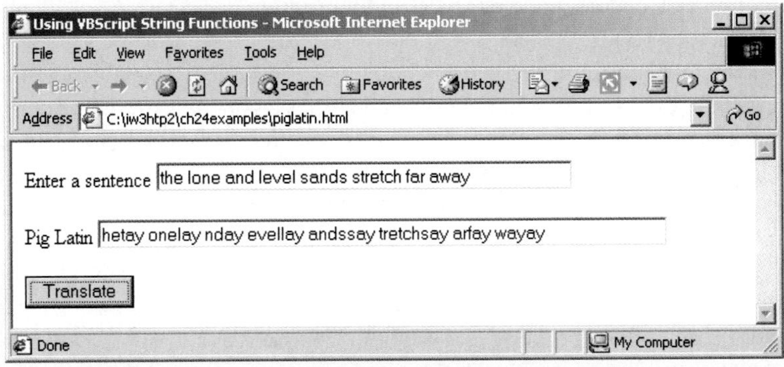

Fig. 24.20 Using VBScript string-processing functions (part 3 of 3).

Lines 34–36 translate an individual word to pig Latin. Function **`Len`** is called to get the number of characters in **`words( k )`**. One is subtracted from the value returned by **`Len`**, to ensure that the first letter in **`words( k )`** is not included in the string returned by **`Right`**. Function **`Left`** is called to get the first letter of **`words( k )`**, which is then concatenated to the string returned by **`Right`**. Finally the contents of **`suffix`** (either **`"ay"`** or **`"y"`**) and a space are concatenated.

Lines 44–51 define an event procedure for **`cmdButton`**'s **`OnClick`** event. Line 50 calls function **`TranslateToPigLatin`**, passing the string input by the user. The pig Latin sentence returned by **`TranslateToPigLatin`** is displayed in a text box (line 49).

24.8 Classes and Objects

In this section, we introduce the concepts (i.e., "object think") and the terminology (i.e., "object speak") of object-oriented programming in VBScript. Objects *encapsulate* (i.e., wrap together) data (*attributes*) and methods (*behaviors*); the data and methods of an object are intimately related. Objects have the property of *information hiding*. This phrase means that, although objects may communicate with one another, objects do not know how other objects are implemented—implementation details are hidden within the objects themselves. Surely it is possible to drive a car effectively without knowing the details of how engines and transmissions work. Information hiding is crucial to good software engineering.

In VBScript, the unit of object-oriented programming is the ***`Class`*** from which objects are *instantiated* (i.e., created). *Methods* are VBScript procedures that are encapsulated with the data they process within the "walls" of classes.

VBScript programmers can create their own *user-defined types* called *classes*. Classes are also referred to as *programmer-defined types*. Each class contains data as well as the set of methods which manipulate that data. The data components of a class are called *instance variables*. Just as an instance of a variant is called a *variable*, an instance of a class is called an *object*. The focus of attention in object-oriented programming with VBScript is on classes rather than methods.

The *nouns* in a system-requirements document help the VBScript programmer determine an initial set of classes with which to begin the design process. These classes are then used to instantiate objects that will work together to implement the system. The *verbs* in a system-requirements document help the VBScript programmer determine what methods to associate with each class.

This section explains how to create and use objects, a subject we call *object-based programming* (*OBP*). VBScript programmers craft new classes and reuse existing classes. Software is then constructed by combining new classes with existing, well-defined, carefully tested, well-documented, widely available components. This kind of *software reusability* speeds the development of powerful, high-quality software. *Rapid applications development* (*RAD*) is of great interest today.

Early versions of VBScript did not allow programmers to create their own classes, but VBScript programmers can now indeed develop their own classes, a powerful capability also offered by such object-oriented languages as C++ and Java.

Packaging software as classes out of which we make objects makes more significant portions of major software systems reusable. On the Windows platform, these classes have been packaged into class libraries, such as Microsoft's *MFC* (*Microsoft Foundation Classes*) that provide C++ programmers with reusable components for handling common programming tasks, such as the creating and manipulating of graphical user interfaces.

Objects are endowed with the capabilities to do everything they need to do. For example, employee objects are endowed with a behavior to pay themselves. Video game objects are endowed with the ability to draw themselves on the screen. This is like a car being endowed with the ability to "go faster" (if someone presses the accelerator pedal), "go slower" (if someone presses the brake pedal) and "turn left" or "turn right" (if someone turns the steering wheel in the appropriate direction). The blueprint for a car is like a class. Each car is like an instance of a class. Each car comes equipped with all the behaviors it needs, such as "go faster," "go slower" and so on, just as every instance of a class comes equipped with each of the behaviors instances of that class exhibit. We will discuss how to create classes and how to add properties and methods to those classes.

Software Engineering Observation 24.2

It is important to write programs that are understandable and easy to maintain. Change is the rule rather than the exception. Programmers should anticipate that their code will be modified. As we will see, using classes improves program modifiability.

Classes normally hide their implementation details from the *clients* (i.e., users) of the classes. This is called *information hiding*. As an example of information hiding, let us consider a data structure called a *stack*.

Think of a stack in terms of a pile of dishes. When a dish is placed on the pile, it is always placed at the top (referred to as *pushing* the dish onto the stack). When a dish is removed from the pile, it is always removed from the top (referred to as *popping* the dish off the stack). Stacks are known as *last-in, first-out* (*LIFO*) *data structures*—the last item *push*ed (inserted) on the stack is the first item *pop*ped (removed) from the stack. So if we push 1, then 2, then 3 onto a stack, the next three pop operations will return 3, then 2, then 1.

The programmer may create a stack class and hide from its clients the implementation of the stack. Stacks can be implemented with arrays and other techniques such as linked lists. A client of a stack class need not know how the stack is implemented. The client simply requires that when data items are placed in the stack with *push* operations, they will be recalled with *pop* operations in last-in, first-out order. Describing an object in terms of behaviors without concern for how those behaviors are actually implemented is called *data abstraction,* and VBScript classes define *abstract data types* (*ADTs*). Although users may happen to know how a class is implemented, users should not write code that depends on these details. This allows a class to be replaced with another version without affecting the rest of the system, as long as the **`Public`** interface of that class does not change (i.e. every method still has the same name, return type and parameter list in the new class definition).

Most programming languages emphasize actions. In these languages, data exists in support of the actions programs need to take. Data is "less interesting" than actions, anyway. Data is "crude." There are only a few built-in data types, and it is difficult for programmers to create their own new data types. VBScript elevates the importance of data. A primary activity in VBScript is creating new data types (i.e., *classes*) and expressing the interactions among *objects* of those classes.

An ADT actually captures two notions, a *data representation of the ADT* and the *operations allowed on the data of the ADT*. For example, subtype integer defines addition, subtraction, multiplication, division and other operations in VBScript, but division by zero is undefined. The allowed operations and the data representation of negative integers are clear, but the operation of taking the square root of a negative integer is undefined.

Software Engineering Observation 24.3

The programmer creates new types through the class mechanism. These new types may be designed to be used as conveniently as built-in types. Thus, VBScript is an extensible language. *Although it is easy to extend the language with these new types, the base language itself cannot be modified.*

Access to **`Private`** data should be carefully controlled by the class's methods. For example, to allow clients to read the value of **`Private`** data, the class can provide a *get method* (also called an *accessor* method or a *query* method).

To enable clients to modify **`Private`** data, the class can provide a *set* method (also called a *mutator* method). Such modification would seem to violate the notion of **`Private`** data. But a *set* method can provide data validation capabilities (such as range checking) to ensure that the data is set properly and to reject attempts to set data to invalid values. A *set* method can also translate between the form of the data used in the interface and the form used in the implementation. A *get* method need not expose the data in "raw" format; rather, the *get* method can edit the data and limit the view of the data the client will see.

Software Engineering Observation 24.4

The class designer need not provide set *or* get *methods for each* **`Private`** *data member; these capabilities should be provided only when it makes sense and after careful thought.*

Classes often provide **`Public`** methods to allow clients of the class to *set* (i.e., assign values to) or *get* (i.e., obtain the values of) **`Private`** instance variables. These methods are special methods in VBScript called ***Property Let***, ***Property Set*** and ***Property Get*** (collectively these methods and the internal class data they manipulate are called *properties*). More specifically, a method that sets variable **mInterestRate** would be named **Property Let InterestRate** and a method that gets the **InterestRate** would be called **Property Get InterestRate**.

Testing and Debugging Tip 24.6

Making the instance variables of a class **Private** *and the methods* **Public** *facilitates debugging because problems with data manipulations are localized to the class's methods.*

Procedures **Property Let** and **Property Set** differ in that **Property Let** is used for non-object subtypes (e.g., integer, string, byte, etc.) and **Property Set** is used for object subtypes.

Testing and Debugging Tip 24.7

Property *procedures should scrutinize every attempt to* set *the object's data and should reject invalid data to ensure that the object's data remains in a consistent state. This eliminates large numbers of bugs that have plagued systems development efforts.*

Software Engineering Observation 24.5

Property Get *procedures can control the appearance of data, possibly hiding implementation details.*

A **Property Let Hour** that stores the hour in universal time as 0 to 23 is shown in Fig. 24.21. Notice the change in the declaration of variable **mHour**—we are using keyword **Private** rather than **Dim**. In this case, **Private** restricts the scope of **mHour** to its class. If **Dim** or **Public** is used, the variable is accessible outside the class. Method definitions that are not preceded by **Public** or **Private** default to **Public**. Variables declared with **Dim** default to **Public**.

Good Programming Practice 24.2

Qualify all class members with either **Public** *or* **Private** *to clearly show their access.*

Suppose **Property Let Hour** is a member of class **CTime1** (we discuss how to create classes momentarily). An object of class **CTime1** is created with the following code

```
Dim wakeUp
Set wakeUp = New CTime1
```

```
Private mHour

Public Property Let Hour( hr )
   If hr >= 0 And hr < 24 Then
      mHour = hr
   Else
      mHour = 0
   End If
End Property
```

Fig. 24.21 Simple **Property Let** procedure.

When creating an object, VBScript keyword ***New*** is used and followed by the class name. When assigning the object to a variable, keyword ***Set*** must be used. When a variable (e.g., **wakeUp**) refers to an object, the variable is called a *reference*.

Common Programming Error 24.18

Attempting to call a method or access a property for a reference that does not refer to an object is an error.

Common Programming Error 24.19

*Attempting to assign a reference a value without using **Set** is an error.*

If we perform the assignments **wakeup.Hour = -6** or **wakeup.Hour = 27**, the **Property Let** procedure would reject these as invalid values and set **theHour** to 0. The **Property Get Hour** procedure is shown in Fig. 24.22.

Using **CTime1** class object **wakeUp**, we can store the value of **Hour** into variable **alarmClockHourValue**, as follows:

```
alarmClockHourValue = wakeup.Hour
```

which call **Property Get Hour** to get the value of **theHour**. The **Class** definition for **CTime1** is shown in Fig. 24.23. Keywords **Class** and **End Class** encapsulate the class members.

Software Engineering Observation 24.6

To implement a read-only property, *simply provide a **Property Get** procedure but no **Property Let** (or **Property Set**) procedure.*

```
Public Property Get Hour()
   Hour = mHour
End Property
```

Fig. 24.22 Simple **Property Get** procedure.

```
Class CTime1
   Private mHour

   Public Property Let Hour( hr )
      If hr >= 0 And hr < 24 Then
         mHour = hr
      Else
         mHour = 0
      End If
   End Property

   Public Property Get Hour()
      Hour = mHour
   End Property
End Class
```

Fig. 24.23 Simple **Class** definition.

Suppose we have a **CEmployee** class that references a **CDate** object named **mBirthDate**. We cannot use a **Property Let** to assign a value to an object. Instead, we must use a **Property Set**, as in each of the following **Property** procedures:

```
Public Property Set BirthDay(bDay)
   Set mBirthDate = bDay
End Property

Public Property Get BirthDay()
   Set BirthDay = mBirthDate
End Property
```

Any **Property Get**, **Property Let** or **Property Set** method may contain the ***Exit Property*** statement that causes an immediate exit from a **Property** procedure.

Accessor methods can read or display data. Another common use for access methods is to test the truth or falsity of conditions—such methods are often called *predicate methods*. An example of a predicate method would be an **IsEmpty** method for any container class—a class capable of holding multiple objects—such as a linked list or a stack. A program might test **IsEmpty** before attempting to remove another item from a container object. A program might test **IsFull** before attempting to insert another item into a container object.

It would seem that providing *set* and *get* capabilities is essentially the same as making the instance variables **Public**. This is another subtlety of VBScript that makes the language desirable for software engineering. If an instance variable is **Public**, it may be read or written at will by any method in the program. If an instance variable is **Private**, a **Public** *get* method certainly seems to allow other methods to read the data at will but the *get* method controls the formatting and display of the data. A **Public** *set* method can—and most likely will—carefully scrutinize attempts to modify the instance variable's value. This ensures that the new value is appropriate for that data item. For example, an attempt to *set* the day of the month to 37 would be rejected, an attempt to *set* a person's weight to a negative value would be rejected, and so on.

Software Engineering Observation 24.7

The benefits of data integrity are not automatic simply because instance variables are made **Private**. *Methods that set the values of* **Private** *data should verify that the intended new values are proper; if they are not, the* set *methods should place the* **Private** *instance variables into an appropriate consistent state.*

Software Engineering Observation 24.8

Every method that modifies the **Private** *instance variables of an object should ensure that the data remains in a consistent state.*

Figure 24.24 demonstrates using a VBScript **Class**. The Web page allows the user to enter a first name, age and social security number which are displayed in a message dialog. This example briefly introduces a VBScript feature for complex pattern matching called *regular expressions*. We use regular expressions to validate the format of the social security number. Client-side scripts often validate information before sending it to the server. In this example, we briefly introduce regular expressions in the context of client-side validation. In Chapter 27, Perl, you will learn more about regular expressions.

Lines 16–69 define **Class Person**, which encapsulates **Private** data members, **Public Property** procedures and a **Private** method. Data members store the person's first name in **name**, the person's age in **yearsOld** and the person's social security number in **ssn**. Both **Property Let** and **Property Get** procedures are provided for the data members.

```
1  <?xml version = "1.0"?>
2  <!DOCTYPE html PUBLIC "-//W3C//DTD XHTML 1.0 Transitional//EN"
3     "http://www.w3.org/TR/xhtml1/DTD/xhtml1-transitional.dtd">
4
5  <!--Fig. 24.24: classes.html -->
6  <!-- VBScript Class          -->
7
8  <html xmlns = "http://www.w3.org/1999/xhtml">
9     <head>
10       <title>Using a VBScript Class</title>
11
12       <script type = "text/vbscript">
13          <!--
14          Option Explicit
15
16          Class Person
17             Private name, yearsOld, ssn
18
19             Public Property Let FirstName( fn )
20                name = fn
21             End Property
22
23             Public Property Get FirstName()
24                FirstName = name
25             End Property
26
27             Public Property Let Age( a )
28                yearsOld = a
29             End Property
30
31             Public Property Get Age()
32                Age = yearsOld
33             End Property
34
35             Public Property Let SocialSecurityNumber( n )
36
37                If Validate( n ) Then
38                   ssn = n
39                Else
40                   ssn = "000-00-0000"
41                   Call MsgBox( "Invalid Social Security Format" )
42                End If
43
44             End Property
45
```

Fig. 24.24 Using VBScript classes and regular expressions (part 1 of 3).

```
            Public Property Get SocialSecurityNumber()
               SocialSecurityNumber = ssn
            End Property

            Private Function Validate( expression )
               Dim regularExpression
               Set regularExpression = New RegExp

               regularExpression.Pattern = "^\d{3}-\d{2}-\d{4}$"

               If regularExpression.Test( expression ) Then
                  Validate = True
               Else
                  Validate = False
               End If

            End Function

            Public Function ToString()
               ToString = name & Space( 3 ) & age & Space( 3 ) _
                    & ssn
            End Function

         End Class   ' Person

         Sub cmdButton_OnClick()
            Dim p                  ' Declare object reference
            Set p = New Person     ' Instantiate Person object

            With p
               .FirstName = Document.Forms(0).txtBox1.Value
               .Age = CInt( Document.Forms(0).txtBox2.Value )
               .SocialSecurityNumber =_
                  Document.Forms(0).txtBox3.Value
               Call MsgBox( .ToString() )
            End With

         End Sub
         -->
      </script>
   </head>

   <body>
      <form action = "">Enter first name
         <input type = "text" name = "txtBox1" size = "10" />
         <p>Enter age
         <input type = "text" name = "txtBox2" size = "5" /></p>
         <p>Enter social security number
         <input type = "text" name = "txtBox3" size = "10" />
         </p><p>
         <input type = "button" name = "cmdButton"
            value = "Enter" /></p>
      </form>
```

Fig. 24.24 Using VBScript classes and regular expressions (part 2 of 3).

```
99      </body>
100  </html>
```

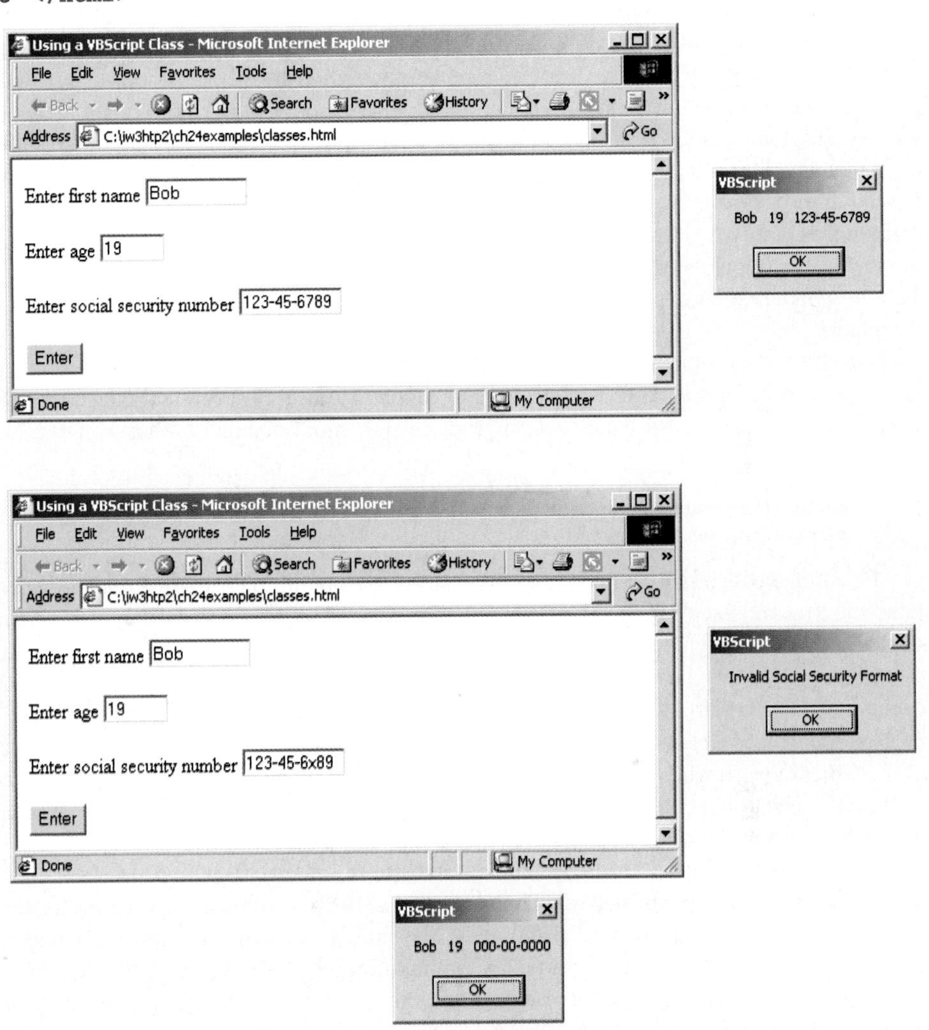

Fig. 24.24 Using VBScript classes and regular expressions (part 3 of 3).

Procedure **`Property Let SocialSecurityNumber`** (lines 35–44) is the most interesting **`Property`** procedure because it calls **`Private`** method **`Validate`** to verify the correct format for the social security number that was input. If **`Validate`** returns **`True`**, the social security number input is assigned to **`ssn`**; if **`Validate`** returns **`False`**, **`ssn`** is assigned the string **`"000-00-0000"`** and a message dialog is displayed.

Method **`Validate`** (line 50–62) checks the format of the social security number by using a so-called regular expression—a concept we explain in the next paragraph. Methods designated as **`Private`** are often called *utility* or *helper* methods. These methods are considered to be part of a class's implementation detail and therefore clients do not have access to them.

The statement in line 52 instantiates a regular expression object (i.e., an object of VBScript class ***RegExp***) and assigns it to reference **regularExpression**. Line 54 sets the ***Pattern*** property to the pattern we wish to match—in this case a social security number which consists of three digits, a hyphen (i.e., **-**), two digits, a hyphen and four digits. This expression reads as follows: the beginning of the string should begin with exactly three digits followed by a hyphen, then two digits followed by a hyphen and end with exactly four digits. The *caret*, **^** indicates the beginning of the string and the **\d** indicates that any digit (i.e., 0–9) is a match. The **{3}**, **{2}** and **{4}** expressions indicate that exactly three occurrences of any digit, exactly two occurrences of any digit and exactly four occurrences of any digit, respectively, are a match. The *dollar sign*, **$** indicates the end of the string. The hyphens are treated as *literal characters* (i.e., a hyphen is not a special character used in a regular expression for pattern matching—so a hyphen literally is treated as a hyphen).

The **If**'s condition (line 56) calls function ***Test*** to determine whether the regular expression's pattern is a match for the string passed into **Test**. A successful match returns **True** and an unsuccessful match returns **False**. For more details on VBScript regular expressions, visit

msdn.microsoft.com/workshop/languages/clinic/scripting051099.asp

Function **ToString** (line 64) returns a string containing the **name**, **age** and **ssn**. Function **Space** (line 65) is called to provide three spaces between words. Keywords ***End Class*** (line 69) designate the end of the class definition.

Lines 71–83 provide an event procedure for **cmdButton**'s **OnClick** event. Line 72 declares **p** as a variant—which can store object subtypes. The statement in line 73 instantiates a **Person** object and assigns it to **p**. As mentioned earlier, VBScript requires the use of the **Set** keyword when assigning an object to a variable. To be more precise, we call **p** a reference, because it is used with an object. At any moment in time, a reference can refer to an object or **Nothing** (i.e., a special value that indicates the absence of an object).

Lines 75–81 use the ***With/End With*** statement to set several property values for **p** and to call **p**'s **ToString** method. The **With/End With** statement is provided for the convenience of the programmer, to minimize the number of times an object's name is written (when setting multiple properties or calling multiple methods). Note that lines 76–79 actually call the appropriate **Property Let** procedures—these lines are not directly accessing **p**'s data. Line 80 calls **p**'s **ToString** method to get the string that the message dialog will display. Although the syntax may appear a bit strange, it is indeed correct.

24.9 Operator Precedence Chart

This section contains the operator precedence chart for VBScript (Fig. 24.25). Operators are shown in decreasing order of precedence from top to bottom.

24.10 Internet and World Wide Web Resources

Although the VBScript language contains far more features than can be presented in one chapter, there are many Web resources available that are related to VBScript. Visit the following sites for additional information.

Operator	Type	Associativity
`()`	parentheses	left to right
`-`	unary minus	left to right
`^`	exponentiation	left to right

`*`
`/`
`\`
	multiplication
	division
	integer division
		left to right

`Mod`	modulus	left to right
`+` `-`	addition subtraction	left to right
`&`	string concatenation	left to right

`=`
`<>`
`<`
`<=`
`>`
`>=`
`Is`
	equality
	inequality
	less than
	less than or equal
	greater than
	greater than or equal
	object equivalence
		left to right

`Not`	logical NOT	left to right
`And`	logical AND	left to right
`Or`	logical OR	left to right
`Xor`	logical exclusive OR	left to right
`Eqv`	logical equivalence	left to right
`Imp`	logical implication	left to right

Fig. 24.25 VBScript operator precedence chart.

msdn.microsoft.com/scripting/VBScript/doc/vbstutor.htm
The *VBScript tutorial* contains a short tutorial on VBScript.

msdn.microsoft.com/scripting/VBScript/doc/vbstoc.htm
The *VBScript language reference* contains links for constants, keywords, functions, etc.

msdn.microsoft.com/vbasic/technical/Documentation.asp
Visual Basic 6 documentation. Use the Visual Basic 6 documentation to get additional information on functions, constants etc. VBScript is a subset of Visual Basic.

msdn.microsoft.com/workshop/languages/clinic/scripting051099.asp
This is an article that discusses regular expressions in VBScript. One substantial example is provided at the end of the article.

SUMMARY

- Visual Basic Script (VBScript) is case-insensitive subset of Microsoft Visual Basic® used in World Wide Web XHTML documents to enhance the functionality of a Web page displayed in a Web browser (such as Microsoft's Internet Explorer) that contains a VBScript scripting engine (i.e., interpreter) and used on servers to enhance the functionality of server-side applications.

- VBScript's arithmetic operators are similar to JavaScript arithmetic operators. Two major differences are the division operator, ****, which returns an integer result, and the exponentiation operator, **^**, which raises a value to a power. VBScript operator precedence differs from that of JavaScript.
- VBScript's symbols for the equality operator and inequality operators are different from JavaScript's symbols. VBScript comparison operators may also be used to compare strings.
- VBScript provides the following logical operators: **And** (logical AND), **Or** (logical OR), **Not** (logical negation), **Imp** (logical implication), **Xor** (exclusive OR) and **Eqv** (logical equivalence).
- Despite the mixture of case in keywords, functions, etc., VBScript is not case-sensitive—uppercase and lowercase letters are treated the same.
- VBScript provides the plus sign, **+**, the and ampersand, **&**, operators for string concatenation. The ampersand is more formally called the string concatenation operator. If both operands of the concatenation operator are strings, these two operators can be used interchangeably. However, if the **+** operator is used in an expression consisting of varying data types, there can be a problem.
- VBScript code is commented either by using a single quote (**'**) or by keyword **Rem**. As with JavaScript's two forward slashes, **//**, VBScript comments are single-line comments.
- Like JavaScript, VBScript has only one data type—variant—and it is capable of storing different types of data (e.g., strings, integers, floating-point numbers, etc.). A variant is interpreted by VBScript in a manner that is suitable to the type of data it contains.
- Variable names cannot be keywords and must begin with a letter. The maximum length of a variable name is 255 characters containing only letters, numbers and underscores.Variables can be declared simply by using their name in the VBScript code. Statement **Option Explicit** forces all variables to be declared before they are used.
- VBScript provides nine control structures for controlling program execution. Many of the control structures provide the same capabilities as their JavaScript counterparts. Syntactically, every VBScript control structure ends with one or more keywords (e.g., **End If**, **Loop**, etc.). Keywords delimit a control structure's body—not curly braces (i.e., **{}**).
- The **If/Then/End If** and **If/Then/Else/End If** control structures behave identically to their JavaScript counterparts. VBScript's multiple selection version of **If/Then/Else/End If** uses a different syntax from JavaScript's version because it includes keyword **ElseIf**.
- VBScript does not use a statement terminator (e.g., a semicolon, **;**). Unlike JavaScript, placing parentheses around conditions in VBScript is optional. A condition evaluates to **True** if the variant subtype is boolean **True** or if the variant subtype is considered non-zero. A condition evaluates to **False** if the variant subtype is boolean **False** or if the variant subtype is considered to be 0.
- VBScript's **Select Case/End Select** structure provides the same functionality as JavaScript's **switch** structure and more. The **Select Case/End Select** structure does not require the use of a statement such as break. One **Case** cannot accidently run into another. The VBScript **Select Case/End Select** structure is equivalent to VBScript's **If/Then/Else/End If** multiple selection structure. The only difference is syntax. Any variant subtype can be used with the **Select Case/End Select** structure.
- VBScript's **While/Wend** repetition structure and **Do While/Loop** behave identically to JavaScript's **while** repetition structure. VBScript's **Do/Loop While** structure behaves identically to JavaScript's **do/while** repetition structure. VBScript contains two additional repetition structures, **Do Until/Loop** and **Do/Loop Until**, that do not have direct JavaScript equivalents. These **Do Until** repetition structures iterate until the condition becomes **True**.
- The **Exit Do** statement, when executed in a **Do While/Loop**, **Do/Loop While**, **Do Until/Loop** or **Do/Loop Until**, causes immediate exit from that structure and execution continues with the next statement in sequence. The fact that a **Do While/Loop** may contain **Exit Do** is the

only difference, other than syntax, between **Do While/Loop** and **While/Wend**. Statement **Exit For** causes immediate exit from the **For/Next** structure.

- Function **IsEmpty** determines whether the variant has ever been initialized by the programmer. If **IsEmpty** returns **True**, the variant has not been initialized by the programmer.
- VBScript math functions allow the programmer to perform common mathematical calculations. Trigonometric functions such as **Cos**, **Sin**, etc. take arguments that are expressed in radians. To convert from degrees to radians use the formula: $radians = degrees \times \pi / 180$.
- Function **InputBox** displays a dialog in which the user can input data.
- VBScript coordinates are measured in units of twips (1440 twips equal 1 Inch). Coordinates are relative to the upper-left corner of the screen, which is position *(0, 0)*. *X* coordinates increase from left to right and *y* coordinates increase from top to bottom.
- Many VBScript functions often take optional arguments.
- The underscore character, _ is VBScript's line continuation character. A statement cannot extend beyond the current line without using this character. A statement may use as many line continuation characters as necessary.
- Function **MsgBox** displays a message dialog.
- In VBScript, function calls that wrap arguments in parentheses must be preceded with keyword **Call**—unless the function call is assigning a value to a variable.
- VBScript provides functions for getting information about the scripting engine (i.e., the interpreter). These functions are **ScriptEngine**—which returns either **"JScript"**, **"VBScript"** or **"VBA"**, **ScriptEngineBuildVersion**—which returns the current build version, **ScriptEngineMajorVersion**—which returns the major version number for the script engine and **ScriptEngineMinorVersion**—which returns the minor release number.
- XHTML comment tags comment out the VBScript code. If the browser understands VBScript, these tags are ignored and the VBScript is interpreted. If the browser does not understand VBScript, the XHTML comment prevents the VBScript code from being displayed as text.
- Procedures that do not return a value begin with keyword **Sub** and end with keywords **End Sub**.
- Variables declared within a VBScript procedure are visible only within the procedure body. Procedures that perform event handling are more properly called event procedures.
- VBScript provides functions **CBool**, **CByte**, **CCur**, **CDate**, **CDbl**, **CInt**, **CLng**, **CSng** and **CStr** for converting between variant subtypes.
- Programmer-defined constants are created by using keyword **Const**.
- Because the **head** section of an XHTML document is decoded first by the browser, VBScript code is normally placed there, so it can be decoded before it is invoked in the document.
- VBScript procedures that return a value are delimited with keywords **Function** and **End Function**. A value is returned from a **Function** procedure by assigning a value to the procedure name. As in JavaScript, a **Function** procedure can return only one value at a time.
- VBScript provides statements **Exit Sub** and **Exit Function** for exiting **Sub** procedures and **Function** procedures, respectively. Control is returned to the caller, and the next statement in sequence after the call is executed.
- A fixed-size array's size does not change during program execution; a dynamic array's size can change during execution. A dynamic array is also called a redimmable array. Array elements may be referred to by giving the array name followed by the element position number in parentheses, **()**. The first array element is at index zero.

- Function **UBound** returns the upper bound (i.e., the highest-numbered index) and function **LBound** returns the lowest-numbered index (i.e., 0).
- Keyword **Public** explicitly indicates that a procedure is public. A procedure may also be marked as **Private**, to indicate that only scripts on the same Web page may call the procedure.
- Statement **ReDim** allocates memory for a dynamic array. All dynamic arrays must receive memory via **ReDim**. Dynamic arrays are more flexible than fixed-sized arrays, because they can be resized anytime using **ReDim** to accommodate new data.
- Function **Array** takes any number of arguments and returns an array containing those arguments.
- Keyword **Preserve** may be used with **ReDim** to maintain the current values in the array. When **ReDim** is executed without **Preserve**, all values contained in the array are lost.
- Arrays can have multiple dimensions. VBScript supports at least 60 array dimensions, but most programmers will need to use no more than two- or three-dimensional arrays. Multidimensional arrays can also be created dynamically.
- Memory allocated for dynamic arrays can be deallocated (released) at run-time using keyword **Erase**. A dynamic array that has been deallocated must be redimensioned with **ReDim** before it can be used again. **Erase** can also be used with fixed-sized arrays to initialize all the array elements to the empty string.
- VBScript strings are case sensitive and begin with an index of 1.
- Objects encapsulate data (attributes) and methods (behaviors); the data and methods of an object are intimately tied together. Objects have the property of information hiding. This means that although objects may communicate with one another, objects do not know how other objects are implemented—implementation details are hidden within the objects themselves.
- In VBScript, the unit of object-oriented programming is the **Class** from which objects are instantiated (i.e., created). Methods are VBScript procedures that are encapsulated with the data they process within the "walls" of classes.
- VBScript programmers can create their own user-defined types called classes. Classes are also referred to as programmer-defined types. Each class contains data as well as the set of methods which manipulate that data. The data components of a class are called instance variables. Just as an instance of a variant is called a variable, an instance of a class is called an object.
- Classes normally hide their implementation details from the clients (i.e., users) of the classes. This is called information hiding.
- Describing an object in terms of behaviors without concern for how those behaviors are actually implemented is called data abstraction, and VBScript classes define abstract data types (ADTs). Although users may happen to know how a class is implemented, users must not write code that depends on these details. This means that a class can be replaced with another version without affecting the rest of the system, as long as the **Public** interface of that class does not change (i.e. every method still has the same name, return type and parameter list in the new class definition).
- Access to **Private** data should be carefully controlled by the class's methods. For example, to allow clients to read the value of **Private** data, the class can provide a get method (also called an accessor method or a query method).
- To enable clients to modify **Private** data, the class can provide a set method (also called a mutator method). A set method can also translate between the form of the data used in the interface and the form used in the implementation. A get method need not expose the data in "raw" format; rather, the get method can edit the data and limit the view of the data the client will see.
- Classes often provide **Public** methods to allow clients of the class to set (i.e., assign values to) or get (i.e., obtain the values of) **Private** instance variables. These methods are special methods

in VBScript called **Property Let**, **Property Set** and **Property Get** (collectively these methods and the internal class data they manipulate are called properties). Procedures **Property Let** and **Property Set** differ in that **Property Let** is used for non-object subtypes (e.g., integer, string, byte, etc.) and **Property Set** is used for object subtypes.

- Method definitions that are not preceded by **Public** or **Private** default to **Public**. Variables declared with **Dim** default to **Public**. Methods designated as **Private** are often called utility or helper methods. These methods are considered to be part of a class's implementation detail, and therefore clients do not have access to them.
- When creating an object, VBScript keyword **New** is used followed by the class name. When assigning the object to a variable, keyword **Set** must be used. When a variable (e.g., **wakeUp**) refers to an object, the variable is called a reference.
- Any **Property Get**, **Property Let** or **Property Set** method may contain the **Exit Property** statement that causes an immediate exit from a **Property** procedure.
- Class **RegExp** may be used to create a regular expression object. A **RegExp** object's **Pattern** property stores a regular expression. Function **Test** determines whether a regular expression's **Pattern** is a match for the string argument passed into it.

TERMINOLOGY

$
\d
^
Abs function
abstract data type (ADT)
accessor method
Active Server Pages (ASP)
addition operator, **+**
And logical operator
Array function
Asc function
Atn function
attribute
behavior
boolean subtype
build version
byte subtype
CBool function
CByte function
CCur function
CDate function
CDbl function
Chr function
CInt function
Class keyword
client
CLng function
comment character, **'**
comparison operator
Const keyword
Cos function
CStr function
currency subtype
date/time subtype
Dim keyword
Do Loop/Until control structure
Do Loop/While control structure
Do Until/Loop control structure
Do While/Loop control structure
double subtype
dynamic array
ElseIf keyword
empty subtype
encapsulation
End Class
End Function
End If
End Property
End Select
End Sub
End With
equality operator, **=**
Eqv logical operator
Erase statement
event procedure
Exit Do statement
Exit For statement
Exit Property statement
Exp function
exponentiation operator, **^**
False keyword
Filter function

Fix function
floating-point division operator, **/**
For/Next control structure
FormatCurrency function
FormateDateTime function
FormatNumber function
FormatPercent function
get method
greater-than operator, **>**
greater-than or equal-to operator, **>=**
If/Then/End If control structure
Imp logical operator
inequality operator, **<>**
input dialog
InputBox function
instantiating an object
InStr function
InStrRev function
Int function
integer division operator, ****
integer subtype
Intranet
IsArray function
IsDate function
IsEmpty function
IsNumeric function
IsObject function
Join function
LBound function
LCase function
Left function
Len function
less-than operator, **<**
less-than or equal-to operator, **<=**
lexicographical comparison
line-continuation character, _
Log function
long subtype
Loop keyword
lower bound
LTrim function
MFC (Microsoft Foundation Classes)
Mid function
modulus operator, **Mod**
MsgBox function
multidimensional array
multiplication operator, *****
mutator method
negation operator, **-**
New keyword
Next keyword
Not logical operator
noun
Now function
object
object subtype
object-based programming (OBP)
Option Explicit
optional argument
Or logical operator
parentheses, **()**
Pattern property
predicate method
Preserve keyword
Private keyword
procedure
programmer-defined type
Property Get method
Property keyword
Property Let method
Property Set method
Public keyword
query method
Randomize function
rapid application development (RAD)
read-only property
ReDim statement
redimmable array
RegExp class
regular expressions
Rem keyword
Replace function
Right function
Rnd function
Round function
RTrim function
ScriptEngine function
ScriptEngineBuildVersion function
ScriptEngineMajorVersion function
ScriptEngineMinorVersion function
Set keyword
set method
Sgn function
Sin function
single subtype
software reusability
Space function
Split function
Sqr function
Step keyword

StrComp function
string concatenation operator, **&**
String function
string subtype
StrReverse function
subtraction operator, **-**
subtype of a variant
Tan function
Test function
To keyword
Trim function
True keyword
twip
TypeName function
UBound function
UCase function
upper bound
user-defined type
variant data type
variant subtype
VarType function
vbLongDate constant
VBScript (Visual Basic Scripting Edition)
VBScript language attribute
VBScript scripting engine
vbShortTime constant
vbTextCompare constant
verb
Wend keyword
While/Wend control structure
With keyword
XOr logical operator

SELF-REVIEW EXERCISES

24.1 State whether the following are *true* or *false*. If the answer is *false*, explain why.
a) VBScript is case-sensitive.
b) **Option Explicit** forces all VBScript variables to be declared.
c) The single quote character indicates a VBScript comment.
d) The exponentiation operator's symbol is the caret, **^**.
e) The starting index for an array may be set to either 0 or 1.
f) Array dimensions begin at 0.

24.2 Fill in the blanks in each of the following:
a) Keyword __________ is required when assigning an object to a reference.
b) Keyword __________ is required when instantiating an object.
c) VBScript variables are of type __________.
d) Function __________ returns a string containing characters from the left side of a string.
e) Class __________ defines a regular expression.
f) Function __________ returns an uppercase string.

24.3 Briefly explain the difference between a **Function** procedure and a **Sub** procedure.

24.4 Fill in the blanks in each of the following statements:
a) Keyword __________ is used to create a constant.
b) By default, script variables declared with **Dim** are __________.
c) Statement **ReDim** is used to allocate memory for a __________ array.
d) **Property** __________ returns a property's value.
e) __________ is the logical AND operator.
f) Function __________ returns the highest numbered array index.

ANSWERS TO SELF-REVIEW EXERCISES

24.1 a) False. VBScript is case-insensitive. b) True. c) True. d) True. e) False. An array's starting index is always 0. f) False. Array dimensions begin at 1.

24.2 a) **Set**. b) **New**. c) variant. d) **Left**. e) **RegExp**. f) **UCase**.

24.3 A **Function** procedure returns a value and a **Sub** procedure does not return a value.

24.4 a) **Const**. b) **Public**. c) dynamic. d) **Get**. e) **And**. f) **UBound**.

EXERCISES

24.5 (*Compound Interest Calculator*) Create an XHTML document that enables the user to calculate compound interest. Provide several **text** components in which the user can enter the *principal amount*, the yearly interest *rate* and the number of *years* (see the compound interest program of Fig. 10.6 for the calculation of interest). Provide a **button** to cause the VBScript to execute and calculate the interest. Display the result in another **text** component. If any **text** component is left empty, display a **MsgBox** indicating the error. Use a **Function** procedure to perform the calculation.

24.6 (*Monthly Compound Interest Calculator*) Modify Exercise 24.5 to calculate the compound interest on a monthly basis. Remember that you must divide the interest rate by 12 to get the monthly rate.

24.7 Write a VBScript that allows the user to enter a name, email address and phone number. Use regular expressions to perform the validation [e.g., names can only contain letters, email must be of the format *username@name.extension* and the phone number must have the format *(555) 555-5555*]. *Note*: You should read the article on regular expression (listed in the Web Resources section) before attempting this exercise.

24.8 Modify the script of Fig. 24.24 to use some of the string-related functions introduced in Section 24.7 to perform the validation instead of a regular expression. How does your new solution compare?

24.9 Write a VBScript that generates from the string **"abcdefghijklmnopqrstuvwxyz{"** the following:

```
             a
            bcb
           cdedc
          defgfed
         efghihgfe
        fghijkjihgf
       ghijklmlkjihg
      hijklmnonmlkjih
     ijklmnopqponmlkji
    jklmnopqrsrqponmlkj
   klmnopqrstutsrqponmlk
  lmnopqrstuvwvutsrqponml
 mnopqrstuvwxyxwvutsrqponm
nopqrstuvwxyz{zyxwvutsrqpon
```

24.10 Law enforcement agencies often get partial descriptions of suspect license plate numbers and have to search for license plate numbers that match the description. Create a program that will allow a local law enforcement agency to determine how many license plate numbers match a partial description. Randomly create 500 6-character long license plate numbers and store them in an array. Allow the user to search for partial plate numbers of 3 or 4 digits. *Note*: License plate numbers can contain both digits and letters. The array should not contain any duplicates.

24.11 Write a program that reads a five-letter word from the user and produces all possible three-letter words that can be derived from the letters of the five-letter word. For example, the three-letter words produced from the word "bathe" include the commonly used words

```
ate    bat    bet    tab    hat    the    tea
```

24.12 Create a class called **CComplex** for performing arithmetic with complex numbers. Write a program to test your class.

Complex numbers have the form

```
realPart + imaginaryPart ∞ i
```

where *i* is

$\sqrt{-1}$

Use floating-point subtypes to represent the **Private** data of the class. Provide **Public** methods for each of the following:

a) Addition of two **CComplex** numbers: The real parts are added together and the imaginary parts are added together.
b) Subtraction of two **CComplex** numbers: The real part of the right operand is subtracted from the real part of the left operand and the imaginary part of the right operand is subtracted from the imaginary part of the left operand.
c) Printing **CComplex** numbers in the form **(A, B)**, where **A** is the real part and **B** is the imaginary part.

24.13 Create a class called **CRational** for performing arithmetic with fractions. Write a program to test your class.

Use integer variables to represent the **Private** instance variables of the class—**mNumerator** and **mDenominator**. The class should store the fraction in reduced form (i.e., the fraction

```
2/4
```

would be stored in the object as 1 in the **mNumerator** and 2 in the **mDenominator**). Provide **Public** methods for each of the following:

a) Addition of two **CRational** numbers. The result is stored in reduced form.
b) Subtraction of two **CRational** numbers. The result is stored in reduced form.
c) Multiplication of two **CRational** numbers. The result is stored in reduced form.
d) Division of two **CRational** numbers. The result is stored in reduced form.
e) Returning **CRational** numbers in the form **mNumerator/mDenominator** (i.e., a string with this format).
f) Returning **CRational** numbers in floating-point format. (Consider providing formatting capabilities that enable the user of the class to specify the number of digits of precision to the right of the decimal point.)

24.14 Use a two-dimensional array to solve the following problem. A company has four salespeople (with salesperson numbers 1 to 4) who sell five different products (with product numbers 1 to 5). Once a day, each salesperson passes in a slip for each different type of product sold. Each slip contains the salesperson number, product number and the total dollar value of that product sold that day.

Write a program that reads this information and summarizes the total sales by salesperson by product. All totals should be stored in the two-dimensional array **sales**. After each input, print the results in tabular format, with each of the columns representing a particular salesperson and each of the rows representing a particular product. Cross-total each row to get the total sales of each product for last month; cross total each column to get the total sales by salesperson for last month. Your neat tabular printout should include these cross-totals to the right of the totaled rows and at the bottoms of the totaled columns. Use VBScript function **FormatCurrency** as part of your solution.

24.15 Use a one-dimensional array to solve the following problem. A company pays its salespeople on a commission basis. The salespeople receive $200 per week plus 9% of their gross sales for that week. For example, a salesperson who grosses $5000 in sales in a week receives $200 plus 9% of

$5000, or a total of $650. Write a program (using an array of counters) that determines how many of the salespeople earned salaries in each of the following ranges (assume that each salesperson's salary is truncated to an integer amount):

Salary Ranges	
1) $200-$299	6) $700-$799
2) $300-$399	7) $800-$899
3) $400-$499	8) $900-$999
4) $500-$599	9) $1000 and over
5) $600-$699	

24.16 Use a one-dimensional dynamic array to solve the following problem. Read in 20 numbers, each of which is between 10 and 100, inclusive. As each number is input, print it only if it is not a duplicate of a number already input. Provide for the "worst case," in which all 20 numbers are different.

24.17 Write a Web page that allows the user to select one or more books by using check boxes. Display the name of each book and its price. Display the current total in a text box at the bottom of the page. When a book is selected (or unselected), update the total. Use VBScript to perform any arithmetic operations and to format the total.

24.18 (*VBScript Calculator*) Write a VBScript calculator that provides addition, subtraction, multiplication and division operations.

24.19 Modify your solution to Exercise 24.18 to include scientific features such as exponentiation, cosine, sine, etc. Use the Windows calculator as a guide.

24.20 In the chapter, we mentioned that VBScript contains various date/time manipulations. Study these date/time capabilities by visiting the resources listed in Section 24.9. Write a program that demonstrates as many of these capabilities as possible.

24.21 Write a **Function** procedure **ToMorseCode** that takes one string argument and returns a string containing the Morse code equivalent. Figure 12.12 lists the Morse code for letters and digits.

24.22 Write a program that plays the "guess the number" game as follows: Your program chooses the number to be guessed by selecting an **Integer** at random in the range 1 to 1000, then displays

```
I have a number between 1 and 1000.
Can you guess my number?
Please enter your first guess.
```

The player then types a first guess. The program responds with one of the following:

```
Excellent! You guessed the number!
Would you like to play again (y or n)?

Too low. Try again.
Too high. Try again.
```

If the player's guess is incorrect, your program should keep telling the player "**Too high**" or "**Too low**" to help the player "zero in" on the correct answer.

25

Active Server Pages (ASP)

Objectives

- To program Active Server Pages using VBScript.
- To understand how Active Server Pages work.
- To understand the differences between client-side scripting and server-side scripting.
- To be able to pass data between Web pages.
- To be able to use server-side include statements.
- To be able to use server-side ActiveX components.
- To be able to create sessions.
- To be able to use cookies.
- To be able to use ActiveX Data Objects (ADO) to access a database.

A client is to me a mere unit, a factor in a problem.
Sir Arthur Conan Doyle

Rule One: Our client is always right.
Rule Two: If you think our client is wrong, see Rule One.
Anonymous

Protocol is everything.
Francoise Giuliani

Outline

25.1 Introduction

Interactive Web pages are created with both client- and server-side scripting. This book has focused on client-side scripting up to this point. The next several chapters discuss server-side technologies, which are essential to programming Internet applications. Server-side scripting uses information sent by clients, information stored on the server, information stored in the server's memory and information from the Internet to dynamically create Web pages. The next two chapters focus on Active Server Pages (ASP), a server-side technology that dynamically builds documents (e.g., XHTML, text, XML, etc.) in response to client requests.

The examples in this chapter illustrate how Active Server Pages use server and client information to create and send dynamic Web pages to clients. Examples in this chapter include a program to display the time and date on a Web server, a guest book, a Web page creator, a user verification system and an advertisement rotator. Chapter 26 builds on this chapter to construct an online message forum that uses Active Server Pages.

25.2 How Active Server Pages Work

Active Server Pages are processed by an *ActiveX component* (i.e., a server-side ActiveX control) called a *scripting engine*. An ASP file has the file extension **`.asp`** and contains XHTML tags and scripting code. Although other languages, like JavaScript, can be used for ASP scripting, VBScript (Chapter 24) is the most widely used.

Software Engineering Observation 25.1

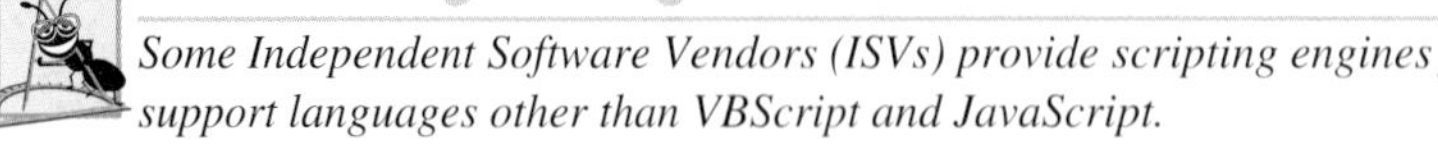

Some Independent Software Vendors (ISVs) provide scripting engines for use with ASP that support languages other than VBScript and JavaScript.

The Active Server Pages in this chapter demonstrate communication between clients and servers via the HTTP protocol of the World Wide Web. When a server receives a client's HTTP request, the server loads the document (or page) requested by the client. XHTML documents are *static documents*—all clients see the same content when the document is requested. ASP is a Microsoft technology for sending to the client dynamic Web content, including XHTML, Dynamic HTML, ActiveX controls, client-side scripts and *Java applets* (i.e., client-side Java programs that are embedded in a Web page). The Active Server Page processes the request (which often includes interacting with a database) and returns the results to the client—normally in the form of an XHTML document, but other data formats (e.g., images, binary data, etc.) can be returned.

When a client requests an ASP document, the document is loaded into memory and parsed (top to bottom) by a scripting engine named **`asp.dll`**. Script code is interpreted as it is encountered.

Portability Tip 25.1

An ASP page that generates pure XHTML may be rendered by any client browser.

Software Engineering Observation 25.2

To take advantage of Active Server Page technology, a Web server must provide a component such as **`asp.dll`** *to interpret ASP instructions.*

25.3 Setup

This chapter contains several examples that require either Internet Information Services (IIS) 5.0 or Personal Web Server (PWS) 4.0 to execute. Before attempting to execute any example, you should make sure PWS or IIS is running. For help installing and running IIS and PWS, see Chapter 21, Web Servers.

If you are going to execute the chapter examples, we recommend that you create a virtual directory (see Chapter 21) named **`Deitel`** on your computer. Copy all the **`.asp`** files from the Chapter 25 examples directory (included on the CD-ROM that accompanies this book), but not any subdirectories, to this directory. Create two other directories beneath **`C:\Inetpub\Wwwroot`** or **`C:\Webshare\Wwwroot`** home directory of your Web server named **`includes`** and **`images`**. Copy all **`.shtml`** files from the CD to **`includes`** and all **`.gif`** (or any other graphic file extension) files to **`images`**.

Some examples access databases. The database files (e.g., **`.mdb`** files) can be copied into any directory on your system. Before executing these examples, you must set up a System Data Source Name (DSN). See the "Setting up a System Data Source Name" at **`www.deitel.com`** for instructions on how to create a DSN.

25.4 Active Server Page Objects

Active Server Pages provide several built-in objects to offer programmers straightforward methods for communicating with a Web browser, gathering data sent by an HTTP request and distinguishing between users. Figure 25.1 provides a brief description of the most commonly used ASP objects.

The ***`Request`*** *object* is commonly used to access the information passed by a get or post request. This information usually consists of data provided by the user in an XHTML form. The **`Request`** object provides access to information, such as "cookies," that are stored on a client's machine. This object also provides access to binary information (e.g., a file upload). The ***`Response`*** *object* sends information, such as XHTML, text, etc. to the client. The ***`Server`*** *object* provides access to methods and properties on the server.

Object Name	Description
Request	Used to access information passed by an HTTP request.
Response	Used to control the information sent to the client.
Server	Used to access methods and properties on the server.

Fig. 25.1 Commonly used ASP objects.

25.5 Simple ASP Examples

In this section, we present simple ASP examples. The first example (Fig. 25.2) sends the Web server's date and time to the client as XHTML markup.

```
<% @LANGUAGE = VBScript %>

<%
   ' Fig. 25.2 : clock.asp
   ' A simple ASP example
   Option Explicit
%>

<!DOCTYPE html PUBLIC "-//W3C//DTD XHTML 1.0 Transitional//EN"
 "http://www.w3.org/TR/xhtml1/DTD/xhtml1-transitional.dtd">

<html xmlns = "http://www.w3.org/1999/xhtml">

   <head>
      <title>A Simple ASP Example</title>

      <style type = "text/css">
         td       { background-color: black;
                    color: yellow }
         strong   { font-family: arial, sans-serif;
                    font-size: 14pt; color: blue }
         p        { font-size: 14pt }
      </style>

   </head>

   <body>

      <p><strong>A Simple ASP Example</strong></p>
         <table border = "6">
            <tr>
               <td>
                  <% =FormatDateTime( Now, vbLongDate ) %>
               </td>

```

Fig. 25.2 Simple Active Server Page (part 1 of 2).

```
36                  <td>
37                     <% =Time() %>
38                  </td>
39               </tr>
40            </table>
41      </body>
42
43   </html>
```

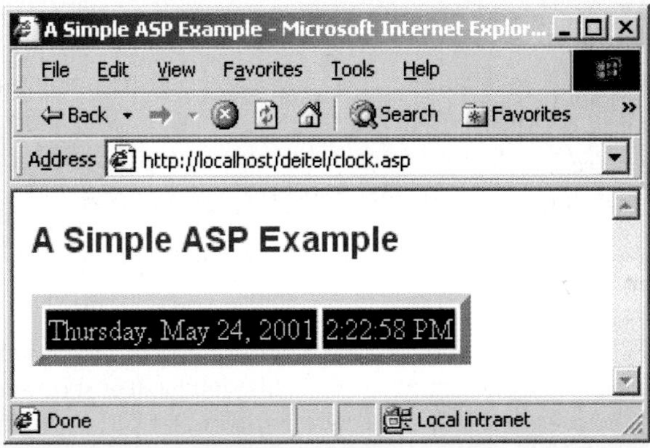

Fig. 25.2 Simple Active Server Page (part 2 of 2).

Notice the *scripting delimiters* `<% and %>` wrapped around the VBScript code—these delimit the scripting code that is executed on the server, not the client. Script enclosed in scripting delimiters is not sent to the client; it is processed by the scripting engine. However, the scripting code inside the delimiters can generate information that is sent to the client. Everything outside `<% and %>` is simply written to the client.

Common Programming Error 25.1

Missing the opening delimiter, `<%`, or closing delimiter, `%>`, or both for a server-side scripting statement is an error.

Line 1 uses the optional **`@LANGUAGE`** *processing directive* to specify VBScript as the scripting language. This indicates the scripting engine needed to interpret the scripting code. In this chapter, we use VBScript exclusively to develop our Active Server Pages, although other scripting languages, such as JavaScript, may be used. If the **`@LANGUAGE`** processing directive is omitted, VBScript is the default.

Good Programming Practice 25.1

*When using VBScript code in an Active Server Page, use the **`@LANGUAGE`** statement for clarity.*

Common Programming Error 25.2

*The **`@LANGUAGE`** directive should always be the first statement in an ASP file. Not placing it there is an error.*

The **`Option Explicit`** statement in line 6 indicates that the programmer must explicitly declare all VBScript variables. Remember that by simply mentioning a new name, VBScript variables are implicitly declared. This can lead to subtle errors. When used, the **Option Explicit** statement must be the first VBScript scripting statement after the **@LANGUAGE** directive. In this particular example, variables are not declared but the **Option Explicit** statement is included as a good programming practice.

Testing and Debugging Tip 25.1

Always include ***Option Explicit*** *even if you are not declaring any VBScript variables. As a script evolves over time, you may need to declare variables and the presence of the* ***Option Explicit*** *statement can help eliminate subtle errors.*

Line 33 calls VBScript function ***FormatDateTime*** to return a string formatted according to the server's date and time. This function accepts two arguments, the date and the format in which to return the date. We call VBScript function **Now** to get the current date and specify the **vbLongDate** format, which indicates that the day, time, month and year should be displayed. This statement is short for

```
<% Call Response.Write( FormatDateTime( Now, vbLongDate ) ) %>
```

which calls the **Response** method ***Write*** to send the formatted date as text to the client.

Line 37 calls VBScript function ***Time*** to get the current time on the server. Function **Time** returns the time in the format, *hh:mm:ss*.This statement is short for

```
<% Call Response.Write( Time() ) %>
```

which calls the **Response** method **Write** to send the time as text to the client.

Fig. 25.3 shows the XHTML generated by **clock.asp** that is rendered in the client browser. This is what the user would see by selecting the **View** menu's **Source** command in Internet Explorer. As you can see, server-side scripts, unlike client-side scripts, are not viewable by the client.

```
<!DOCTYPE html PUBLIC "-//W3C//DTD XHTML 1.0 Transitional//EN"
 "http://www.w3.org/TR/xhtml1/DTD/xhtml1-transitional.dtd">

<html xmlns = "http://www.w3.org/1999/xhtml">

   <head>
      <title>A Simple ASP Example</title>

      <style type = "text/css">
         td       { background-color: black;
                    color: yellow }
         strong   { font-family: arial, sans-serif;
                    font-size: 14pt; color: blue }
         p        { font-size: 14pt }
      </style>

   </head>

   <body>

```

Fig. 25.3 Viewing the XHTML generated by Fig. 25.2 (part 1 of 2).

```
      <p><strong>A Simple ASP Example</strong></p>
         <table border = "6">
            <tr>
               <td>
                  Thursday, May 24, 2001
               </td>

               <td>
                  2:22:58 PM
               </td>
            </tr>
         </table>
   </body>

</html>
```

Fig. 25.3 Viewing the XHTML generated by Fig. 25.2 (part 2 of 2).

ASP is also used to process form input. Data entered into a form can be sent to the server, processed and then sent back to the client in a different format. For example, an e-commerce site may use this to verify a customer's order information. The order information is entered into the form and then sent to the server for processing. Once the information is received, the server may return an order confirmation page, for verification purposes, that displays all the information the customer entered into the form.

Fig. 25.4 shows how to pass information from a form to an **.asp** document using the post method. The **action** attribute of the **form** element indicates the **.asp** file to which the form information is **post**ed.

In line 27 the **Request** object retrieves the form data **post**ed to **name.asp** and returns the contents of the **namebox** field as XHTML to the client.

```
<!DOCTYPE html PUBLIC "-//W3C//DTD XHTML 1.0 Transitional//EN"
 "http://www.w3.org/TR/xhtml1/DTD/xhtml1-transitional.dtd">

<!-- Fig. 25.4 : name.html                           -->
<!-- XHTML document that request an ASP document -->

<html xmlns = "http://www.w3.org/1999/xhtml">

   <head>
      <title>Name Request</title>
   </head>

   <body>

      <p style = "font-family: arial, sans-serif">
         Enter your name:
      </p>

      <!-- request name.asp when posted -->
```

Fig. 25.4 XHTML document that requests an ASP (part 1 of 2).

```
      <form action = "name.asp" method = "post">
         <input type = "text" name = "namebox" size = "20" />
         <input type = "submit" name = "submitButton"
                value = "Enter" />
      </form>

   </body>

</html>
```

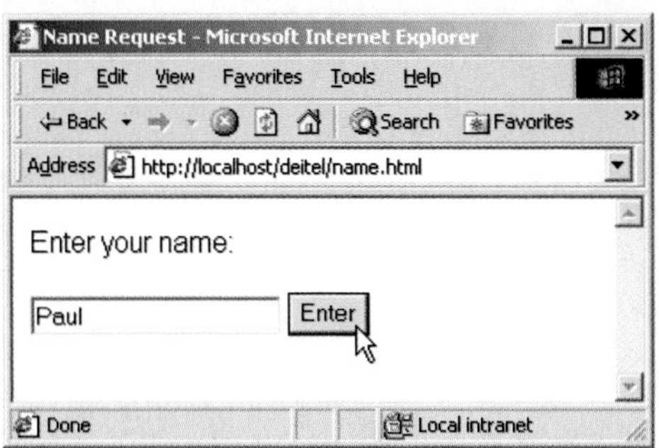

Fig. 25.4 XHTML document that requests an ASP (part 2 of 2).

When the **Enter** button is pressed, the form data is **post**ed to **name.asp** (Fig. 25.5). ASP **name.asp** processes the form data and returns XHTML to the client.

```
<% @LANGUAGE = VBScript %>

<%
   ' Fig. 25.5 : name.asp
   ' Another simple ASP example
   Option Explicit
%>

<!DOCTYPE html PUBLIC "-//W3C//DTD XHTML 1.0 Transitional//EN"
 "http://www.w3.org/TR/xhtml1/DTD/xhtml1-transitional.dtd">

<html xmlns = "http://www.w3.org/1999/xhtml">

   <head>
      <title>Name Information</title>

      <style type = "text/css">
         p        { font-family: arial, sans-serif;
                    font-size: 14pt; color: navy }
         .special { font-size: 20pt; color: green }
      </style>
   </head>

   <body>
```

Fig. 25.5 ASP document that responds to a client request (part 1 of 2).

```

        <!-- retrieve and display namebox's value -->
        <p>Hi <% =Request( "namebox" ) %>, </p><br />
        <p class = "special">Welcome to ASP!</p>

     </body>

  </html>
```

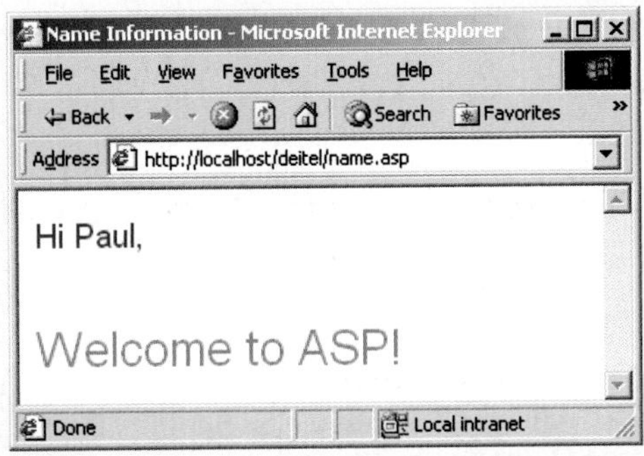

Fig. 25.5 ASP document that responds to a client request (part 2 of 2).

25.6 File System Objects

File System Objects (*FSOs*) provide the programmer with the ability to manipulate files, directories and drives. FSOs also allow the programmer to read and write text and are an essential element for Active Server Pages that persist data. We overview FSO features and then provide a "live-code™" example that uses FSOs.

FSOs are objects in the *Microsoft Scripting Runtime Library*. These FSO types include: ***FileSystemObject***, ***File***, ***Folder***, ***Drive*** and ***TextStream***. Each type is summarized in Fig. 25.6.

Object type	Description
FileSystemObject	Allows the programmer to interact with **File**s, **Folder**s and **Drive**s.
File	Allows the programmer to manipulate **File**s of any type.
Folder	Allows the programmer to manipulate **Folder**s (i.e., directories).
Drive	Allows the programmer to gather information about **Drive**s (hard disks, RAM disks—computer memory used as a substitute for hard disks to allow high-speed file operations, CD-ROMs, etc.). **Drive**s can be local or remote.
TextStream	Allows the programmer to read and write text files.

Fig. 25.6 File System Objects (FSOs).

The programmer can use **FileSystemObject**s to create directories, move files, determine whether a **Drive** exists, etc. Figure 25.7 summarizes some common methods of **FileSystemObject**.

The **File** object allows the programmer to gather information about files, manipulate files and open files. Figure 25.8 lists some common **File** properties and methods.

Methods	Description
CopyFile	Copies an existing **File**.
CopyFolder	Copies an existing **Folder**.
CreateFolder	Creates and returns a **Folder**.
CreateTextFile	Creates and returns a text **File**.
DeleteFile	Deletes a **File**.
DeleteFolder	Deletes a **Folder**.
DriveExists	Tests whether or not a **Drive** exists. Returns a boolean.
FileExists	Tests whether or not a **File** exists. Returns a boolean.
FolderExists	Tests whether or not a **Folder** exists. Returns a boolean.
GetAbsolutePathName	Returns the absolute path as a string.
GetDrive	Returns the specified **Drive**.
GetDriveName	Returns the **Drive** drive name.
GetFile	Returns the specified **File**.
GetFileName	Returns the **File** file name.
GetFolder	Returns the specified **Folder**.
GetParentFolderName	Returns a string representing the parent folder name.
GetTempName	Creates and returns a string representing a file name.
MoveFile	Moves a **File**.
MoveFolder	Moves a **Folder**.
OpenTextFile	Opens an existing text **File**. Returns a **TextStream**.

Fig. 25.7 **FileSystemObject** methods.

Property/method	Description
Properties	
DateCreated	Date. The date the **File** was created.
DateLastAccessed	Date. The date the **File** was last accessed.
DateLastModified	Date. The date the **File** was last modified.

Fig. 25.8 Some common **File** properties and methods (part 1 of 2).

Property/method	Description
`Drive`	**`Drive`**. The **`Drive`** where the file is located.
`Name`	String. The **`File`** name.
`ParentFolder`	String. The **`File`**'s parent folder name.
`Path`	String. The **`File`**'s path.
`ShortName`	String. The **`File`**'s name expressed as a short name.
`Size`	Variant. The size of the **`File`** in bytes.
Methods	
`Copy`	Copy the **`File`**. Same as **`CopyFile`** of **`FileSystemObject`**.
`Delete`	Delete the **`File`**. Same as **`DeleteFile`** of **`FileSystemObject`**.
`Move`	Move the **`File`**. Same as **`MoveFile`** of **`FileSystemObject`**.
`OpenAsTextStream`	Opens an existing **`File`** as a text **`File`**. Returns **`TextStream`**.

Fig. 25.8 Some common **`File`** properties and methods (part 2 of 2).

Property ***`Path`*** contains the **`File`**'s path in *long name format* (the operating system does not abbreviate the name when it exceeds the 8.3 format). Property **`ShortName`** contains, if applicable, the file name in *short name format* (a file name exceeding the 8.3 format is abbreviated). For example, "**`ABCDEFGHIJ.doc`**" is a file name in long name format. That same file name in short name format might be abbreviated as "**`ABCDEF~1.doc`**."

The **`Folder`** object allows the programmer to manipulate and gather information about directories. Figure 25.9 lists some common **`Folder`** properties and methods.

Property/method	Description
Properties	
`Attributes`	Integer. Value indicating **`Folder`**'s attributes (read only, hidden, etc.).
`DateCreated`	Date. The date the folder was created.
`DateLastAccessed`	Date. The date the folder was last accessed.
`DateLastModified`	Date. The date the folder was last modified.
`Drive`	**`Drive`**. The **`Drive`** where the folder is located.
`IsRootFolder`	Boolean. Indicates whether or not a **`Folder`** is a root folder.
`Name`	String. The **`Folder`**'s name.
`ParentFolder`	**`Folder`**. The **`Folder`**'s parent folder.
`Path`	String. The **`Folder`**'s path.
`ShortName`	String. The **`Folder`**'s name expressed as a short name.
`ShortPath`	String. The **`Folder`**'s path expressed as a short path.

Fig. 25.9 Some **`Folder`** properties and methods (part 1 of 2).

Property/method	Description
Size	Variant. The total size in bytes of all subfolders and files.
Type	String. The **Folder** type.
Methods	
Delete	Delete the **Folder**. Same as **DeleteFolder** of **FileSystemObject**.
Move	Move the **Folder**. Same as **MoveFolder** of **FileSystemObject**.
Copy	Copy the **Folder**. Same as **CopyFolder** of **FileSystemObject**.

Fig. 25.9 Some **Folder** properties and methods (part 2 of 2).

Property ***IsRootFolder*** indicates whether the folder is the *root folder* for the **Drive** (i.e., the folder that contains everything on the drive). If the folder is not the root folder, method **ParentFolder** may be called to get the folder's *parent folder* (i.e., the folder in which the selected folder is contained). Method **Size** returns the total number of bytes the folder contains. The size includes *subfolders* (i.e., folders inside the selected folder) and files.

The **Drive** object allows the programmer to gather information about drives. Figure 25.10 lists some common **Drive** properties. Property **DriveLetter** contains the **Drive**'s letter. Property **SerialNumber** contains the **Drive**'s serial number. Property **FreeSpace** contains the number of bytes available.

Property	Description
AvailableSpace	Variant. The amount of available **Drive** space in bytes.
DriveLetter	String. The letter assigned to the **Drive** (e.g., "C").
DriveType	Integer. The **Drive** type. Constants **Unknown**, **Removable**, **Fixed**, **Remote**, **CDRom** and **RamDisk** represent **Drive** types and have the values 0–5, respectively.
FileSystem	String. The file system **Drive** description (FAT, FAT32, NTFS, etc.).
FreeSpace	Variant. Same as **AvailableSpace**.
IsReady	Boolean. Indicates whether or not a **Drive** is ready for use.
Path	String. The **Drive**'s path.
RootFolder	Folder object. The **Drive**'s root **Folder**.
SerialNumber	Long. The **Drive** serial number.
TotalSize	Variant. The total **Drive** size in bytes.
VolumeName	String. The **Drive** volume name.

Fig. 25.10 **Drive** properties.

The **TextStream** object allows the programmer to manipulate text files. Figure 25.11 list **TextStream** properties and methods.

Figure 25.12 is an Active Server Page for a *guest* book, which allows the visitors to enter their name, e-mail and comments. File system objects are used to write the visitor information to a file on the server.

Property/Method	Description
Properties	
AtEndOfLine	Boolean. Indicates whether the end of a line has been encountered.
AtEndOfStream	Boolean. Indicates whether the end of file has been encountered.
Column	Integer. Returns the character's position in a line.
Line	Integer. Returns the current line number.
Methods	
Read	String. Returns a specified number of characters from the file referenced by the **TextStream** object.
ReadAll	String. Returns the entire contents of the file referenced by the **TextStream** object.
ReadLine	String. Returns one line from the file referenced by the **TextStream** object.
Write	String. Writes text to the file referenced by the **TextStream** object.
WriteBlankLines	String. Writes newline characters to the file referenced by the **TextStream** object.
WriteLine	String. Writes one line to the file referenced by the **TextStream** object.
Skip	Variant. Skips a specified number of characters while reading from the file referenced by the **TextStream** object.
SkipLine	Variant. Skips a line of characters while reading from the file referenced by the **TextStream** object.
Close	Close the file referenced by the **TextStream** object.

Fig. 25.11 **TextStream** methods and properties.

```
<% @LANGUAGE = VBScript %>

<% ' Fig. 25.12 : guestbook.asp
   ' Demonstrating File System Objects
   Option Explicit
%>

```

Fig. 25.12 Guest book Active Server Page (part 1 of 5).

```
<!DOCTYPE html PUBLIC "-//W3C//DTD XHTML 1.0 Transitional//EN"
 "http://www.w3.org/TR/xhtml1/DTD/xhtml1-transitional.dtd">

<html xmlns = "http://www.w3.org/1999/xhtml">

   <head>
      <title>GuestBook Example</title>

      <style type = "text/css">
         hr    { size: 1; color: blue }
         table { text-align: center }
         td    { font-size: 12pt }
         p     { font-size: 14pt; color: blue }
         .font { font-family: arial, sans-serif }
      </style>
   </head>
   <body>
<%
   Dim fileObject, textFile, guestBook, mailtoUrl

   ' get physical path for this ASP page and
   ' concatenate guestbook.txt to it
   guestbook = Request.ServerVariables( "APPL_PHYSICAL_PATH" ) _
      & "\guestbook.txt"

   ' instantiate a FileSystemObject
   Set fileObject = Server.CreateObject( _
      "Scripting.FileSystemObject" )

   ' Check if this request is after the user has posted the form
   If Request( "hiddenInput" ) = "true" Then

      ' Print a thank you
      Call Response.Write( "Thanks for your entry, " & _
         Request( "username" ) & "!" )
%>
      <hr />
<%
      ' build the mailtoUrl
      mailtoUrl = Date() & " <a href = " & Chr( 34 ) _
         & "mailto:" & Request( "email" ) & Chr( 34 ) _
         & ">" & Request( "username" ) & "</a>:  "


      ' open the guestbook, 8 is for appending
      ' create the guestbook if it does not exist
      Set textFile = _
         fileObject.OpenTextFile( guestbook, 8, True )

      ' write data to guestbook.txt
      Call textFile.WriteLine( "<hr />" & mailtoUrl & _
         Request( "comment" ) )
      Call textFile.Close()
```

Fig. 25.12 Guest book Active Server Page (part 2 of 5).

```
      End If
   %>

         <p>Please leave a message in our guestbook.</p>

         <!-- write form to the client -->
         <form action = "guestbook.asp" method = "post">
            <table>
               <tr>
                  <td>Your Name:  </td>
                  <td><input class = "font"
                          type = "text" size = "60"
                          name = "username" /></td>
               </tr>

               <tr>
                  <td>Your email address:</td>
                  <td><input class = "font"
                          type = "text" size = "60"
                          name = "email"
                          value = "user@isp.com" />
                  </td>
               </tr>

               <tr>
                  <td>Tell the world:  </td>
                  <td><textarea name = "comment" rows = "3"
                          cols = "50">
Replace this text with the information
you would like to post.</textarea></td>
               </tr>
            </table>

            <input type = "submit" value = "submit" />
            <input type = "reset" value = "clear" />
            <input type = "hidden" name = "hiddenInput"
                   value = "true" />
         </form>

<%
   ' check if the file exists
   If fileObject.FileExists( guestBook ) = True Then


      ' open the guestbook, "1" is for reading
      Set textFile = fileObject.OpenTextFile( guestbook, 1 )

      ' read the entries from the file and write them to
      ' the client.
      Call Response.Write( "Guestbook Entries:<br />" & _
         textFile.ReadAll() )
      Call textFile.Close()

```

Fig. 25.12 Guest book Active Server Page (part 3 of 5).

```
      End If
%>

   </body>

</html>
```

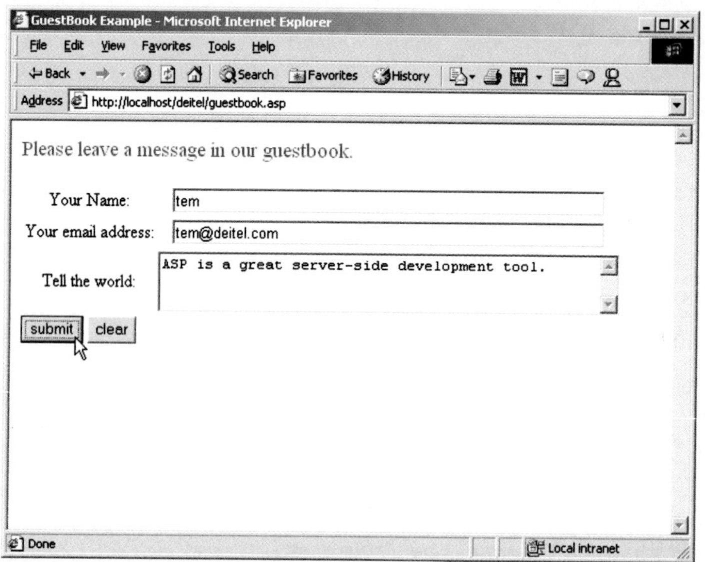

GuestBook Example - Microsoft Internet Explorer
File Edit View Favorites Tools Help
Back Search Favorites History
Address http://localhost/deitel/guestbook.asp

Thanks for your entry, tem!

Please leave a message in our guestbook.

Your Name:
Your email address: user@isp.com
Tell the world: Replace this text with the information you would like to post.
submit clear

Guestbook Entries:

5/24/2001 tem: ASP is a great server-side development tool.

mailto:tem@deitel.com
Local intranet

Fig. 25.12 Guest book Active Server Page (part 4 of 5).

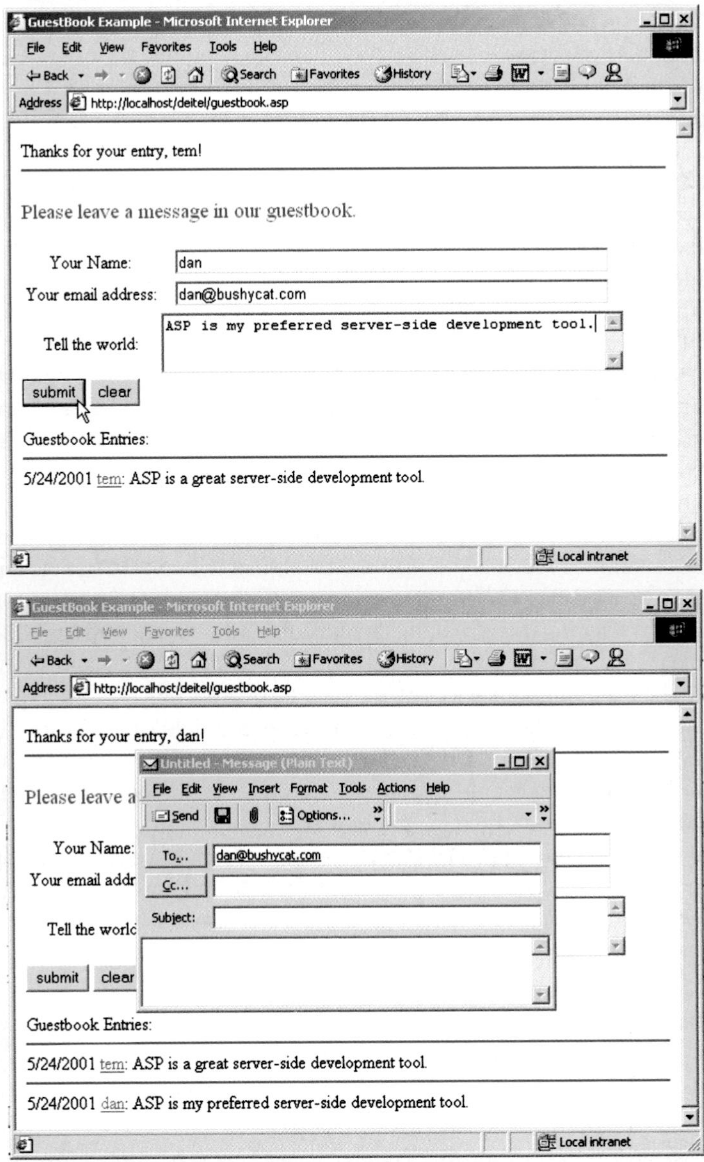

Fig. 25.12 Guest book Active Server Page (part 5 of 5).

The guest book page displayed in the browser consists of a form (to be filled in by the user) and a list of guest book entries (initially, there are no entries in this list). The form (lines 67–98) contains two text fields and a text area for inputting the name, e-mail and user comment.

Line 67 indicates that a post request occurs upon form submission. The action for the form requests the same ASP page in which the form is contained—**`guestbook.asp`**. A form's action is not required to request a different document.

Upon submission, **guestbook.asp** is requested and passes parameter **hiddenInput**—which has the value **"true."** The name **hiddenInput** is programmer-defined—developers of course may choose any name they prefer. We use this technique to determine whether this ASP page is being requested by a form submitted from **guestbook.asp**.

Lines 30–31 pass **Request** method ***ServerVariables*** the *server key* ***APPL_PHYSICAL_PATH*** to retrieve the physical path of the virtual directory where this ASP document resides. We concatenate this with the name of the file, **guestbook.txt**, and assign the result to variable **guestbook**. Fig. 25.13 lists some server variable keys.

Lines 34–35 create an FSO instance (i.e., an object) and assign it to reference **fileObject**. When assigning an object to a reference in VBScript, keyword **Set** is required.

We want only lines 41–60 to execute when the page is loaded with a post request. Line 38 uses the **Request** object to get **hiddenInput**'s value and test it against the string **"true."** When this page is requested by a client for the first time, **hiddenInput** has the value **""** (an *empty string*), and lines 41–60 are not executed. Variable **hiddenInput** is only assigned value **"true"** during the post operation (line 67).

Lines 41–42 print **Thanks for your entry,** followed by the user's name. The **Request** object gets the value **post**ed in the **username** field of the submitted form.

The user's submitted name and e-mail are combined with XHTML tags and assigned to string **mailtoUrl** (lines 47–49). This string, when displayed in the browser, shows the submitted name as a *mailto link*. Clicking this link opens an e-mail message editor with the person's name in the **To:** field. Line 47 calls VBScript function **Date** to assign the current server date to the beginning of **mailtoUrl**. The **Request** object is used to retrieve the values from the **email** field (line 48) and the **username** field (line 49). The value **34** is passed to the VBScript function **Chr** to get a double quote (**"**) character. We call this function because the interpreter would treat a double quote as the end of the **mailtoUrl** string. The XHTML tags are stored in **mailtoUrl**.

Lines 54–55 call method **OpenTextFile** to get a **TextStream** object for accessing the text file **guestbook.txt**. The constant value **8** indicates *append mode* (writing to the end of the file), and **True** indicates that the file will be created if it does not already exist. Read and write modes are specified with constant values **1** and **2**, respectively.

Key Name	Description
APPL_PHYSICAL_PATH	Returns the physical path.
HTTPS	Boolean. Determines if the request came in through SSL (Secure Sockets Layer).
REMOTE_ADDR	Client's DNS name or IP address.
REQUEST_METHOD	Request method (i.e., get and post).
SERVER_NAME	Server's hostname (DNS or IP address).
HTTP_USER_AGENT	Returns information about the client making the request.
HTTP_COOKIE	Returns cookies residing on the client.

Fig. 25.13 Some server variable keys.

Lines 58–59 write text to **guestbook.txt** using the **TextStream** method **WriteLine**. After writing the text to the file, **TextStream** method **Close** is called in line 60 to close the file.

Every time a client requests this Active Server Page, lines 100–115 execute. This VBScript code displays a list of all the users who have made guest book entries. Line 102 uses FSO method **FileExists** to check if the **guestbook.txt** file exists. If this function returns **True**, lines 106–112 execute. In line 106, **guestbook.txt** is opened for reading. Lines 110–111 read the entries from the file and write XHTML to the client. The entire contents of **guestbook.txt** are read by calling **TextStream** method **ReadAll** in line 111. This text is written to the client using **Response.Write**. This text contains XHTML markup which is rendered in the client browser. The **TextStream** method **Close** is called in line 112 to close the file. Fig. 25.14 shows the contents of **guestbook.txt** after two users have submitted comments.

25.7 Session Tracking and Cookies

HTTP does not support persistent information that could help a Web server distinguish between clients. In this section, we introduce two related technologies that enable a Web server to distinguish between clients: *session tracking* and *cookies*.

Many Web sites provide custom Web pages or functionality on a client-by-client basis. For example, some Web sites allow you to customize their home page to suit your needs. An example of this is the *Yahoo!* Web site (**my.yahoo.com**), which allows you to customize how the Yahoo! site appears. [*Note*: You need to get a free Yahoo! ID first.]

Another example of a service that is customized on a client-by-client basis is a *shopping cart* for shopping on the Web. When a purchase is made, the server must distinguish between clients so the business can assign the proper items and charge each client the proper amount.

A third method of customization on a client-by-client basis is marketing to specific audiences. Companies often track the pages people visit so they can display advertisements based on a person's browsing trends. Many people consider tracking to be an invasion of their privacy, an increasingly sensitive issue in our information-based society. See Chapter 32 for more information on this and other legal, ethical and moral issues.

The server performs session tracking by keeping track of when a specific person visits a site. The first time a client connects to the server, the server assigns the user a unique *session ID*. When the client makes additional requests, the client's session ID is compared with the session IDs stored in the server's memory. Active Server Pages use the ***Session*** object to manage sessions. The **Session** object's ***Timeout*** property specifies the number of minutes that a session exists before it expires. The default value for property **Timeout** is 20 minutes. Calling **Session** method ***Abandon*** can also terminate an individual session.

```
<hr />5/24/2001 <a href = "mailto:tem@deitel.com">tem</a>:  ASP is a great tool for server-side development.
<hr />5/24/2001 <a href = "mailto:dan@bushycat.com">dan</a>:  ASP is my preferred server-side development tool.
```

Fig. 25.14 Contents of **guestbook.txt** for Fig. 25.12.

Figure 25.15 is an ASP page generator. Users who are not familiar with ASP may input their information in a form and submit the form, and the ASP page generator will create the user's ASP page. This example consists of two Active Server Pages linked to each other through HTTP post requests. We use session variables in this example to maintain a state between the two ASP pages. Multiple Active Server Pages connected in this manner are sometimes called an *ASP application*. The first page, **instantpage.asp** (Fig. 25.15), consists of a form that requests information from the user. When submitted, the form is **post**ed to **process.asp** (Fig. 25.18). If there are no errors, **process.asp** creates the user's ASP page. Otherwise, **process.asp** redirects the user back to **instantpage.asp**. Also, **process.asp** stores a "welcome back" message in session variable **welcomeBack**. Each time a user submits the form, **process.asp** stores a new "welcome back" message in the session variable. If a file name is not provided, **process.asp** returns an error to **instantpage.asp** (Fig. 25.15). [*Note*: The example presented is IIS specific. PWS users should use the version in the **PWS** folder in the Chapter 25 examples directory (on the CD-ROM that accompanies this book). Separate files are included on the CD for users running Personal Web Server.

Line 30 is a *server-side include* (*SSI*) statement that incorporates the contents of **header.shtml** (Fig. 25.16) into the ASP file. Server-side includes are commands embedded in XHTML documents that add dynamic content. The SSI statement in line 30 is replaced with the contents of the file **header.shtml**. The word ***virtual*** in the SSI refers to the include file's path as it appears below the server's root directory. This is often referred to as a *virtual path*. SSIs can use ***file*** instead of **virtual** to indicate a *physical path* relative to the directory of the current file on the server. For example, line 30 could be rewritten as

```
<!-- #include file = "includes\header.shtml"-->
```

which assumes that **header.shtml** is in the **includes** folder under the directory that contains **instantpage.asp** on the server.

Not all Web servers support the available SSI commands. Therefore, SSI commands are written as XHTML comments. SSI statements always execute before any scripting code executes.

```
1  <% @LANGUAGE = VBScript %>
2
3  <%
4     ' Fig. 25.15 : instantpage.asp
5     ' ASP document that posts data to process.asp
6     Option Explicit
7  %>
8
9  <!DOCTYPE html PUBLIC "-//W3C//DTD XHTML 1.0 Transitional//EN"
10    "http://www.w3.org/TR/xhtml1/DTD/xhtml1-transitional.dtd">
11
12 <html xmlns = "http://www.w3.org/1999/xhtml">
13
```

Fig. 25.15 ASP that posts user information to **process.asp** (part 1 of 4).

```
   <head>
      <title>Instant Page Content Builder</title>

      <style type = "text/css">
         table { text-align: center;
                 font-size: 12pt;
                 color: blue;
                 font-size: 12pt;
                 font-family: arial, sans-serif }
      </style>

   </head>

   <body>

      <!-- include the header                               -->
      <!-- #include virtual = "/includes/header.shtml" -->
      <h2>Instant Page Content Builder</h2>

<% ' if process.asp posted an error, print the error
   ' message.
   If Session( "errormessage" ) <> "no error" Then
      Call Response.Write( Session( "errorMessage" ) )
   ' otherwise, print the welcome back message, if any
   Else
      Call Response.Write( Session( "welcomeBack" ) )
   End If

%>
      <!-- a form to get the information from the user -->
      <form action = "process.asp" method = "post">
         <table>
            <tr>
               <td>Your Name:  </td>

               <td><input type = "text" size = "60"
                          name = "username" /></td>
            </tr>

            <tr>
               <td>Enter the Filename:</td>

               <td><input type = "text" size = "60"
                          name = "filename"
                          value = "yourfilename" /></td>
            </tr>

            <tr>
               <td>Enter the Title:</td>

               <td><input type = "text" size = "60"
                          name = "doctitle"
                          value = "document title" /></td>
```

Fig. 25.15 ASP that posts user information to **process.asp** (part 2 of 4).

```
            </tr>

            <tr>
               <td>Enter the content:</td>

               <td><textarea name = "content" rows = "3"
                     cols = "50">
Replace this text with the
information you would like to post.</textarea></td>
            </tr>
         </table>

         <input type = "submit" value = "submit" />
         <input type = "reset" value = "clear" />
      </form>

      <!-- #include virtual = "/includes/footer.shtml" -->
   </body>
</html>
```

Fig. 25.15 ASP that posts user information to **process.asp** (part 3 of 4).

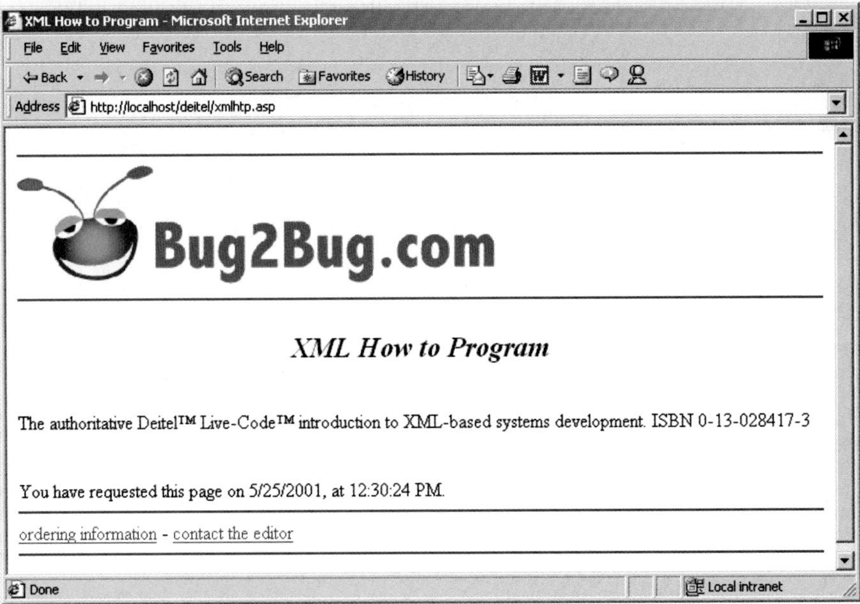

Fig. 25.15 ASP that posts user information to **process.asp** (part 4 of 4).

```
<!-- Fig. 25.16: header.shtml                    -->
<!-- Server-side include file containing XHTML -->
<hr style = "color: blue" />
<img height = "100" src = "/images/bug2bug.gif" alt = "Bug" />
<hr style = "color: blue" />
```

Fig. 25.16 File listing for **header.shtml**.

We also use an SSI in line 83 to include **footer.shtml** (Fig. 25.17).

Software Engineering Observation 25.3

Virtual paths hide the server's internal file structure.

Session variable **errorMessage** is used in this example for error messages, and session variable **welcomeBack** is used to display a "welcome back" message to a returning user. The **If** statement on lines 35–40 tests if the value of session variable **errorMessage** is not equal to **"no error."** If **True**, the value of session variable **errorMessage** is written to the client in line 36. Otherwise, **welcomeBack's** value is written to the client. When the user first requests **instantpage.asp**, session variable **errorMessage** does not have a value, and line 35 returns **True**. A session variable that has not explicitly been given a value contains an empty string. Although line 36 is executed, session variable **errorMessage** has no value, and thus line 36 does not print anything to the client. Note that **Session("errorMessage")** never contains a value unless **process.asp** encounters an error and transfers the user back to **instantpage.asp**. A session variable's value is set and retrieved using the **Session** object.

Line 44 requests Active Server Page **process.asp** when the form is **post**ed. The remainder of **instantpage.asp** is XHTML that defines the form input items and the page footer.

Software Engineering Observation 25.4

Server-side includes may contain any type of information. Text files and XHTML files are two of the most common server-side include files.

Software Engineering Observation 25.5

Server-side includes are performed before any scripting code is interpreted. Therefore, an Active Server Page cannot decide dynamically which server-side includes are used and which are not. Through scripting, an ASP can determine which SSI block is sent to the client.

Testing and Debugging Tip 25.2

Server-side includes that contain scripting code should enclose the scripting code in **<script>** *tags or in* **<% %>** *delimiters to prevent one block of scripting code from running into another block of scripting code.*

Software Engineering Observation 25.6

By convention, server-side include files end with the **.shtml** *extension.*

```
<!-- Fig. 25.17: footer.shtml                     -->
<!-- Server-side include file containing XHTML -->
<hr style = "color: blue" />
<a style = "text-align: center"
   href = "mailto:orders">ordering information</a> -
<a style = "text-align: center"
   href = "mailto:editor">contact the editor</a><br />
<hr style = "color: blue" />
```

Fig. 25.17 File listing for **footer.shtml**.

Software Engineering Observation 25.7

Server-side includes are an excellent technique for reusing XHTML, Dynamic HTML, scripts and other programming elements.

The document **process.asp** (Fig. 25.18) creates the user's ASP document and presents a link to the user's page. This page (**process.asp**) is requested by **instantpage.asp** (line 44).

```
<% @LANGUAGE = VBScript %>

<%
   ' Fig. 25.18 : process.asp
   ' ASP document that creates user's ASP document
   Option Explicit
%>

<%
    Dim message, q

    q = Chr( 34 )   ' assign quote character to q
    Session( "errorMessage" ) = "no error"

   ' check to make sure that they have entered a
   ' valid filename
   If ( LCase( Request( "filename" ) ) = "yourfilename" ) _
      Or Request( "filename" ) = "" Then
      message = "<p style = " & q & "color: red" & q & _
         ">" & "Please enter a valid name or filename.</p>"
      Session( "errorMessage" ) = message
      Call Server.Transfer( "instantpage.asp" )
   End If

   Dim directoryPath, filePath, fileObject, fileName

   ' Create a FileSystem Object
   Set fileObject = Server.CreateObject( _
      "Scripting.FileSystemObject" )

   directoryPath = _
      Request.ServerVariables( "APPL_PHYSICAL_PATH" )

   fileName = Request( "filename" ) & ".asp"

   ' build path for text file
   filePath = directoryPath & "\" & fileName

   ' check if the file already exists
   If fileObject.FileExists( filePath ) Then
      message = "<p style = " & q & "color: red" & q & _
         ">" & "The file name is in use.<br />" & _
         "Please use a different file name.</p>"
```

Fig. 25.18 ASP document that dynamically generates an ASP document (part 1 of 3).

```
         Session( "errorMessage" ) = message
         Call Server.Transfer( "instantpage.asp" )
      End If

      ' save XHTML for the welcome back message
      ' in a session variable
      message = "<p style = " & q & "color: blue" & q & _
         ">" & "Welcome Back, " & Request( "username" ) & _
         "</p><br />"
      Session( "welcomeBack" ) = message

      Dim header, footer, textFile, openMark, closeMark
      openMark = "<" & "%"
      closeMark = "%" & ">"

      ' build the header.
      ' vbCrLf inserts a carriage return/linefeed into the text
      ' string which makes the XHTML code more readable
      header = openMark & " @LANGUAGE = VBScript " & closeMark _
         & vbCrLf & openMark & " ' " & fileName _
         & " " & closeMark & vbCrLf & vbCrLf _
         & "<!DOC" & "TYPE html PUBLIC " & q & _
           "-//W3C//DTD XHTML 1.0 Transitional//EN" & q & _
           vbCrLf & q & "http://www.w3.org/TR/xhtml1/" & _
           "DTD/xhtml1-transitional.dtd" & q & ">" & vbCrLf & _
         "<html xmlns = " & q & "http://www.w3.org/1999/xhtml" & _
         q & ">" & vbCrLf & "<head>" & vbCrLf _
         & "<meta name = " & q & "author" & q & " content = " _
         & q & Request( "username" ) & q & " />" & vbCrLf _
         & "<meta name = " & q & "pubdate" & q & " content = " _
         & q & Date() & q & " />" & vbCrLf _
         & "<title>" & Request( "doctitle" ) & "</title>" _
         & vbCrLf & "</head>" & vbCrLf & "<body>" & vbCrLf _
         & "<!-- #" & "include " & "virtual = " & _
         "/includes/header.shtml -->" _
         & vbCrLf & "<h2 style = " & q & "text-align: center" & _
         q & "><em>" & Request( "doctitle" ) & "</em></h2>" & _
         vbCrLf & "<br />" & vbCrLf

      ' build the footer using a different style for
      ' building the string
      footer = vbCrLf & "<br /><br /><br />" & vbCrLf & _
         "You have requested this page on " & _
         openMark & " =Date() " & closeMark & "," & _
         vbCrLf & "at " & openMark & " =Time() " & _
         closeMark & "." & vbCrLf & _
         "<!-- #" & "include " & "virtual = " & _
         "/includes/footer.shtml -->" _
         & vbCrLf & vbCrLf & "</body>" & vbCrLf & "</html>"

      ' create the ASP file
      Set textFile = fileObject.CreateTextFile( filePath, False )
```

Fig. 25.18 ASP document that dynamically generates an ASP document (part 2 of 3).

```
96       With textFile
97          Call .WriteLine( header & Request( "content" ) & _
98                           footer )
99          Call .Close()
100      End With
101   %>
102
103   <!DOCTYPE html PUBLIC "-//W3C//DTD XHTML 1.0 Transitional//EN"
104    "http://www.w3.org/TR/xhtml1/DTD/xhtml1-transitional.dtd">
105
106   <html xmlns = "http://www.w3.org/1999/xhtml">
107
108      <head>
109         <!-- use the title given by the user -->
110         <title>File Generated: <% =fileName %></title>
111
112         <style type = "text/css">
113            h2 { font-family: arial, sans-serif;
114                 text-align: center }
115         </style>
116
117      </head>
118
119      <body>
120         <!-- #include virtual = "/includes/header.shtml" -->
121         <h2><em>File <% =fileName %>
122            was created successfully.</em>
123         </h2><br />
124
125         <!-- provide a link to the generated page -->
126         <a href = "<% =fileName %>">View your file</a>
127         <!-- #include virtual = "/includes/footer.shtml" -->
128      </body>
129   </html>
```

Fig. 25.18 ASP document that dynamically generates an ASP document (part 3 of 3).

The **`If`** statement in line 17–18 validates the contents of field **Enter the Filename**. If the field is empty or contains the default string **`yourfilename`**, lines 19–21 assign XHTML text containing an error message to the variable **`message`**. Line 21 assigns the value of variable **`message`** to session variable **`errorMessage`**.

Then, line 22 calls **`Server`** method ***`Transfer`*** to request **`instantpage.asp`**. Session variable **`errorMessage`** is accessible by this ASP page.

If the user has entered a valid file name, an FSO object is created in lines 28–29 and assigned to reference **`fileObject`**.

Lines 31–32 specify the path on the server where the ASP file eventually will be written. We call **`Request`** method **`ServerVariables`** to retrieve the physical path. Line 34 builds the file name by concatenating the file name specified by the user to the **`.asp`** file extension. Similarly, line 37 builds the file path by concatenating the file name to the directory path and assigns this value to variable **`filePath`**.

This **`filePath`** is passed to FSO method **`FileExists`**—which is called in line 40 to determine if the file exists. If it does exist, another user has already created an ASP document with the same file name. If this is the case, XHTML containing an error message is set as the value of session variable **errorMessage**. Line 45 calls **Server** method **Transfer** to request **instantpage.asp**.

Lines 50–53 assign XHTML for the "welcome back" message to session variable **welcomeBack**. The format of the message is

```
Welcome back, X!
```

where **X** is the current user's name obtained from the form's **username** field.

Lines 56–57 assign the ASP scripting delimiters to string variables **openMark** and **closeMark**. We use two strings instead of one to represent the opening and closing delimiters (i.e., **"<" & "%"**) because the interpreter treats the single string **"<%"** as a scripting delimiter.

Next, we build the user's ASP file. For clarity, we divide the file into three parts: a header, a footer and the content (provided by the user in the form's **content** field).

Lines 62–81 construct XHTML for the header and assign it to variable **header**. VBScript constant **vbCrLf** is used to insert a carriage-return line-feed combination. The form's values are retrieved using the **Request** object. Lines 85–92 create the page's footer and assign it to variable **footer**.

Lines 95–100 write **header**, text area **content**'s text and **footer** to the text file before closing it. Lines 103–129 send XHTML to the client that contains a link to the created page. Figure 25.19 is a sample ASP file—named **test.asp**—created by Active Server Page **process.asp**. [*Note*: We added lines 1–2 for presentation purposes.]. The screen capture in Fig. 25.20 shows the message displayed when the user returns back to **instantpage.asp**. The screen capture (Fig. 25.21) shows the error message generated when the user does not change the default file name in the **Enter the Filename** field.

Another popular way to customize Web pages is via *cookies*. Cookies store information on the client's computer for retrieval later in the same browsing session or in future browsing sessions. For example, cookies could be used in a shopping application to keep track of the client's shopping-cart items.

```
1   <% @LANGUAGE = VBScript %>
2   <% ' test.asp %>
3
4   <!DOCTYPE html PUBLIC "-//W3C//DTD XHTML 1.0 Transitional//EN"
5   "http://www.w3c.org/TR/xhtml1/DTD/xhtml1-transitional.dtd">
6   <html xmlns = "http://www.w3.org/1999/xhtml">
7   <head>
8   <meta name = "author" content = "tem" />
9   <meta name = "pubdate" content = "2/27/2001" />
10  <title>XML How to Program</title>
11  </head>
12  <body>
13  <!-- Fig. 25.16: header.shtml                    -->
14  <!-- Server-side include file containing XHTML -->
15  <hr style = "color: blue" />
16  <img height = "100" src = "/images/bug2bug.gif" alt = "Bug" />
```

Fig. 25.19 XHTML document generated by **process.asp** (part 1 of 2).

```
<hr style = "color: blue" />
<h2 style = "text-align: center"><em>XML How to Program</em></h2>
<br />

The authoritative Deitel&#8482; Live-Code&#8482;
introduction to XML-based systems development.
ISBN 0-13-028417-3

<br /><br /><br />
You have requested this page on 2/27/2001,
at 10:14:44 PM.
<!-- Fig. 25.17: footer.shtml                  -->
<!-- Server-side include file containing XHTML -->
<hr style = "color: blue" />
<a style = "text-align: center"
   href = "mailto:orders">ordering information</a> -
<a style = "text-align: center"
   href = "mailto:editor">contact the editor</a><br />
<hr style = "color: blue" />

</body>
</html>
```

Fig. 25.19 XHTML document generated by **process.asp** (part 2 of 2).

Cookies are small files sent by an Active Server Page (or another similar technology, such as Perl—discussed in Chapter 27) as part of a response to a client. Every HTTP-based interaction between a client and a server includes a *header* that contains information about either the request (when the communication is from the client to the server) or the response (when the communication is from the server to the client). When an Active Server Page receives a request, the header includes the request type (e.g., **get** or **post**) and cookies stored on the client machine by the server. When the server formulates its response, the header information includes any cookies the server wants to store on the client computer.

Software Engineering Observation 25.8

Some clients do not allow cookies to be written on their machine. A refusal to accept cookies may prevent the client from being able to use the Web site that attempted to write the cookie.

Depending on the *maximum age* of a cookie, the Web browser either maintains the cookie for the duration of the browsing session (i.e., until the user closes the Web browser) or stores the cookie on the client computer for future use. When the browser makes a request to a server, cookies previously sent to the client by that server are returned to the server (if the cookies have not expired) as part of the request formulated by the browser. Cookies are automatically deleted when they *expire* (i.e., reach their maximum age). We use cookies in Section 25.8 to store user IDs.

25.8 Accessing a Database from an Active Server Page

Active Server Pages can communicate with databases through ADO (ActiveX Data Objects—introduced in Chapter 22). ADO provides a uniform way for a program to connect with a variety of databases without having to deal with the specifics of those database systems.

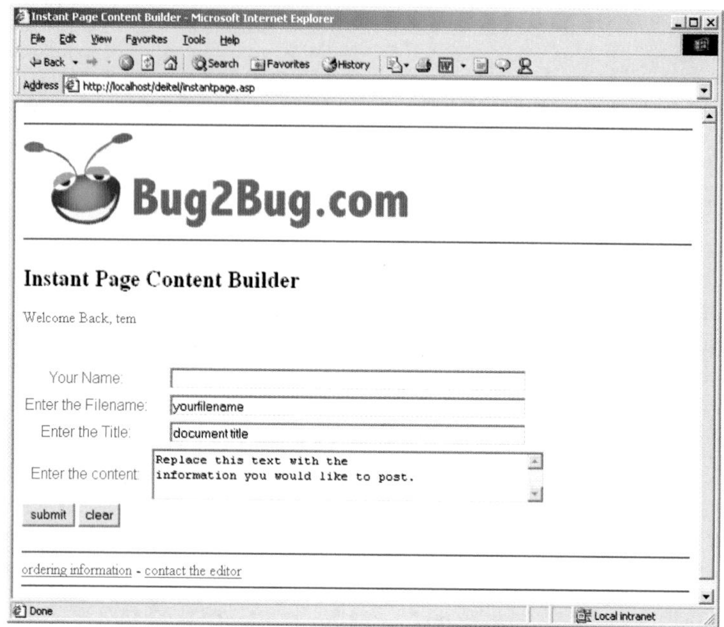

Fig. 25.20 Welcome back message displayed by **`instantpage.asp`**.

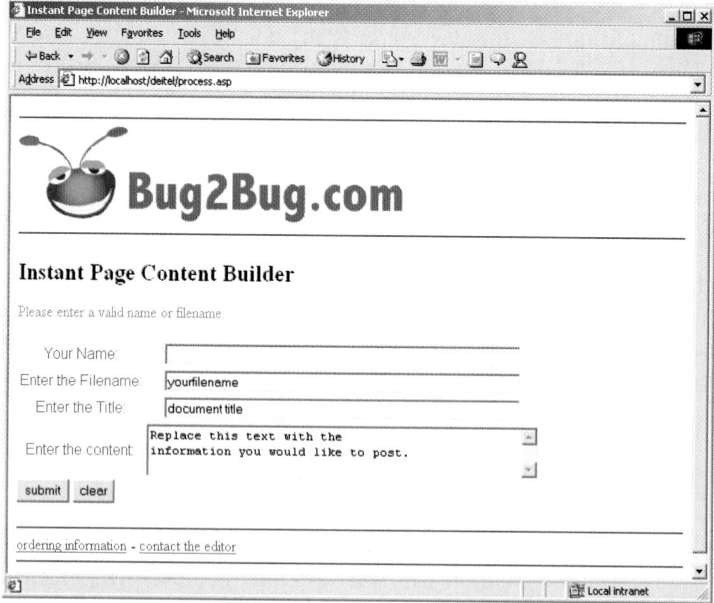

Fig. 25.21 Error message generated by **`instantpage.asp`**.

Web applications are typically *three-tier distributed applications,* consisting of a *user interface*, *business logic* and *database access*. The user interface in such an application is often created using XHTML, Dynamic HTML or XML. The user interface can contain ActiveX controls, client-side scripts and, in some cases, Java applets. XHTML is the preferred mechanism for representing the user interface in systems where portability is a concern. Because most browsers support XHTML, designing the user interface to be accessed through a Web browser guarantees portability across all browser platforms. The user interface can communicate directly with the middle-tier business logic by using the networking provided automatically by the browser. The middle tier can then access the database to manipulate the data. All three tiers may reside on separate computers that are connected to a network or on a single machine.

In multi-tier architectures, Web servers are increasingly used to build the middle tier. They provide the business logic that manipulates data from databases and that communicates with client Web browsers. Active Server Pages, through ADO, can interact with popular database systems. Developers do not need to be familiar with the specifics of each database system. Rather, developers use SQL-based queries, and ADO handles the specifics of interacting with each database system through OLE DB.

Databases enhance applications by providing a data source that can be used to dynamically generate Web pages. Figure 25.15 (**instantpage.asp**) puts the power of Web page creation into the hands of individuals who are not familiar with XHTML or ASP. However, we may want only a certain subset of pre-approved users to be able to access **instantpage.asp**. To restrict access, we use password protection. [*Note*: The example presented here is IIS specific. PWS users should use the version in the Chapter 25 examples directory (on the CD-ROM that accompanies this book). Separate files are included on the CD for users running Personal Web Server.] Before executing this example, an ODBC System DSN for this database must be created. See the "Setting up a System Data Source Name" at **www.deitel.com**.

Fig. 25.22 (**database.asp**) is an ASP document used to connect to and query an Access database.

```
<% @LANGUAGE = VBScript %>

<%
   ' Fig. 25.22 : database.asp
   ' ASP document for interacting with the database
   Option Explicit

   Dim connection, loginData

   ' provide error handling code
   On Error Resume Next
   Session( "errorString" ) = ""

   Set connection = Server.CreateObject( "ADODB.Connection" )
   Call connection.Open( "login" )
   Call errorHandlerLog()

```

Fig. 25.22 ASP document for connecting to a database (part 1 of 2).

```
18        ' create the record set
19        Set loginData = Server.CreateObject( "ADODB.Recordset" )
20        Call loginData.Open( Session( "query" ), connection )
21        Set Session( "loginData" ) = loginData
22
23        Call errorHandlerLog()
24
25        Sub errorHandlerLog()
26           If Err.Number <> 0 Then
27              Dim errorString
28
29              errorString = Session( "errorString" )
30              errorString = errorString & "<p class = " & _
31                 Chr( 34 ) & "error" & Chr ( 34 ) & ">Error (" _
32                 & Err.Number & ") in " & Err.Source & "<br />" & _
33                 Err.Description & "</p><br />"
34              Session( "errorString" ) = errorString
35           End If
36        End Sub
37     %>
```

Fig. 25.22 ASP document for connecting to a database (part 2 of 2).

For simplicity, if an error occurs while the records are being retrieved, we choose to handle the error later in the script. Line 11 specifies that any error caused by a statement from this point onward is ignored, and control is transferred to the statement immediately following the statement that caused the error. Line 12 declares session variable **errorString** and assigns it an empty string as its value.

The **Server** object provides a method (**CreateObject**) to instantiate other objects (e.g., built-in objects, ActiveX components, etc.). Line 14 calls **Server** method **CreateObject** to create an **ADODB.Connection** object and **Set**s it to reference **connection**. An **ADODB.Connection** object encapsulates the functionality necessary to connect to a data source. Line 15 calls method ***Open*** to open the database referenced by the specified ODBC System DSN (i.e., **login**).

Line 16 calls procedure **errorHandlerLog** to process any errors that might have occurred in the script. Lines 25–36 define procedure **errorHandlerLog**. When an error occurs in the script, ***Err*** object's ***Number*** property contains an integer representing which VBScript error has occurred. Line 26 tests if an error has occurred. If **True**, lines 27–34 assign XHTML text containing the error number and a message to session variable **errorString**.

Lines 19–20 **Set** reference **loginData** to an **ADODB.Recordset** object and call method **Open** to execute the query (passed by **login.asp**) against the database referenced by **connection**. Method **Open** is passed a string containing the SQL query and the **ADODB.Connection** object that **connection** references. When **Open** finishes executing, the **ADODB.Recordset** object referenced by **loginData** contains all records that match the SQL query and points to either the first record or *end of file* (***EOF***) if no records were found.

Line 21 **Set**s session variable **loginData** to variable **loginData** referencing the **ADODB.Recordset** object containing all records that matched the SQL query. Line 23 calls procedure **errorHandlerLog** for a second time. Note that in line 30 the error number and message are concatenated to variable **errorString** to ensure that error information is added to previous errors the script has encountered. In Fig. 25.26, we show a sample error.

Fig. 25.23 provides an Active Server Page named **login.asp**, which prompts the user for a login name and password. The login names and passwords are stored in the Access database opened in **database.asp**.

```
<% @LANGUAGE = VBScript %>

<%
   ' Fig. 25.23 : login.asp
   ' ASP document to login to instantpage.asp
   Option Explicit

   ' create the SQL query
   Session( "query" ) = "SELECT loginID FROM Users"
   Call Server.Execute( "database.asp" )
%>

<!DOCTYPE html PUBLIC "-//W3C//DTD XHTML 1.0 Transitional//EN"
 "http://www.w3.org/TR/xhtml1/DTD/xhtml1-transitional.dtd">

<html xmlns = "http://www.w3.org/1999/xhtml">

   <head>
      <title>Login Page</title>

      <style type = "text/css">
         table { text-align: center;
                 font-size: 12pt;
                 color: blue;
                 font-size: 12pt;
                 font-family: arial, sans-serif }
         .error { color: red }
      </style>

   </head>

   <body>

   <!-- #include virtual="/includes/header.shtml" -->
<%
   If Session( "errorString" ) = "" Then
      ' if this is a return after a failed attempt,
      ' print an error
      If Session( "loginFailure" ) = True Then %>
         <p class = "error">Login attempt failed,
                            please try again</p>
<%    End If

```

Fig. 25.23 ASP document that allows the user to log into a site (part 1 of 4).

```
         ' begin the form %>
         <p>Please select your name and enter
            your password to login:</p><br />

         <form action = "submitlogin.asp" method = "post">

            <!-- format the form using a table -->
            <table border = "0">
               <tr>
                  <td>Name:</td>

                  <td>
                     <select name = "loginID">
                        <option value = "noSelection">
                           Select your name</option>

<%
   If Request.Cookies( "loginID" ) <> "" Then
      Call BuildReturning()
   Else
      Call BuildNewUser()
   End If
%>
                     </select>
                  </td>
               </tr>

               <tr>
                  <td>Password:</td>
                  <td><input type = "password"
                          name = "password" /></td>
               </tr>

               <tr>
                  <td></td>
                  <td align = "left">
                     <input type = "submit" value = "Log Me In" />
                  </td>
               </tr>
            </table>
         </form>

         <!-- #include virtual="/includes/footer.shtml" -->
<%
   Else
      Call Response.Write( Session( "errorString" ) )
   End If
%>
   </body>
</html>

<%
   ' builds the option items for loginIDs and writes
```

Fig. 25.23 ASP document that allows the user to log into a site (part 2 of 4).

```
      ' selected for the loginID of the returning user
      Sub BuildReturning()
         Dim found, loginData

         Set loginData = Session( "loginData" )

         ' pull user names from the record set to populate the
         ' dropdown list
         found = False

         While Not loginData.EOF
            ' create this record's dropdown entry
%>          <option
<%          ' if we did not write selected for any option
            ' before
            If ( Not found ) Then

               ' if the current record's loginID is equal to
               ' the loginID cookie, then it is the loginID of
               ' the returning user, and thus we need to write
               ' selected for this option; in this case we also
               ' need to signal that we have written selected
               ' for an option by setting found to True.
               If Request.Cookies( "loginID" ) _
                     = loginData( "loginID" ) Then
                  Call Response.Write( "selected = " & _
                     Chr( 34 ) & "selected" & Chr( 34 ) )
                  found = True
               End If
            End If
%>          value = "<% =loginData( "loginID" ) %>">
            <% =loginData( "loginID" ) %></option>
<%          Call loginData.MoveNext()
         Wend
      End Sub

      ' builds the option items for loginIDs without writing
      ' selected for any loginID
      Sub BuildNewUser()
         Dim loginData

         Set loginData = Session( "loginData" )

         ' pull user names from the record set to populate the
         ' dropdown list
         While Not loginData.EOF
            ' create this record's dropdown entry
%>          <option value = "<% =loginData( "loginID" ) %>">
            <% =loginData( "loginID" ) %></option>
<%          Call loginData.MoveNext()
         Wend
      End Sub
%>
```

Fig. 25.23 ASP document that allows the user to log into a site (part 3 of 4).

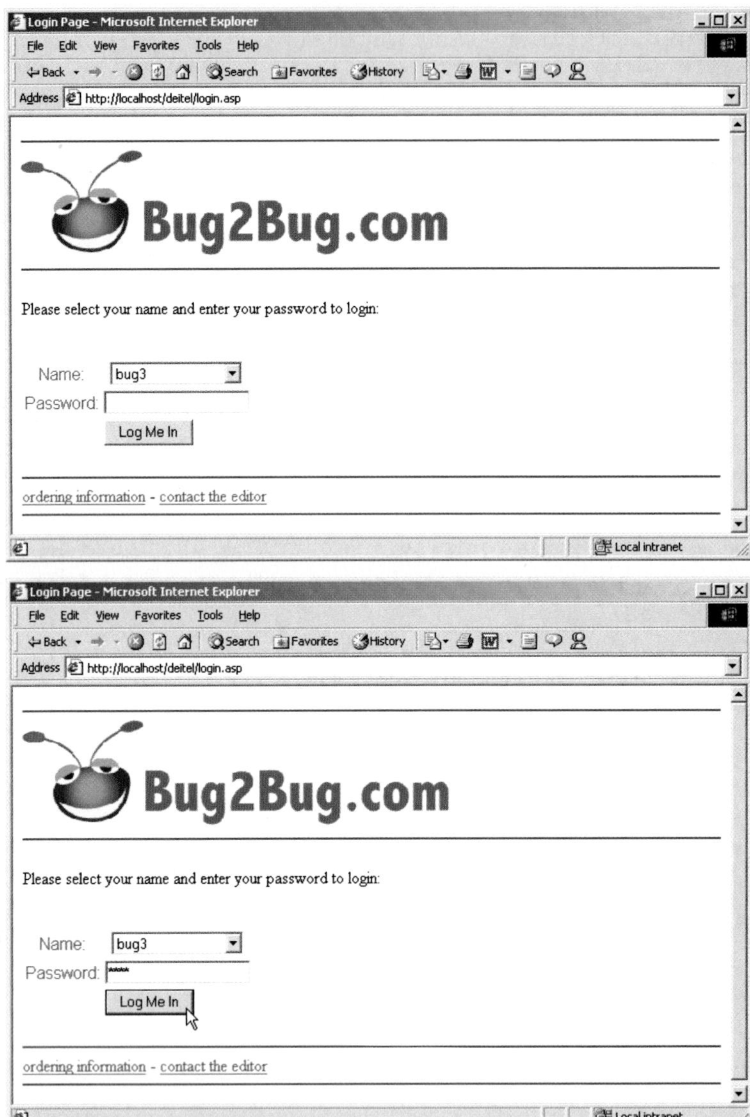

Fig. 25.23 ASP document that allows the user to log into a site (part 4 of 4).

This example uses cookies to identify users. The user's browser must have cookies enabled to run this example. If cookies are disabled, the browser will not permit the example to write a cookie to the client machine, and the example will not be able to identify the user properly. Cookies are enabled in Internet Explorer 5.5 by selecting **Internet Options** from the **Tools** menu, which displays the **Internet Options** dialog. Click the **Security** tab at the top of this dialog to view the current security settings. Select the **Custom Level...** button, scroll down and find **Cookies**, then click **Enable** for both cookie options.

The Active Server Page **login.asp** prompts the user for a login ID and a password while **submitlogin.asp** is responsible for validating the user's login. Both **submitlogin.asp** and **login.asp** use session variable **loginFailure**. If login is successful, **loginFailure** is set to **False**, and the client is transferred to **instantpage.asp**. If login is unsuccessful, the variable is set to **True** and the client is transferred back to **login.asp**. The page recognizes that there was an error in **submitlogin.asp** and displays the error message, because **login.asp** has access to session variable **loginFailure**.

The **loginID** and **password** fields are stored in table **Users** inside an Access database named **login.mdb**. For this example to perform correctly, use for username and password: *bug1*, *bug2*, *bug3* or *bug4*. Users select their **loginID** from a drop-down list populated from the **Users** table. Note that **submitlogin.asp** also accesses the database to verify login information.

The file **submitlogin.asp** writes a cookie (named **loginID**) to the client containing the user's **loginID** string to recognize returning users and to have their **loginID** displayed as selected in the drop-down list. When the user returns, **login.asp** reads the cookie and selects the user's login name from the drop-down list.

Line 9 assigns the SQL query that **SELECT**s all the **loginID**s **FROM** the **Users** table to session variable **query**. We use this session variable in **database.asp** (Fig. 25.22) as a parameter in method **Open** to query the database for each login ID. Line 10 executes **database.asp** to retrieve the login IDs from the database.

Line 36 tests if session variable **errorString** has an empty string as its value. Session variable **errorString** will have an empty string as its value unless an error has occurred in **database.asp**. If this returns **False**, line 89 calls **Response** method **Write** to print the error message to the user.

Lines 39–86 are executed only if **database.asp** has not returned an error. Lines 39–41 determine whether or not the session variable **loginFailure** is **True**, indicating that **submitlogin.asp** has detected an invalid login. If **True**, a message is displayed informing the client that the login attempt failed and prompting for another login.

The **select** structure is included to build the drop-down list of **loginID**s. Lines 57–58 write the first **option** that displays, "Select your name." If no other **option** is marked as **selected**, this **option** is displayed when the page is loaded. The next **option**s are the **loginID**s retrieved from the database. If this is a returning user, we want to display the **loginID** as **selected**.

Line 61 requests the **loginID** cookie. If this is the user's first visit, or if the cookie has expired, **Cookie** returns an empty string. [*Note*: It is possible for a cookie to store an empty string. If this is the case, **Cookie** returns the cookie contents, which is an empty string.] Otherwise, the user's **loginID** is returned. Lines 61–65 call **BuildReturning** if **loginID** contains a login ID and call **BuildNewUser**. Both **BuildReturning** and **BuildNewUser** build the login ID **options**. However, **BuildReturning** selects the returning user's login ID **option** while **BuildNewUser** does not.

BuildReturning's **While** loop (lines 107–130) iterates through **loginData**'s records. Recall that **loginData** contains the **loginID** column (field) of the **Users** table from line 101 and points either to the first record or to **EOF**. Line 107 tests for the end of the record set, indicating that there are no further records. Line 129 increments the record set pointer to the next record.

Each iteration of the **While** loop builds an **option** item for the current record. Line 109 simply writes the opening of the **option** item. Next, we test whether this **option** needs to be **selected** with the **If** statement in lines 120–125. Note that once we have written **selected** for an **option**, there is no need to perform this check in further iterations—**selected** is written for only one **option**. The code that writes **selected** for an option is thus wrapped in another **If** statement (lines 112–126). Variable **found** is set to **False** before the loop, in line 105. Once **selected** is written for an **option**, **found** is assigned **True**. Line 112 prevents the code that writes **selected** for an option from being executed unnecessarily after an **option** is already selected. Lines 120–121 determine whether the current record's **loginID** field is equal to the value of the **loginID** cookie. If so, lines 122–124 write **selected** and set **found** to **True**.

Line 127 sets the **value** for the **option** to the current **loginID**. Finally, line 128 writes the display of this **option** as the current **loginID**.

Active Server Page **submitlogin.asp** (Fig. 25.24) takes the values passed to it by **login.asp** and checks the values against the **Users** table in the database. If a match is found, the user is redirected to **instantpage.asp**. If no match is found, the user is redirected back to **login.asp**. The user never sees or knows about **submitlogin.asp** because the page is pure scripting code (i.e., its entire contents are enclosed in scripting delimiters).

```
<% @LANGUAGE = VBScript %>

<% ' Fig. 25.24 : submitlogin.asp
   ' ASP document to check user's username and password
   Option Explicit

   ' test if a user name and a password were
   ' entered. If not, transfer back to the login page.
   If Request( "password" ) = "" Or _
         Request( "loginID" ) = "noSelection" Then
      Session( "loginFailure" ) = True
      Call Server.Transfer( "login.asp" )
   End If

   Dim connection, loginData

   ' create the SQL query
   Session( "query" ) = _
      "SELECT * FROM Users WHERE loginID = '" & _
      Request( "loginID" ) & "'"

   Call Server.Execute( "database.asp" )
   Set loginData = Session( "loginData" )

   If Request( "password" ) = loginData( "password" ) Then

      ' password is OK, adjust loginFailure
      Session( "loginFailure" ) = False

```

Fig. 25.24 ASP document that validates user login (part 1 of 2).

```
         ' write a cookie to recognize them the next time they
         ' go to login.asp
         Response.Cookies( "loginID" ) = Request( "loginID" )

         ' give it three days to expire
         Response.Cookies( "loginID" ).Expires = Date() + 3

         ' send them to instantpage.asp
         Call Server.Transfer( "instantpage.asp" )
      Else
        Session( "loginFailure" ) = True
        Call Server.Transfer( "login.asp" )
      End If
   %>
```

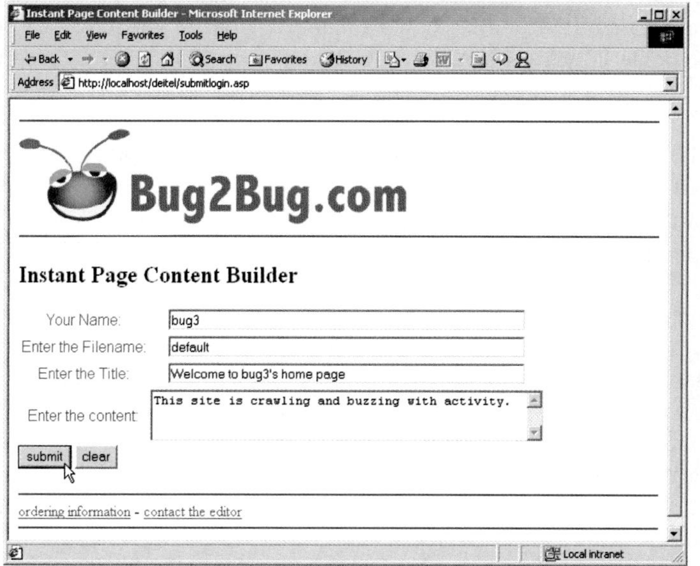

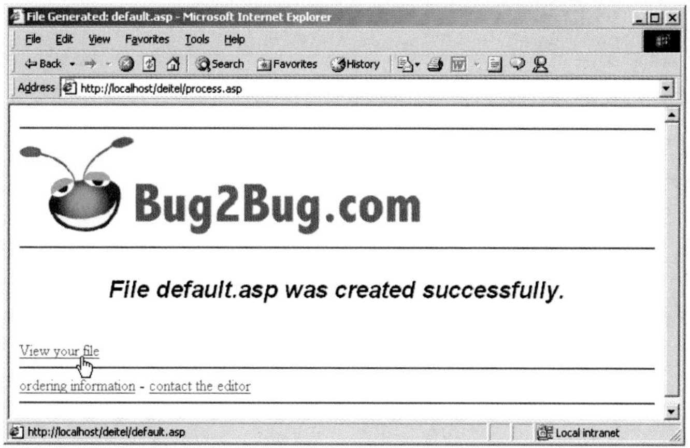

Fig. 25.24 ASP document that validates user login (part 2 of 2).

Lines 9–13 check whether the form's **password** field is empty or if the **loginID** field was submitted with the default value. If so, session variable **loginFailure** is set to **True** and the client is redirected back to **login.asp**.

Lines 18–20 select all the fields from the table. The **WHERE** clause in this SQL statement specifies a condition on which records are selected: Only the record(s) whose **loginID** field has the same value as the form's **loginID** field are selected. Also note that this SQL statement always finds a record because the form's **loginID** values are retrieved from the **Users**' **loginID** field. For example, if **loginID** **bug1** is selected, then session variable **query** contains

```
SELECT * FROM Users WHERE loginID = 'bug1'
```

Line 22 calls **Server** method **Execute** to execute **database.asp** to query the database for the login ID that the user has submitted. Line 23 sets reference **loginData** to session variable **loginData** set in **database.asp** containing the records that have matched our query.

Line 25 checks the password against the password from the record set. Note that the submitted **loginID** is a valid login ID that was selected from the drop-down list. Thus, we only need to check the password to validate a login. If correct, line 32 writes the form's **loginID** value as a cookie named **loginID**.

Line 28 sets the value of session variable **loginFailure** to **False** because the password has been validated. Line 35 sets the expiration date of this cookie to the current date plus three days. If we do not set an expiration date for the cookie when we create it, it is treated as a *session cookie* (i.e., it is destroyed when the browser is closed). [*Note*: If an existing cookie's content is updated, then the expiration date needs to be set again. Otherwise, the cookie is destroyed at the end of the session regardless of the expiration date it had before the update.] The cookie remains on the client's machine until the cookie expires, at which time the browser deletes it.

Next, line 38 calls **Server** method **Transfer** to redirect the client to **instantpage.asp**. Otherwise, the session variable **loginFailure** is set to **True**, and the client is redirected back to **login.asp** (lines 40–41).

25.9 Server-Side ActiveX Components

Server-side script functionality is extended with server-side ActiveX components—ActiveX controls that typically reside on the Web server and do not have a graphical user interface. These components make features accessible to the ASP author. Figure 25.27 summarizes some of the ActiveX components included with Internet Information Services (IIS).

Visit

msdn.microsoft.com/library/default.asp?url=/library/en-us/iisref/html/psdk/asp/comp275c.asp

for more information about Web server technologies.

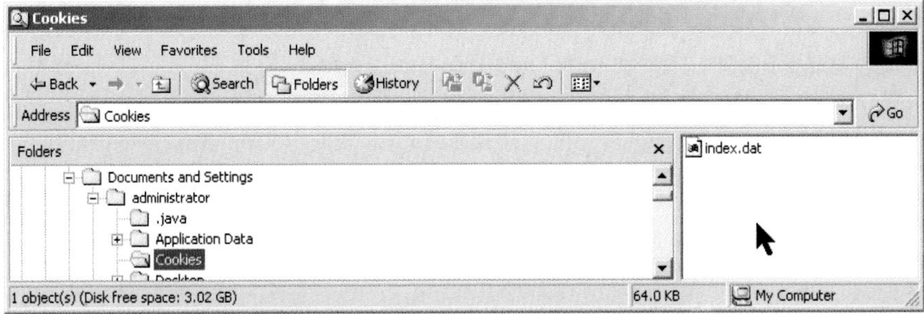

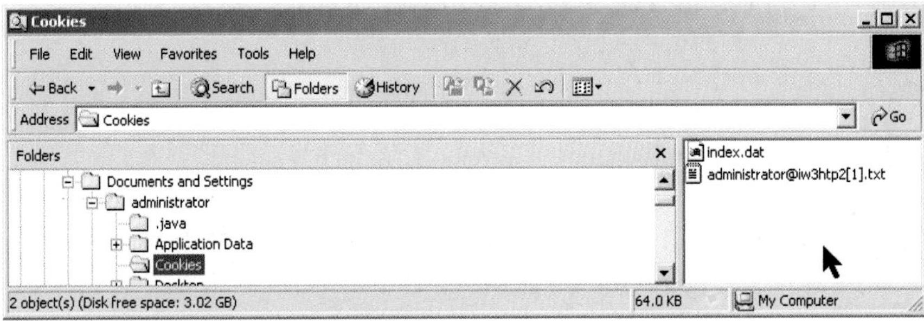

Fig. 25.25 `Cookies` folder before and after cookie creation.

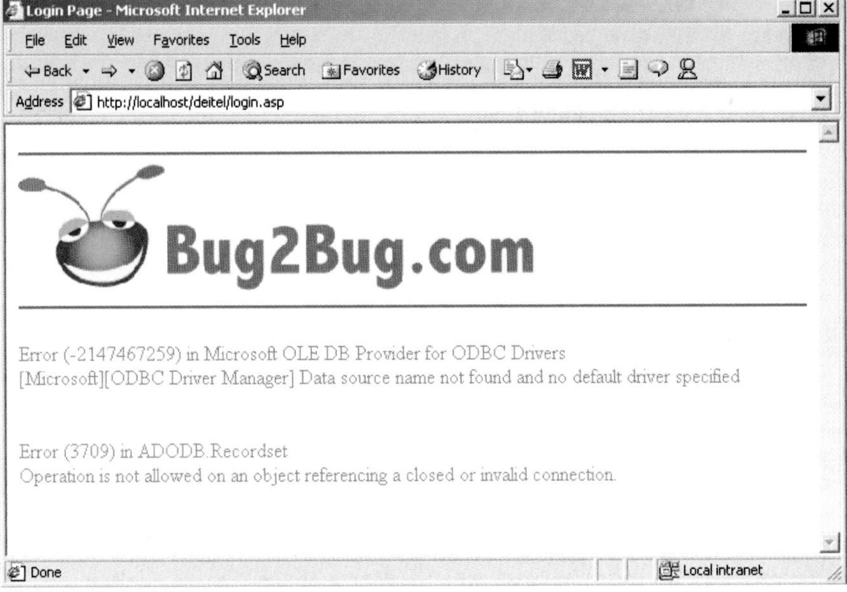

Fig. 25.26 Error messages sent to `login.asp` by `database.asp`.

Component Name	Description
`MSWC.BrowserType`	ActiveX component for gathering information about the client's browser (e.g., type, version, etc.).
`MSWC.AdRotator`	ActiveX component for rotating advertisements on a Web page.
`MSWC.NextLink`	ActiveX component for linking Web pages together.
`MSWC.ContentRotator`	ActiveX component for rotating HTML content on a Web page.
`MSWC.PageCounter`	ActiveX component for storing the number of times a Web page has been requested.
`MSWC.Counters`	ActiveX components that provide general-purpose persistent counters.
`MSWC.MyInfo`	ActiveX component that provides information about a Web site (e.g., owner name, owner address, etc.).
`Scripting.FileSystemObject`	ActiveX component that provides an object library for accessing files on the server or on the server's network.
ActiveX Data Objects (ADO) Data Access Components	ActiveX components that provide an object library for accessing databases.

Fig. 25.27 Some server-side ActiveX components.

Software Engineering Observation 25.9

If the scripting language you are using in an Active Server Page does not support a certain feature, an ActiveX server component can be created using Visual C++, Visual Basic, Delphi, etc., to provide that feature.

Many Web sites sell advertising space—especially Web sites with large numbers of hits. The code in Fig. 25.28 demonstrates the *AdRotator ActiveX component* for rotating advertisements on a Web page. Each time a client requests this Active Server Page, the AdRotator component randomly displays one of several advertisements—in this example, one of five flag images. When the user clicks a country's flag image, the country's corresponding Central Intelligence Agency (CIA) Fact book Web page is displayed. [*Note*: The example presented here is IIS specific. PWS users should use the version in the Chapter 25 examples directory (on the CD-ROM that accompanies this book). Separate files are included on the CD for users running Personal Web Server.]

Line 29 creates an instance of an AdRotator component and assigns it to reference **`rotator`**. Server-side ActiveX components are instantiated by passing the name of the component as a string to the **`Server`** object's method ***`CreateObject`***.

Lines 32–33 call the **`Response`** object's **`Write`** method to send the advertisement as HTML to the client. Method ***`GetAdvertisement`*** is called using reference **`rotator`** to get the advertisements from the file **`config.txt`** (Fig. 25.29).

Performance Tip 25.1

Server-side ActiveX components usually execute faster than their scripting language equivalents.

```
<% @LANGUAGE = VBScript %>

<%
   ' Fig. 25.28 : component.asp
   ' Demonstrating Server-side ActiveX Components
   Option Explicit
%>

<!DOCTYPE html PUBLIC "-//W3C//DTD XHTML 1.0 Transitional//EN"
 "http://www.w3.org/TR/xhtml1/DTD/xhtml1-transitional.dtd">

<html xmlns = "http://www.w3.org/1999/xhtml">

   <head>
      <title>ActiveX Component Example</title>
   </head>

   <body>

      <strong style = "font-family: arial, sans-serif">
         Server-side ActiveX Components
      </strong>

      <p>
<%
   Dim rotator, browser, information, counter

   ' create an AdRotator object
   Set rotator = Server.CreateObject( "MSWC.AdRotator" )

   ' use config.txt to send an advertisement to the client
   Call Response.Write( _
      rotator.GetAdvertisement( "config.txt" ) )

   ' create a BrowserType object
   Set browser = Server.CreateObject( "MSWC.BrowserType" )

   If browser.VBScript = True Then
%>
      <script language = "VBScript">
         Call Msgbox( "Client browser supports VBScript!" )
      </script>
<%
   End If

   If browser.JavaScript = True Then
%>
      <script language = "JavaScript">
         alert( "Client browser supports JavaScript!" );
      </script>
<%
   End If

```

Fig. 25.28 Demonstrating server-side ActiveX components (part 1 of 4).

```
      ' get client's browser information
      information = "<p>Your browser information is:<br />" & _
         Request.ServerVariables( "HTTP_USER_AGENT" ) & _
         "<br />Browser: " & browser.Browser & " Version: " & _
         browser.Version & " Minor version: " & _
         browser.MinorVer & "<br />Cookies are "

      If browser.Cookies Then
         information = information & "enabled</p><br />"
      Else
         information = information & "disabled</p><br />"
      End If

      Call Response.Write( information )

      ' create Page Counter Object
      Set counter = Server.CreateObject( "MSWC.PageCounter" )
      Call counter.PageHit()    ' page has been "hit"
%>
         </p>

         <p style = "color: blue; font-size: 12pt">
            This page has been visited <% =counter.Hits() %>
            times!</p>
      </body>
</html>
```

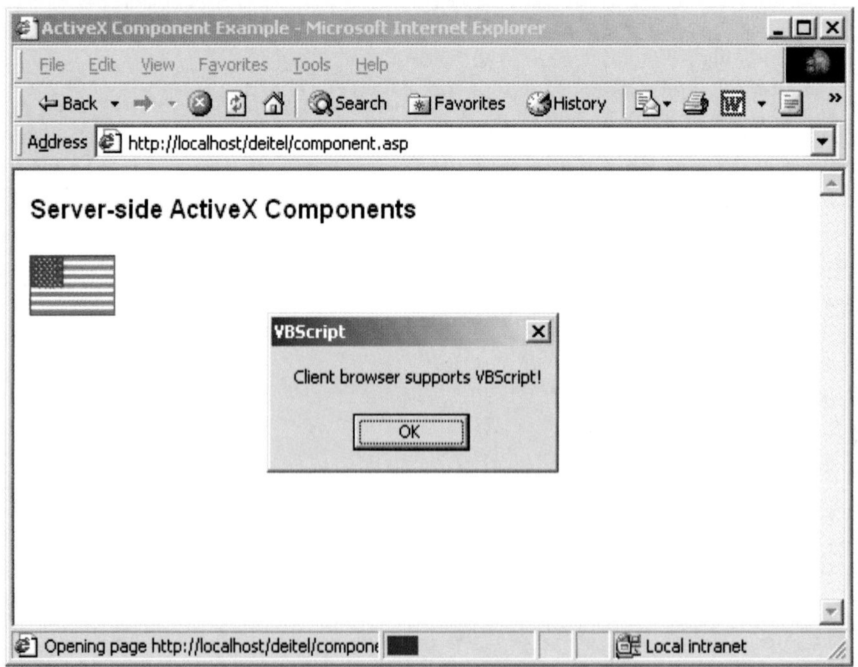

Fig. 25.28 Demonstrating server-side ActiveX components (part 2 of 4).

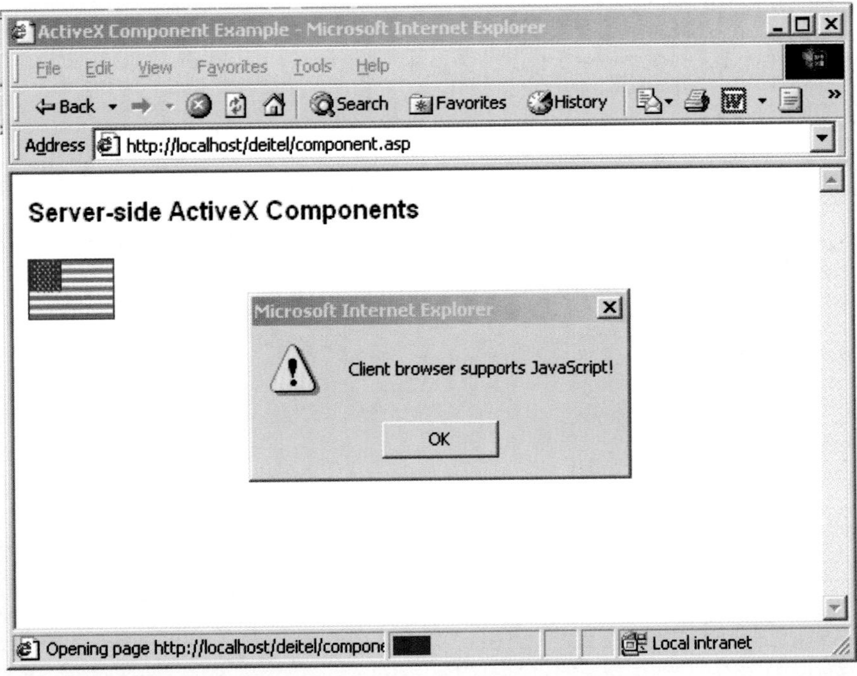

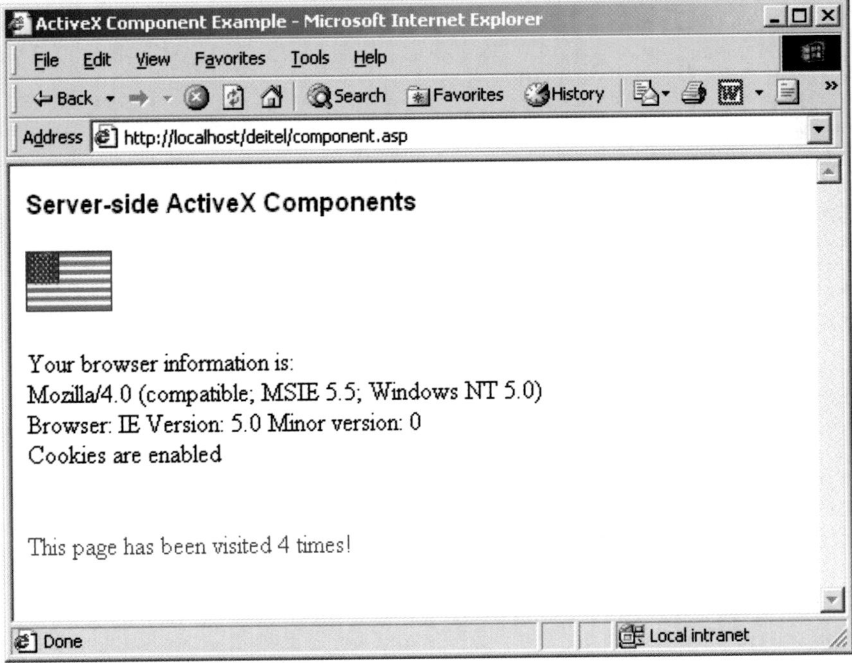

Fig. 25.28 Demonstrating server-side ActiveX components (part 3 of 4).

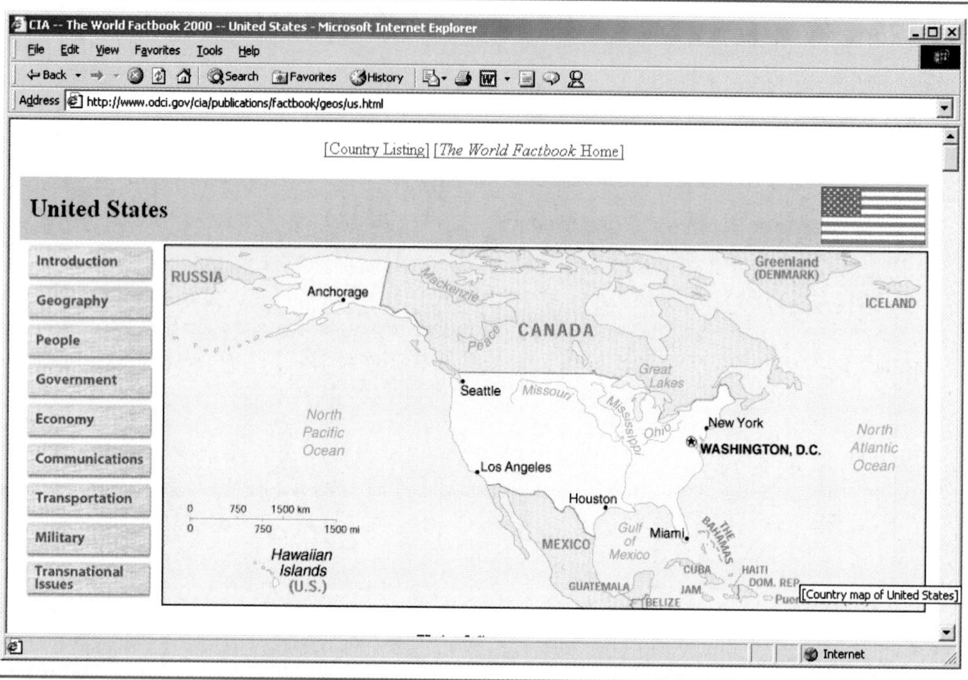

Fig. 25.28 Demonstrating server-side ActiveX components (part 4 of 4).

```
REDIRECT redirect.asp
width 54
height 36
border 1
*
/images/us.gif
http://www.odci.gov/cia/publications/factbook/geos/us.html
United States Information
20
/images/france.gif
http://www.odci.gov/cia/publications/factbook/geos/fr.html
France Information
20
/images/germany.gif
http://www.odci.gov/cia/publications/factbook/geos/gm.html
Germany Information
20
/images/italy.gif
http://www.odci.gov/cia/publications/factbook/geos/it.html
Italy Information
20
/images/spain.gif
http://www.odci.gov/cia/publications/factbook/geos/sp.html
Spain Information
20
```

Fig. 25.29 File **`config.txt`** that describes the advertisements.

Software Engineering Observation 25.10

The AdRotator ActiveX component allows the page author to minimize the amount of space on a Web page committed to advertisements, while at the same time maximizing the number of advertisements to display.

Portability Tip 25.2

Because the AdRotator ActiveX component is executed on the server, clients do not directly interact with the component and, therefore, do not have to support ActiveX technologies.

The file's header (lines 1–4) includes the URL of the **REDIRECT** file, **redirect.asp** (Fig. 25.30), the image **height**, image **width** and image **border** width. The asterisk (line 5) separates the header from the advertisements. Lines 6–9 describe the first advertisement by providing the image's URL (the image's location), the destination URL for redirection upon clicking the ad, a value for the **alt** tag (browsers that cannot display graphics display the specified text) and a number (between 0 and 1000) representing the ratio of time this particular image appears. The ratios must be numbers between 0 and 10,000. For example, if four ads have the ratios 6, 9, 12 and 3, then the time ratios are calculated as 20% (6/30), 30% (9/30), 40% (12/30) and 10% (3/30), respectively. Lines 10–25 list the other four advertisements. [*Note*: If you are executing this example, copy **config.txt** to the **Deitel** virtual directory you created in Section 25.3.]

File **redirect.asp** (Fig. 25.30) redirects the user to the country page when the ad is clicked. Each time the ad is clicked, the document **redirect.asp** is requested and a *query string* is sent with the request. The query string contains an attribute **url** that is equal to the destination URL found in **config.txt** for this ad. Because we are redirecting the user to a different page on the client rather than the server, we call **Response** method **Redirect** to redirect the user to the country page. For example, click the U.S. flag. The resulting behavior is equivalent to typing

```
http://localhost/Deitel/redirect.asp?url=http://www.odci.gov/
cia/publications/factbook/us.html
```

in the browser's **Address** field.

We arbitrarily chose the names **config.txt** and **redirect.asp**. You may choose any name you prefer. The redirect file loads (into the browser) the page referenced by the ad's URL. These files can be placed anywhere in the publishing directory (i.e., they do not have to be under the same directory as **rotate.asp**). For example, if you put **config.txt** under directory **X** in the publishing directory, then Fig 25.28 lines 32–33 would read

```
<% @LANGUAGE = VBScript %>

<%
   ' Fig. 25.30 : redirect.asp
   ' Redirection Page for AdRotator Component
   Option Explicit

   Call Response.Redirect( Request( "url" ) )
%>
```

Fig. 25.30 Code listing for **redirect.asp**.

```
   Call Response.Write( _
      flagChanger.GetAdvertisement( "/X/config.txt" ) )
```

Note that **GetAdvertisement** is passed a URL, not a physical disk path. Hence the use of the forward slash. Also note that **/X/config.txt** is short for **http://localhost/X/config.txt** (the server is **localhost** and the publishing directory is **C:\Inetpub\Wwwroot**). You can replace **localhost** with the IP address **127.0.0.1**, which also refers to the local machine.

Because Web servers respond to a variety of clients, an ASP document often needs to determine who the client is and what features it supports. Line 36 (Fig. 25.28) creates a ***BrowserType*** object to obtain information about the client's browser. Line 38 checks property ***VBScript***'s value to determine if it is **True**. If so, the block (lines 48–50) are written to the client. Lines 46–52 test the ***JavaScript*** property.

Line 56 passes the server variable key **HTTP_USER_AGENT** to **ServerVariables** to obtain a string containing the client's information. The **BrowserType** object's ***Browser***, ***Version*** and ***MinorVer*** properties (lines 57–59) may also be used to obtain similar client information. Line 61 tests the ***Cookies*** property's value to determine if the browser supports cookies.

Many popular Web sites display a "hit" counter that shows how many visitors the site has had. IIS provides the ***PageCounter*** ActiveX component for storing the number of "hits." Method ***PageHit*** (line 71) increments the number of "hits" by one, and method ***Hits*** (line 76) returns the number of "hits."

25.10 Internet and World Wide Web Resources

msdn.microsoft.com/workshop/c-frame.htm?/workshop/server/asp/ASP-over.asp
This Web site is arguably the best ASP resource on the Web. This page, part of the *Microsoft Developers Network*, provides an introduction to ASP technologies.

msdn.microsoft.com/workshop/server/asp/asptutorial.asp
This site is the starting page of an ASP tutorial provided by the *Microsoft Developers Network*. It is one of the most comprehensive ASP tutorials on the Web.

support.microsoft.com/support/default.asp?SD=SO&PR=asp
This site, located on the *Microsoft Personal Online Support Network*, should be your first stop when you are having trouble or are curious about an aspect of ASP. In addition to providing links to other useful help sites, the site also includes a collection of links to ASP technical resources.

www.tcp-ip.com
The *ASP Toolbox* home page is an excellent source for ASP information and resources. The site contains numerous links to free components and other resources helpful in Web development using Active Server Pages. The site tutorials include an overview of Active Server technology as well as helpful hints and demos with source code. Other features of this page include ASP discussion forums and resources.

www.4guysfromrolla.com/webtech/index_asp.shtml
Contains FAQs, ASP-related articles, coding tips, message boards, etc.

www.aspin.com/index
Contains ASP resources including applications, books, forums, references, examples and tutorials, links, etc.

www.kamath.com/default.asp
Contains downloads, FAQs, tutorials, book excerpts, columns, etc.

www.aspwatch.com
Contains ASP-related articles and code examples.

www.developer.com
Great source of information for developers. The ASP section contains working code, troubleshooting techniques and advice.

www.paessler.com/tools/ASPBeautify
Home of a tool that formats ASP pages for readability.

www.asptoday.com
ASPToday contains articles on ASP along with discussion pages and code.

html.about.com/compute/html/msubasp.htm
This page has a list of links to many ASP-related resources on the Web. The site's links range from FAQs pages to tutorials to descriptions of advanced aspects of ASP. The page is a good place to start if you are interested in finding out more about specific ASP-related technologies.

www.w3schools.com/asp
This site is the home of a number of comprehensive ASP tutorials. Topic categories range from ASP objects to general syntax usage. The page is a great place to go to if you are unclear on any individual aspect of ASP programming. Examples are provided at the site.

www.w3scripts.com/asp
This site is the home page of an ASP script repository written to teach different aspects of ASP programming. All script example screens are split into two parts: the script being demonstrated and the script's output. It is a useful site for all levels of ASP programmers.

msdn.microsoft.com/library/default.asp?url=/library/en-us/iisref/html/psdk/asp/comp275c.asp
MSDN site that provides descriptions and links for many server-side ActiveX components.

SUMMARY

- Active Server Pages are processed by an ActiveX component (i.e., a server-side ActiveX control) called a scripting engine.
- An ASP file has the file extension **.asp** and contains XHTML tags and scripting code.
- Although other languages, like JavaScript, can be used for ASP scripting, VBScript is the most widely used.
- ASP is a Microsoft-specific technology for sending dynamic Web content to the client—which includes XHTML, Dynamic HTML, ActiveX controls, client-side scripts and Java applets (i.e., client-side Java programs that are embedded in a Web page).
- An Active Server Page processes the request (which often includes interacting with a database) and returns the results to the client—normally in the form of an XHTML document, but other data formats (e.g., images, binary data, etc.) can be returned, as well.
- When a client requests an ASP document, it is loaded into memory and parsed (top to bottom) by a scripting engine named **asp.dll**. Script code is interpreted as it is encountered.
- Active Server Pages provide several built-in objects to offer programmers straightforward methods for communicating with a Web browser, gathering data sent by an HTTP request and distinguishing between users.

- The **Request** object is commonly used to access the information passed by a get or post request. The **Request** object also provides access to "cookies," which are stored on a client's machine.
- The **Response** object sends information such as XHTML, text, etc. to the client.
- The **Server** object provides access to methods and properties on the server.
- Scripting delimiters **<%** and **%>** wrapped around the VBScript code indicate that the scripting code is executed on the server, not the client.
- The optional **@LANGUAGE** processing directive indicates the scripting engine needed to interpret the scripting code.
- The **Request** object retrieves the form data **post**ed to an ASP document.
- File System Objects (FSOs) provide the programmer with the ability to manipulate files, directories and drives. FSOs also allow the programmer to read and write text and are an essential element for Active Server Pages that persist data.
- FSOs are objects in the Microsoft Scripting Runtime Library. FSO types include: **FileSystemObject**, **File**, **Folder**, **Drive** and **TextStream**.
- The programmer can use **FileSystemObject**s to create directories, move files, determine whether a **Drive** exists, etc.
- The **File** object allows the programmer to gather information about files, manipulate files and open files.
- The **Folder** object allows the programmer to manipulate and gather information about directories.
- The **Drive** object allows the programmer to gather information about drives.
- HTTP does not support persistent information that could help a Web server distinguish between clients.
- The server performs session tracking by keeping track of when a specific person visits a site. The first time a client connects to the server, the server assigns the user a unique *session ID*. When the client makes additional requests, the client's session ID is compared with the session IDs stored in the server's memory.
- Active Server Pages use the **Session** object to manage sessions.
- Multiple Active Server Pages connected are sometimes called an ASP application.
- Server-side includes are commands embedded in XHTML documents that add dynamic content. They are written as XHTML comments. SSI statements always execute before any scripting code executes.
- A session variable that has not explicitly been given a value contains an empty string.
- A session variable's value is set and retrieved using the **Session** object.
- Server-side includes can contain any type of information. Text files and XHTML files are two of the most common server-side include files.
- By convention, server-side include (SSI) files end with the **.shtml** extension.
- Server-side includes are an excellent technique for reusing XHTML, Dynamic HTML, scripts and other programming elements.
- A popular way to customize Web pages is via cookies.
- Cookies store information on the client's computer for retrieval later in the same browsing session or in future browsing sessions.
- Cookies are small files sent by an Active Server Page as part of a response to a client.

- Every HTTP-based interaction between a client and a server includes a header that contains information about either the request (when the communication is from the client to the server) or the response (when the communication is from the server to the client).
- When an Active Server Page receives a request, the header includes the request type (e.g., get or post) and cookies stored on the client machine by the server. When the server formulates its response, the header information includes any cookies the server wants to store on the client computer.
- Depending on the maximum age of a cookie, the Web browser either maintains the cookie for the duration of the browsing session (i.e., until the user closes the Web browser) or stores the cookie on the client computer for future use.
- Active Server Pages can communicate with databases through ADO (ActiveX Data Objects).
- Web applications are typically three-tier distributed applications, consisting of a user interface, business logic and database access.
- Web servers provide the business logic that manipulates data from databases and that communicates with client Web browsers.
- Databases enhance applications by providing a data source that can be used to generate Web pages dynamically.
- **On Error Resume Next** specifies that any error caused by a statement from this point onward is ignored and control is transferred to the statement immediately following the statement that caused the error.
- When an error occurs in the script, **Err** object's **Number** property contains an integer representing which VBScript error has occurred.
- If an expiration date is not set for a cookie when it is created, it is treated as a session cookie (i.e., it is destroyed when the browser is closed).
- The cookie remains on the client's machine until it expires, at which time the browser deletes it.
- Server-side ActiveX components are instantiated by passing the name of the component as a string to the **Server** object's method **CreateObject**.

TERMINOLOGY

%> closing scripting delimiter
<% opening scripting delimiter
Abandon method of **Session**
ActiveX Data Objects (ADO)
ADODB.Command object
ADODB.Connection object
ADODB.RecordSet object
AdRotator ActiveX Control
APP_PHYSICAL_PATH
.asp file
asp.dll
BrowserType ActiveX Component
business logic
cache Web pages
Chr method
client-side scripting
Close method
columns
cookie
cookie expiration
Cookies property
CreateObject method
CreateTextFile method
Drive
EOF constant
Execute method
expiration of a cookie
File
file system object
FileExists method
FileSystemObject
Folder
get HTTP request
GetAdvertisement method
HTTP_USER_AGENT
#include

JavaScript property
@LANGUAGE directive
maximum age of a cookie
MoveFirst method
MoveNext method
On Error Resume Next statement
Open method
OpenTextFile method
Option Explicit statement
physical path
post HTTP request
ReadAll method
record
record set
Redirect method of **Response**
Request object
Response object
script engine
script host
Server object
server variable key
server-side ActiveX component
server-side include (SSI)
server-side scripting
session
session ID
Session object
session tracking
short name format
.shtml file
TextStream
three-tier distributed application
Timeout property of **Session**
Transfer method
vbCrLf constant
VBScript
VBScript property
Version property
virtual path
Write method
WriteLine method

SELF-REVIEW EXERCISES

25.1 State whether each of the following is *true* or *false*. If *false*, explain why.

a) VBScript is the only language that can be used in an Active Server Page.
b) Active Server Page file names typically end in **.asp**.
c) Only Microsoft Internet Explorer can render an Active Server Page.
d) The **<% Option Explicit %>** statement is optional.
e) Variables can be passed from one Active Server Page to another without using a form.
f) VBScript statements cannot be present in a server-side include file.
g) Server-side ActiveX components typically do not have graphical user interfaces.
h) AdRotator is a client-side ActiveX control.
i) Server-side include files end in **.ssi** by convention.
j) Before an ASP can use ADO to access a database, the database must have a System DSN.

25.2 Fill in the blanks for each of the following statements:

a) Processing directive __________ informs **asp.dll** of the scripting language is used.
b) Passing an integer value of __________ to function **Chr** returns the double quote (**"**) character.
c) Session variables retain their value during the duration of the __________.
d) Cookies are files placed on the __________ machine.
e) Constant __________ represents a carriage-return line-feed combination.
f) ASP is an acronym for __________.
g) ActiveX component __________ provides information about the client making the request.
h) **Server** method __________ is called to create an object.
i) The __________ object is used to access information passed by a get or post request.
j) **Server** method __________ is called to transfer the client to a different page.

ANSWERS TO SELF-REVIEW EXERCISES

25.1 a) False. Any scripting language recognized by the server can be used. b) True. c.) False. Most browsers can render XHTML returned by an Active Server Page. d) True. e) True. Variables can be embedded in a URL (e.g., `localhost/page.asp?var=true`). f) False. A server-side include can contain scripting code, XHTML, text, etc. g) True. h) False. AdRotator is a server-side ActiveX component. i) False. Server-side include files end in `.shtml` by convention. j) True.

25.2 a) `@LANGUAGE`. b) `34`. c) session. d) client. e) `vbCrLf`. f) Active Server Page. g) `BrowserType`. h) `CreateObject`. i) `Request`. j) `Transfer`.

EXERCISES

25.3 Create a server-side include file containing the AdRotator code listed in Fig. 25.28. Write an ASP that performs the same action as the AdRotator and uses this server-side include file.

25.4 Modify Fig. 25.2's `clock.asp` to display different time zones.

25.5 Modify Fig. 25.12's `guestbook.asp` to read and write to a database rather than a text file. This exercise requires the use of a database development tool such as Microsoft Access.

25.6 Using the same techniques as Fig. 25.12 (`guestbook.asp`), develop an ASP application for a discussion group. Allow new links to be created for new topics.

25.7 Modify Fig. 25.23's `login.asp` to read and write to a text file rather than a database.

25.8 Create an ASP application that allows the user to customize a Web page. Store the user's name and preferences in a text file. The application should consist of three ASP files: one that asks the user to login and reads from the text file to determine if the user is known. If the user is not known, a second ASP file is loaded asking the user to choose their preference for foreground color, background color and image. Write the new user's name and preferences to the text file. Next, display the page customized to this user using the user's preferences that are stored in the text file. If the user is known at login, the normal page should be displayed.

25.9 Create an Active Server Page that creates an XML document from the following database:

Product ID	Product
152341	Acme Ant
015832	Big Beetle
951324	Candy Caterpillar
765421	Distorted Dragonfly
235231	Easy Earthworm
882312	Foggy Fly
441221	Green Grasshopper
722345	Happy Horsefly
523119	Icky Inchworm
612214	Jumpy Junebug

25.10 Modify Exercise 25.9 to include an XSL document to format and sort (by product ID) the XML document.

26

Case Study: Active Server Pages and XML

Objectives

- To create a Web-based message forum using Active Server Pages.
- To use XML with Active Server Pages.
- To be able to add new forums.
- To be able to post messages to the message forum.
- To use Microsoft's DOM to manipulate an XML document.
- To use XSLT to transform XML documents.

If any man will draw up his case, and put his name at the foot of the first page, I will give him an immediate reply. Where he compels me to turn over the sheet, he must wait my leisure.
Lord Sandwich

They also serve who only stand and wait.
John Milton

A fair request should be followed by a deed in silence.
Dante Alighieri

Outline

26.1 Introduction

In this chapter, we use XML and ASP to create one of the most popular types of Web sites—a *message forum*. Message forums are "virtual" bulletin boards where various topics are discussed. Common features of message forums include discussion groups, questions and answers and general comments. Many Web sites host message forums. For example,

```
messages.yahoo.com/index.html
web.eesite.com/forums
www.deja.com
```

are popular sites that host message forums.

In the case study presented in this chapter, users can post messages and create new forums. We leave the removal of a forum as an exercise for the reader.

26.2 Setup and Message Forum Documents

In this section, we provide the setup instructions for executing the case study. The case study requires the following software:

1. Microsoft Internet Information Services (IIS) or Microsoft Personal Web Server (PWS).
2. Internet Explorer 5.5 (for XML and XSLT processing).
3. msxml 3.0 or higher. Visit **`www.deitel.com`** for download and installation instructions.

Copy the files from the Chapter 26 examples directory (on the CD-ROM that accompanies this book) to the Web directory (e.g., **`c:\inetpub\wwwroot`**). [*Note*: Either IIS or PWS must be installed; otherwise, this Web directory will not exist. This directory must also have **`Write`** permissions to allow users to post messages and add forums. The version presented in this chapter is IIS specific. PWS users should use the version in the examples directory in the **`PWS`** folder.] Each of these files and documents is summarized in Fig. 26.1 and will be discussed later in the chapter.

File Name	Description
forums.xml	XML document listing all available forums and their filenames.
default.asp	Main page, providing navigational links to the forums.
template.xml	Template for a message forum XML document.
addForum.asp	Adds a forum.
forumASP.xml	Sample message forum.
formatting.xsl	Document for transforming message forums into XHTML.
addPost.asp	Adds a message to a forum.
invalid.html	Used to display an error message.
site.css	Style sheet for formatting XHTML documents.
style.css	Style sheet for formatting the message forum site.

Fig. 26.1 Message forum documents.

The main page, **default.asp**, displays the list of available message forums, which are stored in the XML document **forums.xml**. Hyperlinks are provided to each XML message forum document and also to **addForum.asp**, which adds a forum to **forums.xml** and creates a new XML message forum (e.g., **forum2.xml**), using the message forum template **template.xml**.

Each XML message forum document (e.g., **forumASP.xml**) is transformed into an XHTML document using the XSLT document **formatting.xsl**. The CSS document **site.css** formats the XHTML for display. New messages are posted to a forum by **addPost.asp**. If errors occur when the document is processed, **invalid.html** is displayed. Some of these key interactions between documents are illustrated in Fig. 26.2.

26.3 Forum Navigation

This section introduces the documents that organize and display the message forums. Figure 26.3 lists the XML document (**forums.xml**) that marks up each message forum.

Root element **forums** can hold any number of message forums. We provide an initial forum named **forumASP.xml**. An individual message forum is marked up, using element **forum**. Attribute **filename** stores the name of the XML document that contains the forum's markup. We will discuss how this XML document is manipulated momentarily.

Figure 26.4 shows the Active Server Page (**default.asp**) that displays the list of message forums contained in **forums.xml**. CSS document **site.css** is applied to the XHTML sent to the Web browser.

Line 27 gets the absolute path for the file **forums.xml** and stores it in variable **strPath**. Microsoft's XML parser (i.e., msxml) requires an absolute path. Line 29 calls the **Server** object's **CreateObject** method to instantiate a ***DOMDocument*** object (**Microsoft.XMLDOM**) and assigns the object to **xmlFile**. The **DOMDocument** object is the document root of an XML document.

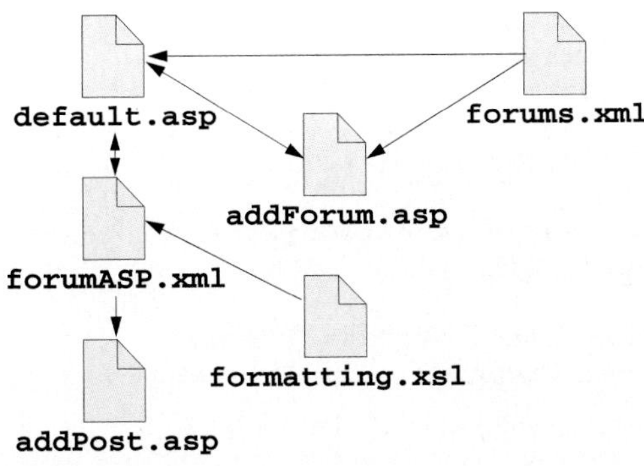

Fig. 26.2 Key interactions between message forum documents.

```
<?xml version = "1.0"?>

<!-- Fig. 26.3 : forums.xml -->
<!-- Creating the ASP forum -->

<forums>

   <forum filename = "forumASP.xml">ASP</forum>

</forums>
```

Fig. 26.3 XML document that marks up the message forums.

```
<% @LANGUAGE = "VBScript" %>

<% ' Fig. 26.4 : default.asp
   ' Forum home page
   Option Explicit
%>

<!DOCTYPE html PUBLIC "-//W3C//DTD XHTML 1.0 Strict//EN"
 "http://www.w3.org/TR/xhtml1/DTD/xhtml1-strict.dtd">

<html xmlns = "http://www.w3.org/1999/xhtml">

   <head>
      <title>Deitel Message Forums</title>
      <link rel = "stylesheet" type = "text/css"
            href = "style.css" />
   </head>

   <body>
      <h1>Deitel Message Forums</h1>
      <p><strong>Available Forums</strong></p>
      <ul>
```

Fig. 26.4 Message forums main page (part 1 of 2).

```
<%
   Dim xmlFile, xmlNodes, xmlItem
   Dim strPath, strTitle, strFileName

   strPath = Server.MapPath( "forums.xml" )

   Set xmlFile = Server.CreateObject( "Microsoft.XMLDOM" )
   xmlFile.Async = False

   If Not xmlFile.Load( strPath ) Then
      Call Server.Transfer( "invalid.html" )
   End If

   Set xmlNodes = xmlFile.DocumentElement.ChildNodes

   For Each xmlItem In xmlNodes
      strFileName = xmlItem.getAttribute( "filename" )
      strTitle = xmlItem.text
%>
      <li>
         <a href = "<% =strFileName %>"><% =strTitle %></a>
      </li>
<%
   Next
%>
      </ul>

      <p><strong>Forum Management</strong></p>

      <ul>
         <li><a href = "addForum.asp">Add a Forum</a></li>
         <li>Delete a Forum</li>
      </ul>

   </body>

</html>
```

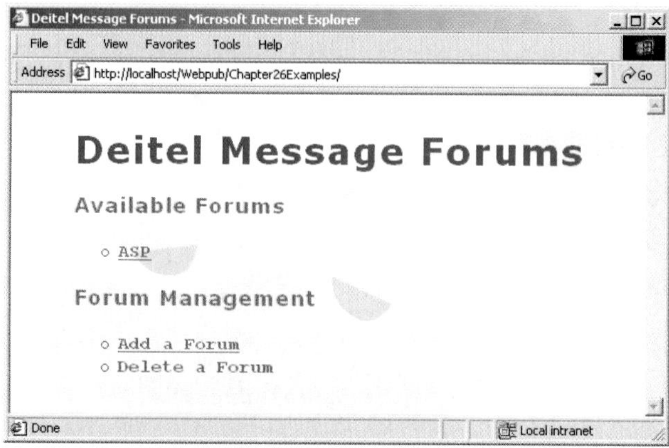

Fig. 26.4 Message forums main page (part 2 of 2).

Line 30 sets the object referenced by **xmlFile** to behave *synchronously* (i.e., when a method is called, it must finish executing before any other method is allowed to execute). We will explain the significance of setting **Async** to **False** momentarily.

Lines 32–34 call method ***Load*** to parse the XML document (e.g., **forums.xml**). If parsing succeeds, **True** is returned; otherwise, **False** is returned. Because **xmlFile** is synchronous, execution does not continue until method **Load** completes. If method calls are not synchronous (i.e., they are *asynchronous*), execution continues despite the fact that the method may not have finished executing, which could result in *logic errors* (i.e., the code does not execute as intended). If parsing fails, we redirect the browser to **invalid.html**, which is discussed in Section 26.7.

Line 36 uses property **DocumentElement** to get the root element's child nodes. Element nodes have property **ChildNodes**, which returns a *collection* (e.g., a list) of the element node's child nodes.

Lines 38–46 contain a **For Each** loop that iterates through all the nodes in the collection of child nodes stored in **xmlNodes**. Line 39 calls method **getAttribute** to get a forum's filename. This method returns the value of the node's **filename** attribute and assigns it to **strFileName**. Line 40 uses property **text** to return the node's text content, which is the forum's name.

Line 43 writes, as an anchor, the value of **strFileName** and writes the value of **strTitle** to describe the anchor. This creates the hyperlinks for the available forums. Each hyperlink references an XML document. For example, the **ASP** forum references **forumASP.xml**.

Line 53 provides a hyperlink to **addForum.asp**, which adds a new forum and is discussed in the next section. Line 54 is a placeholder for a link to delete forums, which is left to the reader as an exercise.

26.4 Adding Forums

In this section, we discuss the documents used to add new forums. Each new forum created is based upon a template XML document named **template.xml** (Fig. 26.5).

This template document contains the bare components for a message forum. It contains a **stylesheet** processing instruction that references **formatting.xsl** (discussed in Fig. 26.8) and **<forum>** tags. The Active Server Page (**addForum.asp**) that modifies the template document is presented in Fig. 26.6. [*Note*: Actually, the copy of the template document loaded into memory is modified and saved to disk with a different name.]

```
<?xml version = "1.0"?>

<!-- Fig. 26.5 : template.xml -->
<!-- Template XML document     -->

<?xml:stylesheet type = "text/xsl" href = "formatting.xsl"?>

<forum>
</forum>
```

Fig. 26.5 Template for message forum XML documents.

```
<% @LANGUAGE = "VBScript" %>
<% Option Explicit %>

<% ' Fig. 26.6 : addForum.asp %>

<%
   Dim xmlFile, xmlRoot, xmlNode
   Dim strTitle, strError, strPath

   If Request( "submit" ) <> Empty Then

      If Request( "name" ) <> Empty And _
         Request( "filename" ) <> Empty And _
         Request( "user" ) <> Empty And _
         Request( "title" ) <> Empty And _
         Request( "text" ) <> Empty Then

         ' Create a new XML file
         strPath = Server.MapPath( Request( "filename" ) )

         Set xmlFile = Server.CreateObject( "Microsoft.XMLDOM" )
         xmlFile.Async = False

         If xmlFile.Load( strPath ) Then
            Call Server.Transfer( "invalid.html" )
         End If

         ' set up the file
         Call xmlFile.Load( Server.MapPath( "template.xml" ) )

         ' get the root element
         Set xmlRoot = xmlFile.DocumentElement

         ' set the filename
         Call xmlRoot.SetAttribute( "filename", _
            Request( "filename" ) )

         ' create Name node
         Set xmlNode = xmlFile.CreateElement( "name" )
         xmlNode.Text = Request( "name" )
         Call xmlRoot.AppendChild( xmlNode )

         ' create first message
         Set xmlNode = xmlFile.CreateElement( "message" )
         Call xmlNode.SetAttribute( "timestamp", Now & " EST" )
         Call xmlRoot.AppendChild( xmlNode )

         Set xmlRoot = xmlNode

         ' create user node
         Set xmlNode = xmlFile.CreateElement( "user" )
         xmlNode.Text = Request( "user" )
         Call xmlRoot.AppendChild( xmlNode )
```

Fig. 26.6 Page to add to a forum (part 1 of 4).

```

            ' create title node
            Set xmlNode = xmlFile.CreateElement( "title" )
            xmlNode.Text = Request( "title" )
            Call xmlRoot.AppendChild( xmlNode )

            ' create text node
            Set xmlNode = xmlFile.CreateElement( "text" )
            xmlNode.Text = Request( "text" )
            Call xmlRoot.AppendChild( xmlNode )

            Call xmlFile.Save( strPath ) ' save the file

            ' load XML file
            strPath = Server.MapPath( "forums.xml" )

            Set xmlFile = Server.CreateObject( "Microsoft.XMLDOM" )
            xmlFile.Async = False

            If Not xmlFile.Load( strPath ) Then
               Call Server.Transfer( "invalid.html" )
            End If

            ' get the root node
            Set xmlRoot = xmlFile.DocumentElement

            ' create nodes
            Set xmlNode = xmlFile.CreateElement( "forum" )
            Call xmlNode.SetAttribute( "filename", _
               Request( "filename" ) )
            xmlNode.Text = Request( "name" )
            Call xmlRoot.AppendChild( xmlNode )

            Call xmlFile.Save( strPath ) ' save the file

            ' finished processing
            Call Server.Transfer( "default.asp" )
         Else
            strError = "ERROR: Invalid input."
         End If

      End If
   %>

   <!DOCTYPE html
      PUBLIC "-//W3C//DTD XHTML 1.0 Strict//EN"
      "http://www.w3.org/TR/xhtml1/DTD/xhtml1-strict.dtd">

   <html xmlns = "http://www.w3.org/1999/xhtml">
   <head>
      <title>Add a Forum</title>
      <link rel = "stylesheet" type = "text/css" href = "style.css" />
   </head>
```

Fig. 26.6 Page to add to a forum (part 2 of 4).

```
<body>
   <p>Create a Forum</p>
   <p><% =strError %></p>

   <form method = "post" action = "addForum.asp">

      <h2>
         Forum Name:<br />
         <input type = "text" size = "40" name = "name"
            value = "<% =Request( "name" ) %>" />
      </h2>

      <h2>
         Forum File Name:<br />
         <input type = "text" size = "40" name = "filename"
            value = "<% =Request( "filename" ) %>" />
      </h2>

      <h2>
         User:<br />
         <input type = "text" size = "40" name = "user"
            value = "<% =Request( "user" ) %>" />
      </h2>

      <h2>
         Message Title:<br />
         <input type = "text" size = "40" name = "title"
            value = "<% =Request( "title" ) %>" />
      </h2>

      <h2>
         Message Text:<br />
         <textarea name = "text" cols = "40"
            rows = "4"><% =Request( "text" ) %></textarea>
      </h2>

      <h2>
         <input type = "submit" name = "submit" value = "Submit" />
         <input type = "reset" value = "Clear" />
      </h2>

   </form>

   <p>
      <a href = "default.asp">Return to Main Page</a>
   </p>

</body>

</html>
```

Fig. 26.6 Page to add to a forum (part 3 of 4).

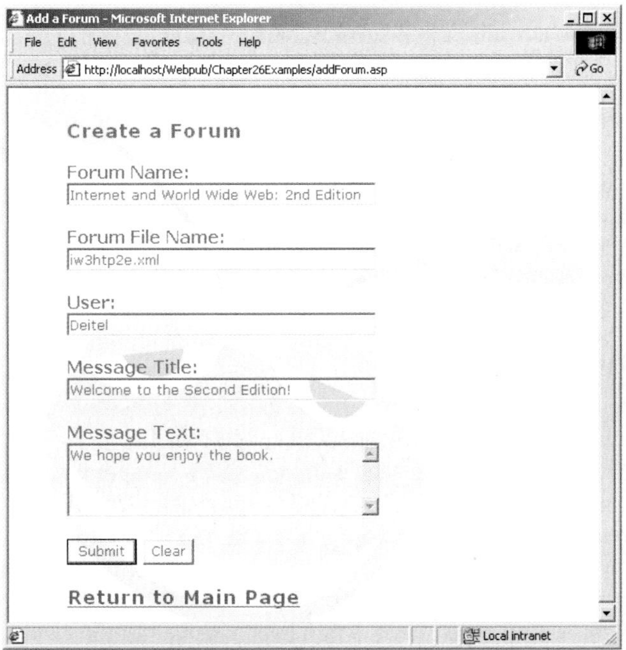

Fig. 26.6 Page to add to a forum (part 4 of 4).

This Active Server Page performs two tasks: First, it displays the form that gets the new forum's information (lines 98–149). Second, it provides the script for creating the forum (lines 1–96). We will discuss the form for getting information first.

Line 110 writes **strError**'s content to the Web browser. Error messages, if they exist, are stored in **strError**. Lines 112–149 create a form to post information back to **addForum.asp**. The form has fields for the forum name, forum file name, user name, message title and message text. The **Request** object is used to retrieve the submitted form's value.

We will now discuss the script logic for the page. Line 10 determines whether the form was submitted by testing the form's **submit** field for a value. If the **submit** field is **Empty**, then the form was not submitted.

Lines 12–16 check the form's fields for values. If any of the fields is **Empty**, the information for the new forum is incomplete, and line 92 sets **strError** to **"ERROR: Invalid input."**.

Lines 24–26 attempt to load the file specified by the user. [*Note*: The name specified in the **Forum File Name** must end in **.xml**.] If the file loads successfully, then the file already exists. Therefore, we transfer to **invalid.html**. Remember, we want to add a new forum, not open an existing one.

Line 29 loads the template XML document (i.e., **template.xml**). We will mark up the form's data and add the data to the in-memory representation of **template.xml**.

Lines 35–36 call method ***SetAttribute*** to create an attribute node named **filename** that has the value contained in form field **filename**. Line 39 creates a new element node named **name**, using **DOMDocument** method ***CreateElement***.

Line 40 assigns form field **name**'s value to the element node's (created in line 39) **Text** property. Line 41 calls method ***AppendChild*** to append the newly created element **name** node to the root element (i.e., **forum**).

Lines 44–46 create and append element **message**, along with attribute **timestamp**, to the root element **forum**. Lines 51–53 create and append element **user** to element **message**. Lines 56–58 create and append element **title**, and lines 61–63 create and append element **text** to the root element.

Line 65 saves the XML document to disk by calling method ***Save***. Variable **strPath** contains the filename provided by the user in line 19. Lines 68–87 open, modify (by adding the new forum just created) and save **forums.xml**.

26.5 Forum XML Documents

This section presents a sample forum (Fig. 26.7) that contains several messages and the XSLT document (Fig. 26.8) that transforms it into XHTML.

Lines 48–53 write an **<a>** tag to the result tree. XSLT element ***xsl:attribute*** creates an attribute named **href** for element **a** and assigns it the value of attribute **filename** concatenated to **addPost.asp?file=**.

```
<?xml version = "1.0"?>

<!-- Fig. 26.7 : forumASP.xml  -->
<!-- Postings on ASP forum     -->

<?xml:stylesheet type = "text/xsl" href = "formatting.xsl"?>

<forum filename = "forumASP.xml">

   <name>ASP Forum</name>

   <message timestamp = "4/28/2001 2:50:34 PM EST">
      <user>D. Bug</user>
      <title>I Love ASP!</title>
      <text>Everyone should use ASP.</text>
   </message>

   <message timestamp = "5/8/2001 11:09:54 AM EST">
      <user>Ms. Quito</user>
      <title>ASP and XML</title>
      <text>What a powerful combination. Try it!</text>
   </message>

   <message timestamp = "5/15/2001 4:39:50 PM EST">
      <user>Sarge Ant</user>
      <title>ASP</title>
      <text>This <em>army ant</em> uses ASP in boot camp.</text>
   </message>

</forum>
```

Fig. 26.7 Sample forum.

```
<?xml version = "1.0"?>

<!-- Fig. 26.8 : formatting.xsl                    -->
<!-- XSL document that transforms XML data to XHTML -->

<xsl:stylesheet version = "1.0"
   xmlns:xsl = "http://www.w3.org/1999/XSL/Transform">

   <xsl:output method = "html" omit-xml-declaration = "no"
      doctype-system =
         "http://www.w3.org/TR/xhtml1/DTD/xhtml1-strict.dtd"
      doctype-public = "-//W3C//DTD XHTML 1.0 Strict//EN" />

   <xsl:template match = "/">

      <html xmlns = "http://www.w3.org/1999/xhtml">
         <xsl:apply-templates select = "*" />
      </html>

   </xsl:template>

   <xsl:template match = "forum">

      <head>
         <title><xsl:value-of select = "name"/></title>
         <link rel = "stylesheet" type = "text/css"
            href = "style.css" />
      </head>

      <body>

         <table width = "100%" cellspacing = "0"
            cellpadding = "2">
            <tr>
               <td class = "forumTitle">
                  <xsl:value-of select = "name" />
               </td>
            </tr>
         </table>

         <table width = "100%" cellspacing = "0"
            cellpadding = "2">
            <xsl:apply-templates
               select = "message" />
         </table>

         <p>
            <a>
               <xsl:attribute
                  name = "href">addPost.asp?file=<xsl:value-of
                     select = "@filename" />
               </xsl:attribute>
               Post a Message</a><br />
```

Fig. 26.8 XSLT to transform XML forum document into HTML (part 1 of 2).

```
               <a href = "default.asp">Return to Main Page</a>
            </p>

         </body>

      </xsl:template>

      <xsl:template match = "message">

            <tr>
               <td class = "msgTitle">
                  <xsl:value-of select = "title" />
               </td>
            </tr>

            <tr>
               <td class = "msgInfo">
                  by
                  <em><xsl:value-of select = "user" /></em>
                  at
                  <span class = "date">
                     <xsl:value-of select = "@timestamp" />
                  </span>
               </td>
            </tr>

            <tr>
               <td class = "msgText">
                  <xsl:value-of select = "text" />
               </td>
            </tr>


      </xsl:template>

   </xsl:stylesheet>
```

Fig. 26.8 XSLT to transform XML forum document into HTML (part 2 of 2).

Figure 26.9 shows the XHTML document rendered by Internet Explorer 5.5 when **forumASP.xml** is transformed by **formatting.xsl**. [*Note*: We have edited the XHTML document for presentation purposes.] Line 66 provides a link to **addPost.asp**, along with the name of the file to which the new message will be added.

```
1  <!DOCTYPE html PUBLIC "-//W3C//DTD XHTML 1.0 Strict//EN"
2  "http://www.w3.org/TR/xhtml1/DTD/xhtml1-strict.dtd">
3
4  <!-- Fig. 26.9 : forumASP_transformed.html -->
5  <!-- Results of transforming forumASP.xml   -->
6
```

Fig. 26.9 Output of the transformation of the forum XML document (part 1 of 3).

```
<html xmlns = "http://www.w3.org/1999/xhtml">

   <head>
      <title>ASP Forum</title>
     <link href = "site.css" type = "text/css" rel = "stylesheet" />
   </head>

   <body>
      <table cellpadding = "2" cellspacing = "0" width = "100%">
         <tr>
            <td class = "forumTitle">ASP Forum</td>
         </tr>
      </table>

      <table cellpadding = "2" cellspacing = "0" width = "100%">
         <tr>
            <td class = "msgTitle">I Love ASP!</td>
         </tr>
         <tr>
            <td class = "msgInfo">
               by
               <em>D. Bug</em>
               at
           <span class = "date">4/28/2001 2:50:34 PM EST</span></td>
         </tr>
         <tr>
            <td class = "msgText">Everyone should use ASP.</td>
         </tr>
         <tr>
            <td class = "msgTitle">ASP and XML</td>
         </tr>
         <tr>
            <td class = "msgInfo">
               by
               <em>Ms. Quito</em>
               at
           <span class = "date">5/8/2001 11:09:54 AM EST</span></td>
         </tr>
         <tr>
            <td class = "msgText">
               What a powerful combination. Try it!</td>
         </tr>
         <tr>
            <td class = "msgTitle">ASP</td>
         </tr>
         <tr>
            <td class = "msgInfo">
               by
               <em>Sarge Ant</em>
               at
           <span class = "date">5/15/2001 4:39:50 PM EST</span></td>
         </tr>
         <tr>
```

Fig. 26.9 Output of the transformation of the forum XML document (part 2 of 3).

```
               <td class = "msgText">
                  This army ant uses ASP in boot camp.</td>
            </tr>
         </table>

         <p>
          <a href = "addPost.asp?file=forumASP.xml">Post a Message</a>
            <br>
            <a href = "default.asp">Return to Main Page</a>
         </p>

      </body>

   </html>
```

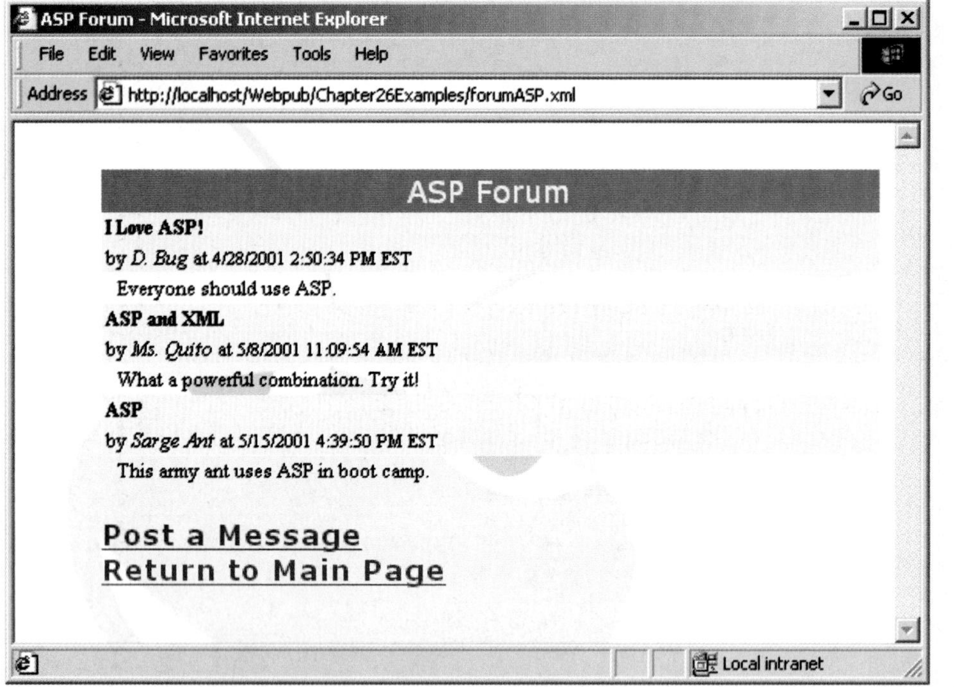

Fig. 26.9 Output of the transformation of the forum XML document (part 3 of 3).

26.6 Posting Messages

In this section, we present the ASP document **addPost.asp** (Fig. 26.10), which posts messages to a forum. This ASP uses much of the same functionality as **addForum.asp**.

Line 23 loads the forum XML document. Lines 31–33 create a **message** element and an associated **timestamp** attribute. Line 38 creates child element **user**; line 41 creates child element **title**; and line 44 creates child element **text** for element **message**. Finally, the forum is saved to disk in line 46.

```
<% @LANGUAGE = "VBScript" %>

<% ' Fig. 26.10 : addPost.asp
   ' ASP document for posting a message

   Option Explicit

   Dim xmlFile, xmlRoot, xmlNode
   Dim strTitle, strError, strPath

   If Request( "submit" ) <> Empty Then

      If Request( "file" ) <> Empty And _
         Request( "userName" ) <> Empty And _
         Request( "messageTitle" ) <> Empty And _
         Request( "messageText" ) <> Empty Then

         strPath = Server.MapPath( Request( "file" ) )

         Set xmlFile = Server.CreateObject( "Microsoft.XMLDOM" )
         xmlFile.Async = False

         If Not xmlFile.Load( strPath ) Then
            Call Server.Transfer( "invalid.html" )
         End If

         ' get the root node
         Set xmlRoot = xmlFile.DocumentElement

         ' create first message
         Set xmlNode = xmlFile.CreateElement( "message" )
         Call xmlNode.SetAttribute( "timestamp", Now & " EST" )
         Call xmlRoot.AppendChild( xmlNode )

         Set xmlRoot = xmlNode

         ' create user node
         Call CreateElementNode( "user", "userName", xmlNode )

         ' create title node
         Call CreateElementNode( "title", "messageTitle", xmlNode )

         ' create text node
         Call CreateElementNode( "text", "messageText", xmlNode )

         Call xmlFile.Save( strPath ) ' save the file

         ' finished processing
         Call Server.Transfer( Request( "file" ) )
      Else
         strError = "ERROR: Invalid input."
      End If

```

Fig. 26.10 Adding a message to a forum (part 1 of 3).

```
   End If

   ' procedure that creates an element node
   Sub CreateElementNode( elementName, formElement, node )
      Set xmlNode = xmlFile.CreateElement( elementName )
      xmlNode.Text = Request( formElement )
      Call xmlRoot.AppendChild( node )
   End Sub
%>

<!DOCTYPE html PUBLIC "-//W3C//DTD XHTML 1.0 Strict//EN"
 "http://www.w3.org/TR/xhtml1/DTD/xhtml1-strict.dtd">

<html xmlns = "http://www.w3.org/1999/xhtml">
   <head>
      <title>Post a Message</title>
      <link rel = "stylesheet" type = "text/css"
            href = "style.css" />
   </head>

   <body>
      <p><% =strError %></p>

      <form method = "post" action = "addPost.asp">
         <p>
            User:<br />
            <input type = "text" size = "40" name = "userName"
                   value = "<% =Request( "userName" ) %>" />
         </p>

         <p>
            Message Title:<br />
            <input type = "text" size = "40" name = "messageTitle"
                   value = "<% =Request( "messageTitle" ) %>" />
         </p>

         <p>
            Message Text:<br />
            <textarea name = "messageText" cols = "40"
                      rows = "4"><% =Request( "messageText" ) %>
            </textarea>
         </p>

         <p>
            <input type = "hidden" name = "file"
                   value = "<% =Request( "file" ) %>"/>
          <input type = "submit" name = "submit" value = "Submit" />
            <input type = "reset" value = "Clear" />
         </p>
      </form>

      <p>
         <a href = "<% =Request( "file" ) %>">Return to Forum</a>
```

Fig. 26.10 Adding a message to a forum (part 2 of 3).

```
      </p>
   </body>

</html>
```

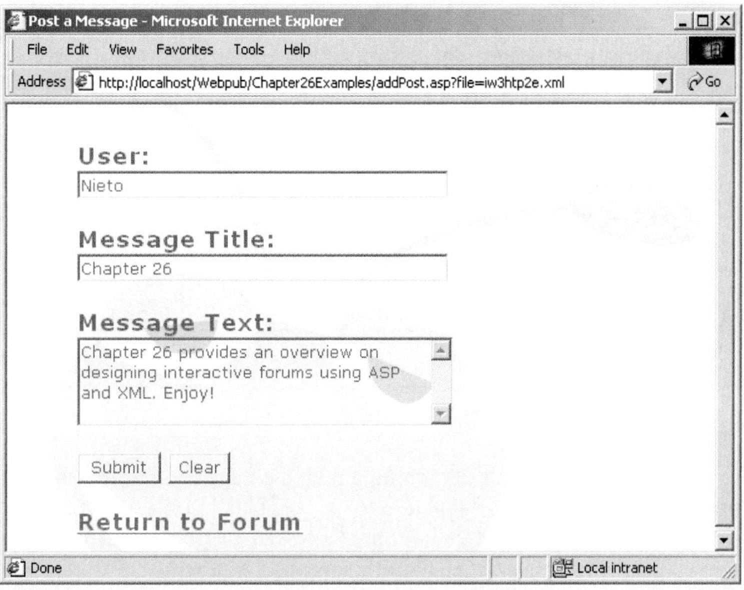

Fig. 26.10 Adding a message to a forum (part 3 of 3).

Figure 26.11 shows a new forum (i.e., **Internet and World Wide Web: 2nd Edition**) added to the message board, while Fig. 26.12 shows the initial content of that forum.

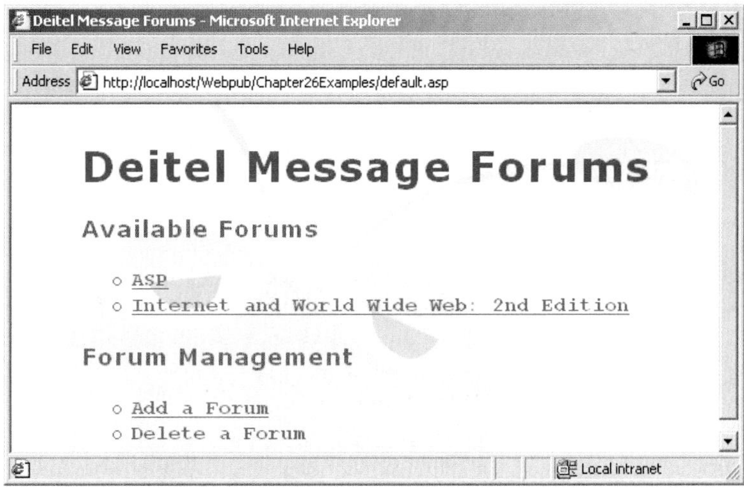

Fig. 26.11 New forum on the message board.

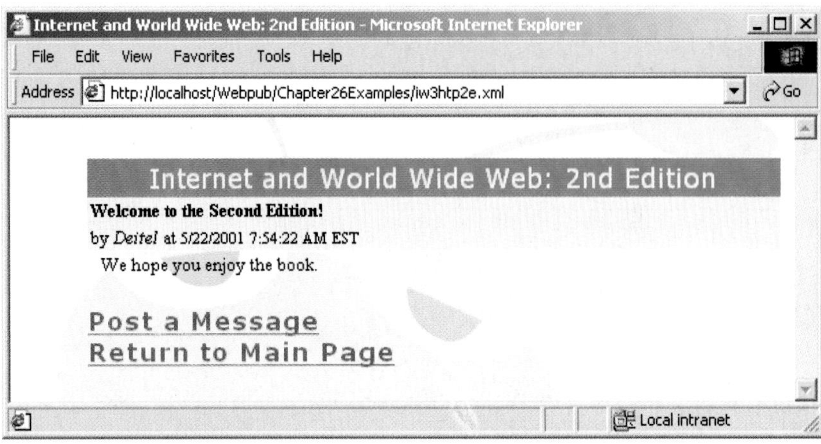

Fig. 26.12 Initial content of the newly added forum.

Figure 26.13 shows the result of posting a new message to the **Internet and World Wide Web: 2nd Edition** forum.

26.7 Other Documents

In this section, we present three other documents used in the case study. Figure 26.14 lists the XHTML document that displays an error message (**`invalid.html`**).

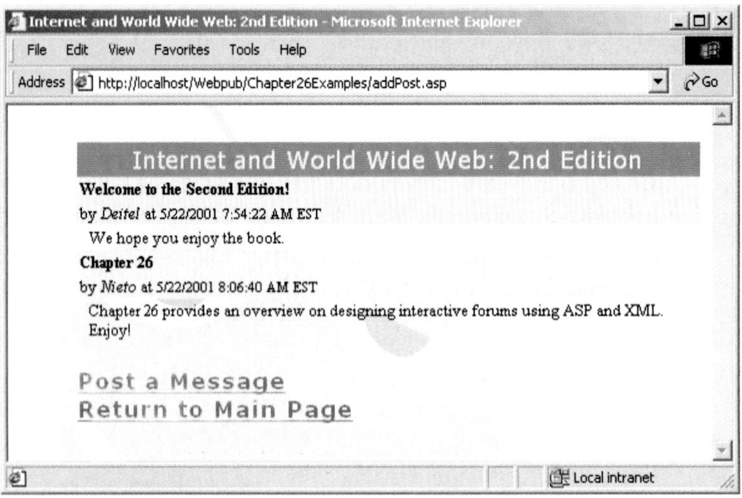

Fig. 26.13 Contents of the **Internet and World Wide Web: 2nd Edition**.

```
<!DOCTYPE html PUBLIC "-//W3C//DTD XHTML 1.0 Strict//EN"
"http://www.w3.org/TR/xhtml1/DTD/xhtml1-strict.dtd">

<!-- Fig. 26.14 : invalid.html             -->
<!-- XHTML document for displaying errors -->

<html xmlns = "http://www.w3.org/1999/xhtml">

   <head>
     <title>Deitel Book Organization</title>
     <link rel = "stylesheet" type = "text/css"
           href = "site.css" />
   </head>

   <body>
      <h1>Invalid Request.</h1>

      <p><a href = "default.asp">Return to Main Page</a></p>
   </body>

</html>
```

Fig. 26.14 Document that displays an error message.

Figure 26.15 lists the CSS document (**site.css**) that formats the XHTML documents. Figure 26.16 lists the CSS document that formats the forum (**style.css**).

```
/* Fig. 26.15 : site.css              */
/* Stylesheet for XHTML documents */

body
{
   background: white;
   color: black;
   font-family: Arial, sans-serif;
   font-size: 10pt;
}

a
{
   background: transparent;
   color: blue;
   text-decoration: none;
}

a:hover
{
   text-decoration: underline;
}
```

Fig. 26.15 CSS document for XHTML pages (part 1 of 2).

```

table
{
   border-width: 1px;
   border-style: solid;
}

.forumTitle
{
   background: lime;
   color: black;
   font-size: 12pt;
   font-weight: bold;
   text-align: center;
}

.msgTitle
{
   background: silver;
   color: black;
   font-size: 10pt;
   font-weight: bold;
}

.msgInfo
{
   background: silver;
   color: black;
   font-size: 10pt;
}

.msgPost
{
   background: silver;
   color: black;
   font-size: 8pt;
}

.msgText
{
   font-size: 10pt;
   padding-left: 10px;
}

.date
{
   font-size: 8pt;
}
```

Fig. 26.15 CSS document for XHTML pages (part 2 of 2).

```
/* Fig. 26.16 : style.css */
/* Stylesheet for forums  */

h1
{
   color: #330099;
   letter-spacing: 2px;
   font-family: Verdana, Geneva, Arial, Helvetica, sans-serif;
   background-color: transparent;
}

h2
{
   color: #6633FF;
   font-family: Verdana, Geneva, Arial, Helvetica, sans-serif;
   font-size: small;
   background-color: transparent;
}

p
{
   font-family: Verdana, Geneva, Arial, Helvetica, sans-serif;
   color: #336666;
   letter-spacing: 1px;
   font-size: larger;
   font-weight: bold;
   background-color: transparent;
}

body
{
   background-image: url(bug2.gif);
   background-repeat: no-repeat;
   margin-top: 5%;
   background-position: 25%;
   margin-left: 10%;
}

li
{
   font-family: "Courier New", Courier, monospace;
   font-weight: bolder;
   list-style-type: circle;
   color: #3333FF;
   background-color: transparent;
}

input
{
   background-color: transparent;
   color: #336666;
   font-family: Verdana, Geneva, Arial, Helvetica, sans-serif;
}
```

Fig. 26.16 CSS document for forums (part 1 of 2).

```

textarea
{
   background-color: transparent;
   color: #336666;
   font-family: Verdana, Geneva, Arial, Helvetica, sans-serif;
}

.forumTitle
{
   color: #FFFFCC;
   font-size: 14pt;
   font-family: Verdana, Geneva, Arial, Helvetica, sans-serif;
   text-align: center;
   background-color: #6666CC;
}

.msgTitle
{
   background: #FFFFCC;
   color: black;
   font-size: 10pt;
   font-weight: bold;
}

.msgInfo
{
   background: #FFFFCC;
   color: black;
   font-size: 10pt;
}

.msgPost
{
   background: silver;
   color: black;
   font-size: 8pt;
}

.msgText
{
   font-size: 10pt;
   padding-left: 10px;
}

.date
{
   font-size: 8pt;
}
```

Fig. 26.16 CSS document for forums (part 2 of 2).

26.8 Internet and World Wide Web Resources

www.4guysfromrolla.com/webtech/101200-1.shtml
This site lists different ways to extract XML data from an ASP page.

www.15seconds.com/focus/XML.htm
The *ASPWatch* site contains many articles on integrating ASP with various technologies. This article focuses on ASP and XML.

TERMINOLOGY

Async property
asynchronous
collection
CreateElement method
CreateObject method
DOMDocument object
Load method
logic error
MapPath method of **Server** object
message forum
Request method
Save method
Server object
synchronous

SELF-REVIEW EXERCISES

26.1 What purpose does the **Async** property of a **DOMDocument** object serve?

26.2 To create child element nodes for elements in an XML document, what needs to be done?

ANSWERS TO SELF-REVIEW EXERCISES

26.1 The **Async** property sets the execution type of **DOMDocument** methods. If **Async** is set to **True**, methods are performed asynchronously, so execution continues even if the method call was not completed. If **Async** is set to **False**, methods are performed synchronously, so execution waits until the method call is completed.

26.2 To create element nodes, call **DOMDocument** object's method **CreateElement**, with the name of the element to be created as a parameter. Next, method **appendChild** is called on the element to which the new element is to be a child, with the child element as the parameter.

EXERCISES

26.3 Create an Active Server Page to delete messages from a forum. This ASP should take a forum's filename and the timestamp of the message as form arguments. Modify **formatting.xsl** to provide a link to the ASP for each message. [*Hint*: To remove an element's child, use **removeChild**, with the node to remove as a parameter.]

26.4 Create an Active Server Page to delete forums. This ASP should list the available forums and allow the user to select one for deletion.

26.5 In lines 98–99 of Fig. 26.10 (**addPost.asp**), what is the value of the **input** element?

26.6 These lines of code are from lines 50–51of **formatting.xsl**. Explain why the **@** in front of **"@filename"** is necessary in the **xsl:value-of** element.

```
<xsl:attribute name = "href">addPost.asp?file=
  <xsl:value-of select = "@filename">Post a Message
</xsl:attribute>
```

26.7 Describe the purpose of Fig. 26.8 (**formatting.xsl**).

26.8 Describe the purpose of lines 19–22 in Fig 26.15 (**site.css**).

27

Perl and CGI (Common Gateway Interface)

Objectives

- To understand basic Perl programming.
- To understand the Common Gateway Interface.
- To understand string processing and regular expressions in Perl.
- To be able to use cookies to read and write client data.
- To be able to construct programs that interact with MySQL databases.

This is the common air that bathes the globe.
Walt Whitman

The longest part of the journey is said to be the passing of the gate.
Marcus Terentius Varro

Railway termini... are our gates to the glorious and unknown. Through them we pass out into adventure and sunshine, to them, alas! we return.
E. M. Forster

There comes a time in a man's life when to get where he has to go—if there are no doors or windows—he walks through a wall.
Bernard Malamud

You ought to be able to show that you can do it a good deal better than anyone else with the regular tools before you have a license to bring in your own improvements.
Ernest Hemingway

Outline

27.1 Introduction

Practical Extraction and Report Language (*Perl*) is one of the most widely used languages for Web programming today. Larry Wall began developing this high-level programming language in 1987 while working at Unisys. His initial intent was to create a programming language to monitor large software projects and generate reports. Wall wanted to create a language that would be more powerful than shell scripting and more flexible than C, a language with rich text-processing capabilities and, most of all, a language that would make common programming tasks straightforward and easy. In this chapter, we discuss Perl 5.6 and examine several practical examples that use Perl for Internet programming.

The *Common Gateway Interface* (*CGI*) is a standard protocol through which users interact with applications on Web servers. Thus, CGI provides a way for clients (e.g., Web browsers) to interface indirectly with applications on the Web server. Because CGI is an interface, it cannot be programmed directly; a script or executable program (commonly called a *CGI script*) must be executed to interact with it. While CGI scripts can be written in many different programming languages, Perl is commonly used due to its power, flexibility and availability of several preexisting programs.

Figure 27.1 illustrates the interaction between client and server when the client requests a document that references a CGI script. Often, CGI scripts process information (e.g., a search-engine query, a credit-card number) gathered from a form. For example, a CGI script might verify credit-card information and notify the client of the results (i.e., accepted or rejected). Permission is granted within the Web server (usually by the *Webmaster* or the author of the Web site) for specific programs on the server to be executed. These programs are typically designated with a certain filename extension (such as **`.cgi`** or **`.pl`**) and/or located within a special directory (such as **`cgi-bin`**). After the application output is sent to the server through CGI, the results may be sent to the client. Information received by the client is usually an HTML or XHTML document, but may contain images, streaming audio, Macromedia Flash files (see Chapter 19), XML (see Chapter 20), etc.

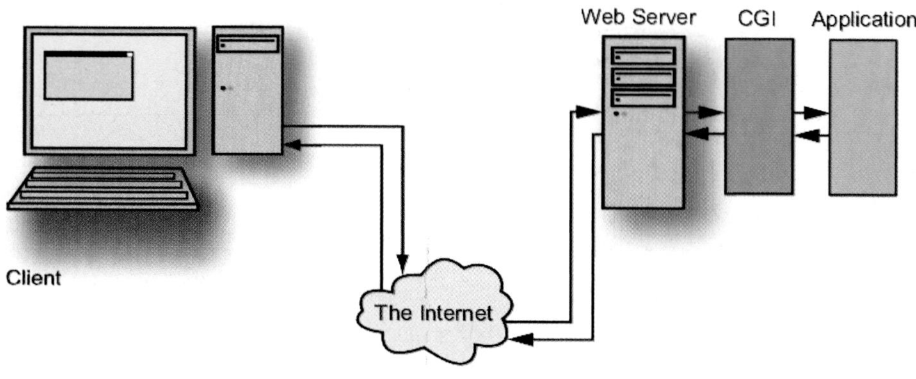

Fig. 27.1 Data path of a typical CGI-based application.

Applications typically interact with the user through *standard input* and *standard output*. Standard input is the stream of information received by a program from a user, typically through the keyboard, but also possibly from a file or another input device. Standard output is the information stream presented to the user by an application; it is typically displayed on the screen, but may be printed, written to a file, etc.

For CGI scripts, the standard output is redirected (or *piped*) through the Common Gateway Interface to the server and then sent over the Internet to a Web browser for rendering. If the server-side script is programmed correctly, the output will be readable by the client. Usually, the output is an HTML or XHTML document that is rendered by a Web browser.

27.2 Perl

With the advent of the World Wide Web and Web browsers, the Internet gained tremendous popularity. This greatly increased the volume of requests users made for information from Web servers. It became evident that the degree of interactivity between the user and the server would be crucial. The power of the Web resides not only in serving content to users, but also in responding to requests from users and generating dynamic content. The framework for such communication already existed through CGI. Most of the information users send to servers is text, thus Perl was a logical choice for programming the server side of interactive Web-based applications. Perl possesses simple, yet powerful, text-processing capabilities and is arguably the most popular CGI scripting language. The Perl community, headed by Wall (who currently works for O'Reilly & Associates as a Perl developer and researcher), continuously works to evolve the language, keeping it competitive with newer server-side technologies, such as Microsoft's Active Server Pages (see Chapter 25).

Figure 27.2 presents a simple Perl program that writes the text **`"Welcome to Perl!"`** to the screen. Because the program does not interact with the Common Gateway Interface, it is not a CGI script. Our initial examples are command-line programs that illustrate fundamental Perl programming.

```
1  #!/usr/bin/perl
2  # Fig. 27.2: fig27_02.pl
3  # A first program in Perl.
4
5  print( "Welcome to Perl!\n" );
```

```
Welcome to Perl!
```

Fig. 27.2 Simple Perl program.

Lines 2–3 use the Perl *comment character* (**#**) to instruct the interpreter to ignore everything on the current line following the **#**. This syntax allows programmers to write descriptive comments inside their programs. The exception to this rule is the *"shebang" construct* (**#!**) on line 1. On Unix systems, this line indicates the path to the Perl interpreter (such as **#!/usr/bin/perl**). On other systems (e.g., Windows), the line may be ignored, or it may indicate to the server (e.g., Apache) that a Perl program follows the statement.

Good Programming Practice 27.1

*While not all servers require the "shebang" construct (**#!**), it is good practice to include it for program portability.*

Common Programming Error 27.1

*Some systems require that the shebang construct indicate the path to the Perl interpreter. If this path is incorrect, the program might not run. For Windows, this path is most likely **#!C:\Perl\bin\perl**. If the reader is unsure as to where the Perl interpreter is, do a search for **perl.exe** and use the path found in the shebang construct.*

The comment (line 2) indicates that the filename of the program is **fig27_02.pl**. Perl program file names typically end with the **.pl** extension. The program can be executed by running the Perl interpreter from the command-line prompt (e.g., the DOS prompt in Windows).

In order to run the Perl script, Perl must first be installed on the system. Windows users should see the "ActiveState Perl Installation" document at **www.deitel.com** for instructions on how to install ActivePerl. ActivePerl is the standard Perl implementation for Windows. For installation on other platforms visit **www.perl.com**.

To run **fig27_02.pl**, type at the command prompt

```
perl fig27_02.pl
```

where **perl** is the interpreter and **fig27_02.pl** is the Perl script. Alternatively, you could type

```
perl -w fig27_02.pl
```

which instructs the Perl interpreter to output warnings to the screen if it finds potential bugs in your code.

On Windows systems, a Perl script may also be executed by double-clicking its program icon. The program window closes automatically once the script terminates, and any screen output is lost. For this reason, it is usually better to run a script from the DOS prompt.

Testing and Debugging Tip 27.1

When running a Perl script from the command line, always use the **-w** *option. Otherwise, the program may seem to execute correctly, while there is actually something wrong with the source code. The* **-w** *option displays warnings encountered while executing a Perl program.*

Line 5 calls function ***print*** to write text to the screen. Note that because Perl is case-sensitive, writing **Print** or **PRINT** instead of **print** yields an error. The text **"Welcome to Perl!\n"** is surrounded in quotes and is called a *string*. The last portion of the string—the newline *escape sequence*, **\n**—moves the output cursor to the next line. The semicolon (**;**) at the end of line 5 terminates Perl statements. Lastly, notice that the argument passed to function **print** (i.e., the string that we wish to print) is enclosed in parentheses **()**. These parentheses are not required; however, we suggest that you use parentheses as often as possible in your programs, to maintain clarity. In this example, we use parentheses to indicate what we want printed. We will demonstrate the use of parentheses throughout the chapter.

Common Programming Error 27.2

Forgetting to terminate a statement with a **;** *is a syntax error in most cases.*

Perl has built-in data types (Fig. 27.3) that represent different kinds of data. Notice that each variable name has a specific character (i.e., **$**, **@** or **%**) preceding it. For example, the **$** character specifies that the variable contains a *scalar* value (i.e., strings, integer numbers, floating-point numbers and references). The script **fig27_04.pl** (Fig. 27.4) demonstrates the manipulation of scalar variables.

Common Programming Error 27.3

Failure to place a preceding **$** *character before a scalar variable name is a syntax error.*

Data type	Format for variable names of this type	Description
Scalar	**$***scalarname*	Can be a string, an integer number, a floating-point number or a reference.
Array	**@***arrayname*	An ordered list of scalar variables that can be accessed using integer indices.
Hash	**%***hashname*	An unordered set of scalar variables whose values are accessed using unique scalar values (i.e., strings) called *keys*.

Fig. 27.3 Perl data types.

```
#!/usr/bin/perl
# Fig. 27.4: fig27_04.pl
# Program to illustrate the use of scalar variables.

```

Fig. 27.4 Using scalar variables (part 1 of 2).

```
5   $number = 5;
6   print( "The value of variable \$number is: $number\n\n" );
7
8   $number += 5;
9   print( "Variable \$number after adding 5 is: $number\n" );
10
11  $number *= 2;
12  print( "Variable \$number after multiplying by 2 is: " );
13  print( "$number\n\n\n" );
14
15  # using an uninitialized variable in the context of a string
16  print( "Using a variable before initializing: $variable\n\n" );
17
18  # using an uninitialized variable in a numeric context
19  $test = $undefined + 5;
20  print( "Adding uninitialized variable \$undefined " );
21  print( "to 5 yields: $test\n" );
22
23  # using strings in numeric contexts
24  $string = "A string value";
25  $number += $string;
26  print( "Adding a string to an integer yields: $number\n" );
27
28  $string2 = "15charactersand1";
29  $number2 = $number + $string2;
30  print( "Adding $number to string \"$string2\" yields: " );
31  print( "$string2\n" );
```

```
The value of variable $number is: 5

Variable $number after adding 5 is: 10
Variable $number after multiplying by 2 is: 20


Using a variable before initializing:

Adding uninitialized variable $undefined to 5 yields: 5
Adding a string to an integer yields: 20
Adding 20 to string "15charactersand1" yields: 15charactersand1
```

Fig. 27.4 Using scalar variables (part 2 of 2).

In Perl, a variable is created the first time it is encountered by the interpreter. Line 5 creates a variable with name **`$number`** and sets its value to **`5`**. Line 8 adds **`5`** to **`$number`**, which results in the value **`10`** being stored in **`$number`**. Notice that we use an *assignment operator* (**`+=`**) to yield an expression equivalent to **`$number = $number + 5`**, which adds **`5`** to the value of **`$number`** and stores the result in **`$number`**. Assignment operators (i.e., **`+=`**, **`-=`**, **`*=`** and **`/=`**) are syntactical shortcuts. Line 9 calls function **`print`** to write text followed by the value of **`$number`**. Note that the actual value of **`$number`** is printed, rather than **`"$number"`**; when a variable is encountered inside a double-quoted (**`""`**) string, Perl uses a process called *interpolation* to replace the variable with its associated data. On line

11, we use a shortcut similar to the one used on line 8: **`*=`**. In this case, we multiply **`$number`** by **`2`** and store the result in **`$number`**.

Testing and Debugging Tip 27.2

*Function **`print`** can be used to display the value of a variable at a particular point during a program's execution. This is often helpful in debugging a program.*

In Perl, uninitialized variables have the value ***`undef`***, which evaluates to different values depending on the variable's context. When **`undef`** is used in a numeric context (e.g., **`$undefined`** on line 19), it evaluates to **`0`**. In contrast, when it is interpreted in a string context (such as **`$variable`** in line 16), **`undef`** evaluates to the empty string (**`""`**).

Lines 24–31 show the results of evaluating strings in numeric context. Unless a string begins with a digit, it is evaluated as **`undef`** in a numeric context. If it begins with a digit, every character up to, but not including, the first nondigit character is evaluated as a number, and the remaining characters are ignored. For example, the string **`"A string value"`** (line 24) does not begin with a digit and, therefore, evaluates to **`undef`**. Because **`undef`** evaluates to **`0`**, variable **`$number`**'s value is unchanged. The string **`"15charactersand1"`** (line 28) begins with a digit and is interpolated as **`15`**. The character **`1`** on the end is ignored, because there are nondigit characters preceding it. Evaluating a string in numeric context does not actually change the value of the string. This rule is shown by line 31's output, which prints the original string, **`"15charactersand1"`**.

Notice that the programmer does not need to differentiate between numeric and string data types, because the interpreter's evaluation of scalar variables depends on the context in which they are used.

Common Programming Error 27.4

*Using an uninitialized variable might make a numerical calculation incorrect. For example, multiplying a number by an uninitialized variable results in **`0`**.*

Testing and Debugging Tip 27.3

*While it is not always necessary to initialize variables before using them, errors can be avoided by doing so. Many Perl programmers use the statements **`use strict`** and **`use warnings`** to catch such errors. For simplicity, we will not initialize variables before using them in this chapter.*

Perl provides the capability to store data in arrays. Arrays are divided into *elements*, each containing a scalar value. The script **`fig27_05.pl`** (Fig. 27.5) demonstrates some techniques for array initialization and manipulation.

```
#!/usr/bin/perl
# Fig. 27.5: fig27_05.pl
# Program to demonstrate arrays in Perl.

@array = ( "Bill", "Bobby", "Sue", "Michelle" );

print( "The array contains: @array\n" );
print( "Printing array outside of quotes: ", @array, "\n\n" );

print( "Third element: $array[ 2 ]\n" );
```

Fig. 27.5 Using arrays (part 1 of 2).

```
11
12  $number = 3;
13  print( "Fourth element: $array[ $number ]\n\n" );
14
15  @array2 = ( 'A' .. 'Z' );
16  print( "The range operator is used to create a list of\n" );
17  print( "all capital letters from A to Z:\n" );
18  print( "@array2 \n\n" );
19
20  $array3[ 3 ] = "4th";
21  print( "Array with just one element initialized: @array3 \n\n" );
22
23  print( 'Printing literal using single quotes: ' );
24  print( '@array and \n', "\n" );
25
26  print( "Printing literal using backslashes: " );
27  print( "\@array and \\n\n" );
```

```
The array contains: Bill Bobby Sue Michelle
Printing array outside of quotes: BillBobbySueMichelle

Third element: Sue
Fourth element: Michelle

The range operator is used to create a list of
all capital letters from A to Z:
A B C D E F G H I J K L M N O P Q R S T U V W X Y Z

Array with just one element initialized:    4th

Printing literal using single quotes: @array and \n
Printing literal using backslashes: @array and \n
```

Fig. 27.5 Using arrays (part 2 of 2).

Line 5 initializes array **`@array`** to contain the strings **`"Bill"`**, **`"Bobby"`**, **`"Sue"`** and **`"Michelle"`**. In Perl, all array variable names must be preceded by the **`@`** symbol. Parentheses are necessary to group the strings in the array assignment; this group of elements surrounded by parentheses is called a *list*. In assigning the list to **`@array`**, each person's name is stored in an individual array element with a unique integer index value, starting at 0.

Common Programming Error 27.5

Although lists in Perl may seem similar to arrays, they are not. A list is simply a group of elements surrounded by parentheses and does not contain the entire functionality of an array.

When **`print`**ing an array inside double quotes (line 7), the array element values are printed with only one space separating them. The values are separated by whatever is in special variable **`$"`**, which, by default, is a space. If this value were changed to the letter **`"a"`**, all the array elements would be printed with the character **`"a"`** between them. If the array name is not enclosed in double quotes when it is **`print`**ed (line 8), the interpreter prints the element values without inserting spaces between them.

Line 10 demonstrates how individual array elements are accessed using square brackets (**[]**). As mentioned previously, if we use the **@** character followed by the array name, we reference the array as a whole. But if the name of the array is prefixed by the **$** character and followed by an index number in square brackets (as in line 10), it refers instead to an individual element of the array, which is a scalar value. Line 13 demonstrates the use of a variable as the index number. The value of **$number[3]** is used to get the value of the fourth element of the array.

Line 15 initializes array **@array2** to contain the capital letters **A** to **Z** inclusive. The *range operator* (**..**) specifies that all values between uppercase **A** and uppercase **Z** be placed in the array. The range operator can be used to create a consecutive series of values, such as **1** through **15** or **a** through **z**.

The Perl interpreter handles memory management. Therefore, it is not necessary to specify an array's size. If a value is assigned to a position outside the range of the array or to an uninitialized array, the interpreter automatically extends the array range to include the new element. Elements that are added by the interpreter during an adjustment of the range are initialized to the **undef** value. Lines 20–21 assign a value to the fourth element in the uninitialized array **@array3**. The interpreter recognizes that memory has not been allocated for this array and creates new memory for the array. The interpreter then sets the value of the first three elements to **undef** and the value of the fourth element to the string **"4th"**. When the array is printed, the first three **undef** values are treated as empty strings and printed with a space between each. This accounts for the three extra spaces in the output before the string **"4th"**.

To print special characters, like ****, **@** and **"** and not have the interpreter treat them as an escape sequence or array, Perl provides two options. The first is to ***print*** (lines 23–24) the characters as a literal string (i.e., a string enclosed in single quotes). When strings are inside single quotes, the interpreter treats the string literally and does not attempt to interpret any escape sequence or variable substitution. The second choice is to use the backslash character (line 26–27) to *escape* special characters.

27.3 String Processing and Regular Expressions

One of Perl's most powerful capabilities is the processing of textual data easily and efficiently, which allows for straightforward searching, substitution, extraction and concatenation of strings. Text manipulation in Perl is usually done with a *regular expression*—a series of characters that serves as a pattern-matching template (or search criterion) in strings, text files and databases. This feature allows complicated searching and string processing to be performed using relatively simple expressions.

Many string-processing tasks can be accomplished by using Perl's *equality* and *comparison* operators (Fig. 27.6, **fig27_06.pl**). Line 5 declares and initializes array **@fruits**. Operator **qw** ("quote word") takes the contents inside the parentheses and creates a comma-separated list, with each element wrapped in double quotes. In this example, **qw(apple orange banana)** is equivalent to **("apple", "orange", "banana")**.

Lines 7–24 demonstrate our first example of Perl *control structures*. The ***foreach*** structure (line 7) iterates sequentially through the elements in **@fruits**. Each element's value is assigned to variable **$item**, and the body of the **foreach** is executed once for each element in the array. Notice that a semicolon does not terminate the **foreach**.

```
1   #!/usr/bin/perl
2   # Fig. 27.6: fig27_06.pl
3   # Program to demonstrate the eq, ne, lt, gt operators.
4
5   @fruits = qw( apple orange banana );
6
7   foreach $item ( @fruits ) {
8
9      if ( $item eq "banana" ) {
10        print( "String '$item' matches string 'banana'\n" );
11     }
12
13     if ( $item ne "banana" ) {
14        print( "String '$item' does not match string 'banana'\n" );
15     }
16
17     if ( $item lt "banana" ) {
18        print( "String '$item' is less than string 'banana'\n" );
19     }
20
21     if ( $item gt "banana" ) {
22        print( "String '$item' is greater than string 'banana'\n" );
23     }
24  }
```

```
String 'apple' does not match string 'banana'
String 'apple' is less than string 'banana'
String 'orange' does not match string 'banana'
String 'orange' is greater than string 'banana'
String 'banana' matches string 'banana'
```

Fig. 27.6 Using the **eq**, **ne**, **lt** and **gt** operators.

Line 9 introduces another control structure: the ***if*** structure. Parentheses surround the condition being tested, and mandatory curly braces surround the block of code that is executed when the condition is true. In Perl, any scalar except the number **0**, the string **"0"** and the empty string (i.e., **undef** values) is defined as true. In our example, when the **$item**'s content is tested against **"banana"** (line 9) for equality, the condition evaluates to true, and the ***print*** command (line 10) is executed.

The remaining **if** statements (lines 13, 17 and 21) demonstrate the other string comparison operators. Operators **eq**, **lt** and **gt** test strings for equality, less-than and greater-than, respectively. These operators are used only with strings. When comparing numeric values, operators **==**, **!=**, **<**, **<=**, **>** and **>=** are used.

Common Programming Error 27.6

Using **==** *for string comparisons or* **eq** *for numerical comparisons can result in errors in the program.*

Common Programming Error 27.7

While the number **0** *and the string* **"0"** *evaluate to false in Perl* **if** *statements, other string values that might look like zero (* **"0.0"***) evaluate to true.*

For more powerful string comparisons, Perl provides the *match operator* (**m//**), which uses regular expressions to search a string for a specified pattern. Figure 27.7 uses the match operator to perform a variety of regular expression tests.

We begin by assigning the string **"Now is is the time"** to variable **$search** (line 5). The expression on line 8 uses the **m//** match operator to search for the *literal characters* **Now** inside variable **$search**. Note that the **m** character preceding the slashes of the **m//** operator is optional in most cases and thus is omitted here.

The match operator takes two operands. The first operand is the regular-expression pattern to search for (**Now**), which is placed between the slashes of the **m//** operator. The second operand is the string within which to search, which is assigned to the match operator using the **=~** operator. The **=~** operator is sometimes called a *binding operator*, because it binds whatever is on its left side to a regular-expression operator on its right.

In our example, the pattern **Now** is found in the string **"Now is is the time"**. The match operator returns true, and the body of the **if** statement is executed. In addition to literal characters like **Now**, which match only themselves, regular expressions can include special characters called *metacharacters*, which specify patterns or contexts that cannot be defined using literal characters. For example, the *caret metacharacter* (**^**) matches the beginning of a string. The next regular expression (line 12) searches the beginning of **$search** for the pattern **Now**.

The **$** metacharacter searches the end of a string for a pattern (line 17). Because the pattern **Now** is not found at the end of **$search**, the body of the **if** statement (line 18) is not executed. Note that **Now$** is not a variable; it is a search pattern that uses **$** to search for **Now** at the end of a string.

```
1  #!/usr/bin/perl
2  # Fig 27.7: fig27_07.pl
3  # Searches using the matching operator and regular expressions.
4
5  $search = "Now is is the time";
6  print( "Test string is: '$search'\n\n" );
7
8  if ( $search =~ /Now/ ) {
9     print( "String 'Now' was found.\n" );
10 }
11
12 if ( $search =~ /^Now/ ) {
13    print( "String 'Now' was found at the beginning of the line." );
14    print( "\n" );
15 }
16
17 if ( $search =~ /Now$/ ) {
18    print( "String 'Now' was found at the end of the line.\n" );
19 }
20
21 if ( $search =~ /\b ( \w+ ow ) \b/x ) {
22    print( "Word found ending in 'ow': $1 \n" );
23 }
24
```

Fig. 27.7 Using the matching operator (part 1 of 2).

```
25  if ( $search =~ /\b ( \w+ ) \s ( \1 ) \b/x ) {
26     print( "Repeated words found: $1 $2\n" );
27  }
28
29  @matches = ( $search =~ / \b ( t \w+ ) \b /gx );
30  print( "Words beginning with 't' found: @matches\n" );
```

```
Test string is: 'Now is is the time'

String 'Now' was found.
String 'Now' was found at the beginning of the line.
Word found ending in 'ow': Now
Repeated words found: is is
Words beginning with 't' found: the time
```

Fig. 27.7 Using the matching operator (part 2 of 2).

The condition on line 21, searches (from left to right) for the first word ending with the letters **ow**. As in strings, backslashes in regular expressions escape characters with special significance. For example, the **\b** expression does not match the literal characters "**\b**." Instead, the expression matches any *word boundary*. A word boundary is a boundary between an *alphanumeric character*—**0**–**9**, **a**–**z**, **A**–**Z** and the underscore character—and something that is not an alphanumeric character. Between the **\b** characters is a set of parentheses, which will be explained momentarily.

The expression inside the parentheses, **\w+ ow**, indicates that we are searching for patterns ending in **ow**. The first part, **\w+**, is a combination of **\w** (an escape sequence that matches a single alphanumeric character) and the **+** *modifier*, which is a *quantifier* that instructs Perl to match the preceding character one or more times. Thus, **\w+** matches one or more alphanumeric characters. The characters **ow** are taken literally. Collectively, the expression **/\b (\w+ ow) \b/** matches one or more alphanumeric characters ending with **ow**, with word boundaries at the beginning and end. See Fig. 27.8 for a description of several Perl regular-expression quantifiers and Fig. 27.9 for a list of regular-expression metacharacters.

Parentheses indicate that the text matching the pattern is to be saved in a special Perl variable (e.g., **$1**, etc.). The parentheses (line 21 of Fig. 27.7) cause **Now** to be stored in variable **$1**. Multiple sets of parentheses may be used in regular expressions, where each match results in a new Perl variable (**$1**, **$2**, **$3**, etc.). The value matched in the first set of parentheses is stored in variable **$1**, the value matched in the second set of parentheses is stored in variable **$2**, and so on.

Quantifier	Matches
`{n}`	Exactly **n** times
`{m,n}`	Between **m** and **n** times inclusive
`{n,}`	**n** or more times

Fig. 27.8 Some of Perl's quantifiers (part 1 of 2).

Quantifier	Matches
`+`	One or more times (same as `{1,}`)
`*`	Zero or more times (same as `{0,}`)
`?`	One or zero times (same as `{0,1}`)

Fig. 27.8 Some of Perl's quantifiers (part 2 of 2).

Symbol	Matches	Symbol	Matches
`^`	Beginning of line	`\d`	Digit (i.e., `0` to `9`)
`$`	End of line	`\D`	Nondigit
`\b`	Word boundary	`\s`	Whitespace
`\B`	Nonword boundary	`\S`	Nonwhitespace
`\w`	Word (alphanumeric) character	`\n`	Newline
`\W`	Nonword character	`\t`	Tab

Fig. 27.9 Some of Perl's metacharacters.

Adding *modifying characters* after a regular expression refines the pattern-matching process. Modifying characters (Fig. 27.10) placed to the right of the forward slash that delimits the regular expression instruct the interpreter how to treat the preceding expression. For example, the **`i`** after the regular expression

```
/computer/i
```

tells the interpreter to ignore case when searching, thus matching **`computer`**, **`COMPUTER`**, **`Computer`**, **`CoMputER`**, etc.

Modifying Character	Purpose
`g`	Perform a global search; find and return all matches, not just the first one found.
`i`	Ignores the case of the search string (case insensitive).
`m`	The string is evaluated as if it had multiple lines of text (i.e., newline characters are not ignored).
`s`	Ignore the newline character and treat it as whitespace. The text is seen as a single line.
`x`	All whitespace characters are ignored when searching the string.

Fig. 27.10 Some of Perl's modifying characters.

When added to the end of a regular expression, the **x** modifying character indicates that whitespace characters are to be ignored. This allows programmers to add space characters to their regular expressions for readability without affecting the search. If the expression were written as

```
$search =~ /\b ( \w+ ow ) \b/
```

—that is, without the **x** modifying character—then the script would be searching for a word boundary, two spaces, one or more alphanumeric characters, one space, the characters **ow**, two spaces and a word boundary. The expression would not match **$search**'s value.

The condition on line 25 uses the *memory function* (i.e., parentheses) in a regular expression. The first parenthetical expression matches any string containing one or more alphanumeric characters. The expression **\1** then evaluates to the word that was matched in the first parenthetical expression. The regular expression searches for two identical, consecutive words, separated by a whitespace character (**\s**), in this case "**is is**."

The condition in line 29 searches for words beginning with the letter **t** in the string **$search**. Modifying character **g** indicates a global search—a search that does not stop after the first match is found. The array **@matches** is assigned the value of a list of all matching words.

27.4 Viewing Client/Server Environment Variables

Knowing information about a client's execution environment allows system administrators to provide client-specific information. *Environment variables* contain information about the execution environment in which script is being run, such as the type of Web browser used, the HTTP host and the HTTP connection. A Web server might use this information to generate client-specific Web pages.

Until now, we have written simple Perl applications that output to the local user's screen. Through the use of CGI, we can communicate with the Web server and its clients, allowing us to use the Internet as a method of input and output for our Perl applications. In order to run Perl scripts as CGI applications, a Web server must be installed and configured correctly for your system. See the "Web Server Installation" document at **www.deitel.com** for information on installing and setting up a Web server.

We place our CGI programs in the **cgi-bin** folder. If this directory does not exist, create it in the Web server's root directory. Other important files (such as **.html** files, **.shtml** files, images, etc.) are normally placed in the root directory of the Web server. For additional information, see your Web server's documentation.

In Fig. 27.11, we present our first CGI program. When creating dynamic Web pages in Perl, we output XHTML by using **print** statements. The XHTML generated in this program displays the client's environment variables. The ***use*** *statement* (line 5) instructs Perl programs to include the contents (e.g., functions) of predefined packages called *modules*. The ***CGI*** *module*, for example, contains useful functions for CGI scripting in Perl, including functions that return strings representing XHTML (or HTML) tags and HTTP headers. With the **use** statement, we can specify which functions we would like to import from a particular module. In line 5, we use the *import tag* ***:standard*** to import a predefined set of standard functions. We use several of these functions in the following examples.

Line 11 instructs the Perl script to **print** a valid *HTTP header,* using function ***header*** from the **CGI** library. Browsers use HTTP headers to determine how to handle incoming data. The **header** function returns the string "**Content-type: text/html\n\n**," indicating to the client that what follows is XHTML. The **text/html** portion of the header indicates that the browser must display the returned information as an XHTML document. Standard output is redirected when a CGI script is executed, so the function **print** outputs to the user's Web browser.

On lines 13–14, we begin to write XHTML to the client by using the ***start_html*** function. This function prints the document type definition for this document, as well as several opening XHTML tags (**<html>**, **<head>**, **<title>**, etc., up to the opening **<body>** tag). Notice that certain information is specified within curly braces (**{}**). In many CGI module functions additional information (e.g., attributes) can be specified within curly braces. The **print** statement on lines 13–14 displays the result returned by **start_html**. Each argument within the curly braces is in the form of a *key–value* pair. A *key* (or *value name*) is assigned a value using the *arrow operator* (**=>**), where the key is to the left of the arrow and the value is to the right. The first argument consists of the key **dtd** and the value **$dtd**. When we include the ***dtd*** argument in the function **start_html**, the default document type definition is changed from HTML's DTD to the value of **$dtd**. This adds the proper XHTML DTD to this file, specified in lines 7–9. The ***title*** argument specifies the value that goes between the opening and closing **<title>** tags. In this example, the title of the Web page is set to **"Environment Variables..."**. Note that the order of these key–value pairs is not important.

The function **start_html**, as well as many other Perl functions, can be used in a variety of ways. All of the arguments to **start_html** are optional, and some arguments can be specified differently than how we see in this program. A good way to find correct syntaxes is to consult *Official Guide to Programming with CGI.pm The Standard for Building Web Scripts* by Lincoln Stein (the creator of the **CGI** library). Information about CGI is also available on the Internet. (See the Web resources at the end of this chapter.)

```
1  #!/usr/bin/perl
2  # Fig. 27.11: fig27_11.pl
3  # Program to display CGI environment variables.
4
5  use CGI qw( :standard );
6
7  $dtd =
8  "-//W3C//DTD XHTML 1.0 Transitional//EN\"
9     \"http://www.w3.org/TR/xhtml1/DTD/xhtml1-transitional.dtd";
10
11 print( header() );
12
13 print( start_html( { dtd => $dtd,
14               title => "Environment Variables..." } ) );
15
16 print( "<table style = \"border: 0; padding: 2;
17             font-weight: bold\">" );
18
```

Fig. 27.11 Displaying CGI environment variables (part 1 of 2).

```
19  print( Tr( th( "Variable Name" ),
20             th( "Value" ) ) );
21
22  print( Tr( td( hr() ), td( hr() ) ) );
23
24  foreach $variable ( sort( keys( %ENV ) ) ) {
25
26     print( Tr( td( { style => "background-color: #11bbff" },
27                    $variable ),
28                td( { style => "font-size: 12pt" },
29                           $ENV{ $variable } ) ) );
30
31     print( Tr( td( hr() ), td( hr() ) ) );
32  }
33
34  print( "</table>" );
35  print( end_html() );
```

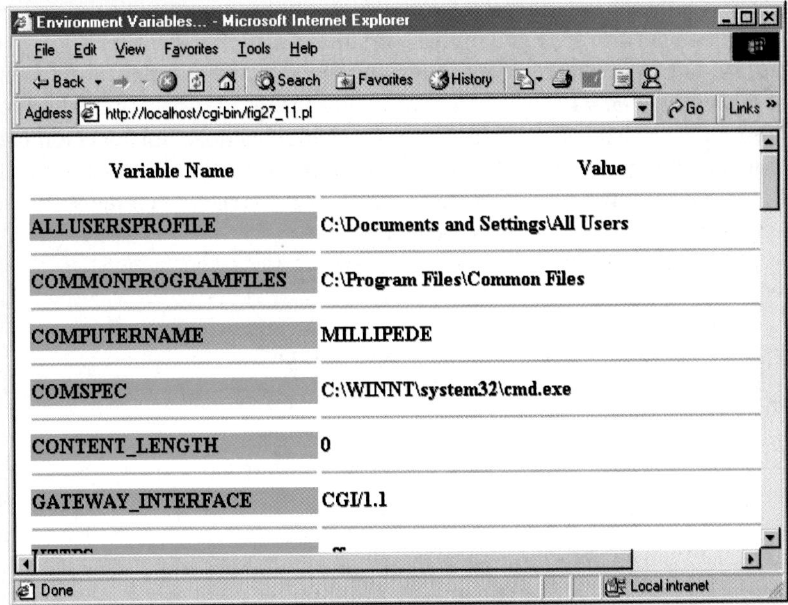

Fig. 27.11 Displaying CGI environment variables (part 2 of 2).

On lines 19–20, we have two more **`CGI.pm`** functions—***`Tr`*** and ***`th`***. These functions place their arguments between table row and table header tags, respectively. The **`print`** statement displays

```
<tr><th>Variable Name</th><th>Value</th></tr>
```

Function **`th`** is called twice, with the arguments **`"Variable Name"`** and **`"Value"`**, causing both of these values to be surrounded by start and end table header tags. [*Note*: This function has a capital "T" because Perl already contains an operator **`tr`**.] We call function **`Tr`** again on line 22 with the ***`hr`*** and ***`td`*** functions, in order to print a row of horizontal rules within **`<td>`** tags.

The **%ENV** *hash* is a built-in table in Perl that contains the names and values of all the environment variables. On lines 24–32, we see a **foreach** structure that uses the **%ENV** hash. The *hash* data type is designated by the **%** character and represents an unordered set of scalar-value pairs. Unlike an array, which accesses elements through integer indices (e.g., **$array[2]**), each element in a hash is accessed using a unique string *key* that is associated with that element's value. For this reason, hashes are also known as *associative arrays*, because the keys and values are associated in pairs. Hash values are accessed using the syntax **$hashName{ keyName }**. In this example, each key in hash **%ENV** is the name of an environment variable name (e.g., **HTTP_HOST**). When this value is used as the key in the **%ENV** hash, that variable's value is returned.

Function ***keys*** returns an unordered array containing all the keys in the **%ENV** hash (line 24), as hash elements have no defined order. We call function ***sort*** to order the array of keys alphabetically. Finally, the **foreach** loop iterates sequentially through the array returned by **sort**, repeatedly assigning the current key's value to scalar **$variable**. Lines 26–31 are executed for each element in the array of key values. In lines 26–29, we output a new row for the table, containing the name of the environment variable (**$variable**) in one column and the value for that variable (**$ENV{ $variable }**) in the next. We call function **td** on line 26 again, using curly-brace notation. This line specifies the value for the attribute **style**. The name of the attribute is specified on the left, followed by its value on the right. When using the **CGI** module functions, this notation is used to specify attribute values. On line 28, we use the hash notation again to specify a **style** attribute. Finally, on line 35, we call the function ***end_html***, which returns the closing tags for the page (**</body>** and **</html>**).

27.5 Form Processing and Business Logic

XHTML forms enable Web pages to collect data from users and send the data to a Web server for processing by server-side programs and scripts. This allows users to purchase products, send and receive Web-based e-mail, participate in a poll, perform online paging or engage in a number of other tasks. This type of Web communication allows users to interact with the server and is vital to Web development.

Figure 27.12 uses an XHTML form to collect information about users before adding them to a mailing list. This type of registration form could be used, by a software company to obtain profile information for a user's company database before allowing the user to download software.

Line 21 contains a **form** element which indicates that, when the user clicks **Register**, the **form** information is **post**ed to the server. The statement **action = "cgi-bin/fig27_13.pl"** directs the server to execute the **fig27_13.pl** Perl script (located in the **cgi-bin** directory) to process the posted form data. We assign a unique name (e.g., **email** on line 33) to each of the form's input fields. When **Register** is clicked, each field's **name** and **value** is sent to the script **fig27_13.pl**, which can then access the submitted value for each specific field.

Good Programming Practice 27.2

Use meaningful XHTML object names for input fields. This practice makes Perl programs easier to understand when processing **form** *data.*

```
<!DOCTYPE html PUBLIC "-//W3C//DTD XHTML 1.0 Transitional//EN"
   "http://www.w3.org/TR/xhtml1/DTD/xhtml1-transitional.dtd">

<!-- Fig. 27.12: fig27_12.html -->

<html>
   <head>
      <title>Sample form to take user input in XHTML</title>
   </head>

   <body style = "font-face: arial; font-size: 12pt">

      <div style = "font-size: 14pt; font-weight: bold">
         This is a sample registration form.
      </div>

      <br />
      Please fill in all fields and click Register.

      <form method = "post" action = "/cgi-bin/fig27_13.pl">

         <img src = "images/user.gif" /><br />

         <div style = "color: blue" >
            Please fill out the fields below.<br />
         </div>

         <img src = "images/fname.gif" />
         <input type = "text" name = "fname" /><br />
         <img src = "images/lname.gif" />
         <input type = "text" name = "lname" /><br />
         <img src = "images/email.gif" />
         <input type = "text" name = "email" /><br />
         <img src = "images/phone.gif" />
         <input type = "text" name = "phone" /><br />

         <div style = "font-size: 10pt">
            Must be in the form (555)555-5555.<br /><br />
         </div>

         <img src = "images/downloads.gif" /><br />
         <div style = "color: blue">
            Which book would you like information about?<br />
         </div>

         <select name = "book">
            <option>Internet and WWW How to Program 2e</option>
            <option>C++ How to Program 3e</option>
            <option>Java How to Program 4e</option>
            <option>XML How to Program 1e</option>
         </select><br /><br />

         <img src = "images/os.gif" /><br />
```

Fig. 27.12 XHTML document with an interactive form (part 1 of 2).

```
         <div style = "color: blue">
            Which operating system are you currently using?
         </div><br />

         <input type = "radio" name = "os"
            value = "Windows NT" checked />
         Windows NT<input type = "radio"
            name = "os" value = "Windows 2000" />
         Windows 2000<input type = "radio"
            name = "os" value = "Windows 98/me" />
         Windows 98/me<br /><input type = "radio"
            name = "os" value = "Linux" />
         Linux<input type = "radio" name = "os"
            value = "Other" />
         Other<br /><input type = "submit"
            value = "Register" />
      </form>
   </body>
</html>
```

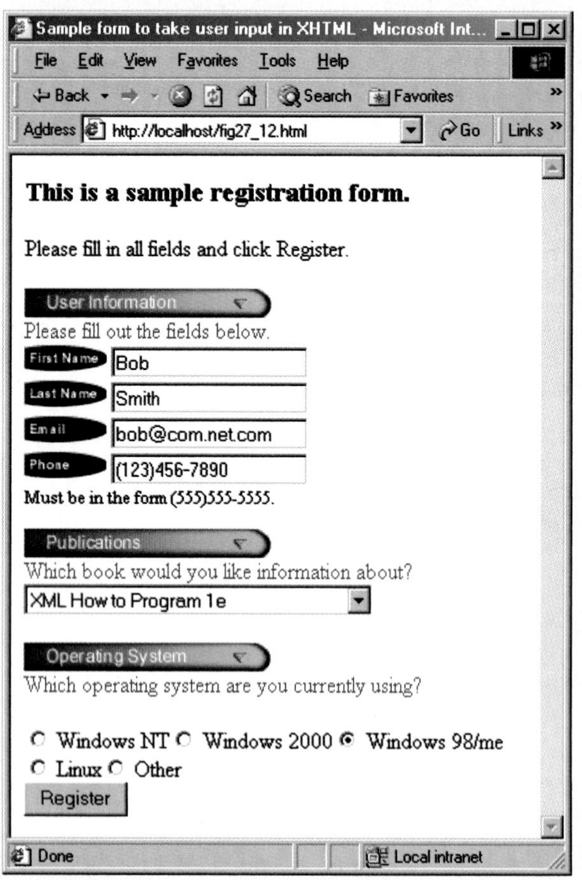

Fig. 27.12 XHTML document with an interactive form (part 2 of 2).

The program in Fig. 27.13 processes the data posted by **`fig27_12.html`** and sends a Web page response back to the client. Function ***`param`*** (lines 8–13) is part of the Perl **`CGI`** module and retrieves values from a form field's value. For example, in line 35 of the previous figure (Fig. 27.12), an XHTML form text field is created with the name **`phone`**. In line 12 of Fig. 27.13, we access the value that the user entered for that field by calling **`param( "phone" )`** and assign the value returned to variable **`$phone`**.

In line 24, we determine whether the phone number entered by the user is valid. In this case, *(555)555-5555* is the only acceptable format. Validating information is crucial when you are maintaining a database, and a great way to do this is using regular expressions. Validation ensures that data is stored in the proper format in a database, that credit-card numbers contain the proper number of digits before encrypting them for submission to a merchant, etc. The design of verifying information is called *business logic*, or *business rules*.

The **`if`** condition in line 24 uses a regular expression to validate the phone number. The expression "**`\(`**" matches the opening parenthesis of the phone number. Because we want to match the literal character **`(`**, we must escape its normal meaning by using the **`\`** character. This sequence must be followed by three digits (**`\d{3}`**), a closing parenthesis, three digits, a hyphen and finally, four more digits. Note that we use the **`^`** and **`$`** metacharacters to ensure that there are no extra characters at the beginning or end of the string.

If the regular expression is matched, then the phone number is valid, and a Web page is sent, thanking the user for completing the form. If the user posts an invalid phone number, the ***`else`*** (lines 63–76) is executed, instructing the user to enter a valid phone number.

```
1  #!/usr/bin/perl
2  # Fig. 27.13: fig27_13.pl
3  # Program to read information sent to the server
4  # from the form in the fig27_12.html document.
5
6  use CGI qw( :standard );
7
8  $os = param( "os" );
9  $firstName = param( "fname" );
10 $lastName = param( "lname" );
11 $email = param( "email" );
12 $phone = param( "phone" );
13 $book = param( "book" );
14
15 $dtd =
16 "-//W3C//DTD XHTML 1.0 Transitional//EN\"
17    \"http://www.w3.org/TR/xhtml1/DTD/xhtml1-transitional.dtd";
18
19 print( header() );
20
21 print( start_html( { dtd => $dtd,
22                      title => "Form Results" } ) );
23
24 if ( $phone =~ / ^ \( \d{3} \) \d{3} - \d{4} $ /x ) {
25    print( "Hi " );
26    print( span( { style => "color: blue; font-weight: bold" },
27                 $firstName ) );
```

Fig. 27.13 Script to process user data from **`fig27_12.html`** (part 1 of 3).

```
   print( "!" );

   print( "\nThank you for completing the survey." );
   print( br(), "You have been added to the " );

   print( span( { style => "color: blue; font-weight: bold" },
                  $book ) );
   print( " mailing list.", br(), br() );

   print( span( { style => "font-weight: bold" },
                 "The following information has
                  been saved in our database: " ), br() );

   print( table(
          Tr( th( { style => "background-color: #ee82ee" },
                      "Name" ),
              th( { style => "background-color: #9370db" },
                      "E-mail" ),
              th( { style => "background-color: #4169e1" },
                      "Phone" ),
              th( { style => "background-color: #40e0d0" },
                      "OS" ) ),

          Tr( { style => "background-color: #c0c0c0" },
              td( "$firstName $lastName" ),
              td( $email ),
              td( $phone ),
              td( $os ) ) ) );

   print( br() );

   print( div( { style => "font-size: x-small" },
            "This is only a sample form. You have not been
             added to a mailing list." ) );
}
else {
   print( div( { style => "color: red; font-size: x-large" },
             "INVALID PHONE NUMBER" ), br() );

   print( "A valid phone number must be in the form " );
   print( span( { style => "font-weight: bold" },
                  "(555)555-5555." ) );

   print( div( { style => "color: blue" },
             "Click the Back button, and enter a
              valid phone number and resubmit." ) );
   print( br(), br() );
   print( "Thank you." );
}

print( end_html() );
```

Fig. 27.13 Script to process user data from **fig27_12.html** (part 2 of 3).

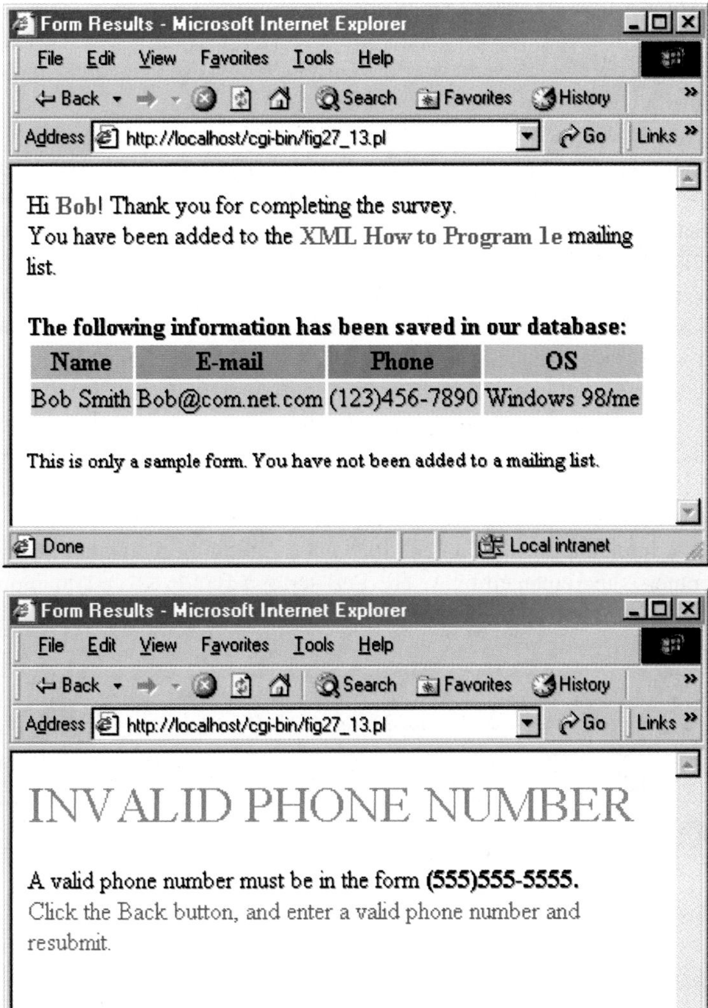

Fig. 27.13 Script to process user data from `fig27_12.html` (part 3 of 3).

Good Programming Practice 27.3

Use business logic to ensure that invalid information is not stored in a database.

The ***br*** function (line 31) adds a break (**`<br />`**) to the XHTML page, while methods ***span*** (line 26) and ***div*** (line 59) add **`<span>`** and **`<div>`** tags to the page, respectively.

27.6 Server-Side Includes

Dynamic content greatly improves the look and feel of a Web page. Pages that include the current date or time, rotating banners or advertisements, a daily message, special offer or company news are attractive, because they are current. Clients see new information on every visit and thus will likely revisit the site in the future.

Server-Side Includes (SSIs) are commands embedded in XHTML documents to allow the creation of simple dynamic content. SSI commands like ***ECHO*** and ***INCLUDE*** enable the inclusion on Web pages of content that is constantly changing (i.e., the current time) or information that is stored in a database. The command ***EXEC*** can be used to run CGI scripts and embed their output directly into a Web page.

Not all Web servers support the available SSI commands. Therefore, SSI commands are written as XHTML comments (e.g., **<!--#ECHO VAR="DOCUMENT_NAME" -->**). Servers that do not recognize these commands treat them as comments. Some servers do support SSI commands, but only if the servers are configured to do so. Check your server's documentation to configure your server appropriately.

A document containing SSI commands is typically given the ***.shtml*** file extension (the **s** at the front of the extension stands for *server*). The **.shtml** files are parsed by the server. The server executes the SSI commands and writes output to the client.

Figure 27.14 implements a *Web page hit counter*. Each time a client requests the document, the counter is incremented by 1. The Perl script **fig27_15.pl** manipulates the counter.

Performance Tip 27.1

Parsing XHTML documents on a server can dramatically increase the load on that server. To increase the performance of a heavily loaded server, try to limit the use of Server Side Includes.

```
<!DOCTYPE html PUBLIC "-//W3C//DTD XHTML 1.0 Strict//EN"
   "http://www.w3.org/TR/xhtml1/DTD/xhtml1-strict.dtd">

<!-- Fig. 27.14: fig27_14.shtml -->

<html>
   <head>
      <title>Using Server Side Includes</title>
   </head>

   <body>
      <h3 style = "text-align: center">
         Using Server Side Includes
      </h3>

      <!--#EXEC CGI="/cgi-bin/fig27_15.pl" --><br />

      The Greenwich Mean Time is
      <span style = "color: blue">
         <!--#ECHO VAR="DATE_GMT" -->.
```

Fig. 27.14 Incorporating a Web-page hit counter and displaying environment variables, using server-side includes (part 1 of 3).

```
         </span><br />

         The name of this document is
         <span style = "color: blue">
            <!--#ECHO VAR="DOCUMENT_NAME" -->.
         </span><br />

         The local date is
         <span style = "color: blue">
            <!--#ECHO VAR="DATE_LOCAL" -->.
         </span><br />

         This document was last modified on
         <span style = "color: blue">
            <!--#ECHO VAR="LAST_MODIFIED" -->.
         </span><br />

         Your current IP Address is
         <span style = "color: blue">
            <!--#ECHO VAR="REMOTE_ADDR" -->.
         </span><br />

         My server name is
         <span style = "color: blue">
            <!--#ECHO VAR="SERVER_NAME" -->.
         </span><br />

         And I am using the
         <span style = "color: blue">
            <!--#ECHO VAR="SERVER_SOFTWARE" -->
            Web Server.
         </span><br />

         You are using
         <span style = "color: blue">
            <!--#ECHO VAR="HTTP_USER_AGENT" -->.
         </span><br />

         This server is using
         <span style = "color: blue">
            <!--#ECHO VAR="GATEWAY_INTERFACE" -->.
         </span><br />

         <br /><br />
         <div style = "text-align: center;
                       font-size: xx-small">
            <hr />
            This document was last modified on
            <!--#ECHO VAR="LAST_MODIFIED" -->.
         </div>
      </body>
   </html>
```

Fig. 27.14 Incorporating a Web-page hit counter and displaying environment variables, using server-side includes (part 2 of 3).

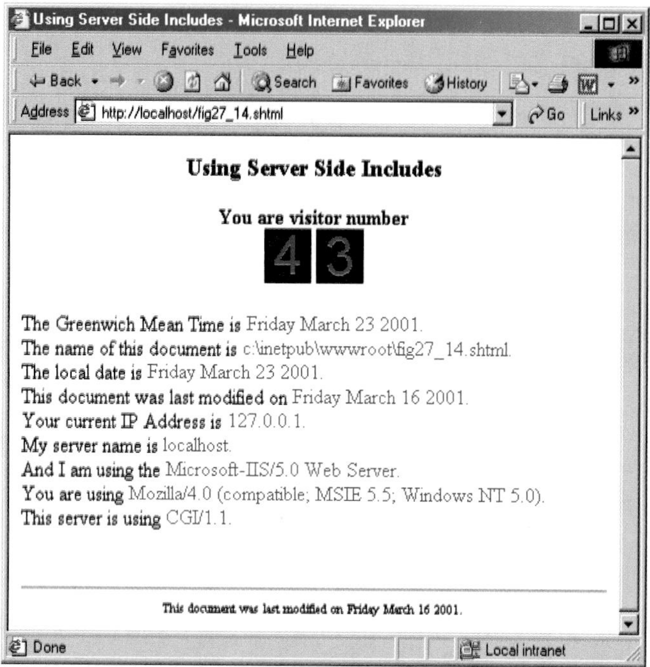

Fig. 27.14 Incorporating a Web-page hit counter and displaying environment variables, using server-side includes (part 3 of 3).

Line 16 of the **fig27_14.shtml** script executes the **fig27_15.pl** script, using the **EXEC** command. Before the XHTML document is sent to the client, the SSI command is executed, and any script output is sent to the client. This technique can increase the load on the server tremendously, depending on how many times the script has to be parsed and the size and workload of the scripts.

Line 20 uses the ***ECHO*** *command* to display variable information. The **ECHO** command is followed by the *keyword* **VAR** and the name of the variable. For example, *variable* ***DATE_GMT*** contains the current date and time in Greenwich Mean Time (GMT). In line 25, the name of the current document is included in the XHTML page with the ***DOCUMENT_NAME*** *variable*. The ***DATE_LOCAL*** *variable* inserts the date on line 30 in local format—different formats are used around the world.

Figure 27.15 (**fig27_15.pl**) introduces file input and output in Perl. Line 8 opens (for input) the file **counter.dat**, which contains the number of hits to date for the **fig27_14.shtml** Web page. Function ***open*** is called to create a *filehandle* to refer to the file during the execution of the script. In this example, the file opened is assigned a filehandle named **COUNTREAD**.

```
1  #!/usr/bin/perl
2  # Fig. 27.15: fig27_15.pl
3  # Program to track the number of times
```

Fig. 27.15 Perl script for counting Web page hits (part 1 of 2).

```
4   # a Web page has been accessed.
5
6   use CGI qw( :standard );
7
8   open( COUNTREAD, "counter.dat" );
9   $data = <COUNTREAD>;
10  $data++;
11  close( COUNTREAD );
12
13  open( COUNTWRITE, ">counter.dat" );
14  print( COUNTWRITE $data );
15  close( COUNTWRITE );
16
17  print( header(), "<div style = \"text-align: center;
18                          font-weight: bold\">" );
19  print( "You are visitor number", br() );
20
21  for ( $count = 0; $count < length( $data ); $count++ ) {
22     $number = substr( $data, $count, 1 );
23     print( img( { src => "images/$number.gif" } ), "\n" );
24  }
25
26  print( "</div>" );
```

Fig. 27.15 Perl script for counting Web page hits (part 2 of 2).

Line 9 uses the *diamond operator*, **<>**, to read one line of the file referred to by filehandle **COUNTREAD** and assign it to the variable **$data**. When the diamond operator is used in a scalar context, only one line is read. If assigned to an array, each line from the file is assigned to a successive element of the array. Because the file **counter.dat** contains only one line (in this case, only one number), the variable **$data** is assigned the value of that number in line 9. Line 10 then increments **$data** by 1. If the file does not yet exist when we try to open it, **$data** is assigned the value **undef**, which will be evaluated as 0 and incremented to 1 on line 10.

Now that the counter has been incremented for this hit, we write the counter back to the **counter.dat** file. In line 13 we open the **counter.dat** file for writing by preceding the file name with a **>** *character* (this is called *write mode*). This immediately truncates (i.e., discards) any data in that file. If the file does not exist, Perl creates a new file with the specified name. Perl also provides an *append mode* (**>>**) for appending to the end of a file. The first argument (**COUNTWRITE**) specifies the *filehandle*, which will be used to refer to the file.

After line 13 is executed, data can be written to the file **counter.dat**. Line 14 writes the counter number back to the file **counter.dat**. The first argument to **print** indicates the filehandle that refers to the file where data are written. If no filehandle is specified, **print** writes to standard out (**STDOUT**). Notice that we need to use a space, rather than a comma, to separate the filehandle from the data. In line 15, the connection to **counter.dat** is terminated by calling function ***close***.

Lines 21–24 use a ***for*** structure to iterate through each digit of the number scalar **$data**. The **for** structure syntax consists of three semicolon-separated statements in parentheses, followed by a body delimited by curly braces. In our example, we iterate until

$count is equal to **length($data)**. Function ***length*** returns the length of a character string, so the **for** iterates once for each digit in the variable **$data**. For instance, if **$data** stores the value **"32"**, then the **for** structure iterates twice, first to process the value **"3"**, and second to process the value **"2"**. In the first iteration, **$count** equals 0 (as initialized on line 21), and the second time **$count** will equal 1. This is because the value of **$count** will be incremented for each loop (as specified by the statement **$count++**, also on line 21). For each iteration, we obtain the current digit by calling function ***substr***. The first parameter passed to function **substr** specifies the string from which to obtain a substring. The second parameter specifies the offset, in characters, from the beginning of the string, so an offset of 0 returns the first character, 1 returns the second and so forth. The third argument specifies the length of the substring to be obtained (one character in this case). The **for** structure then assigns each digit (possibly from a multiple-digit number) to the scalar variable **$number**. Each digit's corresponding image is displayed using the ***img*** function (line 23).

Good Programming Practice 27.4

When opening a text file to read its contents, open the file in read-only mode. Opening the file in other modes increases the risk of overwriting the data accidentally.

Good Programming Practice 27.5

Always close files as soon as you are finished using them.

It is important in this example to think about file permissions and security. This program may not run correctly if the user's default settings do not allow scripts to manipulate files. In order to resolve this issue, the user can change the permissions in the folder where **counter.dat** resides, so that all users have **Write** access. However, the user should be aware that this poses a security risk to the system. Security details are covered in Chapter 32.

27.7 Verifying a Username and Password

It is often desirable to have a *private Web site*—one that is visible only to certain people. Implementing privacy generally involves username and password verification. Figure 27.16 is an XHTML form that queries the user for a username and a password. It posts the fields **username** and **password** to the Perl script **fig27_17.pl** upon submission of the form. Note that for simplicity, this example does not encrypt the data before sending them to the server.

The script **fig27_17.pl** (Fig. 27.17) is responsible for verifying the username and password of the client by crosschecking against values from a database. The database list of valid users and their passwords is a simple text file: **password.txt** (Fig. 27.18).

On line 14 of **fig27_17.pl**, we open the file **password.txt** for reading and assign it to the filehandle **FILE**. To verify that the file was opened successfully, a test is performed using the *logical OR operator* (***or***). Operator **or** returns true if either the left condition or the right condition evaluates to true. If the condition on the left evaluates to true, then the condition on the right is not evaluated. In this case, the function ***die*** executes only if **open** returns false, indicating that the file did not open properly. Function **die** displays an error message and terminates program execution.

```
<!DOCTYPE html PUBLIC "-//W3C//DTD XHTML 1.0 Strict//EN"
   "http://www.w3.org/TR/xhtml11/DTD/xhtml11-strict.dtd">

<!-- Fig. 27.16: fig27_16.html -->

<html>
   <head>
      <title>Verifying a username and a password</title>
   </head>

   <body>
      <p>
         <div style = "font-family = arial">
            Type in your username and password below.
         </div><br />

         <div style = "color: #0000ff; font-family: arial;
                       font-weight: bold; font-size: x-small">
            Note that the password will be sent as plain text.
         </div>
      </p>

      <form action = "/cgi-bin/fig27_17.pl" method = "post">

         <table style = "background-color: #dddddd">
            <tr>
               <td style = "font-face: arial;
                            font-weight: bold">Username:</td>
            </tr>
            <tr>
               <td>
                  <input name = "username" />
               </td>
            </tr>
            <tr>
               <td style = "font-face: arial;
                            font-weight: bold">Password:</td>
            </tr>
            <tr>
               <td>
                  <input name = "password" type = "password" />
               </td>
            </tr>
            <tr>
               <td>
                  <input type = "submit" value = "Enter" />
               </td>
            </tr>
         </table>
      </form>
   </body>
</html>
```

Fig. 27.16 Entering a username and password (part 1 of 2).

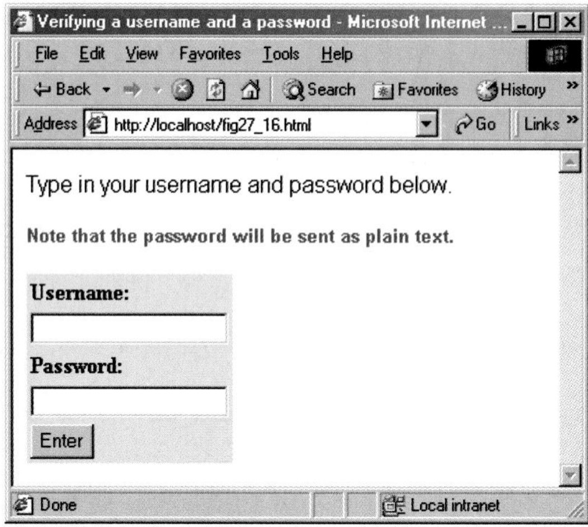

Fig. 27.16 Entering a username and password (part 2 of 2).

Good Programming Practice 27.6

Function **`die`** *can be useful to handle situations in which a program cannot continue. Rather than resulting in program errors, function* **`die`** *will cause the program to end with a message explaining the situation to the user.*

The **`while`** structure (lines 17–29) repeatedly executes the code enclosed in curly braces until the condition in parentheses evaluates to false. In this case, the test condition assigns the next unread line of **`password.txt`** to **`$line`** and evaluates to true as long as a line from the file was successfully read. When the end of the file is reached, **`<FILE>`** returns false and the loop terminates.

```
1  #!/usr/bin/perl
2  # Fig. 27.17: fig27_17.pl
3  # Program to search a database for usernames and passwords.
4
5  use CGI qw( :standard );
6
7  $dtd =
8  "-//W3C//DTD XHTML 1.0 Transitional//EN\"
9     \"http://www.w3.org/TR/xhtml1/DTD/xhtml1-transitional.dtd";
10
11 $testUsername = param( "username" );
12 $testPassword = param( "password" );
13
14 open( FILE, "password.txt" ) or
15    die( "The database could not be opened." );
16
17 while ( $line = <FILE> ) {
18    chomp( $line );
```

Fig. 27.17 Program to analyze the username and password entered into an XHTML form (part 1 of 3).

```
   ( $username, $password ) = split( ",", $line );

   if ( $testUsername eq $username ) {
      $userVerified = 1;

      if ( $testPassword eq $password ) {
         $passwordVerified = 1;
         last;
      }
   }
}

close( FILE );

print( header() );
print( start_html( { dtd => $dtd,
                     title => "Password Analyzed" } ) );

if ( $userVerified && $passwordVerified ) {
   accessGranted();
}
elsif ( $userVerified && !$passwordVerified ) {
   wrongPassword();
}
else {
   accessDenied();
}

print( end_html() );

sub accessGranted
{
   print( div( { style => "font-face: arial;
                           color: blue;
                           font-weight: bold" },
        "Permission has been granted,
        $username.", br(), "Enjoy the site." ) );
}

sub wrongPassword
{
   print( div( { style => "font-face: arial;
                           color: red;
                           font-weight: bold" },
       "You entered an invalid password.", br(),
       "Access has been denied." ) );
}

sub accessDenied
{
   print( div( { style => "font-face: arial;
                           color: red;
```

Fig. 27.17 Program to analyze the username and password entered into an XHTML form (part 2 of 3).

```
71                                       font-size: larger;
72                                       font-weight: bold" },
73            "You have been denied access to this site." ) );
74   }
```

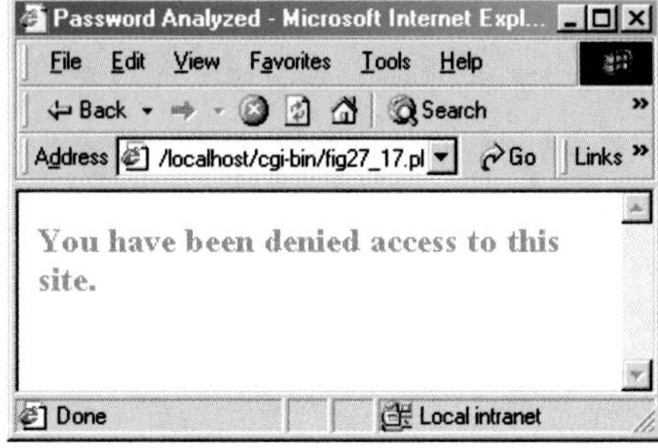

Fig. 27.17 Program to analyze the username and password entered into an XHTML form (part 3 of 3).

```
account1,password1
account2,password2
account3,password3
account4,password4
account5,password5
account6,password6
account7,password7
account8,password8
account9,password9
account10,password10
```

Fig. 27.18 Database **password.txt** containing usernames and passwords.

Each line in **password.txt** (Fig. 27.18) consists of an account name and password pair, separated by a comma, and followed by a newline character. For each line read, function ***chomp*** is called (line 18) to remove the newline character at the end of the line. Then ***split*** is called to divide the string into substrings at the specified separator or *delimiter* (in this case, a comma). For example, the **split** of the first line in **password.txt** returns the list **("account1", "password1")**. The syntax

```
( $username, $password ) = split( ",", $line );
```

sets **$username** and **$password** to the first and second elements returned by **split** (**account1** and **password1**), respectively.

If the username entered is equivalent to the one we have read from the text file, the conditional in line 21 returns true. The **$userVerified** variable is then set to **1**. Next, the value of **$testPassword** is tested against the value in the **$password** variable (line 24). If the password matches, the **$passwordVerified** variable is set to **1**. In this case, because a successful username–password match has been found, the ***last*** statement, used to exit a repetition structure prematurely, allows us to exit the **while** loop immediately in line 26.

We are finished reading from **password.txt**, and we **close** the file on line 31. Line 37 checks if both the username and password were verified, by using the Perl *logical AND operator* (***&&***). If both conditions are true (that is, if both variables evaluate to nonzero values), then the function **accessGranted** is called (lines 49–56), which sends a Web page to the client, indicating a successful login.

If the **if** statement evaluates to false, the condition in the following **elsif** statement is tested. Line 40 tests if the user was verified, but the password was not. In this case, the function **wrongPassword** is called (lines 58–65). The unary *logical negation operator* (***!***) is used in line 40 to negate the value of **$passwordVerified** and test if it is false. If the user is not recognized, function **accessDenied** is called, and a message indicating that permission has been denied is sent to the client (lines 67–74).

Perl allows programmers to define their own *functions* or *subroutines*. Keyword **sub** begins a function definition, and curly braces delimit the function body (lines 49, 58 and 67). To call a function (i.e., to execute the code within the function definition), use the function's name, followed by a pair of parentheses (line 38, 41 and 44).

27.8 Using DBI to Connect to a Database

Database connectivity allows system administrators to maintain information on user accounts, passwords, credit-card information, mailing lists, product inventory, etc. Databases allow companies to enter the world of electronic commerce and maintain crucial data.

In order to access various relational databases in Perl, we need an interface (in the form of software) that allows us to connect to and execute SQL statements (queries). The *Perl DBI* (*Database Interface*) allows us to do this. This interface was created to access different types of databases uniformly. In this section, we access and manipulate a MySQL database. The examples in this section require that MySQL (**www.mysql.org**) be installed. The Perl ***DBI*** module and the MySQL driver, ***DBD::mysql*** (specified on lines 6–7 of Fig. 27.19), are also required.

If you are using ActiveState Perl, you can download these files using the *Perl Package Manager* (PPM), which is part of ActiveState Perl. Using PPM, you can download and install Perl modules and packages (provided that you are connected to the Internet at the time you are running the program). To use PPM, type **ppm** at the command prompt. This command starts the package manager in *interactive mode*, providing you with the **ppm>** prompt. Type **install DBI** and press *Return* to install DBI. To install the MySQL driver, type **install DBD::mysql** and press *Return*.

If you do not have the Perl Package Manager, you can search for the module or package on *CPAN*, the *Comprehensive Perl Archive Network* (**www.cpan.org**). Finally, you will need to use the database **books**. This database is located in the Chapter 27 examples directory on the CD-ROM that accompanies this book. The examples directory contains a subfolder named **books**, which contains all the database files. In your **mysql** directory, there is a **data** directory that contains MySQL databases. Each folder is a database and contains all the files that comprise that database. Copy the **books** folder into this **data** directory.

In Fig. 27.19, the client selects an author from a drop-down list (the authors are numbered according to their ID value). When **Get Info** is clicked, the chosen author and the author's ID are posted to the Perl script in Fig. 27.20 that queries the database for all books published by that author. The results are displayed in an XHTML table. To create and execute SQL queries, we create DBI objects known as *handles*. *Database handles* create and manipulate a connection to a database, while *statement handles* create and manipulate SQL statements (queries) to a database.

```
#!/usr/bin/perl
# Fig. 27.19: fig27_19.pl
# CGI program that generates a list of authors.

use CGI qw( :standard );
use DBI;
use DBD::mysql;

$dtd =
"-//W3C//DTD XHTML 1.0 Transitional//EN\"
   \"http://www.w3.org/TR/xhtml1/DTD/xhtml1-transitional.dtd";

print( header() );

print( start_html( { dtd => $dtd,
                     title => "Authors" } ) );

# connect to "books" database, no password needed
$databaseHandle = DBI->connect( "DBI:mysql:books",
                     "root", "", { RaiseError => 1 } );

# retrieve the names and IDs of all authors
$query = "SELECT FirstName, LastName, AuthorID
             FROM Authors ORDER BY LastName";

# prepare the query for execution, then execute it
# a prepared query can be executed multiple times
$statementHandle = $databaseHandle->prepare( $query );
$statementHandle->execute();

print( h2( "Choose an author:" ) );

print( start_form( { action => 'fig27_20.pl' } ) );

```

Fig. 27.19 Perl script that queries a MySQL database for authors (part 1 of 2).

```
35  print( "<select name = \"author\">\n" );
36
37  # drop-down list contains the author and ID number
38  # method fetchrow_array returns a single row from the result
39  while ( @row = $statementHandle->fetchrow_array() ) {
40     print( "<option>" );
41     print( "$row[ 2 ]. $row[ 1 ], $row[ 0 ]" );
42     print( "</option>" );
43  }
44
45  print( "</select>\n" );
46
47  print( submit( { value => 'Get Info' } ) );
48  print( end_form(), end_html() );
49
50  # clean up -- close the statement and database handles
51  $databaseHandle->disconnect();
52  $statementHandle->finish();
```

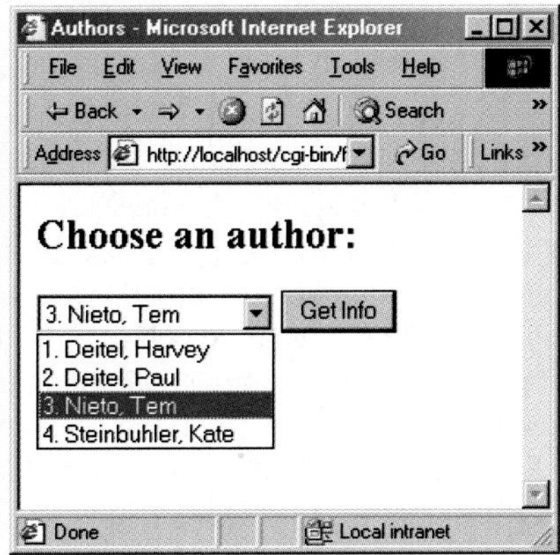

Fig. 27.19 Perl script that queries a MySQL database for authors (part 2 of 2).

On lines 19–20, we connect to the database by calling **`DBI`** method ***`connect`***. The first argument specifies the data source (i.e., the database). Notice that we first specify the interface name (**`DBI`**), followed by a colon (**`:`**), then the database driver (**`mysql`**), followed by another colon and the name of the data source (**`books`**). The second argument specifies the user, and the third argument specifies the password for the database. This database does not require a username or password, so we simply use the empty string (**`""`**). The fourth argument (**`{ RaiseError => 1 }`**) is used for error checking. If an error occurs when trying to connect to the database, function **`die`** is called and passed an error message. Setting this hash reference to **`1`** is like setting a variable to true—this value "turns on" the error checking, saving the programmer from writing extra code to handle this problem or from having the program crash unexpectedly. If the connection succeeds, function **`connect`** returns a database handle that is assigned to **`$databaseHandle`**.

In this example, we query the database for the names and IDs of the authors. We create this query on lines 23–24. On line 28, we use our database handle to prepare the query (using the method ***prepare***). This method prepares the database driver for a statement, which can be executed multiple times. The statement handle returned is assigned to **$statementHandle**. We execute the query by calling method ***execute*** on line 29.

Once the query has been executed, we can access the results by calling method ***fetchrow_array*** (line 39). Each call to this function returns the next set of data in the resulting table until there are no data sets left. A data set, or row in the resulting table, contains one of the elements that satisfied the query. For example, in the first program, a query was executed that returned the ID and name of each author. This query created a table that contained two columns, one for the author's ID and one for the author's name. A row contained the ID and name of a specific author. Each row was returned as an array and assigned to **@row**. We **print** these values as list options on lines 40–42. The option chosen is sent as the parameter **"author"** (line 35) to the Perl script in Fig. 27.20. On lines 51–52,we close the database connection (using method ***disconnect***), and we specify that we are finished with this query by calling method ***finish***. This function closes the statement handle and frees memory, especially if the resulting table was large.

Look-and-Feel Observation 27.1

Using tables to output fields in a database neatly organizes information into rows and columns.

Figure 27.20 presents the script **fig27_20.pl**, which takes the specified author and queries the database for information about that author.

This program creates an XHTML page that displays the title of each book written by the current author, along with the ISBN number and book publisher. In order to obtain this information, we need the author's ID number, because the **AuthorISBN** table contains a field for the author's ID, not the author's name. Recall that the author's ID was posted to this script by **fig27_19.pl**. The ID is the numerical value that precedes the author's name in the **author** parameter. To retrieve the ID and author name, we call method **substr** on lines 16–17. This statement returns the first character in the string (an offset of zero indicates the beginning of the string), which contains the ID value. On line 17, we specify an offset of three, because the author's name begins after the third character. Notice that in this call we do not specify a length, because we want all characters from the offset to the end of the string, inclusive.

```
1  #!/usr/bin/perl
2  # Fig. 27.20: fig27_20.pl
3  # CGI program to query a MySQL database.
4
5  use CGI qw( :standard );
6  use DBI;
7  use DBD::mysql;
8
9  $dtd =
10 "-//W3C//DTD XHTML 1.0 Transitional//EN\"
11    \"http://www.w3.org/TR/xhtml1/DTD/xhtml1-transitional.dtd";
12
13 print( header() );
```

Fig. 27.20 Perl script that queries a MySQL database for author information (part 1 of 3).

```

# retrieve author's ID and name from the posted form
$authorID = substr( param( "author" ), 0, 1 );
$authorName = substr( param( "author" ), 3 );

print( start_html( { dtd => $dtd,
                     title => "Books by $authorName" } ) );

$databaseHandle = DBI->connect( "DBI:mysql:books",
                     "root", "", { RaiseError => 1 } );

# use AuthorID to find all the ISBNs related to this author
$query1 = "SELECT ISBN FROM AuthorISBN
          WHERE AuthorID = $authorID";

$statementHandle1 = $databaseHandle->prepare( $query1 );
$statementHandle1->execute();

print( h2( "$authorName" ) );

print( "<table border = 1>" );
print( th( "Title" ), th( "ISBN" ), th( "Publisher" ) );

while ( @isbn = $statementHandle1->fetchrow_array() ) {
   print( "<tr>\n" );

   # use ISBN to find the corresponding title
   $query2 = "SELECT Title, PublisherID FROM titles
             WHERE ISBN = \'$isbn[ 0 ]\'";
   $statementHandle2 = $databaseHandle->prepare( $query2 );
   $statementHandle2->execute();
   @title_publisherID = $statementHandle2->fetchrow_array();

   # use PublisherID to find the corresponding PublisherName
   $query3 = "SELECT PublisherName FROM Publishers
             WHERE PublisherID = \'$title_publisherID[ 1 ]\'";

   $statementHandle3 = $databaseHandle->prepare( $query3 );
   $statementHandle3->execute();
   @publisher = $statementHandle3->fetchrow_array();


   # print resulting values
   print( td( $title_publisherID[ 0 ] ), "\n" );
   print( td( $isbn[ 0 ] ), "\n" );
   print( td( $publisher[ 0 ] ), "\n" );

   print( "</tr>" );

   $statementHandle2->finish();
   $statementHandle3->finish();
}

```

Fig. 27.20 Perl script that queries a MySQL database for author information (part 2 of 3).

```
67  print( "</table>" );
68
69  print( end_html() );
70
71  $databaseHandle->disconnect();
72  $statementHandle1->finish();
```

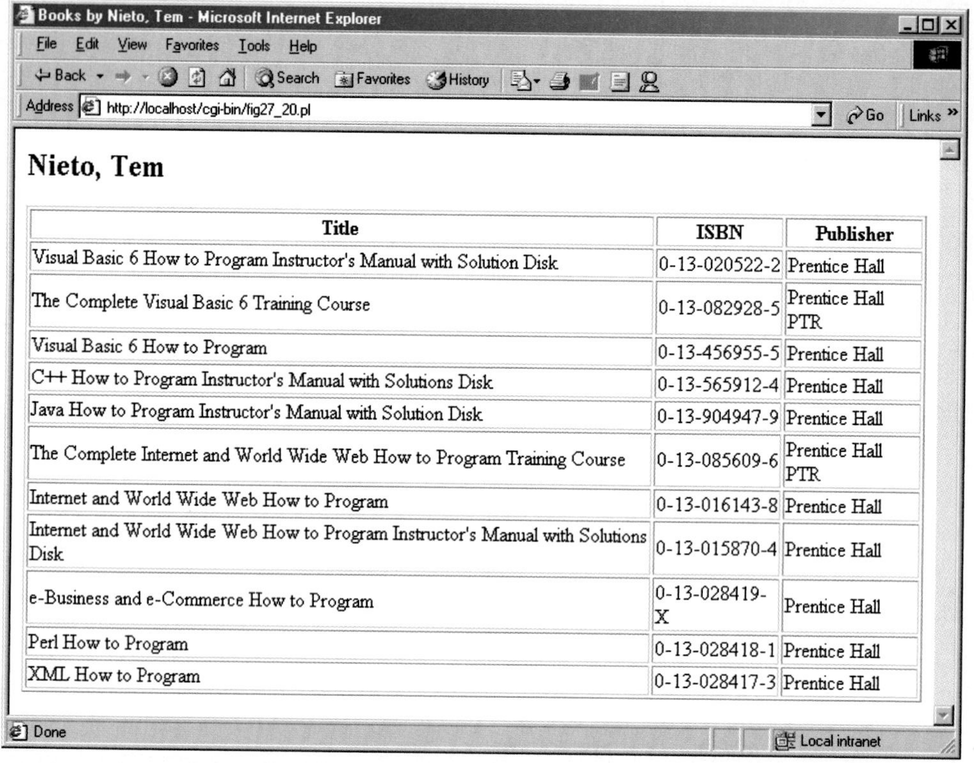

Title	ISBN	Publisher
Visual Basic 6 How to Program Instructor's Manual with Solution Disk	0-13-020522-2	Prentice Hall
The Complete Visual Basic 6 Training Course	0-13-082928-5	Prentice Hall PTR
Visual Basic 6 How to Program	0-13-456955-5	Prentice Hall
C++ How to Program Instructor's Manual with Solutions Disk	0-13-565912-4	Prentice Hall
Java How to Program Instructor's Manual with Solution Disk	0-13-904947-9	Prentice Hall
The Complete Internet and World Wide Web How to Program Training Course	0-13-085609-6	Prentice Hall PTR
Internet and World Wide Web How to Program	0-13-016143-8	Prentice Hall
Internet and World Wide Web How to Program Instructor's Manual with Solutions Disk	0-13-015870-4	Prentice Hall
e-Business and e-Commerce How to Program	0-13-028419-X	Prentice Hall
Perl How to Program	0-13-028418-1	Prentice Hall
XML How to Program	0-13-028417-3	Prentice Hall

Fig. 27.20 Perl script that queries a MySQL database for author information (part 3 of 3).

After connecting to the database, we specify and execute our first query, on lines 26–30. This query returns all the ISBN numbers for the specified author. We place these values in a table. On line 37, we begin a **`while`** loop that iterates through each row matched by the query. The rows are retrieved by calling **`fetchrow_array`**, which returns the current data set as an array. When there are no more data sets to return, the condition evaluates to false. Within the loop, we use the ISBNs to obtain the title and publisher values for the current table row. The query on lines 41–45 uses the ISBN value to determine the book's title and the publisher's ID number. The next query (lines 48–53) uses the publisher's ID to determine the name of the publisher. These values are **`print`**ed on lines 57–59.

27.9 Cookies and Perl

Cookies maintain *state information* for a particular client who uses a Web browser. Preserving this information allows data and settings to be retained even after the execution of a CGI script has ended. Cookies are used to record user preferences (or other information) for the next time a client visits a Web site. For example, many Web sites use cookies to store a client's postal zip code. The zip code is used when the client requests a Web page to send, for instance, current weather information or news updates for the client's region. On the server side, cookies may be used to help track information about client activity, to determine which sites are visited most frequently or how effective certain advertisements and products are.

Microsoft Internet Explorer stores cookies as small text files saved on the client's hard drive. The data stored in the cookies are sent back to the whenever the user requests a Web page from the server. The server can then serve XHTML content to the client, specific to the information stored in the cookie.

Figure 27.21 uses a script to write a cookie to the client's machine. The **fig27_21.html** file is used to display an XHTML form that allows a user to enter a name, height and favorite color. When the user clicks the **Write Cookie** button, the **fig27_22.pl** script (Fig. 27.22) is executed.

Good Programming Practice 27.7

Critical information, such as credit card and password information, should not be stored using cookies. Cookies cannot be used to retrieve information such as e-mail addresses or data on the hard drive of a client's computer.

```
<!DOCTYPE html PUBLIC "-//W3C//DTD XHTML 1.0 Strict//EN"
   "http://www.w3.org/TR/xhtml1/DTD/xhtml1-strict.dtd">

<!-- Fig. 27.21: fig27_21.html -->

<html>
   <head>
      <title>Writing a cookie to the client computer</title>
   </head>

   <body style = "font-face: arial">
         <div style = "font-size: large;
                       font-weight: bold">
            Click Write Cookie to save your cookie data.
         </div><br />

         <form method = "post" action = "cgi-bin/fig27_22.pl"
               style = "font-weight: bold">
            Name:<br />
            <input type = "text" name = "name" /><br />
            Height:<br />
            <input type = "text" name = "height" /><br />
            Favorite Color:<br />
            <input type = "text" name = "color" /><br />
```

Fig. 27.21 XHTML document to read in cookie data from the user (part 1 of 2).

```
               <input type = "submit" value = "Write Cookie" />
            </form>
         </font>
      </body>
   </html>
```

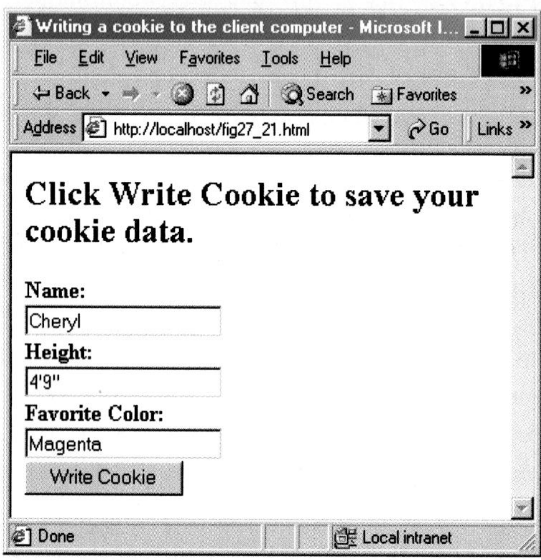

Fig. 27.21 XHTML document to read in cookie data from the user (part 2 of 2).

The **fig27_22.pl** script (Fig. 27.22) reads the data sent from the client on lines 7–9. Line 11 declares and initializes variable **$expires** to contain the expiration date of the cookie. The browser deletes a cookie after it expires. Lines 13–15 call function **print** to output the cookie information. We use the ***Set-Cookie:*** *header* to indicate that the browser should store the incoming data in a cookie. The header sets three attributes for each cookie: A name–value pair containing the data to be stored, the expiration date and the URL path of the server domain over which the cookie is valid. For this example, no path is given, making the cookie readable from anywhere within the server's domain. Lines 21–40 create a Web page indicating that the cookie has been written to the client.

```
1  #!/usr/bin/perl
2  # Fig. 27.22: fig27_22.pl
3  # Program to write a cookie to a client's machine.
4
5  use CGI qw( :standard );
6
7  $name = param( "name" );
8  $height = param( "height" );
9  $color = param( "color" );
10
11 $expires = "Monday, 11-JUN-01 16:00:00 GMT";
12
```

Fig. 27.22 Writing a cookie to the client (part 1 of 2).

```
13  print( "Set-Cookie: Name=$name; expires=$expires; path=\n" );
14  print( "Set-Cookie: Height=$height; expires=$expires; path=\n" );
15  print( "Set-Cookie: Color=$color; expires=$expires; path=\n" );
16
17  $dtd =
18  "-//W3C//DTD XHTML 1.0 Transitional//EN\"
19     \"http://www.w3.org/TR/xhtml1/DTD/xhtml1-transitional.dtd";
20
21  print( header() );
22  print( start_html( { dtd => $dtd,
23                       title => "Cookie Saved" } ) );
24
25  print <<End_Data;
26  <div style = "font-face: arial; font-size: larger">
27     The cookie has been set with the following data:
28  </div><br /><br />
29
30  <span style = "color: blue">
31  Name: <span style = "color: black">$name</span><br />
32  Height: <span style = "color: black">$height</span><br />
33  Favorite Color:</span>
34
35  <span style = "color: $color"> $color</span><br />
36  <br />Click <a href = "fig27_25.pl">here</a>
37  to read saved cookie.
38  End_Data
39
40  print( end_html() );
```

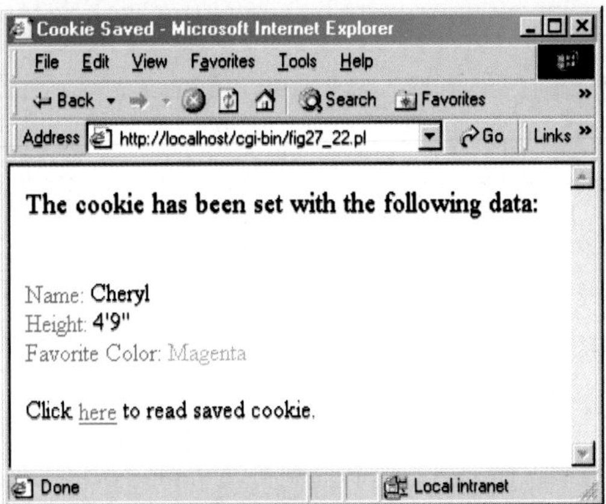

Fig. 27.22 Writing a cookie to the client (part 2 of 2).

On lines 25–38 we see our first *"here" document*. Line 25 instructs the Perl interpreter to print the subsequent lines verbatim (after variable interpolation) until it reaches the **End_Data** label. This label consists simply of the identifier **End_Data**, placed at the beginning of a line, with no whitespace characters preceding it, and followed immediately with a newline. "Here" documents are often used in CGI programs to eliminate the need to call function **print** repeatedly. Notice that we use functions in the **CGI** library, as well as "here" documents, to create a clean program.

If the client is an Internet Explorer browser, cookies are stored in the **Cookies** directory on the client's machine. Figure 27.23 shows the contents of this directory prior to the execution of **fig27_22.pl**. After the cookie is written, a text file is added to this list. The file **cheryl@localhost[1].txt** can be seen in the **Cookies** directory in Fig. 27.24. The domain for which the cookie is valid is **localhost**. The username **cheryl**, however, is only part of the filename Internet Explorer uses for cookies and is not actually a part of the cookie itself. Therefore, a remote server, cannot access the username.

Figure 27.25 (**fig27_25.pl**) reads the cookie written in Fig. 27.22 and displays the information in a table. Environment variable ***HTTP_COOKIE*** contains the client's cookies. Line 25 calls subroutine **readCookies** and places the returned value into hash **%cookies**. The user-defined subroutine **readCookies** splits the environment variable containing the cookie information into separate cookies (using **split**) and stores the cookies as distinct elements in **@cookieArray** (line 39). For each cookie in **@cookieArray**, we call **split** again to obtain the original name–value pair—which, in turn, is stored in **%cookieHash** in line 43.

Note that the **split** function in line 42 makes reference to a variable named ***$_***. The special Perl variable **$_** is used as a default for many Perl functions. In this case, because no variable was provided in the **foreach** loop (line 41), **$_** is used by default. Thus, in this example, **$_** is assigned the value of the current element of **@cookieArray** as a **foreach** structure iterates through it.

Once **%cookieHash** has been created, it is returned from the function on line 46 (using the **return** keyword), and **%cookies** is assigned this value in line 25. A **foreach** loop (lines 28–32) then iterates through the hash with the given key names, printing the key and value for the data from the cookie in an XHTML table.

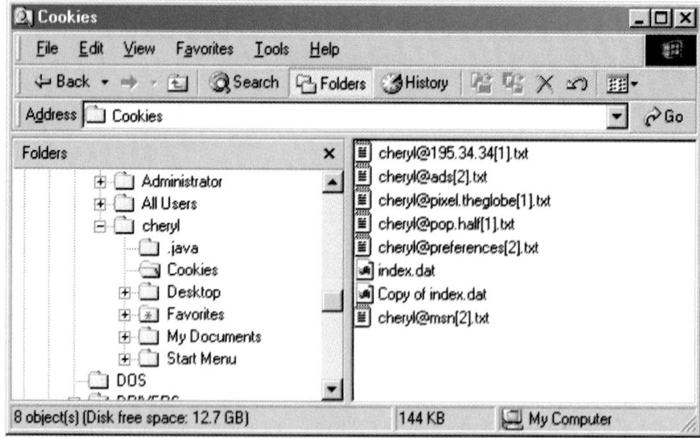

Fig. 27.23 **Cookies** directory before a cookie is written.

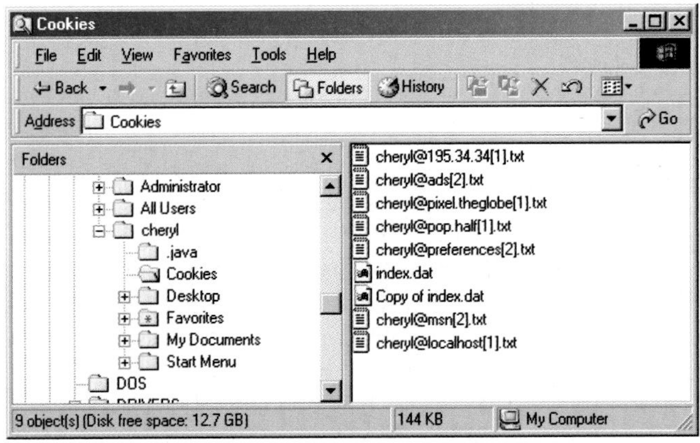

Fig. 27.24 **`Cookies`** directory after a cookie is written.

```
#!/usr/bin/perl
# Fig. 27.25: fig27_25.pl
# program to read cookies from the client's computer.

use CGI qw( :standard );

$dtd =
"-//W3C//DTD XHTML 1.0 Transitional//EN\"
   \"http://www.w3.org/TR/xhtml1/DTD/xhtml1-transitional.dtd";

print( header() );
print( start_html( { dtd => $dtd,
                     title => "Read Cookies" } ) );

print( div( { style => "font-face: arial;
                        font-size: larger;
                        font-weight: bold" },
           "The following data is saved in a
            cookie on your computer." ), br() );

print( "<table style = \"background-color: #aaaaaa\"
             border = 5 cellpadding = 10
             cellspacing = 0>" );

%cookies = readCookies();
$color = $cookies{ Color };

foreach $cookieName ( "Name", "Height", "Color" ) {
   print( Tr( td( { style => "background-color: $color" },
                  $cookieName ),
              td( $cookies{ $cookieName } ) ) );
}
```

Fig. 27.25 Output displaying the cookie's content (part 1 of 2).

```
print( "<table>" );
print( end_html() );

sub readCookies
{
   @cookieArray = split( "; ", $ENV{ 'HTTP_COOKIE' } );

   foreach ( @cookieArray ) {
      ( $cookieName, $cookieValue ) = split( "=", $_ );
      $cookieHash{ $cookieName } = $cookieValue;
   }

   return %cookieHash;
}
```

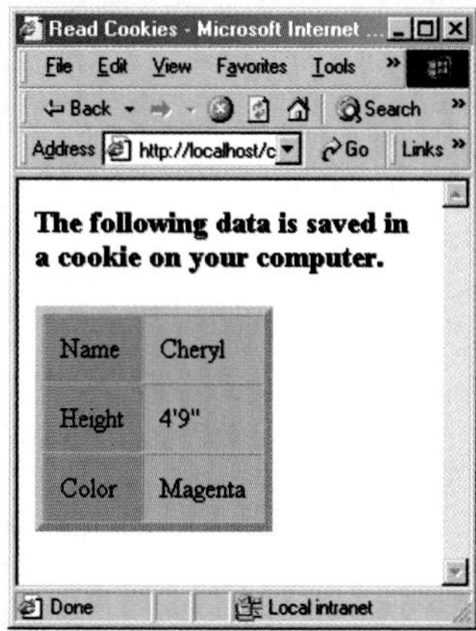

Fig. 27.25 Output displaying the cookie's content (part 2 of 2).

It is important to note that users can disable cookies on their machines. There are a few ways to do this, but the most basic is to create a file similar to a cookie that would be stored on the server's computer, rather than the client's computer. For more information, the reader can visit the Web sites listed at the end of this chapter.

27.10 Operator Precedence Chart

This section contains the operator precedence chart for Perl (Fig. 27.26). The operators are shown in decreasing order of precedence, from top to bottom.

Operator	Type	Associativity
terms and list operators	`print @array` or `sort (4, 2, 7)`	left to right
`->`	member access	left to right

Fig. 27.26 Perl operator precedence chart (part 1 of 3).

Operator	Type	Associativity
++	increment	none
--	decrement	
**	exponentiation	right to left
!	logical NOT	right to left
~	bitwise one's complement	
\	reference	
+	unary plus	
-	unary minus	
=~	matching	left to right
!~	negated match	
*	multiplication	left to right
/	division	
%	modulus	
x	repetition	
+	addition	left to right
-	subtraction	
.	string concatenation	
<<	left shift	left to right
>>	right shift	
named unary operators	unary operators—e.g., **-e** (filetest)	none
<	numerical less than	none
>	numerical greater than	
<=	numerical less than or equal to	
>=	numerical greater than or equal to	
lt	string less than	
gt	string greater than	
le	string less than or equal to	
ge	string greater than or equal to	
==	numerical equality	none
!=	numerical inequality	
<=>	numerical comparison (returns -1, 0 or 1)	
eq	string equality	
ne	string inequality	
cmp	string comparison (returns -1, 0 or 1)	
&	bitwise AND	left to right
|	bitwise inclusive OR	left to right
^	bitwise exclusive OR	
&&	logical AND	left to right
||	logical OR	left to right

Fig. 27.26 Perl operator precedence chart (part 2 of 3).

Operator	Type	Associativity
`..`	range operator	none
`?:`	conditional operator	right to left
`=`	assignment	right to left
`+=`	addition assignment	
`-=`	subtraction assignment	
`*=`	multplication assignment	
`/=`	division assignment	
`%=`	modulus assignment	
`**=`	exponentiation assignment	
`.=`	string concatenation assignment	
`x=`	repetition assignment	
`&=`	bitwise AND assignment	
`|=`	bitwise inclusive OR assignment	
`^=`	bitwise exclusive OR assignment	
`<<=`	left shift assignment	
`>>=`	right shift assignment	
`&&=`	logical AND assignment	
`||=`	logical OR assignment	
`,`	expression separator; returns value of last expression	left to right
`=>`	expression separator; groups two expressions	
`not`	logical NOT	right to left
`and`	logical AND	left to right
`or`	logical OR	left to right
`xor`	logical exclusive OR	

Fig. 27.26 Perl operator precedence chart (part 3 of 3).

27.11 Internet and World Wide Web Resources

There is a strongly established Perl community online that has made available a wealth of information on the Perl language, Perl modules and CGI scripting.

`www.perl.com`
`Perl.com` is the first place to look for information about Perl. The homepage provides up-to-date news on Perl, answers to common questions about Perl and an impressive collection of links to Perl resources on the Internet. The links include sites for Perl software, tutorials, user groups and demos.

`www.perl.org`
This Perl Mongers site is a great one-stop resource for developers. Resources include documentation, links to several other Perl sites and mailing lists.

`www.activestate.com`
From this site you can download ActivePerl—the Perl 5.6 implementation for Windows.

`www.perl.com/CPAN/README.html`
The "Comprehensive Perl Archive Network" includes an extensive listing of Perl-related information.

`www.perl.com/CPAN/scripts/index.html`
This site is the scripts index from the CPAN archive. You will find a wealth of scripts written in Perl.

www.pm.org
This site is the homepage of Perl Mongers, a group dedicated to supporting the Perl community. This site is helpful in finding others in the Perl community with whom to converse; Perl Mongers has established Perl user groups around the globe.

www.speakeasy.org/~cgires
This site is a collection of tutorials and scripts that can provide a thorough understanding of CGI.

www.perlarchive.com
This site features a large number of scripts and guides, as well as a learning center that includes helpful articles.

www.cgi.resourceindex.com
General CGI site including scripts, a list of freelance CGI programmers, documentation, job listings and several other resources.

www.cgi101.com
CGI 101 is a site for those looking to improve their programming ability through familiarity with CGI. The site contains a six-chapter class outlining techniques for CGI programming in the Perl language. The class includes both basic and advanced scripts, with working examples. Also included in the site are script libraries and links to other helpful sources.

www.freeperlcode.com
This site provides a help guide and access to several Perl scripts that can be easily downloaded and installed.

www.jmarshall.com/easy/cgi
This site provides a good, brief explanation of CGI for those with programming experience.

www.stars.com/Authoring/Languages/Perl
This site contains many links to Perl resources.

www.stars.com/Authoring/CGI
The Web Developer's Virtual Library provides tutorials for learning both CGI and Perl.

www.perlmonth.com
Perlmonth is a monthly online periodical devoted to Perl, with featured articles from professional programmers. This site is a good source for those who use Perl frequently and wish to keep up on Perl's latest developments.

tpj.com
The *Perl Journal* is a large magazine dedicated to Perl. Subscribers are provided with up-to-date Perl news and articles, on the Internet or in printed form.

www.1024kb.net/perlnet.html
This page provides a brief tutorial on Perl network programming for those who already know the language. The tutorial uses code examples to explain the basics of network communication.

www.w3.org/CGI
The World Wide Web Consortium page on CGI is concerned with CGI's security issues. This page provides links to CGI specifications, as indicated by the National Center for Super computing Applications (NCSA).

SUMMARY

- The Common Gateway Interface (CGI) is a standard protocol through which applications interact with Web servers. CGI provides a way for clients to interface indirectly with applications on the Web server.

- Because CGI is an interface, it cannot be programmed directly; a script or executable program (commonly called a CGI script) must be executed to interact with it.
- CGI scripts often process information gathered from a form. These programs are typically designated with a certain filename extension (such as **`.cgi`** or **`.pl`**) and/or located within a special directory (such as **`cgi-bin`**). After the application output is sent to the server through CGI, the results may be sent to the client.
- Standard input is the stream of information received by a program from a user, typically through the keyboard, but also possibly from a file or another input device.
- Standard output is the information stream presented to the user by an application; it is typically displayed on the screen, but may also be printed by a printer, written to a file, etc.
- The Perl comment character (**#**) instructs the interpreter to ignore everything on the current line following the **#**. The exception to this rule is the "shebang" construct (**#!**). On Unix systems, this line indicates the path to the Perl interpreter. On other systems, the line may be ignored, or it may indicate to the server that a Perl program follows the statement.
- Perl program file names typically end with the **`.pl`** extension. Programs can be executed by running the Perl interpreter from the command-line prompt (e.g., the DOS prompt in Windows).
- Using the **`-w`** option when running a Perl program instructs the interpreter to output warnings to the screen if it finds bugs in your code.
- Function **`print`** is used to output text.
- Text surrounded by quotes is called a string.
- Escape sequences can be used to output special characters, such as newlines.
- Semicolons (**`;`**) are used to terminate Perl statements.
- Perl has built-in data types that represent different kinds of data, including scalar, hash and array.
- The **`$`** character specifies that a variable contains a scalar value.
- The **`@`** character specifies that a variable contains an array, while the **`%`** character specifies that a variable contains a hash.
- In Perl, a variable is created the first time it is encountered by the interpreter.
- The assignment operators **`+=`**, **`-=`**, **`*=`** and **`/=`** are syntactical shortcuts for other operators.
- When a variable is encountered inside a double quoted (**`""`**) string, Perl uses a process called interpolation to replace the variable with its associated data.
- In Perl, uninitialized variables have the value **`undef`**, which can be evaluated differently depending on context. When **`undef`** is found in a numeric context, it evaluates to **`0`**. When it is interpreted in a string context, **`undef`** evaluates to the empty string (**`""`**).
- Unless a string begins with a digit, it is evaluated as **`undef`** in a numeric context. If the string does begin with a digit, every character up to the first nondigit character is evaluated as a number, and the remaining characters are ignored.
- The programmer does not need to differentiate between numeric and string data types because the interpreter evaluates scalar variables depending on the context in which they are used.
- Several values can be stored in arrays, which are divided into elements, each containing a scalar value. Array variable names are preceded by the **`@`** symbol.
- When **`print`**ing an array inside double quotes, the array element values are printed with only one space separating them.

- Individual array elements are accessed using square brackets (`[]`). If the array name is prefaced by the `$` character and followed by an index number in square brackets, it refers instead to an individual array element, which is a scalar value.
- The range operator (`..`) is used to specify all the values in a range, such as 2–10.
- It is not necessary to specify an array's size. The Perl interpreter recognizes that memory has not been allocated for this array and creates new memory automatically.
- When strings are inside single quotes, the interpreter treats the string literally and does not attempt to interpret any escape sequence or variable substitution.
- Text manipulation in Perl is usually done with regular expressions—a series of characters that serve as pattern-matching templates in strings, text files and databases.
- Operator `qw` ("quote word") takes the contents inside the parentheses and creates a comma-separated list with each element wrapped in double quotes.
- The **`foreach`** structure iterates sequentially through the elements in a specified array, or the elements in a range of values.
- The **`if`** structure is used to execute code depending on a specified condition.
- In Perl, anything except the number `0`, the string `"0"` and the empty string (i.e., **`undef`** values) is defined as true.
- Operators **`ne`**, **`lt`** and **`gt`** test strings for equality, less than and greater than, respectively. These operators are used only with strings. When comparing numeric values, operators `==`, `!=`, `<`, `<=`, `>` and `>=` are used.
- Perl provides the match operator (**`m//`**), which uses regular expressions to search a string for a specified pattern.
- The match operator takes two operands. The first operand is the regular expression pattern for which to search, which is placed between the slashes of the **`m//`** operator. The second operand is the string to search within, which is assigned to the match operator by using the `=~` (binding) operator.
- Regular expressions can include special characters, called metacharacters, that can specify patterns or contexts that cannot be defined using literal characters.
- The caret metacharacter (`^`) searches the beginning of a string for a pattern.
- The **`$`** metacharacter searches the end of a string for a pattern.
- Backslashes are used in regular expressions and strings to escape characters with special significance.
- The **`\b`** expression matches any word boundary.
- The `+` modifier is a quantifier that instructs Perl to match the preceding character one or more times.
- Parentheses indicate that the text matching the pattern is to be saved in a special Perl variable.
- Modifying characters placed to the right of the forward slash that delimits a regular expression instruct the interpreter to treat the expression in different ways.
- Placing an **`i`** after the regular expression tells the interpreter to ignore case when searching.
- Placing an **`x`** after the regular expression indicates that whitespace characters are to be ignored.
- Modifying character **`g`** indicates a global search—a search that does not stop after the first match is found.
- Environment variables contain information about the environment in which a script is being run.

- The **use** statement directs Perl programs to include the contents of predefined packages, called modules.
- The **CGI** module contains many useful functions for CGI scripting in Perl.
- With the **use** statement, we can specify an import tag to include a predefined set of functions.
- We usually specify the import tag **:standard** when importing the **CGI.pm** module to specify the standard **CGI** functions.
- Function **header** directs the Perl program to output a valid HTTP header.
- The **start_html** function begins the output of XHTML. This function will print the document type definition for this document, as well as several opening XHTML tags.
- When using many of the functions in the CGI module, attribute information can be specified within curly braces.
- Each argument within the curly braces is in the form of a key–value pair. A key (or value name) is assigned a value using the arrow operator (**=>**), where the key is to the left of the arrow, and the value is to the right.
- Function **Tr** contains its arguments within table row tags.
- Function **th** contains its arguments within table header tags.
- Function **hr** creates horizontal rules.
- Function **td** contains its arguments within table data tags.
- The hash data type is designated by the **%** character and represents an unordered set of scalar-value pairs.
- Each element in a hash is accessed by using a unique key that is associated with a value.
- Hash values are accessed by using the syntax **$hashName{ keyName }**.
- Function **keys** returns an array of all the keys from a specified hash in no specific order, as hash elements have no defined order.
- We use function **sort** to order the array of keys alphabetically.
- The **%ENV** hash is a built-in table that contains the names and values of all the environment variables.
- Function **end_html** outputs the closing tags for a page (**</body>** and **</html>**).
- Function **param** is used to retrieve values from form field elements.
- Regular expressions can be used to validate information in a CGI script. The design of verifying information is called business logic (also called business rules).
- Function **br** adds a break (**
**) to the XHTML page.
- Function **span** adds **<span>** tags to a page.
- Function **div** adds **<div>** tags to a page.
- Server-Side Includes (SSIs) are commands embedded in HTML documents to allow simple dynamic content creation.
- The command **EXEC** can be used to run CGI scripts and embed their output directly into a Web page. Before the XHTML document is sent to the client, the SSI command **EXEC** is executed and any script output is sent to the client.
- A document containing SSI commands is typically given the **.shtml** file extension. The **.shtml** files are parsed by the server.
- The **ECHO** command is used to display variable information. It is followed by the keyword **VAR** and the name of the variable.

- The variable **DATE_GMT** contains the current date and time in Greenwich Mean Time (GMT).
- The name of the current document is specified the **DOCUMENT_NAME** variable.
- The **DATE_LOCAL** variable inserts the date.
- Function **open** is called to open a file and create a filehandle to be associated with the file.
- The diamond operator (**<>**) is used to read input from the user or a file. When the diamond operator is used in a scalar context, only one line is read. When the operator is used in list context, all the input (or the entire file) is read and assigned to values in the list.
- We open a file for writing by preceding the file name with a **>** character.
- Perl also provides an append mode (**>>**) for appending to the end of a file.
- A **for** structure is similar to a **foreach** structure. It iterates through a set of values, specified in parentheses after the keyword **for**. Within the parentheses, three statements are used to indicate the values through which the structure will iterate.
- Function **length** returns the length of a character string.
- Function **substr** is used to identify a specified substring.
- The **img** function is used to display images.
- Function **die** displays an error message and terminates the program.
- Function **chomp** removes the newline character from the end of a string, if a newline exists.
- Function **split** divides a string into substrings at the specified separator or delimiter.
- The **last** statement is used to exit a loop structure once a desired condition has been satisfied.
- Perl allows programmers to define their own functions or subroutines. Keyword **sub** begins a function definition, and curly braces delimit the function body.
- Database connectivity allows system administrators to maintain crucial data.
- The Perl Database Interface (DBI) allows access to various relational databases in a uniform manner.
- The Perl **DBI** module and the MySQL driver, **DBD::mysql** are required to access and manipulate a MySQL database from a Perl program.
- The Perl Package Manager (PPM) is designed so that the user can easily download and install several Perl modules and packages. Perl modules and packages can also be found on the Comprehensive Perl Archive Network (CPAN).
- To create and execute SQL queries, we create DBI objects, known as handles.
- Database handles create and manipulate a connection to a database.
- Statement handles create and manipulate SQL statements to a database.
- Method **connect** in module **DBI** sets up a database connection and returns a database handle.
- A database handle is used to prepare a database query (using the method ***prepare*** in module **DBI**). This method prepares the database driver for a statement, which can be executed multiple times.
- We execute a query by calling method **execute** in module **DBI**.
- Once a query has been executed, we can access the results using the method **fetchrow_array** in module **DBI**. Each call to this function returns the next set of data in the resulting table until there are no data sets left.
- A database connection can be closed using method **disconnect** in module **DBI**.
- We can indicate that we are no longer using a query by calling method **finish** in module **DBI**.

- Cookies maintain state information for a particular client who uses a Web browser. Microsoft Internet Explorer stores cookies as small text files saved on the client's hard drive.
- We use the **Set-Cookie:** header to indicate that the browser should store the incoming data in a cookie.
- A "here" document is used to output a string verbatim. The string is specified as all the text from the beginning of the document to the closing identifier.
- Environment variable **HTTP_COOKIE** contains the client's cookies.
- The special variable **$_** is used as a default for many Perl functions.

TERMINOLOGY

!= operator
$ metacharacter
$ type symbol
$_ special variable
% type symbol
%ENV hash
***** quantifier
.cgi file extension
.pl file extension
.shtml file extension
:standard import tag
? quantifier
@ type symbol
\b metacharacter
\B metacharacter
\d metacharacter
\D metacharacter
\n escape sequence
\n metacharacter
\s metacharacter
\S metacharacter
\t metacharacter
\w metacharacter
\W metacharacter
\w pattern
^ metacharacter
{} curly braces in **CGI.pm** functions
{m,n} quantifier
{n,} quantifier
{n} quantifier
+ quantifier
< operator
<= operator
<> diamond operator
== operator
> operator
> write mode
>= operator
>> append mode
ActivePerl
ActiveState
alphanumeric character
Apache Web server
append mode (**>>**)
array
assignment operator
associative array
binding operator (**=~**)
br function
built-in metacharacter
business logic
business rules
C programming language
CGI (Common Gateway Interface)
CGI module
CGI script
CGI tutorial
cgi-bin directory
chomp function
close function
comment character (**#**)
comparison operator
connect method
control structure
cookie
Cookies directory
CPAN (Comprehensive Perl Archive Network)
database connectivity
database handle
DATE_GMT variable
DATE_LOCAL variable
DBD::mysql driver
DBI module
delimiter
diamond operator (**<>**)
die function

disconnect method
div function
DOCUMENT_NAME variable
dtd argument in **start_html** function
ECHO command
elements in an array
else clause
empty string
end_html function
environment variable
equality operators
escape sequence
escaping special characters
EXEC command
execute method
fetchrow_array method
filehandle
finish method
for structure
foreach structure
forms
function
g modifying character
gt operator
handle
hash
header function
hr function
HTTP connection
HTTP header
HTTP host
HTTP_COOKIE environment variable
HTTP_HOST environment variable
i modifying character
if structure
img function
import tag
INCLUDE command
interactive mode
interpolation
keys (in a hash)
keys function
last statement
length function
list
literal character
logical AND (**&&**) operator
logical negation operator (**!**)
logical OR (**||**) operator
lt operator
m modifying character
m//
match operator (**m//**)
metacharacter
modifying character
module
MySQL database
mysql directory
MySQL driver
ne operator
numeric context
open function
param function
Perl (Practical Extraction and Report Language)
perl command
Perl data types
Perl interpreter
Perl Package Manager (PPM)
piping
post method
ppm method
prepare method
print function
private Web site
quantifier
qw operator
range operator (**..**)
read-only mode
redirection
regular expression
return keyword
s modifying character
scalar
scalar value
semicolons (**;**) to terminate statement
Set-Cookie: header
shebang construct (**#!**)
sort function
span function
split function
SQL query string
SSI (Server-Side Include)
standard input (**STDIN**)
standard output (**STDOUT**)
start_html function
state information
statement handle
string context
sub keyword
subroutine

substr method
td function
th function
title argument in **start_html** function
tr function
Tr function
undef value
Unisys
use statement
validation
VAR keyword
-w command-line option in Perl
Web server
Webmaster
while structure
word boundary
write mode (**>**)
x modifying character

SELF-REVIEW EXERCISES

27.1 Fill in the blanks in the following statements.

a) The __________ Protocol is used by Web browsers and Web servers to communicate with each other.
b) Typically, all CGI programs reside in directory __________.
c) To output warnings as a Perl program executes, the __________ command-line switch should be used.
d) The three data types in Perl are __________, __________ and __________.
e) __________ are divided into individual elements that can each contain an individual scalar variable.
f) To test the equality of two strings, operator __________ should be used.
g) Business __________ is used to ensure that invalid data are not entered into a database.
h) __________ allow Webmasters to include the current time, date or even the contents of a different HTML document.
i) The __________ control structure iterates once for each element in a list or array.
j) Many Perl functions take special variable __________ as a default argument.

27.2 State whether the following are *true* or *false*. If *false*, explain why.

a) Documents containing Server Side Includes must have a file extension of **.SSI** in order to be parsed by the server.
b) A valid HTTP header must be sent to the client to ensure that the browser correctly displays the information.
c) The numerical equality operator, **eq**, is used to determine if two numbers are equal.
d) The **^** metacharacter is used to match the beginning of a string.
e) Perl has a built-in binding operator, **=**, that tests if a matching string is found within a variable.
f) Cookies can read information, such as e-mail addresses and personal files from a client's hard drive.
g) An example of a valid HTTP header is **Content-type text\html**.
h) CGI environment variables contain such information as the type of Web browser the client is running.
i) The characters **\w** in a regular expression match only a letter or number.
j) CGI is a programming language that can be used in conjunction with Perl to program for the Web.

ANSWERS TO SELF-REVIEW EXERCISES

27.1 a) Hypertext Transfer. b) **cgi-bin**. c) **-w**. d) scalar variable, array, hash. e) Arrays. f) **eq**. g) logic (or rules). h) Server-Side Includes. i) **foreach**. j) **$_**.

27.2 a) False. Documents containing Server-Side Includes usually have a file extension of **.shtml**. b) True. c) False. The numerical equality operator is **==**. d) True. e) False. The built-in binding operator is **=~**. f) False. Cookies do not have access to private information, such as e-mail addresses or private data stored on the hard drive. g) False. A valid HTTP header might be: **Content-type: text/html**. h) True. i) False. **\w** also matches the underscore character. j) False. CGI is an interface, not a programming language.

EXERCISES

27.3 How can a Perl program determine the type of browser a Web client is using?

27.4 Describe how input from an HTML form is retrieved in a Perl program.

27.5 How does a Web browser determine how to handle or display incoming data?

27.6 What is the terminology for a command that is embedded in an HTML document and parsed by a server prior to being sent?

27.7 Write a Perl program named **ex27_07.pl** that creates a scalar value **$states** with the value **"Mississippi Alabama Texas Massachusetts Kansas"**. Using only the techniques discussed in this chapter, write a program that does the following:

a) Search for a word in scalar **$states** that ends in **xas**. Store this word in element 0 of an array named **@statesArray**.
b) Search for a word in **$states** that begins with **k** and ends in **s**. Perform a case-insensitive comparison. Store this word in element 1 of **@statesArray**.
c) Search for a word in **$states** that begins with **M** and ends in **s**. Store this in element 2 of the array.
d) Search for a word in **$states** that ends in **a**. Store this word in element 3 of the array.
e) Search for a word in **$states** at the beginning of the string that starts with **M**. Store this word in element 4 of the array.
f) Output the array **@statesArray** to the screen.

27.8 In this chapter, we have presented CGI environment variables. Develop a program that determines whether the client is using Internet Explorer. If so, determine the version number, and send that information back to the client.

27.9 Modify the programs and documents of Figs. 27.12 and 27.13 to save information sent to the server in a text file.

27.10 Write a Perl program that tests whether an e-mail address is input correctly. A valid e-mail address contains a series of characters followed by the **@** character and a domain name.

27.11 Using CGI environment variables, write a program that logs the IP addresses (obtained with the **REMOTE_ADDR** CGI environment variable) that request information from the Web server.

27.12 Modify the programs of Figs. 27.19 and 27.20 so that there is another column in the resulting table. Each element in that column will be a button that, when clicked, will display a third Web page with a description of the current book. To do this in a straightforward manner, you should create a third program that will query the database for the book's description. This program will be called when one of the buttons is clicked.

28

Python

Objectives

- To understand basic Python data types.
- To understand string processing and regular expressions in Python.
- To use exception handling.
- To perform basic CGI tasks in Python.
- To construct programs that interact with MySQL databases using the Python Database Application Programming Interface (DB-API).

Art is the imposing of a pattern on experience, and our aesthetic enjoyment is recognition of the pattern.
Alfred North Whitehead

No rule is so general, which admits not some exception.
Robert Burton

Outline

28.1 Introduction

Python is an interpreted, cross-platform, object-oriented language that can be used to write large-scale Internet search engines, small administration scripts, GUI applications, CGI scripts and more. The creator of the language, Guido van Rossum, combined a clean syntax with popular elements from several existing languages to produce Python.

Python is a freely distributed technology whose open-source nature has encouraged a wide base of developers to submit modules that extend the language. Using Python's core modules and those freely available on the Web, programmers can develop applications that accomplish a great variety of tasks. Python's interpreted nature facilitates rapid application development (RAD) of powerful programs. GUI applications, in particular, can be tested quickly and developed using Python's interface to Tcl/Tk (among other GUI toolkits).

28.1.1 First Python Program

In this section, we examine a simple Python program and explain how to work with the Python programming environment. For this chapter, we assume the reader has installed Python 2.0 or later. [*Note:* The resources for this book posted at our Web site, **`www.deitel.com`**, include step-by-step instructions on installing Python on Windows and Unix/Linux platforms.] Python can be executed on a program stored in a file, or Python can run in *interactive mode*, where users enter lines of code one at a time. Among other things, interactive mode enables program writers to test small blocks of code quickly and helps contribute to a relatively rapid development time for most Python projects.

Figure 28.1 is a simple Python program that prints the text **`Welcome to Python!`** to the screen. Lines 1–2 contain single-line comments that describe the program. Comments in Python begin with the **`#`** character; Python ignores all text in the current line after this character. Line 4 uses the **`print`** statement to write the text **`Welcome to Python!`** to the screen.

```
# Fig. 28.1: fig28_01.py
# A first program in Python

print "Welcome to Python!"
```

```
Welcome to Python!
```

Fig. 28.1 Simple Python program.

Python statements can be executed in two ways. The first is by typing statements into a file (as in Fig. 28.1). Python files typically end with **.py**, although other extensions (e.g., **.pyw** on Windows) can be used. Python is then invoked on the file by typing

```
python file.py
```

at the command line, where **file.py** is the name of the Python file. [*Note:* To invoke Python, the system path variable must be set properly to include the **python** executable. The resources for this book posted at our Web site, **www.deitel.com**, include step-by-step instructions on how to set the appropriate variable.] The output box of Fig. 28.1 contains the results of invoking Python on **fig28_01.py**.

Python statements can also be interpreted interactively. Typing

```
python
```

at the command prompt runs Python in *interactive mode*.

Testing and Debugging Tip 28.1

In interactive mode, Python statements can be entered and interpreted one at a time. This mode is often useful when debugging a program (i.e., discovering and removing errors in the program).

Figure 28.2 shows Python running in interactive mode on Windows. The first two lines display information about the version of Python being used. The third line begins with the *Python prompt* (**>>>**). A Python statement is interpreted by typing the statement at the Python prompt and pressing the *Enter* or *Return* key.

The **print** statement on the third line prints the text **Welcome to Python!** to the screen. After printing the text to the screen, the Python prompt is displayed again (line 5), and Python waits for the user to enter the next statement. We exit Python by typing *Crtl-Z* (on Microsoft Windows systems) and pressing the *Return* key. [*Note:* On UNIX and Linux systems, *Ctrl-D* exits Python.]

```
Python 2.1 (#15, Apr 16 2001, 18:25:49) [MSC 32 bit (Intel)] on win32
Type "copyright", "credits" or "license" for more information.
>>> print "Welcome to Python!"
Welcome to Python!
>>> ^Z
```

Fig. 28.2 Python in interactive mode.

28.1.2 Python Keywords

Before we discuss Python programming in more detail, we present a list of Python's *keywords* (Figure 28.3). These words have special meanings in Python and cannot be used as variable names, function names or other objects.

A list of Python keywords can also be obtained from the **keyword** *module*. Figure 28.4 illustrates how to obtain the list of Python keywords in interactive mode. [*Note*: We discuss modules further in Section 28.4.]

Python is a case-sensitive language. This means that Python treats variable **x** (lowercase) and variable **X** (upper case) as two different variables. Similarly, the statement

```
Def = 3
```

is a valid Python statement, but the statement

```
def = 3
```

causes a syntax error, because **def** is a keyword and, therefore, not a valid variable name.

Good Programming Practice 28.1

*Using variable or function names that resemble keywords (e.g., variable **Def**) or Python functions (e.g., **list**) may cause confusion to the program writer and readers. Avoid using such variable or function names.*

Line 5 contains the function definition header for function **greatestCommonDivisor**. This function computes the *greatest common divisor* of two numbers—the largest integer that divides evenly into both numbers. The keyword **def** marks the beginning of the function definition. The function takes two parameters: **x** and **y**. The list of parameters is placed inside parentheses (**()**), and the parameter list is followed by a *colon (**:**)*.

Common Programming Error 28.1

Forgetting to place a colon after a function definition header or after a control structure is a syntax error.

28.2 Basic Data Types, Control Structures and Functions

This section introduces basic data types, control structures and functions, using a simple program (Fig. 28.5). In this program, we define two functions that use control structures to perform the operations of those functions.

Python keywords						
`and`	`continue`	`else`	`for`	`import`	`not`	`raise`
`assert`	`def`	`except`	`from`	`in`	`or`	`return`
`break`	`del`	`exec`	`global`	`is`	`pass`	`try`
`class`	`elif`	`finally`	`if`	`lambda`	`print`	`while`

Fig. 28.3 Python keywords.

```
Python 2.1 (#15, Apr 16 2001, 18:25:49) [MSC 32 bit (Intel)] on win32
Type "copyright", "credits" or "license" for more information.
>>> import keyword
>>> print keyword.kwlist
['and', 'assert', 'break', 'class', 'continue', 'def', 'del', 'elif',
'else', 'except', 'exec', 'finally', 'for', 'from', 'global', 'if',
'import', 'in', 'is','lambda', 'not', 'or', 'pass', 'print', 'raise',
'return', 'try', 'while']
>>>
```

Fig. 28.4 Printing Python keywords in interactive mode.

Line 6 calls Python *function* **min** on parameters **x** and **y**. This function returns the smaller of the two values. We assign the value returned by **min** to local variable **gcd**.

Notice that line 6 is indented. Unlike many other languages, Python determines the beginning and end of a statement based on whitespace. Each new line begins a new statement. The indentation in line 6 marks the beginning of the code block that belongs to function **greatestCommonDivisor**. Groups of statements that belong to the same block of code are indented by the same amount. The language does not specify how many spaces to indent, only that the indentation must be consistent.

Common Programming Error 28.2

Inconsistent indentation in a Python program causes a syntax error.

Line 8 describes the beginning of a Python ***while*** *loop*. The code in the **while** block executes as long as **gcd** is greater than or equal to 1.

```
1  # Fig. 28.5: fig28_05.py
2  # Program to illustrate basic data types, control structures and
3  # functions.
4
5  def greatestCommonDivisor( x, y ):
6     gcd = min( x, y )
7
8     while gcd >= 1:
9
10       if ( x % gcd ) == ( y % gcd ) == 0:
11          return gcd
12       else:
13          gcd -= 1
14
15 def determineColor( color ):
16
17    if color == "green":
18       print "You entered green!"
19    elif color == "purple":
20       print "You entered purple!"
21    else:
22       print "You did not enter green or purple."
```

Fig. 28.5 Program illustrating data types, control structures and functions (part 1 of 2).

```
23
24   number1 = int( raw_input( "Enter a positive integer: " ) )
25   number2 = int( raw_input( "Enter a positive integer: " ) )
26
27   print "The greatest common divisor is", \
28      greatestCommonDivisor( number1, number2 )
29
30   for entry in range( 5 ):
31      colorChoice = raw_input( "\nEnter your favorite color: " )
32      determineColor( colorChoice )
```

```
Enter a positive integer: 2
Enter a positive integer: 30
The greatest common divisor is 2

Enter your favorite color: yellow
You did not enter green or purple.

Enter your favorite color: green
You entered green!

Enter your favorite color: black
You did not enter green or purple.

Enter your favorite color: purple
You entered purple!

Enter your favorite color: red
You did not enter green or purple.
```

Fig. 28.5 Program illustrating data types, control structures and functions (part 2 of 2).

Line 10 is a Python ***if*** *statement*. If the specified condition is true (i.e., the condition evaluates to any nonzero value), the code in the **if** block (i.e., the indented code that follows the **if** statement) is executed. The statement in line 10 uses the *modulo operator* (**%**) to determine if parameters **x** and **y** can be divided evenly by variable **gcd**. The statement illustrates the fact that Python comparison expressions can be "chained." This code is identical to

```
if ( x % gcd ) == 0 == ( y % gcd ):
```

and to

```
if x % gcd == 0 and y % gcd == 0:
```

Chaining occurs left to right; therefore, the former expression is more efficient than the expression presented in the code, because the former expression may save a division operation.

If the expression in line 10 is true, we have found the greatest common divisor. The ***return*** *keyword* (line 11) exits the function and returns the specified value.

If the expression in line 10 is false (i.e., the condition evaluates to zero), the code in the **else** block (lines 12–13) executes. This code decrements variable **gcd** by 1, using the **-=** *statement* and has the same effect as the statement

```
gcd = gcd - 1
```

Python defines several such statements, including **+=**, **-=**, ***=**, **/=**, **%=** (modulo division) and ****=** (exponentiation). [*Note:* These statements are new in Python 2.0; using these statements in Python 1.5.2 or less causes a syntax error.]

Function **determineColor** (lines 15–22) takes parameter **color**, which contains a string. Lines 17–22 use the **if/elif/else** *control structure* to evaluate expressions based on the value of the parameter. If the value of parameter **color** is equal to the string **"green"** (line 17), the function prints **"You entered green!"** If the value of **color** is equal to the string **"purple"** (line 19), the function prints **"You entered purple!"** If the value of **name** does not match either of these strings (line 21), the function prints **"You did not enter green or purple."** Function **determineColor** illustrates simple Python string comparisons. We discuss string comparison/manipulation in further detail in Section 28.4.

Line 24 calls Python *function* **raw_input** to get input from the user. This function takes an optional string argument that is displayed as a prompt to the user. The **raw_input** function returns a string. The Python function **int** takes as an argument a noninteger type and returns an integer representation of the argument. We store the integer returned from function **int** in local variable **number1**. Line 25 retrieves a value for **number2** in a similar fashion.

Common Programming Error 28.3

A numerical value obtained via the **raw_input** *function must be converted from a string to the proper numerical type. Manipulating a string representation of a numerical value may result in a logical or syntactical error.*

Lines 27–28 print the greatest common divisor of the two numbers to the screen. The backslash character (****) at the end of line 27 is a *line-continuation character* that allows us to continue a statement on the next line. The *comma* (**,**) that follows the string informs Python that we want to print additional items after the string. In this case, the additional item is the integer value returned by the call to function **greatestCommonDivisor**. Notice from the output that Python automatically inserts a space between the last character in the string and the integer value.

Common Programming Error 28.4

Forgetting to include a line-continuation character (******) at the end of a statement that continues onto the next line is a syntax error.

Line 30 begins a Python **for** *loop*. The call to Python function **range** with an argument of **5** returns the values **0**, **1**, **2**, **3** and **4**. [Note: The function actually returns a *list* that contains these values. We discuss lists in Section 28.3.] The **for** loop iterates through these values and, on each iteration, assigns a value to variable **entry** and then executes the statements in the **for** block (lines 31–32). Thus, the statements in the **for** block are executed five times. These statements retrieve a string from the user and pass that string to function **determineColor**. Notice the "**\n**" *escape sequence* at the beginning of the string in line 31. This is a special Python character that prints a *newline* to the screen. A newline causes the cursor (i.e., the current screen position indicator) to move to the beginning of the next line on the screen. Figure 28.6 lists some common Python escape sequences. After the program calls function **determineColor** on five user-defined strings, the program exits.

28.3 Tuples, Lists and Dictionaries

In addition to basic data types that store numerical values and strings, Python defines three data types for storing more complex data: the *list*—a sequence of related data, the *tuple* (pronounced too-ple)—a list whose elements may not be modified and a *dictionary*—a list of values that are accessed through their associated keys. These data types are high-level implementations of simple data structures that enable Python programmers to manipulate many types of data quickly and easily. Some Python modules (e.g., **Cookie** and **cgi**) use these data types to provide simple access to their underlying data structures. Figure 28.7 is a program that illustrates tuples, lists and dictionaries.

Escape sequence	Meaning
`\n`	Newline (line feed).
`\r`	Carriage return.
`\t`	Tab.
`\'`	Single quote.
`\"`	Double quote.
`\b`	Backspace.
`\\`	Backslash.

Fig. 28.6 Escape sequences.

```
# Fig. 28.7: fig28_07.py
# A program that illustrates tuples, lists and dictionaries.

# tuples
aTuple = ( 1, "a", 3.0 )        # create tuple
firstItem = aTuple[ 0 ]         # first tuple item
secondItem = aTuple[ 1 ]        # second tuple item
thirdItem = aTuple[ 2 ]         # third tuple item

print "The first item in the tuple is", firstItem
print "The second item in the tuple is", secondItem
print "The third item in the tuple is", thirdItem
print

firstItem, secondItem, thirdItem = aTuple
```

Fig. 28.7 Program illustrating tuples, lists and dictionaries (part 1 of 3).

```
print "The first item in the tuple is", firstItem
print "The second item in the tuple is", secondItem
print "The third item in the tuple is", thirdItem
print

aTuple += ( 4, )
print "Used the += statement on the tuple"
print

# print the tuple
print "The raw tuple data is:", aTuple
print "The items in the tuple are:"

for item in aTuple:   # print each item
    print item,

print      # end previous line
print      # blank line

# lists
aList = [ 1, 2, 3 ]      # create list
aList[ 0 ] = 0           # change first element of list
aList.append( 5 )        # add item to end of list

print "The raw list data is:", aList   # print list data
print

aList += [ 4 ]      # add an item to the end of the list
print "Added an item to the list using the += statement"
print

# print each item in the list
print "The items in the list are:"

for item in aList:
    print item,

print      # end previous line
print      # blank line

# dictionaries
aDictionary = { 1 : "January", 2 : "February", 3 : "March",
                4 : "April", 5 : "May", 6 : "June", 7 : "July",
                8 : "August", 9 : "September", 10 : "October",
                11 : "November" }
aDictionary[ 12 ] = "December"          # add item to dictionary

print "The raw dictionary data is:", aDictionary
print "\nThe entries in the dictionary are:"

for item in aDictionary.keys():
    print "aDictionary[ ", item, " ] = ", aDictionary[ item ]
```

Fig. 28.7 Program illustrating tuples, lists and dictionaries (part 2 of 3).

```
The first item in the tuple is 1
The second item in the tuple is a
The third item in the tuple is 3.0

The first item in the tuple is 1
The second item in the tuple is a
The third item in the tuple is 3.0

Used the += statement on the tuple

The raw tuple data is: (1, 'a', 3.0, 4)
The items in the tuple are:
1 a 3.0 4

The raw list data is: [0, 2, 3, 5]

Added an item to the list using the += statement

The items in the list are:
0 2 3 5 4

The raw dictionary data is: {12: 'December', 11: 'November', 10: 'Oc-
tober', 9: 'September', 8: 'August', 7: 'July', 6: 'June', 5: 'May', 4:
'April', 3: 'March', 2: 'February', 1: 'January'}

The entries in the dictionary are:
aDictionary[  12  ] =  December
aDictionary[  11  ] =  November
aDictionary[  10  ] =  October
aDictionary[  9  ] =  September
aDictionary[  8  ] =  August
aDictionary[  7  ] =  July
aDictionary[  6  ] =  June
aDictionary[  5  ] =  May
aDictionary[  4  ] =  April
aDictionary[  3  ] =  March
aDictionary[  2  ] =  February
aDictionary[  1  ] =  January
```

Fig. 28.7 Program illustrating tuples, lists and dictionaries (part 3 of 3).

Line 5 creates a tuple, with elements **1**, **"a"** and **3.0**. Tuples are created as a comma-separated list of values inside parentheses. A tuple is used most often to contain combinations of many data types (e.g., strings, integers, other tuples, etc.). Lines 6–8 use the **[]** *operator* to access specific elements through an index. The first element in a tuple has index 0.

Tuple element contents are *immutable*—they cannot be modified. So, the statement

```
aTuple[ 0 ] = 0
```

produces a run-time error similar to

```
Traceback (innermost last):
  File "<interactive input>", line 1, in ?
TypeError: object doesn't support item assignment
```

Common Programming Error 28.5

Attempting to change an immutable data structure is a syntax error.

Attempting to access a value at a non-existent element is also an error. The statement

```
print aTuple[ 10 ]
```

produces a run-time error similar to

```
Traceback (innermost last):
  File "<interactive input>", line 1, in ?
IndexError: tuple index out of range
```

because **aTuple** does not have a 10th element.

Common Programming Error 28.6

Trying to access an out-of-range element (i.e., an element at an index that does not exist) produces a runtime error.

Line 15 *unpacks* the items of the tuple into three variables. This statement produces the same results as lines 6–8. Line 21 has the effect of adding an element to the end of variable **aTuple**. The right-hand side of the **+=** statement must be a tuple; therefore, we must specify a *one-element tuple* or *singleton* on the right side of the statement. The value **(4,)** is a one-element tuple. The comma after the tuple element value is mandatory, because the value **(4)** is an integer.

Because tuples are immutable, the **+=** statement actually creates a new tuple that combines the tuple on the left side of the **+=** sign (i.e., **aTuple**) with the tuple on the right side of the **+=** sign (i.e., **(4,)**) to create a new tuple. The new tuple is stored in variable **aTuple**.

The output of line 26 shows how the **print** statement handles a variable that is a tuple. Lines 29–30 use a **for** loop to print each element in variable **aTuple**.

The statement in line 29 assigns the first element in **aTuple** (i.e., **aTuple[0]**) to variable **item**. Line 30 then prints the value of variable **item** to the screen. The **for** loop iterates over each element in the tuple, assigns the element to variable **item** and executes the code in line 30.

By default, the **print** statement writes a newline character (e.g., a carriage return) at the end of its output; however, the comma in line 30 tells Python not to print the newline character. In the next iteration of the **for** loop, the **print** statement writes text to the screen on the same line as the previous **print** statement. Lines 32–33 print a new line and a blank line to the screen, respectively, after all the elements in the tuple have been displayed

Line 36 creates a *list* that contains elements **1**, **2** and **3**. Python lists are similar to tuples, except that Python lists are *mutable* (they may be altered). Line 37 demonstrates this fact by assigning the value **0** to the element in the list at index 0. Line 38 adds an element to the end of a list by calling list method **append**. Lists also support several other methods (Fig. 28.8).

Method	Purpose
append(item **)**	Inserts *item* at the end of the list.
count(item **)**	Returns the number of occurrences of *item* in the list.
extend(newList **)**	Inserts *newList* at the end of the list.
index(item **)**	Returns the index of the first occurrence of *item* in the list. If element is not in the list, a **ValueError** exception occurs. [*Note:* We discuss exceptions in Section 28.5]
insert(index, item **)**	Inserts *item* at position *index*.
pop([*index*] **)**	Removes and returns the last element in the list. If parameter *index* is specified, removes and returns the element at position *index*.
remove(item **)**	Removes the first occurrence of *item* from the list. If *item* is not in the list, a **ValueError** exception occurs.
reverse()	Reverses the items in the list.
sort([*function*] **)**	Sorts items of the list. Optional parameter *function* is a comparison function that may be user-defined.

Fig. 28.8 Python list methods.

The output from the statement in line 40 shows how the **print** statement handles a variable that is a list. Line 43 adds the integer **4** to variable **aList**, using the **+=** statement. The value on the right side of the **+=** statement must be a list (or another sequence, such as a string or tuple). In this case, the list contains one element. The **for** statement (lines 50–51) prints each element of the list to the screen.

Lines 57–60 create a Python dictionary. Each entry in a dictionary has two parts—a *key* and a *value*—and a dictionary consists of a set of zero or more comma-separated key-value pairs. A value in a dictionary is manipulated using that value's key. The key must be of an immutable data type (e.g., number, string or a tuple that contains only immutable data types); dictionary values may be any data type. Each key-value pair takes the form *key : value*.

Line 61 illustrates how to add a new element to a dictionary by using the **[]** operator. Because a value must be accessed using its corresponding key, each key in a dictionary must be unique. For example, the statements

```
month = { 11 : "November" }
month[ 11 ] = "Nov."
```

create a dictionary and then change the value associated with key **11** from **"November"** to the abbreviation **"Nov."**.

Lines 66–67 use a **for** loop to print each key-value pair in variable **aDictionary**. Method **keys** returns an unordered list of all keys in the dictionary. Dictionaries also support several other methods (Fig. 28.9). The **for** loop iterates over each key and prints the key and its corresponding value. Each value in the dictionary is accessed using the **[]** operator (line 67).

Method	Description
`clear()`	Deletes all items from the dictionary.
`copy()`	Creates a copy of the dictionary.
get(key [, falseValue] **)**	Returns the value associated with *key*. If *key* is not in the dictionary and if *falseValue* is specified, returns the specified value.
has_key(key **)**	Returns **1** if *key* is in the dictionary; returns **0** if *key* is not in the dictionary.
`items()`	Returns a list of tuples that are key-value pairs.
`keys()`	Returns a list of keys in the dictionary.
setdefault(*key* [, *falseValue*] **)**	Behaves similarly to method **get**. If key is not in the dictionary and *falseValue* is specified, inserts the key and the specified value into dictionary.
update(otherDictionary **)**	Adds all key-value pairs from *otherDictionary* to the current dictionary.
`values()`	Returns a list of values in the dictionary.

Fig. 28.9 Dictionary methods.

28.4 String Processing and Regular Expressions

Programmers use string processing to accomplish a variety of tasks. System administration scripts can use Python modules and strings to process text files. Web programmers can use Python CGI scripts to validate user-entered data from an XHTML form or to aggregate and display data from a variety of sources. This section discusses simple string processing in Python, including the use of *regular expressions*. A regular expression string defines a pattern with which text data can be compared. Regular expressions are used to search through strings, text files, databases, etc. Regular expressions are not part of the core Python language, but regular expression processing capability is available through the standard Python **re** *module*.

Figure 28.10 demonstrates the use of strings in Python. Lines 5–6 assign the value **"This is a string."** to variable **string1** and print that value to the screen. In lines 8–9, we assign a similar value to variable **string2** and print that string.

```
1  # Fig. 28.10: fig28_10.py
2  # Program to illustrate use of strings
3
4  # simple string assignments
5  string1 = "This is a string."
6  print string1
7
8  string2 = "This is a second string."
9  print string2
```

Fig. 28.10 Using strings (part 1 of 2).

```
10
11   # string concatenation
12   string3 = string1 + " " + string2
13   print string3
14
15   # using operators
16   string4 = '*'
17   print "String with an asterisk: " + string4
18   string4 *= 10
19   print "String with 10 asterisks: " + string4
20
21   # using quotes
22   print "This is a string with \"double quotes.\""
23   print 'This is another string with "double quotes."'
24   print 'This is a string with \'single quotes.\''
25   print "This is another string with 'single quotes.'"
26   print """This string has "double quotes" and 'single quotes.'"""
27
28   # string formatting
29   name = raw_input( "Enter your name: " )
30   age = raw_input( "Enter your age: " )
31   print "Hello, %s, you are %s years old." % ( name, age )
```

```
This is a string.
This is a second string.
This is a string. This is a second string.
String with an asterisk: *
String with 10 asterisks: **********
This is a string with "double quotes."
This is another string with "double quotes."
This is a string with 'single quotes.'
This is another string with 'single quotes.'
This string has "double quotes" and 'single quotes.'
Enter your name: Brian
Enter your age: 33
Hello, Brian, you are 33 years old.
```

Fig. 28.10 Using strings (part 2 of 2).

In line 12, three strings—**`string1`**, **`" "`** and **`string2`**—are concatenated with operator **`+`**. We then print this new string (**`string3`**).

Lines 16–17 create and print a string with a single character—an asterisk. Line 18 uses the **`*=`** statement to concatenate **`string4`** to itself 10 times. We print the resulting string in line 19. Python also defines the **`+=`** statement for strings, which effectively concatenates two strings. [*Note:* Because strings are immutable, the **`*=`** and **`+=`** statements actually create new strings to perform their respective operations.]

Lines 22–26 illustrate the use of quotes in a string. Line 22 shows one method of displaying double quotes inside a string. The double quotes are displayed using the *escape character* (**`\`**). If we omit the escape character, then Python interprets the double quote character as marking the end of the string, rather than as a character within the string itself. Line 23 presents another method of displaying double quotes inside a string. Notice that the entire string is contained within single quotes (`'`). Python strings may be contained either within double quotes or single quotes. As line 23 demonstrates, if a string is contained within single quotes, then double quotes within the string do not need to be "escaped" with the backslash character. Similarly, if a string is contained within double quotes (line 25), then single quotes within the string do not need to be escaped.

If we do not want to escape quote characters in a string, we can place the entire string within pairs of three consecutive double quote characters (line 26). This is called a *triple-quoted string*—triple-quoted strings may alternatively be surrounded by sets of three consecutive single quote characters (`'''`). We use triple-quoted strings later in this chapter to output large blocks of XHTML from CGI scripts.

In lines 29–30, we use Python function **`raw_input`** to input the user's name and age. In line 31, we format a string to incorporate the input data. The **`%`** *format character* acts as a place holder in the string. The *format character* **`s`** indicates that we want to place another string within the current string at the specified point. Figure 28.11 lists several *format characters* for use in string formatting. [*Note*: See Appendix D on number systems for a discussion of the numeric terminology in Fig. 28.11.]

At the end of line 31, we use the **`%`** *operator* to indicate that the formatting characters in the string are to be replaced with the values listed between the parentheses. Python constructs the string from left to right by matching a placeholder with the next value specified between parentheses and replacing the formatting character with that value.

Figure 28.12 presents some of Python's regular expression operations. Line 4 *imports* the **`re`** *(regular expression) module.* A *module* contains data and functions that a program can use to accomplish a specific task. After a program imports a module, the program can make use of these data and functions. In our example, importing the **`re`** module enables us to access data and functions that facilitate regular-expression processing.

Line 8 *compiles* the regular expression **`"Test"`**, using the **`re`** module's **`compile`** function. This method returns an object of type **`SRE_Pattern`**, which represents a compiled regular expression.

Symbol	Meaning
`c`	Single character (i.e., a string of length one).
`s`	String.
`d`	Signed decimal integer.
`u`	Unsigned decimal integer.
`o`	Unsigned octal integer.
`x`	Unsigned hexadecimal integer (using format **`abcdef`**).
`X`	Unsigned hexadecimal integer (using format **`ABCDEF`**).
`f`	Floating-point number.
`e`, `E`	Floating-point number (using scientific notation).
`g`, `G`	Floating-point number (using least-significant digits).

Fig. 28.11 String-format characters.

```
# Fig. 28.12: fig28_12.py
# Program searches a string using the regular expression module.

import re

searchString = "Testing pattern matches"

expression1 = re.compile( r"Test" )
expression2 = re.compile( r"^Test" )
expression3 = re.compile( r"Test$" )
expression4 = re.compile( r"\b\w*es\b" )
expression5 = re.compile( r"t[aeiou]", re.I )

if expression1.search( searchString ):
   print '"Test" was found.'

if expression2.match( searchString ):
   print '"Test" was found at the beginning of the line.'

if expression3.match( searchString ):
   print '"Test" was found at the end of the line.'

result = expression4.findall( searchString )

if result:
   print 'There are %d words(s) ending in "es":' % \
      ( len( result ) ),

   for item in result:
      print " " + item,

print
result = expression5.findall( searchString )

if result:
   print 'The letter t, followed by a vowel, occurs %d times:' % \
      ( len( result ) ),

   for item in result:
      print " " + item,

print
```

Fig. 28.12 Using regular expressions to search a string.

If a program uses a particular regular expression string many times, compiling that string can speed up the regular expression comparisons.

Figure 28.13 lists the most popular regular expression symbols recognized by the **re** module. Unless otherwise specified, regular expression characters ***** and **+** match as many occurrences of a pattern as possible. For example, the regular expression **hel*o** matches strings that have the letters **he**, followed by any number of **l**'s, followed by an **o** (e.g., **"heo"**, **"helo"**, **"hello"**, **"helllo"**, etc.).

Character	Matches
`^`	Beginning of string.
`$`	End of string.
`.`	Any character, except a newline.
`*`	Zero or more occurrences of the pattern.
`+`	One or more occurrences of the preceding pattern.
`?`	Zero or one occurrences of the preceding pattern.
`{m, n}`	Between **m** and **n** occurrences of the preceding pattern.
`\b`	Word boundary (i.e., the beginning or end of a word).
`\B`	Non-word boundary.
`\d`	Digit ([**0–9**]).
`\D`	Non-digit.
`\w`	Any alpha-numeric character.
`[...]`	Any character defined by the set.
`[^...]`	Any character not defined by the set.

Fig. 28.13 Some of the **re** module's regular expression characters.

Lines 9–12 use a few of these symbols to compile four regular expression patterns. The expression in line 9 (**expression2**) matches the string **"Test"** at the beginning of a line. The expression in line 10 (**expression3**) matches the string **"Test"** at the end of a line. The expression in line 11 (**expression4**) matches a word that ends with **"es"**. The expression in line 12 (**expression5**) matches the letter **t**, followed by a vowel. Line 12 illustrates the optional second argument that function **compile** may take. This argument is a flag that describes how the regular expression will be used when matching the expression against a string. The ***re.I*** flag means that case is ignored when using the regular expression to process a string.

The **r** character before each string in lines 8–12 indicates that the string is a *raw string*. Python handles backslash characters in raw strings differently than in "normal" strings. Specifically, Python does not interpret backslashes as escape characters. Writing all regular expressions as raw strings can help programmers avoid writing regular expressions that may be interpreted in a way they did not intend. For example, without the raw-string character, the regular-expression string in line 11 would have to be written as **\\b\\w*es\\b**, because **\b** is a backspace to Python, but a word boundary in regular expressions.

Line 14 uses the **SRE_Pattern**'s ***search*** *method* to test **searchString** against the regular expression **expression1**. The **search** method returns an **SRE_Match** object. If **search** does not find any matching substrings, the method returns ***None***. **None** is a Python type whose value indicates that no value exists. In a Python **if** statement, **None** evaluates to false; therefore, we only need to test the return value to determine whether any matches were found. If a match is found, we print an appropriate message.

Line 17 uses **SRE_Pattern**'s ***match*** *method* to test **searchString** against regular expression **expression2**. The **match** method returns an **SRE_Match** object only if the string matches the pattern exactly.

Line 23 uses **SRE_Pattern**'s ***findall*** *method* to store in variable **result** a list of all substrings in **searchString** that match the regular expression **expression4**. If **findall** returns any matches, we print a message that indicates how many words were found (lines 25–27) by using Python *function* **len**. When run on a list, function **len** returns the number of elements in that list. Lines 29–30 print each item in the list, followed by a space.

Lines 34–41 perform similar processing with **expression5** to print all substrings in **searchString** that match the pattern of the letter **t** followed by a vowel. Remember that **expression5** was compiled using the **re.I** flag. Thus the letter **t** or the vowels in **searchString** can be either lower- or uppercase. We end the program by printing a new line.

28.5 Exception Handling

In an interpreted language such as Python, errors pose a unique problem, because many errors caught at compilation time for a compiled language are not caught until run time in an interpreted language. These errors cause *exceptions* in Python. When a program encounters an exception, the program exits and displays an error message.

Exception handling enables programs and programmers to identify an error when it occurs and to take appropriate action. Exception handling is geared to situations in which a code block that detects an error is unable to deal with that error. Such a block of code will *raise an exception*. The programmer can write code that then *catches the exception* and handles the error in a "graceful" manner.

Python accomplishes exception handling through the use of **try/except** blocks. Any code that causes an error raises an exception. If this code is contained in a **try** block, the corresponding **except** block then catches the exception (i.e., handles the error). The core Python language defines a hierarchy of exceptions. A Python **except** block can catch one of these exceptions, or a subset of these exceptions, or it can specify none of these exceptions, in which case the code block catches all exceptions. Figure 28.14 shows how dividing a number by zero raises a **ZeroDivisionError** exception.

Figure 28.15 presents a simple program that illustrates exception handling in Python. The program requests two numbers from the user, then attempts to divide the first number by the second.

```
Python 2.1 (#15, Apr 16 2001, 18:25:49) [MSC 32 bit (Intel)] on win32
Type "copyright", "credits" or "license" for more information.
>>> 1 / 0
Traceback (most recent call last):
  File "<stdin>", line 1, in ?
ZeroDivisionError: integer division or modulo by zero
>>>
```

Fig. 28.14 Interactive session illustrating a **ZeroDivisionError** exception.

```
1  # Fig. 28.15: fig28_15.py
2  # A simple program that illustrates exceptions.
3
4  def getFloat():
5     return float( raw_input( "Enter a number: " ) )
6
7  number1 = number2 = None
8
9  while number1 == None:
10    try:
11       number1 = getFloat()
12    except ValueError:
13       print "Value entered was not a number"
14
15 while number2 == None:
16    try:
17       number2 = getFloat()
18    except ValueError:
19       print "Value entered was not a number"
20
21 try:
22    result = number1 / number2
23 except ZeroDivisionError:
24    print "Cannot divide by zero!"
25 else:
26    print "The result of division is: %f" % result
```

Fig. 28.15 Demonstrating exception handling.

Lines 4–5 define function **getFloat**, which prompts the user for a number and returns the number that the user enters. This function gets user input through Python function **raw_input** and then obtains the user-entered value as a floating-point value with Python function **float**.

Line 7 creates two variables (**number1** and **number2**) and assigns **None** to both. Lines 9–19 use **while** loops to store user-entered values in these variables by using function **getFloat**, with exception handling. In lines 9 and 15, we use the *keyword* **is** to test if the program has received a valid number. Lines 10–11 define a **try** block. Any code in the **try** block that raises an exception will be "caught" and handled in the corresponding **except** block (lines 12–13). The **try** block calls function **getFloat** to get the user input.

If the user does not enter a numerical value at the prompt, the **float** function raises a **ValueError** *exception*, which is caught by the **except** block (lines 12–13). This block prints an appropriate message before program control returns to the top of the **while** loop. Lines 15–19 repeat the same action to get a floating-point value for variable **number2**.

Lines 21-26 print the results of dividing variables **number1** and **number2**. We place the call to **divideNumbers** in the **try** block. As we saw in Fig. 28.14, if a program attempts to divide by zero, the program raises a **ZeroDivisionError**. The **except** block in lines 26–27 catches this exception and prints an appropriate message to the screen.

A **try** block may optionally specify a corresponding **else** block (lines 25–26). If the code in the **try** block does not raise an exception, the program executes the code in the **else** block. If an exception is raised in the **try** block, the **else** block is not executed. In our example, the **else** block prints the result of the division.

Good Programming Practice 28.2

In general, we want to minimize the amount of code contained in a **try** *block. Usually, we only place code in a* **try** *block that could raise an exception that we are capable of handling. In the* **else** *block, we place code that we want to run if no exception is raised in the* **try** *block.*

28.6 Introduction to CGI Programming

Python has many uses on the Web. Modules **cgi** (for access to XHTML forms), **Cookie** (to read and write cookies), **smtplib** (to manipulate SMTP messages), **urllib** (to manipulate Web data), **ftplib** (to perform client-side FTP tasks) and others provide powerful extensions that Web programmers can use to write CGI scripts quickly for almost any task. This section introduces Python CGI programming. Sections 28.7–28.9 present more detailed CGI applications. We assume that the reader has installed and configured the Apache Web server. Apache does not usually need any special configuration to run a Python script; a script need merely be placed in the specified **cgi-bin** directory.

Figure 28.16 gathers all CGI environment variables and values and organizes them in an XHTML table that is displayed in a Web browser. Line 1

```
#!c:\Python\python.exe
```

is a *directive* (sometimes called the *pound-bang* or *Shebang*) that provides the server with the location of the Python executable. This directive must be the first line in a CGI script. For UNIX-based machines, this value might commonly be

`#!/usr/bin/python` or `#!/usr/local/bin/python`

depending on the actual location of the Python executable.

```
1  #!c:\Python\python.exe
2  # Fig 28.16: fig28_16.py
3  # Program to display CGI environment variables
4
5  import os
6  import cgi
7
8  print "Content-type: text/html"
9  print
10
11 print """<!DOCTYPE html PUBLIC
12    "-//W3C//DTD XHTML 1.0 Transitional//EN"
13    "DTD/xhtml1-transitional.dtd">"""
14
15 print """
```

Fig. 28.16 Displaying environment variables (part 1 of 2).

```
16 <html xmlns = "http://www.w3.org/1999/xhtml" xml:lang="en"
17    lang="en">
18    <head><title>Environment Variables</title></head>
19       <body><table style = "border: 0">"""
20
21 rowNumber = 0
22
23 for item in os.environ.keys():
24     rowNumber += 1
25
26     if rowNumber % 2 == 0:
27         backgroundColor = "white"
28     else:
29         backgroundColor = "lightgrey"
30
31     print """<tr style = "background-color: %s">
32     <td>%s</td><td>%s</td></tr>""" \
33           % ( backgroundColor, item,
34               cgi.escape( os.environ[ item ] ) )
35
36 print """</table></body></html>"""
```

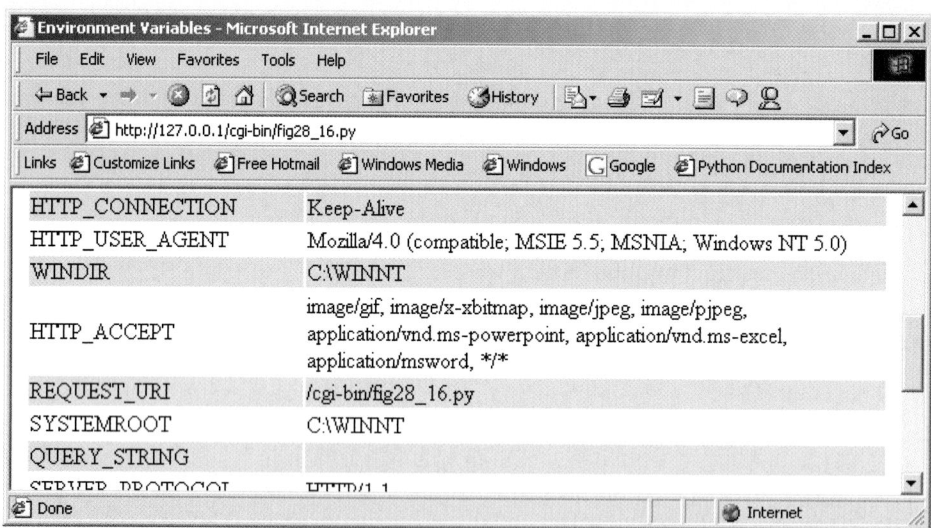

Fig. 28.16 Displaying environment variables (part 2 of 2).

Line 6 imports the **`cgi`** *module* that provides functionalities for writing CGI scripts. In this example, we use the module to format output; in later examples, we use module **`cgi`** to perform more complex CGI tasks.

Lines 8–9 print a valid HTTP header. Browsers use HTTP headers to determine how to handle the incoming data, and a valid header must be sent to ensure that the browser displays the information correctly. The blank line below the header is required; without this line, the content will not be delivered properly to the client. Lines 11–13 print the XHTML **DOCTYPE** string to the browser.

The ***environ*** *data member* (line 23) of module **os** holds all the environment variables. This data member acts like a dictionary; therefore, we can access its keys via the **keys** method and its values via the **[]** operator. In lines 23–34, we print a new row in the table for each item returned by method **os.environment.keys**. This row contains the key and the key's value. Notice that we pass each environment variable to function **cgi.escape**. This function formats text in an "XHTML-safe" way—special XHTML characters such as **<** and **&** are formatted so that they appear in the document as they should. After we have printed all the environment variables, we close the **table**, **body** and **html** tags (line 36).

28.7 Form Processing and Business Logic

XHTML forms allow users to enter data to be sent to a Web server for processing. Once the server receives the form, a server program processes the data. Such a program could help people purchase products, send and receive Web-based e-mail, complete a survey, etc. These types of Web applications allow users to interact with the server. Figure 28.17 uses an XHTML **form** to allow users to input personal information for a mailing list. This type of registration might be used to store user information in a database.

```
<!DOCTYPE html PUBLIC
   "-//W3C//DTD XHTML 1.0 Transitional//EN"
   "DTD/xhtml1-transitional.dtd">
<!-- Fig. 28.17: fig28_17.html -->

<html xmlns = "http://www.w3.org/1999/xhtml" xml:lang="en"
   lang="en">
<head>
   <title>Sample FORM to take user input in HTML</title>
</head>

<body style = "font-family: Arial, sans-serif; font-size: 11pt">

   <div style = "font-size: 15pt; font-weight: bold">
      This is a sample registration form.
   </div>
      Please fill in all fields and click Register.

   <form method = "post" action = "/cgi-bin/fig28_18.py">
      <img src = "images/user.gif" alt = "user" /><br />
      <div style = "color: blue">
         Please fill out the fields below.<br />
      </div>
```

Fig. 28.17 XHTML form to collect information from user (part 1 of 3).

```
        <img src = "images/fname.gif" alt = "firstname" />
        <input type = "text" name = "firstname" /><br />
        <img src = "images/lname.gif" alt = "lastname" />
        <input type = "text" name = "lastname" /><br />
        <img src = "images/email.gif" alt = "email" />
        <input type = "text" name = "email" /><br />
        <img src = "images/phone.gif" alt = "phone" />
        <input type = "text" name = "phone" /><br />

        <div style = "font-size: 8pt">
           Must be in the form (555)555-5555<br/><br/>
        </div>

        <img src = "images/downloads.gif" alt = "downloads" /><br />
        <div style = "color: blue">
           Which book would you like information about?<br />
        </div>

        <select name = "book">
           <option>XML How to Program</option>
           <option>Python How to Program</option>
           <option>E-business and E-commerce How to Program</option>
           <option>Internet and WWW How to Program 2e</option>
           <option>C++ How to Program 3e</option>
           <option>Java How to Program 4e</option>
           <option>Visual Basic How to Program</option>
        </select>
        <br /><br />

        <img src = "images/os.gif" alt = "os" /><br />
        <div style = "color: blue">
           Which operating system are you
           currently using?<br />
        </div>

        <input type = "radio" name = "os" value = "Windows NT"
        checked = "checked" />
        Windows NT
        <input type = "radio" name = "os" value = "Windows 2000" />
        Windows 2000
        <input type = "radio" name = "os" value = "Windows 95_98" />
        Windows 95/98/ME<br />
        <input type = "radio" name = "os" value = "Linux" />
        Linux
        <input type = "radio" name = "os" value = "Other" />
        Other<br />
        <input type = "submit" value = "Register" />

     </form>
  </body>
  </html>
```

Fig. 28.17 XHTML form to collect information from user (part 2 of 3).

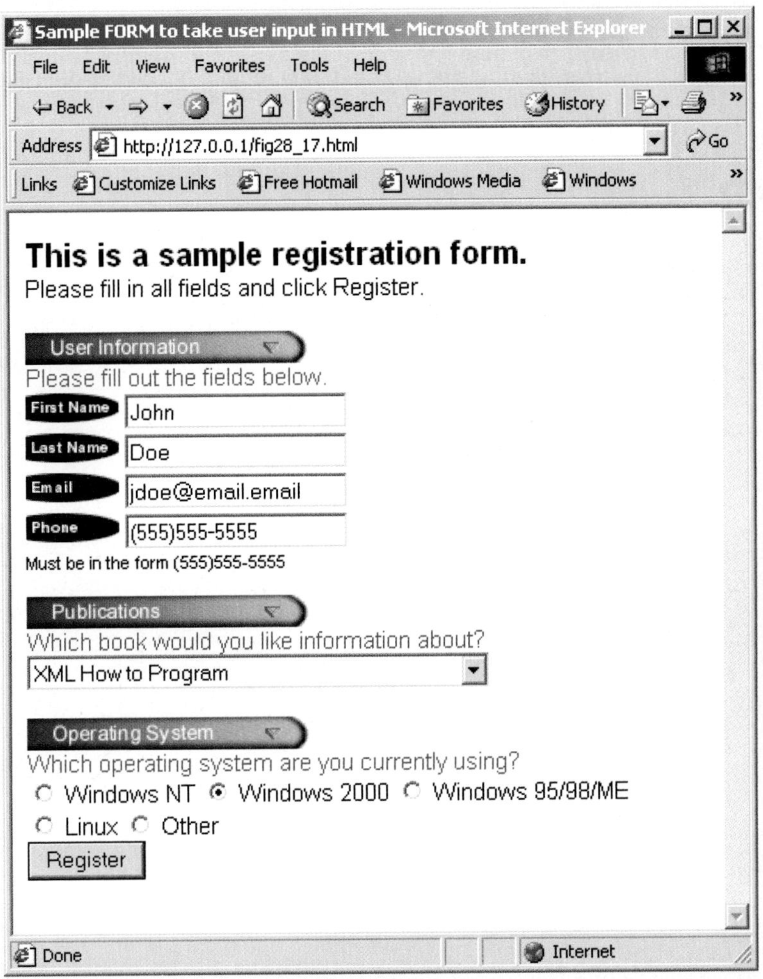

Fig. 28.17 XHTML form to collect information from user (part 3 of 3).

The **`form`** element (line 19) specifies how the information enclosed by tags **`<form>`** and **`</form>`** should be handled. The first attribute, **`method = "post"`**, directs the browser to send the form's information to the server. The second attribute, **`action = "/cgi-bin/fig28_18.py"`**, directs the server to execute the **`fig28_18.py`** Python script, located in the **`cgi-bin`** directory. The **`name`**s given to the input items (e.g., **`firstname`**) in the Web page are important when the Python script is executed on the server. These **`name`**s allow the script to refer to the individual pieces of data the user submits. When the user clicks the button labeled **Register**, both the input items and the names given to the items are sent to the **`fig28_18.py`** Python script.

Figure 28.18 takes user information from **`fig28_17.html`** and sends a Web page to the client indicating that the information was received. Line 6 **`import`**s the **`cgi`** module, which provides functionality for writing CGI scripts in Python, including access to XHTML form values.

```
#!c:\Python\python.exe
# Fig. 28.18: fig28_18.py
# Program to read information sent to the server from the
# form in the form.html document.

import cgi
import re

# the regular expression for matching most US phone numbers
telephoneExpression = \
   re.compile( r'^\(\d{3}\)\d{3}-\d{4}$' )

def printContent():
   print "Content-type: text/html"
   print
   print """
<html xmlns = "http://www.w3.org/1999/xhtml" xml:lang="en"
   lang="en">
   <head><title>Registration results</title></head>
      <body>"""

def printReply():
   print """
      Hi <span style = "color: blue; font-weight: bold">
      %(firstName)s</span>.
      Thank you for completing the survey.<br />
      You have been added to the <span style = "color: blue;
      font-weight: bold">%(book)s </span> mailing list.<br /><br />

      <span style = "font-weight: bold">
      The following information has been saved in our database:
      </span><br />

      <table style = "border: 0; border-width: 0;
         border-spacing: 10">
      <tr><td style = "background-color: yellow">Name </td>
          <td style = "background-color: yellow">Email</td>
          <td style = "background-color: yellow">Phone</td>
          <td style = "background-color: yellow">OS</td></tr>

      <tr><td>%(firstName)s %(lastName)s</td><td>%(email)s</td>
          <td>%(phone)s</td><td>%(os)s</td></tr>
      </table>

      <br /><br /><br />

      <div style = "text-align: center; font-size: 8pt">
      This is only a sample form.
      You have not been added to a mailing list.
      </div></center>
      """ % personInfo

```

Fig. 28.18 XHTML form to get cookie values from user (part 1 of 3).

```
def printPhoneError():

   print """<span style = "color: red; font-size 15pt">
      INVALID PHONE NUMBER</span><br />
      A valid phone number must be in the form
      <span style = "font-weight: bold">(555)555-5555</span>
      <span style = "color: blue"> Click the Back button,
      enter a valid phone number and resubmit.</span><br /><br />
      Thank You."""

def printFormError():

   print """<span style = "color: red; font-size 15pt">
      FORM ERROR</span><br />
      You have not filled in all fields.
      <span style = "color: blue"> Click the Back button,
      fill out the form and resubmit.</span><br /><br />
      Thank You."""

printContent()

form = cgi.FieldStorage()

try:
   personInfo = { 'firstName' : form[ "firstname" ].value,
                  'lastName' : form[ "lastname" ].value,
                  'email' : form[ "email" ].value,
                  'phone' : form[ "phone" ].value,
                  'book' : form[ "book" ].value,
                  'os' : form[ "os" ].value }
except KeyError:
   printFormError()

if telephoneExpression.match( personInfo[ 'phone' ] ):
   printReply()
else:
   printPhoneError()
```

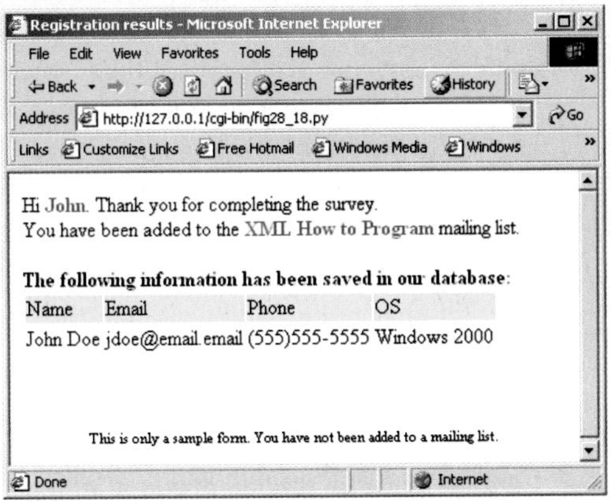
Registration results - Microsoft Internet Explorer
File Edit View Favorites Tools Help
Back Search Favorites History
Address http://127.0.0.1/cgi-bin/fig28_18.py
Go
Links Customize Links Free Hotmail Windows Media Windows
Hi John. Thank you for completing the survey.
You have been added to the XML How to Program mailing list.
The following information has been saved in our database:
Name Email Phone OS
John Doe jdoe@email.email (555)555-5555 Windows 2000
This is only a sample form. You have not been added to a mailing list.
Done
Internet

Fig. 28.18 XHTML form to get cookie values from user (part 2 of 3).

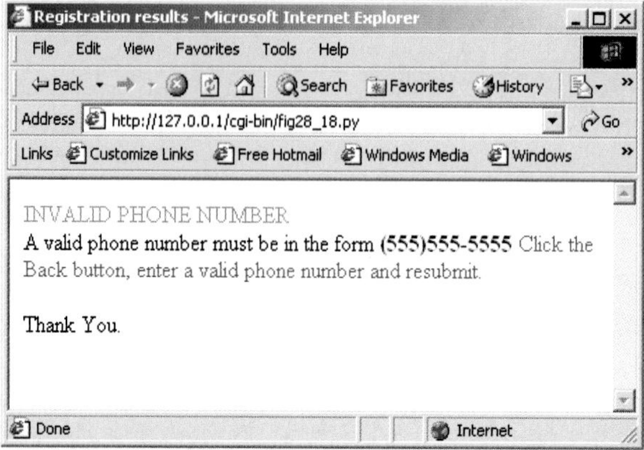

Fig. 28.18 XHTML form to get cookie values from user (part 3 of 3).

Line 72 begins the main portion of the script and calls function **`printContent`** to print the proper HTTP header and XHTML **`DOCTYPE`** string. Line 74 creates an instance of class **`FieldStorage`** and assigns the instance to variable **`form`**. This class contains information about any posted forms. The **`try`** block (lines 76–82) creates a dictionary that contains the appropriate values from each defined element in **`form`**. Each value is accessed via the **`value`** *data member* of a particular **`form`** element. For example, line 78 assigns the **`value`** of the **`lastName`** field of **`form`** to the dictionary key **`'lastName'`**.

If the value of any element in **`form`** is **`None`**, the **`try`** block raises a **`KeyError`** exception, and we call function **`printFormError`**. This function (lines 63–70) prints a message in the browser that tells the user the form has not been completed properly and instructs the user to click the **Back** button to fill out the form and resubmit it.

Line 86 tests the user-submitted phone number against the specified format. We compile the regular expression **`telephoneExpression`** in lines 10–11. If the expression's **`match`** method does not return **`None`**, we call the **`printReply`** function (discussed momentarily). If the **`match`** method does return **`None`** (i.e., the phone number is not in the proper format), we call function **`printPhoneError`**. This function (lines 53–61) displays a message in the browser that informs the user that the phone number is in improper format and instructs the user to click the **Back** button to change the phone number and resubmit the form.

If the user has filled out the form correctly, we call function **`printReply`** (lines 22–51). This function thanks the user and displays an XHTML **`table`** with the information gathered from the form. Notice that we format the output with values from the **`personInfo`** dictionary. For example, the beginning of line 25

```
%(firstName)s
```

inserts the value of the string variable **`firstName`** into the string after the percent sign (**`%`**). Line 51 informs Python that the string variable **`firstName`** is a key in the dictionary **`personInfo`**. Thus, the text at the beginning of line 25 is replaced with the value stored in **`personInfo[ 'firstName' ]`**.

28.8 Cookies

When a client visits a Web site, the server for that Web site may *write a cookie* to the client's machine. This cookie can be accessed by servers within the Web site's domain at a later time. Cookies are usually small text files used to maintain *state information* for a particular client. State information may contain a username, password or specific information that might be helpful when a user returns to a Web site. Many Web sites use cookies to store a client's postal zip code. The zip code is used when the client requests a Web page from the server. The server may send the current weather information or news updates for the client's region. The scripts in this section write cookie values to the client and retrieve the values for display in the browser.

Figure 28.19 is an XHTML **`form`** that asks the user to enter three values. These values are passed to the **`fig28_20.py`** script, which writes the values in a client-side cookie.

Figure 28.20 is the script that retrieves the form values from **`fig28_19.html`** and stores those values in a client-side cookie. Line 6 imports the **`Cookie`** module. This module provides capabilities for reading and writing client-side cookies.

Lines 9–15 define function **`printContent`**, which prints the content header and XHTML **`DOCTYPE`** string to the browser. Line 17 retrieves the form values by using class **`FieldStorage`** from module **`cgi`**. We handle the form values with a **`try/except/else`** block. The **`try`** block (lines 19–22) attempts to retrieve the form values. If the user has not completed one or more of the form fields, the code in this block raises a **`KeyError`** exception. The exception is caught in the **`except`** block (lines 23–28), and the program calls function **`printContent`**, then outputs an appropriate message to the browser.

```
<!DOCTYPE html PUBLIC
   "-//W3C//DTD XHTML 1.0 Transitional//EN"
   "DTD/xhtml1-transitional.dtd">
<!-- Fig. 28.19: fig28_19.html -->

<html xmlns = "http://www.w3.org/1999/xhtml" xml:lang = "en"
   lang = "en">
   <head>
      <title>Writing a cookie to the client computer</title>
   </head>

<body style = "background-image: images/back.gif;
   font-family: Arial,sans-serif; font-size: 11pt" >

   <span style = "font-size: 15pt; font-weight: bold">
      Click Write Cookie to save your cookie data.
   </span><br />

   <form method = "post" action = "/cgi-bin/fig28_20.py">
      <span style = "font-weight: bold">Name:</span><br />
      <input type = "text" name = "name" /><br />
      <span style = "font-weight: bold">Height:</span><br />
      <input type = "text" name = "height" /><br />
      <span style = "font-weight: bold">Favorite Color</span><br />
```

Fig. 28.19 XHTML form to get cookie values from user (part 1 of 2).

```
         <input type = "text" name = "color" /><br />
         <input type = "submit" value = "Write Cookie" />
      </form>

   </body>
   </html>
```

Fig. 28.19 XHTML form to get cookie values from user (part 2 of 2).

The code in the **else** block (lines 29–68) executes after the program successfully retrieves all the form values. Line 32 specifies the format for the expiration value of the cookie. The format characters in this string are defined by the **time** module. For a complete list of **time** tokens and their meanings, visit

www.python.org/doc/current/lib/module-time.html

```
1  #!C:\Python\python.exe
2  # Fig. 28.20: fig28_20.py
3  # Writing a cookie to a client's machine
4
5  import cgi
6  import Cookie
7  import time
8
9  def printContent():
10    print "Content-type: text/html"
11    print
12    print """
13 <html xmlns = "http://www.w3.org/1999/xhtml" xml:lang="en"
14    lang="en">
```

Fig. 28.20 Writing a cookie to a client's machine (part 1 of 3).

```
    <head><title>Cookie values</title></head>"""

form = cgi.FieldStorage()  # get form information

try:  # extract form values
   name = form[ "name" ].value
   height = form[ "height" ].value
   color = form[ "color" ].value
except KeyError:
   printContent()
   print """<body><h3>You have not filled in all fields.
   <span style = "color: blue"> Click the Back button,
   fill out the form and resubmit.<br /><br />
   Thank You. </span></h3>"""
else:

   # construct cookie expiration date and path
   expirationFormat = "%A, %d-%b-%y %X %Z"
   expirationTime = time.localtime( time.time() + 300 )
   expirationDate = time.strftime( expirationFormat,
      expirationTime )
   path = "/"

   # construct cookie contents
   cookie = Cookie.Cookie()

   cookie[ "Name" ] = name
   cookie[ "Name" ][ "expires" ] = expirationDate
   cookie[ "Name" ][ "path" ] = path

   cookie[ "Height" ] = height
   cookie[ "Height" ][ "expires" ] = expirationDate
   cookie[ "Height" ][ "path" ] = path

   cookie[ "Color" ] = color
   cookie[ "Color" ][ "expires" ] = expirationDate
   cookie[ "Color" ][ "path" ] = path

   # print cookie to user and page to browser
   print cookie

   printContent()
   print """<body style = "background-image: /images/back.gif;
   font-family: Arial,sans-serif; font-size: 11pt">
   The cookie has been set with the following data: <br /><br />

   <span style = "color: blue">Name:</span> %s<br />
   <span style = "color: blue">Height:</span> %s<br />
   <span style = "color: blue">Favorite Color:</span>
   <span style = "color: %s"> %s</span><br />""" \
   % ( name, height, color, color )

```

Fig. 28.20 Writing a cookie to a client's machine (part 2 of 3).

```
67      print """<br /><a href= "fig28_21.py">
68      Read cookie values</a>"""
69
70  print """</body></html>"""
```

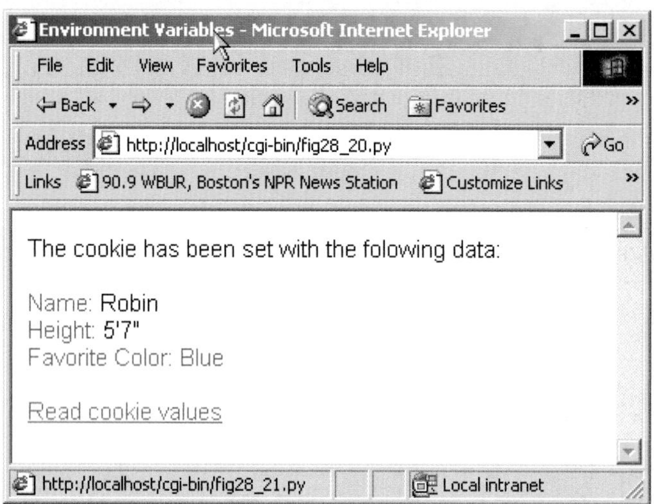

Fig. 28.20 Writing a cookie to a client's machine (part 3 of 3).

The **time** function (line 33) of module **time** returns a floating-point value that is the number of seconds since the *epoch* (i.e., January 1, 1970). We add 300 seconds to this value to set the **expirationTime** for the cookie. We then format the time using the **localtime** function. This function converts the time in seconds to a nine-element tuple that represents the time in local terms (i.e., according to the time zone of the machine on which the script is running). Lines 34–35 call the **strftime** function to format a time tuple into a string. This line effectively formats tuple **expirationTime** as a string that follows the format specified in **expirationFormat**.

Line 39 creates an instance of *class* **Cookie**. An object of class **Cookie** acts like a dictionary, so values can be set and retrieved using familiar dictionary syntax. Lines 41–51 set the values for the cookie, based on the user-entered values retrieved from the XHMTL form.

Line 54 writes the cookie to the browser (assuming the user's browser has enabled cookies) by using the **print** statement. The cookie must be written before we write the content type (line 56) to the browser. Lines 57–65 display the cookie's values in the browser. We then conclude the **else** block by creating a link to a Python script that retrieves the stored cookie values (lines 67–68).

Figure 28.21 is the CGI script that retrieves cookie values from the client and displays the values in the browser. Line 18 creates an instance of class **Cookie**. Line 19 retrieves the cookie values from the client. Cookies are stored as a string in the environment variable **HTTP_COOKIE**. The **load** *method* of class **Cookie** extracts cookie values from a string. If no cookie value exists, then the program raises a **KeyError** exception. We catch the exception in lines 20–22 and print an appropriate message in the browser.

If the program successfully retrieves the cookie values, the code in lines 23–37 displays the values in the browser. Because cookies act like dictionaries, we can use the **keys** method (line 31) to retrieve the names of all the values in the cookie. Lines 32–35 print these names and their corresponding values in a table.

```
1  #!C:\Python\python.exe
2  # Fig. 28.21: fig28_21.py
3  # Program that retrieves and displays client-side cookie values
4
5  import Cookie
6  import os
7
8  print "Content-type: text/html"
9  print
10 print """
11 <html xmlns = "http://www.w3.org/1999/xhtml" xml:lang="en"
12    lang="en">
13    <head><title>Cookie values</title></head>
14    <body style =
15    font-family: Arial, sans-serif; font-size: 11pt">"""
16
17 try:
18    cookie = Cookie.Cookie()
19    cookie.load( os.environ[ "HTTP_COOKIE" ] )
20 except KeyError:
21    print """<span style = "font-weight: bold">Error reading cookies
22    </span>"""
23 else:
24    print """<span style = "font-weight: bold">
25    The following data is saved in a cookie on your computer.
26    </span><br /><br />"""
27
28    print """<table style = "border-width: 5; border-spacing: 0;
29       padding: 10">"""
30
31    for item in cookie.keys():
32       print """<tr>
33          <td style = "background-color: lavender">%s</td>
34          <td style = "background-color: white">%s</td>
35       </tr>""" % ( item, cookie[ item ].value )
36
37    print """</table>"""
38
39 print """</body></html>"""
```

Fig. 28.21 CGI script that retrieves and displays client-side cookie values.

28.9 Database Application Programming Interface (DB-API)

Python's open-source nature encourages independent developers to contribute additions to the language. In earlier versions of Python, many developers contributed modules that provided interfaces to several databases. Unfortunately, these interfaces rarely resembled one another; if an application developer wanted to change the application's database, the whole program had to be rewritten.

The *Python Database Special Interest Group (SIG)* was formed to develop a specification for *Python database application programming interface (DB-API)*. The specification is now in version 2.0, and modules that conform to this specification exist for many databases. In this section we illustrate the Python interface to MySQL (*module* **MySQLdb**).

28.9.1 Setup

The next programming example assumes the user has installed MySQL and the **MySQLdb** module. The **MySQLdb** module must be downloaded and installed. [*Note:* The resources for this book posted at our Web site, **www.deitel.com**, include step-by-step instructions for installing **MySQLdb**.]

28.9.2 Simple DB-API Program

The example in this section lets the user choose an author from an XHTML drop-down list. The user then clicks a button to query the database. The database query returns a list of all books by that author.

Figure 28.22 is a CGI script that creates the XHTML author selection list by querying the database. Line 4 imports the **MySQLdb** module. This provides access to a MySQL database using the Python DB-API.

Lines 6–13 print the HTTP header and XHTML **DOCTYPE** string to the browser. The remainder of the program is contained in a **try/except/else** block. In the **try** block (lines 15–16), we attempt to connect to the MySQL database called **books**. Line 16 connects to the database. The call to **connect** in module **MySQLdb** returns an instance of a **Connection** object. In the call to **connect**, we pass the value **"books"** to the *keyword argument* **db**. A keyword argument is a named argument defined by a function. To pass a value to a named argument, we assign a value to the name inside the function call's parentheses, as in line 16. The **Connection** object returned by the call is stored in local variable **connection**.

```
1  #!c:\Python\python.exe
2  # Fig. 28.22: fig28_22.py
3  # A program to illustrate Python's database connectivity.
4  import MySQLdb
5
6  print "Content-type: text/html"
7  print
8  print """
```

Fig. 28.22 CGI script to create list of authors (part 1 of 2).

```
9  <html xmlns = "http://www.w3.org/1999/xhtml" xml:lang="en"
10    lang="en">
11    <head><title>Select Author</title></head>
12    <body style =
13    font-family: Arial, sans-serif; font-size: 11pt">"""
14
15 try:
16    connection = MySQLdb.connect( db = "books" )
17 except OperationalError:
18    print "Unable to connect to database: %s" % message
19 else:
20    cursor = connection.cursor()
21    cursor.execute( "SELECT * FROM Authors" )
22    authorList = cursor.fetchall()
23
24    cursor.close()                    # close cursor
25    connection.close()                # close connection
26
27    print """
28    <form method = "post" action = "/cgi-bin/fig28_23.py">
29       <select name = "authorID">"""
30
31    for author in authorList:
32       print """<option value = %d>%s, %s</option>"""  \
33             % ( author[ 0 ], author[ 2 ], author[ 1 ] )
34
35    print """
36       </select>
37       <input type = "submit" value = "Execute Query" />
38    </ form>"""
39
40 print """</body></html>"""
```

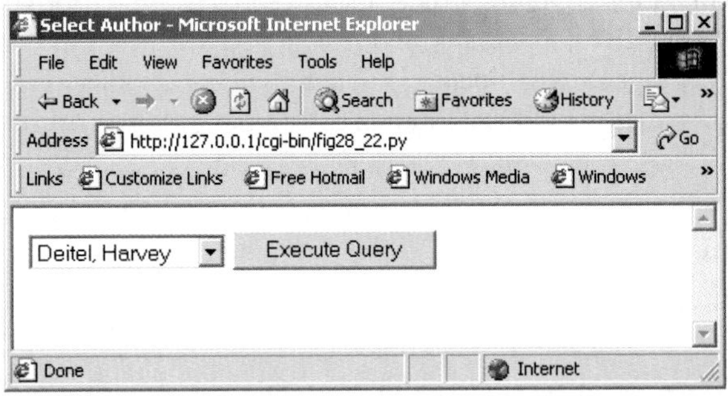

Fig. 28.22 CGI script to create list of authors (part 2 of 2).

If the call to **`MySQLdb.connect`** succeeds, we have connected to the database. If the call does not succeed, the program receives an **`OperationalError`** exception. We catch this exception in lines 17–18, where we print an appropriate error message.

If the program does not encounter an **`OperationalError`** exception, we execute the code in the **`else`** block (lines 19–38). Line 20 calls the **`cursor`** method of object

connection. This method returns a **Cursor** object that allows us to execute queries against the database. We store this object in local variable **cursor**.

Line 21 calls method **execute** to execute an SQL query against the database. The **execute** method takes as an argument a valid SQL string and runs that string against the database. The results of the query are stored in object **cursor**. We retrieve the results by calling method **fetchall** (line 22). This method returns a list of all the records that matched the query string we passed to the **execute** call. In our example, method **fetchall** returns a list of all the records from the **Authors** table in the **books** database. We store this list in local variable **authorList**. In lines 24–25, we close the cursor and the connection by calling their respective **close** methods.

Good Programming Practice 28.3

The Python DB-API implementation automatically closes a connection to a database when the program exits; still, we include this code as a matter of good practice.

The remainder of the **else** block (lines 29–38) writes the XHTML form that lets the user choose an author and query the database. The **form** is posted to **fig28_23.py**, which queries the database for the user-selected author. Lines 27–29 create the XHTML **select** item from which the user will choose an author, named **authorID**. Lines 31–33 contain a **for** loop that creates an **option** for each author in the database. Each record in **authorList** is a tuple with the following format

```
(authorID, firstName, lastName, birthYear)
```

We construct each **option** by assigning a **value** that corresponds to the ID (**author[0]**) and displaying the last name followed by the first name (**author[2]** and **author[1]**, respectively). Lines 35–37 complete the **select** item and add a button to the form, so the user can execute the query.

Figure 28.23 is the CGI script that executes a query against the database based on the author chosen from the form in **fig28_22.html**. Line 10 retrieves the form using the **FieldStorage** class from module **cgi**. Lines 21–30 contain a **try/except** block that attempts to retrieve the **authorID** selected by the user. If the form contains a value for **authorID**, we store that value in local variable **authorID**; otherwise, we print an error message to the browser (lines 24–29). Line 30 calls function **sys.exit**, causing the program to terminate.

```
1  #!c:\Python\python.exe
2  # Fig. 28.23: fig28_23.py
3  # A program to illustrate Python's database connectivity.
4
5  import cgi
6  import MySQLdb
7  import sys
8
9  # get results from form
10 form = cgi.FieldStorage()
11
12 print "Content-type: text/html"
```

Fig. 28.23 CGI script to create table of titles, given an author (part 1 of 3).

```
print
print """
<html xmlns = "http://www.w3.org/1999/xhtml" xml:lang="en"
   lang="en">
   <head><title>Query results</title></head>
   <body style =
   font-family: Arial, sans-serif; font-size: 11pt">"""

try:
   authorID = form[ "authorID" ].value
except KeyError:
   print """<span style = "color: red size = 15pt">
   FORM ERROR</span><br />
   You did not select an author.<br />
   <span style = "color: blue"> Click the Back button,
   fill out the form and resubmit.<br /><br />
   Thank You.</span></body></html>"""
   sys.exit()

# connect to database and get cursor
try:
   connection = MySQLdb.connect( db = 'books' )
except OperationalError:
   print """<span style = "color: red size = 15pt">
   DATABASE ERROR</span><br /> Unable to connect to database.
   </body></html>"""
   sys.exit()

queryString = """select Titles.* from Titles, AuthorISBN
              where AuthorISBN.AuthorID=%s and
              Titles.ISBN=AuthorISBN.ISBN""" % authorID

cursor = connection.cursor()
cursor.execute( queryString )

results = cursor.fetchall()

cursor.close()                  # close cursor
connection.close()              # close connection

# display results
print """<table style = "border: groove 2 pt;
            border-colapse: separate">
         <tr>
            <th>ISBN</th>
            <th>Title</th>
            <th>Edition</th>
            <th>Year</th>
            <th>Description</th>
            <th>Publisher ID</th>
         </tr>"""
```

Fig. 28.23 CGI script to create table of titles, given an author (part 2 of 3).

```
65 for row in results:
66    print "<tr>"
67
68    for entry in row:
69       print '<td style = "border: solid 2pt">%s</td>' % entry
70
71    print "</tr>"
72
73 print """</table></body></html>"""
```

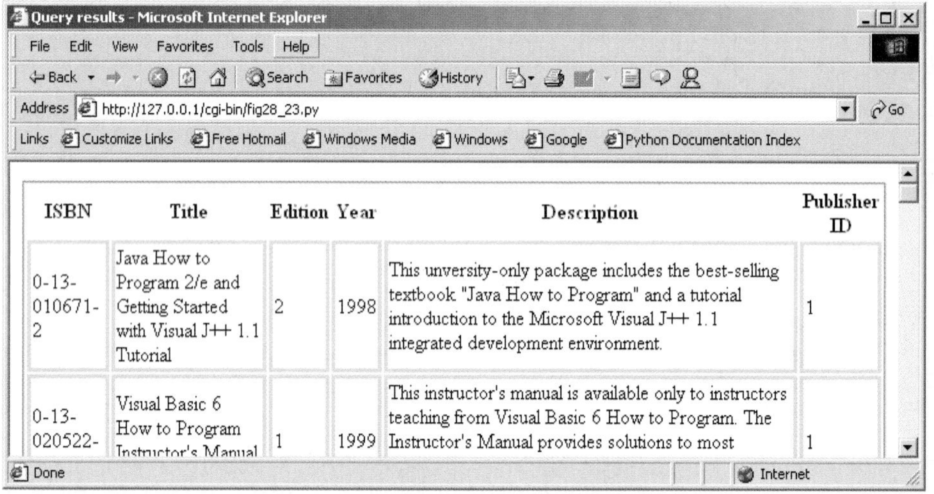

Fig. 28.23 CGI script to create table of titles, given an author (part 3 of 3).

We attempt to connect to the MySQL database called **books** in lines 33–39. If we are unable to obtain a connection, we print an error message and call **sys.exit** to exit the program (lines 36–39).

Lines 41–43 construct a query string to execute against the database. This query selects all columns from table **Title** where the ISBN matches all ISBNs from table **AuthorISBN** that correspond to the **authorID** specified in the form. Lines 45–46 create a cursor for the database and execute the query string against the database. We retrieve the results of the query using method **fetchall** and store the records in local variable **results** (line 48). We then close the cursor and the connection (lines 50–51).

The remainder of the program (lines 54–73) displays the results of the query. We create a table and label the headers with the column names from the database (lines 54–63). Line 65 begins a **for** loop that iterates over each record in local variable **results**. For each record, we create a row in the table (lines 66–71). Each column value has a corresponding entry in the row (lines 68–69). After we have printed all the records, we print a closing table tag (line 73).

In this section we have illustrated Python's DB-API through a specific implementation of the DBI, module **MySQLdb**. Because **MySQLdb** conforms to the DB-API, the code in our examples would not require many changes to work with another module that conforms to the DB-API. In fact, we could use many other databases, such as Microsoft Access or Informix, because their respective modules (**odbc** and **informixdb**) conform to the DB-API.

28.10 Operator Precedence Chart

This section contains the operator precedence chart for Python (Fig. 28.24). The operators are shown in decreasing order of precedence, from top to bottom.

Operator	Type	Associativity
` `	string conversion	left to right
{ }	dictionary creation	left to right
[ ]	list creation	left to right
( )	tuple creation or expression grouping	left to right
( )	function call	left to right
[:]	slicing	left to right
[ ]	subscript access	left to right
.	member access	left to right
**	exponentiation	right to left
~	bitwise NOT	left to right
+ -	unary plus unary minus	right to left
* / %	multiplication division modulus (remainder)	left to right
+ -	addition subtraction	left to right
<< >>	left shift right shift	left to right
&	bitwise AND	left to right
^	bitwise XOR	left to right
|	bitwise OR	left to right
< <= > >= != ==	less than less than or equal greater than greater than or equal not equal equal	left to right
is, **is not**	identity	left to right
in, **not in**	membership tests	left to right

Fig. 28.24 Python operator precedence chart (part 1 of 2).

Operator	Type	Associativity
`not`	boolean NOT	left to right
`and`	boolean AND	left to right
`or`	boolean OR	left to right
`lambda`	lambda expressions (anonymous functions)	left to right

Fig. 28.24 Python operator precedence chart (part 2 of 2).

28.11 Internet and World Wide Web Resources

www.python.org
This is the Python home page. From this site, you can download the latest version of Python for all platforms. The site also posts all the Python documentation and provides links to other resources, such as additional modules, tutorials, search engines, special-interest groups, an event calendar, a job board, mailing lists and archives.

www.zope.com
This is the home page for Zope Corporation, the developers of Zope—a Web application server written in Python.

www.zope.org
This is the home page for Zope and its community.

starship.python.net
This Web site provides resources for Python developers. Site members post Python modules and utilities on this site.

www.python.org/download/download_mac.html
This site provides information on and links to a MacOS version of Python.

www.vex.net/parnassus
This site contains many third-party Python modules, which are freely available for download.

www.pythonware.com
Secret Labs AB is a company that offers application development tools for Python. The Pythonware Web site provides links to Secret Labs AB products and other Python resources.

www.corrt.com/info/pyisp-list.html
This site posts a list of Internet Service Providers (ISPs) that support Python.

starship.python.net/crew/davem/cgifaq
This site posts a Python/CGI FAQ.

www.devshed.com/Server_Side/Python/CGI
This site posts an article/tutorial on writing CGI programs in Python.

starship.python.net/crew/aaron_watters/pws.html
This site provides instructions for configuring IIS/PWS for Python / CGI scripts.

members.nbci.com/alan_gauld/tutor/tutindex.htm
This site contains a Python tutorial geared towards novice programmers. The tutorial's goal is to teach programming fundamentals using Python.

www.python.org/doc/howto/regex/regex.html
This site contains a tutorial on using Python regular expressions.

www.devshed.com/Server_Side/Zope/Intro
This article presents an introduction to Zope, a Web application server written in Python.

www.python.org/windows/win32com
This site contains resources for Python/COM development.

www.pythonware.com/library/tkinter/tkclass/index.htm
This site contains an introduction to **Tkinter**, a Python GUI development library.

www.chordate.com/gadfly.html
This is the home page for Gadfly, a relational database written in Python.

aspn.activestate.com/ASPN/Python/Cookbook
This site contains many Python examples to accomplish a variety of tasks.

www.python.org/windows/win32/odbc.html
An introduction to Python's **odbc** module can be found at this site.

starship.python.net/crew/bwilk/access.html
This site contains a few notes on using Python and Microsoft Access.

www.python.org/doc/Comparisons.html
Guido van Rossum has posted an essay on this page that compares Python with other popular languages, such as Java, C++ and Perl.

www.vic.auug.org.au/auugvic/av_paper_python.html
This article contains an overview of Python and lists many uses and features of the language.

www.networkcomputing.com/unixworld/tutorial/005/005.html
This site contains a tutorial and an introduction to Python.

SUMMARY

- Python is an interpreted, cross-platform, object-oriented language. It is a freely distributed, open-source technology.
- Using Python's core modules and those freely available on the Web, programmers can develop applications that accomplish a variety of tasks.
- Python's interpreted nature facilitates Rapid Application Development (RAD).
- Comments in Python begin with the **#** character; Python ignores all text in the current line after this character.
- Python statements can be executed in two ways. The statements can be typed into a file and then invoking Python on that file. Python statements can also be interpreted dynamically by typing them in at the Python interactive prompt.
- Python keywords have special meanings in Python and cannot be used as variable names, function names and other objects. A list of Python keywords can be obtained from the **keyword** module.
- The keyword **def** marks the beginning of the function definition. The function's parameter list is followed by a colon (**:**).
- Python is a case-sensitive language.
- Python determines the beginning and end of a statement based on whitespace. Each new line begins a new statement, and groups of statements that belong to the same block of code are indented the same amount.
- Keyword **return** causes the program to exit and to return the specified value.

- Python function **raw_input** retrieves input from the program user. This function may optionally take a string argument that is a prompt to the user.
- The Python **int** function converts noninteger data types to integers.
- The backslash character (\) is the line-continuation character. Lines may also be continued freely inside nested parentheses, brackets and braces.
- The "**\n**" escape code is a special Python character that represents a newline character.
- Tuples are created as a comma-separated list of values in parentheses (**( )**). A tuple can contain any data type (e.g., strings, integers, other tuples, etc.) and may contain elements of different types.
- Tuples are immutable—after a tuple is created, an element at a defined index cannot be replaced.
- The **+=** statement adds an element to the end of a tuple.
- By default, the **print** statement writes a newline character (e.g., a carriage return) at the end of its output; however, a comma placed at the end of a **print** statement tells Python to leave out the newline.
- Python lists consist of a sequence of zero or more elements.
- Python lists are mutable—an element at an index that has been defined may be replaced.
- Method **append** adds an element to the end of a list.
- Each entry in a dictionary has two parts—the key and the value—and a dictionary consists of a set of zero or more comma-separated key-value pairs.
- A value in a dictionary is accessed through that value's key. The key must be unique and of an immutable data type (e.g., number, string or tuple that contains only immutable data types); values may be of any data type.
- A regular expression string defines a pattern against which text data can be compared. Regular expression processing capability is available in the standard Python module **re**.
- Unless otherwise specified, regular-expression characters ***** and **+** match as many occurrences of a regular expression as possible.
- Compiling a regular expression string (using **re** method **compile**) speeds up a regular expression comparison that uses that string.
- Strings can be contained in single quotes (**' '**), double quotes (**" "**) or in a set of three single or double quotes (**''' '''** or **""" """**)
- The **%** format character acts like a place holder in the string. Python defines several format characters for use in string formatting
- Importing a module enables programmers to use functions defined by that module.
- An **r** before a string indicates that the string is a raw string. Python handles backslash characters in raw strings differently than in "normal" strings—Python does not interpret backslashes as escape characters in raw strings.
- **re** module's **findall** method returns a list of all substrings in a particular string that match a specified regular expression.
- Exception handling enables programs and programmers to identify an error when the error occurs and to take appropriate action. Python accomplishes exception handling through the use of **try**/**except** blocks.
- Any code that causes an error raises an exception. If the code that raises an exception is contained in a **try** block, the corresponding **except** block catches the exception (i.e., handles the error).
- An **except** block can and should specify a particular exception to catch.

- A **try** block may optionally specify a corresponding **else** block. If the code in the **try** block does not raise an exception, then the program executes the code in the **else** block. If an exception is raised in the **try** block, then the **else** block is skipped.
- The pound-bang (**#!**) directive—the directive that specifies the location of the Python executable— must be the first line in a CGI script.
- The **cgi** module provides functionality for writing CGI scripts in Python, including access to XHTML form values.
- **cgi** method **FieldStorage** provides access to XHTML form values.
- The **Cookie** module provides access to cookies.
- An object of class **Cookie** acts like a dictionary, so values can be set and retrieved using familiar dictionary syntax.
- The **time** function of module **time** returns a floating-point value that is the number of seconds since the "epoch" (i.e., the first day of 1970).
- An object of class **Cookie** acts like a dictionary, so values can be set and retrieved using familiar dictionary syntax.
- The **load** method of module **Cookie** extracts cookie values from a string. If no cookie value exists, then the program raises the **KeyError** exception.

TERMINOLOGY

' (single quote) character
" (double quote) character
""" (triple quote) characters
comment character
#! (pound-bang) directive
% formatting character
% modulo operator
% operator
%= operator
****=** statement
***=** statement
, (comma) character
. (dot) operator
. operator
/= statement
: (colon) character
: (slice) operator
[] operator
**** (backslash) character
\\n escape character
{} characters
"chained" expression
+ operator
+= statement
-= statement
and
Apache Web server
append method
catch an exception
cgi module
CGI scripts
compiling a regular expression
concatenated strings
connection object
constructor
Cookie class
Cookie module
Ctrl-Z/*Ctrl-D* character
cursor object
Database Application Programming Interface
Database Special Interest Group (SIG)
debugging
def
dictionary
else
environ data member of module **os**
epoch
escape character
exception handling
expiration value of a cookie
fetchall method of class **cursor**
FieldStorage class
findall method of module **re**
float function
for
formatting character
get method
greatest common divisor

HTTP header
HTTP_COOKIE environment variable
if
if/elif
if/else
immutable data type
import
importing a module
indentation of statement
int function
interactive mode
key/value pair
KeyError exception
keys
keyword module
list
load method of class **Cookie**
localtime function of module **time**
match method
min function
module
mutable data type
MySQLdb module
newline
None
odbc module
open-source technology
os module
out-of-range element
packing a tuple
pass
pound–bang directive
print statement
Python prompt
query
raise an exception
range
rapid-application development (RAD)
raw string
raw_input
re module
re.I flag
regular expression
replace method
return
search method
self parameter
SRE_Match object
SRE_Pattern object
strftime function of module **time**
string formatting
string manipulation
string processing
Structured Query Language (SQL)
Tcl/Tk
time function
time module
time token
triple-quoted string
try/except
try/except/else
tuple
unpacking a tuple
van Rossum, Guido
while
writing a cookie

SELF-REVIEW EXERCISES

28.1 Fill in the blanks in each of the following statements:

a) Comments in Python begin with the __________ character.

b) Python statements can be executed in two ways. The statements can be typed into a file and then __________, or statements can be __________.

c) The keyword __________ marks the beginning of a Python function definition.

d) Function **raw_input** returns a __________.

e) Python defines three data types for storing complex data: __________, __________ and __________.

f) Tuples are __________ (element values at defined indices may not be changed); whereas lists are __________ (element values at defined indices may be changed).

g) Python implements __________ through the use of **try/except** blocks.

h) The Python module used to obtain XHTML form contents is __________.

i) Cookies are stored in the environment variable __________.

j) The __________ was formed to develop a specification for Python database application-programming interface (DB-API).

28.2 State whether each of the following is *true* or *false*. If *false*, explain why.

a) Python is an interpreted language.
b) To exit Python, type **exit** at the Python prompt.
c) Forgetting to indent after a colon is a style error.
d) The underscore character (_) marks the continuation of a Python statement onto the next line.
e) Elements must be added to a list by calling list method **append**.
f) A tuple is a valid data type for use as a dictionary key.
g) The pound-bang (**#!**) directive—which tells a server where to find the Python executable—must be the first line in a CGI script.
h) An object of class **Cookie** acts like a dictionary, so values can be set and retrieved using familiar dictionary syntax.
i) The syntax needed to manipulate a database is always dependent on that database.
j) A **Cursor** object is needed to execute a query against a database (for DB-API compliant modules).

28.3 How can a Python CGI script determine a client's IP address?

28.4 For each of the following code examples, identify and correct the error(s):

a)
```
print hello
```
b)
```
aTuple = ( 1, 2 )
aTuple[ 0 ] = 2
```
c)
```
if 0 < 3
   print "0 is less than 3."
```
d)
```
for counter in range( 10 ):
print counter
```

28.5 Write a one- to three-line block of code for each of the following tasks:

a) Create a string with 50 exclamation points (**!**) using the ***** operator.
b) Print out even numbers from 0 to 100.
c) Convert a user-entered number from a string to an integer.
d) Determine if a user-entered integer is odd.
e) Concatenate an empty tuple and a singleton with the **+=** statement.

ANSWERS TO SELF-REVIEW EXERCISES

28.1 a) pound (**#**). b) Python is invoked on the file, dynamically interpreted in an interactive session. c) **def**. d) string. e) tuples, lists, dictionaries. f) immutable, mutable. g) exception (or error) handling. h) **cgi**. i) **HTTP_COOKIE**. j) Python Database Special Interest Group.

28.2 a) True. b) False. Type *Crtl-Z* in Microsoft Windows or *Ctrl-D* in Linux/UNIX. c) False. Forgetting to indent after a colon is a syntax error. d) False. The backslash character (****) marks the continuation of a Python statement onto the next line. e) False. Lists can also be augmented by calling the **extend** method or the **+=** statement, for example. f) True. g) True. h) True. i) False. Database modules that conform to the DB-API provide similar syntaxes. j) True.

28.3 A client's IP address is contained in the **REMOTE_ADDR** environment variable of the **os** module.

28.4 a) Logical or syntax error. If the desired result is to output the word "hello," the proper code is **print "hello"**. The code in the problem will print the value of variable **hello**, if a variable by that name exists; the code raises an error if the variable does not exist. b) Runtime error. Tuple values cannot be modified in this way. c) Syntax error. A colon (**:**) must follow the **if** statement. d) Syntax error. The line after the **for** statement must be indented.

28.5 a)
```
theString = '!' * 50
```
b)
```
for item in range( 101 ):
   if item % 2 == 0:
      print item
```
c)
```
number = raw_input( "Enter a number" )
integer = int( number )
```
d)
```
number = int( raw_input( "Enter an integer" ) )
if number % 2 == 1:
   print "The number is odd."
```
e)
```
emptyTuple = ( )
emptyTuple += ( 1, )
```

EXERCISES

28.6 Describe how input from an XHTML **form** is retrieved in a Python program.

28.7 Figure 28.5 defines function **greatestCommonDivisor** that computes the greatest common divisor of two positive integers. Euclid's algorithm is another method of computing the greatest common divisor. The following steps define Euclid's algorithm for computing the greatest common divisor of two positive integers *x* and *y*:

while y > 0
  z = y
  y = x modulo z
  x = z
return x

Write a function **Euclid** that takes two positive integers and computes their greatest common divisor using Euclid's algorithm.

28.8 Modify functions **greatestCommonDivisor** and **Euclid** from Exercise 28.7 so that each function counts the number of modular divisions performed (i.e., the number of times the function uses the **%** operator). Each function should return a tuple that contains the calculated greatest common divisor and the number of modular divisions performed. Run each function on the following pairs of integers in Fig. 28.25, and fill in the rest of the table. Which function takes fewer modular divisions, on average?

28.9 Write a Python program named **states.py** that declares a variable **states** with value **"Mississippi Alabama Texas Massachusetts Kansas"**. Using only the techniques discussed in this chapter, write a program that does the following:

a) Search for a word in variable **states** that ends in **xas**. Store this word in element 0 of a list named **statesList**.
b) Search for a word in **states** that begins with **k** and ends in **s**. Perform a case-insensitive comparison. [*Note:* Passing **re.I** as a second parameter to method compile performs a case-insensitive comparison.] Store this word in element 1 of **statesList**.
c) Search for a word in **states** that begins with **M** and ends in **s**. Store this word in element 2 of the list.
d) Search for a word in **states** that ends in **a**. Store this word in element 3 of the list.
e) Search for a word that begins with **M** in **states** at the beginning of the string. Store this word at element 4 of the list.
f) Output the array **statesList** to the screen.

28.10 In Section 28.6, we discussed CGI environment variables. Write a CGI script that displays a user's IP address in the user's browser.

28.11 Write a CGI script that logs a user into a Web site. The user should be presented with a Web page that contains a form into which users enter their login name and password. The form sends the the user-entered information to a Python script. This script checks a database for the user's login name and validates the user's password. If the login name and password are valid, the Python script writes a **"Login successful"** message to the browser; if the login name and/or password are invalid, the Python script writes a **"Login unsuccessful"** message to the browser.

Integer pairs	Number of modular divisions for `greatestCommonDivisor`	Number of modular divisions for `Euclid`
1, 101	________	________
3, 30	________	________
45, 1000	________	________
13, 91	________	________
100, 1000	________	________
2,2	________	________
777,77	________	________
73,12	________	________
26,4	________	________
99,27	________	________
Average:	________	________

Fig. 28.25 Comparing functions **greatestCommonDivisor** and **Euclid**.

29

PHP

Objectives

- To understand PHP data types, operators, arrays and control structures.
- To understand string processing and regular expressions in PHP.
- To construct programs that process form data.
- To be able to read and write client data using cookies.
- To construct programs that interact with MySQL databases.

Conversion for me was not a Damascus Road experience. I slowly moved into an intellectual acceptance of what my intuition had always known.
Madeleine L'Engle

Be careful when reading health books; you may die of a misprint.
Mark Twain

Reckeners without their host must recken twice.
John Heywood

There was a door to which I found no key; There was the veil through which I might not see.
Omar Khayyam

Outline

29.1 Introduction

PHP, or *PHP Hypertext Preprocessor*, is quickly becoming one of the most popular server-side scripting languages for creating dynamic Web pages. PHP was created in 1994 by Rasmus Lerdorf (who currently works for Linuxcare Inc. as a Senior Open-Source Researcher) to track users at his Web site.[1] In 1995, Lerdorf released it as a package called the "Personal Home Page Tools." PHP 2 featured built-in database support and form handling. In 1997, PHP 3 was released, featuring a rewritten parser, which substantially increased performance and led to an explosion in PHP use. It is estimated that over six million domains now use PHP. The release of PHP 4, which features the new *Zend Engine* and is much faster and more powerful than its predecessor, should further increase PHP's popularity.[2] More information about the Zend engine can be found at **www.zend.com**.

PHP is an *open-source* technology that is supported by a large community of users and developers. Open source software provides developers with access to the software's source code and free redistribution rights. PHP is platform independent; implementations exist for all major UNIX, Linux and Windows operating systems. PHP also provides support for a large number of databases, including MySQL.

After introducing the basics of the scripting language, we discuss viewing environment variables. Knowing information about a client's execution environment allows dynamic content to be sent to the client. We then discuss form processing and business logic, which are vital to e-commerce applications. We provide an example of implementing a private Web site through username and password verification. Next, we build a three-tier, Web-based application that queries a MySQL database. Finally, we show how Web sites use cookies to store information on the client that will be retrieved during a client's subsequent visits to a Web site.

29.2 PHP

When the World Wide Web and Web browsers were introduced, the Internet began to achieve widespread popularity. This greatly increased the volume of requests for information from Web servers. The power of the Web resides not only in serving content to users, but also in responding to requests from users and generating Web pages with dynamic content. It became evident that the degree of interactivity between the user and the server would be crucial. While other languages can perform this function as well, PHP was written specifically for interacting with the Web.

PHP code is embedded directly into XHTML documents. This allows the document author to write XHTML in a clear, concise manner, without having to use multiple **print** statements, as is necessary with other CGI-based languages. Figure 29.1 presents a simple PHP program that displays a welcome message.

In PHP, code is inserted between the scripting delimiters ***<?php*** and **?>**. PHP code can be placed anywhere in XHTML markup, as long as the code is enclosed in these scripting delimiters. Line 8 declares variable **$name** and assigns to it the string **"Paul"**. All variables are preceded by the ***$*** *special symbol* and are created the first time they are encountered by the PHP interpreter. PHP statements are terminated with a *semicolon (**;**)*.

Common Programming Error 29.1

*Failing to precede a variable name with a **$** is a syntax error.*

```
1  <!DOCTYPE html PUBLIC "-//W3C//DTD XHTML 1.0 Strict//EN"
2     "http://www.w3.org/TR/xhtml1/DTD/xhtml1-strict.dtd">
3
4  <!-- Fig. 29.1: first.php -->
5  <!-- Our first PHP script -->
6
7  <?php
8     $name = "Paul";    // declaration
9  ?>
10
11 <html xmlns = "http://www.w3.org/1999/xhtml">
12    <head>
13       <title>A simple PHP document</title>
14    </head>
15
16    <body style = "font-size: 2em">
17       <p>
18          <strong>
19
20             <!-- print variable name's value -->
21             Welcome to PHP, <?php print( "$name" ); ?>!
22          </strong>
23       </p>
24    </body>
25 </html>
```

Fig. 29.1 Simple PHP program (part 1 of 2).

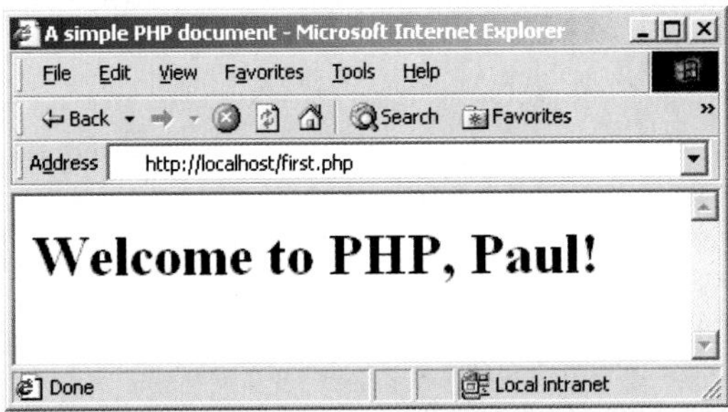

Fig. 29.1 Simple PHP program (part 2 of 2).

Common Programming Error 29.2

Variable names in PHP are case sensitive. Failure to use the proper mixture of case is a syntax error.

Common Programming Error 29.3

Forgetting to terminate a statement with a semicolon (`;`) is a syntax error.

Line 8 contains a *single-line comment*, which begins with two *forward slashes* (`//`). Text to the right of the slashes is ignored by the interpreter. Comments can also begin with the pound sign (`#`). Multiline comments begin with delimiter `/*` and end with delimiter `*/`.

Line 21 outputs the value of variable **`$name`** by calling function **`print`**. The actual value of **`$name`** is printed, instead of **`"$name"`**. When a variable is encountered inside a double-quoted (`""`) string, PHP *interpolates* the variable. In other words, PHP inserts the variable's value where the variable name appears in the string. Thus, variable **`$name`** is replaced by **`Paul`** for printing purposes. PHP variables are "*multitype*", meaning that they can contain different types of data (e.g., *integers*, *doubles* or *strings*) at different times. Figure 29.2 introduces these data types.

Data type	Description
Integer	Whole numbers (i.e., numbers without a decimal point).
Double	Real numbers (i.e., numbers containing a decimal point).
String	Text enclosed in either single (`''`) or double (`""`) quotes.
Boolean	True or false.
Array	Group of elements of the same type.
Object	Group of associated data and methods.
Resource	An external data source.
Null	No value.

Fig. 29.2 PHP data types.

Good Programming Practice 29.1

Whitespace enhances the readability of PHP code. It also simplifies programming and debugging.

PHP scripts usually end with **.php**, although a server can be configured to handle other file extensions. To run a PHP script, PHP must first be installed on your system. Visit **www.deitel.com** for PHP installation and configuration instructions. Although PHP can be used from the command line, a Web server is necessary to take full advantage of the scripting language. Figure 29.3 demonstrates the PHP data types introduced in Fig. 29.2.

```
<!DOCTYPE html PUBLIC "-//W3C//DTD XHTML 1.0 Transitional//EN"
   "http://www.w3.org/TR/xhtml1/DTD/xhtml1-transitional.dtd">

<!-- Fig. 29.3: data.php                -->
<!-- Demonstration of PHP data types -->

<html xmlns = "http://www.w3.org/1999/xhtml">
   <head>
      <title>PHP data types</title>
   </head>

   <body>

      <?php

         // declare a string, double and integer
         $testString = "3.5 seconds";
         $testDouble = 79.2;
         $testInteger = 12;
      ?>

      <!-- print each variable's value -->
      <?php print( $testString ) ?> is a string.<br />
      <?php print( $testDouble ) ?> is a double.<br />
      <?php print( $testInteger ) ?> is an integer.<br />

      <br />
      Now, converting to other types:<br />
      <?php

         // call function settype to convert variable
         // testString to different data types
         print( "$testString" );
         settype( $testString, "double" );
         print( " as a double is $testString <br />" );
         print( "$testString" );
         settype( $testString, "integer" );
         print( " as an integer is $testString <br />" );
         settype( $testString, "string" );
         print( "Converting back to a string results in
            $testString <br /><br />" );
```

Fig. 29.3 Type conversion example (part 1 of 2).

```
42
43          $data = "98.6 degrees";
44
45          // use type casting to cast variables to a
46          // different type
47          print( "Now using type casting instead: <br />
48             As a string - " . (string) $value .
49             "<br />As a double - " . (double) $value .
50             "<br />As an integer - " . (integer) $value );
51       ?>
52    </body>
53 </html>
```

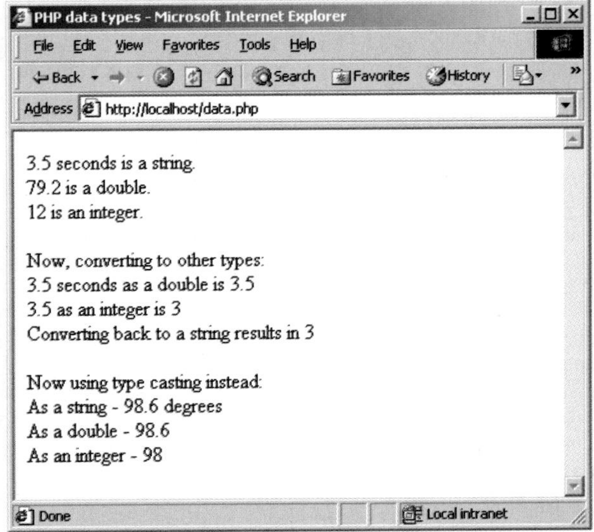

Fig. 29.3 Type conversion example (part 2 of 2).

Conversion between different data types may be necessary when performing arithmetic operations with variables. In PHP, data-type conversion can be performed by passing the data type as an argument to *function* **`settype`**. Lines 17–19 assign a string to variable **`$testString`**, a double to variable **`$testDouble`** and an integer to variable **`$testInteger`**. Variables are converted the to data type of the value they are assigned. For example, variable **`$testString`** becomes a string when assigned the value **`"3.5 seconds"`**. Lines 23–25 **`print`** the value of each variable. Notice that the enclosing of a variable name in double quotes in a **`print`** statement is optional. Lines 34–39 call function **`settype`** to modify the data type of each variable. Function **`settype`** takes two arguments: The variable whose data type is to be changed and the variable's new data type. Calling function **`settype`** can result in loss of data. For example, doubles are truncated when they are converted to integers. When converting between a string and a number, PHP uses the value of the number that appears at the beginning of the string. If no number appears at the beginning of the string, the string evaluates to **`0`**. In line 34, the string **`"3.5 seconds"`** is converted to a double, resulting in the value **`3.5`** being stored in variable

$testString. In line 37, double **3.5** is converted to integer **3**. When we convert this variable to a string (line 39), the variable's value becomes **"3"**.

Another option for conversion between types is *casting* (or *type casting*). Unlike **settype**, casting does not change a variable's content. Rather, type casting creates a temporary copy of a variable's value in memory. Lines 47–50 cast variable **$data**'s value to a **string**, a **double** and an **integer**. Type casting is necessary when a specific data type is required for an arithmetic operation.

The *concatenation operator* (**.**) concatenates strings. This combines multiple strings in the same **print** statement (lines 47–50). A **print** statement may be split over multiple lines; everything that is enclosed in the parentheses, terminated by a semicolon, is sent to the client. PHP provides a variety of arithmetic operators, which we demonstrate in Fig. 29.4.

```
<!DOCTYPE html PUBLIC "-//W3C//DTD XHTML 1.0 Transitional//EN"
   "http://www.w3.org/TR/xhtml1/DTD/xhtml1-transitional.dtd">

<!-- Fig. 29.4: operators.php    -->
<!-- Demonstration of operators -->

<html xmlns = "http://www.w3.org/1999/xhtml">
   <head>
      <title>Using arithmetic operators</title>
   </head>

   <body>
      <?php
         $a = 5;
         print( "The value of variable a is $a <br />" );

         // define constant VALUE
         define( "VALUE", 5 );

         // add constant VALUE to variable $a
         $a = $a + VALUE;
         print( "Variable a after adding constant VALUE
            is $a <br />" );

         // multiply variable $a by 2
         $a *= 2;
         print( "Multiplying variable a by 2 yields $a <br />" );

         // test if variable $a is less than 50
         if ( $a < 50 )
            print( "Variable a is less than 50 <br />" );

         // add 40 to variable #a
         $a += 40;
         print( "Variable a after adding 40 is $a <br />" );

         // test if variable $a is 50 or less
         if ( $a < 51 )
            print( "Variable a is still 50 or less<br />" );
```

Fig. 29.4 Using PHP's arithmetic operators (part 1 of 2).

```

         // test if variable $a is between 50 and 100, inclusive
         elseif ( $a < 101 )
            print( "Variable a is now between 50 and 100,
               inclusive<br />" );
         else
            print( "Variable a is now greater than 100
               <br />" );

         // print an uninitialized variable
         print( "Using a variable before initializing:
            $nothing <br />" );

         // add constant VALUE to an uninitialized variable
         $test = $num + VALUE;
         print( "An uninitialized variable plus constant
            VALUE yields $test <br />" );

         // add a string to an integer
         $str = "3 dollars";
         $a += $str;
         print( "Adding a string to an integer yields $a
            <br />" );
      ?>
   </body>
</html>
```

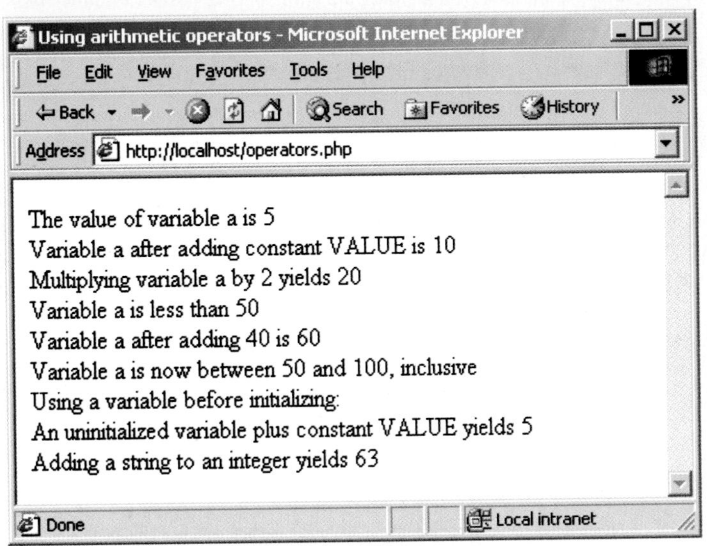

Fig. 29.4 Using PHP's arithmetic operators (part 2 of 2).

Line 14 declares variable **$a** and assigns it the value **5**. Line 18 calls function **define** to create a *named constant*. A constant is a value that cannot be modified once it is declared. Function **define** takes two arguments: the name and value of the constant. An optional third argument accepts a boolean value that specifies whether the constant is case insensitive—constants are case sensitive by default.

Common Programming Error 29.4

Assigning a value to a constant after a constant is declared is a syntax error.

Line 21 adds constant **VALUE** to variable **$a**, which is a typical use of arithmetic operators. Line 26 uses the *assignment operator* ***=** to yield an expression equivalent to **$a = $a * 2** (thus assigning **$a** the value **20**). These assignment operators (i.e., **+=**, **-=**, ***=** and **/=**) are syntactical shortcuts. Line 34 adds **40** to the value of variable **$a**.

In PHP, uninitialized variables have the value ***undef***, which evaluates to different values, depending on its context. For example, when **undef** is used in a numeric context (e.g., **$num** in line 54), it evaluates to **0**. In contrast, when **undef** is interpreted in a string context (such as **$nothing** in line 51), it evaluates to an *empty string* (**""**).

Testing and Debugging Tip 29.1

Always initialize variables before using them. Doing so helps avoid subtle errors.

Strings are converted to integers when they are used in arithmetic operations (lines 59–60). In line 60, the string value **"3 dollars"** is converted to the integer **3** before being added to integer variable **$a**.

Testing and Debugging Tip 29.2

*Function **print** can be used to display the value of a variable at a particular point during a program's execution. This is often helpful in debugging a script.*

Common Programming Error 29.5

*Using an uninitialized variable might result in an incorrect numerical calculation. For example, multiplying a number by an uninitialized variable results in **0**.*

The words **if**, **elseif** and **else** are PHP *keywords* (Fig. 29.5), meaning that they are reserved for implementing language features. PHP provides the capability to store data in arrays. Arrays are divided into *elements* that behave as individual variables. Script **arrays.php** (Fig. 29.6) demonstrates techniques for array initialization and manipulation.

PHP keywords					
and	do	for	include	require	true
break	else	foreach	list	return	var
case	elseif	function	new	static	virtual
class	extends	global	not	switch	xor
continue	false	if	or	this	while
default					

Fig. 29.5 PHP keywords.

Individual array elements are accessed by following the array-variable name with an index enclosed in braces (**[]**). If a value is assigned to an array that does not exist, then the array is created (line 18). Likewise, assigning a value to an element where the index is omitted appends a new element to the end of the array (line 21). The **for** loop (lines 24–25) **print**s each element's value. *Function* ***count*** returns the total number of elements in the array. Because array indices start at 0, the index of the last element is one less than the total number of elements. In this example, the **for** loop terminates once the counter (**$i**) is equal to the number of elements in the array.

Line 31 demonstrates a second method of initializing arrays. Function ***array*** returns an array that contains the arguments passed to it. The first item in the list is stored as the first array element, the second item is stored as the second array element, and so on. Lines 32–33 use another **for** loop to print out each array element's value.

In addition to integer indices, arrays can have nonnumeric indices (lines 39–41). For example, indices **Harvey**, **Paul** and **Tem** are assigned the values **21**, **18** and **23**, respectively. PHP provides functions for *iterating* through the elements of an array (lines 45–46). Each array has a built-in *internal pointer*, which points to the array element currently being referenced. *Function* ***reset*** sets the iterator to the first element of the array. Function ***key*** returns the index of the element to which the iterator points, and function ***next*** moves the iterator to the next element. The **for** loop continues to execute as long as function **key** returns an index. Function **next** returns **false** when there are no additional elements in the array. When this occurs, function **key** cannot return an index, and the script terminates. Line 47 **print**s the index and value of each element.

Function **array** can also be used to initialize arrays with string indices. In order to override the automatic numeric indexing performed by function **array**, use operator **=>** as demonstrated on lines 54–61. The value to the left of the operator is the array index, and the value to the right is the element's value.

The ***foreach*** *loop* is a control structure that is specially designed for iterating through arrays (line 64). The syntax for a **foreach** loop starts with the array to iterate through, followed by the keyword ***as***, followed by the variables to receive the index and the value for each element. We use the **foreach** loop to **print** each element and value of array **$fourth**.

```
1   <!DOCTYPE html PUBLIC "-//W3C//DTD XHTML 1.0 Transitional//EN"
2      "http://www.w3.org/TR/xhtml1/DTD/xhtml1-transitional.dtd">
3
4   <!-- Fig. 29.6: arrays.php -->
5   <!-- Array manipulation     -->
6
7   <html xmlns = "http://www.w3.org/1999/xhtml">
8      <head>
9         <title>Array manipulation</title>
10     </head>
11
12     <body>
13        <?php
14
15           // create array first
```

Fig. 29.6 Array manipulation (part 1 of 3).

```
         print( "<strong>Creating the first array</strong>
            <br />" );
         $first[ 0 ] = "zero";
         $first[ 1 ] = "one";
         $first[ 2 ] = "two";
         $first[] = "three";

         // print each element's index and value
         for ( $i = 0; $i < count( $first ); $i++ )
            print( "Element $i is $first[$i] <br />" );

         print( "<br /><strong>Creating the second array
            </strong><br />" );

         // call function array to create array second
         $second = array( "zero", "one", "two", "three" );
         for ( $i = 0; $i < count( $second ); $i++ )
            print( "Element $i is $second[$i] <br />" );

         print( "<br /><strong>Creating the third array
            </strong><br />" );

         // assign values to non-numerical indices
         $third[ "Harvey" ] = 21;
         $third[ "Paul" ] = 18;
         $third[ "Tem" ] = 23;

         // iterate through the array elements and print each
         // element's name and value
         for ( reset( $third ); $element = key( $third );
            next( $third ) )
            print( "$element is $third[$element] <br />" );

         print( "<br /><strong>Creating the fourth array
            </strong><br />" );

         // call function array to create array fourth using
         // string indices
         $fourth = array(
            "January"   => "first",   "February" => "second",
            "March"     => "third",   "April"    => "fourth",
            "May"       => "fifth",   "June"     => "sixth",
            "July"      => "seventh", "August"   => "eighth",
            "September" => "ninth",   "October"  => "tenth",
            "November"  => "eleventh","December" => "twelfth"
            );

         // print each element's name and value
         foreach ( $fourth as $element => $value )
            print( "$element is the $value month <br />" );
      ?>
   </body>
</html>
```

Fig. 29.6 Array manipulation (part 2 of 3).

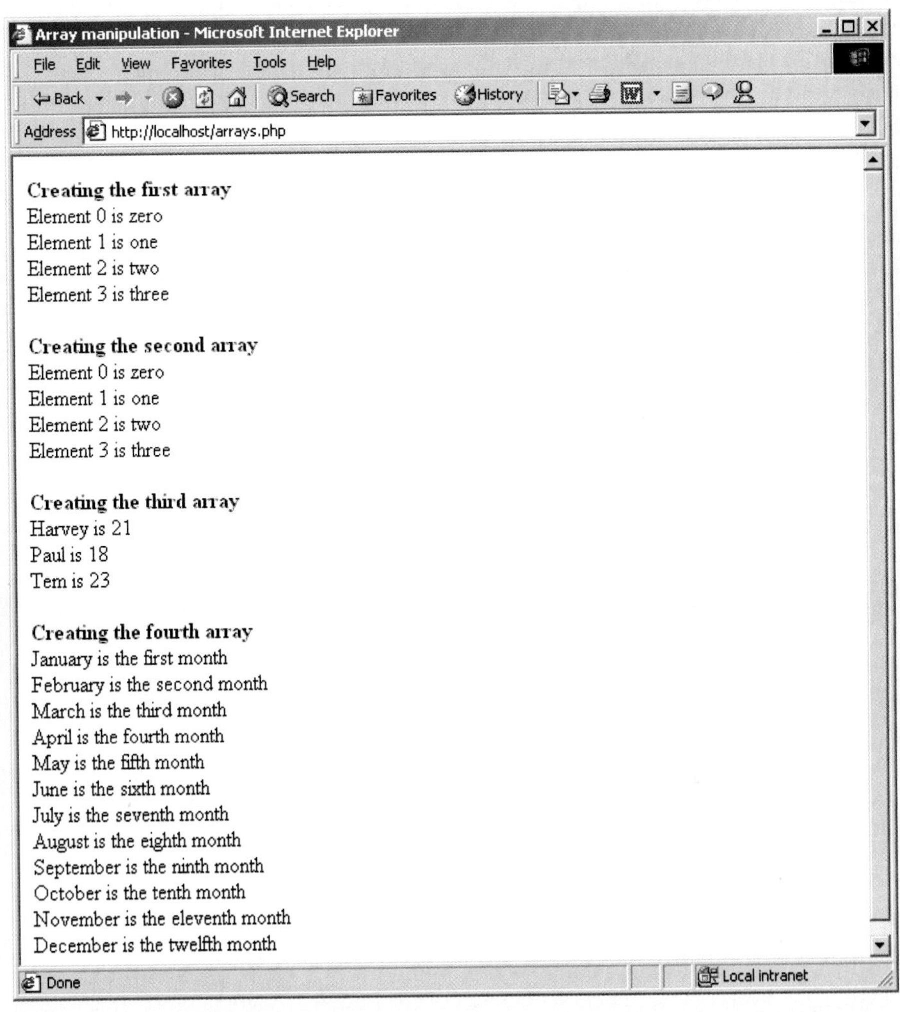

Fig. 29.6 Array manipulation (part 3 of 3).

29.3 String Processing and Regular Expressions

PHP processes text data easily and efficiently, enabling straightforward searching, substitution, extraction and concatenation of strings. Text manipulation in PHP is usually done with *regular expressions*—a series of characters that serve as pattern-matching templates (or search criteria) in strings, text files and databases. This feature allows complex searching and string processing to be performed using relatively simple expressions.

Many string-processing tasks are accomplished by using PHP's *equality* and *comparison* operators (Fig. 29.7). Line 16 declares and initializes array **`$fruits`** by calling function **`array`**. Lines 19–40 iterate through the array, comparing the array's elements to one another.

Lines 23 and 25 call function **`strcmp`** to compare two strings. If the first string alphabetically precedes the second string, then **`-1`** is returned. If the strings are equal, then **`0`** is returned. If the first string alphabetically follows the second string, then **`1`** is returned. The **`for`** loop (line 19) iterates through each element in the **`$fruits`** array. Lines 23–29 compare each element to the string **`"banana"`**, printing the elements that are greater than, less than and equal to the string.

Relational operators (**`==`**, **`!=`**, **`<`**, **`<=`**, **`>`** and **`>=`**) can also be used to compare strings. Lines 33–38 use relational operators to compare each element of the array to the string **`"apple"`**. These operators are also used for numerical comparison with integers and doubles.

```
1  <!DOCTYPE html PUBLIC "-//W3C//DTD XHTML 1.0 Transitional//EN"
2     "http://www.w3.org/TR/xhtml1/DTD/xhtml1-transitional.dtd">
3
4  <!-- Fig. 29.7: compare.php -->
5  <!-- String Comparison      -->
6
7  <html xmlns = "http://www.w3.org/1999/xhtml">
8     <head>
9        <title>String Comparison</title>
10    </head>
11
12    <body>
13       <?php
14
15          // create array fruits
16          $fruits = array( "apple", "orange", "banana" );
17
18          // iterate through each array element
19          for ( $i = 0; $i < count( $fruits ); $i++ ) {
20
21             // call function strcmp to compare the array element
22             // to string "banana"
23             if ( strcmp( $fruits[ $i ], "banana" ) < 0 )
24                print( $fruits[ $i ]." is less than banana " );
25             elseif ( strcmp( $fruits[ $i ], "banana" ) > 0 )
26                print( $fruits[ $i ].
27                   " is greater than banana " );
28             else
29                print( $fruits[ $i ]." is equal to banana " );
30
31             // use relational operators to compare each element
32             // to string "apple"
33             if ( $fruits[ $i ] < "apple" )
34               print( "and less than apple! <br />" );
35             elseif ( $fruits[ $i ] > "apple" )
36               print( "and greater than apple! <br />" );
37             elseif ( $fruits[ $i ] == "apple" )
38                print( "and equal to apple! <br />" );
39
40          }
41       ?>
```

Fig. 29.7 Using the string comparison operators (part 1 of 2).

```
      </body>
   </html>
```

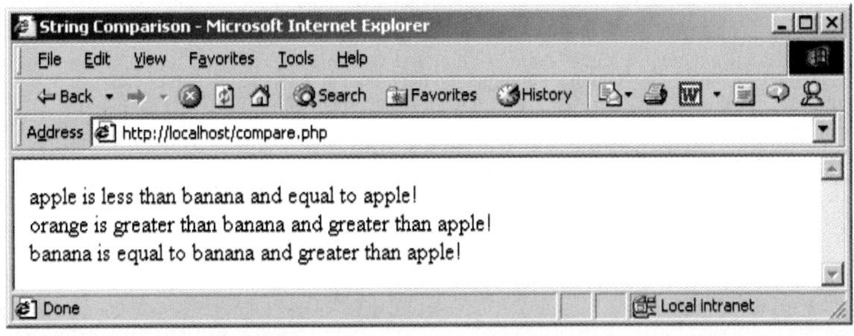

Fig. 29.7 Using the string comparison operators (part 2 of 2).

For more powerful string comparisons, PHP provides functions **ereg** and **preg_match**, which use regular expressions to search a string for a specified pattern. Function **ereg** uses *Portable Operating System Interface (POSIX) extended regular expressions,* whereas function **preg_match** provides *Perl-compatible regular expressions*. POSIX-extended regular expressions are a standard to which PHP regular expressions conform. In this section, we use function **ereg**. Perl regular expressions are more widely used than POSIX regular expressions. Support for Perl regular expressions also eases migration from Perl to PHP. For more information on Perl regular expressions, see Chapter 27, Perl and CGI. Consult PHP's documentation for a list of differences between the Perl and PHP implementations. Figure 29.8 demonstrates some of PHP's regular expression capabilities.

```
<!DOCTYPE html PUBLIC "-//W3C//DTD XHTML 1.0 Transitional//EN"
   "http://www.w3.org/TR/xhtml1/DTD/xhtml1-transitional.dtd">

<!-- Fig. 29.8: expression.php -->
<!-- Using regular expressions -->

<html xmlns = "http://www.w3.org/1999/xhtml">
   <head>
      <title>Regular expressions</title>
   </head>

   <body>
      <?php
         $search = "Now is the time";
         print( "Test string is: '$search'<br /><br />" );

         // call function ereg to search for pattern 'Now'
         // in variable search
         if ( ereg( "Now", $search ) )
            print( "String 'Now' was found.<br />" );
```

Fig. 29.8 Using regular expressions (part 1 of 2).

```
21
22          // search for pattern 'Now' in the beginning of
23          // the string
24          if ( ereg( "^Now", $search ) )
25             print( "String 'Now' found at beginning
26                of the line.<br />" );
27
28          // search for pattern 'Now' at the end of the string
29          if ( ereg( "Now$", $search ) )
30             print( "String 'Now' was found at the end
31                of the line.<br />" );
32
33          // search for any word ending in 'ow'
34          if ( ereg( "[[:<:]]([a-zA-Z]*ow)[[:>:]]", $search,
35             $match ) )
36             print( "Word found ending in 'ow': " .
37                $match[ 1 ] . "<br />" );
38
39          // search for any words beginning with 't'
40          print( "Words beginning with 't' found: ");
41
42          while ( eregi( "[[:<:]](t[[:alpha:]]+)[[:>:]]",
43             $search, $match ) ) {
44             print( $match[ 1 ] . " " );
45
46            // remove the first occurrence of a word beginning
47            // with 't' to find other instances in the string
48            $search = ereg_replace( $match[ 1 ], "", $search );
49          }
50
51          print( "<br />" );
52       ?>
53    </body>
54 </html>
```

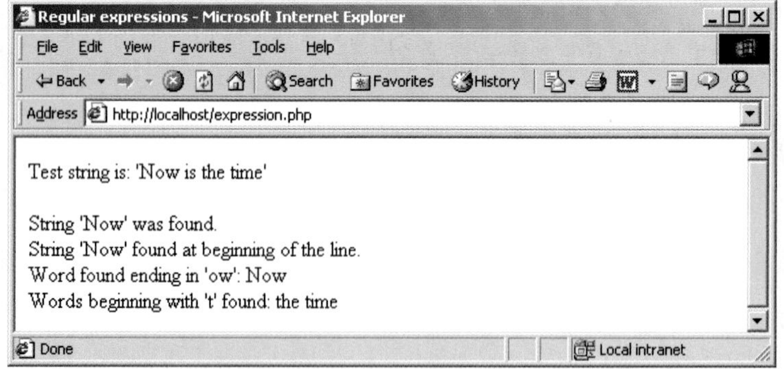

Fig. 29.8 Using regular expressions (part 2 of 2).

We begin by assigning the string **"Now is the time"** to variable **$search** (line 14). Line 19's condition calls function **ereg** to search for the *literal characters* **Now** inside variable **$search**. If the pattern is found, **ereg** returns **true**, and line 20 **print**s a message indicating that the pattern was found. We use single quotes (**''**) inside the **print** statement to emphasize the search pattern. Anything enclosed within single quotes is not interpolated. For example, **'$name'** in a **print** statement would output **$name**. Function **ereg** takes two arguments: a regular expression pattern to search for (**Now**) and the string to search. Although case mixture and whitespace are typically significant in patterns, PHP provides *function* ***eregi*** for specifying case insensitive pattern matches.

In addition to literal characters, regular expressions can include special characters that specify patterns. For example, the *caret (^) special character* matches the beginning of a string. Line 24 searches the beginning of **$search** for the pattern **Now**.

The characters **$**, **^** and **.** are part of a special set of characters called *metacharacters*. A *dollar sign ($)* searches for the specified pattern at the end of the string (line 29). Because the pattern **Now** is not found at the end of **$search**, the body of the **if** statement (lines 30–31) is not executed. Note that **Now$** is not a variable, it is a pattern that uses **$** to search for characters **Now** at the end of a string. Another special character is the period (**.**), which matches any single character.

Lines 34–35 search (from left to right) for the first word ending with the letters **ow**. *Bracket expressions* are lists of characters enclosed in braces (**[ ]**), which match a single character from the list. Ranges can be specified by supplying the beginning and the end of the range separated by a dash (**-**). For instance, the bracket expression **[a-z]** matches any lowercase letter, and **[A-Z]** matches any uppercase letter. In this example, we combine the two to create an expression that matches any letter. The special bracket expressions ***[[:<:]]*** and ***[[:>]]*** match the beginning and end of a word, respectively.

The expression inside the parentheses, **[a-zA-Z]*ow**, matches any word ending in **ow**. It uses the *quantifier* ***** to match the preceding pattern 0 or more times. Thus, **[a-zA-Z]*ow** matches any number of characters followed by the literal characters **ow**. Some PHP quantifiers are listed in Fig. 29.9.

Placing a pattern in parentheses stores the matched string in the array that is specified in the third argument to function **ereg**. The first parenthetical pattern matched is stored in the second array element, the second in the third array element, and so on. The first element (i.e., index 0) stores the string matched for the entire pattern. The parentheses in lines 34–35 result in **Now** being stored in variable **$match[1]**.

Quantifier	Matches
`{n}`	Exactly **n** times.
`{m,n}`	Between **m** and **n** times inclusive.
`{n,}`	**n** or more times.
`+`	One or more times (same as **{1,}**).
`*`	Zero or more times (same as **{0,}**).
`?`	Zero or one times (same as **{0,1}**).

Fig. 29.9 Some PHP quantifiers.

Searching for multiple instances of a pattern in a string is slightly more complicated, because the **ereg** function matches only the first instance of the pattern. To find multiple instances of a given pattern, we must remove any matched instances before calling **ereg** again. Lines 42–49 use a **while** loop and the ***ereg_replace*** *function* to find all the words in the string that begin with **t**. We will say more about this function momentarily.

The pattern used in this example, **[[:<:]](t[[:alpha:]]+)[[:>:]]**, matches any word beginning with the character **t** followed by one or more characters. The example uses the *character class* **[[:alpha:]]** to recognize any alphabetic character. This is equivalent to the **[a-zA-Z]** bracket expression that was used earlier. Figure 29.10 lists some character classes that can be matched with regular expressions.

The quantifier **+** matches one or more instances of the preceding expression. The result of the match is stored in **$match[1]**. Once a match is found, we **print** it on line 44. We then remove it from the string on line 48, using function **ereg_replace**. Function **ereg_replace** takes three arguments: the pattern to match, a string to replace the matched string and the string to search. The modified string is returned. Here, we search for the word that we matched with the regular expression, replace the word with an empty string then assign the result back to **$search**. This allows us to match any other words beginning with the character **t** in the string.

29.4 Viewing Client/Server Environment Variables

Knowledge of a client's execution environment is useful to system administrators who want to provide client-specific information. *Environment variables* contain information about a script's environment, such as the client's Web browser, the HTTP host and the HTTP connection.

Figure 29.11 generates an XHTML document that displays the values of the client's environment variables in a table. PHP stores the environment variables and their values in the ***$GLOBALS*** *array*. Iterating through this array allows us to view all the client's environment variables.

In lines 19–22, we use a **foreach** loop to **print** out the keys and values for each element in the **$GLOBALS** array. Individual array variables can be accessed directly by using an element's key from the **$GLOBALS** array as a variable. For example, to receive information about the user's browser, use the ***$HTTP_USER_AGENT*** *variable*. Figure 29.12 lists some global variables.

Character Class	Description
alnum	Alphanumeric characters (i.e., letters [a-z][A-Z] or digits [0-9]).
alpha	Word characters (i.e., letters [a-z][A-Z]).
digit	Digits.
space	Whitespace.
lower	Lowercase letters.
upper	Uppercase letters.

Fig. 29.10 Some PHP character classes.

```
<!DOCTYPE html PUBLIC "-//W3C//DTD XHTML 1.0 Transitional//EN"
   "http://www.w3.org/TR/xhtml1/DTD/xhtml1-transitional.dtd">

<!-- Fig. 29.11: globals.php                    -->
<!-- Program to display environment variables -->

<html xmlns = "http://www.w3.org/1999/xhtml">
   <head>
      <title>Environment Variables</title>
   </head>

   <body>
      <table border = "0" cellpadding = "2" cellspacing = "0"
         width = "100%">
      <?php

         // print the key and value for each element in the
         // in the $GLOBALS array
         foreach ( $GLOBALS as $key => $value )
            print( "<tr><td bgcolor = \"#11bbff\">
               <strong>$key</strong></td>
               <td>$value</td></tr>" );
      ?>
      </table>
   </body>
</html>
```

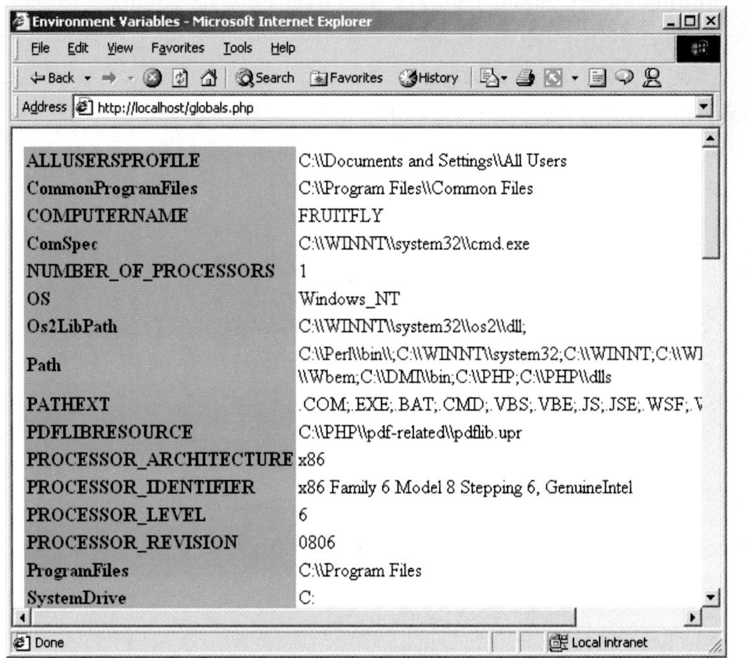

Fig. 29.11 Displaying the environment variables.

Variable Name	Description
$HTTP_USER_AGENT	The client's browser type.
$REMOTE_ADDR	The client's IP address.
$SERVER_NAME	Name of the server on which the script is running.
$SERVER_ADDR	Address of the server on which the script is running.
$HTTP_GET_VARS	Data posted to the server by the *get* method.
$HTTP_POST_VARS	Data posted to the server by the *post* method.
$HTTP_COOKIE_VARS	Data contained in cookies on the client's computer.
$GLOBALS	Array containing all global variables.

Fig. 29.12 Some environment variables.

29.5 Form Processing and Business Logic

XHTML forms enable Web pages to collect data from users and send the data to a Web server for processing. Such interaction between users and Web servers is vital to e-commerce applications, for example. Such capabilities allow users to purchase products, request information, send and receive Web-based e-mail, perform online paging and take advantage of various other online services. Figure 29.13 uses an XHTML **form** to collect information about users for the purpose of adding the users to a mailing list. The type of registration form in this example could be used by a software company to acquire profile information before allowing users to download software.

```
<!DOCTYPE html PUBLIC "-//W3C//DTD XHTML 1.0 Transitional//EN"
   "http://www.w3.org/TR/xhtml1/DTD/xhtml1-transitional.dtd">

<!-- Fig. 29.13: form.html                       -->
<!-- Form for use with the form.php program -->

<html xmlns = "http://www.w3.org/1999/xhtml">
   <head>
      <title>Sample form to take user input in XHTML</title>
   </head>

   <body>

      <h1>This is a sample registration form.</h1>
      Please fill in all fields and click Register.

      <!-- post form data to form.php -->
      <form method = "post" action = "form.php">
         <img src = "images/user.gif" alt = "User" /><br />
         <span style = "color: blue">
            Please fill out the fields below.<br />
         </span>
```

Fig. 29.13 XHTML form for gathering user input (part 1 of 3).

```
         <!-- create four text boxes for user input -->
         <img src = "images/fname.gif" alt = "First Name" />
         <input type = "text" name = "fname" /><br />

         <img src = "images/lname.gif" alt = "Last Name" />
         <input type = "text" name = "lname" /><br />

         <img src = "images/email.gif" alt = "Email" />
         <input type = "text" name = "email" /><br />

         <img src = "images/phone.gif" alt = "Phone" />
         <input type = "text" name = "phone" /><br />

         <span style = "font-size: 10pt">
            Must be in the form (555)555-5555</span>
         <br /><br />

         <img src = "images/downloads.gif"
            alt = "Publications" /><br />

         <span style = "color: blue">
            Which book would you like information about?
         </span><br />

         <!-- create drop-down list containing book names -->
         <select name = "book">
            <option>Internet and WWW How to Program 2e</option>
            <option>C++ How to Program 3e</option>
            <option>Java How to Program 4e</option>
            <option>XML How to Program 1e</option>
         </select>
         <br /><br />

         <img src = "images/os.gif" alt = "Operating System" />
         <br /><span style = "color: blue">
            Which operating system are you currently using?
         <br /></span>

         <!-- create five radio buttons -->
         <input type = "radio" name = "os" value = "Windows NT"
            checked = "checked" />
            Windows NT

         <input type = "radio" name = "os" value =
            "Windows 2000" />
            Windows 2000

         <input type = "radio" name = "os" value =
            "Windows 98" />
            Windows 98<br />

         <input type = "radio" name = "os" value = "Linux" />
```

Fig. 29.13 XHTML form for gathering user input (part 2 of 3).

```
76                  Linux
77
78               <input type = "radio" name = "os" value = "Other" />
79                  Other<br />
80
81                <!-- create a submit button -->
82               <input type = "submit" value = "Register" />
83            </form>
84
85         </body>
86      </html>
```

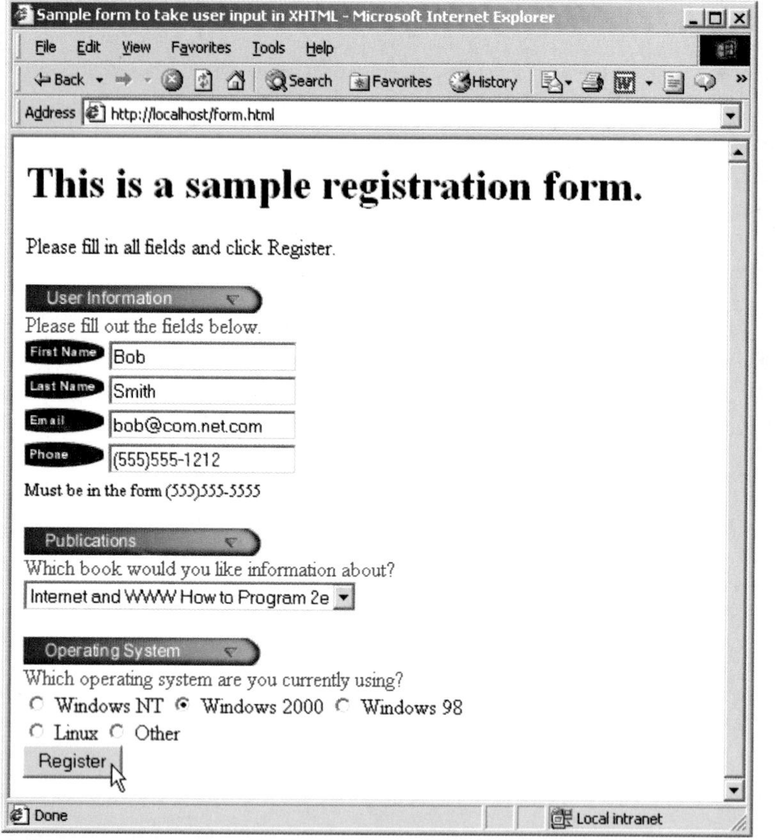

Fig. 29.13 XHTML form for gathering user input (part 3 of 3).

The **`action`** attribute of the **`form`** element (line 18) indicates that, when the user clicks **Register**, the **`form`** data will be **`post`**ed to **`form.php`** (Fig. 29.14) for processing. Using ***`method = "post"`*** appends form data to the browser request which contains the protocol (i.e., HTTP) and the requested resource's URL. Scripts located on the Web server's machine (or on a machine accessible through the network) can access the form data sent as part of the request.

We assign a unique name (e.g., **`email`**) to each of the **`form`**'s **`input`** fields. When **Register** is clicked, each field's **`name`** and **`value`** are sent to the Web server. Script **`form.php`** can then accesses the submitted value for each specific field.

Good Programming Practice 29.2

*Use meaningful XHTML object names for **`input`** fields. This makes PHP scripts that retrieve **`form`** data easier to understand.*

Figure 29.14 (**`form.php`**) processes the data **`post`**ed by **`form.html`** and sends XHTML back to the client. For each **`form`** field **`post`**ed to a PHP script, PHP creates a global variable with the same name as the field. For example, in line 32 of Fig. 29.13, an XHTML text box is created and given the name **`email`**. Later in our PHP script (line 67), we access the field's value by using variable **`$email`**.

In lines 18–19, we determine whether the phone number entered by the user is valid. In this case, the phone number must begin with an opening parenthesis, followed by an area code, a closing parenthesis, an exchange, a hyphen and a line number. It is crucial to validate information that will be entered into databases or used in mailing lists. For example, validation can be used to ensure that credit-card numbers contain the proper number of digits before the numbers are encrypted to a merchant. The design of verifying information is called *business logic* (or *business rules*).

The expression **`\(`** matches the opening parenthesis of the phone number. Because we want to match the literal character **`(`**, we *escape* its normal meaning by preceding it with the **`\`** character. The parentheses in the expression must be followed by three digits (**`[0-9]{3}`**), a closing parenthesis, three digits, a literal hyphen and four additional digits. Note that we use the **`^`** and **`$`** symbols to ensure that no extra characters appear at either end of the string.

```
1  <!DOCTYPE html PUBLIC "-//W3C//DTD XHTML 1.0 Transitional//EN"
2     "http://www.w3.org/TR/xhtml1/DTD/xhtml1-transitional.dtd">
3
4  <!-- Fig. 29.14: form.php                   -->
5  <!-- Read information sent from form.html -->
6
7  <html xmlns = "http://www.w3.org/1999/xhtml">
8     <head>
9        <title>Form Validation</title>
10    </head>
11
12    <body style = "font-family: arial,sans-serif">
13
14       <?php
15
16          // determine if phone number is valid and print
17          // an error message if not
18          if ( !ereg( "^\([0-9]{3}\)[0-9]{3}-[0-9]{4}$",
19             $phone ) ){
20
21             print( "<p><span style = \"color: red;
22                font-size: 2em\">
```

Fig. 29.14 Obtaining user input through forms (part 1 of 3).

```
                INVALID PHONE NUMBER</span><br />
                A valid phone number must be in the form
                <strong>(555)555-5555</strong><br />
                <span style = \"color: blue\">
                Click the Back button, enter a valid phone
                number and resubmit.<br /><br />
                Thank You.</span></p></body></html>" );

            die(); // terminate script execution
         }
      ?>

      <p>Hi
         <span style = "color: blue">
            <strong>
               <?php print( "$fname" ); ?>
            </strong>
         </span>.
         Thank you for completing the survey.<br />

         You have been added to the
         <span style = "color: blue">
            <strong>
               <?php print( "$book " ); ?>
            </strong>
         </span>
         mailing list.
      </p>
      <strong>The following information has been saved
          in our database:</strong><br />

      <table border = "0" cellpadding = "0" cellspacing = "10">
         <tr>
            <td bgcolor = "#ffffaa">Name </td>
            <td bgcolor = "#ffffbb">Email</td>
            <td bgcolor = "#ffffcc">Phone</td>
            <td bgcolor = "#ffffdd">OS</td>
         </tr>

         <tr>
            <?php

               // print each form field's value
               print( "<td>$fname $lname</td>
                  <td>$email</td>
                  <td>$phone</td>
                  <td>$os</td>" );
            ?>
         </tr>
      </table>

      <br /><br /><br />
      <div style = "font-size: 10pt; text-align: center">
```

Fig. 29.14 Obtaining user input through forms (part 2 of 3).

```
76            This is only a sample form.
77            You have not been added to a mailing list.
78         </div>
79      </body>
80   </html>
```

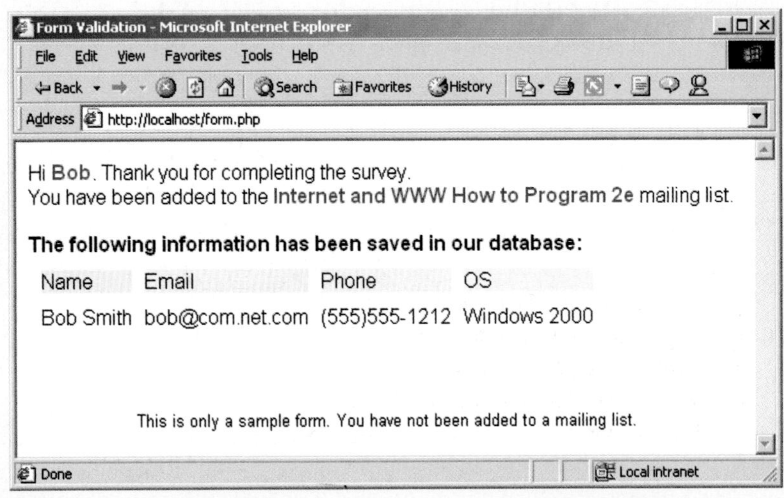

Fig. 29.14 Obtaining user input through forms (part 3 of 3).

If the regular expression is matched, then the phone number is determined to be valid, and an XHTML document is sent to the client, thanking the user for completing the form. Otherwise, the body of the **`if`** statement is executed, and an error message is printed.

Function ***`die`*** (line 31) terminates script execution. In this case, if the user did not enter a correct telephone number, we do not want to continue executing the rest of the script, so we call function **`die`**.

Software Engineering Observation 29.1

Use business logic to ensure that invalid information is not stored in databases. When possible, use JavaScript to validate form data while conserving server resources. However, some data, such as passwords, must be validated on the server-side.

29.6 Verifying a Username and Password

It is often desirable to have a *private Web site*—one that is accessible only to certain individuals. Implementing privacy generally involves username and password verification. Figure 29.15 presents an XHTML **`form`** that queries the user for a username and a password. Fields **`USERNAME`** and **`PASSWORD`** are **`post`**ed to the PHP script **`password.php`** for verification. For simplicity, we do not encrypt the data before sending it to the server. For more information regarding PHP encryption functions, visit

`www.php.net/manual/en/ref.mcrypt.php`

[*Note*: These functions are not available for Windows distributions of PHP.]

```
<!DOCTYPE html PUBLIC "-//W3C//DTD XHTML 1.0 Transitional//EN"
   "http://www.w3.org/TR/xhtml1/DTD/xhtml1-transitional.dtd">

<!-- Fig. 29.15: password.html                        -->
<!-- XHTML form sent to password.php for verification -->

<html xmlns = "http://www.w3.org/1999/xhtml">
   <head>
      <title>Verifying a username and a password.</title>

      <style type = "text/css">
         td { background-color: #DDDDDD }
      </style>
   </head>

   <body style = "font-family: arial">
      <p style = "font-size: 13pt">
         Type in your username and password below.
         <br />
         <span style = "color: #0000FF; font-size: 10pt;
            font-weight: bold">
            Note that password will be sent as plain text
         </span>
      </p>

      <!-- post form data to password.php -->
      <form action = "password.php" method = "post">
         <br />

         <table border = "0" cellspacing = "0"
            style = "height: 90px; width: 123px;
            font-size: 10pt" cellpadding = "0">

            <tr>
               <td colspan = "3">
                  <strong>Username:</strong>
               </td>
            </tr>

            <tr>
               <td colspan = "3">
                  <input size = "40" name = "USERNAME"
                     style = "height: 22px; width: 115px" />
               </td>
            </tr>

            <tr>
               <td colspan = "3">
                  <strong>Password:</strong>
               </td>
            </tr>

```

Fig. 29.15 XHTML form for obtaining a username and password (part 1 of 2).

```
            <tr>
               <td colspan = "3">
                  <input size = "40" name = "PASSWORD"
                     style = "height: 22px; width: 115px"
                     type = "password" />
               <br/></td>
            </tr>

            <tr>
               <td colspan = "1">
                  <input type = "submit" name = "Enter"
                     value = "Enter" style = "height: 23px;
                     width: 47px" />
               </td>
               <td colspan = "2">
                  <input type = "submit" name = "NewUser"
                     value = "New User"
                     style = "height: 23px" />
               </td>
            </tr>
         </table>
      </form>
   </body>
</html>
```

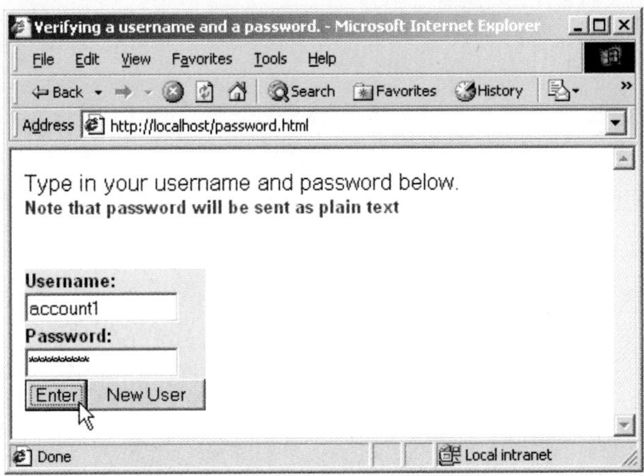

Fig. 29.15 XHTML form for obtaining a username and password (part 2 of 2).

Script **password.php** (Fig. 29.16) verifies the client's username and password by querying a database. The valid user list and each user's respective password is contained within a simple text file named **password.txt** (Fig. 29.17). Existing users are validated against this text file, and new users are appended to it.

First, lines 13–16 check whether the user has submitted a form without specifying a username or password. Variable names, when preceded by the *logical negation operator* (**!**), return **true** if they are empty or are set to **0**. *Logical operator OR* (**||**) returns **true** if either of the variables are empty or are set to **0**. If this is the case, function **fields-Blank** is called (line 144), which notifies the client that all form fields must be completed.

We determine whether we are adding a new user (line 19 in Fig. 29.16) by calling *function* **isset** to test whether variable **$NewUser** has been set. When a user submits the XHTML form in **password.html**, the user clicks either the **New User** or **Enter** button. This sets either variable **$NewUser** or variable **$Enter**, respectively. If variable **$NewUser** has been set, lines 22–36 are executed. If this variable has not been set, we assume the user has pressed the **Enter** button, and lines 42–75 execute.

```
1   <!DOCTYPE html PUBLIC "-//W3C//DTD XHTML 1.0 Transitional//EN"
2      "http://www.w3.org/TR/xhtml1/DTD/xhtml1-transitional.dtd">
3
4   <!-- Fig. 29.16: password.php                              -->
5   <!-- Searching a database for usernames and passwords. -->
6
7   <html xmlns = "http://www.w3.org/1999/xhtml">
8      <head>
9         <?php
10
11           // check if user has left USERNAME
12           // or PASSWORD field blank
13           if ( !$USERNAME || !$PASSWORD ) {
14              fieldsBlank();
15              die();
16           }
17
18           // check if the New User button was clicked
19           if ( isset( $NewUser ) ) {
20
21              // open password.txt for writing using append mode
22              if ( !( $file = fopen( "password.txt",
23                 "append" ) ) ) {
24
25                 // print error message and terminate script
26                 // execution if file cannot be opened
27                 print( "<title>Error</title></head><body>
28                    Could not open password file
29                    </body></html>" );
30                 die();
31              }
32
33              // write username and password to file and
34              // call function userAdded
35              fputs( $file, "$USERNAME,$PASSWORD\n" );
36              userAdded( $USERNAME );
37           }
38           else {
39
40              // if a new user is not being added, open file
41              // for reading
```

Fig. 29.16 Verifying a username and password (part 1 of 4).

```
   if ( !( $file = fopen( "password.txt",
      "read" ) ) ) {
      print( "<title>Error</title></head>
         <body>Could not open password file
         </body></html>" );
      die();
   }

   $userVerified = 0;

   // read each line in file and check username
   // and password
   while ( !feof( $file ) && !$userVerified ) {

      // read line from file
      $line = fgets( $file, 255 );

      // remove newline character from end of line
      $line = chop( $line );

      // split username and password
      $field = split( ",", $line, 2 );

      // verify username
      if ( $USERNAME == $field[ 0 ] ) {
         $userVerified = 1;

         // call function checkPassword to verify
         // user's password
         if ( checkPassword( $PASSWORD, $field )
            == true )
            accessGranted( $USERNAME );
         else
            wrongPassword();
      }
   }

   // close text file
   fclose( $file );

   // call function accessDenied if username has
   // not been verified
   if ( !$userVerified )
      accessDenied();
}

// verify user password and return a boolean
function checkPassword( $userpassword, $filedata )
{
   if ( $userpassword == $filedata[ 1 ] )
      return true;
   else
      return false;
}
```

Fig. 29.16 Verifying a username and password (part 2 of 4).

```

      // print a message indicating the user has been added
      function userAdded( $name )
      {
         print( "<title>Thank You</title></head>
            <body style = \"font-family: arial;
            font-size: 1em; color: blue\">
            <strong>You have been added
            to the user list, $name.
            <br />Enjoy the site.</strong>" );
      }

      // print a message indicating permission
      // has been granted
      function accessGranted( $name )
      {
         print( "<title>Thank You</title></head>
            <body style = \"font-family: arial;
            font-size: 1em; color: blue\">
            <strong>Permission has been
            granted, $name. <br />
            Enjoy the site.</strong>" );
      }

      // print a message indicating password is invalid
      function wrongPassword()
      {
         print( "<title>Access Denied</title></head>
            <body style = \"font-family: arial;
            font-size: 1em; color: red\">
            <strong>You entered an invalid
            password.<br />Access has
            been denied.</strong>" );
      }

      // print a message indicating access has been denied
      function accessDenied()
      {
         print( "<title>Access Denied</title></head>
            <body style = \"font-family: arial;
            font-size: 1em; color: red\">
            <strong>
            You were denied access to this server.
            <br /></strong>" );
      }

      // print a message indicating that fields
      // have been left blank
      function fieldsBlank()
      {
         print( "<title>Access Denied</title></head>
            <body style = \"font-family: arial;
            font-size: 1em; color: red\">
            <strong>
```

Fig. 29.16 Verifying a username and password (part 3 of 4).

```
                    Please fill in all form fields.
                    <br /></strong>" );
            }
        ?>
    </body>
</html>
```

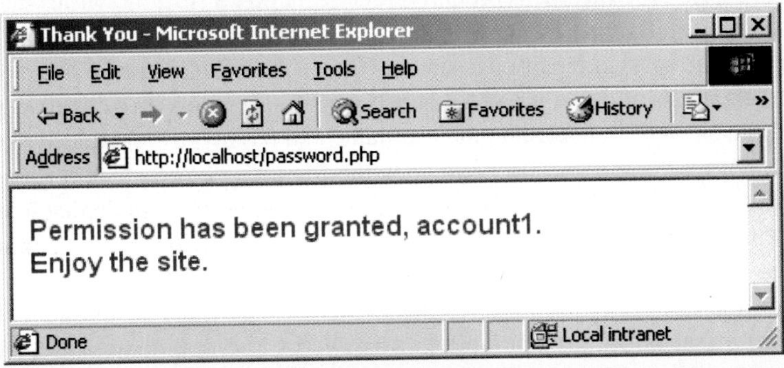

Fig. 29.16 Verifying a username and password (part 4 of 4).

```
account1,password1
account2,password2
account3,password3
account4,password4
account5,password5
account6,password6
account7,password7
account8,password8
account9,password9
account10,password10
```

Fig. 29.17 Database **`password.txt`** containing usernames and passwords.

To add a new user, we open the file **password.txt** by calling *function* **fopen** and assigning the file handle that is returned to variable **$file** (lines 22–23). A *file handle* is a number assigned to the file by the Web server for purposes of identification. Function **fopen** takes two arguments: The name of the file and the mode in which to open it. The possible modes include ***read***, ***write*** and ***append***. Here, we open the file in **append** mode, which opens it for writing, but does not write over the previous contents of the file. If an error occurs in opening the file, function **fopen** does not return a file handle and an error message is printed (lines 27–29), and script execution is terminated by calling *function* ***die*** (line 30). If the file opens properly, function **fputs** (line 35) writes the name and password to the file. To specify a new line, we use the newline character (**\n**). This places each username and password pair on a separate line in the file. On line 36, we pass the variable **$USERNAME** to function **userAdded** (line 98). Function **userAdded prints** a message to the client to indicate that the username and password were added to the file.

If we are not adding a new user, we open the file **password.txt** for reading. This is accomplished by using function **fopen** and assigning the file handle that is returned to variable **$file** (lines 42–43). Lines 44–47 execute if an error occurs in opening the file. The **while** loop (line 54) repeatedly executes the code enclosed in its curly braces (lines 57–75) until the test condition in parentheses evaluates to **false**. Before we enter the **while** loop, we set the value of variable **$userVerified** to **0**. In this case, the test condition (line 54) checks to ensure that the end of the file has not been reached and that the user has not been found in the password file. *Logical operator AND* (**&&**) connects the two conditions. *Function* ***feof***, preceded by the logical negation operator (**!**), returns **true** when there are more lines to be read in the specified file. When the logical negation operator (**!**) is applied to the **$userVerified** variable, **true** is returned if the variable is empty or is set to **0**.

Each line in **password.txt** consists of a username and password pair that is separated by a comma and followed by a newline character. A line from this file is read using function ***fgets*** (line 57) and is assigned to variable **$line**.

This function takes two arguments: The file handle to read, and the maximum number of characters to read. The function reads until a newline character is encountered, the end of the file is encountered or the number of characters read reaches one less than the number specified in the second argument.

For each line read, function ***chop*** is called (line 60) to remove the newline character from the end of the line. Then, function ***split*** is called to divide the string into substrings at the specified separator, or *delimiter* (in this case, a comma). For example, function **split** returns an array containing (**"account1"** and **"password1"**) from the first line in **password.txt**. This array is assigned to variable **$field**.

Line 66 determines whether the username entered by the user matches the one returned from the text file (stored in the variable **$field[0]**). If the condition evaluates to **true**, then the **$userVerified** variable is set to **1**, and lines 71–75 execute. On line 71, function **checkPassword** (line 89) is called to verify the user's password. Variables **$PASSWORD** and **$field** are passed to the function. Function **checkPassword** compares the user's password to the password in the file. If they match, **true** is returned (line 92), whereas **false** is returned if they do not (line 94). If the condition evaluates to **true**, then function **accessGranted** (line 110) is invoked. Variable **$USERNAME** is passed to the function, and a message notifies the client that permission has been granted. However, if the condition evaluates to **false**, then function **wrongPassword** is invoked (line 121), which notifies the client that an invalid password was entered.

When the **while** loop is complete, either as a result of matching a username or of reaching the end of the file, we are finished reading from **password.txt**. We call *function* **fclose** (line 80) to close the file. Line 84 checks whether the **$userVerified** variable is empty or has a value of **0**, which indicates that the username was not found in the **password.txt** file. If this returns **true**, function **accessDenied** is called (line 132). This function notifies the client that access to the server has been denied.

29.7 Connecting to a Database

Databases enable companies to enter the world of e-commerce by maintaining crucial data, and database connectivity allows system administrators to maintain and update such information as user accounts, passwords, credit-card numbers, mailing lists and product inventories. PHP offers built-in support for a wide variety of databases. In this example, we use MySQL. Visit **www.deitel.com** to locate information on setting up a MySQL database. From a Web browser, the client enters a database field name that is sent to the Web server. The PHP script is then executed; the script builds the select query, queries the database and sends a record set in the form of XHTML to the client. The rules and syntax for writing such a query string are discussed in Chapter 22, Database: SQL, MySQL, DBI and ADO.

Figure 29.18 (**data.html**) is a Web page that **post**s form data containing a database field to the server. PHP script **database.php** (Fig. 29.19) processes the form data

Line 17 (Fig. 29.18) creates an XHTML **form**, specifying that the data submitted from the **form** will be sent to script **database.php** (Fig. 29.19). Lines 22–28 add a select box to the **form**, set the name of the select box to **select**, and set its default selection to *****. This value specifies that all records are to be retrieved from the database. Each database field is set as an option in the select box.

```
1   <!DOCTYPE html PUBLIC "-//W3C//DTD XHTML 1.0 Transitional//EN"
2      "http://www.w3.org/TR/xhtml1/DTD/xhtml1-transitional.dtd">
3
4   <!-- Fig. 29.18: data.html      -->
5   <!-- Querying a MySQL Database -->
6
7   <html xmlns = "http://www.w3.org/1999/xhtml">
8      <head>
9         <title>Sample Database Query</title>
10     </head>
11
12     <body style = "background-color: #F0E68C">
13        <h2 style = "font-family: arial color: blue">
14           Querying a MySQL database.
15        </h2>
16
17        <form method = "post" action = "database.php">
18           <p>Select a field to display:
19
```

Fig. 29.18 Form to query a MySQL database (part 1 of 2).

```
                  <!-- add a select box containing options -->
                  <!-- for SELECT query                     -->
                  <select name = "select">
                     <option selected = "selected">*</option>
                     <option>ID</option>
                     <option>Title</option>
                     <option>Category</option>
                     <option>ISBN</option>
                  </select>
               </p>

               <input type = "submit" value = "Send Query"
                  style = "background-color: blue;
                  color: yellow; font-weight: bold" />
            </form>
         </body>
      </html>
```

Fig. 29.18 Form to query a MySQL database (part 2 of 2).

```
<!DOCTYPE html PUBLIC "-//W3C//DTD XHTML 1.0 Transitional//EN"
   "http://www.w3.org/TR/xhtml1/DTD/xhtml1-transitional.dtd">

<!-- Fig. 29.19: database.php         -->
<!-- Program to query a database and -->
<!-- send results to the client.     -->

<html xmlns = "http://www.w3.org/1999/xhtml">
   <head>
      <title>Search Results</title>
   </head>

   <body style = "font-family: arial, sans-serif"
      style = "background-color: #F0E68C">
```

Fig. 29.19 Querying a database and displaying the results (part 1 of 3).

```
      <?php

         // build SELECT query
         $query = "SELECT " . $select . " FROM Books";

         // Connect to MySQL
         if ( !( $database = mysql_connect( "localhost",
            "httpd", "" ) ) )
            die( "Could not connect to database" );

         // open Products database
         if ( !mysql_select_db( "Products", $database ) )
            die( "Could not open Products database" );

         // query Products database
         if ( !( $result = mysql_query( $query, $database ) ) ) {
            print( "Could not execute query! <br />" );
            die( mysql_error() );
         }
      ?>

      <h3 style = "color: blue">
      Search Results</h3>

      <table border = "1" cellpadding = "3" cellspacing = "2"
         style = "background-color: #ADD8E6">

         <?php

            // fetch each record in result set
            for ( $counter = 0;
               $row = mysql_fetch_row( $result );
               $counter++ ){

               // build table to display results
               print( "<tr>" );

               foreach ( $row as $key => $value )
                  print( "<td>$value</td>" );

               print( "</tr>" );
            }

            mysql_close( $database );
         ?>

      </table>

      <br />Your search yielded <strong>
      <?php print( "$counter" ) ?> results.<br /><br /></strong>

      <h5>Please email comments to
         <a href = "mailto:deitel@deitel.com">
```

Fig. 29.19 Querying a database and displaying the results (part 2 of 3).

```
68                  Deitel and Associates, Inc.
69               </a>
70            </h5>
71
72         </body>
73      </html>
```

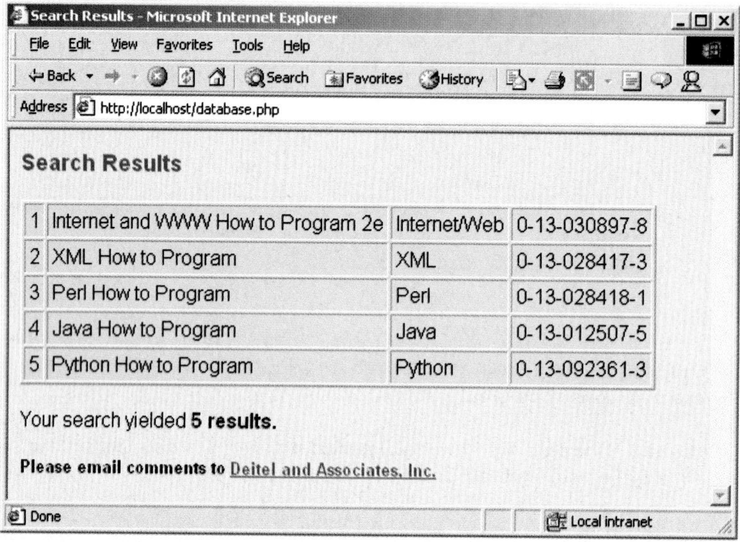

Fig. 29.19 Querying a database and displaying the results (part 3 of 3).

Script **`database.php`** is responsible for building an SQL-query string with the specified field name and sending it to the database-management system. Line 18 concatenates the **`post`**ed field name to a **`SELECT`** query. Line 21 calls *function* **`mysql_connect`** to connect to the MySQL database. We pass three arguments to function **`mysql_connect`**: The server's hostname, a username and a password. This function returns a *database handle*—a reference to the object that is used to represent PHP's connection to the database—which we assign to variable **`$database`**. If the connection to MySQL fails, function **`die`** is called, which outputs an error message and terminates the script. Line 26 calls *function* **`mysql_select_db`** to specify the database to be queried (in this case, **`Products`**). Function **`die`** is called if the database cannot be opened. To query the database, line 30 calls *function* **`mysql_query`**, specifying the query string and the database to query. Function **`mysql_query`** returns an object containing the result set of the query, which we assign to variable **`$result`**. If the query of the database fails, a message is output to the client indicating that the query failed to execute. Function **`die`** is then called, accepting *function* **`mysql_error`** as a parameter instead of a string message. In the event that the query fails, function **`mysql_error`** returns any error strings from the database. Function **`mysql_query`** can also be used to execute SQL statements, such as **`INSERT`** or **`DELETE`**, that do not return results.

Lines 45–56 use a **`for`** loop to iterate through each record in the result set while constructing an XHTML table from the results. The loop condition calls *function*

mysql_fetch_row to return an array containing the elements of each row in the result set of our query (**$result**). The array is then stored in variable **$row**. Lines 52–53 use a **foreach** loop to construct individual cells for each of the elements in the row. The **foreach** loop takes the name of the array (**$row**), iterates through each index value of the array (**$key**) and stores the element in variable **$value**. Each element of the array is then printed as an individual cell. For each row retrieved, variable **$counter** is incremented by one. When the end of the result set has been reached, **undef** (**false**) is returned by function **mysql_fetch_row**, which terminates the **for** loop.

After all rows of the result set have been displayed, the database is closed (line 58), and the table's closing tag is written (line 61). The number of results contained in **$counter** is printed in line 64.

29.8 Cookies

A *cookie* is a text file that a Web site stores on a client's computer to maintain information about that client during and between browsing sessions. A Web site can store a cookie on a client's computer to record user preferences and other information, which the Web site can retrieve during that client's subsequent visits. For example, many Web sites use cookies to store clients' zip codes. The Web site can retrieve the zip code from the cookie and provide weather reports and news updates tailored to the user's region. Web sites also can use cookies to track information about client activity. Analysis of information collected via cookies can reveal the popularity of various Web sites or products. In addition, marketers can use cookies to determine the effects of particular advertising campaigns.

Web sites store cookies on users' hard drives, which raises issues regarding security and privacy. Web sites should not store critical information, such as credit-card numbers or passwords in cookies, because cookies are text files that any program can read. Several cookie features address security and privacy concerns. A particular server can access only the cookies that server placed on the client. For example, a Web application running on **www.deitel.com** cannot access cookies that the Web site **www.prenhall.com/deitel** may have placed on the client's computer. A cookie also has a maximum age, after which the Web browser deletes that cookie. Users who are concerned about the privacy and security implications of cookies can disable cookies in their Web browsers. However, the disabling of cookies can prevent those users from interacting with Web sites that rely on cookies to function properly.

Microsoft Internet Explorer stores cookies as small text files on the client's hard drive. The information stored in the cookie is sent back to the Web server from which it originated whenever the user requests a Web page from that particular server. The Web server can send the client XHTML output that reflects the preferences or information that is stored in the cookie.

Figure 29.20 uses a script to write a cookie to the client's machine. The **cookies.html** file is used to display an XHTML **form** that allows a user to enter a name, height and favorite color. When the user clicks the **Write Cookie** button, the **cookies.php** script (Fig. 29.21) is executed.

Software Engineering Observation 29.2

Some clients do not accept cookies. When a client declines a cookie, the browser application normally informs the client that the site may not function correctly without cookies enabled.

Software Engineering Observation 29.3

Cookies cannot be used to retrieve e-mail addresses or data from the hard drive of a client's computer.

Script **cookies.php** (Fig. 29.21) calls *function* **setcookie** to set the cookies to the values passed from **cookies.html**. Function **setcookie** prints XHTML header information, therefore, it needs to be called before any other XHTML (including comments) is printed.

Function **setcookie** takes the name of the cookie to be set as the first argument, followed by the value to be stored in the cookie. For example, line 7 sets the name of the cookie to **"Name"** and the value to variable **$NAME**, which is passed to the script from **cookies.html**. The optional third argument indicates the expiration date of the cookie. In this example, we set the cookies to expire in five days by taking the current time, which is returned by *function* **time**, and adding the number of seconds after which the cookie should expire (**60** seconds ***** **60** minutes ***** **24** hours ***** **5** days). If no expiration date is specified, the cookie only lasts until the end of the current session, which is the total time until the user closes the browser. If only the **name** argument is passed to function **setcookie**, the cookie is deleted from the cookie database. Lines 12–37 send a Web page to the client indicating that the cookie has been written and listing the values that are stored in the cookie. Lines 34–35 provide a link to **readCookies.php** (Fig. 29.24).

```
<!DOCTYPE html PUBLIC "-//W3C//DTD XHTML 1.0 Transitional//EN"
   "http://www.w3.org/TR/xhtml1/DTD/xhtml1-transitional.dtd">

<!-- Fig. 29.20: cookies.html -->
<!-- Writing a Cookie         -->

<html xmlns = "http://www.w3.org/1999/xhtml">
   <head>
      <title>Writing a cookie to the client computer</title>
   </head>

   <body style = "font-family: arial, sans-serif;
      background-color: #99CCFF">

      <h2>Click Write Cookie to save your cookie data.</h2>

      <form method = "post" action = "cookies.php"
           style = "font-size: 10pt">
         <strong>Name:</strong><br />
         <input type = "text" name = "NAME" /><br />

         <strong>Height:</strong><br />
         <input type = "text" name = "HEIGHT" /><br />

         <strong>Favorite Color:</strong><br />
         <input type = "text" name = "COLOR" /><br />

         <input type = "submit" value = "Write Cookie"
```

Fig. 29.20 Gathering data to be written as a cookie (part 1 of 2).

```
               style = "background-color: #F0E86C; color: navy;
               font-weight: bold" /></p>
         </form>
      </body>
   </html>
```

Fig. 29.20 Gathering data to be written as a cookie (part 2 of 2).

```
<?php
   // Fig. 29.21: cookies.php
   // Program to write a cookie to a client's machine

   // write each form field's value to a cookie and set the
   // cookie's expiration date
   setcookie( "Name", $NAME, time() + 60 * 60 * 24 * 5 );
   setcookie( "Height", $HEIGHT, time() + 60 * 60 * 24 * 5 );
   setcookie( "Color", $COLOR, time() + 60 * 60 * 24 * 5 );
?>

<!DOCTYPE html PUBLIC "-//W3C//DTD XHTML 1.0 Transitional//EN"
   "http://www.w3.org/TR/xhtml1/DTD/xhtml1-transitional.dtd">

<html xmlns = "http://www.w3.org/1999/xhtml">
   <head>
      <title>Cookie Saved</title>
   </head>

   <body style = "font-family: arial, sans-serif">
      <p>The cookie has been set with the following data:</p>

```

Fig. 29.21 Writing a cookie to the client (part 1 of 2).

```
        <!-- print each form field's value -->
        <br /><span style = "color: blue">Name:</span>
           <?php print( $NAME ) ?><br />

        <span style = "color: blue">Height:</span>
           <?php print( $HEIGHT ) ?><br />

        <span style = "color: blue">Favorite Color:</span>

        <span style = "color: <?php print( "$COLOR\">$COLOR" ) ?>
        </span><br />
        <p>Click <a href = "readCookies.php">here</a>
           to read the saved cookie.</p>
     </body>
  </html>
```

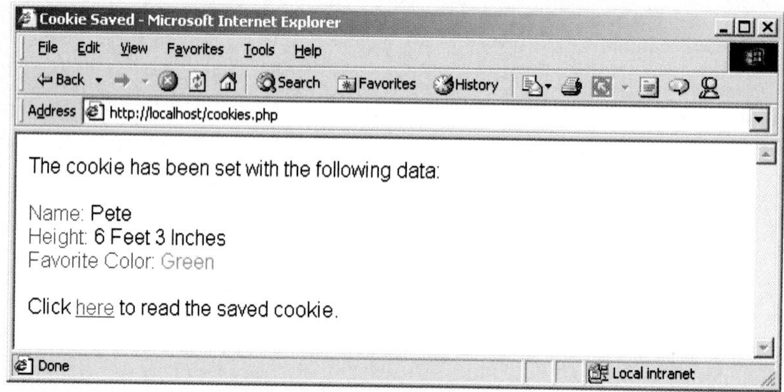

Fig. 29.21 Writing a cookie to the client (part 2 of 2).

If the client is Internet Explorer, cookies are stored in the **Cookies** directory on the client's machine. Figure 29.22 shows the contents of this directory prior to the execution of **`cookies.php`**. After the cookie is written, a text file is added to the directory. In Fig. 29.23, the file **`petel@localhost`** appears in the **Cookies** directory.

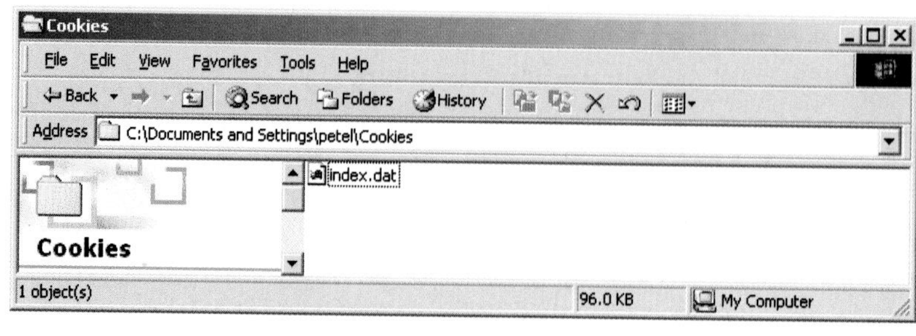

Fig. 29.22 **`Cookies`** directory before a cookie is written.

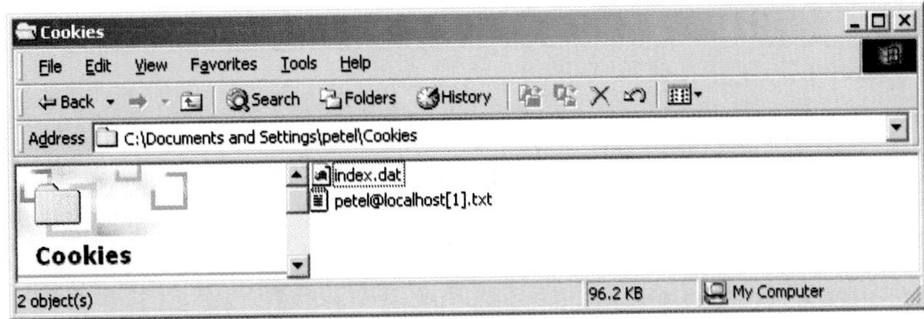

Fig. 29.23 **`Cookies`** directory after a cookie is written.

Figure 29.24 (**`readCookies.php`**) reads the cookie that is written in Fig. 29.21 and displays the cookie's information in a table.

PHP creates variables containing contents of a cookie, similar to when values are posted via forms. Thus, the next time a script is run from a location where the cookie is visible, a cookie set with the name **`"Color"`** is assigned to variable **`$Color`** along with its corresponding value. PHP also creates array **`$HTTP_COOKIE_VARS`**, which contains all the cookie values indexed by their names.

```
<!DOCTYPE html PUBLIC "-//W3C//DTD XHTML 1.0 Transitional//EN"
   "http://www.w3.org/TR/xhtml1/DTD/xhtml1-transitional.dtd">

<!-- Fig. 29.24: readCookies.php                            -->
<!-- Program to read cookies from the client's computer -->

<html xmlns = "http://www.w3.org/1999/xhtml">
   <head><title>Read Cookies</title></head>

   <body style = "font-family: arial, sans-serif">

      <p>
         <strong>
            The following data is saved in a cookie on your
            computer.
         </strong>
      </p>

      <table border = "5" cellspacing = "0" cellpadding = "10">
         <?php

            // iterate through array $HTTP_COOKIE_VARS and print
            // name and value of each cookie
            foreach ( $HTTP_COOKIE_VARS as $key => $value )
               print( "<tr>
                  <td bgcolor=\"#F0E68C\">$key</td>
                  <td bgcolor=\"#FFA500\">$value</td>
                  </tr>" );
         ?>
```

Fig. 29.24 Displaying the cookie's contents (part 1 of 2).

```
30
31          </table>
32       </body>
33    </html>
```

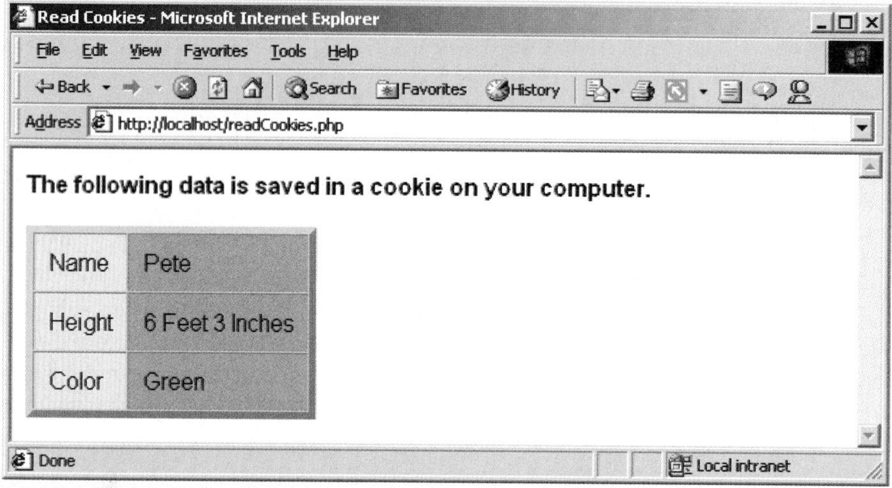

Fig. 29.24 Displaying the cookie's contents (part 2 of 2).

Lines 24–28 iterate through this array using a **`foreach`** loop, printing out the name and value of each cookie in an XHTML table. The **`foreach`** loop takes the name of the array (**`$HTTP_COOKIE_VARS`**) and iterates through each index value of the array (**`$key`**). In this case, the index value is the name of each cookie. Each element is then stored in variable **`$value`**, and these values become the individual cells of the table.

29.9 Operator Precedence

This section contains the operator precedence chart for PHP. In Fig. 29.25, the operators are shown from top to bottom in decreasing order of precedence.

Operator	Type	Associativity
`new`	constructor	none
`[]`	subscript	right to left
`~`	bitwise not	right to left
`!`	not	
`++`	increment	
`--`	decrement	
`-`	unary negative	
`@`	error control	*(This level continued at top of next page)*

Fig. 29.25 PHP operator precedence and associativity (part 1 of 3).

Operator	Type	Associativity
`~`	bitwise not	*(This level continued from bottom of previous page)*
`!`	not	
`++`	increment	
`--`	decrement	
`-`	unary negative	
`@`	error control	
`*`	multiplication	left to right
`/`	division	
`%`	modulus	
`+`	addition	left to right
`-`	subtraction	
`.`	concatenation	
`<<`	bitwise shift left	left to right
`>>`	bitwise shift right	
`<`	less than	none
`>`	greater than	
`<=`	less than or equal	
`>=`	greater than or equal	
`==`	equal	none
`!=`	not equal	
`===`	identical	
`!==`	not identical	
`&`	bitwise AND	left to right
`^`	bitwise XOR	left to right
`|`	bitwise OR	left to right
`&&`	logical AND	left to right
`||`	logical OR	left to right
`=`	assignment	left to right
`+=`	addition assignment	
`-=`	subtraction assignment	
`*=`	multiplication assignment	
`/=`	division assignment	
`&=`	bitwise AND assignment	
`|=`	bitwise OR assignment	
`^=`	bitwise exclusive OR assignment	
`.=`	concatenation assignment	
`<<=`	bitwise shift left assignment	
`>>=`	bitwise shift right assignment	
`and`	logical AND	left to right

Fig. 29.25 PHP operator precedence and associativity (part 2 of 3).

Operator	Type	Associativity
`xor`	exclusive OR	left to right
`or`	logical OR	left to right
`,`	list	left to right

Fig. 29.25 PHP operator precedence and associativity (part 3 of 3).

29.10 Internet and World Wide Web Resources

`www.php.net`
This official PHP site contains the latest versions of PHP, as well as documentation, a list of FAQs, support and links to many other PHP resources.

`www.zend.com`
This site is the home of *Zend Technologies*, the developers of the Zend scripting engine. The site also provides code, tips and applications for PHP developers.

`www.phpbuilder.com`
This site contains resources for PHP developers. The site also includes a search feature and provides links to articles, code and forums.

`www.phpworld.com`
This site provides PHP-related resources, including articles, documentation, links and a help board.

`php.resourceindex.com`
This site provides access to the PHP community, helping visitors find jobs, chats, developer sites and more. The code section of the site contains scripts, functions and classes. In addition, visitors can sign up to receive e-mail updates regarding new resources.

`www.phpwizard.net`
This site contains resources for PHP development. It provides tutorials, links and many other resources.

`phpclub.unet.ru`
This Web page contains manuals, forums, links, books, databases, a FAQ list and other PHP resources.

SUMMARY

- PHP is an open-source technology that is supported by a large community of users and developers. PHP is platform independent; implementations exist for all major UNIX, Linux and Windows operating systems.
- PHP code is embedded directly into XHTML documents and provides support for a wide variety of different databases. PHP scripts typically have the file extension **`.php`**.
- In PHP, code is inserted in special scripting delimiters that begin with **`<?php`** and end with **`?>`**.
- Variables are preceded by the **`$`** special symbol. A variable is created automatically when it is first encountered by the PHP interpreter.
- PHP statements are terminated with a semicolon (**`;`**). Comments begin with two forward slashes (**`//`**). Text to the right of the slashes is ignored by the interpreter.

- When a variable is encountered inside a double-quoted (**""**) string, PHP uses interpolation to replace the variable with its associated data.
- PHP variables are multitype, meaning that they can contain different types of data— integers, floating-point numbers or strings.
- Type casting converts between data types without changing the value of the variable itself.
- The concatenation operator (**.**) appends the string on the right of the operator to the string on the left.
- Uninitialized variables have the value **undef**, which evaluates to different values, depending on the context. When **undef** is used in a numeric context, it evaluates to **0**. When **undef** is interpreted in a string context, it evaluates to an empty string (**""**).
- Strings are automatically converted to integers when they are used in arithmetic operations.
- PHP provides the capability to store data in arrays. Arrays are divided into elements that behave as individual variables.
- Individual array elements are accessed by following the array-variable name with the index number in braces (**[]**). If a value is assigned to an array that does not exist, the array is created. In addition to integer indices, arrays can also have nonnumeric indices.
- Function **count** returns the total number of elements in the array. Function **array** takes a list of arguments and returns an array. Function **array** may also be used to initialize arrays with string indices.
- Function **reset** sets the iterator to the first element of the array. Function **key** returns the index of the current element. Function **next** moves the iterator to the next element.
- The **foreach** loop is a control structure that is specifically designed for iterating through arrays.
- Text manipulation in PHP is usually done with regular expressions—a series of characters that serve as pattern-matching templates (or search criteria) in strings, text files and databases. This feature allows complex searching and string processing to be performed using relatively simple expressions.
- Function **strcmp** compares two strings. If the first string alphabetically precedes the second string, **-1** is returned. If the strings are equal, **0** is returned. If the first string alphabetically follows the second string, **1** is returned.
- Relational operators (**==**, **!=**, **<**, **<=**, **>** and **>=**) can be used to compare strings. These operators can also be used for numerical comparison of integers and doubles.
- For more powerful string comparisons, PHP provides functions **ereg** and **preg_match**, which use regular expressions to search a string for a specified pattern.
- Function **ereg** uses POSIX extended regular expressions, whereas function **preg_match** provides Perl compatible regular expressions.
- The caret (**^**) matches the beginning of a string. A dollar sign (**$**) searches for the specified pattern at the end of the string. The period (**.**) is a special character that is used to match any single character. The **** character is an escape character in regular expressions.
- Bracket expressions are lists of characters enclosed in square brackets (**[ ]**) that match a single character from the list. Ranges can be specified by supplying the beginning and the end of the range separated by a dash (**-**).
- The special bracket expressions **[[:<:]]** and **[[:>:]]** match the beginning and end of a word.
- Character class **[[:alpha:]]** matches any alphabetic character.
- The quantifier **+** matches one or more instances of the preceding expression.

- Function **ereg_replace** takes three arguments: The pattern to search, a string to replace the matched string and the string to search.
- PHP stores environment variables and their values in the **$GLOBALS** array. Individual array variables can be accessed directly by using an element's key from the **$GLOBALS** array as a variable.
- For each **form** field posted to a PHP script, PHP creates a variable with the same name as the field.
- Function **die** terminates script execution.
- Passing a string argument to the **die** function prints that string a message before stopping program execution.
- Function **isset** tests whether a variable has been set.
- Function **fopen** opens a text file.
- A file handle is a number that the server assigns to the file and is used when the server accesses the file.
- Function **fopen** takes two arguments: The name of the file and the mode in which to open the file. The possible modes include **read**, **write** and **append**.
- Function **feof**, preceded by the logical negation operator (**!**), returns **true** when there are more lines to be read in a specified file.
- A line from a text file is read using function **fgets**. This function takes two arguments: The file handle to read and the maximum number of characters to read.
- Function **chop** removes newline characters from the end of a line. Function **split** divides a string into substrings at the specified separator or delimiter. Function **fclose** closes a file.
- Function **mysql_connect** connects to a MySQL database. This function returns a database handle—a reference to the object which is used to represent PHP's connection to the database. Function **mysql_query** returns an object that contains the result set of the query. Function **mysql_error** returns any error strings from the database if the query fails. Function **mysql_fetch_row** returns an array that contains the elements of each row in the result set of a query.
- Cookies maintain state information for a particular client who uses a Web browser. Cookies are often used to record user preferences or other information that will be retrieved during a client's subsequent visits to a Web site. On the server side, cookies can be used to track information about client activity.
- The data stored in the cookie is sent back to the Web server from which it originated whenever the user requests a Web page from that particular server.
- Function **setcookie** sets a cookie. Function **setcookie** takes as the first argument the name of the cookie to be set, followed by the value to be stored in the cookie.
- PHP creates variables containing contents of a cookie, similar to when values are posted via forms.
- PHP creates array **$HTTP_COOKIE_VARS**, which contains all the cookie values indexed by their names.

TERMINOLOGY

$ metacharacter
$GLOBALS variable
$HTTP_COOKIE_VARS
append
array function
array_splice function
as
assignment operator
backslash
bracket expression
caret metacharacter (**^**) in PHP
character class
chomp function
comparison operator

concatenation operator
count function
current function
database connectivity
database handle
delimiter
die function
doubleval function
environment variable
equality operator
ereg function
ereg_replace function
eregi function
fclose function
feof function
fgets function
filehandle
fopen function
foreach loop
fputs function
HTTP connection
HTTP host
Hypertext Preprocessor
index value
interpolation
intval function
isset function
key function
literal character
logical AND operator
logical negation operator (**!**)
metacharacter
MySQL
mysql_connect function
mysql_error function
mysql_fetch_row function
mysql_query function
mysql_selectdb function
newline character
next function
parenthetical memory in PHP
Perl compatible regular expression
PHP (Hypertext Preprocessor)
PHP comment
PHP keyword
pos function
POSIX extended regular expression
preg_match function
print function
printf function
quantifier
read
regular expression
reset
result set
setcookie function
settype function
split function
SQL query string
strcmp function
string context
strval function
typecasting operator
undef
validation
Web server
while loop
write

SELF-REVIEW EXERCISES

29.1 State whether the following are *true* or *false*. If *false*, explain why.

a) PHP code is embedded directly into XHTML.
b) PHP function names are case sensitive.
c) The **strval** function permanently changes the type of a variable into a string.
d) Conversion between data types happens automatically when a variable is used in a context that requires a different data type.
e) The **foreach** loop is a control structure that is designed specifically for iterating over arrays.
f) Relational operators can be used for alphabetic and numeric comparison.
g) The quantifier **+**, when used in a regular expression, matches any number of the preceding pattern.
h) Opening a file in **append** mode causes the file to be overwritten.
i) Cookies are stored on the server computer.
j) The ***** arithmetic operator has higher precedence than the **+** operator.

29.2 Fill in the blanks in each of the following statements:

a) PHP scripts typically have the file extension ________.
b) The two numeric data types that PHP variables can store are ________ and ________.
c) In PHP, uninitialized variables have the value ________.
d) ________ are divided into individual elements, each of which act like individual variables.
e) Function ________ returns the total number of elements in an array.
f) To use Perl compatible regular expressions, use the ________ function.
g) A ________ in a regular expression matches a predefined set of characters.
h) PHP stores all global variables in array ________.
i) Function ________ terminates script execution.
j) ________ can be used to maintain state information on a client's computer.

ANSWERS TO SELF-REVIEW EXERCISES

29.1 a) True. b) False. Function names are not case sensitive. c) False. The **strval** function returns the converted value, but does not affect the original variable. d) True. e) True. f) True. g) False. The quantifier **+** matches one or more of the preceding patterns. h) False. Opening a file in **write** mode causes the file to be overwritten. i) False. Cookies are stored on the client's computer. j) True.

29.1 a) **.php**. b) integers, double. c) **undef**. d) Arrays.
e) **count**. f) **preg_match**. g) character class. h) **$GLOBALS**. i) **die**. j) Cookies.

EXERCISES

29.3 Identify and correct the error in each of the following PHP code examples.

a)

```
<?php print( "Hello World" ); // printing text ?>
```

b)

```
<?php
   $name = "Paul";
   print( "$Name" );
?>
```

29.4 How can a PHP program determine the type of browser that a Web client is using?

29.5 Describe how input from an XHTML **form** is retrieved in a PHP program.

29.6 Describe how a text file can be opened and the different modes that are used to read/write to/from the file.

29.7 Describe how cookies can be used to store information on a computer and how the information can be retrieved by a PHP program. Assume that cookies are not disabled on the client.

29.8 Write a PHP program named **states.php** that creates a scalar value **$states** with the value **"Mississippi Alabama Texas Massachusetts Kansas"**. Write a program that does the following:

a) Search for a word in scalar **$states** that ends in **xas**. Store this word in element 0 of an array named **$statesArray**.
b) Search for a word in **$states** that begins with **k** and ends in **s**. Perform a case-insensitive comparison. Store this word in element 1 of **$statesArray**.

c) Search for a word in **$states** that begins with **M** and ends in **s**. Store this element in element 2 of the array.
d) Search for a word in **$states** that ends in **a**. Store this word in element 3 of the array.
e) Search for a word in **$states** at the beginning of the string that starts with **M**. Store this word in element 4 of the array.
f) Output the array **$statesArray** to the screen.

29.9 In the text, we presented environment variables. Develop a program that determines whether the client is using Internet Explorer. If so, determine the version number and send that information back to the client.

29.10 Modify the program in Fig. 29.14 to save information sent to the server into a text file. Each time a user submits a form, open the text file and print the file's contents.

29.11 Write a PHP program that tests whether an e-mail address is input correctly. Verify that the input begins with series of characters, followed by the **@** character, another series of characters, a period (**.**) and a final series of characters. Test your program, using both valid and invalid email addresses.

29.12 Using environment variables, write a program that logs the address (obtained with the **REMOTE_ADDR** environment variable) requesting information from the Web server.

29.13 Write a PHP program that obtains a URL and a description of that URL from a user and stores the information into a database using **MySQL**. The database should be named **URLs**, and the table should be named **Urltable**. The first field of the database, which is named **URL**, should contain an actual URL, and the second, which is named **Description**, should contain a description of that URL. Use **www.deitel.com** as the first URL, and input **Cool site!** as its description. The second URL should be **www.php.net**, and the description should be **The official PHP site**. After each new URL is submitted, print the complete results of the database in a table.

WORKS CITED

1. S.S. Bakken, et al., "Introduction to PHP," 17 April 2000 **<www.zend.com/zend/hof/rasmus.php>**.

2. S.S. Bakken, et al., "A Brief History of PHP," January 2001 **<www.php.net/manual/en/intro-history.php>**.s

30

Servlets: Bonus for Java™ Developers

Objectives

- To execute servlets with the Apache Tomcat server.
- To be able to respond to HTTP requests from an **`HttpServlet`**.
- To be able to redirect requests to static and dynamic Web resources.
- To be able to maintain session information with cookies and **`HttpSession`** objects.
- To be able to access a database from a servlet.

A fair request should be followed by the deed in silence.
Dante Alighieri

The longest part of the journey is said to be the passing of the gate.
Marcus Terentius Varro

If nominated, I will not accept; if elected, I will not serve.
General William T. Sherman

Me want cookie!
The Cookie Monster, *Sesame Street*

That's the way the cookie crumbles.
Anonymous

Friends share all things.
Pythagoras

If at first you don't succeed, destroy all evidence that you tried.
Newt Heilscher

Outline

30.1 Introduction[1]

There is much excitement over the Internet and the World Wide Web. The Internet ties the "information world" together. The World Wide Web makes the Internet easy to use and gives it the flair and sizzle of multimedia. Organizations see the Internet and the Web as crucial to their information systems strategies. Java provides a number of built-in networking capabilities that make it easy to develop Internet-based and Web-based applications. Not only can Java specify parallelism through multithreading, but it can enable programs to search the world for information and to collaborate with programs running on other computers internationally, nationally or just within an organization. Java can even enable applets and applications running on the same computer to communicate with one another, subject to security constraints.

---

1. We include this chapter as a bonus for Java developers who also are familiar with Java Database Connectivity (JDBC). Of the seven examples in this chapter, six of them will execute using the techniques and software we describe. The last example uses JDBC to interact with an Informix Cloudscape database. Informix provides a developer version of Cloudscape at the Web site **`www.cloudscape.com`**. The installation and configuration instructions are available at the Cloudscape Web site. We provide instructions for creating the database as part of that example.

Networking is a massive and complex topic. Computer science and computer engineering students typically take a full-semester, upper-level course in computer networking and continue with further study at the graduate level. Java provides a rich complement of networking capabilities and will likely be used as an implementation vehicle in computer networking courses. In *Advanced Java 2 Platform How to Program* we introduce several Java networking concepts and capabilities.

Java's networking capabilities are grouped into several packages. The fundamental networking capabilities are defined by classes and interfaces of package **java.net**, through which Java offers *socket-based communications* that enable applications to view networking as streams of data—a program can read from a *socket* or write to a socket as simply as reading from a file or writing to a file. The classes and interfaces of package **java.net** also offer *packet-based communications* that enable individual *packets* of information to be transmitted—commonly used to transmit audio and video over the Internet. Our book *Java How to Program, Fourth Edition* shows how to create and manipulate sockets and how to communicate with packets of data.

Higher-level views of networking[2] are provided by classes and interfaces in packages **java.rmi** (five packages) for *Remote Method Invocation (RMI)* and **org.omg** (seven packages) for *Common Object Request Broker Architecture (CORBA)* that are part of the Java 2 API. The RMI packages allow Java objects running on separate Java Virtual Machines (normally on separate computers) to communicate via remote method calls. Such method calls appear to be to an object in the same program, but actually have built-in networking (based on the capabilities of package **java.net**) that communicates the method calls to another object on a separate computer. The CORBA packages provide similar functionality to the RMI packages. A key difference between RMI and CORBA is that RMI can only be used between Java objects, whereas CORBA can be used between any two applications that understand CORBA—including applications written in other programming languages.

Our discussion of networking over the next two chapters focuses on both sides of a *client-server relationship*. The *client* requests that some action be performed and the *server* performs the action and responds to the client. This request-response model of communication is the foundation for the highest-level views of networking in Java—*servlets* and *JavaServer Pages (JSP)*. A servlet extends the functionality of a server. Packages **javax.servlet** and **javax.servlet.http** provide the classes and interfaces to define servlets. Packages **javax.servlet.jsp** and **javax.servlet.jsp.tagext** provide the classes and interfaces that extend the servlet capabilities for JavaServer Pages. Using special syntax, JSP allows Web-page implementors to create pages that use encapsulated Java functionality and even to write *scriptlets* of actual Java code directly in the page.

A common implementation of the request-response model is between World Wide Web browsers and World Wide Web servers. When a user selects a Web site to browse through their browser (the client application), a request is sent to the appropriate Web server (the server application). The server normally responds to the client by sending the appropriate XHTML Web page. Servlets are effective for developing Web-based solutions that help provide secure access to a Web site, interact with databases on behalf of a client, dynamically generate custom XHTML documents to be displayed by browsers and maintain unique session information for each client.

---

2. Our text *Advanced Java 2 Platform How to Program* discusses several higher-level Java networking capabilities.

Software Engineering Observation 30.1

Although servlets typically are used in distributed Web applications, not all servlets are required to enhance the functionality of a Web server.

This chapter begins our networking discussions with servlets that enhance the functionality of World Wide Web servers—the most common form of servlet today. Chapter 31 discusses JSPs, which are translated into servlets. JSPs are a convenient and powerful way to implement the request/response mechanism of the Web without getting into the lower-level details of servlets. Together, servlets and JSPs form the Web tier of the Java 2 Enterprise Edition (J2EE).

Many developers feel that servlets are the right solution for database-intensive applications that communicate with so-called *thin clients*—applications that require minimal client-side support. The server is responsible for database access. Clients connect to the server using standard protocols available on most client platforms. Thus, the presentation-logic code for generating dynamic content can be written once and reside on the server for access by clients, to allow programmers to create efficient thin clients.

Sun Microsystems, through the *Java Community Process*, is responsible for the development of the servlet and JavaServer Pages specifications. The reference implementation of both these standards is under development by the *Apache Software Foundation* (**`www.apache.org`**) as part of the *Jakarta Project* (**`jakarta.apache.org`**). As stated on the Jakarta Project's home page, "The goal of the Jakarta Project is to provide commercial-quality server solutions based on the Java Platform that are developed in an open and cooperative fashion." There are many subprojects under the Jakarta project to help commercial server-side developers. The servlet and JSP part of the Jakarta Project is called *Tomcat*. This is the official reference implementation of the JSP and servlet standards. We use Tomcat to demonstrate the servlets in this chapter. The most recent implementation of Tomcat at the time of this writing was version 3.2.3. For your convenience, Tomcat 3.2.3 is included on the CD that accompanies *Advanced Java 2 Platform How to Program*. However, the most recent version always can be downloaded from the Apache Group's Web site. To execute the servlets in this chapter, you must install Tomcat or an equivalent servlet and JavaServer Pages implementation. We discuss the set up and configuration of Tomcat in Section 30.3.1 and Section 30.3.2 after we introduce our first example.

In our directions for testing each of the examples in this chapter, we indicate that you should copy files into specific Tomcat directories. All the example files for this chapter are located on the CD that accompanies this book and on our Web site **`www.deitel.com`**.

[*Note*: At the end of Section 30.10, we provide a list of Internet specifications (as discussed in the Servlet 2.2 Specification) for technologies related to servlet development. Each is listed with its RFC (Request for Comments) number. We provide the URL of a Web site that allows you to locate each specification for your review.]

30.2 Servlet Overview and Architecture

In this section, we overview Java servlet technology. We discuss at a high level the servlet-related classes, methods and exceptions. The next several sections present live-code examples in which we build multi-tier client–server systems using servlet and JDBC technology.

The Internet offers many protocols. The *HTTP* (*Hypertext Transfer Protocol*) that forms the basis of the World Wide Web uses *URIs* (*Uniform Resource Identifiers*— sometimes called *Universal Resource Locators* or *URLs*) to locate resources on the Internet. Common URIs represent files or directories and can represent complex tasks such as database lookups and Internet searches. For more information on URL formats, visit

`www.w3.org/Addressing`

For more information on the HTTP protocol, visit

`www.w3.org/Protocols/HTTP`

For information on a variety of World Wide Web topics, visit

`www.w3.org`

JavaServer Pages technology is an extension of servlet technology. Normally, JSPs are used primarily when most of the content sent to the client is static text and markup, and only a small portion of the content is generated dynamically with Java code. Normally, servlets are used when a small portion of the content sent to the client is static text or markup. In fact, some servlets do not produce content. Rather, they perform a task on behalf of the client, then invoke other servlets or JSPs to provide a response. Note that in most cases servlet and JSP technologies are interchangeable. The server that executes a servlet often is referred to as the *servlet container* or *servlet engine*.

Servlets and JavaServer Pages have become so popular that they are now supported directly or with third-party plug-ins by most major Web servers and application servers, including the Netscape iPlanet Application Server, Microsoft's Internet Information Server (IIS), the Apache HTTP Server, BEA's WebLogic application server, IBM's WebSphere application server, the World Wide Web Consortium's Jigsaw Web server, and many more.

The servlets in this chapter demonstrate communication between clients and servers via the HTTP protocol. A client sends an HTTP request to the server or servlet container. The server or servlet container receives the request and directs it to be processed by the appropriate servlet. The servlet does its processing, which may include interacting with a database or other server-side components such as other servlets, JSPs or Enterprise JavaBeans.[3] The servlet returns its results to the client—normally in the form of an HTML, XHTML or XML document to display in a browser, but other data formats, such as images and binary data, can be returned.

30.2.1 Interface `Servlet` and the Servlet Life Cycle

Architecturally, all servlets must implement the ***`Servlet`*** interface. As with many key applet methods, the methods of interface **`Servlet`** are invoked automatically (by the server on which the servlet is installed, also known as the servlet container). This interface defines five methods described in Fig. 30.1.

Software Engineering Observation 30.2

*All servlets must implement the **`Servlet`** interface of package **`javax.servlet`**.*

3. Our text *Advanced Java 2 Platform How to Program* covers Enterprise JavaBeans (EJBs) in detail.

Method	Description
`void init( ServletConfig config )`	This method is automatically called once during a servlet's execution cycle to initialize the servlet. The **ServletConfig** argument is supplied by the servlet container that executes the servlet.
`ServletConfig getServletConfig()`	This method returns a reference to an object that implements interface **ServletConfig**. This object provides access to the servlet's configuration information such as servlet initialization parameters and the servlet's **ServletContext**, which provides the servlet with access to its environment (i.e., the servlet container in which the servlet executes).
`String getServletInfo()`	This method is defined by a servlet programmer to return a **String** containing servlet information such as the servlet's author and version.
`void service( ServletRequest request, ServletResponse response )`	The servlet container calls this method to respond to a client request to the servlet.
`void destroy()`	This "cleanup" method is called when a servlet is terminated by its servlet container. Resources used by the servlet, such as an open file or an open database connection, should be deallocated here.

Fig. 30.1 Methods of interface **Servlet** (package **javax.servlet**).

A servlet's life cycle begins when the servlet container loads the servlet into memory—normally, in response to the first request that the servlet receives. Before the servlet can handle that request, the servlet container invokes the servlet's ***init*** method. After **init** completes execution, the servlet can respond to its first request. All requests are handled by a servlet's ***service*** method, which receives the request, processes the request and sends a response to the client. During a servlet's life cycle, method **service** is called once per request. Each new request typically results in a new thread of execution (created by the servlet container) in which method **service** executes. When the servlet container terminates the servlet, the servlet's **destroy** method is called to release servlet resources.

Performance Tip 30.1

Starting a new thread for each request is more efficient than starting an entirely new process, as is the case in some other server-side technologies such as CGI. [Note: Like servlets, Fast CGI eliminates the overhead of starting a new process for each request.]

The servlet packages define two **abstract** classes that implement the interface **Servlet**—class ***GenericServlet*** (from the package **javax.servlet**) and class ***HttpServlet*** (from the package **javax.servlet.http**). These classes provide default implementations of all the **Servlet** methods. Most servlets extend either **GenericServlet** or **HttpServlet** and override some or all of their methods.

The examples in this chapter all extend class **HttpServlet**, which defines enhanced processing capabilities for servlets that extend the functionality of a Web server. The key method in every servlet is **service**, which receives both a ***ServletRequest*** object and a ***ServletResponse*** object. These objects provide access to input and output streams that allow the servlet to read data from the client and send data to the client. These streams can be either byte based or character based. If problems occur during the execution of a servlet, either **ServletException**s or **IOException**s are thrown to indicate the problem.

Software Engineering Observation 30.3

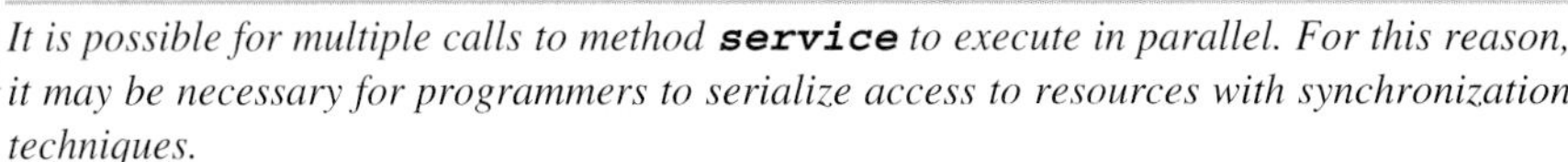

It is possible for multiple calls to method **service** *to execute in parallel. For this reason, it may be necessary for programmers to serialize access to resources with synchronization techniques.*

Software Engineering Observation 30.4

Servlets can implement tagging interface ***javax.servlet.SingleThreadModel*** *to indicate that only one thread of execution may enter method* **service** *on a particular servlet instance at a time. When a servlet implements* ***SingleThreadModel****, the servlet container can create multiple instances of the servlet to handle multiple requests to the servlet in parallel. In this case, you may need to provide synchronized access to shared resources used by method* **service***.*

30.2.2 HttpServlet Class

Web-based servlets typically extend class **HttpServlet**. Class **HttpServlet** overrides method **service** to distinguish between the typical requests received from a client Web browser. The two most common *HTTP request types* (also known as *request methods*) are ***get*** and ***post***. A **get** request *gets* (or *retrieves*) information from a server. Common uses of **get** requests are to retrieve an HTML document or an image. A **post** request *posts* (or *sends*) data to a server. Common uses of **post** requests are to send information to a server—such as authentication information, data from a *form* that obtains user input, information that the server uses to search the Internet or query a database, etc.

Class **HttpServlet** defines methods ***doGet*** and ***doPost*** to respond to **get** and **post** requests from a client, respectively. These methods are called by the **service** method, which is called when a request arrives at the server. Method **service** first determines the request type, then calls the appropriate method for handling such a request. Other less common request types are beyond the scope of this book. Methods of class **HttpServlet** that respond to the other request types are shown in Fig. 30.2. They all receive parameters of type **HttpServletRequest** and **HttpServletResponse** and return **void**. The methods of Fig. 30.2 are not frequently used. For more information on the HTTP protocol, visit

http://www.w3.org/Protocols/

Software Engineering Observation 30.5

Do not override method service in an **HttpServlet** *subclass. Doing so prevents the servlet from distinguishing between request types.*

Method	Description
doDelete	Called in response to an HTTP ***delete*** request. Such a request is normally used to delete a file from a server. This may not be available on some servers, because of its inherent security risks (i.e., the client could delete a file that is critical to the execution of the server or an application).
doOptions	Called in response to an HTTP ***options*** request. This returns information to the client indicating the HTTP options supported by the server, such as the version of HTTP (1.0 or 1.1) and the request methods the server supports.
doPut	Called in response to an HTTP ***put*** request. Such a request is normally used to store a file on the server. This may not be available on some servers, because of its inherent security risks (i.e., the client could place an executable application on the server, which, if executed, could damage the server—perhaps by deleting critical files or occupying resources).
doTrace	Called in response to an HTTP ***trace*** request. Such a request is normally used for debugging. The implementation of this method automatically returns an HTML document to the client containing the request header information (data sent by the browser as part of the request).

Fig. 30.2 Other methods of class **HttpServlet**.

Methods **doGet** and **doPost** receive as arguments an **HttpServletRequest** object and an **HttpServletResponse** object that enable interaction between the client and the server. The methods of **HttpServletRequest** make it easy to access the data supplied as part of the request. The **HttpServletResponse** methods make it easy to return the servlet's results to the Web client. Interfaces **HttpServletRequest** and **HttpServletResponse** are discussed in the next two sections.

30.2.3 HttpServletRequest Interface

Every call to **doGet** or **doPost** for an **HttpServlet** receives an object that implements interface **HttpServletRequest**. The Web server that executes the servlet creates an **HttpServletRequest** object and passes this to the servlet's **service** method (which, in turn, passes it to **doGet** or **doPost**). This object contains the request from the client. A variety of methods are provided to enable the servlet to process the client's request. Some of these methods are from interface ***ServletRequest***—the interface that **HttpServletRequest** extends. A few key methods used in this chapter are presented in Fig. 30.3. You can view a complete list of **HttpServletRequest** methods online at

```
java.sun.com/j2ee/j2sdkee/techdocs/api/javax/servlet/http/
HttpServletRequest.html
```

or you can download and install Tomcat (discussed in Section 30.3.1) and view the documentation on your local computer.

Method	Description
`String getParameter( String name )`	
	Obtains the value of a parameter sent to the servlet as part of a **`get`** or **`post`** request. The **`name`** argument represents the parameter name.
`Enumeration getParameterNames()`	
	Returns the names of all the parameters sent to the servlet as part of a **`post`** request.
`String[] getParameterValues( String name )`	
	For a parameter with multiple values, this method returns an array of **`String`**s containing the values for a specified servlet parameter.
`Cookie[] getCookies()`	
	Returns an array of **`Cookie`** objects stored on the client by the server. **`Cookie`**s can be used to uniquely identify clients to the servlet.
`HttpSession getSession( boolean create )`	
	Returns an **`HttpSession`** object associated with the client's current browsing session. An **`HttpSession`** object can be created by this method (**`true`** argument) if an **`HttpSession`** object does not already exist for the client. **`HttpSession`** objects can be used in similar ways to **`Cookie`**s for uniquely identifying clients.

Fig. 30.3 Some methods of interface **`HttpServletRequest`**.

30.2.4 `HttpServletResponse` Interface

Every call to **`doGet`** or **`doPost`** for an **`HttpServlet`** receives an object that implements interface **`HttpServletResponse`**. The Web server that executes the servlet creates an **`HttpServletResponse`** object and passes it to the servlet's **`service`** method (which, in turn, passes it to **`doGet`** or **`doPost`**). This object provides a variety of methods that enable the servlet to formulate the response to the client. Some of these methods are from interface ***`ServletResponse`***—the interface that **`HttpServletResponse`** extends. A few key methods used in this chapter are presented in Fig. 30.4. You can view a complete list of **`HttpServletResponse`** methods online at

```
java.sun.com/j2ee/j2sdkee/techdocs/api/javax/servlet/http/
HttpServletResponse.html
```

or you can download and install Tomcat (discussed in Section 30.3.1) and view the documentation on your local computer.

30.3 Handling HTTP `get` Requests

The primary purpose of an HTTP **`get`** request is to retrieve the content of a specified URL—normally the content is an HTML or XHTML document (i.e., a Web page). The servlet of Fig. 30.5 and the XHTML document of Fig. 30.6 demonstrate a servlet that handles HTTP **`get`** requests. When the user clicks the **Get HTML Document** button

(Fig. 30.6), a **get** request is sent to the servlet **WelcomeServlet** (Fig. 30.5). The servlet responds to the request by generating dynamically an XHTML document for the client that displays "**Welcome to Servlets!**". Figure 30.5 shows the **WelcomeServlet** source code. Figure 30.6 shows the XHTML document the client loads to access the servlet and shows screen captures of the client's browser window before and after the interaction with the servlet. [*Note*: Section 30.3.1 discusses how to set up and configure Tomcat to execute this example.]

Method	Description
void addCookie(Cookie cookie)	Used to add a **Cookie** to the header of the response to the client. The **Cookie**'s maximum age and whether **Cookie**s are enabled on the client determine if **Cookie**s are stored on the client.
ServletOutputStream getOutputStream()	Obtains a byte-based output stream that enables binary data to be sent to the client.
PrintWriter getWriter()	Obtains a character-based output stream that enables text data to be sent to the client.
void setContentType(String type)	Specifies the MIME type of the response to the browser. The MIME type helps the browser determine how to display the data (or possibly what other application to execute to process the data). For example, MIME type **"text/html"** indicates that the response is an XHTML document, so the browser displays the XHTML page. For more information on

Fig. 30.4 Some methods of interface **HttpServletResponse**.

```java
// Fig. 9.5: WelcomeServlet.java
// A simple servlet to process get requests.
package com.deitel.advjhtp1.servlets;

import javax.servlet.*;
import javax.servlet.http.*;
import java.io.*;

public class WelcomeServlet extends HttpServlet {

   // process "get" requests from clients
   protected void doGet( HttpServletRequest request,
      HttpServletResponse response )
         throws ServletException, IOException
   {
      response.setContentType( "text/html" );
      PrintWriter out = response.getWriter();
```

Fig. 30.5 **WelcomeServlet** handles a simple HTTP **get** request (part 1 of 2).

```
18
19         // send XHTML page to client
20
21         // start XHTML document
22         out.println( "<?xml version = \"1.0\"?>" );
23
24         out.println( "<!DOCTYPE html PUBLIC \"-//W3C//DTD " +
25            "XHTML 1.0 Strict//EN\" \"http://www.w3.org" +
26            "/TR/xhtml1/DTD/xhtml1-strict.dtd\">" );
27
28         out.println(
29            "<html xmlns = \"http://www.w3.org/1999/xhtml\">" );
30
31         // head section of document
32         out.println( "<head>" );
33         out.println( "<title>A Simple Servlet Example</title>" );
34         out.println( "</head>" );
35
36         // body section of document
37         out.println( "<body>" );
38         out.println( "<h1>Welcome to Servlets!</h1>" );
39         out.println( "</body>" );
40
41         // end XHTML document
42         out.println( "</html>" );
43         out.close();  // close stream to complete the page
44      }
45   }
```

Fig. 30.5 **WelcomeServlet** handles a simple HTTP **get** request (part 2 of 2).

Lines 5 and 6 import the **javax.servlet** and **javax.servlet.http** packages. We use several data types from these packages in the example.

Package **javax.servlet.http** provides superclass **HttpServlet** for servlets that handle HTTP **get** requests and HTTP **post** requests. This class implements interface **javax.servlet.Servlet** and adds methods that support HTTP protocol requests. Class **WelcomeServlet** extends **HttpServlet** (line 9) for this reason.

Superclass **HttpServlet** provides method ***doGet*** to respond to **get** requests. Its default functionality is to indicate a "Method not allowed" error. Typically, this error is indicated in Internet Explorer with a Web page that states "This page cannot be displayed" and in Netscape Navigator with a Web page that states "Error: 405." We override method **doGet** (lines 12–44) to provide custom **get** request processing. Method **doGet** receives two arguments—an object that implements interface **HttpServletRequest** and an object that implements interface **HttpServletResponse** (both from package **javax.servlet.http**). The **HttpServletRequest** object represents the client's request, and the **HttpServletResponse** object represents the server's response to the client. If method **doGet** is unable to handle a client's request, it throws an exception of type ***javax.servlet.ServletException***. If **doGet** encounters an error during stream processing (reading from the client or writing to the client), it throws a ***java.io.IOException***.

To demonstrate a response to a **get** request, our servlet creates an XHTML document containing the text "**Welcome to Servlets!**". The text of the XHTML document is the response to the client. The response is sent to the client through the **PrintWriter** object obtained from the **HttpServletResponse** object.

Line 16 uses the **response** object's ***setContentType*** method to specify the content type of the data to be sent as the response to the client. This enables the client browser to understand and handle the content. The content type also is known as the *MIME* type (*Multipurpose Internet Mail Extension*) of the data. In this example, the content type is ***text/html*** to indicate to the browser that the response is an XHTML document. The browser knows that it must read the XHTML tags in the document, format the document according to the tags and display the document in the browser window. For more information on MIME types visit **www.irvine.com/~mime**.

Line 17 uses the **response** object's ***getWriter*** method to obtain a reference to the **PrintWriter** object that enables the servlet to send content to the client. [*Note*: If the response is binary data, such as an image, method ***getOutputStream*** is used to obtain a reference to a **ServletOutputStream** object.]

Lines 22–42 create the XHTML document by writing strings with the **out** object's ***println*** method. This method outputs a newline character after its **String** argument. When rendering the Web page, the browser does not use the newline character. Rather, the newline character appears in the XHTML source that you can see by selecting **Source** from the **View** menu in Internet Explorer or **Page Source** from the **View** menu in Netscape Navigator. Line 43 closes the output stream, flushes the output buffer and sends the information to the client. This commits the response to the client.

The XHTML document in Fig. 30.6 provides a **form** that invokes the servlet defined in Fig. 30.5. The **form**'s **action**

/advjhtp1/welcome1

specifies the URL path that invokes the servlet, and the **form**'s **method** indicates that the browser sends a **get** request to the server, which results in a call to the servlet's **doGet** method. The URL specified as the **action** in this example is discussed in detail in Section 30.3.2 after we show how to set up and configure the *Apache Tomcat server* to execute the servlet in Fig. 30.5.

```
<?xml version = "1.0"?>
<!DOCTYPE html PUBLIC "-//W3C//DTD XHTML 1.0 Strict//EN"
   "http://www.w3.org/TR/xhtml1/DTD/xhtml1-strict.dtd">

<!-- Fig. 9.6: WelcomeServlet.html -->

<html xmlns = "http://www.w3.org/1999/xhtml">
<head>
   <title>Handling an HTTP Get Request</title>
</head>

```

Fig. 30.6 HTML document in which the **form**'s **action** invokes **WelcomeServlet** through the alias **welcome1** specified in **web.xml** (part 1 of 2).

```
<body>
   <form action = "/advjhtp1/welcome1" method = "get">

      <p><label>Click the button to invoke the servlet
         <input type = "submit" value = "Get HTML Document" />
      </label></p>

   </form>
</body>
</html>
```

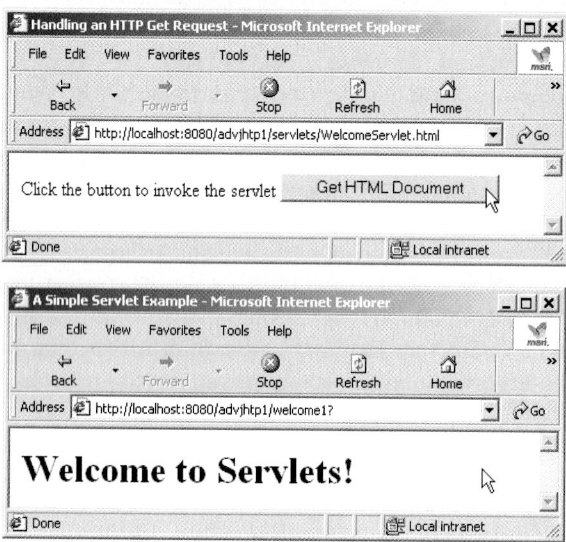

Fig. 30.6 HTML document in which the **`form`**'s **`action`** invokes **`WelcomeServlet`** through the alias **`welcome1`** specified in **`web.xml`** (part 2 of 2).

Note that the sample screen captures show a URL containing the server name ***`localhost`***—a well-known server *host name* on most computers that support TCP/IP-based networking protocols such as HTTP. We often use **`localhost`** to demonstrate networking programs on the local computer, so that readers without a network connection can still learn network programming concepts. In this example, **`localhost`** indicates that the server on which the servlet is installed is running on the local machine. The server host name is followed by **`:8080`**, specifying the TCP port number at which the Tomcat server awaits requests from clients. Web browsers assume TCP port 80 by default as the server port at which clients make requests, but the Tomcat server awaits client requests at TCP port 8080. This allows Tomcat to execute on the same computer as a standard Web server application without affecting the Web server application's ability to handle requests. If we do not explicitly specify the port number in the URL, the servlet never will receive our request and an error message will be displayed in the browser.

Software Engineering Observation 30.6

The Tomcat documentation specifies how to integrate Tomcat with popular Web server applications such as the Apache HTTP Server and Microsoft's IIS.

Ports in this case are not physical hardware ports to which you attach cables; rather, they are logical locations named with integer values that allow clients to request different services on the same server. The port number specifies the logical location where a server waits for and receives connections from clients—this is also called the *handshake point*. When a client connects to a server to request a service, the client must specify the port number for that service; otherwise, the client request cannot be processed. Port numbers are positive integers with values up to 65,535, and there are separate sets of these port numbers for both the TCP and UDP protocols. Many operating systems reserve port numbers below 1024 for system services (such as email and World Wide Web servers). Generally, these ports should not be specified as connection ports in your own server programs. In fact, some operating systems require special access privileges to use port numbers below 1024.

With so many ports from which to choose, how does a client know which port to use when requesting a service? The term *well-known port number* often is used when describing popular services on the Internet such as Web servers and email servers. For example, a Web server waits for clients to make requests at port 80 by default. All Web browsers know this number as the well-known port on a Web server where requests for HTML documents are made. So when you type a URL into a Web browser, the browser normally connects to port 80 on the server. Similarly, the Tomcat server uses port 8080 as its port number. Thus, requests to Tomcat for Web pages or to invoke servlets and JavaServer Pages must specify that the Tomcat server waiting for requests on port 8080.

The client can access the servlet only if the servlet is installed on a server that can respond to servlet requests. In some cases, servlet support is built directly into the Web server, and no special configuration is required to handle servlet requests. In other cases, it is necessary to integrate a servlet container with a Web server (as can be done with Tomcat and the Apache or IIS Web servers). Web servers that support servlets normally have an installation procedure for servlets. If you intend to execute your servlet as part of a Web server, please refer to your Web server's documentation on how to install a servlet. For our examples, we demonstrate servlets with the Apache Tomcat server. Section 30.3.1 discusses the setup and configuration of Tomcat for use with this chapter. Section 30.3.2 discusses the deployment of the servlet in Fig. 30.5.

30.3.1 Setting Up the Apache Tomcat Server

Tomcat is a fully functional implementation of the JSP and servlet standards. It includes a Web server, so it can be used as a standalone test container for JSPs and servlets. Tomcat also can be specified as the handler for JSP and servlet requests received by popular Web servers such as the Apache Software Foundation's Apache Web server or Microsoft's Internet Information Server (IIS). Tomcat is integrated into the Java 2 Enterprise Edition reference implementation from Sun Microsystems.

The most recent release of Tomcat (version 3.2.3) can be downloaded from

```
jakarta.apache.org/builds/jakarta-tomcat/release/v3.2.3/bin/
```

where there are a number of archive files. The complete Tomcat implementation is contained in the files that begin with the name **`jakarta-tomcat-3.2.3`**. Zip, tar and compressed tar files are provided for Windows, Linux and Solaris.

Extract the contents of the archive file to a directory on your hard disk. By default, the name of the directory containing Tomcat is **jakarta-tomcat-3.2.3**. For Tomcat to work correctly, you must define environment variables **JAVA_HOME** and **TOMCAT_HOME**. **JAVA_HOME** should point to the directory containing your Java installation (ours is **d:\jdk1.3.1**), and **TOMCAT_HOME** should point to the directory that contains Tomcat (ours is **d:\jakarta-tomcat-3.2.3**).

Testing and Debugging Tip 30.1

On some platforms you may need to restart your computer for the new environment variables to take effect.

After setting the environment variables, you can start the Tomcat server. Open a command prompt (or shell) and change directories to **bin** in **jakarta-tomcat-3.2.3**. In this directory are the files ***tomcat.bat*** and ***tomcat.sh***, for starting the Tomcat server on Windows and UNIX (Linux or Solaris), respectively. To start the server, type

```
tomcat start
```

This launches the Tomcat server. The Tomcat server executes on TCP port 8080 to prevent conflicts with standard Web servers that typically execute on TCP port 80. To prove that Tomcat is executing and can respond to requests, open your Web browser and enter the URL

```
http://localhost:8080/
```

This should display the Tomcat documentation home page (Fig. 30.7). The host **localhost** indicates to the Web browser that it should request the home page from the Tomcat server on the local computer.

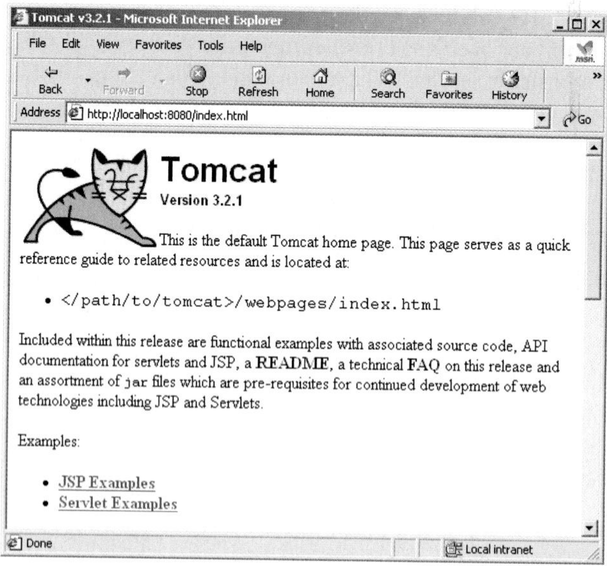

Fig. 30.7 Tomcat documentation home page. (Courtesy of The Apache Software Foundation.)

If the Tomcat documentation home page does not display, try the URL

```
http://127.0.0.1:8080/
```

The host **localhost** translates to the IP address **127.0.0.1**.

Testing and Debugging Tip 30.2

If the host name **localhost** *does not work on your computer, substitute the IP address* **127.0.0.1** *instead.*

To shut down the Tomcat server, issue the command

```
tomcat stop
```

from a command prompt (or shell).

30.3.2 Deploying a Web Application

JSPs, servlets and their supporting files are deployed as part of *Web applications*. Normally, Web applications are deployed in the ***webapps*** subdirectory of **jakarta-tomcat-3.2.3**. A Web application has a well-known directory structure in which all the files that are part of the application reside. This directory structure can be created by the server administrator in the **webapps** directory, or the entire directory structure can be archived in a *Web application archive file*. Such an archive is known as a *WAR file* and ends with the ***.war*** file extension. If a WAR file is placed in the **webapps** directory, then, when the Tomcat server begins execution, it extracts the contents of the WAR file into the appropriate **webapps** subdirectory structure. For simplicity as we teach servlets and JavaServer Pages, we create the already expanded directory structure that will be used for all the examples in this chapter and Chapter 31.

The Web application directory structure has a *context root*—the top-level directory for an entire Web application—and several subdirectories. These are described in Fig. 30.8.

Directory	Description
context root	This is the root directory for the Web application. The name of this directory is chosen by the Web application developer. All the JSPs, HTML documents, servlets and supporting files such as images and class files reside in this directory or its subdirectories. The name of this directory is specified by the Web application creator. To provide structure in a Web application, subdirectories can be placed in the context root. For example, if your application uses many images, you might place an images subdirectory in this directory.
WEB-INF	This directory contains the Web application *deployment descriptor* (***web.xml***).
WEB-INF/ classes	This directory contains the servlet class files and other supporting class files used in a Web application. If the classes are part of a package, the complete package directory structure would begin here.
WEB-INF/lib	This directory contains Java archive (JAR) files. The JAR files can contain servlet class files and other supporting class files used in a Web application.

Fig. 30.8 Web application standard directories.

Common Programming Error 30.1

Using "servlet" or "servlets" as a context root may prevent a servlet from working correctly on some servers.

Before we can deploy our Web application for the **WelcomeServlet** of Fig. 30.5, we must make the servlet container (i.e., Tomcat) aware of the context root for our Web application. We accomplish this by editing the file ***server.xml*** in the **conf** subdirectory of **jakarta-tomcat-3.2.3**. This XML file describes the configuration of the Tomcat server. Open this file, scroll toward the bottom and locate the section that starts with the comment "**Special webapps**." In this section, there are XML ***Context*** elements that describe the context roots for the Tomcat **examples** and **admin** Web applications.

We will create a **Context** called **advjhtp1** to serve as the context root for most of our JSP and servlet examples. To create the **advjhtp1** context root, edit the **server.xml** file, and insert the **Context** element of Fig. 30.9 after the **Context** element for **admin**; then save the **server.xml** file.

Testing and Debugging Tip 30.3

The Tomcat server should be restarted after modifying **server.xml**. *Otherwise, Tomcat will not recognize your new Web application context root.*

Line 2 begins the **Context** element and specifies its ***path*** *attribute*. The server uses the path to determine which Web application receives the request. In particular, attribute **path** specifies the initial part of the path in a URL that requests a Web application. The path is the part of the URL following the host name and optional port number. *Attribute* ***docBase*** specifies the subdirectory of **webapps** in which the Web application files are located.

Now that Tomcat is configured for our context root, we need to configure our Web application to handle the requests. To simplify the deployment of the examples in this chapter, WAR files are not used. Rather, we place the example files in directory **advjhtp1** or the relevant subdirectory. We discuss WAR files in detail as part of the servlet case study in the next chapter.

Deploying a Web application requires the creation of a *deployment descriptor* (stored in a file called ***web.xml***) that specifies various configuration parameters such as the name used to invoke the servlet, a description of the servlet, the class name of the servlet class and a *servlet mapping*, i.e., the path or paths that cause the servlet to be invoked. You must create the **web.xml** file for this example. Many Java Web application deployment tools create this file for you. The **web.xml** file for the first example in this chapter is shown in Fig. 30.10. This file will be enhanced as we add other servlets to the Web application.

```
1  <!-- Advanced Java How to Program JSP/servlet context -->
2  <Context path = "/advjhtp1"
3           docBase = "webapps/advjhtp1"
4           reloadable = "true">
5  </Context>
```

Fig. 30.9 **Context** element for servlet and JSP examples in Chapters 30 and 31.

```
1  <!DOCTYPE web-app PUBLIC
2     "-//Sun Microsystems, Inc.//DTD Web Application 2.2//EN"
3     "http://java.sun.com/j2ee/dtds/web-app_2_2.dtd">
4
5  <web-app>
6
7     <!-- General description of your Web application -->
8     <display-name>
9        Advanced Java How to Program JSP
10       and Servlet Chapter Examples
11    </display-name>
12
13    <description>
14       This is the Web application in which we
15       demonstrate our JSP and Servlet examples.
16    </description>
17
18    <!-- Servlet definitions -->
19    <servlet>
20       <servlet-name>welcome1</servlet-name>
21
22       <description>
23          A simple servlet that handles an HTTP get request.
24       </description>
25
26       <servlet-class>
27          com.deitel.advjhtp1.servlets.WelcomeServlet
28       </servlet-class>
29    </servlet>
30
31    <!-- Servlet mappings -->
32    <servlet-mapping>
33       <servlet-name>welcome1</servlet-name>
34       <url-pattern>/welcome1</url-pattern>
35    </servlet-mapping>
36
37 </web-app>
```

Fig. 30.10 Deployment descriptor for the **advjhtp1** Web application.

Lines 1–3 specify the document type for the Web application deployment descriptor and the location of the DTD for this XML file. Element ***web-app*** (lines 5–37) defines the configuration of each servlet in the Web application and the servlet mapping for each servlet. Element ***display-name*** (lines 8–11) specifies a name that can be displayed to the administrator of the server on which the Web application is installed. Element ***description*** (lines 13–16) specifies a description of the Web application that might be displayed to the administrator of the server.

Element **servlet** (lines 19–29) describes a servlet. Element ***servlet-name*** (line 20) is the name we chose for the servlet (**welcome1**). Element ***description*** (lines 22–24) specifies a description for this particular servlet. Again, this can be displayed to the administrator of the Web server. Element **servlet-class** (lines 26–28) specifies compiled servlet's fully qualified class name. Thus, the servlet **welcome1** is defined by class **com.deitel.advjhtp1.servlets.WelcomeServlet**.

Element ***servlet-mapping*** (lines 32–35) specifies ***servlet-name*** and ***url-pattern*** elements. The *URL pattern* helps the server determine which requests are sent to the servlet (**welcome1**). Our Web application will be installed as part of the **advjhtp1** context root—specified as part of the **Context** element discussed in Fig. 30.9 that we added to the **server.xml** file). Thus, the URL we supply to the browser to invoke the servlet in this example is

```
/advjhtp1/welcome1
```

where **/advjhtp1** specifies the context root that helps the server determine which Web application handles the request and **/welcome1** specifies the URL pattern that is mapped to servlet **welcome1** to handle the request. Note that the server on which the servlet resides is not specified here, although it is possible to do so as follows:

```
http://localhost:8080/advjhtp1/welcome1
```

If the explicit server and port number are not specified as part of the URL, the browser assumes that the form handler (i.e., the servlet specified in the **action** property of the **form** element) resides at the same server and port number from which the browser downloaded the Web page containing the **form**.

There are several URL pattern formats that can be used. The **/welcome1** URL pattern requires an exact match of the pattern. You can also specify *path mappings*, extension mappings and a *default servlet* for a Web application. A path mapping begins with a **/** and ends with a **/***. For example, the URL pattern

```
/advjhtp1/example/*
```

indicates that any URL path beginning with **/advjhtp1/example/** will be sent to the servlet that has the preceding URL pattern. An extension mapping begins with ***.** and ends with a file name extension. For example, the URL pattern

```
*.jsp
```

indicates that any request for a file with the extension **.jsp** will be sent to the servlet that handles JSP requests. In fact, servers with JSP containers have an implicit mapping of the **.jsp** extension to a servlet that handles JSP requests. The URL pattern **/** represents the default servlet for the Web application. This is similar to the default document of a Web server. For example, if you type the URL **www.deitel.com** into your Web browser, the document you receive from our Web server is the default document **index.html**. If the URL pattern matches the default servlet for a Web application, that servlet is invoked to return a default response to the client. This can be useful for personalizing Web content to specific users. We discuss personalization in Section 30.7, Session Tracking.

Finally, we are ready to place our files into the appropriate directories to complete the deployment of our first servlet, so we can test it. There are three files we must place in the appropriate directories—**WelcomeServlet.html**, **WelcomeServlet.class** and **web.xml**. In the **webapps** subdirectory of your **jakarta-tomcat-3.2.3** directory, create the **advjhtp1** subdirectory that represents the context root for our Web application. In this directory, create subdirectories named **servlets** and **WEB-INF**. We place our HTML files for this servlets chapter in the **servlets** directory. Copy the **WelcomeServlet.html** file into the **servlets** directory. In the **WEB-INF** directory, create the subdirectory **classes**, then copy the **web.xml** file into the **WEB-INF** directory, and copy the **WelcomeServlet.class** file, including all its package name directories, into the **classes** directory. Thus, the directory and file structure under the **webapps** directory should be as shown in Fig. 30.11 (file names are in italics).

Testing and Debugging Tip 30.4

Restart the Tomcat server after modifying the **web.xml** *deployment descriptor file. Otherwise, Tomcat will not recognize your new Web application.*

After the files are placed in the proper directories, start the Tomcat server, open your browser and type the following URL—

```
http://localhost:8080/advjhtp1/servlets/WelcomeServlet.html
```

—to load **WelcomeServlet.html** into the Web browser. Then, click the **Get HTML Document** button to invoke the servlet. You should see the results shown in Fig. 30.6. You can try this servlet from several different Web browsers to demonstrate that the results are the same across Web browsers.

Common Programming Error 30.2

Not placing servlet or other class files in the appropriate package directory structure prevents the server from locating those classes properly. This, in turn, results in an error response to the client Web browser. This error response normally is "Not Found (404)" in Netscape Navigator and "The page cannot be found" plus an explanation in Microsoft Internet Explorer.

WelcomeServlet Web application directory and file structure

```
advjhtp1
    servlets
        WelcomeServlet.html
    WEB-INF
        web.xml
        classes
            com
                deitel
                    advjhtp1
                        servlets
                            WelcomeServlet.class
```

Fig. 30.11 Web application directory and file structure for **WelcomeServlet**.

Actually, the HTML file in Fig. 30.6 was not necessary to invoke this servlet. A **get** request can be sent to a server simply by typing the URL in the Web browser. In fact, that is exactly what you are doing when you request a Web page in the browser. In this example, you can type

```
http://localhost:8080/advjhtp1/welcome1
```

in the **Address** or **Location** field of your browser to invoke the servlet directly.

Testing and Debugging Tip 30.5

You can test a servlet that handles HTTP **get** *requests by typing the URL that invokes the servlet directly into your browser's* **Address** *or* **Location** *field.*

30.4 Handling HTTP get Requests Containing Data

When requesting a document or resource from a Web server, it is possible to supply data as part of the request. The servlet **WelcomeServlet2** of Fig. 30.12 responds to an HTTP **get** request that contains a name supplied by the user. The servlet uses the name as part of the response to the client.

```
// Fig. 9.12: WelcomeServlet2.java
// Processing HTTP get requests containing data.
package com.deitel.advjhtp1.servlets;

import javax.servlet.*;
import javax.servlet.http.*;
import java.io.*;

public class WelcomeServlet2 extends HttpServlet {

   // process "get" request from client
   protected void doGet( HttpServletRequest request,
      HttpServletResponse response )
         throws ServletException, IOException
   {
      String firstName = request.getParameter( "firstname" );

      response.setContentType( "text/html" );
      PrintWriter out = response.getWriter();

      // send XHTML document to client

      // start XHTML document
      out.println( "<?xml version = \"1.0\"?>" );

      out.println( "<!DOCTYPE html PUBLIC \"-//W3C//DTD " +
         "XHTML 1.0 Strict//EN\" \"http://www.w3.org" +
         "/TR/xhtml1/DTD/xhtml1-strict.dtd\">" );

      out.println(
         "<html xmlns = \"http://www.w3.org/1999/xhtml\">" );
```

Fig. 30.12 **WelcomeServlet2** handles a **get** request containing data (part 1 of 2).

```
32
33          // head section of document
34          out.println( "<head>" );
35          out.println(
36             "<title>Processing get requests with data</title>" );
37          out.println( "</head>" );
38
39          // body section of document
40          out.println( "<body>" );
41          out.println( "<h1>Hello " + firstName + ",<br />" );
42          out.println( "Welcome to Servlets!</h1>" );
43          out.println( "</body>" );
44
45          // end XHTML document
46          out.println( "</html>" );
47          out.close();  // close stream to complete the page
48       }
49    }
```

Fig. 30.12 **WelcomeServlet2** handles a **get** request containing data (part 2 of 2).

Parameters are passed as name/value pairs in a **get** request. Line 16 demonstrates how to obtain information that was passed to the servlet as part of the client request. The **request** object's ***getParameter*** method receives the parameter name as an argument and returns the corresponding **String** value, or **null** if the parameter is not part of the request. Line 41 uses the result of line 16 as part of the response to the client.

The **WelcomeServlet2.html** document (Fig. 30.13) provides a **form** in which the user can input a name in the text **input** element **firstname** (line 17) and click the **Submit** button to invoke **WelcomeServlet2**. When the user presses the **Submit** button, the values of the **input** elements are placed in name/value pairs as part of the request to the server. In the second screen capture of Fig. 30.13, notice that the browser appended

```
?firstname=Paul
```

to the end of the **action** URL. The **?** separates the *query string* (i.e., the data passed as part of the **get** request) from the rest of the URL in a **get** request. The name/value pairs are passed with the name and the value separated by **=**. If there is more than one name/value pair, each name/value pair is separated by **&**.

```
1  <?xml version = "1.0"?>
2  <!DOCTYPE html PUBLIC "-//W3C//DTD XHTML 1.0 Strict//EN"
3     "http://www.w3.org/TR/xhtml1/DTD/xhtml1-strict.dtd">
4
5  <!-- Fig. 9.13: WelcomeServlet2.html -->
6
7  <html xmlns = "http://www.w3.org/1999/xhtml">
8  <head>
9     <title>Processing get requests with data</title>
10 </head>
```

Fig. 30.13 HTML document in which the **form**'s **action** invokes **Welcome-Servlet2** using alias **welcome2** specified in **web.xml** (part 1 of 2).

```

<body>
   <form action = "/advjhtp1/welcome2" method = "get">

      <p><label>
         Type your first name and press the Submit button
         <br /><input type = "text" name = "firstname" />
         <input type = "submit" value = "Submit" />
      </p></label>

   </form>
</body>
</html>
```

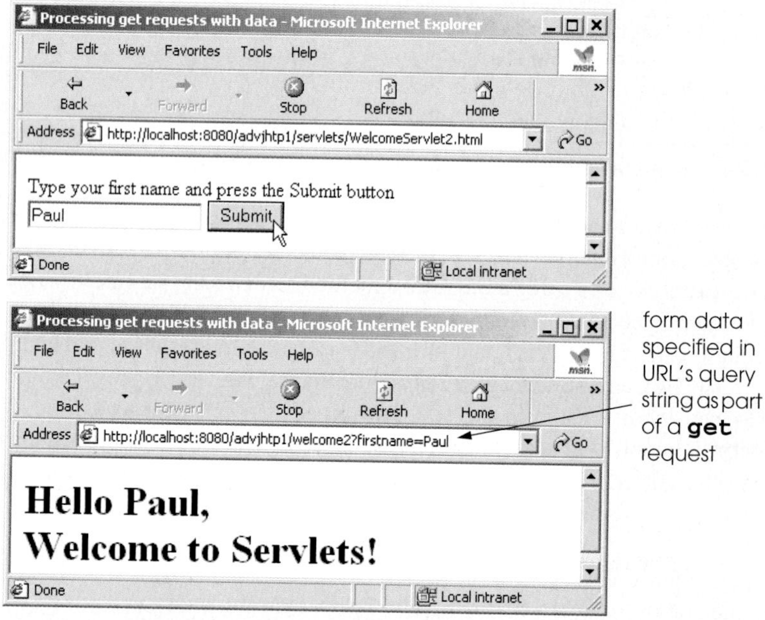

form data specified in URL's query string as part of a **get** request

Fig. 30.13 HTML document in which the **form**'s **action** invokes **WelcomeServlet2** using alias **welcome2** specified in **web.xml** (part 2 of 2).

Once again, we use our **advjhtp1** context root to demonstrate the servlet of Fig. 30.12. Place **WelcomeServlet2.html** in the **servlets** directory created in Section 30.3.2. Place **WelcomeServlet2.class** in the **classes** subdirectory of **WEB-INF** in the **advjhtp1** context root. Remember that classes in a package must be placed in the appropriate package directory structure. Then, edit the **web.xml** deployment descriptor in the **WEB-INF** directory to include the information specified in Fig. 30.14. This table contains the information for the **servlet** and **servlet-mapping** elements that you will add to the **web.xml** deployment descriptor. You should not type the italic text into the deployment descriptor. Restart Tomcat and type the following URL in your Web browser:

```
http://localhost:8080/advjhtp1/servlets/WelcomeServlet2.html
```

Type your name in the text field of the Web page, then click **Submit** to invoke the servlet.

Descriptor element	Value
`servlet` *element*	
`servlet-name`	`welcome2`
`description`	`Handling HTTP get requests with data.`
`servlet-class`	`com.deitel.advjhtp1.servlets.WelcomeServlet2`
`servlet-mapping` *element*	
`servlet-name`	`welcome2`
`url-pattern`	`/welcome2`

Fig. 30.14 Deployment descriptor information for servlet **`WelcomeServlet2`**.

Once again, note that the **`get`** request could have been typed directly into the browser's **Address** or **Location** field as follows:

```
http://localhost:8080/advjhtp1/welcome2?firstname=Paul
```

Try it with your own name.

30.5 Handling HTTP `post` Requests

An HTTP **`post`** request is often used to post data from an HTML form to a server-side form handler that processes the data. For example, when you respond to a Web-based survey, a **`post`** request normally supplies the information you specify in the HTML form to the Web server.

Browsers often *cache* (save on disk) Web pages so they can quickly reload the pages. If there are no changes between the last version stored in the cache and the current version on the Web, this helps speed up your browsing experience. The browser first asks the server if the document has changed or expired since the date the file was cached. If not, the browser loads the document from the cache. Thus, the browser minimizes the amount of data that must be downloaded for you to view a Web page. Browsers typically do not cache the server's response to a **`post`** request, because the next **`post`** might not return the same result. For example, in a survey, many users could visit the same Web page and respond to a question. The survey results could then be displayed for the user. Each new response changes the overall results of the survey.

When you use a Web-based search engine, the browser normally supplies the information you specify in an HTML form to the search engine with a **`get`** request. The search engine performs the search, then returns the results to you as a Web page. Such pages are often cached by the browser in case you perform the same search again. As with **`post`** requests, **`get`** requests can supply parameters as part of the request to the Web server.

The **`WelcomeServlet3`** servlet of Fig. 30.15 is identical to the servlet of Fig. 30.12, except that it defines a **`doPost`** method (line 12) to respond to **`post`** requests rather than a **`doGet`** method. The default functionality of **`doPost`** is to indicate a "Method not allowed" error. We override this method to provide custom **`post`** request processing. Method **`doPost`** receives the same two arguments as **`doGet`**—an object that implements interface **`HttpServletRequest`** to represent the client's request and an object that implements interface **HttpServletResponse** to represent the servlet's response. As with **doGet**, method **doPost** throws a **ServletException** if it is unable to handle a client's request and throws an **IOException** if a problem occurs during stream processing.

```
// Fig. 9.15: WelcomeServlet3.java
// Processing post requests containing data.
package com.deitel.advjhtp1.servlets;

import javax.servlet.*;
import javax.servlet.http.*;
import java.io.*;

public class WelcomeServlet3 extends HttpServlet {

   // process "post" request from client
   protected void doPost( HttpServletRequest request,
      HttpServletResponse response )
         throws ServletException, IOException
   {
      String firstName = request.getParameter( "firstname" );

      response.setContentType( "text/html" );
      PrintWriter out = response.getWriter();

      // send XHTML page to client

      // start XHTML document
      out.println( "<?xml version = \"1.0\"?>" );

      out.println( "<!DOCTYPE html PUBLIC \"-//W3C//DTD " +
         "XHTML 1.0 Strict//EN\" \"http://www.w3.org" +
         "/TR/xhtml1/DTD/xhtml1-strict.dtd\">" );

      out.println(
         "<html xmlns = \"http://www.w3.org/1999/xhtml\">" );

      // head section of document
      out.println( "<head>" );
      out.println(
         "<title>Processing post requests with data</title>" );
      out.println( "</head>" );

      // body section of document
      out.println( "<body>" );
      out.println( "<h1>Hello " + firstName + ",<br />" );
      out.println( "Welcome to Servlets!</h1>" );
      out.println( "</body>" );

      // end XHTML document
      out.println( "</html>" );
      out.close();  // close stream to complete the page
   }
}
```

Fig. 30.15 **WelcomeServlet3** responds to a **post** request that contains data.

The **`WelcomeServlet3.html`** document (Fig. 30.16) provides a **`form`** (lines 13–21) in which the user can input a name in the text **`input`** element **`firstname`** (line 17), then click the **Submit** button to invoke **`WelcomeServlet3`**. When the user presses the **Submit** button, the values of the **`input`** elements are sent to the server as part of the request. However, note that the values are not appended to the request URL. Note that the form's **`method`** in this example is **`post`**. Also, note that a **`post`** request cannot be typed into the browser's **Address** or **Location** field and users cannot bookmark **`post`** requests in their browsers.

```
1  <?xml version = "1.0"?>
2  <!DOCTYPE html PUBLIC "-//W3C//DTD XHTML 1.0 Strict//EN"
3     "http://www.w3.org/TR/xhtml1/DTD/xhtml1-strict.dtd">
4
5  <!-- Fig. 9.16: WelcomeServlet3.html -->
6
7  <html xmlns = "http://www.w3.org/1999/xhtml">
8  <head>
9     <title>Handling an HTTP Post Request with Data</title>
10 </head>
11
12 <body>
13    <form action = "/advjhtp1/welcome3" method = "post">
14
15       <p><label>
16          Type your first name and press the Submit button
17          <br /><input type = "text" name = "firstname" />
18          <input type = "submit" value = "Submit" />
19       </label></p>
20
21    </form>
22 </body>
23 </html>
```

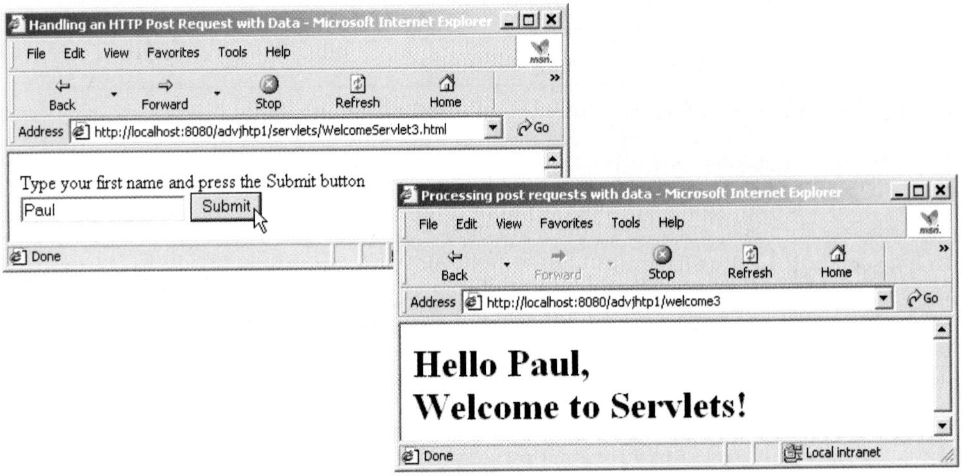

Fig. 30.16 HTML document in which the **`form`**'s **`action`** invokes **`Welcome-Servlet3`** through the alias **`welcome3`** specified in **`web.xml`**.

We use our **advjhtp1** context root to demonstrate the servlet of Fig. 30.15. Place **WelcomeServlet3.html** in the **servlets** directory created in Section 30.3.2. Place **WelcomeServlet3.class** in the **classes** subdirectory of **WEB-INF** in the **advjhtp1** context root. Then, edit the **web.xml** deployment descriptor in the **WEB-INF** directory to include the information specified in Fig. 30.17. Restart Tomcat and type the following URL in your Web browser:

http://localhost:8080/advjhtp1/servlets/WelcomeServlet3.html

Type your name in the text field of the Web page, then click **Submit** to invoke the servlet.

30.6 Redirecting Requests to Other Resources

Sometimes it is useful to redirect a request to a different resource. For example, a servlet could determine the type of the client browser and redirect the request to a Web page that was designed specifically for that browser. The **RedirectServlet** of Fig. 30.18 receives a page parameter as part of a **get** request, then uses that parameter to redirect the request to a different resource.

Descriptor element	Value
servlet *element*	
servlet-name	**welcome3**
description	**Handling HTTP post requests with data.**
servlet-class	**com.deitel.advjhtp1.servlets.WelcomeServlet3**
servlet-mapping *element*	
servlet-name	**welcome3**
url-pattern	**/welcome3**

Fig. 30.17 Deployment descriptor information for servlet **WelcomeServlet3**.

```
// Fig. 9.18: RedirectServlet.java
// Redirecting a user to a different Web page.
package com.deitel.advjhtp1.servlets;

import javax.servlet.*;
import javax.servlet.http.*;
import java.io.*;

public class RedirectServlet extends HttpServlet {

   // process "get" request from client
   protected void doGet( HttpServletRequest request,
      HttpServletResponse response )
         throws ServletException, IOException
   {
```

Fig. 30.18 Redirecting requests to other resources (part 1 of 2).

```
16         String location = request.getParameter( "page" );
17
18         if ( location != null )
19
20            if ( location.equals( "deitel" ) )
21               response.sendRedirect( "http://www.deitel.com" );
22            else
23               if ( location.equals( "welcome1" ) )
24                  response.sendRedirect( "welcome1" );
25
26         // code that executes only if this servlet
27         // does not redirect the user to another page
28
29         response.setContentType( "text/html" );
30         PrintWriter out = response.getWriter();
31
32         // start XHTML document
33         out.println( "<?xml version = \"1.0\"?>" );
34
35         out.println( "<!DOCTYPE html PUBLIC \"-//W3C//DTD " +
36            "XHTML 1.0 Strict//EN\" \"http://www.w3.org" +
37            "/TR/xhtml1/DTD/xhtml1-strict.dtd\">" );
38
39         out.println(
40            "<html xmlns = \"http://www.w3.org/1999/xhtml\">" );
41
42         // head section of document
43         out.println( "<head>" );
44         out.println( "<title>Invalid page</title>" );
45         out.println( "</head>" );
46
47         // body section of document
48         out.println( "<body>" );
49         out.println( "<h1>Invalid page requested</h1>" );
50         out.println( "<p><a href = " +
51            "\"servlets/RedirectServlet.html\">" );
52         out.println( "Click here to choose again</a></p>" );
53         out.println( "</body>" );
54
55         // end XHTML document
56         out.println( "</html>" );
57         out.close();  // close stream to complete the page
58      }
59   }
```

Fig. 30.18 Redirecting requests to other resources (part 2 of 2).

Line 16 obtains the **page** parameter from the request. If the value returned is not **null**, the **if/else** structure at lines 20–24 determines if the value is either "**deitel**" or "**welcome1**." If the value is "**deitel**," the **response** object's ***sendRedirect*** method (line 21) redirects the request to **www.deitel.com**. If the value is "**welcome1**," line 24 redirect the request to the servlet of Fig. 30.5. Note that line 24 does not explicitly specify the **advjhtp1** context root for our Web application. When a servlet uses a relative path to reference another static or dynamic resource, the servlet assumes the same base URL and context root as the one that invoked the servlet—unless a complete URL is specified for the resource. So, line 24 actually is requesting the resource located at

```
http://localhost:8080/advjhtp1/welcome1
```

Similarly, line 51 actually is requesting the resource located at

```
http://localhost:8080/advjhtp1/servlets/RedirectServlet.html
```

Software Engineering Observation 30.7

Using relative paths to reference resources in the same context root makes your Web application more flexible. For example, you can change the context root without making changes to the static and dynamic resources in the application.

Once method **sendRedirect** executes, processing of the original request by the **RedirectServlet** terminates. If method **sendRedirect** is not called, the remainder of method **doPost** outputs a Web page indicating that an invalid request was made. The page allows the user to try again by returning to the XHTML document of Fig. 30.19. Note that one of the redirects is sent to a static XHTML Web page and the other is sent to a servlet.

The **RedirectServlet.html** document (Fig. 30.19) provides two hyperlinks (lines 15–16 and 17–18) that allow the user to invoke the servlet **RedirectServlet**. Note that each hyperlink specifies a **page** parameter as part of the URL. To demonstrate passing an invalid page, you can type the URL into your browser with no value for the **page** parameter.

```
1  <?xml version = "1.0"?>
2  <!DOCTYPE html PUBLIC "-//W3C//DTD XHTML 1.0 Strict//EN"
3     "http://www.w3.org/TR/xhtml1/DTD/xhtml1-strict.dtd">
4
5  <!-- Fig. 9.19: RedirectServlet.html -->
6
7  <html xmlns = "http://www.w3.org/1999/xhtml">
8  <head>
9     <title>Redirecting a Request to Another Site</title>
10 </head>
11
12 <body>
13    <p>Click a link to be redirected to the appropriate page</p>
14    <p>
15    <a href = "/advjhtp1/redirect?page=deitel">
16       www.deitel.com</a><br />
17    <a href = "/advjhtp1/redirect?page=welcome1">
18       Welcome servlet</a>
19    </p>
20 </body>
21 </html>
```

Fig. 30.19 **RedirectServlet.html** document to demonstrate redirecting requests to other resources.

Fig. 30.19 **RedirectServlet.html** document to demonstrate redirecting requests to other resources.

We use our **advjhtp1** context root to demonstrate the servlet of Fig. 30.18. Place **RedirectServlet.html** in the **servlets** directory created in Section 30.3.2. Place **RedirectServlet.class** in the **classes** subdirectory of **WEB-INF** in the **advjhtp1** context root. Then, edit the **web.xml** deployment descriptor in the **WEB-INF** directory to include the information specified in Fig. 30.20. Restart Tomcat, and type the following URL in your Web browser:

```
http://localhost:8080/advjhtp1/servlets/RedirectServlet.html
```

Click a hyperlink in the Web page to invoke the servlet.

Descriptor element	Value
servlet *element*	
servlet-name	**redirect**
description	**Redirecting to static Web pages and other servlets.**
servlet-class	**com.deitel.advjhtp1.servlets.RedirectServlet**
servlet-mapping *element*	
servlet-name	**redirect**
url-pattern	**/redirect**

Fig. 30.20 Deployment descriptor information for servlet **RedirectServlet**.

When redirecting requests, the request parameters from the original request are passed as parameters to the new request. Additional request parameters also can be passed. For example, the URL passed to **sendRedirect** could contain name/value pairs. Any new parameters are added to the existing parameters. If a new parameter has the same name as an existing parameter, the new parameter value takes precedence over the original value. However, all the values are still passed. In this case, the complete set of values for a given parameter name can be obtained by calling method ***getParameterValues*** from interface **HttpServletRequest**. This method receives the parameter name as an argument and returns an array of **String**s containing the parameter values in order from most recent to least recent.

30.7 Session Tracking

Many e-businesses can personalize users' browsing experiences, tailoring Web pages to their users' individual preferences and letting users bypass irrelevant content. This is done by tracking the consumer's movement through the Internet and combining that data with information provided by the consumer, which could include billing information, interests and hobbies, among other things. *Personalization* is making it easier and more pleasant for many people to surf the Internet and find what they want. Consumers and companies can benefit from the unique treatment resulting from personalization. Providing content of special interest to your visitor can help establish a relationship that you can build upon each time that person returns to your site. Targeting consumers with personal offers, advertisements, promotions and services may lead to more customer loyalty—many customers enjoy the individual attention that a customized site provides. Originally, the Internet lacked personal assistance when compared with the individual service often experienced in bricks-and-mortar stores. Sophisticated technology helps many Web sites offer a personal touch to their visitors. For example, Web sites such as MSN.com and CNN.com allow you to customize their home page to suit your needs. Online shopping sites often customize their Web pages to individuals, and such sites must distinguish between clients so the company can determine the proper items and charge the proper amount for each client. Personalization is important for Internet marketing and for managing customer relationships to increase customer loyalty.

Hand in hand with the promise of personalization, however, comes the problem of *privacy invasion*. What if the e-business to which you give your personal data sells or gives those data to another organization without your knowledge? What if you do not want your movements on the Internet to be tracked by unknown parties? What if an unauthorized party gains access to your private data, such as credit-card numbers or medical history? These are some of the many questions that must be addressed by consumers, e-businesses and lawmakers alike.

As we have discussed, the request/response mechanism of the Web is based on HTTP. Unfortunately, HTTP is a *stateless protocol*—it does not support persistent information that could help a Web server determine that a request is from a particular client. As far as a Web server is concerned, every request could be from the same client or every request could be from a different client. Thus, sites like MSN.com and CNN.com need a mechanism to identify individual clients. To help the server distinguish between clients, each client must identify itself to the server. There are a number of popular techniques for distinguishing between clients. We introduce two techniques to track clients individually—*cookies* (Section 30.7.1) and *session tracking* (Section 30.7.2). Two other techniques not discussed in this chapter are using **input** form elements of type **"hidden"** and *URL rewriting*. With **"hidden"** form elements, the servlet can write session-tracking data into a **form** in the Web page it returns to the client to satisfy a prior request. When the user submits the form in the new Web page, all the form data, including the **"hidden"** fields, are sent to the form handler on the server. With URL rewriting, the servlet embeds session-tracking information as **get** parameters directly in the URLs of hyperlinks that the user might click to make the next request to the Web server.

30.7.1 Cookies

A popular way to customize Web pages is via *cookies*. Browsers can store cookies on the user's computer for retrieval later in the same browsing session or in future browsing sessions. For example, cookies could be used in a shopping application to store unique identifiers for the users. When users add items to their online shopping carts or perform other tasks resulting in a request to the Web server, the server receives cookies containing unique identifiers for each user. The server then uses the unique identifier to locate the shopping carts and perform the necessary processing. Cookies could also be used to indicate the client's shopping preferences. When the servlet receives the client's next communication, the servlet can examine the cookie(s) it sent to the client in a previous communication, identify the client's preferences and immediately display products of interest to the client.

Cookies are text-based data that are sent by servlets (or other similar server-side technologies) as part of responses to clients. Every HTTP-based interaction between a client and a server includes a *header* containing information about the request (when the communication is from the client to the server) or information about the response (when the communication is from the server to the client). When an **HttpServlet** receives a request, the header includes information such as the request type (e.g., **get** or **post**) and the cookies that are sent by the server to be stored on the client machine. When the server formulates its response, the header information includes any cookies the server wants to store on the client computer and other information such as the MIME type of the response.

Testing and Debugging Tip 30.6

Some clients do not accept cookies. When a client declines a cookie, the browser application normally informs the client that the site may not function correctly without cookies enabled.

Depending on the *maximum age* of a cookie, the Web browser either maintains the cookie for the duration of the browsing session (i.e., until the user closes the Web browser) or stores the cookie on the client computer for future use. When the browser requests a resource from a server, cookies previously sent to the client by that server are returned to the server as part of the request formulated by the browser. Cookies are deleted automatically when they *expire* (i.e., reach their maximum age).

Figure 30.21 demonstrates cookies. The example allows the user to select a favorite programming language and **post** the choice to the server. The response is a Web page in which the user can select another favorite language or click a link to view a list of book recommendations. When the user selects the list of book recommendations, a **get** request is sent to the server. The cookies previously stored on the client are read by the servlet and used to form a Web page containing the book recommendations.

CookieServlet (Fig. 30.21) handles both the **get** and the **post** requests. The **CookieSelectLanguage.html** document of Fig. 30.22 contains four radio buttons

(**C**, **C++**, **Java** and **VB 6**) and a **Submit** button. When the user presses **Submit**, the **CookieServlet** is invoked with a **post** request. The servlet adds a cookie containing the selected language to the response header and sends an XHTML document to the client. Each time the user clicks **Submit**, a cookie is sent to the client.

```
// Fig. 9.21: CookieServlet.java
// Using cookies to store data on the client computer.
package com.deitel.advjhtp1.servlets;

import javax.servlet.*;
import javax.servlet.http.*;
import java.io.*;
import java.util.*;

public class CookieServlet extends HttpServlet {
   private final Map books = new HashMap();

   // initialize Map books
   public void init()
   {
      books.put( "C", "0130895725" );
      books.put( "C++", "0130895717" );
      books.put( "Java", "0130125075" );
      books.put( "VB6", "0134569555" );
   }

   // receive language selection and send cookie containing
   // recommended book to the client
   protected void doPost( HttpServletRequest request,
      HttpServletResponse response )
         throws ServletException, IOException
   {
      String language = request.getParameter( "language" );
      String isbn = books.get( language ).toString();
      Cookie cookie = new Cookie( language, isbn );

      response.addCookie( cookie );  // must precede getWriter
      response.setContentType( "text/html" );
      PrintWriter out = response.getWriter();

      // send XHTML page to client

      // start XHTML document
      out.println( "<?xml version = \"1.0\"?>" );

      out.println( "<!DOCTYPE html PUBLIC \"-//W3C//DTD " +
         "XHTML 1.0 Strict//EN\" \"http://www.w3.org" +
         "/TR/xhtml1/DTD/xhtml1-strict.dtd\">" );

      out.println(
         "<html xmlns = \"http://www.w3.org/1999/xhtml\">" );

```

Fig. 30.21 Storing user data on the client computer with cookies (part 1 of 3).

```
      // head section of document
      out.println( "<head>" );
      out.println( "<title>Welcome to Cookies</title>" );
      out.println( "</head>" );

      // body section of document
      out.println( "<body>" );
      out.println( "<p>Welcome to Cookies! You selected " +
         language + "</p>" );

      out.println( "<p><a href = " +
         "\"/advjhtp1/servlets/CookieSelectLanguage.html\">" +
         "Click here to choose another language</a></p>" );

      out.println( "<p><a href = \"/advjhtp1/cookies\">" +
         "Click here to get book recommendations</a></p>" );
      out.println( "</body>" );

      // end XHTML document
      out.println( "</html>" );
      out.close();    // close stream
   }

   // read cookies from client and create XHTML document
   // containing recommended books
   protected void doGet( HttpServletRequest request,
      HttpServletResponse response )
         throws ServletException, IOException
   {
      Cookie cookies[] = request.getCookies();  // get cookies

      response.setContentType( "text/html" );
      PrintWriter out = response.getWriter();

      // start XHTML document
      out.println( "<?xml version = \"1.0\"?>" );

      out.println( "<!DOCTYPE html PUBLIC \"-//W3C//DTD " +
         "XHTML 1.0 Strict//EN\" \"http://www.w3.org" +
         "/TR/xhtml1/DTD/xhtml1-strict.dtd\">" );

      out.println(
         "<html xmlns = \"http://www.w3.org/1999/xhtml\">" );

      // head section of document
      out.println( "<head>" );
      out.println( "<title>Recommendations</title>" );
      out.println( "</head>" );

      // body section of document
      out.println( "<body>" );
```

Fig. 30.21 Storing user data on the client computer with cookies (part 2 of 3).

```
100         // if there are any cookies, recommend a book for each ISBN
101         if ( cookies != null && cookies.length != 0 ) {
102            out.println( "<h1>Recommendations</h1>" );
103            out.println( "<p>" );
104
105            // get the name of each cookie
106            for ( int i = 0; i < cookies.length; i++ )
107               out.println( cookies[ i ].getName() +
108                  " How to Program. ISBN#: " +
109                  cookies[ i ].getValue() + "<br />" );
110
111            out.println( "</p>" );
112         }
113         else {    // there were no cookies
114            out.println( "<h1>No Recommendations</h1>" );
115            out.println( "<p>You did not select a language.</p>" );
116         }
117
118         out.println( "</body>" );
119
120         // end XHTML document
121         out.println( "</html>" );
122         out.close();     // close stream
123      }
124   }
```

Fig. 30.21 Storing user data on the client computer with cookies (part 3 of 3).

Line 11 defines **Map books** as a **HashMap** in which we store key/value pairs that use the programming language as the key and the ISBN number of the recommended book as the value. The **CookieServlet init** method (line 14–20) populates books with four key/value pairs of books. Method **doPost** (lines 24–69) is invoked in response to the **post** request from the XHTML document of Fig. 30.22. Line 28 uses method **getParameter** to obtain the user's **language** selection (the value of the selected radio button on the Web page). Line 29 obtains the ISBN number for the selected language from **books**.

Line 30 creates a new ***Cookie*** object (package ***javax.servlet.http***), using the **language** and **isbn** values as the *cookie name* and *cookie value*, respectively. The cookie name identifies the cookie; the cookie value is the information associated with the cookie. Browsers that support cookies must be able to store a minimum of 20 cookies per Web site and 300 cookies per user. Browsers may limit the cookie size to 4K (4096 bytes). Each cookie stored on the client includes a domain. The browser sends a cookie only to the domain stored in the cookie.

Software Engineering Observation 30.8

Browser users can disable cookies, so Web applications that use cookies may not function properly for clients with cookies disabled.

Software Engineering Observation 30.9

By default, cookies exist only for the current browsing session (until the user closes the browser). To make cookies persist beyond the current session, call **Cookie** *method* **setMaxAge** *to indicate the number of seconds until the cookie expires.*

Line 32 adds the cookie to the **`response`** with method ***`addCookie`*** of interface **`HttpServletResponse`**. Cookies are sent to the client as part of the HTTP header. The header information is always provided to the client first, so the cookies should be added to the **`response`** with **`addCookie`** before any data is written as part of the response. After the cookie is added, the servlet sends an XHTML document to the client (see the second screen capture of Fig. 30.22).

Common Programming Error 30.3

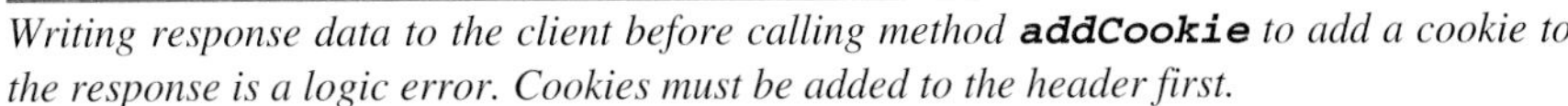

*Writing response data to the client before calling method **`addCookie`** to add a cookie to the response is a logic error. Cookies must be added to the header first.*

The XHTML document sent to the client in response to a **`post`** request includes a hyperlink that invokes method **`doGet`** (lines 73–123). The method reads any **`Cookie`**s that were written to the client in **`doPost`**. For each **`Cookie`** written, the servlet recommends a Deitel book on the subject. Up to four books are displayed on the Web page created by the servlet.

Line 77 retrieves the cookies from the client using **`HttpServletRequest`** method ***`getCookies`***, which returns an array of **`Cookie`** objects. When a **`get`** or **`post`** operation is performed to invoke a servlet, the cookies associated with that server's domain are automatically sent to the servlet.

If method **`getCookies`** does not return **`null`** (i.e., there were no cookies), lines 106–109 retrieve the name of each **`Cookie`** using **`Cookie`** method ***`getName`***, retrieve the value of each **`Cookie`** using **`Cookie`** method ***`getValue`*** and write a line to the client indicating the name of a recommended book and its ISBN number.

Software Engineering Observation 30.10

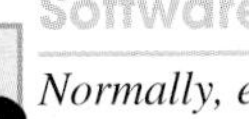

*Normally, each servlet class handles one request type (e.g., **`get`** or **`post`**, but not both).*

Figure 30.22 shows the XHTML document the user loads to select a language. When the user presses **Submit**, the value of the currently selected radio button is sent to the server as part of the **`post`** request to the **`CookieServlet`**, which we refer to as **`cookies`** in this example.

```
<?xml version = "1.0"?>
<!DOCTYPE html PUBLIC "-//W3C//DTD XHTML 1.0 Strict//EN"
   "http://www.w3.org/TR/xhtml1/DTD/xhtml1-strict.dtd">

<!-- Fig. 9.22: CookieSelectLanguage.html -->

<html xmlns = "http://www.w3.org/1999/xhtml">
<head>
   <title>Using Cookies</title>
</head>

<body>
   <form action = "/advjhtp1/cookies" method = "post">

```

Fig. 30.22 **`CookieSelectLanguage.html`** document for selecting a programming language and posting the data to the **`CookieServlet`** (part 1 of 3).

```
        <p>Select a programming language:</p>
        <p>
           <input type = "radio" name = "language"
              value = "C" />C <br />

           <input type = "radio" name = "language"
              value = "C++" />C++ <br />

           <!-- this radio button checked by default -->
           <input type = "radio" name = "language"
              value = "Java" checked = "checked" />Java<br />

           <input type = "radio" name = "language"
              value = "VB6" />VB 6
        </p>

        <p><input type = "submit" value = "Submit" /></p>

     </form>
  </body>
</html>
```

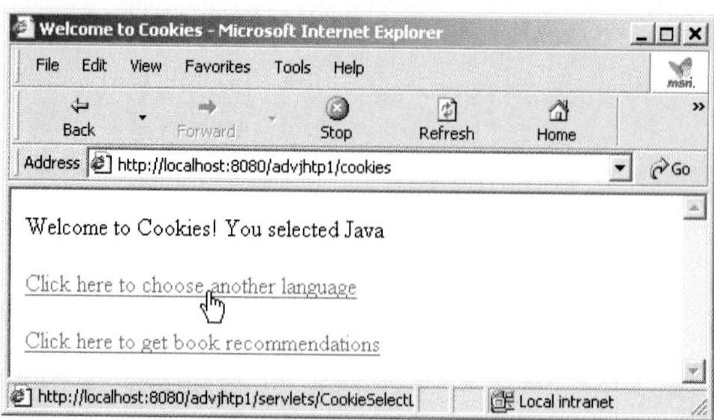

Fig. 30.22 **`CookieSelectLanguage.html`** document for selecting a programming language and posting the data to the **`CookieServlet`** (part 2 of 3).

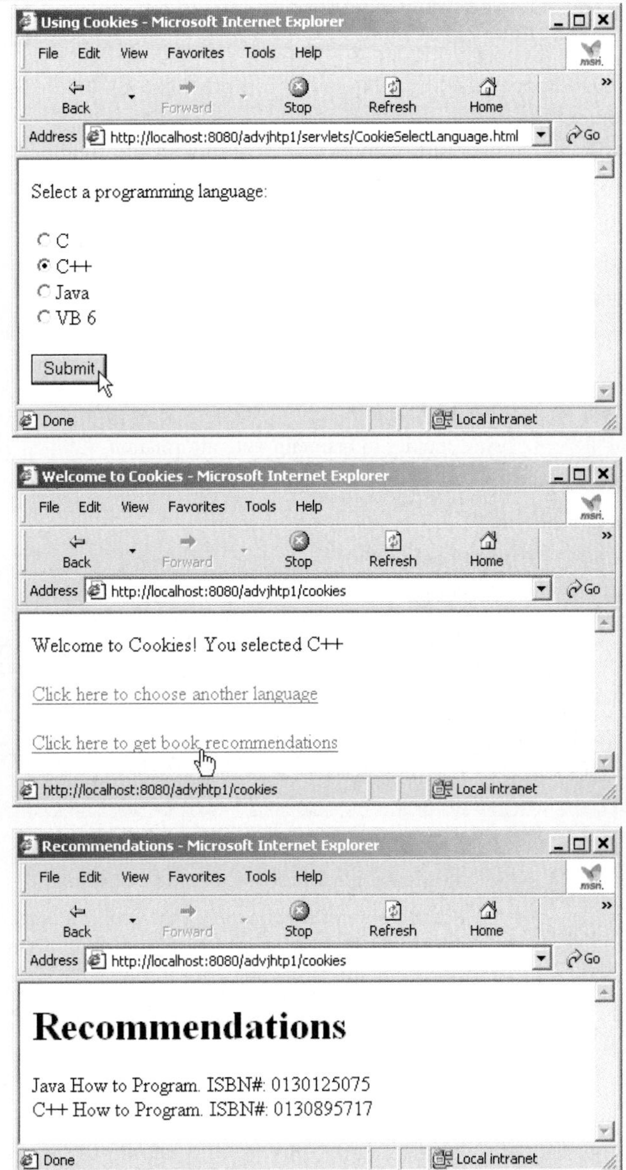

Fig. 30.22 **`CookieSelectLanguage.html`** document for selecting a programming language and posting the data to the **`CookieServlet`** (part 3 of 3).

We use our **`advjhtp1`** context root to demonstrate the servlet of Fig. 30.21. Place **`CookieSelectLanguage.html`** in the **`servlets`** directory created previously. Place **`CookieServlet.class`** in the **`classes`** subdirectory of **`WEB-INF`** in the **`advjhtp1`** context root. Then, edit the **`web.xml`** deployment descriptor in the **`WEB-INF`** directory to include the information specified in Fig. 30.23. Restart Tomcat and type the following URL in your Web browser:

```
http://localhost:8080/advjhtp1/servlets/
CookieSelectLanguage.html
```

When the Web page appears, select a language and press the **Submit** button in the Web page to invoke the servlet.

Various **Cookie** methods are provided to manipulate the members of a **Cookie**. Some of these methods are listed in Fig. 30.24.

Descriptor element	Value
servlet *element*	
servlet-name	**cookies**
description	Using cookies to maintain state information.
servlet-class	**com.deitel.advjhtp1.servlets.CookieServlet**
servlet-mapping *element*	
servlet-name	**cookies**
url-pattern	**/cookies**

Fig. 30.23 Deployment descriptor information for servlet **CookieServlet**.

Method	Description
getComment()	Returns a **String** describing the purpose of the cookie (**null** if no comment has been set with **setComment**).
getDomain()	Returns a **String** containing the cookie's domain. This determines which servers can receive the cookie. By default, cookies are sent to the server that originally sent the cookie to the client.
getMaxAge()	Returns an **int** representing the maximum age of the cookie in seconds.
getName()	Returns a **String** containing the name of the cookie as set by the constructor.
getPath()	Returns a **String** containing the URL prefix for the cookie. Cookies can be "targeted" to specific URLs that include directories on the Web server. By default, a cookie is returned to services operating in the same directory as the service that sent the cookie or a subdirectory of that directory.
getSecure()	Returns a **boolean** value indicating if the cookie should be transmitted using a secure protocol (**true**).
getValue()	Returns a **String** containing the value of the cookie as set with **setValue** or the constructor.

Fig. 30.24 Important methods of class **Cookie** (part 1 of 2).

Method	Description
`getVersion()`	Returns an **`int`** containing the version of the cookie protocol used to create the cookie. A value of 0 (the default) indicates the original cookie protocol as defined by Netscape. A value of 1 indicates the current version, which is based on *Request for Comments (RFC) 2109*.
`setComment( String )`	The comment describing the purpose of the cookie that is presented by the browser to the user. (Some browsers allow the user to accept cookies on a per-cookie basis.)
`setDomain( String )`	This determines which servers can receive the cookie. By default, cookies are sent to the server that originally sent the cookie to the client. The domain is specified in the form **`".deitel.com"`**, indicating that all servers ending with **`.deitel.com`** can receive this cookie.
`setMaxAge( int )`	Sets the maximum age of the cookie in seconds.
`setPath( String )`	Sets the "target" URL prefix indicating the directories on the server that lead to the services that can receive this cookie.
`setSecure( boolean )`	A **`true`** value indicates that the cookie should only be sent using a secure protocol.
`setValue( String )`	Sets the value of a cookie.
`setVersion( int )`	Sets the cookie protocol for this cookie.

Fig. 30.24 Important methods of class **`Cookie`** (part 2 of 2).

30.7.2 Session Tracking with `HttpSession`

Java provides enhanced session tracking support with the servlet API's ***`HttpSession`*** interface. To demonstrate basic session-tracking techniques, we modified the servlet from Fig. 30.21 to use ***`HttpSession`*** objects (Fig. 30.25). Once again, the servlet handles both **`get`** and **`post`** requests. The document **`SessionSelectLanguage.html`** of Fig. 30.26 contains four radio buttons (**C**, **C++**, **Java** and **VB 6**) and a **Submit** button. When the user presses **Submit**, **`SessionServlet`** is invoked with a **`post`** request. The servlet responds by creating an object of type **`HttpSession`** for the client (or using an existing session for the client) and adds the selected language and an ISBN number for the recommended book to the **`HttpSession`** object. Then, the servlet sends an XHTML page to the client. Each time the user clicks **Submit**, a new language/ISBN pair is added to the **`HttpSession`** object.

```
// Fig. 9.25: SessionServlet.java
// Using HttpSession to maintain client state information.
package com.deitel.advjhtp1.servlets;

import javax.servlet.*;
```

Fig. 30.25 Maintaining state information with **`HttpSession`** objects (part 1 of 4).

```
import javax.servlet.http.*;
import java.io.*;
import java.util.*;

public class SessionServlet extends HttpServlet {
   private final Map books = new HashMap();

   // initialize Map books
   public void init()
   {
      books.put( "C", "0130895725" );
      books.put( "C++", "0130895717" );
      books.put( "Java", "0130125075" );
      books.put( "VB6", "0134569555" );
   }

   // receive language selection and create HttpSession object
   // containing recommended book for the client
   protected void doPost( HttpServletRequest request,
      HttpServletResponse response )
         throws ServletException, IOException
   {
      String language = request.getParameter( "language" );

      // Get the user's session object.
      // Create a session (true) if one does not exist.
      HttpSession session = request.getSession( true );

      // add a value for user's choice to session
      session.setAttribute( language, books.get( language ) );

      response.setContentType( "text/html" );
      PrintWriter out = response.getWriter();

      // send XHTML page to client

      // start XHTML document
      out.println( "<?xml version = \"1.0\"?>" );

      out.println( "<!DOCTYPE html PUBLIC \"-//W3C//DTD " +
         "XHTML 1.0 Strict//EN\" \"http://www.w3.org" +
         "/TR/xhtml1/DTD/xhtml1-strict.dtd\">" );

      out.println(
         "<html xmlns = \"http://www.w3.org/1999/xhtml\">" );

      // head section of document
      out.println( "<head>" );
      out.println( "<title>Welcome to Sessions</title>" );
      out.println( "</head>" );

      // body section of document
      out.println( "<body>" );
```

Fig. 30.25 Maintaining state information with **HttpSession** objects (part 2 of 4).

```
      out.println( "<p>Welcome to Sessions! You selected " +
         language + ".</p>" );

      // display information about the session
      out.println( "<p>Your unique session ID is: " +
         session.getId() + "<br />" );

      out.println(
         "This " + ( session.isNew() ? "is" : "is not" ) +
         " a new session<br />" );

      out.println( "The session was created at: " +
         new Date( session.getCreationTime() ) + "<br />" );

      out.println( "You last accessed the session at: " +
         new Date( session.getLastAccessedTime() ) + "<br />" );

      out.println( "The maximum inactive interval is: " +
         session.getMaxInactiveInterval() + " seconds</p>" );

      out.println( "<p><a href = " +
         "\"servlets/SessionSelectLanguage.html\">" +
         "Click here to choose another language</a></p>" );

      out.println( "<p><a href = \"sessions\">" +
         "Click here to get book recommendations</a></p>" );
      out.println( "</body>" );

      // end XHTML document
      out.println( "</html>" );
      out.close();    // close stream
   }

   // read session attributes and create XHTML document
   // containing recommended books
   protected void doGet( HttpServletRequest request,
      HttpServletResponse response )
         throws ServletException, IOException
   {
      // Get the user's session object.
      // Do not create a session (false) if one does not exist.
      HttpSession session = request.getSession( false );

      // get names of session object's values
      Enumeration valueNames;

      if ( session != null )
         valueNames = session.getAttributeNames();
      else
         valueNames = null;

      PrintWriter out = response.getWriter();
      response.setContentType( "text/html" );
```

Fig. 30.25 Maintaining state information with **HttpSession** objects (part 3 of 4).

```

      // start XHTML document
      out.println( "<?xml version = \"1.0\"?>" );

      out.println( "<!DOCTYPE html PUBLIC \"-//W3C//DTD " +
         "XHTML 1.0 Strict//EN\" \"http://www.w3.org" +
         "/TR/xhtml1/DTD/xhtml1-strict.dtd\">" );

      out.println(
         "<html xmlns = \"http://www.w3.org/1999/xhtml\">" );

      // head section of document
      out.println( "<head>" );
      out.println( "<title>Recommendations</title>" );
      out.println( "</head>" );

      // body section of document
      out.println( "<body>" );

      if ( valueNames != null &&
           valueNames.hasMoreElements() ) {
         out.println( "<h1>Recommendations</h1>" );
         out.println( "<p>" );

         String name, value;

         // get value for each name in valueNames
         while ( valueNames.hasMoreElements() ) {
            name = valueNames.nextElement().toString();
            value = session.getAttribute( name ).toString();

            out.println( name + " How to Program. " +
               "ISBN#: " + value + "<br />" );
         }

         out.println( "</p>" );
      }
      else {
         out.println( "<h1>No Recommendations</h1>" );
         out.println( "<p>You did not select a language.</p>" );
      }

      out.println( "</body>" );

      // end XHTML document
      out.println( "</html>" );
      out.close();    // close stream
   }
}
```

Fig. 30.25 Maintaining state information with **`HttpSession`** objects (part 4 of 4).

Most of class **`SessionServlet`** is identical to **`CookieServlet`** (Fig. 30.21), so we concentrate on only the new features here. When the user selects a language from the document **SessionSelectLanguage.html** (Fig. 30.26) and presses **Submit**, method **doPost** (lines 24–90) is invoked. Line 28 gets the user's **language** selection. Then, line 32 uses method ***getSession*** of interface **HttpServletRequest** to obtain the **HttpSession** object for the client. If the server has an existing **HttpSession** object for the client from a previous request, method **getSession** returns that **HttpSession** object. Otherwise, the **true** argument to method **getSession** indicates that the servlet should create a unique new **HttpSession** object for the client. A **false** argument would cause method **getSession** to return **null** if the **HttpSession** object for the client did not already exist. Using a **false** argument could help determine whether a client has logged into a Web application.

Like a cookie, an **HttpSession** object can store name/value pairs. In session terminology, these are called *attributes*, and they are placed into an **HttpSession** object with method ***setAttribute***. Line 35 uses **setAttribute** to put the language and the corresponding recommended book's ISBN number into the **HttpSession** object. One of the primary benefits of using **HttpSession** objects rather than cookies is that **HttpSession** objects can store any object (not just **String**s) as the value of an attribute. This allows Java programmers flexibility in determining the type of state information they wish to maintain for clients of their Web applications. If an attribute with a particular name already exists when **setAttribute** is called, the object associated with that attribute name is replaced.

Software Engineering Observation 30.11

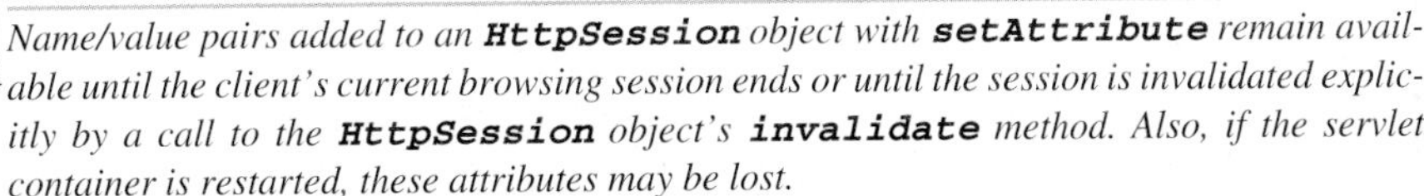

Name/value pairs added to an **HttpSession** *object with* **setAttribute** *remain available until the client's current browsing session ends or until the session is invalidated explicitly by a call to the* **HttpSession** *object's* **invalidate** *method. Also, if the servlet container is restarted, these attributes may be lost.*

After the values are added to the **HttpSession** object, the servlet sends an XHTML document to the client (see the second screen capture of Fig. 30.26). In this example, the document contains various information about the **HttpSession** object for the current client. Line 64 uses **HttpSession** method ***getID*** to obtain the session's unique ID number. Line 67 determines whether the session is new or already exists with method ***isNew***, which returns **true** or **false**. Line 71 obtains the time at which the session was created with method ***getCreationTime***. Line 74 obtains the time at which the session was last accessed with method ***getLastAccessedTime***. Line 77 uses method ***getMaxInactiveInterval*** to obtain the maximum amount of time that an **HttpSession** object can be inactive before the servlet container discards it.

The XHTML document sent to the client in response to a **post** request includes a hyperlink that invokes method **doGet** (lines 94–159). The method obtains the **HttpSession** object for the client with method **getSession** (line 100). We do not want to make any recommendations if the client does not have an existing **HttpSession** object. So, this call to **getSession** uses a **false** argument. Thus, **getSession** returns an **HttpSession** object only if one already exists for the client.

If method **getSession** does not return **null**, line 106 uses **HttpSession** method ***getAttributeNames*** to retrieve an **Enumeration** of the attribute names (i.e., the names used as the first argument to **HttpSession** method **setAttribute**). Each name is passed as an argument to **HttpSession** method ***getAttribute*** (line 141) to retrieve the ISBN of a book from the **HttpSession** object. Method **getAttribute** receives the name and returns an **`Object`** reference to the corresponding value. Next, a line is written in the response to the client containing the title of the recommended book and that book's ISBN number.

Figure 30.26 shows the XHTML document the user loads to select a language. When the user presses **Submit**, the value of the currently selected radio button is sent to the server as part of the **`post`** request to the **`SessionServlet`**, which we refer to as **`sessions`** in this example.

We use our **`advjhtp1`** context root to demonstrate the servlet of Fig. 30.25. Place **`SessionSelectLanguage.html`** in the **`servlets`** directory created previously. Place **`SessionServlet.class`** in the **`classes`** subdirectory of **`WEB-INF`** in the **`advjhtp1`** context root. Then, edit the **`web.xml`** deployment descriptor in the **`WEB-INF`** directory to include the information specified in Fig. 30.27. Restart Tomcat and type the following URL in your Web browser:

```
http://localhost:8080/advjhtp1/servlets/
SessionSelectLanguage.html
```

When the Web page appears, select a language, and press the **Submit** button in the Web page to invoke the servlet.

```
<?xml version = "1.0"?>
<!DOCTYPE html PUBLIC "-//W3C//DTD XHTML 1.0 Strict//EN"
   "http://www.w3.org/TR/xhtml1/DTD/xhtml1-strict.dtd">

<!-- Fig. 9.26: SessionSelectLanguage.html -->

<html xmlns = "http://www.w3.org/1999/xhtml">
<head>
   <title>Using Sessions</title>
</head>

<body>
   <form action = "/advjhtp1/sessions" method = "post">

      <p>Select a programming language:</p>
      <p>
         <input type = "radio" name = "language"
            value = "C" />C <br />

         <input type = "radio" name = "language"
            value = "C++" />C++ <br />

         <!-- this radio button checked by default -->
         <input type = "radio" name = "language"
            value = "Java" checked = "checked" />Java<br />

         <input type = "radio" name = "language"
            value = "VB6" />VB 6
```

Fig. 30.26 **`SessionSelectLanguage.html`** document for selecting a programming language and posting the data to the **`SessionServlet`** (part 1 of 3).

```
      </p>

      <p><input type = "submit" value = "Submit" /></p>

   </form>
</body>
</html>
```

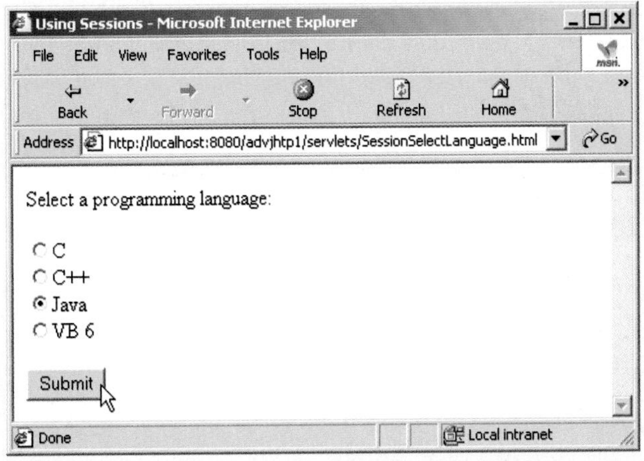

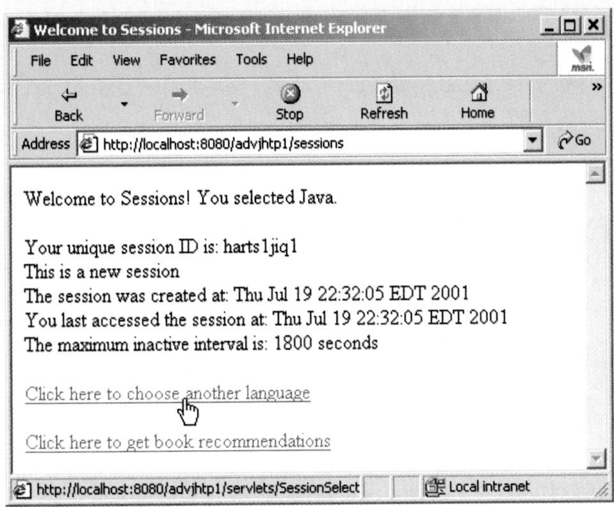

Fig. 30.26 **`SessionSelectLanguage.html`** document for selecting a programming language and posting the data to the **`SessionServlet`** (part 2 of 3).

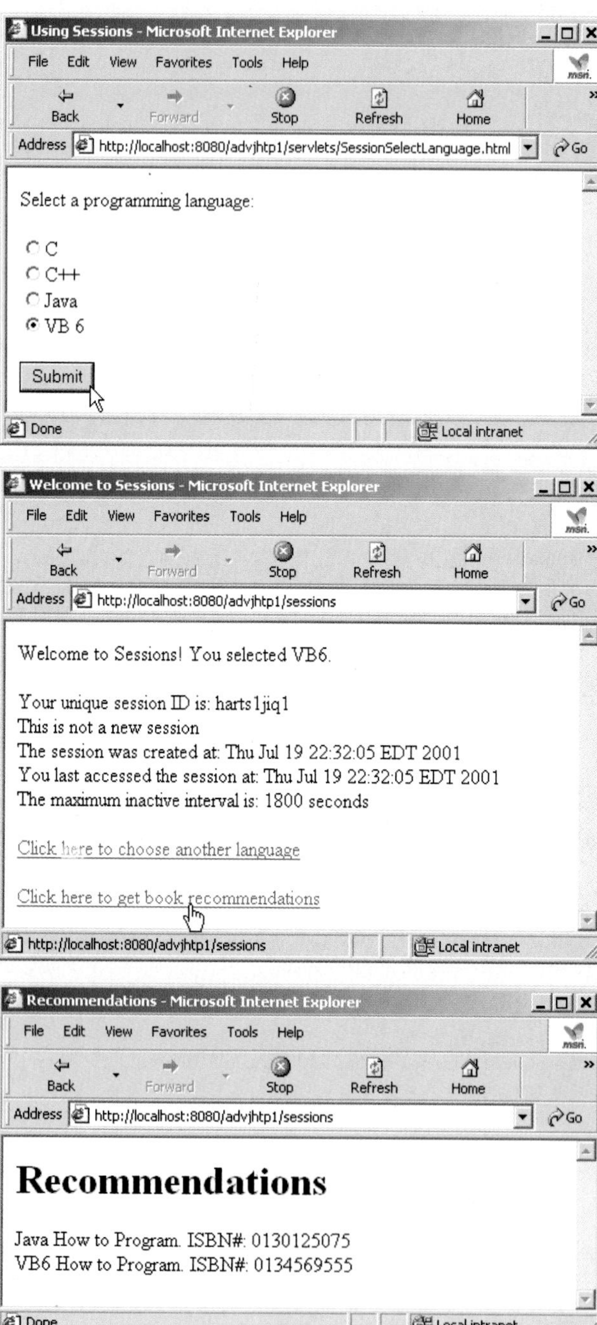

Fig. 30.26 **`SessionSelectLanguage.html`** document for selecting a programming language and posting the data to the **`SessionServlet`** (part 3 of 3).

Descriptor element	Value
servlet *element*	
servlet-name	**sessions**
description	Using sessions to maintain state information.
servlet-class	**com.deitel.advjhtp1.servlets.SessionServlet**
servlet-mapping *element*	
servlet-name	**sessions**
url-pattern	**/sessions**

Fig. 30.27 Deployment descriptor information for servlet **WelcomeServlet2**.

30.8 Multi-tier Applications: Using JDBC from a Servlet

Servlets can communicate with databases via JDBC (Java Database Connectivity), which provides a uniform way for a Java program to connect with a variety of databases in a general manner without having to deal with the specifics of those database systems.

Many of today's applications are *three-tier distributed applications*, consisting of a *user interface*, *business logic* and *database access*. The user interface in such an application is often created using HTML, XHTML (as shown in this chapter) or Dynamic HTML. In some cases, Java applets are also used for this tier. HTML and XHTML are the preferred mechanisms for representing the user interface in systems where portability is a concern. Because HTML is supported by all browsers, designing the user interface to be accessed through a Web browser guarantees portability across all platforms that have browsers. Using the networking provided automatically by the browser, the user interface can communicate with the middle-tier business logic. The middle tier can then access the database to manipulate the data. The three tiers can reside on separate computers that are connected to a network.

In multi-tier architectures, Web servers often represent the middle tier. They provide the business logic that manipulates data from databases and that communicates with client Web browsers. Servlets, through JDBC, can interact with popular database systems. Developers do not need to be familiar with the specifics of each database system. Rather, developers use SQL-based queries and the JDBC driver handles the specifics of interacting with each database system.

The **SurveyServlet** of Fig. 30.28 and the **Survey.html** document of Fig. 30.29 demonstrate a three-tier distributed application that displays the user interface in a browser using XHTML. The middle tier is a Java servlet that handles requests from the client browser and provides access to the third tier—a Cloudscape database accessed via JDBC. The servlet in this example is a survey servlet that allows users to vote for their favorite animal. When the servlet receives a **post** request from the **Survey.html** document, the servlet updates the total number of votes for that animal in the database and returns a dynamically generated XHTML document containing the survey results to the client.

```
// Fig. 9.27: SurveyServlet.java
// A Web-based survey that uses JDBC from a servlet.
package com.deitel.advjhtp1.servlets;

import java.io.*;
import java.text.*;
import java.sql.*;
import javax.servlet.*;
import javax.servlet.http.*;

public class SurveyServlet extends HttpServlet {
   private Connection connection;
   private PreparedStatement updateVotes, totalVotes, results;

   // set up database connection and prepare SQL statements
   public void init( ServletConfig config )
      throws ServletException
   {
      // attempt database connection and create PreparedStatements
      try {
         Class.forName( "COM.cloudscape.core.RmiJdbcDriver" );
         connection = DriverManager.getConnection(
            "jdbc:rmi:jdbc:cloudscape:animalsurvey" );

         // PreparedStatement to add one to vote total for a
         // specific animal
         updateVotes =
            connection.prepareStatement(
               "UPDATE surveyresults SET votes = votes + 1 " +
               "WHERE id = ?"
            );

         // PreparedStatement to sum the votes
         totalVotes =
            connection.prepareStatement(
               "SELECT sum( votes ) FROM surveyresults"
            );

         // PreparedStatement to obtain surveyoption table's data
         results =
            connection.prepareStatement(
               "SELECT surveyoption, votes, id " +
               "FROM surveyresults ORDER BY id"
            );
      }

      // for any exception throw an UnavailableException to
      // indicate that the servlet is not currently available
      catch ( Exception exception ) {
         exception.printStackTrace();
         throw new UnavailableException(exception.getMessage());
      }

```

Fig. 30.28 Multi-tier Web-based survey using XHTML, servlets and JDBC (part 1 of 3).

```
   }  // end of init method

   // process survey response
   protected void doPost( HttpServletRequest request,
      HttpServletResponse response )
         throws ServletException, IOException
   {
      // set up response to client
      response.setContentType( "text/html" );
      PrintWriter out = response.getWriter();
      DecimalFormat twoDigits = new DecimalFormat( "0.00" );

      // start XHTML document
      out.println( "<?xml version = \"1.0\"?>" );

      out.println( "<!DOCTYPE html PUBLIC \"-//W3C//DTD " +
         "XHTML 1.0 Strict//EN\" \"http://www.w3.org" +
         "/TR/xhtml1/DTD/xhtml1-strict.dtd\">" );

      out.println(
         "<html xmlns = \"http://www.w3.org/1999/xhtml\">" );

      // head section of document
      out.println( "<head>" );

      // read current survey response
      int value =
         Integer.parseInt( request.getParameter( "animal" ) );

      // attempt to process a vote and display current results
      try {

         // update total for current survey response
         updateVotes.setInt( 1, value );
         updateVotes.executeUpdate();

         // get total of all survey responses
         ResultSet totalRS = totalVotes.executeQuery();
         totalRS.next();
         int total = totalRS.getInt( 1 );

         // get results
         ResultSet resultsRS = results.executeQuery();
         out.println( "<title>Thank you!</title>" );
         out.println( "</head>" );

         out.println( "<body>" );
         out.println( "<p>Thank you for participating." );
         out.println( "<br />Results:</p><pre>" );

         // process results
         int votes;

```

Fig. 30.28 Multi-tier Web-based survey using XHTML, servlets and JDBC (part 2 of 3).

```
107          while ( resultsRS.next() ) {
108             out.print( resultsRS.getString( 1 ) );
109             out.print( ": " );
110             votes = resultsRS.getInt( 2 );
111             out.print( twoDigits.format(
112                ( double ) votes / total * 100 ) );
113             out.print( "%  responses: " );
114             out.println( votes );
115          }
116 
117          resultsRS.close();
118 
119          out.print( "Total responses: " );
120          out.print( total );
121 
122          // end XHTML document
123          out.println( "</pre></body></html>" );
124          out.close();
125       }
126 
127       // if database exception occurs, return error page
128       catch ( SQLException sqlException ) {
129          sqlException.printStackTrace();
130          out.println( "<title>Error</title>" );
131          out.println( "</head>" );
132          out.println( "<body><p>Database error occurred. " );
133          out.println( "Try again later.</p></body></html>" );
134          out.close();
135       }
136 
137    }  // end of doPost method
138 
139    // close SQL statements and database when servlet terminates
140    public void destroy()
141    {
142       // attempt to close statements and database connection
143       try {
144          updateVo\tes.close();
145          totalVotes.close();
146          results.close();
147          connection.close();
148       }
149 
150       // handle database exceptions by returning error to client
151       catch( SQLException sqlException ) {
152          sqlException.printStackTrace();
153       }
154    }  // end of destroy method
155 }
```

Fig. 30.28 Multi-tier Web-based survey using XHTML, servlets and JDBC (part 3 of 3).

Lines 12 and 13 begin by declaring a **Connection** reference to manage the database connection and three **PreparedStatement** references. The **PreparedStatements** will be used to update the vote count for an animal, to total all the votes and to obtain the complete survey results.

Servlets are initialized by overriding method ***init*** (lines 16–54). Method **init** is called exactly once in a servlet's lifetime, before any client requests are accepted. Method **init** takes a ***ServletConfig*** argument and throws a **ServletException**. The argument provides the servlet with information about its *initialization parameters* (i.e., parameters not associated with a request, but passed to the servlet for initializing servlet variables). These parameters are specified in the **web.xml** deployment descriptor file as part of a **servlet** element. Each parameter appears in an ***init-param*** element of the following form:

```
<init-param>
   <param-name>parameter name goes here</param-name>
   <param-value>parameter value goes here</param-value>
</init-param>
```

Servlets can obtain initialization parameter values by invoking **ServletConfig** method ***getInitParameter***, which receives a string representing the name of the parameter.

In this example, the servlet's **init** method (lines 16–54) performs the connection to the Cloudscape database. Line 21 loads the driver (**COM.cloudscape.core.RmiJdbcDriver**). Lines 22–23 attempt to open a connection to the **animalsurvey** database. The database contains one table (**surveyresults**) that consists of three fields—a unique integer to identify each record called **id**, a string representing the survey option called **surveyoption** and an integer representing the number of votes for a survey option called **votes**. See Section 30.8.1 for instructions on creating the **animalsurvey** database, executing the Cloudscape server and configuring this example to execute in Tomcat.

Lines 27–44 create **PreparedStatement** objects called **updateVotes**, **totalVotes** and **results**. The **updateVotes** statement adds one to the **votes** value for the record with the specified ID. The **totalVotes** statement uses SQL's built-in ***sum*** capability to total all the **votes** in the **surveyresults** table. The results statement returns all the data in the **surveyresults** table.

When a user submits a survey response, method **doPost** (lines 57–137) handles the request. Lines 80–81 obtain the survey response, then the **try** block (lines 84–125) attempts to process the response. Lines 87–88 set the first parameter of **PreparedStatement updateVotes** to the survey response and update the database. Lines 91–93 execute **PreparedStatement totalVotes** to retrieve the total number of votes received. Then, lines 96–123 execute **PreparedStatement results** and process the **ResultSet** to create the survey summary for the client. When the servlet container terminates the servlet, method ***destroy*** (lines 140–154) closes each **PreparedStatement**, then closes the database connection. Figure 30.29 shoes survey.html, which invokes **SurveyServlet** with the alias **animalsurvey** when the user submits the form.

```
<?xml version = "1.0"?>
<!DOCTYPE html PUBLIC "-//W3C//DTD XHTML 1.0 Strict//EN"
   "http://www.w3.org/TR/xhtml1/DTD/xhtml1-strict.dtd">

<!-- Survey.html -->
```

Fig. 30.29 **Survey.html** document that allows users to submit survey responses to **SurveyServlet** (part 1 of 3).

```

<html xmlns = "http://www.w3.org/1999/xhtml">
<head>
   <title>Survey</title>
</head>

<body>
<form method = "post" action = "/advjhtp1/animalsurvey">

   <p>What is your favorite pet?</p>

   <p>
      <input type = "radio" name = "animal"
         value = "1" />Dog<br />
      <input type = "radio" name = "animal"
         value = "2" />Cat<br />
      <input type = "radio" name = "animal"
         value = "3" />Bird<br />
      <input type = "radio" name = "animal"
         value = "4" />Snake<br />
      <input type = "radio" name = "animal"
         value = "5" checked = "checked" />None
   </p>

   <p><input type = "submit" value = "Submit" /></p>

</form>
</body>
</html>
```

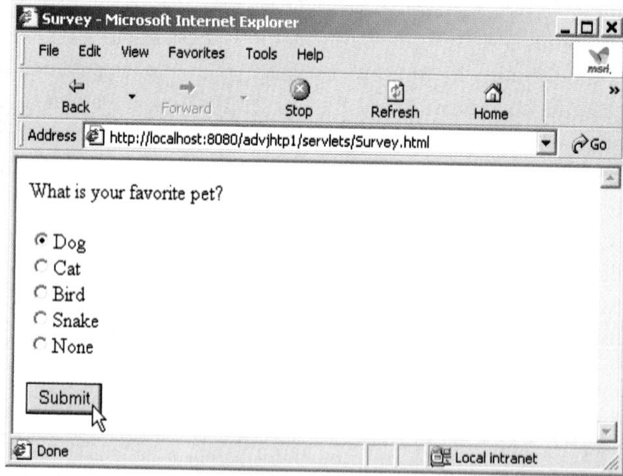

Fig. 30.29 **Survey.html** document that allows users to submit survey responses to **SurveyServlet** (part 2 of 3).

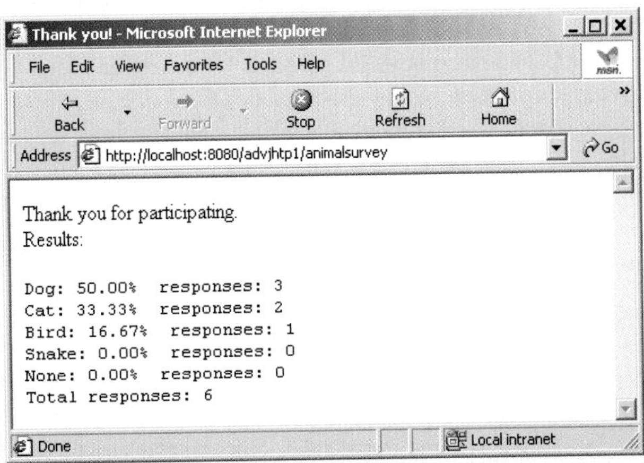

Fig. 30.29 **Survey.html** document that allows users to submit survey responses to **SurveyServlet** (part 3 of 3).

30.8.1 Configuring animalsurvey Database and SurveyServlet

The example in Fig. 30.28 and Fig. 30.29 cannot execute until we create the Cloudscape database **animalsurvey** and configure the **advjhtp1** Web application to recognize **SurveyServlet**. Before proceeding, ensure that you have installed and configured Cloudscape on your system. If you have not, download Cloudscape from the Web site **www.cloudscape.com**. Follow the provided instructions to install Cloudscape. Cloudscape executes on many platforms including Windows, Solaris, Linux, Macintosh and others. For a complete list of platforms on which Cloudscape 3.6 has been tested, visit

```
cloudweb1.cloudscape.com/support/servepage.jsp?
   page=fyi_cert36vms.html
```

The Cloudscape server must be executing to create and manipulate databases in Cloudscape. To execute the server, begin by opening a command window (i.e., an MS-DOS prompt, Command Prompt or UNIX/Linux shell). Change directories to the Cloudscape installation directory (**Cloudscape_3.6**, by default). The installation directory contains a **frameworks** subdirectory. Cloudscape comes with two frameworks in which it can execute—**embedded** and **RmiJdbc**. The **embedded** framework enables Cloudscape to execute as part of a Java application. The **RmiJdbc** framework enables Cloudscape to execute as a standalone database server. We use the standalone database server in this book. Each framework directory has a **bin** subdirectory containing batch files (Windows) and shell scripts (Linux/UNIX) to set environment variables and execute Cloudscape. Change directories to the **bin** directory in the **RmiJdbc** framework. Execute the batch file or shell script starting with the name **setServerCloudscapeCP** to set the environment variables required by the server. Then, execute batch file or shell script starting with the name **startCS** to launch the Cloudscape database server.

The examples for this chapter include a SQL script (**animalsurvey.sql**) that creates the database and its tables. Cloudscape provides an interactive command-line tool called **ij** that can execute this script. We provide a Windows batch file called **createDatabase.bat** that you can use to start **ij** and execute the SQL scripts. Both **animalsurvey.sql** and **createDatabase.bat** are included in the examples directory for this chapter on the CD that accompanies this book. To create database **animalsurvey**, ensure that the Cloudscape server is executing. Next, open a new command prompt and change directories to the **RmiJdbc** framework's **bin** directory in the Cloudscape installation directory. Then, execute the batch file **setClientCloudscapeCP.bat**. In that command prompt, change to the directory containing our examples for this chapter and type

```
createDatabase animalsurvey.sql
```

to execute the SQL script. After completing this task, the **animalsurvey** database is ready for use in **SurveyServlet**. Next, we configure the **advjhtp1** Web application.

We use our **advjhtp1** context root to demonstrate the servlet of Fig. 30.28. Place **Survey.html** in the **servlets** directory created previously. Place **SurveyServlet.class** in the **classes** subdirectory of **WEB-INF** in the **advjhtp1** context root. Then, edit the **web.xml** deployment descriptor in the **WEB-INF** directory to include the information specified in Fig. 30.30. Also, this program cannot execute in Tomcat unless the Web application is aware of the JAR files **cloudscape.jar** and **RmiJdbc.jar** that contain the Cloudscape database driver and its supporting classes. A copy of these files should be placed in the **advjhtp1** context root's **WEB-INF** subdirectory called **lib**. The file **cloudscape.jar** is located in the Cloudscape installation's **lib** subdirectory. The file **RmiJdbc.jar** is located in the **RmiJdbc** framework's **classes** subdirectory. After *copying* these files, restart Tomcat and type the following URL in your Web browser:

```
http://localhost:8080/advjhtp1/servlets/Survey.html
```

When the Web page appears, select a survey response and press the **Submit** button in the Web page to invoke the servlet.

Common Programming Error 30.4

Moving the files **cloudscape.jar** *and* **RmiJdbc.jar** *from their original locations in the Cloudscape installation prevents Cloudscape from executing properly.*

Descriptor element	Value
servlet *element*	
servlet-name	animalsurvey
description	Connecting to a database from a servlet.
servlet-class	com.deitel.advjhtp1.servlets.SurveyServlet
servlet-mapping *element*	
servlet-name	animalsurvey
url-pattern	/animalsurvey

Fig. 30.30 Deployment descriptor information for servlet **SurveyServlet**.

30.9 `HttpUtils` Class

Class **`HttpUtils`** provides three **`static`** utility methods to simplify servlet programming. These methods are discussed in Fig. 30.31.

30.10 Internet and World Wide Web Resources

This section lists a variety of servlet resources available on the Internet and provides a brief description of each.

`java.sun.com/products/servlet/index.html`
The servlet page at the Sun Microsystems, Inc., Java Web site provides access to the latest servlet information and servlet resources.

`jakarta.apache.org`
This is the Apache Project's home page for the *Jakarta Project*. *Tomcat*—the servlets and JavaServer Pages reference implementation— is one of many subprojects of the Jakarta Project.

`jakarta.apache.org/tomcat/index.html`
Home page for the Tomcat servlets and JavaServer Pages reference implementation.

`java.apache.org`
This is the Apache Project's home page for all Java-related technologies. This site provides access to many Java packages useful to servlet and JSP developers.

`www.servlets.com`
This is the Web site for the book *Java Servlet Programming* published by O'Reilly. The book provides a variety of resources. This book is an excellent resource for programmers who are learning servlets.

`theserverside.com`
TheServerSide.com is dedicated to information and resources for Enterprise Java.

`www.servletsource.com`
ServletSource.com is a general servlet resource site containing code, tips, tutorials and links to many other Web sites with information on servlets.

Method	Description
`getRequestURL`	This method takes the **`HttpServletRequest`** object as an argument and returns a **`StringBuffer`** containing the original URL that initiated the request.
`parsePostData`	This method receives an integer and **`ServletInputStream`** as arguments. The integer represents the number of bytes in the **`ServletInputStream`**. The **`ServletInputStream`** contains the key/value pairs **`post`**ed to the servlet from a **`form`**. The method returns a **`Hashtable`** containing the key/value pairs.
`parseQueryString`	This method receives a **`String`** representing the query string in a **`get`** request as an argument and returns a **`Hashtable`** containing the key/value pairs in the query string. The value of each key is an array of **`String`**s. The query string can be obtained with **`HttpServletRequest`** method **`getQueryString`**.

Fig. 30.31 **`HttpUtils`** class methods.

www.cookiecentral.com
A good all-around resource site for cookies.

www.javacorporate.com
Home of the open-source *Expresso Framework*, which includes a library of extensible servlet components to help speed Web application development.

www.servlet.com/srvdev.jhtml
ServletInc's Servlet Developers Forum provides resources for server-side Java developers and information about Web servers that support servlet technologies.

www.servletforum.com
ServletForum.com is a newsgroup where you can post questions and have them answered by your peers.

www.coolservlets.com
Provides free open-source Java servlets.

www.cetus-links.org/oo_java_servlets.html
Provides a list of links to resources on servlets and other technologies.

www.javaskyline.com
Java Skyline is an online magazine for servlet developers.

www.rfc-editor.org
The RFC Editor provides a search engine for RFCs (Request for Comments). Many of these RFCs provide details of Web-related technologies. RFCs of interest to servlet developers include *URIs* (RFC 1630), *URLs* (RFC 1738)URL, *Relative URLs* (RFC 1808), *HTTP/1.0* (RFC 1945), *MIME* (RFCs 2045–2049), *HTTP State Management Mechanism* (RFC 2109), *Use and Interpretation of HTTP Version Numbers* (RFC 2145), *Hypertext Coffee Pot Control Protocol* (RFC 2324), HTTP/1.1 (RFC 2616) and *HTTP Authentication: Basic and Digest Authentication* (RFC 2617).

www.irvine.com/~mime
The *Multipurpose Internet Mail Extensions FAQ* provides information on MIME and a list of many registered MIME types, as well as links to other MIME resources.

SUMMARY

- The classes and interfaces used to define servlets are found in packages **javax.servlet** and **javax.servlet.http**.
- The Internet offers many protocols. The HTTP protocol (Hypertext Transfer Protocol) that forms the basis of the World Wide Web uses URIs (Uniform Resource Identifiers) to locate resources on the Internet.
- Common URLs represent files or directories and can represent complex tasks such as database lookups and Internet searches.
- JavaServer Pages technology is an extension of servlet technology.
- Servlets are normally executed as part of a Web server (also known as the servlet container).
- Servlets and JavaServer Pages have become so popular that they are now supported by most major Web servers and application servers.
- All servlets must implement the **Servlet** interface. The methods of interface **Servlet** are invoked automatically by the servlet container.
- A servlet's life cycle begins when the servlet container loads the servlet into memory—normally in response to the first request to that servlet. Before the servlet can handle the first request, the servlet container invokes the servlet's **init** method. After **init** completes execution, the servlet can respond to its first request. All requests are handled by a servlet's **service** method, which

may be called many times during the life cycle of a servlet. When the servlet container terminates the servlet, the servlet's **destroy** method is called to release servlet resources.

- The servlet packages define two **abstract** classes that implement the interface **Servlet**—class **GenericServlet** and class **HttpServlet**. Most servlets extend one of these classes and override some or all of their methods with appropriate customized behaviors.
- The key method in every servlet is method **service**, which receives both a **ServletRequest** object and a **ServletResponse** object. These objects provide access to input and output streams that allow the servlet to read data from the client and send data to the client.
- Web-based servlets typically extend class **HttpServlet**. Class **HttpServlet** overrides method **service** to distinguish between the typical requests received from a client Web browser. The two most common HTTP request types (also known as request methods) are **get** and **post**.
- Class **HttpServlet** defines methods **doGet** and **doPost** to respond to **get** and **post** requests from a client, respectively. These methods are called by the **HttpServlet** class's **service** method, which is called when a request arrives at the server.
- Methods **doGet** and **doPost** receive as arguments an **HttpServletRequest** object and an **HttpServletResponse** object that enable interaction between the client and the server.
- A response is sent to the client through a **PrintWriter** object returned by the **getWriter** method of the **HttpServletResponse** object.
- The **HttpServletResponse** object's **setContentType** method specifies the MIME type of the response to the client. This enables the client browser to understand and handle the content.
- The server **localhost** (IP address **127.0.0.1**) is a well-known server host name on most computers that support TCP/IP-based networking protocols such as HTTP. This host name can be used to test TCP/IP applications on the local computer.
- The Tomcat server awaits requests from clients on port 8080. This port number must be specified as part of the URL to request a servlet running in Tomcat.
- The client can access a servlet only if that servlet is installed on a server that can respond to servlet requests. Web servers that support servlets normally have an installation procedure for servlets.
- Tomcat is a fully functional implementation of the JSP and servlet standards. It includes a Web server, so it can be used as a stand-alone test container for JSPs and servlets.
- Tomcat can be specified as the handler for JSP and servlet requests received by popular Web servers such as Apache and IIS. Tomcat also is integrated into the Java 2 Enterprise Edition reference implementation from Sun Microsystems.
- JSPs, servlets and their supporting files are deployed as part of Web applications. In Tomcat, Web applications are deployed in the **webapps** subdirectory of the Tomcat installation.
- A Web application has a well-known directory structure in which all the files that are part of the application reside. This directory structure can be set up by the Tomcat server administrator in the **webapps** directory, or the entire directory structure can be archived in a Web application archive file. Such an archive is known as a WAR file and ends with the **.war** file extension.
- If a WAR file is placed in the **webapps** directory, when the Tomcat server starts up it extracts the contents of the WAR file into the appropriate **webapps** subdirectory structure.
- The Web application directory structure is separated into a context root—the top-level directory for an entire Web application—and several subdirectories. The context root is the root directory for the Web application. All the JSPs, HTML documents, servlets and supporting files such as images and class files reside in this directory or its subdirectories. The **WEB-INF** directory contains the Web application deployment descriptor (**web.xml**). The **WEB-INF/classes** directory contains the servlet class files and other supporting class files used in a Web application. The

WEB-INF/lib directory contains Java archive (JAR) files that may include servlet class files and other supporting class files used in a Web application.

- Before deploying a Web application, the servlet container must be made aware of the context root for the Web application. In Tomcat, a **Context** element must be created in the file **server.xml** in the **conf** subdirectory of **jakarta-tomcat-3.2.3**.
- Deploying a Web application requires the creation of a deployment descriptor (**web.xml**).
- HTTP **get** requests can be typed directly into your browser's **Address** or **Location** field.
- Parameters are passed as name/value pairs in a **get** request. A **?** separates the URL from the data passed as part of a **get** request. Name/value pairs are passed with the name and the value separated by **=**. If there is more than one name/value pair, each name/value pair is separated by **&**.
- Method **getParameter** of interface **HttpServletRequest** receives the parameter name as an argument and returns the corresponding **String** value, or **null** if the parameter is not part of the request.
- An HTTP **post** request is often used to post data from an Web-page form to a server-side form handler that processes the data.
- Browsers often cache (save on disk) Web pages so they can quickly reload the pages. Browsers do not cache the server's response to a **post** request.
- Method **doPost** receives the same two arguments as **doGet**—an object that implements interface **HttpServletRequest** to represent the client's request and an object that implements interface **HttpServletResponse** to represent the servlet's response.
- Method **sendRedirect** of **HttpServletResponse** redirects a request to the specified URL.
- When a servlet uses a relative path to reference another static or dynamic resource, the servlet assumes the same context root unless a complete URL is specified for the resource.
- Once method **sendRedirect** executes, processing of the request by the servlet that called **sendRedirect** terminates.
- When redirecting requests, the request parameters from the original request are passed as parameters to the new request. Additional request parameters also can be passed.
- New parameters are added to the existing request parameters. If a new parameter has the same name as an existing parameter, the new parameter value takes precedence over the original value. However, all the values are still passed.
- The complete set of values for a given request-parameter name can be obtained by calling method **getParameterValues** from interface **HttpServletRequest**, which receives the parameter name as an argument and returns an array of **String**s containing the parameter values in order from the most recently added value for that parameter to the least recently added.
- Many Web sites today provide custom Web pages and/or functionality on a client-by-client basis.
- HTTP is a stateless protocol—it does not support persistent information that could help a Web server determine that a request is from a particular client.
- Cookies can store information on the user's computer for retrieval later in the same or in future browsing sessions.
- Cookies are text-based data that are sent by servlets (or other similar technologies) as part of responses to clients.
- Every HTTP-based interaction between a client and a server includes a header containing information about the request (when the communication is from the client to the server) or information about the response (when the communication is from the server to the client).

- When the server receives a request, the header includes information such as the request type (e.g., **get** or **post**) and the cookies stored on the client machine by the server.
- When the server formulates its response, the header information includes any cookies the server wants to store on the client computer and other information such as the MIME type of the response.
- Depending on the maximum age of a cookie, the Web browser either maintains the cookie for the duration of the browsing session or stores the cookie on the client computer for future use. When the browser requests a resource from a server, cookies previously sent to the client by that server are returned to the server as part of the request formulated by the browser. Cookies are deleted automatically when they expire.
- By default, cookies only exist for the current browsing session (until the user closes the browser). To make cookies persist beyond the current session, call **Cookie** method **setMaxAge** to indicate the number of seconds until the cookie expires.
- Method **addCookie** of interface **HttpServletResponse** adds a cookie to the response. Cookies are sent to the client as part of the HTTP header. The header information is always provided to the client first, so the cookies should be added before the response is output.
- **HttpServletRequest** method **getCookies** returns an array of **Cookie** objects. Method **getCookies** returns **null** if there are no cookies in the request.
- **Cookie** method **getName** retrieves the name of a cookie. **Cookie** method **getValue** retrieves the value of a cookie.
- Java provides enhanced session An alternative approach to cookies is to track a session with **HttpSession**s, which eliminate the problems associated with clients disabling cookies in their browsers by making the session-tracking mechanism transparent to the programmer.
- Method **getSession** of interface **HttpServletRequest** obtains an **HttpSession** object for the client.
- Like a cookie, an **HttpSession** object can store name/value pairs. In sessions, these are called attributes, and they are stored with **setAttribute** and retrieved with **getAttribute**.
- Name/value pairs added to an **HttpSession** object with **setAttribute** remain available until the client's current browsing session ends or until the session is explicitly invalidated by a call to the **HttpSession** object's **invalidate** method.
- **HttpSession** method **getID** obtains the session's unique ID number.
- **HttpSession** method **isNew** determines whether a session is new or already exists. Method **getCreationTime** obtains the time at which the session was created.
- **HttpSession** method **getLastAccessedTime** obtains the time at which the session was last accessed.
- **HttpSession** method **getMaxInactiveInterval** obtains the maximum amount of time that an **HttpSession** object can be inactive before the servlet container discards it.
- Many of today's applications are three-tier distributed applications, consisting of a user interface, business logic and database access.
- In multi-tier architectures, Web servers often represent the middle tier. They provide the business logic that manipulates data from databases and that communicates with client Web browsers.
- **Servlet** method **init** takes a **ServletConfig** argument and throws a **ServletException**. The argument provides the servlet with information about its initialization parameters that are specified in a **servlet** element in the deployment descriptor. Each parameter appears in an **init-param** element with child elements **param-name** and **param-value**.

TERMINOLOGY

addCookie method of **HttpServletResponse**
Apache Tomcat server
cache a Web page
commit a response
Context element of **server.xml** file
context root
Cookie class
delete request
deploy a Web application
deployment descriptor
destroy method of **Servlet**
doGet method of **HttpServlet**
doPost method of **HttpServlet**
GenericServlet class
get request
getAttribute method of **HttpSession**
getAttributeNames method of **HttpSession**
getCookies method of **HttpServletRequest**
getCreationTime method of **HttpSession**
getID method of **HttpSession**
getLastAccessedTime method of **HttpSession**
getMaxInactiveInterval method of **HttpSession**
getName method of **Cookie**
getOutputStream method of **HTTPServletResponse**
getParameter method of **HttpServletRequest**
getParameterNames method of **HttpServletRequest**
getParameterValues method of **HttpServletRequest**
getServletConfig method of **Servlet**
getServletInfo method of **Servlet**
getSession method of **HttpServletRequest**
getValue method of **Cookie**
getWriter method of **HTTPServletResponse**
host name
HTTP (Hypertext Transfer Protocol)
HTTP header
HTTP request
HttpServlet interface
HttpServletRequest interface
HttpServletResponse interface
HttpSession interface
init method of **Servlet**
initialization parameter
invalidate method of **HttpSession**
isNew method of **HttpSession**
Jakarta project
JAVA_HOME environment variable
javax.servlet package
javax.servlet.http package
Jigsaw Web server
localhost (**127.0.0.1**)
maximum age of a cookie
MIME type
options request
path attribute
port
post request
put request
redirect a request
request method
request parameter
sendRedirect method of **HttpServletResponse**
server.xml (Tomcat configuration file)
service method of **Servlet**
servlet
servlet container
Servlet interface
servlet life cycle
servlet mapping
ServletConfig interface
ServletContext interface
ServletException class
ServletOutputStream class
ServletRequest interface
ServletResponse interface
session tracking
setAttribute method of **HttpSession**
setContentType method of **HttpServletResponse**
shopping cart
text/html MIME type
thin client
TOMCAT_HOME environment variable
trace request
URL pattern
WAR (Web application archive) file
Web application

Web application deployment descriptor (**web.xml**)
webapps directory
WEB-INF directory
WEB-INF/classes directory
WEB-INF/lib directory
well-known port number

SELF-REVIEW EXERCISES

30.1 Fill in the blanks in each of the following statements:

a) Classes **HttpServlet** and **GenericServlet** implement the ________ interface.

b) Class **HttpServlet** defines the methods ________ and ________ to respond to **get** and **post** requests from a client.

c) **HttpServletResponse** method ________ obtains a character-based output stream that enables text data to be sent to the client.

d) The **form** attribute ________ specifies the server-side *form handler,* i.e., the program that handles the request.

e) ________ is the well-known host name that refers to your own computer.

f) **Cookie** method ________ returns a **String** the name of the cookie as set with ________ or the constructor.

g) **HttpServletRequest** method ***getSession*** returns an ________ object for the client.

30.2 State whether each of the following is *true* or *false*. If *false*, explain why.

a) Servlets usually are used on the client side of a networking application.

b) Servlet methods are executed automatically.

c) The two most common HTTP requests are **get** and **put**.

d) The well-known port number for Web requests is 55.

e) **Cookie**s never expire.

f) **HttpSession**s expire only when the browsing session ends or when the **invalidate** method is called.

g) The **HttpSession** method **getAttribute** returns the object associated with a particular name.

ANSWERS TO SELF-REVIEW EXERCISES

30.1 a) **Servlet**. b) **doGet**, **doPost**. c) **getWriter**. d) **action**. e) **localhost**. f) **getName**, **setName**. g) **HttpSession**.

30.2 a) False. Servlets are usually used on the server side. b) True. c) False. The two most common HTTP request types are **get** and **post**. d) False. The well-known port number for Web requests is 80. e) False. **Cookie**s expire when they reach their maximum age. f) True. g) True.

EXERCISES

30.3 Modify the **Cookie** example of Fig. 30.21 to list prices for each book in the book recommendations. Also, allow the user to select some or all of the recommended books and "order" them. Deploy your Web application on the Tomcat server.

30.4 Modify the **HttpSession** example of Fig. 30.25 to list prices for each book in the book recommendations. Also, allow the user to select some or all of the recommended books and "order" them. Deploy your Web application on the Tomcat server.

30.5 Create a Web application for dynamic FAQs. The application should obtain the information to create the dynamic FAQ Web page from a database that consists of a **Topics** table and an **FAQ** table. The **Topics** table should have two fields—a unique integer ID for each topic (**topicID**) and a name for each topic (**topicName**). The **FAQ** table should have three fields—the **topicID** (a foreign key), a string representing the question (**question**) and the answer to the question (**answer**). When the servlet is invoked, it should read the data from the database and return a dynamically created Web page containing each question and answer, sorted by topic.

30.6 Modify the Web application of Exercise 30.5 so that the initial request to the servlet returns a Web page of topics in the FAQ database. Then, the user can hyperlink to another servlet that returns only the frequently asked questions for a particular topic.

30.7 Modify the Web application of Fig. 30.28 to allow the user to see the survey results without responding to the survey.

30.8 Fig. 30.28 would allow users to vote as many times as they want by simply returning to the survey Web page and submitting additional votes. Modify your solution to Exercise 30.7 such that it uses cookies that last for one day to prevent users from voting more than once a day. When a user returns to the site, the cookie previously stored on their system is sent to the server. The servlet should check for the cookie and, if it exists, indicate that the client already voted in the last 24 hours. The servlet should also return the current survey results.

30.9 Modify the Web application of Fig. 30.28 to make it generic for use with any survey of the appropriate form. Use servlet parameters (as discussed in Section 30.8) to specify the survey options. When the user requests the survey, dynamically generate a **form** containing the survey options. Deploy this Web application twice using different context roots. *Note*: You may need to modify the database in this example so that it can store multiple surveys at once.

30.10 Write a Web application that consists of a servlet (**DirectoryServlet**) and several Web documents. Document **index.html** should be the first document the user sees. In that document, you should have a series of hyperlinks for other Web pages in your site. When clicked, each hyperlink should invoke the servlet with a **get** request that contains a **page** parameter. The servlet should obtain parameter **page** and redirect the request to the appropriate document.

30.11 Modify the Web application of Exercise 30.10 so that the first document the user sees in the browser is dynamically generated from servlet initialization parameters (as discussed in Section 30.8) by servlet **HomePageServlet**. There should be a separate initialization parameter for each page in the Web site. The **HomePageServlet** reads each parameter name and value and creates a **HashMap** of the parameter name/value pairs. This information should be used to create the initial home page dynamically. The **HashMap** also should be placed in the **ServletContext** with method **setAttribute**, so that the **HashMap** can be used in the **DirectoryServlet** to determine where to direct each request. The dynamic home page should have hyperlinks to each document in the Web site. As in Exercise 30.10, when the user clicks a link, servlet **DirectoryServlet** should be invoked and passed a page parameter. Then, the **DirectoryServlet** should obtain the **HashMap** from the **ServletContext**, look up the corresponding document and redirect the user to that document.

31

JavaServer Pages (JSP): Bonus for Java™ Developers (on CD)

Objectives

- To be able to create and deploy JavaServer Pages.
- To use JSP's implicit objects and Java to create dynamic Web pages.
- To specify global JSP information with directives.
- To use actions to manipulate JavaBeans in a JSP, to include other resources dynamically and to forward requests to other JSPs.
- To create custom tag libraries that encapsulate complex functionality in new tags that can be reused by JSP programmers and Web-page designers.

Chapter 31 is included on the CD that accompanies this book in printable Adobe® Acrobat® PDF format. The chapter includes pages 1119–1185.

32

e-Business & e-Commerce (on CD)

Objectives

- To understand how the Internet and World Wide Web are revolutionizing business processes.
- To introduce various business models used on the Web.
- To explore the advantages and disadvantages of creating an online business.
- To examine marketing, payment, security and legal issues that affect e-businesses.

Chapter 32 is included on the CD that accompanies this book in printable Adobe® Acrobat® PDF format. The chapter includes pages 1186–1222.

33

Multimedia: Audio, Video, Speech Synthesis and Recognition

Objectives

- To enhance Web pages with sound and video.
- To use **<bgsound>** to add background sounds.
- To use the **<img>** tag's **dynsrc** property to incorporate video into Web pages.
- To use **<embed>** to add sound or video to Web pages.
- To use the Windows Media Player ActiveX control to play a variety of media formats in Web pages.
- To use the Microsoft Agent ActiveX control to create animated characters that speak to users and respond to spoken commands from users.
- To embed a RealPlayer™ ActiveX control to allow streaming audio and video to appear in a Web page.

The wheel that squeaks the loudest … gets the grease.
John Billings (Henry Wheeler Shaw)

We'll use a signal I have tried and found far-reaching and easy to yell. Waa-hoo!
Zane Grey

TV gives everyone an image, but radio gives birth to a million images in a million brains.
Peggy Noonan

Noise proves nothing. Often a hen who has merely laid an egg cackles as if she had laid an asteroid.
Mark Twain, *Following the Equator*

Outline

33.1 Introduction

Just a few years back, the typical desktop computer's power, although considered substantial at the time, made it impossible to think of integrating high-quality audio and video into applications. Today's computers typically include CD-ROMs, sound cards and other hardware and special software which have make computer multimedia a reality. Economical desktop machines are so powerful that they can store and play DVD-quality sound and video and we expect to see a huge advance in the kinds of programmable multimedia capabilities available through programming languages.

The multimedia revolution occurred first on the desktop computer, with the widespread availability of CD-ROMs. This platform is rapidly evolving towards DVD technology, but our focus in this chapter is on the explosion of sound and video technology that appears on the World Wide Web. In general, we expect the desktop to lead with the technology, because the Web is so dependent on bandwidth, and, for the foreseeable future, Internet bandwidths for the masses are likely to lag considerably behind those available on the desktop. One thing that Deitel has learned—having been in this industry for nearly four decades now—is to plan for the impossible. In the computer and communications fields, the impossible has repeatedly become reality so many times that it is almost routine at this point.

In this chapter, we discuss how to add sound, video and animated characters to Web-based applications. Your first reaction may be a sense of caution because you realize that these are complex technologies and most readers have had little if any education in these areas. This is one of the beauties of today's programming languages. They give the programmer easy access to complex technologies and hide most of the complexity.

Multimedia files can be quite large. Some multimedia technologies require that the complete multimedia file be downloaded to the client before the audio or video begins playing. With streaming technologies, audio and video can begin playing while the files are downloading, to reduce delays. Streaming technologies are becoming increasingly popular.

Performance Tip 33.1

Multimedia is performance intensive. Although processor speed has become less of a concern over the last few years, Internet bandwidth is still a precious resource. Multimedia-based Web applications must be carefully designed to use resources wisely, or they may perform poorly.

Creating audio and video to incorporate into Web pages often requires complex and powerful software such as Adobe™ After Effects® or Macromedia™ Director®. Rather than discuss how to create media clips, this chapter focuses on using existing audio and video clips to enhance Web pages. The chapter also includes an extensive set of Internet and World Wide Web resources. Some of these Web sites display examples of interesting multimedia enhancements, others provide instructional information for developers planning to enhance their own sites with multimedia.

33.2 Audio and Video

Audio and video can be used in Web pages in a variety of ways. Audio and video files can be embedded in a Web page or placed on a Web server such that they can be downloaded "on-demand." A variety of audio and video file formats are available for different uses.

Common video file formats include *MPEG* (*Moving Pictures Experts Group*), *QuickTime*, *RealPlayer*, *AVI* (*Video for Windows*) and *MJPEG* (*Motion JPEG*). Audio formats include *MP3* (*MPEG Layer 3*), *MIDI* (*Musical Instrument Digital Interface*), *WAV* (*Windows Waveform*) and *AIFF* (*Audio Interchange File Format*—Macintosh only).

Encoding and *compression* determine a file's format. An *encoding algorithm* or *CODEC* compresses media files by taking the raw audio or video and transforming it into a format that Web pages can read. Different encoding levels and formats produce file sizes that are ideal for different applications.

Some CODECs are available to the public in the form of *encoding applications*. Most encoding applications compress audio and video files. Some serve as *format converters*, converting one file format into another.

33.3 Adding Background Sounds with the bgsound Element

Some Web sites provide background audio to create a particular "atmosphere" on the site. Various ways exist to add sound to a Web page, the simplest is the ***bgsound*** element.

Portability Tip 33.1

The **bgsound** *element is a Microsoft specific extension to XHTML.*

The **bgsound** element has four key properties—***src***, ***loop***, ***balance*** and ***volume***. To change the property values via a script, assign a scripting name to the **bgsound** element's ***id*** property.

Software Engineering Observation 33.1

The **bgsound** *element should be placed in the* **head** *section of the XHTML document.*

The **src** property specifies the URL of the audio clip to play. Internet Explorer supports a wide variety of audio formats.

Software Engineering Observation 33.2

The audio clip specified with **bgsound**'*s* **src** *property can be any type supported by Internet Explorer.*

The **loop** property specifies the number of times the audio clip will play. The value **-1** (the default) specifies that the audio clip should loop until users browse a different Web page or click the browser's **Stop** button. A positive integer indicates the exact number of times the audio clip should loop. Negative values (except **-1**) and zero values for this property cause the audio clip to play once.

The **balance** property specifies the balance between the left and right speakers. The value for this property is between **-10000** (sound only from the left speaker) and **10000** (sound only from the right speaker). The default value, **0**, indicates that the sound should be balanced between the two speakers.

Software Engineering Observation 33.3

Scripting cannot set **bgsound** *property* **balance**.

The **volume** property determines the volume of the audio clip. The value for this property is between **-10000** (minimum volume) and **0** (maximum volume). The default value is **0**.

Software Engineering Observation 33.4

The volume specified with **bgsound** *property* **volume** *is relative to the current volume setting on the client computer. If the client computer has sound turned off, the* **volume** *property has no effect.*

Portability Tip 33.2

On most computers, the minimum audible volume for **bgsound** *property* **volume** *is a value much greater than* **-10000**. *This value depends on the machine.*

The XHTML document of Fig. 33.1 demonstrates the **bgsound** element and scripting the element's properties. This example's audio clip came from the Microsoft Developer Network's downloads site,

```
msdn.microsoft.com/downloads/default.asp
```

This site contains many free images and sounds. [*Note*: Many of the examples in this chapter require an Internet connection to access certain audio or video files.]

The code in lines 10–12 specify the media source. The **loop** property specifies that the audio clip plays only once. The **balance** and **volume** attributes are omitted so they default to **0**.

Function **changeProperties** lines 16–23 is called in line 49 when the **Set Properties** button is clicked. Lines 18–19 read the new value for property **loop** from the form's **loopit** text field, convert the value to an integer and set the new property value by assigning a value to **audio.loop** (where **audio** is the **id** of the **bgsound** element and **loop** is the scripting name of the property).

Lines 21–22 read the new value for the **volume** property from the form's **vol** text field, convert the value to an integer and set the new property value by assigning a value to **audio.volume** (where **volume** is the scripting name of the property).

```
1  <?xml version = "1.0"?>
2  <!DOCTYPE html PUBLIC "-//W3C//DTD XHTML 1.0 Transitional//EN"
3     "http://www.w3.org/TR/xhtml1/DTD/xhtml1-transitional.dtd">
4
5  <!-- Fig. 33.1: BackgroundAudio.html    -->
6  <!-- Demonstrating the bgsound element -->
7
8  <html xmlns = "http://www.w3.org/1999/xhtml">
9     <head><title>The bgsound Element</title>
10       <bgsound id = "audio" src =
11          "http://msdn.microsoft.com/downloads/sounds/jazzgos.mid"
12          loop = "1"></bgsound>
13
14       <script type = "text/javascript">
15          <!--
16          function changeProperties()
17          {
18             var loop = parseInt( audioForm.loopit.value );
19             audio.loop = ( isNaN( loop ) ? 1 : loop );
20
21             var vol = parseInt( audioForm.vol.value );
22             audio.volume = ( isNaN( vol ) ? 0 : vol );
23          }
24          // -->
25       </script>
26    </head>
27
28    <body>
29       <h1>Background Music via the bgsound Element</h1>
30       <h2>Jazz Gospel</h2>
31
32       This sound is from the free sound downloads at the
33       <a href =
34          "http://msdn.microsoft.com/downloads/default.asp">
35          Microsoft Developer Network</a> downloads site.
36       <hr />
37       Use the fields below to change the number of iterations
38       and the volume for the audio clip<br />
39       Press <strong>Stop</strong> to stop playing the sound.
40       <br />Press <strong>Refresh</strong> to begin playing
41       the sound again.
42
43       <form name = "audioForm" action = "">
44       <p>Loop [-1 = loop forever]</p>
45          <input name = "loopit" type = "text" value = "1" />
46          <br />Volume [-10000 (low) to 0 (high)]
47          <input name = "vol" type = "text" value = "0" /><br />
48          <input type = "button" value = "Set Properties"
49                onclick = "changeProperties()" />
```

Fig. 33.1 Demonstrating background audio with **bgsound** (part 1 of 2).

```
        </form>
    </body>
</html>
```

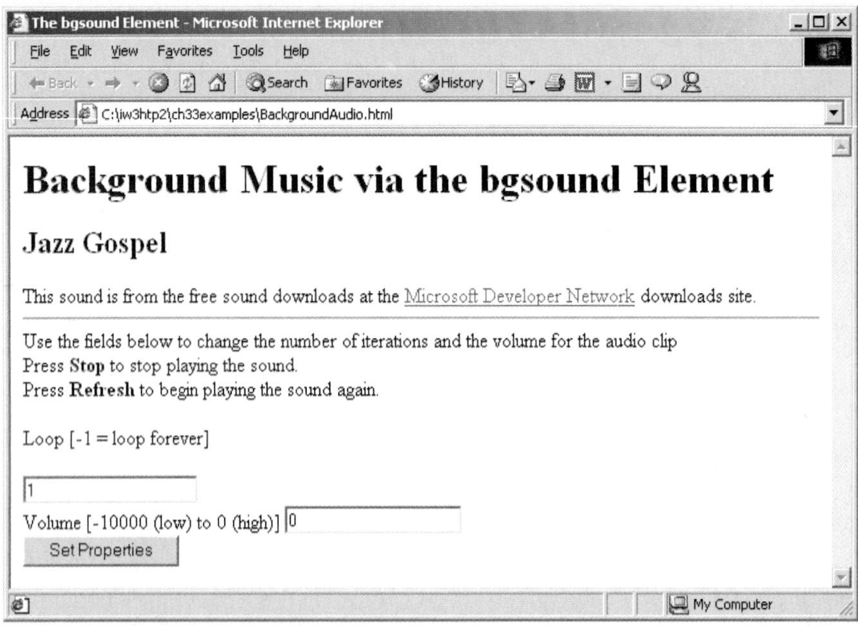

Fig. 33.1 Demonstrating background audio with **bgsound** (part 2 of 2).

33.4 Adding Video with the img Element's dynsrc Property

Users can tremendously enhance the multimedia presentations by incorporating a variety of video formats into their Web pages. The **img** element (introduced in Chapter 4) incorporates both images and videos in a Web page. The **src** property, shown previously, indicates that the source is an image. The ***dynsrc*** (i.e., dynamic source) property indicates that the source is a video clip. The ***dynsrc*** property may have other properties such as **loop**, which is similar to the **bgsound loop** property. The XHTML document of Fig. 33.2 demonstrates the **img** element and its **dynsrc** property.

Portability Tip 33.3

*The **dynsrc** property of the **img** element is specific to Internet Explorer.*

```
<?xml version = "1.0"?>
<!DOCTYPE html PUBLIC "-//W3C//DTD XHTML 1.0 Transitional//EN"
   "http://www.w3.org/TR/xhtml1/DTD/xhtml1-transitional.dtd">

```

Fig. 33.2 Playing a video with the **img** element's **dynsrc** property (part 1 of 2).

```
<!-- Fig. 33.2: Dynamicimg.html                             -->
<!-- Demonstrating the img element's dynsrc property -->

<html xmlns = "http://www.w3.org/1999/xhtml">
   <head>
      <title>An Embedded Video Using the dynsrc Property</title>
      <bgsound src =
         "http://msdn.microsoft.com/downloads/sounds/carib.MID"
         loop = "-1"></bgsound>
   </head>

   <body>
      <h1>An Embedded Video Using the img element's
         dynsrc Property</h1>
      <h2>Car and Carribean Music</h2>
      <table>
         <tr><td><img dynsrc = "car_hi.wmv"
                  start = "mouseover" width = "180"
                  height = "135" loop = "-1"
                  alt = "Car driving in circles" /></td>
            <td>This page will play the audio clip and video
               in a loop.<br />The video will not begin
               playing until you move the mouse over the
               video.<br />Press <strong>Stop</strong> to
               stop playing the sound and the video.</td>
         </tr>
      </table>
   </body>
</html>
```

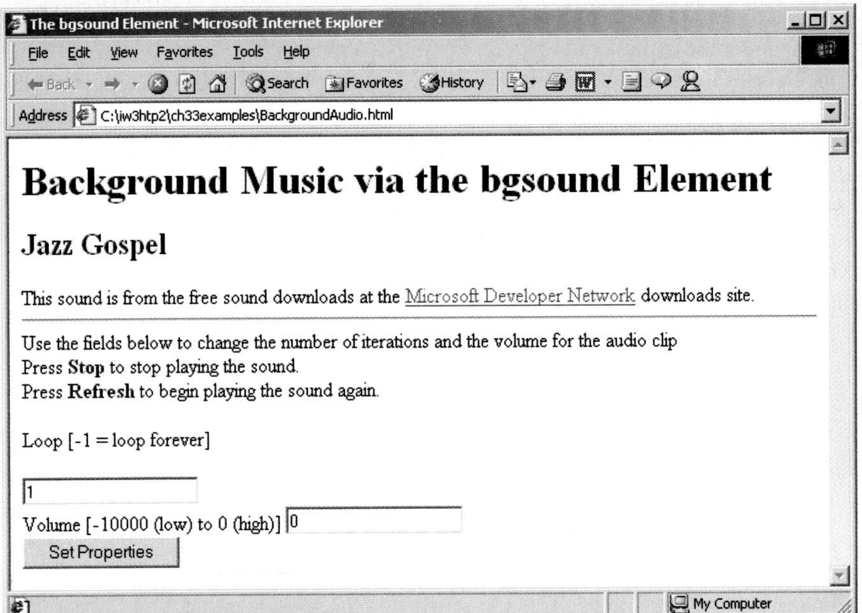

Fig. 33.2 Playing a video with the **`img`** element's **`dynsrc`** property (part 2 of 2).

The **img** element in lines 21–24 uses the **dynsrc** property to load and display the video **car_hi.wmv**. Property ***start*** specifies when the video should start playing. There are two possible start events—***fileopen*** indicates that the video should play as soon as it loads into the browser, and ***mouseover*** indicates that the video should play when users first position the mouse over the video.

33.5 Adding Audio or Video with the embed Element

Previously, we used elements **bgsound** and **img** to embed audio and video in a Web page. In both cases, users of the page have little control over the media clip. In this section, we introduce the ***embed*** element, which embeds a media clip (audio or video) into a Web page. The **embed** element displays a graphical user interface that gives users direct control over the media clip. When the browser encounters a media clip in an **embed** element, the browser plays the clip with the player registered to handle that media type on the client computer. For example, if the media clip is a **wave** file (i.e., a Windows Wave file), Internet Explorer typically uses the Windows Media Player ActiveX control to play the clip. The Windows Media Player has a GUI that enables users to play, pause and stop the media clip. Users can also control the volume of audio and move forward and backward through the clip using the GUI. [*Note*: Section 33.5 discusses embedding the Windows Media Player ActiveX control in a Web page.]

The **embed** element is supported by both Microsoft Internet Explorer and Netscape Communicator, however it is not part of the XHTML 1.0 recommendation. Documents written in XHTML using the **embed** element should render properly in either browser, however, errors may occur when trying to validate the document using the World Wide Web Consortium's XHTML 1.0 validator.

The XHTML document of Fig. 33.3 modifies the **wave** filter example from Chapter 15 by using an **embed** element to add audio to the Web page.

Line 58 uses the **embed** element to specify that the audio file **humming.wav** should be embedded in the Web page. The ***loop*** property indicates that the media clip should loop indefinitely. The **width** and **height** properties define the size of the controls for the sound clip. By default, the GUI for the media player is displayed. To prevent the GUI from appearing in the Web page, add the ***hidden*** property to the **<embed>** element. To script the element, specify a scripting name by adding the **id** property to the **<embed>** element.

The **embed** element can specify video clips as well as audio clips. Figure 33.4 demonstrates an embedded video. The **embed** element that loads and plays the video is located in line 18.

```
1  <?xml version = "1.0"?>
2  <!DOCTYPE html PUBLIC "-//W3C//DTD XHTML 1.0 Transitional//EN"
3     "http://www.w3.org/TR/xhtml1/DTD/xhtml1-transitional.dtd">
4
5  <!-- Fig. 33.3: EmbeddedAudio.html          -->
6  <!-- Background Audio via the embed Element -->
7
```

Fig. 33.3 Embedding audio with the **embed** element (part 1 of 3).

```
<html xmlns = "http://www.w3.org/1999/xhtml">
   <head>
      <title>Background Audio via the embed Element</title>
      <style type = "text/css">
         span    { width: 600 }
         .big    { color: blue;
                   font-family: sans-serif;
                   font-size: 50pt;
                   font-weight: bold }
      </style>

      <script type = "text/javascript">
         <!--
         var TimerID;
         var updown = true;
         var str = 1;

         function start()
         {
            TimerID = window.setInterval( "wave()", 100 );
         }

         function wave()
         {
            if ( str > 20 || str < 1 )
               updown = !updown;

            if ( updown )
               str++;
            else
               str--;

            wft.filters( "wave" ).phase = str * 30;
            wft.filters( "wave" ).strength = str;
         }
         // -->
      </script>
   </head>

   <body onload = "start()">
      <h1>Background Audio via the embed Element</h1>
      <p>Click the text to stop the script.</p>

      <p class = "big" align = "center">
      <span onclick = "window.clearInterval( TimerID )"
         id = "wft" style = "filter:wave(
         add = 0, freq = 3, light = 0, phase = 0, strength = 5)">
         WAVE FILTER EFFECT</p></span>

      <p>These controls can be used to control the audio.</p>
      <embed src = "humming.wav" loop = "true"></embed>
   </body>
</html>
```

Fig. 33.3 Embedding audio with the **embed** element (part 2 of 3).

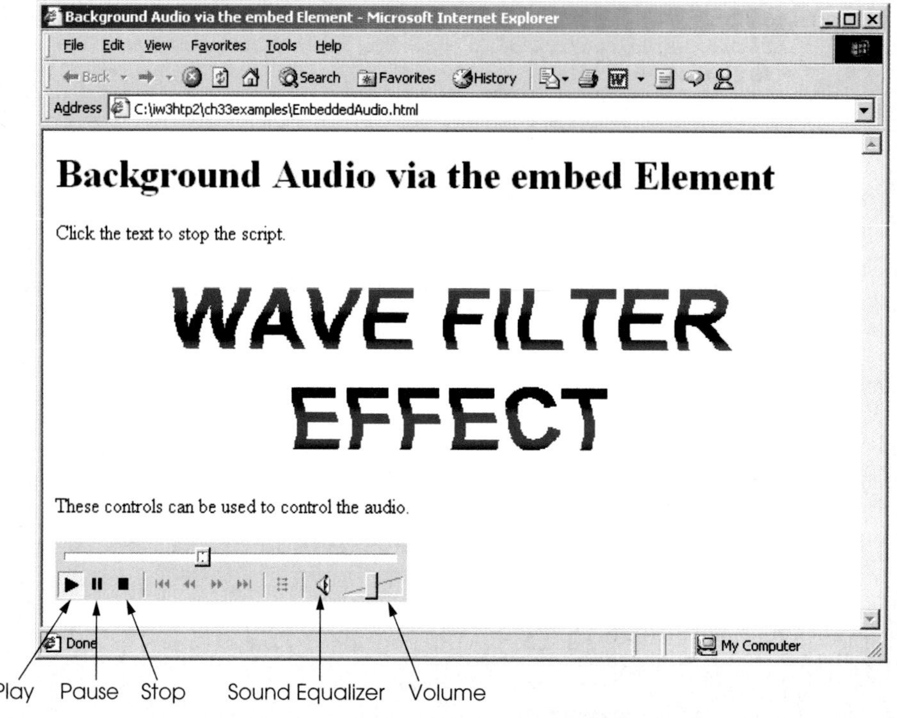

Fig. 33.3 Embedding audio with the **embed** element (part 3 of 3).

33.6 Using the Windows Media Player ActiveX Control

ActiveX controls enhance the functionality of Web pages with interactivity. In this section, we embed the *Windows Media Player ActiveX control* in Web pages, so that we can access a wide range of media formats supported by the Windows Media Player. The Windows Media Player and other ActiveX controls are embedded into Web pages with the ***object*** element.

```
<?xml version = "1.0"?>
<!DOCTYPE html PUBLIC "-//W3C//DTD XHTML 1.0 Transitional//EN"
   "http://www.w3.org/TR/xhtml1/DTD/xhtml1-transitional.dtd">

<!-- Fig. 33.4: EmbeddedVideo.html -->
<!-- Video via the embed Element   -->

<html xmlns = "http://www.w3.org/1999/xhtml">
   <head>
      <title>Video via the embed Element</title>
   </head>

```

Fig. 33.4 Embedding video with the **embed** element (part 1 of 2).

```
   <body>
      <h1>Displaying a Video using the embed Element</h1>
      <h2>Car Driving in Circles</h2>

      <table>
         <tr><td><embed src = "car_hi.wmv" loop = "false"
                    width = "240" height = "176">
                </embed></td>
         </tr></table>
      <hr />
      This page plays the video once.<br />
      Use the controls on the embedded video player to play the
      video again.
   </body>
</html>
```

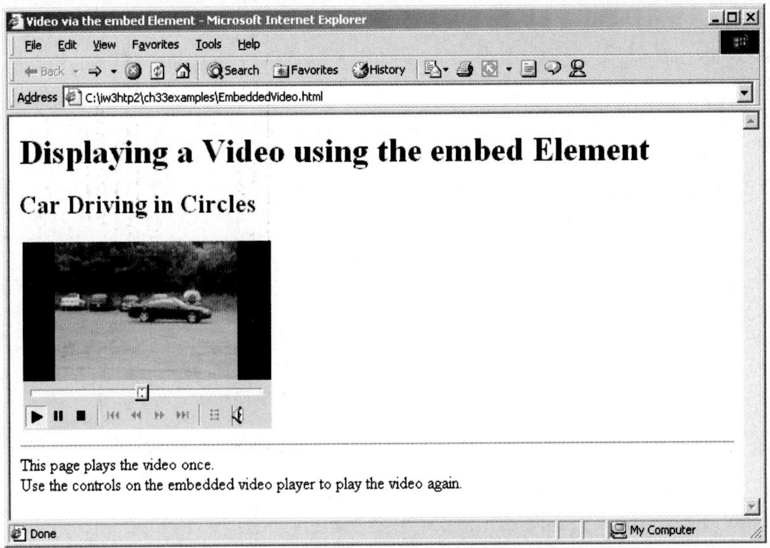

Fig. 33.4 Embedding video with the **embed** element (part 2 of 2).

The XHTML document of Fig. 33.5 demonstrates how to use the **object** element to embed two Windows Media Player ActiveX controls in the Web page. One of the controls plays a video. The other control plays an audio clip.

```
<?xml version = "1.0"?>
<!DOCTYPE html PUBLIC "-//W3C//DTD XHTML 1.0 Transitional//EN"
   "http://www.w3.org/TR/xhtml1/DTD/xhtml1-transitional.dtd">

<!-- Fig. 33.5: MediaPlayer.html    -->
<!-- Embedded Media Player Objects -->
```

Fig. 33.5 Using the **object** element to embed the Windows Media Player ActiveX control in a Web page (part 1 of 3).

```

<html xmlns = "http://www.w3.org/1999/xhtml">
   <head><title>Embedded Media Player Objects</title>
      <script type = "text/javascript">
         <!--
         var videoPlaying = true;

         function toggleVideo( b )
         {
            videoPlaying = !videoPlaying;
            b.value = videoPlaying ?
               "Pause Video" : "Play Video";
            videoPlaying ?
               VideoPlayer.Play() : VideoPlayer.Pause();
         }
         // -->
      </script>
   </head>

   <body>
      <h1>
         Audio and video through embedded Media Player objects
      </h1>
      <hr />
      <table>
         <tr><td valign = "top" align = "center">
         <object id = "VideoPlayer" width = "200" height = "225"
            classid =
               "CLSID:22d6f312-b0f6-11d0-94ab-0080c74c7e95">
            <param name = "FileName" value =
               "car_hi.wmv" />
            <param name = "AutoStart" value = "true" />
            <param name = "ShowControls" value = "false" />
            <param name = "Loop" value = "true" />
         </object></td>
         <td valign = "bottom" align = "center">
         <p>Use the controls below to control the audio clip.</p>
         <object id = "AudioPlayer"
            classid =
               "CLSID:22d6f312-b0f6-11d0-94ab-0080c74c7e95">
            <param name = "FileName" value =
   "http://msdn.microsoft.com/downloads/sounds/carib.mid" />
            <param name = "AutoStart" value = "true" />
            <param name = "Loop" value = "true" />
         </object></td></tr>

         <tr><td valign = "top" align = "center">
            <input name = "video" type = "button" value =
               "Pause Video" onclick = "toggleVideo( this )" />
            </td></tr>
      </table>
   </body>
</html>
```

Fig. 33.5 Using the `object` element to embed the Windows Media Player ActiveX control in a Web page (part 2 of 3).

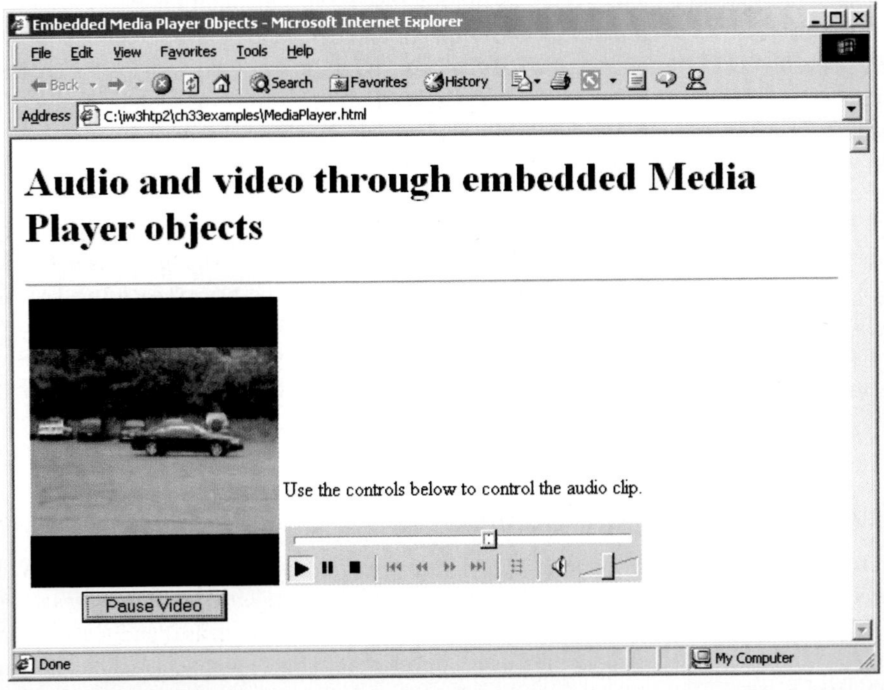

Fig. 33.5 Using the **object** element to embed the Windows Media Player ActiveX control in a Web page (part 3 of 3).

When the **body** of this document loads, two instances of the Windows Media Player ActiveX control are created. The **object** element in lines 33–41 creates a Media Player object for the file **car_hi.wmv** (specified on line 37). Line 33 indicates the start of the embedded **object** definition. The ***id*** property specifies the scripting name of the element (i.e., **VideoPlayer**). The ***width*** and ***height*** properties specify the width and height in pixels that controls occupy in a Web page. On lines 34–35, property ***classid*** specifies the ActiveX control ID for the Windows Media Player. ActiveX controls have unique **classid**s which identify them. A complete list of ActiveX controls available free for download is found at **browserwatch.internet.com/activex/activex-big.html**. Another site that provides information about ActiveX is **www.active-x.com**.

Software Engineering Observation 33.5

Most authoring tools that can embed ActiveX controls allow the user to choose an ActiveX control by selecting it from a list of available controls.

Lines 36–40 specify *parameters* that are passed to the control when it is created in the Web page. Each parameter is specified with a ***param*** element that has ***name*** and ***value*** properties. The ***FileName*** parameter specifies the file containing the media clip. The ***AutoStart*** parameter is a boolean value indicating whether or not the media clip plays when it is loaded. The ***ShowControls*** parameter is a boolean value indicating whether the Media Player controls should be displayed. The **Loop** parameter is a boolean value indicating whether the Media Player should play the media clip indefinitely.

The **object** element in lines 44–51 embeds another Media Player object in the Web page. This Media Player plays the MIDI file **carib.mid** (specified with the **FileName** parameter). A *MIDI* (*Musical Instrument Digital Interface*) file is a sound file that conforms to the MIDI standard for digital music playback. The Media Player starts playing the clip when it is loaded (specified by the **AutoStart** parameter) and infinitely loops the audio clip (specified with the **Loop** parameter).

The script at lines 10–23 shows that the Media Player can be controlled from a script. Clicking **Pause Video** calls function **toggleVideo** (line 14). The button is defined in the XHTML form in lines 54–55. The **onclick** event sets the **toggleVideo** function as the event handler passes **this** as an argument for the function. This event changes the button text in lines 17–18. Lines 19–20 use the boolean variable **videoPlaying** to determine whether to call **VideoPlayer**'s **Play** or **Pause** methods which play or pause the video clip, respectively.

33.7 Microsoft® Agent Control

Microsoft Agent is an exciting technology for *interactive animated characters* in a Windows application or World Wide Web page. The *Microsoft Agent control* provides access to *Agent characters* such as *Peedy* (a parrot), *Genie, Merlin* (a wizard) and *Robby* (a robot)—as well as those created by third-party developers. These Agent characters allow users to interact with the application using more natural human communication techniques. The control accepts both mouse and keyboard interactions, speaks (if a compatible text-to-speech engine is installed) and also supports speech recognition (if a compatible speech recognition engine is installed). With these capabilities, Web pages can speak to users and actually respond to their voice commands. Users can create new characters with the help of the *Microsoft Agent Character Editor* and the *Microsoft Linguistic Sound Editing Tool* (both downloadable from the Microsoft Agent Web site). In this section, we introduce the Microsoft Agent control.

The software for Microsoft Agent is on the CD-ROM that accompanies this book and may be downloaded from Microsoft's Web site **msdn.microsoft.com/library/en-us/dnagent/html/agentdevdl.asp**. This page also provides links to download the *Lernout and Hauspie TruVoice text-to-speech (TTS) engine* and the *Microsoft Speech Recognition engine*, ActiveX controls that power voice integration with Microsoft Agent. [*Note*: The *Lernout and Hauspie TruVoice text-to-speech (TTS) engine* is a 6 MB download. The download process may take some time from the Microsoft Web site. It is advisable to install this component directly from the CD-ROM included with this book.]

Figure 33.6 demonstrates the Microsoft Agent ActiveX control and the Lernout and Hauspie TruVoice text-to-speech engine (also an ActiveX control). This XHTML document embeds each of these ActiveX controls into a Web page that acts as a tutorial for the various types of programming tips presented in this text. Peedy the Parrot displays and speaks text that describes each of the programming tips. When the user clicks the icon for a programming tip, Peedy jumps to that tip and recites the appropriate text.

To run this example, install the Microsoft Agent character Peedy from the accompanying CD. Locate the **Peedy.acs** file on your computer, and change

```
"C:\\WINNT\\msagent\\chars\\Peedy.acs"
```

to reflect the physical path to the file on your computer. [*Note*: make sure all backslashes are preceded by a second backslash.] If you would like to run this example from the Internet, change

```
"C:\\WINNT\\msagent\\chars\\Peedy.acs"
```

to

```
"http://agent.microsoft.com/agent2/chars/peedy/peedy.acf"
```

Performance Tip 33.2

The Microsoft Agent control and the Lernout and Hauspie TruVoice TTS engine will be downloaded automatically from the Microsoft Agent Web site if they are not already installed on your computer. Downloading these controls in advance allows the Web page to use Microsoft Agent and the TTS engine as soon as the Web page is loaded.

Testing and Debugging Tip 33.1

The Microsoft Agent characters and animations are downloadable from the Microsoft Agent Web site. You can download the character information onto your local computer and modify the Microsoft Agent examples to load character data from the local computer for demonstration purposes.

The first screen capture illustrates Peedy finishing his introduction. The second screen capture shows Peedy jumping toward the *Common Programming Error* icon. The last screen capture shows Peedy finishing his discussion of *Common Programming Errors*.

Before using Microsoft Agent or the Lernout and Hauspie TruVoice TTS engine in the Web page, both must load into the Web page via **`object`** elements. Lines 13–16 embed an instance of the Microsoft Agent ActiveX control into the Web page and give it the scripting name **`agent`** via the **`id`** property. Similarly, lines 19–22 embed an instance of the Lernout and Hauspie TruVoice TTS engine into the Web page. This object is not scripted directly by the Web page. The Microsoft Agent uses the TTS engine control to speak the text that Microsoft Agent displays. If either of these controls is not already installed on the computer browsing the Web page, the browser attempts to download that control from the Microsoft Web site. The ***`codebase`*** attribute (lines 15 and 21) specifies the URL from which to download this version of the software (Version 2 for the Microsoft Agent control and Version 6 for the Lernout and Hauspie TruVoice TTS engine). The Microsoft Agent documentation discusses how to place these controls on a server for clients to download. [*Note*: Placing these controls on your own server requires a license from Microsoft.]

The **`body`** of the document (lines 198–250) defines a **`table`** containing the seven programming tip icons. Each tip icon is given a scripting name via its **`img`** element's **`name`** property. The scripting name changes the background color of the **`img`** element when users click it to receive an explanation of that tip type. Each **`img`** element's **`onclick`** event is registered as function **`imageSelectTip`**, defined at line 138. Each **`img`** element passes itself (i.e., **`this`**) to function **`imageSelectTip`** so the function can determine the particular user-selected image.

The XHTML document contains four separate **`script`** elements. The **`script`** element at lines 30–168 defines global variables used in all the **`script`** elements and defines functions **loadAgent** (called in response to the **body** element's **onload** event), **imageSelectTip** (called when users click an **img** element) and **tellMeAboutIt** (called by **imageSelectTip** to speak a few sentences about a tip).

Function **loadAgent** is particularly important because it loads the Microsoft Agent character that is used in this example. Lines 97–98 use the Microsoft Agent control's ***Characters*** collection to load the character information for Peedy. Method ***Load*** of the **Characters** collection takes two arguments. The first argument specifies a name for the character that can be used later to interact with that character, and the second argument specifies the location of the character's data file (**Peedy.acs** in this example).

```
1  <?xml version = "1.0"?>
2  <!DOCTYPE html PUBLIC "-//W3C//DTD XHTML 1.0 Transitional//EN"
3     "http://www.w3.org/TR/xhtml1/DTD/xhtml1-transitional.dtd">
4
5  <!-- Fig. 33.6: tutorial.html -->
6  <!-- Microsoft Agent Control  -->
7
8  <html xmlns = "http://www.w3.org/1999/xhtml">
9     <head>
10       <title>Speech Recognition</title>
11
12       <!-- Microsoft Agent ActiveX Control -->
13       <object id = "agent" width = "0" height = "0"
14          classid = "CLSID:D45FD31B-5C6E-11D1-9EC1-00C04FD7081F"
15          codebase = "#VERSION = 2, 0, 0, 0">
16       </object>
17
18       <!-- Lernout & Hauspie TruVoice text to speech engine -->
19       <object width = "0" height = "0"
20          classid = "CLSID:B8F2846E-CE36-11D0-AC83-00C04FD97575"
21          codebase = "#VERSION = 6, 0, 0, 0">
22       </object>
23
24       <!-- Microsoft Speech Recognition Engine -->
25       <object width = "0" height = "0"
26          classid = "CLSID:161FA781-A52C-11d0-8D7C-00A0C9034A7E"
27          codebase = "#VERSION = 4, 0, 0, 0">
28       </object>
29
30       <script type = "text/javascript">
31          <!--
32
33          var currentImage = null;
34          var tips =
35             [ "gpp", "seo", "perf", "port",
36               "gui", "dbt", "cpe" ];
37          var tipNames = [
38             "Good Programming Practice",
39             "Software Engineering Observation",
40             "Performance Tip", "Portability Tip",
```

Fig. 33.6 Demonstrating Microsoft Agent and the Lernout and Hauspie TruVoice text-to-speech (TTS) engine (part 1 of 7).

```
            "Look-and-Feel Observation",
            "Testing and Debugging Tip",
            "Common Programming Error" ];
         var voiceTips = [
            "Good [Programming Practice]",
            "Software [Engineering Observation]",
            "Performance [Tip]",
            "Portability [Tip]",
            "Look-and-Feel [Observation]",
            "Testing [and Debugging Tip]",
            "Common [Programming Error]" ];
         var explanations = [
            // Good Programming Practice text
            "Good Programming Practices highlight " +
            "techniques for writing programs that are " +
            "clearer, more understandable, more " +
            "debuggable, and more maintainable.",

            // Software Engineering Observation text
            "Software Engineering Observations highlight " +
            "architectural and design issues that affect " +
            "the construction of complex software systems.",

            // Performance Tip text
            "Performance Tips highlight opportunities for " +
            "improving program performance.",

            // Portability Tip text
            "Portability Tips help students write portable " +
            "code that can execute in different Web browsers.",

            // Look-and-Feel Observation text
            "Look-and-Feel Observations highlight graphical " +
            "user interface conventions. These observations " +
            "help students design their own graphical user " +
            "interfaces in conformance with industry " +
            "standards.",

            // Testing and Debugging Tip text
            "Testing and Debugging Tips tell people how to " +
            "test and debug their programs. Many of the " +
            "tips also describe aspects of creating Web " +
            "pages and scripts that reduce the likelihood " +
            "of 'bugs' and thus simplify the testing and " +
            "debugging process.",

            // Common Programming Error text
            "Common Programming Errors focus the students' " +
            "attention on errors commonly made by beginning " +
            "programmers. This helps students avoid making " +
            "the same errors. It also helps reduce the long " +
            "lines outside instructors' offices during " +
```

Fig. 33.6 Demonstrating Microsoft Agent and the Lernout and Hauspie TruVoice text-to-speech (TTS) engine (part 2 of 7).

```
            "office hours!" ];

         function loadAgent()
         {
            agent.Characters.Load( "Peedy",
               "C:\\WINNT\\msagent\\chars\\Peedy.acs" );
            actor = agent.Characters.Character( "Peedy" );
            actor.LanguageID = 0x0409; // sometimes needed

            // get states from server
            actor.Get( "state", "Showing" );
            actor.Get( "state", "Speaking" );
            actor.Get( "state", "Hiding" );

            // get Greet animation and do Peedy introduction
            actor.Get( "animation", "Greet" );
            actor.MoveTo( screenLeft, screenTop - 100 );
            actor.Show();
            actor.Play( "Greet" );
            actor.Speak( "Hello. " +
               "If you would like me to tell you about a " +
               "programming tip, click its icon, or, press " +
               "the 'Scroll Lock' key, and speak the name " +
               "of the tip, into your microphone." );

            // get other animations
            actor.Get( "animation", "Idling" );
            actor.Get( "animation", "MoveDown" );
            actor.Get( "animation", "MoveUp" );
            actor.Get( "animation", "MoveLeft" );
            actor.Get( "animation", "MoveRight" );
            actor.Get( "animation", "GetAttention" );
            actor.Get( "animation", "GetAttentionReturn" );

            // set up voice commands
            for ( var i = 0; i < tips.length; ++i )
               actor.Commands.Add( tips[ i ],
                  tipNames[ i ], voiceTips[ i ], true, true );

            actor.Commands.Caption = "Programming Tips";
            actor.Commands.Voice = "Programming Tips";
            actor.Commands.Visible = true;
         }

         function imageSelectTip( tip )
         {
            for ( var i = 0; i < document.images.length; ++i )
               if ( document.images( i ) == tip )
                  tellMeAboutIt( i );
         }

```

Fig. 33.6 Demonstrating Microsoft Agent and the Lernout and Hauspie TruVoice text-to-speech (TTS) engine (part 3 of 7).

```
         function voiceSelectTip( cmd )
         {
            var found = false;

            for ( var i = 0; i < tips.length; ++i )
               if ( cmd.Name == tips[ i ] ) {
                  found = true;
                  break;
            }

            if ( found )
               tellMeAboutIt( i );
         }

         function tellMeAboutIt( element )
         {
            currentImage = document.images( element );
            currentImage.style.background = "red";
            actor.MoveTo(
               currentImage.offsetParent.offsetLeft,
               currentImage.offsetParent.offsetTop + 30 );
            actor.Speak( explanations[ element ] );
         }
         // -->
      </script>

      <script type = "text/javascript" for = "agent"
            event = "Command( cmd )">
         <!--
         voiceSelectTip( cmd );
         // -->
      </script>

      <script type = "text/javascript" for = "agent"
            event = "BalloonHide">
         <!--
         if ( currentImage != null ) {
            currentImage.style.background = "lemonchiffon";
            currentImage = null;
         }
         // -->
      </script>

      <script type = "text/javascript" for = "agent"
         event = "Click">
         <!--
         actor.Play( "GetAttention" );
         actor.Speak( "Stop poking me with that pointer!" );
         actor.Play( "GetAttentionReturn" );
         // -->
      </script>
   </head>
```

Fig. 33.6 Demonstrating Microsoft Agent and the Lernout and Hauspie TruVoice text-to-speech (TTS) engine (part 4 of 7).

```

   <body style = "background-color: lemonchiffon"
         onload = "loadAgent()">
      <table border = "0">
         <tr>
            <th colspan = "4">
               <h1 style = "color: blue">
                  Deitel Programming Tips
                </h1>
            </th>
         </tr>
         <tr>
            <td align = "center" valign = "top" width = "120">
               <img id = "gpp" src = "GPP_100h.gif"
                    alt = "Good Programming Practice" border =
                    "0" onclick = "imageSelectTip( this )" />
               <br />Good Programming Practices</td>
            <td align = "center" valign = "top" width = "120">
               <img id = "seo" src = "SEO_100h.gif"
                    alt = "Software Engineering Observation"
                    border = "0"
                    onclick = "imageSelectTip( this )" />
               <br />Software Engineering Observations</td>
            <td align = "center" valign = "top" width = "120">
               <img id = "perf" src = "PERF_100h.gif"
                    alt = "Performance Tip" border = "0"
                    onclick = "imageSelectTip( this )" />
               <br />Performance Tips</td>
            <td align = "center" valign = "top" width = "120">
               <img id = "port" src = "PORT_100h.gif"
                    alt = "Portability Tip" border = "0"
                    onclick = "imageSelectTip( this )" />
               <br />Portability Tips</td>
         </tr>
         <tr>
            <td align = "center" valign = "top" width = "120">
               <img id = "gui" src = "GUI_100h.gif"
                    alt = "Look-and-Feel Observation" border =
                    "0" onclick = "imageSelectTip( this )" />
               <br />Look-and-Feel Observations</td>
            <td align = "center" valign = "top" width = "120">
               <img id = "dbt" src = "DBT_100h.gif"
                    alt = "Testing and Debugging Tip" border =
                    "0" onclick = "imageSelectTip( this )" />
               <br />Testing and Debugging Tips</td>
            <td align = "center" valign = "top" width = "120">
               <img id = "cpe" src = "CPE_100h.gif"
                    alt = "Common Programming Error" border =
                    "0" onclick = "imageSelectTip( this )" />
               <br />Common Programming Errors</td>
         </tr>
      </table>
```

Fig. 33.6 Demonstrating Microsoft Agent and the Lernout and Hauspie TruVoice text-to-speech (TTS) engine (part 5 of 7).

```
      <img src = "agent_button.gif" style = "position: absolute;
         bottom: 10px; right: 10px" />
   </body>
</html>
```

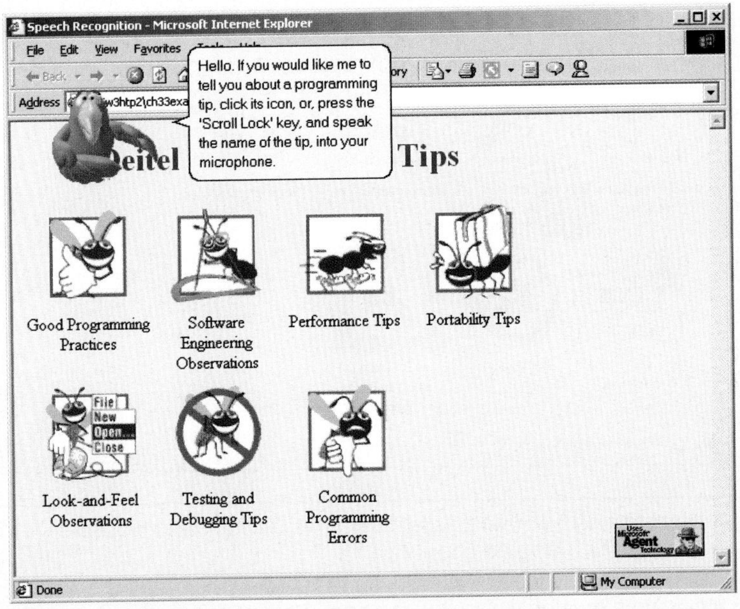

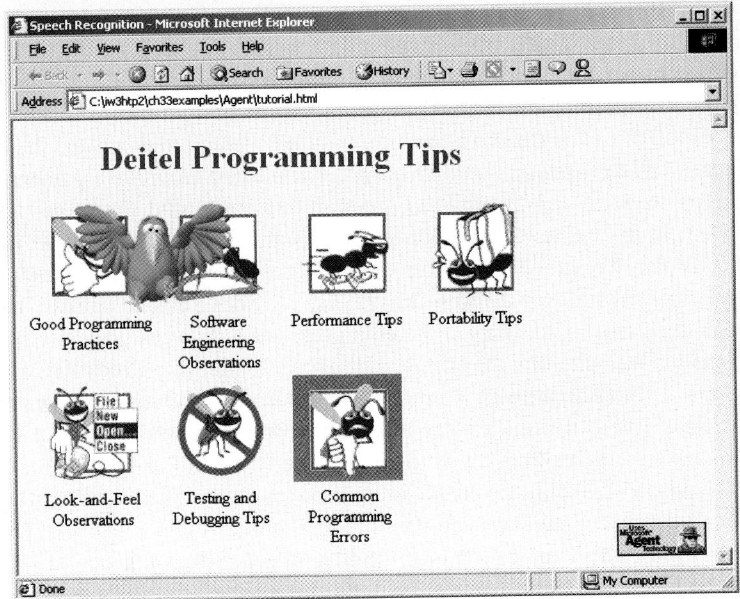

Fig. 33.6 Demonstrating Microsoft Agent and the Lernout and Hauspie TruVoice text-to-speech (TTS) engine (part 6 of 7).

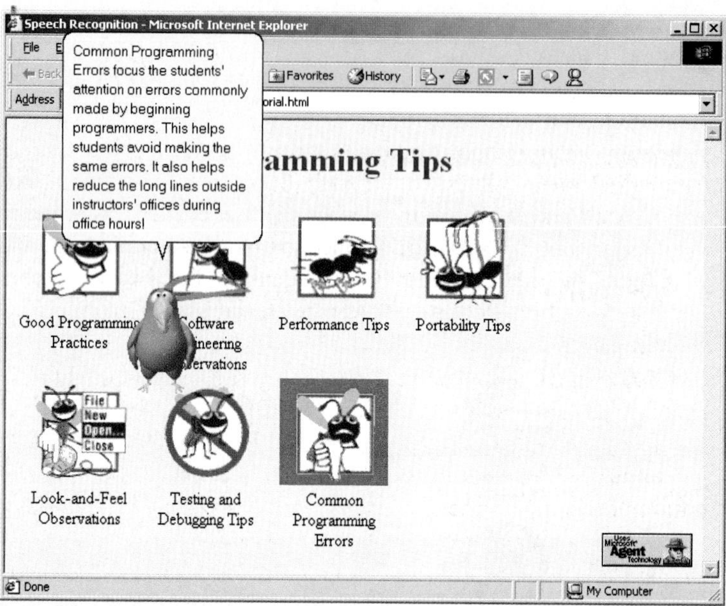

Fig. 33.6 Demonstrating Microsoft Agent and the Lernout and Hauspie TruVoice text-to-speech (TTS) engine (part 7 of 7).

Line 99 assigns to global variable **actor** a reference to the Peedy ***Character*** object. Object **Character** of the **Characters** collection receives as its argument the name that was used to download the character data in lines 97–98. Line 100 sets the **Character**'s ***LanguageID*** property to **0x0409** (English). Microsoft Agent can actually be used with several different languages (see the documentation for more information).

Lines 103–105 use the **Character** object's ***Get*** method to download the ***Showing***, ***Speaking*** and ***Hiding*** states for the character. The method takes two arguments—the *type* of information to download (in this case, state information) and the *name* of the corresponding element (e.g., **Showing**). Each state has animations associated with it. When the character is displayed (i.e., the **Showing** state), its associated animation plays (Peedy flies onto the screen). Downloading the **Speaking** state provides a default animation that makes the character appear to be speaking. When the character hides (i.e., goes into the **Hiding** state), the animations that make the character disappear are played (Peedy flies away).

Line 108 calls **Character** method **Get** to load an animation (**Greet**, in this example). Lines 109–116 use a variety of **Character** methods to interact with Peedy. Line 109 invokes the ***MoveTo*** method to specify Peedy's position on the screen. Line 110 calls method ***Show*** to display the character. When this occurs, the character plays the animation assigned to the **Showing** state (Peedy flies onto the screen). Line 111 calls method ***Play*** to play the **Greet** animation (see the first screen capture). Lines 112–116 invoke method ***Speak*** to make the character speak its string argument. If there is a compatible TTS engine installed, the character displays a bubble containing the text and speaks the text as well. The Microsoft Agent Web site contains complete lists of animations available for each character (some are standard to all characters, others are specific to each character).

Lines 119–125 load several other animations. Line 119 loads the set of ***Idling*** animations that Microsoft Agent uses when users are not interacting with the character. When running this example, be sure to leave Peedy alone for a while to see some of these animations. Lines 120–123 load the animations for moving the character up, down, left and right (***MoveUp***, ***MoveDown***, ***MoveLeft*** and ***MoveRight***, respectively).

Clicking an image calls function **imageSelectTip** (lines 137–142). The method first uses **Character** method ***Stop*** to terminate the current animation. Next, the **for** structure at lines 139–141 determines which image the user clicked. The condition in line 140 calls the **document** object's ***images*** collection which determines the index of the clicked **img** element. If the **tip** number is equal to the image number (**document.images(i)**), then function **tellMeAboutIt** (lines 158–166) is called, where **i** is passed as the argument.

Line 160 of function **tellMeAboutIt** assigns global variable **currentImage** a reference to the clicked **img** element. This function changes the background color of the **img** element that the user clicked by highlighting that image on the screen. Line 161 changes the background color of the image to red. Line 162 invokes **Character** method **MoveTo** to position Peedy above the clicked image. When this statement executes, Peedy flies to the image. The **currentImage**'s ***offsetParent*** property determines the parent element that contains the image (in this example, the **table** cell in which the image appears). The ***offsetLeft*** and ***offsetTop*** properties of the **table** cell determine the location of the cell with respect to the upper left corner of the browser window. The **Character** object's **Speak** method (Line 165) speaks the text that is stored as strings in the array **explanations** for the selected tip.

Lines 177–188 invoke the script for the **agent** control in response to the hiding of the text balloon. If the **currentImage** is not **null**, the background color of the image is changed to **lemonchiffon** (the document's background color) and variable **currentImage** is reset to **null**.

The script for the **agent** control at lines 187–194 is invoked in response to the user's clicking the character. When this occurs, line 190 plays the **GetAttention** animation, line 191 causes Peedy to speak the text "**Stop poking me with that pointer!**" and line 192 plays the last frame of the **GetAttention** animation by specifying **GetAttentionReturn**.

Microsoft provides complete lists of animations as well as recommended standard animation sets for their Agent characters at **msdn.microsoft.com/library/en-us/dnagent/html/characterdata.asp**.

Voice recognition is also included in this example to enable the Agent character to receive voice commands. The first screen capture illustrates Peedy finishing his introduction (Fig. 33.7). The second screen capture shows Peedy after the user presses the *Scroll Lock* key to start issuing voice commands, which initializes the voice-recognition engine (Fig. 33.8). The third screen capture (Fig. 33.9) shows Peedy after receiving a voice command (i.e., "Good Programming Practice", which causes a ***Command*** event for the **agent** control). The last screen capture shows Peedy discussing Good Programming Practices (Fig. 33.10).

To enable Microsoft Agent to recognize voice commands, a compatible voice-recognition engine must be installed. Lines 25–28 use an **object** element to embed an instance of the Microsoft Speech Recognition engine control in the Web page.

Next, the voice commands used to interact with the Peedy must be registered in the **Character** object's ***Commands*** collection. The **for** structure at lines 128–130 uses the **Commands** collection's ***Add*** method to register each voice command. The method receives five arguments. The first argument is a string representing the command *name* (typically used in scripts that respond to voice commands). The second argument is a string that appears in a pop-up menu in response to a right-click on the character. The third argument is a string representing the words or phrase users can speak for this command (stored in array **voiceTips** at lines 44–51). Optional words or phrases are enclosed in square brackets (**[]**). The last two arguments are boolean values indicating whether the command is currently enabled (i.e., whether users can speak the command) and whether the command is currently visible in the pop-up menu and **Voice Commands** window for the character.

Lines 132–134 set the ***Caption***, ***Voice*** and ***Visible*** properties of the **Commands** object. The **Caption** property specifies text that describes the voice command set. This text appears in the small rectangular area that appears below the character when users press the *Scroll Lock* key. The **Voice** property is similar to the **Caption** property except that the specified text appears in the **Voice Commands** window with the set of voice commands the user can speak below it. The **Visible** property is a boolean value that specifies whether the commands of this **Commands** object should appear in the pop-up menu.

After receiving a voice command, the **agent** control's **Command** event handler (lines 170–175) executes. This script calls function **voiceSelectTip** and passes it the name of the received command. Function **voiceSelectTip** (lines 144–156) uses the name of the command in the **for** structure (lines 148–152) to determine the index of the command in the **Commands** object. This value is then passed to function **tellMeAboutIt** (line 158), which causes Peedy to move to the specified tip and discuss that tip.

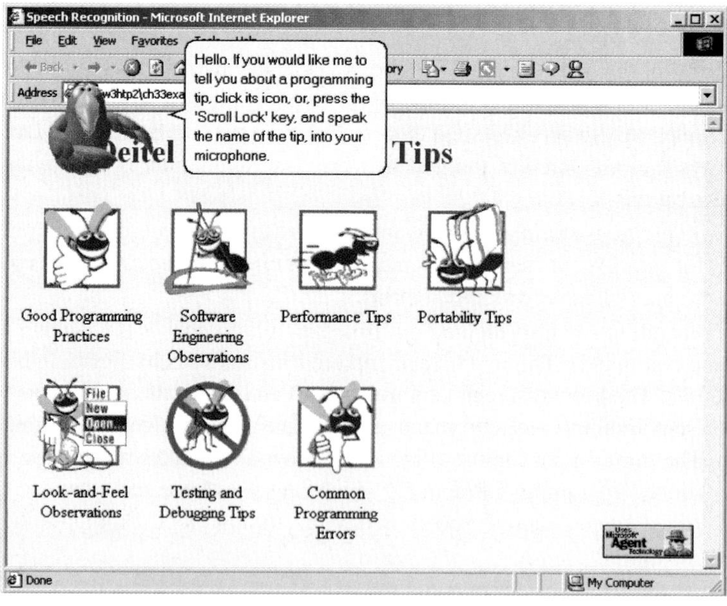

Fig. 33.7 Peedy finishing introduction.

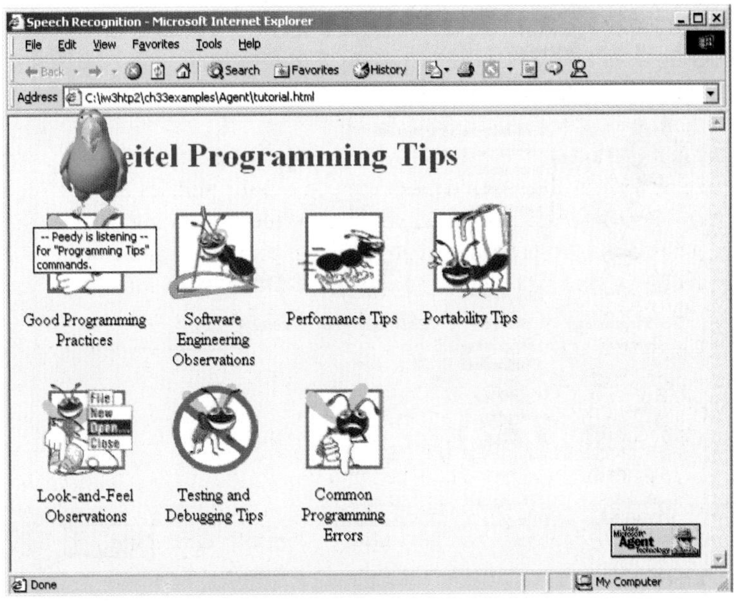

Fig. 33.8 Peedy ready to receive voice commands.

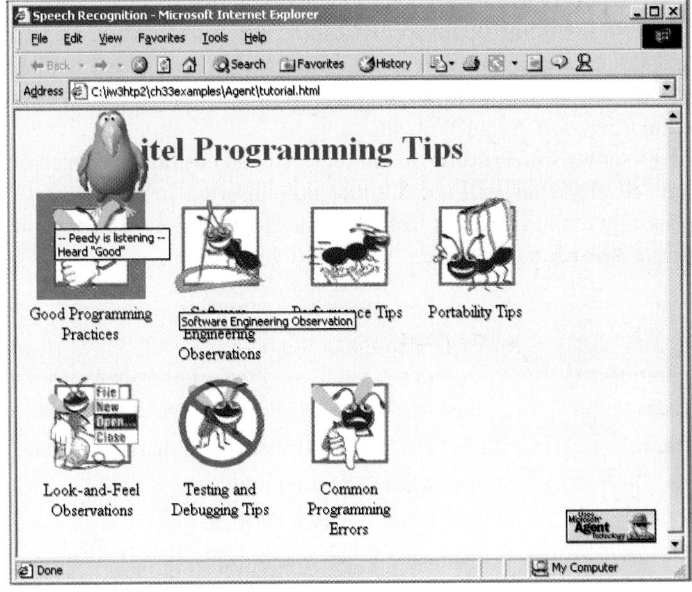

Fig. 33.9 Peedy receiving voice command.

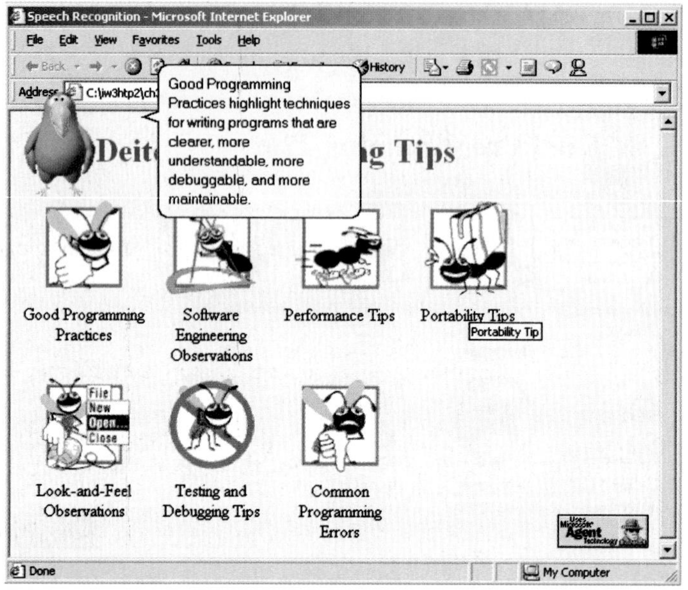

Fig. 33.10 Peedy discussing Good Programming Practice.

This example has covered only the basic features and functionality of Microsoft Agent. Many more features are available. Figure 33.11 lists several other Microsoft Agent events.

Figure 33.12 shows some other properties and methods of the **`Character`** object. Remember that the **`Character`** object represents the character that is displayed on the screen and enables interaction with that character. For a complete listing of properties and methods, see the Microsoft Agent Web site

Figure 33.13 shows some speech output tags that can customize speech output properties. The animated character will speak these tags inserted into the text string. Speech output tags generally remain in effect from the time at which they are encountered until the end of the current **`Speak`** method call.

Event	Description
`BalloonHide`	Called when the text balloon for a character is hidden.
`BalloonShow`	Called when the text balloon for a character is shown.
`Hide`	Called when a character is hidden.
`Move`	Called when a character is moved on the screen.
`Show`	Called when a character is displayed on the screen.
`Size`	Called when a character's size is changed.

Fig. 33.11 Other events for the Microsoft Agent control.

Property or method	Description
Properties	
`Height`	The height of the character in pixels.
`Left`	The left edge of the character in pixels from the left of the screen.
`Name`	The default name for the character.
`Speed`	The speed of the character's speech.
`Top`	The top edge of the character in pixels from the top of the screen.
`Width`	The width of the character in pixels.
Methods	
`Activate`	Sets the currently active character when multiple characters appear on the screen.
`GestureAt`	Specifies that the character should gesture toward a location on the screen that is specified in pixel coordinates from the upper left corner of the screen.
`Interrupt`	Interrupts the current animation. The next animation in the queue of animations for this character is then displayed.
`StopAll`	Stops all animations of a specified type for the character.

Fig. 33.12 Other properties and methods for the **`Character`** object.

Tag	Description
`\Chr=`*string***`\`**	Specifies the tone of the voice. Possible values for *string* are **`Normal`** (the default) for a normal tone of voice, **`Monotone`** for a monotone voice or **`Whisper`** for a whispered voice.
`\Emp\`	Emphasizes the next spoken word.
`\Lst\`	Repeats the last statement spoken by the character. This tag must be the only content of the string in the **`Speak`** method call.
`\Pau=`*number***`\`**	Pauses speech for *number* milliseconds.
`\Pit=`*number***`\`**	Changes the pitch of the character's voice. This value must be within the range 50 to 400 hertz for the Microsoft Agent speech engine.
`\Spd=`*number***`\`**	Changes the speech speed to a value in the range 50 to 250.
`\Vol=`*number***`\`**	Changes the volume to a value in the range 0 (silent) to 65,535 (maximum volume).

Fig. 33.13 Speech output tags.

33.8 RealPlayer™ Plug-in

A RealPlayer object may be embedded into a Web page to enhance the page with streaming audio and video. RealPlayer can also be delivered as a browser plug-in on multiple platforms. Figure 33.14 demonstrates streaming audio in a Web page by embedding a RealPlayer object in the page using **embed** element. Users can select from several different audio sources; this selection then calls a JavaScript which invokes RealPlayer methods to play the selected audio stream.

```
<?xml version = "1.0"?>
<!DOCTYPE html PUBLIC "-//W3C//DTD XHTML 1.0 Transitional//EN"
   "http://www.w3.org/TR/xhtml1/DTD/xhtml1-transitional.dtd">

<!-- Fig. 33.14: real.html                     -->
<!-- Embedding RealPlayer into an XHTML page -->

<html xmlns = "http://www.w3.org/1999/xhtml">
   <head>
      <title>Live Audio!</title>

      <script type = "text/javascript">
         <!--
         var locations =
            [ "http://www.cnn.com/video/audio/cnn.ram",
              "http://www.real.com/showcase/kingredir.ram",
              "http://radio.onlinemusic.com/play/" +
              "jazzsummit.com/rm" ]

         function change( loc )
         {
            raControl.SetSource( locations[ loc ] );
            raControl.DoPlayPause();
         }
         // -->
      </script>
   </head>

   <body>

      <p>Pick from my favorite audio streams:

      <select id = "streamSelect" onchange =
         "change( this.value )">
         <option value = "">Select a station</option>
         <option value = "0">CNN</option>
         <option value = "1">KING-FM</option>
         <option value = "2">Jazz Summit</option>
      </select></p>

      <br />
      <embed id = "raControl" src = ""
         type = "audio/x-pn-realaudio-plugin" width = "275"
         height = "125" controls = "Default"
         autostart = "false" />

   </body>
</html>
```

Fig. 33.14 Embedding RealPlayer in a Web page (part 1 of 2).

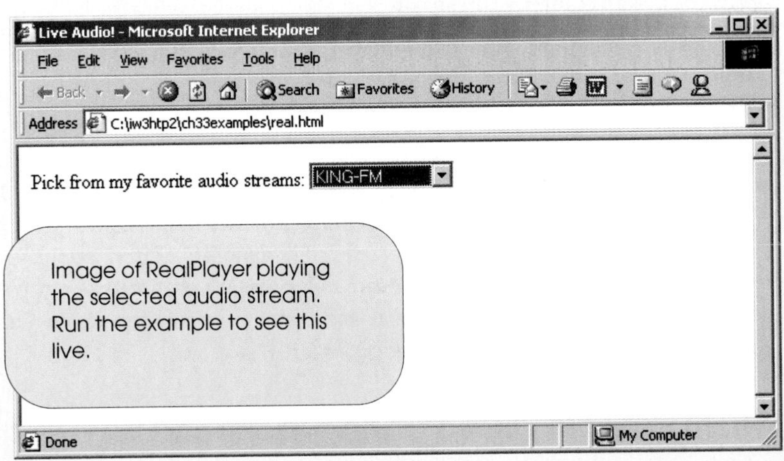

Fig. 33.14 Embedding RealPlayer in a Web page (part 2 of 2).

The **embed** element in lines 42–45 embeds the RealPlayer plug-in into the page. The ***type*** *attribute* specifies the MIME type of the embedded file, which in this case is the MIME type for streaming audio. (Remember that MIME is a standard for specifying the format of content so the browser can determine how to handle the content.) The ***width*** and ***height*** *attributes* specify the dimensions of the space the control occupies on the page. The ***autostart*** *attribute* determines whether the audio starts playing when the page loads (for this example, we set it to **false**). The ***controls*** *attribute* specifies which controls users can access (e.g., *Play* button, *Pause* button and *Volume Control*). Setting **controls** to ***Default*** places the standard control buttons on screen. A list of the available controls can be found at the site

www.real.com/devzone/library/stream/plugtest/plugin.html

We do not set the ***src*** *attribute* of the **embed** element. Normally, this is the location of the streaming audio, but in this example, we use JavaScript to change the source dynamically based on user selections.

Now that the player is embedded in the Web page, we use scripting to activate the streaming audio. The **select** menu (line 33) lists three radio stations, corresponding to the three entries in the array **locations** (defined at line 14), which contain the actual URLs for the live audio of those stations. When the selection changes, function **change** (line 20) is called by the **onchange** event. This function calls methods ***SetSource*** and ***DoPlayPause*** of the RealPlayer object. Method **SetSource** sets the source URL of the audio stream to be played. Then, method **DoPlayPause** toggles between pausing and playing the stream. [*Note*: In this case, the stream is paused because it has not started playing yet, so it begins playing in response to the call to **DoPlayPause**.]

In this example, we only explore streaming audio. The latest versions of RealPlayer support streaming video as well. To view streaming video with RealPlayer, visit the following sites:

www.cnn.com
www.msnbc.com

www.broadcast.com/television

To learn more about programming with RealPlayer, visit the RealPlayer DevZone at

www.realnetworks.com/devzone/index.html

A few years, ago broadcasting personal streaming audio and video required a dedicated server and expensive software. Today, open source software, such as *Darwin Streaming Server* and *RealNetwork's Basic Server G2*, provide "home-made" servers, such as Linux or Apache running on a PC, with streaming capability. These applications are available free for download from **www.shareware.com**. With limited server processor power and Internet bandwidth, this type of set-up cannot support the same number of streams and bit-rates as a dedicated streaming server.

33.9 Synchronized Multimedia Integration Language (SMIL)

The *Synchronized Multimedia Integration Language* (*SMIL*, pronounced "smile") enables Web document authors to coordinate the presentation of a wide range of multimedia elements. SMIL is an XML-based description language that allows static and dynamic text, audio and video to occur simultaneously and sequentially. Like Flash, SMIL provides a time reference for all instances of text and media. A SMIL document specifies the source (i.e., the URL) and presentation of multimedia elements. In XHTML, multimedia elements are autonomous entities that cannot interact without complicated scripts. In SMIL, multimedia elements can work together, enabling document authors to specify when and how multimedia elements appear in a document. For example, SMIL can produce TV-style content, in which static and dynamic text, audio and video occur simultaneously and sequentially. One way to render SMIL documents is with *RealPlayer*. Apple's *Quicktime* plug-in also plays SMIL in both Windows and Mac OS environments.

The example in Fig. 33.15 is a SMIL document that displays **.jpg** images for a variety of *Java How to Program* book covers. The images are displayed sequentially, and sound accompanies each image.

```
<smil>
   <!-- Fig. 33.15: example1.smil -->
   <!-- Example SMIL Document      -->

   <head>
      <layout>
         <root-layout height = "300" width = "280"
            background-color = "#bbbbee" title = "Example" />

         <region id = "image1" width = "177" height = "230"
            top = "35" left = "50" background-color =
            "#ffffff" />
      </layout>
   </head>
   <body>
      <seq>
```

Fig. 33.15 SMIL document with images and sound (part 1 of 2).

```
17
18             <par>
19                <img src = "book1.jpg" region = "image1"
20                   alt = "book 1" dur = "1s" fit = "fill" />
21                <audio src = "bounce.au" dur = ".5s" />
22             </par>
23
24             <par>
25                <img src = "book2.jpg" region = "image1"
26                   alt = "book 2" dur = "1s" fit = "fill" />
27                <audio src = "bounce.au" dur = ".5s" />
28             </par>
29
30             <par>
31                <img src = "book3.jpg" region = "image1"
32                   alt = "book 3" dur = "1s" fit = "fill" />
33                <audio src = "bounce.au" dur = ".5s" />
34             </par>
35
36             <par>
37                <img src = "book4.jpg" region = "image1"
38                   alt = "book4" dur = "1s" fit = "fill" />
39                <audio src = "bounce.au" dur = ".5s" />
40             </par>
41
42             <par>
43                <img src = "book5.jpg" region = "image1"
44                   alt = "book5" dur = "1s" fit = "fill" />
45                <audio src = "bounce.au" dur = ".5s" />
46             </par>
47
48             <par>
49                <img src = "book6.jpg" region = "image1"
50                   alt = "book6" dur = "1s" fit = "fill" />
51                <audio src = "bounce.au" dur = ".5s" />
52             </par>
53          </seq>
54       </body>
55    </smil>
```

Fig. 33.15 SMIL document with images and sound (part 2 of 2).

Element **head** (lines 5–14) contains all the information for setting up the document. Lines 6–13 show element **layout**, which sets the layout attributes for the document.

Lines 7–8 set the document size, color and title using element ***root-layout***. Lines 10–12 set a region for displaying objects (e.g., images) using element **region**. Attribute **id** is a unique identifier for each region. Attributes **width** and **height** specify the size of the region, and attributes **top** and **left** provide its relative position. Attribute **background-color** sets the color of the region's background.

Line 15 begins the element **body**, which encloses the contents of the document. Line 16 starts element **seq**, which sets its child elements to execute sequentially (i.e., in chronological order). A **par** element (starting on Line 18) sets its child elements to execute simultaneously.

Lines 19–20 show element **img**, which references an image. Attribute **src** contains the location of the image, and attribute **alt** provides a description of the image. Attribute **region** specifies the region in which the image is to be displayed; a **fit** value of **fill** sets the image to fill the entire region. Attribute **dur** describes how long the image appears on the screen (e.g., one second). Line 21 shows element **audio**, which references audio file **bounce.au**. The remaining elements in the document (lines 24–52) display different images and play the same audio file.

We can also embed a SMIL document in a Web page. We use the method described in Section 33.7 to embed the RealPlayer. Visitors to a Web site need the RealPlayer plug-in to view SMIL content. The plug-in is installed with RealPlayer basic and is available for download from RealNetworks at

www.real.com/player

Figure 33.16 uses an embedded *RealPlayer* to view our example SMIL document. On lines 14–17 we use the **<embed>** tag to add the RealPlayer to the Web page. The many attributes of this tag determine how our SMIL is displayed. First, set the **src** attribute on line 14 by giving it the location of the SMIL file. The file is located in the same folder so the path is simply the name of the file: **example1.smil**. The **controls** attribute on line 15 is set to **ImageWindow**; hiding the controls from users. The **type** attribute on line 16 allows the specification of the MIME type for the embedded object. In this case, we set **type** to **audio/x-pn-realaudio-plugin** to inform the browser that the Real-Player plug-in will display the SMIL file. Users do not have GUI controls, so the **autostart** attribute set to **true** on line 17 starts the movie automatically.

33.10 Scalable Vector Graphics (SVG)

The *Scalable Vector Graphics (SVG)* markup language describes *vector graphic* data for *JPEG*, *GIF* and *PNG* formats) such that they may be distributed over the Web efficiently. The GIF, JPEG and PNG file formats store images as *bitmaps*. Bitmaps describe the color of every pixel in an image and can take quite a bit of time to download. Due to the method in which bitmap information is stored, images of these file types cannot be enlarged or reduced without a loss of image quality.

Vector graphics are produced by mathematical equations which describe graphical information in terms of lines, curves, etc. Not only do images rendered by vectors require less bandwidth, but these images also can be easily scaled and printed without loss of image clarity. Different graphic formats are discussed in detail in Chapter 3, Photoshop® Elements.

```
1  <?xml version = "1.0"?>
2  <!DOCTYPE html PUBLIC "-//W3C//DTD XHTML 1.0 Transitional//EN"
3     "http://www.w3.org/TR/xhtml1/DTD/xhtml1-transitional.dtd">
4
5  <!-- Fig. 33.16: example1.html          -->
6  <!-- embedding SMIL with RealPlayer   -->
7
```

Fig. 33.16 Using the RealPlayer 8 plug-in to display a SMIL document (part 1 of 2).

```
<html xmlns = "http://www.w3.org/1999/xhtml">
   <head>
      <title>Embedding SMIL with Real Player</title>
   </head>
   <body>
      <div style = "text-align: center">
      <embed src = "example1.smil"
             controls = "ImageWindow"
             type = "audio/x-pn-realaudio-plugin"
             width = "280" height = "300" autostart = "true">
      </embed></div>
   </body>
</html>
```

Fig. 33.16 Using the RealPlayer 8 plug-in to display a SMIL document (part 2 of 2).

Another advantage to using SVG to produce Web graphics is that SVG is an application of XML. This relationship makes it possible for SVG documents to be scripted, searched and dynamically created.

Both Internet Explorer and Netscape Communicator intend to provide native support for SVG in the near future. Currently, Adobe provides a plug-in for Internet Explorer (Version 4.0 or higher for Windows and Version 5.0 for Mac) and for Netscape Communicator (Version 4.0 or higher for both Windows and Mac) that enables SVG documents to be directly rendered in those browsers. This plug-in is available free of charge from Adobe at **www.adobe.com/svg**.

Figure 33.17 is an SVG document that displays some simple shapes in a browser. We use the Adobe plug-in to view the document in Internet Explorer.

```
<?xml version="1.0"?>

```

Fig. 33.17 SVG document example (part 1 of 2).

```
3  <!-- Fig. 33.17: shapes.svg -->
4  <!-- Simple example of SVG  -->
5
6  <svg viewBox = "0 0 300 300" width = "300" height = "300">
7
8     <!-- generate a background -->
9     <g>
10       <path style = "fill: #eebb99"
11          d = "M0,0 h300 v300 h-300 z" />
12    </g>
13
14    <!-- some shapes and colors -->
15    <g>
16
17       <circle style = "fill: green; fill-opacity: 0.5"
18          cx = "150" cy = "150" r = "50" />
19
20       <rect style = "fill: blue; stroke: white"
21          x = "50" y = "50" width = "100" height = "100" />
22
23       <text style = "fill: red; font-size: 24pt"
24          x = "25" y = "250">Welcome to SVG!</text>
25
26    </g>
27 </svg>
```

Fig. 33.17 SVG document example (part 2 of 2).

Line 6 contains the root element for the SVG document. Attribute **viewBox** sets the viewing area for the document. The first two numbers in the value are the *x*- and *y*-coordinates of the upper left corner of the viewing area, and the last two numbers are the width and height of the viewing area. Attribute **width** specifies the width of the image, and attribute **height** specifies the height of the image.

Element **g** groups elements of an SVG document. Lines 10–11 use element **path** to create a box. Attribute **style** uses CSS property **fill** to fill the inside of the box with the color **#eebb99**. Attribute **d** defines the points of the box. Property **M** specifies the starting coordinates *(0, 0)* of the path. Property **h** specifies that the next point is horizontal to the current point and spaced 300 pixels to the right of the current point *(300, 0)*. Property **v** specifies that the next point is vertical to the current point and spaced 300 pixels below it *(300, 300)*. Property **h** then places the point to the left by 300 pixels *(0, 300)*. Property **z** sets the **path** to connect the first and last points, thus closing the box.

Lines 17–24 group three elements: a **circle**, a **rect**angle and a **text** element. Lines 17–18 create a circle with element **circle**. The circle has an *x*-axis center coordinate (attribute **cx**) of 150 pixels, a *y*-axis center coordinate (attribute **cy**) of 150 pixels and a radius (attribute **r**) of 50 pixels. The circle is filled blue, with 50% opacity.

Lines 20 –21 use element **rect**angle to create a rectangle. The rectangle's upper left corner is determined using attributes **x** and **y**. Attribute **width** sets the width of the rectangle, and attribute **height** sets the height of the rectangle.

Lines 23–24 create some text with element **text**. Place the text attributes **x** and **y**. The format of the text is defined using attribute **style**. In this case, the text is red with a font size of 24 points.

Figure 33.18 contains a more complex SVG image that simulates the Earth and Moon rotating around the Sun. This example uses SVG's animation feature.

```
<?xml version = "1.0"?>

<!-- Fig. 33.18: planet.svg     -->
<!-- Planetary motion with SVG -->

<svg viewBox = "-500 -500 1000 1000">
   <g id = "background">
      <path style = "fill: black"
         d = "M -2000,-2000 H 2000 V 2000 H -2000 Z" />
   </g>

   <circle id = "sun" style = "fill: yellow"
      cx = "0" cy = "0" r = "100" />

   <g>
      <animateTransform attributeName = "transform"
         type = "rotate" dur = "80s" from = "0" to = "360"
         repeatCount = "indefinite" />

      <circle id = "earth" style = "fill: blue"
         cx = "400" cy = "0" r = "40" />

      <g transform = "translate( 400 0 )">
         <circle id = "moon" style = "fill: white"
            cx = "70" cy = "0" r = "10">
            <animateTransform attributeName = "transform"
               type = "rotate" dur = "20s" from = "360"
               to = "0" repeatCount = "indefinite" />
```

Fig. 33.18 SVG document with animated elements (part 1 of 2).

```
29             </circle>
30          </g>
31       </g>
32    </svg>
```

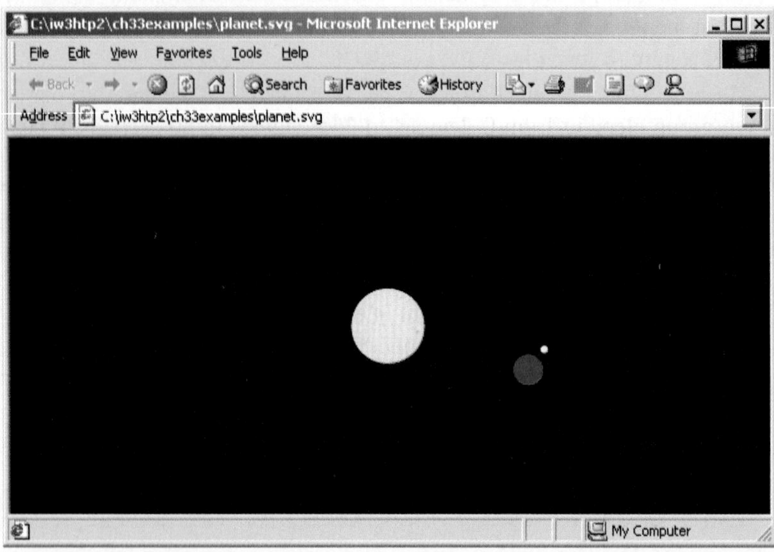

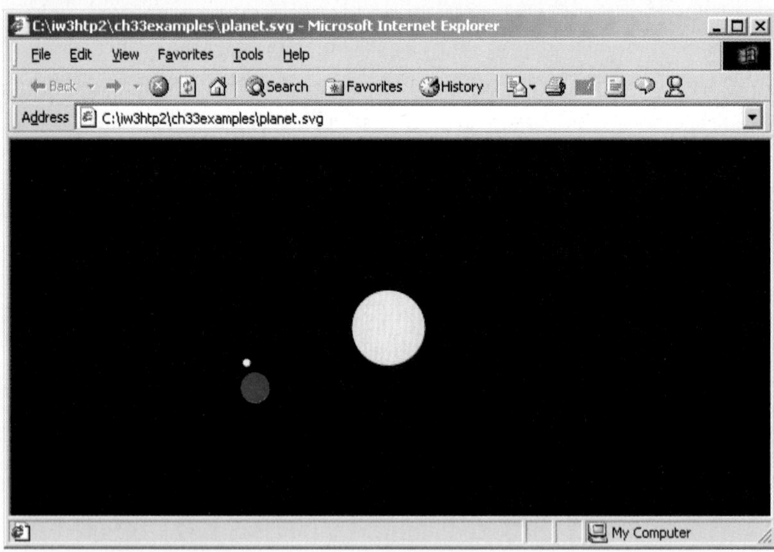

Fig. 33.18 SVG document with animated elements (part 2 of 2).

Lines 8–9 create a box for the background that is much larger than the viewable size. Attribute **`d`** has properties **`H`** and **`V`** that specify absolute coordinates for the **`path`**. Thus, the coordinates of the box are *(-2000, -2000)*, *(2000, -2000)*, *(2000, 2000)* and *(-2000, 2000)*.

Lines 12–13 create a yellow circle with a radius of 100 pixels at coordinate *(0, 0)* to represent the Sun. Line 15 defines element **`g`**, which groups together the circles representing the Earth and Moon. Lines 16–18 use element **`animateTransform`**, which changes the attribute of the parent element specified in attribute **`attributeName`**. Attribute **`type`** defines the property of the attribute that changes. The initial and final values of the transformation are set by attributes **`from`** and **`to`**. Attribute **`dur`** sets the time (i.e., 80 seconds) it takes to change from the initial to the final values, and attribute **`repeatCount`** sets the amount of times to perform this transformation. In our example, we rotate the group element from 0 degrees to 360 degrees in 80 seconds, repeating the rotation indefinitely (i.e., continuously).

Lines 20–21 create a blue circle with a radius of 40 pixels at coordinates *(400, 0)*. When the group rotates, this circle's center stays at a distance of 400 pixels from the origin *(0, 0)*.

Line 23 uses element **`g`** to group the **`circle`** element that represents the Moon. This element has attribute **`transform`**, which **`translate`**s (shifts) the group element 400 pixels to the right, thus centering the group on the blue circle. For other transformations, see the SVG specification. The white circle (the Moon) on lines 24–25 has a child **`animateTransform`** element on lines 26–28 that rotates the Moon 360 degrees counterclockwise around the Earth every 20 seconds.

33.11 Internet and World Wide Web Resources

There are many multimedia-related resources on the Internet and World Wide Web. This section lists a variety of resources that can help you learn about multimedia programming and provides a brief description of each.

`www.microsoft.com/windows/windowsmedia`
The *Windows Media* Web site contains information to help get you started with Microsoft's streaming media technologies. The site also links you to various software.

`www.microsoft.com/ntserver/mediaserv`
The *Windows NT Server site for Windows Media Technology* provides information about serving streaming media over the Internet.

`msdn.microsoft.com/library/en-us/dnagent/html/agentdevdl.asp`
The *Microsoft Agent downloads area* contains all the software downloads you need to build applications and Web pages that use Microsoft Agent.

`msdn.microsoft.com/downloads/default.asp`
The *Microsoft Developer Network Downloads* home page contains images, audio clips and other free downloads.

`www.station.sony.com`
The Station is one of the most popular sites on the Internet today. It is loaded with games that use a variety of multimedia techniques.

`www.broadcast.com`
This is one of the leading Web sites for streaming media on the World Wide Web. From this site, you can access a variety of live and prerecorded audio and video.

`www.real.com`
The *RealNetworks* site is the home of RealPlayer—one of the most popular software products for receiving streaming media over the Web. Also, with their RealJukebox, you can download MP3 files and other digital music.

www.adobe.com/svg
This site provides the latest SVG information for both programmers and designers. It also provides links to SVG enabled sites and SVG relevant downloads.

service.real.com/help/library/guides/extend/embed.htm
This site provides the details of embedding RealPlayer in a Web page and a detailed listing of RealPlayer's methods and events.

www.nasa.gov/gallery/index.html
Visit *NASA's Multimedia Gallery* site to view audio, video and images from NASA's exploration of space and Earth.

www.speech.cs.cmu.edu/comp.speech/SpeechLinks.html
The *Speech Technology Hyperlinks Page* has over 500 links to sites related to computer-based speech and speech recognition.

www.dismusic.com
The *Disney Music Page* offers free Disney music in MIDI (**.mid**) format. MIDI format is particularly useful for embedding sound into a Web page and having it play when someone enters onto the site.

www.Tx-Marketeers.com/musicroom
The Music Room site has a great variety of MIDI format music.

www.spinner.com
The *Spinner* site provides online streaming radio stations, with many genres from which to choose. Either download the player for your computer, or listen to the music through your browser with the RealPlayer plug-in.

www.netradio.com
NetRadio is another online radio station that you can listen to with your browser and the RealPlayer plug-in.

www.discjockey.com
The *DiscJockey.com* site is an on-line radio station with music from the 1940s through the 1990s. The music on this site can be played through RealPlayer or the Windows Media Player.

www.mp3.com
This site is an excellent resource for the MP3 audio format. The site offers files, info on the format, hardware info and software info.

home.cnet.com/category/0-4004.html
CNET is an Internet news group containing a variety of information about today's hottest computer and Internet topics. This page from the *CNET* Web site discusses the MP3 format, MP3 encoders and streaming MP3 format audio over the Internet.

www.mpeg.org
This site is the primary reference site for information on the MPEG video format.

www.winamp.com
Winamp is a popular MP3 player. Winamp can stream MP3 over the Internet.

www.shoutcast.com
SHOUTcast is a streaming audio system. Anyone who has Winamp and a fast Internet connection can broadcast their own net radio.

windowsmedia.com
Visit this site to learn all about Windows Media capabilities such as streaming audio and video over the net.

www.bell-labs.com/project/tts/sable.html
The Sable Markup Language is designed to mark-up text for input into speech synthesizers.

www.w3.org/AudioVideo
This is the W3C Synchronized Multimedia Integration Language (SMIL) home page.

www.w3.org/TR/REC-smil
This site has the most up-to-date W3C SMIL specification.

smw.internet.com/smil/smilhome.html
This site is dedicated to SMIL and includes links, resources and definitions.

SUMMARY

- **bgsound** is an Internet Explorer-specific element that adds background audio to a Web site. The **src** property specifies the URL of the audio clip to play. The **loop** property specifies the number of times the audio clip should play. The **balance** property specifies the balance between the left and right speakers. The **volume** property determines the volume of the audio clip. To change the property values via a script, assign a scripting name to the **id** property.
- The **img** element enables both images and videos to be included in a Web page. The **src** property indicates that the source is an image. The **dynsrc** (i.e., dynamic source) property indicates that the source is a video clip. Property **start** indicates when the video should start playing (specify **fileopen** to play when the clip is loaded or **mouseover** to play when the user first positions the mouse over the video).
- The **embed** element embeds a media clip in a Web page. A graphical user interface can be displayed to give the user control over the media clip. The GUI typically enables the user to play, pause and stop the media clip, to specify the volume and to move forward and backward quickly through the clip. The **loop** property indicates that the media clip should loop forever. To prevent the GUI from appearing in the Web page, add the **hidden** property to the **<embed>** tag. To script the element, specify a scripting name by adding the **id** property to the **<embed>** tag.
- A benefit of Microsoft's ActiveX controls is that they enhance the functionality of Web pages when the controls are incorporated into Web pages that will be displayed in Internet Explorer.
- The **object** element is used to embed ActiveX controls in Web pages. The **width** and **height** properties specify the width and height in pixels that the control occupies in the Web page. Property **classid** specifies the unique ActiveX control ID for the ActiveX control.
- Parameters can be passed to an ActiveX control by placing **param** elements between the **object** element's **<object>** and **</object>** tags. Each parameter is specified with a **param** element that contains a **name** property and a **value** property.
- The Windows Media Player ActiveX control's **FileName** parameter specifies the file containing the media clip. Parameter **AutoStart** is a boolean value indicating whether the media clip plays automatically when it is loaded (**true** if so; **false** if not). The **ShowControls** parameter is a boolean value indicating whether the Media Player controls should be displayed (**true** if so; **false** if not). The **Loop** parameter is a boolean value indicating whether the Media Player should play the media clip in an infinite loop (**true** if so; **false** if not).
- The Windows Media Player ActiveX control's **Play** and **Pause** methods can be called to play or pause a media clip, respectively.
- Microsoft Agent is a technology for interactive animated characters in a Windows application or World Wide Web page. These characters allow users of your application to interact with the application by using more natural human communication techniques. The control accepts both mouse and keyboard interactions, speaks (if a compatible text-to-speech engine is installed) and also supports speech recognition (if a compatible speech-recognition engine is installed). With these capabilities, your Web pages can speak to users and can respond to their voice commands.

- The Microsoft Agent control provides four predefined characters—Peedy the Parrot, Genie, Merlin and Robby the Robot.
- The Lernout and Hauspie TruVoice Text to Speech (TTS) engine is used by the Microsoft Agent ActiveX control to speak the text that Microsoft Agent displays.
- The Microsoft Agent control's **Characters** collection stores information about the characters that are currently available for use in a program. Method **Load** of the **Characters** collection loads character data. The method takes two arguments—a name for the character that can be used later to interact with that character and the URL of the character's data file.
- A **Character** object is used to interact with the character. Method **Character** of the **Characters** collection receives as its argument the name that was used to download the character data and returns the corresponding **Character** object.
- The **Character** object's **Get** method downloads character animations and states.
- Each state has animation effects associated with it. When the character enters a state (such as the **Showing** state), the state's associated animation plays.
- **Character** method **MoveTo** moves the character to a new position on the screen. Method **Show** displays the character. Method **Play** plays the specified animation. Method **Speak** speaks its string argument. If there is a compatible TTS engine installed, the character displays a bubble containing the text and audibly speaks the text as well.
- Many animations have a "**Return**" animation for smooth transitioning between animations.
- The **Idling** animations are displayed by Microsoft Agent when the user is not interacting with the character.
- **Character** method **Stop** terminates the current animation.
- To enable Microsoft Agent to recognize voice commands, a compatible voice-recognition engine, such as the Microsoft Speech-Recognition engine, must be installed.
- The voice commands that the user can speak to interact with a character must be registered in the **Character** object's **Commands** collection.
- The **Commands** collection's **Add** method registers each voice command. The method receives five arguments.
- The **Commands** object's **Caption** property specifies text that describes the voice-command set. This text appears in the small rectangular area that appears below the character when the user presses the *Scroll Lock* key. The **Voice** property is similar to the **Caption** property, except that the specified text appears in the commands window with the set of voice commands the user can speak shown below it. The **Visible** property is a boolean value that specifies whether the commands of this **Commands** object should appear in the pop-up menu.
- When a voice command is received, the **agent** control's **Command** event handler executes.
- A RealPlayer object can be embedded (with the **embed** element) in a Web page to add streaming media to a Web page. The **type** attribute specifies the MIME type of the embedded file. The **width** and **height** attributes specify the dimensions the control will occupy on the page. The **autostart** attribute determines whether the audio should start playing when the page loads. The **controls** attribute specifies which controls are available to the user. Setting **controls** to **Default** places all control buttons on screen. The **src** attribute specifies the location of the streaming audio.
- RealPlayer method **SetSource** sets the source URL of the audio stream to be played. Method **DoPlayPause** toggles between pausing and playing the stream.

TERMINOLOGY

ActiveX control
Add method of **Commands**
animated character
audio
audio format
AutoStart parameter of Media Player
background sound
balance property of the **bgsound** element
bgsound element
Caption property of **Commands**
CD-ROM
character data file
Character method **Characters**
Character object (Microsoft Agent)
Characters collection (Microsoft Agent)
classid property of **object**
codebase property of **object**
Command event (Microsoft Agent)
Commands collection of **Character**
Commands Window
DoPlayPause method of RealPlayer
DVD
Merlin
Microsoft Agent
Microsoft Agent control
Microsoft Speech Recognition engine
MoveTo method **Character**
multimedia
multimedia-based Web application
name property of **param**
natural human communication technique
object element
param element
Pause method of Media Player
Play method of **Character**
Play method of Media Player
"**Return**" animation
SetSource method of RealPlayer
Show method **Character**
ShowControls parameter
Showing state of a character
sound card
Speak method **Character**
Speaking state of a character
dynsrc property of **img**
embed a media clip
embed element
FileName parameter of Media Player
Genie
Get method of **Character**
height property of **object**
hidden property of **embed**
Hiding state of a character
id property of **bgsound**
id property of **embed**
id property of **object**
Idling animations
interactive animated character
Internet bandwidth
Lernout and Hauspie TruVoice TTS engine
load an animation
Load method of **Characters**
Loop parameter of Media Player
loop property of **bgsound**
loop property of **embed**
media clip
speech recognition
src property of **bgsound**
start property of **img**
start property value **fileopen**
start property value **mouseover**
streaming audio
streaming technology
streaming video
text-to-speech (TTS) engine
three-dimensional (3D) object
value property of **param**
video
video clip
video format
Visible property of **Commands**
voice command
Voice property of **Commands**
volume property of **bgsound**
width property of **object**
Windows Media Player
Windows Media Player ActiveX control

SELF-REVIEW EXERCISES

33.1 Fill in the blanks in each of the following statements:

a) _________ is a technology for interactive animated characters.

b) The __________ element plays a background audio in Internet Explorer.
c) The __________ property of the **img** element specifies a video clip that should appear in the **img** element's location in the Web page.
d) The __________ element embeds an ActiveX control on a Web page.
e) The __________ element places an audio or video clip on a Web page.
f) The **img** element's __________ property has values **mouseover** and **fileopen**.
g) The __________ property of the **embed** element prevents a GUI containing media clip controls from being displayed with the media clip.
h) Microsoft Agent's __________ animations enable smooth transitions between animations.
i) When set to **true**, the __________ parameter to the Windows Media Player specifies that a GUI should be displayed so the user can control a media clip.
j) When a compatible __________ engine is available to Microsoft Agent, characters can speak text.
k) The Microsoft Agent control's __________ collection keeps track of the information about each loaded character.

33.2 State whether each of the following is *true* or *false*. If *false*, explain why.
a) The **bgsound** element can be used with any browser.
b) The **img** element enables both images and videos to be included in a Web page.
c) **bgsound** property **balance** cannot be set via scripting.
d) The **name** property of the **object** element specifies a scripting name for the element.
e) The Microsoft Agent **Character** object's **StopAnimation** method terminates the current animation for the character.

ANSWERS TO SELF-REVIEW EXERCISES

33.1 a) Microsoft Agent. b) **bgsound**. c) **dynsrc**. d) **object**. e) **embed**. f) **start**. g) **hidden**. h) "**Return**." i) **ShowControls**. j) text-to-speech. k) **Characters**.

33.2 a) False. The **bgsound** element is specific to Internet Explorer. b) True. c) True. d) False. The **id** property of the **object** element specifies a scripting name. e) False. The **Stop** method terminates the current animation for the character.

EXERCISES

33.3 (*Story Teller*) Store a large number of nouns, verbs, articles, prepositions, etc. in arrays of strings. Then use random number generation to forms sentences and have your script speak the sentences with Microsoft Agent and the Lernout and Hauspie text-to-speech engine.

33.4 (*Limericks*) Modify the limerick-writing script you wrote in Exercise 18.8 to use a Microsoft Agent character and the Lernout and Hauspie text-to-speech engine to speak the limericks your program creates. Use the speech output tags in Fig. 33.10 to control the characteristics of the speech (e.g., emphasis on certain syllables, volume of the voice and pitch of the voice,).

33.5 Modify the script of Exercise 33.4 to play character animations during pauses in the limerick.

33.6 (*Background Audio*) Write an XHTML document and script that allows users to choose from a list of the audio downloads available from the Microsoft Developer Network Downloads site

msdn.microsoft.com/downloads/default.asp

and listen to the chosen audio clip as background music with the **bgsound** element.

33.7 Modify Exercise 33.6 to use the **embed** element to play the audio clips.

33.8 Modify Exercise 33.6 to use the Windows Media Player ActiveX control to play the audio clips.

33.9 (*Video Browser*) Write an XHTML document and script that allows users to choose from a list of the videos available from the NASA Multimedia Gallery site

```
www.nasa.gov/gallery
```

and view that video using the **embed** element.

33.10 Modify Exercise 33.9 to use the Windows Media Player ActiveX control to play the video clips.

33.11 Modify the program of Fig. 33.4 to view videos from the SeaWiFs site

```
seawifs.gsfc.nasa.gov:80/OCEAN_PLANET/HTML/
oceanography_flyby.html
```

Allow users to select which video to play.

33.12 (*Image Flasher*) Create a script that repeatedly flashes an image on the screen. Do this by changing the visibility of the image. Allow users to control the "blink speed."

33.13 (*Digital Clock*) Using features of the Dynamic HTML chapters, implement an application that displays a digital clock in a Web page. You might add options to scale the clock, to display day, month and year, to issue an alarm, to play certain audios at designated times, etc.

33.14 (*Analog Clock*) Create a script that displays an analog clock with hour, minute and second hands that move as the time changes. Use the Structured Graphics Control to create the graphics and play a tick sound every second. Play other sounds to mark every half-hour and hour.

33.15 (*Karaoke*) Create a Karaoke system that plays the music for a song and displays the words for users to sing at the appropriate time.

33.16 (*Calling Attention to an Image*) To emphasize an image, try placing a row of simulated light bulbs around it. You can let the light bulbs flash in unison, or you can let them fire on and off in sequence, one after the other.

33.17 (*Online Product Catalog*) Companies are rapidly realizing the potential for doing business on the Web. Develop an online multimedia catalog from which your customers may select products to be shipped. Use the data binding features of Chapter 16 to load data into tables. Use a Microsoft Agent to announce descriptions of a selected product.

33.18 Modify Exercise 33.17 to support voice commands that allow users to speak a product name to receive a description of the product.

33.19 (*Reaction Time/Reaction Precision Tester*) Create a Web page that moves an image around the screen. The user moves the mouse to catch and click the shape. The shape's speed and size can be varied. Keep statistics on how much time the user typically takes to catch a shape of a given size. The user will probably have more difficulty catching faster moving, smaller shapes.

33.20 (*Animation*) Create an animation by displaying a series of images that represent the frames in the animation. Allow the user to specify the speed at which the images are displayed.

33.21 (*Tortoise and the Hare*) Develop a multimedia version of the Tortoise and Hare simulation of Exercise 11.20. Record an announcer's voice calling the race: "The contenders are at the starting line." "And they're off!" "The Hare pulls out in front." "The Tortoise is coming on strong."—and so forth. As the race proceeds, play the appropriate recorded audios. Play sounds to simulate the animals' running (and the crowd cheering!). Do an animation of the animals racing up the side of the slippery mountain.

33.22 (*Arithmetic Tutor*) Develop a multimedia version of the Computer-Assisted Instruction (CAI) systems you developed in Exercises 10.27, 10.28 and 10.29.

33.23 (*15 Puzzle*) Write a multimedia-based version of the game of 15. There is a 4-by-4 board for a total of 16 slots. One of the slots is empty. The other slots are occupied by 15 tiles, numbered 1 through 15. Any tile next to the currently empty slot can be moved into the currently empty slot by clicking the tile. Your program should create the board with the tiles out of order. The goal is to arrange the tiles into sequential order row by row. Play sounds with the movement of the tiles.

33.24 (*Morse Code*) Modify your solution to Exercise 12.26 to output the morse code using audio clips. Use two different audio clips for the dot and dash characters in Morse code.

33.25 (*Calendar/Tickler File*) Create a general purpose calendar and "tickler" file. The application should sing "Happy Birthday" to you when you use it on your birthday. Have the application display images and play audios associated with important events and remind you in advance of important events. For example, have the application give you a week's warning so you can pick up an appropriate greeting card for that special person. Store the calendar information in a file for use with the data-binding techniques of Chapter 16 to load the calendar information into a table in the Web page.

33.26 *Wartnose* is a character that was developed by e-Clips (`www.e-clips.com.au`)—an Australian company that develops Microsoft Agent characters. Download Wartnose and modify Fig. 33.6 to use Wartnose (as shown in Fig. 33.19). Instructions for installing this character are available on our Web site, `www.deitel.com`. [*Note*: Wartnose is a free download. Before using Wartnose, please read the licensing agreement provided at the e-Clips Web site.]

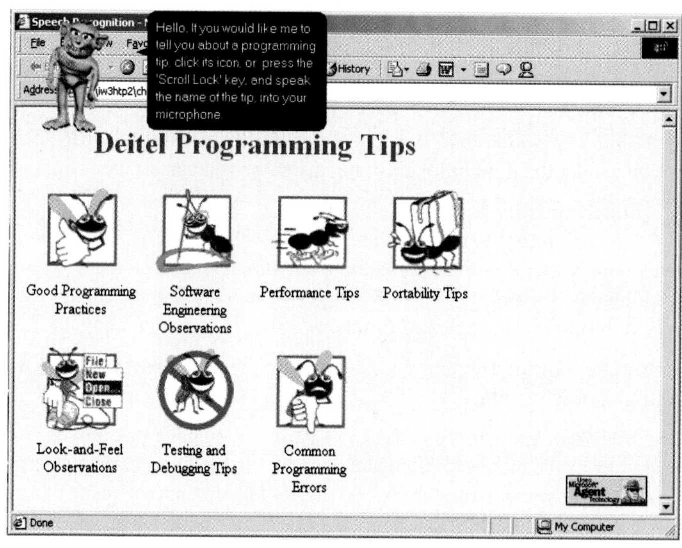

Fig. 33.19 Fig. 33.6 modified to use Wartnose. (Courtesy of e-Clips).

34

Accessibility

Objectives

- To introduce the World Wide Web Consortium's Web Content Accessibility Guidelines 1.0 (WCAG 1.0).
- To understand how to use the **`alt`** attribute of the **`<img>`** tag to describe images to people with visual impairments, mobile-Web-device users, search engines, etc.
- To understand how to make XHTML tables more accessible to page readers.
- To understand how to verify that XHTML tags are used properly and to ensure that Web pages are viewable on any type of display or reader.
- To understand how VoiceXML™ and CallXML™ are changing the way people with disabilities access information on the Web.
- To introduce the various accessibility aids offered in Windows 2000.

'Tis the good reader that makes the good book...
Ralph Waldo Emerson

Outline

34.1 Introduction

Enabling a Web site to meet the needs of individuals with disabilities is a concern for all businesses. People with disabilities are a significant portion of the population, and legal ramifications exist for Web sites that discriminate by not providing adequate and universal access to their resources. In this chapter, we explore the *Web Accessibility Initiative*, its guidelines, various laws regarding businesses and their availability to people with disabilities and how some companies have developed systems, products and services to meet the needs of this demographic.

34.2 Web Accessibility

In 1999, the National Federation for the Blind (NFB) filed a lawsuit against AOL for not supplying access to its services for people with visual disabilities. The *Americans with Disabilities Act (ADA)* and many other efforts address Web accessibility laws (Fig. 34.1).

Act	Purpose
Americans with Disabilities Act	The ADA prohibits discrimination on the basis of disability in employment, state and local government, public accommodations, commercial facilities, transportation and telecommunications.
Telecommunications Act of 1996	The Telecommunications Act of 1996 contains two amendments to Section 255 and Section 251(a)(2) of the Communications Act of 1934. These amendments require that communication devices, such as cell phones, telephones and pagers, be accessible to individuals with disabilities.
Individuals with Disabilities Education Act of 1997	Education materials in schools must be made accessible to children with disabilities.
Rehabilitation Act	Section 504 of the Rehabilitation Act states that college sponsored activities receiving federal funding cannot discriminate against individuals with disabilities. Section 508 mandates that all government institutions receiving federal funding design their Web sites so that they are accessible to individuals with disabilities. Businesses that sell services to the government also must abide by this act.

Fig. 34.1 Acts designed to protect access to the Internet for people with disabilities.

`WeMedia.com`™ (Fig. 34.2) is a Web site dedicated to providing news, information, products and services for the millions of people with disabilities, their families, friends and caregivers. There are 54 million Americans with disabilities, representing an estimated $1 trillion in purchasing power. *We Media* also provides online educational opportunities for people with disabilities.

The Internet enables individuals with disabilities to work in a vast array of new fields. Technologies such as voice activation, visual enhancers and auditory aids, afford more employment opportunities. People with visual impairments may use computer monitors with enlarged text, while people with physical impairments may use head pointers with on-screen keyboards.

Federal regulations, similar to the disability ramp mandate, will be applied to the Internet to accommodate the needs of people with hearing, vision and speech impairments. In the following sections, we explore a variety of products and services that provide Internet access for people with disabilities.

34.3 Web Accessibility Initiative

On April 7, 1997, the World Wide Web Consortium (W3C) launched the *Web Accessibility Initiative* (WAI™). *Accessibility* refers to the usability of an application or Web site by people with disabilities. The majority of Web sites are considered either partially or totally inaccessible to people with visual, learning or mobility impairments. Total accessibility is difficult to achieve because people have varying types of disabilities, language barriers and hardware and software inconsistencies. However, a high level of accessibility is attainable. As more people with disabilities use the Internet, it is imperative that Web site designers increase the accessibility of their sites. The WAI aims for such accessibility, as discussed in its mission statement described at **`www.w3.org/WAI`**.

This chapter explains some of the techniques for developing accessible Web sites. The WAI published the *Web Content Accessibility Guidelines* (*WCAG*) *1.0* to help businesses determine if their Web sites are accessible to everyone. The WCAG 1.0 (**`www.w3.org/TR/WCAG10`**) uses checkpoints to indicate specific accessibility requirements. Each checkpoint has an associated priority indicating its importance. *Priority-one checkpoints* are goals that must be met to ensure accessibility; we focus on these points in this chapter. *Priority-two checkpoints*, though not essential, are highly recommended. These checkpoints must be satisfied, or people with certain disabilities will experience difficulty accessing Web sites. *Priority-three checkpoints* slightly improve accessibility.

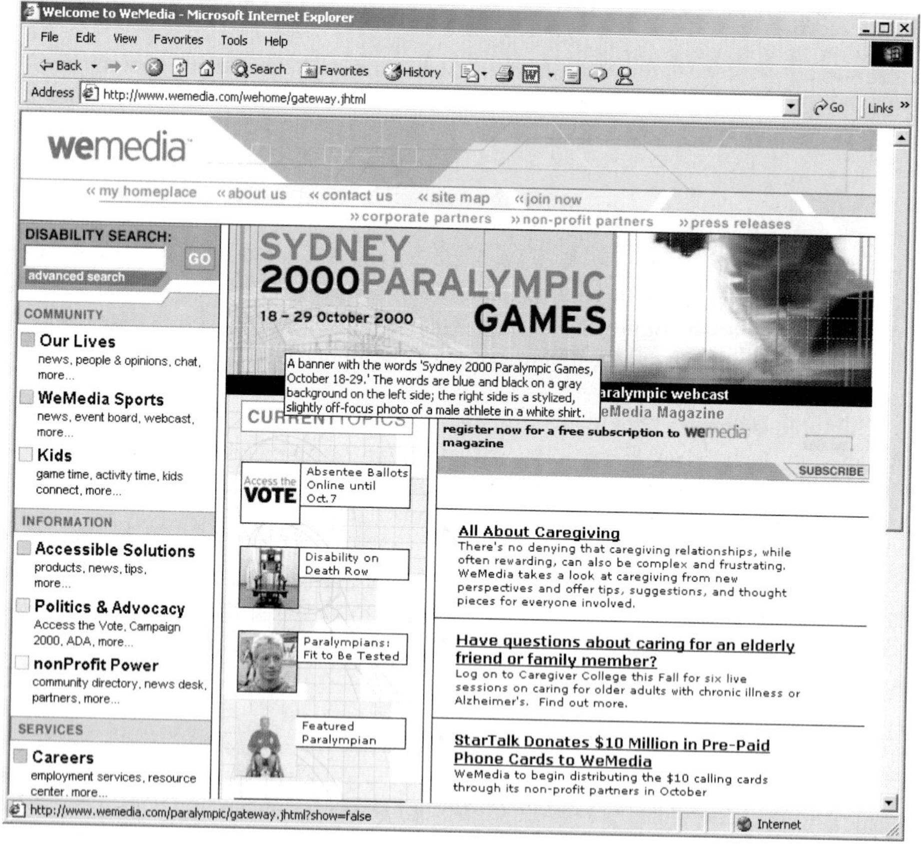

Fig. 34.2 We Media home page. (Courtesy of WeMedia, Inc.)

At the time of this writing, the WAI is working on a *WCAG 2.0* draft. A single checkpoint in the WCAG 2.0 Working Draft may encompass several checkpoints from WCAG 1.0. WCAG 2.0 checkpoints will supersede those in WCAG 1.0. The new version can be applied to a wider range of markup languages (i.e., XML, WML, etc.) and content types than its predecessor. To obtain more information about the WCAG 2.0 Working Draft, visit **www.w3.org/TR/WCAG20**.

The WAI also presents a supplemental checklist of *quick tips*, which reinforce ten important points for accessible Web site design. More information on the WAI Quick Tips can be found at **www.w3.org/WAI/References/Quicktips**.

34.4 Providing Alternatives for Images

One important WAI requirement is to ensure that every image used on a Web page is accompanied by a textual description that clearly defines the purpose of the image. To accomplish this task, include a text equivalent of each item by using the **alt** attribute of the **img** and **input** tags. A text equivalent for images defined using the **object** element is the text between the start and end **<object>** tag.

Web developers who do not use the **alt** attribute to provide text equivalents increase the difficulty people with visual impairments experience in navigating the Web. Specialized *user agents*, such as *screen readers* (programs that allow users to hear all text and text descriptions displayed on their screen) and *braille displays* (devices that receive data from screen-reading software and output the data as braille), allow people with visual impairments to access text-based information that is normally displayed on the screen. A user agent visually interprets Web-page source code and translates it into formatted text and images. Web browsers, such as Microsoft Internet Explorer and Netscape Communicator, and the screen readers mentioned throughout this chapter are examples of user agents.

Web pages that do not provide text equivalents for video and audio clips are difficult for people with visual and hearing impairments to access. Screen readers cannot read images, movies and most other non-XHTML objects from these Web pages. Providing multimedia-based information in a variety of ways (i.e., using the **alt** attribute or providing in-line descriptions of images) helps maximize the content's accessibility.

Web designers should provide useful text equivalents in the **alt** attribute for use in nonvisual user agents. For example, if the **alt** attribute describes a sales growth chart, it should provide a brief summary of the data; it should not describe the data in the chart. Instead, a complete description of the chart's data should be included in the ***longdesc** attribute*, which is intended to augment the **alt** attribute's description. The **longdesc** attribute contains the URL that links to a Web page describing the image or multimedia content. Currently, most Web browsers do not support the **longdesc** attribute. An alternative for the **longdesc** attribute is *D-link*, which provides descriptive text about graphs and charts. More information on D-links can be obtained at the *CORDA Technologies* Web site (**www.corda.com**).

Using a screen reader for Web-site navigation can be time consuming and frustrating, as screen readers cannot interpret pictures and other graphical content. A link at the top of each Web page that provides direct access to the page's content could allow users to bypass a long list of navigation links or other inaccessible elements. This jump can save time and eliminate frustration for individuals with visual impairments.

Emacspeak is a screen interface that allows greater Internet access to individuals with visual disabilities by translating text to voice data. The open source product also implements auditory icons that play various sounds. Emacspeak can be customized with Linux operating systems and provides support for the IBM *ViaVoice* speech engine. The Emacspeak Web site is located at **www.cs.cornell.edu/home/raman/emacspeak/emacspeak.html**.

In March 2001, We Media introduced the "WeMedia Browser," which allows people with poor vision and cognitive disabilities (e.g., dyslexia) to use the Internet more conveniently. The WeMedia Browser improves upon the traditional browser by providing oversized buttons and keystroke commands for navigation. The user can control the speed and volume at which the browser "reads" Web page text. The WeMedia Browser free download is available at **www.wemedia.com**.

IBM Home Page Reader (HPR) is another browser that "reads" text selected by the user. The HPR uses the IBM ViaVoice technology to synthesize a voice. A trial version of HPR is available at **www-3.ibm.com/able/hpr.html**.

34.5 Maximizing Readability by Focusing on Structure

Many Web sites use tags for aesthetic purposes rather than for the appropriate purpose. For example, the **<h1>** heading tag often is used erroneously to make text large and bold rather than as a major section head for content. The desired visual effect may be achieved, but it creates a problem for screen readers. When the screen reader software encounters the **<h1>** tag, it may verbally inform the user that a new section has been reached when it is not the case, which may confuse users. Only use the **h1** in accordance with its XHTML specifications (e.g., as headings to introduce important sections of a document). Instead of using **h1** to make text large and bold, use CSS (discussed in Chapter 6, Cascading Style Sheets) or XSL (discussed in Chapter 20, Extensible Markup Language) to format and style the text. For further examples, refer to the WCAG 1.0 Web site at **www.w3.org/TR/WCAG10**. [*Note:* The **<strong>** tag also may be used to make text bold; however, screen readers emphasize bold text, which affects the inflection of what is spoken.]

Another accessibility issue is *readability*. When creating a Web page intended for the general public, it is important to consider the reading level (i.e., the comprehension and level of understanding) at which it is written. Web site designers can make their sites easier to read by using shorter words. Designers should also limit slang terms and other non-traditional language that may be problematic for users from other countries.

WCAG 1.0 suggests using a paragraph's first sentence to convey its subject. Stating the point of the paragraph in its first sentence makes its easier to find crucial information and allows readers to bypass unwanted material.

The *Gunning Fog Index*, a formula that produces a readability grade when applied to a text sample, evaluates a Web site's readability. More information about the Gunning Fog Index can be obtained from **www.trainingpost.org/3-2-inst.htm**.

34.6 Accessibility in XHTML Tables

Complex Web pages often contain tables for formatting content and presenting data. Many screen readers are incapable of translating tables correctly unless the tables are properly designed. For example, the *CAST eReader*, a screen reader developed by the Center for Applied Special Technology (**www.cast.org**), starts at the top-left-hand cell and reads columns from top to bottom, left to right. This procedure is known as reading a table in a *linearized* manner. The CAST eReader reads the table in Fig. 34.3 as follows:

```
Price of Fruit Fruit Price Apple $0.25 Orange $0.50 Banana
$1.00 Pineapple $2.00
```

```
<?xml version = "1.0"?>
<!DOCTYPE html PUBLIC "-//W3C//DTD XHTML 1.0 Strict//EN"
   "http://www.w3.org/TR/xhtml1/DTD/xhtml1-strict.dtd">

<!-- Fig. 34.3: withoutheaders.html -->
<!-- Table without headers          -->

<html>
   <head>
      <title>XHTML Table Without Headers</title>

      <style type = "text/css">
         body { background-color: #ccffaa;
                text-align: center }
      </style>
   </head>

   <body>

      <p>Price of Fruit</p>

      <table border = "1" width = "50%">

         <tr>
            <td>Fruit</td>
            <td>Price</td>
         </tr>

         <tr>
            <td>Apple</td>
            <td>$0.25</td>
         </tr>

         <tr>
            <td>Orange</td>
            <td>$0.50</td>
         </tr>

         <tr>
            <td>Banana</td>
            <td>$1.00</td>
         </tr>

```

Fig. 34.3 XHTML table without accessibility modifications (part 1 of 2).

```
            <tr>
               <td>Pineapple</td>
               <td>$2.00</td>
            </tr>

         </table>

      </body>
   </html>
```

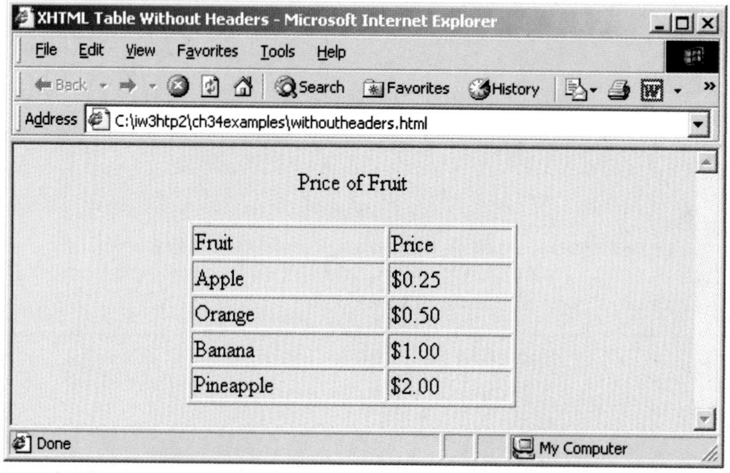

Fig. 34.3 XHTML table without accessibility modifications (part 2 of 2).

This reading does not present the content of the table adequately. WCAG 1.0 recommends using CSS instead of tables, unless the tables' content linearizes in an understandable manner.

If the table in Fig. 34.3 were large, the screen reader's linearized reading would be even more confusing to users. By modifying the **<td>** tag with the **headers** attribute and modifying *header cells* (cells specified by the **<th>** tag) with the **id** attribute, a table will be read as intended. Figure 34.4 demonstrates how these modifications change the way a table is interpreted.

This table does not appear to be different from a standard XHTML table. However, the table is read in a more intelligent manner, when using a screen reader. A screen reader vocalizes the data from the table in Fig. 34.4 as follows:

```
Caption: Price of Fruit
Summary: This table uses th and the id and headers attributes
to make the table readable by screen readers.
Fruit: Apple, Price: $0.25
Fruit: Orange, Price: $0.50
Fruit: Banana, Price: $1.00
Fruit: Pineapple, Price: $2.00
```

Every cell in the table is preceded by its corresponding header when read by the screen reader. This format helps the listener understand the table. The ***headers*** *attribute* is intended specifically for tables that hold large amounts of data. Most small tables linearize well as long as the **<th>** tag is used properly. The **summary** attribute and **caption** element are also suggested. For more examples demonstrating how to make tables accessible, visit **www.w3.org/TR/WCAG**.

```
<?xml version = "1.0"?>
<!DOCTYPE html PUBLIC "-//W3C//DTD XHTML 1.0 Strict//EN"
   "http://www.w3.org/TR/xhtml1/DTD/xhtml1-strict.dtd">

<!-- Fig. 34.4: withheaders.html -->
<!-- Table with headers          -->

<html>
   <head>
      <title>XHTML Table With Headers</title>

      <style type = "text/css">
         body { background-color: #ccffaa;
                text-align: center }
      </style>
   </head>

   <body>

   <!-- this table uses the id and headers attributes to   -->
   <!-- ensure readability by text-based browsers. It also -->
   <!-- uses a summary attribute, used screen readers to   -->
   <!-- describe the table                                 -->

      <table width = "50%" border = "1"
         summary = "This table uses th elements and id and
         headers attributes to make the table readable
         by screen readers">

         <caption><strong>Price of Fruit</strong></caption>

         <tr>
            <th id = "fruit">Fruit</th>
            <th id = "price">Price</th>
         </tr>

         <tr>
            <td headers = "fruit">Apple</td>
            <td headers = "price">$0.25</td>
         </tr>

         <tr>
            <td headers = "fruit">Orange</td>
            <td headers = "price">$0.50</td>
         </tr>

```

Fig. 34.4 Table optimized for screen reading using attribute **headers** (part 1 of 2).

```
            <tr>
               <td headers = "fruit">Banana</td>
               <td headers = "price">$1.00</td>
            </tr>

            <tr>
               <td headers = "fruit">Pineapple</td>
               <td headers = "price">$2.00</td>
            </tr>

         </table>

      </body>
   </html>
```

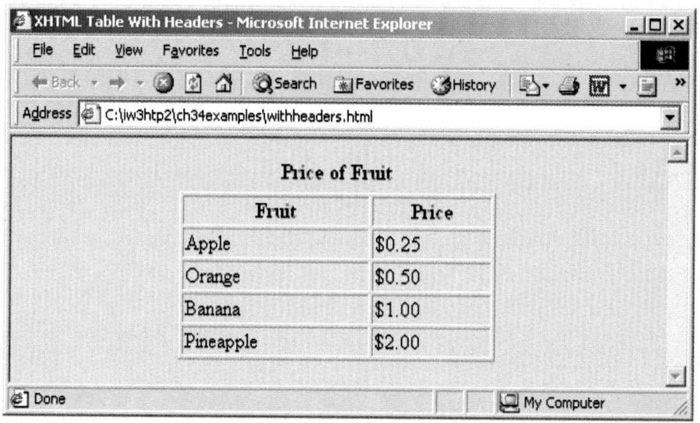

Fig. 34.4 Table optimized for screen reading using attribute **`headers`** (part 2 of 2).

34.7 Accessibility in XHTML Frames

Web designers often use frames to display more than one XHTML file in a single browser window. Frames are a convenient way to ensure that certain content always displays on the screen. Unfortunately, frames often lack proper descriptions, which prevents users with text-based browsers, or users listening with speech synthesizers, from navigating the Web site.

A site with frames must have meaningful descriptions in the **`<title>`** tag for each frame. Examples of good titles include "*Navigation Frame*" and "*Main Content Frame.*" Users with text-based browsers, such as Lynx, must choose which frame they want to open; descriptive titles make this choice simpler. However, assigning titles to frames does not solve all the navigation problems associated with frames. The **`<noframes>`** tag allows Web designers to offer alternative content for browsers that do not support frames.

Good Programming Practice 34.1

Always provide titles for frames to ensure that user agents which do not support frames have alternatives.

Good Programming Practice 34.2

Include a title for each frame's contents with the **frame** *element, and, if possible, provide links to the individual pages within the frameset so that users still can navigate through the Web pages. To provide access to browsers that do not support frames, use the* **<noframes>** *tag. It also provides better access to browsers that have limited support.*

WCAG 1.0 suggests using Cascading Style Sheets (CSS) as an alternative to frames, because CSS can provide similar functionality and are highly customizible. Unfortunately, the ability to display multiple XHTML documents in a single browser window requires the complete support of HTML 4, which is not widespread. However, the second generation of Cascading Style Sheets (CSS2) can display a single document as if it were several documents. However, CSS2 is not yet fully supported by many user agents.

34.8 Accessibility in XML

XML allows developers to create new markup languages, which may not necessarily incorporate accessibility features. To prevent the proliferation of inaccessible languages, the WAI is developing guidelines—the *XML Guidelines (XML GL)*—for creating accessible XML documents. The XML GL recommend including a text description, similar to XHTML's **<alt>** tag, for each non-text object on a page. To facilitate accessibility further, element types should allow grouping and classification and should identify important content. Without an accessible user interface, other efforts to implement accessibility are less effective, so it is essential to create XSLT (Chapter 20) or CSS style sheets that can produce multiple outputs, including document outlines.

Many XML languages, including Synchronized Multimedia Integration Language (SMIL) and Scalable Vector Graphics (SVG) (discussed in Chapter 33), have implemented several of the WAI guidelines. The WAI XML Accessibility Guidelines can be found at **www.w3.org/WAI/PF/xmlgl.htm**.

34.9 Using Voice Synthesis and Recognition with VoiceXML™

A joint effort by AT&T®, IBM®, Lucent™ and Motorola® has created an XML vocabulary that marks up information for *speech synthesizers*, which enable computers to speak to users. This technology, called *VoiceXML*, has tremendous implications for people with visual impairments and for the illiterate. VoiceXML-enabled applications read Web pages to the user, and understand words spoken into a microphone through *speech recognition* technology. An example of a speech recognition tool is IBM's *ViaVoice* (**www-4.ibm.com/software/speech**).

A VoiceXML interpreter and VoiceXML browser process VoiceXML, a platform-independent XML-based technology. Web browsers may incorporate these interpreters in the future. When a VoiceXML document is loaded, a *voice server* sends a message to the VoiceXML browser and begins a conversation between the user and the computer.

IBM *WebSphere Voice Server SDK 1.5* is a VoiceXML interpreter that can be used for testing VoiceXML documents on a desktop computer. To download the VoiceServer SDK, visit **www.alphaworks.ibm.com/tech/voiceserversdk**. [*Note*: To run the VoiceXML program in Fig. 34.5, download *Java 2 Platform Standard Edition* (Java SDK)

1.3 from **www.java.sun.com/j2se/1.3**. To obtain installation instructions for the VoiceServer SDK and the Java SDK, visit the Deitel & Associates, Inc. Web site at **www.deitel.com**.]

Figures 34.5 and 34.6 show examples of VoiceXML that would be appropriate for a Web site. The document's text is spoken to the user, and the text embedded in the VoiceXML tags allows for interactivity between the user and the browser. The output included in Fig. 34.6 demonstrates a conversation that might take place between a user and a computer after loading this document.

```
<?xml version = "1.0"?>
<vxml version = "1.0">

<!-- Fig. 34.5: main.vxml -->
<!-- Voice page          -->

<link next = "#home">
   <grammar>home</grammar>
</link>

<link next = "#end">
   <grammar>exit</grammar>
</link>

<var name = "currentOption" expr = "'home'"/>

<form>
   <block>
      <emp>Welcome</emp> to the voice page of Deitel and
      Associates. To exit any time say exit.
      To go to the home page any time say home.
   </block>
   <subdialog src = "#home"/>
</form>

<menu id = "home">
   <prompt count = "1" timeout = "10s">
      You have just entered the Deitel home page.
      Please make a selection by speaking one of the
      following options:
      <break msecs = "1000" />
      <enumerate/>
   </prompt>

   <prompt count = "2">
      Please say one of the following.
      <break msecs = "1000" />
      <enumerate/>
   </prompt>

   <choice next = "#about">About us</choice>
   <choice next = "#directions">Driving directions</choice>
```

Fig. 34.5 Home page written in VoiceXML (part 1 of 3).

```
      <choice next = "publications.vxml">Publications</choice>
   </menu>

   <form id = "about">
      <block>
      About Deitel and Associates, Inc.
      Deitel and Associates, Inc. is an internationally
      recognized corporate training and publishing organization,
      specializing in programming languages, Internet and World
      Wide Web technology and object technology education.
      Deitel and Associates, Inc. is a member of the World Wide
      Web Consortium. The company provides courses on Java, C++,
      Visual Basic, C, Internet and World Wide Web programming
      and Object Technology.
         <assign name = "currentOption" expr = "'about'"/>
         <goto next = "#repeat"/>
      </block>
   </form>

   <form id = "directions">
     <block>
        Directions to Deitel and Associates, Inc.
        We are located on Route 20 in Sudbury,
        Massachusetts, equidistant from route
      <sayas class = "digits">128</sayas> and route
      <sayas class = "digits">495</sayas>.
      <assign name = "currentOption" expr = "'directions'"/>
      <goto next = "#repeat"/>
     </block>
   </form>

   <form id = "repeat">
      <field name = "confirm" type = "boolean">
         <prompt>
            To repeat say yes. To go back to home, say no.
         </prompt>

         <filled>
            <if cond = "confirm == true">
               <goto expr = "'#' + currentOption"/>
            <else/>
              <goto next = "#home"/>
            </if>
         </filled>

      </field>
   </form>

   <form id = "end">
      <block>
         Thank you for visiting Deitel and Associates voice page.
         Have a nice day.
         <exit/>
```

Fig. 34.5 Home page written in VoiceXML (part 2 of 3).

```
96        </block>
97     </form>
98
99     </vxml>
```

Fig. 34.5 Home page written in VoiceXML (part 3 of 3).

A VoiceXML document contains a series of dialogs and subdialogs which result in spoken interaction between the user and the computer. The **<form>** and **<menu>** tags implement the dialogs. A ***form*** element presents information and gathers data from the user. A ***menu*** element provides users with options and transfers control to other dialogs, based on users' selections.

Lines 7–9 use element ***link*** to create an active link to the home page. Attribute ***next*** specifies the URI navigated to when the link is selected. Element ***grammar*** marks up the text that the user must speak to select the link. In the **link** element, we navigate to the element with **id home** when users speak the word **home**. Lines 11–13 use element **link** to create a link to **id end** when users speak the word **exit**.

Lines 17–24 create a form dialog using element **form**, which collects information from the user. Lines 18–22 present introductory text. Element **block**, which can exist only within a **form** element, groups elements that perform an action or an event. Element **emp** states that a section of text should be spoken with emphasis. If the level of emphasis is not specified, then the default level—*moderate*—is used. Our example uses the default level. [*Note*: To specify an emphasis level, use the **level** attribute. This attribute accepts the following values: *strong*, *moderate*, *none* and *reduced*.]

```
<?xml version = "1.0"?>
<vxml version = "1.0">

<!-- Fig. 34.6: publications.vxml        -->
<!-- Voice page for various publications -->

<link next = "main.vxml#home">
   <grammar>home</grammar>
</link>
<link next = "main.vxml#end">
   <grammar>exit</grammar>
</link>
<link next = "#publication">
   <grammar>menu</grammar>
</link>

<var name = "currentOption" expr = "'home'"/>

<menu id = "publication">

   <prompt count = "1" timeout = "12s">
     Following are some of our publications. For more
     information visit our web page at www.deitel.com.
     To repeat the following menu, say menu at any time.
     Please select by saying one of the following books:
```

Fig. 34.6 Publication page of Deitel's VoiceXML page (part 1 of 4).

```
      <break msecs = "1000" />
      <enumerate/>
   </prompt>

   <prompt count = "2">
      Please select from the following books.
      <break msecs = "1000" />
      <enumerate/>
   </prompt>

   <choice next = "#java">Java.</choice>
   <choice next = "#c">C.</choice>
   <choice next = "#cplus">C plus plus.</choice>
</menu>

<form id = "java">
   <block>
     Java How to program, third edition.
     The complete, authoritative introduction to Java.
     Java is revolutionizing software development with
     multimedia-intensive, platform-independent,
     object-oriented code for conventional, Internet,
     Intranet and Extranet-based applets and applications.
     This Third Edition of the world's most widely used
     university-level Java textbook carefully explains
     Java's extraordinary capabilities.
     <assign name = "currentOption" expr = "'java'"/>
     <goto next = "#repeat"/>
   </block>
</form>

<form id = "c">
   <block>
      C How to Program, third edition.
      This is the long-awaited, thorough revision to the
      world's best-selling introductory C book! The book's
      powerful "teach by example" approach is based on
      more than 10,000 lines of live code, thoroughly
      explained and illustrated with screen captures showing
      detailed output.World-renowned corporate trainers and
      best-selling authors Harvey and Paul Deitel offer the
      most comprehensive, practical introduction to C ever
      published with hundreds of hands-on exercises, more
      than 250 complete programs written and documented for
      easy learning, and exceptional insight into good
      programming practices, maximizing performance, avoiding
      errors, debugging, and testing. New features include
      thorough introductions to C++, Java, and object-oriented
      programming that build directly on the C skills taught
      in this book; coverage of graphical user interface
      development and C library functions; and many new,
      substantial hands-on projects.For anyone who wants to
      learn C, improve their existing C skills, and understand
      how C serves as the foundation for C++, Java, and
```

Fig. 34.6 Publication page of Deitel's VoiceXML page (part 2 of 4).

```
         object-oriented development.
         <assign name = "currentOption" expr = "'c'"/>
         <goto next = "#repeat"/>
      </block>
   </form>

   <form id = "cplus">
      <block>
         The C++ how to program, second edition.
         With nearly 250,000 sold, Harvey and Paul Deitel's C++
         How to Program is the world's best-selling introduction
         to C++ programming. Now, this classic has been thoroughly
         updated! The new, full-color Third Edition has been
         completely revised to reflect the ANSI C++ standard, add
         powerful new coverage of object analysis and design with
         UML, and give beginning C++ developers even better live
         code examples and real-world projects. The Deitels' C++
         How to Program is the most comprehensive, practical
         introduction to C++ ever published with hundreds of
         hands-on exercises, roughly 250 complete programs written
         and documented for easy learning, and exceptional insight
         into good programming practices, maximizing performance,
         avoiding errors, debugging, and testing. This new Third
         Edition covers every key concept and technique ANSI C++
         developers need to master: control structures, functions,
         arrays, pointers and strings, classes and data
         abstraction, operator overloading, inheritance, virtual
         functions, polymorphism, I/O, templates, exception
         handling, file processing, data structures, and more. It
         also includes a detailed introduction to Standard
         Template Library containers, container adapters,
         algorithms, and iterators.
         <assign name = "currentOption" expr = "'cplus'"/>
         <goto next = "#repeat"/>
      </block>
   </form>

   <form id = "repeat">
      <field name = "confirm" type = "boolean">

         <prompt>
            To repeat say yes. Say no, to go back to home.
         </prompt>

         <filled>
            <if cond = "confirm == true">
               <goto expr = "'#' + currentOption"/>
            <else/>
               <goto next = "#publication"/>
            </if>
         </filled>
      </field>
   </form>
</vxml>
```

Fig. 34.6 Publication page of Deitel's VoiceXML page (part 3 of 4).

```
Computer:
Welcome to the voice page of Deitel and Associates. To exit any time
say exit. To go to the home page any time say home.

User:
Home

Computer:
You have just entered the Deitel home page. Please make a selection by
speaking one of the following options: About us, Driving directions,
Publications.

User:
Driving directions

Computer:
Directions to Deitel and Associates, Inc.
We are located on Route 20 in Sudbury,
Massachusetts, equidistant from route 128
and route 495.
To repeat say yes. To go back to home, say no.
```

Fig. 34.6 Publication page of Deitel's VoiceXML page (part 4 of 4).

The **menu** element on line 26 enables users to select the page to which they would like to link. The **choice** element, which is always part of either a **menu** or a **form**, presents the options. The **next** attribute indicates the page to be loaded when a user makes a selection. The user selects a **choice** element by speaking the text marked up between the tags into a microphone. In this example, the first and second **choice** elements on lines 41–42 transfer control to a *local dialog* (i.e., a location within the same document) when they are selected. The third **choice** element transfers the user to the document **publications.vxml**. Lines 27–33 use element ***prompt*** to instruct the user to make a selection. Attribute ***count*** maintains the number of times a prompt is spoken (i.e., each time a prompt is read, **count** increments by one). The **count** attribute transfers control to another prompt once a certain limit has been reached. Attribute **timeout** specifies how long the program should wait after outputting the prompt for users to respond. In the event that the user does not respond before the timeout period expires, lines 35–39 provide a second, shorter prompt to remind the user to make a selection.

When the user chooses the **publications** option, the **publications.vxml** (Fig. 34.6) loads into the browser. Lines 106–111 define **link** elements that provide links to **main.vxml**. Lines 112–114 provide links to the **menu** element (lines 118–138), which asks users to select one of the publications: Java, C or C++. The **form** elements on lines 140–214 describe each of the books on these topics. Once the browser speaks the description, control transfers to the **form** element with an **id** attribute that has a value equal to **repeat** (lines 216–231).

Figure 34.7 provides a brief description of each VoiceXML tag used in the previous example (Fig. 34.6).

VoiceXML Tag	Description
`<assign>`	Assigns a value to a variable.
`<block>`	Presents information to users without any interaction between the user and the computer (i.e., the computer does not expect any input from the user).
`<break>`	Instructs the computer to pause its speech output for a specified period of time.
`<choice>`	Specifies an option in a **menu** element.
`<enumerate>`	Lists all the available options to the user.
`<exit>`	Exits the program.
`<filled>`	Contains elements to be executed when the computer receives user input for a **form** element.
`<form>`	Gathers information from the user for a set of variables.
`<goto>`	Transfers control from one dialog to another.
`<grammar>`	Specifies grammar for the expected input from the user.
`<if>`, `<else>`, `<elseif>`	Control statements used for making logic decisions.
`<link>`	A transfer of control similar to the **goto** statement, but a **link** can be executed at any time during the program's execution.
`<menu>`	Provides user options and transfers control to other dialogs, based on the selected option.
`<prompt>`	Specifies text to be read to the user when a selection is needed.
`<subdialog>`	Calls another dialog. After executing the subdialog, the calling dialog resumes control.
`<var>`	Declares a variable.
`<vxml>`	The top-level tag specifying that the document should be processed by a VoiceXML interpreter.

Fig. 34.7 Some VoiceXML tags.

34.10 CallXML™

Another advancement in voice technology for people with visual impairments is *CallXML*, a technology created and supported by *Voxeo* (**www.voxeo.com**). CallXML creates phone-to-Web applications that control incoming and outgoing telephone calls. Some examples of CallXML applications include voice mail, interactive voice response systems and Internet call waiting. While VoiceXML assists individuals with visual impairments by reading Web pages, CallXML provides individuals with visual impairments access to Web-based content through telephones.

When users access CallXML applications, a *text-to-speech (TTS)* engine reads information contained within CallXML elements. A TTS engine converts text to an automated voice. Web applications respond to the caller's input. [*Note*: A touch-tone phone is required to access CallXML applications.]

Typically, CallXML applications play pre-recorded audio clips or text as output, requesting a response as input. An audio clip may contain a greeting that introduces callers to the application or to a menu of options that requires callers to make touch-tone entries. Certain applications, such as voice mail, may require verbal and touch-tone input. Once the input is received, the application responds by invoking CallXML elements such as **`text`**, which contain the information a TTS engine reads to users. If the application does not receive input within a designated time frame, it prompts the user to enter valid input.

When a user accesses a CallXML application, the incoming telephone call is referred to as a *session*. A CallXML application can support multiple sessions, enabling the application to receive multiple telephone calls at once. Each session is independent of the others and is assigned a unique *sessionID* for identification. A session terminates either when the user hangs up the telephone or when the CallXML application invokes the **`hangup`** element. Our first CallXML example shows the classic Hello World example (Fig. 34.8).

Line 1 contains the optional *XML declaration*.Value ***`version`*** indicates the XML version to which the document conforms. The current XML recommendation is version **`1.0`**. Value ***`encoding`*** indicates the type of *Unicode* encoding to use. For this example we use UTF-8, which requires eight bits to transfer and receive data. More information on Unicode may be found in Appendix G, Unicode®.

```
1  <?xml version = "1.0" encoding = "UTF-8"?>
2
3  <!-- Fig. 34.8: hello.xml              -->
4  <!-- The classic Hello World example -->
5
6  <callxml>
7     <text>Hello World.</text>
8  </callxml>
```

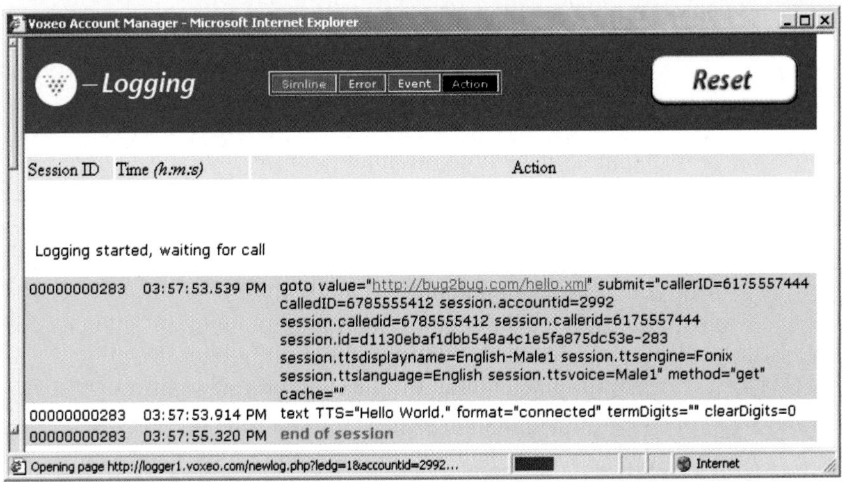

Fig. 34.8 **Hello World** CallXML example. (Courtesy of Voxeo, © Voxeo Corporation 2000–2001.)

The **<callxml>** tag on line 6 declares the contents of a CallXML document. Line 7 contains the **Hello World text**. All text that is to be spoken by a text-to-speech (TTS) engine needs to be placed within **<text>** tags.

To deploy a CallXML application, register with the *Voxeo* Community (**community.voxeo.com**), a Web resource for creating, debugging and deploying phone applications. For the most part, Voxeo is a free Web resource. However, the company charges fees when CallXML applications are deployed commercially. The Voxeo Community assigns a unique telephone number to each CallXML application so that external users may access and interact with the application. [*Note*: Voxeo assigns telephone numbers to applications that reside on the Internet. If you have access to a Web server (IIS, PWS, Apache, etc.), use it to post your CallXML application. Otherwise, open an Internet account using one of the many Internet-service companies (e.g., **www.geocities.com**, **www.angelfire.com**). These companies allow you to post documents on the Internet by using their Web servers.]

Figure 34.8 demonstrates the *logging* feature of the **Voxeo Account Manager**, which is accessible to registered members. The logging feature records and displays the "conversation" between the user and the application. The first row of the logging feature displays the URL of the CallXML application and the *global variables* associated with each session. The application (program) creates and assigns values to global variables at the start of each session, which the entire application can access and modify. The subsequent row(s) display(s) the "conversation." This example shows a one-way conversation (because the application does not accept any input from the user) in which the TTS says **Hello World**. The last row shows the **end of session** message, which states that the phone call has terminated. The logging feature assists developers in debugging their applications. By observing the "conversation," a developer can determine at which point the application terminates. If the application terminates abruptly ("crashes"), the logging feature states the type and location of the error, so that a developer knows the particular section of the application on which to focus.

The next example (Fig. 34.9) shows a CallXML application that reads the ISBN values of three Deitel textbooks—*Internet and World Wide Web How to Program: Second Edition*, *XML How to Program* and *Java How to Program: Fourth Edition*—based on the user's touch-tone input. [*Note*: The following code has been formatted for presentation purposes.]

```
<?xml version = "1.0" encoding = "UTF-8"?>

<!-- Fig. 34.9: isbn.xml                          -->
<!-- Reads the ISBN value of three Deitel books -->

<callxml>
   <block>
      <text>
         Welcome. To obtain the ISBN of the Internet and World
         Wide Web How to Program: Second Edition, please enter 1.
         To obtain the ISBN of the XML How to Program,
```

Fig. 34.9 CallXML example that reads three ISBN values (part 1 of 3). (Courtesy of Voxeo, © Voxeo Corporation 2000–2001.)

```
         please enter 2. To obtain the ISBN of the Java How
         to Program: Fourth Edition, please enter 3. To exit the
         application, please enter 4.
      </text>

      <!-- obtains the numeric value entered by the user and -->
      <!-- stores it in the variable ISBN. The user has 60   -->
      <!-- seconds to enter one numeric value                -->
      <getDigits var = "ISBN"
         maxDigits = "1"
         termDigits = "1234"
         maxTime = "60s" />

      <!-- requests that the user enter a valid numeric -->
      <!-- value after the elapsed time of 60 seconds   -->
      <onMaxSilence>
         <text>
            Please enter either 1, 2, 3 or 4.
         </text>

         <getDigits var = "ISBN"
            termDigits = "1234"
            maxDigits = "1"
            maxTime = "60s" />

      </onMaxSilence>

      <onTermDigit value = "1">
         <text>
            The ISBN for the Internet book is 0130308978.
            Thank you for calling our CallXML application.
            Good-bye.
         </text>
      </onTermDigit>

      <onTermDigit value = "2">
         <text>
            The ISBN for the XML book is 0130284173.
            Thank you for calling our CallXML application.
            Good-bye.
         </text>
      </onTermDigit>

      <onTermDigit value = "3">
         <text>
            The ISBN for the Java book is 0130341517.
            Thank you for calling our CallXML application.
            Good-bye.
         </text>
      </onTermDigit>

      <onTermDigit value = "4">
```

Fig. 34.9 CallXML example that reads three ISBN values (part 2 of 3). (Courtesy of Voxeo, © Voxeo Corporation 2000–2001.)

```
64            <text>
65               Thank you for calling our CallXML application.
66               Good-bye.
67            </text>
68         </onTermDigit>
69      </block>
70
71      <!-- event handler that terminates the call -->
72      <onHangup />
73   </callxml>
```

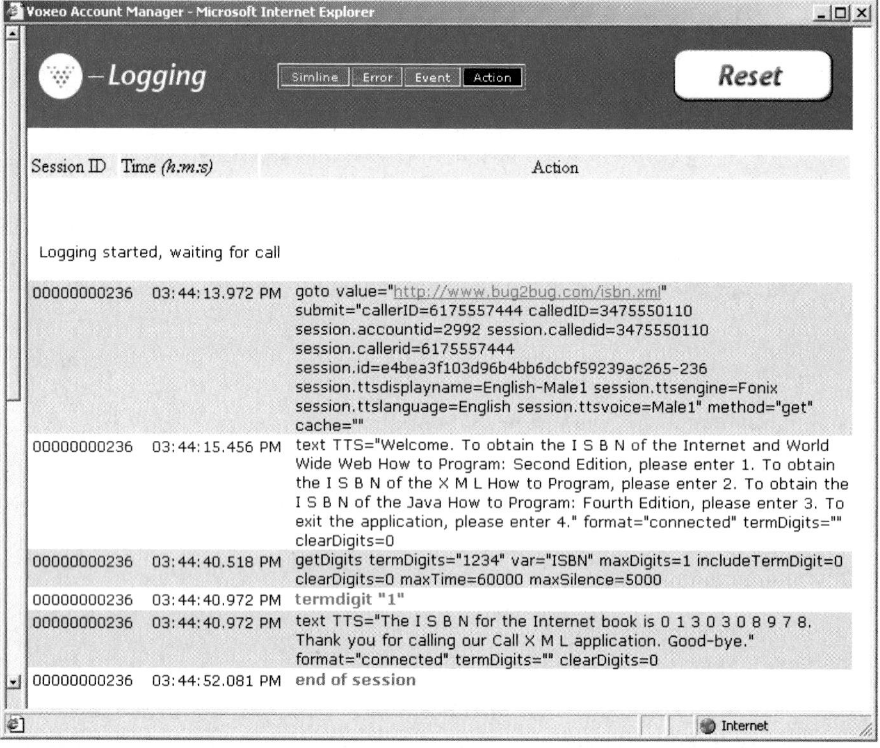

Fig. 34.9 CallXML example that reads three ISBN values (part 3 of 3). (Courtesy of Voxeo, © Voxeo Corporation 2000–2001.)

The ***<block>*** tag (line 7) encapsulates other CallXML tags. Usually, CallXML tags that perform a similar task should be enclosed within **<block>**...**</block>**. The **block** element in this example encapsulates the ***<text>***, ***<getDigits>***, ***<onMaxSilence>*** and ***<onTermDigit>*** tags. A **block** element can also contain nested **block** elements.

Lines 20–23 show some attributes of the **<getDigits>** tag. The **getDigits** element obtains the user's touch-tone response and stores it in the variable declared by the ***var*** attribute (i.e., ISBN). The ***maxDigits*** attribute (line 21) indicates the maximum number of digits that the application can accept. This application accepts only one character. If no number is stated, then the application uses the default value—*nolimit*.

The ***termDigits*** attribute (line 22) contains the list of characters that terminate user input. When a character from this list is received as input, the CallXML application is notified that the last acceptable input has been received and that any character entered after this point is invalid. These characters do not terminate the call; they simply notify the application to proceed to the next step because the necessary input has been received. In our example, the values for **termDigits** are one, two, three or four. The default value for **termDigits** is the null value (**""**).

The ***maxTime*** attribute (line 23) indicates the maximum amount of time to wait for a user response (i.e., 60 seconds). If no input is received within the given time frame, then the CallXML application may terminate—a drastic measure. The default value for this attribute is 30 seconds.

The ***onMaxSilence*** element (lines 27–37) is an *event handler* that is invoked when the **maxTime** (or **maxSilence**) expires. An event handler notifies the application of the appropriate action to perform. In this case, the application asks the user to enter a value because the **maxTime** has expired. After receiving input, **getDigits** (line 32) stores the value in the **ISBN** variable.

The ***onTermDigit*** element (lines 39–68) is an event handler that notifies the application of the appropriate action to perform when users select one of the **termDigits** characters. At least one **<onTermDigit>** tag must be associated with the **getDigits** element, even if the default value (**""**) is used. We provide four actions that the application can perform depending on the user-entered value. For example, if the user enters **1**, the application reads the ISBN value of the *Internet and World Wide Web How to Program: Second Edition* textbook.

Line 72 contains the ***<onHangup/>*** event handler, which terminates the telephone call when the user hangs up the telephone. Our **<onHangup>** event handler is an empty tag (i.e., there is no action to perform when this tag is invoked).

The logging feature in Fig. 34.9 displays the "conversation" between the application and the user. The first row displays the URL of the application and the global variables of the session. The subsequent rows display the "conversation"—the application asks the caller which ISBN value to read, the caller enters **1** (*Internet and World Wide Web How to Program: Second Edition*) and the application reads the corresponding ISBN. The **end of session** message states that the application has terminated.

Brief descriptions of several logic and action CallXML elements are provided in Fig. 34.10. *Logic elements* assign values to, and clear values from, the session variables, and *action elements* perform specified tasks, such as answering and terminating a telephone call during the current session. A complete list of CallXML elements is available at:

www.oasis-open.org/cover/callxmlv2.html

34.11 JAWS® for Windows

JAWS (Job Access with Sound) is one of the leading screen readers on the market today. Henter-Joyce, a division of Freedom Scientific™, created this application to help people with visual impairments use technology.

To download a demonstration version of JAWS, visit **www.hj.com/JAWS/JAWS37DemoOp.htm** and select the **JAWS 3.7 FREE Demo** link. The demo expires after 40 minutes. The computer must be rebooted before another 40-minute session can be started.

Elements	Description
assign	Assigns a **value** to a variable, **var**.
clear	Clears the contents of the **var** attribute.
clearDigits	Clears all digits that the user has entered.
goto	Navigates to another section of the current CallXML application or to a different CallXML application. The **value** attribute specifies the application URL. The **submit** attribute lists the variables that are passed to the invoked application. The **method** attribute states whether to use the HTTP *get* or *post* request types when sending and retrieving information. A *get* request retrieves data from a Web server without modifying the contents, while the *post* request sends modified data.
run	Starts a new CallXML session for each call. The **value** attribute specifies which CallXML application to retrieve. The **submit** attribute lists the variables that are passed to the invoked application. The **method** attribute states whether to use the HTTP *get* or *post* request type. The **var** attribute stores the identification number of the session.
sendEvent	Allows multiple sessions to exchange messages. The **value** attribute stores the message, and the **session** attribute specifies the identification number of the session that receives the message.
answer	Answers an incoming telephone call.
call	Calls the URL specified by the **value** attribute. The **callerID** attribute contains the phone number that is displayed on a CallerID device. The **maxTime** attribute specifies the length of time to wait for the call to be answered before disconnecting.
conference	Connects multiple sessions so that people can participate in a conference call. The **targetSessions** attribute specifies the identification numbers of the sessions, and the **termDigits** attribute indicates the touch-tone keys that terminate the call.
wait	Waits for user input. The **value** attribute specifies how long to wait. The **termDigits** attribute indicates the touch-tone keys that terminate the **wait** element.
play	Plays an audio file or a value that is stored as a number, date or amount of money and is indicated by the **format** attribute. The **value** attribute contains the information (location of the audio file, number, date or amount of money) that corresponds to the **format** attribute. The **clearDigits** attribute specifies whether or not to delete the previously entered input. The **termDigits** attribute indicates the touch-tone keys that terminate the audio file, etc.

Fig. 34.10 List of some CallXML elements (part 1 of 2).

Elements	Description
`recordAudio`	Records an audio file and stores it at the URL specified by **`value`**. The **`format`** attribute indicates the file extension of the audio clip. Other attributes include **`termDigits`**, **`clearDigits`**, **`maxTime`** and **`maxSilence`**.

Fig. 34.10 List of some CallXML elements (part 2 of 2).

The JAWS demo is fully functional and includes an extensive, highly customized help system. Users can select which voice to use and the rate at which text is spoken. Users also can create keyboard shortcuts. Although the demo is in English, the full version of JAWS 3.7 allows the user to choose one of several supported languages.

JAWS also includes special key commands for popular programs such as Microsoft Internet Explorer and Microsoft Word. For example, when browsing in Internet Explorer, JAWS' capabilities extend beyond reading the content on the screen. If JAWS is enabled, pressing *Insert* + *F7* in Internet Explorer opens a **Links List** dialog, which displays all the links available on a Web page. For more information about JAWS and the other products offered by Henter-Joyce, visit **`www.hj.com`**.

34.12 Other Accessibility Tools

Many additional accessibility products are available to assist people with disabilities. This section describes a variety of accessibility products, including hardware items and advanced technologies.

A *braille keyboard*, in addition to having each key labeled with the letter it represents, has the equivalent braille symbol printed on the key. Braille keyboards are combined most often with a speech synthesizer or a braille display, so users can interact with the computer to verify that their typing is correct.

Speech synthesis is another research-intensive area that will benefit people with disabilities. Speech synthesizers have been used for many years to aid those who are unable to communicate verbally. However, the growing popularity of the Web has prompted a great deal of work in the field of speech synthesis and speech recognition. These technologies are allowing individuals with disabilities to use computers more than ever before. The development of speech synthesizers is also enabling the improvement of other technologies, such as VoiceXML and *AuralCSS* (**`www.w3.org/TR/REC-CSS2/aural.html`**). These tools allow people with visual impairment and the illiterate to access Web sites.

Despite the existence of adaptive software and hardware for people with visual impairments, the accessibility of computers and the Internet is still hampered by the high costs, rapid obsolescence and unnecessary complexity of current technology. Moreover, almost all software currently available requires installation by a person who can see. *Ocularis* is a project launched in the open-source community to help address these problems. Open source software for people with visual impairments already exists, and although it is often superior to its proprietary, closed-source counterparts, it has not yet reached its full potential. Ocularis ensures that the blind can use the Linux operating system fully, by providing an Audio User Interface (AUI). Products that integrate with Ocularis include a word processor, calculator, basic finance application, Internet browser and e-mail client. A screen reader will also be included with programs that have a command-line interface. The official Ocularis Web site is located at **ocularis.sourceforge.net**.

People with visual impairments are not the only beneficiaries of the effort being made to improve markup languages. People with hearing impairments also have a number of tools to help them interpret auditory information delivered over the Web, such as *Synchronized Multimedia Integration Language* (SMIL™), discussed in Chapter 33, Multimedia. This markup language is designed to add extra *tracks*—layers of content found within a single audio or video file—to multimedia content. The additional tracks can contain closed captioning.

Technologies also are being designed to help people with severe disabilities, such as *quadriplegia*, a form of paralysis that affects the body from the neck down. One such technology, *EagleEyes*, developed by researchers at Boston College (**www.bc.edu/eagleeyes**), is a system that translates eye movements into mouse movements. Users move the mouse cursors by moving their eyes or heads and thereby can control computers.

The company CitXCorp is developing new technology that translates Web information through the telephone. Information on a specific topic can be accessed by dialing the designated number. The new software is expected to be made available to users for $10 per month. For more information on regulations governing the design of Web sites to accommodate people with disabilities, visit **www.access-board.gov**.

In alliance with Microsoft, GW Micro, Henter-Joyce and Adobe Systems, Inc. are also working on software to aid people with disabilities. JetForm Corp also is accommodating the needs of people with disabilities by developing server-based XML software. The new software allows users to download a format that best meets their needs.

There are many services on the Web that assist e-business owners in designing their Web sites to be accessible to individuals with disabilities. For additional information, the U.S. Department of Justice (**www.usdoj.gov**) provides extensive resources detailing legal issues and current technologies related to people with disabilities.

These examples are just a few of the accessibility projects and technologies that currently exist. For more information on Web and general computer accessibility, see the resources provided in Section 34.14, Internet and World Wide Web Resources.

34.13 Accessibility in Microsoft® Windows® 2000

Beginning with Microsoft *Windows 95*, Microsoft has included accessibility features in its operating systems and many of its applications, including *Office 97*, *Office 2000* and *Netmeeting*. In Microsoft *Windows 2000*, the accessibility features have been significantly enhanced. All the accessibility options provided by Windows 2000 are available through the ***Accessibility Wizard***, which guides users through all the Windows 2000 accessibility features and configures their computers according to the chosen specifications. This section guides users through the configuration of their Windows 2000 accessibility options using the **Accessibility Wizard**.

To access the **Accessibility Wizard**, users must have Microsoft Windows 2000. Click the **Start** button and select **Programs** followed by **Accessories**, **Accessibility** and

Accessibility Wizard. When the wizard starts, the **Welcome** screen is displayed. Click **Next** to display a dialog (Fig. 34.11) that asks the user to select a font size. Click **Next**.

Figure 34.12 shows the next dialog displayed. This dialog allows the user to activate the font size settings chosen in the previous window, change the screen resolution, enable the *Microsoft Magnifier* (a program that displays an enlarged section of the screen in a separate window) and disable personalized menus (a feature which hides rarely used programs from the start menu, which can be a hindrance to users with disabilities). Make selections and click **Next**.

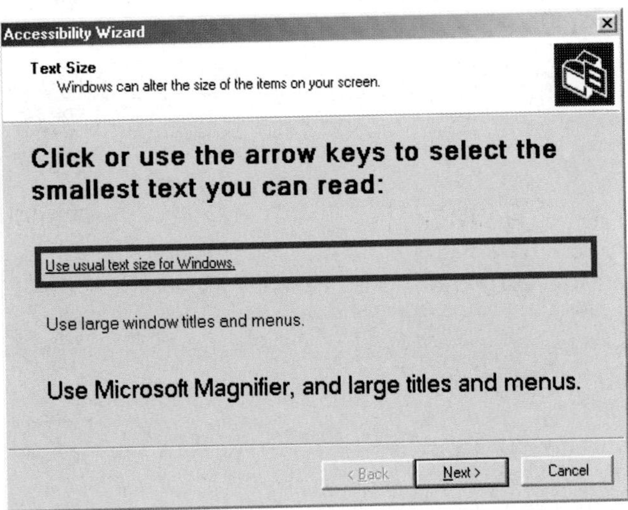

Fig. 34.11 **Font Size** dialog.

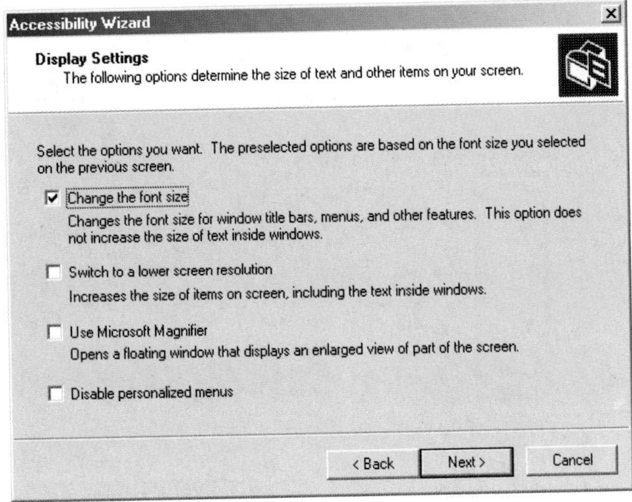

Fig. 34.12 **Display Settings** dialog.

The next dialog (Fig. 34.13) displayed asks questions about the user's disabilities, which allows the **Accessibility Wizard** to customize Windows to better suit their needs. We selected everything for demonstration purposes. Click **Next** to continue.

34.13.1 Tools for People with Visual Impairments

When we checked all the options in Fig. 34.13, the wizard began configuring Windows for people with visual impairments. As shown in Fig. 34.14, this dialog box allows the users to resize the scroll bars and window borders to increase their visibility. Click **Next** to proceed to the next dialog.

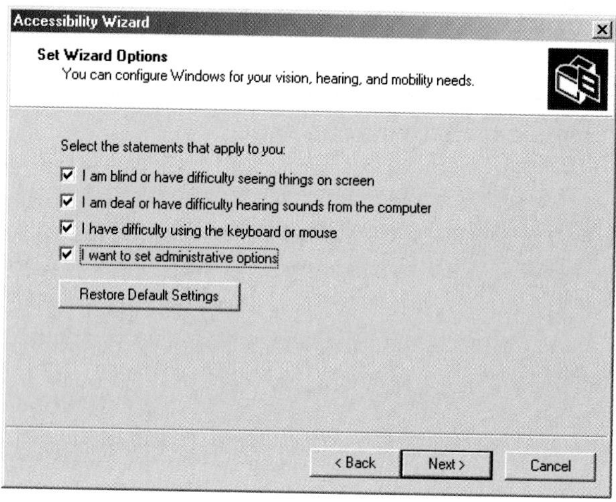

Fig. 34.13 Accessibility Wizard initialization options.

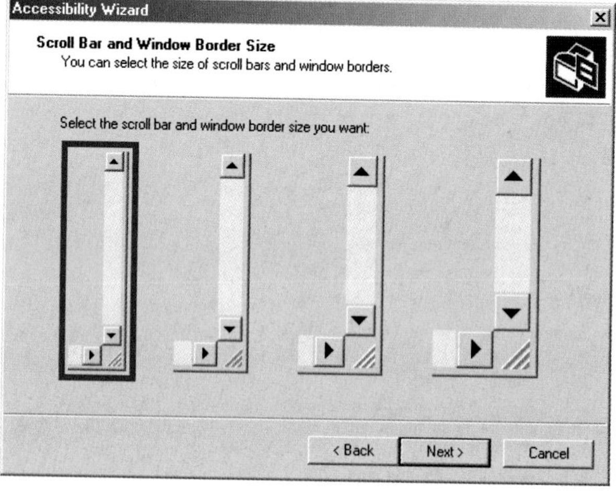

Fig. 34.14 Scroll Bar and Window Border Size dialog.

The dialog in Fig. 34.15's dialog allows the user to resize icons. Users with poor vision, as well as users who have trouble reading, benefit from large icons.

Clicking **Next** displays the **Display Color Settings** dialog (Fig. 34.16). These settings allow users to change Windows' color scheme and resize various screen elements. Click **Next** to view the dialog (Fig. 34.17) for customizing the mouse cursor.

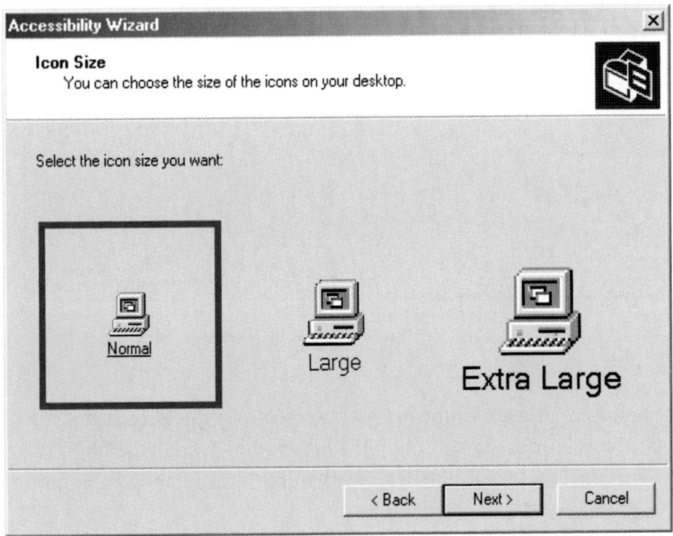

Fig. 34.15 Setting up window element sizes.

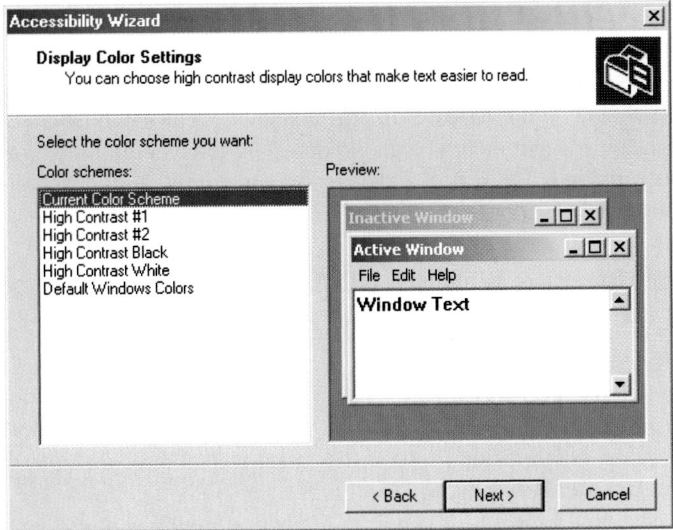

Fig. 34.16 **Display Color Settings** options.

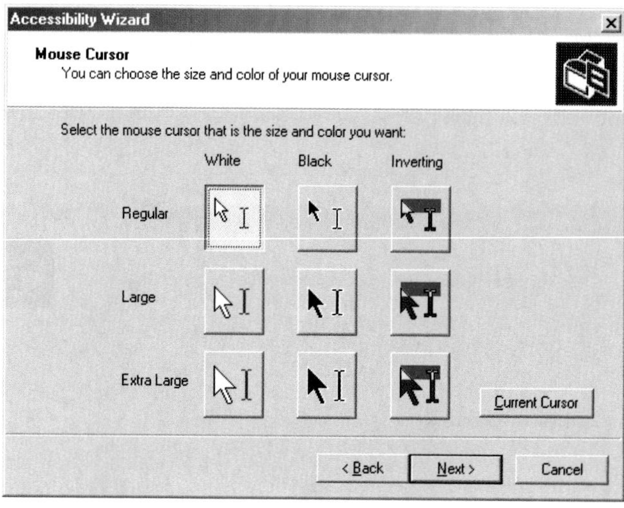

Fig. 34.17 **Accessibility Wizard** mouse cursor adjustment tool.

Anyone who has ever used a laptop computer knows how difficult it is to see the mouse cursor. This is also a problem for people with visual impairments. To help solve this problem, the wizard offers larger cursors, black cursors and cursors that invert the colors of objects underneath them. Click **Next**.

34.13.2 Tools for People with Hearing Impairments

This section, which focuses on accessibility for people with hearing impairments, begins with the ***SoundSentry*** window (Fig. 34.18). **SoundSentry** is a tool that creates visual signals when system events occur. For example, people with hearing impairments are unable to hear the beeps that normally warn users, so **SoundSentry** flashes the screen when a beep occurs. To continue to the next dialog, click **Next**.

The next window is the ***ShowSounds*** window (Fig. 34.19). **ShowSounds** adds captions to spoken text and other sounds produced by today's multimedia-rich software. For **ShowSounds** to work, software developers must provide the captions and spoken text specifically within their software. Make selections and click **Next**.

34.13.3 Tools for Users Who Have Difficulty Using the Keyboard

The next dialog is **StickyKeys** (Fig. 34.20). ***StickyKeys*** is a program that helps users who have difficulty pressing multiple keys at the same time. Many important computer commands can be invoked only by pressing specific key combinations. For example, the reboot command requires pressing *Ctrl+Alt+Delete* simultaneously. **StickyKeys** allows the user to press key combinations in sequence rather than at the same time. Click **Next** to continue to the **BounceKeys** dialog (Fig. 34.21).

Another common problem for certain users with disabilities is accidentally pressing the same key more than once. This problem typically is caused by holding a key down too long. ***BounceKeys*** forces the computer to ignore repeated keystrokes. Click **Next**.

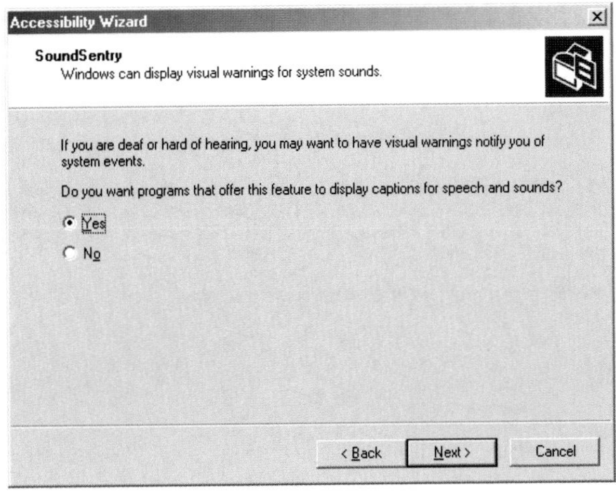

Fig. 34.18 **SoundSentry** dialog.

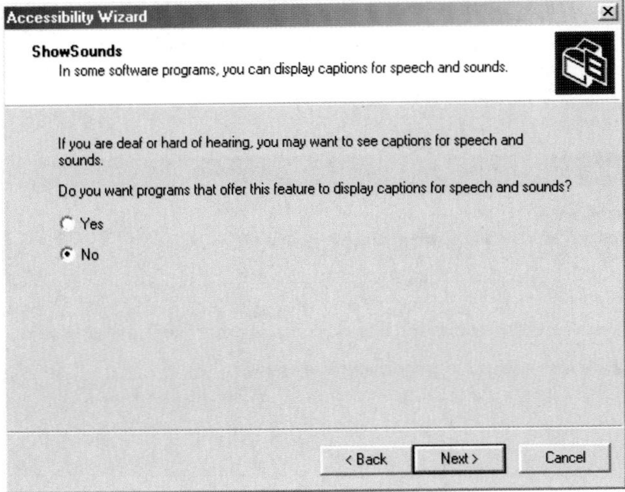

Fig. 34.19 **ShowSounds** dialog.

ToggleKeys (Fig. 34.22) alerts users that they have pressed one of the lock keys (i.e., *Caps Lock*, *Num Lock* and *Scroll Lock*) by sounding an audible beep. Make selections and click **Next**.

Next, the **Extra Keyboard Help** dialog (Fig. 34.23) is displayed. This section activates a tool that displays information such as keyboard shortcuts and tool tips when they are available. Like ShowSounds, this tool requires that software developers provide the content to be displayed. Clicking **Next** will load the **MouseKeys** (Fig. 34.24) customization window.

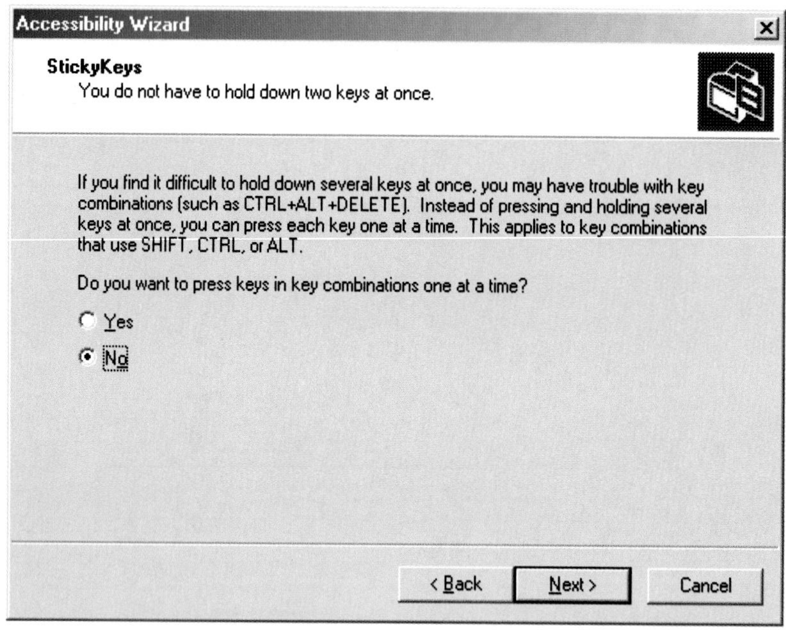

Fig. 34.20 **StickyKeys** window.

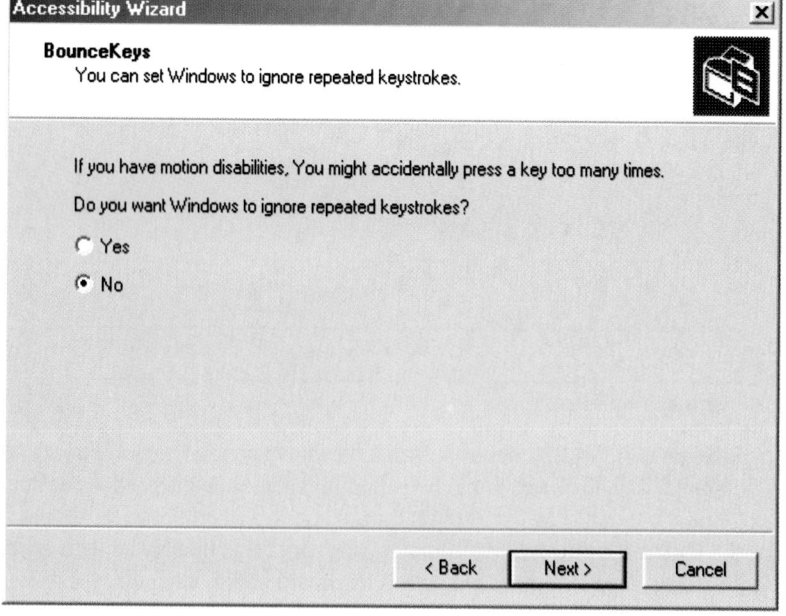

Fig. 34.21 **BounceKeys** dialog.

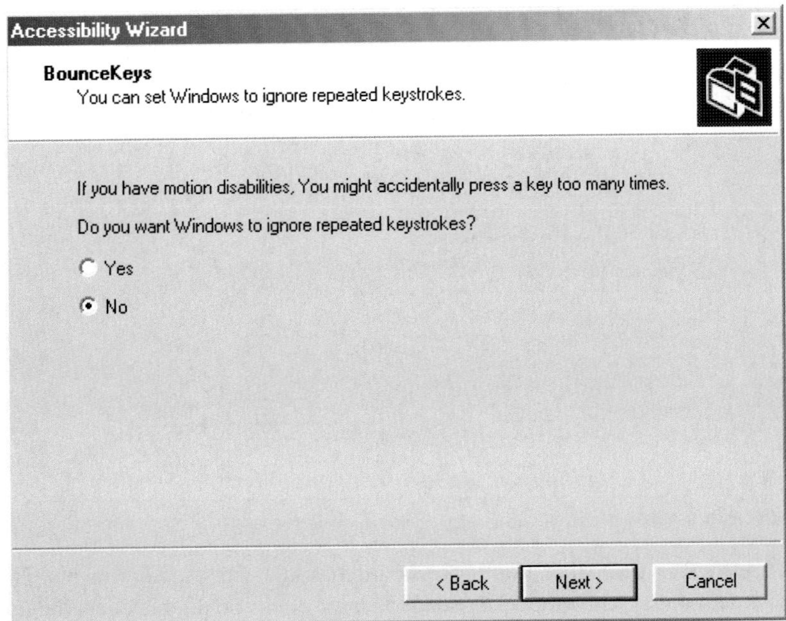

Fig. 34.22 ToggleKeys window.

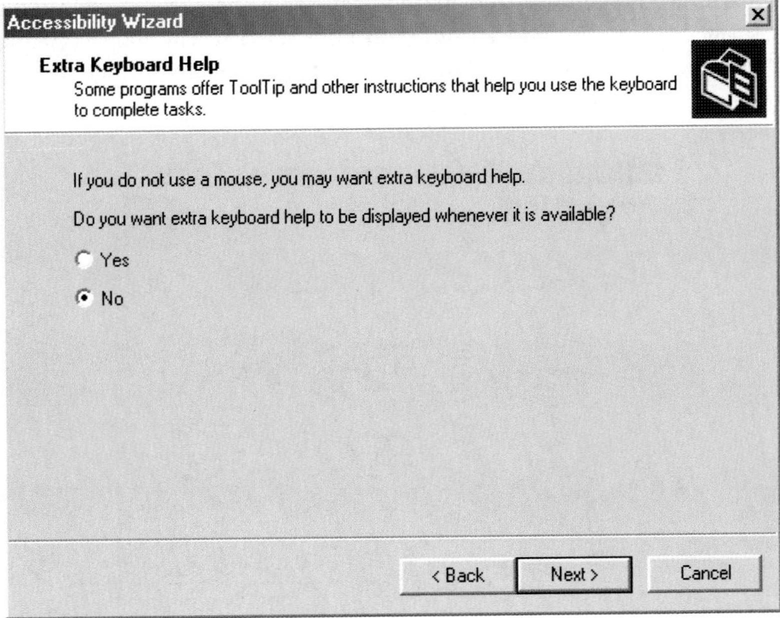

Fig. 34.23 Extra Keyboard Help dialog.

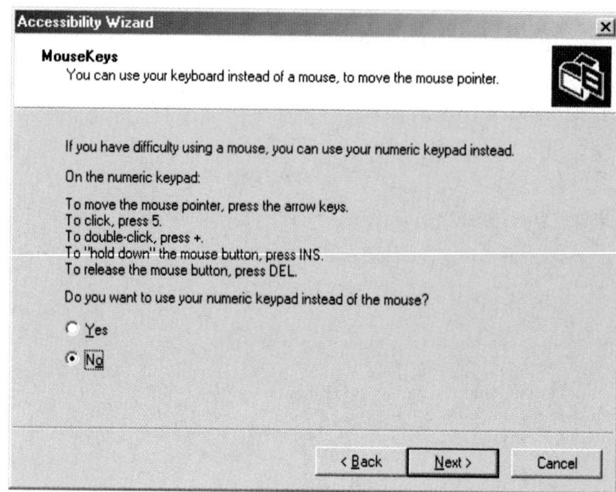

Fig. 34.24 MouseKeys window.

MouseKeys is a tool that uses the keyboard to emulate mouse movements. The arrow keys direct the mouse, while the *5* key sends a single click. To double click, the user must press the + key; to simulate holding down the mouse button, the user must press the *Ins* (Insert) key and to release the mouse button, the user must press the *Del* (Delete) key. To continue to the next screen in the **Accessibility Wizard**, click **Next**.

Today's computer tools are made almost exclusively for right-handed users, including most computer mice. Microsoft recognized this problem and added the ***Mouse Button* Settings** window (Fig. 34.25) to the **Accessibility Wizard**. This tool allows the user to create a virtual left-handed mouse by swapping the button functions. Click **Next**.

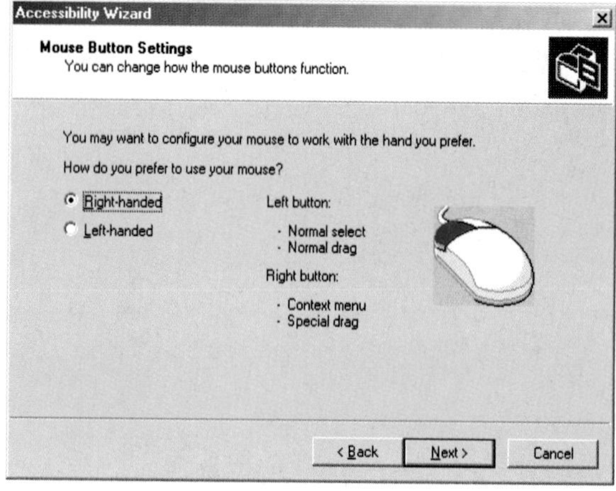

Fig. 34.25 Mouse Button Settings window.

Mouse speed is adjusted by using the **MouseSpeed** (Fig. 34.26) section of the **Accessibility Wizard**. Dragging the scroll bar changes the speed. Clicking the **Next** button sets the speed and displays the wizard's **Set Automatic Timeouts** window (Fig. 34.27).

Although accessibility tools are important to users with disabilities, they can be a hindrance to users who do not need them. In situations where varying accessibility needs exist, it is important that the user be able to turn the accessibility tools off and on as necessary. The ***Set Automatic Timeouts*** window specifies a *timeout* period for the tools. A timeout either enables or disables a certain action after the computer has idled for a specified amount of time. A screen saver is a common example of a program with a timeout period. Here, a timeout is set to toggle the accessibility tools.

Accessibility Wizard
Mouse Speed
You can change the speed of your mouse pointer.
If you have difficulty positioning the mouse pointer to select items on the screen, you can adjust the speed of the pointer.
Mouse pointer speed: Slow Fast
< Back Next > Cancel

Fig. 34.26 **Mouse Speed** dialog.

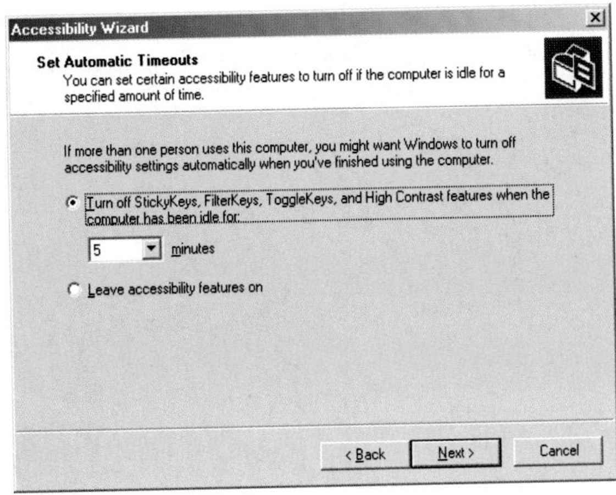

Fig. 34.27 **Set Automatic Timeouts** dialog.

After clicking **Next**, the **Save Settings to File** dialog appears (Fig. 34.28). This dialog determines whether the accessibility settings should be used as the *default settings*, which are loaded when the computer is rebooted, or after a timeout. Set the accessibility settings as the default if the majority of users need them. Users can save the accessibility settings as well, by creating an `.acw` file, which, when clicked, activates the saved accessibility settings on any Windows 2000 computer.

34.13.4 Microsoft Narrator

Microsoft **Narrator** is a text-to-speech program for people with visual impairments. It reads text, describes the current desktop environment and alerts the user when certain Windows events occur. **Narrator** is intended to aid in configuring Microsoft Windows. It is a screen reader that works with Internet Explorer, *Wordpad*, *Notepad* and most programs in the **Control Panel**. Although it is limited outside these applications, **Narrator** is excellent at navigating the Windows environment.

To get an idea of what **Narrator** does, we will explain how to use it with various Windows applications. Click the **Start** button and select **Programs**, followed by **Accessories**, **Accessibility** and **Narrator**. Once **Narrator** is open, it describes the current foreground window. It then reads the text inside the window aloud to the user. Clicking **OK** displays Fig. 34.29's dialog.

Checking the first option instructs **Narrator** to describe menus and new windows when they are opened. The second option instructs **Narrator** to speak the characters you are typing as you type them. The third option moves the mouse cursor to the region being read by **Narrator**. Clicking the **Voice...** button enables the user to change the pitch, volume and speed of the narrator voice.

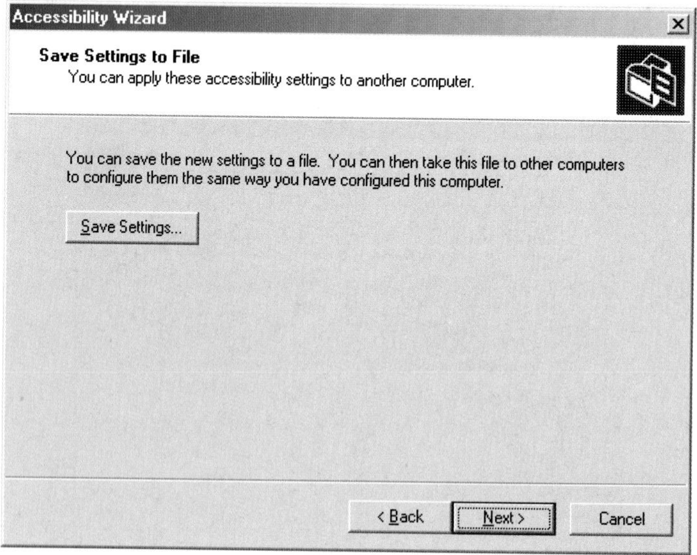

Fig. 34.28 Saving new accessibility settings.

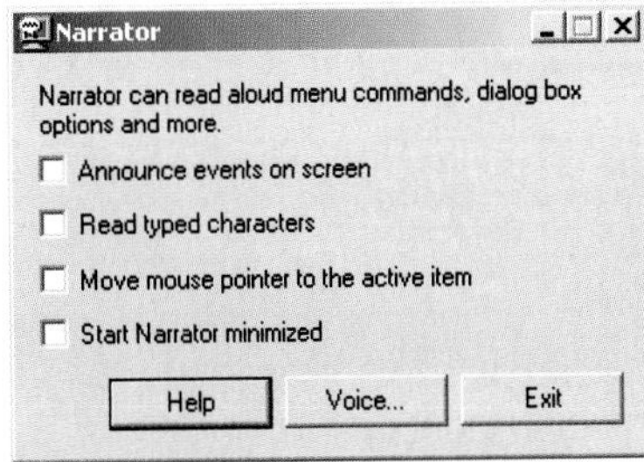

Fig. 34.29 **Narrator** window.

With **Narrator** running, open **Notepad** and click the **File** menu. **Narrator** announces the opening of the program and begins to describe the items in the **File** menu. When scrolling down the list, **Narrator** reads the current item to which the mouse is pointing. Type some text and press *Ctrl-Shift-Enter* to hear **Narrator** read it (Fig. 34.30). If the **Read typed characters** option is checked, **Narrator** reads each character as it is typed. The direction arrows on the keyboard can be used to make **Narrator** read. The up and down arrows cause **Narrator** to speak the lines adjacent to the current mouse position, and the left and right arrows cause **Narrator** to speak the characters adjacent to the current mouse position.

34.13.5 Microsoft On-Screen Keyboard

Some computer users lack the ability to use a keyboard but can use a pointing device such as a mouse. For these users, the *On-Screen Keyboard* is helpful. To access the On-Screen Keyboard, click the **Start** button and select **Programs** followed by **Accessories**, **Accessibility** and **On-Screen Keyboard**. Figure 34.31 shows the layout of the Microsoft On-Screen Keyboard.

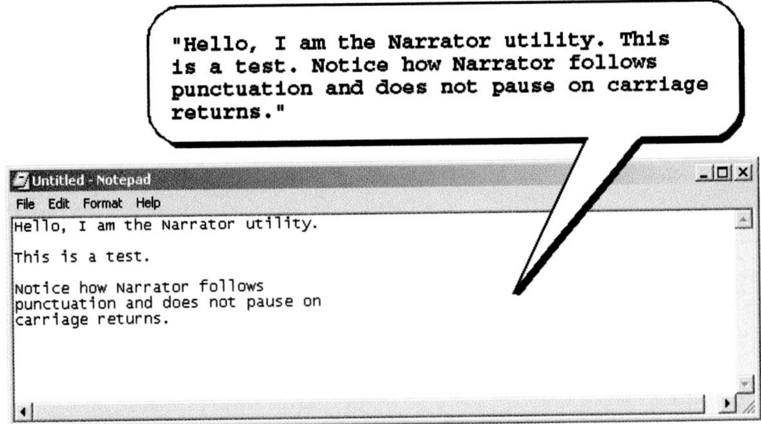

Fig. 34.30 **Narrator** reading **Notepad** text.

Fig. 34.31 Microsoft **On-Screen Keyboard**.

Users who still have difficulty using the On-Screen Keyboard should purchase more sophisticated products, such as *Clicker 4*™ by *Inclusive Technology*. Clicker 4 is an aid for people who cannot effectively use a keyboard. Its best feature is its ability to be customized. Keys can have letters, numbers, entire words or even pictures on them. For more information regarding Clicker 4, visit **`www.inclusive.co.uk/catalog/clicker.htm`**.

34.13.6 Accessibility Features in Microsoft Internet Explorer 5.5

Internet Explorer 5.5 offers a variety of options to improve usability. To access IE5.5's accessibility features, launch the program, click the **Tools** menu and select **Internet Options...**. From the **Internet Options** menu, press the button labeled **Accessibility...** to open the accessibility options (Fig. 34.32).

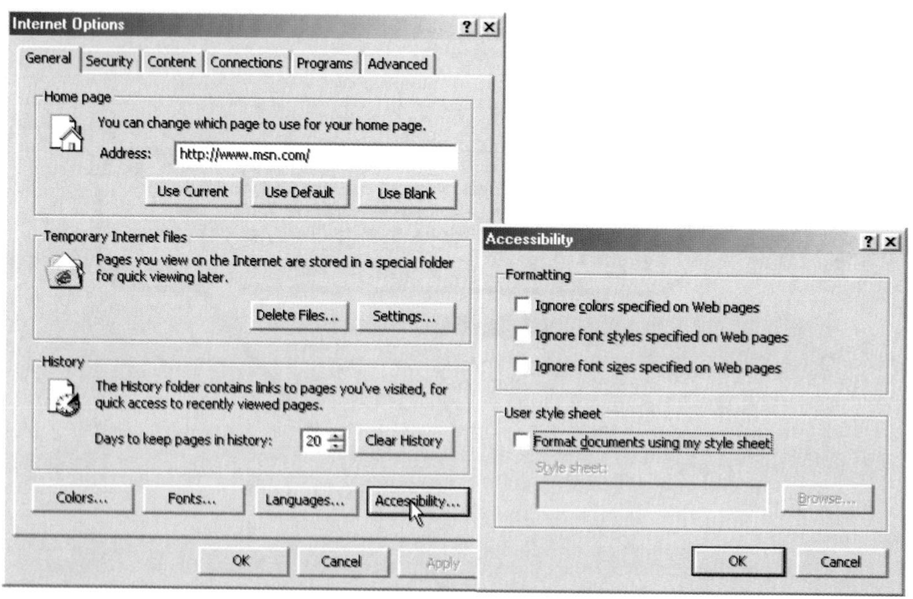

Fig. 34.32 Microsoft Internet Explorer 5.5's accessibility options.

The accessibility options in IE5.5 augment users' Web browsing. Users can ignore Web colors, Web fonts and font size tags. This eliminates problems that arise from poor Web page design and allows users to customize their Web browsing. Users can even specify a *style sheet*, which formats every Web site visited according to users' personal preferences.

These are not the only accessibility options offered in IE5.5. In the **Internet Options** dialog click the **Advanced** tab. This opens the dialog shown in Fig. 34.33. The first option that can be set is labeled **Always expand ALT text for images**. By default, IE5.5 hides some of the `<alt>` text if it exceeds the size of the image it describes. This option forces all the text to be shown. The second option reads: **Move system caret with focus/selection changes**. This option is intended to make screen reading more effective. Some screen readers use the *system caret* (the blinking vertical bar associated with editing text) to decide what is read. If this option is not activated, screen readers may not read Web pages correctly.

Web designers often forget to take accessibility into account when creating Web sites and they use fonts that are too small. Many user agents have addressed this problem by allowing the user to adjust the text size. Click the **View** menu and select **Text Size** to change the font size using IE5.5. By default, the text size is set to **Medium**.

34.14 Internet and World Wide Web Resources

There are many accessibility resources on the Internet and World Wide Web, and this section lists a variety of these resources.

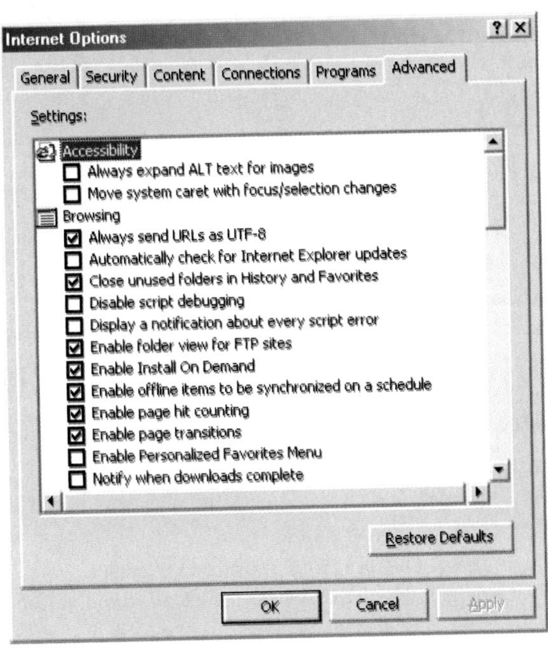

Fig. 34.33 Advanced accessibility settings in Microsoft Internet Explorer 5.5.

www.w3.org/WAI
The World Wide Web Consortium's *Web Accessibility Initiative (WAI)* site promotes the design of universally accessible Web sites. This site contains the current guidelines and forthcoming standards for Web accessibility.

deafness.about.com/health/deafness/msubmenu6.htm
This is the home page of **deafness.about.com**. It is a resource to find information pertaining to deafness.

www.cast.org
CAST (Center for Applied Special Technology) offers software, including a valuable accessibility checker, that help individuals with disabilities use a computer. The accessibility checker is a Web-based program that validates the accessibility of Web sites.

www.trainingpost.org/3-2-inst.htm
This site presents a tutorial on the Gunning Fog Index. The Gunning Fog Index is a method of grading text on its readability.

www.w3.org/TR/REC-CSS2/aural.html
This page discusses Aural Style Sheets, outlining the purpose and uses of this new technology.

laurence.canlearn.ca/English/learn/newaccessguide/indie
INDIE stands for "Integrated Network of Disability Information and Education." This site is home to a search engine that helps users find information on disabilities.

java.sun.com/products/java-media/speech/forDevelopers/JSML
This site outlines the specifications for JSML, Sun Microsystem's Java Speech Markup Language. This language, like VoiceXML, could drastically improve accessibility for people with visual impairments.

www.slcc.edu/webguide/lynxit.html
Lynxit is a development tool that allows users to view any Web site as a text-only browser would. The site's form allows you to enter a URL and returns the Web site in text-only format.

www.trill-home.com/lynx/public_lynx.html
This site allows users to browse the Web with a Lynx browser. Users can view how Web pages appear to users without the most current technologies.

www.wgbh.org/wgbh/pages/ncam/accesslinks.html
This site provides links to other accessibility pages across the Web.

ocfo.ed.gov/coninfo/clibrary/software.htm
This page is the U.S. Department of Education's Web site for software accessibility requirements. It helps developers produce accessible products.

www-3.ibm.com/able/access.html
The homepage of IBM's accessibility site provides information on IBM products and their accessibility and discusses hardware, software and Web accessibility.

www.w3.org/TR/voice-tts-reqs
This page explains the speech synthesis markup requirements for voice markup languages.

www.voicexmlcentral.com
This site contains information about VoiceXML, such as the specification and the document type definition (DTD).

deafness.about.com/health/deafness/msubvib.htm
This site provides information on vibrotactile devices, which allow individuals with hearing impairments to experience audio in the form of vibrations.

web.ukonline.co.uk/ddmc/software.html
This site provides links to software for people with disabilities.

www.hj.com
Henter-Joyce is a division of Freedom Scientific that provides software for people with visual impairments. It is the home of JAWS.

www.abledata.com/text2/icg_hear.htm
This page contains a consumer guide that discusses technologies for people with hearing impairments.

www.washington.edu/doit
The University of Washington's DO-IT (Disabilities, Opportunities, Internetworking and Technology) site provides information and Web development resources for creating universally accessible Web sites.

www.webable.com
WebABLE contains links to many disability-related Internet resources and is geared towards those developing technologies for people with disabilities.

www.webaim.org
The *WebAIM* site provides a number of tutorials, articles, simulations and other useful resources that demonstrate how to design accessible Web sites. The site provides a screen reader simulation.

www.speech.cs.cmu.edu/comp.speech/SpeechLinks.html
The *Speech Technology Hyperlinks* page has over 500 links to sites related to computer-based speech and speech recognition tools.

www.islandnet.com/~tslemko
The *Micro Consulting Limited* site contains shareware speech synthesis software.

www.chantinc.com/technology
This page is the *Chant* Web site, which discusses speech technology and how it works. Chant also provides speech synthesis and speech recognition software.

whatis.techtarget.com/definition
This site provides definitions and information about several topics, including CallXML. Its thorough definition of CallXML differentiates CallXML and VoiceXML, another technology developed by Voxeo. The site contains links to other published articles discussing CallXML.

www.oasis-open.org/cover/callxmlv2.html
This site provides a comprehensive list of the CallXML tags complete with descriptions of each tag. Short examples on how to apply the tags in various applications are provided.

SUMMARY

- Enabling a Web site to meet the needs of individuals with disabilities is an issue relevant to all business owners.
- Legal ramifications exist for Web sites that discriminate against people with disabilities (i.e., by not providing them with adequate access to the site's resources).
- Technologies such as voice activation, visual enhancers and auditory aids enable individuals with disabilities to work in more positions.
- On April 7, 1997, the World Wide Web Consortium (W3C) launched the Web Accessibility Initiative (WAI). The WAI is an attempt to make the Web more accessible; its mission is described at **www.w3.org/WAI**.
- Accessibility refers to the level of usability of an application or Web site for people with disabilities. Total accessibility is difficult to achieve because there are many different disabilities, language barriers, and hardware and software inconsistencies.

- The majority of Web sites are considered either partially or totally inaccessible to people with visual, learning or mobility impairments.
- The WAI publishes the Web Content Accessibility Guidelines 1.0, which assign priorities to a three-tier structure of checkpoints. The WAI currently is working on a draft of the Web Content Accessibility Guidelines 2.0.
- One important WAI requirement is to ensure that every image, movie and sound on a Web site is accompanied by a description that clearly defines the object's purpose; this is called an **`<alt>`** tag.
- Specialized user agents, such as screen readers (programs that allow users to hear what is being displayed on their screen) and braille displays (devices that receive data from screen-reading software and output the data as braille), allow people with visual impairments to access text-based information that is normally displayed on the screen.
- Using a screen reader to navigate a Web site can be time consuming and frustrating, because screen readers are unable to interpret pictures and other graphical content that do not have alternative text.
- Including links at the top of each Web page provides easy access to page's main content.
- Web pages with large amounts of multimedia content are difficult for user agents to interpret unless they are designed properly. Images, movies and most non-XHTML objects cannot be read by screen readers.
- Web designers should avoid misuse of the **`alt`** attribute; it is intended to provide a short description of an XHTML object that may not load properly on all user agents.
- The value of the **`longdesc`** attribute is a text-based URL, linked to a Web page, that describes the image associated with the attribute.
- When creating a Web page intended for the general public, it is important to consider the reading level at which it is written. Web site designers can make their sites more readable through the use of shorter words, as some users may have difficulty reading long words. In addition, users from other countries may have difficulty understanding slang and other nontraditional language.
- Web designers often use frames to display more than one XHTML file at a time and are a convenient way to ensure that certain content is always on screen. Unfortunately, frames often lack proper descriptions, which prevents users with text-based browsers, or users who lack sight, from navigating the Web site.
- The **`<noframes>`** tag allows the designer to offer alternative content to users whose browsers do not support frames.
- VoiceXML has tremendous implications for people with visual impairments and for the illiterate. VoiceXML, a speech recognition and synthesis technology, reads Web pages to users and understands words spoken into a microphone.
- A VoiceXML document is made up of a series of dialogs and subdialogs, which result in spoken interaction between the user and the computer. VoiceXML is a voice-recognition technology.
- CallXML, a language created and supported by Voxeo, creates phone-to-Web applications.
- When a user accesses a CallXML application, the incoming telephone call is referred to as a session. A CallXML application can support multiple sessions that enable the application to receive multiple telephone calls at any given time.
- A session terminates either when the user hangs up the telephone or when the CallXML application invokes the **`hangup`** element.
- The contents of a CallXML application are inserted within the **`<callxml>`** tag.

- CallXML tags that perform similar tasks should be enclosed within the **<block>** and **</block>** tags.
- To deploy a CallXML application, register with the Voxeo Community, which assigns a telephone number to the application so that other users may access it.
- Voxeo's logging feature enables developers to debug their telephone application by observing the "conversation" between the user and the application.
- Braille keyboards are similar to standard keyboards, except that in addition to having each key labeled with the letter it represents, braille keyboards have the equivalent braille symbol printed on the key. Most often, braille keyboards are combined with a speech synthesizer or a braille display, so users can interact with the computer to verify that their typing is correct.
- People with visual impairments are not the only beneficiaries of the effort to improve markup languages. Individuals with hearing impairments also have a great number of tools to help them interpret auditory information delivered over the Web.
- Speech synthesis is another research area that will help people with disabilities.
- Open-source software for people with visual impairments already exists and is often superior to most of its proprietary, closed-source counterparts.
- People with hearing impairments will soon benefit from what is called Synchronized Multimedia Integration Language (SMIL). This markup language is designed to add extra tracks—layers of content found within a single audio or video file. The additional tracks can contain data such as closed captioning.
- EagleEyes, developed by researchers at Boston College (**www.bc.edu/eagleeyes**), is a system that translates eye movements into mouse movements. Users move the mouse cursor by moving their eyes or heads and are thereby able to control computers.
- All of the accessibility options provided by Windows 2000 are available through the **Accessibility Wizard**. The **Accessibility Wizard** takes a user step by step through all of the Windows accessibility features and configures his or her computer according to the chosen specifications.
- Microsoft Magnifier enlarges the section of your screen surrounding the mouse cursor.
- To solve problems seeing the mouse cursor, Microsoft offers the ability to use larger cursors, black cursors and cursors that invert objects underneath them.
- **SoundSentry** is a tool that creates visual signals when system events occur.
- **ShowSounds** adds captions to spoken text and other sounds produced by today's multimedia-rich software.
- **StickyKeys** is a program that helps users who have difficulty pressing multiple keys at the same time.
- **BounceKeys** forces the computer to ignore repeated keystrokes, solving the problem of accidentally pressing the same key more than once.
- **ToggleKeys** causes an audible beep to alert users that they have pressed one of the lock keys (i.e., *Caps Lock*, *Num Lock*, or *Scroll Lock*).
- **MouseKeys** is a tool that uses the keyboard to emulate mouse movements.
- The **Mouse Button Settings** tool allows you to create a virtual left-handed mouse by swapping the button functions.
- A timeout either enables or disables a certain action after the computer has idled for a specified amount of time. A common example of a timeout is a screen saver.
- You can create an **.acw** file, that, when clicked, will automatically activate the saved accessibility settings on any Windows 2000 computer.

- Microsoft **Narrator** is a text-to-speech program for people with visual impairments. It reads text, describes the current desktop environment and alerts the user when certain Windows events occur.

TERMINOLOGY

accessibility
Accessibility Wizard
Accessibility Wizard: Display Color Settings
Accessibility Wizard: Icon Size
Accessibility Wizard: Mouse Cursor
Accessibility Wizard: Scroll Bar and Window Border Size
action element
alt attribute
Americans with Disabilities Act (ADA)
<assign> tag in VoiceXML
AuralCSS
<block> tag in VoiceXML
BounceKeys
braille display
braille keyboard
<break> tag in VoiceXML
<b> tag (bold)
CallXML
<callxml> tag in CallXML
caption
Cascading Style Sheets (CSS)
count attribute in VoiceXML
<choice> tag in VoiceXML
CSS2
D-link
default setting
EagleEyes
encoding
<enumerate> tag in VoiceXML
event handler
<exit> tag in VoiceXML
field variable
<filled> tag in VoiceXML
<form> tag in VoiceXML
frames
get request type
<getDigits> tag in CallXML
global variable
<goto> tag in VoiceXML
<grammar> tag in VoiceXML
Gunning Fog Index
header cells
headers attribute
<h1> tag
IBM ViaVoice
id attribute
<img> tag
JAWS (Job Access With Sound)
level attribute in VoiceXML
linearize
<link> tag in VoiceXML
local dialog
logging feature
logic element
longdesc attribute
Lynx
markup language
maxDigits attribute in CallXML
maxTime attribute in CallXML
<menu> tag in VoiceXML
Microsoft Magnifier
Microsoft Narrator
Mouse Button Settings window
MouseKeys
Narrator
<next> tag in VoiceXML
nolimit (default value)
<noframes> tag
Ocularis
<onHangup> tag in CallXML
<onMaxSilence> tag in CallXML
On-Screen Keyboard
<onTermDigits> tag in CallXML
post request type
priority 1 checkpoint
priority 2 checkpoint
priority 3 checkpoint
<prompt> tag in VoiceXML
quick tip
readability
Read typed characters
screen reader
session
sessionID
Set Automatic Timeout window
ShowSounds
SoundSentry
speech recognition
speech synthesizer
StickyKeys

<strong> tag
style sheet
system carat
<subdialog> tag in VoiceXML
summary attribute
Synchronized Multimedia Integration Language (SMIL)
tables
<td> tag
termDigits attribute in CallXML
<text> tag in CallXML
text-to-speech (TTS)
<th> tag
timeout
<title> tag
ToggleKeys
track
Unicode
user agent
<var> tag in VoiceXML
var attribute in CallXML
version
ViaVoice
voice server
Voice Server SDK
VoiceXML
Voxeo Community
<vxml> tag in VoiceXML
Web Accessibility Initiative (WAI)
Web Content Accessibility Guidelines 1.0
XML declaration
XML Guidelines (XML GL)

SELF-REVIEW EXERCISES

34.1 Expand the following acronyms:
a) W3C.
b) WAI.
c) JAWS.
d) SMIL.
e) CSS.

34.2 Fill in the blanks in each of the following statements.
a) The highest priority of the Web Accessibility Initiative is to ensure that each ________, ________ and ________ is accompanied by a description that clearly defines its purpose.
b) Technologies such as ________, ________ and ________ enable individuals with disabilities to work in a large number of positions.
c) Although they can be used as a great layout tool, ________ are difficult for screen readers to interpret and convey clearly to a user.
d) To make your frame accessible to individuals with disabilities, it is important to include ________ tags on your page.
e) Blind people using computers are often assisted by ________ and ________.
f) CallXML is used to create ________ applications that allow businesses to receive and send telephone calls.
g) A ________ tag must be associated with the **<getDigits>** tag.

34.3 State whether each of the following is *true* or *false*. If *false*, explain why.
a) Screen readers have no problem reading and translating images.
b) When writing pages for the general public, it is important to consider the reading difficulty level of the text you are writing.
c) The **<alt>** tag helps screen readers describe images in a Web page.
d) Left-handed people have been helped by the improvements made in speech-recognition technology more than any other group of people.
e) VoiceXML lets users interact with Web content using speech recognition and speech synthesis technologies.
f) Elements such as **onMaxSilence**, **onTermDigit** and **onMaxTime** are event handlers because they perform a specified task when invoked.

g) The debugging feature of the **Voxeo Account Manager** assists developers in debugging their CallXML application.

ANSWERS TO SELF-REVIEW EXERCISES

34.1 a) World Wide Web Consortium. b) Web Accessibility Initiative. c) Job Access with Sound. d) Synchronized Multimedia Integration Language. e) Cascading Style Sheets.

34.2 a) image, movie, sound. b) voice activation, visual enhancers and auditory aids. c) tables. d) **<noframes>**. e) braille displays, braille keyboards. f) phone-to-Web. g) **<onTermDigit>**.

34.3 a) False. Screen readers have no way of telling a user what is shown in an image. If the programmer includes an **alt** attribute inside the **<img>** tag, the screen reader reads this description to the user. b) True. c) True. d) False. Although left-handed people can use speech-recognition technology as everyone else can, speech-recognition technology has had the largest impact on the blind and on people who have trouble typing. e) True. f) True. g) False. The logging feature assists developers in debugging their CallXML application.

EXERCISES

34.4 Insert XHTML markup into each segment to make the segment accessible to someone with disabilities. The contents of images and frames should be apparent from the context and filenames.

a)
```
<img src = "dogs.jpg" width = "300" height = "250" />
```
b)
```
<table width = "75%">
   <tr><th>Language</th><th>Version</th></tr>
   <tr><td>XHTML</td><td>1.0</td></tr>
   <tr><td>Perl</td><td>5.6.0</td></tr>
   <tr><td>Java</td><td>1.3</td></tr>
</table>
```

34.5 Define the following terms:
a) Action element.
b) Gunning Fog Index.
c) Screen reader.
c) Session.
d) Web Accessibility Initiative (WAI).

34.6 Describe the three-tier structure of checkpoints (priority-one, priority-two and priority-three) set forth by the WAI.

34.7 Why do misused **<h1>** heading tags create problems for screen readers?

34.8 Use CallXML to create a voice mail system that plays a voice mail greeting and records the message. Have friends and classmates call your application and leave a message.

XHTML Special Characters

The table of Fig. A.1 shows many commonly used XHTML special characters—called *character entity references* by the World Wide Web Consortium. For a complete list of character entity references, see the site

`www.w3.org/TR/REC-html40/sgml/entities.html`

Character	HTML encoding	Character	XHTML encoding
non-breaking space	` `	ê	`ê`
§	`§`	ì	`ì`
©	`©`	í	`í`
®	`®`	î	`î`
π	`¼`	ñ	`ñ`
∫	`½`	ò	`ò`
Ω	`¾`	ó	`ó`
à	`à`	ô	`ô`
á	`á`	õ	`õ`
â	`â`	÷	`÷`
ã	`ã`	ù	`ù`
å	`å`	ú	`ú`
ç	`ç`	û	`û`
è	`è`	•	`•`
é	`é`	™	`™`

Fig. A.1 XHTML special characters.

Operator Precedence Chart

This appendix contains the operator precedence chart for JavaScript/JScript/ECMAScript (Fig. B.1). The operators are shown in decreasing order of precedence from top to bottom.

Operator	Type	Associativity
`.`	member access	left to right
`[]`	array indexing	
`()`	function calls	
`++`	increment	right to left
`--`	decrement	
`-`	unary minus	
`~`	bitwise complement	
`!`	logical NOT	
`delete`	delete an array element or object property	
`new`	create a new object	
`typeof`	returns the data type of its argument	
`void`	prevents an expression from returning a value	
`*`	multiplication	left to right
`/`	division	
`%`	modulus	
`+`	addition	left to right
`-`	subtraction	
`+`	string concatenation	

Fig. B.1 JavaScript/JScript/ECMAScript operator precedence and associativity (part 1 of 2).

<table>
<tr><th>Operator</th><th>Type</th><th>Associativity</th></tr>
<tr><td><code><<</code>
<code>>></code>
<code>>>></code></td><td>left shift
right shift with sign extension
right shift with zero extension</td><td>left to right</td></tr>
<tr><td><code><</code>
<code><=</code>
<code>></code>
<code>>=</code>
<code>instanceof</code></td><td>less than
less than or equal
greater than
greater than or equal
type comparison</td><td>left to right</td></tr>
<tr><td><code>==</code>
<code>!=</code>
<code>===</code>
<code>!==</code></td><td>equality
inequality
identity
nonidentity</td><td>left to right</td></tr>
<tr><td><code>&</code></td><td>bitwise AND</td><td>left to right</td></tr>
<tr><td><code>^</code></td><td>bitwise XOR</td><td>left to right</td></tr>
<tr><td><code>|</code></td><td>bitwise OR</td><td>left to right</td></tr>
<tr><td><code>&&</code></td><td>logical AND</td><td>left to right</td></tr>
<tr><td><code>||</code></td><td>logical OR</td><td>left to right</td></tr>
<tr><td><code>?:</code></td><td>conditional</td><td>left to right</td></tr>
<tr><td><code>=</code>
<code>+=</code>
<code>-=</code>
<code>*=</code>
<code>/=</code>
<code>%=</code>
<code>&=</code>
<code>^=</code>
<code>|=</code>
<code><<=</code>
<code>>>=</code>
<code>>>>=</code></td><td>assignment
addition assignment
subtraction assignment
multiplication assignment
division assignment
modulus assignment
bitwise AND assignment
bitwise exclusive OR assignment
bitwise inclusive OR assignment
bitwise left shift assignment
bitwise right shift with sign extension assignment
bitwise right shift with zero extension assignment</td><td>right to left</td></tr>
</table>

Fig. B.1 JavaScript/JScript/ECMAScript operator precedence and associativity (part 2 of 2).

ASCII Character Set

	0	1	2	3	4	5	6	7	8	9
0	nul	soh	stx	etx	eot	enq	ack	bel	bs	ht
1	nl	vt	ff	cr	so	si	dle	dc1	dc2	dc3
2	dc4	nak	syn	etb	can	em	sub	esc	fs	gs
3	rs	us	sp	!	"	#	$	%	&	'
4	(	)	*	+	,	-	.	/	0	1
5	2	3	4	5	6	7	8	9	:	;
6	<	=	>	?	@	A	B	C	D	E
7	F	G	H	I	J	K	L	M	N	O
8	P	Q	R	S	T	U	V	W	X	Y
9	Z	[	\	]	^	_	`	a	b	c
10	d	e	f	g	h	i	j	k	l	m
11	n	o	p	q	r	s	t	u	v	w
12	x	y	z	{	|	}	~	del		

Fig. C.1 ASCII character set.

The digits at the left of the table are the left digits of the decimal equivalent (0-127) of the character code, and the digits at the top of the table are the right digits of the character code. For example, the character code for "F" is 70, and the character code for "&" is 38.

Most users of this book are interested in the ASCII character set used to represent English characters on many computers. The ASCII character set is a subset of the Unicode character set used by scripting languages to represent characters from most of the world's languages. For more information on the Unicode character set, see Appendix G.

Number Systems

Objectives

- To understand basic number systems concepts such as base, positional value, and symbol value.
- To understand how to work with numbers represented in the binary, octal, and hexadecimal number systems
- To be able to abbreviate binary numbers as octal numbers or hexadecimal numbers.
- To be able to convert octal numbers and hexadecimal numbers to binary numbers.
- To be able to covert back and forth between decimal numbers and their binary, octal, and hexadecimal equivalents.
- To understand binary arithmetic, and how negative binary numbers are represented using two's complement notation.

Here are only numbers ratified.
William Shakespeare

Nature has some sort of arithmetic-geometrical coordinate system, because nature has all kinds of models. What we experience of nature is in models, and all of nature's models are so beautiful.

It struck me that nature's system must be a real beauty, because in chemistry we find that the associations are always in beautiful whole numbers—there are no fractions.
Richard Buckminster Fuller

Outline

D.1 Introduction

In this appendix, we introduce the key number systems that JavaScript programmers use, especially when they are working on software projects that require close interaction with "machine-level" hardware. Projects like this include operating systems, computer networking software, compilers, database systems, and applications requiring high performance.

When we write an integer such as 227 or -63 in a JavaScript program, the number is assumed to be in the decimal (base 10) number system. The digits in the decimal number system are 0, 1, 2, 3, 4, 5, 6, 7, 8, and 9. The lowest digit is 0 and the highest digit is 9—one less than the base of 10. Internally, computers use the binary (base 2) number system. The binary number system has only two digits, namely 0 and 1. Its lowest digit is 0 and its highest digit is 1—one less than the base of 2.

As we will see, binary numbers tend to be much longer than their decimal equivalents. Programmers who work in assembly languages and in high-level languages like JavaScript that enable programmers to reach down to the "machine level," find it cumbersome to work with binary numbers. So two other number systems the octal number system (base 8) and the hexadecimal number system (base 16)—are popular primarily because they make it convenient to abbreviate binary numbers.

In the octal number system, the digits range from 0 to 7. Because both the binary number system and the octal number system have fewer digits than the decimal number system, their digits are the same as the corresponding digits in decimal.

The hexadecimal number system poses a problem because it requires sixteen digits—a lowest digit of 0 and a highest digit with a value equivalent to decimal 15 (one less than the base of 16). By convention, we use the letters A through F to represent the hexadecimal digits corresponding to decimal values 10 through 15. Thus in hexadecimal we can have numbers like 876 consisting solely of decimal-like digits, numbers like 8A55F consisting of digits and letters, and numbers like FFE consisting solely of letters. Occasionally, a hexadecimal number spells a common word such as FACE or FEED—this can appear strange to programmers accustomed to working with numbers.

Each of these number systems uses positional notation—each position in which a digit is written has a different positional value. For example, in the decimal number 937 (the 9, the 3, and the 7 are referred to as symbol values), we say that the 7 is written in the ones position, the 3 is written in the tens position, and the 9 is written in the hundreds position.

Notice that each of these positions is a power of the base (base 10), and that these powers begin at 0 and increase by 1 as we move left in the number (Fig. D.3).

Binary digit	Octal digit	Decimal digit	Hexadecimal digit
0	0	0	0
1	1	1	1
	2	2	2
	3	3	3
	4	4	4
	5	5	5
	6	6	6
	7	7	7
		8	8
		9	9
			A (decimal value of 10)
			B (decimal value of 11)
			C (decimal value of 12)
			D (decimal value of 13)
			E (decimal value of 14)
			F (decimal value of 15)

Fig. D.1 Digits of the binary, octal, decimal and hexadecimal number systems.

Attribute	Binary	Octal	Decimal	Hexadecimal
Base	2	8	10	16
Lowest digit	0	0	0	0
Highest digit	1	7	9	F

Fig. D.2 Comparing the binary, octal, decimal and hexadecimal number systems.

Positional values in the decimal number system			
Decimal digit	9	3	7
Position name	Hundreds	Tens	Ones
Positional value	100	10	1
Positional value as a power of the base (10)	10^2	10^1	10^0

Fig. D.3 Positional values in the decimal number system.

For longer decimal numbers, the next positions to the left would be the thousands position (10 to the 3rd power), the ten-thousands position (10 to the 4th power), the hundred-thousands position (10 to the 5th power), the millions position (10 to the 6th power), the ten-millions position (10 to the 7th power), and so on.

In the binary number 101, we say that the rightmost 1 is written in the ones position, the 0 is written in the twos position, and the leftmost 1 is written in the fours position. Notice that each of these positions is a power of the base (base 2), and that these powers begin at 0 and increase by 1 as we move left in the number (Fig D.4).

For longer binary numbers, the next positions to the left would be the eights position (2 to the 3rd power), the sixteens position (2 to the 4th power), the thirty-twos position (2 to the 5th power), the sixty-fours position (2 to the 6th power), and so on.

In the octal number 425, we say that the 5 is written in the ones position, the 2 is written in the eights position, and the 4 is written in the sixty-fours position. Notice that each of these positions is a power of the base (base 8), and that these powers begin at 0 and increase by 1 as we move left in the number (Fig. D.5).

For longer octal numbers, the next positions to the left would be the five-hundred-and-twelves position (8 to the 3rd power), the four-thousand-and-ninety-sixes position (8 to the 4th power), the thirty-two-thousand-seven-hundred-and-sixty eights position (8 to the 5th power), and so on.

In the hexadecimal number 3DA, we say that the A is written in the ones position, the D is written in the sixteens position, and the 3 is written in the two-hundred-and-fifty-sixes position. Notice that each of these positions is a power of the base (base 16), and that these powers begin at 0 and increase by 1 as we move left in the number (Fig. D.6).

Positional values in the binary number system

Binary digit	1	0	1
Position name	Fours	Twos	Ones
Positional value	4	2	1
Positional value as a power of the base (2)	2^2	2^1	2^0

Fig. D.4 Positional values in the binary number system.

Positional values in the octal number system

Decimal digit	4	2	5
Position name	Sixty-fours	Eights	Ones
Positional value	64	8	1
Positional value as a power of the base (8)	8^2	8^1	8^0

Fig. D.5 Positional values in the octal number system.

Positional values in the hexadecimal number system			
Decimal digit	3	D	A
Position name	Two-hundred-and-fifty-sixes	Sixteens	Ones
Positional value	256	16	1
Positional value as a power of the base (16)	16^2	16^1	16^0

Fig. D.6 Positional values in the hexadecimal number system.

For longer hexadecimal numbers, the next positions to the left would be the four-thousand-and-ninety-sixes position (16 to the 3rd power), the sixty-five-thousand-five-hundred-and-thirty-six position (16 to the 4th power), and so on.

D.2 Abbreviating Binary Numbers as Octal Numbers and Hexadecimal Numbers

The main use for octal and hexadecimal numbers in computing is for abbreviating lengthy binary representations. Figure D.7 highlights the fact that lengthy binary numbers can be expressed concisely in number systems with higher bases than the binary number system.

Decimal number	Binary{ representation	Octal representation	Hexadecimal representation
0	0	0	0
1	1	1	1
2	10	2	2
3	11	3	3
4	100	4	4
5	101	5	5
6	110	6	6
7	111	7	7
8	1000	10	8
9	1001	11	9
10	1010	12	A
11	1011	13	B
12	1100	14	C
13	1101	15	D
14	1110	16	E
15	1111	17	F
16	10000	20	10

Fig. D.7 Decimal, binary, octal, and hexadecimal equivalents.

A particularly important relationship that both the octal number system and the hexadecimal number system have to the binary system is that the bases of octal and hexadecimal (8 and 16 respectively) are powers of the base of the binary number system (base 2). Consider the following 12-digit binary number and its octal and hexadecimal equivalents. See if you can determine how this relationship makes it convenient to abbreviate binary numbers in octal or hexadecimal. The answer follows the numbers.

Binary Number	Octal equivalent	Hexadecimal equivalent
`100011010001`	`4321`	`8D1`

To see how the binary number converts easily to octal, simply break the 12-digit binary number into groups of three consecutive bits each, and write those groups over the corresponding digits of the octal number as follows

```
100    011    010    001
4      3      2      1
```

Notice that the octal digit you have written under each group of thee bits corresponds precisely to the octal equivalent of that 3-digit binary number as shown in Fig. D.7.

The same kind of relationship may be observed in converting numbers from binary to hexadecimal. In particular, break the 12-digit binary number into groups of four consecutive bits each and write those groups over the corresponding digits of the hexadecimal number as follows

```
1000   1101   0001
8      D      1
```

Notice that the hexadecimal digit you wrote under each group of four bits corresponds precisely to the hexadecimal equivalent of that 4-digit binary number as shown in Fig. D.7.

D.3 Converting Octal Numbers and Hexadecimal Numbers to Binary Numbers

In the previous section, we saw how to convert binary numbers to their octal and hexadecimal equivalents by forming groups of binary digits and simply rewriting these groups as their equivalent octal digit values or hexadecimal digit values. This process may be used in reverse to produce the binary equivalent of a given octal or hexadecimal number.

For example, the octal number 653 is converted to binary simply by writing the 6 as its 3-digit binary equivalent 110, the 5 as its 3-digit binary equivalent 101, and the 3 as its 3-digit binary equivalent 011 to form the 9-digit binary number 110101011.

The hexadecimal number FAD5 is converted to binary simply by writing the F as its 4-digit binary equivalent 1111, the A as its 4-digit binary equivalent 1010, the D as its 4-digit binary equivalent 1101, and the 5 as its 4-digit binary equivalent 0101 to form the 16-digit 1111101011010101.

D.4 Converting from Binary, Octal or Hexadecimal to Decimal

Because we are accustomed to working in decimal, it is often convenient to convert a binary, octal, or hexadecimal number to decimal to get a sense of what the number is "really" worth. Our diagrams in Section E.1 express the positional values in decimal. To convert a number to decimal from another base, multiply the decimal equivalent of each digit by its positional value, and sum these products. For example, the binary number 110101 is converted to decimal 53 as shown in Fig. D.8.

To convert octal 7614 to decimal 3980, we use the same technique, this time using appropriate octal positional values as shown in Fig. D.9.

To convert hexadecimal AD3B to decimal 44347, we use the same technique, this time using appropriate hexadecimal positional values as shown in Fig. D.10.

D.5 Converting from Decimal to Binary, Octal or Hexadecimal

The conversions of the previous section follow naturally from the positional notation conventions. Converting from decimal to binary, octal, or hexadecimal also follows these conventions.

Suppose we wish to convert decimal 57 to binary. We begin by writing the positional values of the columns right to left until we reach a column whose positional value is greater than the decimal number. We do not need that column, so we discard it. Thus, we first write:

Converting a binary number to decimal

Positional values:	32	16	8	4	2	1
Symbol values:	1	1	0	1	0	1
Products:	1*32=32	1*16=16	0*8=0	1*4=4	0*2=0	1*1=1
Sum:	= 32 + 16 + 0 + 4 + 0 + 1 = 53					

Fig. D.8 Converting a binary number to decimal.

Converting an octal number to decimal

Positional values:	512	64	8	1
Symbol values:	7	6	1	4
Products	7*512=3584	6*64=384	1*8=8	4*1=4
Sum:	= 3584 + 384 + 8 + 4 = 3980			

Fig. D.9 Converting an octal number to decimal.

Converting a hexadecimal number to decimal

Positional values:	4096	256	16	1
Symbol values:	A	D	3	B
Products	A*4096=40960	D*256=3328	3*16=48	B*1=11
Sum:	= 40960 + 3328 + 48 + 11 = 44347			

Fig. D.10 Converting a hexadecimal number to decimal.

Positional values:	64	32	16	8	4	2	1

Then we discard the column with positional value 64 leaving:

Positional values:	32	16	8	4	2	1

Next we work from the leftmost column to the right. We divide 32 into 57 and observe that there is one 32 in 57 with a remainder of 25, so we write 1 in the 32 column. We divide 16 into 25 and observe that there is one 16 in 25 with a remainder of 9 and write 1 in the 16 column. We divide 8 into 9 and observe that there is one 8 in 9 with a remainder of 1. The next two columns each produce quotients of zero when their positional values are divided into 1 so we write 0s in the 4 and 2 columns. Finally, 1 into 1 is 1 so we write 1 in the 1 column. This yields:

Positional values:	32	16	8	4	2	1
Symbol values:	1	1	1	0	0	1

and thus decimal 57 is equivalent to binary 111001.

To convert decimal 103 to octal, we begin by writing the positional values of the columns until we reach a column whose positional value is greater than the decimal number. We do not need that column, so we discard it. Thus, we first write:

Positional values:	512	64	8	1

Then we discard the column with positional value 512, yielding:

Positional values:	64	8	1

Next we work from the leftmost column to the right. We divide 64 into 103 and observe that there is one 64 in 103 with a remainder of 39, so we write 1 in the 64 column. We divide 8 into 39 and observe that there are four 8s in 39 with a remainder of 7 and write 4 in the 8 column. Finally, we divide 1 into 7 and observe that there are seven 1s in 7 with no remainder so we write 7 in the 1 column. This yields:

Positional values:	64	8	1
Symbol values:	1	4	7

and thus decimal 103 is equivalent to octal 147.

To convert decimal 375 to hexadecimal, we begin by writing the positional values of the columns until we reach a column whose positional value is greater than the decimal number. We do not need that column, so we discard it. Thus, we first write

Positional values:	4096	256	16	1

Then we discard the column with positional value 4096, yielding:

Positional values:	256	16	1

Next we work from the leftmost column to the right. We divide 256 into 375 and observe that there is one 256 in 375 with a remainder of 119, so we write 1 in the 256 column. We divide 16 into 119 and observe that there are seven 16s in 119 with a remainder of 7 and write 7 in the 16 column. Finally, we divide 1 into 7 and observe that there are seven 1s in 7 with no remainder so we write 7 in the 1 column. This yields:

```
Positional values:   256  16   1
Symbol values:       1    7    7
```

and thus decimal 375 is equivalent to hexadecimal 177.

D.6 Negative Binary Numbers: Two's Complement Notation

The discussion in this appendix has been focussed on positive numbers. In this section, we explain how computers represent negative numbers using *two's complement notation*. First we explain how the two's complement of a binary number is formed, and then we show why it represents the negative value of the given binary number.

Consider a machine with 32-bit integers. Suppose

```
var value = 13;
```

The 32-bit representation of **value** is

```
00000000 00000000 00000000 00001101
```

To form the negative of **value** we first form its *one's complement* by applying JavaScript's bitwise complement operator (**~**):

```
onesComplementOfValue = ~value;
```

Internally, **~value** is now **value** with each of its bits reversed—ones become zeros and zeros become ones as follows:

```
value:
00000000 00000000 00000000 00001101

~value (i.e., value's ones complement):
11111111 11111111 11111111 11110010
```

To form the two's complement of **value** we simply add one to **value**'s one's complement. Thus

```
Two's complement of value:
11111111 11111111 11111111 11110011
```

Now if this is in fact equal to -13, we should be able to add it to binary 13 and obtain a result of 0. Let us try this:

```
 00000000 00000000 00000000 00001101
+11111111 11111111 11111111 11110011
------------------------------------
 00000000 00000000 00000000 00000000
```

The carry bit coming out of the leftmost column is discarded and we indeed get zero as a result. If we add the one's complement of a number to the number, the result would be all 1s. The key to getting a result of all zeros is that the twos complement is 1 more than the one's complement. The addition of 1 causes each column to add to 0 with a carry of 1. The carry keeps moving leftward until it is discarded from the leftmost bit, and hence the resulting number is all zeros.

Computers actually perform a subtraction such as

```
x = a - value;
```

by adding the two's complement of **value** to **a** as follows:

```
x = a + (~value + 1);
```

Suppose **a** is 27 and **value** is 13 as before. If the two's complement of **value** is actually the negative of **value**, then adding the two's complement of value to a should produce the result 14. Let us try this:

```
a (i.e., 27)          00000000 00000000 00000000 00011011
+(~value + 1)        +11111111 11111111 11111111 11110011
                      -----------------------------------
                      00000000 00000000 00000000 00001110
```

which is indeed equal to 14.

SUMMARY

- When we write an integer such as 19 or 227 or -63 in a JavaScript program, the number is automatically assumed to be in the decimal (base 10) number system. The digits in the decimal number system are 0, 1, 2, 3, 4, 5, 6, 7, 8, and 9. The lowest digit is 0 and the highest digit is 9—one less than the base of 10.
- Internally, computers use the binary (base 2) number system. The binary number system has only two digits, namely 0 and 1. Its lowest digit is 0 and its highest digit is 1—one less than the base of 2.
- The octal number system (base 8) and the hexadecimal number system (base 16) are popular primarily because they make it convenient to abbreviate binary numbers.
- The digits of the octal number system range from 0 to 7.
- The hexadecimal number system poses a problem because it requires sixteen digits—a lowest digit of 0 and a highest digit with a value equivalent to decimal 15 (one less than the base of 16). By convention, we use the letters A through F to represent the hexadecimal digits corresponding to decimal values 10 through 15.
- Each number system uses positional notation—each position in which a digit is written has a different positional value.
- A particularly important relationship that both the octal number system and the hexadecimal number system have to the binary system is that the bases of octal and hexadecimal (8 and 16 respectively) are powers of the base of the binary number system (base 2).
- To convert an octal number to a binary number, simply replace each octal digit with its three-digit binary equivalent.
- To convert a hexadecimal number to a binary number, simply replace each hexadecimal digit with its four-digit binary equivalent.
- Because we are accustomed to working in decimal, it is convenient to convert a binary, octal or hexadecimal number to decimal to get a sense of the number's "real" worth.
- To convert a number to decimal from another base, multiply the decimal equivalent of each digit by its positional value, and sum these products.
- Computers represent negative numbers using two's complement notation.
- To form the negative of a value in binary, first form its one's complement by applying JavaScript's bitwise complement operator (**~**). This reverses the bits of the value. To form the two's complement of a value, simply add one to the value's one's complement.

TERMINOLOGY

base
base 2 number system
base 8 number system
base 10 number system
base 16 number system
binary number system
bitwise complement operator (~)
conversions
decimal number system
digit
hexadecimal number system
negative value
octal number system
one's complement notation
positional notation
positional value
symbol value
two's complement notation

SELF-REVIEW EXERCISES

D.1 The bases of the decimal, binary, octal, and hexadecimal number systems are _________, _________, _________ and _________ respectively.

D.2 In general, the decimal, octal, and hexadecimal representations of a given binary number contain (more/fewer) digits than the binary number contains.

D.3 (True/False) A popular reason for using the decimal number system is that it forms a convenient notation for abbreviating binary numbers simply by substituting one decimal digit per group of four binary bits.

D.4 The (octal / hexadecimal / decimal) representation of a large binary value is the most concise (of the given alternatives).

D.5 (True/False) The highest digit in any base is one more than the base.

D.6 (True/False) The lowest digit in any base is one less than the base.

D.7 The positional value of the rightmost digit of any number in either binary, octal, decimal, or hexadecimal is always _________.

D.8 The positional value of the digit to the left of the rightmost digit of any number in binary, octal, decimal, or hexadecimal is always equal to _________.

D.9 Fill in the missing values in this chart of positional values for the rightmost four positions in each of the indicated number systems:

decimal	`1000`	`100`	`10`	`1`
hexadecimal	`...`	`256`	`...`	`...`
binary	`...`	`...`	`...`	`...`
octal	`512`	`...`	`8`	`...`

D.10 Convert binary 110101011000 to octal and to hexadecimal.

D.11 Convert hexadecimal FACE to binary.

D.12 Convert octal 7316 to binary.

D.13 Convert hexadecimal 4FEC to octal. (Hint: First convert 4FEC to binary then convert that binary number to octal.)

D.14 Convert binary 1101110 to decimal.

D.15 Convert octal 317 to decimal.

D.16 Convert hexadecimal EFD4 to decimal.

D.17 Convert decimal 177 to binary, to octal, and to hexadecimal.

D.18 Show the binary representation of decimal 417. Then show the one's complement of 417, and the two's complement of 417.

D.19 What is the result when the one's complement of a number is added to itself?

SELF-REVIEW ANSWERS

D.1 10, 2, 8, 16.

D.2 Fewer.

D.3 False.

D.4 Hexadecimal.

D.5 False. The highest digit in any base is one less than the base.

D.6 False. The lowest digit in any base is zero.

D.7 1 (the base raised to the zero power).

D.8 The base of the number system.

D.9 Fill in the missing values in this chart of positional values for the rightmost four positions in each of the indicated number systems:

decimal	1000	100	10	1
hexadecimal	4096	256	16	1
binary	8	4	2	1
octal	512	64	8	1

D.10 Octal 6530; Hexadecimal D58.

D.11 Binary 1111 1010 1100 1110.

D.12 Binary 111 011 001 110.

D.13 Binary 0 100 111 111 101 100; Octal 47754.

D.14 Decimal 2+4+8+32+64=110.

D.15 Decimal 7+1*8+3*64=7+8+192=207.

D.16 Decimal 4+13*16+15*256+14*4096=61396.

D.17 Decimal 177
to binary:

```
256 128 64 32 16 8 4 2 1
128 64 32 16 8 4 2 1
(1*128)+(0*64)+(1*32)+(1*16)+(0*8)+(0*4)+(0*2)+(1*1)
10110001
```

to octal:

```
512 64 8 1
64 8 1
(2*64)+(6*8)+(1*1)
261
```

to hexadecimal:

```
256 16 1
16 1
(11*16)+(1*1)
(B*16)+(1*1)
B1
```

D.18 Binary:

```
512 256 128 64 32 16 8 4 2 1
256 128 64 32 16 8 4 2 1
(1*256)+(1*128)+(0*64)+(1*32)+(0*16)+(0*8)+(0*4)+(0*2)+
(1*1)
110100001

One's complement: 001011110
Two's complement: 001011111
Check: Original binary number + its two's complement

110100001
001011111
---------
000000000
```

D.19 Zero.

EXERCISES

D.20 Some people argue that many of our calculations would be easier in the base 12 number system because 12 is divisible by so many more numbers than 10 (for base 10). What is the lowest digit in base 12? What might the highest symbol for the digit in base 12 be? What are the positional values of the rightmost four positions of any number in the base 12 number system?

D.21 How is the highest symbol value in the number systems we discussed related to the positional value of the first digit to the left of the rightmost digit of any number in these number systems?

D.22 Complete the following chart of positional values for the rightmost four positions in each of the indicated number systems:

```
decimal   1000   100    10     1
base 6    ...    ...     6    ...
base 13   ...    169    ...   ...
base 3    27     ...    ...   ...
```

D.23 Convert binary 100101111010 to octal and to hexadecimal.

D.24 Convert hexadecimal 3A7D to binary.

D.25 Convert hexadecimal 765F to octal. (Hint: First convert 765F to binary, then convert that binary number to octal.)

D.26 Convert binary 1011110 to decimal.

D.27 Convert octal 426 to decimal.

D.28 Convert hexadecimal FFFF to decimal.

D.29 Convert decimal 299 to binary, to octal, and to hexadecimal.

D.30 Show the binary representation of decimal 779. Then show the one's complement of 779, and the two's complement of 779.

D.31 What is the result when the two's complement of a number is added to itself?

D.32 Show the two's complement of integer value -1 on a machine with 32-bit integers.

XHTML Colors

Colors may be specified by using a standard name (such as **aqua**) or a hexadecimal RGB value (such as **#00FFFF** for **aqua**). Of the six hexadecimal digits in an RGB value, the first two represent the amount of red in the color, the middle two represent the amount of green in the color, and the last two represent the amount of blue in the color. For example, **black** is the absence of color and is defined by **#000000**, whereas **white** is the maximum amount of red, green and blue and is defined by **#FFFFFF**. Pure **red** is **#FF0000**, pure green (which the standard calls **lime**) is **#00FF00** and pure **blue** is **#00FFFF**. Note that **green** in the standard is defined as **#008000**. Figure E.1 contains the XHTML standard color set. Figure E.2 contains the XHTML extended color set.

Color name	Value	Color name	Value
aqua	#00FFFF	navy	#000080
black	#000000	olive	#808000
blue	#0000FF	purple	#800080
fuchsia	#FF00FF	red	#FF0000
gray	#808080	silver	#C0C0C0
green	#008000	teal	#008080
lime	#00FF00	yellow	#FFFF00
maroon	#800000	white	#FFFFFF

Fig. E.1 XHTML standard colors and hexadecimal RGB values.

Color name	Value	Color name	Value
aliceblue	#F0F8FF	dodgerblue	#1E90FF
antiquewhite	#FAEBD7	firebrick	#B22222
aquamarine	#7FFFD4	floralwhite	#FFFAF0
azure	#F0FFFF	forestgreen	#228B22
beige	#F5F5DC	gainsboro	#DCDCDC
bisque	#FFE4C4	ghostwhite	#F8F8FF
blanchedalmond	#FFEBCD	gold	#FFD700
blueviolet	#8A2BE2	goldenrod	#DAA520
brown	#A52A2A	greenyellow	#ADFF2F
burlywood	#DEB887	honeydew	#F0FFF0
cadetblue	#5F9EA0	hotpink	#FF69B4
chartreuse	#7FFF00	indianred	#CD5C5C
chocolate	#D2691E	indigo	#4B0082
coral	#FF7F50	ivory	#FFFFF0
cornflowerblue	#6495ED	khaki	#F0E68C
cornsilk	#FFF8DC	lavender	#E6E6FA
crimson	#DC1436	lavenderblush	#FFF0F5
cyan	#00FFFF	lawngreen	#7CFC00
darkblue	#00008B	lemonchiffon	#FFFACD
darkcyan	#008B8B	lightblue	#ADD8E6
darkgoldenrod	#B8860B	lightcoral	#F08080
darkgray	#A9A9A9	lightcyan	#E0FFFF
darkgreen	#006400	lightgoldenrodyellow	#FAFAD2
darkkhaki	#BDB76B	lightgreen	#90EE90
darkmagenta	#8B008B	lightgrey	#D3D3D3
darkolivegreen	#556B2F	lightpink	#FFB6C1
darkorange	#FF8C00	lightsalmon	#FFA07A
darkorchid	#9932CC	lightseagreen	#20B2AA
darkred	#8B0000	lightskyblue	#87CEFA
darksalmon	#E9967A	lightslategray	#778899
darkseagreen	#8FBC8F	lightsteelblue	#B0C4DE
darkslateblue	#483D8B	lightyellow	#FFFFE0
darkslategray	#2F4F4F	limegreen	#32CD32
darkturquoise	#00CED1	linen	#FAF0E6
darkviolet	#9400D3	magenta	#FF00FF
deeppink	#FF1493	mediumaquamarine	#66CDAA
deepskyblue	#00BFFF	mediumblue	#0000CD
dimgray	#696969	mediumorchid	#BA55D3

Fig. E.2 XHTML extended colors and hexadecimal RGB values (part 1 of 2).

Color name	Value	Color name	Value
mediumpurple	#9370DB	plum	#DDA0DD
mediumseagreen	#3CB371	powderblue	#B0E0E6
mediumslateblue	#7B68EE	rosybrown	#BC8F8F
mediumspringgreen	#00FA9A	royalblue	#4169E1
mediumturquoise	#48D1CC	saddlebrown	#8B4513
mediumvioletred	#C71585	salmon	#FA8072
midnightblue	#191970	sandybrown	#F4A460
mintcream	#F5FFFA	seagreen	#2E8B57
mistyrose	#FFE4E1	seashell	#FFF5EE
moccasin	#FFE4B5	sienna	#A0522D
navajowhite	#FFDEAD	skyblue	#87CEEB
oldlace	#FDF5E6	slateblue	#6A5ACD
olivedrab	#6B8E23	slategray	#708090
orange	#FFA500	snow	#FFFAFA
orangered	#FF4500	springgreen	#00FF7F
orchid	#DA70D6	steelblue	#4682B4
palegoldenrod	#EEE8AA	tan	#D2B48C
palegreen	#98FB98	thistle	#D8BFD8
paleturquoise	#AFEEEE	tomato	#FF6347
palevioletred	#DB7093	turquoise	#40E0D0
papayawhip	#FFEFD5	violet	#EE82EE
peachpuff	#FFDAB9	wheat	#F5DEB3
peru	#CD853F	whitesmoke	#F5F5F5
pink	#FFC0CB	yellowgreen	#9ACD32

Fig. E.2 XHTML extended colors and hexadecimal RGB values (part 2 of 2).

Career Opportunities (on CD)

Objectives

- To explore the various online career services.
- To examine the advantages and disadvantages of posting and finding jobs online.
- To review the major online career services Web sites available to job seekers.
- To explore the various online services available to employers seeking to build their workforces.

Appendix F is included on the CD that accompanies this book in printable Adobe® Acrobat® PDF format. The appendix includes pages 1333–1356.

G

Unicode®

Objectives

- To become familiar with Unicode.
- To discuss the mission of the Unicode Consortium.
- To discuss the design basis of Unicode.
- To understand the three Unicode encoding forms: UTF-8, UTF-16 and UTF-32.
- To introduce characters and glyphs.
- To discuss the advantages and disadvantages of using Unicode.
- To provide a brief tour of the Unicode Consortium's Web site.

Outline

G.1 Introduction

The use of inconsistent character *encodings* (i.e., numeric values associated with characters) when developing global software products causes serious problems because computers process information using numbers. For instance, the character "a" is converted to a numeric value so that a computer can manipulate that piece of data. Many countries and corporations have developed their own encoding systems that are incompatible with the encoding systems of other countries and corporations. For example, the Microsoft Windows operating system assigns the value 0xC0 to the character "A with a grave accent" while the Apple Macintosh operating system assigns that same value to an upside-down question mark. This results in the misrepresentation and possible corruption of data because data is not processed as intended.

In the absence of a widely-implemented universal character encoding standard, global software developers had to *localize* their products extensively before distribution. Localization includes the language translation and cultural adaptation of content. The process of localization usually includes significant modifications to the source code (such as the conversion of numeric values and the underlying assumptions made by programmers), which results in increased costs and delays releasing the software. For example, some English-speaking programmers might design global software products assuming that a single character can be represented by one byte. However, when those products are localized for Asian markets, the programmer's assumptions are no longer valid, thus the majority, if not the entirety, of the code needs to be rewritten. Localization is necessary with each release of a version. By the time a software product is localized for a particular market, a newer version, which needs to be localized as well, may be ready for distribution. As a result, it is cumbersome and costly to produce and distribute global software products in a market where there is no universal character encoding standard.

In response to this situation, the *Unicode Standard*, an encoding standard that facilitates the production and distribution of software, was created. The Unicode Standard outlines a specification to produce consistent encoding of the world's characters and *symbols*. Software products which handle text encoded in the Unicode Standard need to be localized, but the localization process is simpler and more efficient because the numeric values need not be converted and the assumptions made by programmers about the character encoding are universal. The Unicode Standard is maintained by a non-profit organization called the

Unicode Consortium, whose members include Apple, IBM, Microsoft, Oracle, Sun Microsystems, Sybase and many others.

When the Consortium envisioned and developed the Unicode Standard, they wanted an encoding system that was *universal*, *efficient*, *uniform* and *unambiguous*. A universal encoding system encompasses all commonly used characters. An efficient encoding system allows text files to be parsed easily. A uniform encoding system assigns fixed values to all characters. An unambiguous encoding system represents a given character in a consistent manner. These four terms are referred to as the Unicode Standard *design basis*.

G.2 Unicode Transformation Formats

Although Unicode incorporates the limited ASCII *character set* (i.e., a collection of characters), it encompasses a more comprehensive character set. In ASCII each character is represented by a byte containing 0s and 1s. One byte is capable of storing the binary numbers from 0 to 255. Each character is assigned a number between 0 and 255, thus ASCII-based systems can support only 256 characters, a tiny fraction of world's characters. Unicode extends the ASCII character set by encoding the vast majority of the world's characters. The Unicode Standard encodes all of those characters in a uniform numerical space from 0 to 10FFFF hexadecimal. An implementation will express these numbers in one of several transformation formats, choosing the one that best fits the particular application at hand.

Three such formats are in use, called *UTF-8*, *UTF-16* and *UTF-32*, depending on the size of the units—in *bits*—being used. UTF-8, a variable width encoding form, requires one to four bytes to express each Unicode character. UTF-8 data consists of 8-bit bytes (sequences of one, two, three or four bytes depending on the character being encoded) and is well suited for ASCII-based systems when there is a predominance of one-byte characters (ASCII represents characters as one-byte). Currently, UTF-8 is widely implemented in UNIX systems and in databases. [*Note*: Currently, Internet Explorer 5.5 and Netscape Communicator 6 only support UTF-8, so document authors should use UTF-8 for encoding XML and XHTML documents.]

The variable width UTF-16 encoding form expresses Unicode characters in units of 16-bits (i.e., as two adjacent bytes, or a short integer in many machines). Most characters of Unicode are expressed in a single 16-bit unit. However, characters with values above FFFF hexadecimal are expressed with an ordered pair of 16-bit units called *surrogates*. Surrogates are 16-bit integers in the range D800 through DFFF, which are used solely for the purpose of "escaping" into higher numbered characters. Approximately one million characters can be expressed in this manner. Although a surrogate pair requires 32 bits to represent characters, it is space-efficient to use these 16-bit units. Surrogates are rare characters in current implementations. Many string-handling implementations are written in terms of UTF-16. [*Note*: Details and sample-code for UTF-16 handling are available on the Unicode Consortium Web site at **www.unicode.org**.]

Implementations that require significant use of rare characters or entire scripts encoded above FFFF hexadecimal, should use UTF-32, a 32-bit, fixed-width encoding form that usually requires twice as much memory as UTF-16 encoded characters. The major advantage of the fixed-width UTF-32 encoding form is that it uniformly expresses all characters, so it is easy to handle in arrays.

There are few guidelines that state when to use a particular encoding form. The best encoding form to use depends on computer systems and business protocols, not on the data itself. Typically, the UTF-8 encoding form should be used where computer systems and business protocols require data to be handled in 8-bit units, particularly in legacy systems being upgraded because it often simplifies changes to existing programs. For this reason, UTF-8 has become the encoding form of choice on the Internet. Likewise, UTF-16 is the encoding form of choice on Microsoft Windows applications. UTF-32 is likely to become more widely used in the future as more characters are encoded with values above FFFF hexadecimal. Also, UTF-32 requires less sophisticated handling than UTF-16 in the presence of surrogate pairs. Figure G.1 shows the different ways in which the three encoding forms handle character encoding.

G.3 Characters and Glyphs

The Unicode Standard consists of *characters*, written components (i.e., alphabetic letters, numerals, punctuation marks, accent marks, etc.) that can be represented by numeric values. Examples of characters include: U+0041 LATIN CAPITAL LETTER A. In the first character representation, U+*yyyy* is a *code value*, in which U+ refers to Unicode code values, as opposed to other hexadecimal values. The *yyyy* represents a four-digit hexadecimal number of an encoded character. Code values are bit combinations that represent encoded characters. Characters are represented using *glyphs*, various shapes, fonts and sizes for displaying characters. There are no code values for glyphs in the Unicode Standard. Examples of glyphs are shown in Fig. G.2.

The Unicode Standard encompasses the alphabets, ideographs, syllabaries, punctuation marks, *diacritics*, mathematical operators, etc. that comprise the written languages and scripts of the world. A diacritic is a special mark added to a character to distinguish it from another letter or to indicate an accent (e.g., in Spanish, the tilde "~" above the character "n"). Currently, Unicode provides code values for 94,140 character representations, with more than 880,000 code values reserved for future expansion.

G.4 Advantages/Disadvantages of Unicode

The Unicode Standard has several significant advantages that promote its use. One is the impact it has on the performance of the international economy. Unicode standardizes the characters for the world's writing systems to a uniform model that promotes transferring and sharing data. Programs developed using such a schema maintain their accuracy because each character has a single definition (i.e., *a* is always U+0061, *%* is always U+0025). This enables corporations to manage the high demands of international markets by processing different writing systems at the same time. Also, all characters can be managed in an identical manner, thus avoiding any confusion caused by different character code architectures. Moreover, managing data in a consistent manner eliminates data corruption, because data can be sorted, searched and manipulated using a consistent process.

Another advantage of the Unicode Standard is *portability* (i.e., the ability to execute software on disparate computers or with disparate operating systems). Most operating systems, databases, programming languages and Web browsers currently support, or are planning to support, Unicode.

Character	UTF-8	UTF-16	UTF-32
LATIN CAPITAL LETTER A	0x41	0x0041	0x00000041
GREEK CAPITAL LETTER ALPHA	0xCD 0x91	0x0391	0x00000391
CJK UNIFIED IDEOGRAPH-4E95	0xE4 0xBA 0x95	0x4E95	0x00004E95
OLD ITALIC LETTER A	0xF0 0x80 0x83 0x80	0xDC00 0xDF00	0x00010300

Fig. G.1 Correlation between the three encoding forms.

Fig. G.2 Various glyphs of the character A.

A disadvantage of the Unicode Standard is the amount of memory required by UTF-16 and UTF-32. ASCII character sets are 8 bits in length, so they require less storage than the default 16-bit Unicode character set. However, the *double-byte character set (DBCS)* and the *multi-byte character set (MBCS)* that encode Asian characters (ideographs) require two to four bytes, respectively. In such instances, the UTF-16 or the UTF-32 encoding forms may be used with little hindrance on memory and performance.

Another disadvantage of Unicode is that although it includes more characters than any other character set in common use, it does not yet encode all of the world's written characters. One additional disadvantage of the Unicode Standard is that UTF-8 and UTF-16 are variable width encoding forms, so characters occupy different amounts of memory.

G.5 Unicode Consortium's Web Site

If you would like to learn more about the Unicode Standard, visit **`www.unicode.org`**. This site provides a wealth of information about the Unicode Standard. Currently, the home page is organized into various sections: *New to Unicode*, *General Information*, *The Consortium*, *The Unicode Standard*, *Work in Progress* and *For Members*.

The *New to Unicode* section consists of two subsections: ***What is Unicode?*** and ***How to Use this Site***. The first subsection provides a technical introduction to Unicode by describing design principles, character interpretations and assignments, text processing and Unicode conformance. This subsection is recommended reading for anyone new to Unicode. Also, this subsection provides a list of related links that provide the reader with additional information about Unicode. The **How to Use this Site** subsection contains information about using and navigating the site as well hyperlinks to additional resources.

The *General Information* section contains six subsections: ***Where is my Character?***, ***Display Problems?***, ***Useful Resources***, ***Enabled Products***, ***Mail Lists*** and ***Conferences***. The main areas covered in this section include a link to the Unicode

code charts (a complete listing of code values) assembled by the Unicode Consortium as well as a detailed outline on how to locate an encoded character in the code chart. Also, the section contains advice on how to configure different operating systems and Web browsers so that the Unicode characters can be viewed properly. Moreover, from this section, the user can navigate to other sites that provide information on various topics such as, fonts, linguistics and other standards such as the *Armenian Standards Page* and the *Chinese GB 18030 Encoding Standard.*

The Consortium section consists of five subsections: ***Who we are***, ***Our Members***, ***How to Join***, ***Press Info*** and ***Contact Us***. This section provides a list of the current Unicode Consortium members as well as information on how to become a member. Privileges for each member type—*full*, *associate*, *specialist* and *individual*—and the fees assessed to each member are listed here.

The Unicode Standard section consists of nine subsections: ***Start Here***, ***Latest Version***, ***Technical Reports***, ***Code Charts***, ***Unicode Data***, ***Updates & Errata***, ***Unicode Policies***, ***Glossary*** and ***Technical FAQ***. This section describes the updates applied to the latest version of the Unicode Standard as well as categorizing all defined encoding. The user can learn how the latest version has been modified to encompass more features and capabilities. For instance, one enhancement of Version 3.1 is that it contains additional encoded characters. Also, if users are unfamiliar with vocabulary terms used by the Unicode Consortium, then they can navigate to the **Glossary** subsection.

The *Work in Progress* section consists of three subsections: ***Calendar of Meetings***, ***Proposed Characters*** and ***Submitting Proposals***. This section presents the user with a catalog of the recent characters included into the Unicode Standard scheme as well as those characters being considered for inclusion. If users determine that a character has been overlooked, then they can submit a written proposal for the inclusion of that character. The **Submitting Proposals** subsection contains strict guidelines that must be adhered to when submitting written proposals.

The *For Members* section consists of two subsections: ***Member Resources*** and ***Working Documents***. These subsections are password protected; only consortium members can access these links.

G.6 Using Unicode

The primary use of the Unicode Standard is the Internet; it has become the default encoding system for XML and any language derived from XML such as XHTML. Figure G.3 marks up (as XML) the text "Welcome to Unicode!" in ten different languages: English, French, German, Japanese, Kannada (India), Portuguese, Russian, Spanish, Telugu (India) and Traditional Chinese. [*Note*: The Unicode Consortium's Web site contains a link to code charts that lists the 16-bit Unicode code values.]

Line 1 of the document specifies the XML declaration that contains the Unicode **`encoding`** used. A UTF-8 **`encoding`** indicates that the document conforms to the form of Unicode that uses sequences of one to four bytes. [*Note*: This document uses XML *entity references* to represent characters. Also, UTF-16 and UTF-32 have yet to be supported by Internet Explorer 5.5 and Netscape Communicator 6.] Line 6 defines the root element, **`UnicodeEncodings`**, which contains all other elements (e.g., **`WelcomeNote`**) in the document. The first **`WelcomeNote`** element (lines 9–15) contains the entity references for the English text. The **Code Charts** page on the Unicode Consortium Web site contains the code values for the **Basic Latin** *block* (or category), which includes the English alphabet. The entity reference on line 10 equates to "Welcome" in basic text. When marking up Unicode characters in XML (or XHTML), the entity reference **&#x***yyyy***;** is used, where *yyyy* represents the hexadecimal Unicode encoding. For example, the letter "W" (in "Welcome") is denoted by **W**. Lines 11 and 13 contain the entity reference for the *space* character. The entity reference for the word "to" is on line 12 and the word "Unicode" is on line 14. "Unicode" is not encoded because it is a registered trademark and has no equivalent translation in most languages. Line 14 also contains the **!** notation for the exclamation mark (**!**).

```
1   <?xml version = "1.0" encoding = "UTF-8"?>
2
3   <!-- Fig. G.3: Unicode.xml                        -->
4   <!-- Unicode encoding for ten different languages -->
5
6   <UnicodeEncodings>
7
8      <!-- English -->
9      <WelcomeNote>
10        &#x0057;&#x0065;&#x006C;&#x0063;&#x006F;&#x006D;&#x0065;
11        &#x0020;
12        &#x0074;&#x006F;
13        &#x0020;
14        Unicode&#x0021;
15     </WelcomeNote>
16
17     <!-- French -->
18     <WelcomeNote>
19  &#x0042;&#x0069;&#x0065;&#x006E;&#x0076;&#x0065;&#x006E;&#x0075;&#x0065;
20        &#x0020;
21        &#x0061;&#x0075;
22        &#x0020;
23        Unicode&#x0021;
24     </WelcomeNote>
25
26     <!-- German -->
27     <WelcomeNote>
28  &#x0057;&#x0069;&#x006C;&#x006B;&#x006F;&#x006D;&#x006D;&#x0065;&#x006E;
29        &#x0020;
30        &#x007A;&#x0075;
31        &#x0020;
32        Unicode&#x0021;
33     </WelcomeNote>
34
35     <!-- Japanese -->
36     <WelcomeNote>
```

Fig. G.3 XML document using Unicode encoding (part 1 of 3).

```
         Unicode
         &#x3078;&#x3087;&#x3045;&#x3053;&#x305D;&#x0021;
      </WelcomeNote>

      <!-- Kannada -->
      <WelcomeNote>
         &#x0CB8;&#x0CC1;&#x0CB8;&#x0CCD;&#x0CB5;&#x0C97;&#x0CA4;
         &#x0020;
         Unicode&#x0021;
      </WelcomeNote>

      <!-- Portuguese -->
      <WelcomeNote>
         &#x0053;&#x00E9;&#x006A;&#x0061;
         &#x0020;
&#x0042;&#x0065;&#x006D;&#x0076;&#x0069;&#x006E;&#x0064;&#x006F;
         &#x0020;
         Unicode&#x0021;
      </WelcomeNote>

      <!-- Russian -->
      <WelcomeNote>
         &#x0414;&#x043E;&#x0431;&#x0440;&#x043E;
         &#x0020;
&#x043F;&#x043E;&#x0436;&#x0430;&#x043B;&#x043E;&#x0432;&#x0430;&#x0442;&#x044A;
         &#x0020;
         &#x0432;
         &#x0020;
         Unicode&#x0021;
      </WelcomeNote>

      <!-- Spanish -->
      <WelcomeNote>
&#x0042;&#x0069;&#x0065;&#x006E;&#x0076;&#x0065;&#x006E;&#x0069;&#x0064;&#x0061;
         &#x0020;
         &#x0061;
         &#x0020;
         Unicode&#x0021;
      </WelcomeNote>

      <!-- Telugu -->
      <WelcomeNote>
&#x0C38;&#x0C41;&#x0C38;&#x0C3E;&#x0C35;&#x0C17;&#x0C24;&#x0C02;
         &#x0020;
         Unicode&#x0021;
      </WelcomeNote>

```

Fig. G.3 XML document using Unicode encoding (part 2 of 3).

```
84      <!-- Traditional Chinese -->
85      <WelcomeNote>
86         &#x6B22;&#x8FCE;
87         &#x4F7F;&#x7528;
88         &#x0020;
89         Unicode&#x0021;
90      </WelcomeNote>
91
92   </UnicodeEncodings>
```

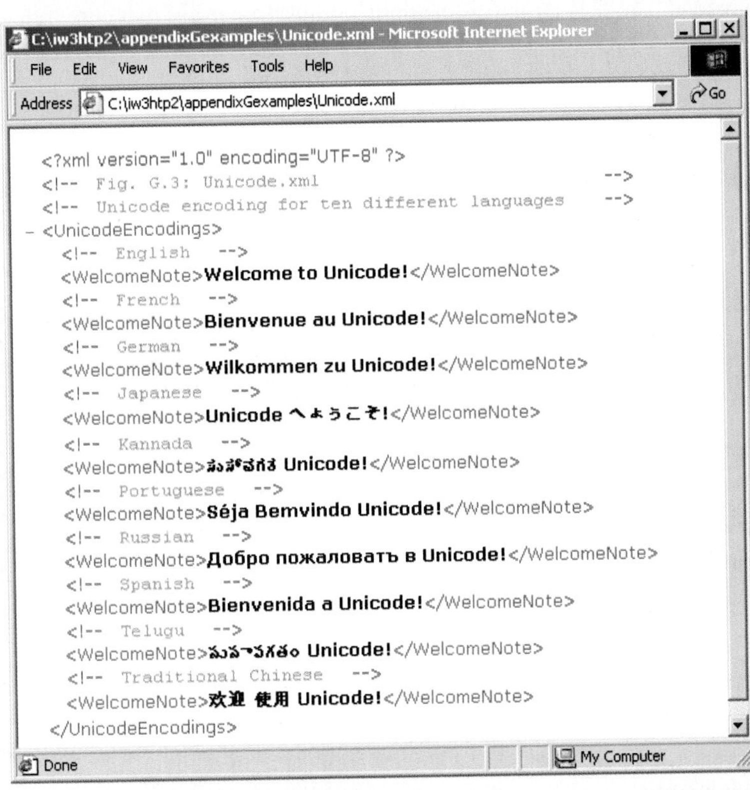

Fig. G.3 XML document using Unicode encoding (part 3 of 3).

The remaining **`WelcomeNote`** elements (lines 18–90) contain the entity references for the other nine languages. The code values used for the French, German, Portuguese and Spanish text are located in the **Basic Latin** block, the code values used for the Traditional Chinese text are located in the **CJK Unified Ideographs** block, the code values used for the Russian text are located in the **Cyrillic** block, the code values used for the Japanese text are located in the **Hiragana** block, and the code values used for the Kannada and Telugu texts are located in their respective blocks.

[*Note*: To render the Asian characters on a Web browser, the proper language files must be installed on your computer. For Windows XP/2000, the language files can be obtained from the Microsoft Web site at **`www.microsoft.com`**. For additional assistance, visit **`www.unicode.org/help/display_problems.html`**.]

G.7 Character Ranges

The Unicode Standard assigns code values, which range from **0000** (**Basic Latin**) to **E007F** (***Tags***), to the written characters of the world. Currently, there are code values for 94,140 characters. To simplify the search for a character and its associated code value, the Unicode Standard generally groups code values by *script* and function (i.e., Latin characters are grouped in a block, mathematical operators are grouped in another block, etc.). As a rule, a script is a single writing system that is used for multiple languages (e.g., the Latin script is used for English, French, Spanish, etc.). The **Code Charts** page on the Unicode Consortium Web site lists all the defined blocks and their respective code values. Figure G.4 lists some blocks (scripts) from the Web site and their range of code values.

SUMMARY

- Before Unicode, software developers were plagued by the use of inconsistent character encoding (i.e., numeric values for characters). Most countries and organizations had their own encoding systems, which were incompatible. A good example is the individual encoding systems on the Windows and Macintosh platforms.

Script	Range of Code Values
Arabic	U+0600–U+06FF
Basic Latin	U+0000–U+007F
Bengali (India)	U+0980–U+09FF
Cherokee (Native America)	U+13A0–U+13FF
CJK Unified Ideographs (East Asia)	U+4E00–U+9FAF
Cyrillic (Russia and Eastern Europe)	U+0400–U+04FF
Ethiopic	U+1200–U+137F
Greek	U+0370–U+03FF
Hangul Jamo (Korea)	U+1100–U+11FF
Hebrew	U+0590–U+05FF
Hiragana (Japan)	U+3040–U+309F
Khmer (Cambodia)	U+1780–U+17FF
Lao (Laos)	U+0E80–U+0EFF
Mongolian	U+1800–U+18AF
Myanmar	U+1000–U+109F
Ogham (Ireland)	U+1680–U+169F
Runic (Germany and Scandinavia)	U+16A0–U+16FF
Sinhala (Sri Lanka)	U+0D80–U+0DFF
Telugu (India)	U+0C00–U+0C7F
Thai	U+0E00–U+0E7F

Fig. G.4 Some character ranges.

- Computers process data by converting characters to numeric values. For instance, the character "a" is converted to a numeric value so that a computer can manipulate that piece of data.
- Without Unicode, localization of global software requires significant modifications to the source code, which results in increased cost and in delays releasing the product.
- Localization is necessary with each release of a version. By the time a software product is localized for a particular market, a newer version, which needs to be localized as well, is ready for distribution. As a result, it is cumbersome and costly to produce and distribute global software products in a market where there is no universal character encoding standard.
- The Unicode Consortium developed the Unicode Standard in response to the serious problems created by multiple character encodings and the use of those encodings.
- The Unicode Standard facilitates the production and distribution of localized software. It outlines a specification for the consistent encoding of the world's characters and symbols.
- Software products which handle text encoded in the Unicode Standard need to be localized, but the localization process is simpler and more efficient because the numeric values need not be converted.
- The Unicode Standard is designed to be universal, efficient, uniform and unambiguous.
- A universal encoding system encompasses all commonly used characters; an efficient encoding system parses text files easily; a uniform encoding system assigns fixed values to all characters; and an unambiguous encoding system represents the same character for any given value.
- Unicode extends the limited ASCII character set to include all the major characters of the world.
- Unicode makes use of three Unicode Transformation Formats (UTF): UTF-8, UTF-16 and UTF-32, each of which may be appropriate for use in different contexts.
- UTF-8 data consists of 8-bit bytes (sequences of one, two, three or four bytes depending on the character being encoded) and is well suited for ASCII-based systems when there is a predominance of one-byte characters (ASCII represents characters as one-byte).
- UTF-8 is a variable width encoding form that is more compact for text involving mostly Latin characters and ASCII punctuation.
- UTF-16 is the default encoding form of the Unicode Standard. It is a variable width encoding form that uses 16-bit code units instead of bytes. Most characters are represented by a single unit, but some characters require surrogate pairs.
- Surrogates are 16-bit integers in the range D800 through DFFF, which are used solely for the purpose of "escaping" into higher numbered characters.
- Without surrogate pairs, the UTF-16 encoding form can only encompass 65,000 characters, but with the surrogate pairs, this is expanded to include over a million characters.
- UTF-32 is a 32-bit encoding form. The major advantage of the fixed-width encoding form is that it uniformly expresses all characters, so that they are easy to handle in arrays and so forth.
- The Unicode Standard consists of characters. A character is any written component that can be represented by a numeric value.
- Characters are represented using glyphs, various shapes, fonts and sizes for displaying characters.
- Code values are bit combinations that represent encoded characters. The Unicode notation for a code value is U+*yyyy* in which U+ refers to the Unicode code values, as opposed to other hexadecimal values. The *yyyy* represents a four-digit hexadecimal number.
- Currently, the Unicode Standard provides code values for 94,140 character representations.
- An advantage of the Unicode Standard is its impact on the overall performance of the international economy. Applications that conform to an encoding standard can be processed easily by computers anywhere.

- Another advantage of the Unicode Standard is its portability. Applications written in Unicode can be easily transferred to different operating systems, databases, Web browsers, etc. Most companies currently support, or are planning to support, Unicode.
- To obtain more information about the Unicode Standard and the Unicode Consortium, visit **`www.unicode.org`**. It contains a link to the code charts, which contain the 16-bit code values for the currently encoded characters.
- The Unicode Standard has become the default encoding system for XML and any language derived from XML, such as XHTML.
- When marking up XML-derived documents, the entity reference **`&#x`***yyyy***`;`** is used, where *yyyy* represents the hexadecimal code value.

TERMINOLOGY

`&#x`*yyyy***`;`** notation
ASCII
block
character
character set
code value
diacritic
double-byte character set (DBCS)
efficient (Unicode design basis)
encode
entity reference
glyph
hexadecimal notation
localization
multi-byte character set (MBCS)
portability
script
surrogate
symbol
unambiguous (Unicode design basis)
Unicode Consortium
Unicode design basis
Unicode Standard
Unicode Transformation Format (UTF)
uniform (Unicode design basis)
universal (Unicode design basis)
UTF-8
UTF-16
UTF-32

SELF-REVIEW EXERCISES

G.1 Fill in the blanks in each of the following.

a) Global software developers had to __________ their products to a specific market before distribution.

b) The Unicode Standard is an __________ standard that facilitates the uniform production and distribution of software products.

c) The four design basis that constitute the Unicode Standard are: __________, __________, __________ and __________.

d) A __________ is the smallest written component the can be represented with a numeric value.

e) Software that can execute on different operating systems is said to be __________.

f) Of the three encoding forms, __________ is currently supported by Internet Explorer 5.5 and Netscape Communicator 6.

G.2 State whether each of the following is *true* or *false*. If *false*, explain why.

a) The Unicode Standard encompasses all the world's characters.

b) A Unicode code value is represented as U+*yyyy*, where *yyyy* represents a number in binary notation.

c) A diacritic is a character with a special mark that emphasizes an accent.

d) Unicode is portable.

e) When designing XHTML and XML documents, the entity reference is denoted by **#U+***yyyy*.

ANSWERS TO SELF-REVIEW EXERCISES

G.1 a) localize. b) encoding. c) universal, efficient, uniform, unambiguous. d) character. e) portable. f) UTF-8.

G.2 a) False. It encompasses the majority of the world's characters. b) False. The *yyyy* represents a hexadecimal number. c) False. A diacritic is a special mark added to a character to distinguish it from another letter or to indicate an accent. d) True. e) False. The entity reference is denoted by **&#x***yyyy*.

EXERCISES

G.3 Navigate to the Unicode Consortium Web site (**www.unicode.org**) and write the hexadecimal code values for the following characters. In which block are they located?

a) Latin letter 'Z.'
b) Latin letter 'n' with the 'tilde (~).'
c) Greek letter 'delta.'
d) Mathematical operator 'less than or equal to.'
e) Punctuation symbol 'open quote (").'

G.4 Describe the Unicode Standard design basis.

G.5 Define the following terms:

a) code value.
b) surrogates.
c) Unicode Standard.
d) UTF-8.
e) UTF-16.
f) UTF-32.

G.6 Describe a scenario where it is optimal to store your data in UTF-16 format.

G.7 Using the Unicode Standard code values, create an XML document that prints your first and last name. The documents should contain the tags **<Uppercase>** and **<Lowercase>** that encode your name in uppercase and lowercase letters, respectively. If you know other writing systems, print your first and last name in those as well. Use a Web browser to render the document.

G.8 Write a JavaScript program that prints "Welcome to Unicode!" in English, French, German, Japanese, Kannada, Portuguese, Russian, Spanish, Telugu and Traditional Chinese. Use the code values provided in Fig. G.3. In JavaScript, a code value is represented through an escape sequence **\u***yyyy*, where *yyyy* is a four-digit hexadecimal number. Call **document.write** to render the text in a Web browser.

Bibliography

Abualsamid, A. "XML: The Big Picture." *Network Computing* 16 April 2001: 85-93.

Alsop, S. "Adios, Netscape! Bye-Bye, Fun." *Fortune* 2 April 2001: 48.

Anderson, R. "The Long and Winding Road to Web-Based Apps." *Network Computing* 19 March 2001: 79-84.

Beazley, D., *Python Essential Reference*. Indianapolis, IN: New Riders Publishing, 2001.

Bleyle, J., et. al., *Macromedia Flash 5 ActionScript Reference Guide.* San Francisco, CA: Macromedia, Inc., 2000.

Boumphrey, F., et. al., *Beginning XHTML.* U.S.: Wrox Press Ltd, 2000.

Choi, W., et. al., *Beginning PHP 4.* US: Wrox Press Ltd, 2000.

Chun, Russell. *Macromedia Flash Advanced.* U.S.: Peachpit Press, 2001.

Chun, W., *Core Python*. Upper Saddle River, NJ: Prentice Hall PTR, 2001.

Cohen, D. "Construct Your E-Commerce Business Tier the Easy Way With XML, ASP, and Scripting." *Microsoft Systems Journal* February 2000: 35-55.

Converse, T. and J. Park, *PHP4 Bible.* Foster City, CA: IDG Books Worldwide, Inc., 2000.

Curtis, H. *Flash Web Design: The Art of Motion Graphics.* U.S.: New Riders Publishing, 2000.

Deitel, H., et. al., *Advanced Java™ 2 Platform How to Program.* Upper Saddle River, NJ: Prentice Hall, 2002.

Deitel, H., et. al., *e-Business & e-Commerce.* Upper Saddle River, NJ: Prentice Hall, 2001.

Deitel, H., et. al., *e-Business & e-Commerce for Managers.* Upper Saddle River, NJ: Prentice Hall, 2001.

Deitel, H. and P. Deitel, *Java How to Program, Fourth Edition.* Upper Saddle River, NJ: Prentice Hall, 2002.

Deitel, H., et. al., *Perl How to Program.* Upper Saddle River, NJ: Prentice Hall, 2001.

Deitel, H., et. al., *XML How to Program.* Upper Saddle River, NJ: Prentice Hall, 2001.

Dick, K. *XML A Manager's Guide.* Reading, MA: Addison Wesley Longman, Inc., 2000.

Dyck, T. "Translating XML Schema." *eWeek* 28 May 2001: 1, 28.

Feiler, J. *Perl 5 Programming Notebook.* Upper Saddle River, NJ: Prentice Hall, 2001.

Floyd, M. *Building Web Sites With XML.* Upper Saddle River, NJ: Prentice Hall, 2000.

Floyd, M. "Generating Style Sheets Dynamically." *Webtechniques* January 2001: 62.

Gibbs, M. "XML Worth A thousand Pics." *Network World* 11 June 2001: 46.

Goldfarb, C. F., et. al., *The XML Handbook, 2nd Edition.* Upper Saddle River, NJ: Prentice Hall, 2000.

Harms, D. and K. McDonald, *The Quick Python Book*, Greenwich: Manning, 2000.

Hoenisch, S. "Structuring Documents with XML." *XML Journal* 31 August 2001: 40-43.

Holzschlag, M.E. "XMHTML Basic: Modularization in Action." *Webtechniques* February 2001: 36-39.

Lamont, J. "Even-handed XML Brings Commonality to Diverse Applications." *KMWorld* June 2000: 10-12.

Lewis, J. "Vendors' Support For XML Is All In The Semantics." *Internet Week 13 November 2000: 44.*

Luh, J. C. "Style and Substance." *Internet Technology* 1 April 2001: 48-51.

Lutz, M., Programming Python. Sebastopol, CA: O'Reilly, 2001.

Marchal, B. *XML By Example.* U.S.: Que Publishing, 2000.

Mohler, J. L. *Flash 5 Graphics, Animation & Interactivity.* Canada: OnWord Press, 2001.

Nairn, G. "Online Collaborations Aim to Speak Same Language." *Financial Times 18 April 2001: 10.*

O'Brien, L. "XSL Plays Important Role In Transformation of XML." *Software Development Times* 1 February 2001: 7.

Orenstein, D. "Time to Talk the Talk." *Business 2.0* 14 November 2000: 108-113.

Patton, T. "XML Schemas In Action." *XML Journal* 31 August 2001: 34-35.

Peschko, E., et. al., *Perl Developers Guide.* U.S.: McGraw-Hill, 2000.

Sebesta, R. W. *A Little Book on Perl.* Upper Saddle River, *NJ: Prentice Hall, 2001.*

Skonnard, A. "Understanding XML Namespaces." *MSDN Magazine* July 2001: 33-43.

"The X-Factor." *Global Technology Business* August 2000: 48-49.

Thomas, O. "Form and Function, Together at Last." *eCompany* July 2001: 92-93.

Wall, L., et. al., *Programming Perl.* U.S.: O'Reilly & Associates, Inc., 2001.

Webster, J. "Transaction Spec Is Proposed." *InternetWeek 13 November 2000: 24.*

Zellen, B. "Apache 2.0 Released In Beta." *Application Development Trends* May 2001: 12.

Index

Symbols

Numerics

A

B

D

E

F

G

H

J

M

P

T

W

X

Y

Z

End User License Agreements

PRENTICE HALL LICENSE AGREEMENT AND LIMITED WARRANTY

READ THE FOLLOWING TERMS AND CONDITIONS CAREFULLY BEFORE OPENING THIS SOFTWARE PACKAGE. THIS LEGAL DOCUMENT IS AN AGREEMENT BETWEEN YOU AND PRENTICE-HALL, INC. (THE "COMPANY"). BY OPENING THIS SEALED SOFTWARE PACKAGE, YOU ARE AGREEING TO BE BOUND BY THESE TERMS AND CONDITIONS. IF YOU DO NOT AGREE WITH THESE TERMS AND CONDITIONS, DO NOT OPEN THE SOFTWARE PACKAGE. PROMPTLY RETURN THE UNOPENED SOFTWARE PACKAGE AND ALL ACCOMPANYING ITEMS TO THE PLACE YOU OBTAINED THEM FOR A FULL REFUND OF ANY SUMS YOU HAVE PAID.

1.GRANT OF LICENSE: In consideration of your purchase of this book, and your agreement to abide by the terms and conditions of this Agreement, the Company grants to you a nonexclusive right to use and display the copy of the enclosed software program (hereinafter the "SOFTWARE") on a single computer (i.e., with a single CPU) at a single location so long as you comply with the terms of this Agreement. The Company reserves all rights not expressly granted to you under this Agreement.

2.OWNERSHIP OF SOFTWARE: You own only the magnetic or physical media (the enclosed media) on which the SOFTWARE is recorded or fixed, but the Company and the software developers retain all the rights, title, and ownership to the SOFTWARE recorded on the original media copy(ies) and all subsequent copies of the SOFTWARE, regardless of the form or media on which the original or other copies may exist. This license is not a sale of the original SOFTWARE or any copy to you.

3.COPY RESTRICTIONS: This SOFTWARE and the accompanying printed materials and user manual (the "Documentation") are the subject of copyright. The individual programs on the media are copyrighted by the authors of each program. Some of the programs on the media include separate licensing agreements. If you intend to use one of these programs, you must read and follow its accompanying license agreement. You may not copy the Documentation or the SOFTWARE, except that you may make a single copy of the SOFTWARE for backup or archival purposes only. You may be held legally responsible for any copying or copyright infringement which is caused or encouraged by your failure to abide by the terms of this restriction.

4.USE RESTRICTIONS: You may not network the SOFTWARE or otherwise use it on more than one computer or computer terminal at the same time. You may physically transfer the SOFTWARE from one computer to another provided that the SOFTWARE is used on only one computer at a time. You may not distribute copies of the SOFTWARE or Documentation to others. You may not reverse engineer, disassemble, decompile, modify, adapt, translate, or create derivative works based on the SOFTWARE or the Documentation without the prior written consent of the Company.

5. TRANSFER RESTRICTIONS: The enclosed SOFTWARE is licensed only to you and may not be transferred to any one else without the prior written consent of the Company. Any unauthorized transfer of the SOFTWARE shall result in the immediate termination of this Agreement.

6. TERMINATION: This license is effective until terminated. This license will terminate automatically without notice from the Company and become null and void if you fail to comply with any provisions or limitations of this license. Upon termination, you shall destroy the Documentation and all copies of the SOFTWARE. All provisions of this Agreement as to warranties, limitation of liability, remedies or damages, and our ownership rights shall survive termination.

7. MISCELLANEOUS: This Agreement shall be construed in accordance with the laws of the United States of America and the State of New York and shall benefit the Company, its affiliates, and assignees.

8.LIMITED WARRANTY AND DISCLAIMER OF WARRANTY: The Company warrants that the SOFTWARE, when properly used in accordance with the Documentation, will operate in substantial conformity with the description of the SOFTWARE set forth in the Documentation. The Company does not warrant that the SOFTWARE will meet your requirements or that the operation of the SOFTWARE will be uninterrupted or error-free. The Company warrants that the media on which the SOFTWARE is delivered shall be free from defects in materials and workmanship under normal use for a period of thirty (30) days from the date of your purchase. Your only remedy and the Company's only obligation under these limited warranties is, at the Company's option, return of the warranted item for a refund of any amounts paid by you or replacement of the item. Any replacement of SOFTWARE or media under the warranties shall not extend the original warranty period. The limited warranty set forth above shall not apply to any SOFTWARE which the Company determines in good faith has been subject to misuse, neglect, improper installation, repair, alteration, or damage by you. EXCEPT FOR THE EXPRESSED WARRANTIES SET FORTH ABOVE, THE COMPANY DISCLAIMS ALL WARRANTIES, EXPRESS OR IMPLIED, INCLUDING WITHOUT LIMITATION, THE IMPLIED WARRANTIES OF MERCHANTABILITY AND FITNESS FOR A PARTICULAR PURPOSE. EXCEPT FOR THE EXPRESS WARRANTY SET FORTH ABOVE, THE COMPANY DOES NOT WARRANT, GUARANTEE, OR MAKE ANY REPRESENTATION REGARDING THE USE OR THE RESULTS OF THE USE OF THE SOFTWARE IN TERMS OF ITS CORRECTNESS, ACCURACY, RELIABILITY, CURRENTNESS, OR OTHERWISE.

IN NO EVENT, SHALL THE COMPANY OR ITS EMPLOYEES, AGENTS, SUPPLIERS, OR CONTRACTORS BE LIABLE FOR ANY INCIDENTAL, INDIRECT, SPECIAL, OR CONSEQUENTIAL DAMAGES ARISING OUT OF OR IN CONNECTION WITH THE LICENSE GRANTED UNDER THIS AGREEMENT, OR FOR LOSS OF USE, LOSS OF DATA, LOSS OF INCOME OR PROFIT, OR OTHER LOSSES, SUSTAINED AS A RESULT OF INJURY TO ANY PERSON, OR LOSS OF OR DAMAGE TO PROPERTY, OR CLAIMS OF THIRD PARTIES, EVEN IF THE COMPANY OR AN AUTHORIZED REPRESENTATIVE OF THE COMPANY HAS BEEN ADVISED OF THE POSSIBILITY OF SUCH DAMAGES. IN NO EVENT SHALL LIABILITY OF THE COMPANY FOR DAMAGES WITH RESPECT TO THE SOFTWARE EXCEED THE AMOUNTS ACTUALLY PAID BY YOU, IF ANY, FOR THE SOFTWARE.

SOME JURISDICTIONS DO NOT ALLOW THE LIMITATION OF IMPLIED WARRANTIES OR LIABILITY FOR INCIDENTAL, INDIRECT, SPECIAL, OR CONSEQUENTIAL DAMAGES, SO THE ABOVE LIMITATIONS MAY NOT ALWAYS APPLY. THE WARRANTIES IN THIS AGREEMENT GIVE YOU SPECIFIC LEGAL RIGHTS AND YOU MAY ALSO HAVE OTHER RIGHTS WHICH VARY IN ACCORDANCE WITH LOCAL LAW.

ACKNOWLEDGMENT

YOU ACKNOWLEDGE THAT YOU HAVE READ THIS AGREEMENT, UNDERSTAND IT, AND AGREE TO BE BOUND BY ITS TERMS AND CONDITIONS. YOU ALSO AGREE THAT THIS AGREEMENT IS THE COMPLETE AND EXCLUSIVE STATEMENT OF THE AGREEMENT BETWEEN YOU AND THE COMPANY AND SUPERSEDES ALL PROPOSALS OR PRIOR AGREEMENTS, ORAL, OR WRITTEN, AND ANY OTHER COMMUNICATIONS BETWEEN YOU AND THE COMPANY OR ANY REPRESENTATIVE OF THE COMPANY RELATING TO THE SUBJECT MATTER OF THIS AGREEMENT.

Should you have any questions concerning this Agreement or if you wish to contact the Company for any reason, please contact in writing at the address below.

Robin Short

Prentice Hall PTR

One Lake Street

Upper Saddle River, New Jersey 07458

END-USER LICENSE AGREEMENT FOR MICROSOFT SOFTWARE

IMPORTANT-READ CAREFULLY: This Microsoft End-User License Agreement ("EULA") is a legal agreement between you (either an individual or a single entity) and Microsoft Corporation ("Microsoft") for the Microsoft software product identified above, which includes computer software and may include associated media, printed materials, and "online" or electronic documentation (collectively, "SOFTWARE PRODUCT"). By installing, copying, or otherwise using the SOFTWARE PRODUCT, you agree to be bound by the terms of this EULA. If you do not agree to the terms of this EULA, you may not use the SOFTWARE PRODUCT.

SOFTWARE PRODUCT LICENSE

The SOFTWARE PRODUCT is protected by copyright laws and international copyright treaties, as well as other intellectual property laws and treaties. The SOFTWARE PRODUCT is licensed, not sold.

INTRODUCTION. The SOFTWARE PRODUCT is comprised of the following components: (i) the core cabinet file components which include Microsoft Agent Server, Microsoft Agent Control and Microsoft Agent Provider; (I) Microsoft Character Animation Data and Image Files; and (IA) Foreign Language .DLL files. The Foreign Language .DLL files provided by Microsoft for use with Microsoft Agent are subject to this EULA, which EULA will only be provided in English. English shall be deemed the language that controls the terms of this EULA.

This EULA describes your rights with respect to the SOFTWARE PRODUCT and its components.

1. GRANT OF LICENSE. This EULA grants you the following rights:

* Standard Use. You may install and use one (1) copy of the SOFTWARE PRODUCT on a single computer.

* Development Use. Microsoft grants you a non-exclusive, limited license, subject to the development use requirements below, to: (i) use the Character Animation Data and Image Files and Foreign Language .DLL files Microsoft has designated at the Microsoft Site (as defined below) for development use with Microsoft Agent, and (ii) create Web pages, scripts or programs that call the Microsoft Agent API to animate the character and display the static or animated images that are provided by Microsoft to enable the end-user selection of an animated image.

* Development Use Requirements.

Software Product. If you exercise the Development Use rights described above, you agree to: (a) only exercise the development rights described above for your Web site or application that uses the SOFTWARE PRODUCT; (b) only allow access to the SOFTWARE PRODUCT by your end-users by (i) providing instructions or a hyperlink URL so that your end-user customers can download the components from Microsoft's Web site located at http://msdn.microsoft.com/msagent/ (the "Microsoft Site") or (ii) including the SOFTWARE PRODUCT's CLSID in an HTML Object tag on your Web site that will automatically download the SOFTWARE PRODUCT for your end-user customers from the Microsoft Site; (c) place one of the following notices on your Web site or application that includes or uses the SOFTWARE PRODUCT: (i) place the notice "Uses Microsoft Agent technology" on your Web site on the introductory page where the SOFTWARE PRODUCT is used or (ii) place the notice "Includes Microsoft Agent technology" in your application's copyright information or packaging; (d) not use Microsoft's name, logo, or trademarks to market your Web site or application; (e) include a valid copyright notice on your Web site or application; and (e) indemnify, hold harmless, and defend Microsoft from and against any claims or lawsuits, including attorney's fees, that arise or result from the use or distribution of your Web site or application.

Microsoft Character Animation Data and Image Files. If you use any of the Character Animation Data and Image Files, you agree to: (a) only use the Character Animation Data and Image Files on your Web site or application that uses the SOFTWARE PRODUCT; (b) display the character's name with the following copyright notice "(c) 1996-1998 Microsoft Corporation. All rights reserved." with the Web site's or application's copyright information or adjacent to the character's image; (c) not use the Character Animation Data and Image Files to disparage Microsoft, its products or services or for promotional goods or for products which, in Microsoft's sole judgment, may diminish or otherwise damage Microsoft's goodwill in the SOFTWARE PRODUCT including but not limited to uses which could be deemed under applicable law to be obscene or pornographic, uses which are excessively violent, unlawful, or which purpose is to encourage unlawful activities; (d) not use the Character Animation Data and Image files to imply Microsoft's sponsorship, endorsement or approval of your software application, service or content provided on your Internet site; (e) not alter the Character Animation Data and Image Files in any way; and (f) not combine the Animated Character(s) or Animation data files with any other object, including, but not limited to, other logos, words, graphics, photos, slogans, numbers, design features or symbols.

2. DESCRIPTION OF OTHER RIGHTS AND LIMITATIONS.

* Support Services. Microsoft may provide you with support services related to the SOFTWARE PRODUCT ("Support Services"). Use of Support Services is governed by the Microsoft policies and programs described in the user manual, in "on line" documentation and/or other Microsoft-provided materials. Any supplemental software code provided to you as part of the Support Services shall be considered part of the SOFTWARE PRODUCT and subject to the terms and conditions of this EULA. With respect to technical information you provide to Microsoft as part of the Support Services, Microsoft may use such information for its business purposes, including for product support and development. Microsoft will not utilize such technical information in a form that personally identifies you.

* Limitations on Reverse Engineering, Decompilation, and Disassembly. You may not reverse engineer, decompile, or disassemble the SOFTWARE PRODUCT, except and only to the extent that such activity is expressly permitted by applicable law notwithstanding this limitation.

* Rental. You may not rent, lease or lend the SOFTWARE PRODUCT.

* Software Transfer. You may permanently transfer all of your rights under this EULA, provided you retain no copies, you transfer all of the SOFTWARE PRODUCT (including all component parts, the media and printed materials, any upgrades, this EULA, and, if applicable, the Certificate of Authenticity), and the recipient agrees to the terms of this EULA.

3. ALL RIGHTS NOT EXPRESSLY GRANTED HEREIN ARE RESERVED BY MICROSOFT.

4. TERMINATION. Without prejudice to any other rights, Microsoft may terminate this EULA if you fail to comply with the terms and conditions of this EULA. In such event, you must destroy all copies of the SOFTWARE PRODUCT and all of its component parts.

5. COPYRIGHT. All title and copyrights in and to the SOFTWARE PRODUCT (including but not limited to any images, photographs, animations, video, audio, music, text, and "applets" incorporated into the SOFTWARE PRODUCT), the accompanying printed materials, and any copies of the SOFTWARE PRODUCT are owned by Microsoft or its suppliers. The SOFTWARE PRODUCT is protected by copyright laws and international treaty provisions. Therefore, you must treat the SOFTWARE PRODUCT like any other copyrighted material. You may not copy the printed materials accompanying the SOFTWARE PRODUCT.

6. U.S. GOVERNMENT RESTRICTED RIGHTS. All SOFTWARE PRODUCT and documentation provided to the U.S. Government pursuant to solicitations issued on or after December 1, 1995 is provided with the commercial rights and restrictions described elsewhere herein. All SOFTWARE PRODUCT provided to the U.S. Government pursuant to solicitations issued prior to December 1, 1995 is provided with RESTRICTED RIGHTS as provided for in FAR, 48 CFR 52.227-14 (JUNE 1987) or FAR, 48 CFR 252.227-7013 (OCT 1988), as applicable.

7. EXPORT RESTRICTIONS. You acknowledge that the SOFTWARE PRODUCT licensed hereunder is subject to the export control laws and regulations of the U.S.A., and any amendments thereof. You confirm that with respect to the SOFTWARE PRODUCT, you will not export or re-export it, directly or indirectly, to any countries that are subject to U.S.A. export restrictions. You further acknowledge that the SOFTWARE PRODUCT may include technical data subject to export and re-export restrictions imposed by U.S.A. law.

MISCELLANEOUS

If you acquired this product in the United States, this EULA is governed by the laws of the State of Washington.

If you acquired this product in Canada, this EULA is governed by the laws of the Province of Ontario, Canada. Each of the parties hereto irrevocably attorns to the jurisdiction of the courts of the Province of Ontario and further agrees to commence any litigation which may arise hereunder in the courts located in the Judicial District of York, Province of Ontario.

If this product was acquired outside the United States, then local law may apply.

If you are interested in additional information on licensing or use of Microsoft Agent, please visit the Microsoft Agent Web site at http://www.microsoft.com/msagent. Should you have any questions concerning this EULA, or if you desire to contact Microsoft for any reason, please contact the Microsoft subsidiary serving your country, or write: Microsoft Sales Information Center/One Microsoft Way/Redmond, WA 98052-6399.

LIMITED WARRANTY

NO WARRANTIES. TO THE MAXIMUM EXTENT PERMITTED BY APPLICABLE LAW, MICROSOFT AND ITS SUPPLIERS DISCLAIM ALL WARRANTIES AND CONDITIONS, EITHER EXPRESS OR IMPLIED, INCLUDING, BUT NOT LIMITED TO, IMPLIED WARRANTIES OF MERCHANTABILITY, FITNESS FOR A PARTICULAR PURPOSE, TITLE AND NON-INFRINGEMENT, WITH REGARD TO THE SOFTWARE PRODUCT, AND THE PROVISION OF OR FAILURE TO PROVIDE SUP-

PORT SERVICES. THIS LIMITED WARRANTY GIVES YOU SPECIFIC LEGAL RIGHTS. YOU MAY HAVE OTHERS, WHICH VARY FROM STATE/JURISDICTION TO STATE/JURISDICTION.

LIMITATION OF LIABILITY. TO THE MAXIMUM EXTENT PERMITTED BY APPLICABLE LAW, IN NO EVENT SHALL MICROSOFT OR ITS SUPPLIERS BE LIABLE FOR ANY SPECIAL, INCIDENTAL, INDIRECT, OR CONSEQUENTIAL DAMAGES WHATSOEVER (INCLUDING, WITHOUT LIMITATION, DAMAGES FOR LOSS OF BUSINESS PROFITS, BUSINESS INTERRUPTION, LOSS OF BUSINESS INFORMATION, OR ANY OTHER PECUNIARY LOSS) ARISING OUT OF THE USE OF OR INABILITY TO USE THE SOFTWARE PRODUCT OR THE PROVISION OF OR FAILURE TO PROVIDE SUPPORT SERVICES, EVEN IF MICROSOFT HAS BEEN ADVISED OF THE POSSIBILITY OF SUCH DAMAGES. IN ANY CASE, MICROSOFT'S ENTIRE LIABILITY UNDER ANY PROVISION OF THIS EULA SHALL BE LIMITED TO THE GREATER OF THE AMOUNT ACTUALLY PAID BY YOU FOR THE SOFTWARE PRODUCT OR US$5.00; PROVIDED HOWEVER, IF YOU HAVE ENTERED INTO A MICROSOFT SUPPORT SERVICES AGREEMENT, MICROSOFT'S ENTIRE LIABILITY REGARDING SUPPORT SERVICES SHALL BE GOVERNED BY THE TERMS OF THAT AGREEMENT. BECAUSE SOME STATES AND JURISDICTIONS DO NOT ALLOW THE EXCLUSION OR LIMITATION OF LIABILITY, THE ABOVE LIMITATION MAY NOT APPLY TO YOU.

Si vous avez acquis votre produit Microsoft au CANADA, la garantie limitée suivante vous concerne :

GARANTIE LIMITÉE

AUCUNE AUTRE GARANTIE - DANS LA MESURE PRÉVUE PAR LA LOI, MICROSOFT ET SES FOURNISSEURS EXCLUENT TOUTE AUTRE GARANTIE OU CONDITION, EXPRESSE OU IMPLICITE, Y COMPRIS MAIS NE SE LIMITANT PAS AUX GARANTIES OU CONDITIONS IMPLICITES DU CARACTÈRE ADÉQUAT POUR LA COMMERCIALISATION OU UN USAGE PARTICULIER EN CE QUI CONCERNE LE LOGICIEL OU CONCERNANT LE TITRE , L'ABSENCE DE CONTREFAÇON DUDIT LOGICIEL, ET TOUTE DOCUMENTATION ÉCRITE QUI L'ACCOMPAGNE, AINSI QUE POUR TOUTE DISPOSITION CONCERNANT LE SUPORT TECHNIQUE OU LA FAÇON DONT CELUI-CI A ÉTÉ RENDU. CETTE GARANTIE LIMITÉE VOUS ACCORDE DES DROITS JURIDIQUES SPÉCIFIQUES.

PAS DE RESPONSABILITÉ POUR LES DOMMAGES INDIRECTS - MICROSOFT OU SES FOURNISSEURS NE SERONT PAS RESPONSABLES EN AUCUNE CIRCONSTANCE POUR TOUT DOMMAGE SPÉCIAL, INCIDENT, INDIRECT, OU CONSÉQUENT QUEL QU'IL SOIT (Y COMPRIS, SANS LIMITATION, LES DOMMAGES ENTRAINÉS PAR LA PERTE DE BÉNÉFICES, L'INTERRUPTION DES ACTIVITÉS, LA PERTE D'INFORMATION OU TOUTE AUTRE PERTE PÉCUNIAIRE) DÉCOULANT DE L'UTILISATION OU DE L'IMPOSSIBILITÉ D'UTILISATION DE CE LOGICIEL AINSI QUE POUR TOUTE DISPOSITION CONCERNANT LE SUPORT TECHNIQUE OU LA FAÇON DONT CELUI-CI A ÉTÉ RENDU ET CE, MÊME SI MICROSOFT A ÉTÉ AVISÉE DE LA POSSIBILITÉ DE TELS DOMMAGES. LA RESPONSABILITÉ DE MICROSOFT EN VERTU DE TOUTE DISPOSITION DE CETTE CONVENTION NE POURRA EN AUCUN TEMPS EXCÉDER LE PLUS ÉLEVÉ ENTRE i) LE MONTANT EFFECTIVEMENT PAYÉ PAR VOUS POUR LE LOGICIEL OU ii) US$5.00. ADVENANT QUE VOUS AYEZ CONTRACTÉ PAR ENTENTE DISTINCTE AVEC MICROSOFT POUR UN SUPPORT TECHNIQUE ÉTENDU, VOUS SEREZ LIÉ PAR LES TERMES D' UNE TELLE ENTENTE.

La présente Convention est régie par les lois de la province d'Ontario, Canada. Chacune des parties à la présente reconnaît irrévocablement la compétence des tribunaux de la province d'Ontario et consent à instituer tout litige qui pourrait découler de la présente auprès des tribunaux situés dans le district judiciaire de York, province d'Ontario.

Au cas où vous auriez des questions concernant cette licence ou que vous désiriez vous mettre en rapport avec Microsoft pour quelque raison que ce soit, veuillez contacter la succursale Microsoft desservant votre pays, dont l'adresse est fournie dans ce produit, ou écrivez à : Microsoft Sales Information Center, One Microsoft Way, Redmond, Washington 98052-6399.

ADOBE SYSTEMS INCORPORATED END USER LICENSE AGREEMENT FOR ADOBE ACROBAT READER

NOTICE TO USER: THIS IS A CONTRACT. BY INSTALLING THIS SOFTWARE YOU ACCEPT ALL THE TERMS AND CONDITIONS OF THIS AGREEMENT.

This Adobe Systems Incorporated ("Adobe") End User License Agreement accompanies the Adobe® Acrobat® Reader product and related explanatory materials ("Software"). The term "Software" also shall include any upgrades, modified versions or updates of the Software licensed to you by Adobe. Please read this Agreement carefully. At the end, you will be asked to accept this agreement and continue to install or, if you do not wish to accept this Agreement, to decline this agreement, in which case you will not be able to use the Software.

Upon your acceptance of this Agreement, Adobe grants to you a nonexclusive license to use the Software, provided that you agree to the following:

1. Use of the Software.

- You may install the Software on a hard disk or other storage device; install and use the Software on a file server for use on a network for the purposes of (i) permanent installation onto hard disks or other storage devices or (ii) use of the Software over such network; and make backup copies of the Software.
- You may make and distribute unlimited copies of the Software, including copies for commercial distribution, as long as each copy that you make and distribute contains this Agreement, the Acrobat Reader installer, and the same copyright and other proprietary notices pertaining to this Software that appear in the Software. If you download the Software from the Internet or similar on-line source, you must include the Adobe copyright notice for the Software with any on-line distribution and on any media you distribute that includes the Software.

2. Copyright and Trademark Rights. The Software is owned by Adobe and its suppliers, and its structure, organization and code are the valuable trade secrets of Adobe and its suppliers. The Software also is protected by United States Copyright Law and International Treaty provisions. You may use trademarks only insofar as required to comply with Section 1 of this Agreement and to identify printed output produced by the Software, in accordance with accepted trademark practice, including identification of trademark owner's name. Such use of any trademark does not give you any rights of ownership in that trademark. Except as stated above, this Agreement does not grant you any intellectual property rights in the Software.

3. Restrictions. You agree not to modify, adapt, translate, reverse engineer, decompile, disassemble or otherwise attempt to discover the source code of the Software. Although you may customize the installer for the Software as documented on the Adobe Acrobat Reader CD-ROM (e.g., installation of additional plug-in and help files), you may not otherwise alter or modify the installer program or create a new installer for the Software. The Software is licensed and distributed by Adobe for viewing, distributing and sharing PDF files. Any plug-in or enhancement that permits you to save modifications to a PDF file is authorized only for use with Acrobat Exchange™ program and may not be used with the Software.

4. No Warranty. The Software is being delivered to you AS IS and Adobe makes no warranty as to its use or performance. ADOBE AND ITS SUPPLIERS DO NOT AND CANNOT WARRANT THE PERFORMANCE OR RESULTS YOU MAY OBTAIN BY USING THE SOFTWARE OR DOCUMENTATION. ADOBE AND ITS SUPPLIERS MAKE NO WARRANTIES, EXPRESS OR IMPLIED, AS TO NONINFRINGEMENT OF THIRD PARTY RIGHTS, MERCHANTABILITY, OR FITNESS FOR ANY PARTICULAR PURPOSE. IN NO EVENT WILL ADOBE OR ITS SUPPLIERS BE LIABLE TO YOU FOR ANY CONSEQUENTIAL, INCIDENTAL OR SPECIAL DAMAGES, INCLUDING ANY LOST PROFITS OR LOST SAVINGS, EVEN IF AN ADOBE REPRESENTATIVE HAS BEEN ADVISED OF THE POSSIBILITY OF SUCH DAMAGES, OR FOR ANY CLAIM BY ANY THIRD PARTY. Some states or jurisdictions do not allow the exclusion or limitation of incidental, consequential or special damages, or the exclusion of implied warranties or limitations on how long an implied warranty may last, so the above limitations may not apply to you.

5. Governing Law and General Provisions. This Agreement will be governed by the laws of the State of California, U.S.A., excluding the application of its conflicts of law rules. This Agreement will not be governed by the United Nations Convention on Contracts for the International Sale of Goods, the application of which is expressly excluded. If any part of this Agreement is found void and unenforceable, it will not affect the validity of the balance of the Agreement, which shall remain valid and enforceable according to its terms. You agree that the Software will not be shipped, transferred or exported into any country or used in any manner prohibited by the United States Export Administration Act or any other export laws, restrictions or regulations. This Agreement shall automatically terminate upon failure by you to comply with its terms. This Agreement may only be modified in writing signed by an authorized officer of Adobe.

6. Notice to Government End Users. If this product is acquired under the terms of a: GSA contract- Use, reproduction or disclosure is subject to the restrictions set forth in the applicable ADP Schedule contract; U.S. Odd contract- Use, duplication or disclosure by the Government is subject to restrictions as set forth in subparagraph (c) (1) (ii) of 252.227-7013; Civilian agency contract- Use, reproduction, or disclosure is subject to 52.227-19 (a) through (d) and restrictions set forth in the accompanying end user agreement.

Unpublished-rights reserved under the copyright laws of the United States. Adobe Systems Incorporated, 345 Park Avenue, San Jose, CA 95110.

Adobe, Acrobat, and Acrobat Exchange are trademarks of Adobe Systems Incorporated.

THE APACHE SOFTWARE LICENSE, VERSION 1.1

Redistribution and use in source and binary forms, with or without modification, are permitted provided that the following conditions are met:

1. Redistributions of source code must retain the above copyright notice, this list of conditions and the following disclaimer.

2. Redistributions in binary form must reproduce the above copyright notice, this list of conditions and the following disclaimer in the documentation and/or other materials provided with the distribution.

3. The end-user documentation included with the redistribution, if any, must include the following acknowledgment: "This product includes software developed by the Apache Software Foundation (http://www.apache.org/)." Alternately, this acknowledgment may appear in the software itself, if and wherever such third-party acknowledgments normally appear.

4. The names "Apache" and "Apache Software Foundation" must not be used to endorse or promote products derived from this software without prior written permission. For written permission, please contact apache@apache.org.

5. Products derived from this software may not be called "Apache", nor may "Apache" appear in their name, without prior written permission of the Apache Software Foundation.

THIS SOFTWARE IS PROVIDED ``AS IS'' AND ANY EXPRESSED OR IMPLIED WARRANTIES, INCLUDING, BUT NOT LIMITED TO, THE IMPLIED WARRANTIES OF MERCHANTABILITY AND FITNESS FOR A PARTICULAR PURPOSE ARE DISCLAIMED. IN NO EVENT SHALL THE APACHE SOFTWARE FOUNDATION OR ITS CONTRIBUTORS BE LIABLE FOR ANY DIRECT, INDIRECT, INCIDENTAL,

SPECIAL, EXEMPLARY, OR CONSEQUENTIAL DAMAGES (INCLUDING, BUT NOT LIMITED TO, PROCUREMENT OF SUBSTITUTE GOODS OR SERVICES; LOSS OF USE, DATA, OR PROFITS; OR BUSINESS INTERRUPTION) HOWEVER CAUSED AND ON ANY THEORY OF LIABILITY, WHETHER IN CONTRACT, STRICT LIABILITY, OR TORT (INCLUDING NEGLIGENCE OR OTHERWISE) ARISING IN ANY WAY OUT OF THE USE OF THIS SOFTWARE, EVEN IF ADVISED OF THE POSSIBILITY OF SUCH DAMAGE.

This software consists of voluntary contributions made by many individuals on behalf of the Apache Software Foundation. Portions of this software are based upon public domain software originally written at the National Center for Supercomputing Applications, University of Illinois, Urbana-Champaign.

The DEITEL & DEITEL Suite of Products...

BOOKS

e-Business & e-Commerce How to Program

BOOK / CD-ROM

©2001, 1254 pp., paper bound w/CD-ROM (0-13-028419-X)

This innovative book explores programming technologies for developing Web-based e-business and e-commerce solutions, and covers e-business and e-commerce models and business issues. Readers learn a full range of options, from "build-your-own" to turnkey solutions. The book examines a number of the top e-businesses (such as Amazon, eBay, Priceline, Travelocity, etc.), explaining the technical details of building successful e-business and e-commerce sites and their underlying business premises. Learn how to implement the dominant e-commerce models — shopping carts, auctions, naming-your-own-price, comparison shopping and bots/ intelligent agents—by using markup languages (HTML, Dynamic HTML and XML), scripting languages (JavaScript, VBScript and Perl), server-side technologies (Active Server Pages and Perl/CGI) and database (SQL and ADO) , security and online payment technologies. Updates are regularly posted to **www.deitel.com** and the book includes a CD-ROM with software tools, source code and live links.

e-Business & e-Commerce for Managers

©2001, 794 pp., paper (0-13-032364-0)

This comprehensive overview of building and managing an e-business explores topics such as the decision to bring a business online, choosing a business model, accepting payments, marketing strategies and security, as well as many other important issues (such as career resources). Features Web resources and online demonstrations that supplement the text and direct readers to additional materials. The book also includes an appendix that develops a complete Web-based shopping cart application using HTML, JavaScript, VBScript, Active Server Pages, ADO, SQL, HTTP, XML and XSL. Plus, company-specific sections provide "real-world" examples of the concepts presented in the book.

Internet & World Wide Web How to Program, Second Edition

BOOK / CD-ROM

©2002, 1300 pp., paper bound w/CD-ROM (0-13-030897-8)

The world's best-selling Internet and Web programming text uses the scripting and markup languages of the Web to present traditional introductory programming concepts. Now you can learn programming fundamentals "wrapped in the metaphor of the Web." Employing the Deitels' signature "live-code™" approach, the book covers markup languages (XHTML, Dynamic HTML), client-side scripting (JavaScript) and server-side scripting (VBScript, ASP, Perl/CGI, Python, PHP, Java servlets, Java Server Pages). The book offers a thorough treatment of programming concepts, with programs that yield visible or audible results in Web pages and Web-based applications. It discusses Internet Explorer, effective Web-based design, multi-tier Web-based applications development, ActiveX® controls and introduces electronic commerce and security. Updated material on **www.deitel.com** and **www.prenhall.com/deitel** provides additional resources for instructors who want to cover Microsoft® or non-Microsoft technologies. The Web site includes an extensive treatment of Netscape® 6 and alternate versions of the code from the Dynamic HTML chapters that will work with non-Microsoft environments as well. The Second Edition also features new and updated material on XHTML, CSS, wireless Internet (WML, WMLScript), Web accessibility, career resources, Python, PHP, XML/XSLT, SVG, SMIL, Web servers, Photoshop Elements, multimedia audio, animation, Macromedia Flash, databases, Perl, CGI, Java servlets, JavaServer Pages, PWS, IIS and Apache.

Python How to Program

BOOK / CD-ROM

©2002, 1000 pp., paper (0-13-092361-3)

This exciting new book provides a comprehensive introduction to Python — a powerful object-oriented programming language with clear syntax and the ability to bring together various technologies quickly and easily. This book covers introductory programming techniques as well as more advanced topics such as graphical user interfaces, databases, wireless Internet programming, networking and multimedia. Readers will learn principles that are applicable to both systems development and Web programming. The book features the outstanding, consistent and applied pedagogy that the *How to Program* series is known for, including the Deitels' signature Live-Code™ Approach, with thousands of lines of code in hundreds of working programs; hundreds of valuable programming tips identified with icons throughout the text; an extensive set of exercises, projects and case studies; two-color four-way syntax coloring and much more.

XML How to Program

BOOK / CD-ROM

©2001, 934 pp., paper (0-13-028417-3)

This book is a complete guide to programming in XML. It explains how to use XML to create customized tags and addresses standard custom markup languages for science and technology, multimedia, commerce and other fields. Concise introductions to Java, JavaServer Pages, VBScript, Active Server Pages and Perl/CGI provide readers with the essentials of these programming languages and server-side development technologies to enable them to work effectively with XML. The book also covers cutting-edge topics such as XQL and SMIL, plus a real-world e-commerce case study and a complete chapter on Web accessibility that addresses Voice XML. It also includes tips such as Common Programming Errors, Software Engineering Observations, Portability Tips and Debugging Hints. Other topics covered include XHTML, CSS, DTD, schema, parsers, DOM, SAX, XPath, XLink, namespaces, XBase, XInclude, XPointer, XSL, XSLT, XSL Formatting Objects, JavaServer Pages, XForms, topic maps, X3D, MathML, OpenMath, CML, BML, CDF, RDF, SVG, Cocoon, WML, XBRL, and BizTalk and SOAP Web resources.

Wireless Internet & Mobile Business How to Program

©2002, 1300 pp., paper (0-13-062226-5)

While the rapid growth of wireless technologies (such as cell phones, pagers and personal digital assistants) offers many new opportunities for businesses and programmers, it also presents numerous challenges related to issues such as security and standardization. This book offers a thorough treatment of both the management and technical aspects of this expanding area, including current practices and future trends. The first half explores the business issues surrounding wireless technology and mobile business, including an overview of existing and developing communication technologies and the application of business principles to wireless devices. It then turns to programming for the wireless Internet, exploring topics such as WAP (including 2.0), WML, WMLScript, XML, XSL, XSLT, XHTML, Wireless Java Programming, Web Clipping and more. Other topics covered include career resources, location-based services, wireless marketing, wireless payments, security, accessibility, international issues, Palm, PocketPC, Windows CE, i-Mode, Bluetooth, J2ME, MIDP, MIDlets, ASP, Perl and PHP. Also discussed are Microsoft .NET Mobile Framework, BREW, multimedia, Flash, VBScript and legal, ethical and social issues.

Perl How to Program

BOOK / CD-ROM

©2001, 1057 pp., paper (0-13-028418-1)

This comprehensive guide to Perl programming emphasizes the use of the Common Gateway Interface (CGI) with Perl to create powerful dynamic Web content for e-commerce applications. The book begins with a clear and careful introduction to programming concepts at a level suitable for beginners, and proceeds through advanced topics such as references and complex data structures. Key Perl topics such as regular expressions and string manipulation are covered in detail. The authors address important and topical issues such as object-oriented programming, the Perl database interface (DBI), graphics and security. Also included is a treatment of XML, a bonus chapter introducing the Python programming language, supplemental material on career resources and a complete chapter on Web accessibility. The text also includes tips such as Common Programming Errors, Software Engineering Observations, Portability Tips and Debugging Hints.

Java How to Program Fourth Edition

BOOK / CD-ROM

©2002, 1100 pp., cloth bound w/CD-ROM (0-13-034151-7)

The world's best-selling Java text is now even better! The Fourth Edition of *Java How to Program* now includes a new focus on object-oriented design with the UML, design patterns, full-color program listings and figures, and the most up-to-date Java coverage available.

Readers will discover key topics in Java programming, such as graphical user interface components, exception handling, multithreading, multimedia, files and streams, networking, data structures, and more. In addition, a new chapter on design patterns explains frequently recurring architectural patterns —information that can help save designers considerable time when building large systems.

The highly detailed optional case study focuses on object-oriented design with the UML and presents fully implemented working Java code.

Updated throughout, the text now includes new and revised discussions on topics such as Swing, graphics, multithreading, multimedia, Java Media Framework, streaming audio, streaming video, socket-and-packet-based networking and career resources. Three introductory chapters heavily emphasize problem solving and programming skills. The chapters on RMI, JDBC, servlets and JavaBeans have been moved to *Advanced Java 2 Platform How to Program*, where they are now covered in much greater depth. (See *Advanced Java 2 Platform How to Program*, at right.)

Advanced Java™ 2 Platform How to Program

BOOK / CD-ROM

©2002, 1000 pp., paper (0-13-089560-1)

Expanding on the world's best-selling Java textbook—*Java How to Program*—*Advanced Java 2 Platform How To Program* presents advanced Java topics for developing sophisticated, user-friendly GUIs; significant, scalable enterprise applications; wireless applications and distributed systems. Focusing on Java 2 Enterprise Edition (J2EE), this textbook integrates technologies such as XML, XSLT, JavaBeans, security, JDBC, JavaServer Pages (JSP), servlets, Remote Method Invocation (RMI), Enterprise JavaBeans (EJB) and design patterns into a significant enterprise case study that leverages J2EE's powerful component model. This textbook also features a case study that integrates Swing, Java2D, drag and drop, XML and design patterns to build a sophisticated drawing application. Additional topics include CORBA, Jini, JavaSpaces, Jiro, Java Management Extensions (JMX) and Peer-to-Peer networking with an introduction to JXTA. This textbook also introduces the Java 2 Micro Edition (J2ME) for building applications for handheld and wireless devices using MIDP and MIDlets. Wireless technologies covered include WAP, WML and i-mode.

C++ How to Program Third Edition

BOOK / CD-ROM

©2001, 1168 pp., paper (0-13-089571-7)

The world's best-selling C++ text teaches programming by emphasizing object-oriented programming, software reuse and component-oriented software construction. This comprehensive book uses the Deitels' signature live-code™ approach, presenting every concept in the context of a complete, working C++ program followed by a screen capture showing the program's output. It also includes a rich collection of exercises and valuable insights in its set of Common Programming Errors, Software Engineering Observations, Portability Tips and Debugging Hints. The Third Edition features an extensive treatment of the Standard Template Library and includes a new case study that focuses on object-oriented design with the UML, illustrating the entire process of object-oriented design from conception to implementation. In addition, it adheres to the latest ANSI/ISO C++ standards. The accompanying CD-ROM contains Microsoft® Visual C++ 6.0 Introductory Edition software, source code for all examples in the text and hyperlinks to C++ demos and Internet resources.

C# How to Program

BOOK / CD-ROM

©2002, 1000 pp., paper (0-13-062221-4)

An exciting new addition to the *How to Program* series, *C# How to Program* provides a comprehensive introduction to Microsoft's new object-oriented language. C# builds on the skills already mastered by countless C++ and Java programmers, enabling them to create powerful Web applications and components—ranging from XML-based Web services on Microsoft's .NET™ platform to middle-tier business objects and system-level applications. Mastering C# will allow programmers to create complex systems—using fewer lines of code and reducing the chance for error. The end result is faster development at a decreased cost—and optimum adaptibility that makes it easy to keep up with the evolving Web.

Look for these related titles in the Deitels' *.NET Series:*

- *Visual Basic® .NET How to Program*
- *Visual C++ .NET How to Program*

C How to Program Third Edition

BOOK / CD-ROM

©2001, 1253 pp., paper (0-13-089572-5)

Highly practical in approach, the Third Edition of the world's best-selling C text introduces the fundamentals of structured programming and software engineering and gets up to speed quickly. This comprehensive book not only covers the full C language, but also reviews library functions and introduces object-based and object-oriented programming in C++ and Java, as well as event-driven GUI programming in Java. The Third Edition includes a new 346-page introduction to Java 2 and the basics of GUIs, and the 298-page introduction to C++ has been updated to be consistent with the most current ANSI/ISO C++ standards. Plus, icons throughout the book point out valuable programming tips such as Common Programming Errors, Portability Tips and Testing and Debugging Tips.

Look for new Visual Studio .NET editions coming soon!

Visual Basic® 6 How to Program

BOOK / CD-ROM

©1999, 1015 pp., paper bound w/CD-ROM (0-13-456955-5)

Getting Started with Microsoft® Visual C++™ 6 with an Introduction to MFC

BOOK / CD-ROM

©2000, 163 pp., paper (0-13-016147-0)

ORDER INFORMATION

SINGLE COPY SALES:
Visa, Master Card, American Express, Checks, or Money Orders only
Toll-Free: 800-643-5506; Fax: 800-835-5327

GOVERNMENT AGENCIES:
Prentice Hall Customer Service
(#GS-02F-8023A)
Phone: 201-767-5994; Fax: 800-445-6991

COLLEGE PROFESSORS:
For desk or review copies, please visit us on the World Wide Web at www.prenhall.com

CORPORATE ACCOUNTS:
Quantity, Bulk Orders totaling 10 or more books. Purchase orders only — No credit cards.
Tel: 201-236-7156; Fax: 201-236-7141
Toll-Free: 800-382-3419

CANADA:
Pearson Education Canada
26 Prince Andrew Place
Don Mills, ON M3C 2T8 Canada
Tel: 416 447 5101; Fax: 416 443 0948
E-mail: phcinfo.pubcanada@pearsoned.com

UK/IRELAND:
Pearson Education
Edinburgh Gate
Harlow, Essex CM20 2JE UK
Tel: 01279 623928; Fax: 01279 414130
E-mail: enq.orders@pearsoned-ema.com

EUROPE, MIDDLE EAST & AFRICA:
Pearson Education
P.O. Box 75598
1070 AN Amsterdam, The Netherlands
Tel: 31 20 5755 800; Fax: 31 20 664 5334
E-mail: amsterdam@pearsoned-ema.com

ASIA:
Pearson Education Asia
317 Alexandra Road #04-01
IKEA Building
Singapore 159965
Tel: 65 476 4688; Fax: 65 378 0370

JAPAN:
Pearson Education
Nishi-Shinjuku, KF Building 101
8-14-24 Nishi-Shinjuku, Shinjuku-ku
Tokyo, Japan 160-0023
Tel: 81 3 3365 9001; Fax: 81 3 3365 9009

INDIA:
Pearson Education Indian Liaison Office
90 New Raidhani Enclave, Ground Floor
Delhi 110 092, India
Tel: 91 11 2059850 & 2059851
Fax: 91 11 2059852

AUSTRALIA:
Pearson Education Australia
Unit 4, Level 2
14 Aquatic Drive
Frenchs Forest, NSW 2086, Australia
Tel: 61 2 9454 2200; Fax: 61 2 9453 0089
E-mail: marketing@pearsoned.com.au

NEW ZEALAND/FIJI:
Pearson Education
46 Hillside Road
Auckland 10, New Zealand
Tel: 649 444 4968; Fax: 649 444 4957
E-mail: sales@pearsoned.co.nz

SOUTH AFRICA:
Pearson Education
P.O. Box 12122
Mill Street
Cape Town 8010 South Africa
Tel: 27 21 686 6356; Fax: 27 21 686 4590

LATIN AMERICA:
Pearson Education Latinoamerica
815 NW 57th Street Suite 484
Miami, FL 33158
Tel: 305 264 8344; Fax: 305 264 7933

Complete Training Courses

Each complete package includes the corresponding *How to Program Series* book and interactive multimedia CD-ROM.*Complete Training Courses* are perfect for anyone interested in learning Java, C++, Visual Basic, XML, Perl, Internet/World Wide Web and e-commerce programming. They are exceptional and affordable resources for college students and professionals learning programming for the first time or reinforcing their knowledge.

Each *Complete Training Course* is compatible with Windows 95, Windows 98, Windows NT and Windows 2000 and includes the following features:

Intuitive Browser-Based Interface

Whether you choose the Web-based *Complete Training Course* or the CD-ROM, you'll love the new browser-based interface, designed to be easy and accessible to anyone who's ever used a Web browser. Every *Complete Training Course* features the full text, illustrations, and program listings of its corresponding *How to Program* book—all in full color—with full-text searching and hyperlinking.

Further Enhancements to the Deitels' Signature Live-Code™ Approach

Every code sample from the main text can be found in the interactive, multimedia, CD-ROM-based *Cyber Classrooms* included in the *Complete Training Courses.* Syntax coloring of code is included for the *How to Program* books that are published in full color. Even the recent two-color books use effective four-way syntax coloring. The *Cyber Classroom* software is provided in full color for all the Deitel books.

Audio Annotations

Hours of detailed, expert audio descriptions of thousands of lines of code help reinforce concepts.

Easily Executable Code

With one click of the mouse, you can execute the code or save it to your hard drive to manipulate using the programming environment of your choice. With selected *Complete Training Courses*, you can also automatically load all of the code into a development environment such as Microsoft® Visual C++™, enabling you to modify and execute the programs with ease.

Abundant Self-Assessment Material

Practice exams test your understanding with hundreds of text questions and answers in addition to those found in the main text. Hundreds of self-review questions, all with answers, are drawn from the text; as are hundreds of programming exercises, half with answers.

Announcing New Web-Based Versions of the Deitels' *Complete Training Courses!*

The same highly acclaimed material found on the *Cyber Classroom* CD-ROMs is now available at the same price via the World Wide Web! When you order the Web-based version of a *Complete Training Course,* you receive the corresponding *How to Program* book with a URL and password that give you six months of access to the *Cyber Classroom* software via the Web.

To explore a demo of this new option, please visit
http://ptgtraining.com

The Complete Advanced Java™ 2 Platform Training Course

CD-ROM version (0-13-091277-8)
Web-based version (0-13-065274-1)

The Complete C++ Training Course, Third Edition

CD-ROM version (0-13-089564-4)
Web-based version (0-13-065156-7)

Bonus! You can run the hundreds of C++ programs with the click of a mouse and automatically load them into Microsoft® Visual C++™, allowing you to modify and execute the programs with ease.

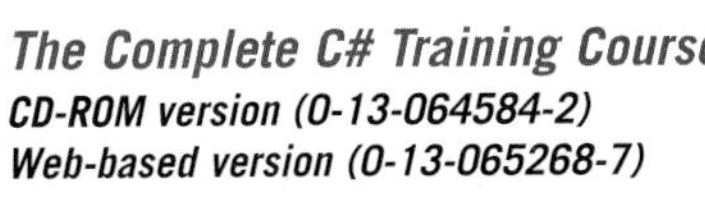

The Complete C# Training Course

CD-ROM version (0-13-064584-2)
Web-based version (0-13-065268-7)

The Complete e-Business & e-Commerce Programming Training Course

CD-ROM version (0-13-089549-0)
Web-based version (0-13-065271-7)

The Complete Internet & World Wide Web Programming Training Course, Second Edition

CD-ROM version (0-13-089550-4)
Web-based version (0-13-065256-3)

The Complete Java Training Course, Fourth Edition

CD-ROM version (0-13-064931-7)
Web-based version (0-13-065259-8)

The Complete Perl Training Course

CD-ROM version (0-13-089552-0)
Web-based version (0-13-066108-2)

The Complete Visual Basic 6 Training Course

CD-ROM version (0-13-082929-3)
Web-based version (0-13-065165-6)

Bonus! You can run the hundreds of Visual Basic programs with the click of a mouse and automatically load them into Microsoft®'s Visual Basic® 6 Working Model edition software, allowing you to modify and execute the programs with ease.

The Complete Wireless Internet & Mobile Business Programming Training Course

CD-ROM version (0-13-062335-0)
Web-based version (0-13-065253-9)

The Complete XML Programming Training Course

CD-ROM version (0-13-089557-1)
Web-based version (0-13-065267-9)

Coming Soon:

- ***The Complete Python Training Course***
  CD-ROM version (0-13-067374-9)
  Web-based version (0-13-067378-1)

All of these ISBNs are retail ISBNs. College and university instructors should contact your local Prentice Hall representative or write to cs@prenhall.com for the corresponding student edition ISBNs.

If you would like to purchase the Cyber Classrooms separately...

Prentice Hall offers Multimedia Cyber Classroom CD-ROMs to accompany the *How to Program* series texts for the topics listed at right. If you have already purchased one of these books and would like to purchase a stand-alone copy of the corresponding *Multimedia Cyber Classroom*, you can make your purchase at the following Web site:

www.informit.com/cyberclassrooms

For **Advanced Java Multimedia Cyber Classroom**, ask for product number 0-13-091276-X

For **C# Multimedia Cyber Classroom**, ask for product number 0-13-064587-7

For **C++ Multimedia Cyber Classroom, 3/E**, ask for product number 0-13-089562-8

For **e-Business & e-Commerce Cyber Classroom**, ask for product number 0-13-089540-7

For **Internet & World Wide Web Cyber Classroom, 2/E**, ask for product number 0-13-089559-8

For **Java Multimedia Cyber Classroom, 4/E**, ask for product number 0-13-064935-X

For **Perl Multimedia Cyber Classroom**, ask for product number 0-13-089553-9

For **Visual Basic 6 Multimedia Cyber Classroom**, ask for product number 0-13-083116-6

For **XML Multimedia Cyber Classroom**, ask for product number 0-13-089555-5

For **Wireless Internet & m-Business Programming Multimedia Cyber Classroom**, ask for product number 0-13-062337-7

www.Deitel.InformIT.com

Deitel & Associates, Inc. is partnering with Prentice Hall's parent company, Pearson PLC, and its information technology Web site, InformIT (`www.informit.com`) to launch the Deitel InformIT site at `www.Deitel.InformIT.com`. The Deitel InformIT site is an online resource center that delivers premium IT content, adding new e-Learning offerings to the established Deitel product suite and the ability to purchase Deitel products. The site will contain information on the continuum of Deitel products, including:

- **Free weekly Deitel Buzz e-mail newsletter**

- **Free informational articles**
- **Deitel e-Matter**
- **Books and new e-Books**
- **Instructor-led training**
- **Web-based training**
- **Complete Training Courses/Cyber Classrooms**

`www.Deitel.InformIT.com` will benefit professionals, professors and students alike. The weekly opt-in Deitel Buzz e-mail newsletter and informational articles offer the reader an up-to-the-minute analysis of trends and technologies as well as insights into programming methodologies. The audio Deitel Buzz is a free opt-in daily e-mail featuring a link to an audio-annotated code sample. One of the authors will provide a detailed walkthrough of the code, offering insights into portability issues, maximizing efficiency and other valuable tips. For more in-depth material, we are pleased to announce the launch of **Deitel e-Matter**. e-Matter consists of sections on leading-edge technologies taken from already published texts, forthcoming texts or pieces written during the Deitel research and development process.

A Sneak Peek at Deitel™ Web-Based Tutorials

Deitel & Associates, Inc. is developing a series of self-paced Web-based tutorials using content from the Cyber Classrooms in their *How to Program Series*. Eventually, it will be possible to access the same cutting-edge content via CD-ROM, the Web, or even wireless devices. New features of these innovative tutorials include:

Five-way Flash animation demonstrating looping.

Interactive Questions

Specialized Q icons are attached to particular lines of code. When clicked, the icon provides a question and—upon pressing a button—an answer relating specifically to that line of code.

Dynamic Glossary

Users click on designated keywords, phrases or programming elements, displaying small windows containing definitions.

Interactive Animations

Deitel Web-based tutorial courses take advantage of the small file sizes of vector-based graphics and advancements in the tools used to produce them such as Macromedia™ Flash®, and use cutting-edge compression techniques and streaming media to deliver abundant audio. The Deitel Java Web-based tutorial features an interactive five-way for-loop animation, as pictured above, which includes an animated flowchart, audio and a simulated output window. Future *Cyber Classrooms* will contain animations illustrating important programming concepts such as flow of control and recursion.

Web-based Labs

Gain hands-on knowledge of the concepts you read about in the text. Deitel Web-based tutorial labs present challenging programming assignments and their solutions.

Abundant Audio

The courses deliver hours of streaming audio-based lectures. All code is syntax colored to make it easier to read and comprehend. Future Cyber Classrooms will contain nearly twice the current amount of audio.

Richer Assessment Types

In addition to the true/false questions found in current *Cyber Classrooms*, future versions will contain richer assessment types including fill-in-the-blank and matching questions.

Multiple Content Paths

Future *Cyber Classrooms* will contain multiple paths through the content, optimized for different users. Students will find an abundance of pedagogy designed just for them, while corporate users will find the content arranged in a way that meets their challenging "just-in-time" learning needs.

FORTHCOMING PUBLICATIONS FROM THE DEITELS

For those interested in

Microsoft® Visual Basic .NET

Visual Basic .NET™ How to Program: This book builds on the pedagogy of the first edition, which was developed for Visual Studio 6. It has a much-enhanced treatment of developing Web-based e-business and e-commerce applications. The book includes an extensive treatment of XML and wireless applications, Web Forms and Web Services.

For those interested in

Python

Python How to Program: This book introduces the increasingly popular Python language which makes many application development tasks easier to accomplish than with traditional object-oriented languages. Many people are touting Python as a more effective first language than C++ or Java.

For those interested in

Flash

Flash 6 How to Program: Hundreds of millions of people browse Flash-enabled Web sites daily. This first book in the Deitel Multimedia series introduces the powerful features of Flash 6 and includes a detailed introduction to programming with the Flash 6 scripting language. The key to the book is that it presents a complete treatment of building Flash-centric multi-tier client/server Web-based applications.

For those interested in

Microsoft® Visual C++ .NET

Visual C++ .NET™ How to Program: This book combines the pedagogy and extensive coverage of *C++ How to Program, Third Edition* with a more in-depth treatment of Windows and Internet programming in Visual Studio .NET. We have carefully culled the best material from each of these areas to produce a solid, two-semester, introductory/intermediate level treatment.

For those interested in

C++

Advanced C++ How to Program: This book builds on the pedagogy of *C++ How to Program, Third Edition,* and features more advanced discussions of templates, multiple inheritance and other key topics. We are co-authoring this book with Don Kostuch, one of the world's most experienced C++ educators.

New & Improved Deitel™ Web Site!

Deitel & Associates, Inc. is constantly upgrading `www.deitel.com`. The new site will feature Macromedia™ Flash® enhancements and additional content to create a more valuable resource for students, professors and professionals. Features will include FAQs, Web resources, e-publications and online chat sessions with the authors. We will include streaming audio clips where the authors discuss their publications. Web-based training demos will also be available at the site.

Turn the page to find out more about Deitel & Associates!